Business Statistics

Business Statistics

Elements and Applications

Mario J. Picconi
School of Business Administration
University of San Diego

•

Albert Romano
Department of Mathematics
San Diego State University

•

Charles L. Olson
School of Business and Public Administration
Governors State University

HarperCollins*CollegePublishers*

Sponsoring Editor: Melissa A. Rosati
Director of Development: Lisa Pinto
Project Editor: Cynthia Funkhouser
Design Supervisor: Dorothy Bungert
Text and Cover Design: Edward Smith Design, Inc.
Cover Photo: Scott, Foresman & Company
Photo Researcher: Judy Ladendorf
Production Administrator: Linda Murray/Valerie A. Sawyer
Compositor: Jonathan Peck Typographers
Printer and Binder: R. R. Donnelley & Sons Company
Cover Printer: The Lehigh Press, Inc.

Photo Credits

Cover photo and Chapters 7, 9, 10, 15: Scott, Foresman & Company. *Chapter 1:* Courtesy Firestone. *Chapter 2:* Superstock. *Chapter 3:* Les Stone/Sygma. *Chapter 4:* Phil Huber/Black Star. *Chapter 5:* Photri, Inc. *Chapter 6:* N. Tully/Sygma. *Chapter 8:* Courtesy Proctor & Gamble.

Chapter 11: Erich Lessing/Magnum Photo. *Chapter 12:* Focus on Sports. *Chapter 13:* Uniphoto. *Chapter 14:* Yvonne Hemsey/Gamma-Liaison. *Chapter 16:* Joseph Nettis/Stock Boston.

Text Credits

"A Big Band Fan: A Research Analyst Uses Moving Average," *Personal Investor*, Sept. 1990, p. 38. Reprinted by permission of Plaza Communications, Inc.

"Up to knees in galoshes, he begs snow" by Jeff Lyons, *Chicago Tribune*, January 24, 1980. Copyrighted January 24, 1980 Chicago Tribune Company. All rights reserved. Used with permission.

Table 3.4: Table adapted from "Industry Norms and Key Business Ratios Desk-Top Edition 1990–1991." Copyright © 1991 Dun & Bradstreet, Inc. All Rights Reserved. Reprinted with permission.

Appendix Table I: Table reprinted from *A Million Random Digits with 100,000 Normal Deviates*, The RAND Corporation (New York: The Free Press, 1955). Copyright © 1955 and 1983 by The RAND Corporation. Used by permission.

Appendix Table II: Table from *Statistics for Management and Economics*, Third Edition, by William Mendenhall and James E. Reinmuth. (Boston: PWS-KENT Publishing Company, 1978), 705–708. Reprinted by permission.

Appendix Table VII: From Table III of Fisher & Yates': *Statistical Tables for Biological, Agricultural and Medical Research* published by Longman Group UK Ltd., London (previously published by Oliver and Boyd Ltd., Edinburgh), and by permission of the authors and publishers.

Appendix Table VIII: Table 8 from *Biometrika Tables for Statisticians*, Vol. 1, 3/E, 1966. Reprinted by permission of the Biometrika Trustees.

Appendix Table IX: "Tables of percentage points of the inverted beta (F) distribution," *Biometrika*, Vol. 33, 1943 with corrections obtained from *Biometrika Tables for Statisticians*, Vol. 2, Table 5, 1972.

Figure Credits

Figure 1.3: "Wendy's mail questionnaire." Reprinted by permission of The Ohio State University.

Figure 5.19: From "Mathematical Models for Financial Management" by Merton H. Miller and Daniel Orr from Selected Paper No. 23. (Chicago: University of Chicago Graduate School of Business, 1966). Reprinted by permission of the author.

Figure 10.1: "Value Lines Calculated Betas for IBM and Lotus" from *Value Line*, Ed. 7 and Ed. 13 by Geo. A. Niemond, May 3 and June 14, 1991, Int'l Bus. Mach. NYSE-IBM; Lotus Development OTC-Lots, pp. 1098 and 2124. Reprinted by permission of Value Line Publishing, Inc.

Business Statistics: Elements and Applications

Library of Congress Cataloging-in-Publication Data

Picconi, Mario J., date–
   Business statistics : elements and applications / Mario J.
Picconi, Albert Romano. Charles L. Olson.
     p.   cm.
   Includes index.
   ISBN 0-06-500174-5
   1. Commercial statistics. 2. Social sciences—Statistical
methods. I. Romano, Albert. II. Olson, Charles L., date–
III. Title.
HF 1017.P43   1993
519.5—dc20

92-16383
CIP

93 94 95 96 9 8 7 6 5 4 3 2

Contents

Appendix

Tables

PREFACE

THE QUALITY CHALLENGE AND THIS TEST'S OBJECTIVE

Everyone who reads a daily newspaper or watches television news knows that business today is obsessed with the idea of quality. Those of us who teach business students are even more aware that our companies must produce quality products to compete in the global market and that the resource necessary to do this is a well-educated, productive work force. Mathematical proficiency and statistical literacy, in particular, are the key, the *lingua franca*, to setting global quality standards. Production workers who are educated in statistics can make and read control charts and track potential problems by recognizing normal variation from statistically significant information. Statistically literate employees are prepared to improve service quality by learning from market-research data, scientific research, and customer feedback.

The message is clear: To offer measurably superior goods and services in a global environment, we must have a statistically literate work force, and that starts with effective teaching.

A critical factor to you and your students is the accuracy of the solutions to problems. To achieve a high standard of accuracy, we participated with carefully selected colleagues in a comprehensive system of creating problems, solving problems, and checking and testing solutions.

Our system also enabled us to achieve a uniformity in problem-solving emphasis and procedure throughout the textbook, the solutions manual, the study guide, and the testbank. You will be able to assure students with confidence that the text and study guide *do* match in problem-solving methodology. So, the time they spend in solving the text exercises and study-guide exercises will give them the practical advantage of being prepared to solve testbank questions.

Our system for ensuring accuracy was implemented for the textbook and its supplements. Textbook problems were written, solved, checked, and tested in the classroom by the three authors. Dirk Yandell of the University of San Diego solved the problems independently and prepared the actual solutions presented in the solutions manual. Barbara McKinney, from Western Michigan University, double-checked the problems and solutions. Barbara served as a reviewer in the manuscript-development process, so she was thoroughly familiar with our approach. Yet a fourth check of the problems and solutions was conducted by Zam Malik while at the University of San Diego.

Dirk Yandell also wrote the study guide and students' solutions manual. The three textbook authors checked all the problems and solutions. Alan Gin, of the University of San Diego, wrote and solved all the problems in the testbank. The three textbook authors and Dirk Yandell checked that material.

As instructors, we understand concern about accuracy and thus implemented a *total quality assurance program*.

By what winning tactic will we help you do this? We propose to forge an alliance among you, the instructor, your students, and the text. By combining your knowledge of the subject matter, your enthusiasm, good humor, and patience, with an effective, practical text with supplements, your students will gain statistical literacy.

OUR TEXT'S STRATEGY

We have two goals: first, to present basic statistical principles in a clear, readable, and pedagogically effective style; and, second, to engage students' interest with real-world situations. To meet the second goal, the text contains the following distinctive elements:

Active Learning. The chapter-opening Headline Issues and the Wendy's Database Analysis both will promote student involvement. The situations and cases are designed to foster class discussions and to direct students to "think and do" in solving problems.

Example Driven. Whenever possible, formulas are derived from examples, thus facilitating students' understanding of generalized mathematical logic. For example, Chapter 9, Analysis of Variance, begins with Herzog, an engineer who must investigate a steel supplier. The ANOVA technique arises out of the situation, and a mathematical generalization follows.

Management Emphasis. The text problems and cases maintain a managerial focus, by linking the statistical solution to a practical business interpretation. For example, the illustrated text problems of Chapters 7 and 8 all conclude with a practical interpretation. The applied case in Chapter 10 shows how a nagging business problem in mail-order houses, when approached by a specific statistical tool, provides management with a time and cost-saving solution.

We present quality control in a comprehensive case, **American Roots of Japanese Product Quality: The Deming Legacy**, after Chapter 6, Sampling Distributions. The case serves two useful purposes. First, it forges the link between the material from earlier descriptive statistics chapters and the material on statistical inference and confidence intervals in Chapter 7. Second, it raises the attention of students to the quality-control issue without imposing the time demands necessary for a full chapter. The case approach affords students the opportunity to get a good introductory view of the subject, leaving a more thorough and comprehensive treatment to courses devoted to production management and quality control.

ORGANIZATION

The content and organization of the text are both traditional and comprehensive. Chapters 1 through 8 are considered core chapters. They cover the descriptive material, probability, probability distributions, sampling, statistical estimation, and hypothesis. Chapters 9 through 16 include additional inference topics (eg., ANOVA, regression, etc.), a descriptive chapter on index numbers, and a chapter on decision theory. This organization offers considerable flexibility in using the individual chapters beyond the core, depending on whether a one-semester (quarter) course or a two-semester (quarter) course sequence is contemplated.

For instance, in a one-semester course, the core chapters can be combined with simple regression and—depending on how many applied cases and Wendy's database exercises are assigned and discussed in class—with an additional two or three chapters that an instructor feels will meet the specific course objectives. In a two-quarter and two-semester course sequence, the instructor should be able to cover all the chapters, at least one Applied Case, and the Wendy's database analysis in all the chapters in which they are discussed.

PEDAGOGICAL FEATURES

The pedagogical features build student interest and confidence in statistics.

Wendy's database is a database of customer response on a Wendy's Corporation marketing survey. It is available as free ASCII diskettes in all student copies, one IBM diskette *and* one Macintosh diskette. The Wendy's database is analyzed in the text to illustrate how statistical tools are employed to answer a firm's critical business questions about its customers and competitive position. The Wendy's database analysis begins in Chapter 1, What Is Statistics?, with the presentation of background information and a copy of the Wendy's survey questionnaire. The authors' statistical analysis of the database appears at the end of most chapters of the text.

Each chapter's Wendy's database discussion ends with a checkpoint exercise that allows students to perform their own statistical analysis on a different variable or set of variables from the database. Using the data diskettes, supplied with the text, and a statistical package such as MINITAB or MYSTAT, the various chapter checkpoint exercises present an ideal vehicle by which the student can gain insight into real-world statistical database analysis.

Headline Issues open each chapter with a vignette describing an article of high interest (eg., dropout rates of college athletes; recall of Perrier bottled water). Lively examples spark students' interest and motivate them to learn statistical concepts covered in the chapter.

Solving applied cases explores a variety of situations, from consulting assignments and management decision-making problems to business-research issues. In each case, the authors' present their analysis, then ask students to perform a similar analysis on a set of data given in a checkpoint exercise. The checkpoint exercise allows students to see how well they understand the case material.

Practice exercises positioned at key points in every chapter help students develop straightforward calculating skills. Full solutions given at the end of the chapter provide immediate feedback on whether students have mastered the procedure.

Chapter exercises that follow a chapter section complement the practice exercises by offering additional practice in the calculating skills for the particular statistical procedure discussed in the section.

Chapter review exercises. Over 1,000 exercises appear in the text. Many of these are at the end of each chapter, starting with straightforward skill problems and then moving to more thorough and thoughtful problems. The latter type require students to "think about, calculate, and interpret" businesslike situations that they may soon be dealing with in the business world.

Numbered examples are presented in the body of the text over several chapters to reinforce the use of statistical methodology in an application setting.

Highlighted equations and theorems within the body of the chapter direct students' attention to important concepts of the chapter.

Boldfaced key terms and concepts placed within the body of the text facilitate easy reference.

Key equations at the end of a chapter summarize the important equations introduced in that chapter in order to facilitate student review.

Computer icon (⌸), next to an exercise, indicates the data is on the free disks accompanying the text.

Study guide icon (▶), next to an exercise, indicates that the full solution of that particular text exercise is available in the study guide. Students can check the problem formulation and determine areas that require additional study.

Summary at the end of a chapter gives the student a concluding overview of the benchmark concepts found in each chapter.

SUPPLEMENTS

Instructor's Resource Manual with over 350 Transparency Masters. Developed by the authors, this manual contains an array of instructional aids for teaching and testing. The resource manual includes for each chapter (1) teacher's notes that include an in-depth discussion with statistical solutions for the Headline Issues, (2) chapter outlines, (3) lecture notes that include demonstration problems not found in the text, (4) supplemental applied cases with solutions not found in the text, (5) a note on the chapter's Wendy's database analysis, and (6) the transparency master section that includes numerous masters illustrating tables and figures from the text, additional masters developed to illustrate concepts, graphics, and demonstration problems and their solutions, and original source material.

Instructor's Solutions Manual, prepared by Dirk Yandell of the University of San Diego with the assistance of the authors, contains fully worked-out solutions and interpretations for all exercises in the text. It is noteworthy that Dirk Yandell has additionally written the student study guide and contributed to the development of the testbank. His involvement guarantees that all three items will exhibit a consistency of language, procedure, and emphasis—a feature generally unavailable in the supplements of other texts. Both students and instructors should find this feature valuable.

Testbank has been class tested and contains 1,600 true/false, multiple-choice, matching, fill-in, and problem-oriented (analytical) questions. The testbank is designed (1) to evaluate a student's recognition and understanding of concepts and (2) to assess a student's ability to solve problems much like the ones illustrated in the text and the student study guide. Answers to all testbank questions are provided.

Testmaster. The testbank is available on $5\frac{1}{4}$- and $3\frac{1}{2}$-inch computer diskettes for the IBM-PC and compatibles and the Macintosh. The HarperCollins TestMaster program is a computerized test generator that lets you construct tests by choosing questions from item banks prepared specifically for this textbook. This program allows you to view test questions on the screen, edit, save, and print questions. In addition, you can add questions to any test or item bank, or even create your own item banks of test questions, which may include graphics.

Transparency acetates. Over one hundred transparencies are available free to adopters. Figures from the book will be four color. The additional 35 transparencies are two-color and will illustrate worked-out headline issue solutions and other supplementary problems.

Student Study Guide and Solutions Manual. Written by Dirk Yandell, this guide contains a chapter outline and review section, an extensive array of concept checks, and full solutions for approximately 20% of the text exercises. These exercises are denoted in the book with a special icon for easy reference [▶]. The study guide contains additional new exercises for student practice and reinforcement. A number of similar multiple-choice questions are also provided. Detailed solutions are provided for every problem. Comments and calculations are given for the correct multiple-choice answer to let students know the "why" for that answer.

Using MINITAB with Business Statistics is a manual written by Denise Dimon and Andrew Allen, both of the University of San Diego. This instructive guide demonstrates the usability and flexibility of the MINITAB system. More specifically, students learn how to manipulate data, how to execute statistical routines, how to obtain statistical results, and how to save and retrieve output and data. One or two problems are solved from each chapter of the book to demonstrate the specific instructions needed to obtain MINITAB output for the statistical techniques discussed in each chapter. The MINITAB manual is available for use with the IBM PC.

MYSTAT Manual—*Using Business MYSTAT in Business Statistics*. Written by Jeff Graham and Mario Picconi of the University of San Diego, this comprehensive guide provides generic information on how to run MYSTAT and presents the implications of MYSTAT for business statistics. Taking a step-by-step approach, the manual demonstrates how MYSTAT can be used to solve 10 problems from the textbook. Problem output is displayed so that students can see the impact of various MYSTAT commands on actual data. When MYSTAT is used with the ASCII disks that accompany the text, the student can solve approximately 114 of the text problems. The MYSTAT manual with software is available in two versions: IBM and Mac.

Grades. HarperCollins offers to adopters this grade-keeping and class-management package for the IBM-PC that maintains data for up to 200 students.

The HarperCollins Business Video Library. Adopters may select from a variety of business videos that are related directly to the book.

Statistical Toolkit 2.0 by Tony Patricelli of Northeastern Illinois University (IBM or Apple) is designed for students who wish to get help with tedious calculations or see step-by-step solutions. Graphic portions of the program can be used by instructors for classroom demonstrations illustrating such concepts as probability defined as area under curves or Central Limit Theorem. The *Toolkit* is available on a site license arrangement with permission to duplicate disks for student use.

ACKNOWLEDGMENTS

Learning how to reach students and motivate them to excel in statistics takes time. Six years of development have produced an ambitious package of text and supplements. Fortunately, we had the academic and personal support to accomplish our goals. A special note of thanks to Dean Jim Burns at the University of San Diego for his continuing support and for saving the day with a printer and PC at a critical hour.

A special thank you to Judy Mersino, who translated and typed without complaint the hieroglyphics I handed to her over and over again. A thank you to Barbara Mersino for pinch-hitting on short notice. Dirk Yandell has become a constant source of competent work and advice. His part in the total quality-control system deserves special recognition, along with the part played by Alan Gin, Barbara McKinney, and Zam Malik. Our gratitude also to the following reviewers who over these years have not only spotted our inelegancies and mistakes but have also been helpful by offering us pedagogical tips:

Mary S. Alguire, University of Arkansas
Deborah J. Gougeon, University of Scranton
Irwin Greenberg, George Mason University
Gary Kelley, West Texas State University
Barbara McKinney, Western Michigan University
Barbara K. Mardis, University of Northern Iowa

Buddy L. Myers, Kent State University
Thomas E. Obremski, University of Denver
Diane L. Petersen, Northern Illinois University
Harrison Reinken, Phoenix College
Edwin S. Shapiro, University of San Francisco
William C. Struning, Seton Hall University
Lee J. Van Scyoc, University of Wisconsin–Oshkosh
Rick Low Wing, San Francisco State University

We are grateful to the literary executor of the late Sir Ronald A. Fisher, F.R.S., to Dr. Frank Yates, F.R.S., and the Longman Group Ltd., London, for permission to reprint Table III from their book *Statistical Tables for Biological, Agricultural, and Medical Research*, Sixth Edition, 1974.

A note of thanks on the home front to our wives, who bent their schedules and commitments so that we could stay the course. Their good meals and conversation were a welcome break in the day's writing.

At HarperCollins, we are grateful for the good cheer and support of many people: Melissa Rosati, Acquisitions Editor, and her assistant, Pamela Wilkie; Lisa Pinto, Director of Development for Business and Economics; Maurice Prater, Marketing Manager; and Evelyn Owens, Supplements Editor. Also, a special note of thanks to Development Editors Mary Konstant and Elaine Silverstein, who worked daily with us in sorting out the reviewers' comments and making sure our responses answered their concerns. Finally, special thanks to our Project Editor, Cynthia Funkhouser, who made all the pieces come together for us.

USING MINITAB ON THE WENDY'S DATABASE

The Wendy's database analysis shown in the text is an analysis using the MINITAB statistical package of the responses from 406 respondents on a 148 question survey. To perform the analysis shown in the text, the entire Wendy's database (406 rows × 148 columns) was brought into the mainframe version of MINITAB and was available in columns C1 to C148. When operations were performed that generated additional columns of data, they were placed in columns designated C150 or greater. For the user of the PC version MINITAB (as well as the user of the student PC version), space limitations will not permit the MINITAB worksheet to hold the entire 148 column database. To alleviate this problem, the data diskette provided with the text is designed so that each question is given a separate file, e.g., the 406 responses for survey question 1 is in file Q001.DAT, and the 406 responses on survey question 148 is in file Q148.DAT. The creation of 148 separate files allows the PC user to use the MINITAB READ command to bring into the MINITAB worksheet only the individual files needed for a particular analysis.

For example, if the analysis calls for question 126, question 137, and question 145, then the commands would be:

```
MTB> READ 'Q126.DAT' C1
MTB> READ 'Q137.DAT' C2
MTB> READ 'Q145.DAT' C3
```

Now the responses for question 126 would be in column C1 (column 1), responses for question 137 in C2 (column 2), and responses for question 145 in C3 (column 3). To avoid losing track of which survey question you are dealing with and which is now being stored in C1, C2, or C3, it would be helpful to use the MINITAB NAME command to reinstate the question number to C1, C2, C3, e.g., MTB> Name C1 'Q126', or perhaps give C1 a more descriptive label as 'WUSAGE' since survey question 126 refers to Wendy's usage. You will notice that the text will often execute operations by referring to the descriptive label of the column rather than the "C" notation. Operationally, it is a bit more cumbersome to use descriptive labels rather than the "C" notation, but it is more appealing for following the operations and reading the results.

WHAT IS STATISTICS?

F ederal government testing of passenger car tires produced some disconcerting evidence—a failure rate of 6% among the tires tested. The tire manufacturers pooh-poohed the evidence, arguing that the few thousand tested tires amounted to only a few hundredths of a percent of the 180 million tires produced annually. But a Senate inquiry into the matter did not accept the tire manufacturers' arguments. After examining the statistical study, a noted senator stated that hundreds of thousands of inadequate or defective tires manufactured annually leave unsuspecting drivers traveling around the country on a time bomb.

The time bomb blew up for the Firestone Tire and Rubber Company. The consistently high failure rate on their popular 500 model steel-belted radial tires led to costly lawsuits, and eventually forced a massive recall. The net result was millions of dollars of red ink on the firm's profit and loss statement and a tarnished reputation besides.

How could a sample representing such a small percentage of tires manufactured signal the developing failure-rate problem? Confidence in the signal is warranted because the sample was designed, taken, and analyzed using modern statistical tools—tools that very often don't require the sample to be a large percentage of the population studied.

Overview

This chapter begins with a definition of statistics in its broadest terms and then discusses the three distinct, but highly complementary, branches of statistics: statistical design, statistical description, and statistical inference. The important role that each plays in conducting a statistical investigation is then examined. The design is shown to be concerned with efficient ways of gathering data; the descriptive branch summarizes and reports the data collected; statistical inference specifies the proper procedure for making statistical statements that are valid generalizations (inferences) about the entire collection of items under investigation. The chapter concludes with a discussion of the different types of data, both categorical and quantitative, that are available. Illustrations are given as to what constitutes proper arithmetical and logical operations in dealing with the different types of data.

The final item in the chapter presents the history of the Wendy's franchise, the competetive situation Wendy's faces, and the 148 item mail questionnaire Wendy's used to obtain information on 406 fast food customers. The Wendy's database used throughout the text is the responses by the 406 customers on the 148 items. The worksheet for the responses shows 406 rows with 148 columns.

1.1
INTRODUCTION TO STATISTICS

Statistics is a field of study concerned with gathering, transforming, and analyzing data for the purpose of making intelligent statements and drawing appropriate conclusions. Given such a definition, statistics can be relevant to many disciplines—medicine, education, business, etc. Business is our concern.

Let's now examine the major branches of statistics that interact in an effective statistical investigation. There are three major branches of statistics: (1) design, (2) description, and (3) inference.

STATISTICAL DESIGN

Statistical design deals with procedures for efficiently gathering data suitable for statistical analysis. Numerous designs offer procedures for gathering necessary data. The appropriateness of a design depends upon the circumstances of an individual problem. No single design is always best in all circumstances.

The importance of a good statistical design cannot be overemphasized. The data collection procedure must comply with the assumptions which underlie the statistical techniques that will be used. Only then can we use the results for valid conclusions.

In the government test of automobile tire failures, it seems that a *simple random sampling design* (which we shall describe fully in a later chapter) was used. The objective of this design is similar to the objective in card games of insisting that cards be picked from a well-shuffled deck. Collecting data according to such a design assures that selection of the tires will not be biased for or against the ones that are defective. If the statistical design doesn't stipulate random sampling, sample selection bias may creep in. False hazardous generalizations may result, for example, from the sample tires to the entire lot of tires. Random sampling ensures that sample results will be governed by mathematical laws of probability. If this is so, we will be able to make a valid generalization from the sample of a few thousand tires to the entire lot of 180 million tires.

STATISTICAL DESCRIPTION

Statistical description is concerned with techniques for communicating statistical information. Such techniques involve condensing, summarizing, and reporting data in order to distinguish important regularities and patterns underlying an ever present variation. This is sometimes called "number crunching." By reporting the proportion of defective tires among the tested tires, the federal agency engaged in statistical description. The agency provided one number, the percent defective, that summarized the results of the tests.

Graphs, charts, and other pictorial devices can be very helpful descriptive tools for highlighting important features of the data. In Chapter 2, we shall study several of these tools, learning both how to construct them and how to apply and interpret them.

STATISTICAL INFERENCE

Statistical inference is the branch of statistics that provides us with methods for making valid generalizations about specific characteristics in the entire collection of items or objects under investigation by examining only some selected items from the collection. The entire collection under investigation is called the **statistical population**. The process of selecting some members to be studied is called **sampling**, and the selected members constitute a **sample** from the population. A numerical value that describes the magnitude or extent of the specific characteristic in the population is called a **population parameter**. The comparable numerical value that describes the magnitude or extent of the specific characteristic in the sample is called the **sample statistic**. The parameter or the statistic can be an average, a proportion, or a measure of variability. In our tire example, the 180 million tires made annually constitute the statistical population. The true proportion of defective tires among the 180 million is the population parameter. The 6% failure rate found for the tires sampled is the sample statistic. In this case it is a sample proportion.

When we make a generalization, we make a predictive statement about a population parameter based on the sample statistic. Making a predictive statement about the population parameter from the corresponding sample statistic is referred to as a *statistical inference*. The word *inference* indicates that we proceed from the particular to the general; the word *statistical* indicates that we rely on a sample statistic to draw the inference.

$$\text{Sample statistic} \quad \xrightarrow{\text{Inference}} \quad \text{Population parameter}$$

In our tire example, the 6% failure rate found among tires examined in the sample is the sample statistic that can be used to draw an inference about the population parameter, the failure rate among the 180 million tires in the population. That is,

$$\begin{pmatrix} \text{6\% failure rate of tires} \\ \text{tested (the sample)} \end{pmatrix} \quad \xrightarrow{\text{Inference}} \quad \begin{pmatrix} \text{Failure rate among} \\ \text{all tires produced} \end{pmatrix}$$

Making a statement about the population characteristic by using statistical inference based on sampling is an alternative to making a statement by gathering all the data on that characteristic in the entire population. The latter is known as a **population census**. Sampling has two clear potential advantages over a census: lower cost and more timely information. However, there exist other important reasons for sampling. For example, gathering data for a population census may be physically impossible or destructive (imagine the damage done to automobiles subjected to the collision and impact tests to determine crashworthiness). Surprisingly, even when a census is taken, sampling is sometimes used to evaluate and improve census methods. This has been particularly true in the case of the U.S. Census of Population conducted every decade. Certain groups, notably low-income residents and illegal aliens, are difficult to count accurately. Sampling methods have been helpful in reducing the error.

Our objective in statistical inference is to know the true values of the population parameters (that is, the relevant characteristics of the entire collection of items, objects, or measurements). However, the limitations of data gathering usually restrict us to the use of sample values. Since samples provide only partial views of populations, the sample values are only estimates of the corresponding population parameter values. These estimates, like all estimates, are ordinarily subject to error (known technically as **sampling error**). The basic methodology of statistical inference requires knowledge about the patterns of the estimation errors that arise from the sampling process.

THE RELATIONSHIPS AMONG THE THREE BRANCHES

Figure 1.1 is a flowchart that portrays the interrelationships among the three branches of statistics. (Again, we use our tire example.) All three branches are needed to properly conduct statistical investigations.

Figure 1.1
Flowchart for conducting
statistical research

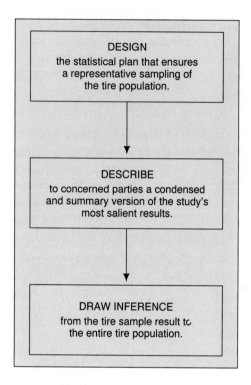

The data we encounter can be classified as either *categorical data* or *quantitative data*. These two different kinds of data reflect the underlying variable type and can be further classified according to the measurement scale used. That is, the measurement scale defines the kind of comparison that can be made. Such a classification scheme is shown in Figure 1.2. The figure shows the various possible combinations.

1.2
TYPES OF DATA

CATEGORICAL DATA

When the data collected refer to a described characteristic of the items or objects under study, the recordings are on a **categorical variable**. An item is placed in one and only one category. That is, the categories within a variable are mutually exclusive; for example, agreeing with an opinion rules out disagreeing with the opinion and with having no opinion at all. Furthermore, each recording is associated with a measurement scale that can be designated as either *nominal* or *ordinal*.

Nominal

The **nominal scale** is a scale of names that merely describe the object as a member of a particular category. For example, a calculator may be identified with a particular brand as Casio, Sharp, or Texas Instruments; or a company may be described by type of organization as a sole proprietorship, a partnership, or a corporation. No value judgment is made on which is more meritorious. The only arithmetic operation that can be performed on nominal data is counting. For instance, consider the prevalence of the three types of business organizations listed in Table 1.1. As the table illustrates, a comparison of nominal data may involve a comparison of counts that can be stated alternatively in terms of percentages.

Figure 1.2
Classification scheme for variable type and measurement scale

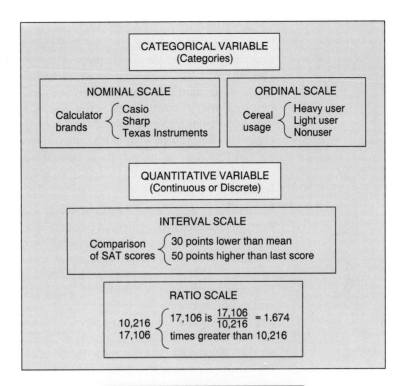

TABLE 1.1	U.S. Business Organizations	
TYPE	**NUMBER**	**PERCENTAGE**
	Thousands	**%**
Proprietorship	12,394	70.7
Partnership	1,703	9.7
Corporation	3,429	19.6

Source: *Statistical Abstracts of the United States*, 110th ed., 1990, U.S. Department of Commerce, Bureau of the Census Table No. 858.

Ordinal

The **ordinal scale**, on the other hand, indicates relative order or rank in addition to description. For instance, consumers of a product (say cereal) may be ranked according to usage categories: heavy user, light user, or nonuser. Each category of usage is more or less than another category, but there is no indication how much more or how much less. A danger of interpretation arises when ranked categories are assigned numerical values. Suppose "heavy user" is given the value 2, "light user" is given the value 1, and "nonuser" is given the value 0. Can we safely say that the heavy user consumed twice as much as the light user? Unfortunately, such comparisons are sometimes suggested, but they should be avoided.

QUANTITATIVE DATA

When the data collected refer to a numerically measured characteristic of the items or objects under investigation, the recordings are on a **quantitative variable**. The numerical values of a quantitative variable are either **discrete** or **continuous values**. For example, the price of a share of stock on the New York Stock Exchange is a quantitative variable that assumes discrete values, since price changes are in discrete jumps of $\frac{1}{8}$ point or multiples of $\frac{1}{8}$ point. However, numerically measured dimensions such as time, weight, or length are continuous and so can always be recorded with more precision. For instance, the thickness of the silicon wafer in a computer chip coming off the production line can always be measured to a more refined level.

Two types of measurement scales may be used for making comparisons between values of a quantitative variable: the *interval scale* and the *ratio scale*. The ratio scale is considered the stronger scale of measurement since the permissible operations for ratio scaled measurements includes those permissible for interval scaled measurements.

Interval

An **interval scale** indicates the magnitude of whatever is measured, and the differences between measured magnitudes can be computed. For example, your Scholastic Aptitude Test (SAT) score might be 30 points higher than the mean and 50 points higher than it was last year. With an intervally scaled measurement we know not only that one number is higher than another (as we would know from an ordinal scale), but also *how much* higher. That is, differencing (subtraction) or addition are always permissible arithmetical operations for interval scale values, even when the unit of measurement and the zero point are arbitrarily set. For instance, the freezing point of water on the Celsius temperature scale is arbitrarily set at 0° (32° on the Fahrenheit scale). The 0° on the Celsius scale does not mean the absence of heat (and neither does the 32° on the Fahrenheit scale). It is then permissible to say that 90°C is 60°C more than 30°C but not that 90°C is three times hotter than 30°C.

Ratio

A **ratio scale** possesses a natural zero point. For example, the zero assigned to no sales is a natural zero point. This means that the numbers assigned to sales are ratio-scaled numbers. For example, we can compare 30 units of sales made by salesperson A to 90 units of sales made by salesperson B, set up the ratio 90:30, and say that salesperson B sold three times as much as salesperson A.

Table 1.2 summarizes the four scales of measurement, the arithmetic operations that can be applied, and the comparisons that can be made.

TABLE 1.2 Overview of the Types of Measurement Scales and Their Implications		
SCALE	**ARITHMETIC OPERATION**	**IMPLICATION**
Categorical		
Nominal	Counting	Categorizes
Ordinal	Counting	Categorizes
	Ranking	Ranks
Quantitative		
Interval	Counting	Categorizes
	Ranking	Ranks
	Addition	Has equal measurement units
	Subtraction	Arbitrary zero or base point
Ratio	Counting	Categorizes
	Ranking	Ranks
	Addition	Has equal measurement units
	Subtraction	Has absolute or natural zero
	Multiplication	
	Division	

Many statistical pitfalls await the person who doesn't carefully consider the measurement scale of the data being investigated.

● ●

PRACTICE EXERCISE

1.1 In an attempt to determine what direction to take in promoting fresh pineapples, a pineapple growers' trade association commissioned an opinion study among pineapple users, which led to the following response table:

Percentage of General Agreement* about Certain Characteristics of Fresh Pineapples by the 2344 Respondents				
CHARACTERISTIC	**TOTAL** **%**	**HEAVY USERS** **%**	**MODERATE USERS** **%**	**LIGHT USERS** **%**
Qualities				
Low-calorie fruit	62	65	61	59
Extra special/gourmet fruit	56	63	57	60
Rich in vitamin C	49	50	52	45
Most delicious flavor of any fruit	48	53	49	42
Spoils more quickly than other fruits	74	69	76	77
Expensive compared with most fresh fruit	43	40	43	48
Season				
Best ones come in the spring	73	72	75	72
Except in springtime, almost never in the stores	57	52	55	63
Uses/versatility				
More ways to use than most other fruit	67	71	68	61
Very few recipes for using them	13	11	13	16
Hawaiian quality				
Best pineapples come from Hawaii	20	23	16	21
Flavor–appearance relationship				
Very difficult to judge their taste by how they look	65	66	64	65
(Number of respondents)	(2344)	(852)	(734)	(758)

*The difference between the percentages shown and the total 100% is accounted for by "disagree" or "don't know" answers.

a. Are the variables on the characteristics categorical or are they quantitative in nature? Name three variables.
b. Do the six characteristics or attributes under the heading "Qualities" represent mutually exclusive attributes? Explain.
c. Heavy, moderate, and light can be viewed as mutually exclusive user designations. How would you interpret the percentages under each designation across the row "Rich in vitamin C" (or any other row)? (Hint: Read carefully the footnote at the bottom of the table.)

● ●

SUMMARY

Why study statistics? Knowledge of statistical principles and methods is an aid in making better business decisions. How can we be confident about the procedures we use for gathering, presenting, and analyzing data? The set of ground rules statisticians have developed in order to ensure that there is a consistent and logical way to treat data and reach defensible conclusions about statistical results is called *statistical theory*. Its exposition and application to solving business problems is the goal of this text.

PRACTICE EXERCISE ANSWERS

1.1 a. Categorical. Low-calorie fruit, Extra special/gourmet fruit, Rich in vitamin C, etc.

b. No. Each quality attribute is a different categorical variable. Thus, the qualities are not mutually exclusive; fresh pineapples may possess the quality "Low-calorie" and the quality "Rich in vitamin C." Generalizing, we can say that for each individual attribute considered, a fresh pineapple may or may not possess that attribute. Conceivably, a fresh pineapple may possess all six attributes.

c. This question emphasizes the importance of understanding the classification scheme. It is true that heavy, moderate, and light represent mutually exclusive user categories, and data classified according to this scheme should account for all users and therefore should add up to 100% of all users (they do, as you can see from the number of respondents row). But the percentages shown in the table refer to the presence of that attribute tabulated from the responses for a specified type of user. For example, in the row "Rich in vitamin C," the value 52% under "Moderate users" means that among the moderate users, 52% agreed that fresh pineapples are rich in vitamin C. The other 48% of the moderate users must not have agreed. Fully reported, the percentages would appear as follows:

CHARACTERISTIC	TOTAL	HEAVY USERS	MODERATE USERS	LIGHT USERS
Quality				
Rich in vitamin C				
Percent who agree	49	50	52	45
Percent who disagree or don't know	51	50	48	55
	100	100	100	100

If the classification scheme is understood, figures in the last two rows of the above table are implied; they are not usually reported, because they add unnecessary clutter to the table.

CHAPTER REVIEW EXERCISES

▶ **1.1** Give examples of applications of statistics in fields known to you.

1.2 Find examples of statistical inference in your daily newspaper or on television news.

▶ **1.3** A drug manufacturer claims that a new drug can relieve the symptoms of flu without any undesirable side effects at least 98% of the time it is used in treating these symptoms. In a random sample of 225 subjects suffering the symptoms of flu, 217 showed relief without undesirable side effects. Identify aspects of statistical design, statistical description, and statistical inference.

1.4 An oceanographic expedition took 12 random readings of ocean temperatures at the surface location A and recorded temperatures between 51.5°F and 64.1°F, with an average temperature of 57.3°F. They took 15 random readings of ocean temperature at the surface location B and recorded temperatures between 53.2°F and 65.3°F, with an average temperature of 59.5°F. The expedition leader would like to know whether it is reasonable on the basis of this sample information to conclude that the true average temperature at location B is higher than at location A. Identify aspects of statistical design, statistical description, and statistical inference. Is the average temperature of 57.3°F at location A a statistic of the sample or a parameter of the population?

1.5 A consumer agency claims that the nicotine intake from cigarettes increases as the cigarette gets shorter. A sample of 5 cigarettes is tested for nicotine in their smoke when they are full sized and then when they have been smoked halfway. Results (in milligrams) are as follows:

FULL SIZE	19.4	21.6	22.8	20.4	24.3
HALF SMOKED	20.4	25.7	21.5	27.1	23.8

The director of the test wants to know whether it is reasonable to conclude that nicotine intake is greater with half smoked cigarettes. Before the conclusion can be statistically validated, what assumption would you need to make about the data collection, that is, with respect to the statistical design of the experiment?

1.6 At one radar checkpoint, 24 cars out of a random sample of 324 cars exceeded the speed limit, and at a second radar checkpoint, 36 cars out of a random sample of 361 cars exceeded the speed limit. A highway patrol officer wants to know whether it is reasonable to report that the true proportion of speeding cars is the same at both checkpoints. Identify aspects of statistical design, statistical description, and statistical inference.

▶ **1.7** For each of the measurements described, indicate whether a nominal, ordinal, interval, or ratio scale was used. Explain why you think your answer is correct.
   a. A measurement of brand preference between Peak and Shell antifreeze
   b. A compilation of total Peak antifreeze sales in Ohio in 1990
   c. A determination of the temperature at which the mixture of 2 gallons of Peak and 2 gallons of water will freeze

1.8 What kind of measurement scale is implied by the following statement? "A sample of 600 adults was asked to rank aspirin, Anacin, Bufferin, Excedrin, Emperin, and Tylenol in order of preference for relief of headaches. The most preferred was given a ranking of 1 and least preferred a ranking of 6. The average for Tylenol was 2.76."

▶ **1.9** Two stores, profiled below by their customers, are attempting to sell to the same target customers, using basically the same approach (merchandise, advertising, and price).

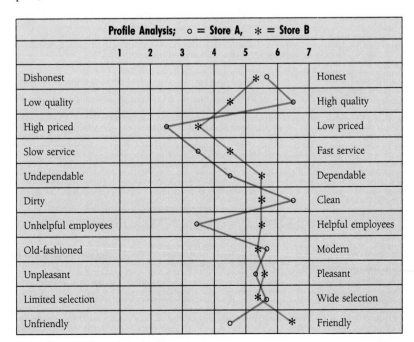

a. Are the variables that comprise the profile categorical or quantitative? Indicate whether a numerical, ordinal, interval, or ratio scale was used. Can we say that the employees in store B are about 50% more helpful than the employees in store A?

b. Since store A appears to be the higher-quality, higher-priced store, is it in a good competitive position with respect to the other profile variables? What does the profile suggest about the competitive position of store B?

WENDY'S DATABASE ANALYSIS

Wendy's database is a case study that is developed in various chapters of this text. The intention is to tie the material in the chapters to a common thread. Each chapter's material illustrates a statistical technique presented in that chapter. Computer output, a discussion, and an analysis of the results are included. Follow-up exercises direct you to perform a similar analysis for a different data block from the Wendy's survey.

In this chapter, the Wendy's material contains two items:

1. The background of Wendy's and of the "hamburger wars" that prompted Wendy's to agree to survey the fast food user market for customer demographics and preferences. Who is the Wendy's type of customer?
2. The questionnaire used to generate the survey data.

Wendy's International, Inc.

"Hamburgers are the great American love affair," a New York financial analyst once observed. But a key question posed to 43-year-old R. David Thomas and his management team of franchise veterans in 1969 was, "Does America really need *another* hamburger chain?" Thomas, sometimes described as "David following the hamburger Goliaths," was convinced he could play in the competitive hamburger game with the likes of McDonald's and Burger King. More than two decades and billions of Wendy's International, Inc. hamburgers later, we know that Thomas was right.

Background

Thomas founded Wendy's in 1969 as Wendy's Old-Fashioned Hamburgers, Inc. (later changed to Wendy's International, Inc.), just when it appeared to some that America could not absorb one more hamburger outlet, much less an entire chain. Some skeptical observers believed the entire fast food growth curve had already peaked and that the rapid expansion of franchised restaurants in the 1960s would cease.

Product Line

Thomas' goal was to bring a "better" hamburger stand to Americans. After several years of food service experience, including a brief stint as vice-president of operations in Arthur Treacher's Fish and Chips organization, Thomas opened the first Wendy's store in downtown Columbus, Ohio, in 1969. Thomas tested a number of ideas in the first store, which resulted in the recipe he thought would help Wendy's succeed.

1. The $\frac{1}{4}$ pound hamburger was designed as the basic menu item. This avoided head-to-head competition with McDonald's or Burger King's $\frac{1}{10}$ pound hamburger. Also, Wendy's used only fresh (not frozen) 100% beef hamburger meat converted into patties daily; this contrasted with McDonald's and Burger King's frozen patties. French fries complemented the hamburger entree.
2. Wendy's decided to offer lots of different condiments to customers. The various combinations of condiments were promoted intensely in Wendy's advertising.
3. "Frosty" was selected as the main drink to promote. It was a 100% dairy product—a cross between chocolate and vanilla flavors, and halfway between soft ice cream and a really thick milkshake. Shakes sold by McDonald's, by contrast, were not made from milk.
4. The final key menu decision was chili. Wendy's chili is particularly mild but can be made more spicy by adding hot sauces and pepper.

These were the basics of Wendy's limited menu: freshly ground hamburger, french fries, condiments, Frosty, and chili. Other items have been added over the years: salad bar, hot potatoes with stuffing, kid's boxes, chicken fillet sandwiches.

Buildings

All Wendy's restaurants were built to company specifications as to exterior style and interior decor. Most were free-standing one-story brick buildings constructed on 25,000 square foot sites with parking for 35–40 cars. Some downtown restaurants were of a storefront type, which varied according to available locations, but they generally retained the standard red, yellow, and white decor and sign. Wendy's put substantial effort into designing a building that reflected the old-fashioned theme. Large plate-glass windows let diners look out and let prospective customers get a taste of the interior of the restaurant.

The restaurant design also stressed great flexibility. With a few minor changes, Wendy's could sell almost any kind of food in these buildings. The theme and decor could be changed almost overnight. Wendy's doesn't have any booths, only tables with two or four standardized chairs around them.

Positioning Strategy

The Wendy's strategy was described by one analyst as "selling better hamburgers than McDonald's or Burger King at a cheaper price per ounce." As he commented, it takes no more labor to prepare a larger hamburger at a higher price. "McDonald's labor cost is about 22% of sales; Wendy's is only 15% because of its larger sandwiches."

In support of the higher-priced hamburger strategy, Thomas stressed the freshness and quality of Wendy's product. According to him, "quality is our recipe" was more than Wendy's slogan. "This is the way we think about every part of our operation. We do this by quality of raw materials, people, and delivery system."

Wendy's in the 1980s

The early forecasts of doom for Wendy's proved groundless. During the 1970s, Wendy's experienced steady growth, and growth continued well into the 1980s.

But now the hamburger wars that started in the 1970s continue to make competition extremely tough. Sophisticated and successful marketing strategies used by McDonald's and Burger King to maintain their positions in the industry have forced Wendy's to evaluate its own position in the business.

Wendy's Marketing Strategy for the 1990s

Wendy's performance in the 1990s will depend upon how well Wendy's understands its customers and plans its future marketing strategy. Market surveys through questionnaires mailed to a random sample of households are an important source of information. One example of a questionnaire that was sent out appears in Figure 1.3. It received 620 responses. From those 620 questionnaires, 406 had complete demographic information (variables 136–148) useful for computer analysis. Such survey data can be used to identify target market segments that Wendy's should focus on and to suggest marketing actions to reach those segments.

Figure 1.3
Wendy's mail questionnaire: fast food survey*

*Used by permission of Ohio State University. The cases do not reflect Wendy's market position as appraised by Wendy's International. This is a modified and updated version of the original questionnaire and data.

PLEASE TAKE YOUR TIME AND BE SURE TO ANSWER EVERY QUESTION. YOU WILL NOTICE THAT YOU ARE NOT ASKED TO IDENTIFY YOURSELF ANYWHERE IN THE QUESTIONNAIRE. THIS INSURES THAT ALL RESPONSES REMAIN STRICTLY CONFIDENTIAL.

1. Do you ever eat at FAST FOOD RESTAURANTS?   1. __ Yes   2. __ No
2. IF YOU DO

   About how often do you use them?

   1. __ More than once a WEEK   4. __ Once a MONTH
   2. __ Once a WEEK   5. __ Less than once a MONTH
   3. __ Two or three times a MONTH

IF YOU DON'T please go to item 136.

Figure 1.3
Wendy's mail questionnaire:
fast food survey* (*continued*)

Please indicate how familiar you are with each of the following fast food restaurants. Circle "6" if you have never heard of the restaurant, "1" if you are very familiar with the restaurant, or somewhere in between depending upon how familiar you are with the restaurant.

	Very Familiar with It					Have Never Heard of It
3. ARBY'S	1	2	3	4	5	6
4. BORDEN BURGER	1	2	3	4	5	6
5. HARDEE'S	1	2	3	4	5	6
6. BURGER KING	1	2	3	4	5	6
7. HUNGRY HERMAN'S	1	2	3	4	5	6
8. MC DONALD'S	1	2	3	4	5	6
9. WENDY'S	1	2	3	4	5	6
10. WHITE CASTLE	1	2	3	4	5	6
11. KENTUCKY FRIED CHICKEN	1	2	3	4	5	6
12. LUM'S	1	2	3	4	5	6
13. FRISCH'S	1	2	3	4	5	6
14. ARTHUR TREACHER'S	1	2	3	4	5	6
15. LONG JOHN SILVER'S	1	2	3	4	5	6

How important is it to you that a fast food restaurant satisfy you on the following characteristics? Circle "1" if the characteristic is very important, "6" if the characteristic is very unimportant, or somewhere in between depending on how important it is to you that the restaurant satisfy you on the characteristic.

	Very Important					Very Unimportant
16. Speed of service	1	2	3	4	5	6
17. Variety of menu	1	2	3	4	5	6
18. Popularity with children	1	2	3	4	5	6
19. Cleanliness	1	2	3	4	5	6
20. Convenience	1	2	3	4	5	6
21. Taste of food	1	2	3	4	5	6
22. Price	1	2	3	4	5	6
23. Drive-in window	1	2	3	4	5	6
24. Friendliness of personnel	1	2	3	4	5	6
25. Quality of french fries	1	2	3	4	5	6
26. Taste of hamburgers	1	2	3	4	5	6

Please indicate how much you think each of the fast food restaurants *has* of the following characteristics. Circle "1" if you think the restaurant is high in the characteristic, "6" if you believe it is low in the characteristic, or somewhere in between depending on how much of the characteristic you think the restaurant has. Please give your opinion of every restaurant on each characteristic even if you have to guess.

	FOOD					
	Taste Very Good					Taste Very Bad
27. BORDEN BURGER	1	2	3	4	5	6
28. HARDEE'S	1	2	3	4	5	6
29. BURGER KING	1	2	3	4	5	6
30. MC DONALD'S	1	2	3	4	5	6
31. WENDY'S	1	2	3	4	5	6
32. WHITE CASTLE	1	2	3	4	5	6

Figure 1.3
Wendy's mail questionnaire:
fast food survey* (*continued*)

CLEANLINESS

	Extremely Clean				Not Clean at All	
33. BORDEN BURGER	1	2	3	4	5	6
34. HARDEE'S	1	2	3	4	5	6
35. BURGER KING	1	2	3	4	5	6
36. MC DONALD'S	1	2	3	4	5	6
37. WENDY'S	1	2	3	4	5	6
38. WHITE CASTLE	1	2	3	4	5	6

CONVENIENCE

	Close to Where I Am				Out of the Way	
39. BORDEN BURGER	1	2	3	4	5	6
40. HARDEE'S	1	2	3	4	5	6
41. BURGER KING	1	2	3	4	5	6
42. MC DONALD'S	1	2	3	4	5	6
43. WENDY'S	1	2	3	4	5	6
44. WHITE CASTLE	1	2	3	4	5	6

PRICE

	Low Cost Menu				High Cost Menu	
45. BORDEN BURGER	1	2	3	4	5	6
46. HARDEE'S	1	2	3	4	5	6
47. BURGER KING	1	2	3	4	5	6
48. MC DONALD'S	1	2	3	4	5	6
49. WENDY'S	1	2	3	4	5	6
50. WHITE CASTLE	1	2	3	4	5	6

SERVICE

	Very Fast Service				Often a Long Wait	
51. BORDEN BURGER	1	2	3	4	5	6
52. HARDEE'S	1	2	3	4	5	6
53. BURGER KING	1	2	3	4	5	6
54. MC DONALD'S	1	2	3	4	5	6
55. WENDY'S	1	2	3	4	5	6
56. WHITE CASTLE	1	2	3	4	5	6

POPULARITY WITH CHILDREN

	Children Like the Food Extremely Well				Children Don't Like the Food at All	
57. BORDEN BURGER	1	2	3	4	5	6
58. HARDEE'S	1	2	3	4	5	6
59. BURGER KING	1	2	3	4	5	6
60. MC DONALD'S	1	2	3	4	5	6
61. WENDY'S	1	2	3	4	5	6
62. WHITE CASTLE	1	2	3	4	5	6

Figure 1.3
Wendy's mail questionnaire:
fast food survey* (*continued*)

		MENU				
	Wide Variety Menu				Narrow Variety Menu	
63. BORDEN BURGER	1	2	3	4	5	6
64. HARDEE'S	1	2	3	4	5	6
65. BURGER KING	1	2	3	4	5	6
66. MC DONALD'S	1	2	3	4	5	6
67. WENDY'S	1	2	3	4	5	6
68. WHITE CASTLE	1	2	3	4	5	6

Following are a series of questions regarding your attitudes toward fast food restaurants. To each question, please indicate whether you STRONGLY AGREE, AGREE, DON'T KNOW (NEUTRAL), DISAGREE, STRONGLY DISAGREE. There are no right or wrong answers: we only want to know what YOU think.

	Strongly Agree	Agree	Don't Know	Disagree	Strongly Disagree
69. If I eat out at all these days, I usually go to a fast food restaurant.	1	2	3	4	5
70. The hardest thing is to get everyone to agree where to go to eat.	1	2	3	4	5
71. Our children usually like to eat where their parents do.	1	2	3	4	5
72. Our children decide at what fast food restaurant we eat.	1	2	3	4	5
73. Going to a fast food hamburger restaurant is OK on weekends but not during the week.	1	2	3	4	5
74. The easiest way to judge a fast food hamburger restaurant is the quality of the french fries.	1	2	3	4	5
75. All fast food hamburgers taste the same.	1	2	3	4	5
76. The way a fast food store is decorated is important to me.	1	2	3	4	5
77. I tend to go to the same fast food restaurant all the time.	1	2	3	4	5
78. If a fast food restaurant has an atmosphere similar to that of a regular restaurant I feel more comfortable going to it.	1	2	3	4	5
79. I am more interested in the taste of a hamburger, not if the meat were frozen or ground fresh daily.	1	2	3	4	5
80. I would rather specify what toppings I want on a hamburger than buy one that is pre-cooked and pre-wrapped.	1	2	3	4	5
81. As long as the food tastes good and I can get what I want, a place does not have to be nice.	1	2	3	4	5

Figure 1.3
Wendy's mail questionnaire:
fast food survey* (*continued*)

	Strongly Agree	Agree	Don't Know	Disagree	Strongly Disagree
82. I consider a hamburger made of frozen meat to taste better than one where the meat is fresh.	1	2	3	4	5
83. I find that I go to fast food restaurants more now than full-service restaurants.	1	2	3	4	5
84. I prefer fast food restaurants that have a drive-in window so I don't have to get out of my car.	1	2	3	4	5

People go to fast food restaurants for many different reasons and on many different occasions. If you sometimes eat at a fast food hamburger restaurant, *circle* the number in the column below that tells how often you go to this type of restaurant on the following occasions.

	Never					Almost Always
85. I go there for breakfast.	1	2	3	4	5	6
86. I go there for lunch.	1	2	3	4	5	6
87. I go there for a mid-afternoon snack.	1	2	3	4	5	6
88. I go there for supper (or dinner).	1	2	3	4	5	6
89. I go there for an evening snack.	1	2	3	4	5	6
90. I go there on weekdays.	1	2	3	4	5	6
91. I go there primarily on weekends.	1	2	3	4	5	6
92. I go there when I'm too busy to cook for others.	1	2	3	4	5	6
93. I go there with friends.	1	2	3	4	5	6
94. I go there with members of my family.	1	2	3	4	5	6
95. I go there by myself.	1	2	3	4	5	6
96. I go there when I get a taste for something special.	1	2	3	4	5	6
97. I'll go there after a show or an evening out.	1	2	3	4	5	6
98. I go there when I'm traveling away from home.	1	2	3	4	5	6
99. I go there during a shopping trip.	1	2	3	4	5	6
100. I go there and eat in the car.	1	2	3	4	5	6
101. I'll go there to eat in their dining room.	1	2	3	4	5	6
102. I buy food to go.	1	2	3	4	5	6

Please indicate your preference for all six fast food restaurants listed below. This is done in the following manner: rank the restaurants 1 through 6 by writing "1" beside the most preferred restaurant, "2" beside the next most preferred restaurant, and so forth. Rank all six restaurants even if you have limited knowledge about them.

103. BORDEN BURGER _____
104. HARDEE'S _____
105. BURGER KING _____
106. MC DONALD'S _____
107. WENDY'S _____
108. WHITE CASTLE _____

Figure 1.3
Wendy's mail questionnaire:
fast food survey* (*continued*)

Please indicate how likely it is that you would go to each of the following places for dinner.

	Very Likely				Not at All Likely	
109. PONDEROSA	1	2	3	4	5	6
110. MC DONALD'S	1	2	3	4	5	6
111. STEAK AND ALE	1	2	3	4	5	6
112. WENDY'S	1	2	3	4	5	6
113. YORK STEAK HOUSE	1	2	3	4	5	6
114. BURGER KING	1	2	3	4	5	6
115. WHITE CASTLE	1	2	3	4	5	6

How important do you consider each of the following as sources of information about fast food restaurants? Check for each item listed.

Important Information Obtained Through	Important Source of Information	Somewhat Important Source of Information	Not a Source of Information
116. Television	_____	_____	_____
117. Radio	_____	_____	_____
118. Newspapers	_____	_____	_____
119. Magazines	_____	_____	_____
120. Billboards	_____	_____	_____
121. Friends or relatives	_____	_____	_____
122. Mail	_____	_____	_____

123. Approximately how much do you spend for an average meal when eating out? (Check One)

    1. __ Less than $1.00   4. __ $3.00 to $4.00
    2. __ $1.00 to $2.00   5. __ $4.00 to $5.00
    3. __ $2.00 to $3.00   6. __ Over $5.00

124. Which item do you feel is the best buy in terms of giving you the most for your money?

    1. __ Wendy's single burger
    2. __ McDonald's Quarter Pounder
    3. __ Burger King Whopper
    4. __ Hardee's Burger

125. Have you ever eaten at Wendy's?   1. __ Yes   2. __ No

If *No*, go to item 136.

If *Yes*, how often do you go to Wendy's?

126. 1. __ More than once a week   4. __ Once a month
       2. __ Once a week   5. __ Less than once a month
       3. __ Two or three times a month   6. __ Only once

Figure 1.3
Wendy's mail questionnaire:
fast food survey* (*continued*)

When you go to Wendy's, what do you generally order? (Check *Yes* or *No* for each item)

127. Single $\frac{1}{4}$ pound	1. __ Yes	2. __ No
128. Double $\frac{1}{2}$ pound	1. __ Yes	2. __ No
129. Triple $\frac{3}{4}$ pound	1. __ Yes	2. __ No
130. French fries	1. __ Yes	2. __ No
131. Chili	1. __ Yes	2. __ No
132. Frosty	1. __ Yes	2. __ No
133. Soft drink or other beverage	1. __ Yes	2. __ No

134. Have you ever used Wendy's fast drive-thru window
service?   1. __ Yes   2. __ No
135. Do you enjoy the opportunity to garnish your
hamburgers your own way?   1. __ Yes   2. __ No
136. Are you: 1. __ Single   2. __ Married   3. __ Other (widowed or divorced)
137. Are you: 1. __ Male   2. __ Female
138. How many children 18 and under live in your home?
(Circle One)   0   1   2   3   4   5   6   7

IF YOU HAVE children in the home, please indicate how many children are of the following ages: (Circle one number in each category)

139. Under 2 years	0	1	2	3	4
140. 2–5	0	1	2	3	4
141. 6–11	0	1	2	3	4
142. 12–17	0	1	2	3	4

143. Do you own or rent the apartment or house in which you are currently living?
1. __ Rent   2. __ Own
144. In what type of dwelling are you now living?
1. __ House   2. __ Apartment   3. __ Duplex
145. Which of the following classifications comes closest to describing your occupation?
1. __ Managerial   6. __ Professional
2. __ Skilled trade   7. __ Housewife
3. __ General laborer   8. __ Student
4. __ Office worker   9. __ Retired
5. __ Technical
146. What was the last grade you completed in school?
1. __ Less than 8 years   4. __ 1–2 years college (or technical school)
2. __ 9–11 years   5. __ 3–4 years college
3. __ High school graduate   6. __ Graduate or professional degree
147. Please check your age bracket.
1. __ 15–19   5. __ 35–39   9. __ 70 or over
2. __ 20–24   6. __ 40–49
3. __ 25–29   7. __ 50–59
4. __ 30–34   8. __ 60–69
148. Finally, please check your approximate total family income (before taxes).**
1. __ Under $10,000   5. __ $25,000–$29,999
2. __ $10,000–$14,999   6. __ $30,000–$34,999
3. __ $15,000–$19,999   7. __ $35,000–$39,999
4. __ $20,000–$24,999   8. __ $40,000–Over

AGAIN THANK YOU FOR TAKING TIME TO COMPLETE THIS QUESTIONNAIRE

**Authors' explanatory note: Question 148 asks family income of the survey respondent. The first seven categories represent the lower and moderate income levels, whereas the moderately

continued at the top of next page

Figure 1.3
Wendy's mail questionnaire: fast food survey* (*continued*)

high and high incomes are lumped together in one open-ended category, $40,000 and over. Two reasons can be offered as an explanation of why the survey was designed with the last category open-ended beyond $40,000. First, it is clear that families who fall into the highest income category on the survey have the financial means to easily afford to patronize fast food restaurants. The real interest of the questionnaire then must be centered on learning more about the patronage behavior and attitudes of families who have income below that level and have to stretch their budgets to eat out, even at a fast food restaurant. The second explanation is psychological. Lower and moderate income respondents may find it less intimidating to report their income status if they see that their income falls in the middle of the categories listed rather than at the lowest or near the lowest category.

Wendy's: Looking Ahead

The analysis of the Wendy's survey data carried out in this book allows you to explore many important and interesting business issues in the fast food industry. Your exploration will help you realize that your newly acquired statistical tools are a useful aid in understanding the nature of the fast food business—or any business—and possibly gaining an edge on your competitors. Here are some of those issues and the chapter in which the discussion will be found:

- What perceptions do consumers have of industry leader McDonald's concerning food taste, cleanliness, menu price? Do most people have similar perceptions? What are the perceptions about other competitors regarding these same characteristics? What are the perceptions about Wendy's? (Chapter 2)

- How dependent are fast food restaurants on frequent users—people who patronize fast food restaurants once a week or more? (Chapter 2)

- On what dimensions of image do consumers see McDonald's most favorably? On what dimensions is McDonald's most vulnerable? How does McDonald's image profile compare with that of other fast food competitors? With Wendy's? (Chapter 3)

- How sharp is McDonald's image? Do other competitors have a fuzzier image? What about the sharpness of Wendy's own image? (Chapter 3)

- How much do people spend when they go to a fast food restaurant? (Chapter 7)

- What proportion of fast food customers are frequent users? (Chapter 7)

- By how much (if at all) is Wendy's food preferred to that of Burger King? Other competitors? (Chapter 8)

- Can the observed sample rating differences plausibly be attributed to sampling error? (Chapter 8)

- Is there something in Wendy's product offering (e.g., "do your own garnishing") that discriminates between people who like Wendy's ("Wendy's kind of people") and those who have a low preference for Wendy's? (Chapter 8)

- What factors differentiate "Wendy's kind of people" from people who prefer McDonald's or Burger King (e.g., attitudes toward fresh rather than frozen meat, importance of french fries, etc.)? (Chapter 9)

- How strong is the relationship between food taste image and brand preference? (Chapter 10)

- Are people more likely to recognize the "Wendy's difference" the more familiar they are with Wendy's? (Chapter 10)

- How closely linked in the fast food industry are brand familiarity and locational convenience? (Chapter 10)

- How well can brand preference be predicted and explained by food taste image, brand convenience image, and menu price image? (Chapter 11)

- Is there a relationship between brand preference and preference for specific features that differentiate the brands? (Chapter 12)
- Is family size a distinguishing factor that differentiates "Wendy's kind of people" from people who prefer McDonald's or White Castle? (Chapter 13)
- Lastly, in Chapter 15, we use the historical sales data for Wendy's to describe and analyze Wendy's historical growth path of sales revenue.

Our analysis of the Wendy's database directs you to what you might like to do—and probably would do—if you were a Wendy's marketing executive. The discussion and the step-by-step procedure will enable you to see how logical conclusions are drawn from analyzing actual business information. Of course, you are encouraged to explore other interesting questions on your own.

DATA REDUCTION
Descriptive Representations

The big supermarket chains in southern California are in intense competition for the consumer food dollar. Because these chains carry the same or a very similar assortment of products, they compete on the basis of price, convenience, and customer service. To keep customers aware of their chain's weekly price specials, convenient shopping hours, and fast checkout service, supermarket chains mail out multicolored circulars in addition to purchasing full-page ads in local newspapers. Each chain attempts to establish a distinct, favorable image to gain and maintain customer loyalty. For instance, a chain claiming to be the price leader (lowest prices) must clearly present ads to demonstrate that its prices can't be beat.

Suppose you are the person assigned to design the newspaper ads of the Lucky supermarket account—the chain reported to be the price leader. You are unhappy with the current ads. They present a blizzard of store price comparisons across the four major chains for a long list of branded items (see Table 2.1). You are concerned that because of all the fine print, the ads will neither draw enough attention nor hold it long enough for readers to absorb the message that Lucky's prices are lowest. You are particularly concerned because Lucky's prices aren't always the lowest of the four stores compared, and if the reader's eye happened to fall first on one of these items, attention might be short and the wrong message conveyed. You are anxious to organize and display the price differences so that the big picture quickly emerges; it should show the dominance of Lucky as the price leader. One of the possible statistical devices suggested to you are graphical presentations. This chapter will present various graphical techniques that might serve well to clearly highlight the price superiority of Lucky.

Overview

In this chapter and the next, we'll discuss some very effective statistical methods for data reduction that highlight, rather than hide, important features of the data. In this chapter, we'll show how to take a blizzard of unorganized data and construct tables, graphs, and charts that extract and present messages hidden by the profusion of data. As a result, we'll see pictorial representations with patterns or trends, and then we'll reorganize the pictorial representations to gain greater insight into these patterns and trends. In Chapter 3, we'll discuss how to reduce the data to single numerical values that actually summarize the important characteristics of the pictorial representations.

TABLE 2.1 An Illustration of Price Comparisons on Similar Brands Across Various Chains				
CANNED AND PACKAGED PRODUCTS	**LUCKY**	**BIG BEAR**	**RALPHS**	**VONS**
Moore Onion Rings, frozen, 16 oz pkg.	1.29	1.79	NA	1.59
Birdseye Broccoli Spears, frozen, 10 oz pkg.	0.99	NA	1.07	1.09
C&W Petite Corn, frozen, 16 oz pkg.	1.59	1.89	1.77	1.69
Birdseye Cut Corn, frozen, 16 oz pkg.	1.19	1.39	1.19	1.29
Country Crock Classic Margarine, 16 oz ctn.	0.69	0.92	1.09	NA
I Can't Believe It's Not Butter! sticks, 16 oz pkg.	1.49	1.67	1.67	1.69
Country Crock Corn Oil Margarine, 16 oz pkg.	1.09	1.24	NA	1.19
Land O'Lakes Butter, 16 oz pkg.	1.99	2.59	2.19	1.99
Imperial Margarine, 16 oz pkg.	0.50	0.45	0.79	0.87
Promise Spread Sticks, 16 oz pkg.	1.29	1.49	1.47	NA
Imperial Soft Margarine, 2 ct., 8 oz ctns.	1.39	1.59	1.57	1.59
Light Imperial Spread, 32 oz ctn.	1.59	1.79	1.77	1.59
Dole Pineapple Orange Juice, 64 oz ctn.	2.49	2.85	2.63	NA
Kraft Light Neufchatel, 8 oz pkg.	0.99	NA	1.39	1.41
Lake to Lake Extra Sharp Cheese, 9 oz pkg.	2.29	2.69	NA	2.39
Lake to Lake Sharp Cheddar Cheese, 9 oz pkg.	2.19	2.37	2.09	2.35
Bob's Seafood Sauce, 12 oz jar	1.49	1.79	1.57	1.49
Bob's Tartar Sauce, 12 oz jar	1.49	NA	1.57	1.49
Lake to Lake Monterey Jack Cheese, 9 oz pkg.	1.50	2.19	2.05	1.69
Bordens Lite Line Sharp Cheddar Cheese, 8 oz pkg.	2.19	2.19	2.09	NA
Lake to Lake Mild Cheddar Cheese, 9 oz pkg.	1.50	2.19	2.05	1.69
Heart Beat American Cheese Slices, 8 oz pkg.	1.79	1.89	NA	1.99
Kraft American Cheese Slices, 16 oz pkg.	2.99	2.87	3.05	3.49
Bordens Lite Line American Cheese, 8 oz pkg.	2.19	NA	2.09	2.29
Reddi Wip Whipped Topping, 7 oz can	0.79	NA	1.67	0.79
Knudsen Nice N' Lite Cottage Cheese, 16 oz ctn.	1.49	1.49	1.67	1.69
Rod's Real Whipped Cream, 7 oz can	1.29	1.59	1.49	1.19
Pillsbury Crescent Rolls, 4 oz ctn.	0.83	NA	1.25	0.78
Pillsbury Cinnamon Rolls, 6 oz ctn.	0.93	1.39	0.98	0.99
Pillsbury Hungry Jack Honey Biscuits, 10 oz tube	0.79	0.85	0.88	0.85
Sunny Delight Citrus Punch, chilled, 64 oz btl.	0.99	1.19	1.29	1.29
Tropicana Orange Juice, chilled, 64 oz ctn.	2.59	2.65	2.99	NA
Tropicana Pure Premium Orange Juice, chilled, 96 oz ctn.	4.99	4.69	5.59	5.29
Jell-O Pudding Snacks, chocolate and vanilla, 6 ct., pkg.	2.29	2.49	2.57	2.59
Yoplait Yogurt Snack, strawberry and blueberry, 16 oz ctn.	1.79	1.85	1.69	1.89
Kissle Creamy Blend, chocolate, 6 oz pkg.	0.59	0.71	0.68	0.69
Dubuque Canned Ham, pear shape, 5 lb can	8.99	12.99	NA	13.99
Messana Mozzarella Cheese Ball, 16 oz pkg.	1.99	2.89	NA	2.29
Ball Park Beef Franks, 16 oz pkg.	1.89	NA	2.45	2.67
Shofar Kosher Beef Franks, 12 oz pkg.	2.29	2.57	2.65	2.69
Grillmaster Chicken Franks, 16 oz pkg.	0.99	1.39	1.37	0.89
Hebrew National Beef Dinner Franks, 16 oz pkg.	2.99	NA	3.39	3.69
Butterball Smoked Chicken Breast, 6 oz pkg.	1.89	2.19	1.89	2.19
Gallo Lite Dry Italian Salami, 16 oz pkg.	3.99	NA	5.17	4.99
Gallo Deli Style Salami, 16 oz pkg.	3.99	5.19	5.17	5.19
Bell Park Knockwurst, 1 lb pkg.	1.89	2.59	2.35	2.39
Butterball Bun Size Turkey Franks, 16 oz pkg.	1.39	NA	1.55	1.64
Ball Park Meat Franks, 16 oz pkg.	1.89	2.49	2.35	2.47
Gallo Deli Style Ham, 8 oz pkg.	2.99	NA	2.99	3.19
Danola Sliced Ham, 12 oz pkg.	2.89	NA	3.49	2.99
Jones Sliced Liverwurst, 8 oz pkg.	1.45	1.79	1.39	2.29
Matchlight Charcoal Briquets, 8 lb bag	4.45	4.49	4.51	4.59
Kingsford Charcoal Briquets, 20 lb bag	5.89	NA	6.59	6.99
Kingsford Charcoal Briquets, 10 lb bag	3.29	3.79	3.57	3.69
Cascade Liquid Dishwasher Detergent, 65 oz btl.	3.09	NA	3.59	3.29
All Concentrated Laundry Detergent, 49 oz box	1.99	2.45	2.09	2.29
Cascade Dishwasher Detergent Powder, 65 oz box	3.09	2.99	3.59	3.29
Joy Dishwashing Liquid Detergent, 22 oz btl.	1.29	1.29	1.39	1.49
Tide Laundry Detergent, 136 oz box	6.99	9.55	8.79	8.79

NA = Not available

2.1
FREQUENCY DISTRIBUTIONS

Numerical data collected and presented in their original form are **raw data**. There are many ways to sort and organize the raw data collected on a particular characteristic common to a group of items. For example, consider data on the waiting time of patients in the emergency room of a particular hospital. One way to organize this or any other set of raw data is to place similar numerical values into categories called **classes** and count the number of items that fall into each class. The latter number is called the **class frequency**. Thus, one class might include waiting times up to 10 minutes. Another class might include waiting times beyond 10 minutes and up to 20 minutes. The entire collection of classes and their respective class frequencies is a **frequency distribution**. Frequency distributions can be presented in either tabular or graphic form. The purpose of either form is to reveal an underlying pattern of variation for a particular characteristic (as in the supermarket pricing example). Often the pattern is unrecognizable in the original (raw) form, but is readily recognizable in the tabular or graphic form. First, we'll consider the tabular form of a frequency distribution, and then the graphic form.

Suppose the Joint Committee for Accreditation of Hospitals requires that reasonable standards be set for various hospital services. The administrators at a group of large city hospitals agree that an "ideal" hospital should be able to treat certain types of emergency cases within 30 minutes of arrival. To encourage hospitals to move toward this ideal, the administrators want to set a standard that can realistically be met by hospitals putting forth a sincere effort, and at the same time result in a significant reduction in patient waiting time. To determine the standard, hospitals are asked to suppy data on the waiting times presently experienced by their patients.

The data in Table 2.2 give the excess waiting times (beyond the 30 minute ideal) for 200 patients. No negative values are shown since no waiting time was less than 30 minutes.

TABLE 2.2	Raw Data: 200 Recordings on *Excess* Patient Waiting Time at a Hospital Emergency Room (Nearest Minute)																			
39	41	53	54	85	69	81	36	32	51	41	49	23	53	46	48	27	45	15	61
40	79	50	39	59	46	52	51	0	33	33	38	51	34	40	57	47	56	79	41
100	45	49	60	76	49	66	48	73	15	6	31	44	48	29	41	68	62	46	70
72	40	60	44	56	46	92	36	74	25	78	52	37	24	35	54	26	52	33	73
47	88	63	14	30	51	26	25	53	46	49	53	63	64	43	48	64	1	29	22
74	32	87	60	26	59	53	23	50	41	58	36	32	33	51	44	31	58	74	50
62	60	42	32	51	31	89	30	55	60	9	61	12	0	80	25	41	78	61	66
69	49	63	76	97	79	52	69	54	49	67	59	55	48	23	81	25	59	89	51
71	50	62	87	34	43	40	31	27	65	51	78	36	73	50	45	36	52	69	31
85	77	68	58	56	29	29	64	49	71	41	37	44	54	64	36	66	62	42	36

Left in this form, the raw data set does not reveal the information necessary for the accreditation committee. We can, however, turn to a frequency table for help. The construction of a frequency table with defined classes and frequencies requires a two-stage process. Stage one is to determine the classes, and stage two is to assign individual data items to the classes.

STAGE ONE: DETERMINE THE CLASSES

Stage one requires three steps:

Step 1

Find the range. From the value of the largest observation, L, and the value of the smallest observation, S, find the difference, $L - S$. This difference is called the **range**, R. For our data, $L - S = 100 - 0 = 100$, so the value of R is 100.

Step 2

Determine the number of classes and their lengths. Partition the range into a specific number of intervals of equal size. (Later, we shall discuss exceptional situations in which you might want to break the rule of equal size intervals.)

A rule of thumb is to use from 5 to 20 equal sized intervals. A small number of intervals is appropriate when there are few observations. It doesn't make sense to use 20 intervals when there are only 10 or 20 observations. Increase the number of intervals as the number of observations increases. The length of the intervals defines the size of the **class interval**.

Don't hesitate to make a small adjustment to the class interval length so the interval is convenient to work with. If we choose 11 equal sized class intervals for the waiting time data, we divide the range, 100, by the chosen number of intervals, 11, and obtain 9.09 for the length of each class interval. Since 9.09 is not a convenient unit to work with, we shall increase it slightly to 10. This gives us 11 classes, each with an equal class interval length of 10.

Step 3

Determine the class intervals. Each class interval has an upper and lower limit. Before individual observations can be assigned to particular class intervals, the upper and lower limits (called **class limits**) of each class interval must be specified. As soon as any one class interval is specified, the upper and lower limits of all the other class intervals follow automatically once we have determined the size of the class interval.

Usually, the lower limit of the first class interval is the first limit to be specified. Considerable discretion is allowed in the choice of a lower limit, but it is preferable to start relatively close to, but smaller than, the smallest raw data value, S. The uppermost class interval should be relatively close to, but larger than, the largest raw data value, L.

Since $S = 0$ for the waiting time data, let's consider 0, and then, alternatively, -1 and -5 as possible values for the lower limit of the first class. Suppose we choose 0 as the lower limit of the first interval and construct 11 equal sized class intervals of size 10, as listed below. We find that the largest observation ($L = 100$) is equal to the lower limit of the last interval.

Smallest	0– 9
observation	10– 19
is 0	20– 29
	30– 39
	40– 49
	50– 59
	60– 69
	70– 79
Largest	80– 89
observation	90– 99
is 100	100–109

If -1 is chosen as the lower limit of the first class, the largest observation still lies near the lower end of the last interval.

To improve the balance let's set the lower limit of the first class interval at -5.

Now we find that $L = 100$ falls well within the last constructed interval, and $S = 0$ also falls well within its interval. Because the balance is better this way, we let -5 be the lower limit of the first class.

Smallest observation,	$-5-$	4
0, is now well within	5–	14
the first interval	15–	24
	25–	34
	35–	44
	45–	54
	55–	64
	65–	74
Largest observation,	75–	84
100, is now well within	85–	94
the last interval	95–	104

The lower and upper class limits for the 11 class intervals are listed above. In general, to establish the lower limits of the other 10 classes, we start by defining the interval length as the difference between the lower limits of successive class intervals. Then we can determine the lower limit of the second class interval as follows:

a. Since we have decided in Step 2 to use 10 as the size of the class interval, we know that

$$\left(\begin{array}{c}\text{Lower limit of}\\ \text{second class}\end{array}\right) - \left(\begin{array}{c}\text{Lower limit of}\\ \text{first class}\end{array}\right) = 10$$

b. By substituting -5 for the lower limit of the first class, we can write

$$\left(\begin{array}{c}\text{Lower limit of}\\ \text{second class}\end{array}\right) - (-5) = 10$$

c. Therefore, the lower limit of the second class must be $5 = 10 + (-5)$.

To establish the upper limit of each class, we first note that in this particular example the stated limits are measured in integers. The lower limit of the second class is 5, so the upper limit of the first class must be set at 4, the next integer just below 5. Since the interval length is also equal to the difference between upper limits of successive class intervals, the complete set of class intervals is -5–4, 5–14, 15–24, 25–34, 35–44, 45–54, 55–64, 65–74, 75–84, 85–94, 95–104.

STAGE TWO: ASSIGN INDIVIDUAL DATA ITEMS TO CLASSES, AND TALLY THE OBSERVATIONS

Assign each recorded value to the class interval in which it belongs. A tally mark is made for each observation assigned to an interval. The number of observations recorded in each class interval is the *class frequency*. Table 2.3 is the excess patient waiting time frequency table.

CLASS MIDPOINTS

The midpoint of a class interval, or its **class mark**, can be viewed as the typical or representative value of that interval. An interval's midpoint may be obtained by dividing the sum of the interval's lower and upper class limits by 2. For example, the midpoint

	TABLE 2.3 Frequency Table (Using Class Limits) for Excess Patient Waiting Times			
LOWER CLASS LIMIT	**CLASS MIDPOINT**	**UPPER CLASS LIMIT**	**TALLY**	**CLASS FREQUENCY**
−5	−0.5	4	|||	3
5	9.5	14	||||	4
15	19.5	24	++++ ||	7
25	29.5	34	++++ ++++ ++++ ++++ ++++ ++++	30
35	39.5	44	++++ ++++ ++++ ++++ ++++ ++++ ||	32
45	49.5	54	++++ ++++ ++++ ++++ ++++ ++++ ++++ ++++ ++++ ||||	49
55	59.5	64	++++ ++++ ++++ ++++ ++++ ++++ ||	32
65	69.5	74	++++ ++++ ++++ ++++		21
75	79.5	84	++++ ++++ ||	12
85	89.5	94	++++ |||	8
95	99.5	104	||	2

for the first class interval in Table 2.3 is $(−5 + 4)/2 = −0.5$. The midpoints for the other intervals in Table 2.3 are listed between the class limits.

USING THE FREQUENCY DISTRIBUTION

Excess patient waiting times will vary from one patient situation to another, and the reasons may be beyond the control of hospital administrators. Thus, it would be premature to conclude on the basis of a single, or even a few, long waiting time observation(s) that improvement is needed in the operation of the emergency room. There are, however, important patterns in the frequency table of the waiting time data that, if understood, would be useful in determining how standards should be set. For example, notice in Table 2.3 that more than half (113) of the excess waiting times are clustered within the three middlemost classes (from 35 to 64 minutes), whereas only 22.51% [$(43 \div 200) \times 100\%$] of the excess waiting times exceed 64 minutes. Suppose the administrators have reason to believe that this particular emergency room is well run, and the observed excess waiting times are typical of what might be expected for an efficiently run emergency room. Then the frequency table can be used to develop realistic guidelines for excess waiting times. For instance, one guideline may be that not more than 25% of the excess waiting times should exceed 64 minutes. By computing the percentages for the various waiting times, the performance of any emergency room can be compared with values of the emergency rooms that are regarded as efficient. Later in this section we show how to convert a frequency table to a *relative frequency table* to facilitate such comparisons.

PRACTICE EXERCISE

2.1 The following data represent exam grades obtained by 45 students in an elementary statistics class:

72	70	60	85	78		100	55	76	100	37		25	71	76	80	17
96	70	51	100	91		98	72	69	58	25		91	70	84	70	98
85	50	100	47	49		67	58	56	66	93		31	60	83	93	62

a. Construct a frequency table using 9 equal sized class intervals. Start with a lower class limit of 15 for the first class.

b. It would also be correct to start with a lower class limit of 14 for the first class. Perform the tally for this second set of intervals and compare with the preceding solution.

CUMULATIVE FREQUENCY TABLE

It can be useful to know how many observations lie above a particular value or how many lie below a particular value. Adding together successive class frequencies allows us to determine the **cumulative frequency** for values that are "less than" or "more than" any particular value. A **cumulative frequency table** presents in tabular form the designated "less than" classes (or "more than" classes) with their corresponding cumulative frequencies. Look again at the excess waiting time data of Table 2.3. Here's how to construct the cumulative frequency table. Start with the lower class limit of the first class. We find no observation qualifies for the "less than −5" class; therefore, the cumulative frequency for the "less than −5" class is 0. With 3 observations in the next class, the cumulative frequency would be $0 + 3 = 3$ for the "less than 5" class. The cumulative frequency is $0 + 3 + 4 = 7$ for the "less than 15" class, and so on. Organizing the "less than" classes and their respective cumulative frequencies in a tabular form, we obtain the "less than" cumulative frequency table given in Table 2.4. The last "less than" class shows that all 200 observations have an excess waiting time less than 105 minutes.

TABLE 2.4 "Less than" Cumulative Frequency Table of Excess Patient Waiting Times	
LOWER CLASS LIMIT	**CUMULATIVE FREQUENCY**
Less than −5	0
Less than 5	3
Less than 15	7
Less than 25	14
Less than 35	44
Less than 45	76
Less than 55	125
Less than 65	157
Less than 75	178
Less than 85	190
Less than 95	198
Less than 105	200

PRACTICE EXERCISE

2.2 Construct a cumulative "less than" frequency table from the frequency table shown in the solution to Practice Exercise 2.1a.

RELATIVE FREQUENCY TABLE

Showing only the frequency in each interval may not be as desirable as showing the percentage, proportion, or **relative frequency** of items in each interval. This is especially true if we want to compare two hospitals in which the recorded total number of items are different. For example, suppose we want to draw a comparison between excess waiting times at two hospitals, A and B. It would be more informative to say that 24.5% of the excess waiting times in hospital A were in the 45–54 minute interval, while in hospital B, only 19% fell into the same interval than it would be if we said that 49 of 200 excess waiting times in hospital A and 57 of 300 times in hospital B were in the 45–54 minute interval. A percentage comparison in this case allows the relative performance to be seen easily.

A frequency table converts to a **relative frequency table** simply by dividing each class frequency by the total number of items. To express a relative frequency in percentage terms, simply multiply the relative frequency by 100. Table 2.5 shows comparable figures for both the relative frequency and percentage relative frequency.

TABLE 2.5 Relative Frequency Distribution of 200 Recordings on Excess Patient Waiting Time at a Hospital Emergency Room (Nearest Minute)			
CLASS INTERVAL	**FREQUENCY**	**RELATIVE FREQUENCY**	**% RELATIVE FREQUENCY**
−5– 4	3	$(3 \div 200) = .015$	$(.015 \times 100) = $ 1.5
5– 14	4	.020	2.0
15– 24	7	.035	3.5
25– 34	30	.150	15.0
35– 44	32	.160	16.0
45– 54	49	.245	24.5
55– 64	32	.160	16.0
65– 74	21	.105	10.5
75– 84	12	.060	6.0
85– 94	8	.040	4.0
95–104	2	.010	1.0

PRACTICE EXERCISE

2.3 Using the solution of Practice Exercise 2.1a, construct a relative frequency table including the percentage relative frequency.

CUMULATIVE RELATIVE FREQUENCY TABLE

To construct a **cumulative relative frequency table** from a cumulative frequency table, divide each cumulative frequency in the cumulative frequency table by the total number of observations. Table 2.6 was constructed from the cumulative frequency table given in Table 2.4.

TABLE 2.6 Cumulative Relative Frequency Distribution of 200 Recordings on Excess Patient Waiting Time at a Hospital Emergency Room (Nearest Minute)			
LOWER LIMIT OF CLASS INTERVAL	**CUMULATIVE FREQUENCY**	**CUMULATIVE RELATIVE FREQUENCY**	**% CUMULATIVE RELATIVE FREQUENCY**
Less than −5	0	.000	0.0
Less than 5	3	$(3 \div 200) = $ .015	$(.015 \times 100) = $ 1.5
Less than 15	7	.035	3.5
Less than 25	14	.070	7.0
Less than 35	44	.220	22.0
Less than 45	76	.380	38.0
Less than 55	125	.625	62.5
Less than 65	157	.785	78.5
Less than 75	178	.890	89.0
Less than 85	190	.950	95.0
Less than 95	198	.990	99.0
Less than 105	200	1.000	100.0

• •

PRACTICE
EXERCISE

2.4 Construct a cumulative "less than" relative frequency table from the solution shown in Practice Exercise 2.2.

• •

AN EXCEPTION TO EQUAL SIZED INTERVALS

It is generally more difficult to analyze the frequency across unequal class intervals, so equal sized intervals should be used whenever possible. Some circumstances, however, warrant the use of unequal sized intervals. For instance, suppose the range of the values is large, and yet the data are concentrated at one end of the range. The distribution of such data is said to be highly **skewed**. One example of a skewed distribution is shown in Table 2.7, which lists the annual salaries of 36 wage earners surveyed in San Diego.

TABLE 2.7 Reported Annual Salaries (in Dollars) of 36 Surveyed San Diego Workers					
71,893	5,563	26,843	16,919	11,761	14,470
8,254	36,429	17,713	33,101	24,530	41,730
53,544	14,320	32,903	20,356	66,805	21,359
20,215	15,075	44,114	26,888	90,095	29,791
177,388	21,287	25,410	20,083	13,269	17,151
18,829	19,647	26,591	10,503	18,346	15,428

Looking over the data in Table 2.7, we see that the largest value is $L = \$177,388$, the smallest value is $S = \$5563$, and the range is $R = L - S = \$177,388 - \$5563 = \$171,825$. Suppose we specify 10 equal sized intervals over the range. Then each interval length should equal $17,182.5$. With a slight adjustment to a more convenient value, we have an interval length of $\$17,190$. If we start at $\$5501$ as the lower class limit for the first interval, we get the frequency distribution shown in Table 2.8.

TABLE 2.8 Frequency Table of Reported Annual Salaries of 36 Surveyed San Diego Workers			
LOWER CLASS LIMIT	UPPER CLASS LIMIT	TALLY	CLASS FREQUENCY
5,501	22,690	╫╫ ╫╫ ╫╫ ╫╫	20
22,691	39,880	╫╫ ‖‖‖‖	9
39,881	57,070	‖‖‖	3
57,071	74,260	‖‖	2
74,261	91,450	‖	1
91,451	108,640		0
108,641	125,830		0
125,831	143,020		0
143,021	160,210		0
160,211	177,400	‖	1

The class frequencies show that practically all the observations lie in the first 5 class intervals. Because of one extreme observation, the sixth through ninth class intervals are empty. The combination of a heavy concentration of items in the first 2 intervals along with empty intervals 6–9 indicates that using 10 equal sized intervals is not appropriate in this case.

Suppose that instead of constructing 10 equal sized intervals to cover the entire range, we set up 9 equal sized intervals and 1 additional interval that is open-ended; that is, there will be no upper limit on the highest class. The 9 equal sized intervals can accommodate the bulk of the observations, which presently lie in the first 5 intervals. The tenth and last interval will be open-ended to accommodate the one extreme value. Now we use $L^* = \$90,095$, the largest value in what was originally the fifth interval, as a plausible alternate "largest value" and calculate the modified range, $R^* = \$90,095 - \$5563 = \$84,532$. Using the modified range, we find the interval length to be $\$84,532 \div 9 = \$9392.44$, which we round up to $\$9400$ for convenience. Thus, the lower limit of the first interval is $\$5501$ as before, and the upper limit of the ninth interval is $\$90,100$. The tenth interval includes all values greater than $\$90,100$ (in this particular example the only value in this tenth interval would be $\$177,388$). In conclusion, we can say that:

1. Equal sized intervals are preferred in classifying the data.
2. One open-ended interval is often helpful in classifying extreme observations.

The modified, or open-ended, frequency table constructed is shown in Table 2.9.

TABLE 2.9 Modified Frequency Table of Reported Annual Salaries of 36 Surveyed San Diego Workers			
LOWER CLASS LIMIT	**UPPER CLASS LIMIT**	**TALLY**	**CLASS FREQUENCY**
5,501	14,900	‖‖ ‖	7
14,901	24,300	‖‖ ‖‖ ‖‖‖	13
24,301	33,700	‖‖ ‖‖‖	8
33,701	43,100	‖	2
43,101	52,500	‖	1
52,501	61,900	‖	1
61,901	71,300	‖	1
71,301	80,700	‖	1
80,701	90,100	‖	1
90,101 or more		‖	1

Table 2.9 clearly shows that incomes are highly concentrated in the second class, $14,901–$24,300, with a sharp frequency falloff for incomes higher than $33,700. A drawback of having an open-ended class interval in a frequency table is that there is no way to surmise the magnitude of the value of the one income placed in the last class.

One acceptable way to avoid using an open-ended class is to simply list the extreme values separately. To do this for the distribution in Table 2.9 means dropping the interval "90,101 or more" and reporting the extreme value $177,388. This type of reporting permits the reader to inquire further into possible explanations for the extreme value's occurrence and magnitude.

• •

PRACTICE EXERCISE

2.5 The following data represent, for 40 precincts, the percentage of registered voters (to the nearest percent) who voted in the last election:

49	35	7	32	29	98	30	27	26	16
44	24	35	27	33	45	27	31	14	35
38	31	40	32	39	2	36	7	36	6
13	19	38	20	6	29	9	29	38	48

Construct a frequency table using 8 equal sized intervals plus 1 open-ended interval.

• •

ROUNDED MEASUREMENTS

Recorded values are often rounded up or rounded down values of the original values that actually occurred. Nevertheless, the lower and upper limits of a class interval are always constructed from the recorded values. This means that when the recorded values are rounded values the stated class limits do not define the boundaries for the original (unrounded) values that are in the interval. For example, consider the data on emergency room waiting times in Table 2.2. These data have been rounded to the nearest minute; an actual waiting time between 4 and 5 minutes would be rounded up and recorded as 5 minutes or rounded down and recorded as 4 minutes, depending on which integer the actual value was closer to. By convention, the integer 4 is the rounded value for actual values from 3.5 up to but not including 4.5. The integer 5 is the rounded value for actual values from 4.5 up to but not including 5.5.

Because of the gaps between the upper class limit of one class interval and the lower class limit of the next, the values 4.5, 14.5, . . . , 94.5 are the true end points dividing the classes. These end points are called the **class boundaries**. The upper class boundary of the first class extends up to 4.5, a half unit above the stated upper class limit; the lower class boundary of this first class will begin at −5.5, a half unit below the stated lower class limit of −5. Likewise, the upper class boundary for the last class will extend up to 104.5, a half unit above the stated upper class limit of 104. Beginning with the first class, the complete set of class boundaries consists of the pairs: −5.5 up to 4.5, 4.5 up to 14.5, 14.5 up to 24.5, . . . , 94.5 up to 104.5. Also, by looking at our previously stated class intervals, you can now see that the lower class limit for each interval is the rounded up lower class boundary of that interval; likewise the upper class limit is the rounded down upper class boundary.

• •

EXERCISES   ❑ ▶ 2.1 An agency that advocates consumer rights assigns one of its personnel to look at what is happening with variable interest rate home equity loans. According to a procedure that is prevalent in the industry, payments are made monthly and the variable interest rate is changed quarterly in concert with the market rate in effect at the beginning of each quarter. Also, the interest charge for the month is calculated by first dividing the current interest rate by 365 days (to put the interest rate on a per day basis), and then multiplying the result by the number of days in the billing period and by the average principal during the billing period. In terms of a formula, this would read:

$$\text{Interest charge} = \left(\frac{\text{Current interest rate}}{365}\right)\left(\begin{array}{c}\text{Number}\\\text{of days}\end{array}\right)\left(\begin{array}{c}\text{Average}\\\text{principal}\end{array}\right)$$

The consumer's bill shows the values for the current interest rate, the number of days in the billing period, and the average principal during the billing period.

The consumer advocate sends out a mailer to 430 persons who have either contributed funds to the agency or have answered prior consumer questionnaires. In the mailer the investigator asks if the respondent has taken out a variable rate home equity loan and, if so, to please mail a copy of one month's billing statement to the agency. In all, 47 billing statements are received from 47 different respondents. To analyze the data, the investigator records the actual interest charged the respondent and then calculates the interest that should be charged according to the information on the bill, using the interest charge formula. The difference in these two values is then obtained by subtracting the interest that should be charged from the actual interest charged. If the difference is positive, the consumer has been overcharged; if the difference is negative, the consumer has been undercharged. The raw data on the interest differences (in actual dollars and cents) follow:

6.90	6.28	6.33	5.63	5.25		8.18	8.11	5.20	6.13	8.17
6.25	7.62	7.06	4.78	7.32		5.62	6.29	5.64	6.97	7.30
6.45	5.67	6.39	6.42	5.28		5.00	7.80	5.22	7.20	5.95
5.79	6.28	7.76	5.84	8.63		4.42	6.33	5.12	5.61	6.96
5.55	6.15	6.19	6.83	5.13		4.50	7.79			

a. Construct a frequency table using 7 intervals; start with a lower class boundary of 4.085.
b. Construct a cumulative "less than" frequency table from the frequency table in part a.
c. Construct a relative frequency table from the frequency table in part a.
d. Construct a cumulative "less than" relative frequency table from the table in part b or the table in part c.
e. When you examine your constructions in parts a–d, what impression(s) do you get?

□ 2.2 Newly developed techniques in the field of genetic engineering provide a wide variety of potential economic applications. In one particular study, a gene that controls growth in rainbow trout was introduced into 21 catfish. Normally, this variety of catfish reaches full growth in 18 months. If the introduction of this growth gene into the catfish could speed up its growth, it would be a boon to catfish farmers and to consumers. The lengths of time (in months) it took the 21 catfish to reach full growth are given below.

15.9	7.6	11.3	15.4		13.9	10.6	11.6	13.1
13.1	10.6	10.8	13.2		12.2	9.7	10.8	9.4
9.8	11.4	14.8	16.5		16.8			

a. Construct a frequency table using 5 intervals; start with a lower class limit of 7.6.
b. Construct a cumulative "less than" frequency table from the frequency table in part a.
c. Construct a relative frequency table from the frequency table in part a.
d. Construct a cumulative "less than" relative frequency table from the table in part b or the table in part c.
e. When you examine your constructions in parts a–d, what impression(s) do you get?

□ 2.3 The professional resume services industry wants to promote resume writing services among "yuppies," young, urban, professionally oriented persons. A spokesperson for the industry claims that yuppies seeking jobs in their professions have very high success rates when their resumes are designed, written, and printed by professional resume services. A survey company is hired to determine the proportions of yuppies who got jobs in their professions using resumes composed by professional resume services. The survey company looked at 37 different professional fields. The young professional people working in these fields were asked if they had used a resume service. The results, showing the percent of young working professionals who used a resume service, are given below.

89.7	90.3	61.4	60.9	97.2	73.2	69.5	94.6	65.9	76.1
99.6	83.8	69.1	97.7	68.4	90.9	76.2	70.7	88.3	61.7
70.5	60.9	63.0	54.2	87.1	92.0	73.2	67.9	67.6	78.7
61.3	73.3	67.9	38.3	62.8	80.5	56.6			

a. Construct a frequency table using 6 intervals; start with a lower class limit of 36.9.
b. Construct a cumulative "less than" frequency table from the frequency table in part a.
c. Construct a relative frequency table from the frequency table in part a.
d. Construct a cumulative "less than" relative frequency table from the table in part b or the table in part c.
e. When you examine your constructions in parts a–d, what impression(s) do you get?

● ●

2.2
FREQUENCY CURVES

The intent of a graph or a diagram is to obtain a visual image of the variation in data values. Two types of graphs that may be constructed from frequency tables are *frequency polygons* and *ogives*.

FREQUENCY POLYGONS

A **frequency polygon** is a line graph representation of a frequency table. It is developed by plotting the class midpoints and the respective frequencies of the class intervals. Follow this procedure:

Step 1
On a sheet of graph paper, mark midpoints on the horizontal axis.

Step 2
Scale the vertical axis for the frequencies.

Step 3
Above each class midpoint, plot a point whose height represents the frequency of that class.

Step 4
Join the points with straight line segments.

Step 5
Connect the line drawing to the horizontal axis by setting two additional class midpoints, one above and one below the existing midpoints.

Here's how to construct a frequency polygon from Table 2.3, the frequency table for excess patient waiting times. Table 2.10 shows the class midpoints and frequencies taken from Table 2.3.

TABLE 2.10 Modified Frequency Table of Excess Patient Waiting Times	
CLASS MIDPOINT	**CLASS FREQUENCY**
−0.5	3
9.5	4
19.5	7
29.5	30
39.5	32
49.5	49
59.5	32
69.5	21
79.5	12
89.5	8
99.5	2

Mark off the class midpoints on the horizontal axis. Above each midpoint put a dot at the height representing the class frequency, and connect the dots. Now go to the left side of the horizontal axis. Additionally, mark off −10.5; this is the class midpoint of the interval that precedes our first stated interval. Draw a line that connects the −10.5 point on the horizontal axis and the first midpoint dot. On the right side of the horizontal axis mark off 109.5, the class midpoint of the interval that follows our last stated interval. Connect by a line the horizontal axis from this point and the last midpoint dot. The two new lines anchor the tails of the frequency polygon to the horizontal axis. The resultant frequency polygon is shown in Figure 2.1.

Figure 2.1
Frequency polygon of excess patient waiting times

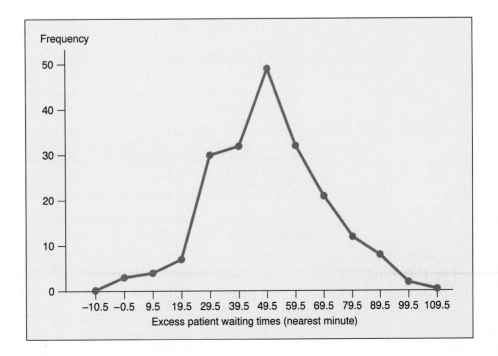

Figure 2.2
Ogive of excess patient waiting times

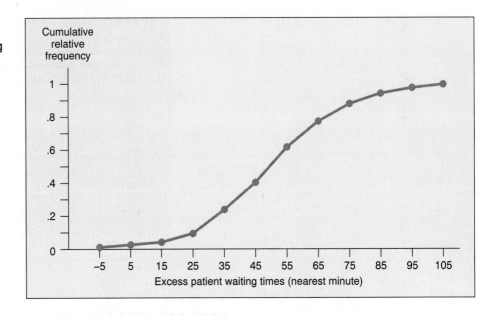

2.6 From the solution to Practice Exercise 2.1a, construct a frequency polygon.

OGIVES

An **ogive** is a line graph representation of a "less than" cumulative frequency table or a "less than" cumulative relative frequency table. It is constructed by plotting the "less than" class limits and their respective cumulative frequencies or cumulative relative frequencies. Follow this procedure:

Step 1
On a sheet of graph paper, mark off the lower class limits on the horizontal axis.

Step 2
Mark the vertical axis for the cumulative frequencies or corresponding cumulative relative frequencies.

Step 3
Above each class limit on the horizontal axis, plot a point to represent the corresponding cumulative frequency or cumulative relative frequency.

Step 4
Join the plotted points with straight line segments.

The ogive from the "less than" cumulative relative frequency table of Table 2.6 is shown in Figure 2.2.

EXERCISES

2.4 Construct an ogive from the pairs of values in the solution of Practice Exercise 2.4.

▶ **2.5** Refer to Exercise 2.1, and use the data and results.
   a. Construct a frequency polygon.
   b. Construct an ogive.
   c. Examine your constructions in parts a and b. Do you get the same or similar impressions as you had in Exercise 2.1?

2.6 Refer to Exercise 2.2, and use the data and results.
   a. Construct a frequency polygon.
   b. Construct an ogive.
   c. Examine your constructions in parts a and b. Do you get the same or similar impressions as you had in Exercise 2.2?

2.7 Refer to Exercise 2.3, and use the data and results.
   a. Construct a frequency polygon.
   b. Construct an ogive.
   c. Examine your constructions in parts a and b. Do you get the same or similar impressions as you had in Exercise 2.3?

2.3

OTHER GRAPHICAL AND PICTORIAL REPRESENTATIONS

Computer graphics have revolutionized the publication industry. Magazines, newspapers, and government, industrial, management, and scientific reports increasingly use a wide and varied array of graphical and pictorial representations to summarize data. Four popular types are *histograms*, *bar charts*, *pie charts*, and *three-dimensional graphs*. The type of graphical representation chosen in a given situation is generally dictated by taste or convenience. We should, however, be careful that the representation be accurate and without distortion.

HISTOGRAMS

A **histogram** is a bar graph representation that is plotted using the class boundaries and respective frequencies from a frequency table. Construct a histogram in the following way:

Step 1
On a sheet of graph paper, use the class boundaries to mark off class intervals on the horizontal axis.

Step 2
Fill each class interval with a vertical bar so that the height of the bar equals the corresponding class frequency.

The histogram in Figure 2.3 is constructed from the class boundaries and frequencies for the excess patient waiting time data presented in Table 2.3.

BAR CHARTS

A **bar chart** is a histogram with the bars separated. The bars are placed over the intervals designated by the class limits, not the class boundaries. Bar charts can be shown in a horizontal or vertical position. Figure 2.4 is a vertical bar chart and Figure 2.5 is a horizontal bar chart for the excess patient waiting time data.

Discrete versus Continuous Variables

In deciding whether to use a bar chart or a histogram, consider the type of variable on which measurements are recorded. A variable can assume values from either a discrete scale or a continuous scale. For example, the number of nurses absent daily

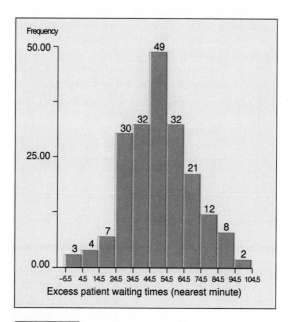

Figure 2.3
Histogram of excess patient
waiting times

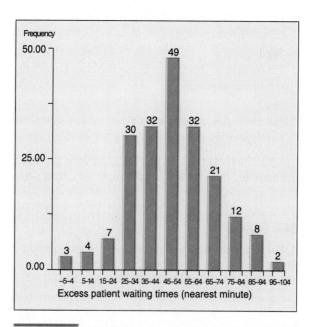

Figure 2.4
Vertical bar chart of excess
patient waiting times

Figure 2.5
Horizontal bar chart of excess patient waiting times

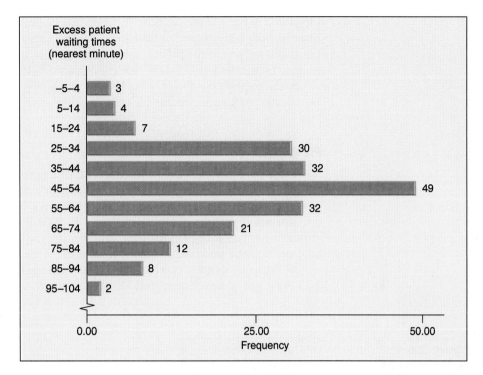

in a hospital would be a discrete variable; the possible values of the variable would be only integers, since you couldn't have 13.79 nurses absent. The values of a discrete variable change in discrete steps or jumps. For discrete variables, bar graphs are appropriate (remember that bar graphs should show a gap between intervals). Continuous variables, on the other hand, are measured on a continuous scale. For example, the excess patient waiting time data is measured on a time scale, and time is a continuous scale. Frequency distributions for continuous variables should be represented by a histogram.

Categorical Variables

Up to this point all the data considered have been based on variables that are quantitative in nature: each observation has been a number. Quantitative variables distinguish objects according to some numerical characteristic. For example, people waiting in line at the bank for 1 minute, 2 minutes, or 3 minutes have waiting time in line as a quantitative (variable) characteristic. Qualitative, or categorical, variables, on the other hand, provide only nonnumeric descriptions, that is, names or labels that identify the category to which the item belongs. Brand of tire purchased, a person's gender, and one's favorite NFL football team are qualitative variables. For example, the people who go to see the Chargers, Giants, or Dolphins play have the names of NFL football teams as a categorical variable and may be described as Charger, Giant, or Dolphin fans, respectively.

When the data are recordings of a categorical variable (e.g., monthly unit sales of types of tires, weekly production of makes of automobiles), bar graphs are particularly appropriate. Sometimes in these cases caricatures of the described items (such as dollars, tires, people, or factories) are used, with the size of the caricature representing the proportion of items in the category. In the not too distant past, bar graph construction required both patience and at least some minimal degree of graphical skills. Today, bar graphs are generated routinely using spreadsheet or graphics software for personal computers (such as Lotus 1-2-3™, Excel™, Quattro™, Harvard Graphics™).

A bar graph is not the only method for graphically presenting categorical data. Frequently, you'll encounter the pie chart, an alternative to the bar graph.

PIE CHARTS

A **pie chart** is a pictorial device that conveys the proportion of the recorded data that falls in each category. The pie chart in Figure 2.6, for example, shows the proportions of various ethnic groups in a certain large city. Figure 2.7 presents two pie charts that compare actual proportional computer usage in 1988 in one pie and projected proportional computer usage in 2000 in the other. In such comparisons, the pie chart approach is useful since the sizes of the sections of the pies give a quick visual overview of how computer usage is expected to grow and change from 1988 to 2000. Exercise 2.35 at the end of this chapter gives a general approach to construction of a pie chart.

Figure 2.6
Pie chart showing the proportions of various ethnic groups in a certain large city

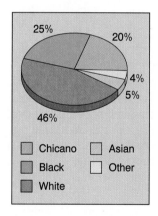

Figure 2.7
Actual 1988 and projected 2000 total value of worldwide shipments by U.S. manufacturers and market share of computer categories

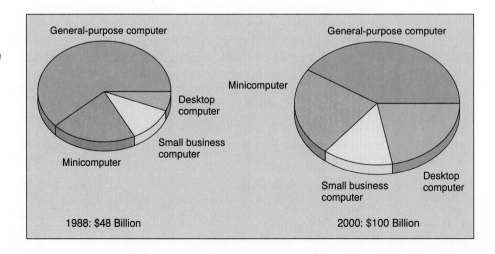

However, as a practical matter, pie charts, like bar graphs, are routinely generated by spreadsheet or graphics software for personal computers.

THREE-DIMENSIONAL GRAPHS

Three-dimensional histograms are used to portray how two variables are jointly related to the frequency of a third variable. For example, consider a manufacturer of automobile brake linings testing a sample of 407 linings. The manufacturer may wish to show how miles traveled and years in use are jointly related to the frequency of failures. The manufacturer's test results of this relationship are shown in Figure 2.8.

FLOWCHARTS

Planning the statistical analysis of a data set requires making several choices, including which device to use in organizing and presenting data. The choices and the sequence of the various steps in the process can be sketched as a flowchart as shown in Figure 2.9.

Figure 2.8
Three-dimensional graph showing frequency of brake lining failure (wearout) as it relates to time in use and to miles traveled

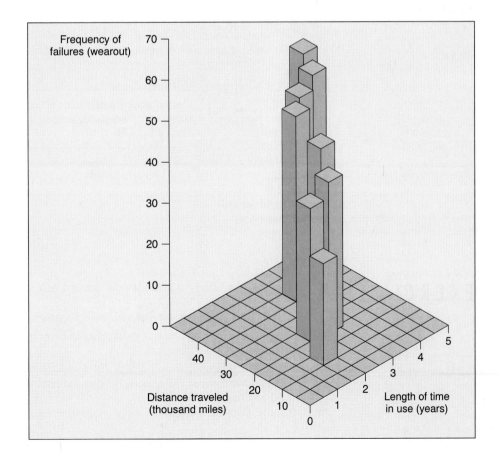

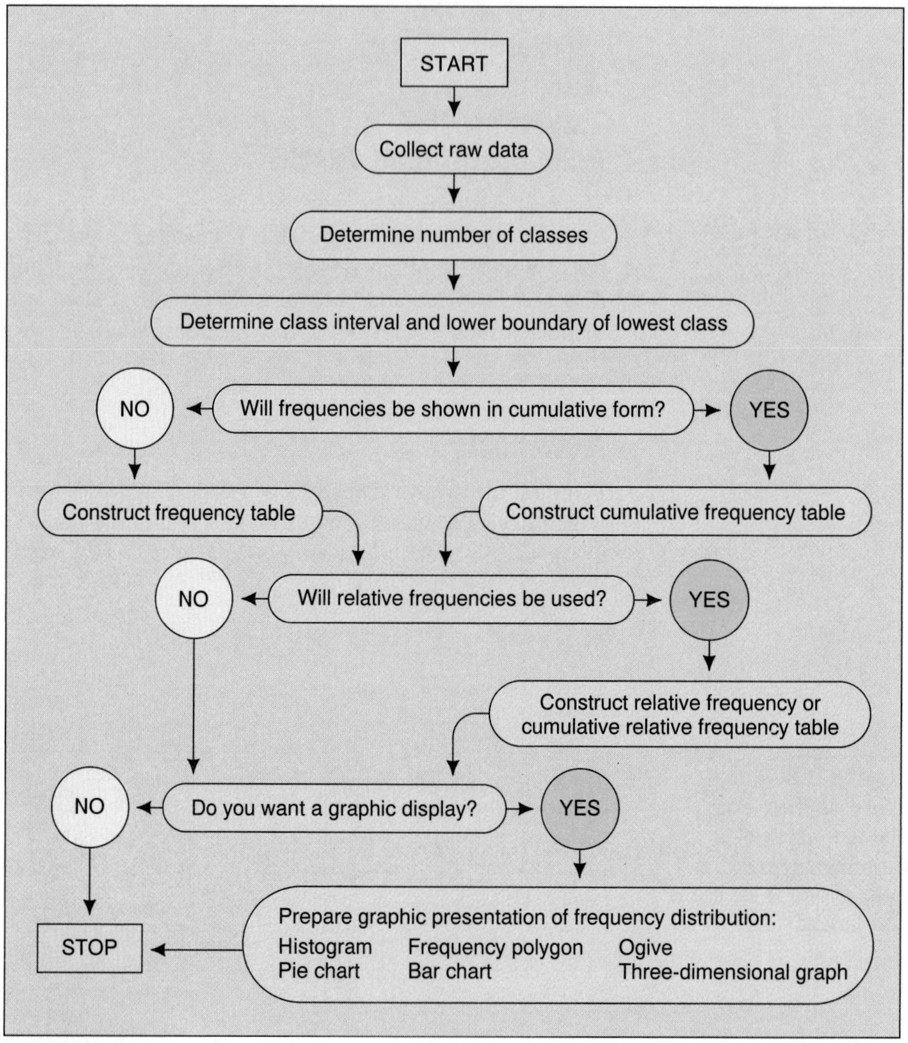

Figure 2.9
Flowchart for tabular and
graphical presentations

• •

EXERCISES ❏ ▶ **2.8** Refer to Exercise 2.1, and use the data and results.
a. Construct a histogram.
b. Does the histogram alter your earlier impressions? Why?

❏ **2.9** Refer to Exercise 2.2, and use the data and results.
a. Construct a histogram.
b. Does the histogram alter your earlier impressions? Why?

❏ **2.10** Refer to Exercise 2.3, and use the data and results.
a. Construct a histogram.
b. Does the histogram alter your earlier impressions? Why?

• •

2.4
EXPLORATORY DATA ANALYSIS

To assist in examining data, the traditional graphical methods for analyzing data have recently been supplemented by a new class of techniques referred to as **exploratory data analysis (EDA)**. Two of the most popular of these techniques are the *stem-and-leaf display* and the *boxplot*, or *box-and-whiskers plot*.

STEM-AND-LEAF DISPLAY

A **stem-and-leaf display** is a graphical device that has features similar to the histogram but with an additional attractive feature. First, the data are grouped into classes, and then tallies are made of the class frequencies. When graphed, however, the bars are formed by stacking side by side the actual integer values of the original observations. This feature allows us to retrieve the values of the original observations.

The classes of a stem-and-leaf display are generally designated by one- or two-digit values listed vertically in a column on the left-hand side of the display. The digits of each class represent the number of tens, hundreds, or thousands in each data recording. For example, data recordings with three-digit numbers ranging from 100 to 250 would use 10, 11, 12, . . . , 25 class integers to represent the number of tens in each recording. These class integers are the "stem" of the stem-and-leaf display. Each recording falls in one and only one of the listed classes. Once the data recording class is specified, the last digit is plotted horizontally in line with that class. For example, a data value of 114 would be plotted as a 4 in line with class 11; a value of 200 would be plotted as a 0 in line with class 20. The string of last digits shows up as a horizontal bar; the values comprising the bar are plotted according to sequence of occurrence or according to magnitude. The digits in the bars constitute the "leaves" of the stem-and-leaf display.

The stem-and-leaf display shown in Figure 2.10 is for the excess waiting time data given in Table 2.2. It was constructed as follows:

1. Since the data values range from 0 to 100, integer values from 0 through 10 serve as the tens classes and are listed to the left of the vertical line.
2. The last digit on each recording forms the horizontal bar in line with the class. The first data value, 39, has 3 tens so its last digit, 9, is placed in class 3; the second value, 40, requires a 0 in line with class 4; the third value, 100, requires a 0 in line with class 10; and so on.

Figure 2.10
Stem-and-leaf plot of excess patient waiting times

```
 0 | 06109
 1 | 4552
 2 | 655349769255373996
 3 | 9906623381745316166326670 11422
 4 | 07150946968619948603818756121458411990329
 5 | 3049612131231374620189210459810543291680
 6 | 0309634842161926417059403280 29
 7 | 2963489034838196741
 8 | 8519109775
 9 | 27
10 | 0
```

Some data sets require judgment and flexibility in constructing a stem-and-leaf display. Suppose we wish to construct a stem-and-leaf display for the following data:

71.27	64.01	43.74	34.51	56.29
59.68	95.01	65.20	2.11	0.88
89.36	99.78	92.02	82.86	11.28
68.67	24.88	21.74	46.90	92.68
98.74	11.46	76.97	67.35	34.08

The values cover a very broad range from a minimum of 0.88 to a maximum of 99.78. To attempt to deal with these values in the manner just described would require a stem-and-leaf display that would be too long and too dispersed to be effective. One possible solution would be to ignore the decimal portion of each value, form 10 classes ranging from 0 to 9 to the left of the vertical line, and use the units digit to form the horizontal bars. The resultant stem-and-leaf plot effectively presents the range and concentration of the data:

0	20
1	11
2	41
3	44
4	36
5	96
6	8457
7	16
8	92
9	85922

Depending on the range of values in the data set, several stem-and-leaf displays are possible and acceptable in portraying the variation of the data recording. A major feature of the stem-and-leaf plot is the recovery of the original data.

PRACTICE EXERCISE

2.7 The following data represent exam grades obtained by 45 students in an elementary statistics class:

72	70	60	85	78	100	55	76	100	37	25	71	76	80	17
96	70	51	100	91	98	72	69	58	25	91	70	84	70	98
85	50	100	47	49	67	58	56	66	93	31	60	83	93	62

Construct a stem-and-leaf plot.

MEASURES OF RELATIVE POSITION: PERCENTILES, QUARTILES, AND THE FIVE-NUMBER SUMMARY

Percentiles

Percentiles, like ranks, indicate the relative positions of data values within a distribution. But percentiles use percentages from 0% to 100% with the ranking scale starting at the smallest number. So the 0th percentile starts at the smallest number and the 100th percentile ends at the largest. There are three things to remember about percentiles:

1. A percentile is a number used to specify rank, measured in the same units as values in the data set. For the excess patient waiting time example, all percentiles would be measured in minutes of excess waiting time.
2. A percentile can be used to find the data value at a given percentage ranking, as in "the 50th percentile is 49 minutes" (see Figure 2.11).
3. A percentile also can be used to indicate the percentage ranking of a given data value, as in "the excess waiting time of hospital H, 65 minutes, was in the 75th percentile" (see Figure 2.11).

An ogive constructed by plotting cumulative percentage relative frequencies on the vertical axis and the data values on the horizontal axis is a useful device for finding percentiles. Figure 2.11 shows the percentage ogive constructed from the cumulative relative frequency distribution given in Table 2.6. Figure 2.11 is identical to Figure 2.2 except that values on the vertical axis have been multiplied by 100. Percentiles displayed in this figure are approximate, since the ogive is constructed from grouped data.

Finding the approximate percentile ranking for a given number is easy:

Step 1
Find the data value along the horizontal axis.

Step 2
Move vertically up to meet the ogive.

Step 3
Move horizontally to the left, and read the percentile ranking.

In the example shown in Figure 2.11, the number 49 is the 50th percentile.

Finding the approximate value for a given percentile ranking is just as easy:

Step 1
Find the percentage along the vertical axis.

Step 2
Move right horizontally to the ogive.

Step 3
Move straight down, and read the number on the horizontal axis.

In the example shown in Figure 2.12, the 25th percentile is 37.

Quartiles

Certain percentiles can be very useful in describing the shape of the frequency distribution. For example, the 25th, 50th, and 75th percentiles are often used for this purpose. These three specific percentiles are referred to as the first, second, and third **quartiles**, Q_1, Q_2, and Q_3, of the frequency distribution. The quartiles represent the values at the three positions that divide the number of observations of the distribution into quarters.

To compute approximate quartiles from a data array, the following procedure may

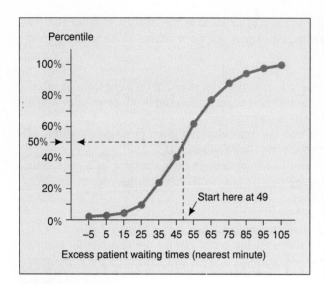

Figure 2.11
Locating the approximate
percentile for a given number

Figure 2.12
Locating the approximate
number for a given percentile

be used (the letter N is used to define the population size, and the letter n is used to define the sample size):

Step 1
Locate the positions for Q_1, Q_2, and Q_3 as follows:

Quartile	Population	Sample
1	$\dfrac{N + 1}{4}$	$\dfrac{n + 1}{4}$
2	$\dfrac{2(N + 1)}{4}$	$\dfrac{2(n + 1)}{4}$
3	$\dfrac{3(N + 1)}{4}$	$\dfrac{3(n + 1)}{4}$

Step 2
Determine the quartile values by applying the following rules:

a. If the quartile position is found to be an integer, then the quartile value is the numerical value of the particular observation at that position.
b. If the quartile value is found to be halfway between two integer positions, then the quartile value is the average of the numerical values for the two observations at the two integer positions.
c. If the quartile value is found to be neither an integer nor a value halfway between two other integer positions, then round off the quartile position to the nearest integer and let the numerical value of the particular observation at that position be the quartile value.

Using the salary data given in Table 2.7 on 36 San Diego workers, we proceed as follows:

Step 1

First, arrange the observations starting with the lowest salary and ending with the highest salary. The array would be:

5,563	8,254	10,503	11,762	13,269	14,320
14,470	15,075	15,428	16,919	17,151	17,713
18,346	18,829	19,647	20,083	20,215	20,356
21,287	21,359	24,530	25,410	26,591	26,843
26,888	29,791	32,903	33,101	36,429	41,730
44,114	53,544	66,805	71,893	90,095	177,388

Now, determine the quartile positions:

$$\frac{36 + 1}{4} = 9.25 \quad \rightarrow \text{9th position in the array}$$

$$\frac{2(36 + 1)}{4} = 18.50 \quad \rightarrow \text{between 18th and 19th positions in the array}$$

$$\frac{3(36 + 1)}{4} = 27.75 \quad \rightarrow \text{28th position in the array}$$

Step 2

Determine the quartile values: The 9th numerical value of annual salary, starting from the lowest, is \$15,428, so \$15,428 is the first quartile value, Q_1. The value of Q_2 is the average of the values at the 18th and 19th positions, that is,

$$\frac{\$20,356 + \$21,287}{2} = \$20,821.50$$

The 28th numerical value of salary is \$33,101, so \$33,101 is the third quartile value, Q_3.

Five-Number Summary

When the two extreme values of a distribution (i.e., the smallest value and the largest value) are reported along with the three quartiles, we have a set of positional values known as the **five-number summary**. Each of these five numbers gives some perspective about the raw data. The two extreme values indicate the range of values spanned by the data; the second quartile indicates the center of the data; the first and third quartiles define the location of the "middle half" of the data. Taken together they provide a thumbnail sketch of the main features of the data. For the salary data given in Table 2.7, the five-number summary is 5,563, 15,428, 20,821.50, 33,101, 177,388. That is, 5,563 is the smallest value of the range; 15,428 is Q_1; 20,821.50 is Q_2, the center of the data; 33,101 is Q_3; and 177,388 is the largest value of the range. The middle half of the values range from 15,428 to 33,101.

BOXPLOTS, OR BOX-AND-WHISKERS PLOTS

A **boxplot**, or **box-and-whiskers plot**, is another graphical EDA device designed to show the range and concentration of the data. In its simplest form a boxplot is a graphical presentation of the five-number summary. It consists of a box with dashed lines (whiskers) that extend out from the left and right sides of the box. The purpose of this display is to divide the data recordings into three groups: the lower 25% group, the middle 50% group, and the upper 25% group. Since the format is standard for every boxplot, comparisons give a quick visual assessment of the differences in range and concentration for various distributions of data.

The box itself portrays the range and concentration of the middle 50% group. The placement and length of the box show the location and concentration, respectively, of the middle 50% group recordings; the smaller the length of the box, the greater the concentration. The left whisker represents the range of the data recordings for the lower 25% group, and the right whisker represents the upper 25% group. The shorter the whiskers, the more concentrated are the data values for the group. A long whisker is an indication of a wide dispersion of values for that 25% group. A vertical slash (or plus sign) placed in the box designates the value that splits the middle 50% group into its two 25% subgroupings. If the slash (or plus sign) appears in the middle of the box, creating two equal sized inner boxes, it indicates that the two inner 25% groupings are distributed symmetrically.

Figure 2.13 shows boxplots corresponding to six different shapes of frequency polygons. Notice how the location of the box changes as the direction of skewness changes. Notice also that the width of the box increases as the dispersion of the distribution increases.

Constructing Box-and-Whiskers Plots

Using the five-number summary to construct a box-and-whisker plot, proceed as follows:

Step 1
On the horizontal axis, plot the values of the variable under study.

Step 2
Draw a box on the horizontal axis such that the left end of the box is aligned

Figure 2.13
Boxplots describing various frequency polygons

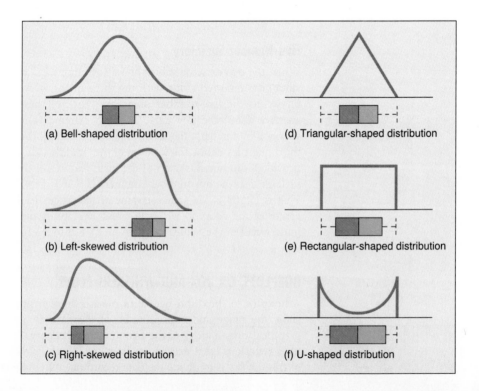

(a) Bell-shaped distribution

(b) Left-skewed distribution

(c) Right-skewed distribution

(d) Triangular-shaped distribution

(e) Rectangular-shaped distribution

(f) U-shaped distribution

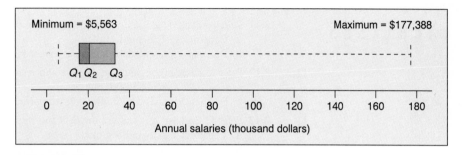

Figure 2.14
Boxplot for annual salary data for San Diego workers;
$Q_1 = \$15,428,$
$Q_2 = \$20,821.50,$
$Q_3 = \$33,101$

with the first quartile, Q_1, and the right end of the box is aligned with the third quartile, Q_3.

Step 3
Split the box with a vertical line at Q_2, the center of the data set.

Step 4
Extend a line (a whisker) from the left end of the box to a point that aligns with the smallest value in the data set.

Step 5
Lastly, extend another line (or whisker) from the right end of the box to a point that aligns with the largest value in the data set.

Figure 2.14 illustrates the boxplot constructed from the five-number summary for the annual salary data in Table 2.7. Note that the vertical mark inside the box is much closer to the left side of the box than to the right side. This shows that the data recordings for the two inner 25% groups are not equally balanced. Finding the two whiskers unequal in length also suggests a lack of symmetry for the outer groups. Had there been symmetry, we would have found whiskers of approximately equal length and a box mark nearly in the middle of the box. Since we found a long inner box on the right side and a long whisker on the right side, we can conclude that the distribution of data recordings is highly skewed to the right side.

PRACTICE EXERCISE

2.8 The following data represent exam grades obtained by 45 students in an elementary statistics class:

72	70	60	85	78	100	55	76	100	37	25	71	76	80	17
96	70	51	100	91	98	72	69	58	25	91	70	84	70	98
85	50	100	47	49	67	58	56	66	93	31	60	83	93	62

a. Find the quartiles of the distribution.
b. Give the five-number summary for the data.
c. Construct the boxplot.

● ●

EXERCISES

▶ **2.11** Refer to Exercise 2.1, and use the data and results.
   a. Construct a stem-and-leaf plot.
   b. Do these representations alter your earlier impressions? Why?

□ **2.12** Refer to Exercise 2.2, and use the data and results.
   a. Construct a stem-and-leaf plot.
   b. Do these representations alter your earlier impressions? Why?

□ **2.13** Refer to Exercise 2.3, and use the data and results.
   a. Construct a stem-and-leaf plot.
   b. Do these representations alter your earlier impressions? Why?

● ●

2.5

SAMPLE COMPUTER OUTPUT

A variety of computer software packages are specifically designed to manipulate data and perform statistical analyses. MINITAB, SYSTAT, SAS, and SPSS are some of the most popular packages. Many are now available for personal computers as well as for mainframe computers (e.g., business MYSTAT is a personal computer version of SYSTAT). General-purpose data manipulation software, such as Lotus 1-2-3, offer excellent graphical capabilities for preparing charts and graphs, even though their statistical analysis capabilities may be limited.

Terminology and features of the statistical software packages are not standardized. While each package aims to be "user-friendly," differences in nomenclature for the same operation make it difficult to switch back and forth between packages. However, MINITAB output can be read by Lotus 1-2-3, so it is possible to combine the statistical analysis power of MINITAB with the graphical capabilities of Lotus.

Computer pictures of boxplots can be more informative than the simple boxplots described in the preceding section. For instance, the whiskers of computer boxplots are not set to extend to the extreme values (called **outliers**) of the upper and lower 25% groupings. Instead, the whiskers extend only as far as the greatest concentration of the upper and lower 25% groupings. Detailed **boxplots** of this kind typically have whiskers that extend from the box about 1.5 times the length of the box. The computer printout shows symbols for the extreme values, such as asterisks (possible outliers) and zeros (likely outliers).

Figure 2.15 shows computer-generated depictions from the MINITAB and business MYSTAT programs for the excess patient waiting times data. Differences in the two depictions for the same data arise because of the differences in each program's internal logic for selecting the number of intervals to be used and then assigning observations to the selected intervals. MINITAB and business MYSTAT boxplots for annual salaries for 36 San Diego workers are presented in Figure 2.16.

Compare Figures 2.5 and 2.15, and Figures 2.14 and 2.16. You'll find that both the computer printouts closely resemble their respective graphs, which we constructed earlier. But the computer-generated boxplots in Figure 2.16 reveal more detail than Figure 2.14 about the extreme values (possible and likely outliers) by showing asterisks and zeros in the upper 25% grouping.

Extensive discussions of the MINITAB and business MYSTAT statistical packages, with detailed instructions on how to use each package and obtain output keyed to this text, are available in separate supplements.

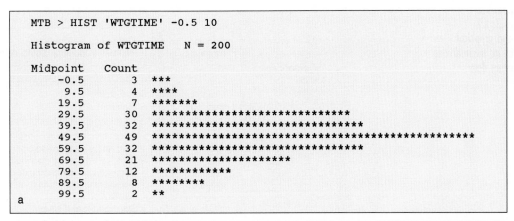

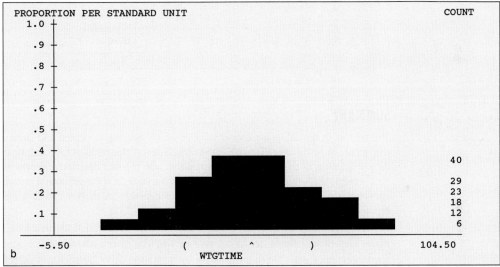

Figure 2.15
(a) MINITAB bar chart and (b) business MYSTAT histogram of excess patient waiting time data

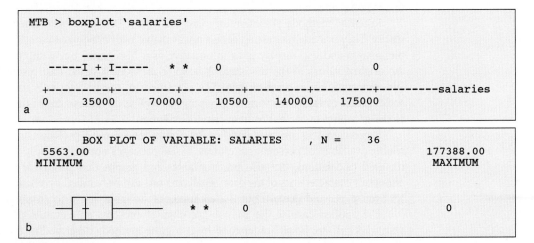

Figure 2.16
(a) MINITAB output and (b) business MYSTAT output: annual salaries of 36 San Diego workers

Figure 2.17
Tabular and graphical
procedures for summarizing
and reporting data

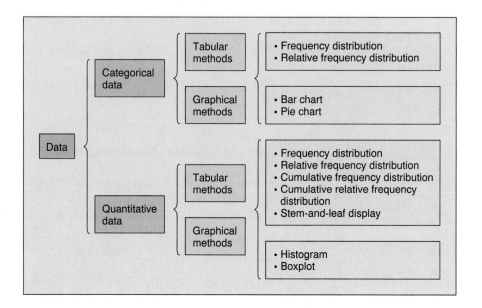

SUMMARY

The tabular, graphical, and pictorial ways in which data are presented and summarized in this chapter are by no means exhaustive of the wide variety of the methods for reducing and describing data. Regardless of the method, the principle in constructing descriptive representations of the data remains the same: to depict the underlying variation and concentration present in the data. However, the most appropriate method to use depends on the type of data under study, as Figure 2.17 indicates.

To organize raw data in a frequency table several questions must be asked. How many classes will there be? What will be the size of the class interval, and where will the lowest class start? Will cumulative or noncumulative frequencies be reported? Will relative frequencies be used? If a graphical presentation is considered desirable to portray the variation and concentration in the data, what form will it take? Among the choices are the frequency polygon, ogive, histogram, bar chart, pie chart, and three-dimensional graph.

Recently, methods of exploratory data analysis (EDA) have been gaining in popularity. They provide interesting details not available with previous methods. For example, a stem-and-leaf display is as informative as a histogram, but without sacrificing the original values of the raw data. A boxplot provides a visual impression of range and concentration of a set of data. The placement of the boxplot tells us the degree and location of values for various groupings as well as an assessment of the symmetry of the grouping in the entire frequency distribution.

Large data sets are best handled by computer software packages that are now readily available for personal computers. These packages not only rapidly perform the required calculations, but also prepare tables and graphs that effectively present the important characteristics of the data. Small data sets can be handled by a hand calculator (or even paper and pencil), but if a computer is available, use it to ensure accuracy.

The applied case at the end of this chapter presents an example of the many situations that are better understood by using the methods described in this chapter. The Wendy's Database Analysis that follows the applied case gives the first hands-on look at the large survey of data that was introduced in Chapter 1 and will be further treated and analyzed in subsequent chapters.

PRACTICE EXERCISE ANSWERS

2.1 By examining the 45 data values, we find that the largest observation, L, is 100; the smallest observation, S, is 17. The range, R, is

$$R = L - S$$
$$= 100 - 17 = 83$$

Nine equal sized intervals are requested, but the range of 83 is not evenly divisible by 9. Adjust the range to 90 so that 9 equal sized intervals of length 10 can be used. The 7 units added to the range allows the first interval to extend a few units below the smallest observation and the ninth interval to extend above the largest observation. The choice of lower limit for the first interval is somewhat arbitrary.

a. The frequency table if the lower limit for the first class is chosen to be 15 is:

LOWER CLASS LIMIT	UPPER CLASS LIMIT	FREQUENCY
15	24	1
25	34	3
35	44	1
45	54	4
55	64	7
65	74	10
75	84	6
85	94	6
95	104	7
		45

b. If the limit of the first class is chosen to be 14, then the frequency table is:

LOWER CLASS LIMIT	UPPER CLASS LIMIT	FREQUENCY
14	23	1
24	33	3
34	43	1
44	53	4
54	63	7
64	73	10
74	83	5
84	93	7
94	103	7
		45

2.2 If the lower limit of the first class is chosen to be 15, then the cumulative "less than" frequency table is:

LOWER LIMIT OF CLASS INTERVAL	CUMULATIVE "LESS THAN" FREQUENCY
Less than 15	0
Less than 25	1
Less than 35	4
Less than 45	5
Less than 55	9
Less than 65	16
Less than 75	26
Less than 85	32
Less than 95	38
Less than 105	45

2.3

CLASS INTERVAL	FREQUENCY	RELATIVE FREQUENCY	% RELATIVE FREQUENCY
15– 24	1	1/45 = .0222	2.22
25– 34	3	3/45 = .0667	6.67
35– 44	1	1/45 = .0222	2.22
45– 54	4	4/45 = .0889	8.89
55– 64	7	7/45 = .1556	15.56
65– 74	10	10/45 = .2222	22.22
75– 84	6	6/45 = .1333	13.33
85– 94	6	6/45 = .1333	13.33
95–104	7	7/45 = .1556	15.56
	45	1.0000	100.00

2.4

LOWER LIMIT OF CLASS INTERVAL	CUMULATIVE "LESS THAN" FREQUENCY	CUMULATIVE "LESS THAN" RELATIVE FREQUENCY
Less than 15	0	0/45 = .0000
Less than 25	1	1/45 = .0222
Less than 35	4	4/45 = .0889
Less than 45	5	5/45 = .1111
Less than 55	9	9/45 = .2000
Less than 65	16	16/45 = .3556
Less than 75	26	26/45 = .5778
Less than 85	32	32/45 = .7111
Less than 95	38	38/45 = .8444
Less than 105	45	45/45 = 1.0000

2.5 By examining the 40 data values, we find that the largest observation is 98; the second largest value is 49; the smallest observation is 2. Omitting the largest value, the remaining range is $R = 49 - 2 = 47$. Eight equal sized intervals are requested, but the range of 47 is not evenly divisible by 8. Adjust the range to 48 so that 8 equal sized intervals of length 6 can be used. The 1 unit added to the range allows the first interval to extend 1 unit below the lowest value or the last closed interval to extend 1 unit above 49. One solution is:

LOWER CLASS LIMIT	UPPER CLASS LIMIT	FREQUENCY
2	7	5
8	13	2
14	19	3
20	25	2
26	31	10
32	37	8
38	43	5
44	49	4
50 or more		1
		40

2.6 The frequency polygon is obtained by plotting the following pairs of values:

CLASS MIDPOINT	FREQUENCY
9.5	0
19.5	1
29.5	3
39.5	1
49.5	4
59.5	7
69.5	10
79.5	6
89.5	6
99.5	7
109.5	0

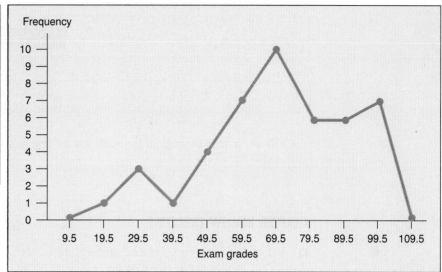

2.7

1	7
2	55
3	71
4	79
5	015868
6	079602
7	2008261060
8	55430
9	6183138
10	0000

2.8 a. To find the quartiles, first order the observations of exam grades:

17 25   25   31   37   47   49   50   51   55   56   58   58   60   60
62 66   67   69   70   70   70   70   71   72   72   76   76   78   80
83 84   85   85   91   91   93   93   96   98   98   100   100   100   100

Quartile positions:

$$Q_1 = \frac{45 + 1}{4} = 11.5\text{, so use the midpoint between the 11th and 12th positions in the ordered array}$$

$$Q_2 = \frac{2(45 + 1)}{4} = 23\text{, so use the 23rd position in the ordered array}$$

$$Q_3 = \frac{3(45 + 1)}{4} = 34.5\text{, so use the midpoint between the 34th and 35th positions in the ordered array}$$

So the quartile values are $Q_1 = (56 + 58)/2 = 57$, $Q_2 = 70$, and $Q_3 = (85 + 91)/2 = 88$.

b. The five-number summary includes the minimum and maximum data values in addition to the quartile values shown in part a: 17, 57, 70, 88, 100.

c. The boxplot is:

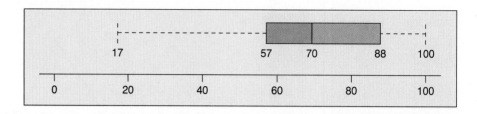

The bulk of the class did well on the exam, but the lowest 25% of the scores had a wide spread, from 17 to 57.

CHAPTER REVIEW EXERCISES

☐ **2.14** The following set of data represents the number of automobiles passing through an intersection each hour over a 30 hour period.

> 38 99 70 43 10 73 90 86 70 60 68 30 26 79 50
> 84 81 95 94 95 42 64 14 19 17 56 10 6 45 21

a. Find the value of the range.
b. Use 6 equal sized intervals and construct a frequency table.
c. Use the result in part b to construct a "less than" cumulative frequency table.
d. Use the result in part b to construct a relative frequency table.
e. Use the result in part c to construct a "less than" cumulative relative frequency table.

☐ **2.15** The following set of data represents the number of hamburgers sold by Campus Food Services during lunch hour each day over a 30 day period.

> 44 51 51 53 50 52 44 55 54 52 51 55 46 49 49
> 50 44 37 50 49 55 52 57 49 53 45 43 54 53 53

a. Find the value of the range.
b. Use 6 equal sized intervals and construct a frequency table.
c. Use the result in part b to construct a "less than" cumulative frequency table.
d. Use the result in part b to construct a relative frequency table.
e. Use the result in part c to construct a "less than" cumulative relative frequency table.

☐ **2.16** The following set of data represents the number of burglaries in 30 cities in the United States during one weekend.

> 128 20 18 50 1 46 111 95 82 39 19 97 73 18 11
> 1 123 260 3 28 106 44 146 21 55 97 145 90 53 52

a. Find the value of the range.
b. Use 6 equal sized intervals and construct a frequency table.
c. Use the result in part b to construct a "less than" cumulative frequency table.
d. Use the result in part b to construct a relative frequency table.
e. Use the result in part c to construct a "less than" cumulative relative frequency table.

▶ **2.17** Suppose we are given the following frequency table for salaries (in thousands of dollars) of 95 teachers:

SALARY	FREQUENCY
14.55–18.55	4
18.55–22.55	4
22.55–26.55	10
26.55–30.55	27
30.55–34.55	3
34.55–38.55	12
38.55–42.55	15
42.55–46.55	11
46.55–50.55	9
Total	95

Note that the class intervals are given in terms of the class boundaries.
a. Find (1) the length of the class interval, (2) the class limits, and (3) the class midpoints.
b. Is it possible to determine the number of salaries that are: (1) More than $17,000? (2) Less than $46,550? (3) Less than $35,000? (4) More than $30,550? (5) At most $38,550? (6) At least $42,550?

2.18 Suppose we are given the following frequency table for property losses (in thousands of dollars) of 63 burglaries in one city:

PROPERTY LOSS	FREQUENCY
3.65– 9.65	10
9.65–15.65	6
15.65–21.65	22
21.65–27.65	15
27.65–33.65	9
33.65–39.65	1
Total	63

Note that the class intervals are given in terms of the class boundaries.
a. Find (1) the length of the class interval, (2) the class limits, and (3) the class midpoints.
b. Is it possible to determine the number of property losses that are: (1) More than $17,000? (2) Less than $30,000? (3) Less than $33,650? (4) More than $21,650? (5) At most $27,650? (6) At least $15,650? (7) At least $31,000? (8) At most $10,000?

2.19 Suppose we are given the following measurements (in millimeters) of 69 roaches collected in a trap:

LENGTH mm	FREQUENCY
1– 3	1
4– 6	6
7– 9	11
10–12	23
13–15	16
16–18	7
19–21	4
22–24	1
Total	69

Note that the class intervals are given in terms of the class limits.

a. Find (1) the length of the class interval, (2) the class boundaries, and (3) the class midpoint.

b. Is it possible to determine the number of roaches whose lengths are: (1) More than 17 mm? (2) Less than 18 mm? (3) Less than 19 mm? (4) More than 9 mm? (5) At most 12 mm? (6) At least 15 mm? (7) At least 16 mm? (8) At most 10 mm?

2.20 Suppose we are given the following weights (in grams) of 245 pumpkin seedlings:

WEIGHTS g	FREQUENCY
16–20	43
21–25	36
26–30	25
31–35	14
36–40	8
41–45	16
46–50	29
51–55	33
56–60	41
Total	245

Note that the class intervals are given in terms of class limits.

a. Find (1) the length of the class interval, (2) the class boundaries, and (3) the class midpoints.

b. Is it possible to determine the number of seedlings whose weights are: (1) More than 17 g? (2) Less than 18 g? (3) Less than 31 g? (4) More than 45 g? (5) At most 21 g? (6) At least 46 g? (7) At least 30 g? (8) At most 20 g?

2.21 The numbers of automobiles that pass through a red light at a certain intersection during a given week are grouped into a frequency table with the following classes: −0.5–2.5, 2.5–5.5, 5.5–8.5, 8.5–11.5, and 11.5–14.5. Find:

a. The length of the class interval   b. The class midpoints
c. The class limits

2.22 The lengths (in inches) of a sample of a certain species of small mammal are grouped into a frequency table with the following classes: 1.35–1.65, 1.65–1.95, 1.95–2.25, 2.25–2.55, 2.55–2.85, and 2.85–3.15. Find:

a. The length of the class interval   b. The class midpoints
c. The class limits

2.23 Refer to Exercise 2.14, and use the data and results.

a. Construct a frequency polygon.   b. Construct an ogive.

2.24 Refer to Exercise 2.15, and use the data and results.

a. Construct a frequency polygon.   b. Construct an ogive.

2.25 Refer to Exercise 2.16, and use the data and results.

a. Construct a frequency polygon.   b. Construct an ogive.

▶ **2.26** Use the frequency table in Exercise 2.17.

a. Construct a frequency polygon.   b. Construct an ogive.

2.27 Use the frequency table in Exercise 2.18.

a. Construct a frequency polygon.   b. Construct an ogive.

2.28 Use the frequency table in Exercise 2.19.

a. Construct a frequency polygon.   b. Construct an ogive.

2.29 Use the frequency table in Exercise 2.20.
   a. Construct a frequency polygon.   b. Construct an ogive.

2.30 The following set of data represents the number of athletic injuries at 45 high schools during the past academic year.

75	64	11	41	61	65	8	91	86	95	97	42	76	87	67
14	94	39	78	74	94	88	54	81	27	83	34	13	96	32
65	73	24	91	52	58	36	95	75	72	28	55	77	99	16

Use 7 equal sized intervals and construct:
   a. A frequency polygon   b. An ogive

2.31 Use the data in Exercise 2.30.
   a. Construct a histogram.   b. Construct a bar chart.

▶ **2.32** Use the frequency table in Exercise 2.17.
   a. Construct a histogram.   b. Construct a bar chart.

2.33 Use the frequency table in Exercise 2.18.
   a. Construct a histogram.   b. Construct a bar chart.

2.34 The following set of data represents the number of videocassette recorders sold at 60 retail outlets during the last Christmas shopping season.

69	41	20	81	86	79	92	90	22	26	37	26	57	88	83
9	18	83	58	71	76	3	25	29	44	22	11	92	8	17
95	41	6	72	77	57	1	76	13	79	75	45	52	92	17
16	1	75	49	83	28	81	74	46	22	40	84	23	18	85

Use 8 equal sized intervals and construct:
   a. A histogram   b. A bar chart

▶ **2.35** To construct a pie chart, subdivide a circle into sectors that are proportional to the frequencies or percentages of the corresponding groups. Since a circle has 360° (degrees), we use 3.6° to represent 1%. Thus, if a category represents 10% of the whole, it is represented in the pie chart by a sector whose central angle is 36°. Given this information, construct a pie chart for the data in the following table.

TYPE OF TREE	NUMBER
Acacia	50
Eucalyptus	100
Mulberry	125
Podocarpus	75
Sycamore	150
Total	500

2.36 Construct a pie chart for the data in the following table.

PROFESSION	NUMBER
Accountant	80
Biologist	20
Carpenter	40
Dentist	40
Doctor	120
Engineer	80
Teacher	20
Total	400

▷ **2.37** Use the data in Exercise 2.14, and construct a stem-and-leaf plot.

2.38 Use the data in Exercise 2.15, and construct a stem-and-leaf plot.

2.39 The following table lists the sodium content (in milligrams) in 1 oz servings of breakfast cereals, based on the published content labeling on the package.

SODIUM CONTENT mg/oz	BRAND OF CEREAL
160	General Foods Raisin Bran
45	General Foods Super Sugar Crisp
65	General Foods New Horizon Trail Mix
150	General Foods Fruity Pebbles
180	General Foods Alpha Bits
160	General Foods Honey Comb
230	General Foods Natural Bran Flakes
180	General Mills Lucky Charms
370	General Mills Wheaties
170	General Mills Trix
200	General Mills Cocoa Puffs
280	General Mills Golden Grahams
70	Kellogg Honey Smacks
125	Kellogg Apple Jacks
125	Kellogg Froot Loops
90	Kellogg Sugar Corn Pops
0	Kellogg Raisin Squares
200	Kellogg Sugar Frosted Flakes
320	Kellogg Product 19
190	Kellogg Cracklin' Bran (Oat)
220	Kellogg Raisin Bran
5	Kellogg Frosted Mini Wheats
190	Kellogg Cocoa Krispies
260	Kellogg All Bran
290	Kellogg Corn Flakes
170	Kellogg Nutri Grain (Wheat)
230	Kellogg Special K
190	Nabisco 100% Bran
180	Nabisco Team
0	Nabisco Spoon Size Shredded Wheat
180	Post Grape Nuts
200	Quaker Oats Cap'n Crunch with Crunchberries
0	Quaker Oats Puffed Rice
220	Quaker Oats Cap'n Crunch
180	Quaker Oats Cinnamon Life
180	Quaker Oats Life
190	Ralston Purina Chocolate Chip Cookie Crisp
115	Ralston Purina Ghostbusters
310	Ralston Purina Corn Chex

a. Construct a stem-and-leaf display for the data.
b. Group the data into 7 classes of equal width, and construct a frequency table.
c. What advantage does the stem-and-leaf display have (if any) over the frequency table?

2.40 The village of Park Forest sponsored a 10 km scenic race. The ages of male participants, at their last birthday, are listed below. Construct a stem-and-leaf display of the data. Use 10 years as the stem unit.

Men

19	37	22	46	29	27	35	30
48	18	25	29	57	26	34	13
23	44	30	38	45	21	55	43
28	26	37	42	63	14	48	33
35	22	20	33	19	52	41	25
21	44	36	27	34	40	28	26
11	27	39	22	31	35	26	30

2.41 The 10 km scenic race in Exercise 2.40 included female participants also. Their ages are given below.

Women

32	25	29	37	18	34	28
30	41	33	29	44	19	50
22	36	25	32	38	24	47
28	32	31	17	26	40	23

a. To the stem-and-leaf display already constructed in Exercise 2.40 for male participants (with leaves drawn to the right of the stem), add a stem-and-leaf display for the women by drawing the leaves to the left of the stem.
b. Construct separate frequency tables for the male and female ages.
c. Compare the distributions of the ages of the male and female participants. In making this comparison, do the stem-and-leaf plots show an advantage over the frequency tables?
d. Construct separate boxplots for the male and female age data.
e. In comparing the male and female age distributions, do the boxplots provide an advantage over both the stem-and-leaf displays and the frequency tables?

2.42 One measure of a corporation's attitude toward business risk is the amount of cash and near-cash (called *cash equivalents*) assets the corporation holds to meet its daily cash requirements to operate its business. An important measure that describes a company's cash position relative to its current needs is *cash turnover*, the number of days of cash outlays due to sales the corporation can cover with the amount in its cash or cash equivalents account. The smaller the cash turnover figure, the higher the risk taking attitude of the corporation. Large cash turnover values, on the other hand, indicate a very conservative position, since this reflects a stockpiling of cash to meet the corporation's daily requirements.

Even in the same industry, where firms usually expect similar business risk, different cash turnover policies are evident. Cash turnover data for 20 pharmaceutical companies are presented below.

Pharmaceutical Companies

49	39	52	45	47	10	33	11	14	51
28	55	98	62	85	89	29	38	76	36

a. Construct a stem-and-leaf display for the data. Use 10 days as the stem unit.
b. Construct a boxplot for these data.
c. Write a brief statement summarizing cash turnover concentration in the pharmaceutical industry. Write it so that it will be helpful to a financial analyst who is interested in the risk taking position of a firm, but who does not understand stem-and-leaf displays or boxplots.

2.43 As an extension to Exercise 2.42, listed below are cash turnover data for 36 energy companies specializing in fossil fuels.

Energy Resources Companies

37	17	7	10	10	62	39	16	8	19	41	5
11	20	11	54	6	13	10	28	26	42	37	28
54	12	8	30	4	42	25	31	2	45	13	80

a. Construct a stem-and-leaf display for the energy companies. Do this by extending the leaves for the energy industries leftward from the stem already constructed in Exercise 2.42 for the pharmaceutical company data. (This is called a *back-to-back* stem-and-leaf display.)

b. Construct a boxplot for the energy company data.

c. Comment on how the pharmaceutical and energy industries compare on cash turnover; for example, in which industry is there a tendency for cash turnover to assume larger values?

□ **2.44** The data collected on the sale of hamburgers by Campus Food Services during the lunch hour in Exercise 2.38 included data for the sale of hamburgers during the dinner hour. The data are given below:

17	57	35	43	74	56	88	95	77	76	50	24	78	15	48
10	8	99	85	62	55	13	36	87	17	12	25	59	17	32

a. To the stem-and-leaf display already constructed in Exercise 2.38 for the lunch hour data (with leaves to the right of the stem), add a stem-and-leaf display for the dinner hour data by drawing the leaves to the left of the stem.

b. Construct separate frequency tables for the lunch and dinner hour data.

c. Compare the distributions of lunch and dinner sales of hamburgers. In making this comparison, do the stem-and-leaf plots show an advantage over the frequency table?

d. Construct separate, but adjacent, boxplots for the lunch and dinner hour data.

e. In comparing the lunch and dinner hour distributions, do the boxplots provide an advantage over both the stem-and-leaf displays and the frequency tables?

SOLVING APPLIED CASES

The techniques presented in this chapter are invaluable aids in organizing and interpreting data. An example of their use is illustrated here.

80/20 Rule Using the Ogive

You will encounter a phenomenon known as the "80/20 rule" in many situations. The rule refers to the circumstance where a small percentage of persons or objects account for a large share of whatever is being measured (20% or less of the persons or objects account for 80% or more of whatever is being measured). For example, marketing people frequently find that 20% of the customers account for 80% of sales or profits; universities find that 20% or less of their courses generate 80% or more of their student credit hours.

Table 2.11 shows a specific breakdown of the sales importance of 13 inventoried items. The first column is the item code used for identification. The second column lists the number of units of sales, and the third column lists the price or value per unit of sales. The fourth column lists the results of multiplying the second and third columns, and represents the total sales value of each item; for example, item 647BQ has 40,100 units sold at $20 per unit, for a total sales value of $802,000. The fifth column lists the cumulative sales; that is, the cumulation for items 647BQ and 8944C is $802,000 + $282,000 = $1,084,000, and this represents 73.2% of total sales (sixth column). As we proceed down the fifth column, each new cumulative sales entry is added to the previous total for a new cumulative total. Notice that the items are listed

TABLE 2.11		Cumulative Distribution of Sales of Inventoried Items			
ITEM CODE	SALES VOLUME Units	PRICE PER UNIT $	SALES × PRICE $	CUMULATIVE SALES $	CUMULATIVE PERCENT
647BQ	40,100	20.00	802,000	802,000	54.2
8944C	282	1,000.00	282,000	1,084,000	73.2
6869R	1,730	100.00	173,000	1,257,000	84.9
1287B	5,100	200.00	102,000	1,359,000	91.8
2246R	595	100.00	59,500	1,418,500	95.0
4973Z	8	4,000.00	32,000	1,450,500	98.0
8924A	83	2,000.00	16,600	1,467,100	99.1
9937D	796	100.00	7,960	1,475,060	99.6
5321J	3,270	1.00	3,270	1,478,330	99.89
6777K	118	10.00	1,180	1,479,510	99.97
4222F	31	10.00	310	1,479,820	99.99
5664G	3	10.00	30	1,479,850	100.00
8437F	10	0.10	1	1,479,851	100.00

in descending order according to sales revenue (i.e., fourth column). This is how they should be listed for the kind of data analysis representation illustrated in this example.

An ogive of the distribution given in Table 2.11 is shown in Figure 2.18. The straight line indicates what the ogive would look like if all items had equal sales revenue. The large gap between the actual ogive and the straight line indicates the concentration of sales among a few items. Both Table 2.11 and Figure 2.18 confirm the 80/20 rule, since they show that 3 out of 13 items (23%) represent over 80% (approx. 85%) of the dollar sales volume.

Checkpoint Exercise

1. The Wilmington Corporation, a large producer of consumer merchandise, was considering entry into a lucrative pressed glass–ceramic segment of the cooking and bakeware market. This segment has been monopolized by Corning Glass Works, which markets its products under the trade name Corningware, but the Corning patent was due to expire in 18 months, and Wilmington had the technical and manufacturing capabilities to produce a competitive product. A question Wilmington needed to consider was whether its distribution strength

Figure 2.18
Ogive of sales of inventoried items

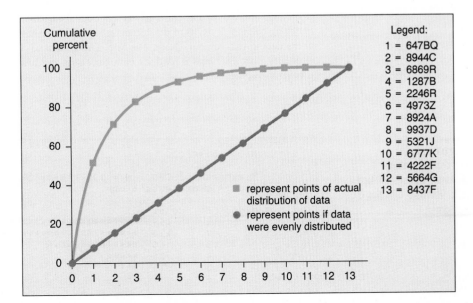

was in the type of outlets where pressed glass–ceramic cookware was likely to be purchased. A profile of distribution strength based on a percentage ogive can be helpful in studying this question. The breakdown of Wilmington sales by type of outlet is given in the table.

TYPE OF OUTLET	SALES $ million
Department stores	32.1
Supermarkets	18.4
Discount stores	36.5
Hardware stores	16.8
Chain stores	12.2
Premium	10.7
Institutional	6.1
Government	12.3
Mail order	6.2
Other	1.7
	153.0

a. Arrange the data in decreasing order according to sales.
b. Compute the cumulative sales and the cumulative percentage sales for the ordered data.
c. Construct an ogive based on the cumulative percentage sales.
d. What percentage of outlets accounts for 80% of sales?

WENDY'S DATABASE ANALYSIS

In this set of exercises we first examine the image fast food restaurants have among consumers on such characteristics as food taste, cleanliness of the restaurant, and menu price. Then we examine another aspect of importance to the fast food restaurants, namely patronage frequency.

Image

1. What do consumers think of the taste of McDonald's food?

Food taste of the six chains studies is rated in Questions 27–32 of the survey (see Chapter 1); Question 30 refers to McDonald's. Thus, the data for answering this question are found in column 30 of the database. Our analysis was done using the MINITAB software package. After retrieving column 30 (C30 to the computer) from the Wendy's file, we asked for a histogram of the data in this column. (Note: The MINITAB command, HISTOGRAM, gives a graph that resembles a bar chart and is used for both bar charts and histograms.) The resulting bar chart is given in Figure 2.19.

Figure 2.19
Bar chart describing McDonald's image on food taste (MINITAB calls this a histogram)

```
MTB > hist c30

Histogram of C30    N = 391    N* = 15
Each * represents 5 obs.

Midpoint    Count
       1      158    ********************************
       2      119    ************************
       3       66    *************
       4       26    ******
       5       13    ***
       6        9    **
```

The chart shows that 15 of the 406 respondents to the survey did not answer the question on taste of McDonald's food. But the remaining 391 persons who did answer this question gave McDonald's high marks on food taste. The most common rating was number 1 (the best possible), 158 people; this was followed in frequency by response number 2, 119 people. Only 9 persons gave McDonald's the poorest rating (number 6).

2. Is McDonald's as favorably perceived on other important dimensions?

One important dimension is cleanliness. McDonald's periodically sends unannounced inspectors to check on the cleanliness of the washrooms, outside litter removal, tables that have not been cleared, and other sanitary and housekeeping items that customers might notice.

Cleanliness of the food chains is rated in Questions 33–38 of the survey, with Question 36 referring to McDonald's. This means the data we want is found in column 36 (C36) of the database. Again using the HISTOGRAM command, we find the results given in Figure 2.20, and again we see that McDonald's is perceived very favorably.

More than three decades ago McDonald's got its start as the "15¢ hamburger" place. Since then, inflation, among other factors, has helped push hamburger prices higher by several times those original McDonald's prices. Moreover, menu expansion has made many other higher-priced items available. Is McDonald's still perceived as having a low-priced menu?

Question 48 is the one that rates McDonald's on price, so the data we want are found in column 48 (C48). The chart given in Figure 2.21 depicts the results.

Although not as one-sided as the food taste and cleanliness ratings, McDonald's image on price is nevertheless extremely favorable. Ninety persons gave McDonald's a 1 rating; and more than half the respondents rated McDonald's as 1 or 2. So, yes, McDonald's is still perceived as having a low-priced menu.

3. How do percents of other fast food chains on these same characteristics compare with percents of McDonald's?

Figure 2.20
Bar chart describing McDonald's image on cleanliness

```
MTB > hist c36

Histogram of C36   N = 388   N* = 18
Each * represents 5 obs.

Midpoint    Count
       1      164    ********************************
       2      146    *****************************
       3       60    ************
       4       13    ***
       5        4    *
       6        1    *
```

Figure 2.21
Bar chart describing McDonald's image on menu price

```
MTB > hist c48

Histogram of C48   N = 387   N* = 19
Each * represents 5 obs.

Midpoint    Count
       1       90    *****************
       2      123    ************************
       3       96    *******************
       4       56    ***********
       5       17    ****
       6        5    *
```

Let us consider White Castle, a much smaller regional competitor with a different operating strategy. The White Castle data on food taste, cleanliness, and price reputation are found in columns C32, C38, and C50, respectively. The corresponding bar charts are shown in Figures 2.22, 2.23, and 2.24.

Overall, it is clear from the bar charts that far fewer people rate the taste of White Castle food or the cleanliness of their establishments as favorably as McDonald's. Figure 2.22 shows that the common response on food taste was number 6, "taste very bad." Still, note the spike at 1 on the food taste chart. Despite the preponderance of low ratings, it appears that White Castle has a following. Perhaps these are consumers who comprise a market segment having substantially different preferences from the majority of consumers, and to whom White Castle has a strong appeal.

The White Castle price perception bar chart presents a different story. Consumer responses are highly clustered on the lower numbers, indicating a strong perception of a low-priced menu.

We can summarize the images consumers have of these two fast food chains by the following comparisons: McDonald's restaurants are seen as cleaner and serving better tasting food at somewhat higher prices than White Castle.

Wendy's Database Student Exercises

1. Use the MINITAB statistical software package (or an alternate package designated by your instructor) to generate frequency tables, bar charts and/or histograms, and boxplots on food taste image, cleanliness image, and price image for the following chains: Wendy's, Burger King, Hardee's, and Borden Burger.
2. Using your frequency distributions for the four chains, which chain would you say has the most favorable image on (a) food taste, (b) cleanliness, and (c) price?

Patronage Frequency

(Note: This is a more advanced database analysis than the previous one. It requires you to code a column of data.)

How pervasive among consumers is their patronage of fast food restaurants?

Everyone knows that fast food restaurants are big business these days, but what is the source of that business? Does a majority of the population patronize these restaurants? Or does most of the business come from a small percentage of the population who patronize the restaurants very frequently, say several times per week?

Fast food advertising plans hinge on the answers to these questions. A mass media "shotgun" approach is more desirable the more pervasive the consumer patronage. A "rifle" approach targeted at the frequent users is more advantageous the more concentrated the fast food spending is among a small percentage of consumers. A frequency distribution and its histogram provide statistical evidence on patronage frequency that can be very useful in making the choice between a rifle approach and a shotgun approach.

The bar chart in Figure 2.25 organizes the responses (1–5) to Question 2 (C2) given by the 406 respondents on their fast food usage. It indicates the largest frequency is for answer 3, "two or three times a month."

Now let's define a frequent fast food user as anyone who answers 1 or 2 on Question 2, and code these to 1. Also, let's define an occasional fast food user as anyone who answers 3, 4, or 5, and code these to 0. The bar chart of the coded values is given in Figure 2.26, which shows that frequent users of fast food (coded 1) are nearly as common as the occasional users (coded 0).

Wendy's Database Student Exercises

1. Construct a histogram for Question 126 (C126), Wendy's fast food usage, and comment on the results.

Figure 2.22
Bar chart describing White
Castle's image on food taste

```
MTB > hist c32

Histogram of C32    N = 392    N* = 14
Each * represents 2 obs.

Midpoint    Count
       1       62    *******************************
       2       45    ***********************
       3       54    **************************
       4       66    *********************************
       5       76    **************************************
       6       89    ********************************************
```

Figure 2.23
Bar chart describing White
Castle's image on cleanliness

```
MTB > hist c38

Histogram of C38    N = 390    N* = 16
Each * represents 2 obs.

Midpoint    Count
       1       64    ******************************
       2       74    *************************************
       3       93    **********************************************
       4       74    *************************************
       5       61    ******************************
       6       24    ***********
```

Figure 2.24
Bar chart describing White
Castle's image on menu price

```
MTB > hist c50

Histogram of C50    N = 387    N* = 19
Each * represents 5 obs.

Midpoint    Count
       1      226    *********************************************
       2       91    ******************
       3       46    *********
       4       13    ***
       5        3    *
       6        8    **
```

Figure 2.25
Bar chart describing frequency
of usage

```
MTB > hist c2

Histogram of C2    N = 395    N* = 11
Each * represents 5 obs.

Midpoint    Count
       1       88    *****************
       2       91    ******************
       3      132    **************************
       4       41    ********
       5       43    ********
```

```
MTB > code (1:2)1 (3:5)0 c2 c200
MTB > hist c200

Histogram of C200   N = 395   N* = 11
Each * represents 5 obs.

Midpoint   Count
       0    216  ********************************************
       1    179  ***********************************
```

──────
Figure 2.26
Bar chart comparing usage by occasional and frequent users; 0 = occasional fast food user, 1 = frequent fast food user

2. Now define as a frequent Wendy's fast food user anyone who answers 1 or 2, and code these to 1. Define as an occasional Wendy's fast food user anyone who answers 3, 4, 5, or 6, and code these to 0. Construct a histogram for the coded values, and comment on the results.
3. Which of the two advertising approaches, rifle or shotgun, do you think Wendy's should use?

Numerical Summary Measures

Junk bonds were the financial rage of the 1980s. They were not only the "hot issue" for institutional investors to achieve higher returns, but also the money machine devised by Michael Milken (the former Drexel Burnham Lambert junk bond dealer), who reportedly earned over $100 million in one year for his services to Drexel's junk bond department. But if a bond is really thought of as "junk," why would anyone want to buy it? And why did both the supply and demand for junk bonds show a phenomenal growth in the 1980s?

Typically, these bonds are issued by either a growing small business looking to borrow money for expansion or a large company looking to borrow money to finance a merger or an acquisition—also called a *leveraged buyout (LBO)*. These bonds come with fairly high interest rates, and place a heavy interest payment obligation on the issuing firm (enough so that it could cause a nonpayment default). Because of this heavy interest payment burden, these bonds receive a B or lower rating grade compared to the AAA, AA, and A ratings of safer corporate bonds. The name "junk" comes from these low ratings. Their offshoots, junk bond mutual funds, are portfolios of junk bonds. Let's take a close look at junk bond mutual funds to see what junk bonds have to offer to the investing public.

Junk bond mutual funds are professionally managed well-diversified collections of the low-rated bonds paying fairly high interest rates. Investors who place investment dollars in junk bond mutual funds must face a higher risk than those who place their money in a bond mutual fund composed of, say, U.S. government securities. U.S. government securities mutual funds also are professionally managed well-diversified bond collections, but their composition is solely U.S. government backed bonds. These bonds pay a lower interest rate, but because the issuer is the U.S. government investors are guaranteed their interest payments. For this reason U.S. government securities mutual funds are at the other end of the investment safety spectrum compared to junk bond mutual funds. Why do investors place their money in junk bonds? Common sense tells us that investors willing to assume the higher risk of junk bonds must do so because they expect to earn a higher return. Therefore, in an intuitive way we know that return must follow risk. But for better understanding, can we be more precise in defining risk, measure it statistically, and then perhaps assess the risk–return relationship?

In financial circles risk is commonly viewed as the chance of experiencing adverse events different from what is expected. For a financial instrument such as bonds, it must mean experiencing returns that differ negatively from the financial return expected. The more frequent and the wider the differences from the expected for a given type of financial instrument, the greater must be the underlying risk of that instrument. But how can we determine what is to be expected and the risk we are taking? One common approach to this problem accepted by most financial analysts is to look back at historical returns.

Table 3.1 presents 11 years of annual returns for two diversified bond mutual funds: the Kemper High Yield Fund (a junk bond fund) and the Kemper U.S. Government Securities Fund. The annual return columns of the table show that considerable volatility exists for both funds among the annual returns over this 11 year period. There are some years when high returns are registered, while returns in other years are near zero or slightly negative. A perspective on the degree of volatility that exists for these two bond mutual funds can be obtained from the graphical displays shown in Figure 3.1. But a graphical presentation can't accurately describe the "typical" average return for these two funds, nor the difference in risk that exists between the two funds (if there is a difference). Exact numerical measures of risk and expected return derived from the historical returns are needed.

TABLE 3.1	Annual Returns on Two Bond Mutual Funds, 1979–1989		
	KEMPER HIGH YIELD FUND*		**KEMPER U.S. GOVERNMENT SECURITIES FUND†**
Year	**Annual Return, %**	**Year**	**Annual Return, %**
1979	2.40	1979	0.90
1980	−0.90	1980	−0.10
1981	8.70	1981	0.60
1982	39.70	1982	28.40
1983	17.70	1983	8.90
1984	10.20	1984	12.20
1985	23.10	1985	22.30
1986	18.30	1986	16.20
1987	8.90	1987	2.70
1988	14.40	1988	6.30
1989	−1.10	1989	14.00

*Formed 1979; total net assets 1989: $1,406.3 mil.; portfolio maturity: 10.2 years.
†Formed 1979; total net assets 1989: $4,590.0 mil.; portfolio maturity: 8.9 years.

To estimate the *expected return*, financial analysts commonly calculate the *average (mean) return*, computed over the number of periods for which past data are available. In this case, an estimate of the expected return can be computed from the sample of 11 years of annual returns (from 1979 to 1989). Likewise, since what makes an investment risky is that there is some volatility, or spread of the annual returns from the average return, a measure of volatility is needed. One measure of this volatility is called the *standard deviation*, a statistical measure we shall learn more about later in this chapter. A risk estimate also can be calculated for the sample of 11 years of returns from 1979 to 1989.

The calculated means and standard deviations of the two Kemper funds, derived from the 11 year sample of annual returns, are given below.

	MEASURE OF EXPECTED RETURN (MEAN)	MEASURE OF VOLATILITY (STANDARD DEVIATION)
KEMPER HIGH YIELD FUND	12.85%	11.34%
KEMPER U.S. GOVERNMENT SECURITIES FUND	10.22%	9.43%

Figure 3.1
Graphic display of annual returns, 1979–1989

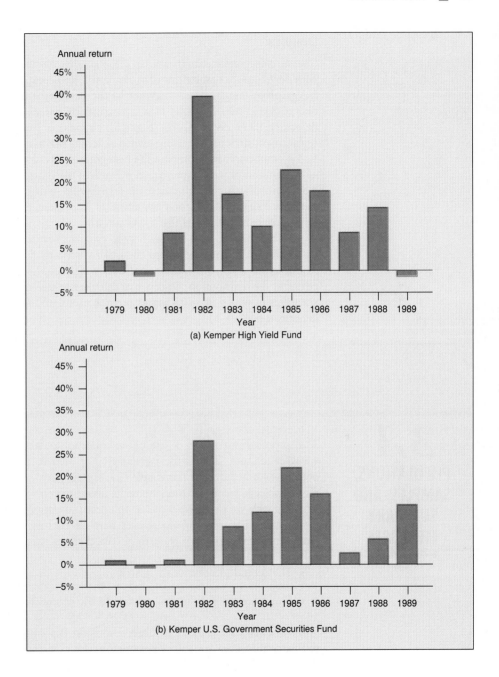

Annual return

(a) Kemper High Yield Fund

Annual return

(b) Kemper U.S. Government Securities Fund

If these calculated values can be viewed as a fair indication of the expected return and risk that are present in these funds, then the computed values do confirm the notion that return follows risk. The Kemper High Yield Fund does show a higher expected (average) return, but the price paid is a greater volatility of returns.

In this chapter we'll get very specific about how to compute the *summary measures* of expected return and risk, and how to compute a summary measure that is useful when a comparison between the two distributions is being made.

Overview

The various graphical and tabular presentations discussed in Chapter 2 provide us with devices that organize raw data into usable and comprehensive forms. But, at times, the graph or tabular report may not be the best statistical device, even if it is easy to obtain. Sometimes, just one or a few numerical values may provide the information necessary for a decision. For example, suppose a car rental dealer is considering replacement tires produced by several different tire manufacturers. The dealer would find it cumbersome to compare the histograms (if available) depicting the distribution of the amount of wear experienced by each of the different brands of tires. The dealer would probably much rather have the distribution information on tire mileage concisely stated by a single number or a few numbers. For instance, how much wear "on average" to expect? How reliable is that expectation?

In this chapter, we'll discuss how to calculate several numerical *summary measures* that further condense the information of a distribution. These measures describe the *central location* of a distribution and how widely *dispersed* the data are relative to the center of the distribution. Once we've calculated these measures, we'll look into some situations in which these measures provide useful and appropriate information to the investigator.

3.1 POPULATIONS, SAMPLES, AND SUMMARY MEASURES

As mentioned in Chapter 1, the entire collection of items, objects, or measurements we wish to study defines the *population*. The information recorded about the actual objects examined defines the *sample*. The sample may (but generally does not) include all the objects, items, or measurements about which we wish to draw a conclusion. which is why we distinguish the sample from the population.

The main features of a data set may be captured by numerical values called **summary measures**. Two features of data that are often wanted are:

- The central location of the distribution of the data

- The dispersion of the data relative to the central location

When the data set consists of observations on the entire population, the numerical summary measures are called **parameters**; by convention, parameters are generally denoted by letters from the Greek alphabet. When observations are from a sample, the numerical summary measures are called **statistics**, which are denoted by letters from the Roman alphabet.

Generally, time and cost limit us to deal with information on samples and statistics, not with populations and parameters. Much of this text is devoted to making the important connection linking the numerical summary measure of the sample to the corresponding numerical summary measure of the population. In the following sections we discuss methods for computing summary numerical measures for both population and sample observations. Since the methods described apply to both, the symbols assigned will designate whether we are computing the summary measure for a population or for a sample.

3.2
MEASURES OF CENTRAL LOCATION

Suppose a questionnaire was distributed to the senior classes at two small rural high schools, and it was filled out by 40 students at each institution. One piece of information solicited by the questionnaire was the annual expenditure these 80 students felt was needed in order to attend a public college or university in their state. Let's assume that these 80 responses are the entire collection of responses we wish to study. They constitute two populations of data, one for the first school and one for the second school. The raw data on student responses (in thousands of dollars) are reported in Table 3.2.

TABLE 3.2 Eighty Student Responses on Annual Expenditure Needed for College (in Thousands of Dollars)									
POPULATION OF OBSERVATIONS FROM SCHOOL 1									
7.5	8.3	6.7	6.8	9.5	8.5	7.9	11.2	9.9	8.4
6.8	7.8	7.4	9.2	8.3	8.9	7.2	5.8	6.0	10.3
9.8	12.5	9.5	9.9	8.5	5.5	6.7	5.5	6.1	5.8
7.9	7.8	11.4	5.6	7.3	8.1	6.8	7.3	8.0	8.3
POPULATION OF OBSERVATIONS FROM SCHOOL 2									
3.1	3.2	3.4	4.4	2.5	7.0	3.9	3.7	3.2	3.9
5.2	4.6	3.4	6.2	3.9	2.2	5.3	4.7	4.9	3.7
3.9	3.4	4.6	2.6	3.2	4.0	3.6	1.9	4.8	3.3
2.8	2.6	4.1	5.0	4.3	1.8	4.1	5.8	1.7	7.6

The histograms presented in Figures 3.2 and 3.3 show the distributions of the reported values for the two populations. A comparison of the two histograms immediately makes clear an important difference. Figure 3.2 is centered at a higher value

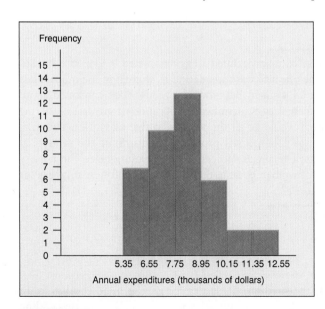

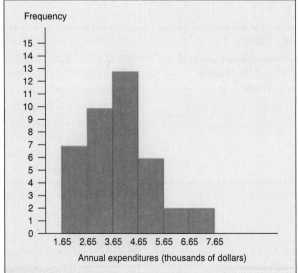

Figure 3.2
Histogram of responses on annual expenditures needed for school 1

Figure 3.3
Histogram of responses on annual expenditures needed for school 2

along the horizontal axis than Figure 3.3. *Is there a tangible numerical value that will describe "where the distribution is located"? If so, it should have a higher value for school 1 than for school 2.* A measure of this type is called a measure of **central location**, or *central tendency*. By comparing the numerical measures of central location for two distributions, we expect the distribution that has a histogram centered at a higher value along the horizontal axis to have the higher-valued numerical measure of central location. We are not restricted to one measure of central location; there are many numerical summary measures, and we shall consider three of them. Each provides a different perspective on the location of the center of a distribution. These measures are the *mode*, *median*, and *mean*.

MODE

Whether we are dealing with data representing a sample or a population, the **mode** is simply the most common value. For example, suppose the number of children in each family on a tiny remote island of seven families is: 1, 2, 3, 2, 4, 2, 1. The mode is 2, since that value occurs most frequently. For data grouped into classes, where the identities of the original observations are lost, the class with the highest frequency is considered the **modal class** (assuming equal class intervals).

Sometimes the mode is not a unique value. For instance, if we are dealing with the raw data in Table 3.2 for the 40 students at school 1, the values 6.8 and 8.3 are both modes. When the distribution of data has two modes, it is referred to as a *bimodal distribution*. In such cases the mode is of limited usefulness as a measure of central location. But there are situations that require that the decision making summary measure for the central location of the distribution be the mode. Here is one example of such a situation.

■ **EXAMPLE 3.1**

Pantyhose Dimensions and the "Average Woman"

In the 1970s, a new pantyhose company named L'eggs marketed a "one size fits all" type of pantyhose. Actually, the one size was intended to fit women in the modal class and was never intended to fit all women. But since the modal class contained about 70% of the population of women, L'eggs identified the location of greatest clustering and produced a single size that would fit all the women in that class. Concentrating only on this one size, L'eggs was able to mass produce and distribute the product at very low cost, guaranteeing itself financial success. L'eggs revolutionized the hosiery business, and to a generation of women became the thrifty, good-fitting pantyhose for the "average" woman.

MEDIAN

For samples or populations, the **median**, M, is defined as the middle value in an **ordered array**. That is, when all the items are arranged in ascending or descending order, the median is the middle value that divides the items into two equal groups. If the number of items is odd, the determination of the median is simple. It is the value of the middlemost item.

■ **EXAMPLE 3.2**
Grade-Point Averages of Seven Students

The grade-point averages (based on a scale from 0 to 4) for a group of seven students are

$$3.8 \quad 1.1 \quad 2.1 \quad 2.7 \quad 1.7 \quad 3.3 \quad 2.2$$

Ranking these observations from smallest to largest, we get

$$1.1 \quad 1.7 \quad 2.1 \quad 2.2 \quad 2.7 \quad 3.3 \quad 3.8$$

The fourth item is a unique middle item that separates the data into two equal groups of three items. Its value is 2.2; thus, 2.2 is the value of the median for these seven observations.

If there is an even number of items, then by convention the median is the value "in between," that is, it is equal to the sum of the two middlemost values divided by 2. Let's examine a situation in which the number of items is even and determine the median.

■ **EXAMPLE 3.3**
Profitability Analysis: A Drug/Alcohol Abuse Treatment Center

Total KompKare, an all-purpose treatment center, has overexpanded and is financially strapped for cash. Consequently, KompKare is searching for a friendly merger candidate that will infuse new cash into KompKare's operations. In the treatment center business the length of a patient's stay is a crucial element for maintaining profitability. An analyst for Uni Hospital Corp., an interested merger prospect, is examining KompKare's business records. A sample of 14 patient files reveals the following length of stay (in days):

$$12 \quad 10 \quad 9 \quad 10 \quad 14 \quad 12 \quad 5 \quad 15 \quad 9 \quad 13 \quad 18 \quad 12 \quad 10 \quad 9$$

To find the value of the median for this set of data we first array the 14 observations from the smallest to the largest value:

$$5 \quad 9 \quad 9 \quad 9 \quad 10 \quad 10 \quad 10 \quad 12 \quad 12 \quad 12 \quad 13 \quad 14 \quad 15 \quad 18$$

Since 14 items is an even number of items, there is no unique middle item. The two middlemost values are the seventh and eighth items from either end. Starting from the low end, the value of the seventh observation is 10, and the value of the eighth item is 12. Any value between 10 and 12 may be considered the median value. One of the values in this range is halfway between 10 and 12; that is, $(10 + 12) \div 2 = 11$. By convention this midpoint of the range between the two middlemost items is identified as the median value. In this case, the value of the median is equal to 11.

In summary, the following is a procedure for finding the value of the median for a set of raw data:

Step 1
Rank the observations from the smallest value to the largest value.

Step 2
If the number of observations is odd, find the value of the unique middle observation.

Step 3

If the number of observations is even, locate the two middlemost observations and simply average their values (the sum of their values divided by 2).

When the number of observations is relatively small, this procedure can be followed easily. For large sets of observations, it is best to use computer statistical packages. These are designed to assign a rank to each data value and from the ranked values locate the median value, or at least locate the middlemost observations.

THE MEAN, OR ARITHMETIC AVERAGE

Another commonly used measure of central location is the arithmetic mean, generally referred to as the **mean**, or arithmetic average. To find the value of the mean for a set of observations we simply add up the values of the observations and divide by the total number of observations. For the 14 observations on length of stay in Example 3.3, the value of the mean is

$$\frac{5 + 9 + 9 + 9 + 10 + 10 + 10 + 12 + 12 + 12 + 13 + 14 + 15 + 18}{14} = 11.286$$

You'll see later that it's useful to have a formula expressing the operations involved in computing an arithmetic mean. To develop a formula, consider again the data given in Example 3.2. If we let X_1 represent 3.8, X_2 represent 1.1, X_3 represent 2.1, and so on, then

$$\text{Mean} = \frac{3.8 + 1.1 + 2.1 + 2.7 + 1.7 + 3.3 + 2.2}{7}$$

$$= \frac{X_1 + X_2 + X_3 + X_4 + X_5 + X_6 + X_7}{7}$$

$$= 2.414$$

We'll use μ (the Greek letter mu) to represent the mean of a population of numerical observations, and we'll use the symbol $\bar{X}$ (read, X bar) to represent the mean of a sample of numerical observations. These symbols are not interchangeable. In general, if N represents the number of observations in a population, then:

Population Mean

$$\mu = \text{Population mean} = \frac{X_1 + X_2 + \cdots + X_N}{N} = \frac{\sum_{i=1}^{N} X_i}{N} \qquad \textbf{(3-1)}$$

where the notation Σ means to sum a group of numbers. If you are not familiar with this **summation notation**, consult a college algebra textbook or the *Student Study Guide and Solutions Manual*, by Dirk Yandell, that accompanies this text.

If n represents the number of observations in a sample, then the sample mean formula is:

Sample Mean

$$\bar{X} = \text{Sample mean} = \frac{X_1 + X_2 + \cdots + X_n}{n} = \frac{\sum_{i=1}^{n} X_i}{n} \qquad \text{(3-2)}$$

Now let's calculate a sample mean. Suppose an amateur collector has obtained a relatively rare rock specimen on one of her weekend collecting trips. She wishes to weigh the rock to determine its value, but knows that her scale is inaccurate; it does not register the same measurement each time the same rock is weighed. To compensate for the variation in measurements, she decides to average five weighings. Her assumption is that the magnitude and direction of the error at each weighing is unrelated to the magnitude and direction of error of the previous weighings. Her thinking is that if she makes several weighings, the overestimates and underestimates will effectively cancel each other out, so that the average for the weighings will be very close to the true weight. She obtains the following measurements (in ounces): 3.7, 3.5, 3.4, 3.9, 3.6. Then she calculates the mean:

$$\bar{X} = \frac{3.7 + 3.5 + 3.4 + 3.9 + 3.6}{5} = 3.62$$

Thus, the amateur collector uses $\bar{X} = 3.62$ as an estimate of the rock's true weight. The value $\bar{X}$ should not itself be considered the true weight since it is an averaging of five values that are inaccurate. The five weighings represent a sample from the population of items (all possible weighings) of interest to us.

The mean is by far the most available measure of central location. Its availability on pocket calculators and portable computers make it the "average" most people refer to. But since it is the computational average of all the values of the data set, *the mean is sensitive to the values of extreme observations.* The median and mode, on the other hand, are virtually unaffected by the values of extreme observations, and this is frequently an advantage. For example, let's determine the mode, median, and mean for the following set of seven items:

$$1 \quad 2 \quad 3 \quad 3 \quad 3 \quad 4 \quad 5$$

For this set of data,

$$\text{Mode} = 3 \qquad \text{Median} = 3 \qquad \text{Mean} = 3$$

These values of the measures of central location tell us the most frequent value is 3 (mode); it is also the middle value (median); and it is the value that mathematically balances all the values in the data set (mean).

Now let's look at another set of seven items:

$$1 \quad 2 \quad 3 \quad 3 \quad 3 \quad 4 \quad 97$$

We find that

$$\text{Mode} = 3 \qquad \text{Median} = 3 \qquad \text{Mean} = 16.14$$

The two sets of seven items differ in only one item value: 97 replaces 5. Six items out of the seven retain the same value. But as we can see, the mean has been dramatically affected and presents a distorted view of the "typical" value of the data set. In using the mean we must be careful not to assume it is a middlemost value (unless we know that the histogram or frequency distribution is symmetrically shaped about the mean). Because of this sensitivity of the mean to extreme values, financial rating services such as Dun & Bradstreet use the median to report the average sized financial ratio across different sized firms.

Despite this disadvantage of the mean in some situations, the mean is a popular summary measure of central location. It is used in the development of statistical theory, and it possesses mathematical properties useful in determining other summary measures. We will soon see that the measure of variability called the standard deviation (referred to in the introduction to this chapter) relies for its computation on the mean. At least part of the popularity of the arithmetic mean is the algebraic relationship that makes it possible to go from a mean to a total. This is an especially desirable property when sample surveys are used instead of a population census. The following example illustrates why the mean serves as the key summary measure to estimate the size of the market for a product.

■ **EXAMPLE 3.4**

Estimating the Number of Cameras in Michigan

A camera manufacturer wants to estimate the total number of cameras in existence among Michigan households. The manufacturer surveys a sample of Michigan households and calculates the mean number of cameras per household in the sample. Using the sample mean of the survey as an estimate of the mean for the entire state of Michigan is the key to the problem. Then, all the manufacturer needs to do is multiply the sample survey mean by the number of all households, N, in Michigan to get an estimate of the total number of cameras in Michigan. For example, if the sample survey mean number of cameras per household is 1.2 and the number of Michigan households is 2 million, the estimated number of cameras in Michigan is (1.2)(2 million) = 2.4 million.

Since both the median and the mode are positional measures, there is no simple algebraic relationship between the median and the total or between the mode and the total. In survey work, especially in business and economics, the real interest often centers on the total for some population, and this unquestionably contributes to the popularity of the mean as a summary measure.

• •

PRACTICE EXERCISES

3.1 The following data represent exam grades obtained by 45 students in an elementary statistics class (these data were first seen in Practice Exercise 2.1):

72	70	60	85	78		100	55	76	100	37		25	71	76	80	17
96	70	51	100	91		98	72	69	58	25		91	70	84	70	98
85	50	100	47	49		67	58	56	66	93		31	60	83	93	62

Find the values of the mode, median, and mean.

3.2 "We expect purchasers to wait an average of 10 weeks after the product hits the market before making the purchase."

Suppose you are in charge of distributing this product. You would like to know when peak demand is likely to occur so that you can estimate how long you have to build a distribution system that can handle peak demand. You think the 10 week average mentioned in the preceding statement might be useful for this purpose, but you are uncertain whether the average mentioned is a mean, median, or mode. For your purposes, which type of average would be most useful? Explain.

● ●

3.3

MEASURES OF VARIABILITY, OR DISPERSION

Central location is only one of the characteristics of a histogram for which we might want a numerical summary measure. Another characteristic is the **variability**, **dispersion**, or spread of values in a distribution. What is true about a comparison between central location measures of two populations is not necessarily true about a comparison of their spreads. For example, in comparing the central location of two school populations in Section 3.2, we said school 1 should have a numerical central location measure that is higher in value than the one for school 2. The situation is quite different when it comes to variability. Both histograms in Figures 3.2 and 3.3 are the same shape and appear to have the same spread of values around their respective centers, so we expect to find very similar values for their summary numerical measures of dispersion.

Are the values of the observations clustered closely about the center, or are they widely dispersed? In drawing comparisons between two sets of data, we may find that the two sets of data have the same center but differ dramatically in how observations cluster about the center. To distinguish between such data sets, another numerical measure is needed—one that measures the dispersion of observations.

Suppose that the same questionnaire sent to the 80 students at the two small rural high schools was also sent to another 40 students at a third small rural high school. The third school's responses for the question on annual college expenditures needed are shown in Table 3.3 (in thousands of dollars). A histogram representation for these data is given in Figure 3.4.

TABLE 3.3 Forty Student Responses on Annual Expenditure Needed for College (in Thousands of Dollars)									
POPULATION OF OBSERVATIONS FROM SCHOOL 3									
6.7	7.5	8.3	9.2	8.3	8.8	10.1	7.3	8.1	6.8
9.9	8.1	6.7	6.6	8.8	6.7	9.0	7.2	6.8	9.5
7.8	8.5	7.9	11.2	9.8	8.4	6.7	7.9	7.8	8.2
10.2	7.1	9.5	7.3	8.0	7.4	9.9	8.5	8.3	7.8

Now compare Figure 3.4 to Figure 3.2. Both histograms have the same general central location and shape, but they differ in the spread along the horizontal axis. The distribution of student responses for school 3 appears to have a much narrower spread than the distribution of student responses for school 1.

Six numerical summary measures are commonly used to quantify the spread, or dispersion, of a distribution: *range, interquartile range, mean absolute deviation, variance, standard deviation,* and *coefficient of variation.*

Figure 3.4
Histogram of responses on annual expenditures needed for school 3

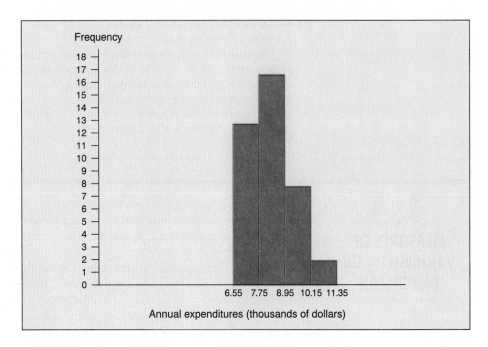

RANGE

The **range** is the numerical summary measure already mentioned in Chapter 2. It is calculated by obtaining the difference between the value of the largest observation and the value of the smallest observation. Looking at the values in Table 3.2, the range for school 1 is equal to 12.5 − 5.5 = 7. Looking at Table 3.3, the value of the range for school 3 is equal to 11.2 − 6.6 = 4.6. The smaller value for school 3 is indicative of the narrower spread of the distribution for school 3 compared to the distribution for school 1. The value of the range is a quick and easy numerical summary measure to calculate; it requires only two values—the largest and smallest values of the distribution. But, unfortunately, since it relies on only two values, *the range can give no hint as to whether a concentration of values in the distribution exists or not.*

There are situations in which the range can serve as a very useful measure of dispersion, such as in quality control procedures. To assure uniformity in the measurements of a product from a production process, the range of the measurements must be kept within prescribed limits. If the range exceeds the limits, the product is considered to lack uniformity, and the production process is not meeting product specifications and may be deemed out of control. A detailed discussion of quality control and procedures used to determine when a production process is out of control is given in the Comprehensive Case Study following Chapter 6.

Since the range considers only the value of the observation at the lowest position in the distribution and the value of the observation at the highest position in the distribution, the range is also classified as a summary measure of relative position. Computationally simple to obtain, the range is also conceptually the most easily understood of all summary measures of dispersion.

INTERQUARTILE RANGE

Another positional measure of dispersion is the **interquartile range (IQR)**. The interquartile range is the width of the boxplots discussed in Chapter 2. Like the range, it is the difference between two values: the value beyond which lies the highest 25% of the observations (the third or upper quartile, Q_3 or UQ), and the value below which lies the lowest 25% (the first or lower quartile, Q_1 or LQ) of the observations. For the annual salary data for San Diego workers discussed in Chapter 2, the IQR can be obtained from the boxplot shown in Figure 2.14. The IQR is $Q_3 - Q_1 = \text{UQ} - \text{LQ}$, or $\$33,101 - \$15,428 = \$17,673$. Table 3.4 illustrates how the financial service agency Dun & Bradstreet reports the IQR for different types of retailing, wholesaling, manufacturing, and construction industries as standards of comparison or norms for selected financial ratios, against which individual firms in the industry can be compared.

TABLE 3.4			Examples of Dun & Bradstreet's 14 Financial Ratios for Selected Industries*											
LINE OF BUSINESS (NUMBER OF CONCERNS REPORTING)	QUICK RATIO (×)	CURRENT RATIO (×)	CURRENT LIABILITIES TO NET WORTH (%)	CURRENT LIABILITIES TO INVENTORY (%)	TOTAL LIABILITIES TO NET WORTH (%)	FIXED ASSETS TO NET WORTH (%)	COLLECTION PERIOD (DAYS)	SALES TO INVENTORY (×)	TOTAL ASSETS TO SALES (%)	SALES TO NET WORKING CAPITAL (×)	ACCOUNTS PAYABLE TO SALES (%)	RETURN ON SALES (%)	RETURN ON TOTAL ASSETS (%)	RETURN ON NET WORTH (%)
CREDIT REPORTING SERVICES (130)	6.1 2.3 1.0	9.9 3.4 1.4	7.3 20.8 62.3	186.1 260.7 335.4	9.2 29.4 83.5	14.0 31.8 67.8	28.0 42.9 54.9	71.0 47.6 24.1	27.6 44.2 66.9	9.4 5.4 2.7	1.5 2.5 4.0	15.0 4.6 2.8	18.3 8.3 0.8	68.0 19.5 1.5
HIGHWAY AND STREET CONSTRUCTION (2455)	2.4 1.4 0.9	3.1 1.8 1.3	24.6 56.1 114.0	198.4 348.3 577.2	39.1 88.2 175.1	38.0 71.0 116.5	26.7 47.5 71.0	136.7 55.0 21.7	32.9 46.0 65.4	15.8 8.4 4.5	2.8 5.8 9.9	7.5 2.9 0.6	12.4 5.4 0.7	24.9 11.2 1.7
TIRES AND TUBES (565)	1.2 0.8 0.5	2.4 1.6 1.2	50.3 122.5 262.7	77.0 119.5 183.8	61.6 154.8 330.9	16.6 33.1 70.2	23.4 35.4 50.7	11.7 7.3 5.3	27.2 35.2 45.5	17.5 9.2 5.4	7.3 10.9 16.5	3.7 1.5 0.4	7.8 3.5 0.7	24.7 9.5 2.2
LABORATORY APPARATUS (71)	2.2 1.1 0.8	4.6 2.3 1.6	18.1 53.5 113.4	47.5 99.4 163.9	20.2 73.0 152.6	12.7 37.1 67.2	39.4 58.8 74.5	12.3 6.0 4.2	42.4 56.8 90.4	6.9 4.4 3.1	3.8 5.7 8.7	12.3 3.6 0.8	11.8 5.4 0.6	33.1 12.9 1.4
NONRESIDENTIAL CONSTRUCTION (1885)	2.2 1.4 1.0	2.9 1.7 1.3	35.0 90.1 190.5	103.8 253.9 595.7	48.1 109.0 220.0	10.8 22.9 50.6	26.3 47.1 67.2	237.3 82.2 25.9	21.9 30.3 44.6	17.8 9.9 5.7	3.7 7.5 12.2	6.8 2.7 0.7	15.0 6.3 1.8	33.6 15.6 4.3
MANAGEMENT SERVICES (1022)	2.9 1.3 0.7	4.0 1.9 1.1	15.2 48.0 133.6	90.0 247.5 532.1	26.2 73.9 195.5	12.2 34.7 79.4	16.4 45.8 90.9	140.5 55.6 17.1	25.9 47.4 109.2	15.6 6.6 3.0	1.7 4.2 9.7	16.0 4.6 1.1	20.2 6.9 1.2	50.9 16.8 3.3

Source: "Industry Norms & Key Business Ratios Desk-Top Edition 1990–91," Dun & Bradstreet Business Credit Services.
*Industry average ratios (1990) for selected lines of business. The center value is the median, and the values immediately above and below it are the upper and lower quartiles, respectively.

MEASURES OF DISPERSION BASED ON ARITHMETIC CALCULATIONS

All positional measures of dispersion such as the range and IQR have the same key drawback. Individually, they don't provide information on the density of observations and so give little idea as to the concentration of the observations around some central point. This drawback is somewhat alleviated by graphical devices such as the boxplot (discussed in Chapter 2), constructed from five key positions within the distribution (the highest and lowest values; the middlemost value, or median; and the upper and lower quartiles).

However, to provide information on the density of observations there are numerical measures of dispersion that take into account every observation. We'll consider three such measures: the mean absolute deviation, variance, and standard deviation. These measures require arithmetic calculations on each observation rather than finding the relative position of only one or two observations.

How should a measure of dispersion be constructed using all the data? When asked this question, students often suggest constructing a measure of dispersion for the "total difference" between individual observations and a measure of central location, say, the arithmetic mean. Using the mean, the idea would be that the more dispersed the values from the mean, the greater should be the "total difference." Let's examine this suggestion more closely with the following example.

Suppose company A has two branches, one in San Diego and one in Phoenix. The monthly salaries of the five employees working in its San Diego branch are $1498, $1764, $1291, $1117, and $1650. The mean salary for these five employees is $1464.

The monthly salaries of the five employees working in the Phoenix branch are $1333, $1587, $1455, $1564, and $1381. The mean salary for these five employees is also $1464. The distribution of the salaries, relative to the mean, for both branches is shown graphically in Figure 3.5. Clearly, there is a wider spread among the San Diego branch employees' monthly salaries than among the Phoenix branch employees' monthly salaries.

But let's see what happens when we follow the approach suggested above. Following the suggested approach, the total of the numerical differences for the San Diego employees is

$$(\$1498 - \$1464) + (\$1764 - \$1464) + (\$1291 - \$1464) + (\$1117 - \$1464) + (\$1650 - \$1464) = 0$$

For the Phoenix employees, we have

$$(\$1333 - \$1464) + (\$1587 - \$1464) + (\$1455 - \$1464) + (\$1564 - \$1464) + (\$1381 - \$1464) = 0$$

In both cases, the total (sum) of the differences is 0. By definition of the mean this result must always hold true. This is because the sum of the positive differences from the mean must always be equal to the sum of the negative differences from the

Figure 3.5
A comparison of the dispersion of salaries of ten employees working for the same company, but at two different branches

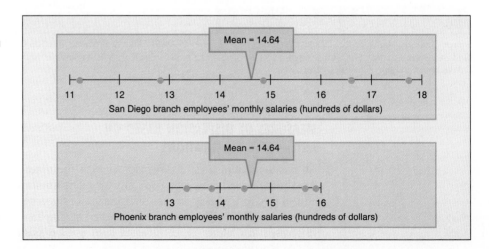

mean. Adding all the differences together will always yield 0. One way to avoid this result is to eliminate the signs of the differences. The next summary measure of variation that we'll discuss does just that.

MEAN ABSOLUTE DEVIATION

If we decide to eliminate the signs of the differences by using the absolute values of the differences, we obtain a summary measure of dispersion called the **mean absolute deviation (MAD)**. The mean absolute deviation requires us to take the absolute value of the numerical difference between each observational value and the mean, sum the absolute values, and then divide the sum by the number of observations.

For the San Diego employees, the mean absolute deviation is

$$\frac{|\$1498 - \$1464| + |\$1764 - \$1464| + |\$1291 - \$1464| + |\$1117 - \$1464| + |\$1650 - \$1464|}{5} = \$208$$

For the Phoenix employees, the mean absolute deviation is

$$\frac{|\$1333 - \$1464| + |\$1587 - \$1464| + |\$1455 - \$1464| + |\$1564 - \$1464| + |\$1381 - \$1464|}{5} = \$89.20$$

Judging from the values of the mean absolute deviations, the San Diego employees' salaries are more than twice as dispersed as the salaries of the Phoenix employees. This statement agrees with our visual conclusion from Figure 3.5.

The formula that describes the mean absolute deviation is:

Population Mean Absolute Deviation

$$\text{MAD} = \frac{\sum_{i=1}^{N} |X_i - \mu|}{N} \tag{3-3}$$

The corresponding formula for the sample is:

Sample Mean Absolute Deviation

$$\text{MAD} = \frac{\sum_{i=1}^{n} |X_i - \bar{X}|}{n} \tag{3-4}$$

The MAD is an appropriate summary error measure to use when the business and economic consequences are tied directly to the deviations from the mean in either direction. For this reason, several economic forecasting systems use the MAD as an error measure.

VARIANCE AND STANDARD DEVIATION

The second way to eliminate signs is to square the differences before summing. The resulting summary measure of dispersion obtained by summing the squared differences between each value and the mean and then dividing the sum by the number of observations is called the **variance**.

For the San Diego employees, the value of the variance is

$$\frac{(1498 - 1464)^2 + (1764 - 1464)^2 + (1291 - 1464)^2 + (1117 - 1464)^2 + (1650 - 1464)^2}{5} = 55,218$$

and for the Phoenix employees, the value of the variance is

$$\frac{(1333 - 1464)^2 + (1587 - 1464)^2 + (1455 - 1464)^2 + (1564 - 1464)^2 + (1381 - 1464)^2}{5} = 9852$$

These two variance values (55,218 and 9852) reflect the difference in the dispersions of the two groups in squared terms. *The variance can be interpreted as the average of the squared differences.* The formula for the population variance, denoted by the symbol σ^2 (the Greek letter sigma squared), is:

Population Variance

$$\sigma^2 = \frac{\sum\limits_{i=1}^{N} (X_i - \mu)^2}{N} \tag{3-5}$$

An equivalent computational formula for the variance helps avoid some of the lengthy computations of squared terms in the defining formula (3-5). It comes in handy when the observational values involve several digits.

Computational Formula for Population Variance

$$\sigma^2 = \frac{\sum\limits_{i=1}^{N} X_i^2 - N\mu^2}{N} = \frac{\sum\limits_{i=1}^{N} X_i^2 - \dfrac{\left(\sum\limits_{i=1}^{N} X_i\right)^2}{N}}{N} \tag{3-6}$$

Using the computational formula (3-6) for the salaries of the San Diego employees, we have

$$\sum X^2 = (1498)^2 + (1764)^2 + (1291)^2 + (1117)^2 + (1650)^2$$
$$= 10,992,570$$

and

$$\sigma^2 = \frac{10,992,570 - 5(1464)^2}{5} = 55,218$$

A comparison of the variance values shows that the variance of the San Diego employees' salaries (55,218) exceeds that of the Phoenix employees (9852). Although we can clearly conclude that the San Diego employees face a greater dispersion of salaries than do the Phoenix employees, we should keep in mind that the variance uses squared terms (in this case, squared dollar terms), and therefore actual differences tend to be magnified.

We would expect the formula for the sample variance to parallel the formula for the population variance, simply using $\bar{X}$ instead of μ and n instead of N. However, statisticians prefer to use the following formula, and this is the sample variance formula we will use in this text:

Sample Variance

$$S^2 = \frac{\sum\limits_{i=1}^{n} (X_i - \bar{X})^2}{n - 1} \qquad (3\text{-}7)$$

Why use $n - 1$ instead of n in the denominator? Although the proof is beyond the scope of this text, the purpose of dividing by $n - 1$, and not n, is to ensure that the sample variance will be an unbiased estimate of the population variance. The sample variance defined using n in the denominator would, on average, underestimate the population variance. This is especially true when the sample size n is small. By using $n - 1$ we appropriately compensate for this underestimation.

As for the population variance, we have a computational formula for the sample variance, S^2, that substitutes for formula (3-7) and eliminates lengthy calculations, particularly if noninteger data are given.

Computational Formula for Sample Variance

$$S^2 = \frac{n \sum\limits_{i=1}^{n} X_i^2 - \left(\sum\limits_{i=1}^{n} X_i\right)^2}{n(n - 1)} = \frac{\sum\limits_{i=1}^{n} X_i^2 - \dfrac{\left(\sum\limits_{i=1}^{n} X_i\right)^2}{n}}{n - 1} \qquad (3\text{-}8)$$

Another commonly used numerical summary measure of variability is the **standard deviation**. The population standard deviation is the square root of the population variance and is represented by the Greek letter σ.

The defining and computational formulas for the population standard deviation are:

Population Standard Deviation

$$\sigma = \sqrt{\frac{\sum\limits_{i=1}^{N} (X_i - \mu)^2}{N}} \qquad (3\text{-}9)$$

Computational Formula

$$\sigma = \sqrt{\frac{\sum\limits_{i=1}^{N} X_i^2 - \dfrac{\left(\sum\limits_{i=1}^{N} X_i\right)^2}{N}}{N}} \tag{3-10}$$

The standard deviation and the variance are very prevalent measures of dispersion, especially in discussions and reports where the reader can be assumed to be acquainted with elementary statistics. The standard deviation is the more widely used of the two. Since the standard deviation value is expressed in the same measurement units as the observations and the mean, it lends itself to direct use and interpretation. For example, when observations are measured in pounds, the mean and standard deviation will also be measured in pounds, but the variance will be measured in pounds squared.

For the salaries of the San Diego employees, the value of the population standard deviation is the square root of 55,218, that is, $\sqrt{55,218} = \$234.985$. For the salaries of the Phoenix employees, the value of the population standard deviation is the square root of 9852, that is, $\sqrt{9852} = \$99.257$. The large numerical difference between the two standard deviations is clear evidence that the salaries of the San Diego employees are substantially more spread out than those of the Phoenix employees, a fact consistent with Figure 3.5.

The sample standard deviation is simply the square root of the sample variance. The computational formula for the sample standard deviation is simply the square root of the computational formula for the sample variance.

Computational Formula for Sample Standard Deviation

$$S = \sqrt{\frac{n \sum\limits_{i=1}^{n} X_i^2 - \left(\sum\limits_{i=1}^{n} X_i\right)^2}{n(n-1)}} = \sqrt{\frac{\sum\limits_{i=1}^{n} X_i^2 - \dfrac{\left(\sum\limits_{i=1}^{n} X_i\right)^2}{n}}{n-1}} \tag{3-11}$$

We are now ready to examine a situation in which measuring variability becomes the critical element of the business decision.

■ **EXAMPLE 3.5**

Measuring Delivery Time Dependability

A Chicago produce distributor wants to cut physical distribution costs, a major component of total costs. With a good estimate of transit time, storage and holding costs can be cut. The sooner the order is met, the lower will be the physical costs of storing and holding. Transit time tends to increase with increasing distance between origin and Chicago. For produce originating in California, an estimate of mean transit time for shipments going 2000 miles to Chicago enables the Chicago produce distributor to plan how much lead time to allow in placing orders. Shorter average transit time guarantees fresher produce on arrival. But there still remains concern about the variability of the transit times around the estimated mean transit time for 2000 mile trips. The greater the variation in transit times, the more uncertain is the arrival time for any particular shipment. An actual transit time substantially different from the average will cause disastrous operating problems. For instance, lettuce from California arriving too early may wilt on the loading dock while waiting to be processed. Late arriving lettuce is likely to disrupt scheduled service to restaurants and supermarkets, which depend on receiving daily delivery. Confronted with possible spoilage costs or unserviced customers, the Chicago produce distributor may forego using one mode of transit with a lower average transit time in favor of another offering greater dependability, even if the latter, on the average, delivers produce that is somewhat less fresh.

For example, say one mode of transit schedules 9 days on average, but transit time varies from 7 to 15 days, a range of 8 days. Another mode of transit has an average of 10 days, but transit time varies between 8 and 12 days, a range of only 4 days. The latter transit mode appears to provide a more dependable service since it has a smaller range than that shown by the first transit mode.

However, the standard deviation of delivery time might be a better measure of delivery time variability than the range, since the standard deviation takes into account the density of clustering around the mean. Thus, looking at S as the measure of dependability, what if $S = 1.6$ for the first mode of transit and $S = 0.7$ for the second mode? Again, the second mode would be judged the more reliable supplier and is better suited to the produce distributor's needs, but this time we also have taken into account a measure of the density of clustering around the mean, so we feel more certain that this is the better choice.

Now, here is a practice exercise to help sharpen your skills in calculating the various measures of dispersion.

PRACTICE EXERCISE

3.3 The following data represent exam grades obtained by 45 students in an elementary statistics class:

72	70	60	85	78	100	55	76	100	37	25	71	76	80	17
96	70	51	100	91	98	72	69	58	25	91	70	84	70	98
85	50	100	47	49	67	58	56	66	93	31	60	83	93	62

Find the values of the range, variance, and standard deviation.

COEFFICIENT OF VARIATION

The common measures of dispersion—the range, interquartile range, mean absolute deviation, variance, and standard deviation—are called *absolute measures of dispersion* since they are computed without reference to any other summary measure. But there is a *relative* measure of dispersion that has become widely used: the **coefficient of variation (CV)**. The coefficient of variation is a relative measure since it makes a relative comparison of the standard deviation of the distribution to the mean of the distribution in the form of a ratio. The expression for the population coefficient of variation (in percentage terms) is:

Coefficient of Variation

$$CV = \frac{\sigma}{\mu}(100) \qquad (3\text{-}12)$$

Because standard deviation (σ) and mean (μ) are measured in the same units, the coefficient of variation ratio is a pure number without units of measurement. This allows us to use the coefficient of variation to *compare the relative variation* shown by two sets of measurement data without regard for the units or the magnitudes of measurement of the two data sets. For example, if twenty measurements are found to have a mean of 1000 lb and a standard deviation of 100 lb, they will have the same relative variation as twenty measurements that yield a mean of 10 in. and a standard deviation of 1 in.

Let's now see how the coefficient of variation can be applied in a business situation.

■ **EXAMPLE 3.6**

Sales Consistency

Suppose two store managers of a supermarket chain are competing for a promotion on the basis of sales performance. Manager A shows that for the past 3 months her store showed average (arithmetic mean) sales of $27,000 per day, with a standard deviation of $4500 per day. Manager B shows that for the past 3 months his store showed average (arithmetic mean) sales of $37,000 per day, with a standard deviation of $5200 per day. The district supervisor is impressed by manager B's higher daily average sales, but is concerned with his higher variability. Consistency, in the form of steady, narrowly fluctuating sales, is highly desirable for a firm dealing with perishables.

To make a more quantitative appraisal of the relative variabilities of the sales in the two stores, the district supervisor calculates their respective coefficients of variation. For manager A's store, the coefficient of variation is

$$CV = \frac{4500}{27,000}(100) = 16.67\%$$

For manager B's store, the coefficient of variation is

$$CV = \frac{5200}{37,000}(100) = 14.05\%$$

So the district supervisor concludes that although manager B's store shows more *absolute variation* in sales than manager A's store, manager B's store actually shows less *relative variation* in sales, considering the higher level of sales. The supervisor now feels more confident that manager B has a better sales performance and therefore is in line for the promotion.

We can also calculate the coefficient of variation for samples (cv). It is the ratio of the sample standard deviation to the sample mean and is expressed as:

Sample Coefficient of Variation

$$cv = \frac{S}{\bar{X}}(100) \qquad (3\text{-}13)$$

3.4
SAMPLE COMPUTER OUTPUT

Computers are commonly used to organize raw data and calculate descriptive statistical measures. For example, the data on excess patient waiting times discussed in Chapter 2 consisted of 200 observations, so making these calculations by hand is very tedious. A computer can perform all the calculations very quickly once the data are typed in. Outputs from the MINITAB and business MYSTAT statistical software packages are shown in Figure 3.6 for the excess waiting time data. Notice that neither system calculates the mode as a central location measure. Both systems provide the standard deviation as a measure of dispersion, but neither system gives the interquartile range, MAD, or coefficient of variation. Both systems treat all data as sample data, so the standard deviation values are given as sample standard deviations. MINITAB reports the first and third quartile values as Q1 and Q3, respectively, so the interquartile range can be found·by taking the difference between Q1 and Q3. The coefficient of variation also can be determined from the MINITAB and MYSTAT results by dividing the standard deviation by the mean and multiplying by 100. The MAD cannot be determined from either output.

```
MTB > desc 'wtgtime'

                  N      MEAN    MEDIAN    TRMEAN     STDEV    SEMEAN
wtgtime         200     50.09     50.00     50.14     19.32      1.37

                MIN       MAX        Q1        Q3
wtgtime        0.00    100.00     36.00     62.75

a
```

```
TOTAL OBSERVATIONS:     200


                        WTGTIME


        N OF CASES                 200
        MINIMUM                  0.000
        MAXIMUM                100.000
        RANGE                  100.000
        MEAN                    50.090
        STANDARD DEV            19.323
        STD. ERROR              1.366
        SKEWNESS(G1)             0.014
        KURTOSIS(G2)            -0.085
        SUM                  10018.000

        b
```

MINITAB and MYSTAT both provide only sample standard deviations. If the 200 data values are considered a population, then we find the value for the population standard deviation σ as $19.323\sqrt{199}/\sqrt{200} = 19.27 = \sigma$.

Figure 3.6
(a) MINITAB and (b) business MYSTAT output for excess patient waiting time data

3.5

SOME USES OF THE MEAN AND STANDARD DEVIATION

We have described several measures of central location and dispersion for data. Two of these measures, the mean as a measure of central location and the standard deviation as a measure of dispersion, will be used extensively in the remainder of this book. Using only these two measures we can learn much about a data set.

CHEBYSHEV'S THEOREM

There is a mathematical theorem that uses the mean and standard deviation to make a remarkable statement about the concentration of observations around the mean for any set of data. The theorem is called **Chebyshev's theorem** and it states:

Chebyshev's Theorem

> For any set of data (numerical observations), the proportion of the data that lie within a specified distance of k standard deviations on either side of the mean is *at least* equal to $1 - 1/k^2$, where $k > 1$.

According to the theorem, therefore, for any data set we can expect to find the following:

1. At least $1 - 1/2^2 = .7500$ of the observations lie within a distance of ± 2 standard deviations of the mean. Commonly, a proportion of .75 is reported as 75% of the observations.
2. At least $1 - 1/3^2 = .8889$ of the observations lie within a distance of ± 3 standard deviations of the mean.
3. At least $1 - 1/4^2 = .9375$ of the observations lie within a distance of ± 4 standard deviations of the mean.

Letting X represent the value of an observation, the theorem may be represented by the expression below:

Chebyshev's Theorem

$$P(\mu - k\sigma < X < \mu + k\sigma) \geq 1 - \frac{1}{k^2} \qquad \text{for } k > 1 \qquad (3\text{-}14)$$

This inequality reads, "The proportion of observed values that lie between $\mu - k\sigma$ and $\mu + k\sigma$ is at least equal to $1 - 1/k^2$." Note that the value of k need not be an integer. Chebyshev's theorem gives only the *minimum* estimate of the percentage of observations that lie within k standard deviations of the mean. In actuality, Chebyshev's theorem is generally a rather conservative estimate of the actual percentage of observations that lie within k standard deviations of the mean.

To demonstrate the applicability of Chebyshev's theorem, let's look back at the patient waiting time data of Table 2.2. We restate the data for convenience, as shown in Table 3.5.

TABLE 3.5	Raw Data: 200 Recordings on Excess Patient Waiting Time at a Hospital Emergency Room (Nearest Minute)																			
39	41	53	54		85	69	81	36		32	51	41	49		23	53	46	48		27	45	15	61
40	79	50	39		59	46	52	51		0	33	33	38		51	34	40	57		47	56	79	41
100	45	49	60		76	49	66	48		73	15	6	31		44	48	29	41		68	62	46	70
72	40	60	44		56	46	92	36		74	25	78	52		37	24	35	54		26	52	33	73
47	88	63	14		30	51	26	25		53	46	49	53		63	64	43	48		64	1	29	22
74	32	87	60		26	59	53	23		50	41	58	36		32	33	51	44		31	58	74	50
62	60	42	32		51	31	89	30		55	60	9	61		12	0	80	25		41	78	61	66
69	49	63	76		97	79	52	69		54	49	67	59		55	48	23	81		25	59	89	51
71	50	62	87		34	43	40	31		27	65	51	78		36	73	50	45		36	52	69	31
85	77	68	58		56	29	29	64		49	71	41	37		44	54	64	36		66	62	42	36

For the data in Table 3.5, we find that $\mu = 50.09$ and $\sigma = 19.2744$. Suppose the Joint Committee for Accreditation of Hospitals wishes to set k to determine the guideline that one would expect to encompass nearly 90% of the patient waiting times. According to Chebyshev's theorem, for $k = 3$, at least $1 - 1/3^2 = .8889$ (88.89%) of the observations should lie between

$$\mu - 3\sigma = 50.09 - 3(19.2744) = -7.7332$$

and

$$\mu + 3\sigma = 50.09 + 3(19.2744) = 107.9132$$

If the emergency room of this hospital can be considered typical of a well-run emergency room, it would be appropriate for the committee to apply Chebyshev's theorem to the mean and standard deviation of this distribution and set a reasonable standard for maximum waiting time. For example, rounding off 107.9132 to 108 minutes, the committee could recommend that all accredited hospitals set 108 minutes as a maximum waiting time for patients. This stipulation could be implemented since at least 88.89% of the waiting times meet this standard (108 minutes or less). This example illustrates that important statements about the set of data can be made from the summary values of μ and σ without the need of the individual observations.

PRACTICE EXERCISE

3.4 The following data represent exam grades obtained by 45 students in an elementary statistics class:

72	70	60	85	78		100	55	76	100	37		25	71	76	80	17
96	70	51	100	91		98	72	69	58	25		91	70	84	70	98
85	50	100	47	49		67	58	56	66	93		31	60	83	93	62

According to Chebyshev's theorem, at least 75% of the observations should lie within 2 standard deviations of the mean. That is, at least 75% of the observations should lie within the bounds $\mu - 2\sigma$ and $\mu + 2\sigma$.

a. Find the values of these two bounds for the given data.
b. Find the actual percentage of the observations that lie within these bounds.

STANDARDIZED SCORE, OR *Z* SCORE

The difference between an observation's value, X, and its mean, μ, is often standardized by dividing the difference by the value of the standard deviation, σ. The difference is then expressed in terms of standard deviation units, and the result is called a **standardized score**, or **Z score**:

Standard Z Score

$$\text{For populations} \quad Z = \frac{X - \mu}{\sigma}$$

$$\text{For samples} \quad Z = \frac{X - \bar{X}}{S}$$

(3-15)

The value of a Z score may be positive or negative, depending on whether the value X lies above or below μ or $\bar{X}$. By expressing Chebyshev's theorem in terms of the standardized, or Z, score we can write:

Chebyshev Inequality

$$P(-k < Z < +k) \geq 1 - \frac{1}{k^2} \qquad \text{for } k > 1$$

(3-16)

This equation reads, "The proportion of Z scores with values between $\pm k$ is at least equal to $1 - 1/k^2$."

When Z scores are reported to an audience that is not familiar with statistical terminology, a transformation is sometimes made so that the scores are (supposedly) more comprehensible. One common transformation reads: transformed standardized score $= 100Z + 500$. A transformation of this kind is used to report SAT verbal and math scores.

PRACTICE EXERCISE

3.5 Suppose a class of 35 students had an average score of 60.8, with a standard deviation of 14, on a final exam.
  a. If a student scored 72 on the final exam, what was the standardized Z score?
  b. If a student has a standardized Z score of -1.2, what was the actual score on the final exam?

OUTLIERS

As explained in Chapter 2, an outlier is an observation in a data set that does not lie within the general range of all the other values. One way to determine whether a value is an outlier is to use the Z score along with Chebyshev's theorem. Sometimes the outlier is found to be the result of a recording error or a misclassification error.

According to Chebyshev's theorem, the proportion of all the calculated Z scores that lie between -5 and $+5$ is at least

$$P(-5 < Z \text{ score} < +5) \geq 1 - \frac{1}{5^2} = .96$$

This means that not more than 4% of the time should a Z score be less than −5 or greater than +5. Thus, finding a Z score value greater than +5 or less than −5 is good evidence that the observation is an outlier. Detecting and identifying the cause of an outlier is an important issue in production and quality control, as the following example illustrates.

Suppose a large corporation's quality control inspector examines the data reported on the percentage of defective items produced on five production lines over three shifts on the previous day. The data are presented in Table 3.6.

TABLE 3.6 The Percent Defective for Five Production Lines Over Three Shifts					
		PRODUCTION LINE			
		1	**2**	**3**	**4**	**5**
SHIFT	**1**	1.1	1.9	0.9	1.2	1.9
	2	1.9	1.1	1.7	11.1	1.1
	3	1.0	2.0	1.8	1.8	0.9

The inspector spots a rather high percentage value (11.1%) for production line 4 on shift 2. It is not a typical value, and it may not be plausible given the distribution of the other values. If the value is found to be inconsistent with the distribution of the other values, there is just cause to investigate further the reason for its occurrence. The inspector analyzes the data:

1. Excluding the 11.1% value, the mean and standard deviation of the distribution of the other 14 values are $\mu = 1.45$ and $\sigma = 0.4188$.
2. With respect to the mean and standard deviation of the 14 item distribution, the percentage 11.1 has a Z score value of

$$Z = \frac{11.1 - 1.45}{0.4188} = 23 \quad \text{(approx.)}$$

3. A Z score of 23 indicates that the value 11.1 lies 23 standard deviations away from the mean of the distribution of the other values. This is a very strong indication that 11.1 is an outlier.

Armed with this evaluation, the inspector approaches the technician who wrote the report. Fortunately their discussion reveals that the 11.1 value was the result of a transcription error and not a system failure. The technician had written 1.1 on his inspection sheet, but someone had accidentally inserted an extra "1" when the data were transferred to the report.

SYMMETRY AND SKEWNESS

The skewness characteristic of a distribution reflects the asymmetry of the spread of values. The magnitude of the differences among the values of the mean, mode, and median signal the degree of skewness that exists. The greater the gap between the median and mean values, the greater the tendency toward skewness in the direction of the mean.

● ●

EXERCISES ❏

3.1 A census of the incomes in a certain affluent neighborhood revealed the following recent annual gross incomes (in dollars) for all 29 families living there:

247,919	285,983	234,994	264,916	286,789	319,331
237,949	272,290	247,604	287,280	279,043	272,333
334,561	277,340	277,534	258,180	302,751	278,391
317,594	248,426	266,364	285,085	300,649	292,394
259,456	264,455	281,118	246,746	250,356	

a. Find the values of the mean, median, and mode.
b. Find the values of the range, mean absolute deviation, variance, standard deviation, and coefficient of variation.
c. Use Chebyshev's theorem to determine, at the least, how many of the raw data values should lie within 1.8 standard deviations of the mean. Compare your answer with an actual count of the raw data values that do lie within 1.8 standard deviations of the mean. How does the result using Chebyshev's theorem compare with the actual count?
d. What impressions do you get from these results?

❏ ▶ **3.2** A salesperson makes a 5% commission on every sale she makes. In the past 25 working days her daily sales (in dollars) were

2864	4913	5058	3432	3350	4491	4873	1640	2980	4591
3965	4361	3771	5172	4451	3424	3496	3479	3929	4527
4036	4095	5122	3833	3808					

a. Find the values of the mean, median, and mode.
b. Find the values of the range, mean absolute deviation, variance, standard deviation, and coefficient of variation.
c. Use Chebyshev's theorem to determine, at the least, how many of the raw data values should lie within 2.4 standard deviations of the mean. Compare your answer with an actual count of the raw data values that do lie within 2.4 standard deviations of the mean. How does the result using Chebyshev's theorem compare with the actual count?
d. What impressions do you get from these results?
e. Since the raw data represent sales, and since the salesperson makes a 5% commission, what was her average daily earnings for the 25 day period?
f. Suppose the salesperson earned a 5% commission on all sales up to $2500, a 6% commission on all sales from $2500 to $3000, and a 7% commission on all sales over $3000. What was her total earnings for the 25 day period? What was her average commission for the 25 day period?

● ●

3.6

MEASURES OF CENTRAL LOCATION AND DISPERSION FROM GROUPED DATA

Often, data are published in the form of frequency tables, with the original raw data unavailable. Without access to the raw data it is impossible to calculate exactly the values of such summary measures as the mean and standard deviation. It is possible, however, to obtain approximate measures of central location and dispersion from data presented in the frequency table. To illustrate, we shall use the frequency table for the excess patient waiting times given previously in Table 2.3 and reproduced in modified form as Table 3.7. The techniques that are applied to obtain the summary measures require the class midpoint for each interval.

TABLE 3.7 Frequency Table for Excess Patient Waiting Times			
LOWER CLASS BOUNDARY	**CLASS MIDPOINT** m_i	**UPPER CLASS BOUNDARY**	**CLASS FREQUENCY** f_i
−5.5	−0.5	4.5	3
4.5	9.5	14.5	4
14.5	19.5	24.5	7
24.5	29.5	34.5	30
34.5	39.5	44.5	32
44.5	49.5	54.5	49
54.5	59.5	64.5	32
64.5	69.5	74.5	21
74.5	79.5	84.5	12
84.5	89.5	94.5	8
94.5	99.5	104.5	2

MEAN

The mean for grouped data of a frequency table is calculated in the following way:

Step 1
Multiply each class midpoint, m_i, by the class frequency, f_i, of its corresponding class interval.

Step 2
Sum all the products obtained in Step 1.

Step 3
Divide the sum by the number of observations.

We apply this procedure to the data in Table 3.7:

$$m_i \times f_i$$

$$
\begin{aligned}
(-0.5)\ (3) &= \ -1.5 \\
(9.5)\ (4) &= \ \ \ 38.0 \\
(19.5)\ (7) &= \ \ 136.5 \\
(29.5)(30) &= \ \ 885.0 \\
(39.5)(32) &= 1264.0 \\
(49.5)(49) &= 2425.5 \\
(59.5)(32) &= 1904.0 \\
(69.5)(21) &= 1459.5 \\
(79.5)(12) &= \ \ 954.0 \\
(89.5)\ (8) &= \ \ 716.0 \\
(99.5)\ (2) &= \ \ 199.0 \\
\hline
\text{Sum} &= 9980.0
\end{aligned}
$$

Mean for grouped data of the 200 excess patient waiting times $= \dfrac{9980}{200} = 49.9$

In general, the expression for obtaining an approximate value for the mean using grouped data is:

Grouped Data: Mean for a Population of N Values

$$\mu_g = \frac{\sum_{i=1}^{k} m_i f_i}{N}$$ (3-17)

where

μ_g is the mean for the grouped data,

N is the number of values in the population,

k is the number of class intervals,

m_i is the class midpoint for the ith class interval,

f_i is the frequency of values belonging to the ith class interval.

If the values we are working with are sample observations, the formula will be:

Grouped Data: Mean for a Sample of Size n

$$\bar{X}_g = \frac{\sum_{i=1}^{k} m_i f_i}{n}$$ (3-18)

where

$\bar{X}_g$ is the mean for the grouped data,

n is the number of values in the sample,

k is the number of class intervals,

m_i is the class midpoint for the ith class interval,

f_i is the frequency of values belonging to the ith class interval.

MODE

The mode for grouped data is determined by the value of the class midpoint of the interval with the highest frequency—the modal class. For the data in Table 3.7, the mode is 49.5.

VARIANCE

If the grouped data represent a population of N values, then the variance is approximated by:

Grouped Data: Variance for a Population of N Values

$$\sigma_g^2 = \frac{\sum_{i=1}^{k} (m_i - \mu_g)^2 f_i}{N} \tag{3-19}$$

where

σ_g^2 is the variance for the grouped data, μ_g is the mean for the grouped data, N is the number of values in the population, k is the number of class intervals for the grouped data, m_i is the class midpoint for the ith class interval, f_i is the frequency of values in the ith class interval.

Using the excess patient waiting time data in Table 3.7 and the mean for grouped data found above, the following illustrates a procedure for computing the variance from a frequency table:

$(m_i - \mu_g)$	$(m_i - \mu_g)^2$	f_i	$(m_i - \mu_g)^2 f_i$
$-0.5 - 49.9$	2540.16	3	7,620.48
$9.5 - 49.9$	1632.16	4	6,528.64
$19.5 - 49.9$	924.16	7	6,469.12
$29.5 - 49.9$	416.16	30	12,484.80
$39.5 - 49.9$	108.16	32	3,461.12
$49.5 - 49.9$	0.16	49	7.84
$59.5 - 49.9$	92.16	32	2,949.12
$69.5 - 49.9$	384.16	21	8,067.36
$79.5 - 49.9$	876.16	12	10,513.92
$89.5 - 49.9$	1568.16	8	12,545.28
$99.5 - 49.9$	2460.16	2	4,920.32
		200	75,568.00

Now we find

$$\sigma_g^2 = \frac{75,568}{200} = 377.84$$

For samples of size n, the sample variance is approximated by:

Grouped Data: Variance for a Sample of Size n

$$S_g^2 = \frac{\sum_{i=1}^{k} (m_i - \bar{X}_g)^2 f_i}{n - 1} \tag{3-20}$$

where

S_g^2 is the sample variance for the grouped data, $\bar{X}_g$ is the sample mean for the grouped data, n is the number of values in the sample, k is the number of class intervals for the grouped data, m_i is the class midpoint for the ith class interval, f_i is the frequency of values in the ith class interval.

As before, the standard deviation for grouped data is simply the square root of the variance, that is, $\sigma_g = \sqrt{\sigma_g^2}$ and $S_g = \sqrt{S_g^2}$. Therefore, for the data in Table 3.7, we have $\sigma_g = \sqrt{377.84} = 19.44$.

ORIGINAL DATA VERSUS GROUPED DATA

The need to use formulas for grouped data to calculate summary measures arises only when the entire data set is unavailable. Because the individual values in the data set are lost in grouping, some amount of error can be expected when the formulas for grouped data are used to calculate the summary measures. To illustrate, consider the case of the excess patient waiting time data. Since we have calculated the actual values of the mean and standard deviation from the entire data set, we can see the error involved in using the formulas for grouped data. Table 3.8 gives a comparison of the summary measures for the excess patient waiting times using the original raw data versus the grouped data.

TABLE 3.8 Summary Measures for Excess Patient Waiting Times, Raw versus Grouped Data		
SUMMARY MEASURE	**RAW DATA**	**GROUPED DATA**
Mean	50.09	49.9
Median	50	Not computed
Mode	51	49.5
Variance	371.50	377.84
Standard deviation	19.27	19.44

The discrepancy between the measures for raw data and grouped data will vary, depending on how well the grouped data assumption (that all the values in an interval may be represented uniquely by the class midpoint) actually holds. Generally, that assumption introduces an error into the calculations.

EXERCISES

3.3 Refer to Exercise 2.2 in Chapter 2, where we discussed the potential economic application of speeding up the growth rate of catfish through genetic engineering. We repeat the data (lengths of times, in months) here for convenience. Consider the data to be a sample of what could happen if we apply the genetic engineering technique to all catfish.

15.9	7.6	11.3	15.4	13.9	10.6	11.6	13.1
13.1	10.6	10.8	13.2	12.2	9.7	10.8	9.4
9.8	11.4	14.8	16.5	16.8			

a. Find the values of the mean, median, and mode.
b. Find the values of the range, mean absolute deviation, variance, standard deviation, and coefficient of variation.
c. Use Chebyshev's theorem to determine at least how many of the raw data values should lie within 1.5 standard deviations of the mean. Compare your answer

with the actual count of the raw data values that do lie within 1.5 standard deviations of the mean. How does the result using Chebyshev's theorem compare with the actual count?

d. What impressions do you get from these results?

e. Compare your impressions here with the impressions you obtained from the descriptive procedures in Chapter 2.

3.4 Refer to Exercise 2.1 in Chapter 2, where we discussed the matter of overcharging on a variable interest rate home equity loan. We repeat the data (interest differences, in actual dollars and cents) here as a matter of convenience. Consider the data to be a sample of what may be happening to all persons with variable rate home equity loans.

6.90	6.28	6.33	5.63	5.25	8.18	8.11	5.20	6.13	8.17
6.25	7.62	7.06	4.78	7.32	5.62	6.29	5.64	6.97	7.30
6.45	5.67	6.39	6.42	5.28	5.00	7.80	5.22	7.20	5.95
5.79	6.28	7.76	5.84	8.63	4.42	6.33	5.12	5.61	6.96
5.55	6.15	6.19	6.83	5.13	4.50	7.79			

a. Find the values of the mean, median, and mode.

b. Find the values of the range, mean absolute deviation, variance, standard deviation, and coefficient of variation.

c. Use Chebyshev's theorem to determine at least how many of the raw data values should lie within 2.7 standard deviations of the mean. Compare your answer with an actual count of the raw data values that do lie within 2.7 standard deviations of the mean. How does the result using Chebyshev's theorem compare with the actual count?

d. What impressions do you get from these results?

e. Compare your impressions here with the impressions you obtained from the descriptive procedures in Chapter 2.

3.5 Recall the discussion in Exercise 2.3 in Chapter 2 concerning the use of resumes by young professionally oriented persons working in 37 different professional fields. For convenience, we repeat the data (percents of young working professionals who used a resume service) here. Consider the data to be the population of percentages for the 37 different professional fields.

89.7	90.3	61.4	60.9	97.2	73.2	69.5	94.6	65.9	76.1
99.6	83.8	69.1	97.7	68.4	90.9	76.2	70.7	88.3	61.7
70.5	60.9	63.0	54.2	87.1	92.0	73.2	67.9	67.6	78.7
61.3	73.3	67.9	38.3	62.8	80.5	56.6			

a. Find the values of the mean, median, and mode.

b. Find the values of the range, mean asbolute deviation, variance, standard deviation, and coefficient of variation.

c. Use Chebyshev's theorem to determine at least how many of the raw data values should lie within 2.2 standard deviations of the mean. Compare your answer with an actual count of the raw data values that do lie within 2.2 standard deviations of the mean. How does the result using Chebyshev's theorem compare with the actual count?

d. What impressions do you get from these results?

e. Compare your impressions here with the impressions you obtained from the descriptive procedures in Chapter 2.

SUMMARY

Summary measures of central location and dispersion provide valuable, descriptive information about the main features of the distribution of values in a data set.

The arithmetic mean, median, and mode are all summary measures of central location. But one measure may be more appropriate for a particular situation than the others. For instance, the mean can be used to determine a population total (as in estimating the number of cameras in Michigan). The median is used when a middle-most measure is desired, and is influenced only by how many—and not by how far—values are above and below it. This property allows the median to be computed for open-ended distributions, whereas the mean cannot.

The variation in the data values is described by the summary measures of dispersion. Some measures of dispersion are based upon the position of values within the distribution—the range and interquartile range (IQR). Although fairly easy to compute, these measures don't indicate the concentration of observations around some central point. The measures of variation that do provide such an indication require arithmetic calculations on each observation. They are the mean absolute deviation (MAD), variance, and standard deviation. The coefficient of variation is useful in describing the dispersion of a distribution relative to its mean.

Sometimes it is important to determine the maximum percentage of observations (population or sample) that can lie beyond a given distance from the mean in either direction. Chebyshev's inequality provides this information if the mean and standard deviation are known.

Although summary measures are valuable aids in describing the distribution of values, they should be interpreted with caution. For example, if only the mean height of the players on the basketball team is given, an erroneous conclusion might be reached about the typical height of the players on the team. Mean and standard deviation alone give no information about skewness of the distribution. An analysis can be viewed more confidently when some measure of central location, dispersion, and skewness are provided.

KEY EQUATIONS

Population Mean

$$\mu = \text{Population mean} = \frac{X_1 + X_2 + \cdots + X_N}{N} = \frac{\sum_{i=1}^{N} X_i}{N} \tag{3-1}$$

where $X_1, X_2, \ldots, X_N$ represent the N values in the population.

Sample Mean

$$\bar{X} = \text{Sample mean} = \frac{X_1 + X_2 + \cdots + X_n}{n} = \frac{\sum_{i=1}^{n} X_i}{n} \tag{3-2}$$

where $X_1, X_2, \ldots, X_n$ represent the n values in the sample.

Population Mean Absolute Deviation

$$\text{MAD} = \frac{\sum_{i=1}^{N} |X_i - \mu|}{N} \tag{3-3}$$

where $X_1, X_2, \ldots, X_N$ represent the N values in the population, and μ is the population mean.

Sample Mean Absolute Deviation

$$\text{MAD} = \frac{\sum_{i=1}^{n} |X_i - \bar{X}|}{n} \tag{3-4}$$

where $X_1, X_2, \ldots, X_n$ represent the n values in the sample, and $\bar{X}$ is the sample mean.

Population Variance

$$\sigma^2 = \frac{\sum_{i=1}^{N} (X_i - \mu)^2}{N} \tag{3-5}$$

where $X_1, X_2, \ldots, X_N$ represent the N values in the population, and μ is the population mean.

Computational Formula for Population Variance

$$\sigma^2 = \frac{\sum_{i=1}^{N} X_i^2 - N\mu^2}{N} = \frac{\sum_{i=1}^{N} X_i^2 - \frac{\left(\sum_{i=1}^{N} X_i\right)^2}{N}}{N} \tag{3-6}$$

where $X_1, X_2, \ldots, X_N$ represent the N values in the population, and μ is the population mean.

Sample Variance

$$S^2 = \frac{\sum_{i=1}^{n} (X_i - \bar{X})^2}{n - 1} \tag{3-7}$$

where $X_1, X_2, \ldots, X_n$ represent the n values in the sample, and $\bar{X}$ is the sample mean.

Computational Formula for Sample Variance

$$S^2 = \frac{n\sum_{i=1}^{n} X_i^2 - \left(\sum_{i=1}^{n} X_i\right)^2}{n(n - 1)} = \frac{\sum_{i=1}^{n} X_i^2 - \frac{\left(\sum_{i=1}^{n} X_i\right)^2}{n}}{n - 1} \tag{3-8}$$

where $X_1, X_2, \ldots, X_n$ represent the n values in the sample.

Population Standard Deviation

$$\sigma = \sqrt{\frac{\sum_{i=1}^{N} (X_i - \mu)^2}{N}} \tag{3-9}$$

where $X_1, X_2, \ldots, X_N$ represent the N values in the population, and μ is the population mean.

Computational Formula for Population Standard Deviation

$$\sigma = \sqrt{\frac{\sum_{i=1}^{N} X_i^2 - \frac{\left(\sum_{i=1}^{N} X_i\right)^2}{N}}{N}} \tag{3-10}$$

where $X_1, X_2, \ldots, X_N$ represent the N values in the population, and μ is the population mean.

Computational Formula for Sample Standard Deviation

$$S = \sqrt{\frac{\sum_{i=1}^{n} X_i^2 - \frac{\left(\sum_{i=1}^{n} X_i\right)^2}{n}}{n - 1}} \tag{3-11}$$

where $X_1, X_2, \ldots, X_n$ represent the n values in the sample.

Population Coefficient of Variation

$$CV = \frac{\sigma}{\mu}(100) \tag{3-12}$$

where σ is the population standard deviation, and μ is the population mean.

Sample Coefficient of Variation

$$cv = \frac{S}{\bar{X}}(100) \tag{3-13}$$

where S is the sample standard deviation, and $\bar{X}$ is the sample mean.

Chebyshev's Theorem

$$P(\mu - k\sigma < X < \mu + k\sigma) \geq 1 - \frac{1}{k^2} \tag{3-14}$$

where X represents a single population value, μ is the population mean, σ is the population standard deviation, k is any value greater than 1 that we may choose, and P is the proportion of population values that lie between $\mu - k\sigma$ and $\mu + k\sigma$.

Standard Z Score

$$\text{For populations} \quad Z = \frac{X - \mu}{\sigma}$$

$$\text{For samples} \quad Z = \frac{X - \bar{X}}{S} \tag{3-15}$$

where X represents a single population or sample value, μ is the population mean, σ is the population standard deviation, $\bar{X}$ is the sample mean, and S is the sample standard deviation.

Chebyshev Inequality

$$P(-k < Z < +k) \geq 1 - \frac{1}{k^2} \tag{3-16}$$

where Z is the standardized Z score, k is any value greater than 1, and P is the proportion of Z scores with values between $\pm k$.

Grouped Data: Mean for a Population of N Values

$$\mu_g = \frac{\sum\limits_{i=1}^{k} m_i f_i}{N} \tag{3-17}$$

where μ_g is the mean for the grouped data, N is the number of values in the population, k is the number of class intervals, m_i is the class midpoint for the ith class interval, and f_i is the frequency of values belonging to the ith class interval.

Grouped Data: Mean for a Sample of Size n

$$\bar{X}_g = \frac{\sum\limits_{i=1}^{k} m_i f_i}{n} \tag{3-18}$$

where $\bar{X}_g$ is the mean for the grouped data, n is the number of values in the sample, k is the number of class intervals, m_i is the class midpoint for the ith class interval, and f_i is the frequency of values belonging to the ith class interval.

Grouped Data: Variance for a Population of N Values

$$\sigma_g^2 = \frac{\sum\limits_{i=1}^{k} (m_i - \mu_g)^2 f_i}{N} \tag{3-19}$$

where σ_g^2 is the variance for the grouped data, μ_g is the mean for the grouped data, N is the number of values in the population, k is the number of class intervals for the grouped data,

m_i is the class midpoint for the ith class interval, and f_i is the frequency of values in the ith class interval.

Grouped Data: Variance for a Sample of Size n

$$S_g^2 = \frac{\sum_{i=1}^{k} (m_i - \bar{X}_g)^2 f_i}{n - 1} \tag{3-20}$$

where S_g^2 is the sample variance for the grouped data, $\bar{X}_g$ is the sample mean for the grouped data, n is the number of values in the sample, k is the number of class intervals for the grouped data, m_i is the class midpoint for the ith class interval, and f_i is the frequency of values in the ith class interval.

PRACTICE EXERCISE ANSWERS

3.1 First, order the values from smallest to largest. The mode is the most frequently observed value. For this data set, there are two modes, since the data values 70 and 100 each occur four times.

The median is the value of the middlemost observation in the ordered list. Since there are 45 values, the middle value is in the 23rd position. The median is 70. Twenty-two data values are less than or equal to 70 in magnitude, and twenty-two values are greater than or equal to 70.

The mean is found by adding the 45 values and dividing the sum by 45. The sum of all 45 data values is 3145, so the mean is $3145/45 = 69.889$.

3.2 The mode, if it is singular, would be the most useful since it reflects where the point of peak demand occurs. The value of the mean would be affected by extreme values and thus could miss, by a wide margin, the point of peak demand. The value of the median simply reflects the point where half the demand has already occurred, and the peak may already have been passed.

3.3 The range is found by subtracting the value of the lowest observation from the value of the highest observation. From this set of 45 exam scores, the lowest score is 17 and the highest score is 100, so the range is $100 - 17 = 83$.

If the 45 exam scores represent scores for the entire class, the data should be thought of as a population. The population variance is given by the formula

$$\sigma^2 = \frac{\sum_{i=1}^{N} (X_i - \mu)^2}{N}$$

where the mean μ was found in Practice Exercise 3.1 to be 69.889. The variance is

$$\sigma^2 = \frac{\sum_{i=1}^{N} (X_i - \mu)^2}{N}$$

$$= \frac{(72 - 69.889)^2 + (70 - 69.889)^2 + \cdots + (62 - 69.889)^2}{45}$$

$$= \frac{21{,}042.444}{45}$$

$$= 467.61$$

The computational formula also could be used to compute the variance:

$$\sigma^2 = \frac{\sum_{i=1}^{N} X_i^2 - N\mu^2}{N} = \frac{240{,}843 - (45)(69.889)^2}{45} = 467.59$$

(The correct answer of 467.61 would be obtained if we used the more exact value of $\mu = 69.8888889$ instead of the rounded 69.889.)

The standard deviation is the square root of the variance:

$$\sigma = \sqrt{\sigma^2} = \sqrt{467.61} = 21.624$$

3.4 a. In Practice Exercise 3.1 we found that the mean is $\mu = 69.889$ and in Practice Exercise 3.3 we found that the standard deviation is $\sigma = 21.624$. The boundaries are

$$\mu - 2\sigma = 69.889 - (2)21.624 = 26.64$$
$$\mu + 2\sigma = 69.889 + (2)21.624 = 113.14$$

  b. Looking at the actual 45 data values, we see that 42 are greater than 26.64 but less than 113.14. Expressed as a percentage, $\frac{42}{45} = .9333$, or 93.33%.

3.5 a. The standardized value of a score of 72 is $(72 - 60.8)/14 = 0.8$. The positive Z score of 0.8 means that the value 72 lies 0.8 standard deviations above the mean score of 60.8.

  b. An unknown score X is 1.2 standard deviations below the mean, so

$$\frac{X - \mu}{\sigma} = \frac{X - 60.8}{14} = -1.2$$
$$X = 60.8 - (1.2)(14) = 44$$

The student received a 44 on the exam.

CHAPTER REVIEW EXERCISES

3.6 What does the population consist of if an Internal Revenue Service agent wishes to examine some of the tax returns prepared by:
  a. A tax preparer working out of her home?
  b. A tax preparer working out of a small office?
  c. A tax preparer working for a large chain of tax preparers?
  d. A large chain of tax preparers?

3.7 What does the population consist of if a physiologist wishes to examine electrocardiograms of some of the persons who:
  a. Run regularly along Mission Bay in San Diego?
  b. Run regularly on the boardwalk in Rockaway Beach in New York?
  c. Run regularly along Lake Shore Drive in Chicago?
  d. Run regularly in the United States?

3.8 The following set of data represents a population of the number of automobiles passing through an intersection each hour over a 30 hour period.

| 38 | 99 | 70 | 43 | 10 | 73 | 90 | 86 | 70 | 60 | 68 | 30 | 26 | 79 | 50 |
| 84 | 81 | 95 | 94 | 95 | 42 | 64 | 14 | 19 | 17 | 56 | 10 | 6 | 45 | 21 |

  a. Find the value (or values) of the mode (or modes).
  b. Find the value of the median. c. Find the value of the mean.

3.9 The following set of data represents a population of the number of hamburgers sold by Campus Food Services during lunch hour each day over a 30 day period.

| 44 | 51 | 51 | 53 | 50 | 52 | 44 | 55 | 54 | 52 | 51 | 55 | 46 | 49 | 49 |
| 50 | 44 | 37 | 50 | 49 | 55 | 52 | 57 | 49 | 53 | 45 | 43 | 54 | 53 | 53 |

  a. Find the value (or values) of the mode (or modes).
  b. Find the value of the median. c. Find the value of the mean.

3.10 The following set of data represents a population of the number of burglaries in 30 cities in the United States during one weekend.

| 128 | 20 | 18 | 50 | 1 | 46 | 111 | 95 | 82 | 39 | 19 | 97 | 73 | 18 | 11 |
| 1 | 123 | 260 | 3 | 28 | 106 | 44 | 146 | 21 | 55 | 97 | 145 | 90 | 53 | 52 |

a. Find the value (or values) of the mode (or modes).
b. Find the value of the median.   c. Find the value of the mean.

3.11 The following set of data represents a population of the number of videocassette recorders sold at 60 retail outlets during the last Christmas shopping season.

69	41	20	81	86	79	92	90	22	26	37	26	57	88	83
9	18	83	58	71	76	3	25	29	44	22	11	92	8	17
95	41	6	72	77	57	1	76	13	79	75	45	52	92	17
16	1	75	49	83	28	81	74	46	22	40	84	23	18	85

a. Find the value (or values) of the mode (or modes).
b. Find the value of the median.   c. Find the value of the mean.

3.12 For the automobile data in Exercise 3.8:
a. Find the value of the range.   b. Find the value of the variance.
c. Find the value of the standard deviation.

▶ **3.13** For the hamburger data in Exercise 3.9:
a. Find the value of the range.   b. Find the value of the variance.
c. Find the value of the standard deviation.

3.14 For the burglary data in Exercise 3.10:
a. Find the value of the range.   b. Find the value of the variance.
c. Find the value of the standard deviation.

3.15 For the videocassette recorder data in Exercise 3.11:
a. Find the value of the range.   b. Find the value of the variance.
c. Find the value of the standard deviation.

3.16 Using the results for the automobile data in Exercises 3.8 and 3.12, apply Chebyshev's theorem to determine the minimum percentage of the observations that should lie within:
a. 2 standard deviations of the mean; and then determine the actual percentage of observations that do lie within 2 standard deviations of the mean.
b. 1.5 standard deviations of the mean; and then determine the actual percentage of observations that do lie within 1.5 standard deviations of the mean.

3.17 Using the results for the burglary data in Exercises 3.10 and 3.14, apply Chebyshev's theorem to determine the minimum percentage of the observations that should lie within:
a. 2.3 standard deviations of the mean; and then determine the actual percentage of observations that do lie within 2.3 standard deviations of the mean.
b. 1.8 standard deviations of the mean; and then determine the actual percentage of observations that do lie within 1.8 standard deviations of the mean.

3.18 The following data are a population of scores obtained by 40 job applicants on an aptitude test designed to measure manual dexterity skills:

69	90	61	73	62	45	26	40	54	35	43	60	48	80	39
25	51	55	62	43	52	75	61	22	56	39	51	69	57	83
51	88	60	36	54	71	81	73	56	91					

a. Find the value of the mean, variance, and standard deviation.
b. Use Chebyshev's theorem to determine the minimum percentage of the observations that should lie within:
    i. 1.5 standard deviations of the mean; and then determine the actual percentage of observations that do lie within 1.5 standard deviations of the mean.
    ii. 1.8 standard deviations of the mean; and then determine the actual per-

centage of observations that do lie within 1.8 standard deviations of the mean.

iii. 2 standard deviations of the mean; and then determine the actual percentage of observations that do lie within 2 standard deviations of the mean.

iv. 2.3 standard deviations of the mean; and then determine the actual percentage of observations that do lie within 2.3 standard deviations of the mean.

v. 3 standard deviations of the mean; and then determine the actual percentage of observations that do lie within 3 standard deviations of the mean.

▶ **3.19** The mean and standard deviation for a set of numbers are 13.1 and 2.7, respectively. At least what percentage of the set of numbers lies between:

a. 5.108 and 21.092?   b. 7.808 and 18.392?
c. 6.215 and 19.985?   d. 9.563 and 16.637?

3.20 The mean and standard deviation for a set of numbers are 13.1 and 2.7, respectively. *At most* what percentage of the set of numbers lies *outside* the interval from:

a. 5.108 to 21.092?   b. 7.808 to 18.392?
c. 6.215 to 19.985?   d. 9.563 to 16.637?

▶ **3.21** According to Chebyshev's theorem, at least what proportion of a set of measurements should lie within 1.69 standard deviations of their mean?

3.22 According to Chebyshev's theorem, at most what proportion of a set of measurements should differ from their mean by more than 1.69 standard deviations?

3.23 Suppose an Internal Revenue Service agent is given 133 tax returns prepared by a certain tax preparer. Describe a situation where the tax returns would be considered:

a. A sample   b. A population

3.24 Suppose a physiologist is given 1100 electrocardiograms from the files at a certain hospital. Describe a situation where the electrocardiograms would be considered:

a. A sample   b. A population

▶ **3.25** The following is a sample of percent differences between actual and forecasted sales volume by the sales force of a very large corporation:

$$+10.4 \quad -4.4 \quad -15.3 \quad -31.5 \quad +20.8$$
$$+22.7 \quad -19.7 \quad -5.5 \quad +14.3 \quad -9.9$$

a. Find the value of the median.   b. Find the value of the mean.

3.26 The following is a sample of sales performance data for sales executives (in millions of dollars):

$$7 \quad 9 \quad 6 \quad 3 \quad 10 \quad 17 \quad 11 \quad 4 \quad 8 \quad 5 \quad 20$$

a. Find the value of the median.   b. Find the value of the mean.

3.27 The following data represent the percentage of yolk (to the nearest percent) in a sample of eggs from a certain species of turtle:

$$43 \quad 41 \quad 44 \quad 39 \quad 38 \quad 44 \quad 39 \quad 40 \quad 43 \quad 42 \quad 42 \quad 45 \quad 42$$

a. Find the value of the median.   b. Find the value of the mean.

3.28 With respect to the sample data in Exercise 3.26, find the value of:

a. The range   b. The variance   c. The standard deviation

⬛ ▶ **3.29** The grade-point averages for a sample of 50 college students at a large college are as follows:

2.2	3.4	2.5	3.3	3.2		2.8	2.5	3.7	2.3	1.6		3.1	3.8	3.5	3.1	3.4
3.7	3.2	3.3	3.6	2.6		1.9	1.9	3.3	2.8	2.1		3.2	3.8	2.9	3.2	3.9
2.7	3.8	1.8	2.0	2.5		2.6	3.5	3.4	3.7	3.1		1.9	1.9	3.2	3.0	3.0
2.4	3.3	3.1	3.7	2.5											

   a. Find the values of the sample mean and sample standard deviation.
   b. Use Chebyshev's theorem to determine the minimum proportion of the observations that should lie within 1.21 standard deviations of the mean. Compare this result with the proportion of observations that actually do lie within 1.21 standard deviations of the mean.
   c. Use Chebyshev's theorem to determine the maximum proportion of the observations that should differ from the mean by more than 1.21 standard deviations.
   d. Use Chebyshev's theorem to determine at least how many of the observations should lie between 1.932 and 3.948. Compare this result with the number that actually lie between 1.932 and 3.948.
   e. Use Chebyshev's theorem to determine at most how many of the observations should be less than 1.932 or greater than 3.948. Compare this result with the number that actually do satisfy this condition.

⬛ **3.30** The following numbers are the class midpoints and class frequencies for grouped data for a sample of seedling weights, in grams.

Class Midpoint	Class Frequency
18	43
23	36
28	25
33	14
38	8
43	16
48	29
53	33
58	41

Calculate the value of:
   a. The mean   b. The variance   c. The standard deviation

⬛ **3.31** The following numbers are the class midpoints and class frequencies for grouped data for a sample of roach lengths, in millimeters.

Class Midpoint	Class Frequency
2	1
5	6
8	11
11	23
14	16
17	7
20	4
23	1

Calculate the value of:
   a. The mean   b. The variance   c. The standard deviation

□ 3.32 The following numbers are the class midpoints and class frequencies for grouped data for a sample of property losses, in thousands of dollars.

Class Midpoint	Class Frequency
6.65	10
12.65	6
18.65	22
24.65	15
30.65	9
36.65	1

Calculate the value of:
a. The mean   b. The variance   c. The standard deviation

□ ▶ 3.33 The following numbers are the class midpoints and class frequencies for grouped data for a population of salaries, in thousands of dollars.

Class Midpoint	Class Frequency
16.55	4
20.55	4
24.55	10
28.55	27
32.55	3
36.55	12
40.55	15
44.55	11
48.55	9

Calculate the value of:
a. The mean   b. The variance   c. The standard deviation

SOLVING APPLIED CASES
Replacing Light Bulbs

Replacing light bulbs in large office buildings can be an expensive proposition if it is done on an individual basis each time a bulb burns out. To save on labor costs, many firms replace all the light bulbs in a given section of the building (including the ones that are still working) at regularly scheduled intervals. This policy makes the most sense when there is not much variability in the length of lamp life, because then all bulbs can be replaced shortly before they start burning out.

Suppose a large office building uses two types of bulbs, and suppose the owner of the building wishes to establish an economical strategy for bulb replacement. The owner hires a testing service to determine the longevity characteristics of the two types of bulbs. The testing service takes a random sample of 16 bulbs of each type, and records the number of hours each bulb lasts before burning out. The test results are given in Table 3.9.

Summarizing the data numerically, the testing service finds

$$\bar{X}_A = 1009.625 \qquad S_A = 42.32$$
$$\bar{X}_B = 1100.625 \qquad S_B = 182.88$$

Apparently, type B bulbs last longer, on the average, than type A bulbs. But type B bulbs also exhibit greater variability in their longevity, and it would be interesting to determine how

TABLE 3.9 Longevity of Light Bulbs (Measured to the Nearest Hour)	
TYPE A	**TYPE B**
999	1131
940	687
1004	939
966	1255
1007	1115
1027	1197
983	1363
988	1154
1004	1161
1011	962
1089	1157
1018	1133
971	782
995	1018
1104	1269
1048	1287

this could affect not only the strategy for replacing bulbs, but also a choice between the two types of bulbs.

If we use Chebyshev's theorem, we note that when $k = 2$, then $\bar{X}_A - 2S_A = 925$, $\bar{X}_A + 2S_A = 1094$, $\bar{X}_B - 2S_B = 735$, and $\bar{X}_B + 2S_B = 1466$. Thus, if these sampled bulbs are considered typical of all the bulbs in the building, then at least 75% of the type A bulbs in the building should last more than 925 hours, whereas at least 75% of the type B bulbs in the building should last more than 735 hours. Similarly, when $k = 3$, then $\bar{X}_A - 3S_A = 883$, $\bar{X}_A + 3S_A = 1137$, $\bar{X}_B - 3S_B = 552$, and $\bar{X}_B + 3S_B = 1649$. This suggests that at least 89% of the type A bulbs should last more than 883 hours, whereas at least 89% of the type B bulbs should last more than 552 hours. These results are summarized in Table 3.10.

TABLE 3.10 Chebyshev Bounds on Light Bulb Longevity Data ($X \pm kS$)			
		TYPE A	**TYPE B**
k	$1 - (1/k^2)$	hr	hr
2	75%	925–1094	735–1466
3	89%	883–1137	552–1649

Chebyshev's theorem guarantees that at least 89% of type A bulbs last 883 hours or more, but for the type B bulbs the guarantee is that at least 89% of them last only 552 hours or more. Thus, assuming the bulbs sell at the same price, the owner replacing bulbs at regular intervals would probably be better off using type A bulbs even though they have a shorter mean life. However, if the owner elects to replace bulbs only when they burn out, type B bulbs might be the better choice because of their greater average longevity.

Checkpoint Exercises

1. Suppose three types of identically priced light bulbs have longevity distributions described by the summary statistics given below (longevity measured to the nearest hour).

Type of Bulb	Mean	Standard Deviation
A	1500	300
B	1300	200
C	1400	100

a. If the average longevity is the only criterion, which type of bulb should be selected?

b. Based on Chebyshev's inequality, which type of bulb has the best record for lasting more than 1000 hours?

c. Which type of bulb should be selected if replacement is at regular intervals? Only when a bulb burns out?

2. Suppose three identically priced common stocks have earnings per share (EPS) distributions described by the summary statistics given below.

Stock	Mean EPS	Standard Deviation of EPS
A	$3.00	$0.30
B	$2.60	$0.20
C	$2.80	$0.10

a. Which stock has the best track record on total earnings over the period measured?

b. Based on Chebyshev's inequality, which stock has the best track record on earning more than $2.00 per share per period?

c. Can we say which stock has the worst track record in terms of keeping EPS above $2.00?

WENDY'S DATABASE ANALYSIS

The Wendy's database analysis in Chapter 2 considered a fast food chain's image. The image of a fast food chain was constructed by looking at the distribution of consumer perceptions about the fast food chain on each image dimension. For example, we considered McDonald's image on food taste, White Castle's image on menu price, etc. This chapter extends the image theme, but adds to it the variation concept often encountered in marketing and consumer research.

Image Profile

1. What do consumers believe are McDonald's strong points and weak points?

To explore this question we need to construct an image profile for McDonald's across the relevant dimensions. By reporting the mean rating of each dimension, we summarize consumer perceptions of that attribute. Each mean value is plotted on a separate line showing a scale of the possible values. The mean values recorded on separate lines are then connected by straight lines, tracing out the image profile of the fast food chain as shown in Figure 3.7.

Figure 3.7
Image profile for McDonald's

ATTRIBUTE	VARIABLE	MEAN	1......2......3......4......5......6
Food taste	30	2.0895	
Cleanliness	36	1.8402	
Convenience	42	1.9380	
Menu price	48	2.4884	
Fast service	54	1.8497	
Popularity with children	60	1.4568	
Menu variety	66	2.9351	

```
MTB > desc c30, c36, c42, c48, c54, c60, c66

              N     N*      MEAN     MEDIAN      TRMEAN       STDEV      SEMEAN
C30         391     15    2.0895     2.0000      1.9601      1.2257      0.0620
C36         388     18    1.8402     2.0000      1.7543      0.9066      0.0460
C42         387     19    1.9380     1.0000      1.7765      1.3317      0.0677
C48         387     19    2.4884     2.0000      2.4183      1.1944      0.0607
C54         386     20    1.8497     2.0000      1.7241      1.0336      0.0526
C60         359     47    1.4568     1.0000      1.3220      0.8892      0.0469
C66         385     21    2.9351     3.0000      2.8732      1.3876      0.0707

              MIN        MAX         Q1         Q3
C30         1.0000     6.0000     1.0000     3.0000
C36         1.0000     6.0000     1.0000     2.0000
C42         1.0000     6.0000     1.0000     2.0000
C48         1.0000     6.0000     2.0000     3.0000
C54         1.0000     6.0000     1.0000     2.0000
C60         1.0000     6.0000     1.0000     2.0000
C66         1.0000     6.0000     2.0000     4.0000
```

Figure 3.8
MINITAB output for McDonald's image profile

The image profile provides a quick graphic display of McDonald's strengths and weaknesses as perceived by consumers. Since the entire profile line lies on the left side of the diagram, it seems fair to say that McDonald's overall image is favorable. However, the zigzagging profile line indicates some differences among image components. The leftmost point indicates the most favorable image component (popularity with children), while the rightmost point indicates the least favorable image component (menu variety). Cleanliness and fast service are also seen as McDonald's strong points, while menu price appears as a relative weakness in McDonald's image.

By using a single summary measure to represent an image component, the image profile facilitates comparisons of the overall images of several different components. Of course, information on the distribution of individual differences among consumers in image perception is lost with the image profile technique.

The MINITAB command to obtain the mean of a variable is DESCRIBE. Thus, the command

DESCRIBE C30

directs the computer to compute the mean and other descriptive measures of the data in column 30 (McDonald's food taste responses).

The means needed for the McDonald's image profile can be computed simultaneously if the command

DESCRIBE C30, C36, C42, C48, C54, C60, C66

is given. The results are shown in Figure 3.8.

2. How does McDonald's image profile compare with that of Burger King?

To generate the means required for the Burger King image profile we type the command:

DESCRIBE C29, C35, C41, C47, C53, C59, C65

where C29 represents the Burger King food taste variable, C35 represents the Burger King cleanliness variable, etc. The results are shown in Figure 3.9.

```
MTB > desc c29, c35, c41, c47, c53, c59, c65

              N        N*      MEAN    MEDIAN    TRMEAN    STDEV   SEMEAN
C29         390        16    2.4231    2.0000    2.3257   1.2899   0.0653
C35         388        18    2.1933    2.0000    2.1314   0.9890   0.0502
C41         385        21    2.7377    2.0000    2.6542   1.6587   0.0845
C47         381        25    3.0761    3.0000    3.0554   1.2126   0.0621
C53         385        21    2.0857    2.0000    1.9827   1.1136   0.0568
C59         356        50    2.1320    2.0000    2.0469   1.0990   0.0582
C65         383        23    3.1384    3.0000    3.0986   1.3141   0.0671

             MIN       MAX        Q1        Q3
C29       1.0000    6.0000    1.0000    3.0000
C35       1.0000    6.0000    1.0000    3.0000
C41       1.0000    6.0000    1.0000    4.0000
C47       1.0000    6.0000    2.0000    4.0000
C53       1.0000    6.0000    1.0000    3.0000
C59       1.0000    6.0000    1.0000    3.0000
C65       1.0000    6.0000    2.0000    4.0000
```

Figure 3.9
MINITAB output for Burger King image profile

The Burger King image profile can be plotted on the same graph with the McDonald's image profile to facilitate an accurate comparison of the two profiles. We show this in Figure 3.10.

Plotting both image profiles on the same graph makes comparison of the two profiles relatively easy. On any attribute, the image profile located further to the left is the one with the better image. The horizontal distance between the two image profile lines indicates the amount of superiority on that attribute. Noting that the McDonald's image profile line is everywhere to the left of the Burger King image profile line, we quickly see that McDonald's has a more favorable image on every listed attribute. Relative to McDonald's image profile, Burger King's strongest attributes are menu variety and fast service, since the two restaurants are closest on these attributes. Popularity with children and menu price are two weak points in Burger King's image compared to McDonald's. In absolute terms, Burger King is seen most favorably on service, although even here McDonald's comes out ahead. Construction of the image profile lines makes such comparisons relatively simple.

Image Sharpness

3. Is the image profile line reflecting a consensus of opinion on the image of a brand?

The image profile line measures only the average value of a brand's image; it does not give any clue to the amount of agreement among consumers on the brand image. We say that a brand's image is *sharp* on a given attribute when consumers rate similarly, and we say the image

Figure 3.10
Image profiles for McDonald's and Burger King;
x's = McDonald's,
o's = Burger King

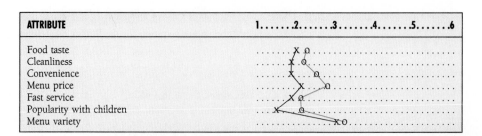

ATTRIBUTE	1......2......3......4......5......6
Food taste	
Cleanliness	
Convenience	
Menu price	
Fast service	
Popularity with children	
Menu variety	

Figure 3.11
Image sharpness profile for McDonald's

ATTRIBUTE	VARIABLE	STDEV	0......1......2......3......4......5
Food taste	30	1.2557	.........X..........................
Cleanliness	36	0.9066	.......X............................
Convenience	42	1.3317	.........X..........................
Menu price	48	1.1944	........X...........................
Fast service	54	1.0336	.......X............................
Popularity with children	60	0.8892	......X.............................
Menu variety	66	1.3876	.........X..........................

is *blurred* when they don't. We use the standard deviation to measure sharpness. The lower the value of the standard deviation, the sharper the image.

The MINITAB command DESCRIBE provides the standard deviation of the column number (variable) identifying the data. Looking back at Figure 3.8, we find the standard deviation for McDonald's on food taste C30 to be 1.2257. An image sharpness profile can be constructed by plotting the value of the standard deviation for each attribute listed in Figure 3.8 and connecting the points with straight lines, as in Figure 3.11. The farther the line is to the left, the sharper the image that the consumer public has of the given feature. For example, McDonald's has the sharpest image on popularity with children (STDEV = 0.8892) and the fuzziest image on menu variety (STDEV = 1.3876). Comparing McDonald's and Burger King on image sharpness (Figures 3.11 and 3.12), we find McDonald's has a sharper image than Burger King on most attributes, especially convenience and popularity with children.

Wendy's Database Student Exercises

1. Use the MINITAB statistical software package and its DESCRIBE command (or an alternate package designated by your instructor) to generate means and standard deviations on food taste, cleanliness, convenience image, menu price, fast service, popularity with children, and menu variety for McDonald's, Wendy's, Burger King, and White Castle.

   DESCRIBE C30, C36, C42, C48, C54, C60, C66 (for McDonald's)
   DESCRIBE C31, C37, C43, C49, C55, C61, C67 (for Wendy's)
   DESCRIBE C29, C35, C41, C47, C53, C59, C65 (for Burger King)
   DESCRIBE C32, C38, C44, C50, C56, C62, C68 (for White Castle)

2. Use the computed means from Exercise 1 to graph image profiles for:
   a. Wendy's versus McDonald's   b. Wendy's versus Burger King
   c. Wendy's versus White Castle

   Comment on the strengths and weaknesses of Wendy's versus each competing brand. Which brand would you say has the best overall image?

3. Use the computed standard deviations to graph Wendy's image sharpness profile. On which attribute would you say that Wendy's has the sharpest image? Does Wendy's have a sharper image on more attributes than McDonald's?

Figure 3.12
Image sharpness profile for Burger King

ATTRIBUTE	VARIABLE	STDEV	0......1......2......3......4......5
Food taste	29	1.2899	.........o..........................
Cleanliness	35	0.9890	........o...........................
Convenience	41	1.6587	..............o.....................
Menu price	47	1.2126	.........o..........................
Fast service	53	1.1136	........o...........................
Popularity with children	59	1.0990	........o...........................
Menu variety	65	1.3141	..........o.........................

PROBABILITY

Headline Issue

THE STING OF UNCERTAINTY: HERE TO STAY

The sting of uncertainty isn't pleasant. You know it's touched the people on the street when they mumble, "There's no such thing as a sure thing." Football coaches know the feeling, too, when their premier placekicker misses the point after a touchdown. The emotion reaches Wall Street brokers when "Black Tuesday" type days hit, and the market takes a nosedive. As unpleasant as it may be, uncertainty is here to stay and needs to be considered when we make decisions.

Some people deal with uncertainty on a professional basis. The old riverboat gambler, stereotyped by a green eyeshade and fancy shirt, is a classic example. Modern risk takers are found in the executive offices of financial institutions such as savings and loans (S&Ls) and commercial banks. The pin-striped suit has replaced the green eyeshade and fancy shirt. But the conservative look shouldn't fool you. Financial institution lending officers take risks for bigger stakes than the riverboat gambler ever dreamed of. And they take risks with the public's money, as the bailout of the S&Ls of the 1980s and 1990s has shown us.

The source of a financial institution's loan and investment funds is the money deposited by customers who seek to earn interest on their deposited money. This pool of money represents the loanable funds that the lending officer has available to lend to business enterprises that need the cash and are willing to pay interest on the borrowed amount. The difference between the interest rate charged to the business borrower and the interest rate paid to the depositor is one source of profit for the financial institution.

This all seems very simple. Where is the risk for the lending institution? One source of risk is that the financial institution has an obligation to come up with cash when the depositor demands it. Since most of the cash will typically be lent out by the financial institution, it cannot all be on hand. The lending institution is always uncertain of the exact time and size of depositor withdrawals. A second source of risk is that the institution faces the uncertainty of a borrower who may not pay back the loan.

How does the financial institution deal with this uncertainty? Based on past records, the amount of defaulting loans combined with the size of depositor cash withdrawals are estimated. The amount of the cash drain is typically estimated by the financial institution to be within specified upper and lower limits with *calculable probablilty*. To meet the possible range of cash drain, cash reserves are held as standard practice (a practice also required by government regulations). When financial institutions take a conservative approach toward lending and loans, these ranges work quite well and cash reserves are adequate. But in the 1980s, risky loans appeared on the books of some financial institutions (e.g., Arizona land speculation, junk bond investments). When unforeseen events appeared in the market (e.g., dramatic drop in Arizona real estate prices, the bankruptcy filing of Drexel Burnham Lambert, which supported the junk bond market), borrowers defaulted on their principal and interest. The notorious financial institution, Lincoln Savings & Loan of Irvine, California, headed by Charles Keating was seized by federal regulators because of its risk ventures into Arizona real estate and subsequent nonperforming loans.

Also, in 1988, the collapse of the price of oil in world markets caused the Federal Regulatory Agency to use over a billion dollars of insurance funds to consolidate several troubled Texas financial institutions that had made risky loans to the oil industry.

The reports of what happened in these cases usually cite "imprudent" loans and investments. But to anyone familiar with probability and gambling, it's just a case of high-stakes gambling with depositors' money.

Overview

We have seen in Chapters 2 and 3 that an important reason for examining data is to gain information that will help make good decisions. But even with accurate and plentiful data, decision makers face uncertainty. The connection between the data summaries covered in the previous two chapters and decisions made in the face of uncertainty is *probability*, the topic introduced in this chapter. Probabilities describe our uncertainty about a possible occurrence of something, which we call *events*.

In this chapter, we'll write event descriptions in symbolic form, combine events, assign probabilities to events, and determine probabilities for combinations of events while maintaining a connection with real-life experiences. In particular, we'll discuss how to use the probabilities we do know to help find the probabilities we don't know but want to know. Later in this chapter we'll show how the notion of probability can be applied to business situations. In subsequent chapters, we extend probability to a wider variety of applications.

4.1

PROBABILITIES AND EVENTS

A stock is ready for a nosedive, car loans go into default, people win lotteries. What do all these have in common? They are real-world items that can be viewed as events whose occurrence or nonoccurrence is of considerable interest. Since there is a chance of occurrence or nonoccurrence, it seems natural to ask "What is the probability a stock will nosedive?", "What is the probability a loan will default?", or "What is the probability I will win a lottery?" To answer each of these probability questions, we must consider the possible outcomes that collectively form an event.

Before working with events, we need several definitions: An **experiment** is any method for obtaining observations or measurements that can be repeated in the same way. The possible observations that result from each performance of the experiment are called **possible outcomes**. At any performance of the experiment, one and only one of the possible outcomes occurs and is called the **actual outcome**. The set of *all* possible outcomes of an experiment is called the **sample space** and is denoted *S*. An **event** is any collection of the possible outcomes from *S*. If any of the possible outcomes defined in an event occurs, the event is said to have occurred. Because events are what probabilities are assigned to, understanding events is very important. The first example considers a source of uncertainty familiar to game players—rolling a die.

Figure 4.1
Venn diagram showing the sample space and events described in Example 4.1

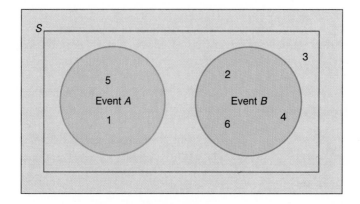

■ **EXAMPLE 4.1**

Rolling a Single Die

As a *model* describing all the possible outcomes of the roll of a six-sided die, we have $S = \{1, 2, 3, 4, 5, 6\}$. Suppose the die is fair—that is, perfectly balanced so that when the die is rolled repeatedly each possible outcome is expected to occur one-sixth of the time. Then each possible outcome is **equally likely to occur** one-sixth of the time. With this in mind we can define the events $E_1 = \{1\}$, $E_2 = \{2\}$, $E_3 = \{3\}$, $E_4 = \{4\}$, $E_5 = \{5\}$, and $E_6 = \{6\}$; then we should expect each event to occur in one-sixth of the rolls. Alternatively, these expectations can be understood as *probabilities*. In that case we write $P(E_1) = P(E_2) = P(E_3) = P(E_4) = P(E_5) = P(E_6) = \frac{1}{6}$, read as "the probability of the event E_1 is equal to the probability of the event E_2 is equal to . . . the probability of the event E_6, and each of these probabilities is each equal to $\frac{1}{6}$."

Now consider the events $A = \{1, 5\}$ and $B = \{2, 4, 6\}$. A Venn diagram showing the sample space for the die-rolling experiment, and showing events A and B, is given in Figure 4.1. **Venn diagrams** are pictorial representations of relationships among events. In a Venn diagram the sample space is generally represented by a rectangle, and events are represented by circles, parts of circles, or other representations within the rectangle.

Since event A includes two of the six equally likely possible outcomes, it is reasonable to expect that event A will occur twice as often as event E_1, which includes only one of the six possible outcomes. Similarly, our expectation is that event B will occur three times as often as E_1. In summary, we can conclude that $P(A) = \frac{2}{6}$ and $P(B) = \frac{3}{6}$. What we are saying, in effect, is that $P(A)$ is equal to $P(E_1) + P(E_5)$ and $P(B)$ is equal to $P(E_2) + P(E_4) + P(E_6)$. Moreover, we can expect that $P(S) = 1$ $\left(\text{i.e., } \frac{6}{6} = 1\right)$, since we must get either a 1 or 2 or 3 or 4 or 5 or 6 when a six-sided die is rolled. This means that we are *certain* to get one of the possible outcomes in S when the experiment is carried out.

Before proceeding, we need to explain what is meant by the *occurrence of an event*. An **event occurs** if and only if it contains the possible outcome that occurs. For example, suppose four persons, Tom, Jane, Mary, and Hal, are available for promotion. Now suppose that A is the event "a man gets promoted" (i.e., $A = \{$Tom, Hal$\}$) and suppose B is the event "either Tom or Mary gets promoted" (i.e., $B = \{$Tom, Mary$\}$). If Tom gets promoted, then both events, A and B, occur. If Mary gets promoted, then only event B occurs. If Hal gets promoted, then only event A occurs. And if Jane gets promoted then neither event A nor event B occurs.

What we have discussed thus far provides an intuitive justification for the following three **probability postulates** associated with the occurrence of events:

Probability Postulates, First Set

> For any sample space S containing at least one possible outcome:
>
> a. $P(S) = 1$, always.
> b. For any event A in S, $0 \leq P(A) \leq 1$.   (4-1)
> c. The probability of an event A is calculated by summing the probabilities associated with the possible outcomes defined in A. That is, if $A = \{e_1, e_2, \ldots, e_k\}$, then $P(A) = P(\{e_1\}) + P(\{e_2\}) + P(\{e_3\}) + \cdots + P(\{e_k\})$, where $e_1, e_2, \ldots, e_k$ represent possible outcomes.

For any valid assignment of probabilities to events, these simple rules must be followed:

1. Define the experiment.
2. List the possible outcomes.
3. Assign probabilities to the possible outcomes.
4. Determine the collection of possible outcomes contained in the event of interest.
5. Sum the probabilities associated with the possible outcomes in the event to obtain the event probability.

Although the probability postulates are useful and provide ground rules for working with given probabilities, they aren't much help in supplying specific probability values for individual events. Let's now look at that issue.

4.2
ASSIGNING PROBABILITIES TO EVENTS

Thus far, our exploration of probability has paid little attention to the origin of the probability values stated in the simple case of rolling a single die in Example 4.1. By assuming that the die was fair, we explicitly assumed that all possible outcomes in the sample space have the same probability (i.e., the possible outcomes are equally likely). Let's now consider an everyday business situation where it makes sense to assign the same probability to every possible outcome in the sample space.

■ **EXAMPLE 4.2**

Assigning Probabilities to Winning a Sundae Combination

Your local yogurt parlor advertises a "build your own sundae" with several choices at the same price. You can choose from 3 styles of container (sugar waffle cone, plain cone, or paper cup), 3 flavors (vanilla, chocolate, or strawberry), 7 toppings (granola, coconut, peanuts, carob, chocolate chips, rainbow sprinkles, or banana chips), and 4 syrups (fudge, maple, butterscotch, or cherry). To promote the parlor's "bring along a friend free" theme, the parlor gives each sundae patron an "instant winner" lottery card upon paying the bill. The card entitles every customer to invite a friend to a free sundae with the customer's next purchase of a "build your own sundae." The free offer is for one specific combination from the sundae bar. To determine which specific combination the friend is entitled to, the customer scrapes off a thin silver screen on the card, which then reveals the sundae combination to be served free to the friend. What is the probability that the customer will win a sundae combination of plain waffle cone, vanilla flavored yogurt, granola topping, and maple syrup?

Assuming that every customer wins some sundae combination, let A represent the event that the customer wins one consisting of plain cone, vanilla-flavored yogurt, granola topping, and maple syrup. Based on the probability postulates listed in Section 4.1, we know that $0 \leq P(A) \leq 1$; the probability that a customer will win a unique sundae combination is some value between 0 and 1. But the earlier discussion doesn't tell us *what specific probability value* within the range from 0 to 1 we should assign to $P(A)$. Let's assume that equal numbers of lottery cards have been printed for each sundae combination so that on any one draw a customer is just as likely to win any combination. Within this framework there is a unique, reasonable, valid, and correct value for $P(A)$; it is $P(A) = \frac{1}{252}$. Although the value for $P(A)$ was not stated explicitly, we were able to deduce it from the given information once the stipulation was made that all possible sundae combinations are equally likely. In the remainder of this section we'll explain the equally likely procedure for assigning probabilities to events, and we'll explain two other methods of making probability assignments to events.

PROCEDURE ONE: EQUALLY LIKELY POSSIBLE OUTCOMES

Define the possible outcomes in a sample space in a way that makes plausible the assumption that the possible outcomes are equally likely. Then count the number of possible outcomes in the sample space S [this count is denoted $n(S)$] and the number of possible outcomes in the event A [this count is denoted $n(A)$]; assign $P(A) = n(A)/n(S)$. The "build your own sundae" example used this procedure. The value $P(A) = \frac{1}{252}$ is uniquely correct, given the assumption that there are 252 equally likely possible outcomes.

Now suppose the free sundae promotion is changed so that the customer paying the bill receives a 20% discount coupon toward a "build your own sundae" of his or her choice. In this case, there is no lottery, and it would not be plausible to assume that every possible sundae combination is as likely as any other to be chosen by a randomly selected customer using the discount coupon. Some combinations will almost certainly be more popular than others. Therefore, we need to consider alternative procedures for assigning probabilities to the possible combinations.

PROCEDURE TWO: KNOWN RELATIVE FREQUENCIES

Rely on known relative frequencies of possible outcomes (or relative frequencies of events).

Not every experiment yields possible outcomes that are equally likely. How often something happened in the past can be used as a number to estimate the probability that it will happen again in the future. Let's look at a situation where past performance can be used to estimate a probability.

Suppose an insurance company knows from past actuarial data that among all females who are 30 years old, about 50 out of every 100,000 will die within a 1 year period. Using the relative frequency method, the company estimates the probability of death for someone in that age group as

$$\frac{50}{100,000} = .0005$$

An illustration of the importance of the relative frequency approach for making probability assessments for scheduling hospital beds is given in the Beth Israel Hospital applied case at the end of this chapter.

PROCEDURE THREE: SUBJECTIVE JUDGMENT

Quantify your subjective judgment about possible outcomes (or events).

What procedure should be followed in situations where we have little or no justification to assume equally likely possible outcomes and where there is no directly available information on the relative frequencies associated with the possible outcomes or events? In these cases we may use our judgment to quantify qualitative aspects of the situation and assign *subjective probabilities* to the possible outcomes or events. For example, suppose a restaurant owner opens a second restaurant in another, culturally different, part of the city. The owner is concerned because she lacks information on the eating preferences of the potential customers in that area. She may resort to a reasonable hunch or "gut feeling" and conclude that half the customers will order a combination made up of scrambled eggs, bacon, hash browns, and orange juice. "Half the customers" implies assigning a probability of $\frac{1}{2}$ that a customer whose preference she does not know will order this combination. This third procedure is different from the first two procedures. It differs from the first procedure because the subjective value was not formulated on the assumption that this combination has the same probability as every other possible combination. It differs from the second procedure because the basis of the subjective value is neither from past history at previous locations nor from past experience at the new location. Hence, there is no known relative frequency upon which to base a projection of the relative frequency that may actually exist.

Other examples of subjective probabilities abound. Las Vegas odds quoted for sporting events, such as football or horse racing, are examples. So are the odds that you will make money when you invest in newly issued stocks or bonds, and the odds that you will correctly guess which topics your professor will include on the next exam. Subjective probabilities do not necessarily exclude relative frequency information or experience. In fact, properly assessed subjective probabilities will take relevant prior information or experience into account.

In this text we will not pursue subjective probabilities beyond this discussion, but the following example does illustrate how subjective probabilities play a critical role in decisions made at important financial institutions. It shows how disagreement, in the form of expectations of what the future interest rate would be, led not to one best estimate but to a (subjective) probability distribution expressing how probable various possible values were thought to be.

■ **EXAMPLE 4.3**

The Morgan Guaranty Trust and Subjective Probabilities

The Sources and Uses Committee of the Morgan Guaranty Trust Company, a large New York City bank, was composed of top-ranking executives. The committee met about twice a month to receive information and recommendations concerning basic asset and liability policy decisions. Typical topics considered were the buying and selling of bonds and notes for the firm's investment portfolio, the quantity of CDs (certificates of deposit) to be issued, and their maturity period.

At each meeting the committee received information and recommendations on anticipated money market developments. The presentation was made by a group of seven financial market specialists who closely monitored changes in market conditions. Considerable discussion among this group of specialists normally preceded their presentation. Opinions typically differed among the specialists about the likely value of interest rate changes. Yet the discussion had always concluded with a single-valued estimate of the future interest rate. Thus, the specialist group might report they expected a 10% prime rate in 3 months, or an 8% certificate of deposit rate in 1 month, and so forth. Thus, even though the group members all had their individual expectations about the rate, they simply substituted one number for their diverse expectations. There was no formal procedure for quantifying into one value the collective judgment of interest rate expectations of the participants. Thus, one time the reported rate might be a median of the individual expectations, and the next time it might be the mode or median. Nor was there any procedure for describing how much uncertainty surrounded the single value reported as the group's expectation. There was no attempt to report that one time they were quite certain their estimate was accurate, but another time they knew their estimate was shaky. Eventually, management resolved to correct this situation.

In the early 1970s, the bank's top management set about introducing an element of quantification for the uncertainty that existed. They wanted some way to tie probabilities into the range of possible interest rates. The procedure they decided upon employed subjective probabilities. First, an interest rate range was established within which all seven specialists were convinced the actual rate would be included. Then the range was subdivided, and probabilities were assigned to each interval in accordance with the consensus of the financial market specialist group. To illustrate how this works, let's say this week the group of financial market specialists meets to express a view as to what the 90 day CD rate would be 3 months from now. The meeting might result in the following subjective probability assignments:

INTEREST RATE RANGE		PROBABILITY
At least:	But less than:	
7.875%	8.125%	.15
8.125%	8.375%	.30
8.375%	8.625%	.30
8.625%	8.875%	.20
8.875%	9.125%	.05

Notice that the group believes that there is an 80% chance that interest rates for 90 day CDs will fall between 8.125% and 8.875%.

4.3

PROBABILITIES FOR COMBINED EVENTS

Events can be combined in various ways. In considering the combinations, it is important to know that *when a possible outcome is listed in an event, it is always listed exactly once.* With this in mind, we shall define the *union of events, intersection of events, empty event, mutually exclusive events,* and *complement of an event.* The definitions are then illustrated in Example 4.4.

UNION OF EVENTS

An event *C* representing the **union** of two events *A* and *B* contains all the possible outcomes, and only those possible outcomes, in one or the other or both of the two events *A* and *B*. Symbolically, we write *C* = *A* ∪ *B*, with the symbol ∪ indicating union. We read *A* ∪ *B* as "*A* union *B*" or as "*A* or *B*."

The definition of union can be extended to more than two events. For example, an event *F* representing the union of the events *A*, *B*, *C*, and *D* contains all the possible outcomes, and only those possible outcomes, in the events A, B, C, and D. Symbolically, we write $F = A \cup B \cup C \cup D$.

INTERSECTION OF EVENTS

An event C representing the **intersection** of two events A and B contains those possible outcomes, and only those possible outcomes, common to both A and B. Symbolically, we write $C = A \cap B$, with the symbol $\cap$ indicating intersection. We read $A \cap B$ as "A intersect B" or as "A and B." The definition of intersection can be extended to more than two events. For example, an event F representing the intersection of the events A, B, C, and D contains those possible outcomes, and only those possible outcomes, common to A, B, C, and D. Symbolically, we write $F = A \cap B \cap C \cap D$.

EMPTY EVENT

An event is **empty** if it contains no possible outcomes. An empty event is denoted by $\varnothing$.

MUTUALLY EXCLUSIVE EVENTS

If two nonempty events A and B have no possible outcomes in common, we say their intersection is empty and the events are **mutually exclusive**. Symbolically, we write that two nonempty events A and B are mutually exclusive if and only if $A \cap B = \varnothing$.

COMPLEMENT OF AN EVENT

An event A is defined to be the **complement** of an event B if and only if $A \cap B = \varnothing$ and $A \cup B = S$. The complement of an event A is sometimes denoted by A'. Thus, $A \cup A' = S$ and $A \cap A' = \varnothing$. We may also note that $S' = \varnothing$. In words, the complement of an event A, denoted A', is an event consisting of all those elements, and only those elements, contained in S but not contained in A.

In the following example, the definitions of union of events, intersection of events, empty event, mutually exclusive events, and complement of an event are applied to events in the sample space of rolling a pair of dice.

■ **EXAMPLE 4.4**

Rolling a Pair of Dice

The experiment consists of rolling a pair of dice and counting the number of dots on each upface. The sample space S consists of all 36 possible ordered pairs (possible outcomes): (1, 1), (1, 2), . . . , (1, 6), (2, 1), . . . , (2, 6), . . . , (6, 1), . . . , (6, 6). An outcome listed as an ordered pair means that the pair of numbers must occur in a particular sequence. An ordered pair is indicated by separating the numbers by a comma and enclosing the pair within parentheses. The sample space may be written as

$$S = \{(1, 1), (1, 2), \ldots, (1, 6), (2, 1), \ldots, (2, 6), \ldots, (6, 1), \ldots, (6, 6)\}$$

This is shown pictorially (Venn diagram) in Figure 4.2.

Figure 4.2
Pictorial illustration of the sample space for rolling a pair of dice. The event A_7 consists of the possible outcomes where the sum of the dots on the two upfaces is equal to 7. The event R consists of the possible outcomes where at least one upface shows 6 dots.

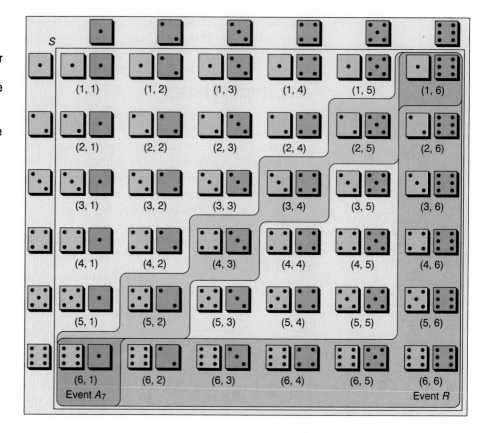

a. If the event A_7 is defined as "the sum of the dots on the two upfaces is equal to 7," it may be represented as $A_7 = \{(1, 6), (6, 1), (2, 5), (5, 2), (3, 4), (4, 3)\}$. The event A_7 contains 6 possible outcomes, and is indicated in Figure 4.2 by the diagonal shading of dice.

b. By defining the event A_{11} as "the sum of the dots on the two upfaces is equal to 11," we encompass only 2 possible outcomes. The event may be represented as $A_{11} = \{(5, 6), (6, 5)\}$.

c. The event A_e, defined as "the sum of the dots on the upfaces is an even value," has 18 possible outcomes. The event may be represented as

$$A_e = \{(1, 1), (1, 3), (1, 5), (2, 2), (2, 4), (2, 6), (3, 1), (3, 3), (3, 5),$$
$$(4, 2), (4, 4), (4, 6), (5, 1), (5, 3), (5, 5), (6, 2), (6, 4), (6, 6)\}$$

d. The event A_o, defined as "the sum of the dots on the upfaces is odd," may be represented as

$$A_o = \{(1, 2), (1, 4), (1, 6), (2, 1), (2, 3), (2, 5), (3, 2), (3, 4), (3, 6),$$
$$(4, 1), (4, 3), (4, 5), (5, 2), (5, 4), (5, 6), (6, 1), (6, 3), (6, 5)\}$$

The event A_o has 18 possible outcomes.

e. The event R, defined as "the number of dots on at least one of the upfaces is equal to 6," may be represented by

$$R = \{(1, 6), (6, 1), (2, 6), (6, 2), (3, 6), (6, 3),$$
$$(4, 6), (6, 4), (5, 6), (6, 5), (6, 6)\}$$

The event R has 11 possible outcomes, and is indicated in Figure 4.2 by the bottom and right border shadings.

f. The event that contains those possible outcomes where the sum of the dots on the two upfaces is equal to *either* 7 *or* 11 may be represented by

$$T = \{(1, 6), (6, 1), (2, 5), (5, 2), (3, 4), (4, 3), (5, 6), (6, 5)\}$$

Note that the event T consists of all the possible outcomes in the two events A_7 and A_{11}. Event T is the union of events A_7 and A_{11}. Symbolically, this is represented as $T = A_7 \cup A_{11}$.

g. Note that events A_7 and A_{11} have no possible outcomes in common. Thus, A_7 and A_{11} are mutually exclusive events. That is, $A_7 \cap A_{11} = \varnothing$

h. Consider the event containing those possible outcomes where the sum of the dots on the two upfaces is equal to 7 (i.e., event A_7) *or* at least one of the upfaces has 6 dots (i.e., event R). The combined event may be represented as

$$W = \{(1, 6), (6, 1), (2, 5), (5, 2), (3, 4), (4, 3), (2, 6), (6, 2),$$
$$(3, 6), (6, 3), (4, 6), (6, 4), (5, 6), (6, 5), (6, 6)\}$$

Note that event W consists of all possible outcomes in both the events A_7 and R, and only those possible outcomes. Thus, $W = A_7 \cup R$. Here are some important things to note about the union W:

  ■ Figure 4.2 shows that A_7 has 6 possible outcomes, R has 11 possible outcomes, and their union W has 15 possible outcomes. The number of possible outcomes in W is less than the sum of the number in A_7 and in R, which form the union!
  ■ Note in Figure 4.2 that A_7 and R have two possible outcomes in common, namely the ordered pairs $(1, 6)$ and $(6, 1)$. That A_7 and R have possible outcomes in common means A_7 and R are not mutually exclusive events. That is, $A_7 \cap R = \{(1, 6), (6, 1)\}$.
  ■ Note also that the possible outcomes $(1, 6)$ and $(6, 1)$ are each listed only once in the event W.

i. An event containing those possible outcomes where the sum of the dots on the two upfaces is equal to 7 *and* at least one of the upfaces has 6 dots may be represented as $D = \{(1, 6), (6, 1)\}$. Note that since event D consists of those possible outcomes, and only those possible outcomes, found in part h to be common to A_7 and R, it is the intersection of A_7 and R; that is, $D = A_7 \cap R$.

j. An event containing those possible outcomes where the sum of the dots on the upfaces of the two dice is either an even number or an odd number may be represented as

$$A_e \cup A_o = \{\text{all the ordered pairs that could occur}\} = S$$

Thus, the union of the mutually exclusive events A_e and A_o yields an event that is equal to the original sample space. By definition, A_o is the complement of A_e; thus, $A_o = A_e'$.

EXHAUSTIVE EVENTS

When the union of nonempty events results in an event equal to the sample space, the given events are said to be **exhaustive**. An event A and its complement A' are always exhaustive.

EVENT EQUALITY

Two events are **equivalent**, **equal**, or **identical** if and only if they contain exactly the same possible outcomes. For example, if event A is defined as $A = \{1, 2, 3\}$ and event B is defined as $B = \{2, 1, 3\}$, then A and B are identical events, even though the possible outcomes are listed in different orders; A and B contain exactly the same possible outcomes. However, A and B would not be identical if $A = \{1, 2, 3\}$ and $B = \{1, 2, 4\}$, since they do not have exactly the same possible outcomes. Additionally, $A = \{(1, 1), (1, 2)\}$ and $B = \{(1, 2), (1, 1)\}$ are equal events, but $A = \{(1, 1), (1, 2)\}$ and $B = \{(1, 1), (2, 1)\}$ are not equal, since the ordered pair $(1, 2)$ and the ordered pair $(2, 1)$ indicate a different sequence in the outcomes of the experiment. In summary, by writing $A = B$, we indicate that A and B are equal events. When they are not identical, we write $A \neq B$

PRACTICE EXERCISE

4.1 Suppose the sample space is given by $S = \{1, 3, 5, 7, 9, 11, 13, 15, 17\}$, and suppose $A = \{5, 9, 13, 17\}$, $B = \{3, 5, 7, 15, 17\}$, and $C = \{1, 3, 7\}$. Find:

a. A' b. B' c. C' d. $A \cup B$
e. $A \cup C$ f. $B \cup C$ g. $A \cup B \cup C$ h. $A \cap B$
i. $A \cap C$ j. $B \cap C$ k. $A \cap B \cap C$ l. $A \cup B'$
m. $A' \cup B$ n. $A' \cup B'$ o. $A \cap B'$ p. $A' \cap B$
q. $A' \cap B'$ r. $(A \cup B)'$ s. $(A \cap B)'$

ADDITIONAL PROBABILITY POSTULATES

We are now ready for two additional probability postulates.

Probability Postulates, Second Set

For any nonempty sample space S:

d. $P(\emptyset) = 0$, always.   (4-2)

e. If A and B are two nonempty events in S, then $P(A \cup B) = P(A) + P(B)$ if and only if $A \cap B = \emptyset$.

The following are useful corollaries and may be verified with Venn diagrams.

f. $P(A') = 1 - P(A)$ (4-3)

g. $P(A) = P(A \cap B) + P(A \cap B')$ (4-4a)

h. $P(B) = P(A \cap B) + P(A' \cap B)$ (4-4b)

The last two corollaries refer to events A and B and say that the probability of an event equals the sum of the probabilities of the events that partition it.

PROBABILITY OF THE UNION OF TWO EVENTS

It is important to know how to find the probability of the union of two nonempty events even when the two events are not mutually exclusive. To do this, add the probabilities associated with the two events and subtract the probability associated with their intersection. From the single die experiment discussed in Section 4.1, let's define the events $A = \{1, 2\}$, $B = \{1, 3, 5\}$, and $C = \{1, 2, 3, 5\}$. From their descriptions and from the properties of events, it can be seen that $C = A \cup B$. That is, the union of A and B is an event consisting of the four elements found in either or both of A and B. With equally likely outcomes it can also be stated that $P(C) = \frac{4}{6}$, $P(A) = \frac{2}{6}$, and $P(B) = \frac{3}{6}$. But note that $P(C) \neq P(A) + P(B)$. Since $A \cap B = E_1$, where $P(E_1) = \frac{1}{6}$, it turns out that

$$P(C) = P(A) + P(B) - P(A \cap B)$$

Numerically, $\frac{4}{6} = \frac{2}{6} + \frac{3}{6} - \frac{1}{6}$. In other words,

$$P(A \cup B) = P(A) + P(B) - P(A \cap B)$$

When the intersection of the two events is empty, its probability is 0, so we subtract 0 and then have the special case of postulate e, Equation (4-2). If the intersection is not empty, we subtract the value of the probability associated with the intersection and follow the **general addition rule**.

General Addition Rule for Probabilities

If A and B are any two events in the sample space S, then

$$P(A \cup B) = P(A) + P(B) - P(A \cap B) \tag{4-5}$$

In some probability problems, every possible outcome in the sample space is equally likely to occur. In other cases, the possible outcomes are not equally likely. In both cases, however, the general additional rule for probabilities is applicable.

■ **EXAMPLE 4.5**

Event Probabilities for Sample Spaces with Possible Outcomes That Are Not Equally Likely

Let $S = \{a, b, c, d, e, f, g\}$, where the possible outcomes a and b are each associated with a probability of $\frac{1}{14}$, the possible outcomes c, d, and e are each associated with a probability of $\frac{1}{21}$, the possible outcome f is associated with a probability of $\frac{3}{7}$, and the possible outcome g is associated with a probability of $\frac{2}{7}$. Let $A = \{a, c, f\}$, $B = \{c, d\}$, and $C = \{a, c, d, g\}$. Then:

a. $P(A) = P(\{a\} \cup \{c\} \cup \{f\}) = P(\{a\}) + P(\{c\}) + P(\{f\}) = \frac{1}{14} + \frac{1}{21} + \frac{3}{7} = \frac{23}{42}$

b. Similarly, $P(B) = \frac{2}{21}$, $P(C) = \frac{19}{42}$, and $P(S) = 1$

c. $A \cap B = \{c\}$ and $P(A \cap B) = \frac{1}{21}$

d. $A \cup B = \{a, c, d, f\}$ and $P(A \cup B) = \frac{25}{42}$

e. $P(A \cup B) = P(A) + P(B) - P(A \cap B)$

f. $A' = \{b, d, e, g\}$ and $P(A') = \frac{19}{42}$

g. $P(A') = 1 - P(A)$

h. $A \cap B' = \{a, f\}$ and $P(A \cap B') = \frac{7}{14}$

i. $A' \cap B = \{d\}$ and $P(A' \cap B) = \frac{1}{21}$

j. $P(A) = P(A \cap B) + P(A \cap B')$

k. $P(B) = P(A \cap B) + P(A' \cap B)$

l. $A' \cup B' = \{a, b, d, e, f, g\}$ and $P(A' \cup B') = \frac{40}{42}$

m. $A' \cup B' = (A \cap B)'$, so $P(A' \cup B') = P(A \cap B)'$

n. $A' \cap B' = \{b, e, g\}$ and $P(A' \cap B') = \frac{17}{42}$

o. $A' \cap B' = (A \cup B)'$, so $P(A' \cap B') = P(A \cup B)'$

In the Chapter Review Exercises, you will be asked to find similar properties and probabilities involving the event C (see Exercise 4.22).

In the previous example the probabilities of all the possible outcomes were known at the beginning of the problem, and they were used to find the probabilities of the various events. However, many situations arise in which we do not know the probabilities of the individual possible outcomes. It is important to understand that in many probability problems it is not necessary to know the probabilities of individual possible outcomes. Example 4.6 illustrates the application of the various probability rules to events when there is no specific knowledge of the probabilities associated with their respective possible outcomes.

■ **EXAMPLE 4.6**

Event Probabilities Without Knowledge of the Possible Outcomes

Let A and B be two nonempty events in a sample space S such that $P(A) = .5$, $P(B) = .7$, and $P(A \cap B) = .4$. Then:

a. $P(A \cup B) = .5 + .7 - .4 = .8$

b. $P(A \cap B') = .5 - .4 = .1$

c. $P(A' \cap B) = .7 - .4 = .3$

d. $P(A' \cap B') = P(A \cup B)' = 1 - .8 = .2$

e. $P(A' \cup B') = P(A \cap B)' = 1 - .4 = .6$

CAUTION: In calculating probabilities you should never obtain a final answer whose value is negative or greater than 1. If you do, then either (1) the problem was stated incorrectly, or (2) you made a conceptual error, or (3) you made an arithmetic error.

● ●

PRACTICE EXERCISE

4.2 Suppose the sample space is given by $S = \{1, 3, 5, 7, 9, 11, 13, 15, 17\}$, where we associate each possible outcome with a probability of $\frac{1}{9}$. Let $A = \{5, 9, 13, 17\}$, $B = \{3, 5, 7, 15, 17\}$, and $C = \{1, 3, 7\}$. Find:

a. $P(A)$ b. $P(B)$ c. $P(C)$ d. $P(A')$
e. $P(B')$ f. $P(C')$ g. $P(A \cup B)$ h. $P(A \cup C)$
i. $P(B \cup C)$ j. $P(A \cup B \cup C)$ k. $P(A \cap B)$ l. $P(A \cap C)$
m. $P(B \cap C)$ n. $P(A \cap B \cap C)$ o. $P(A \cup B')$ p. $P(A' \cup B)$
q. $P(A' \cup B')$ r. $P(A \cap B')$ s. $P(A' \cap B)$ t. $P(A' \cap B')$
u. $P(A \cup B)'$ v. $P(A \cap B)'$

● ●

EXERCISES

4.1 Consider the affluent families in Exercise 3.1 in Chapter 3. We repeat their annual gross incomes (in dollars):

$247,919   285,983   234,994   264,916   286,789   319,331
$237,949   272,290   247,604   287,280   279,043   272,333
$334,561   277,340   277,534   258,180   302,751   278,391
$317,594   248,426   266,364   285,085   300,649   292,394
$259,456   264,455   281,118   246,746   250,356

Now suppose that among these families there are families with 0, 1, 2, 3, or 4 children, but we don't know who they are. And suppose that a local financial report states that the annual gross incomes of:

- The families with 0 children or 1 child range from $234,000 to $264,000.
- The families with 1 child or 2 children range from $247,000 to $280,000.
- The families with 2 or 3 children range from $260,000 to $300,000.
- The families with 3 or 4 children range from $270,000 to $340,000.

Let S be the sample space consisting of the annual gross incomes for the 29 families; let A be the event consisting of the possible annual gross incomes of the families with 0 children or 1 child; let B be the event consisting of the possible annual gross incomes of the families with 1 child or 2 children; let C be the event consisting of the possible annual gross incomes of the families with 2 or 3 children; and let D be the event consisting of the possible annual gross incomes of the families with 3 or 4 children. In each of the following, list the possible outcomes included in the given event:

a. A b. B c. C d. D
e. C' f. D' g. $C \cup D$ h. $C \cap D$
i. $(C \cup D)'$ j. $(C \cap D)'$ k. $C' \cap D$
l. $(C \cap D) \cup (C' \cap D)$ Is this event equal to any of the preceding events?
m. $C' \cap D'$ Is this event equal to any of the preceding events?
n. $C' \cup D'$ Is this event equal to any of the preceding events?
o. $A \cap D$ What kind of event do you get? What can you say about the events A and D?

4.2 With respect to the sample space and events in Exercise 4.1, list the possible outcomes in the following sets:
  a. A'
  b. $A' \cap D$ Are these two events mutually exclusive?
  c. $A \cap C$ Are these two events mutually exclusive?
  d. $A \cap C'$ Are these two events mutually exclusive?

▶ **4.3** With respect to the sample space and events in Exercise 4.1, construct a Venn diagram to show the sample space and the events A, B, C, and D.

4.4 Suppose $P(A) = .33$, $P(B) = .19$, and $A \cap B = \varnothing$. What is the value of $P(A \cup B)$?

▶ **4.5** Suppose $P(A) = .33$, $P(B) = .19$, and $P(A \cup B) = .49$. What is the value of $P(A \cap B)$?

4.6 With respect to the sample space and events described in Exercise 4.1, we have

$S = \{247{,}919, \ldots, 319{,}331, 237{,}949, \ldots, 272{,}333, \ldots, 250{,}356\}$

$A = \{234{,}994, 237{,}949, 246{,}746, 247{,}604, 247{,}919, 248{,}426, 250{,}356,$
$258{,}180, 259{,}456\}$

$B = \{247{,}604, 247{,}919, 248{,}426, 250{,}356, 258{,}180, 259{,}456, 264{,}455,$
$264{,}916, 266{,}364, 272{,}290, 272{,}333, 277{,}340, 277{,}534, 278{,}391, 279{,}043\}$

$C = \{264{,}455, 264{,}916, 266{,}364, 272{,}290, 272{,}333, 277{,}340, 277{,}534,$
$278{,}391, 279{,}043, 281{,}118, 285{,}085, 285{,}983, 286{,}789, 287{,}280, 292{,}394\}$

$D = \{272{,}290, 272{,}333, 277{,}340, 277{,}534, 278{,}391, 279{,}043, 281{,}118,$
$285{,}085, 285{,}983, 286{,}789, 287{,}280, 292{,}394, 300{,}649, 302{,}751, 317{,}594,$
$319{,}331, 334{,}561\}$

Now suppose a TV talk show host wishes to arbitrarily select one of these 29 families for a personal interview. (By using the word "arbitrary" our intent is to make all the possible outcomes in the sample space equally likely for selection; that is, the probability associated with each possible outcome in the sample space is $\frac{1}{29}$.)
  a. What is the probability that the host selects a person from event A? That is, what is the value of $P(A)$?
Similarly, what is the value of each of the following?
  b. $P(B)$ c. $P(C)$ d. $P(D)$ e. $P(C')$
  f. $P(D')$ g. $P(C \cup D)$ h. $P(C \cap D)$ i. $P(C \cup D)'$
  j. $P(C \cap D)'$ k. $P(C' \cap D)$
  l. $P(C \cap D) + P(C' \cap D)$ Is this value equal to $P(D)$?
  m. $P(C' \cap D')$ Is this value equal to $P(C \cup D)'$?
  n. $P(C' \cup D')$ Is this value equal to $P(C \cap D)'$?
  o. $P(A \cap D)$

● ●

4.4
CONDITIONAL PROBABILITY

There are circumstances where our knowledge of the occurrence of one event alters our perspective about how likely we think that some other event will occur. For example, suppose you are an insurance agent with a prospective 45-year-old male customer for a very large amount of life insurance. Through routine questioning you discover the following:

1. One-fourth of the males on his father's side died by the age of 50 from a rare disease.
2. One-third of the males on his mother's side died by the age of 53 from a heart attack.

Prior to learning about the family history, the life expectancy of this man may be considered a random selection from the population of life expectancies of all 45-year-old men. That population would be the sample space for the experiment of selecting the life expectancy of a 45-year-old man about whom nothing else is known. It would include men whose male ancestors did not have a high incidence of early death as well as those whose male ancestors did have a high incidence of early death. Once it is known that the male ancestors of the man in question had a high incidence of early death, the entire sample space is no longer relevant. *Of relevance now is only that part of the sample space that pertains to life expectancies of men whose male ancestors have a high incidence of early death.*

Do you think your company will insure this person, and should you devote any more time writing up a policy for him? On the basis of the information about his family history, it would appear that this man's life expectancy might be less than the normal life expectancy for men of his age. In terms of probabilities based on known sample spaces, *how can we adjust our probabilities when we know that only part of the sample space is involved?* For example, let event B represent the part of the sample space that includes only 45-year-old men with a family history as described in items 1 and 2 above. Let event A represent the event that at the end of this year the person is still alive. We can then define $P(A \mid B)$ as the **conditional probability** event A occurs *given that* event B occurs. The next example illustrates conditional probability in a sampling context.

■ **EXAMPLE 4.7**

Random Selection of Slips of Paper from a Hat

NOTE: When we speak of a **random** selection from a given finite sample space, unless specific probability values are given, we mean that the possible outcomes in the given sample space are equally likely.

Suppose we have 8 slips of paper in a hat, each with only one of the letters a, b, c, d, e, f, g, h written on it. If we *randomly* select one slip of paper, the probability is $\frac{1}{8}$ that it will have the letter f written on it.

Now suppose we want to randomly select a second piece of paper without returning the first slip. If we know that the first slip has f written on it, then we know that now only 7 slips of paper are left, none of which has the letter f on it. Thus, the sample space for the second selection is only a part of the original sample space; it has been reduced to 7 possible outcomes. Also, we know that (1) the probability is 0 that the second slip will also have the letter f written on it; and (2) the probability is $\frac{1}{7}$ that the second slip will have the letter d written on it.

Let

$$A_1 = \{\text{The letter } f \text{ appears on the first slip}\}$$

$$A_2 = \{\text{The letter } f \text{ appears on the second slip}\}$$

$$B_2 = \{\text{The letter } d \text{ appears on the second slip}\}$$

Figure 4.3
Illustrating conditional
probability for 8 slips of paper

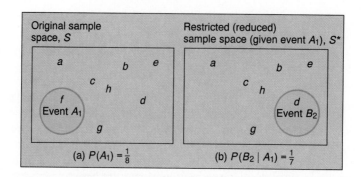

Then $P(A_2 \mid A_1)$ is the conditional probability that event A_2 occurs given that event A_1 occurs. Similarly, $P(B_2 \mid A_1)$ is the conditional probability that B_2 occurs given that A_1 occurs. And we know from the above discussion that

$$P(A_1) = \tfrac{1}{8} \qquad P(A_2 \mid A_1) = 0 \qquad P(B_2 \mid A_1) = \tfrac{1}{7}$$

The original and reduced sample spaces are illustrated in Figure 4.3.

Let's next show an example of the conditional probability in an investment context.

■ **EXAMPLE 4.8**

**An Investors'
Convention**

Suppose there is a local convention of investors with 773 investors attending; 139 of them invest only in real estate (event A), and 634 invest only in the stock market (event A'). None of these investors invest in both real estate and the stock market. Of the 139 who invest in real estate, 41 have made a profit on their investment and 98 have lost money. Of the 634 who invest in the stock market, 163 have made a profit and 471 have lost money. Thus, 204 have made a profit (event B), and 569 have lost money (event B'). This information is summarized in Table 4.1.

TABLE 4.1	Investors in Real Estate and the Stock Market		
	PROFIT **B**	**LOSS** **B'**	**ROW TOTAL**
REAL ESTATE **A**	41	98	139
STOCK MARKET **A'**	163	471	634
COLUMN TOTAL	204	569	773

If an individual is randomly selected from the entire group of 773 investors, then:

a. The probability is $\frac{139}{773}$ that he or she will have invested in real estate; that is, $P(A) = \frac{139}{773}$.

b. The probability is $\frac{634}{773}$ that he or she will have invested in the stock market; that is, $P(A') = \frac{634}{773}$.

c. The probability is $\frac{204}{773}$ that the investor will have made a profit; that is, $P(B) = \frac{204}{773}$.

d. The probability is $\frac{569}{773}$ that the investor will have lost money; that is, $P(B') = \frac{569}{773}$.

The probabilities of the intersection (joint) events are:

e. The probability that a randomly selected individual will have invested in real estate *and* made a profit is $\frac{41}{773}$, or $P(A \cap B) = \frac{41}{773}$.

f. The probability that a randomly selected individual will have invested in real estate *and* lost money is $\frac{98}{773}$, or $P(A \cap B') = \frac{98}{773}$.

g. The probability that a randomly selected individual will have invested in the stock market *and* made a profit is $\frac{163}{773}$, or $P(A' \cap B) = \frac{163}{773}$.

h. The probability that a randomly selected individual will have invested in the stock market *and* lost money is $\frac{471}{773}$, or $P(A' \cap B') = \frac{471}{773}$.

Now suppose we will be introduced to an investor to be randomly chosen from the 634 persons who invest in the stock market. What is the probability that he or she will have made a profit? It can't be $P(B) = \frac{163}{773}$, because that value refers to the situation in which all 773 investors are included in the sample space. According to Table 4.1, of the 634 individuals who invest in the stock market, 163 have made a profit. Thus, the probability is $\frac{163}{634}$ that the stock market investor we are going to meet has made a profit; that is, $P(B \mid A') = \frac{163}{634}$. Clearly, $P(B \mid A')$ does not necessarily equal $P(B)$. Similarly, the probability is $\frac{471}{634}$ that the stock market investor we are going to meet will have lost money, or $P(B' \mid A') = \frac{471}{634}$.

Suppose we will be introduced to another investor, to be randomly chosen from the 139 persons who invest in real estate. Of the 139 individuals who invest in real estate, 41 have made a profit. Thus, the probability is $\frac{41}{139}$ that the chosen real estate investor will have made a profit, or $P(B \mid A) = \frac{41}{139}$. Similarly, the probability is $\frac{98}{139}$ that the chosen real estate investor will have lost money, or $P(B' \mid A) = \frac{98}{139}$.

Examples 4.7 and 4.8 dealt with restricted sample spaces. That is, given some prior information it was found that we no longer had to deal with the entire original sample space. Instead, our consideration could be restricted to some subset from the original sample space and we could deal with that subset as though it was all the sample space needed. A problem is encountered, however, if all the probabilities on which we have information refer to the entire sample space S, but the probability we seek is a conditional probability defined on a restricted sample space. That is, suppose we are given not only $P(A)$ but also other values defined on the entire sample space, such as $P(B)$ and $P(A \cap B)$, and we want the probability of B adjusted for the restriction on the sample space [i.e., suppose we want $P(B \mid A)$]. Fortunately, such adjustments can be made from values defined on the entire sample space. *To find the probability that an event B occurs given that an event A occurs, we need to know the probability that both events occur relative to the probability that event A occurs.* Symbolically, the relationship is

$$P(B \mid A) = \frac{P(A \cap B)}{P(A)}$$

We see that the results in Example 4.8 are consistent with this:

$$P(B \mid A) = \frac{P(A \cap B)}{P(A)} = \frac{\frac{41}{773}}{\frac{139}{773}} = \frac{41}{139}$$

$$P(B \mid A') = \frac{P(A' \cap B)}{P(A')} = \frac{\frac{163}{773}}{\frac{634}{773}} = \frac{163}{634}$$

and so on.

In general, given any two nonempty events A and B in a sample space S, we define conditional probability for a restricted sample space in terms of probabilities from the original sample space.

Conditional Probability

$$P(A \mid B) = \frac{P(A \cap B)}{P(B)} \qquad \text{where } P(B) \neq 0 \qquad (4\text{-}6)$$

where the conditional probability that event A occurs given that event B occurs (restricted sample space) is equal to the probability (on the entire sample space) that events A and B occur together divided by the probability that event B occurs.

Similarly,

$$P(B \mid A) = \frac{P(A \cap B)}{P(A)} \qquad \text{where } P(A) \neq 0 \qquad (4\text{-}7)$$

where the conditional probability that event B occurs given that event A occurs is equal to the probability that events A and B occur together divided by the probability that event A occurs.

The ordinary probabilities such as $P(A)$ and $P(B)$ are referred to as *marginal* or *unconditional probabilities*.

By simple algebraic manipulation of equations (4-6) and (4-7), we get the **general multiplication rule**:

General Multiplication Rule

$$P(A \cap B) = P(B)P(A \mid B) = P(A)P(B \mid A) \qquad (4\text{-}8)$$

When working with restricted sample spaces and conditional probabilities, it is useful to know that for any nonempty events A and B in a sample space S,

$$P(B \mid A) = 1 - P(B' \mid A)$$

$$P(B \mid A') = 1 - P(B' \mid A')$$

You may verify these equations with the values given in Example 4.8. In the exercises, you will be asked to verify them as a general rule (see Exercise 4.39). Note, however, that $P(B \mid A) \neq 1 - P(B \mid A')$, and $P(B \mid A') \neq 1 - P(B' \mid A)$. One should be very careful about extrapolating mathematical rules.

INDEPENDENT EVENTS

There are situations where the value of the probability of an event is not changed when the sample space is restricted by the knowledge that some other event has occurred. That is, there are situations where $P(B \mid A) = P(B)$. When that happens we say that events A and B are *independent*. Formally: For any two nonempty events A and B in a sample space S, the events A and B are **independent** if and only if $P(A \mid B) = P(A)$. This definition immediately leads to the **special multiplication rule**:

Special Multiplication Rule

For any two nonempty events A and B in the sample space S, with $P(A) \neq 0$ and $P(B) \neq 0$, the events A and B are independent if and only if

$$P(A \cap B) = P(A)P(B) \tag{4-9}$$

DEPENDENT VERSUS INDEPENDENT EVENTS

Events that are not independent are **dependent**. The following example illustrates the difference between independent and dependent events.

■ **EXAMPLE 4.9**

Independent Events versus Dependent Events

Let $S = \{a, b, c, d, e, f, g, h\}$, where each possible outcome is associated with a probability of $\frac{1}{8}$. Let $A = \{a, b, c, d\}$, $B = \{b, c, f, g\}$, and $C = \{c, e, f, h\}$. Then

$$P(A) = \tfrac{4}{8} = \tfrac{1}{2}$$

$$P(B) = \tfrac{4}{8} = \tfrac{1}{2}$$

$$P(C) = \tfrac{4}{8} = \tfrac{1}{2}$$

$$P(A \cap B) = \tfrac{2}{8} = \tfrac{1}{4}$$

$$P(A \cap C) = \tfrac{1}{8}$$

Now we can compute

$$P(A \mid B) = \frac{P(A \cap B)}{P(B)} = \frac{\tfrac{1}{4}}{\tfrac{1}{2}} = \frac{1}{2} = P(A)$$

Thus, events A and B are independent. Notice that the special multiplication rule does apply to the independent events A and B since

$$P(A \cap B) = \tfrac{1}{4} = P(A)\,P(B) = \left(\tfrac{1}{2}\right)\left(\tfrac{1}{2}\right)$$

Also,

$$P(A \mid C) = \frac{P(A \cap C)}{P(C)} = \frac{\tfrac{1}{8}}{\tfrac{1}{2}} = \frac{1}{4} \neq P(A)$$

Thus, events A and C are not independent; they are dependent. Notice that the special multiplication rule does not apply to dependent events. That is,

$$P(A \cap C) = \tfrac{1}{8} \neq P(A)P(C) = \left(\tfrac{1}{2}\right)\left(\tfrac{1}{2}\right)$$

CAUTION: Many students have difficulty distinguishing between mutually exclusive events and independent events. Briefly, *if two nonempty events A and B are independent, they cannot be mutually exclusive.* And *if two nonempty events A and B are mutually exclusive, they cannot be independent.* That is, if A and B are nonempty events:

a. When A and B are mutually exclusive, then $P(A \mid B) = 0 \neq P(A)$.
b. When A and B are independent, then $P(A \mid B) = P(A) \neq 0$.

PRACTICE EXERCISES

4.3 As in Practice Exercise 4.2, suppose the sample space is $S = \{1, 3, 5, 7, 9, 11, 13, 15, 17\}$, where we associate each element with a probability of $\frac{1}{9}$. Let $A = \{5, 9, 13, 17\}$, $B = \{3, 5, 7, 15, 17\}$, and $C = \{1, 3, 7\}$. Find:

a. $P(A \mid B)$ b. $P(B \mid A)$ c. $P(A \mid C)$ d. $P(C \mid A)$
e. $P(A \mid B')$ f. $P(A' \mid B)$ g. $P(A' \mid B')$ h. $P(B \mid A')$
i. $P(B' \mid A)$ j. $P(B' \mid A')$ k. $P(A \mid C')$ l. $P(A' \mid C)$
m. $P(A' \mid C')$ n. $P(C \mid A')$ o. $P(C' \mid A)$ p. $P(C' \mid A')$
q. Are events A and B independent? Are events A and C independent?

4.4 With respect to Example 4.9, show that

a. $P(A \mid B') = P(A)$ b. $P(A' \mid B) = P(A')$ c. $P(A' \mid B') = P(A')$
d. $P(B \mid A) = P(B)$ e. $P(B \mid A') = P(B)$ f. $P(B' \mid A) = P(B')$
g. $P(B' \mid A') = P(B')$ h. $P(A \cap B) = P(A)P(B)$

EXERCISES

4.7 With respect to Exercises 4.1 and 4.6, and with the type of selection discussed in Exercise 4.6:

a. If a local news reporter discovers that the talk show host selected a family whose income is a possible outcome in the set D, what is the conditional probability that the family's income is also a possible outcome in the event C? That is, what is the value of $P(C \mid D)$?
Similarly, what is the value of each of the following?
b. $P(D \mid C)$ c. $P(A \mid D)$ d. $P(D \mid A)$
e. Are events C and D independent?
f. Are events A and D independent?

▶ **4.8** Suppose we are given a sample space S with 8 equally likely possible outcomes. That is, suppose $S = \{a, b, c, d, e, f, g, h\}$ with each possible outcome having probability $\frac{1}{8}$. Let $A = \{a, b\}$, $B = \{a, d, e, f\}$, and $C = \{b, g, h\}$. What is the value of each of the following?

a. $P(A)$ b. $P(B)$ c. $P(C)$ d. $P(A \cap B)$
e. $P(A \cap C)$ f. $P(B \cap C)$ g. $P(A \mid B)$ h. $P(A \mid C)$
i. $P(B \mid C)$ j. $P(B \mid A)$ k. $P(C \mid A)$ l. $P(C \mid B)$
m. Are events A and B independent?   n. Are events A and C independent?
o. Are events B and C independent?   p. Which events are mutually exclusive?

4.5
BAYES' THEOREM

Often we know the value of the conditional probability of the occurrence of one event, B, given that an event A has occurred or will occur [i.e., $P(B \mid A)$], but we would rather know the inverse conditional probability. That is, we know $P(B \mid A)$, but we would rather know the value of $P(A \mid B)$. Ordinarily these two probabilities differ. For example, suppose an agency claims that by using a certain diagnostic technique it can correctly identify 85% of the individuals in a group of known cancer patients. The claim states, "Given that a person has cancer, this diagnostic technique will correctly identify that person 85% of the time." What the individual being tested really wants to know, however, is, "Given that the diagnostic technique says that I have cancer, what is the chance that I actually do have cancer?" A conditional probability is known, but the inverse conditional probability is desired.

An inverse probability such as this one can be found by using a simple manipulation of the general multiplication rule. Recall that

$$P(A \cap B) = P(A)P(B \mid A) = P(B)P(A \mid B)$$

Thus, $P(A)P(B \mid A) = P(B)P(A \mid B)$, so that

$$P(A \mid B) = \frac{P(A)P(B \mid A)}{P(B)} \qquad \text{if } P(B) \neq 0$$

If the values for $P(A)$, $P(B \mid A)$, and $P(B)$ are known, the value for $P(A \mid B)$ can be found from this equation. If we do not know the value for $P(B)$, however, it may be possible to determine it from other relationships. First, we must recognize that B is the union of $A \cap B$ and $A' \cap B$. Then from the special addition rule (probability postulate), it follows that $P(B) = P(A \cap B) + P(A' \cap B)$, and $P(B)$ is then found by applying the multiplication rule:

$$P(B) = P(A \cap B) + (P(A' \cap B) = P(A)P(B \mid A) + P(A')P(B \mid A')$$

The latter expression is used in **Bayes' theorem**.

Bayes' Theorem

$$P(A \mid B) = \frac{P(A)P(B \mid A)}{P(A)P(B \mid A) + P(A')P(B \mid A')} \qquad \text{(4-10)}$$

From Bayes' theorem we can find the value for $P(A \mid B)$ if we know the values for $P(A)$, $P(B \mid A)$, and $P(B \mid A')$. Thus, if we are given $P(B \mid A)$ but really want the inverse probability $P(A \mid B)$, we can calculate it if $P(A)$ and $P(B \mid A')$ are also known. In the following example, exactly this type of situation is encountered.

■ **EXAMPLE 4.10**

Evaluating a Diagnostic Test for Cancer

An agency claims that by using a certain diagnostic technique (examining skin and bone cultures, measuring respiratory rate, and measuring the amount of a certain compound in the blood) it can correctly identify as having cancer 85% of the individuals in a group of known cancer patients. If we let $A = \{$Individual has cancer$\}$ and $B = \{$Diagnostic test asserts the individual has cancer$\}$, then the agency's claim may be represented by $P(B \mid A) = .85$. What is of concern to the person being tested may be represented by $P(A \mid B)$; that is, "If the test says I have cancer, do I really have cancer?" Now suppose the test mistakenly indicates cancer 20% of the time with individuals who do not have cancer; this asserts that $P(B \mid A') = .20$. Suppose also that 10% of the population is expected to have cancer; that is, suppose $P(A) = .10$. With this information we can use Bayes' theorem to evaluate the probability that the person has cancer given that the diagnostic test indicates cancer:

$$P(A \mid B) = \frac{(.10)(.85)}{(.10)(.85) + (.90)(.20)} = .321 \text{ (approx.)}$$

Thus, in this situation, if the individual is told that the test indicates cancer, then there is approximately only a 32% chance that cancer is actually present. Surely this would offer some hope to the person who is told that a test that is 85% reliable indicates cancer!

An alternate, tabular approach to solving this type of problem is illustrated in Figure 4.4.

$$P(A \mid B) = \frac{P(A \cap B)}{P(B)} = \frac{.085}{.265} = .321 \text{ (approx.)}$$

A tree diagram approach, as in Figure 4.5, offers another way to evaluate the inverse conditional probabilities.

Each branch probability is the product of the probabilities along the branch. To find the inverse probability, $P(A \mid B)$:

Step 1

The branch in which both A and B occur has probability $(.10)(.85)$.

Step 2

The other branch in which B occurs has probability $(.90)(.20)$.

Step 3

The denominator of the inverse (Bayes' theorem) probability is the sum of the probabilities in Steps 1 and 2.

Step 4

Then

$$P(A \mid B) = \frac{P(A)P(B \mid A)}{P(A)P(B \mid A) + P(A')P(B \mid A')}$$

$$= \frac{(.10)(.85)}{(.10)(.85) + (.90)(.20)} = 0.321 \text{ (approx.)}$$

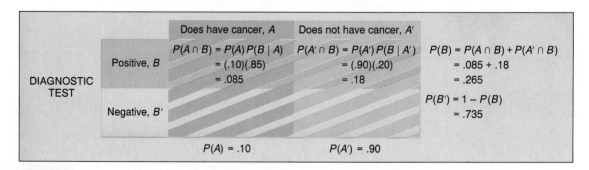

Figure 4.4
Tabular approach to solving a
Bayes' theorem problem

Figure 4.5
Tree diagram to evaluate a
diagnostic test for cancer

Let A = {person has cancer} and B = {diagnostic test is positive}

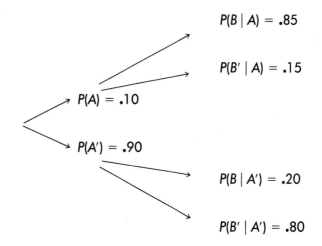

$P(B \mid A) = .85$

$P(B' \mid A) = .15$

$P(A) = .10$

$P(A') = .90$

$P(B \mid A') = .20$

$P(B' \mid A') = .80$

Before closing this section we point out that Bayes' theorem may also be interpreted as the recomputing of the probability of an event A when new information about an event B is available or becomes available. That is, equation (4-10) also may be written as

$$P(A \mid B) = \left[\frac{P(B \mid A)}{P(A)P(B \mid A) + P(A')P(B \mid A')} \right] P(A)$$

By looking at the right-hand side of this expression, we can see that the probability of event A is modified by the conditional probabilities of B with A and of B with A'.

PRACTICE EXERCISE

4.5 Suppose A is the event that a person shops at a discount warehouse, and suppose B is the event that a shopper spends more than $200 at one time. If 90% of all shoppers shop at discount warehouses, then $P(A) = .9$. If 70% of all those who shop at discount warehouses spend more than $200 at one time, then $P(B \mid A) = .7$. And if 20% of all those who do not shop at discount warehouses spend more than $200 at one time, then $P(B \mid A') = .2$. Find:
a. $P(A \mid B)$, the probability that a person who spent more than $200 at one time shopped at a discount warehouse.
b. $P(A \mid B')$, the probability that a person who did not spend more than $200 at one time shopped at a discount warehouse.

EXERCISES

▶ 4.9 Suppose a bank examiner finds that 2% of the customers at a certain bank are overcharged on their loans, 5% are underpaid on their savings interest, and 0.1% are both overcharged on loans and underpaid on savings interest. Let A represent the set of customers who are overcharged on loans, and let B represent the set of customers who are underpaid on their interest. Now suppose we arbitrarily select a customer. (By the word "arbitrarily" we mean that all the customers at the bank are equally likely to be selected.) In that case we have $P(A) = .02$, $P(B) = .05$, and $P(A \cap B) = .001$. What is the value of each of the following?

  a. $P(A \mid B)$ b. $P(B \mid A)$

  c. $P(A' \mid B)$ Is this value equal to $1 - P(A \mid B)$?

  d. $P(B' \mid A)$ Is this value equal to $1 - P(B \mid A)$?

  e. $P(A \mid B')$ Is this value equal to $1 - P(A \mid B)$?

  f. $P(B \mid A')$ Is this value equal to $1 - P(B \mid A)$?

4.10 Suppose a bank examiner at another bank finds that 3% of the customers at that bank are overcharged on their loans. And suppose that of those customers who are overcharged on their loans, 40% are underpaid on their savings interest, whereas of those who are not overcharged on their loans only 1% are underpaid on their savings interest. Now suppose we arbitrarily select a customer.

  a. What is the probability that the customer is overcharged on loans and underpaid on interest?

  b. What is the probability that the customer is not overcharged on loans but is underpaid on interest?

  c. What is the probability that the customer is overcharged on loans but is not underpaid on interest?

  d. What is the probability that the customer is neither overcharged on loans nor underpaid on interest?

  e. Now suppose we are informed that the selected customer is underpaid on interest. What is the conditional probability that this customer is overcharged on loans?

  f. Suppose we are informed that the selected customer is not underpaid on interest. What is the conditional probability that this customer is overcharged on loans?

SUMMARY

When we apply probability theory in varied settings, we have to decide on the method by which probabilities will be assigned to the possible outcomes and to their related events. Because the rules of probability only restrict and do not dictate the actual values that may be assigned, an assignment method must be chosen.

    Of the three procedures available for making probability assignments, the choice rests upon (1) the nature of the events, (2) the availability of historical data, and (3) the use of the probabilities.

    In the equally likely possible outcomes approach, we must have reason or justification to assert that the possible outcomes are equally likely. If they are, the probability of the event is determined by how many possible outcomes are included in the event.

    In the relative frequency approach, the probability assignment is based on empirical evidence and may represent the historical frequency of the events.

    We make subjective probability assignments when possible outcomes cannot plausibly be treated as equally likely, and there are no (or inadequately documented) historical relative frequencies that would permit objective assignments.

KEY EQUATIONS
Probability Postulates

For any nonempty sample space S:

a. $P(S) = 1$, always.

b. For any event A in S, $0 \leq P(A) \leq 1$.

(4-1)

c. The probability of an event A is calculated by summing the probabilities associated with the possible outcomes defined in A.

d. $P(\emptyset) = 0$, always. **(4-2)**

e. If A and B are any two nonempty events in S, then $P(A \cup B) = P(A) + P(B)$ if and only if $A \cap B = \emptyset$.

Probability of the Complement of an Event

$$P(A') = 1 - P(A) \tag{4-3}$$

Partitioning the Probability of an Event

$$P(A) = P(A \cap B) + P(A \cap B') \tag{4-4a}$$

$$P(B) = P(A \cap B) + P(A' \cap B) \tag{4-4b}$$

General Addition Rule for Probabilities

If A and B are any two events in the sample space S, then

$$P(A \cup B) = P(A) + P(B) - P(A \cap B) \tag{4-5}$$

This represents the probability that either event A or event B, or both, occurs.

Conditional Probability

$$P(A \mid B) = \frac{P(A \cap B)}{P(B)} \qquad \text{where } P(B) \neq 0 \tag{4-6}$$

This represents the conditional probability that event A occurs given that event B occurs.

$$P(B \mid A) = \frac{P(A \cap B)}{P(A)} \qquad \text{where } P(A) \neq 0 \tag{4-7}$$

This represents the conditional probability that event B occurs given that event A occurs.

General Multiplication Rule

$$P(A \cap B) = P(B)P(A \mid B) = P(A)P(B \mid A) \tag{4-8}$$

This represents the probability that events A and B both occur.

Special Multiplication Rule

$$P(A \cap B) = P(A)P(B) \tag{4-9}$$

This represents the probability that events A and B both occur when, and only when, the events A and B are independent.

Bayes' Theorem

$$P(A \mid B) = \frac{P(A)P(B \mid A)}{P(A)P(B \mid A) + P(A')P(B \mid A')} \tag{4-10}$$

This represents a relationship between the conditional probability that event A occurs given that event B occurs and the inverse conditional probabilities that event B occurs given that event A occurs and that event B occurs given that event A' occurs.

PRACTICE EXERCISE ANSWERS

4.1 a. {1, 3, 7, 11, 15}   b. {1, 9, 11, 13}

c. {5, 9, 11, 13, 15, 17}   d. {3, 5, 7, 9, 13, 15, 17}

e. {1, 3, 5, 7, 9, 13, 17}   f. {1, 3, 5, 7, 15, 17}

g. {1, 3, 5, 7, 9, 13, 15, 17}   h. {5, 17}

i. ∅

j. {3, 7}

k. ∅

l. {1, 5, 9, 11, 13, 17}

m. {1, 3, 5, 7, 11, 15, 17}

n. {1, 3, 7, 9, 11, 13, 15}

o. {9, 13}

p. {3, 7, 15}

q. {1, 11}

r. {1, 11}   Note that $(A \cup B)' = A' \cap B'$.

s. {1, 3, 7, 9, 11, 13, 15}   Note that $(A \cap B)' = A' \cup B'$.

4.2 a. $\frac{4}{9}$ b. $\frac{5}{9}$ c. $\frac{3}{9}$ d. $\frac{5}{9}$ e. $\frac{4}{9}$

f. $\frac{6}{9}$ g. $\frac{7}{9}$ h. $\frac{7}{9}$ i. $\frac{6}{9}$ j. $\frac{8}{9}$

k. $\frac{2}{9}$ l. 0   m. $\frac{2}{9}$ n. 0   o. $\frac{6}{9}$

p. $\frac{7}{9}$ q. $\frac{7}{9}$ r. $\frac{2}{9}$ s. $\frac{3}{9}$ t. $\frac{2}{9}$

u. $\frac{2}{9}$ Note that $P(A \cup B)' = P(A' \cap B') = 1 - P(A \cup B)$.

v. $\frac{7}{9}$ Note that $P(A \cap B)' = P(A' \cup B') = 1 - P(A \cap B)$.

4.3 a. In Practice Exercise 4.2 we found $P(A \cap B) = \frac{2}{9}$ and $P(B) = \frac{5}{9}$. To find

$$P(A \mid B) = \frac{P(A \cap B)}{P(B)}$$

substitute the appropriate values. The final answer is $\frac{2}{5}$.

b. $\frac{2}{4}$

c. In Practice Exercise 4.2 we found $P(A \cap C) = 0$ and $P(C) = \frac{3}{9}$. To find

$$P(A \mid C) = \frac{P(A \cap C)}{P(C)}$$

substitute the appropriate values. The answer is 0.

d. 0   e. $\frac{2}{4}$ f. $\frac{3}{5}$ g. $\frac{2}{4}$

h. $\frac{3}{5}$ i. $\frac{2}{4}$ j. $\frac{2}{5}$ k. $\frac{4}{6}$

l. First we note that $A' \cap C = \{1, 3, 7\}$, so $P(A' \cap C) = \frac{3}{9}$. In Practice Exercise 4.2 we found $P(C) = \frac{3}{9}$. To find

$$P(A' \mid C) = \frac{P(A' \cap C)}{P(C)}$$

substitute the appropriate values. The answer is 1. Note that $P(A' \mid C) = 1 - P(A \mid C)$.

m. $\frac{2}{6}$ n. $\frac{3}{5}$ o. 1   p. $\frac{2}{5}$

Events A and B are not independent. Events A and C are not independent.

4.4 a. We first find $A \cap B' = \{a, d\}$, so $P(A \cap B') = \frac{2}{8}$. And we find $P(B') = 1 - P(B) = 1 - \frac{4}{8} = \frac{4}{8}$. To find

$$P(A \mid B') = \frac{P(A \cap B')}{P(B')}$$

substitute the appropriate values:

$$P(A \mid B') = \frac{\frac{1}{4}}{\frac{1}{2}} = \frac{1}{2} = P(A)$$

b. To find $P(A' \mid B)$ find $A' \cap B$ and $P(A' \cap B)$. Then

$$P(A' \mid B) = \frac{P(A' \cap B)}{P(B)}$$

and substitute the appropriate values:

$$P(A' \mid B) = \frac{\frac{1}{4}}{\frac{1}{2}} = \frac{1}{2} = P(A') = 1 - P(A)$$

c. To find $P(A' \mid B')$ find $A' \cap B'$ and $P(A' \cap B')$. Then

$$P(A' \mid B') = \frac{P(A' \cap B')}{P(B')}$$

and substitute the appropriate values:

$$P(A' \mid B') = \frac{\frac{1}{4}}{\frac{1}{2}} = \frac{1}{2} = P(A')$$

d. $P(B \mid A) = \frac{\frac{1}{4}}{\frac{1}{2}} = \frac{1}{2} = P(B)$

e. $P(B \mid A') = \frac{\frac{1}{4}}{\frac{1}{2}} = \frac{1}{2} = P(B)$

f. $P(B' \mid A) = \frac{\frac{1}{4}}{\frac{1}{2}} = \frac{1}{2} = P(B') = 1 - P(B)$

g. $P(B' \mid A') = \frac{\frac{1}{4}}{\frac{1}{2}} = \frac{1}{2} = P(B')$

h. $P(A \cap B) = \frac{1}{4} = \left(\frac{1}{2}\right)\left(\frac{1}{2}\right) = P(A)P(B)$

4.5 a. $P(A \mid B) = \dfrac{P(A \cap B)}{P(B)} = \dfrac{P(A)P(B \mid A)}{P(A)P(B \mid A) + P(A')P(B \mid A')}$

$= \dfrac{(.9)(.7)}{(.9)(.7) + (.1)(.2)} = .969$

b. $P(A \mid B') = \dfrac{P(A \cap B')}{P(B')} = \dfrac{P(A)P(B' \mid A)}{P(A)P(B' \mid A) + P(A')P(B' \mid A')}$

$= \dfrac{(.9)(.3)}{(.9)(.3) + (.1)(.8)} = .771$

CHAPTER REVIEW EXERCISES

4.11 Give an event description that lists the coins used as money by the United States.

4.12 Give an event description that lists the major brands of gasoline in your area.

▶ **4.13** Give an event description that lists all the integers with a value greater than 11.

4.14 Give an event description that lists all the real numbers with a value greater than 11.

4.15 Give an event description listing all the possible outcomes of the experiment of tossing two coins.

4.16 Four persons are eligible for promotion: Tom, Jane, Mary, and Hal. Of these, only 2 can be promoted at this time. What do the following events represent?
a. $A = \{\{\text{Tom, Jane}\}\}$
b. $C = \{\{\text{Jane, Mary}\}, \{\text{Jane, Hal}\}, \{\text{Mary, Hal}\}\}$

▶ **4.17** In Exercise 4.16, if:
a. Tom and Jane get promoted, which events occur?
b. Jane and Hal get promoted, which events occur?
c. Tom and Jane, or Jane and Hal, get promoted, which events occur?
d. Tom and Hal get promoted, which events occur?
e. Tom and Jane or Tom and Hal get promoted, which events occur?

4.18 Suppose we have a sample space $S = \{a, b, c, d, e, f, g, h, i\}$ and events
$A = \{b, d, f, h, i\}$, $B = \{a, c, f, g, h\}$, and $C = \{a, b, c, d, e\}$.
  a. Depict S, A, B, and C in terms of a Venn diagram.
  Give an event description listing the possible outcomes in each of the following:

b. A'	c. C'	d. $A \cap B$	e. $A \cup B$
f. $B \cap C$	g. $B \cup C$	h. $A \cap B \cap C$	i. $A \cup B \cup C$
j. $A \cap C'$	k. $A \cup C'$	l. $B \cap C'$	m. $B \cup C'$
n. $A' \cap B$	o. $A' \cup B$	p. $A' \cap C$	q. $A' \cup C$
r. $A' \cap C'$	s. $A' \cup C'$		

  t. Does $(A \cup C)' = A' \cap C'$?
  u. Does $(A \cap C)' = A' \cup C'$?
  v. Does $(A \cup B \cup C)' = A' \cap B' \cap C'$?
  w. Does $(A \cap C) \cup (A \cap C') = A$?
  x. Does $(A' \cap C) \cup (A' \cap C') = A'$?
  y. Does $(B \cap C) \cup (B \cap C') = B$?
  z. Does $(B' \cap C) \cup (B' \cap C') = B'$?

4.19 Suppose $S = \{-4, -3, -2, -1, 0, 1, 2, 3, 4, 5, 6, 7, 8\}$ is the sample space and
the events are $A = \{-4, -3, 3, 4\}$, $B = \{-1, 1, 3, 4, 5\}$, and $C = \{-2, 0, 3, 4, 8\}$.
  a. Depict S, A, B, and C in terms of a Venn diagram. Give an event description
  listing the possible outcomes in each of the following:

b. A'	c. B'	d. $A \cap C$	e. $A \cup C$
f. $B \cap C$	g. $B \cup C$	h. $A \cap B \cap C$	i. $A \cup B \cup C$
j. $A \cap B'$	k. $A \cup B'$	l. $A' \cap B$	m. $A' \cup B$
n. $B' \cap C$	o. $B' \cup C$	p. $A' \cap C$	q. $A' \cup C$
r. $A' \cap B'$	s. $A' \cup B'$		

  t. Does $(A \cup B)' = A' \cap B'$?
  u. Does $(A \cap B)' = A' \cup B'$?
  v. Does $(A \cap B \cap C)' = A' \cup B' \cup C'$?
  w. Does $(A \cap B) \cup (A \cap B') = A$?
  x. Does $(A' \cap B) \cup (A' \cap B') = A'$?
  y. Does $(A \cap B) \cap (A \cap B') = \varnothing$?
  z. Does $(A \cap B) \cap (A' \cap B) = \varnothing$?

4.20 Use general Venn diagrams to show:
  a. The region for $A' \cap B$ b. The region for $A \cap B'$
  c. That $(A \cap B) \cup (A \cap B') = A$ d. That $(A \cap B) \cap (A \cap B') = \varnothing$
  e. That $(A \cap B) \cup (A' \cap B) = B$ f. That $(A \cap B) \cap (A' \cap B) = \varnothing$
  g. The region for $A' \cap B'$ h. That $(A \cup B)' = A' \cap B'$
  i. The region for $A' \cup B'$ j. That $(A \cap B)' = A' \cup B'$

4.21 An experiment consists of randomly selecting 2 adults from San Diego County
and recording whether each is Republican, Democrat, Independent, or none of
these. List the possible outcomes in the:
  a. Sample space
  b. Event where neither person is a Republican
  c. Event where neither person is a Democrat
  d. Event where neither person is a Democrat nor a Republican

▶ **4.22** Refer to Example 4.5 (page 124) in the text, and find:

a. $B \cap C$	b. $P(B \cap C)$	c. $P(B \cap C)'$
d. $B \cup C$	e. $P(B \cup C)$	f. $P(B \cup C)'$
g. $B \cap C'$	h. $(B \cap C) \cup (B \cap C')$	i. $P(B \cap C')$
j. $P[(B \cap C) \cup (B \cap C')]$	k. $B' \cap C$	l. $P(B' \cap C)$
m. $(B \cap C) \cup (B' \cap C)$	n. $P[(B \cap C) \cup (B' \cap C)]$	o. $B' \cup C'$
p. $P(B' \cup C')$	q. $B' \cap C'$	r. $P(B' \cap C')$

s. Are events B and C mutually exclusive?

t. Are events B and C' mutually exclusive?

u. Are events B' and C mutually exclusive?

v. Are events B' and C' mutually exclusive?

4.23 Let $P(A) = .5$, $P(B) = .7$, and $P(A \cup B) = .9$. Find the value of:

a. $P(A \cap B)$ b. $P(A \cap B')$ c. $P(A' \cap B)$ d. $P(A' \cap B')$

e. $P(A' \cup B')$ f. $P(A \cup B')$ g. $P(A' \cup B)$

4.24 Let S be a sample space with 11 equally likely possible outcomes. That is, let $S = \{a, b, c, d, e, f, g, h, i, j, k\}$, where $P[\{a\}] = P[\{b\}] = \cdots = P[\{k\}] = \frac{1}{11}$. Let $A = \{g, k\}$, $B = \{b, c, k\}$, and $C = \{b, d, f, h, j, k\}$. Find the value of:

a. $P(A \cup B)$ b. $P(A \cup B)'$ c. $P(A \cap B)$

d. $P(A \cap B)'$ e. $P(A' \cup B')$ f. $P(A' \cap B')$

g. $P(A \cup C)'$ h. $P(A \cap C)'$ i. $P(A' \cap C')$

j. $P(A' \cup C')$ k. $P(A \cup B \cup C)$ l. $P(A \cap B \cap C)$

m. $P(A' \cap B' \cap C')$ n. $P(A' \cup B' \cup C')$

4.25 Let $S = \{a, b, c, d, e, f, g, h, i, j, k, l, m, n, o, p, q, r, s, t\}$, where we associate the possible outcomes $a, b, c, d, e, f, g, h, i, j$ each with probability .04, the possible outcome k with probability .40, the possible outcome l with probability .12, and the rest each with probability .01. Let $A = \{a, b, c, m, s, t\}$, $B = \{c, q, r, t\}$, and $C = \{b, m, o, t\}$. Find the value of:

a. $P(A)$ b. $P(B)$ c. $P(C)$

d. $P(A \cap B)$ e. $P(A \cap C)$ f. $P(B \cap C)$

g. $P(A \cap B \cap C)$ h. $P(A \cup B)$ i. $P(A \cup C)$

j. $P(B \cup C)$ k. $P(A \cup B \cup C)$ l. $P(A' \cap B')$

m. $P(A' \cup B')$ n. $P(A' \cap C')$ o. $P(A' \cup C')$

p. $P(B' \cap C')$ q. $P(B' \cup C')$ r. $P(A' \cap B' \cap C')$

s. $P(A' \cup B' \cup C')$

4.26 If $P(A) = .3$, $P(B) = .5$, and $P(A \cup B) = .8$, are the events A and B mutually exclusive?

▶ **4.27** Let $P(A) = .6$, $P(A \cap B') = .2$, and $P(A' \cap B) = .3$. Find the value of:

a. $P(A \cap B)$ b. $P(B)$ c. $P(A \cup B)$ d. $P(A' \cap B')$

e. $P(A' \cup B')$ f. $P(A \cup B')$ g. $P(A' \cup B)$

4.28 If $P(A) = .5$, $P(B) = .7$, and $P(A \cup B) = .6$, would these values lead to an inconsistency with the properties and postulates of probability?

4.29 If $P(A) = .36$, $P(B) = .47$, and $P(A \cup B) = .83$, would these values lead to an inconsistency with the properties and postulates of probability?

4.30 Refer to Exercise 4.18, where $S = \{a, b, c, d, e, f, g, h, i\}$, $A = \{b, d, f, h, i\}$, $B = \{a, c, f, g, h\}$, and $C = \{a, b, c, d, e\}$. Suppose the possible outcomes in S are equally likely; that is, each possible outcome is associated with a probability of $\frac{1}{9}$. Find the value of:

a. $P(A)$ b. $P(B)$ c. $P(C)$ d. $P(A \cap B)$

e. $P(A \cap C)$ f. $P(B \cap C)$ g. $P(A \cup B)$ h. $P(A \cup C)$

i. $P(B \cup C)$ j. $P(A \mid B)$ k. $P(A \mid C)$ l. $P(B \mid C)$

m. $P(B \mid A)$ n. $P(C \mid A)$ o. $P(C \mid B)$

p. Are events A and B independent?

q. Are events A and C independent?

r. Are events B and C independent?

4.31 Consider the same sample space and events as in Exercise 4.30, but suppose the possible outcomes are associated with the following respective probabilities: $\frac{1}{18}$, $\frac{1}{18}$, $\frac{1}{18}$, $\frac{1}{18}$, $\frac{4}{9}$, $\frac{1}{18}$, $\frac{1}{9}$, $\frac{1}{18}$, $\frac{1}{9}$. Find the value of:

a. $P(A)$ b. $P(B)$ c. $P(C)$ d. $P(A \cap B)$

e. $P(A \cap C)$ f. $P(B \cap C)$ g. $P(A \cup B)$ h. $P(A \cup C)$
i. $P(B \cup C)$ j. $P(A \mid B)$ k. $P(A \mid C)$ l. $P(B \mid C)$
m. $P(B \mid A)$ n. $P(C \mid A)$ o. $P(C \mid B)$
p. Are events A and B independent?
q. Are events A and C independent?
r. Are events B and C independent?

4.32 Suppose A and B are nonempty independent events with $P(A) = .2$ and $P(B) = .3$. Find the value of:

a. $P(A \cap B)$ b. $P(A \mid B)$ c. $P(B \mid A)$ d. $P(A \cup B)$
e. $P(A')$ f. $P(A' \cap B)$ g. $P(A' \mid B)$ h. $P(B \mid A')$
i. $P(B')$ j. $P(A \cap B')$ k. $P(A \mid B')$ l. $P(B' \mid A)$
m. $P(A' \mid B')$ n. $P(B' \mid A')$ o. $P(A' \cup B)$ p. $P(A \cup B')$
q. $P(A' \cap B')$ r. $P(A' \cup B')$

▶ **4.33** If $P(A) = .3$, $P(B) = .5$, and $P(A \cup B) = .8$, are the events A and B independent?

▶ **4.34** The following table lists 400 students according to whether they showed interest in a subject and whether they received a grade of C or better in that subject:

	INTERESTED	NOT INTERESTED
C OR BETTER	83	105
LESS THAN C	41	171

If the name of one of the 400 students is picked at random, find the probability that:

a. The student had been interested and received a grade of C or better.
b. The student had not been interested and received a grade of C or better.
c. The student received a grade of C or better, given the student had been interested.
d. The student had been interested, given the student received a grade of C or better.
e. The student received a grade less than C, given the student had been interested.
f. The student received a grade less than C, given the student had not been interested.
g. The student received a grade of C or better, given the student had not been interested.

4.35 A sample space has 5 points a, b, c, d, e with associated probabilities of .20, .15, .25, .25, .20, respectively. Is this possible? Why?

▶ **4.36** Suppose A and B are nonempty independent events with $P(A) = .31$, $P(B) = .62$, $P(A \cap B) = .1922$, $P(A \cup B) = .7378$, $P(A' \mid B') = .69$, $P(B \mid A') = .62$, $P(A \mid B') = .1178$, and $P(A \mid B) = .31$. Would these values lead to an inconsistency with the properties and postulates of probability?

4.37 Suppose 70% of all food handlers in supermarkets have been properly trained to understand the danger in refreezing thawed frozen meat products. Suppose also that 90% of all food handlers in supermarkets are knowledgeable about sanitary procedures in the handling of packaged, as well as unpackaged, foods. And suppose that 68% of the food handlers are both trained to understand the handling of frozen meat products and are knowledgeable about sanitary procedures in the handling of foods. If a food handler is randomly selected, what is the probability that she:

a. Has been trained in the handling of frozen meat products or is knowledgeable about sanitary procedures in the handling of foods?
b. Has been trained in the handling of frozen meat products or is not knowledgeable about sanitary procedures in the handling of foods?

c. Has not been trained in the handling of frozen meat products or is knowledgeable about sanitary procedures in the handling of foods?

d. Has not been trained in the handling of frozen meat products or is not knowledgeable about sanitary procedures in the handling of foods?

e. Has been trained in the handling of frozen meat products, given that she is knowledgeable about sanitary procedures in the handling of foods?

f. Is knowledgeable about sanitary procedures in the handling of foods, given that she has been trained in the handling of frozen meat products?

g. Has not been trained in the handling of frozen meat products, given that she is knowledgeable about sanitary procedures in the handling of foods?

h. Has been trained in the handling of frozen meat products, given that she is not knowledgeable about sanitary procedures in the handling of foods?

i. Has not been trained in the handling of frozen meat products, given that she is not knowledgeable about sanitary procedures in the handling of foods?

4.38 The probability is .11 that an automobile insurance policyholder will be involved in an accident leading to a liability claim; the probability is .23 that the accident leads to a collision damage claim; the probability is .04 that the accident leads to both a liability and collision damage claim. What is the probability of an accident leading to:

a. Either a liability or a collision damage claim?

b. Neither a liability nor a collision damage claim?

c. A liability claim given that a collision damage claim is made?

d. A collision damage claim given that a liability claim is made?

4.39 Verify that:

a. $P(B \mid A) = 1 - P(B' \mid A)$ b. $P(B \mid A') = 1 - P(B' \mid A')$

▶ **4.40** Show that if A and B are nonempty events with $P(A \mid B) = P(A) \neq 0$ and $P(B) \neq 0$, then:

a. $P(A \cap B) = P(A)P(B)$ b. $P(A \mid B') = P(A)$

c. $P(A' \mid B) = P(A')$ d. $P(A \cap B') = P(A)P(B')$

e. $P(A' \cap B) = P(A')P(B)$ f. $P(A' \cap B') = P(A')P(B')$

g. $P(A' \mid B') = P(A')$ h. $P(B \mid A) = P(B)$

i. $P(B \mid A') = P(B)$ j. $P(B' \mid A) = P(B')$

k. $P(B' \mid A') = P(B')$

4.41 Refer to Example 4.10 (page 133). Use a tree diagram to find $P(A \mid B')$, the probability that the person has cancer given that the test is negative.

4.42 Forty percent of all students in a certain course are procrastinators. If the probability is .8 that a procrastinator will fail the course, whereas the probability is .95 that a nonprocrastinator will fail the course, what is the probability that if a student fails the course he or she is a procrastinator?

4.43 Assume that 1% of the inhabitants of a country suffer from a certain disease. A new diagnostic test is developed that gives a positive indication 98% of the time when an individual has this disease and a negative indication 90% of the time when the disease is absent. An individual is randomly selected, given the test, and reacts positively. What is the probability that he or she has the disease?

4.44 A corporation uses a selling aptitude test to aid it in the selection of its sales force. Past experience has shown that only 60% of all persons applying for a sales position achieved a classification of satisfactory in actual selling, whereas the remainder were classified as unsatisfactory. Of those classified as satisfactory, 90% had scored a passing grade on the aptitude test. Only 30% of those classified as unsatisfactory had passed the test. On the basis of this information, what is the probability that a candidate would be a satisfactory salesperson, given a passing grade on the aptitude test?

▶ **4.45** Suppose there is a very small one-industry (i.e., one-factory) town with a total population of 1300 people. Suppose that 800 of these people work in the factory, 350 of whom are female, and suppose the town has a total female population of 550. If the name of one of the male townspeople is randomly selected as a grand prize winner in a national contest, what is the probability that he does not work in the factory?

4.46 An auto parts dealer receives a shipment of 2 rebuilt carburetors and 3 new carburetors. He also has in stock 2 rebuilt carburetors and 2 new carburetors. A clerk, unfamiliar with new and rebuilt carburetors, randomly selects one carburetor from the shipment and puts it with the stock carburetors. A customer comes in to purchase a carburetor, and the clerk randomly selects one from the stock. Given that the carburetor selected from the stock is a rebuilt carburetor, what is the conditional probability that the carburetor transferred from the shipment to the stock was rebuilt?

▶ **4.47** a. A box contains 7 coins, 3 of which are fair (or honest) coins, but the others have heads on both sides. If a coin is randomly selected from the box and then tossed twice, what is the probability that 2 heads will be obtained?
  b. Given that 2 heads are obtained in the experiment in part a, what is the probability that the coin selected is a fair coin?
  c. Given that 2 heads are not obtained in the experiment in part a, what is the probability that the coin selected is a fair coin?
  d. Suppose the coin is tossed 10 times and the result is 9 heads and 1 tail. What is the probability that the coin is fair?

4.48 Proponents and opponents of the Equal Rights Amendment argue about the popularity of the amendment. The two sides provide numbers to "prove" the popularity or unpopularity of the issue. If the numbers presented are proportions (probabilities) in favor of or against the amendment, describe a situation where the proportions (probabilities) would be based on:
  a. An assumption of equally likely possible outcomes
  b. Relative frequencies of possible outcomes or events
  c. A subjective judgment

4.49 A prospective investor is presented with a scheme that will give her a 20% return on her investment within 1 year. The investor wishes to determine the probability that the investment will succeed in its objective. Describe a situation where a statement for the probability of success would be based on:
  a. An assumption of equally likely possible outcomes
  b. Relative frequencies of possible outcomes or events
  c. A subjective judgment

▶ **4.50** An employer interviews 6 candidates for a single position. After reading their resumes and letters of recommendation, the employer estimates each candidate's success potential and rolls a fair die to decide on which candidate to hire. What does this action suggest about the probabilities assigned by the employer toward the success potential of these candidates?

4.51 In Exercise 4.50, if the employer decides to personally interview only 2 of the 6 candidates (and disqualifies the other 4), what would this suggest about the probability assignment procedure used by the employer?

4.52 In Exercise 4.50, if the employer requests that the 6 candidates take an in-plant aptitude test and then uses the results to compare with success frequencies of past and present employees with similar scores, what would this suggest about the probability assignment procedure used by the employer?

SOLVING APPLIED CASES
Scheduling at Beth Israel Hospital: Probability Assessment for Maternity Bed Demand

Boston's Beth Israel Hospital administration faces a scheduling situation familiar to hospitals everywhere. One of the hospital administrator's chief responsibilities is to schedule staff, bed space, and other facilities to accommodate the day-to-day flow of patients. The task would be simple if all daily patient admissions were controllable, thus permitting schedule coordination between the surgeon/physician and the hospital administrator. But patient admissions come from uncontrollable as well as controllable sources. Controllable sources are elective admissions, such as planned surgery, or other medical procedures for which the time and date of a patient's entrance to the hospital is scheduled by the surgeon/physician in consultation with the hospital administrator. The uncontrollable source comes from nonelective admissions, such as maternity ward admissions, since they cannot be preset for any given day nor postponed. This type of admission would not create a scheduling problem for the hospital administrator if the number of such admissions varied only slightly from day to day or if the variations follow a predictable pattern. Under the latter circumstances, scheduling problems would be minimal. But scheduling frequently is perplexing because maternity ward admissions fluctuate over a wide range from day to day, and the sequence and timing of births is unpredictable. Admissions to the ward follow no predictable day-to-day pattern.

In addition to the unpredictability of maternity ward admissions, there exists another planning and scheduling complication. An ideal situation would be that when maternity ward admissions slacked, the beds and staff on hand to meet peak maternity ward admissions would be used to alleviate the unmet beds and staffing needs elsewhere in the hospital. This "lending" of excess maternity ward beds and staff would permit full utilization of personnel and facilities, if it could be done. However, obstetrical beds are by law restricted to obstetrical patients. Likewise, maternity ward nurses specially trained in obstetrics cannot routinely be interchanged with medical/surgical nurses because of training and health-related issues.

Consequently, in order to make plans for the overall usage of facilities and staff, the hospital administrator must find a way to deal effectively with the uncontrollable demand coming from the maternity ward. A practical solution is to recognize the unpredictable variations by using a probability distribution. The administrator can obtain an estimate of the probability distribution of demand for maternity beds working with the records of maternity ward occupancy over a 6 month period. And the administrator can use the estimated probability distribution to answer such questions as:

a. What is the probability of running into particular levels of high demand?

b. What is the chance of experiencing a dramatic slump in demand?

c. What is the bed occupancy rate most likely to occur?

From the records given in Table 4.2 we can see that 17 patients were admitted on 5 (2.7%) of the days, 18 patients on 3 (1.6%) of the days, and 19 patients on 1 (0.5%) of the days. A staircase, or step, ogive based on the cumulative "less than" frequencies and percentages given in Table 4.3 is shown in Figure 4.6.

The vertical scale in Figure 4.6 shows the cumulative percentage of days as well as the corresponding cumulative frequencies. For example, the dot at the top of the staircase at 28 patients aligns with a cumulative frequency of 91 days, and a cumulative percentage of 50%. This means that on 50% of the days there were 28 or fewer patients in the ward.

Now let's smooth the staircase ogive by fitting a smooth curve through the steps, as shown in Figure 4.7. The smoothing procedure produces an S-shaped curve (smooth ogive) super-imposed on the steps, and we use the smooth ogive to make probability assessments.

TABLE 4.2 Daily Number of Patients in the Obstetrics Ward: Frequency Distribution, During 6-Month Period		
NUMBER OF PATIENTS	**FREQUENCY**	**PERCENT OF DAYS**
	Days	
13	2	1.1
14	2	1.1
17	5	2.7
18	3	1.6
19	1	0.5
20	5	2.7
21	7	3.8
22	6	3.3
23	8	4.4
24	4	2.2
25	9	4.9
26	12	6.6
27	12	6.6
28	15	8.2
29	10	5.5
30	11	6.0
31	7	3.8
32	10	5.5
33	11	6.0
34	9	4.9
35	5	2.7
36	5	2.7
37	1	0.5
38	6	3.3
39	5	2.7
40	3	1.6
41	2	1.1
42	3	1.6
43	2	1.1
45	1	0.5

Source: Beth Israel Hospital Daily Census, published in the Harvard Business School Case, "Beth Israel Hospital, Boston."

TABLE 4.3 Cumulative Figures on the Daily Number of Patients in the Obstetrics Ward: Cumulative Frequency Distribution, During 6-Month Period		
NUMBER OF PATIENTS	**CUMULATIVE "LESS THAN" FREQUENCY**	**CUMULATIVE "LESS THAN" PERCENTAGE**
	Days	
12 or less	0	0.0
13 or less	2	1.1
14 or less	4	2.2
17 or less	9	4.9
18 or less	12	6.5
19 or less	13	7.1
20 or less	18	9.9
21 or less	25	13.7
22 or less	31	17.0
23 or less	39	21.4
24 or less	43	23.6
25 or less	52	28.5
26 or less	64	35.2
27 or less	76	41.8
28 or less	91	50.0
29 or less	101	55.4
30 or less	112	61.5
31 or less	119	65.4
32 or less	129	70.9
33 or less	140	76.9
34 or less	149	81.9
35 or less	154	84.6
36 or less	159	87.4
37 or less	160	87.9
38 or less	166	91.2
39 or less	171	93.9
40 or less	174	95.5
41 or less	176	96.7
42 or less	179	98.4
43 or less	181	99.5
45 or less	182	100.0

To convert the smooth ogive so that it reads as a probability curve, we divide the cumulative percentages on the vertical scale by 100, as shown in Figure 4.8. The vertical scale in the figure now shows values that may be used as probabilities. The small squares on the ogive in Figure 4.8 indicate the height of the ogive for various integer values on the horizontal axis.

Let's make a probability assessment, calculating the probability, say, of demand not exceeding 40 patients in a day nor falling as low as 19 patients in a day. We first draw a vertical line from 19 on the horizontal axis upward to the small square at point A on the curve; then from point A we extend a horizontal line to the left intersecting the vertical axis at .066. The value .066 is the estimated probability of 19 patients or less. A second vertical line is drawn from 40 on the horizontal axis upward to the small square at point B on the curve. Extending a horizontal line from point B to the vertical axis gives the intersection at .945. This means that the value .945 is the estimated probability of 40 or fewer patients, which is another way of saying that demand

Figure 4.6
Step function ogive for Beth
Israel Hospital data

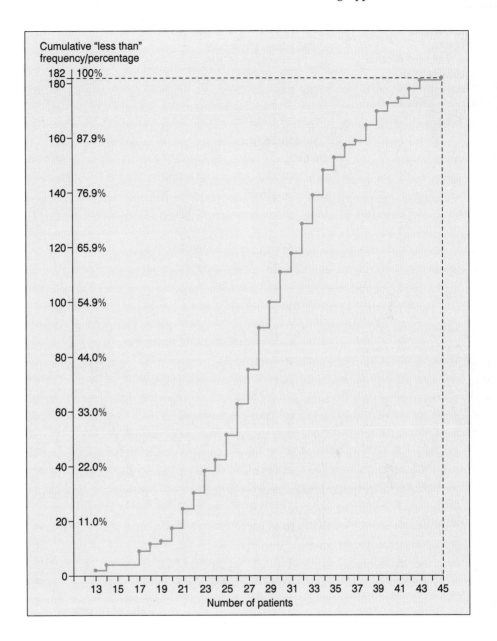

does not exceed 40. We find the difference .945 − .066 = .879, or approximately .88. Therefore, the estimated probability is .88 that demand will not exceed 40 patients nor be as low as 19 patients on a given day.

Checkpoint Exercises

1. Estimate the probability that Beth Israel Hospital will handle more than 38 obstetrics patients.
2. If the hospital administration needs an estimate of the range of patients that encompass 50% of daily demand, we need to consider the middlemost 50% of the probability. What range of numbers of patients would you suggest?

Figure 4.7
Smoothed ogive to obtain
probability values

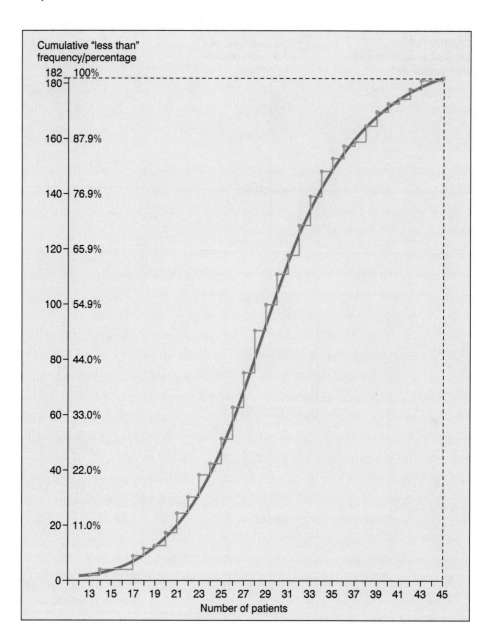

Figure 4.8
Cumulative probabilities

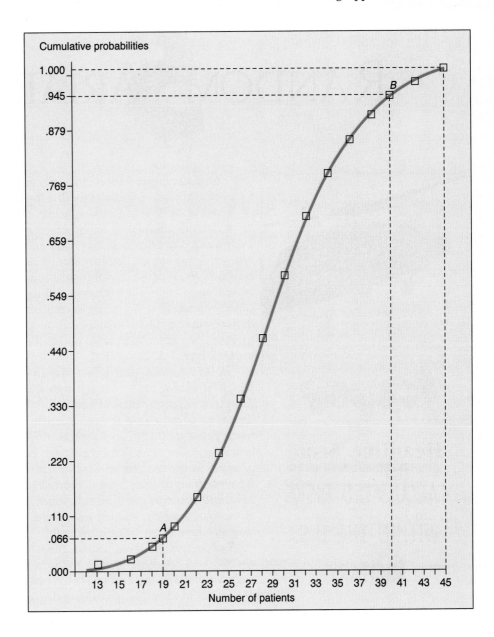

RANDOM 5 VARIABLES

merican military leaders can hardly avoid decisions that involve "calculated risks." Sometimes the decision is to act and take the calculated risk in the hope of achieving an important military objective. At other times the decision is to not act, so as to deliberately avoid the calculated risk of a military disaster. Little attention is paid to this calculated risk activity of our U.S. military leaders until the decision (to act or not act) backfires, as decisions will eventually do. When that happens, decision makers come under close scrutiny, and their judgment and expertise are called into question. There are several instances in which U.S. military decision makers have been subjected to public and congressional interrogation. One instance occurred during the era of the late Ayatollah Khomeini in Iran.

In 1979, Iranians seized the American embassy in Tehran and held its personnel hostage. In an attempt to rescue the hostages, a difficult and dangerous helicopter mission was set up. The plan called for eight helicopters to fly more than 800 miles at low altitude during the night over sandy desert to a designated rendezvous point. When three of the eight helicopters failed to reach the rendezvous point in workable condition, the mission was aborted. The mission commander required six helicopters at the rendezvous point in order to proceed with the mission. A debate soon developed over whether more helicopters should have been sent, in view of the known mechanical and navigational hazards that accompany such long nighttime desert flying missions.

Headline Issue

CALCULATED RISKS WITHIN THE U.S. MILITARY

Let's pursue this issue, assuming that the military planners had accumulated evidence from practice missions about low-altitude flying over sand at night. This information should have allowed the military planners to be quite aware of the probability that an individual helicopter would not be successful in reaching the rendezvous point. Knowing the number sent (eight) and the number required (six), let's further assume that each helicopter has a .75 probability of getting to the rendezvous point in satisfactory condition. What would be the probability that a sufficient number of helicopters (at least six) make the trip successfully? According to the appropriate (binomial) probability model presented in this chapter, the probability of six or more helicopters reaching the rendezvous point is a modest .6786. This means there was nearly 1 chance in 3 that the mission would be aborted because of too few helicopters reaching the rendezvous point. How much risk reduction would be gained by sending a few extra helicopters? With just three additional helicopters, the calculations indicate that the risk of failure is reduced by a factor of 10, that is, cut from .3214 to .0343 (less than 1 chance in 29).

Should we have used a much higher probability of success for an individual helicopter than the .75 we assumed, say .95? A high probability of .95 would certainly make it more reasonable to send only eight helicopters for the mission. But such a high probability of success is not consistent with the statements issued by the military at the time. In the statements released, the military planners stressed the fact that the mission was *highly risky*.

Hindsight tells us that more helicopters should have been sent. But the point of this discussion is that appropriate statistical thinking and calculation should have aided this decision, given the time and information at hand. Had the formulation of military strategy by military planners taken into account the appropriate probabilities, the quality of the military decisions would have been enhanced, possibly avoiding the needless loss of men and material that occurred and averting the disastrous national and international repercussions that followed.

Overview

In Chapters 2 and 3 we examined procedures and devices that showed us how to deal with past data, that is, recordings on events that have already happened. Frequency distributions gave shape to the data, and summary measures described the central location of the data and the spread and concentration of the data. We now want to examine the procedures and devices that can describe future events, that is, what *may* happen, rather than what has already happened. The rules for dealing with what may happen are the probability rules, and the direct counterpart of the frequency distribution is the *probability distribution*. The probability distribution has shape and can be broadly described by its summary measures, its mean and its variance. Probability distributions now become our model representations of the range of possible values that may occur along with a measure of the chances that their values will occur. Like cars, probability distributions come in various models, but a few models are the most popular and useful. We will begin our investigation of probability distributions by describing a generalized model. Then we will turn to specialized probability models that are particularly useful in business situations.

All probability distributions are distinguished by a variable, called a *random variable*, a range of possible values for the random variable, and the respective probabilities associated with those values. The probability distribution in this way identifies the existence of different degrees of uncertainty with different values of the random variable. We will also see early in the chapter that random variables translate descriptive events to numerical values.

In summary, this chapter introduces the concept of a random variable and several probability distributions that serve as models for the behavior of certain common types of data. When we introduce the various probability distributions, we'll show the kinds of data for which they work as models and we'll state the conditions that make them work. The purpose of this chapter is twofold: (1) to connect a probability distribution with data behavior and (2) to evaluate probabilities from probability distributions.

5.1
RANDOM VARIABLES AND THEIR DISTRIBUTIONS

The discussion of probability in Chapter 4 was based on sample spaces comprised of descriptive elements. In this section, we introduce the concept of a *random variable* to *summarize numerically* the descriptive elements of a sample space, and then go on to describe the probability distribution of the random variable and the summary measures of the probability distribution.

RANDOM VARIABLES

Consider a fair coin experiment in which we intend to toss the coin three times. The collection of all the possible outcomes, or elements, can be described by the eight ordered triples (H, H, H), (H, H, T), (H, T, H), (T, H, H), (H, T, T), (T, H, T), (T, T, H), and (T, T, T), where H means a head turns up and T means a tail turns up. The sample space may then be represented by

$$S = \{(H, H, H), (H, H, T), (H, T, H), (T, H, H),$$
$$(H, T, T), (T, H, T), (T, T, H), (T, T, T)\}$$

If we have properly defined the sample space, one of these eight possible outcomes must occur. Since the coin is a fair coin, each of the eight possible outcomes is considered equally likely and has a corresponding probability of $\frac{1}{8}$. Let's define the events A, B, C, D as follows: $A = \{(H, H, H)\}$, $B = \{(H, H, T), (H, T, H), (T, H, H)\}$, $C = \{(H, T, T), (T, H, T), (T, T, H)\}$, and $D = \{(T, T, T)\}$. Notice that A and D each contain one possible outcome, whereas B and C each contain three possible outcomes. Since each possible outcome has a probability of $\frac{1}{8}$, then $P(A) = \frac{1}{8}$, $P(B) = \frac{3}{8}$, $P(C) = \frac{3}{8}$, and $P(D) = \frac{1}{8}$. The expression $P(A) = \frac{1}{8}$ means the probability that event A occurs (i.e., the coin showing heads in all three tosses) is equal to 1 chance in 8.

Now let's redefine the possible outcomes stated descriptively above in terms of a number, say, the number of heads. This means that the descriptive element (H, H, H) is replaced by the numerical value 3, the descriptive element (H, H, T) by the numerical value 2, the descriptive element (H, T, H) by the numerical value 2, and so on. Also, let X represent the number of heads. This process can be pictured as follows:

Descriptive Elements		Numerical Values
HHH	Redefined as ⟶	3
HHT ⎫ HTH ⎬ ⟶ THH ⎭		2
HTT ⎫ THT ⎬ ⟶ TTH ⎭		1
TTT ⟶		0
Sample space		Sample space

This is a perfectly legitimate approach, since the numerical values 3, 2, 1, 0 are mutually exclusive possibilities (3 heads can't be 2 heads) and collectively comprise a sample space. Now event A can be written equivalently as $X = 3$, event B as $X = 2$, event C as $X = 1$, and event D as $X = 0$; the result is

$$P(A) = P(X = 3) = \tfrac{1}{8} \qquad P(B) = P(X = 2) = \tfrac{3}{8}$$
$$P(C) = P(X = 1) = \tfrac{3}{8} \qquad P(D) = P(X = 0) = \tfrac{1}{8}$$

Notice that there is no probability rule that says the values of X must be equally likely. Organizing the values of X (the number of heads) and their corresponding probabilities into a table, we have the **probability distribution of X**:

NUMBER OF HEADS X	0	1	2	3
PROBABILITY $P(X = x)$	$\frac{1}{8}$	$\frac{3}{8}$	$\frac{3}{8}$	$\frac{1}{8}$

Figure 5.1 shows a graphical presentation of the number of heads and the corresponding probabilities from tossing a coin three times.

To summarize briefly, by letting X represent the number of heads, numerical values of X replace the descriptive elements and the probabilities of the descriptive elements are condensed to the appropriate probabilities of the numerical values. The four values of X along with their four probabilities comprise the entire probability distribution of X. The conversion of a descriptive element to a unique numerical value is accomplished by a function called a **random variable**. The letter X denotes that random variable. The probabilities assigned to the values of X, $P(X = x)$, condense the probability assignments given to the original descriptive elements and, importantly, are consistent with the rules of probability.

Although the concept of a random variable has been shown to be applicable to descriptive sample spaces with equally likely possible outcomes, this is not required. Suppose a biased coin rather than a fair coin was used. This would make the equally likely assumption invalid, and it would be improper to link values of the random variable with equally likely descriptive elements of the sample space. In this case, probabilities assigned to the values of the random variable will depend directly on long-run historical relative frequencies of finding 3, 2, 1, or 0 heads. The linkage of the random variable concept with the descriptive sample space is an informative approach and will prove to be very useful in developing sophisticated probability models representing real-world situations that involve uncertainty.

PROBABILITY DISTRIBUTIONS OF RANDOM VARIABLES

From our preliminary look at probability distributions, we can readily surmise that there are two conditions that must be met by the values of a probability distribution. The individual probability values must all lie between 0 and 1, inclusive; and their sum must equal 1. This is summarized by the following **probability postulates for random variables**:

Probability Postulates for Random Variables

1. $0 \leq P(X = x) \leq 1$ for all x
2. $\sum P(X = x) = 1$ when summed over all x

(5-1)

Figure 5.1
Graphic version of the number of heads and corresponding probabilities resulting from three tosses of a fair coin

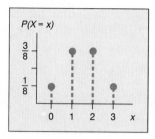

The postulates state that the random variable X will assume a value x with a probability between 0 and 1, inclusive, and the sum of all the probabilities must be exactly equal to 1. The following illustrative example shows the conversion of a 36 element descriptive sample space to a random variable with 11 values and its probability distribution.

■ **EXAMPLE 5.1**

Rolling a Pair of Dice

Consider the case of rolling a pair of fair dice. If all the possible outcomes are listed as ordered pairs, the sample space is found to consist of 36 equally likely ordered pairs: $\{(1, 1), (1, 2), \ldots , (6, 6)\}$. Redefining the possible outcomes in terms of the sum of the dots on the upfaces of the two dice, the descriptive element $(1, 1)$ is redefined as 2, the descriptive element $(1, 2)$ is redefined as 3, and so on. We have, in effect, performed the function of a random variable and redefined the sample space to be $S = \{x \mid x = 2, 3, \ldots , 12\}$. Although the 36 ordered pairs are equally likely, the 11 values in the newly defined sample space are not. The probability assigned to each value x depends upon how many of the equally likely descriptive elements are linked to that value. Only one of the ordered pairs yields a sum of 2, but two of the ordered pairs each yield a sum of 3; so it follows that the value 3 will be twice as probable as the value 2. Three of the ordered pairs each yield a sum of 4; thus, the value 4 will be three times as probable as the value 2. Continuing in this fashion, the probability distribution for the random variable X is given by the following table:

$X = x$	2	3	4	5	6	7	8	9	10	11	12
$P(X = x)$	$\frac{1}{36}$	$\frac{2}{36}$	$\frac{3}{36}$	$\frac{4}{36}$	$\frac{5}{36}$	$\frac{6}{36}$	$\frac{5}{36}$	$\frac{4}{36}$	$\frac{3}{36}$	$\frac{2}{36}$	$\frac{1}{36}$

Check to see if the values assigned to $P(X = x)$ conform with the two probability postulates. That is, does each probability value fall in the interval from 0 to 1, and does the sum equal 1?

Summary measures found useful in describing a frequency distribution in Chapters 2 and 3 are also useful in describing a probability distribution. Just as the mean, or average, served as the summary measure of central location for a frequency distribution, the mean also provides a measure of central location for the probability distribution. By convention, the mean is called the **expected value** of the random variable X and is represented by the symbol $E(X)$.

Expected Value of the Random Variable X

$$E(X) = \sum xP(X = x) \qquad \text{summed over all values of } x \qquad (5\text{-}2)$$

For the distribution of dots on the roll of two dice, we have

$$E(X) = (2)\left(\tfrac{1}{36}\right) + (3)\left(\tfrac{2}{36}\right) + (4)\left(\tfrac{3}{36}\right) + \cdots + (12)\left(\tfrac{1}{36}\right)$$
$$= 7$$

Note that the value 7 is the expected value *not* because it is the single value of the distribution that is most probable to occur, but because it is the numerical value that results from the expected value computation we just described. Furthermore, the value of $E(X)$ may or may not be one of the possible values of X. The expected value of X is strictly an average that serves as a measure of central location. It may not even be a realistic value, as when a report states that "the expected value of the distribution for the number of children per household is 1.9."

The important parameters that describe the behavior of a random variable are customarily assigned the same Greek letters used to describe the parameters of a population. Therefore, the mean, variance, and standard deviation for the distribution of a random variable X are defined as follows:

CALCULATOR NOTE: The μ, σ^2, and σ keys on a pocket calculator provide the mean, variance, and standard deviation for a set of data that has been entered, not for a random variable. Pocket calculators are not designed to provide means, variances, and standard deviations for probability distributions of random variables.

Mean

$$\mu = E(X) = \sum xP(X = x) \qquad \text{summed over all } x \qquad (5\text{-}3)$$

Variance

$$\sigma^2 = \sum (x - \mu)^2 P(X = x) \qquad \text{summed over all } x \qquad (5\text{-}4)$$

Standard Deviation

$$\sigma = \sqrt{\sigma^2} \qquad\qquad (5\text{-}5)$$

An alternative formula for the computation of σ^2 is given by:

Computational Formula for Variance

$$\sigma^2 = \sum x^2 P(X = x) - \mu^2 \qquad \text{summed over all } x$$

This computational formula avoids the tedious operation of subtracting the value of μ from each value x when σ^2 is computed by hand. Except for rounding error, both formulas for σ^2 will yield the same numerical result.

Now let's see how the computational formula is used to calculate the variance and standard deviation of a random variable. Consider once again the distribution of the sum of the dots on the upfaces of two dice. Having found that $\mu = 7$, the value of σ^2 and σ are

$$\sigma^2 = (2)^2\left(\tfrac{1}{36}\right) + (3)^2\left(\tfrac{2}{36}\right) + \cdots + (12)^2\left(\tfrac{1}{36}\right) - (7)^2$$

$$= 5.83333$$

$$\sigma = \sqrt{5.8333} = 2.415$$

Applying Chebyshev's Theorem

Once the two summary measures μ and σ are known, Chebyshev's theorem can be applied to the distribution of the sum of the dots on the upfaces of the two dice. Recall from Chapter 3 that Chebyshev's theorem states that at least $(1 - 1/k^2)100\%$ of all the values in a set of data (population) will be within $\mu \pm k\sigma$. By setting $k = 2$, we know that at least $(1 - 1/2^2)100\%$, or 75%, of the values will be within 2 standard deviations of the mean. For mean $\mu = 7$ and standard deviation $\sigma = 2.415$, at least 75% of the time the sum of the dots on the upfaces of the two dice should be a value in the interval $7 \pm 2(2.415)$, that is, between the values of 2.17 and 11.83. In terms of probabilities, we can state that there is a probability of (1) at least .75 that the sum will be greater than 2 and less than 12; and (2) at most .25 that 2 and 12 occur.

PRACTICE EXERCISE

5.1 A probability distribution model for the random variable reflecting the elements of the roll of a fair die is given by

$X = x$	1	2	3	4	5	6
$P(X = x)$	$\frac{1}{6}$	$\frac{1}{6}$	$\frac{1}{6}$	$\frac{1}{6}$	$\frac{1}{6}$	$\frac{1}{6}$

a. Find the value of $\mu = E(X)$.   b. Find the value of σ^2.

EXERCISES

The following information applies to Exercises 5.1–5.4. Suppose there are three features in a sales presentation that may independently go wrong:

1. The salesperson may unknowingly offend the client by discussing a sensitive topic.
2. The product itself may not perform to expectations when demonstrating its function.
3. The client may have had a very negative experience just prior to the sales presentation.

Suppose the probability is .01 that the salesperson unknowingly offends a client on a sensitive issue; the probability is .003 that the product does not perform to expectations when demonstrating its function; and the probability is .025 that the client had a very negative experience just prior to the sales presentation. If we let A represent the first possibility, B represent the second possibility, and C represent the third possibility, then P(A) = .01, P(B) = .003, and P(C) = .025, where A, B, and C are independent events.

▶ **5.1** Find the values of each of the following:
a. $P(A' \cap B' \cap C')$ b. $P(A \cap B' \cap C')$ c. $P(A' \cap B \cap C')$
d. $P(A' \cap B' \cap C)$ e. $P(A \cap B \cap C')$ f. $P(A \cap B' \cap C)$
g. $P(A' \cap B \cap C)$ h. $P(A \cap B \cap C)$

5.2 Noting that A, B, and C are not mutually exclusive, there are as many as 3 things that could go wrong in one sales presentation. Let the random variable X represent the number of features that can go wrong in a sales presentation. Find the values of each of the following:
a. $P(X = 0)$ b. $P(X = 1)$ c. $P(X = 2)$ d. $P(X = 3)$

5.3 List the probability distribution of the random variable X in Exercise 5.2.

5.4 a. Find the mean and variance of the random variable X in Exercise 5.3.
b. On the average, how many features can a salesperson expect to go wrong in a sales presentation?

c. If the information describes a real-world situation, should the salesperson be concerned with any of the 3 features going wrong in a sales presentation?

●   ● ● ● ●

5.2

SOME DISCRETE PROBABILITY DISTRIBUTIONS

Games of chance date back to early human history and are the origins of the subjects we today call probability and statistics. But the formal study of the subject did not begin until the seventeenth century, when wealthy gamblers asked their mathematician friends to explain the patterns they witnessed in games of chance. Mathematicians soon discovered that the mathematical structures developed to explain the patterns went far beyond the gaming parlors and could be used to explain real-world phenomena. But it wasn't until the twentieth century that the applications of probability and statistics to modeling real-world phenomena associated with uncertainty became widespread. We begin our discussion with probability distributions associated with **discrete random variables**, that is, random variables whose values change by discrete steps or jumps, not over a continuum of values. For example, on a roll of a single die, the random variable X can assume a value of 1, 2, 3, 4, 5, or 6 (the number of dots on the upface of the die). That is, the value of X steps from 1 to 2, 2 to 3, and so on; X cannot assume any values between them, such as 1.5 or 2.9.

BINOMIAL DISTRIBUTION

A specialized discrete probability distribution that has been very useful in describing many real-world phenomena is the *binomial distribution*. Let's consider a situation that will enable us to intuitively understand the expression for the binomial distribution.

Suppose an unprepared student taking a surprise 10 question true–false test decides to answer each question by flipping a fair coin: If the coin turns up heads, the student marks the question "true"; if the coin turns up tails, the student marks the question "false." Then the probability of getting exactly 6 correct answers is equal to the expression $_{10}C_6\left(\frac{1}{2}\right)^{10}$. Let's examine this expression. The coefficient of the expression, $_{10}C_6$, represents the total number of ways (combinations) of selecting 6 correct answers out of the 10 questions. Since the probability is $\frac{1}{2}$ that a particular question will be answered correctly, and the probability is $\frac{1}{2}$ that a particular question will be answered incorrectly, then the probability of obtaining one combination of 6 questions independently answered correctly and the other 4 questions independently answered incorrectly will be $\left(\frac{1}{2}\right)^6\left(\frac{1}{2}\right)^4 = \left(\frac{1}{2}\right)^{10}$. By multiplying the one combination probability by $_{10}C_6$, the total number of combinations possible, we get the probability that the student will get exactly 6 correct answers. Similar probabilities can be derived for exactly 3 correct answers, $_{10}C_3\left(\frac{1}{2}\right)^{10}$; or for exactly 0 correct answers, $_{10}C_0\left(\frac{1}{2}\right)^{10}$.

Generalizing, let the random variable X represent the number of correct answers possible. Then the probability distribution of the random variable X is given by

$$P(X = x) = {}_{10}C_x\left(\frac{1}{2}\right)^{10} = {}_{10}C_x\left(\frac{1}{2}\right)^x\left(\frac{1}{2}\right)^{10-x}$$

where $_{10}C_x$ represents the number of ways that x correct answers can be obtained out of the 10 questions. The expression $_{10}C_x$ also can be written in factorial form.

$$_{10}C_x = \frac{10!}{x!(10-x)!}$$

The symbol ! signifies the factorial operation. Thus, 10! is read, "ten factorial," $x!$ is read, "x factorial," and $(10 - x)!$ is read, "ten minus x factorial." The computed value of 10! is $10 \times 9 \times 8 \times 7 \times 6 \times 5 \times 4 \times 3 \times 2 \times 1 = 3{,}628{,}800$. (By definition, $0! = 1$.) Written in factorial form, the expression for $P(X = x)$ is

$$P(X = x) = \frac{10!}{x!(10 - x)!}\left(\frac{1}{2}\right)^{x}\left(\frac{1}{2}\right)^{10-x} \qquad \text{for } x = 0, 1, \ldots, 10$$

This specific expression is one member of a family of specialized distributions called *binomial probability distributions*.

Five conditions characterize a binomial probability distribution. To illustrate each condition, we have linked each one to an appropriate characteristic in the 10 question true–false test example.

1. There is a sequence of n trials (e.g., questions, tosses of a coin, rolls of a die, deaths, or persons reacting to a drug).
   For the true–false test illustration: There are $n = 10$ questions on the test.
2. There are exactly two possibilities for each trial (i.e., correct versus not correct, true versus false, plus versus minus, defective versus nondefective, yes versus no, or success versus failure).
   For the true–false test illustration: For each question there are two possibilities—the student can answer correctly or incorrectly.
3. The trials are independent. What actually happens on one trial does not change the probability of what can happen on any subsequent trial.
   For the true–false test illustration: The answer to one question does not influence the answer to any other question. For instance, the probability of answering the second question correctly is not affected by the answer given to the first question; the probability of answering the third question correctly is not affected by the answers given to the first two questions; and so on. The answers to the questions are independent of each other because the student's choice is determined solely by the flip of a coin, and the coin has no memory of previous results.
4. If p is the probability of one possibility occurring on one trial, then the probability for that possibility remains unchanged at p for any subsequent trial. This condition of unchanged probability p is sometimes stated as "the probability of a 'success' is the same for each trial."
   For the true–false test illustration: The probability that the student answers a question correctly is the same for each question since the same fair coin is tossed and the same decision procedure is used for each question.
5. The random variable X represents the number of same type occurrences of the two possibilities over the n trials. Generally, we speak of the number of "successes." A "success" may be the number of correct responses, the number of defectives, or the number of deaths for the n trials considered.
   For the true–false test illustration: The random variable X represents the number of correct answers in 10 questions.

All five conditions must be met for the binomial distribution to be the appropriate model for the probabilistic behavior of the random variable X. A general expression for the **binomial distribution** is given by the following equation:

Binomial Distribution

$$P(X = x) = \frac{n!}{x!(n-x)!} \, p^x(1-p)^{n-x} \qquad \text{for } x = 0, 1, 2, \ldots, n \quad (5\text{-}6)$$

where n represents the number of independent two-valued "success" versus "failure" trials; p represents the probability of a "success" on a given trial; x represents number of "successes" among the n trials; and $P(X = x)$ represents the probability of getting exactly x "successes" among the n trials.

The next two examples are applications of the binomial distribution. The first example applies the binomial distribution to the outcomes of a sample survey.

■ **EXAMPLE 5.2**

A Television Survey

A television survey conducted in a large city finds that 90% of the TV viewing households watched a certain miniseries. If a random sample of 11 TV households from a complete listing of all TV households in the city had been taken during that time:

a. What is the probability that none of the households watched the series?
b. What is the probability that at least 1 household watched the series?

Discussion

Let's first see how the facts of the problem match the conditions of the binomial distribution:

1. The 11 households constitute 11 trials ($n = 11$).
2. The trials have two possibilities: Each household is either watching the miniseries or not watching the miniseries.
3. The trials are independent since random selection of different households across the city presumably allows each household to be geographically separated and to independently select its own programs.
4. The probability of watching the miniseries is $p = .90$ for each household.
5. The random variable X represents the number of TV households watching the miniseries ($0 \leq X \leq 11$).

The factual statements of the problem appear to satisfy the five conditions required for the binomial distribution to serve as an applicable model. The probability distribution is therefore given by

$$P(X = x) = \frac{11!}{x!(11 - x)!} \, (.9)^x(.1)^{11-x} \qquad \text{for } x = 0, 1, 2, \ldots, 11$$

Solution

a. $P(X = 0) = (1)(.9)^0(.1)^{11} = 0$ (to four-decimal-place accuracy)
b. $P(X \geq 1) = 1 - P(X = 0) = 1$ (to four-decimal-place accuracy)

For the conditions specified, the sample almost certainly would include at least 1 household watching the miniseries.

The second example applies the binomial distribution to a faulty machine that is shortchanging its customers.

■ **EXAMPLE 5.3**

An Automatic Teller Machine

An automatic teller machine has developed the quirk of randomly shortchanging customers. If it shortchanges 2% of its customers, what is the probability that:

a. None of 50 customers get shortchanged?
b. At least 1 out of 50 customers gets shortchanged?
c. At most 1 out of 50 customers gets shortchanged?

Discussion

Comparing the facts of the problem to the binomial distribution conditions, we note the following:

1. The 50 customers constitute 50 trials ($n = 50$).
2. The 50 trials each have two possibilities: Each customer either will be shortchanged or will not be shortchanged.
3. The trials are independent since we are told that the machine *randomly* shortchanges a customer.
4. The probability is .02 that a customer will be shortchanged ($p = .02$).
5. The random variable X represents the number of shortchanged customers ($0 \leq X \leq 50$).

The facts of the problem appear to meet the conditions of the binomial distribution. The probability distribution is therefore given by

$$P(X = x) = \frac{50!}{x!(50 - x)!}(.02)^x(.98)^{50-x} \qquad \text{for } x = 0, 1, 2, \ldots, 50$$

Solution

a. $P(X = 0) = (1)(.02)^0(.98)^{50} = .36$
b. $P(X \geq 1) = 1 - P(X = 0) = .64$
c. $P(X \leq 1) = P(X = 0) + P(X = 1) = .74$

The final answers show that there is a 74% chance that at most 1 of the 50 customers will be shortchanged; a 64% chance that at least 1 will be shortchanged; but only a 36% chance that none of the 50 customers will be shortchanged. This suggests an unacceptably high probability of shortchanging 1 customer out of every 50 who use the machine.

The mean and variance for the binomial distribution are given by the following equations:

Mean and Variance of the Binomial Distribution

$$\mu = np \qquad\qquad (5\text{-}7)$$
$$\sigma^2 = np(1 - p)$$

For the automatic teller machine example (Example 5.3), we have $n = 50$, $p = .02$, and $1 - p = .98$. Thus,

$$\mu = (50)(.02) = 1$$
$$\sigma^2 = (50)(.02)(.98) = .98$$

PRACTICE EXERCISE

5.2 A person playing a certain strategy at a gaming table in Las Vegas has a .49 probability of winning on each play. In 15 plays:
a. What is the probability the person wins 5 times?
b. What is the probability the person wins at most 5 times?

Using the Binomial Probability Table

Probability values for the binomial distribution can be obtained from Table II in the Appendix at the end of this book. This table lists the probabilities that the value of the random variable will be less than or equal to x for various values of x, n, and p. In the next example we use the table to find the probabilities for selected values of the random variable, given values of n and p.

EXAMPLE 5.4

Using the Binomial Probability Table

Suppose $n = 12$ and $p = .30$. Find:

a. $P(X = 0)$ b. $P(X \le 1)$ c. $P(X = 1)$ d. $P(X \le 5)$
e. $P(X = 5)$ f. $P(X > 5)$ g. $P(X \ge 5)$

Solution

On the left-hand side of Table II find $n = 12$. Having located $n = 12$:

a. Find the row corresponding to $x = 0$. Moving across the row to the column headed by $p = .30$, locate the entry .014 in the table. It is at the intersection of the row $x = 0$ and the column $p = .30$. This table value is the answer for $P(X \le 0)$; that is, $P(X \le 0) = .014$. However, there can't be fewer than 0 successes, so $P(X < 0) = 0$. Therefore, since $P(X = 0) = P(X \le 0) - P(X < 0)$, it follows that $P(X = 0) = .014$.
b. Find the row corresponding to $x = 1$. Moving across the row to the column headed by $p = .30$, observe the entry .085. This is the value for $P(X \le 1)$. That is,
   $P(X \le 1) = .085$.
c. $P(X = 1) = P(X \le 1) - P(X = 0) = .085 - .014 = .071$
d. Find the intersection of the row corresponding to $x = 5$ and the column $p = .30$. The entry .882 is the value for $P(X \le 5)$. That is, $P(X \le 5) = .882$.
e. $P(X = 5) = P(X \le 5) - P(X \le 4) = .882 - .724 = .158$
f. $P(X > 5) = 1 - P(X \le 5) = 1 - .882 = .118$
g. $P(X \ge 5) = 1 - P(X < 5) = 1 - P(X \le 4) = 1 - .724 = .276$

PRACTICE EXERCISE

5.3 If the random variable X has a binomial distribution with $n = 16$ and $p = .7$, find:
a. $P(X \le 7)$ b. $P(X \le 6)$ c. $P(X = 7)$ d. $P(X \ge 7)$ e. $P(X > 7)$

POISSON DISTRIBUTION

A discrete probability distribution that has wide use in management science and production is the *Poisson distribution*. Let's first briefly state one situation that prompts the use of the Poisson distribution and then give an example for obtaining the Poisson probability. Suppose the number of trials, n, is very large, and the binomial distribution probabilities become difficult to evaluate. Here's an illustration of how this situation can arise in a business environment.

■ **EXAMPLE 5.5**

Reliability of Guidance Systems

Guidance systems for space programs require highly reliable components. To ensure reliability, redundancies are included so that if one component should fail, another equivalent component assumes its function. Suppose redundancies are built in so that failures are independent, and suppose a guidance system can tolerate up to 5 failures before there is a real concern over the performance of the system. If there are 15,000 components, each with a probability equal to .00001 of failing, what is the probability that fewer than 5 will fail?

Discussion

The facts of the problem indicate that the five binomial distribution conditions are met:

1. The 15,000 components constitute 15,000 trials.
2. Each trial has two possibilities, that is, each component will either fail or not fail.
3. The failures are independent.
4. The probability of failure is $p = .00001$ for each component.
5. The random variable X represents the number of component failures among the 15,000 components.

With the conditions of the binomial distribution met, the probability distribution is given by

$$P(X = x) = \binom{15,000}{x}(.00001)^x(.99999)^{15,000-x} \qquad \text{for } x = 0, 1, 2, \ldots, 15,000$$

Solution

$$P(X < 5) = \sum_{x=0}^{4}\left[\binom{15,000}{x}(.00001)^x(.99999)^{15,000-x}\right]$$

We can quickly see from the above solution that the numbers and the operations involved are a computational nightmare. Even if a pocket calculator is available, the number of digits involved rules out its use. The alternative route to take is to approximate the binomial distribution by using the **Poisson distribution**. The Poisson distribution approximation for the binomial distribution is reasonably good when n is very large and p is small (as a rule of thumb, when $n > 100$ and $p < .01$). The Poisson distribution, when used as an approximation to the binomial distribution, is written as follows:

Poisson Distribution
Approximation to the Binomial Distribution

$$P(X = x) = \frac{(np)^x e^{-np}}{x!} \qquad \text{for } x = 0, 1, 2, \ldots \qquad \text{(5-8)}$$

where $e \approx 2.718281828459$ is the base for natural logarithms (to 12 decimal places; like π, e is an irrational number with a nonrepeating decimal representation); n represents the number of independent trials; p represents the probability of success on each trial; and x represents the number of successes.

Notice in the Poisson expression that there is no restriction on the upper limit of x. This means that the values of x are countably infinite despite the fact that n is finite. This condition doesn't present a difficulty since the probability of success diminishes rapidly toward 0 as the value of x increases towards n.

To use the Poisson distribution as an approximation, the value of np must be calculated. For Example 5.5, we have

$$np = (15{,}000)(.00001) = .15$$

Thus,

CALCULATOR NOTE: Find the e^x key on a scientific or business calculator. This key can be used to evaluate $e^{-.15}$. Consult the manual that comes with the calculator for specific information on how to use the e^x key.

$$P(X < 5) = \sum_{x=0}^{4} \frac{(.15)^x e^{-.15}}{x!}$$

$$= .860708 + .129106 + .009683 + .000484 + .000018$$

$$= .999999$$

So, it is almost certain (probability .999999) that fewer than 5 of the 15,000 components will fail. Given the high probability of nonfailure, we can conclude that the guidance system will be reliable.

The mean and variance of the Poisson distribution when used for a binomial distribution approximation are

$$\mu = E(X) = np \qquad \text{Var}(X) = \sigma^2 = np$$

Interestingly, the values of the mean and variance of the Poisson distribution are identical.

The Poisson distribution is not only a useful approximation for the binomial distribution, but also an appropriate model for situations that involve (1) counting specific occurrences over a continuum, such as volume, time, area, or distance; and (2) counting a low number of occurrences for the defined volume, time, area, or distance considered. Several types of situations meet these conditions:

- The number of red blood cells in a volume of blood
- The number of incoming calls over a specified period of time
- The number of particles of pollutants present in a given volume of city air
- The number of defects in a bolt of cloth

If X represents the number of occurrences, then the Poisson probability distribution is given by the following equation:

Poisson Distribution

$$P(X = x) = \frac{\lambda^x e^{-\lambda}}{x!} \qquad \text{for } x = 0, 1, 2, \ldots \qquad (5\text{-}9)$$

where λ is actually the average number of occurrences *per unit* of volume, time, area, or distance.

The mean and variance for this form of the Poisson distribution are, respectively,

$$\mu = E(X) = \lambda \qquad \text{Var}(X) = \sigma^2 = \lambda$$

Let's examine an example where area is the continuum over which occurrences are counted.

■ **EXAMPLE 5.6**

Defects in Bolts of Cloth

Suppose the production of a certain type of cloth averages 2 defects per bolt. If a bolt is randomly selected and inspected, what is the probability that:

a. The bolt has no defects?　　b. The bolt has at least 1 defect?

Solution

To solve this problem using the Poisson distribution model, we must assume that equal areas of cloth all have the same probability of containing a defect. Now let X represent the number of defects in the bolt. The probability distribution of X is given by

$$P(X = x) = \frac{2^x e^{-2}}{x!} \qquad \text{for } x = 0, 1, 2, \ldots$$

a. $P(X = 0) = \dfrac{2^0 e^{-2}}{0!} = .1353$　　b. $P(X \geq 1) = 1 - P(X = 0) = .8647$

The Poisson distribution possesses the important property that $E(X) = \lambda$ (per unit of volume, time, area, or distance) stays constant. This means that:

1. If we double the units of volume, time, area, or distance, then we can double the value of $E(X)$.
2. If we halve the units, we can halve the value of $E(X)$.
3. In general, if we change the units by a multiple of k, then we change the value of $E(X)$ by a multiple of k.

In the next example we'll illustrate how to calculate the probability of a specific occurrence as $E(X)$ is changed.

■ **EXAMPLE 5.7**

Defects in Bolts of Cloth, Continued

Suppose that in Example 5.6, only half the bolt is to be inspected. If 2 defects are expected per full bolt, then on the average only 1 defect should be expected per half bolt; that is, $\lambda = 1$ per half bolt. If only half a bolt is inspected, what is the probability that:

a. The half bolt has no defects?　　b. The half bolt has at least 1 defect?

Solution

Let X represent the number of defects in the half bolt. The Poisson probability distribution of X is given by

$$P(X = x) = \frac{(1)^x e^{-1}}{x!} \qquad \text{for } x = 0, 1, 2, \ldots$$

a. $P(X = 0) = .3679$ b. $P(X \geq 1) = 1 - P(X = 0) = .6321$

Using the Poisson Probability Table

To obtain probability values for the Poisson distribution without a calculator, consult Table III in the Appendix at the end of this book. The table lists the probabilities that the value of the random variable will be less than or equal to x for various values of λ and x. If a binomial distribution is being approximated by the Poisson distribution, let $\lambda = np$ when using the table. We now show how to use the table for a specific value of λ.

Suppose $\lambda = 7.4$. Using the Poisson probability table, the following is the procedure for finding the probabilities for $P(X = 0)$, $P(X \leq 6)$, $P(X = 6)$, $P(X > 6)$, and $P(X \geq 6)$.

Procedure

Step 1
Locate the column in the table for $\lambda = 7.4$.

Step 2
Locate the row for $x = 0$.

Step 3
The intersection of this row and column shows the entry .0006. This is the value for $P(X \leq 0)$; that is, $P(X \leq 0) = .0006$. However, note that there cannot be fewer than 0 successes, so $P(X < 0) = 0$. Then, since $P(X = 0)$ can be expressed as $P(X \leq 0) - P(X < 0)$, it follows that $P(X = 0) = .0006$.

Step 4
The value for $P(X \leq 6)$ is the entry at the junction of $x = 6$ and $\lambda = 7.4$; that is, $P(X \leq 6) = .3920$.

Step 5
$P(X = 6) = P(X \leq 6) - P(X \leq 5) = .3920 - .2526 = .1394$

Step 6
$P(X > 6) = 1 - P(X \leq 6) = 1 - .3920 = .6080$

Step 7
$P(X \geq 6) = 1 - P(X < 6) = 1 - P(X \leq 5) = 1 - .2526 = .7474$

Now, here are some practice exercises to develop your skill in identifying and solving problems involving the Poisson distribution.

PRACTICE EXERCISES

5.4 On a certain day in the United States it is expected that there will be 1,000,000 cars on the highways. If the probability is .0000015 that any one automobile traveling on the highways that day will be involved in an accident involving a fatality, what is the probability that:
   a. Exactly 2 automobiles will be involved in a fatality that day?
   b. Less than 2 automobiles will be involved in a fatality that day?

5.5 A traffic counter at a certain intersection finds that on the average, 7 automobiles pass through the intersection every 5 minutes.
a. In a randomly selected 5 minute period, what is the probability that exactly 3 cars will pass through the intersection?
b. In a randomly selected 10 minute period, what is the probability that exactly 3 cars will pass through the intersection?

EXERCISES

▶ **5.5** Suppose that 1% of the automobiles on the road have smog control devices that have been tampered with. At a checkpoint, 20 automobiles are randomly stopped for a smog control device check.
a. What is the probability that none of the 20 smog control devices have been tampered with?
b. What is the probability that less than 2 of the 20 smog control devices have been tampered with?
c. What is the probability that at most 2 of the 20 smog control devices have been tampered with?
d. What is the mean for this distribution?
e. What is the standard deviation for this distribution?

5.6 Suppose that 40% of all the professional athletes in the United States earn annual salaries of $80,000 or more. If an athlete's agent is involved in contract negotiations with management and randomly selects the salaries of 17 professional athletes as examples of other players' worth:
a. What is the probability that fewer than 9 of the 17 earn $80,000 or more?
b. What is the probability that exactly 10 of the 17 earn $80,000 or more?
c. What is the probability that more than 3 of the 17 earn $80,000 or more?
d. What is the mean for this distribution?
e. What is the standard deviation for this distribution?
f. What is the probability that fewer than 9 of the 17 earn less than $80,000?

5.7 Suppose that according to records, 0.01% of the motorists crossing the Mexico/ United States border at Tijuana/San Diego violate some federal law.
a. What is the approximate probability that among 4000 randomly selected motorists crossing the Tijuana/San Diego border, none violate any federal laws?
b. What is the approximate probability that among 4000 randomly selected motorists crossing the Tijuana/San Diego border, at least 1 violates some federal law?
c. What is the mean for this distribution?
d. What is the standard deviation for this distribution?

5.8 With respect to Exercise 5.7:
a. What is the approximate probability that among 33,000 randomly selected motorists crossing the Tijuana/San Diego border, none violate any federal laws?
b. What is the approximate probability that among 33,000 randomly selected motorists crossing the Tijuana/San Diego border, at least 1 violates some federal law?
c. What is the mean for this distribution?
d. What is the standard deviation for this distribution?

▶ **5.9** Between the hours of 8 am and 10 am on a Saturday morning, the traffic bureau in a certain city estimates there are 5000 cars on the road. Traffic records show that between 8 am and 10 am, on average, 1 car in 4000 is involved in a traffic fatality. What is the probability that next Saturday between 8 am and 10 am there will be fewer than 3 traffic fatalities?

5.10 The average number of red blood corpuscles in a healthy person is 5,000,000 per cubic millimeter (mm³). Red blood counts are used to diagnose diseases and nutritional problems. To make accurate blood counts, a sample of blood is diluted one-hundredfold to a density of 50,000 red blood corpuscles per cubic millimeter. Then a glass slide with a drop of the diluted sample is covered with a calibrated cover slip and placed under a microscope. The field of vision under the microscope represents a volume of $\frac{1}{5000}$ mm³. Thus, for a healthy person, the average number of red blood corpuscles in the field of vision seen under the microscope should be 10. However, there is variation in the number seen from one field of vision to the next. If X represents the actual number of red blood corpuscles in a field of vision, then its probability distribution is given by

$$P(X = x) = \frac{10^x e^{-10}}{x!} \qquad \text{for } x = 0, 1, 2, \ldots$$

In order for this expression to be applicable, we must assume that equal volumes of blood all have the same probability of being occupied by a red blood corpuscle. Taking a sample of blood from a healthy person, what is the probability that the number of red blood corpuscles in the field of vision will be less than 5?

5.3
CONTINUOUS PROBABILITY DISTRIBUTIONS

DISCRETE VERSUS CONTINUOUS DISTRIBUTIONS

Probability distributions may be *discrete* or *continuous*. The binomial distribution presented in Section 5.2 is an example of a discrete probability distribution. That is, the random variable defined by the binomial probability distribution can assume only discrete numerical values: 0, 1, 2, . . . , n.

Many situations exist, however, in which a random variable, at least theoretically, is not restricted to assuming only discrete numerical values. For example, theoretically there is no limit to the precision of the measurements for the diameter of a ball bearing, the speed of information transmission, or the life expectancy of a microchip. These measurements are made on a continuous scale in which theoretically there are no gaps, or discontinuities, between the potential measurements. A random variable that defines a set of values in which theoretically there are no gaps or discontinuities is referred to as a **continuous random variable**. Its corresponding probability distribution is known as a **continuous probability distribution**.

The fact that a continuous probability distribution has no gaps, or discontinuities, introduces a new feature to probability assessments. To illustrate, take the discrete probability distribution representing probabilities associated with the roll of a fair die. In that case we found that $P(X = 1) = \frac{1}{6}$ (the probability is $\frac{1}{6}$ that the upface will show 1 dot when the die is rolled). But for a continuous probability distribution, it is true that $P(X = a) = 0$ for any specific value a. (We shall see why in Example 5.8.) The only possible way to get a nonzero value for a probability with a continuous probability distribution is to look at *intervals* such as $a < X < b$. That is, for continuous probability distributions it is possible for $P(a < X < b)$ to be different from 0, but it is never possible for $P(X = a)$ to be different from 0. We examine this issue in the next example, where X is defined as a continuous random variable.

■ **EXAMPLE 5.8**

A Dart-Throwing Target

The diagram in Figure 5.2 represents a rectangular dart-throwing target. The target is 2 ft wide and 0.5 ft high. The area of this target is equal to 1 (the width times the height). The bull's-eye region is shaded. Suppose a blindfolded person throws darts at the target, and we consider only those darts that hit the target.

a. What proportion of the darts should we expect to land in the bull's-eye region?
b. What proportion of the darts should we expect to land in the rectangle of the target region above the interval from $X = 1.25$ to $X = 2$?
c. What proportion of the darts should we expect to land on the line $X = 1.25$?

Solution

a. If the person throwing the darts is blindfolded, then one part of the target is just as likely to be hit as any other part. Thus, the proportion of darts expected to land in the bull's-eye region is equal to the ratio of the area of the bull's-eye region to the entire area of the target region. The former is equal to $(0.5)(1.25 - 0.75) = 0.25$, and the latter is equal to 1. Thus, of the darts that hit the target, the proportion landing in the rectangle over the interval from $X = 0.75$ to $X = 1.25$ is equal to .25. We may translate this to say that the probability is .25 that a thrown dart that hits the target region will land in the bull's-eye region $[P(0.75 < X < 1.25) = .25]$. In Figure 5.2, this probability is represented by the area under the relative frequency curve between $X = 0.75$ and $X = 1.25$.

b. Since a blindfolded person throwing the darts is just as likely to hit any part of the target, the proportion of darts landing in the target region above the interval from $X = 1.25$ to $X = 2$ is equal to the ratio of the area of the rectangle in the interval (1.25, 2) to the area of the entire target region. The former is equal to $0.5(2 - 1.25) = 0.375$, and the latter is equal to 1. Therefore, the proportion expected to land in the rectangle over the interval from $X = 1.25$ to $X = 2$ is .375. This tells us that for the darts that hit the target, the probability is .375 of landing in the rectangle over the interval from $X = 1.25$ to $X = 2$ $[P(1.25 < X < 2) = .375]$. This probability is represented by the area under the relative frequency curve in Figure 5.2 between the values $X = 1.25$ and $X = 2.00$.

c. In a like manner, the proportion of darts landing in the target region on the line $X = 1.25$ is equal to the ratio of the area of the line $X = 1.25$ to the area of the entire target region. The area of the line is equal to $(0.5)(1.25 - 1.25) = 0$. This implies that the proportion expected to land on the line $X = 1.25$

Figure 5.2
Dart-throwing target

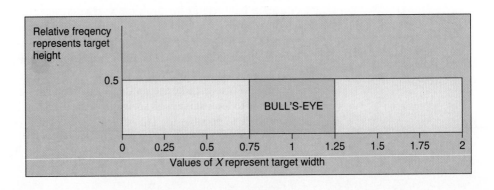

is equal to 0. So, for the darts that hit the target, the probability of landing on the line $X = 1.25$ (or on any line) is equal to 0 [$P(X = 1.25) = 0$].

The essential principles to remember from the calculations in Example 5.8, are:

1. Probabilities must be calculated over areas.
2. Points and lines have 0 areas.

Therefore, the probabilities associated with points and lines must equal 0. This will be true whenever the random variable is continuous.

NORMAL PROBABILITY DENSITY FUNCTION

The *normal probability density function* is a model for the behavior of many naturally occurring phenomena. Measurements such as heights, weights, grades, IQ measurements, and beak lengths of bird types all tend to appear normally distributed, or have a **normal distribution**. Even measurements of concentrations of minerals in human blood have been found to be nearly normally distributed. A general expression for the **normal probability density function** is given by the following equation:

Normal Probability Density Function

$$f(x;\ \mu,\ \sigma^2) = \frac{1}{\sqrt{2\pi}\sigma}\, e^{-(1/2)[(x-\mu)/\sigma]^2} \qquad \text{for } -\infty < x < \infty \qquad \textbf{(5-10)}$$

where $-\infty < \mu < \infty$, $\sigma > 0$, $e \approx 2.718281828459$, and $\pi \approx 3.1415926$.

When graphed, the normal probability density function is a **bell-shaped curve**, symmetrical about its mean, μ. The symmetry informs us that the median and mode are equal to μ. The standard deviation is symbolized by σ. *Both tails of the normal curve extend outward indefinitely, moving toward but never quite reaching the horizontal axis; nevertheless, the area under the curve above the horizontal axis is finite and always equal to 1.* A graph of the normal probability density function for $\mu = 0$ and $\sigma = 1$ is given in Figure 5.3.

STANDARD NORMAL PROBABILITY DENSITY FUNCTION

The normal probability density function with mean $\mu = 0$ and standard deviation $\sigma = 1$ is referred to as the **standard normal probability density function**, or the **standard normal distribution**. A normal probability calculation for a normal curve with designated values for μ and σ involves finding the area under the curve over a specified interval on the horizontal axis. Computers can help do this, but tables are generally easy enough to use and are extremely helpful in calculating a normal probability.

Fortunately, only one table is needed to cover all possible values of μ and σ. All normal density functions can be linked to the standard normal probability density

Figure 5.3
Normal probability density
function with $\mu = 0$, $\sigma = 1$

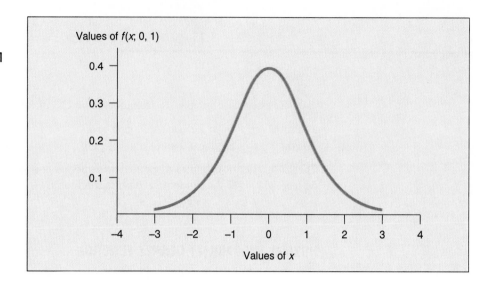

function. The area under any normal curve always can be equated to a corresponding area under the standard normal curve. Using a table of probabilities (areas) for the standard normal curve, such as Appendix Table IV, probabilities can be found for any normal probability density function.

In this text the capital letter Z represents the random variable whose probability density function is the standard normal probability density function. This function produces a symmetric curve around $Z = 0$, and Appendix Table IV makes use of this fact. The table provides areas under the normal curve only for the right side of the curve between $Z = 0$ and values of Z greater than 0. Thus, if a and b are both positive, we can use the table to evaluate probabilities such as $P(Z < a)$, $P(Z > a)$, and $P(a < Z < b)$. The condition of symmetry about $Z = 0$ also enables us to use the table to find areas under the curve on the left side of the curve, that is, for $P(Z < -a)$, $P(Z > -a)$, and $P(-b < Z < -a)$. For example, consider any positive value a. The table lists values for $P(0 < Z < a)$. Because of the symmetry about $Z = 0$, $P(-a < Z < 0) = P(0 < Z < a)$.

In the examples that follow, refer to Appendix Table IV to see how we use that table to evaluate a variety of probabilities involving different intervals for Z.

■ **EXAMPLE 5.9**

Using the Standard Normal Probability Table

Find the probability that the value of the standard normal random variable Z will be a value between 0 and 1.39. That is, evaluate $P(0 < Z < 1.39)$.

Solution

Step 1
Use Table IV and find the value 1.3 in the leftmost column, titled Z.

Step 2
Follow the row at 1.3 across to the right until you reach the entry in the column headed by .09.

Step 3
The entry .4177 represents the probability that the value of Z will be a value between 0 and 1.39.

Figure 5.4
Finding probabilities with the standard normal probability table

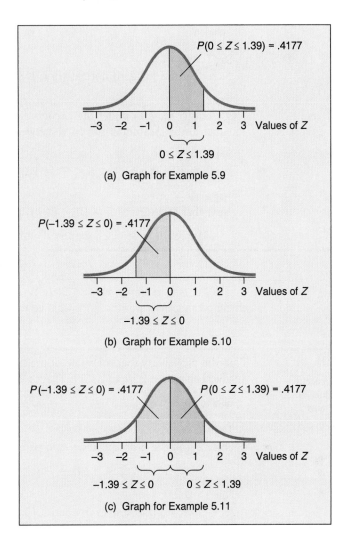

$P(0 \leq Z \leq 1.39) = .4177$

$0 \leq Z \leq 1.39$

(a) Graph for Example 5.9

$P(-1.39 \leq Z \leq 0) = .4177$

$-1.39 \leq Z \leq 0$

(b) Graph for Example 5.10

$P(-1.39 \leq Z \leq 0) = .4177$ $P(0 \leq Z \leq 1.39) = .4177$

$-1.39 \leq Z \leq 0$ $0 \leq Z \leq 1.39$

(c) Graph for Example 5.11

Step 4
Symbolically, $P(0 < Z < 1.39) = P(0 \leq Z \leq 1.39) = .4177$.

The result is depicted graphically in Figure 5.4a.

In the next example, we take advantage of the symmetrical nature of the normal curve. Table IV, which shows areas under the curve for positive values of Z, is used to find the probability corresponding to an area under the curve for a negative value of Z.

■ **EXAMPLE 5.10**

Using the Standard Normal Probability Table, Continued

Find the probability that the value of the standard normal random variable Z will be a value between -1.39 and 0. That is, evaluate $P(-1.39 < Z < 0)$.

Solution

Step 1
Note that the standard normal curve is symmetric about $Z = 0$.

Step 2
Therefore, the area under the curve between $Z = -1.39$ and $Z = 0$ is exactly equal to the area·under the curve between $Z = 0$ and $Z = 1.39$.

Step 3
Symbolically, $P(-1.39 < Z < 0) = P(0 < Z < 1.39) = .4177$.

Step 4
Note that $P(-1.39 \leq Z \leq 0) = P(-1.39 < Z < 0)$.

The result is depicted graphically in Figure 5.4b.

In the next example, we use Table IV to find the probability for an interval of Z encompassing both positive and negative values.

■ **EXAMPLE 5.11**

Using the Standard Normal Probability Table, Continued

Find the probability that the value of the standard normal random variable Z will be a value between -1.39 and 1.39. That is, evaluate $P(-1.39 < Z < 1.39)$.

Solution

Step 1
First, break the problem down into parts we can find from Table IV:

$$P(-1.39 < Z < 1.39) = P(-1.39 < Z < 0) + P(0 < Z < 1.39)$$

Step 2
Therefore, from Examples 5.9 and 5.10, $P(-1.39 < Z < 1.39) = .4177 + .4177 = .8354$.

Step 3
Note that $P(-1.39 < Z < 1.39) = P(-1.39 \leq Z \leq 1.39)$.

The result is depicted graphically in Figure 5.4c.

In the following example, we'll use Table IV to find the probability corresponding to an interval between two positive values.

■ **EXAMPLE 5.12**

Using the Standard Normal Probability Table, Continued

Find the probability that the value of the standard normal random variable Z will be a value between 1.39 and 2.63. That is, evaluate $P(1.39 < Z < 2.63)$.

Solution

Step 1
First, break the problem down into parts we can find in Table IV:

$$P(1.39 < Z < 2.63) = P(0 < Z < 2.63) - P(0 < Z < 1.39)$$

Step 2

We have already determined that $P(0 < Z < 1.39) = .4177$.

Step 3

In order to find the value for $P(0 < Z < 2.63)$, we find the value 2.6 in the leftmost column of Table IV, headed Z. Then we follow the row at 2.6 across to the right until we reach the entry in the column headed by .03. The entry .4957 represents the probability that the value of Z will be between 0 and 2.63. Symbolically, we have $P(0 < Z < 2.63) = .4957$. Note that $P(0 \leq Z \leq 2.63) = P(0 < Z < 2.63)$.

Step 4

Therefore, $P(1.39 < Z < 2.63) = .4957 - .4177 = .0780$.

Step 5

Note that $P(1.39 \leq Z \leq 2.63) = P(1.39 < Z < 2.63)$.

The result is depicted graphically in Figure 5.5.

Figure 5.5
Finding probabilities with the standard normal probability table (continued)

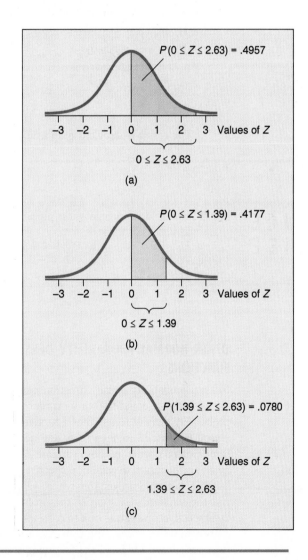

By virtue of the fact that the standard normal curve is symmetric about $Z = 0$, we also know that $P(-2.63 < Z < -1.39) = P(1.39 < Z < 2.63)$. In general, $P(a < Z < b) = P(-b < Z < -a)$.

In the final example, we use Table IV to find a right-tail probability, that is, a probability corresponding to an interval to the right of a positive value.

■ **EXAMPLE 5.13**

Using the Standard Normal Probability Table, Continued

Find the probability that the value of the standard normal random variable Z will be a value greater than 1.39. That is, evaluate $P(Z > 1.39)$.

Solution

We can take two approaches to find this probability. Both approaches rely on the fact that the area under the entire curve is equal to 1 and the curve is symmetric about $Z = 0$. Then half the area lies to the right of $Z = 0$ and half the area lies to the left of $Z = 0$. In other words, $P(Z > 0) = P(Z < 0) = .5$.

a. One approach is

$$P(Z > 1.39) = P(Z > 0) - P(0 < Z < 1.39) = .5 - .4177 = .0823$$

Note that $P(Z \geq 1.39) = P(Z > 1.39)$ and that $P(Z < 0) = P(Z \leq 0) = P(Z > 0) = P(Z \geq 0) = .5$.

b. An alternate approach is

$$P(Z > 1.39) = 1 - P(Z \leq 1.39) = 1 - [P(Z < 0) + P(0 \leq Z \leq 1.39)]$$
$$= 1 - (.5 + .4177) = 1 - .9177 = .0823$$

The result is depicted graphically in Figure 5.6.

PRACTICE EXERCISE

5.6 If Z is a random variable whose probability density function is the standard normal probability density function, find:

a. $P(0 < Z < 1)$ b. $P(-1 < Z < 0)$ c. $P(-1 < Z < 1)$
d. $P(Z > 1)$ e. $P(Z < -1)$ f. $P(Z < 1)$
g. $P(Z > -1)$

OTHER NORMAL PROBABILITY DENSITY FUNCTIONS

Normal probability density function models for real-world phenomena do not usually have a mean μ equal to 0 or a standard deviation σ equal to 1. The standard normal probability density function as a model is the exception rather than the rule. For this reason it is useful to show how any normal random variable X is transformed into a standardized normal random variable Z. We'll use the symbols μ and σ to identify the mean and standard deviation, respectively, of the distribution of the random variable X.

If X is a random variable whose values are normally distributed with the mean μ and the standard deviation σ, the probabilities associated with values of X are found by first converting values of X to corresponding values of Z, and then using the standard normal table as before. The conversion from values of X to corresponding values of Z is accomplished by using the following relationship:

Figure 5.6
Finding probabilities with the
standard normal probability
table (continued)

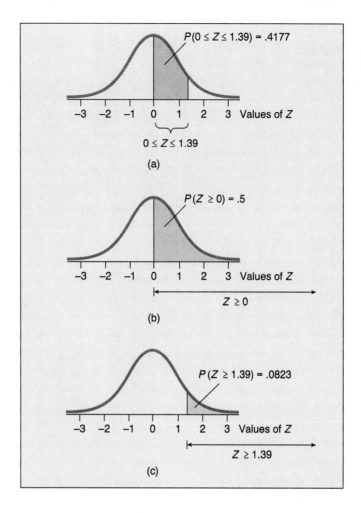

Standardizing a Normal Random Variable

$$Z = \frac{X - \mu}{\sigma} \qquad (5\text{-}11)$$

The examples below illustrate the procedure.

■ **EXAMPLE 5.14**

**Converting a Normal
Random Variable to
the Standard Normal
Random Variable**

If the random variable X is normally distributed with mean $\mu = 10$ and standard deviation $\sigma = 3$, evaluate $P(X < 7.6)$.

Solution

Step 1
With $\mu = 10$ and $\sigma = 3$, $X = 7.6$ translates to

$$Z = \frac{7.6 - 10}{3} = -.8$$

Step 2
We assert that $P(X < 7.6) = P(Z < -.8)$ and illustrate the equality in Figure 5.7.

Figure 5.7
Finding probabilities for a
normal random variable

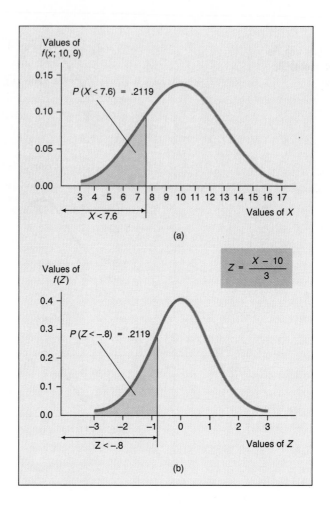

Step 3

Evaluate $P(Z < -.8)$: Since the standard normal curve is symmetric about $Z = 0$, we can assert that $P(Z < -.8) = P(Z > .8)$. Then

$$P(Z > .8) = P(Z > 0) - P(0 < Z < .8)$$

Since $P(Z > 0) = .5$ and $P(0 < Z < .8) = .2881$, according to Table IV, we have $P(Z > .8) = .5 - .2881 = .2119$. Also, $P(Z < -.8) = P(Z > .8) = .2119$.

Step 4

Therefore, $P(X < 7.6) = P(Z < -.8) = .2119$.

In the next example, the solution requires subdividing the interval into two parts, with a Z transformation for each part.

■ **EXAMPLE 5.15**

**Converting a Normal
Random Variable to
the Standard Normal
Random Variable,
Continued**

If the random variable X is normally distributed with mean $\mu = 10$ and standard deviation $\sigma = 3$, evaluate $P(7.6 < X < 10.3)$.

Solution

Step 1

Again, with $\mu = 10$ and $\sigma = 3$, $X = 7.6$ translates to

$$Z = \frac{7.6 - 10}{3} = -.8$$

Also, $X = 10.3$ translates to

$$Z = \frac{10.3 - 10}{3} = .1$$

Step 2
We assert that $P(7.6 < X < 10.3) = P(-.8 < Z < .1)$ and illustrate the equality in Figure 5.8.

Step 3
Evaluate $P(-.8 < Z < .1)$: First,

$$P(-.8 < Z < .1) = P(-.8 < Z < 0) + P(0 < Z < .1)$$

Since the standard normal curve is symmetric about $Z = 0$, we can assert that $P(-.8 < Z < 0) = P(0 < Z < .8)$. Then, according to Appendix Table IV, $P(0 < Z < .8) = .2881$ and $P(0 < Z < .1) = .0398$, and we have

$$P(-.8 < Z < .1) = .2881 + .0398 = .3279$$

Step 4
Therefore, $P(7.6 < X < 10.3) = P(-.8 < Z < .1) = .3279$.

Figure 5.8
Finding probabilities for a
normal random variable
(continued)

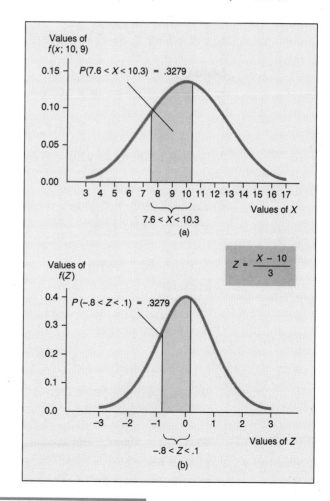

In the next example, calculations are made in the context of a business example in which probabilities are interpreted as relative frequencies.

■ **EXAMPLE 5.16**

Lifetimes of Light Bulbs

A certain type of light bulb manufactured by company A has a lifetime that is normally distributed with a mean of 1000 hr and a standard deviation of 50 hr. What proportion of bulbs of this type have lifetimes of:

a. More than 950 hr?   b. Less than 880 hr?   c. Between 950 and 1050 hr?

Discussion

Letting X represent the random variable, the problem can be restated in terms of X:

1. The random variable X represents the length of life of a randomly selected light bulb.
2. The random variable X is normally distributed with mean $\mu = 1000$ and standard deviation $\sigma = 50$.

We are asked to find:

a. $P(X > 950)$ b. $P(X < 880)$ c. $P(950 < X < 1050)$

Solution

a. With $\mu = 1000$ and $\sigma = 50$, $X = 950$ translates to

$$Z = \frac{950 - 1000}{50} = -1$$

We assert that $P(X > 950) = P(Z > -1)$; see Figure 5.9. Also,

$$P(Z > -1) = P(-1 < Z < 0) + P(Z > 0)$$

Since $P(Z > 0) = .5$ and $P(-1 < Z < 0) = P(0 < Z < 1) = .3413$, according to Table IV, we have

$$P(Z > -1) = .3413 + .5 = .8413$$

and $P(X > 950) = P(Z > -1) = .8413$. Therefore, approximately 84% of the bulbs have a lifetime of more than 950 hr.

b. To evaluate $P(Z < 880)$, we begin as usual. With $\mu = 1000$ and $\sigma = 50$, $X = 880$ translates to

$$Z = \frac{880 - 1000}{50} = -2.4$$

We can assert that $P(X < 880) = P(Z < -2.4)$; see Figure 5.10. Also,

$$P(Z < -2.4) = P(Z < 0) - P(-2.4 < Z < 0)$$

Since $P(Z < 0) = .5$ and $P(-2.4 < Z < 0) = P(0 < Z < 2.4) = .4918$, according to Table IV, we have

$$P(Z < -2.4) = .5 - .4918 = .0082$$

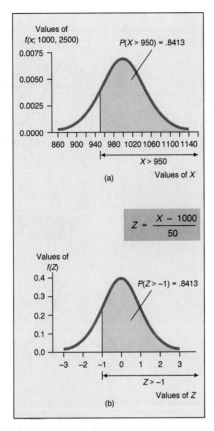

Figure 5.9
Finding probabilities for a
normal random variable
(continued)

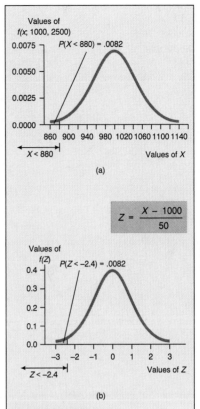

Figure 5.10
Finding probabilities for a
normal random variable
(continued)

and $P(X < 880) = P(Z < -2.4) = .0082$. Therefore, less than 1% (actually, 0.82%) of the bulbs have a lifetime less than 880 hr.

c. To evaluate $P(950 < X < 1050)$, we translate $X = 950$ to $Z = -1$ (see the solution to part a) and $X = 1050$ to

$$Z = \frac{1050 - 1000}{50} = 1$$

Therefore, $P(950 < X < 1050) = P(-1 < Z < 1)$; see Figure 5.11. Now,

$$P(-1 < Z < 1) = P(-1 < Z < 0) + P(0 < Z < 1)$$

And $P(-1 < Z < 0) = P(0 < Z < 1) = .3413$, according to Table IV, so that

$$P(-1 < Z < 1) = .3413 + .3413 = .6826$$

The result is $P(950 < X < 1050) = P(-1 < Z < 1) = .6826$. Therefore, approximately 68% of the bulbs have a lifetime between 950 and 1050 hr.

Figure 5.11
Finding probabilities for a
normal random variable
(continued)

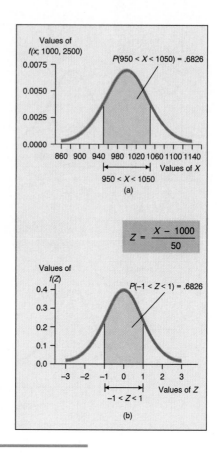

The next example also has a business context, but with an interesting twist. We are given the standard deviation of the distribution, but not the mean. Using Table IV, we will be able to find the mean of the distribution.

■ **EXAMPLE 5.17**

Videocassette Recorders: Finding the Mean Lifetime

Suppose we are told that 0.82% of the recording heads of videocassette recorders produced by a certain company will fail in less than 880 hr, and we are to assume that the lifetime distribution of these heads is normal with a standard deviation of 50 hr. What is the mean life of these heads (in hours)?

Discussion

Letting X represent the random variable, the problem can be stated in terms of X and then restated in terms of Z:

1. The random variable X represents the length of life of a randomly selected recording head.
2. The random variable X is normally distributed with an unknown mean μ and standard deviation $\sigma = 50$.
3. $P(X < 880) = .0082$

We are asked to find the value of μ.

Solution

We begin as before by translating $P(X < 880) = .0082$ to

$$P\left(Z < \frac{880 - \mu}{50}\right) = .0082$$

According to Table IV, $P(Z < -2.4) = .5 - .4918 = .0082$. Therefore,

$$\frac{880 - \mu}{50} = -2.4$$

Solving for μ, we find $\mu = 1000$ hr.

In the following example, the mean of the distribution is given, but not the standard deviation. However, if we use the formula provided in the problem in conjunction with Table IV, we will be able to find the standard deviation.

■ **EXAMPLE 5.18**

Annual Sick Leave: Finding the Standard Deviation

In a certain very large corporation, 84.13% of the employees take more than 13 hr of sick leave each year. If the number of hours of annual sick leave taken by the employees is normally distributed with a mean of 17.4 hr, what is the value of the standard deviation (in hours) of the distribution?

Discussion

Letting X represent the random variable, the problem can be stated in terms of X and then restated in terms of Z:

1. The random variable X represents the number of hours of annual sick leave taken by a randomly selected employee.
2. The random variable X is normally distributed with mean $\mu = 17.4$ and an unknown value for the standard deviation σ.
3. $P(X > 13) = .8413$

Solution

First, $P(X > 13) = .8413$ translates to

$$P\left(Z > \frac{13 - 17.4}{\sigma}\right) = .8413$$

According to Table IV, $P(Z > -1) = .5 + .3413 = .8413$. Therefore,

$$\frac{13 - 17.4}{\sigma} = -1$$

Solving for σ, we find $\sigma = 4.4$ hr.

PRACTICE EXERCISES

5.7 If the random variable X, representing an electrical measurement characteristic of a transistor, is normally distributed with mean $\mu = 10$ and standard deviation $\sigma = 3$, evaluate:
a. $P(10 < X < 13)$ b. $P(7 < X < 10)$ c. $P(7 < X < 13)$
d. $P(X > 13)$ e. $P(X < 7)$ f. $P(X < 13)$
g. $P(X > 7)$

5.8 If the random variable X, representing the weight (in pounds) of cartons transported by a certain carrier, is normally distributed with mean $\mu = 233$ and standard deviation $\sigma = 17$, evaluate:

a. $P(233 < X < 250)$ b. $P(216 < X < 233)$ c. $P(216 < X < 250)$
d. $P(X > 250)$ e. $P(X < 216)$ f. $P(X < 250)$
g. $P(X > 216)$

5.9 If the random variable X, representing the weight (in pounds) of cartons transported by a certain carrier, is normally distributed with mean $\mu = 233$ and standard deviation $\sigma = 17$, evaluate:

a. $P(233 < X < 267)$ b. $P(216 < X < 267)$
c. $P(250 < X < 267)$ d. $P(199 < X < 216)$

NORMAL DISTRIBUTION
APPROXIMATION TO THE BINOMIAL DISTRIBUTION

In Section 5.2, the Poisson distribution was discussed as an approximation to the binomial distribution when the number of trials, n, is very large and the probability of a "success," p, is small. But what happens when n is very large and p is not small? For example, suppose $n = 1000$ and $p = .39$. How difficult would it be to evaluate the following expression?

$$P(X = 231) = \frac{1000!}{231!769!}(.39)^{231}(.61)^{769}$$

In such situations, we use the normal distribution as an approximation to the binomial distribution. As a rule of thumb: *The normal distribution is a reasonable approximation to the binomial distribution when $np \geq 5$ and $n(1 - p) \geq 5$. Furthermore, for a given value of n, the approximation will be better the closer p is to .5.*

To use the normal distribution to approximate probabilities for the binomial random variable X, a transformation of the binomial random variable X to the standard normal random variable Z is required. The transformation is made using the following relationship:

Standard Normal Distribution
Approximation to the Binomial Distribution

$$Z = \frac{X - np}{\sqrt{np(1 - p)}} \qquad (5\text{-}12)$$

where np and $np(1 - p)$ represent the mean and variance, respectively, for the binomial distribution.

However, since X is a discrete random variable and Z is a continuous random variable, a **continuity correction factor** is needed. The examples below illustrate the procedure for using the normal distribution to obtain approximate probabilities for the binomial distribution.

In the first example, n is small enough that exact binomial probabilities can be obtained from Appendix Table II (the binomial probability table). Then the standard normal distribution approximation is made. A comparison of the exact and approximate probabilities reveals that even for values of n as small as 16, the normal distribution may give good approximations to the exact binomial probabilities.

■ **EXAMPLE 5.19**

Normal Distribution Approximation to the Binomial Distribution

A balanced coin is tossed 16 times. Let X represent the number of heads. A histogram representation for the distribution of X is given in Figure 5.12. The values for the probabilities were obtained from the binomial probability table (Table II) with $n = 16$ and $p = .5$.

Now we'll use the normal distribution to evaluate each of the following:

a. $P(X = 10)$ b. $P(X \geq 10)$ c. $P(X > 10)$
d. $P(6 < X \leq 10)$ e. $P(6 \leq X < 10)$

Solution

Since the discrete binomial distribution is going to be approximated by a normal curve, which is continuous, a continuity correction is needed. The continuity correction is accomplished by superimposing a normal curve, with $\mu = np = (16)(.5) = 8$ and $\sigma = \sqrt{np(1 - p)} = \sqrt{16(.5)(.5)} = 2$, over the histogram representing the binomial distribution with $n = 16$ and $p = .5$. This is done so that we can see which regions of the normal curve coincide with the specified regions of the binomial distribution.

a. In the histogram in Figure 5.13, the shaded area of the rectangle from $X = 9.5$ to $X = 10.5$ represents $P(X = 10)$; this is approximated by the area under the normal curve from $X = 9.5$ to $X = 10.5$. Thus, to find $P(X = 10)$ using the normal approximation we evaluate

$$P\left(\frac{9.5 - 8}{2} \leq Z \leq \frac{10.5 - 8}{2}\right) = P(.75 \leq Z \leq 1.25)$$

$$= .3944 - .2734 = .121$$

The approximation compares favorably with the value $.895 - .773 = .122$ obtained from the binomial probability table (Table II).

Figure 5.12
Histogram representation for the distribution of the random variable X having the binomial distribution with $n = 16$ and $p = .5$

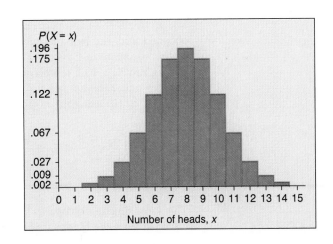

Figure 5.13
Comparing the normal
distribution with the binomial
distribution

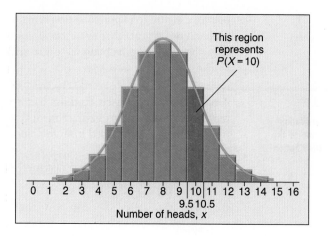

This region
represents
$P(X = 10)$

9.5 10.5
Number of heads, x

b. In the histogram in Figure 5.14a, the shaded area of the rectangles from
$X = 9.5$ to $X = 16.5$ represents $P(X \geq 10)$; this is approximated by the
area under the normal curve from $X = 9.5$ to $X = 16.5$. Thus, to find
$P(X \geq 10)$ using the normal approximation we evaluate

$$P\left(\frac{9.5 - 8}{2} \leq Z \leq \frac{16.5 - 8}{2}\right) = P(.75 \leq Z \leq 4.25)$$

$$= .5 - .2734 = .2266$$

The approximation compares favorably with the value $1 - .773 = .227$
obtained from the binomial probability table (Table II).

c. In the histogram in Figure 5.14b, the shaded area of the rectangles from
$X = 10.5$ to $X = 16.5$ represents $P(X > 10)$; this is approximated by the
area under the normal curve from $X = 10.5$ to $X = 16.5$. Thus, to find
$P(X > 10)$ using the normal approximation we evaluate

$$P\left(\frac{10.5 - 8}{2} \leq Z \leq \frac{16.5 - 8}{2}\right) = P(1.25 \leq Z \leq 4.25)$$

$$= .5 - .3944 = .1056$$

The approximation compares favorably with the value $1 - .895 = .105$
obtained from the binomial probability table (Table II).

d. In the histogram in Figure 5.15a, the shaded area of the rectangles from
$X = 6.5$ to $X = 10.5$ represents $P(6 < X \leq 10)$; this is approximated by
the area under the normal curve from $X = 6.5$ to $X = 10.5$. Thus, to find
$P(6 < X \leq 10)$ using the normal approximation we evaluate

$$P\left(\frac{6.5 - 8}{2} \leq Z \leq \frac{10.5 - 8}{2}\right) = P(-.75 \leq Z \leq 1.25)$$

$$= .2734 + .3944 = .6678$$

The approximation compares favorably with the value $.895 - .227 = .668$
obtained from the binomial probability table (Table II).

e. In the histogram in Figure 5.15b, the shaded area of the rectangles from $X = 5.5$ to $X = 9.5$ represents $P(6 \leq X < 10)$; this is approximated by the area under the normal curve from $X = 5.5$ to $X = 9.5$. Thus, to find $P(6 \leq X < 10)$ using the normal approximation we evaluate

$$P\left(\frac{5.5 - 8}{2} \leq Z \leq \frac{9.5 - 8}{2}\right) = P(-1.25 \leq Z \leq .75)$$
$$= .2734 + .3944 = .6678$$

The approximation compares favorably with the value $.773 - .105 = .668$ obtained from the binomial probability table (Table II).

The rationale underlying the use of the continuity correction is based on three points:

1. The probability of getting k successes in n independent trials may be represented by the area of a rectangle whose base boundary values are $k - \frac{1}{2}$ and $k + \frac{1}{2}$, and whose height is equal to the probability.
2. The area is approximated by computing the probability that a normal random variable with mean $\mu = np$ and standard deviation $\sigma = \sqrt{np(1 - p)}$ will assume values between the boundary values $k - \frac{1}{2}$ and $k + \frac{1}{2}$.

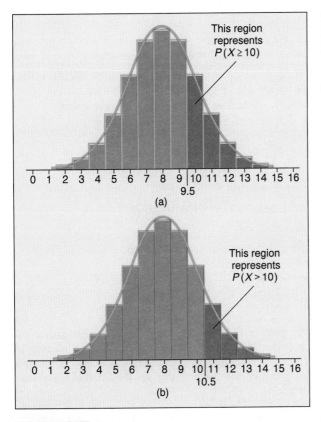

Figure 5.14
Comparing the normal distribution with the binomial distribution (continued)

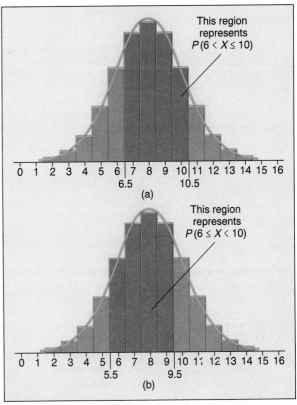

Figure 5.15
Comparing the normal distribution with the binomial distribution (continued)

3. In making the normal approximation, we adjust to the appropriate boundary values, depending on whether we wish to include or exclude the event {k successes}.

The final example of this section is a business application in which the value of n is too large for the binomial probability table (Table II) and the calculations are too complex to do by hand.

■ **EXAMPLE 5.20**

Luncheon Choice on an Airline Flight

A passenger airline offers all 160 passengers on a Chicago/San Diego flight a luncheon choice of boneless breast of chicken or sirloin tips of beef in burgundy sauce. Because the passengers don't select their meal until the flight is in progress, there is no way to be sure in advance how many will choose chicken and how many will choose beef. Yet, to avoid excess food waste and cost, the airline can't afford to carry many excess meals on the flight. A careful study of historical records reveals that:

1. 60% of the passengers have chosen beef when offered the choice between chicken and beef.
2. Passenger choices appeared to be independent, so that a binomial distribution is appropriate.

What is the probability that on this particular flight, the number of passengers choosing beef will be more than 110?

Solution

Let X represent the number of passengers who select beef. Then X has a binomial distribution with mean $\mu = np = (160)(.6) = 96$ and standard deviation $\sigma = \sqrt{np(1 - p)} = \sqrt{(160)(.6)(.4)} = 6.197$. We are asked to evaluate $P(X > 110)$. The normal distribution approximation to the binomial distribution can be used to evaluate this probability. (Note that $X > 110$ excludes the event {110 successes}.) The normal approximation is found from

$$P(X > 110) = P\left(Z \geq \frac{110.5 - 96}{6.197}\right) = P(Z \geq 2.34)$$

From Appendix Table IV, $P(Z \geq 2.34)$ is found to be

$$P(Z \geq 2.34) = .5 - .4904 = .0096$$

Thus, there is approximately only 1 chance in 100 (.0096 probability) that more than 110 passengers would choose the beef in burgundy sauce on that flight.

PRACTICE EXERCISE

5.10 Suppose that 40% of all family practice doctors in the United States have had to deal with malpractice suits. Also, suppose that 24 family practice doctors are randomly selected. Let X represent the number of family practice doctors in our sample who have had to deal with malpractice suits. Then X is a random variable that has the binomial distribution with $n = 24$ and $p = .40$. Find:
a. $P(X = 8)$ using Table II.
b. $P(X = 8)$ using the normal distribution approximation, and compare this result with the result obtained in part a.
c. $P(X \leq 8)$ using Table II.
d. $P(X \leq 8)$ using the normal distribution approximation, and compare this result with the result obtained in part c.

e. $P(X < 8)$ using Table II.

f. $P(X < 8)$ using the normal distribution approximation, and compare this result with the result obtained in part e.

EXERCISES

▶ **5.11** A well-known breakfast cereal claims to have 3 g of protein in 1 oz of cereal. Suppose the weight of protein per ounce of cereal is normally distributed with a mean of 3 g and a standard deviation of 0.13 g. What is the probability that in a randomly selected ounce of cereal the amount of protein will:

a. Exceed 2.779 g? b. Exceed 3.221 g?

c. Be between 2.779 g and 3.26 g? d. Be less than 3.182 g?

5.12 A young stockbroker claims to handle transactions amounting to $175,000 daily. Suppose the amount handled daily is normally distributed with a mean of $175,000 and a standard deviation of $30,000. What is the probability that on a randomly selected day the amount the stockbroker handles is:

a. Less than $160,000? b. Less than $224,500?

c. More than $238,300? d. Between $112,600 and $160,000?

5.13 Suppose that 10% of all companies listed on the New York Stock Exchange (NYSE) are ripe for a stock takeover. If you randomly select 121 companies listed on the NYSE, what is the approximate probability that:

a. 12 of the selected companies are ripe for a stock takeover?

b. 15 of the selected companies are ripe for a stock takeover?

c. From 7 to 11, inclusive, of the selected companies are ripe for a stock takeover?

d. From 9 to 13, inclusive, of the selected companies are ripe for a stock takeover?

e. Fewer than 10 of the selected companies are ripe for a stock takeover?

5.14 Suppose that 4% of all the passenger aircraft flown by the commercial airlines in the United States have suffered serious structural stress. If the Federal Aviation Administration (FAA) randomly inspects 144 passenger aircraft, what is the approximate probability that it will find:

a. More than 7 aircraft that have suffered serious structural stress?

b. Exactly 0 aircraft that have suffered serious structural stress?

c. More than 1 aircraft that have suffered serious structural stress?

d. Fewer than 5 aircraft that have suffered serious structural stress?

5.4

SAMPLE COMPUTER OUTPUT

Many problems involving probability distributions also can be solved on a computer using MINITAB or one of the other statistical software systems. For example, Figure 5.16 shows MINITAB output for the binomial distribution problem first encountered in Example 5.4, in which $n = 12$ and $p = .30$. The MINITAB command PDF, followed by the subcommand BINOMIAL, used with the values $n = 12$ and $p = .30$ gives the complete probability distribution.

Figure 5.17 shows MINITAB output for the Poisson distribution problem discussed in Example 5.6. Again, the MINITAB command PDF is used, this time followed by the subcommand POISSON, used with the value $\lambda = 2$.

Normal distribution probabilities also can be computed using the MINITAB system. For example, reconsider the problem in Example 5.16, which involves a normal distribution with a mean light bulb life of 1000 hr and a standard deviation of 50 hr. In part a of that example we found that $P(X > 950) = .8413$ for a lifetime of more than 950 hr. The MINITAB system can be used to check this answer; the output shown in

Figure 5.16
MINITAB output: binomial distribution

```
MTB > pdf;
SUBC> binomial n =12, p = .30

          BINOMIAL WITH N = 12   P = 0.300000
             K              P(X = K)
             0               0.0138
             1               0.0712
             2               0.1678
             3               0.2397
             4               0.2311
             5               0.1585
             6               0.0792
             7               0.0291
             8               0.0078
             9               0.0015
            10               0.0002
            11               0.0000
```

Figure 5.17
MINITAB output: Poisson distribution

```
     MTB > pdf;
     SUBC> poisson mean=2

     POISSON WITH MEAN = 2.000
   K        P(X = K)
   0         0.1353
   1         0.2707
   2         0.2707
   3         0.1804
   4         0.0902
   5         0.0361
   6         0.0120
   7         0.0034
   8         0.0009
   9         0.0002
  10         0.0000
```

Figure 5.18
MINITAB output: normal distribution

```
MTB > cdf 950;
SUBC> normal mu=1000,  sigma=50

 950.0000     0.1587
```

Figure 5.18 was obtained using the command CDF 950, followed by the subcommand NORMAL 1000, 50. The first value printed is 950, the value up to which the cumulative probability is being evaluated. The second value printed is the cumulative probability $P(X < 950) = .1587$. This value must be subtracted from 1.00 to find $P(X > 950) = 1 - .1587 = .8413$, exactly the answer we calculated in Example 5.16.

SUMMARY

Random variables provide a link between the descriptive sample spaces in Chapter 4 and events that are expressible as numerical values. Probabilities associated with the descriptive sample spaces are uniquely identified with probabilities associated with the corresponding numerical values. We discussed two kinds of probability distributions for numerical values: (1) discrete probability distributions, such as the binomial probability distribution, in which the probabilities are associated with specific numerical values; and (2) continuous random variables, such as the normal probability distribution, in which the nonzero probabilities are associated only with intervals. Random variables are important because we can now construct and examine models to describe the behavior of real-world phenomena. When a probability distribution model applies, we can use it to determine the probability that some realization will take place. For example, you can determine the chance that you can fake your way on a 20 question true–false test by flipping a fair coin to answer each question and guessing "true" if the coin comes up heads and "false" if it comes up tails. If you have to get at least 10 questions correct in order to pass the test, you can determine the probability that you will pass with your coin-flipping strategy by employing the binomial distribution as a model with $n = 20$ and $p = .5$. Your probability of passing would then be

$$\sum_{x=10}^{20} \frac{20!}{x!(20 - x)!} .5^x(1 - .5)^{20-x} = .5881$$

In other words, you would have almost a 59% chance of passing the true–false test simply by guessing. Does this surprise you? But if the model applies, the answer is correct!

What we'll be doing in subsequent chapters will be to examine some probability distribution models that frequently occur in the real world, and we shall use the models to make probabilistic inferences that some kinds of events will take place or could have taken place.

KEY EQUATIONS

Probability Postulates for Random Variables

The random variable counterpart to sample spaces is given by the following two postulates:

$$
\begin{array}{ll}
1.\ 0 \le P(X = x) \le 1 & \text{for all } x \\
2.\ \Sigma\, P(X = x) = 1 & \text{when summed over all } x
\end{array}
\tag{5-1}
$$

Expected Value of the Random Variable X

$$E(X) = \Sigma\, xP(X = x) \quad \text{summed over all values of } x \tag{5-2}$$

Mean

$$\mu = E(X) = \Sigma\, xP(X = x) \quad \text{summed over all } x \tag{5-3}$$

Variance

$$\sigma^2 = \Sigma\,(x - \mu)^2 P(X = x) \quad \text{summed over all } x \tag{5-4}$$

An alternative computational formula for the variance is given by

$$\sigma^2 = \Sigma\, x^2 P(X = x) - \mu^2 \quad \text{summed over all } x$$

Standard Deviation

$$\sigma = \sqrt{\sigma^2} \tag{5-5}$$

Binomial Distribution

$$P(X = x) = \frac{n!}{x!(n - x)!}\, p^x(1 - p)^{n-x} \quad \text{for } x = 0, 1, 2, \ldots, n \tag{5-6}$$

where n represents the number of independent two-valued "success" versus "failure" trials; p represents the probability of a "success"; and x represents the number of "successes" among the n trials.

Mean and Variance of the Binomial Distribution

$$\mu = np \tag{5-7}$$

$$\sigma^2 = np(1 - p)$$

Poisson Distribution Approximation to the Binomial Distribution

$$P(X = x) = \frac{(np)^x e^{-np}}{x!} \quad \text{for } x = 0, 1, 2, \ldots \tag{5-8}$$

where $e \approx 2.718281828459$; n represents the number of independent trials; p represents the probability of success on each trial; and x represents the number of successes. The mean and variance for this form of the Poisson distribution are, respectively,

$$\mu = E(X) = np \quad \sigma^2 = np$$

Poisson Distribution

$$P(X = x) = \frac{\lambda^x e^{-\lambda}}{x!} \quad \text{for } x = 0, 1, 2, \ldots \tag{5-9}$$

where λ is actually the average number of occurrences per unit of volume, time, area, or distance. The mean and variance for this form of the Poisson distribution are, respectively,

$$\mu = E(X) = \lambda \quad \text{Var}(X) = \sigma^2 = \lambda$$

Normal Probability Density Function

$$f(x; \mu, \sigma^2) = \frac{1}{\sqrt{2\pi}\sigma} e^{-(1/2)[(x-\mu)/\sigma]^2} \quad \text{for } -\infty < x < \infty \tag{5-10}$$

where $-\infty < \mu < \infty$, $\sigma > 0$, $e \approx 2.718281828459$, and $\pi \approx 3.1415926$.

Standardizing a Normal Random Variable

$$Z = \frac{X - \mu}{\sigma} \tag{5-11}$$

where X is a normal random variable with mean μ and standard deviation σ and Z is the standard normal random variable with mean equal to 0 and standard deviation equal to 1.

Standard Normal Distribution Approximation to the Binomial Distribution

$$Z = \frac{X - np}{\sqrt{np(1 - p)}} \tag{5-12}$$

where X represents the number of successes among n independent two-valued trials; p represents the probability of a success in each trial; Z is the standard normal random variable with mean equal to 0 and standard deviation equal to 1; and np and $np(1 - p)$ represent the mean and variance, respectively, for the binomial distribution.

PRACTICE EXERCISE ANSWERS

5.1 a. $\mu = E(X) = 1\left(\frac{1}{6}\right) + 2\left(\frac{1}{6}\right) + \cdots + 6\left(\frac{1}{6}\right) = 3.5$

b. $\sigma^2 = (1 - 3.5)^2\left(\frac{1}{6}\right) + (2 - 3.5)^2\left(\frac{1}{6}\right) + \cdots + (6 - 3.5)^2\left(\frac{1}{6}\right) = 2.9167$

5.2 a. $P(X = 5 \mid p = .49, n = 15) = \frac{n!}{x!(n - x)!} p^x(1 - p)^{n-x}$

$$= \frac{15!}{5!10!} (.49)^5(.51)^{10} = .10098$$

b. $P(X \le 5) = \sum_{x=0}^{5}\left[\frac{15!}{x!(15 - x)!} (.49)^x(.51)^{15-x}\right]$

$$= .00004 + .00059 + .00398 + .01657 + .04777 + .10098$$

$$= .16993$$

5.3 Using the cumulative binomial probability table, find the block of rows for which $n = 16$ and look down the column for $p = .7$.

a. $P(X \le 7) = .026$

b. $P(X \le 6) = .007$

c. $P(X = 7) = P(X \le 7) - P(X \le 6) = .026 - .007 = .019$

d. $P(X \ge 7) = 1 - P(X \le 6) = 1 - .007 = .993$

e. $P(X > 7) = 1 - P(X \le 7) = 1 - .026 = .974$

5.4 Using the theoretically correct (but computationally cumbersome) binomial distribution with $n = 1,000,000$ and $p = .0000015$:

a. $P(X = 2) = \dfrac{n!}{x!(n-x)!} p^x(1-p)^{n-x}$

$= \dfrac{1,000,000!}{2!\,999,998!} (.0000015)^2(1 - .0000015)^{999,998} = .2510$

An alternative is to use the Poisson distribution approximation to the binomial distribution with $n = 1,000,000$, $p = .0000015$, and use the Poisson probability table with $\lambda = np = 1.5$:

$$P(X = 2) = P(X \le 2) - P(X \le 1) = .8088 - .5578 = .2510$$

b. $P(X < 2) = P(X = 0) + P(X = 1) = .2231 + .3347 = .5578$

5.5 a. Use the Poisson distribution with $\lambda = 7$:

$$P(X = 3) = \frac{\lambda^x e^{-\lambda}}{x!} = \frac{7^3 e^{-7}}{3!} = .05213$$

b. If the time interval doubles, the mean number of occurrences will double. Use the Poisson distribution with $\lambda = 14$:

$$P(X = 3) = \frac{\lambda^x e^{-\lambda}}{x!} = \frac{14^3 e^{-14}}{3!} = .00038$$

5.6 a. $P(0 < Z < 1) = .3413$

b. $P(-1 < Z < 0) = .3413$

c. $P(-1 < Z < 1) = P(-1 < Z < 0) + P(0 < Z < 1) = .3413 + .3413 = .6826$

d. $P(Z > 1) = .5 - P(0 \le Z \le 1) = .5 - .3413 = .1587$

e. $P(Z < -1) = .5 - P(-1 \le Z \le 0) = .5 - .3413 = .1587$

f. $P(Z < 1) = .5 + P(0 < Z < 1) = .5 + .3413 = .8413$

g. $P(Z > -1) = .5 + P(-1 < Z < 0) = .5 + .3413 = .8413$

5.7 In each part below, the random variable X is transformed to a standard normal variable Z using the transformation

$$Z = \frac{X - \mu}{\sigma} \qquad \text{where } \mu = 10 \text{ and } \sigma = 3$$

a. $P(10 < X < 13) = P\left(\dfrac{10 - 10}{3} < \dfrac{X - \mu}{\sigma} < \dfrac{13 - 10}{3}\right)$

$= P(0 < Z < 1) = .3413$

b. $P(7 < X < 10) = P\left(\dfrac{7 - 10}{3} < \dfrac{X - \mu}{\sigma} < \dfrac{10 - 10}{3}\right)$

$= P(-1 < Z < 0) = .3413$

Similarly,

c. $P(7 < X < 13) = P(-1 < Z < 1) = .6826$

d. $P(X > 13) = P(Z > 1) = .5 - P(0 \le Z \le 1) = .5 - .3413 = .1587$

e. $P(X < 7) = P(Z < -1) = .5 - P(-1 \le Z \le 0) = .5 - .3413 = .1587$

f. $P(X < 13) = P(Z < 1) = .5 + P(0 < Z < 1) = .5 + .3413 = .8413$

g. $P(X > 7) = P(Z > -1) = .5 + P(-1 < Z < 0) = .5 + .3413 = .8413$

5.8 In each part below, the random variable X is transformed to a standard normal variable Z using the transformation

$$Z = \frac{X - \mu}{\sigma} \quad \text{where } \mu = 233 \text{ and } \sigma = 17$$

a. $P(233 < X < 250) = P\left(\frac{233 - 233}{17} < \frac{X - \mu}{\sigma} < \frac{250 - 233}{17}\right)$

$= P(0 < Z < 1) = .3413$

b. $P(216 < X < 233) = P\left(\frac{216 - 233}{17} < \frac{X - \mu}{\sigma} < \frac{233 - 233}{17}\right)$

$= P(-1 < Z < 0) = .3413$

Similarly,

c. $P(216 < X < 250) = P(-1 < Z < 1) = .6826$
d. $P(X > 250) = P(Z > 1) = .5 - P(0 \le Z \le 1) = .5 - .3413 = .1587$
e. $P(X < 216) = P(Z < -1) = .5 - P(-1 \le Z \le 0) = .5 - .3413 = .1587$
f. $P(X < 250) = P(Z < 1) = .5 + P(0 < Z < 1) = .5 + .3413 = .8413$
g. $P(X > 216) = P(Z > -1) = .5 + P(-1 < Z < 0) = .5 + .3413 = .8413$

5.9 In each part below, use the same standard normal transformation as in Practice Exercise 5.8.

a. $P(233 < X < 267) = P\left(\frac{233 - 233}{17} < \frac{X - \mu}{\sigma} < \frac{267 - 233}{17}\right)$

$= P(0 < Z < 2) = .4772$

b. $P(216 < X < 267) = P\left(\frac{216 - 233}{17} < \frac{X - \mu}{\sigma} < \frac{267 - 233}{17}\right)$

$= P(-1 < Z < 2)$

$= P(-1 < Z \le 0) + P(0 \le Z < 2)$

$= .3413 + .4772 = .8185$

Similarly,

c. $P(250 < X < 267) = P(1 < Z < 2) = P(0 < Z < 2) - P(0 \le Z \le 1)$
$= .4772 - .3413 = .1359$
d. $P(199 < X < 216) = P(-2 < Z < -1)$
$= P(-2 < Z < 0) - P(-1 \le Z \le 0)$
$= .4772 - .3413 = .1359$

5.10 a. $P(X = 8) = P(X \le 8) - P(X \le 7) = .328 - .192 = .136$
b. An approximation can be made by considering a normally distributed variable X with mean $\mu = np = 9.6$ and standard deviation $\sigma = \sqrt{np(1 - p)} = \sqrt{24(.4)(.6)} = 2.4$. Approximate $P(X = 8)$ by evaluating

$$P(7.5 < X < 8.5) = P\left(\frac{7.5 - 9.6}{2.4} < Z < \frac{8.5 - 9.6}{2.4}\right)$$

$$= P(-.875 < Z < .458)$$

$$= P(-.88 < Z < -.46) \text{ (approx.)}$$

$$= P(-.88 < Z < 0) - P(-.46 < Z < 0)$$

$$= .3106 - .1772 = .1334 \text{ (approx.)}$$

c. $P(X \le 8) = .328$
d. As in part b, approximate $P(X \le 8)$ by evaluating

$$P(X < 8.5) = P\left(Z < \frac{8.5 - 9.6}{2.4}\right)$$

$$= P(Z < -.458)$$
$$= P(Z < -.46) \text{ (approx.)}$$
$$= .5 - P(-.46 \le Z \le 0)$$
$$= .5 - .1772 = .3228 \text{ (approx.)}$$

e. $P(X < 8) = P(X \le 7) = .192$

f. As in part b, approximate $P(X < 8)$ by evaluating

$$P(X < 7.5) = P\left(Z < \frac{7.5 - 9.6}{2.4}\right)$$
$$= P(Z < -.875)$$
$$= P(Z < -.88) \text{ (approx.)}$$
$$= .5 - P(-.88 \le Z \le 0)$$
$$= .5 - .3106 = .1894 \text{ (approx.)}$$

CHAPTER REVIEW EXERCISES

5.15 Suppose we have a sample space

$$S = \{(a, a, a), (a, a, b), (a, b, a), (a, b, b), (b, b, b)\}$$

with equally likely possible outcomes. Let the random variable X represent the number of a's in the possible outcome. Find:

a. The probability distribution of X b. $E(X)$ c. σ^2

5.16 Suppose we have a sample space

$$S = \{(a, a, a), (a, a, b), (a, b, a), (a, b, b), (b, b, b)\}$$

where the possible outcomes (a, a, a) and (a, a, b) are each associated with a probability of .1, the possible outcome (a, b, a) is associated with a probability of .4, and the possible outcomes (a, b, b) and (b, b, b) are each associated with a probability of .2. Let the random variable X represent the number of a's in the outcome. Find:

a. The probability distribution of X b. $E(X)$ c. σ^2

▶ **5.17** Suppose we have a sample space

$$S = \{(1, 2, 3), (3, 2, 1), (1, 3, 1), (2, 4, 6), (4, 6, 2), (1, 2, 4), (3, 4, 5), (1, 3, 5)\}$$

with equally likely possible outcomes. Let the random variable X represent the sum of the values in each possible outcome. Find:

a. The probability distribution of X b. $E(X)$ c. σ^2

5.18 Suppose we have a sample space

$$S = \{(1, 2, 3), (3, 2, 1), (1, 3, 1), (2, 4, 6), (4, 6, 2), (1, 2, 4), (3, 4, 5), (1, 3, 5)\}$$

where the possible outcome $(1, 2, 3)$ is associated with a probability of .125; the possible outcomes $(3, 2, 1)$, $(1, 3, 1)$, $(2, 4, 6)$, and $(4, 6, 2)$ are each associated with a probability of .0625; the possible outcomes $(1, 2, 4)$ and $(3, 4, 5)$ are each associated with a probability of .25; and the possible outcome $(1, 3, 5)$ is associated with a probability of .125. Let the random variable X represent the sum of the values in each possible outcome. Find:

a. The probability distribution of X b. $E(X)$ c. σ^2

5.19 Suppose a cage contains 8 mice, each with an identification tag numbered 1–8. A laboratory assistant randomly selects 2 mice. Let the random variable X represent the sum of the numbers on the identification tags of the 2 selected mice. Find the probability distribution of X.

5.20 A class of 20 students has 5 students of age 21, 4 students of age 20, 8 students of age 19, and 3 students of age 18. Suppose we randomly select 1 student from this class, and let the random variable X represent the age of the chosen student. Find:
a. The probability distribution of the random variable
b. The expected value of the random variable
c. The standard deviation of the distribution of the random variable

▶ **5.21** Five candidates apply for two positions with a certain company. The respective ages of the given candidates are 27, 31, 43, 52, and 36. Suppose the candidates are considered equally qualified and equally desirable, and two are then randomly selected for the two positions. Let the random variable X represent the sum of the ages of the two persons hired, and find:
a. The probability distribution of the random variable
b. The expected value of the random variable
c. The standard deviation of the random variable

5.22 An insurance company makes the following assessment of the chance of fire damage during the next year for a certain house:

DAMAGE	$50,000	$30,000	$10,000	$0
PROBABILITY	.0001	.001	.05	?

What premium should the company charge in order to expect a profit of $50? [Hint: Let the random variable X represent the cost of the damage. Then determine the value for $P(X = 0)$ and find $E(X)$.]

▶ **5.23** A personnel manager is asked to provide information concerning the amount of excess time certain employees take for lunch. After studying all their records, the personnel manager set up the following table (excess time is in minutes):

EXCESS TIME	0	1	2	3	4	5	6	7
PROBABILITY	.0025	.0149	.0446	?	.1339	.1606	.1606	.3937

a. Determine the probability that excess time is equal to 3 minutes.
b. Find the average excess time taken by these employees.
c. Find the standard deviation for this distribution.
d. According to Chebyshev's theorem, about how much excess lunch time should we expect these employees to take at least 75% of the time?

5.24 A student is totally unprepared for a 10 question multiple choice test, with 5 choices per question. She decides to answer each question by tossing a fair five-sided die, and she will mark "a" if the upface shows 1 dot, "b" if the upface shows 2 dots, and so on. What is the probability she will get exactly:
a. No correct answers?   b. 1 correct answer?   c. 2 correct answers?
d. 3 correct answers?   e. 6 correct answers?
f. Give a general expression for the probability distribution of the random variable in this case.

▶ **5.25** In a certain neighborhood there are 210 registered voters, 42 of whom are registered Democrats. Fifteen different surveyors go through the neighborhood, independent of each other, and each randomly selects 1 registered voter. What is the probability that among the 15 surveys exactly:
a. No Democrats are selected?   b. 1 Democrat is selected?
c. 7 Democrats are selected?   d. 12 Democrats are selected?

e. Give a general expression for the probability distribution of the random variable in this case.

f. Find the mean and standard deviation of the distribution.

g. Use Chebyshev's theorem to determine approximately how many Democrats should be included in the 15 surveys at least 50% of the time.

5.26 Suppose $n = 5$ and $p = .20$. Use the binomial probability table to find:
  a. $P(X = 0)$ b. $P(X = 1)$ c. $P(X \leq 1)$ d. $P(X < 1)$
  e. $P(X \geq 0)$ f. $P(X > 0)$ g. $P(X > 1)$ h. $P(X \geq 1)$

5.27 Suppose $n = 7$ and $p = .20$. Use the binomial probability table to find:
  a. $P(X = 0)$ b. $P(X = 1)$ c. $P(X \leq 1)$ d. $P(X < 1)$
  e. $P(X \geq 0)$ f. $P(X > 0)$ g. $P(X > 1)$ h. $P(X \geq 1)$

5.28 Suppose $n = 10$ and $p = .90$. Use the binomial probability table to find:
  a. $P(X = 5)$ b. $P(X \leq 5)$ c. $P(X \geq 5)$ d. $P(X > 5)$
  e. $P(X = 9)$ f. $P(X \leq 9)$ g. $P(X < 9)$ h. $P(X \geq 9)$
  i. $P(X > 9)$

5.29 Suppose $n = 11$ and $p = .60$. Use the binomial probability table to find:
  a. $P(X = 5)$ b. $P(X \leq 5)$ c. $P(X \geq 5)$ d. $P(X > 5)$
  e. $P(X = 9)$ f. $P(X \leq 9)$ g. $P(X < 9)$ h. $P(X \geq 9)$
  i. $P(X > 9)$ j. $P(X = 10)$ k. $P(X \leq 10)$ l. $P(X < 10)$
  m. $P(X \geq 10)$ n. $P(X > 10)$

5.30 Suppose $n = 19$ and $p = .95$. Use the binomial probability table to find:
  a. $P(X \leq 18)$ b. $P(X = 18)$ c. $P(X \leq 19)$
  d. $P(X < 19)$ e. $P(X = 19)$ f. $P(16 \leq X \leq 18)$
  g. $P(16 < X \leq 18)$ h. $P(16 \leq X < 18)$ i. $P(16 < X < 18)$
  j. $P(16 < X < 19)$

5.31 Suppose that 20% of the items produced by a certain process are rated as being of excellent quality. If 11 items are randomly selected from a very large output, what is the probability that the sample will contain:
  a. No items of excellent quality?
  b. Exactly 1 item of excellent quality?
  c. Exactly 6 items of excellent quality?
  d. Exactly 9 items of excellent quality?
  e. At least 2 items of excellent quality?
  f. At most 2 items of excellent quality?
  g. Less than 2 items of excellent quality?
  h. More than 2 items of excellent quality?
  i. At most 7 items of excellent quality?
  j. Give a general expression for the probability distribution of the random variable in this case.
  k. Find the mean and standard deviation of the distribution.

5.32 Historically, 95% of the applicants at a university pass a physical exam upon entering the university. In a group of 14 new applicants, what is the probability that:
  a. Exactly none fail the physical exam?
  b. Exactly 1 fails the physical exam?
  c. Exactly 6 fail the physical exam?
  d. Exactly 11 fail the physical exam?
  e. At most 3 fail the physical exam?
  f. At least 2 fail the physical exam?
  g. Give a general expression for the probability distribution of the random variable in this case.
  h. Find the mean and variance of the distribution.

5.33 Suppose that 10% of those passing through U.S. Customs are in violation of a federal statute. If 207 passengers from an overseas plane pass through Customs, what is the probability that:

a. Exactly none are in violation of a federal statute?

b. Exactly 100 are in violation of a federal statute?

c. At least 150 are in violation of a federal statute?

d. At most 87 are in violation of a federal statute?

e. Less than 120 are in violation of a federal statute?

f. More than 170 are in violation of a federal statute?

g. Give a general expression for the probability distribution of the random variable in this case.

h. Find the mean and variance of the distribution.

i. Use Chebyshev's theorem to determine approximately how many of the passengers should be in violation of a federal statute at least 60% of the time.

▶ **5.34** In the manufacture of commercial semiconductor devices (used in almost all types of electronic appliances, such as microwave ovens, computers, automobile ignition systems, intruder warning devices, stereos, videorecorders, and so on), an objective is to have a reliability of at least .999. That is, an objective is to have a probability of at most .001 (0.1%) that a semiconductor will be defective. If a manufacturer succeeds in producing only 0.1% defective semiconductors, what is the probability that the company will ship exactly 11 defective semiconductors among a group of 10,000 semiconductors?

a. Solve the problem using the binomial distribution.

b. Solve the problem using the Poisson distribution.

c. Obtain numerical values for the solutions in parts a and b.

d. Compare the two numerical solutions in part c. How close are they? What can you say about the Poisson distribution approximation to the binomial distribution?

5.35 The probability is .002 that a person will be a carrier of a certain disease. In a city of 550,000 persons, what is the probability that there are:

a. Exactly 1000 carriers?   b. At least 1000 carriers?

c. Fewer than 1200 carriers?

d. Find the mean and variance for this distribution.

5.36 The probability is .007 that a home in a certain city has been burglarized. In a random sample of 500 homes, what is the probability that:

a. Exactly 1 of the homes has been burglarized?

b. Exactly 2 of the homes have been burglarized?

c. At least 2 of the homes have been burglarized?

d. Fewer than 2 of the homes have been burglarized?

e. Find the mean and variance for this distribution.

▶ **5.37** At a certain gas station, automobile arrivals at a pump have a Poisson distribution with an average arrival frequency of 3.8 automobiles per 20 minute period. What is the probability that during a 20 minute period:

a. 2 automobiles arrive at the pump?

b. 4 automobiles arrive at the pump?

c. More than 3 automobiles arrive at the pump?

d. Give a general expression for the probability distribution of the random variable in this case.

5.38 At a certain savings and loan institution, customer arrivals have a Poisson distribution with an average arrival frequency of 1.3 customers per 5 minute period. What is the probability that during a 5 minute period:

a. No customers arrive at the savings and loan?

b. 3 customers arrive at the savings and loan?

c. 6 customers arrive at the savings and loan?

d. Give a general expression for the probability distribution of the random variable in this case.

5.39 With respect to Exercise 5.37, what is the probability that during a 10 minute period:

a. 2 automobiles arrive at the pump?

b. 4 automobiles arrive at the pump?

c. More than 3 automobiles arrive at the pump?

d. Give a general expression for the probability distribution of the random variable in this case.

5.40 With respect to Exercise 5.38, what is the probability that during a 10 minute period:

a. No customers arrive at the savings and loan?

b. 3 customers arrive at the savings and loan?

c. 6 customers arrive at the savings and loan?

d. Give a general expression for the probability distribution of the random variable in this case.

5.41 Suppose $n = 1000$ and $p = .0002$. Use the Poisson probability table to find:

a. $P(X = 0)$ b. $P(X < 1)$ c. $P(X \leq 1)$ d. $P(X > 1)$

e. $P(X \geq 1)$ f. $P(X = 4)$ g. $P(X < 4)$ h. $P(X \leq 4)$

i. $P(X > 4)$ j. $P(X \geq 4)$

5.42 Suppose $n = 1000$ and $p = .0007$. Use the Poisson probability table to find:

a. $P(X = 0)$ b. $P(X < 1)$ c. $P(X \leq 1)$ d. $P(X > 1)$

e. $P(X \geq 1)$ f. $P(X = 4)$ g. $P(X < 4)$ h. $P(X \leq 4)$

i. $P(X > 4)$ j. $P(X \geq 4)$

5.43 If the random variable X has a Poisson distribution with mean equal to 3.3, use the Poisson probability table to find:

a. $P(X = 4)$ b. $P(X \leq 4)$ c. $P(X < 4)$

d. $P(X > 4)$ e. $P(X \geq 4)$ f. $P(4 \leq X \leq 7)$

g. $P(4 < X \leq 7)$ h. $P(4 \leq X < 7)$ i. $P(4 < X < 7)$

5.44 If the random variable X has a Poisson distribution with mean equal to 7.1, use the Poisson probability table to find:

a. $P(X = 0)$ b. $P(X = 1)$ c. $P(X \leq 1)$

d. $P(X > 4)$ e. $P(X \geq 4)$ f. $P(X = 11)$

g. $P(4 \leq X \leq 7)$ h. $P(4 < X \leq 7)$ i. $P(4 \leq X < 7)$

j. $P(4 < X < 7)$ k. $P(5 < X < 16)$ l. $P(5 \leq X \leq 13)$

5.45 If Z is a standard normal random variable, evaluate:

a. $P(0 < Z < 1.55)$ b. $P(-1.55 < Z < 0)$ c. $P(0 < Z < 2.55)$

d. $P(-2.55 < Z < 0)$ e. $P(0 < Z < 3.55)$ f. $P(-3.55 < Z < 0)$

g. $P(0 < Z < .55)$ h. $P(-.55 < Z < 0)$ i. $P(0 < Z < 1.12)$

j. $P(-1.71 < Z < 0)$ k. $P(0 < Z < 3.08)$ l. $P(-2.47 < Z < 0)$

m. $P(0 < Z < 1.96)$ n. $P(-2.33 < Z < 0)$ o. $P(0 < Z < 1.65)$

p. $P(-2.57 < Z < 0)$

▶ **5.46** If Z is a standard normal random variable, evaluate:

a. $P(-1.55 < Z < 1.55)$ b. $P(-2.55 < Z < 2.55)$

c. $P(-3.55 < Z < 3.55)$ d. $P(-.55 < Z < .55)$

e. $P(-1.12 < Z < 1.12)$ f. $P(-1.71 < Z < 1.71)$

g. $P(-3.08 < Z < 3.08)$ h. $P(-2.47 < Z < 2.47)$

i. $P(-1.96 < Z < 1.96)$ j. $P(-2.33 < Z < 2.33)$

k. $P(-1.65 < Z < 1.65)$ l. $P(-2.57 < Z < 2.57)$

5.47 If Z is a standard normal random variable, evaluate:

a. $P(-1.46 < Z < -.32)$ b. $P(-1.96 < Z < -.19)$

   c. $P(.19 < Z < 1.46)$ d. $P(.19 < Z < .32)$
   e. $P(-2.77 < Z < -1.96)$ f. $P(1.96 < Z < 2.77)$
   g. $P(.59 < Z < 2.81)$ h. $P(-2.81 < Z < -.59)$
   i. $P(2.22 < Z < 3.08)$ j. $P(-3.08 < Z < -2.22)$
   k. $P(1.65 < Z < 2.93)$ l. $P(-2.89 < Z < -.76)$

5.48 If Z is a standard normal random variable, evaluate:

   a. $P(Z < 1.96)$ b. $P(Z < 1.65)$ c. $P(Z < 2.57)$
   d. $P(Z < 2.33)$ e. $P(Z < 3.08)$ f. $P(Z < 2.77)$
   g. $P(Z < .19)$ h. $P(Z < .32)$ i. $P(Z < 1.46)$
   j. $P(Z < 2.22)$ k. $P(Z > 1.96)$ l. $P(Z > 1.65)$
   m. $P(Z > 2.57)$ n. $P(Z > 2.33)$ o. $P(Z > 3.08)$
   p. $P(Z > 2.77)$ q. $P(Z > .19)$ r. $P(Z > .32)$
   s. $P(Z > 1.46)$ t. $P(Z > 2.22)$

5.49 If Z is a standard normal random variable, evaluate:

   a. $P(Z < -1.96)$ b. $P(Z < -1.65)$ c. $P(Z < -2.57)$
   d. $P(Z < -2.33)$ e. $P(Z < -3.08)$ f. $P(Z < -2.77)$
   g. $P(Z < -.19)$ h. $P(Z < -.32)$ i. $P(Z < -1.46)$
   j. $P(Z < -2.22)$ k. $P(Z > -1.96)$ l. $P(Z > -1.65)$
   m. $P(Z > -2.57)$ n. $P(Z > -2.33)$ o. $P(Z > -3.08)$
   p. $P(Z > -2.77)$ q. $P(Z > -.19)$ r. $P(Z > -.32)$
   s. $P(Z > -1.46)$ t. $P(Z > -2.22)$

5.50 If Z is a standard normal random variable, find the value a such that:

   a. $P(0 < Z < a) = .4750$ b. $P(0 < Z < a) = .4901$
   c. $P(0 < Z < a) = .4505$ d. $P(0 < Z < a) = .4949$
   e. $P(a < Z < 0) = .4750$ f. $P(a < Z < 0) = .4901$
   g. $P(a < Z < 0) = .4505$ h. $P(a < Z < 0) = .4949$

▶ **5.51** If Z is a standard normal random variable, find the value a such that:

   a. $P(Z < a) = .9750$ b. $P(Z < a) = .9901$
   c. $P(Z < a) = .9505$ d. $P(Z < a) = .9949$
   e. $P(Z > a) = .9750$ f. $P(Z > a) = .9901$
   g. $P(Z > a) = .9505$ h. $P(Z > a) = .9949$

5.52 If Z is a standard normal random variable, find the value a such that:

   a. $P(Z > a) = .0250$ b. $P(Z > a) = .0099$
   c. $P(Z > a) = .0495$ d. $P(Z > a) = .0051$
   e. $P(Z < a) = .0250$ f. $P(Z < a) = .0099$
   g. $P(Z < a) = .0495$ h. $P(Z < a) = .0051$

5.53 If Z is a standard normal random variable, find the value a such that:

   a. $P(-a < Z < a) = .95$ b. $P(-a < Z < a) = .9802$
   c. $P(-a < Z < a) = .901$ d. $P(-a < Z < a) = .9898$
   e. $P(-a < Z < a) = .8836$ f. $P(-a < Z < a) = .9606$

5.54 If the random variable X is normally distributed with mean $\mu = 10$ and standard deviation $\sigma = 3$, evaluate:

   a. $P(10 < X < 14.65)$ b. $P(5.35 < X < 10)$
   c. $P(10 < X < 17.65)$ d. $P(2.35 < X < 10)$
   e. $P(10 < X < 15.88)$ f. $P(4.12 < X < 10)$

5.55 If the random variable X is normally distributed with mean $\mu = 10$ and standard deviation $\sigma = 3$, evaluate:

   a. $P(5.35 < X < 14.65)$ b. $P(2.35 < X < 17.65)$
   c. $P(4.12 < X < 15.88)$ d. $P(5.05 < X < 14.95)$
   e. $P(3.01 < X < 16.99)$ f. $P(2.29 < X < 17.71)$

▶ **5.56** If the random variable X is normally distributed with mean $\mu = 10$ and standard deviation $\sigma = 3$, evaluate:
   a. $P(14.65 < X < 17.65)$ b. $P(14.65 < X < 15.88)$
   c. $P(15.88 < X < 17.71)$ d. $P(14.95 < X < 16.99)$
   e. $P(15.13 < X < 19.33)$ f. $P(2.29 < X < 5.05)$

5.57 If the random variable X is normally distributed with mean $\mu = 10$ and standard deviation $\sigma = 3$, evaluate:
   a. $P(2.35 < X < 5.05)$ b. $P(2.29 < X < 4.12)$
   c. $P(3.01 < X < 5.35)$ d. $P(2.35 < X < 4.87)$
   e. $P(4.87 < X < 7.39)$ f. $P(2.29 < X < 7.39)$

5.58 If the random variable X is normally distributed with mean $\mu = 10$ and standard deviation $\sigma = 3$, evaluate:
   a. $P(X < 14.65)$ b. $P(X > 17.65)$ c. $P(X < 15.88)$
   d. $P(X > 19.33)$ e. $P(X > 7.39)$ f. $P(X < 2.29)$
   g. $P(X > 4.87)$ h. $P(X < 4.12)$

5.59 If the random variable X is normally distributed with mean $\mu = 10$ and standard deviation $\sigma = 3$, evaluate:
   a. $P(X > 14.65)$ b. $P(X < 17.65)$ c. $P(X > 15.88)$
   d. $P(X < 19.33)$ e. $P(X < 7.39)$ f. $P(X > 2.29)$
   g. $P(X < 4.87)$ h. $P(X > 4.12)$

▶ **5.60** If the random variable X is normally distributed with mean $\mu = 10$ and standard deviation $\sigma = 3$, find the value a such that:
   a. $P(X < a) = .9750$ b. $P(X < a) = .9901$
   c. $P(X < a) = .9505$ d. $P(X < a) = .9949$
   e. $P(X > a) = .8438$ f. $P(X > a) = .9750$
   g. $P(X > a) = .9505$ h. $P(X > a) = .9901$

5.61 If the random variable X is normally distributed with mean $\mu = 10$ and standard deviation $\sigma = 3$, find the value a such that:
   a. $P(X < a) = .0250$ b. $P(X < a) = .0099$
   c. $P(X < a) = .0495$ d. $P(X < a) = .0051$
   e. $P(X > a) = .1562$ f. $P(X > a) = .0250$
   g. $P(X > a) = .0495$ h. $P(X > a) = .0099$

5.62 A well-known brand of size D batteries has a lifetime that is normally distributed with a mean of 105 hr and a standard deviation of 20 hr.
   a. What proportion of the batteries have a lifetime of less than 95 hr?
   b. If a person buys 1 battery of this type, what would be the probability that its lifetime would be between 70 and 90 hr?
   c. Find a value a such that 89.97% of the batteries of this type will have a lifetime of more than a hours.

5.63 Suppose that the lengths of steel beams produced by a certain company are normally distributed with a mean of 99 in. and a standard deviation of 5 in.
   a. What proportion of the beams produced by this company have a length greater than 84 in.?
   b. What is the probability that a beam randomly selected from the output of this company will have a length between 96.8 and 106.8 in.?
   c. Find the length a such that 95.05% of the beams are greater than a.

5.64 The average annual rainfall in a certain region is normally distributed with a mean of 31.3 in. and a standard deviation of 7.2 in.
   a. In any given year, what is the probability that the amount of rain will exceed 24.82 in.?

b. In any given year, what is the probability that the amount of rain will be between 31.3 and 51.172 in.?

c. Find a value *a* such that the probability is .0495 that the amount of rain in any given year will exceed *a* inches.

▶ **5.65** Suppose a consumer agency provides the following information in comparing two brands of automobile batteries: brand A has an average life expectancy of 44.1 months, with a standard deviation of 6.7 months; brand B has an average life expectancy of 53.9 months, with a standard deviation of 14.5 months. Assuming the life expectancies for the two brands of batteries are normally distributed, which of the two brands would provide fewer batteries with a life expectancy of less than 30.7 months?

5.66 Suppose X is a normally distributed random variable with mean $\mu = 19$. Find the value of the standard deviation of the distribution if 6.06% of the area under the curve lies to the left of 14.35.

5.67 Suppose X is a normally distributed random variable with variance $\sigma^2 = 81$. Find the value of the mean of the distribution if 13.35% of the area under the curve lies to the right of 89.99.

5.68 Suppose X is a normally distributed random variable with mean $\mu = 24$. If 0.62% of the area under the curve lies to the left of 14, find the area to the right of 34.

5.69 Suppose X is a normally distributed random variable with variance $\sigma^2 = 25$. If 2.5% of the area under the curve lies to the right of 100, find the area to the right of 79.7.

5.70 A balanced coin is tossed 14 times, and we let X represent the number of heads. In each of the following use the binomial probability table to find the exact probability. Then use the normal approximation to the binomial distribution to find the approximate probability, and compare the two answers.

a. $P(X = 10)$ b. $P(X \leq 10)$ c. $P(X < 10)$
d. $P(X \geq 10)$ e. $P(X > 10)$ f. $P(6 \leq X \leq 10)$
g. $P(6 < X \leq 10)$ h. $P(6 \leq X < 10)$ i. $P(6 < X < 10)$

▶ **5.71** Suppose that 20% of the output of a certain machine is rated as being of inferior quality. If we randomly select 90 items from the output of the machine, what is the approximate probability that we will get:

a. Either 17, 18, or 19 items in the sample that are of inferior quality?
b. At most 19 items in the sample that are of inferior quality?
c. At least 19 items in the sample that are of inferior quality?

5.72 Suppose that 95% of the calculators produced by a certain manufacturer will have fewer than 3 malfunctions in 10,000,000 calculations. If we randomly select 36 of these machines, what is the approximate probability that:

a. More than 2 of these machines will have fewer than 3 malfunctions in 10,000,000?
b. Exactly 7 of these machines will have fewer than 3 malfunctions in 10,000,000?
c. Exactly 33 of these machines will have fewer than 3 malfunctions in 10,000,000?
d. More than 26 of these machines will have fewer than 3 malfunctions in 10,000,000?
e. Less than 20 of these machines will have fewer than 3 malfunctions in 10,000,000?
f. At most 29 of these machines will have fewer than 3 malfunctions in 10,000,000?
g. At least 30 of these machines will have fewer than 3 malfunctions in 10,000,000?

5.73 If 49% of the automobiles in a certain state have defective mufflers and if the state highway patrol randomly stops 90 motorists to check for safety violations, what is the approximate probability that:

a. More than 40 but less than 43 of the automobiles will have defective mufflers?

b. More than 43 of the sampled automobiles will have defective mufflers?

c. Exactly 50 will have defective mufflers?

d. At least 45 will have defective mufflers?

e. The proportion of the automobiles in the sample with defective mufflers will exceed .40?

f. The proportion of the automobiles in the sample with defective mufflers will be anywhere from .1 to .6, inclusive?

5.74 Suppose that 15% of all manuscripts submitted to publishers are deemed worthy of publication. If we randomly select 80 manuscripts, what is the probability that:

a. At least 15 of them will be deemed worthy of publication?

b. At most 12 will be deemed worthy of publication?

c. Between 10 and 15, inclusive, will be deemed worthy of publication?

d. Exactly 13 will be deemed worthy of publication?

e. More than 11 will be deemed worthy of publication?

f. The proportion of the 80 manuscripts deemed worthy of publication will be between .15 and .20, inclusive?

g. The proportion of the 80 manuscripts deemed worthy of publication will not exceed .10?

5.75 If 65% of the people who drive automobiles are required to wear corrective lenses, what is the approximate probability that in a random sample of 100 motorists:

a. Between 59 and 67, inclusive, of those sampled will wear corrective lenses?

b. Exactly 60 of those sampled will wear corrective lenses?

c. Less than 63 of those sampled will wear corrective lenses?

d. At most 58 of those sampled will wear corrective lenses?

▶ **5.76** Twenty percent of the parts produced by a machine are defective. If a random sample of 144 parts produced by this machine is taken, what is the approximate probability that:

a. Exactly 28 of the sampled parts will be defective?

b. Between 20 and 30, inclusive, of the sampled parts will be defective?

c. Fewer than 25 of the sampled parts will be defective?

d. At least 29 of the sampled parts will be defective?

▶ **5.77** A manufacturer knows from experience that the diameters of pins produced have a normal distribution with mean 0.25000 in. and standard deviation 0.00020 in.

a. What percent of the pins have diameters less than 0.24980 in.?

b. What is the approximate probability that two pins randomly picked will both have diameters less than 0.24980 in.?

5.78 Eighty percent of a large shipment of tomatoes are ripe tomatoes. A cannery inspector randomly selects 100 tomatoes from the shipment. What is the approximate probability that the sample proportion of ripe tomatoes exceeds .905?

5.79 The proportion of voters favoring a zoning change is .40. If a random sample of 150 voters is taken, what is the approximate probability that:

a. At most 80 in the sample favor the zoning change?

b. Between 50 and 70, inclusive, in the sample favor the zoning change?

5.80 With respect to a production line producing toaster-ovens, an entire day's production will be held up for individual inspection of each toaster-oven if more than 10 defective toaster-ovens are found in a random sample of 64 toaster-ovens. What is the probability an entire day's production will:

a. Be held up if the production line is producing 20% defective toaster-ovens?

b. Be held up if the production line is producing 10% defective toaster-ovens?

c. Not be held up if the production line is producing 36% defective toaster-ovens?

SOLVING APPLIED CASES

The probability models considered in this chapter have many applications in business and management practice. The case below considers a problem that every business organization has to deal with: how to manage its cash.

Controlling Cash Balances: An Application of the Normal Probability Model

A prime concern of the controller of a firm is to prevent technical insolvency (a shortage of cash), because the condition adversely affects the firm's credit position with its creditors and thereby the firm's profitability. Avoiding technical insolvency requires the firm to have the cash on hand when debt obligations become due. However, holding too much cash in reserve means losing the interest that otherwise would be earned if the excess cash were in marketable securities. It is important, therefore, to balance the risk of insolvency against the loss of interest and hold an optimal amount of cash on hand.

Traditional guidelines to cash reserves are often inaccurate; they do not necessarily take into account the actual daily cash changes of a particular company. Let's suppose a firm has accounts payable and other current obligations that average $10,000 daily. As these short-term obligations mature, they must be paid from cash balances replenished each day by receipts from customers who have accumulated accounts receivable balances averaging $10,000 daily. To buffer mismatches of daily payment obligations against daily receipts, an average cash balance of $10,000 is maintained. This gives a 2-to-1 ratio of cash and nearcash assets to current obligations, a ratio which some financial analysts think is appropriate.

Is it really necessary to stockpile that much cash? Perhaps not. Miller and Orr* have developed a decision rule on the amount of cash to hold, given that the cash drawn to meet maturing obligations follows a normal distribution. Suppose that the firm's corporate records of daily cash changes resulting from the difference between cash inflow from account receipts and cash outflow from account payments that day are examined for 189 consecutive days. The records show that the daily changes have a mean of $66.37 and a standard deviation of $355.18. A histogram showing the frequency (number of days) that daily cash change ranges occurred is given in Figure 5.19. Superimposed on the histogram is a normal curve having the same mean and standard deviation. For the normal distribution to be applicable as a model, the shape of the histogram should conform to the expectations based on the given normal distribution. Visually, we can see a reasonable correspondence in the figure.

Another requirement for the application we are leading up to is that the daily cash changes be independent of each other. This requires testing the daily cash changes for randomness. We shall presume randomness in this example as a reasonable assumption, since the cash changes from one day to another can be attributed to many independent factors.

Once we agree to use the normal distribution as a model, we can use the computed mean and standard deviation to substitute for the normal distribution parameters μ and σ, and we can use the normal probability table to calculate probabilities. For example, to find the probability of a negative daily cash change of -288.81 or worse:

*M. H. Miller and D. Orr, "An Application of Control Limit Models to the Management of Corporate Cash Balances," in A. A. Robichek, ed., *Financial Research and Management Decisions*. New York: Wiley, 1967.

Figure 5.19
Daily cash changes

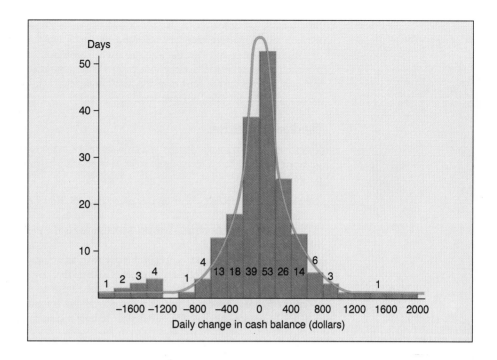

1. Convert -288.81 to a Z value:

$$Z = \frac{X - \mu}{\sigma}$$

$$= \frac{-\$288.81 - 66.37}{355.18}$$

$$= -1$$

2. Express the required probability for X in terms of a corresponding value for Z:

$$P(X < -288.81) = P(Z < -1) = .1587$$

A negative value for daily cash change indicates a cash inflow insufficient to cover the cash payment outflow; this circumstance reflects what would be a shortage of cash were it not for a cash balance buffer on hand.

We can also find the probability of a negative daily cash flow of $-\$999.17$ or worse; that is, $P(X < -999.17) = P(Z < -3) = .0014$. And we can find the probability of a negative daily cash flow of $-\$1709.53$ or worse; that is, $P(X < -1709.53) = P(Z < -5)$. This represents a probability of .000003, or 3 chances in 1 million. In other words, there are only 3 chances in 1 million of a negative cash outflow of $1709.53 or worse. To protect against this we would need to keep a cash balance of less than $2000! Thus, even allowing for some inadequacy in the fit of the normal distribution as a model, keeping an actual cash balance of $10,000 seems an unnecessarily large and wasteful amount to hold as a buffer against cash outflows.

Of course, the actual amount of the buffer required will depend upon how fast cash can be shifted into earning assets, such as treasury bills, and back to cash again. If this round-trip conversion takes, say, 3 days, then the firm would need a buffer sufficient to offset the maximum cash outflow that would occur over 3 days. Fortunately, it is possible to make the round-trip conversion in 1 day, so only a 1 day buffer is needed.

Finally, we would like to note that the business significance of using the normal model in this case comes from the fact that it offers a mechanical decision rule that can be handled by the clerical staff as an alternative to the expensive use of the controller's time and involvement.

Additionally, the decision rule that results serves as a benchmark of performance against which the controller's performance can be compared. It is interesting that in the actual situation described by Miller and Orr, the firm's controller proved not to be equal to the challenge. The mechanical normal model decision rule proved to be more effective in monitoring and managing the cash reserves of the firm than the firm's controller, who made decisions on the basis of insight gained from years of experience.

Checkpoint Exercises

Suppose that a firm's daily changes in cash balance are independent from one day to the next, and suppose the distribution is normal with mean $\mu = \$500$ per day and standard deviation $\sigma = \$5000$ per day.

1. What is the probability that on any given day, the firm's cash flow will be negative (i.e., a net cash outflow)?
2. If a day starts with a cash balance of $1000, what is the probability of running short of cash that day?
3. Suppose the firm decides to begin the day with an amount of cash so that there would be only a .001 probability of running short of cash on that day. What should be the cash balance at the beginning of the day? The intent of the firm is to invest, at the end of the day, the excess cash not needed to maintain that probability condition.
4. If the firm ends the day with $20,000 cash, how much cash should be invested in order to maintain the condition just described in Exercise 3?

SAMPLING DISTRIBUTIONS

I n 1990 another St. Valentine's Day massacre occurred. This one did not involve unsavory characters on the streets of Chicago, but rather a notable firm in the town of Vergeze in southern France. The victim this time was the stock price, profits, and public image of Source Perrier, the French firm dominant worldwide in the bottled water market. The company had to recall and destroy 160 million bottles of Perrier water from 120 countries at a cost of $35 million.

What caused the Perrier recall? Twelve days prior to St. Valentine's Day, the U.S. Food and Drug Administration (FDA) had sent a letter to Source Perrier telling them to check closely the purity of the water used in its bottled carbonated water. Perrier immediately began testing the water. But events quickly unfolded. By the following week, the FDA announced publicly that tested bottles of Perrier water contained 12.3–12.9 parts per billion (ppb) of benzene, a cancer-causing agent, compared to the maximum permissible of 5 ppb.

Perrier's own tests confirmed the findings! On Friday, February 9, the contamination was confirmed by Source Perrier, blaming a cleanser mistakenly used by a worker to remove grease from bottling machinery. The company claimed its well in southern France, heavily promoted in advertisements for its purity, was not tainted. Perrier announced that as a preventive measure it was withdrawing 72 million bottles from the North American market. Supplies of Perrier elsewhere in the world were said to be unaffected, and Perrier hoped to gain good will by its prompt recall of the product in North America.

But over the weekend, traces of benzene were found in Perrier water that had been shipped to other countries. On Wednesday, St. Valentine's Day, the company recalled all stocks of Perrier worldwide. Source Perrier retracted its original statement of the cause of the contamination, saying now that it was due to filters on the incoming water supply that had not been changed for 6 weeks. Tests run in the United States indicated that the beverage had been contaminated with benzene for about 6 months.

With the product withdrawal, and with the changing stories about the extent and cause of the problem, the public credibility of Perrier came under question. Sold at a premium price because of its supposed purity, it was now revealed to have been impure. The more damaging evidence was the revelation that Source Perrier had been lax in monitoring the equipment that assures purity, and lacked the quality control procedures to detect the problem when it did arise.

*New York Times, February 13 and 15, 1990; *Financial Times*, February 15, 1990.

Surprisingly, the results from a sample of just 13 bottles of contaminated water were enough evidence to start the entire recall process. By studying this chapter you will have a better understanding of how and why a small sample could lead to valid conclusions about a population of 160 million bottles. Moreover, the Comprehensive Case Study following this chapter will acquaint you with the techniques of statistical process control that can prevent disasters of this kind.

Overview

In Chapter 5 we saw that several specific types of probability distributions are useful presentations, or models, for the variability found in real-world data. In this chapter we focus on sampling experiments, and we will find that our knowledge of the normal probability distribution will be useful in dealing with sampling results. We'll start by discussing different sampling procedures from populations. Then we'll calculate sample means and sample standard deviations, construct frequency tables for sample means, and see that the frequency tables for sample means give us bell-shaped curves like a normal probability distribution with a mean and variance related to the mean and variance of the original population. We'll also discuss sample proportions and their relationships to the binomial distribution and to the normal distribution. In short, the purpose of this chapter is to examine closely the nature of the distribution of sampling results obtained by performing sampling experiments in the hope that the distribution of sampling results reveals the nature of the underlying population (mean and variance) from which the sample results are derived.

6.1
SAMPLING PROCEDURES

Suppose we draw a sample from a population and compute two sample statistics:

1. The sample mean, $\bar{X}$
2. The sample standard deviation, S

We'd like to use these sample statistics to make valid statements about their respective population counterparts, the population mean (μ) and the population standard deviation (σ). To do so we have to account for the fact that different samples will give different values for $\bar{X}$ and S. In other words, because of the variability of sample statistics, precise statements specifying the exact values of μ and σ are not possible. However, it is possible to make probabilistic statements of the "closeness" between the value of a sample statistic and the value of the corresponding population parameter. But to make valid probabilistic statements we have to be sure that the rules of probability apply, and that depends on the type of procedure used in taking samples from the population. This brings us to a discussion of *random sampling* procedures.

RANDOM SAMPLING

Suppose you manufacture equipment measuring blood cholesterol. You are negotiating with a prospective customer who wants you to demonstrate that your product will have a longer working life than that of any of your competitors. You have the longevity data on your own blood cholesterol measuring equipment, but you lack comparative data on your competitors. The longevity seems the critical factor for your prospective customer's decision, so you propose the following plan: (1) Define the longevity data of all the product you have been producing as one population of interest, and similarly define the longevity data of your competitors' products as the other populations of interest. (2) Select specified subsets (samples) from each of the blood cholesterol measuring equipment populations (i.e., brands). (3) Compare the longevity recordings among the brand samples. (4) Conclude that the comparison among the samples is an accurate reflection of the comparison that would have resulted if the respective populations had been used. To ensure an unbiased drawing of the samples, you hire an independent testing and sampling service to perform the sampling and evaluate the results.

To convince the prospective customer of the validity and objectivity of your method, you and the customer would have to agree on the following:

1. The populations of interest (the equipment longevity recordings for each brand)
2. That sampling is a necessity
3. That a sampling procedure be used that has a high chance of closely mirroring the longevity present in the respective populations

Once the first two issues have been resolved, there may be some difficulty in reaching agreement on a satisfactory sampling procedure. For example, the customer may feel the sampling service you hire might be inclined to tilt the sample in your favor. This could be done by deliberately selecting items of your product that your production manager knows are of better quality. Meanwhile, the selection of samples of your competitors' products might be simply ordinary purchases at a retail outlet. Any scheme in which the judgment of the testing service would play a large part would suggest the possibility of "stacking the deck" in your favor; this possibility undermines the credibility of the sampling results. To forestall any hint of favoritism, you propose collection of results by *random sampling*. Properly implemented, this should eliminate the suspicion of favoritism. There are several ways random sampling can be accomplished.

SIMPLE RANDOM SAMPLING

Suppose the prospective customer agrees to let the testing service purchase the samples of blood cholesterol measuring equipment from retail outlets, but with one stipulation: The determination of the retail outlets to be visited and the purchases must be made on the same day. This stipulation eliminates the possibility of the production manager shipping better than usual products to the retail outlets designated for purchases. To assure that the selection of retail outlets will not be predictable, the testing service decides to use a random selection procedure, or random sampling plan. Any one of the following is an acceptable method:

1. Drawing names out of a hat: Obtain a list of all retail outlets that carry the product; put each name on a separate piece of paper and put the names in a hat or bowl; mix the papers thoroughly; select the retail outlets from which the purchases are to be made. The selected outlets for the purchases comprise a random sample from the population of outlets.
2. Computer selection: The selection procedure just described can be computerized by programming a computer to:
   a. Assign each outlet a distinct number.

　　b. Generate a specified number of random numbers using the computer's random number generator.

　　c. Match the generated numbers with the numbers assigned to the outlets.

　　d. Print the names of the outlets with numbers corresponding to the selected random numbers.

　　e. Make the purchases from the selected outlets.

3. Using a table of random numbers: When a computer is not readily available to generate random numbers, a table of random numbers, as shown in Appendix Table I can be used. Table I is simply a printout of the random numbers generated by a computer programmed to simulate the tossing of a fair, ten-sided die. One legitimate (but arbitrary) way to use Table I for the selection of a random sample is outlined below:

　　a. Assign a distinct number to each individual in the population.

　　b. Toss a coin and set up a prespecified scheme for the possible coin outcomes to determine which page of the table to start on. For example, toss a coin 3 times and if it turns up HHH, start on the first page of the table; if it turns up HHT, start on the second page; and so on.

　　c. Toss a die and set up a prespecified scheme for the possible die outcomes to determine in which direction to read the random numbers. For example, toss a die once and if a 1 appears on the face of the die, read the numbers down the page; if a 2 appears on the face of the die, read the numbers up the page; if a 3 appears, read the numbers across the page to the right and then down; and so on.

　　d. To determine the number of digits to read, select four-digit numbers ranging from 0000 to 9999 if the number of individuals in the population does not exceed 10,000. Select five-digit numbers ranging from 00000 to 99999 if the number of individuals in the population does not exceed 100,000.

　　e. Now start reading the selected digit size number from anywhere on the page you selected in the direction you determined.

　　f. Match the numbers selected from the table with the numbers assigned to the members of the population; the members of the population whose numbers match those selected from the random number table become the sample of retail outlets from which purchases are to be made.

　　The procedure we have just detailed is a **simple random sampling** plan, a method we first mentioned in Chapter 1 in the automobile tire application. The result of using this procedure is a **random sample**. It should be clear by now that the purpose of selection by simple random sampling is to afford every member listed in the population the same chance as any other member of being included in a sample and provides that the selection of any member of the population in the sample in no way affects the chance of any other member of the population being selected. Every combination of members from the population has the same chance of sample inclusion as any other combination. This procedure eliminates the possibility of sample results being influenced by judgment or selection bias.

　　Throughout the remainder of this text, a sample shall mean a simple random sample unless otherwise indicated. The inferential procedures discussed in subsequent chapters of this text all assume a simple random sample.

　　We should be aware, however, that there are alternative random sampling plans available that are more efficient for certain situations than simple random sampling. A few of these methods are described below.

STRATIFIED SAMPLING

Sometimes it is advantageous to subdivide a population into several distinct non-overlapping subpopulations, or strata, and then take a simple random sample from each stratum. Taking random samples from each stratum is called **stratified random sampling**. This type of sampling is most useful when the subpopulations, or strata, show a small dispersion relative to the overall dispersion in the entire population.

Suppose a food expert wished to determine the effects of a low-fat, high-carbohydrate diet on college students. The expert believes that the diet may have a different effect on students of different ages and sexes, so the population of college students is subdivided into four nonoverlapping subpopulations: women students 21 years of age or under; women students over 21 years of age; men students 21 years of age or under; and men students over 21 years of age. A simple random sample from each of these four nonoverlapping subpopulations is taken. Notice in this case that two variables (sex and age) were used for the classification of the subpopulations, or strata. Whenever two or more variables are used for the classification of the subpopulations, the procedure is called **cross-stratification**. By obtaining random samples from each stratum, we have applied a cross-stratified random sampling procedure.

What about the size of samples from the subpopulations? Should they all be of the same size? If the sizes of the samples drawn from the strata are made proportional to the respective sizes of the subpopulations, the procedure is called **proportional sampling**. Proportional sampling is usually more efficient than simply taking equal size samples from each stratum. A sample is considered more efficient than another sample if the sample yields a smaller overall standard deviation than the other sample. However, proportional allocation can lead us astray from the optimal allocation of the subsample sizes. For instance, it will be better (more efficient) to oversample from strata that have observations with wide dispersions, and to undersample from strata that have low dispersions.

CLUSTER SAMPLING

Cluster sampling is another sampling procedure which, like stratified sampling, investigates the subpopulations of the population once that population has been subdivided into many, small, nonoverlapping subpopulations, or clusters. But unlike stratified sampling, which requires the investigation of each subpopulation, cluster sampling requires only a random selection from the collection of clusters. Thus, the procedure results in only some of the clusters being investigated and most of the clusters not being investigated.

There are two distinct benefits from cluster sampling: First, it is typically cheaper to sample a given number of persons from the same cluster than to sample the same number of persons geographically scattered. Second, cluster sampling avoids the need to have a complete listing of all the population members. Let's consider a school study to illustrate these points.

Suppose an educator wishes to determine the effects of the introduction of micro-computers into a 6th grade classroom in a very large city. The educator could obtain a complete listing of the 6th graders in the city school system and randomly draw the required sample from that list. On the other hand, the educator could view the population of 6th graders in the city as subdivided into individual elementary school clusters and draw a random selection from the number of elementary schools. Knowing the benefits of cluster sampling, the educator has decided to deal with a random sample of the schools (clusters) and not with a simple random sampling from the list of all individual students. At this point, the educator has decided which schools will be studied, but not which students. Two alternative procedures are available for selecting the students at the selected schools. One alternative is to study the effects of the microcomputer on all the 6th grade students at each of the selected schools. The other alternative requires drawing a random sample of 6th grade students at each of the selected schools (clusters) and then studying the effects of the microcomputer introduction on the students in these samples. In either case, the educator has taken advantage of cluster sampling and has not needed to know how many students there are nor who they are in each of the schools *not* selected for the investigation.

SYSTEMATIC SAMPLING

Another random sampling method uses a **systematic sampling** scheme to facilitate selection. The procedure begins with randomly selecting one person or item; then every kth person or item (i.e., every 2nd or every 3rd or every 4th) is systematically picked from the list of the population members until the prescribed sample size is reached. For example, a reporter working for a local television station during election time may pick from the population of polling places a particular polling place, then interview every $k = 10$th voter coming out of the polling location. Or a food demonstrator may select a local supermarket from the population of local supermarkets and offer food to and then interview an initial customer; then the demonstrator offers food to and interviews every third person entering the supermarket. Or an Internal Revenue Service auditing agent first separates the tax forms according to income classes, then picks a particular class, and after selecting the initial tax return to review decides to take every 67th return in the class to examine in detail. The reporter, the food demonstrator, and the Internal Revenue Service agent are all using a systematic sampling procedure to provide an objective way of selection.

Unfortunately, if there is an underlying systematic pattern in the data that happens to correspond to the sampling system (repeats itself every kth item), this procedure will produce larger sampling errors than would simple random sampling. Suppose a university administrator is anxious to keep in touch with students' attitudes toward the university during an academic year. The administrator decides to sample from the student body every 4 weeks; that is, the fourth week of the semester is chosen for the first assessment, and assessments are made every 4 weeks thereafter. Unknowingly, this systematic sampling plan coincides exactly with scheduled exams that are routinely administered every 4 weeks, thereby prompting students to have negative attitudes every time the assessment is taken. It would have been much better to have administered the assessment during a simple random sampling plan for the dates selected.

E X E R C I S E S

Use the following profile in Exercises 6.1–6.4: An electronic device permits a calling service to dial automatically up to 10,000 preprogrammed telephone numbers and announce a specific message on each call. Suppose a home remodeling contractor hires a calling service to call 10,000 numbers listed in the phone directory (there are 1,233,000 phone numbers listed in this directory) and announce that the home remodeling contractor "will be working in your neighborhood and, because his men will already be there, he can offer you a substantial discount on your home remodeling project."

6.1 If the contractor requests a random sample from the phone directory, how should the calling service program in the 10,000 numbers?

6.2 If the contractor specifies a stratified random sample from the phone directory, how might the calling service program in the 10,000 numbers?

6.3 If the contractor specifies a cluster sample from the phone directory, how might the calling service program in the 10,000 numbers?

6.4 If the contractor specifies a systematic sample from the phone directory, how might the calling service program in the 10,000 numbers?

6.2
SAMPLING DISTRIBUTIONS

If you own an automobile and have it serviced regularly at the same service station with good results, you may tend to conclude that all, or most, services stations belonging to the same chain provide reliable service. You may well be inclined to stop at service stations belonging to the same chain on business trips or vacations. Or, if in contrast, you have a bad experience with one service station, you may tend to stay away from all service stations belonging to the same chain.

Situations like this point out the fact that we sometimes reach a conclusion about all items on the basis of limited information. In statistics, an observed sample is analogous to limited information. It provides only partial information on the population from which it was drawn. The degree of informational content offered by a sample depends on the size of the sample—smaller samples offer less information than larger samples. Regardless of the sample size (small or large), we do make and will continue to make statements and draw conclusions (inferences) that generalize from the information on a sample of items to the population of all items.

But how can a conclusion be valid if we know that sample results vary? The limited information we obtain from one sample is not expected to be exactly the same as the limited information we obtain from another sample. What assurance do we have that the limited information from a sample will not be misleading? One possibility is to consider the accumulated information of "all possible samples" drawn from the population while holding the sample size unchanged (we hold the sample size unchanged so that sample size is not a complicating factor). The accumulated information of "all possible samples" will show the inevitable variation of sample results from sample to sample, which can then be organized into a distribution. We'll see that this distribution assumes an important pattern and shows characteristics that are vital in developing objective methods for drawing inferences about the underlying population characteristics (parameters).

FORMING SAMPLING DISTRIBUTIONS: EXPERIMENT 1

Let's now concentrate on the **sampling distribution of the sample mean,** $\bar{X}$, in repeated random sampling. One particular pattern tends to emerge for the distribution of the sample mean for equal size samples drawn from the same population.

Suppose students on a research project surveyed all 10 households that live in a new housing development to learn about their breakfast cereal consumption habits. The recordings taken are the number of days ready-to-eat breakfast cereal had been served to at least one member of the household during the previous 2 weeks. The 10 household responses for the number of days are:

$$1, \quad 5, \quad 9, \quad 7, \quad 6, \quad 0, \quad 3, \quad 8, \quad 2, \quad 4$$

These data on breakfast cereal consumption days constitute a population of 10 items. The values of the population mean and population variance are given by

$$\mu = \frac{\sum\limits_{i=1}^{N} X_i}{N}$$

$$\sigma^2 = \frac{\sum\limits_{i=1}^{N} (X_i - \mu)^2}{N}$$

where $N = 10$. The results are

$\mu = 4.5$ days per 2 weeks, on the average, per household

$\sigma^2 = 8.25$

Suppose that about the same time the student research group conducted their survey, a professional marketing firm decided to survey the entire city to obtain the same type of information. In the particular housing development surveyed by the students, the marketing firm surveyed just 2 households, which were selected randomly. Let's examine the possible sampling results for the marketing firm in that one housing development. Their sampling procedure for breakfast cereal usage could have yielded any one of 90 equally likely ordered pairs of sample results. These equally likely ordered pairs of observations are listed in Table 6.1.

TABLE 6.1 Ninety Equally Likely Ordered Pairs of Sample Results When Sampling from a Small Finite Population and $n = 2$								
(1, 5)	(1, 9)	(1, 7)	(1, 6)	(1, 0)	(1, 3)	(1, 8)	(1, 2)	(1, 4)
(5, 1)	(5, 9)	(5, 7)	(5, 6)	(5, 0)	(5, 3)	(5, 8)	(5, 2)	(5, 4)
(9, 1)	(9, 5)	(9, 7)	(9, 6)	(9, 0)	(9, 3)	(9, 8)	(9, 2)	(9, 4)
(7, 1)	(7, 5)	(7, 9)	(7, 6)	(7, 0)	(7, 3)	(7, 8)	(7, 2)	(7, 4)
(6, 1)	(6, 5)	(6, 9)	(6, 7)	(6, 0)	(6, 3)	(6, 8)	(6, 2)	(6, 4)
(0, 1)	(0, 5)	(0, 9)	(0, 7)	(0, 6)	(0, 3)	(0, 8)	(0, 2)	(0, 4)
(3, 1)	(3, 5)	(3, 9)	(3, 7)	(3, 6)	(3, 0)	(3, 8)	(3, 2)	(3, 4)
(8, 1)	(8, 5)	(8, 9)	(8, 7)	(8, 6)	(8, 0)	(8, 3)	(8, 2)	(8, 4)
(2, 1)	(2, 5)	(2, 9)	(2, 7)	(2, 6)	(2, 0)	(2, 3)	(2, 8)	(2, 4)
(4, 1)	(4, 5)	(4, 9)	(4, 7)	(4, 6)	(4, 0)	(4, 3)	(4, 8)	(4, 2)

For each ordered pair or sample result, a sample mean, $\bar{X}$, can be computed. How close do the means of these pairs of observations reflect the true mean (μ) for the entire housing development? To answer the question, we'll compute and list a sample mean for each pair, construct a frequency distribution of the sample means, and see how closely the frequency distribution clusters about the true mean μ. Then we'll calculate the mean and variance of the frequency distribution of the sample means and see how these two values relate to the mean and variance of the original population. The means, $\bar{X}_i$, for the equally likely ordered pairs given in Table 6.1 are listed in Table 6.2.

TABLE 6.2		Ninety Sample Means of the Sample Results Shown in Table 6.1						
3	5	4	3.5	0.5	2	4.5	1.5	2.5
3	7	6	5.5	2.5	4	6.5	3.5	4.5
5	7	8	7.5	4.5	6	8.5	5.5	6.5
4	6	8	6.5	3.5	5	7.5	4.5	5.5
3.5	5.5	7.5	6.5	3	4.5	7	4	5
0.5	2.5	4.5	3.5	3	1.5	4	1	2
2	4	6	5	4.5	1.5	5.5	2.5	3.5
4.5	6.5	8.5	7.5	7	4	5.5	5	6
1.5	3.5	5.5	4.5	4	1	2.5	5	3
2.5	4.5	6.5	5.5	5	2	3.5	6	3

The lowest value among the 90 mean values is 0.5; the highest value is 8.5. Very few of the means (10, to be exact) are on target and actually equal the calculated population mean value of 4.5. Discouraging? Inferences about population structures depend upon sampling, and here 80 of the 90 possible sample results are off the mark! But how far off the mark are they? To find out, the sample means themselves must be organized and presented in a distribution so that the pattern of variability becomes evident. The steps to obtain this sample mean distribution are the following:

Step 1
Make a list of the sample means.

Step 2
Construct a frequency table.

Step 3
Plot a histogram.

Step 4
Compute a mean for the 90 means.

Step 5
Compute a variance for the 90 means.

TABLE 6.3 A Frequency Table for All 90 Possible Sample Means (for Samples of Size 2, Taken Without Replacement from a Population Consisting of the Values 0, 1, 2, 3, 4, 5, 6, 7, 8, 9)		
CLASS INTERVAL	**TALLY**	**FREQUENCY**
−0.7–1.3	||||	4
1.4–3.4	⊞ ⊞ ⊞ ⊞	20
3.5–5.5	⊞ ⊞ ⊞ ⊞ ⊞ ⊞ ⊞ ⊞ ||	42
5.6–7.6	⊞ ⊞ ⊞ ⊞	20
7.7–9.7	||||	4
	Total	90

The frequency table given in Table 6.3 and the corresponding histogram given in Figure 6.1b both reveal a pattern of variability. Many of the sample means cluster close to the value $\mu = 4.5$, an encouraging sign. But to be more precise about the apparent central location and variability, we need to calculate two key measures, the mean $\mu_{\bar{X}}$ and the variance $\sigma^2_{\bar{X}}$ of this distribution. Notice that we have subscripted μ and σ^2 to indicate that we are dealing with the distribution of $\bar{X}$.

Figure 6.1
Frequency distribution of
sample means of sampling
($n = 2$) for experiment I and
original population distribution

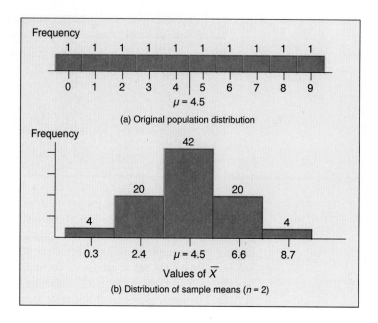

(a) Original population distribution

(b) Distribution of sample means ($n = 2$)

The formula for the mean $\mu_{\bar{X}}$ for the 90 sample means is

$$E(\bar{X}) = \mu_{\bar{x}} = \frac{\sum\limits_{i=1}^{90} \bar{X}_i}{90}$$

The formula for the variance $\sigma_{\bar{X}}^2$ for the 90 sample means is

$$\text{Var}(\bar{X}) = \sigma_{\bar{X}}^2 = \frac{\sum\limits_{i=1}^{90} (\bar{X}_i - \mu_{\bar{x}})^2}{90}$$

The computed mean value for the 90 means is

$$\mu_{\bar{x}} = \frac{3 + 5 + 4 + \cdots + 3.5 + 6 + 3}{90} = 4.5$$

and the computed variance for the 90 means is

$$\sigma_{\bar{X}}^2 = \frac{(3 - 4.5)^2 + (5 - 4.5)^2 + \cdots + (6 - 4.5)^2 + (3 - 4.5)^2}{90} = 3.6666667$$

Two points need to be made: (1) The original population mean μ and the mean of the distribution of $\bar{X}$'s, $\mu_{\bar{x}}$, are identical and equal to the value 4.5, that is, $\mu_{\bar{x}} = \mu$. (2) The variance of the distribution of $\bar{X}$'s, $\sigma_{\bar{X}}^2$ is related to the population variance σ^2 in the following way:

$$\sigma_{\bar{X}}^2 = \left(\frac{\sigma^2}{2}\right)\left(\frac{10 - 2}{10 - 1}\right)$$

Having previously found that $\sigma^2 = 8.25$, we can substitute this value into the expression above and solve. The result equals 3.6666667, the same value obtained for $\sigma_{\bar{X}}^2$. We should note that the value 2 in the expression for $\sigma_{\bar{X}}^2$ is the sample size n, and the value 10 is the population size N. So what we have found is that the frequency distribution of the sample means clusters close to the value of the original population mean. But more importantly, the mean of the frequency distribution of the sample means is exactly equal to the original population mean, and the variance is related to, but less than, the original population variance. Both of these points are supported by comparing parts a and b of Figure 6.1. This evidence prompts the following generalization:

Mean and Variance of Sampling Distributions of Sample Means for Finite Populations

For finite populations of size N, when random samples of size n are drawn without replacement, the following relationships hold true:

Mean

$$\mu_{\bar{X}} = \mu \tag{6-1}$$

Variance

$$\sigma_{\bar{X}}^2 = \left(\frac{\sigma^2}{n}\right)\left(\frac{N-n}{N-1}\right) \tag{6-2}$$

In these expressions, μ and σ^2 are the mean and variance of the original population, and $\mu_{\bar{X}}$ and $\sigma_{\bar{X}}^2$ are the mean and variance of the frequency distribution of all possible sample means of sample size n taken from the original population. Thus, μ and σ are the mean and standard deviation, respectively, of the data on the population of 10 households in the subdivision. The values of $\mu_{\bar{X}}$ and $\sigma_{\bar{X}}$ are the mean and standard deviation, respectively, of the 90 ordered pairs given in Table 6.1. The standard deviation $\sigma_{\bar{X}}$ is simply the square root of $\sigma_{\bar{X}}^2$ and is known as the **standard error of the mean**.

When the finite population size N is large relative to the sample size n, a modification of the formula for $\sigma_{\bar{X}}^2$ is appropriate. Let's look at the effect on the factor $(N - n)/(N - 1)$ as N becomes much larger than n:

If $N = 100$ and $n = 10$, then: $\dfrac{100 - 10}{100 - 1} = 0.909$

If $N = 10,000$ and $n = 50$, then: $\dfrac{10,000 - 50}{10,000 - 1} = 0.995$

If $N = 1,000,000$ and $n = 120$, then: $\dfrac{1,000,000 - 120}{1,000,000 - 1} = 0.99988$

We can conclude that the ratio $(N - n)/(N - 1)$ will be very close to 1 when the size N of the original population is very large relative to the sample size n.

This leads to the assertion that if the population size N is very large relative to the sample size n, the approximate relationship between $\sigma_{\bar{X}}^2$ and σ^2 is as follows:

Relationship Between Population Variance and Variance of Sampling Distributions for $\bar{X}$ for Very Large Finite Populations, or Infinitely Large Populations

$$\sigma_{\bar{X}}^2 = \frac{\sigma^2}{n} \tag{6-3}$$

Use the following rule of thumb to judge the appropriateness of equation (6-3). Given a finite population of size N from which random samples of size n are drawn without replacement:

$$\text{Use} \quad \sigma_{\bar{X}}^2 = \frac{\sigma^2}{n} \quad \text{instead of} \quad \left(\frac{\sigma^2}{n}\right)\left(\frac{N-n}{N-1}\right) \quad \text{when} \quad N \geq 20n.$$

That is, use equation (6-3) when the sample size is less than 5% of the population size.

SAMPLING FROM A VERY LARGE POPULATION: EXPERIMENT II

We can demonstrate the validity of the rule of thumb given above by performing a sampling simulation from a very large population. Returning to the new housing development, let's now actually suppose that the development consists of a large number of homes. Additionally, suppose one-tenth of these households served ready-to-eat breakfast cereal 0 days during the previous 2 weeks; one-tenth served ready-to-eat breakfast cereal 1 day during the previous 2 weeks; one-tenth served ready-to-eat breakfast cereal 2 days during the previous 2 weeks; and so on, up to one-tenth of the households served ready-to-eat breakfast cereal 9 days during the previous 2 weeks.

Randomly drawing 2 households, the possible sample results would be the 100 equally likely ordered pairs (0, 0), (0, 1), . . . , (9, 9) shown in Table 6.4. Ninety of these ordered pairs are identical to the pairs shown in Table 6.1. These 90 possible outcomes are shown on the right side of the vertical line in Table 6.4.

TABLE 6.4 One Hundred Equally Likely Ordered Pairs When Sampling from a Very Large Finite Population and $n = 2$									
(1, 1)	(1, 5)	(1, 9)	(1, 7)	(1, 6)	(1, 0)	(1, 3)	(1, 8)	(1, 2)	(1, 4)
(5, 5)	(5, 1)	(5, 9)	(5, 7)	(5, 6)	(5, 0)	(5, 3)	(5, 8)	(5, 2)	(5, 4)
(9, 9)	(9, 1)	(9, 5)	(9, 7)	(9, 6)	(9, 0)	(9, 3)	(9, 8)	(9, 2)	(9, 4)
(7, 7)	(7, 1)	(7, 5)	(7, 9)	(7, 6)	(7, 0)	(7, 3)	(7, 8)	(7, 2)	(7, 4)
(6, 6)	(6, 1)	(6, 5)	(6, 9)	(6, 7)	(6, 0)	(6, 3)	(6, 8)	(6, 2)	(6, 4)
(0, 0)	(0, 1)	(0, 5)	(0, 9)	(0, 7)	(0, 6)	(0, 3)	(0, 8)	(0, 2)	(0, 4)
(3, 3)	(3, 1)	(3, 5)	(3, 9)	(3, 7)	(3, 6)	(3, 0)	(3, 8)	(3, 2)	(3, 4)
(8, 8)	(8, 1)	(8, 5)	(8, 9)	(8, 7)	(8, 6)	(8, 0)	(8, 3)	(8, 2)	(8, 4)
(2, 2)	(2, 1)	(2, 5)	(2, 9)	(2, 7)	(2, 6)	(2, 0)	(2, 3)	(2, 8)	(2, 4)
(4, 4)	(4, 1)	(4, 5)	(4, 9)	(4, 7)	(4, 6)	(4, 0)	(4, 3)	(4, 8)	(4, 2)

The pairs on the left side of the line represent sample results that are possible in the present case and not in the case presented in Table 6.1. The corresponding sample means for the sample results of Table 6.4 are listed in Table 6.5.

TABLE 6.5 One Hundred Sample Means of the Sample Results Shown in Table 6.4									
1	3	5	4	3.5	0.5	2	4.5	1.5	2.5
5	3	7	6	5.5	2.5	4	6.5	3.5	4.5
9	5	7	8	7.5	4.5	6	8.5	5.5	6.5
7	4	6	8	6.5	3.5	5	7.5	4.5	5.5
6	3.5	5.5	7.5	6.5	3	4.5	7	4	5
0	0.5	2.5	4.5	3.5	3	1.5	4	1	2
3	2	4	6	5	4.5	1.5	5.5	2.5	3.5
8	4.5	6.5	8.5	7.5	7	4	5.5	5	6
2	1.5	3.5	5.5	4.5	4	1	2.5	5	3
4	2.5	4.5	6.5	5.5	5	2	3.5	6	3

A frequency table of these 100 possible sample means is given in Table 6.6, and the corresponding histogram is shown in Figure 6.2.

TABLE 6.6 A Frequency Table for All 100 Possible Sample Means (for Samples of Size 2, Taken With Replacement from a Population Consisting of the Values 0, 1, 2, 3, 4, 5, 6, 7, 8, 9)		
CLASS INTERVAL	**TALLY**	**FREQUENCY**
−0.7–1.3	卌 |	6
1.4–3.4	卌 卌 卌 卌 ||	22
3.5–5.5	卌 卌 卌 卌 卌 卌 卌 卌 ||||	44
5.6–7.6	卌 卌 卌 卌 ||	22
7.7–9.7	卌 |	6
	Total	100

The mean $\mu_{\bar{X}}$ and variance $\sigma_{\bar{X}}^2$ of the sample means of Table 6.5 are obtained, as before, from the formulas

$$\mu_{\bar{X}} = \frac{\sum_{i=1}^{100} \bar{X}_i}{100}$$

$$\sigma_{\bar{X}}^2 = \frac{\sum_{i=1}^{100} (\bar{X}_i - \mu_{\bar{X}})^2}{100}$$

Figure 6.2
Frequency distribution of sample means of sampling ($n = 2$) for experiment II

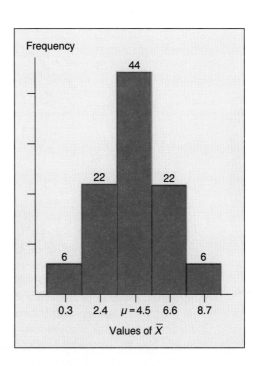

The calculated values are $\mu_{\bar{X}} = 4.5$ and $\sigma_{\bar{X}}^2 = 4.125$; these represent the mean and variance of the frequency distribution of sample means when $n = 2$. Comparing these calculated values to the mean μ and variance σ^2 for the original population, we find that the frequency distribution of all possible sample means has a mean $\mu_{\bar{X}}$ equal to the population mean μ and a variance $\sigma_{\bar{X}}^2 = \sigma^2/2$, as predicted by equation (6-3). This empirical demonstration supports the generalization we made about the sampling process and the relationship between the features of the frequency distribution of sample means and the features of the original population distribution. In summary:

- **The process.** Given a population with a mean μ and variance σ^2, consider all possible random samples of the same size n and calculate their respective sample means, $\bar{X}_i$.

- **The sampling distribution.** The frequency distribution of all possible sample means of sample size n obtained in the preceding process is the sampling distribution of $\bar{X}$ values. This sampling distribution can be characterized by a measure for the central location of the $\bar{X}$ values and by a measure for the variation shown by the $\bar{X}$ values. The sampling distribution mean $\mu_{\bar{X}}$ is a measure of the central location, and the sampling distribution variance $\sigma_{\bar{X}}^2$ is a measure of the variation. For random samples of the same size n, the sampling distribution of $\bar{X}$ shows a mean $\mu_{\bar{X}}$ such that

$$\mu_{\bar{X}} = \mu$$

This indicates that the mean of the sampling distribution of the sample means coincides exactly with the mean of the population distribution from which the samples are taken.

The variance of the sampling distribution is determined by one of two formulas, depending on the sampling procedure and the population size relative to the sample size.

1. The first expression,

$$\sigma_{\bar{X}}^2 = \left(\frac{\sigma^2}{n}\right)\left(\frac{N-n}{N-1}\right)$$

   is used when (a) the population size N is not very large relative to the sample size n, and (b) the sampling is without replacement.

2. The second expression

$$\sigma_{\bar{X}}^2 = \frac{\sigma^2}{n}$$

   is used when (a) the population size N is very large relative to the sample size n (i.e., when $N \geq 20n$), or (b) the sampling is taken from a population that is theoretically infinite in size.

We'd like to point out that sampling distributions (frequency distributions) are not restricted only to sample means. For each possible sample of size n from a population we can also calculate a variance, standard deviation, proportion, or any other sample statistic, and for each of these statistics we can construct a frequency table, plot a histogram, examine its frequency distribution, and find the mean and standard deviation of its frequency distribution. In other words, every statistic has a sampling distribution, but the distributions do not all necessarily look alike nor do they necessarily have the same characteristics as the sampling distribution of the sample means.

In general, the **sampling distribution of a statistic** is the probability distribution, or behavior pattern, of the values of a statistic for all possible samples of the same size n from the original population.

LOOKING AHEAD

The parent population distribution from which the sample values are drawn is the probability distribution of the random variable X. Likewise, the resulting sampling distribution of $\bar{X}$ can be viewed as the probability distribution of the random variable $\bar{X}$. Each observed sample mean then represents one drawing from the possible $\bar{X}$ values defined by the sampling (probability) distribution of $\bar{X}$. By knowing about the type of probability distribution we are dealing with, we could make probability statements about getting a value of $\bar{X}$ within a specified interval. This would be extremely useful in describing the probability and magnitude of the discrepancy we should expect in using the value of the sample mean $\bar{X}$ to estimate the value of the population mean μ. A better understanding of the nature of the sampling (probability) distribution of $\bar{X}$ is the subject of the next section.

PRACTICE EXERCISE

6.1 Suppose a population consists of the values 1, 3, 5, 7.
   a. Find the mean and variance for this population.
   b. List all 6 possible samples of size 2, taken without replacement, from this population (or you may list all 12 equally likely ordered pairs). Then find the mean of each pair; and compute the mean and variance of the 6 (or 12) means using the summation formulas in the text.
   c. Compare the results in part b with the corresponding results in part a.
   d. List all 16 possible samples of size 2 (16 equally likely ordered pairs), taken with replacement, from this population. Then find the mean of each pair; and compute the mean and variance of the 16 means using the summation formulas in the text.
   e. Compare the results in part d with the corresponding results in parts a and b.

EXERCISES

▶ 6.5 Suppose that 31 students in a class purchase their textbooks at different prices (depending on whether the books are used or new, and where the books are purchased), and suppose their average cost is $38.60 with a standard deviation of $4.50. If we were to take all possible samples of size 3 (without replacement, of course) from the 31 students and find the average cost for each sample, what can we say about the values of the mean and variance of the distribution of these sample averages?

6.6 Suppose that, theoretically, the average cost for textbooks per semester is $282 with a standard deviation of $53. Now suppose a college administrator wishes to estimate the actual average cost of textbooks for each student at the college. To do this, the administrator considers interviewing 100 of the 49,000 students at the college and asking how much the student spent on textbooks for the current semester. The administrator will then obtain a cost average based upon the figures given by the 100 interviewed students. If we consider all possible cost averages based upon all possible samples of 100 taken from the 49,000 students, what would be the values of the mean and standard deviation of the distribution of these cost averages?

6.7 Suppose an automobile manufacturing company claims that its automobiles have an average drag coefficient of 0.33 with a standard deviation of 0.02. If a consumer agency were to check this claim by obtaining an average based on a random sample of 4 automobiles, what would be the mean and standard deviation of the distribution of all possible random samples of size 4 from this company's automobiles? Assume this company produces 100,000 automobiles each year.

6.3

DISTRIBUTION OF SAMPLE MEANS

In evaluating the results of our empirical experiments in the preceding section, we noted that only 10 of the 90 possible means had a value equal to the mean of the original population—a clear indication that sample means usually differ from the mean of the original population. But we also noted that the sample means tend to cluster about the value of the population mean. This clustering aspect of the sample means about the population mean value should not be underplayed nor is it an accident. Rather, it is an extremely important phenomenon that needs to be understood. The shapes of the histograms presented in Figures 6.1 and 6.2 confirm the fact that the distribution of $\bar{X}$ values tends to cluster and peak at the value where $\mu_{\bar{X}}$ is equal to μ. Now let's further examine what happens to the shape of the sampling distribution of $\bar{X}$ when the sample size n is large.

CENTRAL LIMIT THEOREM

A statement of the shape and characteristics of the sampling distribution of $\bar{X}$ when the sample size is large is given by the **central limit theorem**.

Central Limit Theorem

> If from a large (or, theoretically, infinite) population with finite values for the mean μ and variance σ^2, we take all possible random samples of the same size n, where n is large, then the probability (sampling) distribution of the random variable $\bar{X}$ is approximately normal (with mean $\mu_{\bar{X}} = \mu$ and variance $\sigma_{\bar{X}}^2 = \sigma^2/n$).

Special case. If the population distribution from which samples are taken is itself normally distributed with mean μ and variance σ^2, then the sampling distribution of all possible sample means of samples of the same size n is *exactly a normal distribution* with mean $\mu_{\bar{X}} = \mu$ and variance $\sigma_{\bar{X}}^2 = \sigma^2/n$. This holds true regardless of whether n is small or large.

But the remarkable fact about the central limit theorem is that it is not restrictive about the shape of the population distribution from which we sample. No matter what the shape of the population distribution, as long as the population distribution has finite values for the mean and variance, the sampling distribution for the mean of a large sample drawn from that population will end up looking like a normal curve—even if the population distribution bears no resemblance to the shape of a normal curve!

Some insight into the tendency toward normality in the sampling distribution of the sample mean $\bar{X}$ as n increases can be gained by examining four populations and the sampling distributions of their sample means for samples of size 2, 4, and 25, as shown in Figure 6.3.

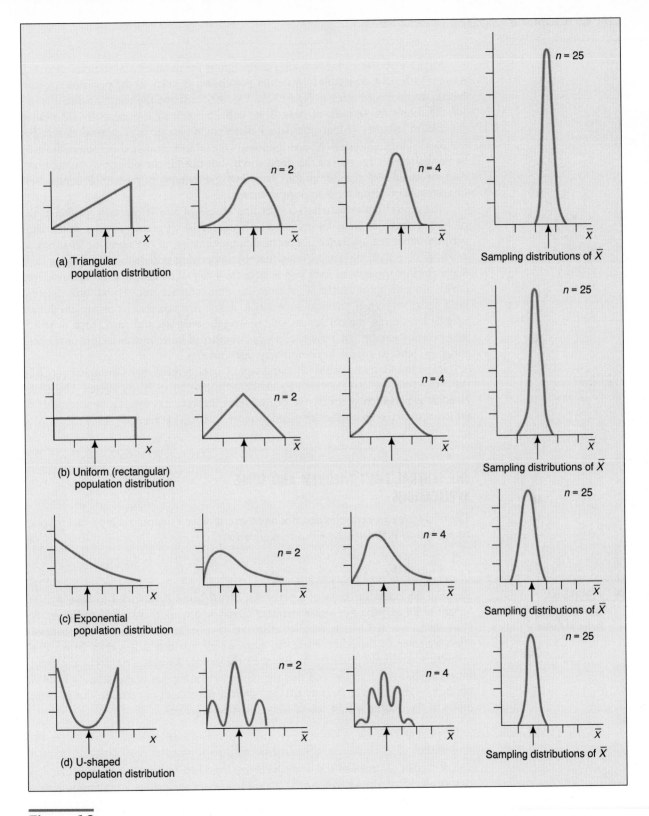

Figure 6.3
The central limit theorem: the tendency of the sampling distribution of $\bar{X}$ toward normality as n increases for different population distributions

Figure 6.3b shows the sampling distributions for the means of samples of size 2, 4, and 25 from a uniformly distributed population (similar to the population distribution we have been using in Figure 6.1). Figure 6.3c shows the sampling distributions for the means of samples of sizes 2, 4, and 25 from an exponentially distributed population. Neither parent population distribution resembles a normal curve. For samples of size 4, the sampling distributions of the sample means exhibit some similarity to normal curves for two of the populations, but not for the other two populations. And for samples of size 25, all four sampling distributions of the sample means bear unmistakable resemblances to normal curves.

The central limit theorem is a sweeping statement and is generally viewed as the most important theorem for statistical inference. The theorem provides statisticians with an important assurance; the normal approximation of the sampling distribution of $\bar{X}$ will be reasonably good even when the underlying population distribution does depart from symmetry, as long as n is large (as a rule of thumb, $n \geq 30$ is considered large). Since samples of size 30 or more are commonplace, the central limit theorem becomes of very great practical importance. In fact, the theorem helps explain in part why data on measurement errors, grades, heights, weights, and such (each of which may be considered as an average of a large number of independent factors or random variables) tend to appear to be normally distributed.

It is interesting to note that this tendency of measurement errors to appear normally distributed was noticed even before a mathematical explanation was offered. The mathematical explanation given by the central limit theorem has undergone a number of refinements since its earliest formulation more than 100 years ago.

THE CENTRAL LIMIT THEOREM AND SOME APPLICATIONS

The following two examples describe situations in which the central limit theorem can be applied to help evaluate a business situation.

■ **EXAMPLE 6.1**

Short-Weighting Boxes of Cereal

Suppose the cereal in boxes of a particular cereal brand is intended to have a mean weight of 24 oz per box, with a standard deviation among the weights of 0.6 oz. An FDA official is asked to determine whether the boxes of cereal have been systematically short-weighted to the point where the mean weight per box is less than 24 oz. FDA inspectors randomly purchase 36 boxes of the cereal. Assume that deliberate short-weighting has *not* occurred and that the mean weight for this brand actually is 24 oz per box. What is the probability that the average net weight of cereal in the 36 cereal boxes in the sample will be found to be less than 23.8 oz?

Discussion

The weight of cereal in the boxes will vary from box to box. But if deliberate short-weighting has not occurred, then the average weight for a random sample of 36 boxes should be fairly close to 24 oz. The issue then is: Is it reasonable to expect the sample average to be less than 23.8 oz if there is no deliberate short-weighting? More specifically, what is the value of $P(\bar{X} < 23.8)$ if the underlying population mean $\mu = 24$? A very low probability indicates that it is not reasonable to expect such a sample average.

Although we are sampling without replacement, the sample can be assumed to be a very small fraction of the very large population of boxes of cereal of that specified type.

Solution

Step 1
The population distribution of cereal weights has an assumed mean $\mu = 24$ and a standard deviation $\sigma = 0.6$. An example of what the population distribution could look like is illustrated in Figure 6.4.

Step 2
The average weight of the sample of size $n = 36$ cereal boxes is a random variable, $\bar{X}$.

Step 3
The mean $\mu_{\bar{X}}$ is equal to $\mu = 24$, and the standard error of the mean $\sigma_{\bar{X}}$ is equal to

$$\frac{\sigma}{\sqrt{n}} = \frac{0.6}{\sqrt{36}} = 0.1$$

Step 4
With $n = 36$ we have $n \geq 30$, and thus n is large enough to justify the assertion that the random variable $\bar{X}$ is approximately normally distributed. In this case the population distribution of the sample means could appear as illustrated in Figure 6.5.

Step 5
Notice how the distribution of the sample means very closely clusters about the original population mean, $\mu = 24$, when you compare Figures 6.4 and 6.5.

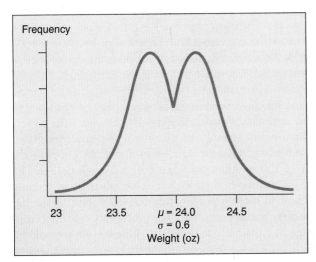

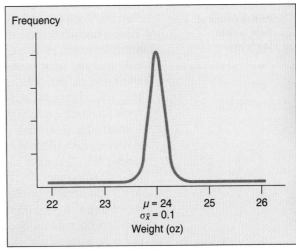

Figure 6.4
An example of what the population distribution of cereal box weights could look like

Figure 6.5
Sampling distribution of $\bar{X}$, the average weight of samples of 36 cereal boxes

Step 6

Knowing that the sampling distribution of $\bar{X}$ is approximately normally distributed with mean $\mu_{\bar{X}} = 24$ and standard deviation $\sigma_{\bar{X}} = 0.1$, and using a procedure comparable to that described in Chapter 5, Section 5.3, we can convert $\bar{X}$ to the standard normal random variable Z using the expression

$$Z = \frac{\bar{X} - \mu_{\bar{X}}}{\sigma_{\bar{X}}} = \frac{\bar{X} - \mu}{\sigma/\sqrt{n}}$$
$$= \frac{\bar{X} - 24}{0.1}$$

Step 7

For $\bar{X} = 23.8$, we get a value of

$$Z = \frac{23.8 - 24}{0.1} = -2$$

Step 8

Using Appendix Table IV, we can now write $P(\bar{X} < 23.8) = P(Z < -2) = .5 - .4772 = .0228$.

Step 9

The probability calculated indicates that there is only a small probability (2.28% chance) that the average weight of a random sample of 36 boxes will be less than 23.8 oz if the cereal boxes are not being deliberately short-weighted (i.e., true $\mu = 24$ oz).

Note that the concluding probability statement refers to hypothetical sample results, not to sample results obtained after an actual sampling. This is appropriate since probability properly describes the chances before the experiment is conducted.

Now consider another similar application of the central limit theorem.

■ **EXAMPLE 6.2**

Portion Control of Meat in Hero Sandwiches

Suppose the delicatessen department in a large supermarket advertises that its family hero sandwich contains a full pound of whatever sandwich meat the customer prefers. The perennial favorites are the expensive cuts: roast beef, ham, and turkey. About 1000 sandwiches are made each week. Because customers ask for different thicknesses of meat and also want to see the meat sliced fresh for the sandwich, the deli can't precut and preweigh each pound portion. The manager of the deli believes that the servers are consistently a bit generous in making up the sandwiches and have a tendency to add a few slices over the pound mark rather than to underweigh the meat. The servers acknowledge that some variation exists among the weights of the sandwich meat. However, they insist that the overweight sandwiches balance out the underweight sandwiches. A random sample of 100 weighings is taken over a 2 week period. The deli manager comes to you, the store manager, since with your formal statistical training you might be able to suggest how to make a proper statistical evaluation. Assuming the historical $\sigma = 0.03$ lb (slightly under $\frac{1}{2}$ oz), find the probability that the mean sample weight would be as large as 1 lb and $\frac{1}{2}$ oz (1.031 lb) if the servers are holding to a true mean weight of 1.00 lb.

Discussion

The weight of meat cut for the sandwiches will vary from sandwich to sandwich. But if the servers are holding to the 1 lb standard, then the average weight for a random sample of 100 weighings should be fairly close to 1 lb. The question then is: Is it reasonable to expect the sample average to be more than 1.031 lb if the servers are operating at the intended 1 lb level? More specifically, what is the value of $P(\bar{X} > 1.031)$ if the underlying population mean $\mu = 1.00$?

Solution

Step 1
The population distribution of sandwich meat weighings has a mean of $\mu = 1$ and a population standard deviation $\sigma = 0.03$. An example of what the population distribution of the weighings could look like is illustrated in Figure 6.6.

Step 2
The average of the sample of $n = 100$ weighings is a random variable, $\bar{X}$.

Step 3
The mean $\mu_{\bar{X}}$ is equal to $\mu = 1$, and the standard deviation $\sigma_{\bar{X}}$ is equal to

$$\frac{\sigma}{\sqrt{n}} = \frac{0.03}{\sqrt{100}} = 0.003$$

Step 4
With $n = 100$ we have $n \geq 30$, and thus it is reasonable to assert that the random variable $\bar{X}$ is approximately normally distributed. In this case the population distribution of the sample means could appear as illustrated in Figure 6.7.

Step 5
Notice again how the distribution of the sample means very closely clusters about the original population mean, $\mu = 1$, when you compare Figures 6.6 and 6.7.

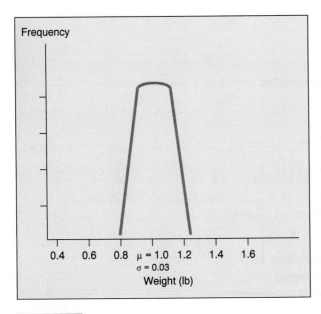

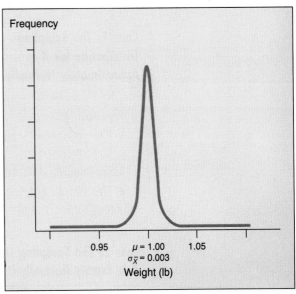

Figure 6.6
An example of what the population distribution of sandwich meat weighings could look like

Figure 6.7
Sampling distribution of $\bar{X}$, the average weight of samples of 100 meat weighings

Step 6

With the sampling distribution of $\bar{X}$ approximately normal with mean $\mu_{\bar{X}} = 1$ and standard deviation $\sigma_{\bar{X}} = 0.003$, we can convert $\bar{X}$ to the standard normal random variable Z using the formula

$$Z = \frac{\bar{X} - \mu_{\bar{X}}}{\sigma_{\bar{X}}}$$

$$= \frac{\bar{X} - 1}{0.003}$$

Step 7

For $\bar{X} = 1.031$, the corresponding value of

$$Z = \frac{1.031 - 1}{0.003} = 10.33$$

Step 8

We can now write $P(\bar{X} > 1.031) = P(Z > 10.33) = 0$, to four decimal places.

Step 9

The probability calculation shows that finding a sample of 100 weighings to yield an average above 1.031 lb would be extremely unusual if the servers are holding true to a mean weight of 1 lb.

SUMMARY FOR THE SAMPLING DISTRIBUTION OF SAMPLE MEANS

We'll now summarize the main points so far. We distinguish two cases, one in which the sampling distribution for $\bar{X}$ is only approximately normally distributed, and the other in which $\bar{X}$ is exactly normally distributed.

Case 1: The Sampling Distribution for $\bar{X}$ Is Approximately Normally Distributed

- The population distribution from which the sampling is done is not a normal population.
- The population is large (or theoretically infinite) with a finite mean μ and a finite variance σ^2.
- Repeated random samples are taken of the same size $n \geq 30$.
- The sampling distribution of $\bar{X}$ is approximately a normal distribution with mean $\mu_{\bar{X}} = \mu$ and variance $\sigma_{\bar{X}}^2 = \sigma^2/n$.

Case 2: The Sampling Distribution for $\bar{X}$ Is Exactly Normally Distributed

- The population distribution from which the sampling is done is a normal population with mean μ and variance σ^2.
- Repeated random samples are taken of the same size $n > 1$.

- The sampling distribution of $\bar{X}$ is exactly a normal distribution with mean $\mu_{\bar{X}} = \mu$ and variance $\sigma_{\bar{X}}^2 = \sigma^2/n$.

In either case, the procedure described in this section for evaluating probabilities for sample means is applicable. The procedure relies on the following relationship:

Standard Normal Conversion for Sample Means

$$Z = \frac{\bar{X} - \mu_{\bar{X}}}{\sigma_{\bar{X}}} = \frac{\bar{X} - \mu}{\sigma/\sqrt{n}} \qquad (6\text{-}4)$$

This equation allows us to obtain probabilities for $\bar{X}$ via the standard normal probability table.

PRACTICE EXERCISES

6.2 Let a continuous random variable X represent lifetimes (in hours) of a certain catalyst used in an industrial process. Suppose X has a probability distribution with mean $\mu = 117$ and standard deviation $\sigma = 58$; and suppose a random sample of size $n = 841$ is taken from the population. What is the probability that the value of the sample mean $\bar{X}$ will exceed 121.72?

6.3 Let a random variable X represent the monthly rent for a one bedroom apartment in a certain city. Suppose X is normally distributed with mean $\mu = 466$ and standard deviation $\sigma = 24$. A random sample of size $n = 9$ is taken from the population. What is the probability that the value of the sample mean $\bar{X}$ will be less than 452.64?

CENTRAL LIMIT THEOREM AND CHEBYSHEV'S THEOREM

Chebyshev's theorem was first introduced and applied in Chapter 3. Chebyshev's theorem states that for any set of data (whether a population or sample) the proportion of observations that lie within k standard deviations of the mean is at least equal to $1 - (1/k^2)$, where $k > 1$. For populations, this can be expressed as a probability statement:

$$P(\mu - k\sigma < X < \mu + k\sigma) \geq 1 - \frac{1}{k^2}$$

For samples, we write

$$P(\bar{X} - kS < X < \bar{X} + kS) \geq 1 - \frac{1}{k^2}$$

where S is the sample standard deviation. Does Chebyshev's theorem offer a better description of the probability distribution of sample means than the central limit theorem? If the central limit theorem provides a better description of the distribution of the sample means, we should expect that the proportion of sample means $\bar{X}$ that lie within k standard deviations of the mean $\mu_{\bar{X}}$ will more closely conform to the normal distribution value suggested by the central limit theorem than the conservative range suggested by Chebyshev's theorem. More specifically, does the normal distribution formula give a more exact value for $P(\mu_{\bar{X}} - k\sigma_{\bar{X}} < \bar{X} < \mu_{\bar{X}} + k\sigma_{\bar{X}})$ than the conservative lower bound of $1 - 1/k^2$ of Chebyshev's theorem? To evaluate, let's examine the data presented previously in Table 6.2 and repeated here in Table 6.7.

TABLE 6.7	List of Possible Sample Means from Student Survey of 10 Households When $n = 2$							
*3	*5	*4	*3.5	0.5	*2	*4.5	*1.5	*2.5
*3	*7	*6	*5.5	*2.5	*4	*6.5	*3.5	*4.5
*5	*7	*8	*7.5	*4.5	*6	8.5	*5.5	*6.5
*4	*6	*8	*6.5	*3.5	*5	*7.5	*4.5	*5.5
*3.5	*5.5	*7.5	*6.5	*3	*4.5	*7	*4	*5
0.5	*2.5	*4.5	*3.5	*3	*1.5	*4	*1	*2
*2	*4	*6	*5	*4.5	*1.5	*5.5	*2.5	*3.5
*4.5	*6.5	8.5	*7.5	*7	*4	*5.5	*5	*6
*1.5	*3.5	*5.5	*4.5	*4	*1	*2.5	*5	*3
*2.5	*4.5	*6.5	*5.5	*2	*5	*3.5	*6	*3

*Asterisks mark values that are within 2 standard deviations of the mean.

Recall that the data reveal that $\mu_{\bar{X}} = 4.5$ and $\sigma_{\bar{X}} = \sqrt{3.6666667} = 1.915$. According to Chebyshev's theorem, for $k = 2$ the percentage of the means that lie between $4.5 - 2(1.915) = 0.67$ and $4.5 + 2(1.915) = 8.33$ should be at least 75%. By comparison, applying the central limit theorem gives us the following percentage under the normal curve for the range 0.67–8.33:

$$P(0.67 < \bar{X} < 8.33) = P(-2 < Z < 2) = .9544, \quad \text{or approx. } 95.44\%$$

A count of the sample means with values greater than 0.67 and less than 8.33 (marked by asterisks in Table 6.7) totals 86. In percentage terms we have $\left(\frac{86}{90}\right) \times 100\% = 95.55\%$, a figure in much closer conformity with the central limit theorem's normal curve value of 95.44% than with the Chebyshev's theorem value of 75%.

In summary, Chebyshev's theorem provides a rather conservative estimate of the percentage of observations that lie within k standard deviations of the mean. When the normal distribution approximation is applicable, a much closer estimate is obtained. Since the normal distribution is widely applicable and widely used, it has become a common practice to provide percentages for values within 1, 2, and 3 standard deviations of the mean for normal distributions. These percentages are given in the form of the **empirical rule**:

The Empirical Rule

1. Approximately 68% of the values will lie within 1 standard deviation of the mean (i.e., approx. 68% of the values will lie within the interval from $\mu - \sigma$ to $\mu + \sigma$).
2. Approximately 95% of the values will lie within 2 standard deviations of the mean (i.e., approx. 95% of the values will lie within the interval from $\mu - 2\sigma$ to $\mu + 2\sigma$).
3. Approximately 99.7% of the values will lie within 3 standard deviations of the mean (i.e., approx. 99.7% of the values will lie within the interval from $\mu - 3\sigma$ to $\mu + 3\sigma$).

CENTRAL LIMIT THEOREM AND THE NORMAL DISTRIBUTION APPROXIMATION TO THE BINOMIAL DISTRIBUTION

Let's refer back to the binomial distribution discussed in Chapter 5. We have a series of n independent trials. The outcome of each trial will be something we call either a "success" or a "failure." There will be a probability p of success on each trial. If we have n such trials, we estimate p with the sample proportion of successes. For example, if you want to estimate the probability that a coin toss will lead to a head (success), you could toss the coin 100 times and count the number of times it comes up heads. You would then estimate the probability of getting heads by calculating the proportion of observed heads (i.e., the number of observed heads divided by 100). So, if we let X represent the observed number of successes and n represent the number of trials, the proportion of successes X/n is an estimate of the probability of getting a success on any trial.

But the proportion of successes is really a disguised mean. Why? Because it is the average of 1's and 0's, where the 1's are assigned to successes and the 0's are assigned to failures. This means that the sample proportion X/n represents the average number of successes among the n trials. Therefore, according to the central limit theorem, the distribution of sample proportions X/n may be approximated by a normal distribution when the value of n is sufficiently large. The mean and standard deviation of the distribution of sample proportions are given by

$$\mu = E\left(\frac{X}{n}\right) = p \qquad \text{and} \qquad \sigma = \sqrt{\text{Var}\left(\frac{X}{n}\right)} = \sqrt{\frac{p(1-p)}{n}}$$

Figure 6.8 shows the histograms for the binomial distributions with $n = 5$, 10, and 40, when $p = .5$. Notice that the shapes of these distributions approach the shape of a normal curve as n increases. For small n ($n = 5$), the distribution of X shows little resemblance to the normal curve. But at $n = 40$, we find that the distribution of X closely resembles a normal curve.

This tendency of the distribution of a binomial random variable X to approach a normal distribution as n increases is quite general and is consistent with the distribution of proportions X/n. Since the distributions of X/n and X both approach normal distributions as the number of trials n increases, we can evaluate binomial distribution probabilities for large values of n by using the normal distribution as an approximation. The procedure for approximating the binomial distribution by the normal distribution was first discussed in Chapter 5, and now we have additional support from the central limit theorem that the approximation works. The rule of thumb given in Chapter 5 is repeated here:

Rule of Thumb

The normal distribution is a reasonable approximation to the binomial distribution when $np \geq 5$ and $n(1 - p) \geq 5$. Furthermore, for a given value of n, the approximation will be better the closer p is to .5.

Figure 6.8
Histograms of binomial
distributions for different
values of n

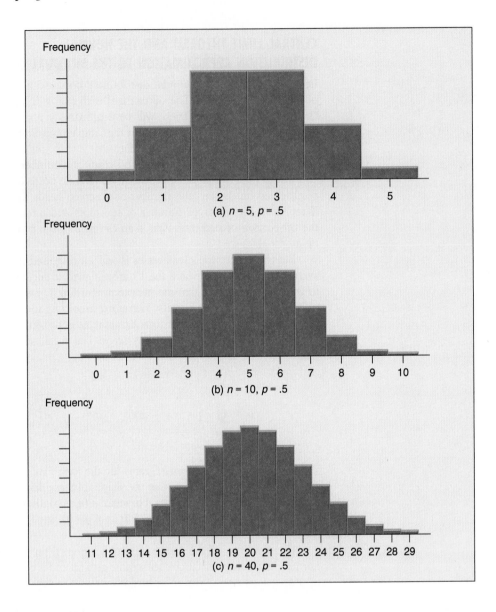

To use a normal distribution to approximate probabilities for the binomial random variable X, the variable X is converted to the standard normal random variable Z using the following formula (from Chapter 5):

Normal Distribution
Approximation to the Binomial Distribution

$$Z = \frac{X - np}{\sqrt{np(1 - p)}} \tag{6-5}$$

where np and $np(1 - p)$ represent the mean and variance, respectively, for the binomial distribution.

Equivalently, the expression for proportions is:

$$Z = \frac{\frac{X}{n} - p}{\sqrt{\frac{p(1-p)}{n}}} \qquad \text{(6-6)}$$

where X/n represents the sample proportion, and p and $p(1-p)/n$ represent the mean and variance, respectively, for the distribution of X/n.

Let's examine the use of equations (6-5) and (6-6) in a gaming situation.

■ **EXAMPLE 6.3**

Sampling Distribution for Proportion

Suppose a gambler believes his probability of winning with a certain strategy at a gaming table in Las Vegas is $p = .51$. If his belief is correct and if he plays 400 times in one day using his strategy each time, what is the approximate probability that the proportion of his wins on that day will exceed .50?

Solution

Step 1
We seek to evaluate $P(X/n) > .50) = P(X/400 > .50)$.

Step 2
Alternatively, we can write $P(X/400) > .50) = P(X > 200)$. That is, the gambler must win more than 200 times out of 400 trials to obtain a proportion that exceeds .50.

Step 3
Incorporating the required continuity correction discussed in Section 5.3, we restate $P(X > 200)$ as $P(X \geq 200.5)$.

Step 4
Calculating the terms np and $n(1-p)$, we find that $np = 400(.51) = 204$, and $n(1-p) = 400(.49) = 196$. Since both terms are greater than 5, we meet the condition of our rule of thumb for using the normal distribution to approximate the binomial distribution.

Step 5
The equivalent Z expression for $X = 200.5$ is

$$Z = \frac{X - np}{\sqrt{nP(1-np)}}$$
$$= \frac{200.5 - 204}{\sqrt{400(.51)(.49)}}$$
$$= -.35$$

Therefore, we can write $P(X \geq 200.5) = P(Z \geq -.35)$.

Step 6
According to Appendix Table IV, $P(Z \geq -.35) = .6368$.

Step 7

Thus, on a day that the gambler plays and uses his strategy, the probability is .6368 that the proportion of his wins will exceed .50. (Or, he will win more than half the time on approx. 63.68% of the days he uses his strategy.)

PRACTICE EXERCISE

6.4 An educator claims that 20% of all college students in the United States would fail a standard spelling test. If her claim is true and if a random sample of 500 students is selected from the population of all college students in the United States, what is the probability that more than 15% of the selected students will fail the standard spelling test?

EXERCISES

▶ **6.8** An automobile manufacturer has offered a 6 yr/60,000 mi powertrain warranty. If the powertrain has a life expectancy of 61,000 mi with a standard deviation of 8000 mi, what is the probability that the average life of powertrains from 625 randomly selected automobiles will be:
   a. Less than 60,497.6 mi?   b. More than 62,748.8 mi?
   c. From 61,428.8 to 61,771.2 mi?   d. From 60,472 to 60,708.8 mi?

6.9 The manager of a fast food franchise claims that her store averages $313,000 per week in receipts, with a standard deviation of $11,500 per week. Suppose the weekly averages are approximately normally distributed. What is the probability that if you take a random sample of 25 weekly receipts, they will show an average:
   a. Less than $317,393?   b. More than $307,963?
   c. Between $311,528 and $317,071?   d. Between $315,484 and $319,808?

6.10 An automobile manufacturer offers a 6 yr/60,000 mi powertrain warranty. If the manufacturer expects 3% of the powertrains to fail within the warranty period and if 10,000 of these automobiles have been sold, what is the approximate probability that:
   a. More than 266 of these powertrains will fail within the warranty period?
   b. More than 333 of these powertrains will fail within the warranty period?
   c. Fewer than 265 of these powertrains will fail within the warranty period?
   d. Fewer than 335 of these powertrains will fail within the warranty period?
   e. Between 265 and 323, inclusive, of these powertrains will fail within the warranty period?
   f. If it costs the manufacturer an average of $473 to honor the warranty on a failed powertrain, what is the approximate probability that it will cost the manufacturer more than $125,345 to honor the warranties on the 10,000 automobiles?

SUMMARY

Sampling procedures are not to be taken lightly. Improper sampling procedures can lead to misleading information. Proper sampling procedures, on the other hand, can provide relatively accurate information. Sample means and sample proportions, for example, will have frequency distributions that can be approximated by the normal distribution. Moreover, the frequency distribution of sample means clusters closely about the original true population mean. The clustering is closer when the population standard deviation σ is small and the sample size n is large. We saw this clustering of sample means $\bar{X}$ around μ when we compared Figure 6.4 with Figure 6.5, and Figure 6.6 with Figure 6.7. This should give us a fairly comfortable feeling that sample means are good estimators of population means.

Also, we can use the normal distribution to calculate the probability that the sample mean or proportion value we observe will be within a specified distance from the corresponding population parameter. For the 36 cereal boxes in Example 6.1, there is only a 2.28% chance that the average weight of the 36 boxes would be more than 0.2 oz less than the population mean of 24 oz; for the gambler in Example 6.3, there is a 63.68% chance that he will win more than 50% of his plays.

As we progress through this text we'll find other useful ways to utilize the behavior properties of the frequency distributions of sample means and other sample statistics.

KEY EQUATIONS

Mean and Variance of Sampling Distributions of Sample Means:

Mean

$$\mu_{\bar{X}} = \mu \tag{6-1}$$

Variance (1)

$$\sigma_{\bar{X}}^2 = \left(\frac{\sigma^2}{n}\right) \left(\frac{N - n}{N - 1}\right) \tag{6-2}$$

when the population size N is not very large relative to the sample size n, and we sample without replacement.

Variance (2)

$$\sigma_{\bar{X}}^2 = \frac{\sigma^2}{n} \tag{6-3}$$

when the population size N is very large relative to the sample size n (i.e., when $N \geq 20n$); or when the population size is theoretically infinite; or when we sample with replacement from a finite population. Note, μ and σ^2 are the mean and variance, respectively, of the original population; and $\mu_{\bar{X}}$ and $\sigma_{\bar{X}}^2$ are the mean and variance, respectively, of the distribution of all possible sample means of same size n that can be taken from the original population.

Standard Error of the Mean

The standard deviation $\sigma_{\bar{X}}$ is also known as the standard error of the mean.

Standard Normal Conversion for Sample Means

$$Z = \frac{\bar{X} - \mu_{\bar{X}}}{\sigma_{\bar{X}}} = \frac{\bar{X} - \mu}{\sigma/\sqrt{n}} \tag{6-4}$$

Normal Distribution
Approximation to the Binomial Distribution

$$Z = \frac{X - np}{\sqrt{np(1 - p)}} \tag{6-5}$$

or, equivalently for proportions:

$$Z = \frac{\frac{X}{n} - p}{\sqrt{\frac{p(1 - p)}{n}}} \tag{6-6}$$

where np and $np(1 - p)$ represent the mean and variance, respectively, for the binomial distribution, X/n represents the sample proportion of successes, and p and $p(1 - p)/n$ represent the mean and variance, respectively, for the distribution of X/n.

PRACTICE EXERCISE ANSWERS

6.1 a. $\mu = \dfrac{1 + 3 + 5 + 7}{4} = 4.0$;

$$\sigma_X^2 = \dfrac{(1 - 4)^2 + (3 - 4)^2 + (5 - 4)^2 + (7 - 4)^2}{4} = 5.0$$

b. The unordered pairs are $\{1, 3\}, \{1, 5\}, \{1, 7\}, \{3, 5\}, \{3, 7\}, \{5, 7\}$. The means are 2, 3, 4, 4, 5, 6.

$$\mu_{\bar{X}} = \dfrac{2 + 3 + 4 + 4 + 5 + 6}{6} = 4.0;$$

$$\sigma_{\bar{X}}^2 = \dfrac{(2 - 4)^2 + (3 - 4)^2 + \cdots + (6 - 4)^2}{6} = 1.67$$

c. $\mu_{\bar{X}} = \mu$ and $\sigma_{\bar{X}}^2 = \dfrac{\sigma^2}{2}\left(\dfrac{4 - 2}{4 - 1}\right)$

d. The ordered pairs are (1, 1), (1, 3), (1, 5), (1, 7), (3, 1), (3, 3), (3, 5), (3, 7), (5, 1), (5, 3), (5, 5), (5, 7), (7, 1), (7, 3), (7, 5), (7, 7). The means are 1, 2, 3, 4, 2, 3, 4, 5, 3, 4, 5, 6, 4, 5, 6, 7.

$$\mu_{\bar{X}} = \dfrac{1 + 2 + 3 + \cdots + 6 + 7}{16} = 4.0;$$

$$\sigma_{\bar{X}}^2 = \dfrac{(1 - 4)^2 + (2 - 4)^2 + \cdots + (7 - 4)^2}{16} = 2.5$$

e. $\mu_{\bar{X}} = \mu$ and $\sigma_{\bar{X}}^2 = \sigma^2/2$

6.2 $\bar{X}$ is approximately normally distributed with mean $\mu_{\bar{X}} = 117$ and standard deviation $\sigma_{\bar{X}} = \sigma/\sqrt{n} = 58/\sqrt{841} = 2$.

$$P(\bar{X} > 121.72) = .5 - P(117 \le \bar{X} \le 121.72)$$

$$= .5 - P\left(\dfrac{117 - 117}{2} \le Z \le \dfrac{121.72 - 117}{2}\right)$$

$$= .5 - P(0 \le Z \le 2.36)$$

$$= .5 - .4909 = .0091$$

6.3 $\bar{X}$ is exactly normally distributed with mean $\mu_{\bar{X}} = 466$ and standard deviation $\sigma_{\bar{X}} = \sigma/\sqrt{n} = 24/\sqrt{9} = 8$.

$$P(\bar{X} < 452.64) = .5 - P(452.64 \le \bar{X} \le 466)$$

$$= .5 - P\left(\dfrac{452.64 - 466}{8} \le Z \le \dfrac{466 - 466}{8}\right)$$

$$= .5 - P(-1.67 \le Z \le 0)$$

$$= .5 - .4525 = .0475$$

6.4 X/n is distributed approximately normally with mean .2 and standard deviation

$$\sigma_{X/n} = \sqrt{\dfrac{p(1 - p)}{n}} = \sqrt{\dfrac{(.2)(.8)}{500}} = 0.01789$$

$$P\left(\dfrac{X}{500} > .15\right) = P(X > 75) = P(X \ge 75.5)$$

$$= P\left(Z \ge \dfrac{75.5 - 100}{\sqrt{(500)(.2)(.8)}}\right)$$

$$= P(Z \ge -2.74)$$

$$= .5 + P(-2.74 \le Z \le 0)$$

$$= .5 + .4969 = .9969$$

CHAPTER REVIEW EXERCISES

▶ **6.11** Suppose you work for the county health agency and you are told that, on the average, 62% of the emergency cases coming into the county-supported emergency clinic are minor injuries. You wish to check on this figure, but you don't want to look at all the records. Suggest a procedure for taking a random sample from the clinic's emergency records during the past month.

6.12 A professor claims that over the 25 years she has been teaching, her students have an average score of 67% over all the group final exams given by her department. She says that all her records are intact and are available for scrutiny. Suggest a procedure for taking a random sample from these records.

6.13 Refer to Exercise 6.11.
   a. Suggest a systematic sampling procedure.
   b. Suppose there are 10 emergency clinics in the county. Suggest (1) a stratified random sampling procedure, and (2) a cluster sampling procedure.

6.14 Refer to Exercise 6.12.
   a. Suggest a systematic sampling procedure.
   b. Suggest a stratified random sampling procedure.
   c. Suggest a cluster sampling procedure.

6.15 If we have a population consisting of 10 numbers, with a mean of 4.5 and a variance of 8.25, and if we take all possible samples of size 2 without replacement from that population and calculate their means, then the distribution of these sample means has a mean and a variance equal to what values?

6.16 If we have a population consisting of 10 numbers, with a mean of 4.5 and variance of 8.25, and if we take all possible samples of size 4 without replacement from that population and calculate their means, then the distribution of these sample means has a mean and a variance equal to what values?

6.17 If we have a population consisting of 1 million members, with a mean of 4.5 and a variance of 8.5, and if we take all possible samples of size 2 from that population and calculate their means, then the distribution of these sample means has a mean and a variance equal to what values? For the variance, use the exact formula and the approximate formula, and compare the two answers.

6.18 If we have a population consisting of 1 million members, with a mean of 4.5 and a variance of 8.5, and if we take all possible samples of size 4 from that population and calculate their means, then the distribution of these sample means has a mean and a variance equal to what values? For the variance, use the exact formula and the approximate formula, and compare the two answers.

▶ **6.19** Suppose a population consists of the numbers 1, 3, 5, 7, and 9.
   a. Compute the mean for this population.
   b. Compute the variance for this population.
   c. List all possible ordered samples of size 2 taken without replacement from this population.
   d. List the means of all the samples in part c.
   e. Compute the mean of the values listed in part d, and compare with the value of the mean found in part a.
   f. Compute the variance of the values listed in part d, and compare with the value of the variance obtained by using the exact formula.

6.20 Suppose a population consists of the numbers 0, 2, 4, 6, and 8.
   a. Compute the mean for this population.
   b. Compute the variance for this population.
   c. List all possible unordered samples of size 4 taken without replacement from this population.

d. List the means of all the samples in part c.

e. Compute the mean of the values listed in part d, and compare with the value of the mean found in part a.

f. Compute the variance of the values listed in part d, and compare with the value of the variance obtained by using the exact formula.

6.21 If we take samples of size 11 from a theoretically infinite population with mean and variance equal to 71 and 19, respectively, then:

a. What is the mean of the distribution of the sample means?

b. What is the variance of the distribution of the sample means?

c. If we take samples of size 22, what happens to the value of the mean of the distribution of the sample means relative to the answer given in part a?

d. If we take samples of size 22, what happens to the value of the variance of the distribution of the sample means relative to the answer given in part b?

▶ **6.22** If we take samples of size 36 from a theoretically infinite population with mean and variance equal to 221 and 44, respectively, then:

a. What is the mean of the distribution of the sample means?

b. What is the variance of the distribution of the sample means?

c. If we take samples of size 9, what happens to the value of the mean of the distribution of the sample means relative to the answer given in part a?

d. If we take samples of size 9, what happens to the value of the variance of the distribution of the sample means relative to the answer given in part b?

▶ **6.23** If the distribution of sample means, for samples of size 36, has mean equal to 24 and standard deviation equal to 0.1, use the central limit theorem to find:

a. $P(\bar{X} < 23.8)$ b. $P(\bar{X} > 24.2)$ c. $P(\bar{X} < 24.165)$

d. $P(\bar{X} < 23.804)$ e. $P(\bar{X} > 24.257)$ f. $P(\bar{X} < 24.305)$

6.24 If the distribution of sample means, for samples of size 25, has mean equal to 10 and standard deviation equal to 0.08, use the central limit theorem to find:

a. $P(\bar{X} < 9.8592)$ b. $P(\bar{X} > 10.1864)$ c. $P(\bar{X} < 9.8136)$

d. $P(\bar{X} > 10.132)$ e. $P(\bar{X} > 9.7944)$ f. $P(\bar{X} < 10.232)$

6.25 If the original, theoretically infinite, population has a mean of 1 and a standard deviation of 0.03, then, based on samples of size 100, use the central limit theorem to find:

a. $P(\bar{X} > 1.031)$ b. $P(\bar{X} < 1.003)$ c. $P(\bar{X} < 0.994)$

d. $P(\bar{X} > 0.9925)$ e. $P(\bar{X} > 1.00588)$ f. $P(\bar{X} < 1.00528)$

6.26 If the original, theoretically infinite, population has a mean of 19.5 and a standard deviation of 2.71, then, based on samples of size 100, use the central limit theorem to find:

a. $P(\bar{X} > 20.28861)$ b. $P(\bar{X} < 18.98239)$ c. $P(\bar{X} < 20.01761)$

d. $P(\bar{X} > 18.71139)$ e. $P(\bar{X} > 19.24255)$ f. $P(\bar{X} < 19.41057)$

6.27 A federal agency claims that the average weekly grocery bill for a husband and wife living alone comes to $65, with a standard deviation of $9. If we randomly select 36 households consisting of just a husband and wife living alone, what is:

a. The approximate probability that the average weekly grocery bill for these 36 households is between $62.55 and $68.10?

b. The amount A such that the probability is .9505 that the average weekly grocery bill for these 36 households is more than A?

c. The probability that the average weekly grocery bill for these 36 households is at least $62?

d. The probability that the total grocery bill for the 36 households will exceed $2213.64?

e. According to Chebyshev's theorem, at least what percentage of the households consisting of just a husband and wife should have a weekly grocery bill between $50.15 and $79.85? If we assume these costs are normally distributed, what percentage of these households should have a weekly grocery bill between $50.15 and $79.85? Compare the two answers.

f. According to Chebyshev's theorem, at least what percentage of the samples of size 36 should have a weekly grocery bill between $62 and $68? Using the normal distribution, what percentage of the samples of size 36 should have an average weekly grocery bill between $62 and $68? Compare the two answers.

6.28 Assume the average gross weight of tractor-trailer trucks traveling through the San Joaquin Valley in California is 47,000 lb, with a standard deviation of 3600 lb. Assume also that the weights are normally distributed, and suppose we randomly select four such trucks traveling through the San Joaquin Valley. What is:

a. The probability that the average weight of these four trucks is between 42,608 and 51,428 lb?

b. The weight W such that the probability is .8997 that the average weight of the four trucks is less than W?

c. The probability that the average weight of these four trucks is at most 50,006 lb?

d. The probability that the combined weight of the four trucks will be less than 199,304 lb?

e. According to Chebyshev's theorem, at least what proportion of the tractor-trailer trucks traveling through the San Joaquin Valley should weigh from 39,800 to 54,200 lb? Using the normal distribution, what proportion should weigh from 39,800 to 54,200 lb? Compare the two answers.

f. According to Chebyshev's theorem, at least what proportion of samples of size 4 should have an average weight from 41,600 to 52,400 lb? Using the normal distribution, what proportion should weigh from 41,600 to 52,400 lb? Compare the two answers.

▶ **6.29** Assume that the net weight of cereal in a box of a certain type of cereal is normally distributed with a mean weight of 16 oz and a standard deviation of 0.5 oz. If a random sample of size 25 is taken of boxes of cereal of this type, what is:

a. The probability that the average net weight of cereal in the 25 boxes is less than 15.6 oz?

b. The probability that the average net weight of cereal in the 25 boxes will be between 15.7 and 16.7 oz?

c. The probability that the average net weight of cereal in the 25 boxes will be at most 16.17 oz?

d. The probability that the average net weight of cereal in the 25 boxes will be at least 15.935 oz?

e. The weight W such that the probability is .9901 that the average net weight of the 25 boxes is greater than W?

f. The probability that the net weight of the 25 boxes will be less than 397.75 oz?

6.30 A machine can be adjusted so that the amount of flour it pours into a bag is a normally distributed random variable with a mean of 10 lb and a standard deviation of 0.4 lb. What is:

a. The probability that a bag of flour filled by the machine will weigh between 9.6 and 10.4 lb?

b. The probability that the average weight of 25 randomly selected bags filled by the machine will be less than 9.8592 lb?

c. The probability that the total weight of 25 randomly selected bags filled by the machine will be more than 254 lb?

d. The weight W such that the probability is .975 that the weight of one bag filled by the machine is greater than W?

e. The weight W such that the probability is .975 that the average weight of 25 randomly selected bags is greater than W?

6.31 Suppose we have a very large lot of 300,000 automobile tires, 1% of which have defective sidewalls, and suppose we take all possible samples of size 400 from that population.

a. On the average, how many tires in the samples should have defective sidewalls?

b. On the average, what proportion of the tires in the samples should have defective sidewalls?

6.32 Suppose we take all possible samples of size 500 from the population in Exercise 6.31.

a. On the average, how many tires in the samples should have defective sidewalls?

b. On the average, what proportion of the tires in the samples should have defective sidewalls?

▶ **6.33** The highway patrol claims that at a certain checkpoint they catch 4 drunk drivers per every 100 automobiles that they stop.

a. How many drunk drivers should they expect to see among the next 25 automobiles they stop?

b. What proportion of drunk drivers should they expect to see among the next 50 automobiles they stop?

c. With respect to the distribution of sample proportions for groups of 50 automobiles stopped by the highway patrol at the checkpoint, what is the standard deviation?

6.34 With respect to the population of tires in Exercise 6.31, use the central limit theorem to find the approximate probabilities for:

a. $P(X > 5)$ b. $P\left(\dfrac{X}{400} < .0075\right)$

6.35 With respect to the conditions specified in Exercise 6.32, use the central limit theorem to find the approximate probabilities for:

a. $P(X > 3)$ b. $P\left(\dfrac{X}{500} < .014\right)$

6.36 If the highway patrol claims that at a certain checkpoint they catch 4 drunk drivers per every 100 automobiles that they stop, then:

a. What is the approximate probability that they will catch more than 1 drunk driver among the next 25 automobiles that they stop?

b. What is the approximate probability that they will catch more than 1 drunk driver among the next 50 automobiles they stop?

c. What is the approximate probability that the proportion of drunk drivers they catch among the next 100 automobiles they stop will be at most .06?

6.37 According to past records, 2% of the milk shakes sold at a certain fast food chain in Goodyear, Arizona, are date shakes (made from fresh dates). If they sell 150 shakes on a given day, then:

a. How many date shakes should they expect to sell?

b. What proportion of the shakes should they expect to be date shakes?

c. What is the probability that more than 1% of the shakes they sell will be date shakes?

▶ **6.38** Suppose that on the national level 88% of entering college students will continue with their college education and graduate. In a first year class of 1000 students, what is the probability that:

a. At least 864 will complete their college education and graduate?

b. At least 85% will complete their college education and graduate?

SOLVING APPLIED CASES
Statistical Distribution of Averages: The Basis of Wholesaling Strategy

Near the cash register in his restaurant concession at a northeastern Ohio truck stop, Frank Cazmier has a display of giant stuffed toy animals, which some truckers purchase for their children. The animals cost Frank $50 each, and he sells them for $90 each.

Like many other small retailers, Frank orders conservatively. He invariably orders four of the stuffed toy animals, fewer than he could sell. "Turnover," he says, "I could sell, *on average*, about nine of these stuffed toy animals a month. But if I have a bad month with the stuffed animals and only one of them sells, I still have to come up with $450 when the toy sales representative stops by. That really hurts."

Burt Crowley, a tobacco and candy wholesaler, told Frank he had decided to add stuffed toy animals to his line of merchandise and would be interested in supplying Frank with stuffed toy animals. "I have to pay $50 just like you do, and so I'll have to charge you $60. But with a $90 selling price you'll clear $30 per stuffed toy animal, which, for nine animals, comes to an average of $270 per month, a definite improvement over the previous $160. You'll have the big advantage of animals in stock, since I can deliver to you on my regular twice weekly calls. You won't have to wait until the end of the month for replenishment. With a fresh supply of stuffed animals in your hands quickly, you'll never run low, but instead be in position to capture about five extra sales a month without putting up your own money for inventory. It's like having your cake and eating it too." Frank did some quick figuring and said, "It looks good, Burt. The only thing I don't understand is why you want to do it for $10 profit per animal. You know how sporadic the sales are, and you don't like having your cash tied up in inventory any more than I do."

And Burt replied, "You are only one of 36 customers I'll have. Your monthly sales vary a lot. Mine won't, thanks to the *statistical distribution of averages*. If you want to be a good wholesaler, you have to know about the statistical behavior of averages."

Assume that each of Burt's customers has the same sales distribution as Frank; that is, they each have a probability distribution for sales of stuffed toy animals with a mean μ of 9 per month and a standard deviation σ of 3 per month. Let's also assume that risk can be measured in terms of the variability, σ.

a. For Frank, and for each of the other 35 retailers, the monthly probability distribution of sales has a standard deviation of $\sigma = 3$.

b. For Burt, the corresponding monthly probability distribution per retailer is the probability distribution of $\bar{X}$, the average monthly sales per retailer. The probability distribution has the mean $\mu_{\bar{X}} = 9$ and, importantly, its standard deviation is only

$$\sigma_{\bar{X}} = \frac{\sigma}{\sqrt{n}} = \frac{3}{\sqrt{36}} = .5$$

c. Therefore, Frank's variability relative to Burt's variability is

$$\frac{\sigma}{\sigma_{\bar{X}}} = \frac{3}{.5} = 6$$

We see that Frank, as a single retailer, has a monthly average sales potential of 9, whereas Burt has a monthly average of 9 *per retailer* over 36 retailers. Moreover, Burt encounters considerably less variation of monthly mean sales (per retailer) than Frank. In fact, on a relative basis, Frank's variation is 6 times greater than Burt's. This shows that Burt faces much less downside sales risk than Frank, even though both stock to meet their average demands. To put this into a numbers perspective, consider first what Frank's sales would look like on a monthly basis if his sales vary over 2 standard deviations from month to month. His low sales month would result in $9 - 2(3) = 3$ sales, and his high sales month would yield $9 + 2(3) = 15$ sales. How should he stock for such a wide variation? In contrast, consider what Burt's sales *per retailer* would look like on a monthly basis if his sales vary over 2 standard deviations from month to month. His low sales month would result in $9 - 2(.5) = 8$ sales, and his high sales month would yield $9 + 2(.5) = 10$ sales. Clearly, there is much less variable risk, per retailer, for Burt than for the individual retailer operating on his own.

d. Can we explain how the behavior of statistical averages relates to Burt's wholesaling strategy? Burt's wholesaling strategy appeals to customers like Frank because it helps them capture sales they presently lose, without increasing their risk of cash shortage. Burt carries, and makes available to his customers, the inventory they want on short notice but are unwilling to risk holding. It is a common notion that middlemen like Burt sell and profit without benefitting anyone else. This simply is not true. Manufacturers, retailers (like Frank), and customers (such as Frank's customers) all benefit from Burt's wholesaling operation. There is an increased profit for the manufacturer and for the retailer (Frank) from the larger sales volume. Additionally, customers find a greater availability of the product to better suit their purchase time preferences. It is of particular interest to note that Burt's strategy does not depend at all on volume price discounts from the manufacturer as is commonly believed. If discounts are available because of volume production and shipping, it is an additional benefit of the wholesaling system. The key to Burt's wholesaling strategy is that the individual retailer's holding risk is diversified and reduced by Burt's inventory holding operation. The 36 retailers' demand fluctuations are not perfectly linked with each other, so if one retailer's demand slumps, another retailer's demand may increase. Otherwise, there would be no net gain from Burt's wholesaling strategy. As long as the 36 retailers' demands exhibit independent movements, one retailer's demand slump would likely be offset by another's rise. This averaging out process lowers the per unit risk of Burt to a level that is lower than any of the retailers. The statistical distribution of averages is a foundation for the risk advantage. Burt and other wholesalers recognize why it is critical to understand how the statistical behavior of averages works for them.

Checkpoint Exercise

1. Assume that Frank and all of Burt's other retailers have a probability distribution for sales of stuffed toy animals with a mean $\mu = 13$ per month and a standard deviation $\sigma = 4$ per month. And assume that Burt serves 25 retailers.
   a. Let $\bar{X}$ represent the mean sales per retailer in a given month. What are the values of the mean $\mu_{\bar{X}}$ and the standard deviation $\sigma_{\bar{X}}$ of the sampling distribution of $\bar{X}$?
   b. What is the ratio of Frank's variability (measured by σ) to Burt's variability (measured by $\sigma_{\bar{X}}$)?
   c. What would be Frank's high and low monthly sales if his sales vary over 2 standard deviations from month to month?
   d. What would be Burt's high and low monthly sales if his sales vary over 2 standard deviations from month to month?

COMPREHENSIVE CASE STUDY

AMERICAN ROOTS OF JAPANESE PRODUCT QUALITY: THE DEMING LEGACY*

We would be hard-pressed to find an example in recent industrial history that dramatically matches Japan's post-World War II turnaround in the quality, productivity, and competitive position of its manufactured goods industries. Pre- and early post-World War II Japanese export products were cheap and poorly made. But this changed during the 1950s. Japan's business community and its government made a long-term commitment to upgrade the quality of its products and to gain a foothold in world markets. Today, virtually everyone recognizes Japanese exports as high-quality products that are competitively priced. In fact, Japanese photographic, electronic, and automotive products have been able to dominate some markets. What few people realize is that Japan's meteoric rise has American roots and that statistical analysis has played a pivotal role.

A key person in this manufacturing turnaround was the American statistician W. E. Deming. What was his secret weapon in the quality control wars that developed? Statistical process control—a statistical methodology that had been developed and advocated by American and British statisticians prior to and during World War II.

While American manufacturers reacted complacently to the production and managerial implications of this quality revolution, Japanese manufacturers listened eagerly and implemented this production philosophy wholeheartedly. Benefits flowed in the form of increased productivity and stronger competitive positions. The slow reaction of American businesses was a consequence of their conventional belief that higher quality would always result in higher costs, due to more frequent and more stringent inspections. In contrast, the Japanese pursued the new belief that *higher quality goes hand in hand with lower costs* when the source of the improved quality is the implementation of statistical process control rather than increased inspection. Japanese production workers were taught how to make their own statistical charts of product variability. Excess product variability was easily spotted and quickly corrected. This early detection procedure led to the discovery and correction of faults in the production process, fewer overall defects, and fewer inspectors needed at the end of the production line. For instance, Japanese automobile manufacturers have one final inspection, while U.S. automobile manufacturers have inspections at several intermediate steps—and end up producing more lemons! In conclusion, the modern Japanese miracle testifies to the power of statistical principles applied to the manufacturing process and confirms what statisticians have been saying for decades: Quality improvement through statistical process control translates to increases in productivity and lower inspection costs.

As an expression of gratitude, the Emperor of Japan awarded Deming the Imperial Medal, and Japanese industry instituted an annual Deming Prize to be awarded to the individual who contributed most to the advancement of precision and dependability of product. Now, decades later, American manufacturers are frantically trying to implement the American know-how exported to Japan. The methodology isn't a secret and usually can be understood by persons who don't have strong technical backgrounds, so perhaps this is a case of "better late than never."

Paradoxically, the slide of American-made goods into the quality doldrums occurred even though the needed expertise was available among American statisticians

---

*W. Edwards Deming. *Quality, Productivity, and Competitive Position*, MIT Center for Advanced Engineering Study, 1982.

as well as among quality control professionals in most large American industrial organizations. Additionally, new managers were graduating from American business schools with increasingly stronger technical backgrounds and training in statistics. American top management had everything it needed to know about quality control and statistics at its fingertips. What it lacked, however, was the concern and sense of urgency to see what was important in the quality arena.

This case study discusses the methodology of statistical process control, the means for achieving uniform quality that American manufacturing initially let pass by. To understand this methodology, we need to understand the nature of sampling processes.

AIMING FOR UNIFORMITY OF MANUFACTURING: CONTROL CHARTS AND STATISTICAL PROCESS CONTROL

Uniformity of output is one hallmark of excellence in mass production processes. For example, consider the manufacturing process for bolts. Uniformity of output of the bolts allows for greater interchangeability of bolts and less concern about which bolt is picked to be used. Otherwise, each bolt would require custom fitting to each nut and washer. Custom fitting is extremely costly and time-consuming. Unfortunately, however, 100% uniformity is not possible in a mass production environment. There will always be some variability in output due to such things as wear and tear on the manufacturing system, differences in operators, and variations in raw materials. The issue is how to inspect each finished part, sorting out the good from the bad parts. From Deming's perspective this is time-consuming and costly, and as inefficient as custom fitting each bolt to a nut and washer.

Background: Statistical Process Control

An alternative and potentially more efficient approach relies on statistical process control. This approach involves close monitoring of the output and a clear understanding of the different types of variability found in the production process. One type of variability is inherent in the system, *common cause variability*. An example is variation in raw materials. Its presence in the system causes the system to produce output showing only a random pattern of variability. This type of variability is considered to be uncontrollable, because it can't be eliminated without improving the quality of the raw material or revamping the production process itself. A second type of variability is external to the system and is called *specific*, or *assignable*, *cause variability*. For example, wear and tear on machines can cause a wider variability in the product from the manufacturing system. When discovered, the source of this variability can be identified, isolated, and eliminated.

The key objective of statistical process control is to achieve and maintain a system's capability by eliminating sources of specific cause variability. This leaves only common cause variability acting within a range permitted by production specifications. Four different situations linking common cause and specific cause variation to product specifications are presented in Figure 1. Let's now discuss these situations using Figure 1 as a guideline.

Figure 1
Four in control and out of
control situations

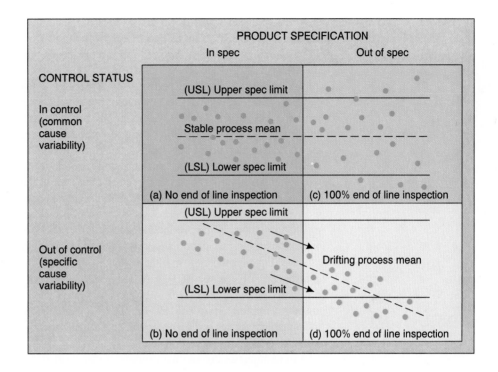

Consider the situation in which production shows output variation that is entirely random (i.e., only common cause at work, no specific cause variation) and well within the range considered acceptable according to product specifications. This situation is portrayed in Figure 1a. This is the best of all worlds because there wouldn't be any defective product output. It would be pointless to inspect the individual parts produced by the production process. All production output, in this ideal situation, could be labeled "good," so there wouldn't be any need to look for bad ones. Not having to inspect all the individual parts could result in considerable savings. This savings implies a lower average unit cost of production, which has the effect of putting the manufacturer in a stronger competitive position.

But what assurance do we have that the output variation of the manufacturing process will continue to be as portrayed in Figure 1a? Unfortunately, none whatsoever, because process parameters can, and frequently do, shift in value. So how should this ideal production system be monitored to be sure that it continues to produce only random output variations consistent with product specification? Here is where inspection comes in. Not to sort out good product output from bad, but to detect shifts in the parameters of the process. For this, statistical sampling is required. By taking small samples of the process, the manufacturer can obtain estimates of the parameters (process mean and process variability) to detect whether any undesirable change in the parameters due to a specific cause is occurring. Figure 1b indicates what appears to be a downward drifting pattern of output variation, which would result from a downward drifting mean. In the language of statistical process control, the manufacturer wants to be able to distinguish between a production process remaining "in control," as in Figure 1a, and one heading "out of control," as in Figure 1b. When a process is in control, the parameters of the process are stable, and the output shows only random variation occurring. A process heading out of control may mean one or more parameters are shifting too far, causing the product dimension to move outside the product specifications. Early identification of the parameter shift is the key to quality control. Once identified, the manufacturer can attempt to correct the specific cause affecting the production process.

What device did Deming teach the Japanese to use in detecting the statistical process control situations? Deming taught the Japanese worker how to construct simple *control charts* to detect and monitor the in control and out of control situations. The control charts shown in Figure 2 are illustrative of the format used. The graphs are simply sequence plots of key sample statistics, usually the sample mean $\bar{X}$ (to monitor the process mean parameter) and the sample range (to monitor the process variability parameter) over the production run. If the chart indicates a rapidly worsening out of control situation, as shown in Figure 1d, immediate action is necessary, possibly stopping the production process. Swift detection and elimination of the specific cause would forestall a major production disruption and avoid wasting labor and material on unacceptable products that soon would be coming off the production line.

Deming pointed out another problem situation. In this case, the process is in control (i.e., no specific cause variation), but there is no guarantee that output meets product specifications. It is possible that a process can be stable, but have too much random variation. An in control process with too much variation, even though stable, will still necessitate 100% inspection to sort out the good parts from the bad. This situation is shown in Figure 1c.

To summarize the six main points of statistical process control:

- The purpose of sampling in statistical process control is to determine whether the production process is in control or out of control.
- If the process is out of control, action must be taken to find and eliminate the cause, possibly shutting down production in order to find the cause.
- If the process variation is in control, the action taken will depend upon whether variation is within product specifications or not within product specifications.
- If variation is within product specifications, no action is taken (i.e., no inspection except periodic monitoring of the process).
- If variation is not within product specifications, then 100% inspection is required to sort out acceptable output. In the latter case, there is an obvious incentive to invest in efforts to reduce variability until it is within product specifications.
- A basic tool in monitoring and detecting the various control situations is in the control chart, a sequence plot of a key statistic, say $\bar{X}$ or R (the sample range), measured for small samples taken at periodic intervals from the process.

A SITUATION REQUIRING 100% INSPECTION: A COMPUTATIONAL EXAMPLE

An example will illustrate some key ideas about statistical quality control. Let's suppose we are considering the production of small steel springs used in an automobile engine. A critical feature of these springs is the amount of elongation they show when subjected to a predetermined amount of tension. The current production system performing at its best (i.e., in control) will produce individual springs, which, when tested for elongation, show elongations that vary randomly around the value of 10 (ten-thousandths

Figure 2
Control chart (a)

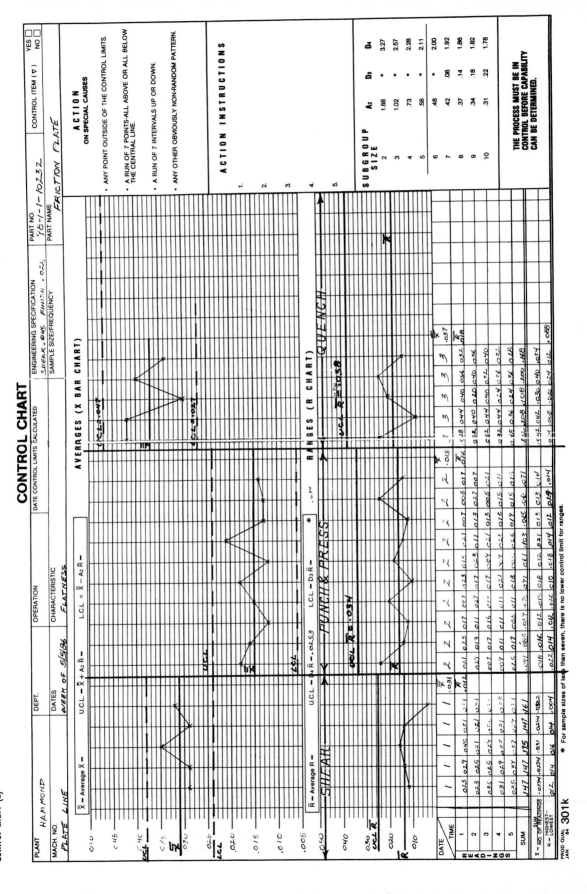

Figure 2
Control chart (b)

Upper chart

	ENTERED	MEASURED
BP HI SPEC:	11.880	
BP LO SPEC:	11.630	
UCL X =	11.855	11.841
UCL R =	11.761	11.777
LCL X =	.150	.120
LCL R =	.000	.000

SAMPLE SIZE: 5
FREQUENCY: # RUNS: 30
COUNT: 151

		STD DEV =	.024
XDBAR =	11.809		
R BAR =	.057		.59
CP =	1.71/		1.04
CPK HI =	.97/		.40
CPK LO =	2.46/		

ACTION ON SPECIAL CAUSES
• ANY POINT OUT OF CONTROL LIMITS
• 7 SUCCESSIVE POINTS, ALL ABOVE OR BELOW THE CENTERLINE
• 7 SUCCESSIVE POINTS, UP OR DOWN
• ANY OTHER NON-RANDOM PATTERN

Columns: TIME / RANGE | $\bar{R}$ | UCL-R | SAMPLE | LCL-$\bar{X}$ | $\bar{\bar{X}}$ | $\bar{X}$ | UCL-$\bar{X}$ | AVERAGE

Lower chart

CUSTOMER
PART NO. 31504-4125
ORDER NO. AFTER GAUGE
CONTROL NO.
CHARACTERISTIC: FINAL FREE HEIGHT
MEASUREMENT:
SAMPLE FREQ: 5
DATE: 11/13/85   CLOCK#

	ENTERED	MEASURED
BP HI SPEC:	11.880	
BP LO SPEC:	11.630	
UCL X =	11.855	11.841
UCL R =	11.761	11.777
LCL X =	.150	.120
LCL R =	.000	.000

SAMPLE SIZE: 5
FREQUENCY: # RUNS: 30
COUNT: 151

		STD DEV =	.024
XDBAR =	11.809		
R BAR =	.057		.59
CP =	1.71/		1.04
CPK HI =	.97/		.40
CPK LO =	2.46/		

ACTION ON SPECIAL CAUSES
• ANY POINT OUT OF CONTROL LIMITS
• 7 SUCCESSIVE POINTS, ALL ABOVE OR BELOW THE CENTERLINE
• 7 SUCCESSIVE POINTS, UP OR DOWN
• ANY OTHER NON-RANDOM PATTERN

TIME	RANGE	SAMPLE	AVERAGE
09:15	.053	1	11.819
09:15	.042	2	11.823
09:15	.056	3	11.818
09:15	.073	4	11.814
09:15	.053	5	11.825
09:15	.071	6	11.843
09:15	.079	7	11.808
09:15	.073	8	11.808
09:15	.012	9	11.820
09:15	.041	10	11.806
09:15	.077	11	11.822
09:15	.041	12	11.810
09:15	.076	13	11.813
09:15	.064	14	11.808
09:15	.032	15	11.799
09:15	.080	16	11.802
09:15	.047	17	11.812
09:15	.050	18	11.818
09:15	.088	19	11.797
09:15	.050	20	11.816
09:15	.078	21	11.779
09:15	.079	22	11.809
09:15	.027	23	11.793
09:15	.047	24	11.790
09:15	.050	25	11.821
09:15	.037	26	11.792
09:15	.083	27	11.805
09:15	.048	28	11.806
09:15	.072	29	11.811
09:15	.046	30	11.789

of an inch). The variation has not been confined within product specifications (the situation portrayed in Figure 1c), so 100% inspection has been used to identify the good springs.

The random variation of the manufactured output is further studied to learn more about the distribution of elongation measurements. It is learned that the distribution can be described by a normal probability distribution with mean $\mu = 10$ (ten-thousandths of an inch) and standard deviation $\sigma = 1$ (ten-thousandths of an inch). The values of μ and σ are the *process parameters*.

We define the *system capability* as the spread between values 3 standard deviations above and 3 standard deviations below the process mean. Thus, in our example, the system capability is the spread between

$$\mu + 3\sigma = 10 + 3(1) = 13$$

and

$$\mu - 3\sigma = 10 - 3(1) = 7$$

(ten-thousandths of an inch), or an estimated spread of $13 - 7 = 6$ (ten-thousandths of an inch). System capability is determined by the variability of individual elongation measurements. The process mean μ is not a factor in determining system capability, because ordinarily we can position the mean wherever we please by properly adjusting the production equipment.

Next, we need to know the *system requirements* specified for a properly functioning spring. Let's suppose the product specifications require elongation not to exceed 11 nor fall below 9 (ten-thousandths of an inch); that is, the system requirement allows a spread of $11 - 9 = 2$ (ten-thousandths) centered at a mean of 10 (ten-thousandths).

Finally, we must compare system requirements with system capability. In this example, the system requirement of 2 (ten-thousandths) maximum spread is more stringent than the 6 (ten-thousandths) range capability of the system. So, even though this current production system is in control (giving the best output that can be expected of it), unacceptable parts are going to be produced. Now, here is the key implication for quality control: *Since the elongation variation is random (no predictable sequence), the only way to find acceptable parts (those with elongation within system requirements) is 100% inspection, that is, inspecting each and every spring.* Costly as this might prove to be, a lower inspection percentage will let unacceptable springs slip through, perhaps ending up malfunctioning in a produced automobile and thus creating a poor quality reputation for the automobile manufacturer. Another alternative, of course, is to develop a new production system capable of producing product that meets the specifications.

THE ARITHMETIC OF LOWER COST FOR HIGHER QUALITY

The financial burden of maintaining a 100% inspection system in the situation just described provides a strong incentive to invest time and effort to change the system for the better. Here we must choose one or both of two different approaches. We can either find a way to relax the system requirements without adversely affecting quality or improve the system capabilities, or some combination of both.

Let's first get a better understanding of the extent of the unacceptable parts problem. Using the normal distribution table and the process parameters $\mu = 10$ and $\sigma = 1$, we can determine the percentage of springs that will have acceptable elongation measurements (between 9 and 11). For this determination we need the values of the standard normal random variable corresponding to the upper and lower ends of the acceptable elongation values. At the upper end of the acceptable elongation values, we have

$$Z = \frac{X - \mu}{\sigma}$$

$$= \frac{11 - 10}{1} = 1$$

The probability that the elongation measurement will be between 10 and 11 is equal to the probability that Z will be between 0 and 1. From the normal table we see that this probability is equal to .3413. Thus, the probability that the elongation measurement will be between 10 and 11 is equal to .3413.

At the lower end of the acceptable elongation values, we have

$$Z = \frac{X - \mu}{\sigma}$$

$$= \frac{9 - 10}{1} = -1$$

Thus, there is also a probability of .3413 that the elongation measurement will be between 9 and 10. Therefore, between 9 and 11 we have a probability of .3413 + .3413 = .6826. Multiplying by 100 to convert to a percentage, we see that in the long run 68.26% of the springs produced are expected to be acceptable. Unfortunately, this means that 100% − 68.26% = 31.74% of the parts are expected to be unacceptable—a very substantial portion.

To see the financial bonus for improving the system, let's consider some cost figures. Because cost per individual spring is very low, it will be easiest to see the point if costs are figured for 1000 springs. Suppose the labor and material cost per 1000 springs (good and bad) averages $80, excluding inspection, and suppose inspection can be done for $120 per 1000. Finally, let's assume the unacceptable springs will simply be discarded rather than reworked. (This is likely a realistic assumption, and we make it here to simplify our calculations.) Thus, to figure the average cost per 1000 parts produced, we add $80 to the $120 inspection, for a total average cost of $200 per 1000. However, only 68.26% of the springs, or an average of 682.6 per 1000, are expected to be acceptable. So the cost per 1000 acceptable springs is ($200/682.6) × 1000 = $292.99, or approx. $293.

Now suppose through diligent effort the system capability is improved to a spread of 3 (ten-thousandths of an inch), instead of the 6 ten-thousandths originally specified, and assume a way is found to relax the system requirement to a spread of 4 (ten-thousandths of an inch) without any adverse effect on the functionality of the springs. That is, we now have a system capability improved so that $\sigma = 0.5$ (ten-thousandths of an inch) instead of $\sigma = 1$ (ten-thousandth), and a relaxed requirement that permits a spread from 8 to 12 (ten-thousandths of an inch) instead of from 9 to 11 (ten-thousandths). Then, at the upper end, we have

$$Z = \frac{X - \mu}{\sigma}$$

$$= \frac{12 - 10}{0.5} = 4$$

and at the lower end, we have

$$Z = \frac{X - \mu}{\sigma}$$

$$= \frac{8 - 10}{0.5} = -4$$

For all practical purposes, all the springs produced will be acceptable. In this situation, inspection for the purpose of sorting out acceptable from unacceptable parts can be eliminated, and having eliminated inspection cost, the new cost per 1000 acceptable springs will be $80. The production cost decline from $293 to $80 per 1000 acceptable springs is an astounding incentive for system improvement. Project this rate of savings over hundreds of thousands, much less millions, of springs, and project this savings over several thousand other parts needed for an automobile, and you can sense the gains that can be made by system improvement compared with 100% inspection of every component at every intermediate stage of production. Manufacturers who do not opt for system improvement and attempt to remain cost competitive by curtailing 100% inspection, open themselves to using unacceptable parts. The eventual result is a lowering of quality image in the marketplace and possible class action suits from disgruntled customers or the federal government.

Checkpoint Exercises

1. Assume, for the questions that follow, that the production process is in control, and that the springs have a mean elongation of 20 (ten-thousandths of an inch) and standard deviation of 2 (ten-thousandths of an inch). The system requirement for acceptable parts is the range 17–23 (ten-thousandths of an inch). Labor and material cost $90 per 1000 springs produced, and inspection cost is $0.15 per spring inspected.
   a. What percentage of the produced springs are acceptable given the current system capability?
   b. What percentage of the produced springs should be individually inspected and sorted to ensure acceptability?
   c. What is the expected cost per 1000 acceptable parts?
   d. What savings per 1000 parts would be obtained if the system could be improved to the point where system capability exceeds the system requirements?
   e. An out-of-control situation is indicated on a control chart by which of the following condition(s)? (1) Random sequence variation, (2) stable trend upward, (3) stable trend downward, (4) persistent sawtooth pattern trend downward, (5) frequent observations outside control limit.
2. In quality control work, samples are selected from a production line and various quality characteristics are measured in order to check that the process is in control. Suppose that a bottling process is intended to fill bottles with, on average, 21 fluid ounces (fl oz) of beverage. Variation around this average follows the normal distribution pattern with a standard deviation of 0.5 fl oz.
   a. If a technician samples 25 bottles (when the process is in control) and measures the amount of beverage in each, what is the probability that the sample average (for the 25 bottles) will exceed 21.2 fl oz?
   b. A technician would like to determine the "1 σ limits" (an interval extending 1 standard deviation above and below the mean) within which the sample average from 25 bottles should fall about two-thirds of the time. What is the appropriate set of limits?

PROCESS VARIABILITY AT AN AUTOMOBILE FACTORY

Data were recorded over a 10 day period on the thickness of primer paint sprayed on new automobiles. Recordings were made on a sample of 10 cars each morning and on 10 more cars each afternoon. These data are shown in Table 1. The values of $\bar{X}$ and S were recorded for each sample, $n = 10$. These values are also shown in Table 1.

	DAY 1		DAY 2		DAY 3		DAY 4		DAY 5	
SAMPLE	1	2	1	2	1	2	1	2	1	2
1	1.30	1.01	1.22	1.08	0.98	1.12	0.92	1.04	1.08	1.20
2	1.10	1.10	1.05	1.12	1.30	1.30	1.10	1.14	0.92	1.13
3	1.20	1.15	0.93	1.11	1.31	1.01	1.13	1.18	1.11	1.19
4	1.25	0.97	1.08	1.28	1.12	1.20	1.02	1.12	1.20	1.16
5	1.05	1.25	1.15	1.00	1.08	1.11	0.92	1.00	1.01	1.03
6	0.95	1.12	1.27	0.95	1.10	0.93	1.17	1.02	1.04	1.25
7	1.10	1.10	0.95	1.15	1.15	1.02	1.24	1.05	0.94	1.20
8	1.16	0.90	1.11	1.14	1.35	1.25	0.98	1.34	1.05	1.24
9	1.37	1.04	1.12	1.28	1.12	1.05	1.34	1.12	1.12	1.10
10	0.98	1.08	1.10	1.31	1.26	1.10	1.12	1.05	1.06	1.03
$\bar{X}$	1.15	1.07	1.10	1.14	1.18	1.11	1.10	1.11	1.06	1.15
S	0.136	0.098	0.106	0.120	0.121	0.115	0.136	0.101	0.086	0.079

TABLE 1 Primer Paint Thickness (Mils) Data for $n = 200$

Legend: 1 = Morning, 2 = Afternoon

	DAY 6		DAY 7		DAY 8		DAY 9		DAY 10	
SAMPLE	1	2	1	2	1	2	1	2	1	2
1	1.25	1.24	1.13	1.08	1.08	1.14	1.06	1.14	1.07	1.13
2	0.91	1.34	1.16	1.31	1.26	1.02	1.12	1.22	1.05	0.90
3	0.96	1.40	1.12	1.12	1.13	1.14	0.98	1.18	0.97	1.12
4	1.04	1.26	1.22	1.18	0.94	0.94	1.12	1.27	1.05	1.04
5	0.93	1.13	1.12	1.15	1.30	1.30	1.20	1.17	1.16	1.40
6	1.08	1.15	1.07	1.17	1.15	1.08	1.02	1.26	1.02	1.12
7	1.29	1.08	1.04	0.98	1.07	0.94	1.19	1.15	1.02	1.15
8	1.42	1.02	1.28	1.05	1.02	1.12	1.03	1.07	1.14	1.01
9	1.10	1.05	1.12	1.00	1.22	1.15	1.02	1.02	1.07	1.30
10	1.00	1.18	1.10	1.26	1.18	1.36	1.09	1.36	1.00	1.14
$\bar{X}$	1.10	1.19	1.14	1.13	1.14	1.12	1.08	1.18	1.06	1.13
S	0.170	0.125	0.070	0.107	0.111	0.137	0.074	0.099	0.059	0.141

Legend: 1 = Morning, 2 = Afternoon

A frequency distribution showing the variability of primer paint thickness for the 200 automobiles was constructed and is shown in Table 2. A histogram for these data is given in Figure 3. The primer thickness in the frequency table, Table 2, ranges from 0.90 to 1.44 mils, with more than half the measurements being between 1.00 and 1.14 mils.

A frequency distribution of the 20 sample means is given in Table 3, and the corresponding histogram is graphed in Figure 4. Notice how much more tightly clustered are the sample means compared to the individual observations graphed in Figure 3.

TABLE 2 Frequency Distribution for Primer Paint Thickness (Mils) for $n = 200$	
THICKNESS OF PAINT	**FREQUENCY**
0.90–0.94	13
0.95–0.99	11
1.00–1.04	28
1.05–1.09	27
1.10–1.14	47
1.15–1.19	25
1.20–1.24	13
1.25–1.29	16
1.30–1.34	13
1.35–1.39	4
1.40–1.44	3
	200

TABLE 3 Frequency Distribution for 20 Sample Means, Primer Paint Thickness Data (Mils)	
VALUE OF $\bar{X}$	**FREQUENCY**
1.050–1.074	3
1.075–1.099	1
1.100–1.124	6
1.125–1.149	5
1.150–1.174	2
1.175–1.199	3
	20

Figure 3
Histogram for primer paint thickness data, $n = 200$

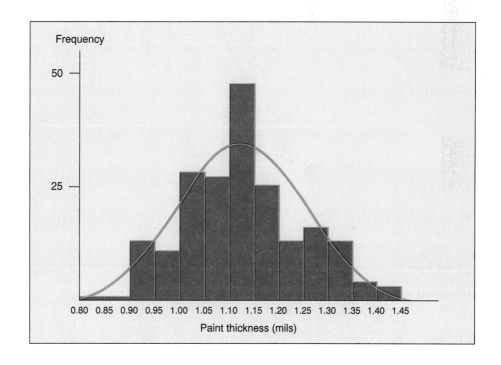

The mean of the 20 sample means is calculated from

$$\bar{\bar{X}} = \frac{\sum \bar{X}_i}{20} = 1.12 \text{ mils}$$

where $\bar{\bar{X}}$ is read as "X double bar".

Likewise, the mean of the 20 sample standard deviations is calculated from

$$\bar{S} = \frac{\sum S_i}{20} = 0.110 \text{ mil}$$

Figure 4
Histogram for 20 means for primer paint thickness data

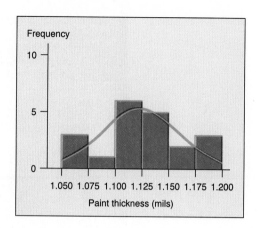

and the upper (UCL) and lower control limits (LCL) for the process mean are found from the expressions

$$\text{UCL} = \bar{\bar{X}} + A_3 \bar{S} \qquad \text{and} \qquad \text{LCL} = \bar{\bar{X}} - A_3 \bar{S}$$

where A_3 is a constant varying by sample size and is obtained from a firm's quality control specifications manual. (The concept and construction of the UCL and LCL values will be discussed in Chapter 7, but with a different perspective.) For sample sizes 2–10, the values of A_3 are

n	2	3	4	5	6	7	8	9	10
A_3	2.66	1.95	1.63	1.43	1.29	1.18	1.10	1.03	0.98

In our example, the sample size is 10, so the value used for the term A_3 is 0.98. Applying the formula for the upper control limit, we get

$$\text{UCL} = 1.12 + (0.98)(0.110) = 1.23 \text{ mil}$$

Figure 5
Control chart for $\bar{X}$: all 20 samples

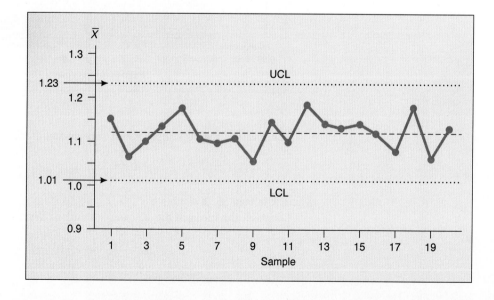

and for the lower control limit, we get

$$\text{LCL} = 1.12 - (0.98)(0.110) = 1.01 \text{ mil}$$

The upper and lower control limits are also known as "3 σ limits for $\bar{X}$," because essentially the A terms are set so that the limits are $\pm 3 S_{\bar{x}}$ above and below $\bar{\bar{X}}$. The control limits are shown in Figure 5. With the 20 values of $\bar{X}$ plotted on the same graph, we see that all lie well within the control limits. Also note that there does not appear to be any distinct upward or downward drift to the points, nor a pattern or cycle that might suggest nonrandomness. Consequently, we can conclude that the process appears to be in statistical control.

Checkpoint Exercises

3. Prepare separate control charts for (1) the morning data and for (2) the afternoon data.
4. How would you interpret these charts?
5. Should separate control charts be kept for the morning data and the afternoon data? Explain.

STATISTICAL INFERENCE: CONFIDENCE INTERVALS

E very month a highly competitive battle is fought among the major television networks to win the TV ratings war for their programming. But the months of May, November, and February are especially important because these are the "sweepstakes" months of the TV ratings contest. It is critical for the major networks to do well in the ratings war during these months because advertisers use the results of these sweepstakes months to decide which network will receive the bulk of advertising dollars spent in the coming months. In the lucrative Los Angeles TV market, a permanent loss of a single rating point could cost a network as much as $1 million in annual advertising revenue.

Since the first years of television, A. C. Nielsen has been considered the expert in compiling accurate TV ratings. But in the last few years the validity of the Nielson rating system has come into question. A major criticism is aimed at Nielsen's statistical methodology. The growing dissatisfaction with Nielsen has brought new firms, such as Arbitron, into the market with their own rating services. To gain a better perspective on the nature of the criticism leveled against Nielsen, let's examine the statistical methodology that Nielsen uses in computing the ratings.

Nielsen ratings are based on a secret sample of 1170 TV homes, which Nielsen statisticians pick randomly from a U.S. Census Bureau master list. Homes are geographically spread across the country. For a typical week, Nielsen reports ratings derived from viewing information from about 933 homes (of the 1170 available homes). A rating published by Nielsen is the percentage of those 993 homes tuned to a particular show. For example, let's assume The Cosby Show received a rating of 20 for the week. This means 20% of the sample homes had tuned in that show for at least 6 minutes—about 199 sets in all. Nielsen then assumes that the same percentage of all 73 million American TV households were watching that show and thus claims that an estimated 15 million homes (rounded) were tuned in. The company compiles such ratings for every show on the air (Table 7.1).

When a research firm sets up a panel of 1170 homes from a total of 73 million and uses 993 of them to measure television viewing for everyone else, the accuracy of the method naturally comes into question. The issue of accuracy of the Nielsen rating system may be addressed by a combination of two statistical numbers that Nielsen uses. One statistical number is the *estimated sampling error*, which can be calculated from the variation of the sample results and the size of the sample. The other statistical number is the *level of confidence*; this value is set by Nielsen. Typically, the level of confidence is set anywhere between 66 and 99%. The combination of the sampling error and the level of confidence that Nielsen sets determines the *margin of error*. The margin of error for the 66% confidence level for the Nielsen sample is 1.3 rating points. The margin of error allows us to construct a *confidence interval* around the

TABLE 7.1 Example of a Nielsen TV Ratings Chart					
PROGRAM	**NETWORK**	**RATING**	**PROGRAM**	**NETWORK**	**RATING**
1. Roseanne	ABC	20.8	41. MacGyver	ABC	10.6
2. Cheers	NBC	18.4	42. Thirtysomething	ABC	10.3
3. The Cosby Show	NBC	17.4	43. Fair Game	NBC	10.1
4. A Different World	NBC	17.0	44. 48 Hours	CBS	9.9
5. Dear John	NBC	16.0	45. Perfect Strangers	ABC	9.8
6. The Wonder Years	ABC	16.1	46. Murphy Brown	CBS	9.8
7. Murder, She Wrote	CBS	15.4	47. 227	NBC	9.7
8. Have Faith	ABC	15.3	48. Club Med	ABC	9.5
9. Who's the Boss?	ABC	14.8	49. Rocky III	CBS	9.5
10. 60 Minutes	CBS	14.5	50. Warm Hearts, Cold Feet	CBS	9.3
11. Shannon's Deal	NBC	14.5	51. Tony Awards	CBS	9.3
12. Empty Nest	NBC	14.2	52. Wiseguy	CBS	9.1
13. Hunter	NBC	14.1	53. America's Most Wanted	FOX	8.9
14. The Golden Girls (Mon.)	NBC	14.1	54. Married . . . With Children	FOX	8.9
15. The Golden Girls	NBC	13.8	55. Day by Day	NBC	8.7
16. Unsolved Mysteries	NBC	13.6	56. Lying, Cheating, Stealing	ABC	8.5
17. Matlock	NBC	13.5	57. Coach	ABC	8.3
18. 20/20	ABC	13.1	58. Beauty and the Beast	CBS	8.1
19. L.A. Law	NBC	12.9	59. Family Ties	NBC	7.7
20. Hogan Family	NBC	12.9	60. Highway to Heaven	NBC	7.4
21. Night Court	NBC	12.9	61. International Rock Awards	ABC	7.3
22. ALF	NBC	12.9	62. Hard Time on Planet Earth	CBS	6.7
23. Little Girl Lost	ABC	12.8	63. Earth-Star Voyager, Part 2	ABC	6.7
24. Midnight Caller	NBC	12.7	64. Mission Impossible	ABC	6.6
25. Mr. Belvedere	ABC	12.4	65. West 57th	CBS	6.5
26. Just the Ten of Us	ABC	12.4	66. Tour of Duty	CBS	6.5
27. My Two Dads	NBC	12.0	67. Charlie Brown Special	CBS	6.4
28. Super Bloopers & Practical Jokes	NBC	11.9	68. Real Genius	CBS	6.0
29. In the Heat of the Night	NBC	11.9	69. North & South, Book II, Part 4	ABC	6.0
30. Full House	ABC	11.6	70. World in Turmoil	ABC	5.7
31. Assault and Matrimony	NBC	11.6	71. 21 Jump Street	FOX	5.5
32. Newhart	CBS	11.6	72. Live-In	CBS	5.3
33. Growing Pains	ABC	11.5	73. It's Gary Shandling's Show	FOX	4.8
34. Mortons by the Bay	NBC	11.5	74. Cops	FOX	4.7
35. NBA Playoff Chicago vs. Detroit	CBS	11.4	75. Tracey Ullman Show	FOX	4.5
36. Designing Women	CBS	11.4	76. Gang of Four	ABC	4.0
37. Amen	NBC	11.2	77. Duet	FOX	3.5
38. Head of the Class	ABC	11.1	78. Beyond Tomorrow	FOX	2.9
39. Kate & Allie	CBS	10.8	79. Summer Blockbusters	FOX	2.9
40. Jake and the Fatman	CBS	10.7			

rating published by Nielsen. That is, the confidence interval estimate is the rating plus or minus the margin of error. Using the assumed 20 rating for the The Cosby Show, the 66% confidence interval would be written as 20 ± 1.3. Therefore, the 66% confidence interval for The Cosby Show would have a lower limit of 18.7 (20 − 1.3) and an upper limit of 21.3 (20 + 1.3). The range of the 66% confidence interval goes from 18.7 to 21.3—a width of 2.6 rating points. The 66% confidence level attached to a constructed interval means that the interval constructed by this procedure is on average accurate 2 out of 3 times and inaccurate 1 out of 3 times. For this particular interval, we can then say that we are 66% confident that between 18.7 and 21.3% of all American homes actually watched The Cosby Show.

If similar 66% confidence interval estimates are constructed around the published Nielsen ratings for the various TV shows, we find that many of the 66% confidence interval ranges overlap. Moreover, if Nielsen raised the level of confidence to the industry standard of 95%, the margin of error would need to be increased by a factor of 2, that is, 2(1.3) = 2.6. Again using the assumed 20 rating for The Cosby Show, the 95% confidence interval would be 20 ± 2.6. Therefore, the 95% confidence interval for The Cosby Show would have a lower limit of 17.4 and an upper limit of 22.6. Notice that the 95% confidence interval would cover a wider range of 5.2 rating points instead of the previous 2.6 rating points for the 66% confidence interval. If we construct a 95% confidence interval around each Nielsen rating for the individual TV shows, we find that a substantial number of the 95% confidence interval ranges overlap. The disturbing aspect of this high percentage of overlapping is that it suggests that the true differences between the program rankings could possibly *not exist at all* if all American homes had been surveyed. This means that programs canceled because of poor ratings could simply be victims of unfavorable statistical sampling error rather than truly poor ratings. In the 1978 sweepstakes, for example, The Love Boat show ranked number 20 and managed to survive. If it had been the victim of sampling error in the sweepstakes and ranked lower, it might have been canceled, never getting the opportunity to prove that the durability of its popularity would last well into the 1980s.

In this chapter we will examine more completely the statistical foundations of the margin of error and confidence level concepts, along with their practical interpretation as an aid on making decisions.

Overview

This chapter begins the study of statistical inference—the statistical methods used for estimating population parameters. This chapter builds on the probability and sampling concepts we studied in Chapters 4–6, where we found that (1) probability concepts quantify the chance of something happening; (2) a probability distribution tells us what outcomes are possible and how probable they are. The particular types of probability distributions we studied in Chapter 5 were special because the relationships between possible outcomes and their probabilities can be expressed by mathematical equations. The equations for these distributions (e.g., normal, binomial) have only a few parameters. Knowing the parameters and the equations, the outcome possibilities and their probabilities can be determined by consulting tables. Chapter 6 links the probability distribution concept to sampling. Sampling from a parent population (a parent probability distribution), we were able to specify (1) the shape of the probability distribution of the possible sample results and (2) the parameters of that distribution. In brief, we now know:

$$\begin{pmatrix} \text{Given a probability} \\ \text{distribution and its} \\ \text{population parameters} \end{pmatrix} \xrightarrow[\text{to}]{\text{Probability leads us}} \begin{pmatrix} \text{What possibly} \\ \text{and probably} \\ \text{can happen} \end{pmatrix}$$

In this and the next three chapters, we employ the methodology of statistical inference to invert the process. That is, the methodology of statistical inference is:

$$\begin{pmatrix} \text{From what did} \\ \text{happen (e.g.,} \\ \text{an observed} \\ \text{sample mean)} \end{pmatrix} \xrightarrow[\text{leads us back to}]{\substack{\text{Statistical} \\ \text{inference}}} \begin{pmatrix} \text{The likely value of the population} \\ \text{parameter (e.g., population mean)} \\ \text{of the probability distribution that} \\ \text{generated the value of the sample} \\ \text{statistic (e.g., sample mean)} \end{pmatrix}$$

NOTE TO THE INSTRUCTOR AND STUDENT: We have placed all the basic material on confidence intervals in one chapter, but we recognize that instructors' preferences vary. Some will teach only confidence intervals for a single population at this point, and then proceed to hypothesis testing for single populations. To accommodate this approach, we have designed the material so that Sections 8.1–8.3 can follow Sections 7.1–7.4. A similar consideration was given two-population inferences: the confidence interval estimation material of Sections 7.5–7.7 can be followed by the hypothesis testing material in Sections 8.4–8.6. Similarly, Sections 7.8 and 7.9 can be followed by Sections 8.7 and 8.8.

7.1

CONFIDENCE INTERVAL ESTIMATES FOR ONE POPULATION MEAN, μ

We will begin our study of statistical inference with methods for estimating the population mean μ. The methodology for making these estimates depends on whether the population standard deviation σ is known or unknown and also on the sample size. Three variations on the methodology result.

CASE 1: WHEN THE VALUE FOR σ IS KNOWN

The mean $\bar{X}$ from sample data provides a single-valued, or **point estimate**, of the population mean μ. Now we want to construct an interval around the point estimate $\bar{X}$, letting the entire interval rather than a single point be our estimate of μ. This is an **interval estimate**. The construction procedure requires that we use our knowledge (acquired in Chapter 6) of the properties of the sampling distribution of $\bar{X}$. We learned in Chapter 6 that we can measure in probability terms how close a sample value $\bar{X}$ is expected to be to the value μ. Our objective now is to develop a procedure, based on the sampling distribution, that constructs intervals around $\bar{X}$. The construction methodology will enable us to justify our confidence that the intervals will contain μ. The procedure for constructing these **confidence intervals** relies on two statistical concepts:

1. The central limit theorem (discussed in Section 6.3), which validates treating the distribution of sample means as normal, or nearly normal, as long as the sample size is large.
2. The standard normal random variable Z for which we can write the following expression for an upper tail area:

Standard Normal Upper Tail Area

$$P(Z \geq +Z_\alpha) = \alpha \qquad \text{(7-1)}$$

Equation (7-1) states that α is the area under the curve to the right beyond the value $+Z_\alpha$. The corresponding expression for the lower tail area is the following:

Standard Normal Lower Tail Area

$$P(Z \leq -Z_\alpha) = \alpha \qquad \text{(7-2)}$$

This says that α is also the area under the curve to the left beyond the value $-Z_\alpha$.

In Figure 7.1, $\alpha = .025$ is the shaded area under the curve *to the right* of the point $+Z_{.025} = 1.96$. The unshaded area to the left of the point $+Z_{.025}$ represents $P(Z \leq +Z_{.025}) = 1 - .025 = .975$.

Figure 7.1
Illustration of the $+Z_\alpha$ notation: $P(Z \geq +Z_{.025}) = P(Z \geq 1.96) = .025$

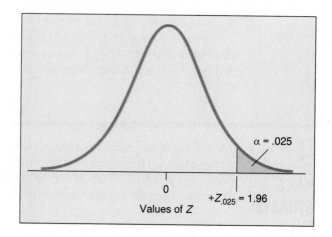

$\alpha = .025$

0

$+Z_{.025} = 1.96$

Values of Z

In Figure 7.2, $\alpha = .025$ is the shaded area under the curve *to the left* of the point $-Z_{.025} = -1.96$. The unshaded area to the right of $-Z_{.025}$ represents $P(Z \geq -Z_{.025}) = 1 - .025 = .975$.

Figure 7.2
Illustration of the $-Z_\alpha$ notation: $P(Z \leq -Z_{.025}) = P(Z \leq -1.96) = .025$

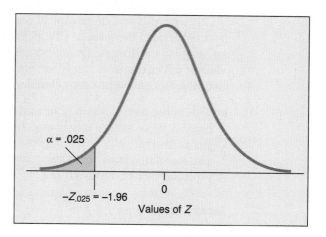

$\alpha = .025$

$-Z_{.025} = -1.96$

0

Values of Z

How do we adapt the standard notation for confidence interval estimates so that we can deal with a two tail area under the curve? Since α represents the total area in both tails, to indicate that the total tail area is split into two equal amounts between the lower and upper tail areas, we specify that the area in each tail is $\alpha/2$. As we can see in Figure 7.3, the area between these tails is equal to $1 - \alpha$. That is,

$$P(-Z_{\alpha/2} \leq Z \leq Z_{\alpha/2}) = 1 - \alpha$$

Now to check your understanding of the $\alpha/2$ notation, let's solve the following expression:

$$P(-Z_{\alpha/2} \leq Z \leq +Z_{\alpha/2}) = ? \qquad \text{where } \alpha = .05$$

that is,

$$P(-Z_{.025} \leq Z \leq +Z_{.025}) = ?$$

Did you get .950? Here's how this probability is determined.

Figure 7.3
Illustration of the
$\pm Z_{\alpha/2}$ notation

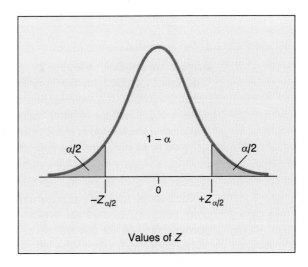

Step 1
Note that the area we want lies between the lower tail point (denoted by $-Z_{.025}$) and the upper tail point (denoted by $Z_{.025}$).

Step 2
Start by finding the area to the left of the upper tail point. This is
$P(Z \leq +Z_{.025}) = 1 - .025 = .975$.

Step 3
Now we'll have to subtract the area to the left of the lower tail point, which is
$P(Z \leq -Z_{.025}) = .025$.

Step 4
The difference between the areas found in Steps 2 and 3 is the area between the lower and upper tail points: $.975 - .025 = .950$.

The shaded region in Figure 7.4 represents $P(-Z_{.025} \leq Z \leq +Z_{.025}) = .950$.

Figure 7.4
Illustration of the $\pm Z_{\alpha/2}$
notation:
$P(-Z_{.025} \leq Z \leq +Z_{.025})$
$= P(-1.96 \leq Z \leq +1.96)$
$= .950$

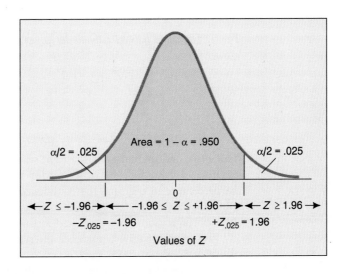

Here are some concluding points to remember about the terms α, Z_α, and $Z_{\alpha/2}$:

- The α symbol always indicates the total tail probability under the curve.
- When we are dealing with only one tail of the distribution, the symbol $+Z_\alpha$ designates a point on the horizontal axis located in the right tail of the Z distribution, with α representing the area under the curve to the right of the point $+Z_\alpha$; and the symbol $-Z_\alpha$ designates a point on the horizontal axis located in the left tail of the Z distribution, with α representing the area under the curve to the left of the point $-Z_\alpha$.
- When we are dealing with two tails of the distribution, the symbol $+Z_{\alpha/2}$ designates a point on the horizontal axis located in the right tail of the Z distribution, with $\alpha/2$ representing the area under the curve to the right of the point $+Z_{\alpha/2}$; and the symbol $-Z_{\alpha/2}$ specifies a point on the horizontal axis located in the left tail of the Z distribution, with $\alpha/2$ representing the area under the curve to the left of the point $-Z_{\alpha/2}$.

Now suppose that sampling is from a normally distributed population, or we can invoke the central limit theorem. In either case the sampling distribution of $\bar{X}$ is normally distributed with mean $\mu_{\bar{X}} = \mu$ and standard deviation $\sigma_{\bar{X}} = \sigma/\sqrt{n}$, where μ and σ are the *original* population mean and standard deviation, respectively. When this is the case, then

$$Z = \frac{\bar{X} - \mu}{\dfrac{\sigma}{\sqrt{n}}}$$

is a standard normal random variable with mean $\mu = 0$ and standard deviation $\sigma = 1$. Substituting for Z, the above expression may be expressed alternately as

$$P\left(-Z_{\alpha/2} \le \frac{\bar{X} - \mu}{\dfrac{\sigma}{\sqrt{n}}} \le Z_{\alpha/2}\right) = 1 - \alpha$$

Rearranging the terms inside the parentheses, we have the standard expression for a $1 - \alpha$ confidence interval estimate for μ:

$1 - \alpha$ Confidence Interval Estimate for μ, σ Known

$$\bar{X} - Z_{\alpha/2}\left(\frac{\sigma}{\sqrt{n}}\right) \le \mu \le \bar{X} + Z_{\alpha/2}\left(\frac{\sigma}{\sqrt{n}}\right) \tag{7-3}$$

The terms $\bar{X} - Z_{\alpha/2}(\sigma/\sqrt{n})$ on the left side of (7-3) compute the **lower confidence limit** of μ, and the terms on the right side give the **upper confidence limit** of μ. By specifying a value for $1 - \alpha$, we set the two limits so that $(1 - \alpha)100\%$ represents the percentage of the time the confidence limits will include the true value of μ. A confidence level may be referred to in terms of $1 - \alpha$, or in percentage terms as $(1 - \alpha)100\%$. Both forms are used in this book.

Let's consider 95% confidence intervals. First, with $1 - \alpha$ set at .95, the value of $\alpha = .05$, $\alpha/2 = .025$, and $Z_{\alpha/2} = Z_{.025} = 1.96$ (from Appendix Table IV). Next, we take independent random samples of size n, and find $\bar{X}$ for each sample. Finally, we construct upper and lower confidence limits with each $\bar{X}$ using $+Z_{.025}$ and $-Z_{.025}$ so that 95% of the constructed intervals should include the true value μ. Of course, since μ is unknown, we never know if any one particular interval constructed actually contains the true value of μ within its limits. But the construction process ensures that 95% of them do. Before construction there is a .95 probability that the interval limits of any one interval being constructed will include the true value of μ. The result of this procedure is illustrated in Figure 7.5.

To be more specific about the process let's now suppose we took a random sample of 49 observations from a normally distributed population with $\sigma = 7$ that yields $\bar{X} = 9$. Using equation (7-3), what would be the 95% confidence interval for μ? To solve this problem we first note that the confidence level of 95% implies $1 - \alpha = .95$, so that $\alpha = .05$, $\alpha/2 = .025$, and $Z_{\alpha/2} = Z_{.025}$. From the standard normal probability table (Table IV), we find $Z_{.025} = 1.96$, as before. The standard deviation of the population is given as $\sigma = 7$, so the standard deviation of the sampling distribution for $\bar{X}$ is $\sigma_{\bar{X}} = \sigma/\sqrt{n} = 7/\sqrt{49} = 1$.

The upper limit of the 95% confidence interval for μ is thus $\bar{X} + Z_{\alpha/2}(\sigma/\sqrt{n})$, or $9 + (1.96)(7/\sqrt{49}) = 10.96$. The lower limit is $\bar{X} - Z_{\alpha/2}(\sigma/\sqrt{n})$, or $9 - (1.96)(7/\sqrt{49}) = 7.04$. The expression $\pm Z_{\alpha/2}(\sigma/\sqrt{n}) = \pm(1.96)(7/\sqrt{49})$ represents what we referred to as the **margin of error** in the TV ratings opening scenario.

Let's now look at an example where the manager of a fast food franchise wishes to obtain an interval estimate of the amount of meat the sandwich makers are putting into sandwiches.

Figure 7.5
Illustration of the interval estimate concept

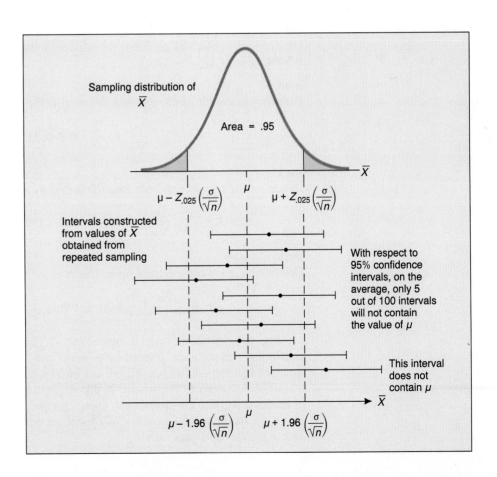

Fast food sandwich franchises depend on high volume and maintaining cost control over food. Cost control is particularly important on the expensive items in the sandwiches, such as meat. If the amount of meat in sandwiches is not closely monitored, the food costs can skyrocket. Suppose the manager of one store in the Subs Inc. chain is monitoring the portions of meat put into the sandwiches. Although food preparers are instructed to put only a specific number of ounces of meat into a sandwich, variations in the actual weights occur because of the difficulty of adhering to rigid standards. Subs Inc. records show that even when care is taken, the weight of the meat put into the sandwiches is normally distributed with a standard deviation of $\frac{1}{2}$ oz. To monitor meat costs under current conditions in which meat costs 30¢ per ounce, a random sample of $n = 64$ sandwiches is selected and the meat portions weighed. The sample mean is $\bar{X} = 5.20$ oz. Find a 95% confidence interval estimate of the true mean weight of the portions of meat put into sandwiches at this branch of Subs Inc.

Statistical Solution

Step 1
Specify the level of confidence and $1 - \alpha$: The problem stipulates a 95% confidence interval, which implies $1 - \alpha = .95$.

Step 2
Determine the values of α and $\alpha/2$: $1 - \alpha = .95$ implies that $\alpha = .05$. Thus, $\alpha/2 = .025$.

Step 3
Determine the value of $Z_{\alpha/2}$: From the standard normal probability table (Table IV) the value of $Z_{.025} = 1.96$.

Step 4
Determine the value of the standard deviation of the sampling distribution for $\bar{X}$:

$$\frac{\sigma}{\sqrt{n}} = \frac{\frac{1}{2}}{\sqrt{64}} = 0.0625$$

Step 5
Determine the upper confidence limit: This is given by

$$\bar{X} + Z_{\alpha/2}\left(\frac{\sigma}{\sqrt{n}}\right) = 5.20 + 1.96(0.0625) = 5.32 \text{ oz}$$

Step 6
Determine the lower confidence limit: This is given by

$$\bar{X} - Z_{\alpha/2}\left(\frac{\sigma}{\sqrt{n}}\right) = 5.20 - 1.96(0.0625) = 5.08 \text{ oz}$$

The 95% confidence interval then is 5.08–5.32 oz. We cannot say for certain that this particular interval includes the true (actual) mean weight of the meat put into the sandwiches, but we can be 95% confident it does. On average, 95 out of 100 intervals constructed in this way will include the true mean weight of the meat put into the sandwiches. Using cost per ounce figures for these meats, the manager can obtain a 95% confidence interval estimate of the average cost of the meat per sandwich.

Practical Interpretation

We are 95% confident that the interval from 5.08 to 5.32 oz contains the true average amount of meat put into the sandwiches. Knowing that the meat costs 30¢ per ounce, then we can say with 95% confidence that the interval estimate between $5.08 \times \$0.30 = \$1.52$ and $5.32 \times \$0.30 = \$1.60$ covers the true average meat cost per sandwich. The Subs Inc. manager can compare this cost estimate to the price charged for each sandwich to determine a range for the profitability per sandwich.

TRADEOFF BETWEEN LEVEL OF CONFIDENCE AND LENGTH OF INTERVAL

The length of a confidence interval is the difference between the upper and lower confidence limits. That is,

$$\text{Length of interval} = 2Z_{\alpha/2}\left(\frac{\sigma}{\sqrt{n}}\right)$$

The length of the confidence interval is inversely related to the level of confidence. Let's observe what happens to the length of the interval as α is decreased. We'll start with $\alpha = .10$:

1. If $\alpha = .10$, then $\alpha/2 = .05$, $Z_{.05} = 1.645$, and the length of the interval is equal to $3.29(\sigma/\sqrt{n})$.

Now reduce α to .01:

2. If $\alpha = .01$, then $\alpha/2 = .005$, $Z_{.005} = 2.58$, and the length of the interval is equal to $5.16(\sigma/\sqrt{n})$.

Thus, the increased confidence gained by moving from a 90% confidence level to a confidence level of 99% results in a larger interval length, by the ratio $5.16/3.29 = 1.57$, an increase of more than 50%. The conclusion that can be drawn from these computations is that *when the values of σ and n remain unchanged, a lowering of α (e.g., from .10 to .01) increases the level of confidence $1 - \alpha$, but the unfortunate consequence is an increase in the margin of error, which is reflected in the increased length of the interval.*

Before we proceed any further with our discussion of confidence intervals for μ, we would like to point out that certain values of $1 - \alpha$ are very commonly used in practice in constructing confidence intervals. These values are $1 - \alpha = .80, .90, .95, .98,$ and $.99$. In Appendix Table V and in the table below, we list these values of $1 - \alpha$ and their corresponding Z values for easy reference:

CONFIDENCE LEVEL $1 - \alpha$	$\alpha/2$	VALUES OF $Z_{\alpha/2}$
.80	.100	1.282
.90	.050	1.645
.95	.025	1.960
.98	.010	2.326
.99	.005	2.576

Notice that the $Z_{\alpha/2}$ values in this table are given to three decimal places; for example, for $1 - \alpha = .80$ we have $Z_{\alpha/2} = Z_{.100} = 1.282$. This level of precision is not obtainable from Appendix Table IV, which gives Z values to only two decimal places.

Using Appendix Table V, a 99% confidence interval estimate for μ is given by

$$\bar{X} - 2.576\frac{\sigma}{\sqrt{n}} \leq \mu \leq \bar{X} + 2.576\frac{\sigma}{\sqrt{n}}$$

and a 90% confidence interval estimate for μ is given by

$$\bar{X} - 1.645\frac{\sigma}{\sqrt{n}} \leq \mu \leq \bar{X} + 1.645\frac{\sigma}{\sqrt{n}}$$

PRACTICE EXERCISE

7.1 Suppose the random variable X represents monthly home equity loan payments and is normally distributed with standard deviation $\sigma = \$24$. A random sample of size $n = 9$ is taken from the population, and the sample mean is $\$459.13$. Find a 95% confidence interval for the population mean μ.

We now illustrate the construction of confidence intervals for the case in which the population is not necessarily assumed normally distributed.

CASE 2: WHEN THE VALUE FOR σ IS UNKNOWN: LARGE SAMPLES

In these applications we rely only on the available sample evidence to calculate the sample standard deviation S as an estimate of the value of σ. When the sample size n is large (30 or more will be considered large), the central limit theorem allows us to state that

$$Z = \frac{\bar{X} - \mu}{\dfrac{S}{\sqrt{n}}}$$

has approximately a normal distribution. *This implies that the basic procedure previously discussed using the Z distribution can again be followed, when the value of S, the sample standard deviation, is substituted for the value of σ, and the sample is large.* The next example illustrates this situation.

■ **EXAMPLE 7.2**

Effective Scheduling of Checkout Personnel

Managers of large supermarkets have to deal with the problem of scheduling checkout personnel. For effective scheduling, each supermarket manager needs to know how long it takes, on the average, for a well-trained clerk to handle a customer at the checkout counter. Suppose a manager decides to collect this information by randomly selecting 100 transactions handled by well-trained clerks. She finds that the mean time per transaction is $\bar{X} = 3.25$ min, with a standard deviation of $S = 1.50$ min. Find a 99% confidence interval for the mean time per customer transaction by the well-trained clerks.

Statistical Solution

The central limit theorem (discussed in Section 6.3) is a mathematical statement of the fact that distributions of sample means in the real world tend toward normality as the sample sizes increase, regardless of the shape of the original population distribution. Thus, whether or not checkout times themselves are normally distributed, a sample size of 100 is usually large enough to justify assuming a normal, or nearly normal, distribution for the sample mean.

Step 1
Specify the level of confidence and $1 - \alpha$: A 99% confidence interval (stated in the problem) implies that $1 - \alpha = .99$.

Step 2
Determine α and $\alpha/2$: $1 - \alpha = .99$ implies that $\alpha = .01$. Thus, $\alpha/2 = .005$.

Step 3
Determine the value of $Z_{\alpha/2}$: The value of $Z_{.005} = 2.576$ (from the table).

Step 4
Calculate the estimated standard deviation of the sampling distribution of $\bar{X}$:

$$\frac{S}{\sqrt{n}} = \frac{1.50}{\sqrt{100}} = 0.15 \text{ min}$$

Step 5
Determine the upper confidence limit: This is given by

$$\bar{X} + Z_{\alpha/2}\left(\frac{S}{\sqrt{n}}\right) = 3.25 + 2.576(0.15) = 3.64 \text{ min}$$

Step 6
Determine the lower confidence limit: This is given by

$$\bar{X} - Z_{\alpha/2}\left(\frac{S}{\sqrt{n}}\right) = 3.25 - 2.576(0.15) = 2.86 \text{ min}$$

The constructed 99% confidence interval covers the values 2.86–3.64 min. It is not certain that this particular interval includes the true mean checkout time for an efficient clerk; but since an interval constructed this way has a 99% chance of including the true mean, we are 99% confident that this particular interval does. The manager can use this result to establish guidelines for all the checkout clerks.

Practical Interpretation

The manager can be 99% confident that the interval from 2.86 to 3.64 min contains the true average checkout time for a well-trained clerk. Two possible ways the manager can use this result are the following:

1. After a new checkout clerk has been trained and has completed a probationary period, the manager can compare the new checkout clerk's average transaction time with the interval for the efficient clerks. (If you were the manager and found that the new clerk's average transaction time was 4.5 min, what would you do?)
2. The manager can grade the current checkout clerks on transaction efficiency using the confidence interval as a standard.

```
• • • • • • • • • • • • • • • • • • • • • • • • • • • • • • • •
```

P R A C T I C E
E X E R C I S E

7.2 Suppose the random variable X represents the time it takes on the production line for a well-trained team of auto mechanics to assemble the automobile engine, and suppose the assembly times for a random sample of 100 assemblies ($n = 100$) are recorded. A sample mean of 498 min and a sample standard deviation of 72 min are obtained from the recorded observations. Find a 95% confidence interval for the population mean μ. Suggest a practical use for the information found.

```
• • • • • • • • • • • • • • • • • • • • • • • • • • • • • • •
```

A generalization can now be made about confidence intervals for large samples ($n > 30$) when the value for the population variance σ is unknown.

1 − α Confidence Interval Estimate
for μ, σ Unknown: Large Sample

$$\bar{X} - Z_{\alpha/2}\left(\frac{S}{\sqrt{n}}\right) \leq \mu \leq \bar{X} + Z_{\alpha/2}\left(\frac{S}{\sqrt{n}}\right) \tag{7-4}$$

CASE 3: WHEN THE VALUE FOR σ IS UNKNOWN: SMALL SAMPLES

When the size of the sample is small (i.e., less than or equal to 30), and *we are sampling from a normally distributed* population, then it is appropriate to say that the test statistic follows a **Student t distribution**:

Student t Statistic

$$t_{(n-1)} = \frac{\bar{X} - \mu}{S/\sqrt{n}} \tag{7-5}$$

Let's examine the characteristics of the Student t distribution.

The Student *t* Distribution

In the early 1900s, the Student t probability density function was derived by W. S. Gossett, who published under the pseudonym Student. It has become an important probability density function with wide applications for situations where the normal distribution is only an approximate model. Values for this probability function are given in Appendix Table VII. The notation $t_{(\alpha,\nu)}$, which appears in Table VII, refers to values in the table where the subscript α represents the right or left tail probability and the subscript ν represents the **degrees of freedom (d.f.)**. In this section, $\nu = n - 1$. That is, the degrees of freedom determine the correct row to read in Table VII, and α determines the correct column to read. Expression (7-6) below gives the right tail probability for a positive t value, and expression (7-7) gives the left tail probability for a negative t value.

A graph of the Student t probability density function changes for different degrees of freedom ν and produces a bell-shaped curve, symmetrical about its mean value of

Student t Tail Probabilities

Right Tail Probability

$$P(t_\nu \geq +t_{(\alpha,\nu)}) = \alpha \qquad (7\text{-}6)$$

Left Tail Probability

$$P(t_\nu \leq -t_{(\alpha,\nu)}) = \alpha \qquad (7\text{-}7)$$

0. The curve looks very much like a standard normal probability density function, but with fatter tails and slightly more rounded peak. The similarity between the Student t probability density function and the standard normal probability density function increases rapidly as the value of the degrees of freedom for the Student t probability density function increases, and the two distributions are virtually indistinguishable when the degrees of freedom exceed 30. This is why for large samples we can safely use $S/\sqrt{n}$ as a substitute for $\sigma/\sqrt{n}$. You can verify that the standard normal distribution is the limiting form of the Student t distribution by comparing the bottom row of the t table (Appendix Table VII) with corresponding $Z_{\alpha/2}$ table values (see Table V). The values are identical. A graph of the Student t probability density function, with 9 d.f., is given in Figure 7.6. It is a bell-shaped curve, symmetric about 0, but it is not a standard normal curve. In general, the mean for the Student t probability density function is equal to 0; and its variance, for $\nu > 2$, is equal to $\nu/(\nu - 2)$.

The Student t table (Appendix Table VII) is constructed so that (1) the degrees of freedom (d.f.) column is on the left; (2) the body of the table lists the $t_{(\alpha,\nu)}$ values; and (3) the top row of the table gives the tail probabilities α (or areas under the curve starting at the listed $t_{(\alpha,\nu)}$ value and going to infinity). The following examples illustrate how Table VII is used to find t values corresponding to specified values of α and ν, and various probability values α (area under the curve) for specified values of ν. Example 7.3 provides practice in using the Student t distribution with $\nu = 9$ d.f., and Example 7.4 illustrates the use of the table to find t values for a variety of problems with different degrees of freedom.

Figure 7.6
Student t distribution with 9 d.f.

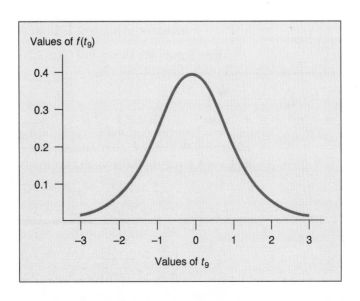

Figure 7.7
Using the Student *t* probability
table

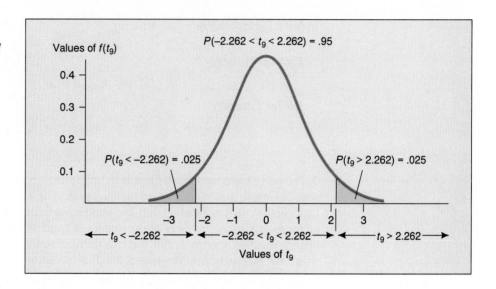

■ **EXAMPLE 7.3**

**Using the Student *t*
Distribution Table**

In the examples below note the relationship between the *t* value given (2.262 or −2.262 in most cases) and either the corresponding value of α or a probability on the Student *t* distribution. The expressions pertain to the row corresponding to d.f. = 9 in Table VII.

a. $P(t_9 \geq 2.262) = P(t_9 > 2.262) = .025$
b. $+t_{(.025,9)} = 2.262$
c. $P(t_9 \leq 2.262) = P(t_9 < 2.262) = 1 - .025 = .975$
d. $P(0 \leq t_9 \leq 2.262) = P(0 < t_9 < 2.262) = .5 - .025 = .475$
e. $P(t_9 \leq -2.262) = P(t_9 < -2.262) = .025$
f. $-t_{(.025,9)} = -2.262$
g. $P(t_9 \geq -2.262) = P(t_9 > -2.262) = 1 - .025 = .975$
h. $P(-2.262 \leq t_9 \leq 0) = P(-2.262 < t_9 < 0) = .5 - .025 = .475$
i. $P(-2.262 \leq t_9 \leq 2.262) = P(-2.262 < t_9 < 2.262) = .95$
j. $P(|t_9| \leq 2.262) = P(|t_9| < 2.262) = .95$
k. $P(|t_9| \geq 2.262) = P(|t_9| > 2.262) = .05$

These regions are shown in Figure 7.7.

Now compare probability values for t_{infinity} (t_{inf}) with corresponding probability values of Z. Five cases for comparison are presented below, using right tail probabilities for t_{inf} and matching them with the corresponding Z values in Table V.

$$P(t_{\text{inf}} > 1.282) = .100 = P(Z > Z_{.100}) = P(Z > 1.282)$$

$$P(t_{\text{inf}} > 1.645) = .050 = P(Z > Z_{.050}) = P(Z > 1.645)$$

$$P(t_{\text{inf}} > 1.960) = .025 = P(Z > Z_{.025}) = P(Z > 1.960)$$

$$P(t_{\text{inf}} > 2.326) = .010 = P(Z > Z_{.010}) = P(Z > 2.326)$$

$$P(t_{\text{inf}} > 2.576) = .005 = P(Z > Z_{.005}) = P(Z > 2.576)$$

Note that the t values in the row at 29 d.f. in Table VII do not differ by much from the t values in the last row (i.e., d.f. at infinity). We can thus conclude that *when the number of degrees of freedom exceeds 29, we may use values of the standard normal random variable Z to approximate values of t and to obtain probabilities for values of t.*

In the next example the use of the t table is reversed. We start with a given probability value, and we are asked to find the corresponding $t_{(\alpha,\nu)}$ value.

■ **EXAMPLE 7.4**

Using the Student t Distribution Table (Continued)

Find the tabular value of $t_{(\alpha,\nu)}$, where:

a. $P(0 < t_{17} < t_{(\alpha,17)}) = .490$
b. $P(-t_{(\alpha,13)} < t_{13} < 0) = .495$
c. $P(t_{11} < -t_{(\alpha,11)}) = .025$
d. $P(|t_{12}|) < t_{(\alpha,12)}) = .980$

Solution

a. In the row corresponding to d.f. = 17, we first recognize that
$P(t_{17} > 2.567) = .010$ so that $P(0 < t_{17} < 2.567) = .5 - .010 = .490$.
Therefore, $t_{(\alpha,17)} = 2.567 = t_{(.010,17)}$.

b. In the row corresponding to d.f. = 13, we first recognize that
$P(t_{13} < -3.012) = .005$ so that $P(-3.012 < t_{13} < 0) = .5 - .005 = .495$. Therefore, $t_{(\alpha,13)} = 3.012 = t_{(.005,13)}$.

c. In the row corresponding to d.f. = 11, we recognize that $P(t_{11} < -2.201) = .025$. Therefore, $t_{(\alpha,11)} = 2.201 = t_{(.025,11)}$.

d. In the row corresponding to d.f. = 12, we recognize that $P(|t_{12}| < 2.681) = P(-2.681 < t_{12} < 2.681) = .980$, since $P(t_{12} > 2.681) = P(t_{12} < -2.681) = .010$ and $P(-2.681) < t_{12} < 2.681) = 1 - 2(.010)$. Therefore, $t_{(\alpha,12)} = 2.681 = t_{(.010,12)}$.

P R A C T I C E   E X E R C I S E

7.3 If the random variable t_5 has the Student t distribution with 5 d.f., find:

a. $P(t_5 > 1.476)$ b. $P(t_5 < 1.476)$
c. $P(t_5 < -1.476)$ d. $P(t_5 > -1.476)$
e. $P(-1.476 < t_5 < 1.476)$ f. $t_{(.01,5)}$
g. $t_{(.025,5)}$ h. $P(1.476 < t_5 < 4.032)$
i. $P(-4.032 < t_5 < -1.476)$

The Student t distribution is the probability distribution used in constructing a confidence interval estimate for μ when we sample from a normally distributed population, σ is unknown, and the sample size is small (less than or equal to 30). The Z distribution is not appropriate when n is small and σ is unknown.

In general, with $\nu = n - 1$, we can write

$$P(-t_{(\alpha/2,n-1)} \le t_{(n-1)} \le +t_{(\alpha/2,n-1)}) = 1 - \alpha$$

In this expression we may substitute

$$\frac{\bar{X} - \mu}{S/\sqrt{n}} \quad \text{for} \quad t_{(n-1)}$$

and then we may write

$$P\left(-t_{(\alpha/2, n-1)} \le \frac{\bar{X} - \mu}{S/\sqrt{n}} \le +t_{(\alpha/2, n-1)}\right) = 1 - \alpha$$

From this expression it is possible to derive the following expression for a $1 - \alpha$ confidence interval for μ:

$1 - \alpha$ Confidence Interval
Estimate for μ, σ Unknown: Small Sample

$$\bar{X} - t_{(\alpha/2, n-1)}\left(\frac{S}{\sqrt{n}}\right) \le \mu \le \bar{X} + t_{(\alpha/2, n-1)}\left(\frac{S}{\sqrt{n}}\right) \qquad (7\text{-}8)$$

The calculation of the lower and upper confidence limits using equation (7-8) is demonstrated in the following example.

■ **EXAMPLE 7.5**

Estimating Bridge Construction Costs

Suppose a construction company executive is assigned the task of estimating construction costs for a bid on a large bridge project. The executive believes the cost estimation errors are normally distributed, but knows neither the mean size of the error to be expected nor the standard deviation of the distribution of errors. The company has recently completed seven bridge projects, and the executive believes the errors in estimating the cost for these projects may be regarded as a random sample from the distribution of cost estimation errors.

For this sample of $n = 7$, the mean estimation error (expressed as a percentage of true completed cost) is -14.3% and the standard deviation is 9.1%. Both the negative sign and the magnitude of the estimation error are important pieces of information for the company. The negative sign indicates that the estimates are generally too low; the value 14.3 indicates that the underestimation is a considerable percentage. Find a 90% confidence interval for the construction cost error percentage.

Statistical Solution

Step 1
Specify the confidence level and $1 - \alpha$: The problem asks for a 90% confidence interval, which implies that $1 - \alpha = .90$.

Step 2
Determine $\alpha/2$: $1 - \alpha = .90$ implies that $\alpha = .10$. Thus, $\alpha/2 = .05$.

Step 3
Find ν: $\nu = n - 1 = 7 - 1 = 6$

Step 4
Find $t_{(\alpha/2, \nu)}$: The t table value for $t_{(.05, 6)}$ is 1.943.

Step 5
Determine the value of $S/\sqrt{n}$:

$$\frac{S}{\sqrt{n}} = \frac{9.1}{\sqrt{7}} = 3.44\%$$

Step 6
Find the upper confidence limit: This is given by

$$\bar{X} + t_{(\alpha/2, n-1)}\left(\frac{S}{\sqrt{n}}\right) = -14.3 + 1.943(3.44) = -7.62\%$$

Step 7
Find the lower confidence limit: This is given by

$$\bar{X} - t_{(\alpha/2, n-1)}\left(\frac{S}{\sqrt{n}}\right) = -14.3 - 1.943(3.44) = -20.98\%$$

The 90% confidence interval covers the range from -20.98 to -7.62%. Although we can't be certain that this particular interval includes the true mean estimation error percentage, we do know that the process of constructing such intervals assures us that 90% of the intervals include μ. Therefore, we are 90% confident that this interval does include the true mean.

Practical Interpretation

Because the upper and lower limits of the 90% confidence interval are negative, the executive can be fairly certain that the company is, on average, underestimating its costs by at least 7.62%. If the company persists in underestimating its construction costs, it will likely be winning bids and getting lots of construction contracts, but how long can it stay in business?

In the above example note the explicit statement or assumption that the random variable is normally distributed. Note also the absence of information on σ from any previous studies, necessitating reliance on S computed from the sample; and since $n \leq 30$, the Student t distribution is required.

PRACTICE EXERCISE

7.4 In Practice Exercise 7.1 the random variable X, representing home equity loan payments, was normally distributed with $\sigma = 24$. A random sample of $n = 9$ was taken from the population, resulting in a sample mean of \$459.13. This led to a 95% confidence interval for the population mean μ with a lower confidence limit of \$443.45 and an upper confidence limit of \$474.81. Now suppose the value of σ had been unknown, but the value of the standard deviation of the sample turned out to be 24. Find the 95% confidence interval for μ.

Flowchart I

The flowchart shown in Figure 7.8 is presented to help you determine the appropriate statistic in a particular situation. The following example leads us through the chart and shows how to make the correct choice.

Figure 7.8
Flowchart I, for a $1 - \alpha$ confidence interval for one population mean

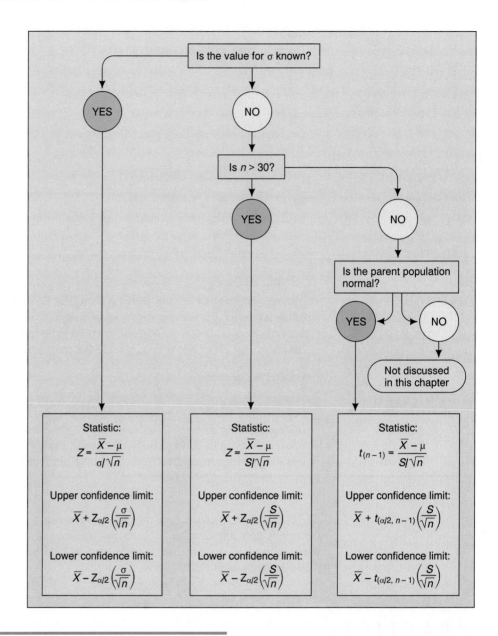

EXAMPLE 7.6

Student IQs

Assume that the IQs of students at a very large university are normally distributed. Construct a 95% confidence interval for the average IQ of this population of students if a random sample of 49 students has an average IQ of 110 and a standard deviation of 10.8.

Statistical Solution

Step 1

Is the value for σ known? The values 110 and 10.8 are the mean and standard deviation of the sample; therefore, the answer to this question is no.

Step 2

Since the answer in Step 1 is no, the next determination is whether n is greater than 30. With the sample size of 49, the answer is yes.

Step 3
Following the center path of the flowchart, we find the appropriate statistic to use. This is

$$Z = \frac{\bar{X} - \mu}{S/\sqrt{n}}$$

Step 4
Specify the confidence level and $1 - \alpha$: The 95% confidence interval implies $1 - \alpha = .95$.

Step 5
Determine $\alpha/2$: $1 - \alpha = .95$ implies that $\alpha = .05$. Thus, $\alpha/2 = .025$.

Step 6
Find the value of $Z_{\alpha/2}$: The value of $Z_{.025} = 1.96$.

Step 7
Determine the value of $S/\sqrt{n}$:

$$\frac{S}{\sqrt{n}} = \frac{10.9}{\sqrt{49}} = 1.543$$

Step 8
Find the upper confidence limit: The upper confidence limit is given by $110 + (1.96)(1.543) = 113.02$.

Step 9
Find the lower confidence limit: The lower confidence limit is given by $110 - (1.96)(1.543) = 106.98$.

The 95% confidence interval spans the values from 106.98 to 113.02. Because we know that the procedure constructs intervals that have a 95% chance of including the true average IQ, we can be 95% confident that this particular interval includes the true average IQ for this student body.

Practical Interpretation

The dean of admissions at this university can be 95% confident that the interval from 106.98 to 113.02 contains the true average IQ of the university's students. If the dean is proud of this figure, he can have the information put into the university's promotional literature; otherwise, he might leave it out.

The next example provides additional practice in the use of the flowchart in Figure 7.8 for making the correct choice of estimation procedure.

■ **EXAMPLE 7.7**

Tooth Plaque Buildup

A dental researcher working in the laboratory of an oral products manufacturer wants to estimate the amount of plaque buildup on teeth when a certain food component is heavily consumed. She administers a heavy diet of the food component to 16 mice for 30 days, and finds an average plaque buildup of 3.5 units. Assume prior extensive experience has shown that the distribution of the amount of plaque buildup is normal with a standard deviation of 1.2 units. Find a 95% confidence interval for the average plaque buildup when the food component diet is used for 30 days.

Statistical Solution

Since we are told to assume the plaque buildup is normally distributed, we can proceed with the following sequence of steps:

Step 1

Is the value for σ known? The answer to this question is yes, since prior extensive experience indicates a population characteristic, $\sigma = 1.2$.

Step 2

Since the answer in Step 1 is yes, we follow the path on the left in the flowchart. The chart indicates that the appropriate statistic to use is given by

$$Z = \frac{\bar{X} - \mu}{\sigma/\sqrt{n}}$$

Step 3

The 95% confidence interval stated in the problem implies that $1 - \alpha = .95$.

Step 4

$1 - \alpha = .95$ implies that $\alpha = .05$. Thus, $\alpha/2 = .025$.

Step 5

The value of $Z_{.025} = 1.96$.

Step 6

$$\frac{\sigma}{\sqrt{n}} = \frac{1.2}{\sqrt{16}} = 0.3$$

Step 7

The upper confidence limit is given by $3.5 + (1.96)(0.3) = 4.088$.

Step 8

The lower confidence limit is given by $3.5 - (1.96)(0.3) = 2.912$.

The 95% confidence interval limits are from 2.912 to 4.088 units. Since we know that the procedure used in constructing the interval has a 95% chance of including the true mean, we can be 95% confident that this interval includes the true average plaque buildup using the food component diet for 30 days.

Practical Interpretation

The dental researcher can be 95% confident that the interval from 2.912 to 4.088 units contains the true average amount of plaque buildup. If plaque buildup of this magnitude is undesirable, then the researcher could recommend that the company develop a product directed toward plaque removal for heavy users of that food component.

PRACTICE EXERCISE

7.5 Suppose the random variable X, representing monthly food expenditures, is normally distributed, and suppose we take a random sample from the population. Find a 95% confidence interval for the population mean μ if:
   a. $\sigma^2 = 729$, $\bar{X} = \$531.43$, and $n = 9$
   b. $S^2 = 729$, $\bar{X} = \$531.43$, and $n = 100$
   c. $S^2 = 729$, $\bar{X} = \$531.43$, and $n = 9$

7.2

DETERMINING SAMPLE SIZE FOR ESTIMATING μ

Often, it is the task of the practitioner or researcher to determine the size of the sample needed. Such a task requires prior specification of the desired level of confidence and the acceptable margin of error between the values of $\bar{X}$ and μ. The margin of error, or **error of estimate**, is often called the **error tolerance** to reflect the imprecision a decision maker is willing to tolerate. The elements that determine the sample size are:

- The discrepancy between $\bar{X}$ and μ measured by the absolute value of their difference:

$$|\bar{X} - \mu| = E$$

  The value of E is the magnitude of the error of estimate, the error tolerance, or the margin of error.

- The predetermined level of confidence is measured by $1 - \alpha$.

- Either of two presumptions are made:
  a. The population from which we are sampling is normal.
  b. Or the size of the sample we will have to take will be large enough so that the distribution of the sample mean will be normal, or nearly normal.

The expression we shall use to determine the sample size is given by:

Determining Sample Size for Estimating μ

$$n = \left(\frac{Z_{\alpha/2}\sigma}{E}\right)^2 \tag{7-9}$$

This formula is derived from the expression for constructing confidence intervals. In solving the formula, two items must be considered: (1) When the solution for the formula doesn't result in an exact integer value, we *round up* so that the confidence level will be *at least* $1 - \alpha$. (2) In order to use this particular formula, *we must have a known value for* σ, gained either from past experience or from some theoretical considerations.

We are now ready to illustrate examples in which formula (7-9) is used to solve for n.

■ **EXAMPLE 7.8**

Lifetimes of Light Bulbs

Suppose past evidence shows that the lifetimes of light bulbs from a certain production line have a standard deviation of 100 hr. But a modification has been made in the gas surrounding the filaments in the bulbs, and we now wish to estimate the average lifetime of the light bulbs with this modification. It is believed that the modification won't affect the standard deviation of the lifetimes, just the average life. How large a sample should be taken if we want to be 98% confident that the average lifetime estimate will be within 5 hr of the true average lifetime for these bulbs?

Solution

Step 1
Specify the level of confidence and $1 - \alpha$: The level of confidence is 98%, which implies that $1 - \alpha = .98$.

Step 2

Determine $\alpha/2$: A value of $1 - \alpha = .98$ implies that $\alpha = .02$, and $\alpha/2 = .01$.

Step 3

Given that σ is known, find $Z_{\alpha/2}$: From Appendix Table V we have $Z_{.01} = 2.326$. (Alternatively, see the bottom row of the Student t table, Table VII, under column .01.).

Step 4

Specify σ: The value of $\sigma = 100$ is given in the problem.

Step 5

Specify E: The value of $E = 5$ is given in the problem.

Step 6

Calculate n using the sample size formula:

$$n = \left[\frac{(2.326)(100)}{5} \right]^2 = 2164.11$$

Step 7

Round up to the next higher integer: Thus, to be at least 98% confident that the observed average lifetime will be within 5 hr of the true average lifetime of these bulbs, we would need to take a random sample of 2165 bulbs from the population.

The sample size of 2165 in Example 7.8 is larger than you might have expected. Yet this is what is required to achieve the stipulated precision and level of confidence. In the next example the required sample size will probably be seen as surprisingly small. The point is that the sample size formula is easy to apply, so there is no reason to guess wrongly.

■ **EXAMPLE 7.9**

Treadlife of Tires

Suppose records indicate that a certain manufacturer's production process produces tires with a treadlife standard deviation of 2000 mi. Now, suppose as area manager that you want to obtain a reliable estimate of the average treadlife of tires produced by this manufacturer, and that your estimate is to be in error by not more than 500 mi with a probability of at least .90. How large a sample should we take?

Solution

Step 1

Specify the level of confidence and $1 - \alpha$: The level of confidence is 90%. This implies that $1 - \alpha = .90$.

Step 2

Determine $\alpha/2$: The value $1 - \alpha = .90$ means that $\alpha = .10$, and $\alpha/2 = .05$.

Step 3

Given that σ is known, find $Z_{\alpha/2}$: From Table V, $Z_{.05} = 1.645$. (Alternatively, see the bottom row of the Student t table, Table VII, under column .05.)

Step 4

Specify σ: The value of $\sigma = 2000$.

Step 5

Specify E: The value of $E = 500$.

Step 6
Calculate n using the sample size formula:

$$n = \left[\frac{(1.645)(2000)}{500} \right]^2 = 43.3$$

Step 7
Round up to the next higher integer: Thus, to be at least 90% confident that the observed average treadlife is within 500 mi of the true average treadlife of these tires, you would need to take a random sample of 44 tires from the population. Note that here we are dealing with a very large, or infinite, target population. Thus, it is noteworthy that such a small sample of 44 is sufficient to attain the stated error tolerance and confidence objectives even when the population consists of millions of tires.

PRACTICE EXERCISE

7.6 Suppose the random variable X, representing watch battery life, is normally distributed with standard deviation equal to 21 hr. How large a sample should we take if we want our estimate of μ to be in error by not more than 10 hr with a probability of at least .95?

EXERCISES

7.1 Find the value of the probability in each case:
a. $P(Z > Z_{.0475})$ b. $P(Z > Z_{.01})$ c. $P(Z > Z_{.005})$
d. $P(Z < Z_{.05})$ e. $P(Z < Z_{.01})$ f. $P(Z < Z_{.005})$
g. $P(Z > -Z_{.05})$ h. $P(Z > -Z_{.01})$ i. $P(Z > -Z_{.005})$
j. $P(Z < -Z_{.05})$ k. $P(Z < -Z_{.01})$ l. $P(Z < -Z_{.005})$

7.2 Find the value of the probability in each case:
a. $P(-Z_{.0129} < Z < Z_{.0129})$ b. $P(-Z_{.05} < Z < Z_{.05})$
c. $P(-Z_{.005} < Z < Z_{.005})$ d. $P(-Z_{.0129} < Z < Z_{.0475})$
e. $P(-Z_{.01} < Z < Z_{.025})$ f. $P(-Z_{.05} < Z < Z_{.005})$

▶ 7.3 Find the value Z in each case:
a. $Z_{.025}$ b. $Z_{.0051}$ c. $Z_{.0495}$ d. $Z_{.4522}$ e. $Z_{.0027}$

7.4 Find the value Z in each case:
a. $Z_{.4286}$ b. $Z_{.0188}$ c. $Z_{.0694}$ d. $Z_{.0287}$ e. $Z_{.0207}$

7.5 A random sample of 81 observations from a normally distributed population with $\sigma = 9$ yields $\bar{X} = 2.000$. Find a 95.96% confidence interval for the population mean μ.

▶ 7.6 The daily business at a local restaurant is said to be normally distributed with a standard deviation of $571. Find a 95% confidence interval for μ if a random sample of 17 days' receipts shows an average daily income of $9832. Would it be reasonable for the restaurant owner to claim to the IRS that her average daily income is $9400?

7.7 It is believed that the IQ scores of fourth graders are normally distributed with a standard deviation of 15 IQ points. Find a 98.68% confidence interval for μ if a random sample of 100 fourth graders had an average IQ score of 110.

7.8 The increase in girth of 3-year-old maple trees in a 1 yr period is believed to be normally distributed with a standard deviation of 0.6 in. Find a 91.98% confidence interval for μ, the theoretical average increase in girth in a given 1 yr period, if 100 randomly selected 3-year-old maple trees have an average increase in girth of 2.3 in. in the 1 yr period to age 4 yr.

7.9 If the random variable t_7 has the Student t distribution with 7 d.f., evaluate:
  a. $P(t_7 < 1.415)$ b. $P(t_7 < 3.499)$
  c. $P(t_7 < -1.415)$ d. $P(t_7 < -3.499)$
  e. $P(-1.415 < t_7 < 1.415)$ f. $P(-3.499 < t_7 < 3.499)$
  g. $P(-3.499 < t_7 < 2.365)$ h. $P(-3.499 < t_7 < 2.998)$
  i. $P(1.415 < t_7 < 2.365)$ j. $P(2.998 < t_7 < 3.499)$

7.10 A foreman in a manufacturing plant wishes to estimate the average amount of time it takes a worker to assemble a certain device. He randomly selects 81 workers and discovers that they take an average of 29 min with a standard deviation of 4.5 min. Assuming the times are normally distributed, find a 90.10% confidence interval for the average amount of time it takes the workers in this plant to assemble the device. What can you tell the foreman?

7.11 Assume that the IQs of students at a very large university are normally distributed. Construct an 89.90% confidence interval for the average IQ of all the students at this college if a random sample of 49 students has an average IQ of 119 and a standard deviation of 10.8.

7.12 Assume that the time it takes to assemble the parts of an electric lamp is normally distributed. Construct a 95% confidence interval for the average assembly time if a random sample of 16 trials has an average assembly time of 400 sec with a standard deviation of 10 sec. Is it reasonable to suppose that the average assembly time will not exceed 410 sec?

▶ **7.13** An attempt was made to estimate the amount of plaque buildup on teeth when a certain food component is introduced into the diet. An experimenter subjected 25 randomly selected mice to the diet for 30 days and found an average plaque buildup of 3.5 units, with a standard deviation of 1.1 units. Find a 99% confidence interval for the average plaque buildup in mice subjected to the diet for 30 days. Suppose any food component that produces a plaque buildup in excess of 4.2 units is to be stricken from the diet. Should this food component be stricken from the diet?

7.14 The mean and variance for a random sample of 64 measurements are 14.1 and 10.24, respectively. If we assume the population of measurements from which the sample is taken is normal, find a 99% confidence interval for the mean of the population.

7.15 A vacuum cleaner manufacturer claims that her top-of-the-line model has superior cleaning capability. She claims her machine will pick up 9 oz of dirt in 5 min of vacuuming a 12×12 ft carpet that hasn't been vacuumed in 3 days. A total of 36 independent trials of 5 min of vacuuming different 12×12 ft carpets that hadn't been vacuumed for 3 days were conducted. The average weight of the dirt picked up was 8.69 oz with a standard deviation of 1.05 oz. Assume that the weight of the vacuumed dirt is normally distributed. Find an 80% confidence interval for the average weight of dirt picked up by this model of vacuum cleaner under the specified conditions.

7.16 A newly developed genetic engineering technique produces large quantities of somatotropin, a growth hormone. In a field experiment, 16 randomly selected cows are injected daily with a specified dosage of somatotropin. Milk production for these cows had been recorded for a period of 2 months prior to the injections, and then is recorded for 2 months after the inception of the injections. The improvement in milk production (converted to percent) associated with the injections is recorded for each cow. The results are:

| .152 | .324 | .383 | .327 | .347 | | .283 | .175 | .239 | .261 | .275 |
| .380 | .191 | .218 | .336 | .210 | | .328 | | | | |

Assume that the percent improvements are normally distributed. Use the sample results to find a 95% confidence interval for the true average improvement in milk production associated with injections of somatotropin.

▶ **7.17** The following data represent monthly payments (in dollars) made by 51 randomly selected VISA® credit card holders:

181.78	157.39	142.45	140.92	166.98	128.48	149.46	108.61	122.72	112.86
157.35	116.25	167.46	138.95	106.89	113.53	147.03	136.28	162.70	150.13
117.32	125.57	166.06	152.61	160.39	112.66	137.06	125.60	200.29	107.78
134.56	185.24	118.63	202.61	110.79	149.05	132.60	165.51	112.29	180.77
123.30	200.76	122.32	84.29	144.97	151.52	156.13	153.41	149.13	110.26
161.97									

Assume the monthly payments are normally distributed. Use the sample results to find a 99% confidence interval for the true average monthly payments made by VISA® credit card holders.

▶ **7.18** An agency that monitors the legal profession has noted that although lawyers' incomes change with time, the variance has remained fairly stable with time [with a value of ($27,000)^2]. Suppose the agency wishes to estimate the current average income for lawyers. How large a random sample should it take if it wants its estimate to be within $10,000 of the true average income with a confidence level of 0.98? Assume the incomes are normally distributed with a standard deviation of $27,000.

7.19 Suppose the agency in Exercise 7.18 takes a preliminary random sample of size 9 and gets a sample average of $101,500. Construct a 98% confidence interval for the true average income based on the sample result.

7.20 The treadlife of tires produced by a certain manufacturer is normally distributed with a standard deviation of 2000 mi. We wish to estimate the average treadlife of tires produced by this manufacturer. With a probability of at least .90, we want our estimate to err by not more than 100 mi. How large a sample should we take?

7.21 The shelf life of a certain canned product is known to have a standard deviation of 12 days. Shelf life is normally distributed. How large a sample would be needed to determine the average shelf life to within 7 days with probability at least equal to .90?

● ●

7.3

CONFIDENCE INTERVAL ESTIMATES FOR A POPULATION PROPORTION

We shall represent the observed sample proportion, X/n, with the symbol $\hat{p}$. The **sample proportion** $\hat{p}$ is a point estimate of the true population proportion p. Although $\hat{p}$ provides us with a working estimate of p, how reliably close is $\hat{p}$ to the true (population) value of p? To gain some indication, we refer to the sampling distribution of $\hat{p}$. Fortunately, from the discussion of sampling distributions in Chapter 6, we know that there are circumstances in which it is permissible to use a normal approximation. The number of independent trials n must be large (i.e., $n > 30$), and *both* $n\hat{p}$ and $n(1 - \hat{p})$ must be greater than or equal to 5. When these conditions are met, the Z statistic is expressed as

$$Z = \frac{\hat{p} - p}{\sqrt{\dfrac{\hat{p}(1 - \hat{p})}{n}}}$$

It then follows that

$$P\left(-Z_{\alpha/2} \le \frac{\hat{p} - p}{\sqrt{\dfrac{\hat{p}(1 - \hat{p})}{n}}} \le Z_{\alpha/2}\right) = 1 - \alpha$$

We should first verify that both $n\hat{p}$ and $n(1 - \hat{p})$ exceed 5. Only large samples will be considered, and for large samples the continuity correction (discussed in Section 5.3) makes little difference and will not be used. For the construction of approximate $1 - \alpha$ confidence limits for p we will use the following expressions:

$1 - \alpha$ Confidence Interval Estimate for p

$$\hat{p} - Z_{\alpha/2}\sqrt{\frac{\hat{p}(1 - \hat{p})}{n}} \le p \le \hat{p} + Z_{\alpha/2}\sqrt{\frac{\hat{p}(1 - \hat{p})}{n}} \qquad \text{(7-10)}$$

The upper $1 - \alpha$ confidence limit is given by

$$\hat{p} + Z_{\alpha/2}\sqrt{\frac{\hat{p}(1 - \hat{p})}{n}} \qquad \text{(7-11)}$$

and the lower $1 - \alpha$ confidence limit is given by

$$\hat{p} - Z_{\alpha/2}\sqrt{\frac{\hat{p}(1 - \hat{p})}{n}} \qquad \text{(7-12)}$$

The following example demonstrates a situation in which the required conditions are met.

■ **EXAMPLE 7.10**

Credit Card Usage Among College Students

Suppose a credit card manager at a large New York bank wishes to assess the potential in appealing to the college student segment of the market. She proposes to estimate the proportion of regular credit card users among college students in the United States. Funding is approved for the market research. After interviewing 2416 students who were randomly selected from around the country, only 151 are found to be regular users. The manager decides to present the findings by constructing a 97% confidence interval estimate for the true proportion of credit card users among college students in the United States.

To verify the validity of the normal distribution approximation to the binomial distribution, $n\hat{p} = 2416\left(\frac{151}{2416}\right)$ and $n(1 - \hat{p}) = 2416\left(1 - \frac{151}{2416}\right)$ must be computed and must exceed 5, which they do.

Statistical Solution

Step 1
Specify the confidence interval and $1 - \alpha$: The 97% confidence interval stated in the problem implies that $1 - \alpha = .97$.

Step 2
Determine $\alpha/2$: $1 - \alpha = .97$ implies that $\alpha = .03$. Thus, $\alpha/2 = .015$.

Step 3
Determine $Z_{\alpha/2}$: From Table IV, $Z_{.015} = 2.17$.

Step 4
From the sample result calculate $\hat{p}$:

$$\hat{p} = \frac{151}{2416} = .0625$$

Step 5
From the sample result calculate:

$$\sqrt{\frac{\hat{p}(1 - \hat{p})}{n}} = \sqrt{\frac{(.0625)(1 - .0625)}{2416}} = .004925$$

Step 6
Determine the upper confidence limit: This is equal to

$$.0625 + (2.17)(.004925) = .073$$

Step 7
Determine the lower confidence limit: This is equal to

$$.0625 - (2.17)(.004925) = .052$$

The credit card manager can claim that she is 97% confident that the interval from 5.2% to 7.3% includes the true measure of the proportion of regular credit card users among college students in the United States. Her claim is valid because these intervals are constructed using a procedure that produces intervals that contain the true proportion 97% of the time.

Practical Interpretation

The low percentage of current users (given the high level of confidence) suggests that there is a large segment of the college student market that has yet to be tapped.

PRACTICE EXERCISE

7.7 Let the random variable X represent the number of times a person in a gambling casino wins at roulette using a strategy that is the same for each play, regardless of a win or loss on previous plays. Also suppose that the probability of winning is the same on each play. In that case, the random variable X follows a binomial distribution with a probability p of winning on each trial. Find a 95% confidence interval for p if the gambler wins 100 times in 225 independent trials.

7.4

DETERMINING SAMPLE SIZE FOR ESTIMATING p

Practitioners and researchers often need to determine the size of the sample required to estimate p, given a specified level of confidence and margin of error. The margin of error E is specified as the absolute value of the difference between the point estimate $\hat{p}$ and the true population proportion p; it is written as

$$|\hat{p} - p| = E$$

The expression for determining the sample size requires the value of E, the value of $Z_{\alpha/2}$ (determined from the level of confidence specified), and an *initial estimate of p*, denoted by p^*:

Determining Sample Size for Estimating p

$$n = \left(\frac{Z_{\alpha/2}}{E}\right)^2 p^*(1 - p^*) \tag{7-13}$$

When, prior to sampling, we have some available information about p based on past experience or theoretical considerations, we may base the value specified for p^* on that information. If there is no reasonable basis for specifying p^* prior to sampling, then we set $p^* = .5$. In the latter case, we use $p^* = .5$ because it can be shown that the product $p^*(1 - p^*)$ reaches a maximum value of .25 when $p^* = .5$. [You can verify this claim by trying various values of p^* between 0 and 1 in the $p^*(1 - p^*)$ product.] When $p^*(1 - p^*)$ is set at .25, equation (7-13) maximizes the value for n, the needed sample size, thereby assuring us that the margin of error will be within the specified range with at least the specified level of confidence, no matter what the actual value of p. If the numerical value for n found from equation (7-13) is not an integer, the result is rounded up to guarantee that the confidence level will be at least $1 - \alpha$. The following example illustrates the determination of the sample size.

EXAMPLE 7.11

Network Television and Sampling

As described in the Headline Issue at the beginning of this chapter, TV ratings represent the percentage of the sampled television viewers in specific geographical areas who watch a particular program. Advertising revenues and the fortunes of a network typically depend on the ratings of the network, so networks pay constant attention to the ratings. These ratings are calculated from sample information. What simple random sample size should be used so that the margin of error in estimating the true percentage of viewers watching a particular program will not be greater than 2% with 95% confidence?

Solution

Step 1
Specify the level of confidence and $1 - \alpha$: The problem stipulates 95% confidence, which implies that $1 - \alpha = .95$.

Step 2
Determine $\alpha/2$: $1 - \alpha = .95$ implies that $\alpha = .05$. Thus, $\alpha/2 = .025$.

Step 3
Determine the value of $Z_{\alpha/2}$: From Table IV or V, $Z_{.025} = 1.960$.

Step 4
Specify the margin of error, E: The problem stipulates 2%, which translates to the value of $E = .02$.

Step 5
Determine the value of n: We are not given a value for p. Hence, use the expression

$$n = \left(\frac{Z_{\alpha/2}}{E}\right)^2 (.25) = \left(\frac{1.960}{.02}\right)^2 (.25) = 2401$$

Thus, in order to claim, with at least 95% confidence, that the observed value of our sample proportion is within 2% of the true proportion of viewers watching a particular telecast, we need a random sample of 2401 viewers.

PRACTICE EXERCISES

7.8 This exercise revisits the roulette strategy problem considered in Practice Exercise 7.7. The random variable X represents the number of times a person in a gambling casino wins at roulette using a particular strategy. The strategy is the same for each play regardless of a win or loss on previous plays, and the probability of winning is the same on each play. So X has the binomial distribution with probability p of winning on each trial. How large a sample should we take so that the margin of error of the estimate of p will not be greater than 5% with probability .95?

7.9 Suppose we take a random sample of homes in the United States and count the number, X, of homes in the sample with solar water heaters. In that case, X is a random variable that follows the binomial distribution with the parameter p. The value p represents the true proportion of homes in the United States with solar water heaters. If prior experience indicates that p is approximately equal to .2, how large a sample should we take to ensure that the margin of error in estimating p will not be greater than 5% with probability .95?

EXERCISES

▶ **7.22** A chain photo service claims that only 3% of its customers complain about the prints they get from the rolls of film they bring in for developing and printing. Suppose a random sample of 196 customers reveals that 5 of the customers were dissatisfied with the prints they had received. Use this sample result to find an approximate 95% confidence interval for the true proportion of dissatisfied customers.

7.23 An interstate savings institution claims that 94% of its depositors have both a savings account and a checking account with the institution. Suppose a random sample of 234 customers shows that 226 have both a savings account and a checking account, whereas the other 8 have either only a savings account or only a checking account, but not both. Use this sample result to construct an approximate 90% confidence interval for the true proportion of depositors who have both types of accounts with this institution.

7.24 In the manufacture of fish sticks it was noticed that 8 packages out of a random sample of 64 packages were adulterated with fly parts and mouse waste. Find a 99% confidence interval for the proportion of adulterated fish stick packages produced. The Food and Drug Administration (FDA) is authorized to seize a lot if there is evidence that the lot contains in excess of 13% adulterated packages. Should the lot from which this sample was taken be seized?

▶ **7.25** In a random sample of 2000 registered California voters, 1132 favored legislation to liberalize import quotas on alcoholic beverages. Construct a 90% confidence interval for the proportion of all registered California voters who favor legislation to liberalize import quotas. If it takes more than 50% of all registered California voters to pass the legislation, would it be reasonable to suppose that the legislation to liberalize import quotas on alcoholic beverages will pass?

7.26 A manufacturer of buttons believes that 5% of the buttons he produces are defective. How large a sample should he take so that his error of estimation will be less than .01 with a probability equal to .98?

7.27 An opinion survey is to be taken to estimate the true proportion of families who have at least one family member who watches television on Saturday night. What size sample should be taken to give a 5% margin of error with 99% confidence? Suppose that prior estimates indicate 63% of families have at least one family member who watches television on Saturday night.

7.28 What size sample should an auditor take of a very large firm's accounts in order to estimate the true proportion of mismanaged accounts, if the auditor wants the estimate to be within 7% of the true proportion with 98% confidence?

● ●

7.5
CONFIDENCE INTERVAL ESTIMATES FOR THE DIFFERENCE BETWEEN TWO POPULATION MEANS, $\mu_1 - \mu_2$

In many instances a comparison between two populations requires a measure of the difference between the two population means. Are the two population means different from each other or are they equal to each other? If they differ, then by how much do they differ? Here are several examples:

- A government agency is purchasing water filtration equipment. The agency is interested in determining the difference in the average amount of particulates remaining in the filtered water from two machines, each produced by a company competing for the contract.

- A company's personnel group wishes to use a new training program for its assembly line employees and decides to try a pilot program to estimate the mean difference in the assembly time between the new pilot program and the current program.

- An industrial chemist is interested in comparing the average yields of a compound produced by two different methods.

- An investor wants to internationalize his stock portfolio. He compares the average returns for a representative group of stocks on two different foreign stock exchanges.

- A plastics manufacturer is interested in comparing the average rates of rejection for extrusions on the same type of material from two different suppliers.

The basic step-by-step procedure we'll use for obtaining confidence intervals for the difference between two population means closely resembles the procedure used in obtaining confidence intervals for one population mean. But there are some differences and issues that arise that need to be clarified.

1. Are the values of the population variances known or unknown? There are three cases that we will consider:
   Case 1: The values of the two population variances are both known.
   Case 2: The values of the two population variances are unknown, but are assumed to be equal.
   Case 3: The values of the two population variances are unknown, but are assumed not equal.
2. What are the assumptions about the distributions of the populations from which we are sampling? Must the sampling be from a normal distribution or approximately normal distribution? Are there sample size limitations?
3. Can the standard normal Z statistic always be used?

In our discussion of the various cases, we will use the standard notation summarized in Table 7.2 for population means, sample means, population standard deviations, sample standard deviations, and sample sizes.

TABLE 7.2 Notation for Two-Sample Inferences				
	POPULATION 1	**SAMPLE 1**	**POPULATION 2**	**SAMPLE 2**
MEAN	μ_1	$\bar{X}_1$	μ_2	$\bar{X}_2$
STANDARD DEVIATION	σ_1	S_1	σ_2	S_2
SAMPLE SIZE	n_1	n_1	n_2	n_2

CASE 1: WHEN THE VALUES OF σ_1 AND σ_2 ARE BOTH KNOWN

When the values of σ_1 and σ_2 are both known, when the populations are normal or approximately normal, and when independent random sampling is conducted on both populations to obtain $\bar{X}_1$ and $\bar{X}_2$, then the sampling distribution of $\bar{X}_1 - \bar{X}_2$ will be normally, or approximately normally, distributed. The appropriate Z statistic is given by

$$Z = \frac{(\bar{X}_1 - \bar{X}_2) - (\mu_1 - \mu_2)}{\sqrt{\dfrac{\sigma_1^2}{n_1} + \dfrac{\sigma_2^2}{n_2}}}$$

Additionally it can be stated that

$$P\left(-Z_{\alpha/2} \leq \frac{(\bar{X}_1 - \bar{X}_2) - (\mu_1 - \mu_2)}{\sqrt{\dfrac{\sigma_1^2}{n_1} + \dfrac{\sigma_2^2}{n_2}}} \leq Z_{\alpha/2}\right) = 1 - \alpha$$

From this expression we can derive the following expression for a $1 - \alpha$ confidence interval estimate for $\mu_1 - \mu_2$:

$1 - \alpha$ Confidence Interval Estimate for $\mu_1 - \mu_2$: Both Population Standard Deviations Known

$$(\bar{X}_1 - \bar{X}_2) - Z_{\alpha/2}\sqrt{\frac{\sigma_1^2}{n_1} + \frac{\sigma_2^2}{n_2}} \leq \mu_1 - \mu_2 \leq (\bar{X}_1 - \bar{X}_2) + Z_{\alpha/2}\sqrt{\frac{\sigma_1^2}{n_1} + \frac{\sigma_2^2}{n_2}} \quad \text{(7-14)}$$

The term on the left side of the inequality is the lower confidence limit of the difference between two population means, and the term on the right side of the inequality is the upper confidence limit.

We are now ready to analyze situations that involve two populations and make an inference about the difference between their means.

■ **EXAMPLE 7.12**

The Reliability of Two Independent Testing Laboratories

A large food processing company wants to determine the quantity of a certain chemical in the shipments of food it receives. Two reputedly reliable testing laboratories are asked to analyze food samples. From past experience with substances of this type, it is known that laboratory 1 will have a standard deviation of 0.0013 parts per million (ppm), and laboratory 2 will have a standard deviation of 0.0015 ppm. Laboratory 1 is given 12 food samples to analyze, and laboratory 2 is given 15 food samples. The mean obtained by laboratory 1 is 0.0161 ppm, and the mean obtained by laboratory 2 is 0.0176 ppm. Find a 98% confidence interval for the difference between the two laboratory population means. Assume the measurements made by the two laboratories both come from normal distributions. This assumption is not unreasonable if their measurement errors generally tend to appear normally, or approximately normally, distributed.

Statistical Solution

Step 1
Specify the level of confidence and $1 - \alpha$: The problem stipulates a 98% confidence interval, which implies $1 - \alpha = .98$.

Step 2
Determine $\alpha/2$: $1 - \alpha = .98$ implies that $\alpha = .02$. Thus, $\alpha/2 = .01$.

Step 3
Determine $Z_{\alpha/2}$: From Table V, $Z_{.01} = 2.326$.

Step 4
Establish the values of σ_1 and σ_2: These are stated in the problem as $\sigma_1 = 0.0013$ and $\sigma_2 = 0.0015$.

Step 5
Establish n_1 and n_2: These are stated in the problem as $n_1 = 12$ and $n_2 = 15$.

Step 6
Establish $\bar{X}_1$ and $\bar{X}_2$: These are stated in the problem as $\bar{X}_1 = 0.0161$ and $\bar{X}_2 = 0.0176$.

Step 7
Determine the upper confidence limit for $\mu_1 - \mu_2$: This is equal to

$$(0.0161 - 0.0176) + 2.326\sqrt{\frac{(0.0013)^2}{12} + \frac{(0.0015)^2}{15}} = -0.0002456$$

Step 8
Determine the lower confidence limit for $\mu_1 - \mu_2$: This is equal to

$$(0.0161 - 0.0176) - 2.326\sqrt{\frac{(0.0013)^2}{12} + \frac{(0.0015)^2}{15}} = -0.0027544$$

We are 98% confident that the interval from -0.0027544 to -0.0002456 includes the true discrepancy between the two laboratories in determining the average quantity of the specified chemical found in the food.

Practical Interpretation

If both laboratories are reliable, there should be statistical agreement between their test results. This means that the confidence interval should contain the value 0 (no underlying difference in the true mean results). But in this case the upper and lower limits of the interval are both negative and the confidence interval doesn't contain the value 0 (no difference). The absence of 0 in the interval indicates a lack of agreement between the two laboratories. As a matter of fact, since we are 98% confident that the interval contains the true value of the difference, and since 0 is not contained in the interval, then we can be at least 98% confident that the two laboratories are not in agreement, and laboratory 2 provides a higher estimate of the amount of the chemical in the food. This discrepancy would have a clear practical consequence if it has been established that the chemical poses a health hazard at levels exceeding 0.0161 ppm, since in that case laboratory 1 would indicate no health hazard whereas laboratory 2 would indicate there is a health hazard. Which laboratory's estimate should we accept? Clearly, it would be important for the two laboratories to investigate the discrepancy and make the necessary changes that would ensure accuracy and consistency to restore credibility.

PRACTICE EXERCISE

7.10 Suppose the random variable X_1 represents the balance sheet valuation of assets of small businesses filing bankruptcy in San Diego County. Historically, the valuation figures are found to be normally distributed with variance $\sigma_1^2 = 25$ (thousand)^2. A random sample of 9 small businesses ($n_1 = 9$) from the population is found to have a sample mean of $469.41 (thousand). Additionally, random variable X_2 represents the balance sheet valuation of assets of small businesses filing bankruptcy in Los Angeles County. Historically, these figures show a normal distribution with variance $\sigma_2^2 = 21$ (thousand)^2. A random sample of $n_2 = 9$ small businesses from the population yields a sample mean of $455.01 (thousand). Find a 95% confidence interval for the difference $\mu_1 - \mu_2$ between the two population means.

In Example 7.12, the Case 1 procedure was followed because σ_1 and σ_2 were known and because we were told to assume both populations were normally distributed. Given these conditions, it was irrelevant that the sample sizes happened to be small. However, suppose the population normality assumption is removed. In that case, both sample sizes must be large enough—each more than 30—to justify assuming the sample means are normally, or approximately normally, distributed.

CASE 2: WHEN THE VALUES OF σ_1 AND σ_2 ARE UNKNOWN, BUT PRESUMED EQUAL

When the two values for the population standard deviations are unknown, but information exists that allows us to presume their values are equal, a confidence interval for $\mu_1 - \mu_2$ may still be computed. However, the values of the corresponding sample standard deviation S_1 and S_2 substitute for σ_1 and σ_2, respectively. Consequently, the procedure just described in Case 1 must be modified.

By presuming $\sigma_1 = \sigma_2$, it follows that

$$\sigma_1 = \sigma_2$$

$$\searrow \swarrow$$

$$\sigma \quad \text{Common standard deviation}$$

That is, by presuming $\sigma_1 = \sigma_2$ we presume a common standard deviation σ. In this case, the sample values S_1 and S_2 are estimates of the common value σ. We can thus combine them into a single *pooled estimate*, S_p:

Pooled Estimate of σ

$$S_p = \sqrt{\frac{(n_1 - 1)S_1^2 + (n_2 - 1)S_2^2}{n_1 + n_2 - 2}} \tag{7-15}$$

By substituting S_p for both σ_1 and σ_2, and assuming the two populations are normal or approximately normal, we can use the Z statistic or the Student t statistic to calculate the upper and lower confidence limits. We shall first formulate the expressions for the large sample case and then for the small sample case.

Large Samples

When $n_1 + n_2 - 2 > 30$, the following Z statistic is appropriate:

$$Z = \frac{(\bar{X}_1 - \bar{X}_2) - (\mu_1 - \mu_2)}{\sqrt{\frac{S_p^2}{n_1} + \frac{S_p^2}{n_2}}} = \frac{(\bar{X}_1 - \bar{X}_2) - (\mu_1 - \mu_2)}{S_p\sqrt{\frac{1}{n_1} + \frac{1}{n_2}}}$$

Computed in this way, the Z statistic can be used to develop the approximate $1 - \alpha$ confidence limits for $\mu_1 - \mu_2$.

$1 - \alpha$ Confidence Limits for $\mu_1 - \mu_2$, Population Variances Unknown, but Presumed Equal: Large Samples

The upper $1 - \alpha$ confidence limit is given by

$$(\bar{X}_1 - \bar{X}_2) + Z_{\alpha/2}S_p\sqrt{\frac{1}{n_1} + \frac{1}{n_2}} \tag{7-16}$$

and the lower $1 - \alpha$ confidence limit is given by

$$(\bar{X}_1 - \bar{X}_2) - Z_{\alpha/2}S_p\sqrt{\frac{1}{n_1} + \frac{1}{n_2}} \tag{7-17}$$

We will now use these limits to analyze the difference in academic achievement of students who own cars versus those who don't own cars.

■ **EXAMPLE 7.13**

Car Ownership and Academic Achievement

A university investigation was conducted to determine whether car ownership was detrimental to academic achievement. The investigation was based upon two random samples of 20 students, each drawn from the student body. The grade-point average for the 20 non-car owners was 2.75 with a sample variance of 0.36, as opposed to a grade-point average of 2.51 with a variance of 0.40 for the 20 car owners. Find a 90% confidence interval for the difference in grade-point averages for car owners versus non-car owners. Assume that grade-point averages are normally distributed and that the population variances for the two groups are unknown but equal.

Statistical Solution

Step 1
Specify the level of confidence and $1 - \alpha$: The problem stipulates a 90% confidence interval, which implies $1 - \alpha = .90$.

Step 2
Determine $\alpha/2$: $1 - \alpha = .90$ implies that $\alpha = .10$. Thus, $\alpha/2 = .05$.

Step 3
Calculate the pooled sample standard deviation S_p:

$$S_p = \sqrt{\frac{19(0.36) + 19(0.40)}{20 + 20 - 2}} = 0.6164 \text{ (approx.)}$$

Step 4
Verify that the pooled degrees of freedom exceeds 30:

$$n_1 + n_2 - 2 = 38 > 30$$

Step 5
Determine $Z_{\alpha/2}$: $Z_{.05} = 1.645$ (from Table V).

Step 6
Determine the upper confidence limit: The upper confidence limit is equal to

$$(2.75 - 2.51) + (1.645)(0.6164)\sqrt{\frac{1}{20} + \frac{1}{20}} = 0.5606$$

Step 7
Determine the lower confidence limit: The lower confidence limit is equal to

$$(2.75 - 2.51) - (1.645)(0.6164)\sqrt{\frac{1}{20} + \frac{1}{20}} = -0.0806$$

We are 90% confident that the interval from -0.0806 to 0.5606 contains the true difference in grade-point averages between the two groups.

Practical Interpretation

Since the upper limit is positive and the lower limit is negative, the value 0 is contained in the interval. Since the difference of 0 is contained within these bounds, it is possible that there is no difference in grade-point averages between the two groups. Since the sample information suggests that it is statistically plausible that both groups have equivalent grade-point averages, would you as president of this university take actions that discourage students from owning cars to improve students' grade-point averages?

PRACTICE EXERCISE

7.11   The random variables X_1 and X_2 represent monthly water usage in North County and in Orange County, respectively. Suppose they are independently normally distributed with the same variance σ^2. Independent random samples of sizes $n_1 = 20$ and $n_2 = 15$ are taken in each county and the values $\bar{X}_1 = 622$, $S_1^2 = 561$, $\bar{X}_2 = 501$, $S_2^2 = 429$ are obtained. Find a 95% confidence interval for the difference $\mu_1 - \mu_2$ between the two population means and interpret the results.

Small Samples

When $n_1 + n_2 - 2 \leq 30$, the following Student t statistic is appropriate:

$$t_\nu = t_{n_1+n_2-2} = \frac{(\bar{X}_1 - \bar{X}_2) - (\mu_1 - \mu_2)}{\sqrt{\dfrac{S_p^2}{n_1} + \dfrac{S_p^2}{n_2}}} = \frac{(\bar{X}_1 - \bar{X}_2) - (\mu_1 - \mu_2)}{S_p \sqrt{\dfrac{1}{n_1} + \dfrac{1}{n_2}}}$$

where $\nu = n_1 + n_2 - 2$ is the number of degrees of freedom for the Student t statistic in this section. This statistic can be used to develop $1 - \alpha$ confidence limits for $\mu_1 - \mu_2$.

$1 - \alpha$ Confidence Limits for $\mu_1 - \mu_2$, Population Variances Unknown, but Presumed Equal: Small Samples

The upper $1 - \alpha$ confidence limit is given by

$$(\bar{X}_1 - \bar{X}_2) + t_{(\alpha/2,n_1+n_2-2)}S_p \sqrt{\frac{1}{n_1} + \frac{1}{n_2}} \qquad (7\text{-}18)$$

and the lower $1 - \alpha$ confidence limit is given by

$$(\bar{X}_1 - \bar{X}_2) - t_{(\alpha/2,n_1+n_2-2)}S_p \sqrt{\frac{1}{n_1} + \frac{1}{n_2}} \qquad (7\text{-}19)$$

We are now ready to consider the following example, which compares the tensile strengths of wires produced by two production lines.

■ **EXAMPLE 7.14**

Wire Production Lines

Two production lines that produce the same type of wire are being evaluated. We need to find a 98% confidence interval for the difference in the average tensile strengths of the wires for the two lines. The mean and standard deviation of the tensile strengths of a random sample of 9 wires from one line are 10 and 2.1 units, respectively; and the corresponding values of a random sample of 8 wires from the second line are 11.4 and 1.9 units, respectively. Assume the two populations of tensile strength measurements from the two production lines have the same variance and that both populations are normally distributed.

Statistical Solution

Step 1
Specify the level of confidence and $1 - \alpha$: The problem stipulates 98% confidence, which implies $1 - \alpha = .98$.

Step 2
Determine $\alpha/2$: $1 - \alpha = .98$ implies that $\alpha = .02$. Thus, $\alpha/2 = .01$.

Step 3
Determine the pooled sample standard deviation S_p:

$$S_p = \sqrt{\frac{8(2.1)^2 + 7(1.9)^2}{9 + 8 - 2}} = 2.0091 \text{ (approx.)}$$

Step 4
Verify that the pooled degrees of freedom does not exceed 30:

$$n_1 + n_2 - 2 = 15$$

(Note: If $n_1 + n_2 - 2 > 30$, the large sample procedure previously discussed is applicable.)

Step 5
Determine $t_{(\alpha/2,\nu)} = t_{(\alpha/2,n_1+n_2-2)}$: From Table VII, $t_{(.01,15)} = 2.602$.

Step 6
Determine the upper confidence limit: The upper confidence limit is equal to

$$(10 - 11.4) + (2.602)(2.0091)\sqrt{\frac{1}{9} + \frac{1}{8}} = 1.14$$

Step 7
Determine the lower confidence limit: The lower confidence limit is equal to

$$(10 - 11.4) - (2.602)(2.0091)\sqrt{\frac{1}{9} + \frac{1}{8}} = -3.94$$

The interval from -3.94 to 1.14 units has been constructed from a process that 98% of the time produces intervals that include the true difference in the average tensile strengths of the wires produced by the two production lines. Therefore, we are 98% confident that this constructed interval includes the true difference.

Practical Interpretation

Since 0 is contained within these bounds, the statistical evidence suggests that there is no difference in the average tensile strengths of wires produced by the two production lines. With this result is there any basis for singling out one of the two production lines for a production award for higher tensile strength?

PRACTICE EXERCISE

7.12 The random variables X_1 and X_2 represent customer monthly credit card balances at the San Bernardino branch and Ventura branch, respectively, of an appliance store chain. Suppose the variables are independently normally distributed with the same variance σ^2. Independent random samples of sizes $n_1 = n_2 = 9$ were taken and it was found that $\bar{X}_1 = \$263$, with $S_1^2 = 336$, and $\bar{X}_2 = \$342$, with $S_2^2 = 432$. Find a 95% confidence interval for the difference $\mu_1 - \mu_2$ between the two population means. Interpret the meaning of the fact that 0 is not contained within the limits.

CASE 3: WHEN THE VALUES OF σ_1 AND σ_2 ARE UNKNOWN, BUT PRESUMED UNEQUAL

When the values for the population standard deviations are unknown, S_1 replaces σ_1 and S_2 replaces σ_2 in the estimating formulas. In this section we shall describe the adjustments necessary under the inequality of population variance conditions for the large sample situation and for the small sample situation. But because the two population standard deviations are not assumed equal, the procedure previously described is no longer directly applicable.

Large Samples

When $n_1 \geq 30$ and $n_2 \geq 30$, the following Z statistic is appropriate:

$$Z = \frac{(\bar{X}_1 - \bar{X}_2) - (\mu_1 - \mu_2)}{\sqrt{\dfrac{S_1^2}{n_1} + \dfrac{S_2^2}{n_2}}}$$

This Z statistic can be used to develop the $1 - \alpha$ confidence intervals for $\mu_1 - \mu_2$.

$1 - \alpha$ Confidence Limits for $\mu_1 - \mu_2$, Population Variances Unknown, but Presumed Unequal: Large Samples

The upper $1 - \alpha$ confidence limit is given by

$$(\bar{X}_1 - \bar{X}_2) + Z_{\alpha/2} \sqrt{\frac{S_1^2}{n_1} + \frac{S_2^2}{n_2}} \qquad \text{(7-20)}$$

and the lower $1 - \alpha$ confidence limit is given by

$$(\bar{X}_1 - \bar{X}_2) - Z_{\alpha/2} \sqrt{\frac{S_1^2}{n_1} + \frac{S_2^2}{n_2}} \qquad \text{(7-21)}$$

We shall now use these limits to compare tire wear between two brands of tires.

■ **EXAMPLE 7.15**

Tire Brand Longevity

Fifty tires of each of two brand name tire manufacturers are tested for longevity by recording the number of miles of wear before reaching minimum tread specifications. The data yield $\bar{X}_1 = 30,500.6$ mi, $\bar{X}_2 = 33,617.8$ mi, $S_1^2 = 21,678.4$, and $S_2^2 = 24,812.5$. Find a 90% confidence interval for the true average difference in miles of wear for the two brands of tires. (Note that the sample sizes are both large enough—greater than 30—to justify assuming the sample means are normally, or approximately normally, distributed.)

Statistical Solution

Step 1
Specify the level of confidence and $1 - \alpha$: The problem stipulates 90% confidence, which implies $1 - \alpha = .90$.

Step 2
Determine $\alpha/2$: $1 - \alpha = .90$ implies that $\alpha = .10$. Thus, $\alpha/2 = .05$.

Step 3
Establish large sample status:

$$n_1 = n_2 = 50 > 30$$

Step 4
Determine the value of $Z_{\alpha/2}$: From Table V, $Z_{.05} = 1.645$.

Step 5
Determine the upper confidence limit: The upper confidence limit is equal to

$$(30,500.6 - 33,617.8) + 1.645 \sqrt{\frac{21,678.4}{50} + \frac{24,812.5}{50}} = -3067 \text{ mi (approx.)}$$

Step 6

Determine the lower confidence limit: The lower confidence limit is equal to

$$(30{,}500.6 - 33{,}617.8) - 1.645\sqrt{\frac{21{,}678.4}{50} + \frac{24{,}812.5}{50}} = -3167 \text{ mi (approx.)}$$

We can be 98% confident that the interval from -3167 to -3067 mi includes the true average difference in the miles of tread wear between the two brands of tires.

Practical Interpretation

The upper and lower bounds are both negative, and the value 0 is not contained in the interval. This means we are highly confident that the tire wear is not the same for both brands. The confidence interval suggests that brand 2 tires last, on the average, 3000 mi more than brand 1. If the two brands are priced the same and offer the same warranty, which tire brand would you buy?

PRACTICE EXERCISE

7.13 The random variables X_1 and X_2 represent (in hours) the storage life before spoilage of refrigerated cheese, newly packaged by two different dairy producers. Suppose previous testing of this type of cheese from these two producers suggests that the storage lives are normally distributed with unequal variances σ_1^2 and σ_2^2, respectively. Suppose we take independent random samples of sizes $n_1 = n_2 = 30$ and get $\bar{X}_1 = 459.13$, $S_1^2 = 576$, $\bar{X}_2 = 455.01$, and $S_2^2 = 441$. Find a 95% confidence interval for the difference $\mu_1 - \mu_2$ between the two population means. Interpret the significance of finding 0 within the bounds.

Small Samples

When either one (or both) of n_1 or n_2 is less than 30 and $\sigma_1^2 \neq \sigma_2^2$, the following Student t statistic is appropriate:

$$t_\nu = \frac{(\bar{X}_1 - \bar{X}_2) - (\mu_1 - \mu_2)}{\sqrt{\dfrac{S_1^2}{n_1} + \dfrac{S_2^2}{n_2}}}$$

where ν represents the number of degrees of freedom for the Student t statistic. To determine the value of ν in this section, we will select the smaller of $n_1 - 1$ and $n_2 - 1$.* We can use this Student t statistic to develop $1 - \alpha$ confidence limits for $\mu_1 - \mu_2$.

*A more precise, but much more cumbersome, expression for ν is

$$\nu = \frac{(S_1^2/n_1 + S_2^2/n_2)^2}{\dfrac{(S_1^2/n_1)^2}{n_1 - 1} + \dfrac{(S_2^2/n_2)^2}{n_2 - 1}}$$

This value of ν is then rounded to the nearest integer.

1 − α Confidence Limits for μ₁ − μ₂, Population
Variances Unknown, but Presumed Unequal: Small Samples

The upper $1 - \alpha$ confidence limit is given by

$$(\bar{X}_1 - \bar{X}_2) + t_{(\alpha/2, \nu)} \sqrt{\frac{S_1^2}{n_1} + \frac{S_2^2}{n_2}} \qquad \text{(7-22)}$$

and the lower $1 - \alpha$ confidence limit is given by

$$(\bar{X}_1 - \bar{X}_2) - t_{(\alpha/2, \nu)} \sqrt{\frac{S_1^2}{n_1} + \frac{S_2^2}{n_2}} \qquad \text{(7-23)}$$

The following example illustrates the application of these limits to a situation comparing the competency scores of students who used two different textbooks.

▪ **EXAMPLE 7.16**

Textbook Advertising Claims

In advertising a new textbook, a publisher claims that students who receive instruction based on the new textbook will score higher on a certain competency exam than students using another text. A random sample of 8 students who have used only the new textbook and a random sample of 8 students who have used only the other text are given the competency exam. The mean competency score for the 8 students who used the publisher's new textbook is $\bar{X}_1 = 76.5$ with a standard deviation of 13.959; and the mean competency score for the other 8 students is $\bar{X}_2 = 72.375$ with a standard deviation of 24.372. Find a 95% confidence interval for the true average difference in scores between the two groups. (We may assume that the competency scores are normally distributed.)

Statistical Solution

Step 1
Specify the level of confidence and $1 - \alpha$: The problem stipulates 95% confidence, which implies $1 - \alpha = .95$.

Step 2
Determine $\alpha/2$: $1 - \alpha = .95$ implies that $\alpha = .05$. Thus, $\alpha/2 = .025$.

Step 3
Establish small or large sample status: $n_1 = n_2 = 8 < 30$, which implies small sample status.

Step 4
Determine the degrees of freedom ν. To get the value for the number of degrees of freedom, we note that both $n_1 - 1$ and $n_2 - 1 = 8 - 1 = 7$, so we shall use $\nu = 7$ as the degrees of freedom.

Step 5
Determine the value of $t_{(\alpha/2, \nu)}$: From Table VII, $t_{(.025, 7)} = 2.365$.

Step 6
Determine the upper confidence limit: The upper confidence limit is equal to

$$(76.5 - 72.375) + 2.365 \sqrt{\frac{(13.959)^2}{8} + \frac{(24.372)^2}{8}} = 27.61$$

Step 7

Determine the lower confidence limit: The lower confidence limit is equal to

$$(76.5 - 72.375) - 2.365\sqrt{\frac{(13.959)^2}{8} + \frac{(24.372)^2}{8}} = -19.36$$

We can claim with 95% confidence that the true average difference in competency exam scores for the two groups of students lies in the interval from -19.36 to 27.61.

Practical Interpretation

With 0 contained within these bounds, it seems reasonable from the evidence to assert there is no difference in mean competency scores between the two groups. Would you be inclined to pay a premium price for the new textbook or even reach a decision on which text to use based on these results?

PRACTICE EXERCISE

7.14 The random variables X_1 and X_2 represent monthly balances of defaulting accounts for a clothing chain in Oakland and in Santa Barbara, respectively. Because of merchandise differences in the two cities, X_1 and X_2 are assumed independently normally distributed but with unequal variances. Suppose we take independent random samples of sizes $n_1 = 10$ and $n_2 = 5$ from the respective populations and get $\bar{X}_1 = \$173.42$, $S_1 = 24$, $\bar{X}_2 = \$158.75$, and $S_2 = 21$. Find a 95% confidence interval for the difference $\mu_1 - \mu_2$ between the two population means. Interpret the significance of finding 0 within the bounds of this interval.

Flowchart II

The flowchart provided in Figure 7.9 is designed to help you determine the appropriate statistic to use to obtain confidence limits for $\mu_1 - \mu_2$. The examples that follow show the step-by-step procedures.

■ **EXAMPLE 7.17**

Job Testing

E.T. Systems administers aptitude tests for client corporations who want to test job applicants' math skills. Math aptitude scores tend to be normally distributed with a mean of 57 and a standard deviation of 22. E.T. Systems decided to modify the format of the testing procedure, anticipating that the change will affect the applicants' average, but leave the standard deviation unaffected. To verify that the modification has no regional bias, tests were given to applicants on the East coast and West coast. The average final test score of 21 randomly selected East coast applicants is 62.3, and the average final test score of 27 randomly selected West coast applicants is 64.7. Find a 95% confidence interval for the true difference in mean math scores between the two groups.

Statistical Solution

Step 1

Are the values for σ_1 and σ_2 known? The answer to this question is yes, since the given value of 22 is based on past experience, is presumed to be unaffected by the changes, and applies to both populations.

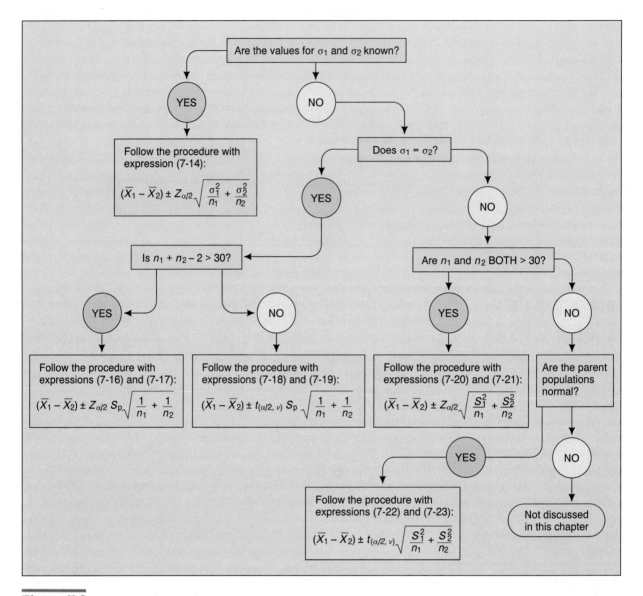

Figure 7.9
Flowchart II, for a $1 - \alpha$ confidence interval for $\mu_1 - \mu_2$

Step 2
Since the answer in Step 1 is yes, we follow the procedure with expression (7-14).

Step 3
95% confidence implies $1 - \alpha = .95$.

Step 4
$1 - \alpha = .95$ implies that $\alpha = .05$. Thus, $\alpha/2 = .025$.

Step 5
From Table V, $Z_{.025} = 1.960$.

Step 6

$$\sigma_1 = \sigma_2 = 22$$

Step 7

$$n_1 = 21 \quad \text{and} \quad n_2 = 27$$

Step 8

$$\bar{X}_1 = 62.3 \quad \text{and} \quad \bar{X}_2 = 64.7$$

Step 9

The upper confidence limit for $\mu_1 - \mu_2$ is equal to

$$(62.3 - 64.7) + 1.960\sqrt{\frac{(22)^2}{21} + \frac{(22)^2}{27}} = 10.1 \text{ (approx.)}$$

Step 10

The lower confidence limit for $\mu_1 - \mu_2$ is equal to

$$(62.3 - 64.7) - 1.960\sqrt{\frac{(22)^2}{21} + \frac{(22)^2}{27}} = -14.9 \text{ (approx.)}$$

We can be 95% confident that the interval from -14.9 to 10.1 includes the true difference in mean math scores between the two groups of applicants.

Practical Interpretation

Finding 0 within the bounds means that the sample evidence strongly suggests no true difference in the average math scores between the groups of applicants. How does this result render the concern that regional bias exists in the new testing format?

In Example 7.17 the values for σ_1 and σ_2 were known. Now let's see what happens when the values for σ_1 and σ_2 are not known.

■ **EXAMPLE 7.18**

Forest Management

As part of its forest management program, the Department of the Interior monitors the growth of the various types of trees across state boundaries. For instance, the Joshua tree found in northwestern Arizona and in California is periodically checked. Suppose height measurements on a random sample of 35 mature Joshua trees in California are found to have an average height of 24.7 ft with a standard deviation of 10.4 ft, and a random sample of 32 mature Joshua trees in Arizona are found to have an average height of 19.1 ft with a standard deviation of 9.9 ft. Find a 98% confidence interval for the average difference in height between the Joshua trees in California and Arizona. Assume that the heights are normally distributed.

Statistical Solution

Step 1

Are the values for σ_1 and σ_2 known? Since the available values are sample values, the answer to this question is no.

Step 2
Although the answer in Step 1 is no, is it permissible or valid to assert that $\sigma_1 = \sigma_2$? The answer to this question is also no, since there are no theoretical, or assumed, reasons to believe that they are equal.

Step 3
Since the answers in Steps 1 and 2 are both no, we must next determine if both n_1 and n_2 are greater than 30. With $n_1 = 35$ and $n_2 = 32$, the answer to this question is yes, both are greater than 30.

Step 4
These answers put us on the path in the flowchart (Figure 7.9) that leads to the procedure involving expressions (7-20) and (7-21).

Step 5
98% confidence implies $1 - \alpha = .98$.

Step 6
$1 - \alpha = .98$ implies that $\alpha = .02$. Thus, $\alpha/2 = 0.01$.

Step 7
From Table V, $Z_{.01} = 2.326$.

Step 8

$$S_1 = 10.4 \qquad \text{and} \qquad S_2 = 9.9$$

Step 9

$$n_1 = 35 \qquad \text{and} \qquad n_2 = 32$$

Step 10

$$\bar{X}_1 = 24.7 \qquad \text{and} \qquad \bar{X}_2 = 19.1$$

Step 11
The upper confidence limit for $\mu_1 - \mu_2$ is equal to

$$(24.7 - 19.1) + 2.326\sqrt{\frac{(10.4)^2}{35} + \frac{(9.9)^2}{32}} = 11.4 \text{ ft (approx.)}$$

Step 12
The lower confidence limit for $\mu_1 - \mu_2$ is equal to

$$(24.7 - 19.1) - 2.326\sqrt{\frac{(10.4)^2}{35} + \frac{(9.9)^2}{32}} = -0.2 \text{ ft (approx.)}$$

We can be 98% confident that the interval from -0.2 to 11.4 ft includes the average difference in height between the Joshua trees in California and Arizona.

Practical Interpretation

With the value of 0 contained within the confidence interval bounds, it is statistically reasonable to conclude that there is no difference in the average height of the Joshua trees in California and Arizona.

In Example 7.18 the values for σ_1 and σ_2 were not known, and σ_1 was not equal to σ_2. We'll now look at an example where σ_1 and σ_2 are not known, but where we assume that σ_1 is equal to σ_2.

■ **EXAMPLE 7.19**

PC Testing

KOMPAC, a rapidly growing innovative PC manufacturer, claims a superior operating performance for its machine compared to the leading machines in that category. You decide to design a test to determine the relative speed of performance with respect to a certain very complex task. It is believed that speed measurements are normally distributed and have the same variance for the two machines. A random sample of 5 time measurements with KOMPAC's advertised machine yields an average time of 4.8 min with a standard deviation of 1.1 min, and a random sample of 7 time measurements with the competing machine yields an average time of 7.2 min with a standard deviation of 1.9 min. Find a 95% confidence interval for the average difference in time the two machines take to perform the given task.

Statistical Solution

Step 1
Are the values for σ_1 and σ_2 known? Since the values given are sample values, the answer to this question is no.

Step 2
Since the answer in Step 1 is no, the next step is to determine whether it is permissible or valid to assert that $\sigma_1 = \sigma_2$. Since it is stated that there are reasons to believe that they are equal, we must conclude that the answer to this question is yes.

Step 3
Since the answer to Step 1 is no, and the answer to Step 2 is yes, the next step is to check whether $n_1 + n_2 - 2 > 30$. We see that $n_1 + n_2 - 2 = 10$ and, hence, the answer to this question is no.

Step 4
The path in the flowchart (Figure 7.9) traced by the results above directs us to use the procedure given by expressions (7-18) and (7-19).

Step 5
95% confidence implies $1 - \alpha = .95$.

Step 6
$1 - \alpha = .95$ implies that $\alpha = .05$. Thus, $\alpha/2 = .025$.

Step 7

$$S_p = \sqrt{\frac{4(1.1)^2 + 6(1.9)^2}{5 + 7 - 2}} = 1.6279$$

Step 8

$$n_1 + n_2 - 2 = 10$$

Step 9
From Table VII, $t_{(.025,10)} = 2.228$.

Step 10
The upper confidence limit for $\mu_1 - \mu_2$ is equal to

$$(4.8 - 7.2) + (2.228)(1.6279)\sqrt{\frac{1}{5} + \frac{1}{7}} = -0.3 \text{ min}$$

Step 11
The lower confidence limit for $\mu_1 - \mu_2$ is equal to

$$(4.8 - 7.2) - (2.228)(1.6279)\sqrt{\frac{1}{5} + \frac{1}{7}} = -4.5 \text{ min}$$

We can be 95% confident that the interval from -4.5 to -0.3 min includes the average difference in time the two PC machines take to perform the assigned task.

Practical Interpretation

Since the upper and lower bounds are both negative, we can be 95% confident that KOMPAC's machine is at least 0.3 min faster than the competing machine at the assigned task. If you have a long report that is due, and if writing the report requires the use of a personal computer performing the given task a minimum of 1000 times, would it matter to you which of these two computers you use?

PRACTICE EXERCISE

7.15 A medical testing lab is monitoring the growth of two varieties of the same species of a medicinal shrub. The random variables X_1 and X_2 represent the heights (in inches) to which the two varieties grow at maturity. Suppose the two varieties are independently normally distributed, and independent random samples of sizes $n_1 = 10$ and $n_2 = 5$ are taken from the respective populations. Find a 95% confidence interval for the difference $\mu_1 - \mu_2$ between the two population means if:
a. $\sigma_1^2 = 121$, $\sigma_2^2 = 169$, $\bar{X}_1 = 39$, and $\bar{X}_2 = 57$
b. $\sigma_1^2 = \sigma_2^2 = \sigma^2$, $S_1^2 = 121$, $S_2^2 = 169$, $\bar{X}_1 = 39$, and $\bar{X}_2 = 57$
c. $\sigma_1^2 \neq \sigma_2^2$, $S_1^2 = 121$, $S_2^2 = 169$, $\bar{X}_1 = 39$, and $\bar{X}_2 = 57$

7.6
PAIRED OBSERVATIONS

When sample observations are taken from populations that are not independent, pairing the observations for observed differences can be useful. For instance, before and after measurements on the same subjects are paired observations that are useful in many fields. For example:

- In medical research, a study of the before and after effects of a new drug on blood pressure
- In psychological research, a study of the before and after effects of different stress factors on work performance
- In marketing research, a study of the before and after effects of consumer advertising on buying behavior

The pairing procedure takes advantage of the existing natural pairings. By analyzing the paired observed differences, d, we can make inferences about the true mean difference, μ_d, between the "before" population and the "after" population. Had the before and after measurements not been paired (i.e., observations not taken on the same subjects), the estimation procedure used would be required to deal not only with the before and after variability, but also with the variability among subjects. By assuming that the two underlying populations for the measurements are normally, or nearly normally, distributed, the following Student t statistic may be used:

$$t_{(n-1)} = \frac{\bar{d} - \mu_d}{S_d/\sqrt{n}}$$

where

$t_{(n-1)}$ is the Student t statistic with $n - 1$ degrees of freedom;

n represents the number of paired differences;

$d_i = X_{1,i} - X_{2,i}$ represents the ith paired difference ($i = 1, \ldots, n$);

$\bar{d} = \dfrac{\Sigma\, d_i}{n}$;

$S_d = \sqrt{\dfrac{n\Sigma\, d_i^2 - (\Sigma\, d_i)^2}{n(n - 1)}}$;

$\mu_d = \mu_1 - \mu_2$, the true difference between the two population means.

This statistic can be used to develop $1 - \alpha$ confidence limits for μ_d.

$1 - \alpha$ Confidence Limits for μ_d: Paired Observations

The upper $1 - \alpha$ confidence limit is given by

$$\bar{d} + t_{(\alpha/2, n-1)}\left(\frac{S_d}{\sqrt{n}}\right) \qquad\qquad (7\text{-}24)$$

and the lower $1 - \alpha$ confidence limit is given by

$$\bar{d} - t_{(\alpha/2, n-1)}\left(\frac{S_d}{\sqrt{n}}\right) \qquad\qquad (7\text{-}25)$$

Let's now use this approach to analyze the change in efficiency, if any, resulting from a retraining program.

■ **EXAMPLE 7.20**

Production Efficiency and Retraining

In an efficiency move, a large corporation is considering retraining its production personnel to reduce the time it takes to perform a certain task. Before embarking on a costly retraining program for all its production personnel, the corporation decides to experiment by selecting a random sample of 5 persons from its production personnel, and time their performance of the task before going through the retraining schedule and then again 1 week after having completed the training. Let $X_{1,i}$ represent the time it takes the ith employee to perform the task before the retraining, and let $X_{2,i}$ represent the time it takes the same employee to perform the task after the retraining. The change in time for the ith employee to perform the task is given by the difference $X_{1,i} - X_{2,i}$. The results are given in Table 7.3.

Find a 99% confidence interval for the mean difference μ_d in time to perform the given task. Assume that performance times are normally distributed. The solution uses paired observations because before and after measurements were taken on the same person. A Student t distribution is used because (1) the population of performance

∘TABLE 7.3 The Time (in Minutes) to Perform a Task				
EMPLOYEE	**BEFORE RETRAINING** $X_{1,i}$	**AFTER RETRAINING** $X_{2,i}$	**PAIRED DIFFERENCE** d_i	d_i^2
1	45	34	11	121
2	57	50	7	49
3	39	37	2	4
4	38	33	5	25
5	55	41	14	196
			$\Sigma\, d_i = 39$	$\Sigma\, d_i^2 = 395$

$$\bar{d} = \frac{\Sigma\, d_i}{n} = \frac{39}{5} = 7.8$$

$$S_d = \sqrt{\frac{n\Sigma\, d_i^2 - (\Sigma\, d_i)^2}{n(n-1)}} = \sqrt{\frac{5(395) - (39)^2}{5(4)}} = 4.76$$

times is assumed to be normally distributed for both populations, (2) the population standard deviations are not known, and (3) the sample size is small.

Statistical Solution

Step 1
Specify the level of confidence and $1 - \alpha$: 99% confidence implies $1 - \alpha = .99$.

Step 2
Determine $\alpha/2$: $1 - \alpha = .99$ implies that $\alpha = .01$. Thus, $\alpha/2 = .005$.

Step 3
Determine the degrees of freedom:

$$n - 1 = 5 - 1 = 4$$

Step 4
Determine the value of $t_{(\alpha/2, n-1)}$: From Table VII, $t_{(.005,4)} = 4.604$.

Step 5
Determine the value of $S_d/\sqrt{n}$:

$$\frac{S_d}{\sqrt{n}} = \frac{4.76}{\sqrt{5}} = 2.129 \text{ min}$$

Step 6
Determine the upper confidence limit:

$$7.8 + (4.604)(2.129) = 17.6 \text{ min}$$

Step 7
Determine the lower confidence limit:

$$7.8 - (4.604)(2.129) = -2.0 \text{ min}$$

The procedure for constructing the interval produces intervals that 99 times out of 100 contain the true mean difference. Knowing this, we can be 99% confident that the interval from -2.0 to 17.6 min contains the true mean difference in time before and after retraining to perform the given task.

Practical Interpretation

Since the difference of 0 is contained within the bounds of the interval, it is statistically reasonable to conclude that there is no difference in the before and after times to perform the task. If you were the person in charge, would you have the corporation undertake the costly retraining program?

● ●

EXERCISES

▶ **7.29** Two very reliable laboratories are asked to analyze food samples from a given manufacturer to determine the quantity of a certain chemical in the food. From past experience with substances of this type, it is known that the distribution of the quantity of the chemical in the food will have a standard deviation of 0.0017 ppm. Laboratory 1 is given 34 food samples to analyze and finds a mean of 0.0061 ppm; laboratory 2 is given 45 food samples and finds a mean of 0.0069 ppm. Find a 98% confidence interval for the difference between the population means for the two laboratories. Assume the distribution of the quantity of the chemical in the food is normal. Is it reasonable to assert that the two laboratories are in agreement?

7.30 A random sample of 61 of last year's model of a certain make of car showed an average of 27.3 miles per gallon (mpg) with a standard deviation of 4.4 mpg in freeway driving when the cars were new. A random sample of 61 of this year's model of the same make of car shows an average of 32.5 mpg with a standard deviation of 3.5 mpg in freeway driving. Assume that the distributions of the miles per gallon for automobiles of this model and make for both years are normal. Construct a 99% confidence interval for the true difference in the average miles per gallon between this year's model and last year's model.

7.31 A random sample of 22 policies from insurance company A shows a net profit of $39 per policy, with a standard deviation of $3.70 per policy. A random sample of 31 policies from insurance company B shows a net profit of $47 per policy with a standard deviation of $3.90 per policy. Assume the policy profits are normally distributed, and assume that the variances are equal for the policy profits for both insurance companies. Find a 90% confidence interval for the true difference in the average net profit per policy between the two insurance companies.

▶ **7.32** Suppose the management team of a very large office building finds that replacing light bulbs is a costly operation. In deciding between two different types of bulbs that have the same unit cost, management considers the information that 10 bulbs of type A had an average longevity of 4372 hr, with a standard deviation of 66.5 hr; and 11 bulbs of type B had an average longevity of 4191 hr, with a standard deviation of 64.8 hr. Assume that the longevity of these bulbs is normally distributed, and assume that the population variances are equal for both types of bulbs. Find a 99% confidence interval for the true difference in the average longevity of the two types of bulbs.

7.33 A computer manufacturer purchases RAM chips from two different suppliers. The specifications for the chips are the same for the two suppliers. In particular, the chips are supposed to operate at a speed of 8 megahertz (MHz). In actuality, the speed varies among the chips, but the average is supposed to be 8 MHz with a standard deviation of 0.1 MHz. The computer manufacturer notices, however, that although the variability among the chips appears to reflect a standard deviation of 0.1 MHz for both suppliers, the average speeds among the chips don't appear to be equal to 8 MHz for both suppliers. As a preliminary check, the manufacturer takes independent random samples of 12 chips from each supplier and gets an average speed of 8.1 MHz for the chips from the first supplier and a speed of 7.9

MHz for the chips from the second supplier. Assume the speeds are normally distributed and use the sample results to find a 98% confidence interval for the true difference in the average speeds of the chips from the two suppliers.

7.34 A new sports stadium is being constructed and is to have a domed roof designed to be opened during fair weather but closed during inclement weather. The material for the roof is to be aluminum in sheet form. The specifications call for sheets with an average thickness of 2 mm and a standard deviation of 0.15 mm. The architect narrows down her choice to two suppliers and, to make a choice between them, she wants to see how close they come to satisfying the specifications. She takes a random sample of 15 sheets from one supplier and gets a mean thickness of 1.97 mm with a standard deviation of 0.23 mm. She then takes a random sample of 13 sheets from the second supplier and gets a mean of 2.01 mm with a standard deviation of 0.14 mm. Assume the thicknesses are normally distributed, and find a 95% confidence interval for the true difference in the average thicknesses between the two suppliers.

7.35 A random sample of 40 people are asked to estimate the price of a new model automobile based on a series of picture slides presented to them. These same 40 people are then brought into a showroom where they can inspect the new model by direct contact, and they are again asked to estimate the price of the automobile. The manufacturer then assesses the data by matching the "before direct contact" and "after direct contact" price estimates. He then subtracts the "before" price estimate from the "after" price estimate. A positive difference would indicate that the viewer had a higher price opinion of the automobile after direct contact with the automobile, and a negative difference would indicate that the viewer had a lower price opinion after direct contact. The average for the 40 differences was $2085, and the standard deviation was $976. Assume the differences come from a normally distributed population and construct a 98% confidence interval for the true average difference.

7.36 An oceanographic expedition took 12 random readings of ocean temperatures at surface location A and recorded an average temperature of 57.3°F with a standard deviation of 6.1°F. They also took 15 random readings of ocean temperatures at surface location B and recorded an average temperature of 59.5°F with a standard deviation of 5.9°F. Assuming readings are normally distributed with equal variances at the two locations, find a 99% confidence interval for the difference in the average temperature at the two locations. Would it be reasonable to conclude that the average temperatures at the two locations are equal?

7.37 Magnets produced by a certain production process are required to have a specified average magnetic strength. The overall variability of the strengths of the magnets is also required to be within certain specifications. Two production lines produce magnets with strengths that are known to be normally distributed with the same standard deviation of 1.25 units. A sample of size 11 from one production line shows an average magnetic strength of 9.37 units, and a sample of size 7 from the second production line shows an average magnetic strength of 8.55 units. Find a 90% confidence interval for the difference in the average magnetic strengths of the populations of magnets from the two production lines. Would it be reasonable to conclude that the average magnetic strengths are the same for magnets produced by the two production lines?

▶ **7.38** A certain stimulus is tested for its effect on blood pressure. Nine patients have their blood pressures measured before and after the stimulus. The results are given in the table. Construct a 98% confidence interval for the average before–after difference in blood pressure. Assume that blood pressures are normally distributed. Is it reasonable to conclude that the stimulus has an effect on blood pressure?

					PATIENT				
	1	**2**	**3**	**4**	**5**	**6**	**7**	**8**	**9**
BEFORE	127	128	124	140	135	125	130	118	121
AFTER	127	120	128	136	133	127	131	127	128

● ●

7.7

CONFIDENCE INTERVAL ESTIMATES FOR THE DIFFERENCE BETWEEN TWO POPULATION PROPORTIONS, $p_1 - p_2$

Comparisons between two populations may focus on the difference in the proportion of members in each population possessing a specific quality or attribute. A point (single-valued) estimate of the difference between the two population proportions is simply the difference between the two sample proportions. However, to make an interval estimate, a confidence interval for the difference must be constructed. For example, consider a production manager examining two different assembly lines. The manager may want a confidence interval to estimate the difference in proportions of defective items produced by each group. Or a gambling casino operator may want to obtain an interval estimate of the difference in proportions of wins for two brands of slot machines. The necessary conditions for the estimating procedure are similar to the conditions for the procedure described in Section 7.3. For instance, let p_1 and p_2 represent the true proportions of "successes" in their respective populations, and let $\hat{p}_1 = X_1/n_1$ and $\hat{p}_2 = X_2/n_2$ represent their respective sample point estimates. If n_1 and n_2 are both greater than or equal to 30, then the standard normal statistic Z can be used to construct $1 - \alpha$ confidence intervals for $p_1 - p_2$.

More specifically, we define

p_1 as the probability of a success from the first population;

p_2 as the probability of a success from the second population;

n_1 as the number of observations (i.e., the number of independent trials) from the first population;

n_2 as the number of observations (i.e., the number of independent trials) from the second population;

X_1 as the number of successes among the n_1 trials;

X_2 as the number of successes among the n_2 trials;

$\hat{p}_1 = X_1/n_1$ as a point estimate of p_1;

$\hat{p}_2 = X_2/n_2$ as a point estimate of p_2;

S_1 as the sample standard deviation for the proportion of successes observed in the sample from the first population, calculated as $S_1 = \sqrt{\hat{p}_1(1 - \hat{p}_1)/n_1}$;

S_2 as the sample standard deviation for the proportion of successes observed in the sample from the second population, calculated as $S_2 = \sqrt{\hat{p}_2(1 - \hat{p}_2)/n_2}$.

The Z statistic for constructing $1 - \alpha$ confidence interval estimates for $p_1 - p_2$ is

$$Z = \frac{(\hat{p}_1 - \hat{p}_2) - (p_1 - p_2)}{\sqrt{S_1^2 + S_2^2}}$$

The $1 - \alpha$ confidence interval estimate for $p_1 - p_2$ is then defined by the upper and lower confidence limits:

$1 - \alpha$ Confidence Limits for $p_1 - p_2$: Large Samples

The upper $1 - \alpha$ confidence limit is given by

$$(\hat{p}_1 - \hat{p}_2) + Z_{\alpha/2}\sqrt{S_1^2 + S_2^2} \tag{7-26}$$

and the lower $1 - \alpha$ confidence limit is given by

$$(\hat{p}_1 - \hat{p}_2) - Z_{\alpha/2}\sqrt{S_1^2 + S_2^2} \tag{7-27}$$

Let's now compare the percentage of D and F grades received by division I and division II college athletes.

■ **EXAMPLE 7.21**

Grades of D and F Received by College Athletes

The percentage of D and F grades received by collegiate athletes in division I universities and division II universities was duly noted by the National Collegiate Athletic Association (NCAA). In a random sample of 50 students from division I universities over the past 3 yr, 16 received overall grades in the D–F range; and in a random sample of 40 students from division II universities over the same period, 8 had overall grades in the D–F range. Find a 95% confidence interval for the difference in the proportion of D and F grades received in the two divisions.

Statistical Solution

Step 1
Specify the confidence level and $1 - \alpha$: The problem stipulates 95% confidence, which implies $1 - \alpha = .95$.

Step 2
Determine $\alpha/2$: $1 - \alpha = .95$ implies that $\alpha = .05$. Thus, $\alpha/2 = .025$.

Step 3
Establish that n_1 and n_2 meet the large sample requirements:

$$n_1 = 50 > 30 \quad \text{and} \quad n_2 = 40 > 30$$

Step 4
Determine $Z_{\alpha/2}$: From Table V, $Z_{.025} = 1.96$.

Step 5
Calculate the point estimates $\hat{p}_1$ and $\hat{p}_2$:

$$\hat{p}_1 = \frac{16}{50} = 0.32 \quad \text{and} \quad \hat{p}_2 = \frac{8}{40} = 0.20$$

Step 6
Determine the upper confidence limit: The upper confidence limit is equal to

$$(0.32 - 0.20) + 1.960\sqrt{\frac{(0.32)(0.68)}{50} + \frac{(0.20)(0.80)}{40}} = 0.299$$

Step 7
Determine the lower confidence limit: The lower confidence limit is equal to

$$(0.32 - 0.20) - 1.960\sqrt{\frac{(0.32)(0.68)}{50} + \frac{(0.20)(0.80)}{40}} = -0.059$$

There is 95% confidence that the interval from -0.059 to 0.299 includes the true difference in the proportions of student grades in the D–F range between the two divisions.

Practical Interpretation

A difference of 0 is contained within the bounds. Thus, it is statistically reasonable to conclude that there is no difference in the proportions of D or F grades received in the two divisions. Suppose you are a high school athlete evaluating offers by universities in the two divisions. Does the sample evidence suggest to you that division I universities are (statistically) academically tougher than division II universities?

PRACTICE EXERCISE

7.16 Based on computer simulations, a gambler has developed two strategies for playing the roulette table at an Atlantic City casino. The gambler intends to use one strategy in 64 independent plays at the roulette table (i.e., the probability of winning is the same for each play). Then, after dinner, a second strategy will be used in 81 independent plays (i.e., the probability of winning is the same for each play, but may be different from the probability of winning with the first strategy). Let the random variable X_1 represent the number of times the gambler wins using the first strategy and let the random variable X_2 represent the number of wins using the second strategy. Then X_1 and X_2 are independently, binomially distributed. They have probabilities p_1 and p_2, respectively, of winning on each play. If the gambler wins 47 times with the first strategy and 51 times with the second strategy, find a 95% confidence interval for the difference $p_1 - p_2$ between the two proportions.

EXERCISES

7.39 At one large university, 21 out of a random sample of 325 students didn't pass a hearing test. At a second large university, 19 out of a random sample of 280 students didn't pass the hearing test. Find a 95% confidence interval for the difference in the proportions of students at the two universities who didn't pass the hearing test. Is it reasonable to infer that both universities have the same proportion of students who can't pass the hearing test?

7.40 At one radar checkpoint, 24 cars out of a random sample of 324 cars exceeded the speed limit. At a second radar checkpoint, 36 cars out of a random sample of 361 cars exceeded the speed limit. Construct a 90% confidence interval for the difference in the proportions of cars that exceed the speed limit at the two locations. Is it reasonable to report that the proportion of speeding cars is the same at both checkpoints?

▶ **7.41** A quality control manager notices that the day and night shifts operating on a certain production line may not be equally productive. In particular, she senses that the day shift may be producing a higher proportion of rejects. To check this out, she randomly selects 75 items from the day shift's production and 75 items from the night shift's production. Of the 75 from the day shift's production, 7 are rejects; of the 75 from the night shift's production, 3 are rejects. Find an approximate 95% confidence interval for the true difference in the proportions of rejects produced by the day and night shifts.

7.42 An Hispanic lawyer is concerned about possible biased composition of juries in capital punishment trials. He claims that jury composition in capital punishment trials has a consistently lower percentage of Hispanics than jury composition in civil cases. To illustrate his contention, he takes a random sample of 40 juries in capital punishment trials and finds 2 of the juries had at least one Hispanic member. He also takes a random sample of 54 juries in civil cases and finds 17 of the juries had at least one Hispanic member. Find an approximate 98% confidence interval for the true difference in the proportions of juries with at least one Hispanic member.

7.8

CONFIDENCE INTERVAL ESTIMATES FOR POPULATION VARIANCE

The sample variance S^2 calculated from a random sample of the population is a *point estimate* of the population variance σ^2. As with the other point estimates we studied ($\bar{X}$ for μ, $\hat{p}$ for p), S^2 provides a working value to use when we don't know the actual value of σ^2. But how reliable an estimate for σ^2 is S^2? A level of confidence can be assigned to intervals for σ^2 as we did for the confidence intervals for μ and p. The procedure for constructing confidence intervals for σ^2 requires a statement about the appropriate sampling distribution (probability density function) for the random variable S^2. Without providing a mathematical proof and without offering an intuitive argument, we shall simply state that if the random sampling is from a normally distributed population, then the random variable $(n-1)S^2/\sigma^2$ has a **chi-square distribution** with $n-1$ degrees of freedom. That is,

$$\frac{(n-1)S^2}{\sigma^2} = \chi^2_{(n-1)}$$

where χ is the Greek letter chi.

THE CHI-SQUARE DISTRIBUTION

Probability values for this probability function are given in Tables VIIIa and VIIIb in the Appendix. To use these tables we shall use the notation $\chi^2_{(\alpha,\nu)}$, where $\nu = n-1$, the degrees of freedom; and α represents the right tail probability. The degrees of freedom designate the correct row to use in the table. Notice that negative values for χ^2 do not exist. This means that probabilities in the left tail cannot be designated by negative χ^2 terms as we were able to do by using negative Z and negative t terms. Instead, we shall adapt the subscript notation of the χ^2 symbol to accommodate for this. The following two chi-square expressions illustrate the adaptation (they are illustrated in Tables VIIIa and VIIIb).

Chi-Square Tail Probabilities

Right Tail Probability

$$P(\chi_\nu^2 \geq \chi_{(\alpha,\nu)}^2) = \alpha \tag{7-28}$$

Left Tail Probability

$$P(\chi_\nu^2 \leq \chi_{(1-\alpha,\nu)}^2) = \alpha \tag{7-29}$$

The graphs of the chi-square probability density functions shown in Figure 7.10 are skewed (asymmetrical) curves, starting at 0 and extending to the right toward infinity. Although the right tails extend to infinity, the area under the curve in each case is finite and is equal to 1. As the number of degrees of freedom increases, the curve takes on a more symmetrical shape and approaches the shape of a normal probability density function. Graphs for the chi-square distribution are given in Figure 7.10 for 2, 3, and 5 d.f. The mean for a chi-square distribution is equal to ν, and its variance is equal to 2ν.

Reading the Chi-Square Table

The chi-square table is constructed so that the first column gives the degrees of freedom, ν; the body of the table lists the particular value of chi-square for each specified $\chi_{(\alpha,\nu)}^2$ or $\chi_{(1-\alpha,\nu)}^2$ condition; and the top row of the table gives information on α, the probability (or area under the curve) for intervals starting from the value of chi-square given in the table to infinity.

The following examples provide practice in using Tables VIIIa and VIIIb to find probabilities for a chi-square distribution. To use the tables, values of ν must be specified, along with either a specified χ^2 value or a specified value of α. Example 7.22 uses $\nu = 9$ d.f. and specifies either a right or left tail χ^2 value or both. We are

Figure 7.10
Chi-square distributions

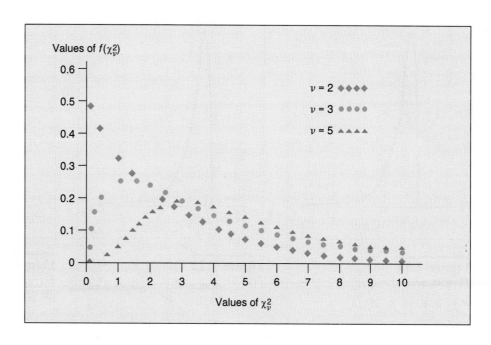

asked either for a probability related to the one tail or for the probability between two specified χ^2 values.

■ **EXAMPLE 7.22**

Using the Chi-Square Probability Tables

From the chi-square table rows corresponding to $\nu = 9$ d.f., we find:

a. $P(\chi_9^2 \geq 2.700) = P(\chi_9^2 > 2.700) = .975$
b. $P(\chi_9^2 \leq 2.700) = P(\chi_9^2 < 2.700) = 1 - .975 = .025$
c. $P(\chi_9^2 \geq 3.325) = P(\chi_9^2 > 3.325) = .95$
d. $P(\chi_9^2 \leq 19.023) = P(\chi_9^2 < 19.023) = 1 - .025 = .975$
e. $P(2.7 \leq \chi_9^2 \leq 19.023) = P(2.7 < \chi_9^2 < 19.023) = .975 - .025 = .95$
f. $P(\chi_9^2 \leq 16.919) = P(\chi_9^2 < 16.919) = 1 - .05 = .950$

Example 7.23 specifies the degrees of freedom and either the right tail area or two specific locations on the distribution. We are asked for the corresponding χ^2 value, using tail areas for the probability between the two values specified.

■ **EXAMPLE 7.23**

Using the Chi-Square Probability Tables (Continued)

a. $P(\chi_3^2 \geq \chi_{(.10,3)}^2) = P(\chi_3^2 \geq 6.251) = .10$
   This is shown graphically in Figure 7.11.

b. $P(\chi_3^2 \geq \chi_{(.95,3)}^2) = P(\chi_3^2 \geq 0.352) = .950$
   This is shown graphically in Figure 7.12.

c. $P(\chi_{(.95,3)}^2 \leq \chi_3^2 \leq \chi_{(.10,3)}^2) = .95 - .10 = .85$
   This is shown graphically in Figure 7.13.

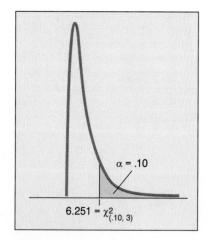

Figure 7.11
$P(\chi_3^2 \geq \chi_{(.10,3)}^2) =$
$P(\chi_3^2 \geq 6.251) = .10$

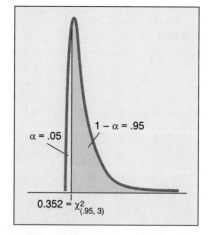

Figure 7.12
$P(\chi_3^2 \geq \chi_{(.95,3)}^2) =$
$P(\chi_3^2 \geq 0.352) = .95$

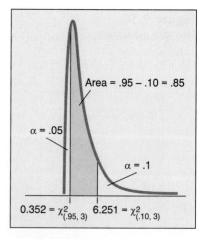

Figure 7.13
$P(\chi_{(.95,3)}^2 \leq \chi_3^2 \leq \chi_{(.10,3)}^2)$
$= .85$

7.17 If the random variable χ^2_{21} has the chi-square distribution with 21 d.f., find:

a. $P(\chi^2_{21} > 35.4789)$
b. $P(\chi^2_{21} < 35.4789)$
c. $P(\chi^2_{21} > 10.28293)$
d. $P(\chi^2_{21} < 10.28293)$
e. $P(10.28293) < \chi^2_{21} < 35.4789)$
f. $\chi^2_{(.90,21)}$
g. $\chi^2_{(.005,21)}$

DERIVING THE $1 - \alpha$ CONFIDENCE INTERVAL ESTIMATE FOR σ^2

In keeping with our convention of dividing the probability α of confidence intervals equally between the two tails, the following probability statement can be written:

$$P(\chi^2_{(1-\alpha/2,\nu)} \leq \chi^2_\nu \leq \chi^2_{(\alpha/2,\nu)}) = 1 - \alpha$$

Since the term $(n - 1)S^2/\sigma^2$ follows a chi-square distribution, we may make the appropriate substitutions and write the following:

$$P\left(\chi^2_{(1-\alpha/2,n-1)} \leq \frac{(n - 1)S^2}{\sigma^2} \leq \chi^2_{(\alpha/2,n-1)}\right) = 1 - \alpha$$

where $\nu = n - 1$. From this statement, the $1 - \alpha$ confidence interval for σ^2 follows:

$1 - \alpha$ Confidence Interval Estimate for σ^2

$$\frac{(n - 1)S^2}{\chi^2_{(\alpha/2,n-1)}} \leq \sigma^2 \leq \frac{(n - 1)S^2}{\chi^2_{(1-\alpha/2,n-1)}} \tag{7-30}$$

The left term is the lower confidence limit for σ^2, and the right term is the upper confidence limit for σ^2.

It is important to note that taking the square root of each of the three terms in inequality (7-30) results in a $1 - \alpha$ confidence interval for the population standard deviation σ.

We are now ready to use this approach to analyze the variability among drivers in response to a particular driving hazard.

■ **EXAMPLE 7.24**

Time Responses to Driving Hazards

Automotive companies are aware that the driving public places a high importance on automotive safety. Thus, the basic design of autos today must include many safety features. To design these safety features auto firms must be aware that human beings vary in their response times to driving hazards. Therefore, the auto companies are constantly gathering data to measure the amount of variation for which allowances must be made. Suppose an automotive firm conducts an experiment in which 91 healthy adults of both sexes between the ages of 21 and 30 are subjected to a certain driving hazard, and the sample variance of the observed response times is found to be 0.0196. Find a 95% confidence interval for the population variance in response times to the given driving hazard. Assume that response times are normally distributed.

Statistical Solution

Step 1

Specify the confidence level and $1 - \alpha$: The problem stipulates a 95% confidence interval, which implies $1 - \alpha = .95$.

Step 2

Determine $\alpha/2$: $1 - \alpha = .95$ implies that $\alpha = .05$. Thus, $\alpha/2 = .025$.

Step 3

Determine $\chi^2_{(1-\alpha/2,\nu)}$: From Table VIIIa, $\chi^2_{(.975,90)} = 65.6466$.

Step 4

Determine $\chi^2_{(\alpha/2,\nu)}$: From Table VIIIb, $\chi^2_{(.025,90)} = 118.136$.

Step 5

Determine the upper confidence limit: The upper confidence limit of the population variance is given by

$$\frac{(90)(0.0196)}{65.6466} = 0.0269$$

Step 6

Determine the lower confidence limit: The lower confidence limit of the population variance is given by

$$\frac{(90)(0.0196)}{118.136} = 0.0149$$

The corresponding confidence limits for the population standard deviation are $\sqrt{0.0269} = 0.1640$ sec and $\sqrt{0.0149} = 0.1221$ sec, respectively.

Thus, we can be 95% confident that the interval from 0.0149 to 0.0269 includes the true variance in response times. Equivalently, we can be 95% confident that the interval from 0.1221 to 0.1640 sec includes the true value of the standard deviation.

Practical Interpretation

According to these observations, we can be 95% confident that the interval from 0.1221 to 0.1640 sec contains the true standard deviation in response times to a driving hazard. In a practical sense this means that whatever is found to be the average adult response time to the driving hazard, we can be at least 95% confident that the distribution of response times has a standard deviation at least equal to 0.1 sec. If 0.1 sec variability is deemed too large for safety standards (meaning that those with slower than average reaction time face significant driving risk), then automobile producers must engineer a car with safety modifications that compensate for those of us who react too slowly.

P R A C T I C E
E X E R C I S E

7.18 Suppose we can assume that the population of monthly home equity loan payments in San Diego County are normally distributed; and suppose a random sample of size $n = 71$ from the population results in a sample variance of 441. Find a 95% confidence interval for the population variance.

EXERCISES

7.43 If the random variable χ_9^2 has the chi-square distribution with 9 d.f., evaluate:
  a. $P(\chi_9^2 > 1.735)$
  b. $P(\chi_9^2 > 21.666)$

7.44 If the random variable χ_9^2 has the chi-square distribution with 9 d.f., evaluate:
  a. $P(\chi_9^2 < 1.735)$
  b. $P(\chi_9^2 < 21.666)$
  c. $P(2.088 < \chi_9^2 < 21.666)$
  d. $P(1.735 < \chi_9^2 < 21.666)$

▶ **7.45** The variance of a random sample of size 41 taken from a normally distributed population is equal to 13.4. Find the 95% confidence interval for the population variance.

7.46 With respect to hand grenades, assume that the time to explosion from the time the pin is pulled and the safety released is a normally distributed random variable. Clearly, a very small variance is highly desired. Find a 98% confidence interval for the population variance if a random sample of 71 grenades is tested and found to have a variance of 0.09. What can you say about this confidence interval?

7.47 With respect to the data in Exercise 7.16, which is repeated here, find a 99% confidence interval for the population variance.

| .152 | .324 | .383 | .327 | .347 | | .283 | .175 | .239 | .261 | .275 |
| .380 | .191 | .218 | .336 | .210 | | .328 | | | | |

7.48 With respect to the data in Exercise 7.17, which is repeated here, find a 98% confidence interval for the population variance.

181.78	157.39	142.45	140.92	166.98		128.48	149.46	108.61	122.72	112.86
157.35	116.25	167.46	138.95	106.89		113.53	147.03	136.28	162.70	150.13
117.32	125.57	166.06	152.61	160.39		112.66	137.06	125.60	200.29	107.78
134.56	185.24	118.63	202.61	110.79		149.05	132.60	165.51	112.29	180.77
123.30	200.76	122.32	84.29	144.97		151.52	156.13	153.41	149.13	110.26
161.97										

▶ **7.49** A young couple wishes to purchase a fast food franchise store, and they are told that daily sales at the store have been fairly consistent over the past 2 yr. To check this out, the couple takes a random sample of 17 days from the records of the past 2 yr and gets a variance of 155,236. Assume the daily receipts are normally distributed. Find a 95% confidence interval for the population variance.

7.9

CONFIDENCE INTERVAL ESTIMATES FOR THE RATIO OF TWO POPULATION VARIANCES

Interval estimates that compare two population variances require a *ratio* of the two population variances rather than a difference. The general procedure for confidence interval construction assumes the two populations from which we are sampling are normal, or nearly normal. The samples are also assumed to be independent. Under these conditions, an **F statistic** can be constructed as follows:

$$F_{(n_1-1, n_2-1)} = \frac{S_1^2/\sigma_1^2}{S_2^2/\sigma_2^2}$$

where

$n_1 - 1$ and $n_2 - 1$ each identify a particular member of the family of F probability distributions;

$F_{(n_1-1,n_2-1)}$ is a random variable that has an F distribution identified by the subscripts $n_1 - 1$ and $n_2 - 1$;

S_1^2 represents the variance of a sample of size n_1 taken from a normal population whose variance is equal to σ_1^2;

S_2^2 represents the variance of a sample of size n_2 taken from a normal population whose variance is equal to σ_2^2.

THE *F* DISTRIBUTION

Probability values for the F distribution are given in Tables IXa and IXb in the Appendix. The use of these tables follows directly from the subscripts shown in the table notation $F_{(\alpha,\nu_1,\nu_2)}$, where the subscript $\nu_1 = n_1 - 1$ is referred to as the *degrees of freedom for the numerator*, and the subscript $\nu_2 = n_2 - 1$ is referred to as the *degrees of freedom for the denominator*. The degrees of freedom for the numerator, ν_1, guides us to the correct column to use in the table, and the degrees of freedom for the denominator, ν_2, guides us to the correct row to use in the table. The value of α directs us to either Table IXa or IXb. Table IXa provides the F values for the upper 5% tail, and Table IXb provides the F values for the upper 1% tail. More formally, the value of α is defined as follows:

F Distribution (Right) Tail Probability

$$P(F_{(\nu_1,\nu_2)} \geq F_{(\alpha,\nu_1,\nu_2)}) = \alpha \qquad (7\text{-}31)$$

When graphed, the F probability density function is a skewed (asymmetrical) curve, starting at 0 and extending to the right toward infinity. Although the right tail extends to infinity, the area under the curve is finite and is equal to 1. The curve becomes more symmetrical as the number of degrees of freedom for the rows and columns increase. Graphs for the F distribution are given in Figure 7.14 for $\nu_1 = 2$, $\nu_2 = 2$ and $\nu_1 = 10$, $\nu_2 = 10$ degrees of freedom. By convention, we can use ordered pairs to represent this as (2, 2) and (10, 10), where the first entry is ν_1 and the second entry is ν_2.

Reading the *F* Table

The table is constructed so that the numerator degrees of freedom ($\nu_1 = n_1 - 1$) identify the columns; the denominator degrees of freedom ($\nu_2 = n_2 - 1$) identify the rows; the value of α indicates the right tail area of the distribution; and the body of the table lists the unique values of F for the specified $F_{(\alpha,\nu_1,\nu_2)}$ condition. Table IXa provides the values of F that cut off the upper 5% of the area under the curve. Table IXb provides the values of F that cut off the upper 1% of the area under the curve.

The following examples provide practice in using Tables IXa and IXb to find probability values on a particular F distribution for specified values of F (Example 7.25), and to find values of F for specified values of α, ν_1, and ν_2 (Example 7.26).

Figure 7.14
F distributions

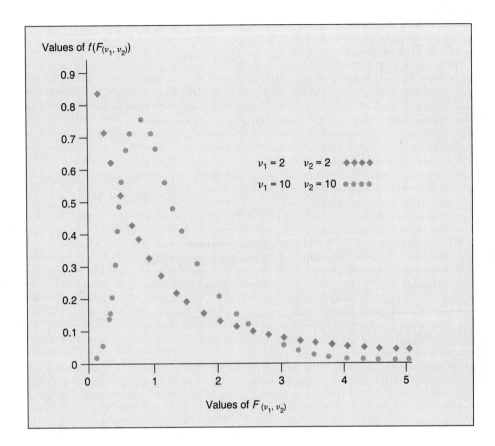

EXAMPLE 7.25

Using the F Probability Table

We use Table IXa to find the following F values for the upper 5% of the F curve:

a. $P(F_{(3,5)} < 5.41) = .95$
b. $P(F_{(3,5)} > 5.41) = .05$
c. $P(F_{(15,10)} < 2.85) = .95$
d. $P(F_{(6,24)} > 2.51) = .05$
e. $P(F_{(24,6)} > 3.84) = .05$

Now let's look at finding the appropriate value of F when we are given the values for α, ν_1, and ν_2.

EXAMPLE 7.26

Using the F Probability Table (Continued)

Table IXa provides the F values for the upper 5% of the F curve, and Table IXb provides the F values for the upper 1% of the F curve:

a. $P(F_{(9,7)} \geq F_{(.05,9,7)}) = .05$, and $F_{(.05,9,7)} = 3.68$
b. $P(F_{(7,9)} \geq F_{(.05,7,9)}) = .05$, and $F_{(.05,7,9)} = 3.29$
c. $P(F_{(9,7)} \geq F_{(.01,9,7)}) = .01$, and $F_{(.01,9,7)} = 6.72$
d. $P(F_{(7,9)} \geq F_{(.01,7,9)}) = .01$, and $F_{(.01,7,9)} = 5.61$

7.19 If the random variable $F_{(12,17)}$ has the F distribution with 12 and 17 d.f. for numerator and denominator, respectively, find:

   a. $P(F_{(12,17)} > 2.38)$ b. $P(F_{(12,17)} < 2.38)$

7.20 If the random variable $F_{(15,25)}$ has the F distribution with 15 and 25 d.f. for numerator and denominator, respectively, find:

   a. $F_{(.05,15,25)}$ b. $F_{(.01,15,25)}$

Without providing a mathematical justification, we shall simply state that the expression for a $1 - \alpha$ confidence interval for the ratio of two population variances is the following:

$1 - \alpha$ Confidence Interval
Estimate for the Ratio of Two Variances

$$\left(\frac{S_2^2}{S_1^2}\right)\left(\frac{1}{F_{(\alpha/2,n_2-1,n_1-1)}}\right) \leq \frac{\sigma_2^2}{\sigma_1^2} \leq \left(\frac{S_2^2}{S_1^2}\right)F_{(\alpha/2,n_1-1,n_2-1)} \qquad \text{(7-32)}$$

The term on the left is the lower confidence limit of the ratio of two variances, and the term on the right is the upper confidence limit.

We'll now use inequality (7-32) to compare the variability in longevity between two different ethnic groups.

■ **EXAMPLE 7.27**

Length of Life Among Ethnic Groups

An executive with a large insurance company has been studying some data and charts. After separating data according to two specific ethnic groups, it appears to her that the data for one group has nearly twice the variance in length of life as the other. Assume length of life is normally distributed, or nearly so. A random sample of $n_1 = 41$ taken from all available data of one ethnic group has a variance of 136.89, and a random sample of $n_2 = 61$ taken from all available data of the second ethnic group has a variance of 204.49. Find a 98% confidence interval for the ratio of the two population variances.

Statistical Solution

Step 1
Specify the level of confidence and $1 - \alpha$: The problem stipulates 98% confidence, which implies $1 - \alpha = .98$.

Step 2
Determine $\alpha/2$: $1 - \alpha = .98$ implies that $\alpha = .02$. Thus, $\alpha/2 = .01$.

Step 3
Determine the degrees of freedom for numerator and denominator:

$$\nu_1 = n_1 - 1 = 40 \quad \text{and} \quad \nu_2 = n_2 - 1 = 60$$

Step 4
Find values of $F_{(\alpha/2,\nu_1,\nu_2)}$ and $F_{(\alpha/2,\nu_2,\nu_1)}$: From Table IXb, $F_{(.01,40,60)} = 1.94$ and $F_{(.01,60,40)} = 2.02$.

Step 5

Determine the upper confidence limit: The upper confidence limit is given by

$$\left(\frac{204.49}{136.89}\right)(1.94) = 2.90$$

Step 6

Determine the lower confidence limit: The lower confidence limit is given by

$$\left(\frac{204.49}{136.89}\right)\left(\frac{1}{2.02}\right) = 0.74$$

Although there is no certainty that the interval from 0.74 to 2.90 contains the true value of the ratio of the two population variances, we can be 98% confident that it does.

Practical Interpretation

With the value of the lower limit less than 1 and the value of the upper limit greater than 1, the confidence interval contains the value 1. A value of 1 indicates that the two population variances are equal (i.e., $\sigma_1^2 = \sigma_2^2$). Thus, it is statistically reasonable to assert that the data do not identify which (if either) of the two ethnic groups has the greater variability in length of life.

PRACTICE EXERCISE

7.21 The random variables X_1 and X_2 represent the heights (in inches) to which two varieties of the same species of a certain shrub grow at maturity. Suppose these variables are independently normally distributed. We take independent random samples of sizes $n_1 = 9$ and $n_2 = 6$, respectively, from each population and get $S_1^2 = 121$ and $S_2^2 = 169$. Find a 90% confidence interval for the ratio of the two population variances.

EXERCISES

7.50 Find the values of the random variable F that satisfy the following relationships:

a. $P(F_{(5,3)} > F) = .05$ b. $P(F_{(5,3)} > F) = .01$

c. $P(F_{(5,3)} < F) = .95$ d. $P(F_{(5,3)} < F) = .99$

e. $P(F_{(24,16)} > F) = .05$ f. $P(F_{(15,25)} < F) = .99$

g. $P(F_{(60,11)} < F) = .99$ h. $P(F_{(9,25)} < F) = .95$

▶ **7.51** A manufacturer of electronic components believes that the variance of the lifetime distribution of components she manufactures is equal to that of her major competitor; that is, she believes that the ratio of the two population variances is equal to 1. A random sample of size 31 from the first manufacturer has a variance of 21.7, and a random sample of size 25 from the competitor has a variance of 32.6. Assume the lifetimes of the electronic components produced by these two manufacturers are normally distributed. Find a 90% confidence interval for the ratio of the two population variances. Is it reasonable for the manufacturer to express her belief as an advertising claim?

7.52 With respect to Exercise 7.31, where a random sample of 22 policies from company A had a standard deviation of $3.70 and a random sample of 31 policies from company B had a standard deviation of $3.90, find a 90% confidence interval for the true ratio of the two population variances.

7.53 With respect to Exercise 7.33, where independent random samples of 12 chips were taken from each supplier, find a 98% confidence interval for the true ratio of the two population variances if the respective sample standard deviations were 0.09 and 0.11 MHz.

7.54 With respect to Exercise 7.32, where a random sample of 10 type A bulbs had a standard deviation of 66.5 hr and a random sample of 11 type B bulbs had a standard deviation of 64.8 hr, find a 98% confidence interval for the true ratio of the two population variances.

SUMMARY

We have encountered in this chapter many business situations in which it is important to be able to make a reliable statement that generalizes from sample data to the population. This process of generalizing is called *statistical inference*. Our main focus has been on the type of statistical inference involving the *confidence interval procedure*. By constructing a confidence interval we found an estimating range of values within which the population parameter is expected to occur. Our confidence in the procedure is based in probability theory and is expressed by the confidence level attached to the confidence interval estimate—typically set at a high level such as 95 or 99%. For the businessperson the attractiveness of setting a high confidence level comes at the price of a wide (and less useful) estimating interval. The practicing businessperson must balance the objective of getting rid of as much uncertainty as possible with the objective of getting as exact an estimate as possible. In the next chapter, we will examine a second type of statistical inference called *hypothesis testing*.

KEY EQUATIONS

Standard Normal Upper Tail Area

$$P(Z \geq +Z_\alpha) = \alpha \tag{7-1}$$

Standard Normal Lower Tail Area

$$P(Z \leq -Z_\alpha) = \alpha \tag{7-2}$$

$1 - \alpha$ Confidence Interval Estimate for μ, σ Known

$$\bar{X} - Z_{\alpha/2}\left(\frac{\sigma}{\sqrt{n}}\right) \leq \mu \leq \bar{X} + Z_{\alpha/2}\left(\frac{\sigma}{\sqrt{n}}\right) \tag{7-3}$$

The term on the left is the lower confidence limit, and the term on the right is the upper confidence limit.

$1 - \alpha$ Confidence Interval Estimate for μ, σ Unknown: Large Sample

$$\bar{X} - Z_{\alpha/2}\left(\frac{S}{\sqrt{n}}\right) \leq \mu \leq \bar{X} + Z_{\alpha/2}\left(\frac{S}{\sqrt{n}}\right) \tag{7-4}$$

where S is the sample standard deviation, the term on the left is the lower confidence limit, and the term on the right is the upper confidence limit.

Student t Statistic

When the size of the sample is small (i.e., ≤ 30), and the sampling is from a normally distributed population, then it can be shown that

$$t_{(n-1)} = \frac{\bar{X} - \mu}{S/\sqrt{n}} \tag{7-5}$$

where $t_{(n-1)}$ has the Student t distribution with $n - 1$ degrees of freedom.

Student t Tail Probabilities

Right Tail Probability

$$P(t_\nu \geq +t_{(\alpha,\nu)}) = \alpha \tag{7-6}$$

Left Tail Probability

$$P(t_\nu \leq -t_{(\alpha,\nu)}) = \alpha \tag{7-7}$$

where ν represents the number of degrees of freedom.

$1 - \alpha$ Confidence Interval
Estimate for μ, σ Unknown: Small Sample

$$\bar{X} - t_{(\alpha/2, n-1)}\left(\frac{S}{\sqrt{n}}\right) \leq \mu \leq \bar{X} + t_{(\alpha/2, n-1)}\left(\frac{S}{\sqrt{n}}\right) \tag{7-8}$$

The term on the left is the lower confidence limit, the term on the right is the upper confidence limit, and the number of degrees of freedom is equal to $n - 1$.

Determining Sample Size for Estimating μ

$$n = \left(\frac{Z_{\alpha/2}\sigma}{E}\right)^2 \tag{7-9}$$

where $E = |\bar{X} - \mu|$ is the error of estimate for the mean.

$1 - \alpha$ Confidence Interval Estimate for p

$$\hat{p} - Z_{\alpha/2}\sqrt{\frac{\hat{p}(1 - \hat{p})}{n}} \leq p \leq \hat{p} + Z_{\alpha/2}\sqrt{\frac{\hat{p}(1 - \hat{p})}{n}} \tag{7-10}$$

The upper $1 - \alpha$ confidence limit is given by

$$\hat{p} + Z_{\alpha/2}\sqrt{\frac{\hat{p}(1 - \hat{p})}{n}} \tag{7-11}$$

and the lower $1 - \alpha$ confidence limit is given by

$$\hat{p} - Z_{\alpha/2}\sqrt{\frac{\hat{p}(1 - \hat{p})}{n}} \tag{7-12}$$

and where $\hat{p} = X/n$.

Determining Sample Size for Estimating p

$$n = \left(\frac{Z_{\alpha/2}}{E}\right)^2 p^*(1 - p^*) \tag{7-13}$$

where p^* represents an initial estimate of p based on past experience or theoretical considerations. When there is no initial estimate for p^*, we use $p^* = .5$. Also, $|\hat{p} - p| = E$ is the error of estimate for the population proportion.

$1 - \alpha$ Confidence Interval Estimate for
$\mu_1 - \mu_2$: Both Population Standard Deviations Known

$$(\bar{X}_1 - \bar{X}_2) - Z_{\alpha/2}\sqrt{\frac{\sigma_1^2}{n_1} + \frac{\sigma_2^2}{n_2}} \leq \mu_1 - \mu_2 \leq (\bar{X}_1 - \bar{X}_2) + Z_{\alpha/2}\sqrt{\frac{\sigma_1^2}{n_1} + \frac{\sigma_2^2}{n_2}} \tag{7-14}$$

The term on the left side of the inequality is the lower confidence limit, and the term on the right side of the inequality is the upper confidence limit.

Pooled Estimate of σ

$$S_p = \sqrt{\frac{(n_1 - 1)S_1^2 + (n_2 - 1)S_2^2}{n_1 + n_2 - 2}} \tag{7-15}$$

$1 - \alpha$ Confidence Limits for $\mu_1 - \mu_2$, Population Variances Unknown, but Presumed Equal: Large Samples

The upper $1 - \alpha$ confidence limit is given by

$$(\bar{X}_1 - \bar{X}_2) + Z_{\alpha/2}S_p \sqrt{\frac{1}{n_1} + \frac{1}{n_2}} \tag{7-16}$$

and the lower $1 - \alpha$ confidence limit is given by

$$(\bar{X}_1 - \bar{X}_2) - Z_{\alpha/2}S_p \sqrt{\frac{1}{n_1} + \frac{1}{n_2}} \tag{7-17}$$

$1 - \alpha$ Confidence Limits for $\mu_1 - \mu_2$, Population Variances Unknown, but Presumed Equal: Small Samples

The upper $1 - \alpha$ confidence limit is given by

$$(\bar{X}_1 - \bar{X}_2) + t_{(\alpha/2, n_1 + n_2 - 2)}S_p \sqrt{\frac{1}{n_1} + \frac{1}{n_2}} \tag{7-18}$$

and the lower $1 - \alpha$ confidence limit is given by

$$(\bar{X}_1 - \bar{X}_2) - t_{(\alpha/2, n_1 + n_2 - 2)}S_p \sqrt{\frac{1}{n_1} + \frac{1}{n_2}} \tag{7-19}$$

where the number of degrees of freedom is $\nu = n_1 + n_2 - 2$.

$1 - \alpha$ Confidence Limits for $\mu_1 - \mu_2$, Population Variances Unknown, but Presumed Unequal: Large Samples

The upper $1 - \alpha$ confidence limit is given by

$$(\bar{X}_1 - \bar{X}_2) + Z_{\alpha/2} \sqrt{\frac{S_1^2}{n_1} + \frac{S_2^2}{n_2}} \tag{7-20}$$

and the lower $1 - \alpha$ confidence limit is given by

$$(\bar{X}_1 - \bar{X}_2) - Z_{\alpha/2} \sqrt{\frac{S_1^2}{n_1} + \frac{S_2^2}{n_2}} \tag{7-21}$$

$1 - \alpha$ Confidence Limits for $\mu_1 - \mu_2$, Population Variances Unknown, but Presumed Unequal: Small Samples

The upper $1 - \alpha$ confidence limit is given by

$$(\bar{X}_1 - \bar{X}_2) + t_{(\alpha/2, \nu)} \sqrt{\frac{S_1^2}{n_1} + \frac{S_2^2}{n_2}} \tag{7-22}$$

and the lower $1 - \alpha$ confidence limit is given by

$$(\bar{X}_1 - \bar{X}_2) - t_{(\alpha/2, \nu)} \sqrt{\frac{S_1^2}{n_1} + \frac{S_2^2}{n_2}} \tag{7-23}$$

where we select the smaller of $n_1 - 1$ and $n_2 - 1$, and set that equal to ν.

$1 - \alpha$ Confidence Limits for μ_d: Paired Observations

The upper $1 - \alpha$ confidence limit is given by

$$\bar{d} + t_{(\alpha/2, n-1)}\left(\frac{S_d}{\sqrt{n}}\right) \tag{7-24}$$

and the lower $1 - \alpha$ confidence limit is given by

$$\bar{d} - t_{(\alpha/2, n-1)}\left(\frac{S_d}{\sqrt{n}}\right) \tag{7-25}$$

$1 - \alpha$ Confidence Limits for $p_1 - p_2$: Large Samples

The upper $1 - \alpha$ confidence limit is given by

$$(\hat{p}_1 - \hat{p}_2) + Z_{\alpha/2}\sqrt{S_1^2 + S_2^2} \tag{7-26}$$

and the lower $1 - \alpha$ confidence limit is given by

$$(\hat{p}_1 - \hat{p}_2) - Z_{\alpha/2}\sqrt{S_1^2 + S_2^2} \tag{7-27}$$

where $\hat{p}_1 = X_1/n_1$ represents a point estimate of p_1; $\hat{p}_2 = X_2/n_2$ represents a point estimate of p_2; S_1 represents the sample standard deviation for the proportion of successes observed in the sample from the first population, calculated as $S_1 = \sqrt{\hat{p}_1(1 - \hat{p}_1)/n_1}$; and S_2 represents the sample standard deviation for the proportion of successes observed in the sample from the second population, calculated as $S_2 = \sqrt{\hat{p}_2(1 - \hat{p}_2)/n_2}$.

Chi-Square Tail Probabilities

Right Tail Probability

$$P(\chi_\nu^2 \geq \chi_{(\alpha,\nu)}^2) = \alpha \tag{7-28}$$

Left Tail Probability

$$P(\chi_\nu^2 \leq \chi_{(1-\alpha,\nu)}^2) = \alpha \tag{7-29}$$

where ν represents the number of degrees of freedom.

$1 - \alpha$ Confidence Interval Estimate for σ^2

$$\frac{(n-1)S^2}{\chi_{(\alpha/2, n-1)}^2} \leq \sigma^2 \leq \frac{(n-1)S^2}{\chi_{(1-\alpha/2, n-1)}^2} \tag{7-30}$$

The term on the left is the lower confidence limit, the term on the right is the upper confidence limit, and the number of degrees of freedom is $\nu = n - 1$.

F Distribution (Right) Tail Probability

$$P(F_{(\nu_1, \nu_2)} \geq F_{(\alpha, \nu_1, \nu_2)}) = \alpha \tag{7-31}$$

where ν_1 is the numerator degrees of freedom, and ν_2 is the denominator degrees of freedom.

$1 - \alpha$ Confidence Interval Estimate for the Ratio of Two Variances

$$\left(\frac{S_2^2}{S_1^2}\right)\left(\frac{1}{F_{(\alpha/2, n_2-1, n_1-1)}}\right) \leq \frac{\sigma_2^2}{\sigma_1^2} \leq \left(\frac{S_2^2}{S_1^2}\right)F_{(\alpha/2, n_1-1, n_2-1)} \tag{7-32}$$

The term on the left is the lower confidence limit, and the term on the right is the upper confidence limit.

PRACTICE EXERCISE ANSWERS

7.1   The sample size is small but the population standard deviation is known, so the standard normal distribution is used. For 95% confidence, use $Z_{.025} = 1.960$. The upper and lower confidence limits are given by $\bar{X} \pm Z_{\alpha/2}\sigma/\sqrt{n}$, so

$$459.13 + 1.960\left(\frac{24}{3}\right) = 474.81$$

$$459.13 - 1.960\left(\frac{24}{3}\right) = 443.45$$

With 95% confidence, the average monthly home equity loan payment is between $443.45 and $474.81, approx.

7.2   The population standard deviation is unknown, but the sample size is greater than 30, so a normal distribution is used. For 95% confidence, $Z_{.025} = 1.960$, and the confidence limits are given by $\bar{X} \pm Z_{\alpha/2}S/\sqrt{n}$, so

$$498 + 1.960\left(\frac{72}{10}\right) = 512.112$$

$$498 - 1.960\left(\frac{72}{10}\right) = 483.888$$

With 95% confidence, the average assembly time for a well-trained team is between 512.112 min and 483.888 min. This information could be used in a number of ways: for labor cost estimation; for information during wage negotiations with company or union representatives; or for motivating new teams to improve productivity.

7.3   a. $P(t_5 > 1.476) = .10$
    b. $P(t_5 < 1.476) = .90$
    c. $P(t_5 < -1.476) = .10$
    d. $P(t_5 > -1.476) = .90$
    e. $P(-1.476 < t_5 < 1.476) = .80$
    f. $t_{(.01,5)} = 3.365$
    g. $t_{(.025,5)} = 2.571$
    h. $P(1.476 < t_5 < 4.032) = P(t_5 < 4.032) - P(t_5 < 1.476) = .995 - .90 = .095$
    i. $P(-4.032 < t_5 < -1.476) = P(t_5 < -1.476) - P(t_5 < -4.032) = .10 - .005 = .095$

7.4   The sample mean is 459.13 and the sample standard deviation is 24. Since the value of the population variance is not known and since the sample size is not greater than 30, use the Student t distribution with $n - 1 = 8$ d.f. For a 95% confidence interval, we have $t_{(.025,8)} = 2.306$, and the upper and lower confidence limits are given by $\bar{X} \pm t_{(\alpha/2,n-1)}(S/\sqrt{n})$, so

$$459.13 + 2.306\left(\frac{24}{3}\right) = 477.578$$

$$459.13 - 2.306\left(\frac{24}{3}\right) = 440.682$$

With 95% confidence the average monthly home equity loan payment is between $440.68 and $477.58, approx.

7.5   a. Since the population variance is known, the appropriate statistic is the Z statistic, $Z_{.025} = 1.960$, so the confidence limits are given by $\bar{X} \pm Z_{\alpha/2}(\sigma/\sqrt{n})$, and

$$531.43 + 1.960\left(\frac{27}{3}\right) = 549.07$$

$$531.43 - 1.960\left(\frac{27}{3}\right) = 513.79$$

b. The population variance is unknown, but the sample size is greater than 30, so the appropriate statistic is the Z statistic, $Z_{.025} = 1.960$, so the confidence limits are given by $\bar{X} \pm Z_{\alpha/2}(S/\sqrt{n})$, and

$$531.43 + 1.960\left(\frac{27}{10}\right) = 536.722$$

$$531.43 - 1.960\left(\frac{27}{10}\right) = 526.138$$

c. The population variance is unknown and the sample size is less than 30, so the appropriate statistic is the t statistic, with $n - 1 = 8$ d.f., $t_{(.025,8)} = 2.306$, so the confidence limits are given by $\bar{X} \pm t_{(\alpha/2,n-1)}(S/\sqrt{n})$, and

$$531.43 + 2.306\left(\frac{27}{3}\right) = 552.184$$

$$531.43 - 2.306\left(\frac{27}{3}\right) = 510.676$$

7.6 It is known that $\sigma = 21$, $1 - \alpha = .95$ so $Z_{.025} = 1.960$, and $E = 10$. Using the required sample size formula,

$$n = \left(\frac{Z\sigma}{E}\right)^2 = \left[\frac{(1.960)(21)}{10}\right]^2 = 16.941$$

Use $n = 17$.

7.7 $n = 225$; $\hat{p} = \frac{100}{225} = .4444$; $1 - \alpha = .95$ so $Z_{.025} = 1.960$; and

$$S_{\hat{p}} = \sqrt{\frac{\hat{p}(1 - \hat{p})}{n}} = \sqrt{\frac{(.4444)(.5556)}{225}} = .0331$$

The confidence limits are given by $\hat{p} \pm Z_{\alpha/2}S_{\hat{p}} = .4444 \pm (1.960)(.0331)$, so the upper limit is .5094 and the lower limit is $= .3795$.

7.8 No information exists to provide an estimate of p, so use $p^* = .5$ as an estimate; $E = .05$ and $Z_{.025} = 1.960$. The required sample size is

$$n = \left(\frac{Z_{\alpha/2}}{E}\right)^2(p^*)(1 - p^*) = \left(\frac{1.960}{.05}\right)^2(.5)(.5) = 384.16$$

Use $n = 385$.

7.9 Experience indicates that $p = .2$; $E = .05$ and $Z_{.025} = 1.960$. The required sample size is

$$n = \left(\frac{Z_{\alpha/2}}{E}\right)^2(p)(1 - p) = \left(\frac{1.960}{.05}\right)^2(.2)(.8) = 245.86$$

Use $n = 246$.

7.10 It is known that $\sigma_1^2 = 25$, $\sigma_2^2 = 21$, $\bar{X}_1 = 469.41$, $\bar{X}_2 = 455.01$, $n_1 = 9$, $n_2 = 9$, and $1 - \alpha = .95$ so $Z_{.025} = 1.960$. The upper and lower confidence limits are given by

$$(\bar{X}_1 - \bar{X}_2) \pm Z_{\alpha/2}\sqrt{\frac{\sigma_1^2}{n_1} + \frac{\sigma_2^2}{n_2}} = (469.41 - 455.01) \pm 1.960\sqrt{\frac{25}{9} + \frac{21}{9}}$$

so the upper limit is \$18.83 and the lower limit is \$9.97. Zero is not in this interval, so it is reasonable to assert that the two means are not equal.

7.11 $n_1 = 20$, $n_2 = 15$, $\bar{X}_1 = 622$, $\bar{X}_2 = 501$, $S_1^2 = 561$, and $S_2^2 = 429$. Since $n_1 + n_2 - 2 = 33 > 30$, the Z statistic is used to construct the confidence limits. $1 - \alpha = .95$ so

$Z_{.025} = 1.960$. Since the distributions of the two groups are assumed to have the same variance, a pooled estimate of σ will be used:

$$S_p = \sqrt{\frac{(n_1 - 1)S_1^2 + (n_2 - 1)S_2^2}{n_1 + n_2 - 2}}$$

$$= \sqrt{\frac{(19)(561) + (14)(429)}{20 + 15 - 2}} = 22.4722$$

The upper and lower confidence limits are given by

$$(\bar{X}_1 - \bar{X}_2) \pm Z_{\alpha/2}S_p\sqrt{\frac{1}{n_1} + \frac{1}{n_2}} = (622 - 501) \pm 1.960(22.4722)\sqrt{\frac{1}{20} + \frac{1}{15}}$$

so the upper limit is 136.044 and the lower limit is 105.956. We are 95% confident that the mean water usage in North County exceeds the mean water usage in Orange County by between approx. 106 and 136 units.

7.12 $n_1 = 9$, $n_2 = 9$, $\bar{X}_1 = 263$, $\bar{X}_2 = 342$, $S_1^2 = 336$, and $S_2^2 = 432$. Since $n_1 + n_2 - 2 = 16 < 30$, a t statistic with $\nu = n_1 + n_2 - 2 = 16$ d.f. is used to construct the confidence limits. $1 - \alpha = .95$ so $t_{(.025,16)} = 2.120$. Since the distributions of the two groups are assumed to have the same variance, a pooled estimate of σ will be used:

$$S_p = \sqrt{\frac{(n_1 - 1)S_1^2 + (n_2 - 1)S_2^2}{n_1 + n_2 - 2}}$$

$$= \sqrt{\frac{(8)(336) + (8)(432)}{9 + 9 - 2}} = 19.5959$$

The upper and lower confidence limits are given by

$$(\bar{X}_1 - \bar{X}_2) \pm t_{(\alpha/2,\nu)}S_p\sqrt{\frac{1}{n_1} + \frac{1}{n_2}} = (263 - 342) \pm 2.120(19.5959)\sqrt{\frac{1}{9} + \frac{1}{9}}$$

so the upper limit is $-\$59.42$ and the lower limit is $-\$98.58$. This interval does not contain 0, so it is reasonable to conclude that the average monthly credit card balances at the two branches are not equal.

7.13 The population variances are unknown, but sample results show $S_1^2 = 576$, $S_2^2 = 441$, $\bar{X}_1 = 459.13$, $\bar{X}_2 = 455.01$, and $n_1 = n_2 = 30$. Since $n_1 \geq 30$ and $n_2 \geq 30$, a Z statistic is used. $1 - \alpha = .95$ so $Z_{025} = 1.960$. The upper and lower confidence limits are given by

$$(\bar{X}_1 - \bar{X}_2) \pm Z_{\alpha/2}\sqrt{\frac{S_1^2}{n_1} + \frac{S_2^2}{n_2}} = (459.13 - 455.01) \pm 1.960\sqrt{\frac{576}{30} + \frac{441}{30}}$$

so the upper limit is 15.532 and the lower limit is -7.292. Zero is in this interval, so it is reasonable to assert that the two means are equal.

7.14 Let $n_1 = 10$, $n_2 = 5$, $\bar{X}_1 = 173.42$, $\bar{X}_2 = 158.75$, $S_1 = 24$, and $S_2 = 21$. Since n_1 and n_2 are less than 30, a t statistic is used to construct the confidence limits, with $1 - \alpha = .95$. The number of degrees of freedom can be chosen conservatively as the smaller of $n_1 - 1$ and $n_2 - 1$. This conservative approach yields $\nu = 4$ d.f. Note that the theoretically correct formula for ν generates a larger number of degrees of freedom:

$$\nu = \frac{[(S_1^2/n_1) + (S_2^2/n_2)]^2}{\dfrac{(S_1^2/n_1)^2}{n_1 - 1} + \dfrac{(S_2^2/n_2)^2}{n_2 - 1}}$$

$$= \frac{[(576/10) + (441/5)]^2}{\dfrac{(576/20)^2}{9} + \dfrac{(441/5)^2}{4}} = 9.189$$

which is rounded to $\nu = 9$. Using the conservative value of $\nu = 4$, the t statistic is $t_{(.025,4)}, = 2.776$, and the upper and lower confidence limits are given by

$$(\bar{X}_1 - \bar{X}_2) \pm t_{(\alpha/2,\nu)} \sqrt{\frac{S_1^2}{n_1} + \frac{S_2^2}{n_2}} = (173.42 - 158.75) \pm 2.776 \sqrt{\frac{(24)^2}{10} + \frac{(21)^2}{5}}$$

so the upper limit is $48.19 and the lower limit is $-$18.85.

7.15 Let $n_1 = 10$, $n_2 = 5$, $\bar{X}_1 = 39$, $\bar{X}_2 = 57$, and $1 - \alpha = .95$.

a. The population standard deviations are known, so a Z statistic is used. The confidence limits are given by

$$(\bar{X}_1 - \bar{X}_2) \pm Z_{\alpha/2} \sqrt{\frac{\sigma_1^2}{n_1} + \frac{\sigma_2^2}{n_2}} = (39 - 57) \pm 1.960 \sqrt{\frac{121}{10} + \frac{169}{5}}$$

so the upper limit is -4.721 and the lower limit is -31.278. Zero is not in this interval, so we are 95% confident that the two means are not equal.

b. The population variances are equal but unknown, so a pooled estimated will be used. Since $n_1 + n_2 - 2 = 16 < 30$, a t statistic with $\nu = n_1 + n_2 - 2 = 13$ d.f. is used to construct the confidence limits; $t_{(.025,13)} = 2.160$.

$$S_p = \sqrt{\frac{(n_1 - 1)S_1^2 + (n_2 - 1)S_2^2}{n_1 + n_2 - 2}}$$

$$= \sqrt{\frac{(9)(121) + (4)(169)}{10 + 5 - 2}} = 11.652$$

The upper and lower confidence limits are given by

$$(\bar{X}_1 - \bar{X}_2) \pm t_{(\alpha/2,\nu)} S_p \sqrt{\frac{1}{n_1} + \frac{1}{n_2}} = (39 - 57) \pm 2.160(11.652) \sqrt{\frac{1}{10} + \frac{1}{5}}$$

so the upper limit is -4.2147 and the lower limit is -31.7853.

c. A t statistic is used to construct the confidence limits. The number of degrees of freedom can conservatively be chosen as the smaller of $n_1 - 1$ and $n_2 - 1$. This conservative approach yields $\nu = 4$ d.f. Note that the theoretically correct formula for ν generates a larger number of degrees of freedom:

$$\nu = \frac{[(S_1^2/n_1) + (S_2^2/n_2)]^2}{\frac{(S_1^2/n_1)^2}{n_1 - 1} + \frac{(S_2^2/n_2)^2}{n_2 - 1}}$$

$$= \frac{[(121/10) + (169/5)]^2}{\frac{(121/10)^2}{9} + \frac{(169/5)^2}{4}} = 6.979$$

which is rounded to $\nu = 7$. Using 4 d.f., the t statistic is $t_{(.025,4)} = 2.776$. The confidence limits are given by

$$(\bar{X}_1 - \bar{X}_2) \pm t_{(\alpha/2,\nu)} \sqrt{\frac{S_1^2}{n_1} + \frac{S_2^2}{n_2}} = (39 - 57) \pm 2.776 \sqrt{\frac{121}{10} + \frac{169}{5}}$$

so the upper limit is 0.807 and the lower limit is -36.807.

7.16 Let $\hat{p}_1 = \frac{47}{64}$, $\hat{p}_2 = \frac{51}{81}$. Since n_1 and n_2 are greater than 30, a Z statistic is used: $1 - \alpha = .95$, so $Z_{\alpha/2} = Z_{.025} = 1.960$.

$$S_1 = \sqrt{\frac{\hat{p}_1(1 - \hat{p}_1)}{n_1}} = \sqrt{\frac{(47/64)(17/64)}{64}} = 0.05521$$

$$S_2 = \sqrt{\frac{\hat{p}_2(1 - \hat{p}_2)}{n_2}} = \sqrt{\frac{(51/81)(30/81)}{81}} = 0.05366$$

The upper and lower confidence limits are given by

$$(\hat{p}_1 - \hat{p}_2) \pm Z_{\alpha/2}\sqrt{S_1^2 + S_2^2} = \left(\frac{47}{64} - \frac{51}{81}\right) \pm 1.960\sqrt{(0.05521)^2 + (0.05366)^2}$$

so the upper limit is 0.2556 and the lower limit is -0.0462.

7.17 a. $P(\chi_{21}^2 > 35.4789) = .025$

b. $P(\chi_{21}^2 < 35.4789) = .975$

c. $P(\chi_{21}^2 > 10.28293) = .975$

d. $P(\chi_{21}^2 < 10.28293) = .025$

e. $P(10.28293 < \chi_{21}^2 < 35.4789) = P(\chi_{21}^2 < 35.4789) - P(\chi_{21}^2 < 10.28293) = .975 - .025 = .950$

f. $\chi_{(.90,21)}^2 = 13.2396$

g. $\chi_{(.005,21)}^2 = 41.4010$

7.18 $S^2 = 441$ and $n = 71$; $1 - \alpha = .95$, so

$$\chi_{(1-\alpha/2,n-1)}^2 = \chi_{(.975,70)}^2 = 48.7576$$

$$\chi_{(\alpha/2,n-1)}^2 = \chi_{(.025,70)}^2 = 95.0231$$

The upper confidence limit is

$$\frac{(n-1)S^2}{\chi_{(1-\alpha/2,n-1)}^2} = \frac{(70)(441)}{48.7576} = 633.132$$

The lower confidence limit is

$$\frac{(n-1)S^2}{\chi_{(\alpha/2,n-1)}^2} = \frac{(70)(441)}{95.0231} = 324.868$$

7.19 a. $P(F_{(12,17)} > 2.38) = .05$ b. $P(F_{(12,17)} < 2.38) = .95$

7.20 a. $F_{(.05,15,25)} = 2.09$ b. $F_{(.01,15,25)} = 2.85$

7.21 Let $n_1 = 9$, $S_1^2 = 121$, $n_2 = 6$, $S_2^2 = 169$; $1 - \alpha = .90$, so use $F_{(\alpha/2,n_1-1,n_2-1)} = F_{(.05,8,5)} = 4.82$ and $F_{(\alpha/2,n_2-1,n_1-1)} = F_{(.05,5,8)} = 3.69$. The upper confidence limit is

$$\left(\frac{S_2^2}{S_1^2}\right)F_{(\alpha/2,n_1-1,n_2-1)} = \left(\frac{169}{121}\right)(4.82) = 6.732$$

The lower confidence limit is

$$\left(\frac{S_2^2}{S_1^2}\right)\left(\frac{1}{F_{(\alpha/2,n_2-1,n_1-1)}}\right) = \left(\frac{169}{121}\right)\left(\frac{1}{3.69}\right) = 0.379$$

CHAPTER REVIEW EXERCISES

7.55 Find the value of the probability in each case:

a. $P(Z > Z_{.0475})$ b. $P(Z > Z_{.0129})$ c. $P(Z > Z_{.025})$

d. $P(Z < Z_{.0475})$ e. $P(Z < Z_{.0129})$ f. $P(Z < Z_{.025})$

g. $P(Z > -Z_{.0475})$ h. $P(Z > -Z_{.0129})$ i. $P(Z > -Z_{.025})$

j. $P(Z < -Z_{.0475})$ k. $P(Z < -Z_{.0129})$ l. $P(Z < -Z_{.025})$

7.56 Find the value of the probability in each case:

a. $P(-Z_{.0475} < Z < Z_{.0475})$

b. $P(-Z_{.025} < Z < Z_{.025})$

c. $P(-Z_{.01} < Z < Z_{.01})$

d. $P(-Z_{.0475} < Z < Z_{.0129})$

e. $P(-Z_{.025} < Z < Z_{.01})$

f. $P(-Z_{.005} < Z < Z_{.05})$

7.57 Find the value of Z in each case:

a. $Z_{.0475}$

b. $Z_{.0129}$

c. $Z_{.0099}$

d. $Z_{.2946}$

7.58 Find the value of Z in each case:

a. $Z_{.0367}$

b. $Z_{.3372}$

c. $Z_{.0033}$

d. $Z_{.0968}$

7.59 A random sample of 64 observations from a normally distributed population with $\sigma = 8$ yields $\bar{X} = 1.326$. Find a 98.02% confidence interval for the population mean μ.

7.60 The treadlife of a certain brand and grade of tire is believed to be normally distributed with a standard deviation of 2600 mi. Find a 98.54% confidence interval for μ if a random sample of 81 tires has an average treadlife of 41,300 mi. Would it be reasonable for the tire manufacturer to offer a 40,000 mi warranty?

▶ **7.61** A packager of canned nuts presumes that the distribution of the weights of the nuts going into the cans is normal with a standard deviation of 0.1 oz. Find a 94.26% confidence interval for μ if a random sample of 20 cans had an average of 7.92 oz. Is it reasonable for the packager to label the cans as containing 8 oz. of nuts?

7.62 Suppose it is known that the lifetimes of light bulbs produced using a certain process have a normal distribution with a standard deviation of 80 hr. Find a 96.16% confidence interval for μ, the average lifetime of the light bulbs, if a random sample of 16 observations has a mean of 299.2 hr. Should the distributor of these bulbs advertise them as having life expectancies of 275 hr?

7.63 Suppose the weights of baseballs produced by a certain company are normally distributed with a standard deviation of 0.5 oz. If a random sample of 10 balls taken from the output of this company has an average weight of 6.25 oz, find a 93.28% confidence interval for the average weight of baseballs produced by this company. What can you say about your confidence interval?

7.64 Suppose the monthly amounts charged by people who possess a certain credit card are normally distributed with a standard deviation of $27.22. Construct an 89.90% confidence interval for the average monthly amount charged by people who possess this credit card if a random sample of 23 of these people have an average monthly charge of $95.32. What can you say about your confidence interval?

7.65 If the random variable t_7 has the Student t distribution with 7 d.f., evaluate:

a. $P(t_7 > 2.365)$ b. $P(t_7 > 1.415)$

c. $P(t_7 > 2.998)$ d. $P(t_7 > 3.499)$

7.66 If the random variable t_7 has the Student t distribution with 7 d.f., evaluate:

a. $P(t_7 < 2.365)$

b. $P(t_7 < 2.998)$

c. $P(t_7 < -2.365)$

d. $P(t_7 < -2.998)$

e. $P(-2.365 < t_7 < 2.365)$

f. $P(-2.998 < t_7 < 2.998)$

g. $P(-2.365 < t_7 < 1.415)$

h. $P(-2.998 < t_7 < 3.499)$

i. $P(-2.365 < t_7 < -1.415)$

j. $P(-3.499 < t_7 < -2.998)$

7.67 If the random variable t_{16} has the Student t distribution with 16 d.f., evaluate:
a. $P(t_{16} > 2.921)$
b. $P(t_{16} < 2.921)$
c. $P(-1.746 < t_{16} < 2.583)$
d. $P(-2.921 < t_{16} < -1.337)$
e. $P(2.120 < t_{16} < 2.583)$

7.68 If the random variable t_ν has the Student t distribution with ν degrees of freedom, find the tabular value of t where:
a. $P(t_{17} > t) = .05$
b. $P(t_{11} < t) = .01$
c. $P(t_{22} < t) = .99$
d. $P(t_5 > t) = .90$
e. $P(-t < t_{28} < t) = .98$
f. $P(-t < t_4 < t) = .80$

7.69 A gambler wishes to estimate her average gains or losses in a certain game of chance. Going over her records, she randomly selects a sample of 64 playing times and finds an average loss of $335.01 with a standard deviation of $197.24. Construct a 99.50% confidence interval for her true average gain or loss. What can you say about the confidence interval?

▶ **7.70** The National Bureau of Standards tested a random sample of 100 bottles of a chemical reagent taken at random from a warehouse. It found the mean pH of the sample to be 8.2 with a sample standard deviation of 0.16. (The pH is a measure of acidity or alkalinity; values below 7 indicate acidity and values above 7 indicate alkalinity. The lower the value, the more acid is the reagent; and the higher the value, the more alkaline is the reagent.) Find a 98.96% confidence interval for the true average pH of bottles of this reagent at this warehouse. Would you say that the reagent in question is an alkaline product?

7.71 Assume the weights of male students at a certain large university are normally distributed. Construct an 80% confidence interval for the average weight of male students at this university if a random sample of 25 male students has an average weight of 153.15 lb with a standard deviation of 18.49 lb.

7.72 In order to estimate the amount of delinquent property taxes, a county clerk takes a random sample of 9 records from the records of all delinquent accounts. The mean debt is $432.72 with a standard deviation of $90.24. Assume that delinquent property tax debts are normally distributed and find a 98% confidence interval for the average delinquent property tax debt. Would it be reasonable for the county clerk to assert that delinquent accounts average $450?

7.73 The roadrunner is a swift-footed bird of the cuckoo family. A random sample of 40 roadrunners showed an average length of 23.11 in. with a standard deviation of 2.7 in. Find a 90% confidence interval for the average length of these birds. Assume the lengths are normally distributed. What can you say about your confidence interval?

▶ **7.74** Suppose the life expectancy for a certain type of semiconductor device is a normally distributed random variable. A random sample of 16 semiconductors has an average life of 9937 hr with a standard deviation of 100 hr. Find a 98% confidence interval for the average life expectancy of this type of semiconductor device. Would it be reasonable for the manufacturer of the semiconductor device to claim that the average life expectancy is better than 9900 hr?

7.75 Assume that the diameters of logs cut by a lumber mill are normally distributed. Construct a 95% confidence interval for the average diameter of the logs cut by the mill if a random sample of 5 cut logs have the following diameters (in inches): 24.5, 24.3, 25.0, 24.0, and 24.7.

7.76 A random sample of 13 ball bearings taken from a large population of ball bearings had the following diameters (in inches): 0.053, 0.051, 0.048, 0.057, 0.039, 0.056, 0.051, 0.053, 0.057, 0.050, 0.047, 0.055, 0.052. Assuming the diameters are normally distributed, find a 99% confidence interval for the average diameter of the bearings in this population. What can you say about a permissible tolerance range for the housing for the bearings?

7.77 A distributor of fuses tested 15 randomly selected fuses at a 10% overload condition. The fuses blew at an average time of 7.4 sec with a standard deviation of 2.1 sec. Assuming that the times to blowing out at this condition are normally distributed, find a 90% confidence interval for the average time to blow out for the distributor's population of fuses. If fuses should blow out with an average time of less than 7 sec at a 10% overload, are the distributor's fuses within specifications?

7.78 A betta is a tropical fish known for its beautiful fin array and fierce attitude. In a random sample of 64 full-grown male bettas, the average length is 4.3 cm with a standard deviation of 0.8 cm. Find a 95% confidence interval for the average length of full-grown male bettas. Assume the lengths are normally distributed. What can you say about your confidence interval?

7.79 The lifetimes of light bulbs produced using a certain process are normally distributed with a standard deviation of 100 hr. Suppose we wish to estimate the average lifetime of bulbs produced by this process. How large a sample should we take if we want the probability to be at least .98 that our estimate will be within 5 hr of the true average lifetime of bulbs produced by this process?

7.80 Assume that the monthly amounts charged by people who possess a certain credit card are normally distributed with a standard deviation of $24.51. We wish to estimate the average monthly amount charged by using the mean of a random sample of 23 card holders. What can we say, with probability .95, about the maximum size of our error? [Hint: Consider the expression $n = (Z_{\alpha/2}\sigma/E)^2$ and solve for E.]

7.81 Suppose the time it takes a worker to assemble a certain device is normally distributed, and suppose a random sample of 81 workers take an average of 29 min with a standard deviation of 4.5 min. Using the sample mean to estimate the corresponding population mean, what can we assert, with a probability of .99, about the maximum size of our error? [Hint: Consider the expression $n = (Z_{\alpha/2}S/E)^2$ and solve for E.]

7.82 The weights of women students at a very large university are normally distributed. Suppose a random sample of 25 women students has an average weight of 119 lb with a standard deviation of 16 lb. Using the sample mean to estimate the corresponding population mean, what can we say, with a probability of .90, about the maximum size of our error? [Hint: Consider the expression $n = (t_{(\alpha/2,n-1)}S/E)^2$ and solve for E.]

7.83 A prospective purchaser of a fast food franchise is told that the earnings for the franchise have a standard deviation of $100 a day. The purchaser wishes to estimate the actual average daily earnings to within $40 with a probability of at least .98. How large a sample of daily earnings from the franchise's records should she take? Assume the daily earnings are normally distributed.

▶ **7.84** A washing machine manufacturer claims his machines are of such excellent quality that their life expectancies are quite uniform and have a standard deviation of only 40 days. How large a sample should a consumer agency take if it wants to be within 40 days of the true average life expectancy of these machines with a probability of at least .95? Assume the life expectancies are normally distributed. Based on your result, would you say that it would be economically feasible for the agency to attempt to be this accurate if the cost per machine is $375?

7.85 Suppose we assume that the income distribution of persons having served on juries during the past year is normal with a standard deviation of $2155. If a lawyer wishes to determine the average income of persons who have served on juries during the past year, how large a sample should she take if she wishes her estimate to be within $1500 of the actual average with a probability of .9534?

7.86 A manufacturer believes that the distribution of thicknesses of disks produced by a particular process is normal with variance equal to 0.0025. How large a sample should be taken if the manufacturer wishes to be within 0.025 in. of the true average thickness of the disks with a probability of .9862?

▶ **7.87** At a certain radar checkpoint it was noticed that 24 cars out of a random sample of 256 cars exceeded the speed limit. Find a 90% confidence interval for the proportion of cars that exceed the speed limit at this checkpoint. What can you say about your confidence interval?

7.88 In a random sample of 144 families of size 4, 121 were found to have spent more than $130 on their weekly grocery bill. Find a 95% confidence interval for the proportion of families who spend more than $130 on their weekly grocery bill. What can you say about your confidence interval?

7.89 In the manufacture of a certain kind of button it was noticed that 8 buttons, out of a random sample of 400 buttons, were defective. Find a 98% confidence interval for the proportion of defective buttons produced.

7.90 Suppose there is some question as to whether or not a given coin is honest—that is, balanced evenly. After 1600 tosses it is noted that heads turned up exactly 576 times. Construct a 98% confidence interval for p, the probability of a head. Is it reasonable to suppose that the coin is not honest?

7.91 Suppose we wish to estimate the proportion p of cars that exceed the speed limit on a certain section of freeway. How large a sample should we take if we wish our estimate to be within 2% of p with a probability of at least .98?

7.92 With respect to Exercise 7.91, suppose we have some prior evidence to indicate that the proportion is close to .75. With this information, how large a sample should we take if we wish our estimate to be within 2% of p with a probability of at least .99?

7.93 If a quality control engineer believes that 15% of the company's product is of premium quality, what size sample should he take so that the error of estimation will be less than .05 with probability at least equal to .95?

7.94 Suppose we wish to estimate the proportion of registered California voters who favor liberalizing import quotas on alcoholic beverages. If we wish our estimate to be correct to within 5% with a probability of at least .99, how large a sample should we take?

▶ **7.95** With respect to jury composition during the past year, a lawyer wishes to determine the percentage of juries composed entirely of persons over the age of 50. If he has access to the data, how many juries should he review (i.e., what size sample should he take) if he wishes his estimate to be within 10% of the true value with a probability of at least .9372?

7.96 A laboratory is asked to determine the quantity of a certain impurity in a drug manufactured by two different pharmaceutical companies. From past experience with this impurity, it is known that the standard deviation of the amount of the specified impurity is the same for both companies and is equal to 0.00072 parts per million (ppm). Thirty seven samples from the first manufacturer and 36 samples from the second manufacturer are analyzed and the respective means are found to be 0.0033 and 0.0028. Find a 90% confidence interval for the difference between the population means for the two pharmaceutical companies. Assume the distribution of the quantity of impurity is normal. Is it reasonable to regard the average amount of impurities in the drug produced by the two pharmaceutical companies as being equal?

7.97 A government agency conducts an investigation to determine whether the salaries of men and women in a certain profession are equal. The salaries of a random sample of 27 women in the profession are recorded and compared with the salaries of an independently drawn random sample of 22 men in the profession. For the 27 women, the average annual salary is $27,495 with a standard deviation of $2259. For the 22 men, the average annual salary is $32,975 with a standard deviation of $2573. Assume the salaries for both groups are normally distributed with the same variance. Find a 90% confidence interval for the difference in the average annual salaries of men and women in the given profession. Is it reasonable to conclude that the salaries for men and women are equal?

7.98 A study is conducted to determine the difference in the average yield of a synthetic hormone produced by two different genetic engineering procedures. A random sample of 11 batches produced by one procedure has an average yield of 39.2 g with a standard deviation of 7.8 g. An independent random sample of 10 batches produced by the second procedure has an average yield of 42.1 g with standard deviation of 7.3 g. Assume the yields for both procedures are normally distributed with the same variance, and find a 90% confidence interval for the difference in the average yield of the synthetic hormone produced by the two procedures. Is it reasonable to conclude that the average yields are the same for the two procedures?

7.99 A random sample of 10 boxes of a certain type of cereal of one brand has an average of 7.6 g of sugar per box with a standard deviation of 2.3 g of sugar per box. An independent random sample of 11 boxes of the same type (and weight per box) of cereal from another brand has an average of 4.9 g of sugar per box with a standard deviation of 0.9 g of sugar per box. Assume the weight of sugar in the boxes for each group is normally distributed, but do not assume the variances are equal. Find a 98% confidence interval for the difference in the average weight of sugar per box between the two brands. Can we reasonably conclude that the average amount of sugar per box is the same for both brands?

▶ **7.100** A publishing company claims that students who receive instruction based on their new textbook will score higher on a certain competency exam than students who use the current text. To examine this claim, 16 students were assigned to two classes, 8 in each, with one class using the new book and the other using the current text. The grades obtained on a standard competency exam given at the end of the semester are given in the table. Find a 95% confidence interval for the true difference in the mean grades for the two groups of students. Assume the scores are normally distributed for both groups. Is it reasonable to suppose that students using the new textbook scored higher on the average than students using the current text?

NEW BOOK	56	61	72	74	81	80	90	98
CURRENT TEXT	31	46	60	74	88	89	94	97

7.101 A random sample of 40 packages of frozen fish sticks distributed by one manufacturer has an average of 17.3 parts per million (ppm) of contamination with a standard deviation of 4.6 ppm. An independent random sample of 50 packages of frozen fish sticks distributed by a second manufacturer has an average of 9.7 ppm contamination with a standard deviation of 1.1 ppm. Assume the concentration of contaminant for each manufacturer's frozen fish sticks is normally distributed, but do not assume the variances are equal. Find a 99% confidence interval for the difference in the average concentration of contaminant in the frozen fish stick packages distributed by the two manufacturers. If you have a strong desire to eat frozen fish sticks, would you be just as likely to purchase fish sticks from one manufacturer as from the other?

7.102 A random sample of 6 automobiles of one brand yields an average of 27 miles per gallon (mpg) of gasoline with a standard deviation of 4.7 mpg. A random sample of 8 automobiles of another brand yields an average of 24 mpg with a standard deviation of 5.0 mpg. Construct a 99% confidence interval for the difference in the average miles per gallon of gasoline in operating the two brands of automobiles. Assume the populations are normally distributed with equal variances. Is it reasonable for both brands of automobile to claim the same gas mileage?

7.103 A production process is supposed to produce semiconductors with an average amperage characteristic of 100 microamps (μA) with a standard deviation of 2 μA. From past experience, a quality control manager knows that the standard deviation remains stable, but the average fluctuates. With respect to a given 24 hr period the manager decides to compare the averages between the day and night shifts. A random sample of 9 transistors from the day shift's production yields an average of 100.3 μA, and a random sample of 12 transistors from the night shift's production yields an average of 99.6 μA. Assuming the amperage characteristics for the two shifts are normally distributed with equal variances, find a 95% confidence interval for the difference in the average amperage for semiconductors produced by the two shifts. Is it reasonable for the quality control manager to conclude that both shifts are operating equally with respect to average amperage?

7.104 An accountant analyzed delinquent accounts for two companies, company A and company B. The accountant found that for a random sample of 35 delinquent accounts from company A, the average delinquent amount was $123.35 with a standard deviation of $29.94. For a random sample of 41 delinquent accounts from company B, the average delinquent amount was $96.17 with a standard deviation of $14.34. Assuming the delinquent amounts are normally distributed, find a 90% confidence interval for the difference in the average amounts in the two delinquent accounts. Is it reasonable to assert that the average delinquent accounts are the same for both companies?

▶ **7.105** An auditor for a brokerage house takes a random sample of 7 accounts from account executive A and 9 accounts from account executive B. With respect to the former, the auditor finds an average gain of $3.33 per share with a standard deviation of $0.875 per share; and with respect to account executive B, the auditor finds an average gain of $2.875 per share with a standard deviation of $1.25 per share. Assume the gains (losses) are normally distributed with equal variances for the two account executives. Find a 95% confidence interval for the difference in the average per share gain between the two account executives. If the auditor decides to open an account, should preference be given to one of the account executives?

7.106 A consumer agency claims that the nicotine intake from cigarettes increases as the cigarette gets shorter. Five cigarettes are tested for nicotine in the smoke when they are full sized and then when they have been smoked halfway. The results (in milligrams) are given in the table. Construct a 90% confidence interval for the average full–half nicotine intake. Assume that nicotine intake is normally distributed. Is it reasonable to conclude that nicotine intake is greater with half-smoked cigarettes?

FULL SIZE	19.4	21.6	22.8	20.4	24.3
HALF SMOKED	20.4	25.7	21.5	27.1	23.8

7.107 On a question concerning library hours on a college campus, 84 out of 100 men interviewed favored the proposal to increase the hours of operation; 156 out of 160 women favored the proposal. Find a 98% confidence interval for the difference in proportions of men and women who favor the proposal. Is it reasonable to conclude that the proportions favoring the proposal are the same for men as for women?

7.108 In a random sample of 225 families of size 4 in one state, 72 families were found to have spent more than $130 on their weekly grocery bill. In a random sample of 256 families of size 4 in a second state, 135 families were found to have spent more than $130 on their weekly grocery bill. Find a 95% confidence interval for the difference in the proportions of families of size 4 that spend more than $130 on weekly grocery bills in the two states. Is it reasonable to report that the proportion of families of size 4 who spend more than $130 weekly on groceries is the same for both states?

7.109 In a random sample of 64 packages of fish sticks produced by manufacturer A, 8 packages were found to be adulterated; and in a random sample of 81 packages produced by manufacturer B, 9 packages were found to be adulterated. Find a 98% confidence interval for the difference in the proportions of adulterated packages of fish sticks between the two manufacturers. Can it reasonably be said that both manufacturers produce the same proportion of adulterated packages of fish sticks?

7.110 In a random sample of 100 tires produced by manufacturer A, 81 tires exceeded the mileage guaranteed by the manufacturer; and in a random sample of 200 tires produced by manufacturer B, 140 tires exceeded the mileage guaranteed by the manufacturer. Construct a 99% confidence interval for the difference in the proportions of tires exceeding the manufacturers' guarantees. Based on this result would it be reasonable to infer that the proportion of tires exceeding the guaranteed mileage is the same for both manufacturers?

▶ 7.111 One hundred cans of brand A tuna and 50 cans of brand B tuna are tested for mercury contamination. Twenty cans of brand A and 10 cans of brand B are found to be contaminated. Find a 90% confidence interval for the difference in the proportions of contaminated cans for the two brands. Would it be reasonable to conclude that both brands have the same proportion of mercury contaminated cans?

7.112 A random sample of 300 castings produced on mold A contain 19 defectives, while a random sample of 250 castings produced on mold B contain 27 defectives. Find a 90% confidence interval for the difference in the proportions of defectives produced by the two molds. Is it reasonable to conclude that the proportion of defectives is the same for both molds?

7.113 If the random variable χ_9^2 has the chi-square distribution with 9 d.f., evaluate:
a. $P(\chi_9^2 > 23.589)$
b. $P(\chi_9^2 > 2.088)$

7.114 If the random variable χ_9^2 has the chi-square distribution with 9 d.f., evaluate:
a. $P(\chi_9^2 < 23.589)$
b. $P(\chi_9^2 < 2.088)$
c. $P(1.735 < \chi_9^2 < 23.589)$
d. $P(2.088 < \chi_9^2 < 23.589)$

7.115 If the random variable χ_ν^2 has the chi-square distribution with ν degrees of freedom, evaluate:
a. $P(\chi_{21}^2 < 11.591)$
b. $P(\chi_{21}^2 > 35.479)$
c. $P(\chi_{15}^2 < 5.229)$
d. $P(\chi_{15}^2 > 30.578)$
e. $P(7.015 < \chi_{18}^2 < 34.805)$
f. $P(0.412 < \chi_5^2 < 12.832)$
g. $P(42.557 < \chi_{29}^2 < 49.588)$
h. $P(4.075 < \chi_{14}^2 < 5.629)$

7.116 The variance of a random sample of size 91 taken from a normally distributed population is equal to 10. Find a 95% confidence interval for the population variance.

▶ **7.117** A manufacturer of electronic components believes that the lifetimes of the components she manufactures are normally distributed. Find a 99% confidence interval for the variance of that distribution if a random sample of 30 components has a variance of 21.3. What can you say about your confidence interval?

7.118 An automotive engineer claims that the voltage produced across a certain type of sparkplug has a normal distribution with a very small variance. Find a 95% confidence interval for the variance of the distribution if a random sample of 27 sparkplugs has a variance of 0.0026. What can you say about your confidence interval?

7.119 The diameters of platinum leads into a semiconductor device should have a very small variance. (The greater the variability, the greater the number of defective semiconductors.) Assume the diameters are normally distributed. Find a 90% confidence interval for the population variance if a random sample of 22 platinum leads has a variance of 0.009. If the variance of the distribution of platinum lead diameters should not exceed 0.008, is it reasonable to suppose the population of platinum leads from which this sample was taken will have a large number of semiconductor rejects?

7.120 Find the values of the random variable F that satisfy the following relationships:
a. $P(F_{(3,5)} > F) = .05$
b. $P(F_{(3,5)} > F) = .01$
c. $P(F_{(3,5)} < F) = .95$
d. $P(F_{(3,5)} < F) = .99$
e. $P(F_{(20,20)} > F) = .01$
f. $P(F_{(12,21)} < F) = .95$
g. $P(F_{(60,30)} > F) = .05$
h. $P(F_{(15,60)} > F) = .05$

▶ **7.121** A neurologist notices that a certain type of mentally retarded person is capable of learning specific tasks, but cannot associate tasks according to principle. That is, a person with this type of mental retardation can be taught two very similar tasks, but each task must be taught step-by-step as though the two tasks have nothing in common. A normal person can be taught either one of the two tasks step-by-step, and then can be taught the other task simply by pointing out the principles behind the two tasks and by indicating the differences. This phenomenon causes the neurologist to think that perhaps some part, or pattern, of the brain is associated with the ability to associate by principle. To determine this, she performs an experiment using a sample of 41 mentally retarded persons and 41 normal persons. She measures the variance in the amplitude of a certain wave pattern. She finds that for the mentally retarded persons the variance is 17.3, and for the normal persons the variance is 2.4. Find a 98% confidence interval for the ratio of the two population variances. Is it reasonable for the neurologist to conclude that the variance in the amplitude is greater for mentally retarded persons?

SOLVING APPLIED CASES

One purpose of confidence intervals is to use sample information to provide interval estimates (as an added dimension to point estimates) of population parameters. The length or precision of an interval depends upon two factors: the sample size used and the designated level of confidence. The following case study involves a business situation in which confidence intervals are used to aid management in decision making.

Confidence Interval Estimates for 7-Eleven Price Premiums

The Southland Corporation conducted a price survey in a southwestern city on a sampling of items sold in its chain of 7-Eleven convenience food stores, and compared those prices with prices for the same items at two leading supermarket chains in that city. Southland executives knew that 7-Eleven prices tended to be higher than their supermarket competition. Prices typically charged at supermarket chains are set weekly, and apply simultaneously to all the stores in the chain; but 7-Eleven top management permits each franchise to use some discretion on prices set. Prior to the survey, 7-Eleven top management did not have objective information as to the size of the price premium being charged. (The price premiums are, for given items, the 7-Eleven price minus the matched supermarket price.) It was management's objective, based on the results of a random sampling scheme of 45 items, to generalize the sample findings to the entire population of approximately 3200 items sold in the typical 7-Eleven store. A confidence interval based on the sample mean price premium provides an objective interval estimate of the mean price premium for all 3200 items. An interval estimate at the 95% confidence level would be calculated as follows:

$$\text{Upper limit:} \quad \bar{d} + 1.96\left(\frac{S}{\sqrt{n}}\right)$$

$$\text{Lower limit:} \quad \bar{d} - 1.96\left(\frac{S}{\sqrt{n}}\right)$$

where $\bar{d}$ and S are the mean and standard deviation, respectively, of the price premiums in the sample. Let's compute this confidence interval for the 7-Eleven data presented in Table 7.4.

We find

$$\text{Upper confidence limit} = 0.4249 + 1.96\left(\frac{0.389}{\sqrt{45}}\right) = 0.5386$$

$$\text{Lower confidence limit} = 0.4249 - 1.96\left(\frac{0.389}{\sqrt{45}}\right) = 0.3112$$

Using these lower and upper bounds, we are 95% confident that the mean price of items purchased at 7-Eleven is from \$0.3112 to \$0.5386 higher than the price of the same items at Kroger. Using the lower limit of \$0.3112 to represent the mean price premium of 7-Eleven compared with Kroger, we see that a purchase of two items at 7-Eleven would cost 62¢ (2 × 0.3112) extra, on average, and three items would cost 93¢ extra, on average, and so on. We can surmise from these estimates why, in places where both stores are available, most customers buy only one or two items at 7-Eleven. For a few items, customers are willing to pay the extra money for the greater convenience, but relatively few customers will shop at 7-Eleven for a dozen or more items.

TABLE 7.4 Price Premiums for 7-11 Merchandise				
	7-ELEVEN	**SKAGGS**	**KROGER**	**DIFFERENCE** **7-Eleven minus Kroger**
Groceries				
Ragu Spaghetti Sauce with meat, 1.5 oz	$1.29	$0.99	$0.91	$0.38
Starkist Tuna (solid white), 7 oz	2.19	1.49	1.59	0.60
Ranch Style Pinto Beans, 15 oz	0.59	0.45	0.43	0.16
Del Monte Sweet Peas, 17 oz	0.75	0.49	0.49	0.26
Ocean Spray Jellied Cranberry Sauce, 16 oz	0.89	0.57	0.57	0.32
Maxwell House Instant Coffee, 6 oz	4.25	2.95	2.93	1.32
Nabisco Oreo Cookies, 15 oz	1.99	1.79	1.47	0.52
Log Cabin Syrup, 12 oz	1.55	1.19	1.13	0.42
Kellogg's Corn Flakes, 12 oz	1.35	0.91	0.83	0.52
Oscar Mayer Bologna, 8 oz	1.39	1.23	1.19	0.20
Beer/wine				
Cella Bianco, 750 ml	3.59 (cold)	3.09	2.99	0.60
Mateus Rose, 750 ml	4.29 (cold)	3.39	3.69	0.60
Miller Lite, 12 oz, 6 pack	2.75	2.39	2.49	0.26
Schlitz, 12 oz, 6 pack	2.65	2.39	2.45	0.20
Budweiser, 12 oz, 6 pack	2.65	2.29	1.89	0.76
Candy				
M&M's, 7.5 oz	1.59	1.29	1.25	0.34
Tootsie Roll, 38 g	0.30	0.23	0.23	0.07
Certs	0.35	0.23	0.25	0.10
Health/beauty aids				
Contac, 10 capsules	2.19	1.79	1.79	0.40
Pepto Bismol, 8 oz	3.05	2.29	1.89	1.16
Flex Shampoo, 16 oz	3.39	1.79	1.69	1.70
Dry Idea Anti-perspirant, 1.5 oz	2.85	1.89	1.79	1.06
Bayer Aspirin, 50 tablets	1.89	1.19	1.19	0.70
Kleenex, 125	0.89	0.79	0.62	0.27
Nonfoods				
Tide, 49 oz	2.39	2.05	1.84	0.55
Clorox, 64 oz	1.05	0.73	0.73	0.32
SOS, 10 pads	0.99	0.69	0.59	0.40
Pampers, 12 toddler	2.49	2.09	2.19	0.30
Hefty Trash Bags, 10	2.25	1.79	1.59	0.66
Purina Dog Chow, 5 lb	2.69	2.09	2.13	0.56
Kodak Film, 35mm, color print, 36	4.69	2.89	3.29	1.40
Baked goods				
Mrs. Baird's Honey Bun	0.49	0.41 (Hostess)	0.41 (Hostess)	0.08
Dolly Madison Variety Donuts, 12	1.59	1.39 (Hostess)	1.39 (Hostess)	0.20
Mrs. Baird's Xtra Thin White, 24 oz	0.99	0.89	0.89	0.10
Beverages/soft drinks				
6 pack, 12 oz cans	2.39	2.29	2.25	0.14
6 pack, 16 oz nonreturnable	2.49	2.39	2.45	0.04
2 liter bottle	1.69	1.53	1.55	0.14
Hawaiian Punch, red, 46 oz	1.35	0.85	0.85	0.50
Dairy products				
Oak Farm Milk, $\frac{1}{2}$ gal	1.33	1.23 (Pure)	1.45 (Borden's)	−0.12
Oak Farm Half & Half Cream, pt	0.79	0.69 (Quality)	0.83 (Borden's)	−0.04
Minute Maid OJ, carton, 32 oz	1.19	0.99	0.89	0.30
Farm Field Lowfat Yogurt, 8 oz	0.45	0.39 (Swiss Style)	0.39 (Yubi)	0.06
Tobacco products				
Copenhagen Snuff, 1.2 oz	1.05	0.59	0.75	0.30
Levi Garrett Chewing Tobacco, large	0.99	0.75	0.88	0.11
Single pack cigarettes	0.95	0.80	0.75	0.20
		Total price difference for 45 items sampled		$19.12
		Mean price difference, $\bar{d}$		.4249
		Standard deviation of price difference, S		.3890

With this objective information on the mean 7-Eleven item price premium, top management now knows the extra cost shoppers are paying for the convenience of shopping at 7-Eleven. They need the information if they contemplate instituting a reduction in the price premium in an attempt to stimulate an increase in the number of purchased items.

Checkpoint Exercise

1. Use the 7-Eleven price and the Skaggs price for the simple random sample of merchandise items reported in Table 7.4 to calculate a 95% confidence interval for the mean price premium.

WENDY'S DATABASE ANALYSIS

In the Chapter 3 Wendy's Database Student Exercises we used summary descriptive measures to form image profiles of the fast food brands. Wendy's, you may recall, was perceived as offering good tasting food at comparatively high prices, with stores that were less conveniently located than some of the other fast food restaurants. The analysis in Chapter 3 was done with the understanding that the data represented a random sample from the population of customers. Under that assumption we can use the survey's observed sample values to estimate the population values of interest. In this section we shall focus on the confidence interval procedure and use MINITAB to construct the confidence intervals.

Let's begin with the question of how much consumers spend, on average, when they go to a fast food restaurant.

■ PROBLEM 1

Construct a 95% confidence interval for the average fast food expenditure, variable C123.

a. Use the MINITAB command CODE to recode variable 123 responses to a quantitative variable that represents a point estimate of a customer's expenditure average, replacing the expenditure range given in the questionnaire, and place the new variable in column 200. The recoding gives the following:

Variable C123 Responses	become	Point Estimate of Expenditure Average
1		$0.75
2		$1.50
3		$2.50
4		$3.50
5		$4.50
6		$6.00

Then use the 95% confidence interval command TINT on the value in C200. The appropriate MINITAB commands and the resultant output are given in Figure 7.15.

b. Interpret the 95% confidence interval for average fast food expenditure.

```
MTB > code (1)0.75 (2)1.5 (3)2.5 (4)3.5 (5)4.5 (6)6.0 c123, c200
MTB > name c200 'AvgFFexp'
MTB > tint 95 c200

                   N      MEAN    STDEV   SE MEAN    95.0 PERCENT C.I.
AvgFFexp         382    3.0825   1.5184    0.0777   ( 2.9297,   3.2352)
```

Figure 7.15
A 95% confidence interval for fast food expenditures

Solution

At the 95% confidence level, the interval from $2.93 to $3.24 per meal contains the true average fast food expenditure per meal.

Our next problem is to estimate the proportion of frequent fast food users. A fast food user is defined in terms of how often a customer goes to a fast food restaurant during a fixed time period.

■ **PROBLEM 2**

Construct a 95% confidence interval for the proportion of frequent fast food users as measured by variable C2.

a. Use the MINITAB command CODE to recode variable C2 to separate the frequent fast food users from the occasional fast food users. Place the new variable in column 200. The results are the following:

Variable C2 Responses	Type of Usage	Coded
1–2	Frequent	1
3–5	Occasional	0

Then construct a 95% confidence interval using the MINITAB command TINT.* The MINITAB commands and the resultant output are shown in Figure 7.16.

b. Interpret the 95% confidence interval for the proportion of fast food users who are frequent fast food users.

Solution

At the 95% level of confidence the interval from 0.404 to 0.503 contains the true proportion of frequent fast food users. That is, between 40 and 50% of fast food users are estimated to be frequent fast food users.

```
MTB > code (1:2)1 (3:5)0 c2 c200
MTB > name c200 'propfreq'
MTB > tint 95 'propfreq'

                  N       MEAN     STDEV   SE MEAN    95.0 PERCENT C.I.
propfreq        395     0.4532    0.4984   0.0251   ( 0.4038,   0.5025)
```

Figure 7.16
A 95% confidence interval for the proportion of frequent fast food users

---

*Because the data used in this analysis is the result of coding the characteristic into two classifications, 0 or 1, for each respondent (i.e., each trial), the theoretical underlying distribution for the number of 1's (X) among the n trials is a binomial distribution. However, since the sample size is large ($n = 395$), the central limit theorem applies, and we can say that the sampling distribution of the sample proportion (X/n) is approximately normal. For large values of n the t and normal distributions are approximately equal, so we rely on the TINT MINITAB command to obtain the necessary interval calculations.

Notice that the calculation of the standard error of the mean (SE MEAN) using TINT is slightly different from the theoretically correct calculation of the standard error of the proportion. TINT provides a slightly larger value (in this example the difference is in the fourth decimal place), which slightly increases the length of the interval.

```
MTB > subt c29 c31 c150
MTB > name c150 'TasteB/W'
MTB > tint 95 c150

                N      MEAN    STDEV   SE MEAN    95.0 PERCENT C.I.
TasteB/W       382   -0.4817   1.6373   0.0838   ( -0.6464, -0.3169)
```

Figure 7.17
A 95% confidence interval for the average taste difference between Wendy's and Burger King

---

■ **PROBLEM 3**

Use the paired difference procedure to construct a 95% confidence interval for the mean ratings difference between Burger King and Wendy's for food taste by the same respondent.

a. Use the MINITAB command SUBTRACT to create the taste difference variable C150 between Wendy's and Burger King. That is, subtract the Burger King taste variable C29 from the Wendy's taste variable C31. Construct a 95% confidence interval using the command TINT as shown in Figure 7.17.

b. Interpret the 95% confidence interval for the mean taste difference between Wendy's and Burger King.

Solution

At the 95% confidence level the interval from -0.646 to -0.317 rating points contains the true average taste difference between Wendy's and Burger King. The negative values indicate that Wendy's received the more favorable ratings of the two brands. Since the interval does not contain the value 0, it suggests that there may be a true difference in the average taste between Wendy's and Burger King.

■ **PROBLEM 4**

Use the two independent samples procedure to construct a 95% confidence interval for the proportional difference in ratings of the high versus low preference Wendy's customers with respect to the opportunity to garnish, variable C135 (stored in C201 after coding).

a. Use the MINITAB command CODE to recode variable C107 (stored in C200 after coding) so that high preference Wendy's customers and low preference Wendy's customers can be separated. Accordingly, we have:

Variable C123		
Responses	Type of Customer	Coded
1–2	High preference	1
3–6	Low preference	0

Now construct a 95% confidence interval using the MINITAB command TWOT.* The appropriate MINITAB commands and the corresponding output are shown in Figure 7.18.

b. Interpret the 95% confidence interval for the proportional difference between high versus low preference Wendy's customers with respect to variable C135.

---

*Again we can rely on the TWOT MINITAB command and the underlying t distribution approximation to the normal distribution to obtain the necessary interval calculations since n_1 and n_2 are both large.

```
MTB > code (1:2)1 (3:6)0 c107 c200
MTB > code (1)1 (2)0 c135 c201
MTB > name c200 'h/1prew'
MTB > name c201 'y/ngarn'
MTB > twot 95 c201 c200

TWOSAMPLE T FOR y/ngarn
h/1prew    N      MEAN     STDEV    SE MEAN
1         209     0.938    0.242    0.0167
0         118     0.822    0.384    0.0354

95 PCT CI FOR MU 1 - MU 0: (0.03851, 0.1930)

TTEST MU 1 = MU 0 (VS NE): T= 2.96  P=0.0035  DF=  170
```

Figure 7.18
A 95% confidence interval between high preference and low preference Wendy's customers

Solution

At the 95% confidence level, the interval from 0.03851 to 0.1930 contains the true difference in proportions between high versus low preference Wendy's customers with respect to the opportunity to garnish. Since the mean for high preference Wendy's customers is slightly higher (0.938 versus 0.822), it indicates more high preference customers answer yes. This suggests that "enjoy the opportunity to garnish" is favored slightly more by high preference Wendy's customers than by low preference Wendy's customers.

Wendy's Database Student Exercise

1. Construct a 95% confidence interval for the average family income, variable C148.
    a. Use the MINITAB command CODE to recode variable C148 from a range response to a point estimate of the average value and place in C225. Use the following scheme:

Variable C148 Response	becomes	Income Point Estimate
1		$ 7,500
2		$12,500
3		$17,500
4		$22,500
5		$27,500
6		$32,500
7		$37,500
8		$45,000

Then construct a 95% confidence interval using the MINITAB command TINT. That is, use the following sequence commands:

MTB > CODE (1)7500, (2)12500, (3)17500, (4)22500,
          (5)27500, (6)32500, (7)37500, (8)45000,
          C148, C225

MTB > TINT 95 C225

    b. Interpret the resulting confidence interval.

2. Construct a 95% confidence interval for the proportion of Wendy's fast food users that are frequent fast food users. That is, construct a 95% confidence interval using the data in variable C126.

a. Use the MINITAB command CODE to recode variable C126 so that frequent Wendy's fast food users can be separated from occasional Wendy's fast food, where the latter are placed in C226. Accordingly, we have:

Variable C126 Responses	Type of Wendy's User	Coded
1–2	Frequent	1
3–6	Occasional	0

Now construct a 95% confidence interval. That is, use the following series of commands:

MTB > CODE (1:2)1, (3:6)0, C126, C226

MTB > TINT 95 C226

b. Interpret the resulting confidence interval.

3. Use the paired difference in ratings to construct 95% confidence intervals for the mean rating differences between McDonald's and Wendy's on the following characteristics and variables:

Characteristic	McDonald's	Wendy's
Food Taste	C30	C31
Cleanliness	C36	C37
Convenience	C42	C43
Price	C48	C49
Service	C54	C55
Popularity with children	C60	C61
Menu	C66	C67

a. For food taste, use the commands

MTB > SUBT C30 C31 C150

MTB > NAME C150 'tasteM/W'

MTB > TINT 95 'tasteM/W'

and repeat the procedure for each of the above characteristics.

b. Interpret the meaning of each confidence interval constructed.

4. Use the two independent samples procedure to construct a 95% confidence interval for the proportional difference in ratings of the high versus low preference McDonald's customers on variable C135, the responses on the opportunity to garnish.

a. Use the MINITAB command CODE to define the variable high/low preference McDonald's customers placed in C200. Then construct the 95% confidence interval using the command TWOT.

Variable C106 Responses	Type of Customer	Coded
1–2	High preference	1
3–6	Low preference	0

MTB > CODE (1:2)1 (3:6)0 C106 C200

MTB > CODE (1)1 (2)0 C135 C201

MTB > NAME C200 'h/1prem'

MTB > NAME C201 'y/ngarn'

MTB > TWOT 95 C201 C200

b. Interpret the meaning of the confidence interval.

STATISTICAL INFERENCE: TESTING HYPOTHESES

Headline Issue

CRISIS AT PROCTER & GAMBLE: THE RELY NIGHTMARE

It was a business nightmare for one of America's oldest and largest corporations. After 15 years of developmental and test marketing, Procter & Gamble launched its Rely® brand of feminine tampons. Consumer approval quickly gave the brand significant market share. Rely showed every sign of becoming a market leader, joining the company's stable of household-word brands, such as Tide, Crest, Pampers, Folgers, and Prell. Then, in September 1980, Procter & Gamble withdrew its successful new entry from the market. This was a stunning reversal. The decision was the culmination of several days of intensive deliberations by the company's top management.

What triggered such a drastic move? A study published by the U.S. Center for Disease Control linked Rely usage with the alarming increase in reported cases of toxic shock syndrome (TSS). This newly discovered, potentially serious disease mainly affects women under 30 who use tampons during their menstrual periods.

The initial reaction of Procter & Gamble executives to the publication of this study was to save the Rely brand. The evidence was entirely statistical and circumstantial, and involved only a few dozen reported cases among millions of users. Morever, the disease occurred among users of other brands as well. But newspapers quickly began to publish articles linking Rely tampons to TSS deaths. By mid-September, Rely's troubles had become a front page story. One big headline read, "Rely Causes 35 Deaths." There was extensive radio and television coverage of the issue. Facing potentially monumental liability suits, a persistent negative press, and threats of government (FDA) action, Procter & Gamble capitulated and withdrew the product from the market. Top management ordered a halt in production and the removal of Rely from dealers' shelves. Paid ads appeared in newspapers urging women to discontinue their use of Rely because of the possible risk involved and to send back the unused product for a refund. Rely as a brand was dead, killed by statistical ammunition Procter & Gamble was unable to defeat.

We might wonder, "What evidence singled out Rely among all other brands of tampons?" How could the Center for Disease Control be sure of its results? How could it eliminate "coincidence" from consideration? What is the likelihood that the results of its investigation were in error? These are questions that can be stated and evaluated by the statistical procedures of hypothesis testing. The objective of this chapter is to present the elements of hypothesis testing and illustrate various situations to which it can be applied.

Overview

The previous chapter presented statistical inference by interval estimation. We used sample data to estimate the value of a population parameter. The estimate provided a range of values—an interval—within which the population parameter was estimated to occur. Implicit in the construction of the interval estimate from a random sample is the assumption that the sample is a source of all the relevant information about the parameter. No effort is made on the part of an investigator to indicate a particular belief about the population parameter prior to collecting the sample evidence. This chapter presents another way to draw a statistical inference about the population parameter. This method of drawing an inference is called *hypothesis testing*. The purpose of this type of statistical inference is to determine whether the sample results support (or fail to support) a particular belief, or hypothesis, about the population parameter value specified by the investigator.

Here are some circumstances in which this type of inference would be applied:

■ A firm is marketing a new product to a particular consumer segment. The firm requires a 3% market share of the targeted consumer segment to achieve successful market penetration. The firm's market research department conducts test marketing to a random sample of the targeted consumer segment to determine whether the sample results indicate that a 3% market share has been achieved.

■ A financial services firm is evaluating a new order processing system to determine whether it is performing more efficiently than the old system. The firm takes random samples of orders processed to compare processing time against the known processing time of the old system.

■ The manager of a clothing store in a large city has announced that a major credit card will be accepted for customer purchases as well as the store's own card. The manager believes that the average expenditure by major credit card customers will be higher than the average amount spent by the store's own credit card holders. A random sample of customer purchases charged by the major credit card is taken and compared to the records of the store's own credit card average.

Hypothesis testing is used to reach conclusions on these questions and others similar to it. In this chapter we will examine the elements necessary for the hypothesis testing procedure.

8.1

THE BASICS OF HYPOTHESIS TESTING

The objective of hypothesis testing is captured by this question:

Is the sample evidence consistent with a particular hypothesized value for the population parameter, or does the sample evidence contradict the hypothesized value?

By rejecting the plausibility of the initially hypothesized value, we indirectly establish the plausibility of an alternative hypothesized value or range of values. In this way, the investigator makes an inference about the value of the population parameter.

HYPOTHESIS TESTING AND JURY TRIALS

The logic used in hypothesis testing is similar to that used in jury trials. The hypothesis is comparable to the starting trial premise in the American legal system—that the defendant is innocent. By discrediting the starting premise, we establish the credibility of the alternative hypothesis that the defendant is guilty. This is the job of the prosecutor, who must present relevant evidence to show the jury that beyond a reasonable doubt the hypothesis of innocence is no longer tenable. The phrase "beyond a reasonable doubt" acknowledges that the defendant's innocence is still a possibility, but also that the prosecutor's evidence must be very strong so that the possibility of innocence becomes highly unlikely. It is important that the possibility of innocence be highly unlikely because of the jury's intent to minimize the risk of wrongly condemning the defendant. The evidence must convince the 12 independent jurors that the defendant's innocence is no longer a plausible position to maintain. Once the initial hypothesis of innocence is discredited, the prosecutor can get the jury to turn to the alternative hypothesis of guilty. Failure to present such convincing evidence brings a "not guilty" verdict.

In summary, to "prove" the alternative hypothesis of guilty—the hypothesis the prosecutor wishes to establish—the prosecutor proceeds indirectly by "disproving" the initial hypothesis of innocence. This type of reasoning is a *proof by contradiction*.

In a statistical hypothesis test, the observed sample results are equivalent to the evidence in a jury trial. Evidence represented by a prosecuting attorney is to discredit the innocence hypothesis, and an objective of using sample evidence is to evaluate the credibility of the initially hypothesized value of the population parameter. In both cases, the objective is to determine whether the initial or starting hypothesis is consistent with the evidence.

EVIDENCE OF UNUSUALNESS: THE TEST STATISTIC AND ITS *p*-VALUE

The strength of sample evidence in statistical hypothesis testing is connected with the idea of "unusualness." We start by assuming that the initial hypothesis about the particular value of the parameter is true. If the observed sample evidence is "extremely unusual" given that the stated value of the parameter is true, then we have a basis for rejecting the plausibility of the initially hypothesized parameter value.

Assuming the initial hypothesized parameter value is true, what sample result is unusual or highly unlikely? An unusual or highly unlikely result is one we expect to appear rarely and has a very small probability of appearing if the initial hypothesized parameter value is true. We'll illustrate this point by an example. Let's initially assume a coin to be fair so that we can hypothesize that the probability of heads on any one toss is one-half, that is, $p = .5$. We'll obtain sample results and use these results as the **test statistic** for the hypothesized value. Suppose we toss the coin 600 times, getting 338 heads for a sample proportion of heads of $338/600 = .563$. Assuming the hypothesis that "The coin is fair" is true, how unusual is it to get 338 heads or more? To find a measure of the aggregate unusualness of finding such a sample result, we need to calculate the probability of getting 338 or more heads in 600 tosses. Since the underlying probability distribution is binomial, we need to determine the probability of obtaining 338 or more successes (heads appearing) for $n = 600$ trials when $p =$

.5. Using a normal distribution approximation to the binomial distribution with the continuity correction as discussed in Chapter 6, we let

$$\mu = np = 600(.5) = 300 \quad \text{and} \quad \sigma = \sqrt{np(1 - p)} = \sqrt{600(.5)(.5)}$$

The calculation is then

$$P(X \geq 338) = P\left(Z \geq \frac{337.5 - 300}{\sqrt{600(.5)(.5)}}\right)$$

$$= P(Z \geq 3.06) = .5 - .4989 = .0011$$

In this case, we have converted the X test statistic, which is binomially distributed, to the Z test statistic, which is standard normally distributed. This allows us to consult the standard normal distribution table (Appendix Table IV) for probability calculations. The numerical value 3.06 is the computed value of the Z test statistic. So the probability of a Z value as extreme as 3.06 is a measure of the unusualness of the sample results in testing the hypothesis. This probability value, found in Appendix Table IV, is a *conditional probability,* which we call the **p-value** of the test statistic. It represents the probability of finding sample results as unusual (extreme) as the one that was actually observed, assuming that the hypothesized parameter value is correct. The p-value of the test statistic is automatically printed out by many computer statistical software packages.

Is the p-value found above consistent with the notion of a fair coin? The p-value of .0011 indicates that the probability is very small (only 11 chances in 10,000) that 338 or more heads would occur in 600 tosses of a fair coin. This very low probability says that the observed value of 338 heads in 600 tosses is an implausible sample result for a fair coin. With a p-value near 0, the fair coin hypothesis may now be rejected with confidence, and the alternative hypothesis, that the coin is biased, is indirectly supported.

The rejection of the fair coin hypothesis is statistically supportable, but there is no iron-clad guarantee that it is correct. The small (near 0) p-value suggests that there still exists some chance (no matter how small) that the conclusion to reject the fair coin hypothesis is erroneous. We shall have more to say about the possibility of error shortly.

The p-value calculated above is appropriate when our concern is a bias toward too many heads. A different p-value must be determined when our concern is with bias in either direction—that is, too many heads or too few heads. More specifically, if bias in either direction is the hypothesis under investigation, then the p-value calculated must be appropriate for the condition *at least as extreme as the result actually observed in either direction.* Remembering that a fair coin has an equal chance of producing an extreme result below the expected value of 300 heads as it has of producing a similar extreme result above the expected value, we can state that the probability of 262 and less must be identical to the probability of 338 and more. Therefore, the overall p-value for finding either extreme given a fair coin would be twice .0011, or .0022. The latter value is called a **two-sided p-value,** whereas the value .0011 is called a **one-sided p-value.** The choice of a one-sided or two-sided p-value depends entirely on the way the investigator wishes to conduct the hypothesis test.

● ●

PRACTICE
EXERCISES

8.1 State lottery officials claim that lottery revenue can increase $100,000 with each game if the odds of winning are reduced, thereby letting the prize money accumulate for bigger jackpots. Now suppose that the odds of winning are reduced for 6 months. We observe a

$20,000 increase in revenue per game, and we are able to calculate its *p*-value, that is, we are able to calculate the probability of the observed $20,000 increase assuming an expected increase of $100,000.

  a. If the calculated *p*-value is found to be .001, would you say that it is consistent with the hypothesis that the increased lottery revenue is $100,000 per game? Remember that the calculated *p*-value measures how unusual the observed $20,000 increase is when you expect a $100,000 increase.

  b. If the calculated *p*-value is equal to .276, would you say that it is consistent with the hypothesis that the increased lottery revenue is $100,000 per game?

8.2 An airline claims that its planes arrive on schedule at least 95% of the time. A sample study of their plane arrival times shows an on-schedule rate of 86%.

  a. If the *p*-value associated with this sample result is .39, would you be inclined to conclude that the sample result is not consistent with the airline claim?

  b. What if the *p*-value is .00235?

8.3 A manufacturer of frozen fish sticks claims that his product does not average any more than 2 parts per million (ppm) of insect waste. If a sample of his product shows an average of 2.3 ppm and the *p*-value associated with this result is equal to .00085, would you say that this result is consistent with the manufacturer's claim?

NULL AND ALTERNATIVE HYPOTHESES

We will need some special terms in our discussion of hypothesis testing. The challenged hypothesis upon which evidence is brought to bear is called the **null hypothesis** and is denoted by H_o. The null hypothesis always expresses a value of the parameter of a probability distribution we intend to subject to scrutiny by the weight of sample evidence.

For the fair coin example, the null hypothesis is written

$$H_o: \quad p = .5$$

The value of p is the parameter of the probability distribution that defines the chance of obtaining a head on each toss of the coin. Equivalently, the value of p can be interpreted as a long-run relative frequency—that is, the proportion of heads expected after a substantial number of tosses.

The purpose of scrutinizing the null hypothesis is to determine whether there is support for the **alternative hypothesis**, denoted by the symbol H_A. The form of the alternative hypothesis determines whether a one-sided or two-sided testing procedure is to be conducted.

In the fair coin example, the two possible one-sided alternative hypotheses are written as

$$(1)\ H_A: \quad p > .5$$
$$(2)\ H_A: \quad p < .5$$

The form

$$H_A: \quad p \neq .5$$

is the two-sided alternative hypothesis. The first one-sided alternative states that the coin is biased toward heads (favoring heads); the second one-sided alternative states that the coin is biased against heads. The two-sided alternative allows for a bias in either direction (favoring heads or against heads).

PRACTICE EXERCISES

8.4 Suppose an educator claims that introducing a computer with a powerful word processor into an English class will help the students become more proficient at reading as well as writing. If a research group decides to test the null hypothesis given below with an experiment involving students at a variety of schools around the country, how should the research group express the alternative hypothesis?

> H_o: A computer with a powerful word processor will increase student proficiency at reading and writing.

8.5 An investment broker claims that over the past 10 years her clients have earned an average return of 10% per year on their investments. To convince you, she will let you randomly select a sample of 80 clients and you can draw your own conclusion.

a. If you state your null hypothesis as

> H_o: The broker's clients earn an average return of 10% per year on their investments.

what is your alternative hypothesis?

b. If you state your null hypothesis as

> H_o: The broker's clients earn an average return of at least 10% per year on their investments.

what is your alternative hypothesis?

c. If you state your null hypothesis as

> H_o: The broker's clients earn an average return of at most 10% per year on their investments.

what is your alternative hypothesis?

8.6 A market analyst claims that a market crash will follow if a specific index consisting of 10 economic indicators turns negative. What should be the alternative hypothesis if the null hypothesis is given as follows?

> H_o: A market crash will follow if the index of 10 economic indicators turns negative.

IDENTIFYING TYPE I AND TYPE II ERRORS

An hypothesis test concludes with a decision about whether or not to reject the null hypothesis. This decision in combination with whether the null hypothesis is true or not results in any one of four possible situations.

1. The null hypothesis is true and the decision is not to reject it.
2. The null hypothesis is false and the decision is to reject it.
3. The null hypothesis is true and the decision is to reject it.
4. The null hypothesis is false and the decision is not to reject it.

In the first two situations, the hypothesis testing procedure leads to a correct decision about the null hypothesis. In the last two situations, an erroneous decision is made with respect to the null hypothesis. However, the two errors are not of the same type.

The erroneous decision of situation 3 is to reject the null hypothesis when (unknown to the investigator) it is actually true. This is called a **Type I error.**

The erroneous decision of situation 4 is not to reject the null hypothesis when (again, unknown to the investigator) it is actually false. This is called a **Type II error.**

Table 8.1 shows the relationship between the decision and the actual status of H_o. It also indicates the different types of error that may arise and the applicable probability designations.

TABLE 8.1	A Generalized Decision Table Showing Correct and Incorrect Decision Making	
DECISION	**ACTUAL SITUATION**	
	H_o **Is True**	H_o **Is False**
Do Not Reject H_o	Correct decision Probability is at least equal to $1 - \alpha$	Type II error Probability is a value β that depends on several factors
Reject H_o	Type I error Probability is at most equal to α	Correct decision Probability is equal to $1 - \beta$

Let's examine these circumstances and consequences more closely. A Type I error is committed only if the null hypothesis, H_o, is true and the decision is to reject it. The probability or risk of a Type I error is designated by the **Greek letter α**. The investigator typically sets the maximum level of α in the hypothesis testing procedure. This value is called the **level of significance** of the test.

A Type II error is committed only if the null hypothesis is false and the decision is not to reject it. The probability or risk of a Type II error is designated by the **Greek letter β**. The probability of committing a Type II error is determined by three elements:

1. The value chosen for the level of significance, α
2. The size of the sample, n
3. The true (but unknown) value of the population parameter.

By holding two of these three elements unchanged and changing the third element, we change the probability of committing a Type II error. More specifically, the probability of a Type II error becomes *larger:* (1) the smaller the value chosen for the level of significance, α; (2) the smaller the sample size, n; (3) the closer the true value is to the hypothesized value given in H_o.

Type I and Type II errors cannot occur simultaneously. We can be in only one of the four situations at any given time. However, when the sample size is fixed, lowering the risk of one type of error raises the risk of incurring the other. In other words, for a fixed n, there is a direct tradeoff between the level of α and the level of β, so a choice must be made as to which type of error is more important to avoid. The consequences of both types of errors must be considered before selecting the level of significance of the test.

To reduce both α and β simultaneously requires an increase in the sample size. For instance, in the Rely tampon case of the opening scenario it is critical that the values for both α and β be small. To commit a Type I error and mistakenly accuse Rely tampons of being the cause of toxic shock syndrome could have led to a lawsuit by Procter & Gamble. On the other hand, to commit a Type II error and mistakenly permit the sale of Rely tampons could have led to deaths, illnesses, and lawsuits by affected consumers and their families. To keep both α and β at acceptably low levels, the Center for Disease Control had to withhold a decision until enough cases were collected to meet the appropriate sample size requirement.

Although both Type I and Type II errors are considered in this chapter, the stronger emphasis is on Type I errors. This is consistent with widespread hypothesis testing practice for statistical investigations of many kinds. Nevertheless, there are many types of problems in which the serious consequences of Type II errors necessitate that Type II errors be formally incorporated into the hypothesis testing procedure. A discussion entitled "Determining β" at the end of Section 8.2 explains how this can be done.

PRACTICE EXERCISES

8.7   Suppose we conduct an experiment to test an educator's claim that introducing a computer with a powerful word processor into an English class will help students become more proficient at reading and writing, and suppose the null and alternative hypotheses are given as follows:

> H_o: A computer with a powerful word processor will increase student proficiency at reading and writing.
>
> H_A: A computer with a powerful word processor will not increase student proficiency at reading and writing.

a. What would be our conclusion if we decide to reject the null hypothesis?
b. What would be our conclusion if we decide not to reject the null hypothesis?
c. What would be our conclusion if we commit a Type I error?
d. What would be our conclusion if we commit a Type II error?

8.8   Suppose an investment broker's claim is stated in the null hypothesis as:

> H_o: My clients earn an average return of at least 10% per year on their investments.

The corresponding alternative hypothesis is stated as:

> H_A: My clients earn an average return of less than 10% per year on their investments.

a. What type of error would you be making if you invested with that broker and his claim is false? Would this be a serious error?
b. What type of error would you be making if you did not invest with that broker and his claim is true? Would this be a serious error?

8.9   You are in a high stakes poker game with five other players. You have a fairly good hand, but the other players are betting high. There are four mutually exclusive possibilities, two of which are: you have the winning hand and you continue playing the hand; you have the winning hand but you don't continue playing the hand (you fold).
a. What are the other two possibilities?
b. Suppose you set up your null and alternative hypotheses as follows.

> H_o: I have the winning hand.
>
> H_A: I don't have the winning hand.

What error could you commit if you continue playing? Would that be a Type I or a Type II error? What error could you commit if you fold? Would that be a Type I or a Type II error?

8.10   A company grants you a job interview assuming you have the proper qualifications. But, after interviewing you and looking over your resume, the company decides not to hire you because you don't have the proper qualifications.
a. What were the company's null and alternative hypotheses in granting you the job interview?
b. If you do have the proper qualifications, the company made a mistake in not hiring you. What type of error did they make?

DECISION RULE AND REJECTION REGION

In testing a statistical hypothesis, a decision must eventually be made as to whether to reject the null hypothesis or not. That decision should be based upon a **decision rule** established before sample results have become known; otherwise, the decision would always be open to the suspicion that the results might have influenced the decision rule. The decision rule anticipates possible values of the test statistic and establishes within the range of possible values an interval called the **rejection region.** If the value of the test statistic falls in the rejection region, the null hypothesis is rejected; otherwise, it is not rejected.

For example, in the fair coin example, we might have established the following rejection region for a two-sided test of H_o:

$$Z < -1.96 \quad \text{or} \quad Z > +1.96$$

Using this rule, the null hypothesis would be rejected if the computed Z test statistic has a value less than -1.96 or if it has a value greater than $+1.96$. Since the computed Z test statistic in the fair coin example has a value of $Z = 3.06$, it falls within the rejection region. Therefore, the null hypothesis H_o that the coin is fair is rejected. In general, the value of the test statistic that separates the rejection region from the nonrejection region is identified by using the subscript c, as in $Z_c = +1.96$ and $Z_c = -1.96$ in the fair coin example. These boundary values are also called **critical values** of the test statistic.

The decision rule and its Z_c value(s) are inextricably linked to the risk of Type I error, α, set by the investigator. In a two-sided test of the fair coin hypothesis, setting the level of significance α at 5% puts 2.5% in the upper tail and 2.5% in the lower tail of the standardized normal Z distribution. The corresponding Z values that mark off 2.5% in each tail are $Z_c = +1.96$ and $Z_c = -1.96$. When the value of the Z test statistic either exceeds the Z_c value ($Z > +Z_c$) or is less than $-Z_c$ ($Z < -Z_c$), it falls in the rejection region. Therefore, changing the level of significance changes the Z_c values, the rejection region, and the decision rule.

For a two-sided test, the general expressions identifying the boundary values for the rejection region in relationship to α are

$$Z < -Z_{\alpha/2} \quad \text{or} \quad Z > +Z_{\alpha/2}$$

and

$$P(Z < -Z_{\alpha/2}) + P(Z > +Z_{\alpha/2}) = \alpha$$

where the Z_c values are $+Z_{\alpha/2}$ and $-Z_{\alpha/2}$, which are determined by the level of α set.

PRACTICE EXERCISES

8.11 If the decision rule for a two-sided hypothesis test sets the level of risk of a Type I error at $\alpha = .01$, what are the values of Z from the standard normal distribution that mark off each tail?

8.12 If the value of Z from the standard normal distribution that marks off the tail in a one-sided hypothesis test is equal to $+1.96$, what is the value of α?

8.13 If the value of Z from the standard normal distribution that marks off the tail in a one-sided hypothesis test is equal to -1.96, what is the value of α?

8.14 If the value of Z from the standard normal distribution that marks off the tails in a two-sided test is equal to ±2.04, what is the value of α?

8.15 If the rejection region is given by $Z > +2.04$, what does our decision rule say we should do if:
a. The value of the test statistic is equal to 1.98?
b. The value of the test statistic is equal to 10.98?

8.16 If the rejection region is given by $Z < -2.04$, what does our decision rule say we should do if:
a. The value of the test statistic is equal to -1.33?
b. The value of the test statistic is equal to -2.43?
c. The value of the test statistic is equal to 1.98?
d. The value of the test statistic is equal to 10.98?

REPORTING TEST RESULTS

Once the decision rule has been applied, the conclusion reached about the null hypothesis completes the statistical part of the hypothesis test. But there remains the issue of properly reporting the results of the test. For reporting purposes statisticians use the key phrase **statistically significant**, which indicates whether or not the computed test statistic falls in the rejection region. When the computed test statistic falls in the rejection region and the null hypothesis is rejected, it means that the difference between the observed value of the sample statistic and the hypothesized value of the null hypothesis H_o is too large to be attributed simply to sampling variation. Therefore, it is declared a statistically significant difference. When the test statistic does not fall in the rejection region, the difference is described as "not statistically significant." Along with the phrase statistically significant, the level of significance should be made clear in reporting test results. For example, in the fair coin test we can report the results as being statistically significant at the 5% level.

It is also important to note that when the p-value is available, it provides very useful information since it indicates the level of significance at which the null hypothesis can be rejected. Also, a smaller p-value indicates greater significance; that is, a p-value of 1% is more significant than a p-value of 5%.

In addition to the formal statistical findings of an investigation there always should be some account of the practical importance of the test results. This account should provide the reader with information as to what the investigator sees as the practical importance of the findings. Many of the examples in this chapter conclude with an explanation of the practical importance of the findings.

PRACTICE EXERCISES

8.17 In a test of hypothesis, would the result be considered statistically significant if the p-value is equal to .0034? Would you reject the null hypothesis?

8.18 Suppose the null hypothesis states

H_o: The company has not committed fraud.

What conclusion would you come to if you reject H_o?

8.19 Suppose the null and alternative hypotheses are given as

H_o: The weight of the meat in a $\frac{1}{4}$ lb burger is $\frac{1}{4}$ lb.

H_A: The weight is less than $\frac{1}{4}$ lb.

a. What conclusion would you state if you reject H_o?
b. What conclusion would you state if you do not reject H_o?

8.20 Suppose the null and alternative hypotheses are given as

H_o: The company is financially solvent.

H_A: The company is not financially solvent.

a. What conclusion would you state if you reject H_o?
b. What conclusion would you state if you do not reject H_o?
c. Would a Type I error be serious?
d. Would a Type II error be serious?

● ●

PROBLEM SOLVING BY HYPOTHESIS TESTING: AN OVERVIEW

Several steps should be kept in mind when considering problem solving by hypothesis testing. The first step always is to understand the problem. The following questions help define and outline the important features of the problem:

- What constitutes the population under study?

- What is it we wish to know about that population?

- What is already known about the population?

- Is there need to resort to sampling?

- Is the cost of sampling high?

- Is sampling destructive?

- Is the sample obtained a random sample?

- Does a completely random sample suffice, or is some alternate procedure (such as stratified sampling, cluster sampling, and so on) more appropriate?

- What specific statistical procedure is applicable to the analysis of the data to be gathered?

The next step is to formulate the null and alternative hypotheses and select the method of testing. That is:

- State the null hypothesis H_o to be tested along with any H_o assumptions (often asserted without proof).

- State the alternative hypothesis H_A, a specified alternative to H_o that is plausible to consider.

- Select the statistical decision making procedure along with the decision rule to be applied.

After the hypotheses are stated the last step is to get the sample, calculate the value of the sample statistic, perform the statistical test, draw a conclusion, and give a practical interpretation. The procedure would be: (1) obtain a sample, (2) calculate a test statistic from the sample values used in the statistical decision procedure, (3) apply the decision rule of the procedure and reach a decision on the status of the null hypothesis, (4) reach a conclusion and give a practical interpretation to the results.

The basic elements and procedure of problem solving by hypothesis testing have now been covered. The remainder of this chapter will apply hypothesis testing methodology to population means, population proportions, and population variances.

PRACTICE EXERCISE

8.21 Test the null hypothesis that for the coin referred to in this section the probability of heads on each toss is .5, against the alternative hypothesis that the probability of heads is greater than .5. Use a 1% level of significance and the same findings as reported earlier, that is, 338 heads in 600 tosses.
   a. Write symbolically the null and alternative hypotheses.
   b. What is the value of Z_c?
   c. What is the rejection region?
   d. What is the decision rule?
   e. What is the value of the test statistic?
   f. What decision should be made about the null hypothesis?
   g. What is the maximum level of significance at which H_o could be rejected.

EXERCISES

▶ **8.1** A clinic claims it has a miracle cure for a certain disease that is fatal in 99% of cases. In each of the cases below, indicate whether the result is more likely a matter of significance or a matter of coincidence.
   a. A person contracts the stated disease that is fatal in 99% of cases. The person hears about the clinic's miracle cure, goes for it, and survives.
   b. Twenty persons independently contract the stated disease. They independently hear about the clinic's miracle cure, go for it, and all survive.
   c. Twenty persons who have been diagnosed as having the stated disease independently decide to go to the clinic for their miracle treatment. Of these 20 persons, 10 survive.

8.2 Suppose a clinic claims it has a cure for a disease that is fatal in 99% of cases. Suppose we decide to test the clinic's claim (using volunteers who have the disease) with the null hypothesis specifying that the claim is true.
   a. What kind of error would we make if we fail to reject the null hypothesis, and the null hypothesis is actually false?
   b. What consequences are there in making the error in part a?
   c. What kind of error would we make if we reject the null hypothesis, and the null hypothesis is actually true?
   d. What consequences are there in making the error in part c?

8.3 Suppose an automobile mechanic tells you that you need to replace an engine part on your car at a total cost of $120, and suppose he tells you that if you don't replace the part you will get engine exhaust in your car when you have either the heater or air-conditioner on. If we set up the null hypothesis as specifying that the mechanic's diagnosis is correct:
   a. What kind of error would you make if you fail to reject the null hypothesis, and the null hypothesis is actually false?
   b. What consequences are there in making the error in part a?
   c. What kind of error would you make if you reject the null hypothesis, and the null hypothesis is actually true?
   d. What consequences are there in making the error in part c?

8.2

TEST OF HYPOTHESIS: ONE POPULATION MEAN

Hypothesis testing for one population mean will use the sample mean $\bar{X}$ to formulate the test statistics for the testing. There are two cases with different test statistics: in one case the value of σ is known; in the other case the value of σ is unknown.

CASE 1: WHEN THE VALUE FOR σ IS KNOWN

Where the value for σ, the population standard deviation, is known, two situations result in the same test statistic: In the first situation we are sampling from a normal population, in which case the sampling distribution of $\bar{X}$ is exactly normal regardless of the sample size. In the second situation, we are not necessarily sampling from a normal population, but the sample size n is large enough for the central limit theorem to apply, so that the sampling distribution for $\bar{X}$ is approximately normal. The appropriate test statistic in both situations is given below.

Test Statistic for One Population Mean: σ Known

$$Z = \frac{\bar{X} - \mu_o}{\sigma/\sqrt{n}} \qquad (8\text{-}1)$$

where μ_o is the hypothesized value of the population mean μ specified in H_o.

This expression tells us that the test statistic is distributed as the standard normal random variable Z for which we have table values (Appendix Table IV).

The null hypothesis for tests of one population mean will always be of the form H_o: $\mu = \mu_o$. But the form of the alternative hypothesis determines whether we will be conducting a two-sided or one-sided hypothesis test on the population mean. Two-sided tests, by definition, always deal with both tails of the testing probability distribution. One-sided tests can be an upper tail test or a lower tail test. Let's first consider the one-sided test and then the two-sided test.

For the upper tail test, the hypotheses are

$$H_o: \quad \mu = \mu_o$$
$$H_A: \quad \mu > \mu_o$$

The corresponding rejection region is:

Rejection Region for (One-Sided) Upper Tail Test, One Population Mean: σ Known

Reject H_o if

$$Z = \frac{\bar{X} - \mu_o}{\sigma/\sqrt{n}} > +Z_\alpha \qquad (8\text{-}2)$$

For the lower tail test, the hypotheses are

$$H_o: \quad \mu = \mu_o$$
$$H_A: \quad \mu < \mu_o$$

The corresponding rejection region is:

Rejection Region for (One-Sided) Lower Tail Test, One Population Mean: σ Known

Reject H_o if

$$Z = \frac{\bar{X} - \mu_o}{\sigma/\sqrt{n}} < -Z_\alpha \qquad\qquad (8\text{-}3)$$

The respective rejection regions are shown in Figures 8.1 and 8.2

For a two-sided test, the hypotheses are

$$H_o: \quad \mu = \mu_o$$
$$H_A: \quad \mu \neq \mu_o$$

The corresponding two-sided rejection region is:

Rejection Region for Two-Sided Test, One Population Mean: σ Known

Reject H_o if

$$Z = \frac{\bar{X} - \mu_o}{\sigma/\sqrt{n}} < -Z_{\alpha/2} \qquad \text{or} \qquad Z = \frac{\bar{X} - \mu_o}{\sigma/\sqrt{n}} > +Z_{\alpha/2} \qquad (8\text{-}4)$$

The rejection region is shown in Figure 8.3.

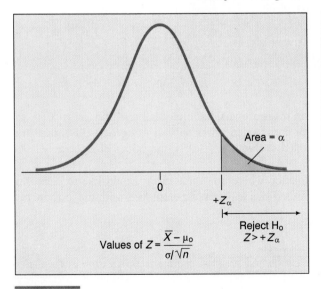

Figure 8.1
Distribution of Z test statistic showing one-sided rejection region (upper tail), $Z > +Z_\alpha$

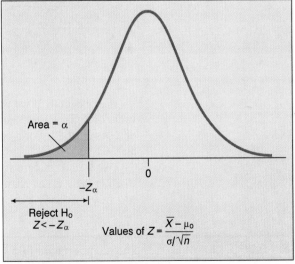

Figure 8.2
Distribution of Z test statistic showing one-sided rejection region (lower tail), $Z < -Z_\alpha$

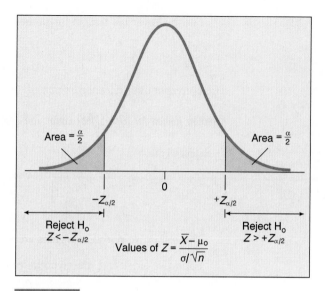

Figure 8.3
Distribution of Z test statistic showing two-sided rejection region (upper and lower tails), $Z < -Z_{\alpha/2}$ and $Z > +Z_{\alpha/2}$

There are certain values of α that are very commonly used in hypothesis testing. These values are $\alpha = .100, .050, .025, .010,$ and $.005$. For easy reference we list these values and their corresponding Z values for one-sided and two-sided tests below and in Appendix Table VI.

SIGNIFICANCE LEVEL α	VALUE OF Z_α (ONE-SIDED)	SIGNIFICANCE LEVEL α	VALUE OF $Z_{\alpha/2}$ (TWO-SIDED)
.100	1.282	.100	1.645
.050	1.645	.050	1.960
.025	1.960	.025	2.240
.010	2.326	.010	2.576
.005	2.576	.005	2.810

For example, if we wish to make a one-sided upper tail test using $\alpha = .050$, the value of Z_α is $+1.645$; and for a one-sided lower tail test using $\alpha = .050$, the value of Z_α is -1.645. For a two-sided test with $\alpha = .050$, the values of $Z_{\alpha/2}$ are -1.960 and $+1.960$.

We'll now analyze the situation where a hospital chain would like to determine whether there is any change in used sick leave among employees with the introduction of a new sick leave plan.

■ **EXAMPLE 8.1**

Sick Leave Compensation

The administration of a publicly owned hospital chain that hires thousands of new employees annually has decided to introduce a new delayed compensation sick leave plan. The plan pays no compensation for the first few sick days, but pays extended benefits for longer sick leaves. The plan is modeled after the "deductible" type of insurance plans, which provide no compensation up to a prespecified deductible amount, but compensate for all loss beyond the deductible amount. The plan will apply (for the time being at least) only to newly hired employees. The administration decides, because of a limited budget and costly record keeping, to monitor closely the absenteeism behavior of a random sample of 100 nurses hired under the new sick leave plan. Personnel records for the past few years show that, in the past, newly hired nurses averaged 8.8 sick days with a standard deviation of 4 days during their first year. If the random sample of 100 newly hired nurses averages 7.2 sick days during their first year under the new sick leave plan, does this indicate a significant departure from the average shown in the records of the past few years? Choose a level of significance of .01.

Statistical Solution

Step 1
Set up H_o and H_A: First, state H_o. Usually, H_o reflects the assumption of no change. In this example, no change means that the average number of sick days is the same under the new plan as under the old plan. Thus, H_o: $\mu = \mu_o$ becomes H_o: $\mu = 8.8$, where 8.8 is the average number of sick days under the old plan.

Now state H_A. H_A reflects the investigator's interest in the possibility of a change in the average number of sick days. The investigator would be delighted with a decrease in the average, and would be unhappy with an increase. This two-sided alternative hypothesis is symbolized by H_A: $\mu \neq 8.8$.

In summary, we write

H_o: $\mu = 8.8$ (Absenteeism behavior is unchanged under the new plan.)

H_A: $\mu \neq 8.8$ (Absenteeism behavior has changed under the new plan.)

Step 2
Select a level of significance: In this case $\alpha = .01$ is given in the description of the problem.

Step 3
Determine the value of σ: Since the reported standard deviation is derived from past records, not from the sample of the 100 nurses hired under the new plan, we should consider the reported value as the known population value. Hence, $\sigma = 4$.

Step 4
Determine the sample size, n: This is given as $n = 100$.

Step 5
Check the applicability of the normal distribution for the sampling distribution of $\bar{X}$: Since the sample size $n = 100$ is large, we may assume that the central limit theorem applies and the sampling distribution of the sample mean is approximately normal.

Step 6
Write the expression for the test statistic: The test statistic is

$$Z = \frac{\bar{X} - 8.8}{4/\sqrt{100}}$$

Step 7

Determine the rejection region: The rejection region $Z < -Z_{\alpha/2}$ or $Z > +Z_{\alpha/2}$ is given by

$$Z = \frac{\bar{X} - 8.8}{4/\sqrt{100}} < -Z_{.005} = -2.576 \quad \text{or} \quad Z = \frac{\bar{X} - 8.8}{4/\sqrt{100}} > +Z_{.005} = +2.576$$

This is shown in Figure 8.4.

Step 8

Determine the value of the sample statistic, $\bar{X}$: The problem states that $\bar{X} = 7.2$.

Step 9

Determine the value of the test statistic and apply the decision rule: Substituting 7.2 for $\bar{X}$ in the test statistic, the observed value of the test statistic is equal to -4. This value is less than -2.576 and, hence, lies in the rejection region. So we reject H_o of no change in absenteeism.

Step 10

Calculate the p-value: In this example, the p-value is obtained from

$$P(\bar{X} < 7.2 \mid \mu = 8.8) = P\left(Z < \frac{7.2 - 8.8}{4/\sqrt{100}}\right)$$

$$= P(Z < -4) = 0 \quad \text{To four decimal places}$$

where $P(\bar{X} < 7.2 \mid \mu = 8.8)$ is the conditional probability that $\bar{X}$ would be less than 7.2 given that the true mean is equal to 8.8. Since this is a two-sided test, the p-value required is the probability of finding either a value of Z less than -4 or greater than $+4$. Having found the probability for one side, we merely double the result to obtain the probability for two sides. With the probability of 0 to four decimal places on one side, twice that value still yields a result close to 0.

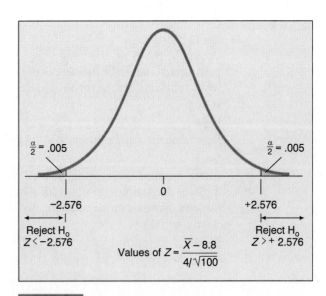

Figure 8.4
Distribution of Z test statistic with $\mu = 8.8$

The near 0 value virtually rules out the chance that we could have obtained such a result if the null hypothesis were true.

Practical Interpretation

At an $\alpha = .01$ level of significance the difference between $\bar{X} = 7.2$ and $\mu_o = 8.8$ is statistically significant. Thus, we conclude that there is a statistically significant change in the absenteeism behavior under the new sick leave plan relative to the absenteeism behavior for the past few years. The fact that the change reflects fewer days of sick leave means that absenteeism for newly hired nurses has decreased with the implementation of the delayed compensation sick leave plan. Since absenteeism is costly in terms of lost productivity, the hospital administration would be very pleased to hear about it and would be favorably inclined to implement the delayed compensation sick leave plan to all employees. However, the administration should not expect that long-time employees will react the same way as newly hired employees, so the hospital administration should be cautioned against a hasty generalized implementation.

PRACTICE EXERCISES

8.22 Suppose we wish to test, with $\alpha = .05$, the hypothesis that checks written on checking accounts with a local bank average \$40; that is, $H_o: \mu = 40$. Assume we already know that $\sigma = \$8$ and we wish to take a random sample of $n = 16$ checks.
   a. With the alternative that they average more than \$40, that is, $H_A: \mu > 40$, we have

$$H_o: \quad \mu = 40$$
$$H_A: \quad \mu > 40$$

   Use $\alpha = .05$, and find the rejection region.
   b. Find the rejection region for a two-sided test, again using $\alpha = .05$.

8.23 Suppose we wish to test the hypothesis in Practice Exercise 8.22 against the alternative that the checks average less than \$40. Use $\alpha = .05$. Now we have

$$H_o: \quad \mu = 40$$
$$H_A: \quad \mu < 40$$

Suppose we already know that $\sigma = \$8$. If we take a random sample of $n = 16$ checks and find $\bar{X} = 35$, then:
   a. Should we reject H_o?
   b. What is the p-value?

CASE 2: WHEN THE VALUE FOR σ IS UNKNOWN

When a random sample is taken from a normal population whose variance is unknown, we must estimate the value of σ. As in the case for confidence intervals, an estimate of the population standard deviation σ is the sample standard deviation S. When σ is unknown and S is used as its estimate, the sample size determines the appropriate test statistic. The test statistic for a large sample has a different sampling distribution than the test statistic for the small sample case. Let's begin with the large sample case.

Large Samples

When the sample size exceeds 30, an appropriate test statistic is given by the following:

Test Statistic for One Population Mean: σ Unknown, Large Sample

$$Z = \frac{\bar{X} - \mu_o}{S/\sqrt{n}} \tag{8-5}$$

The same procedure outlined earlier in this section is followed for one-sided tests and two-sided tests.

The following example illustrates a situation in which the Z test statistic would be used for a one-sided test.

■ **EXAMPLE 8.2**

"Shaving" Meat Patties

Millions of "Big Burgers," advertised as containing $\frac{1}{4}$ lb of beef, are sold each year by a chain of fast food restaurants in a large city. The meat is purchased in patties from a local meat dealer, who guarantees that the patties weigh an average of 0.250 lb. The variations in density of beef and other factors simply make it unfeasible to require every patty to weigh exactly 0.250 lb.

The relatively low wholesale mark-up on meat (say, 10%), combined with the fact that it is impractical for the restaurant chain to weigh each and every patty purchased, encourages unscrupulous meat dealers to fraudulently increase their profit margin by "shaving" just a little meat from each patty. If some of the patties are weighed upon receipt by the restaurants and found to be underweight, the unscrupulous dealer simply claims it was due to a "bad (unusual) sample" that happened by chance. Often, fast food chains are reluctant to change dealers merely on the suspicion that a particular dealer is cheating on the weight, because good meat dealers are hard to find. The retailer doesn't want to stop doing business with a dealer unless there is strong evidence that the dealer is dishonest. That is, the retailer wants to keep low the risk of a Type I error—in this case, the error of wrongly accusing a dealer who in fact is not cheating.

Suppose the retailer does become suspicious of a meat dealer. The retailer then decides to take a random sample of 100 hamburger patties from a large shipment received from the suspected dealer. If the mean weight of these 100 patties is 0.249 lb with a standard deviation of 0.020 lb, does this provide significant evidence that the dealer is "shaving" just a little meat from each patty? Use a level of significance of .01.

Statistical Solution

Step 1
Set up H_o and H_A: First, state H_o. H_o reflects the assumption of no change, which in this case means that the dealer doesn't shave the meat. That is, $\frac{1}{4}$ lb patties on average weigh $\frac{1}{4}$ lb. This is symbolized by H_o: $\mu = 0.250$.

Now state H_A. H_A reflects concern that shaving of the meat occurs and $\frac{1}{4}$ lb patties weigh on average less than $\frac{1}{4}$ lb. This is a one-sided alternative, symbolized by H_A: $\mu < 0.250$.

In summary, we can write

$$H_o: \quad \mu = 0.25 \quad \text{(No shaving of the meat occurs.)}$$
$$H_A: \quad \mu < 0.25 \quad \text{(Some shaving of the meat occurs.)}$$

Step 2
Select a level of significance: In this case $\alpha = .01$.

Step 3

Determine the value of σ, if possible: The standard deviation given in the example is based on a sample of 100 patties, so the value given is the sample standard deviation S, and not a population standard deviation σ.

Step 4

Determine the sample size, n: This is given as $n = 100$.

Step 5

Check the applicability of the normal distribution for the sampling distribution of $\bar{X}$: Since the sample size $n = 100$ is considered large, the central limit theorem applies and we may consider the sampling distribution of the sample mean to be approximately normal.

Step 6

Write the expression for the test statistic: The test statistic is

$$Z = \frac{\bar{X} - 0.250}{S/\sqrt{100}}$$

Step 7

Determine the rejection region: The rejection region for the one-sided test is given by

$$Z = \frac{\bar{X} - 0.250}{S/\sqrt{100}} < -2.326$$

The rejection region is formed to the left of $Z = -2.326$, as shown in Figure 8.5.

A Type I error would result from a conclusion that the dealer is shaving the meat patties when in fact he is not shaving, and a Type II error would result from a conclusion that the dealer is not shaving the patties when in fact he is shaving.

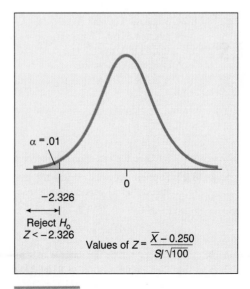

Figure 8.5
Distribution of Z test statistic with $\mu = 0.250$

Step 8

Determine the values of the sample statistics, $\bar{X}$ and S: The observed value of $\bar{X}$ is 0.249, and the observed value of S is 0.020.

Step 9

Determine the value of the test statistic and apply the decision rule: Substituting 0.249 for $\bar{X}$ and 0.020 for S in the test statistic, we compute a calculated Z value equal to -0.5. Since the calculated Z value is not less than -2.326, it doesn't lie in the rejection region. So we can't reject H_o (no meat shaving).

Step 10

Calculate the p-value: In this example, the p-value is

$$P(\bar{X} < 0.249 \mid \mu = 0.25) = P\left(Z < \frac{0.249 - 0.25}{0.020/\sqrt{100}}\right)$$

$$= P(Z < -.5) = .5 - .1915 = .3085$$

The large p-value suggests that the observed difference between the sample value of 0.249 and the assumed mean value of 0.250 is likely the result of chance variation. The evidence is consistent with the allegation that no real change in the mean weight for all meat patties has occurred.

Practical Interpretation

At the .01 level of significance we conclude that there is not significant evidence of "shaving" by this dealer. The retailer's suspicions appear to be unfounded, at least at this time. Unless other reasons exist to discontinue purchasing, the retailer should continue purchasing from this dealer. Of course, if the retailer's suspicions are aroused again at a later date, he can repeat the test with another independent random sample.

PRACTICE EXERCISES

8.24 Suppose we wish to test the hypothesis that checks written on money market accounts average \$160, that is, H_o: $\mu = \$160$, against the alternative that the checks average less than \$160, that is, H_A: $\mu < 160$. A sample of size $n = 64$ is taken. The sample standard deviation is $S = 20$.

a. Give the rejection region with the alternative that:

$$H_o: \quad \mu = 160$$
$$H_A: \quad \mu < 160$$

Use $\alpha = .05$.

b. Give the rejection region for a two-sided test of H_o, again using $\alpha = .05$.

8.25 Suppose we wish to test the hypothesis that checks written on money market accounts average \$160 versus the alternative that they average more than \$160. Then

$$H_o: \quad \mu = 160$$
$$H_A: \quad \mu > 160$$

Use $\alpha = .05$. If a sample of size $n = 64$ has the sample standard deviation $S = 20$ and the sample mean $\bar{X} = \$164.31$, then:

a. Should we reject H_o?

b. What is the p-value?

Determining β

The value of β is the probability of committing a Type II error. In some problems it is important to calculate the β values corresponding to various alternative values of the population parameter. We'll illustrate a procedure for finding a value for β using the situation described in Example 8.2.

Suppose that unknown to the retailer, the meat dealer in Example 8.2 is selling beef patties that on average actually weigh 0.240 lb. Then, applying the decision rule (with $\alpha = .01$) in Example 8.2 to the circumstance in which the true average weight of the meat patties is 0.240 lb, what is the value of β, the probability of not rejecting H_o: $\mu = 0.250$ if H_A is true, where H_A is defined as $\mu = 0.240$.

Statistical Solution

Step 1

State the nonrejection region for H_o in terms of $\bar{X}$: In Example 8.2 the nonrejection region for H_o: $\mu = 0.250$ is $Z > -2.326$. This can be expressed in terms of $\bar{X}$ by solving the following expression for $\bar{X}$:

$$Z = \frac{\bar{X} - 0.250}{0.020/\sqrt{100}} > -2.326$$

We obtain $\bar{X} > 0.245348$.

NOTE: The additional decimal places in 0.245348 are needed so that the numerical result obtained here will be in agreement with the numerical result obtained by using the more general expression given by equation (8-6).

Step 2

Specify a value for μ in H_A for which β is to be calculated: For this example, the value of β is obtained given that H_A: $\mu = 0.240$.

Step 3

Calculate β: This means finding the probability for the expression

$$\beta = P(\bar{X} > 0.245348 \mid \mu = 0.240; S = 0.020)$$

$$= P\left(Z > \frac{0.245348 - 0.240}{0.020/\sqrt{100}}\right)$$

$$= P(Z > 2.67) = .5 - .4962 = .0038$$

Thus, a meat dealer who decides to cheat by shaving his patties down to as low as 0.240 lb will stand very little chance (only 38 chances in 10,000) of going undetected if the decision rule in Example 8.2 is applied.

The relationship between α and β in the above example is illustrated in Figure 8.6. Note that with respect to the point 0.245348, the value of β is the right tail area under the normal curve with $\mu_A = 0.240$, and the value of α is the left tail area under the normal curve with $\mu_o = 0.250$.

In calculating the value of β in the example, we arbitrarily chose the alternative H_A: $\mu = 0.240$. Suppose, instead, the meat dealer decides to cheat only a little and shaves his patties so that they weigh on average 0.247 lb, which is much closer to 0.250 lb. In that case, applying the decision rule of Example 8.2 would yield a probability of

$$\beta = P(\bar{X} > 0.245348 \mid \mu = 0.247; S = 0.020)$$

$$= P\left(Z > \frac{0.245348 - 0.247}{0.020/\sqrt{100}}\right)$$

$$= P(Z > -0.83) = .5 + .2967 = .7967$$

This very high probability shows that a meat dealer who is not too greedy and shaves

Figure 8.6
Determining β, the probability of a Type II error

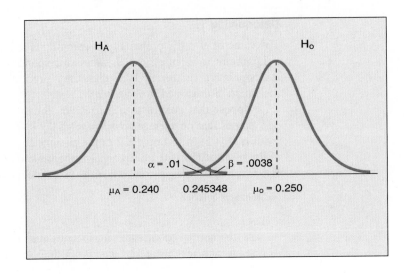

the patties only slightly to 0.247 lb, will very likely (approx. .80 probability) go undetected! This is a dramatic shift from the slim chance (38 in 10,000) of going undetected if he gets too greedy and shaves his patties to 0.240 lb.

We now generalize this discussion to show how to find the value of β for a one-sided test where H_o: $\mu = \mu_o$ versus H_A: $\mu_A < \mu_o$. For the case where the sample size n is greater than 30, the value of β is calculated by evaluating the following probability:

Value of β for the One-Sided Test Where H_o: $\mu = \mu_o$ versus H_A: $\mu_A < \mu_o$

$$\beta = P\left(Z > \frac{\mu_o - \mu_A}{S/\sqrt{n}} - Z_\alpha\right) \tag{8-6}$$

where μ_A is a specified alternative value for μ. If we know the value of σ, we use its value instead of S.

The same procedure can be used to derive the expression for finding the value of β for the one-sided test where H_o: $\mu = \mu_o$ versus H_A: $\mu_A > \mu_o$:

Value of β for the One-Sided Test Where H_o: $\mu = \mu_o$ versus H_A: $\mu_A > \mu_o$

$$\beta = P\left(Z < \frac{\mu_o - \mu_A}{S/\sqrt{n}} + Z_\alpha\right) \tag{8-7}$$

where μ_A is a specified alternative value for μ.

Finally, we use the following expression to find the value of β for a two-sided test where H_o: $\mu = \mu_o$ versus H_A: $\mu_A \neq \mu_o$:

Value of β for the Two-Sided Test Where H_o: $\mu = \mu_o$ versus H_A: $\mu_A \neq \mu_o$

$$\beta = P\left(\frac{\mu_o - \mu_A}{S/\sqrt{n}} - Z_{\alpha/2} < Z < \frac{\mu_o - \mu_A}{S/\sqrt{n}} + Z_{\alpha/2}\right) \tag{8-8}$$

where μ_A is a specified alternative value for μ.

Power Curves

The value of β is the probability of not rejecting H_o when H_o is false. The value $1 - \beta$ is the probability that we will reject H_o when H_o is false. So the value $1 - \beta$ represents our ability to detect a false null hypothesis; this value is referred to as the **power of the test**. A value close to 1 represents strong power; a value close to 0 represents weak power.

In the meat patties example we noticed that the value of β changed with μ_A, the alternative values for μ. This in turn implies that the value of $1 - \beta$ will also change with the alternative values for μ. To illustrate this, we have constructed Table 8.2 showing the changing values of β and $1 - \beta$ for various alternative values for μ for the meat patties example. Values from this table are plotted in Figure 8.7, where they form a *power curve*. The power curve for a one-sided test where the alternative hypothesis is stated as H_A: $\mu_A < \mu_o$ appears as a reverse S-shaped curve.

We notice from Table 8.2 and Figure 8.7 that the power of the test increases as the value of μ_A is more distant from the value of μ_o. This means that the power to

TABLE 8.2	Values of β and 1 - β for Selected Alternative Values of μ for the Meat Patties Case	
VALUES OF μ_A	**β, THE PROBABILITY YOU WILL NOT REJECT H_o: $\mu = 0.250$**	**$1 - \beta$, THE PROBABILITY YOU WILL REJECT H_o: $\mu = 0.250$**
0.250	.99	.01
0.249	.9664	.0336
0.248	.9082	.0918
0.247	.7967	.2033
0.246	.6293	.3707
0.245	.4325	.5675
0.244	.2514	.7486
0.243	.1210	.8790
0.242	.0475	.9525
0.241	.0150	.9850
0.240	.0038	.9962

Figure 8.7
Power curve for the meat patties example
(H_A: $\mu_A < \mu_o$)

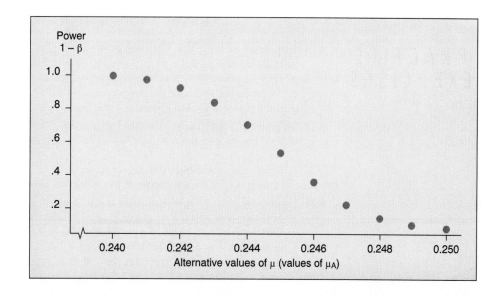

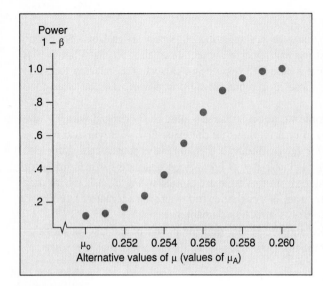

Figure 8.8
Power curve for H_A: $\mu_A > \mu_o$

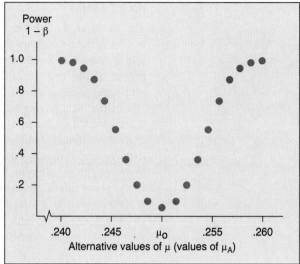

Figure 8.9
Power curve for H_A: $\mu_A \neq \mu_o$

discriminate between μ_o and μ_A increases as the difference between μ_o and μ_A increases. It should also be pointed out that the shape of the power curve changes with the type of alternative hypothesis considered. If the alternative hypothesis had been stated as H_A: $\mu_A > \mu_o$, the power curve for this one-sided test would appear as a regular S-shaped curve, as shown in Figure 8.8.

However, if the alternative hypothesis is stated as H_A: $\mu_A \neq \mu_o$, the power curve for the two-sided test is U-shaped, as shown in Figure 8.9. The narrowness of the U is an indicator of the ability of the two-sided test to discriminate between the value of the parameter stated in H_o and the alternative values stated in H_A. A narrow U indicates good discrimination; a wide U-shaped curve indicates a poor discriminator.

PRACTICE EXERCISES

8.26 Suppose we have H_o: $\mu = 1215$ versus H_A: $\mu_A < 1215$.
   a. Find the value of β if $n = 100$, $S = 250$, $\alpha = .05$, and $\mu_A = 1200$.
   b. Find the power of the test if $n = 100$, $S = 250$, $\alpha = .05$, and $\mu_A = 1200$.
   c. Repeat parts a and b for the case where $\mu_A = 1190$.
   d. Is the power of the test greater in part c than in part b?

8.27 Suppose we have H_o: $\mu = 37$ versus H_A: $\mu > 37$.
   a. Find the value of β if $n = 225$, $S = 15$, $\alpha = .05$, and $\mu_A = 38$.
   b. Find the power of the test if $n = 225$, $S = 15$, $\alpha = .05$, and $\mu_A = 38$.
   c. Repeat parts a and b for the case where $\mu_A = 39$.
   d. Is the power of the test greater in part c than in part b?

8.28 Suppose we have H_o: $\mu = 499$ versus H_A: $\mu \neq 499$.
   a. Find the value of β if $n = 144$, $S = 36$, $\alpha = .05$, and $\mu_A = 496$.
   b. Find the power of the test if $n = 144$, $S = 36$, $\alpha = .05$, and $\mu_A = 496$.
   c. Repeat parts a and b for the case where $\mu_A = 502$.
   d. Is the power of the test greater in part c than in part b?

Small Samples

When the sample size does not exceed 30 and we do not know the population value σ, but the underlying population from which we sample is normally distributed, an appropriate test statistic to use for testing hypotheses concerning μ is given by:

Test Statistic for One Population
Mean: σ Unknown, Small Sample

$$t_{n-1} = \frac{\bar{X} - \mu_o}{S/\sqrt{n}} \qquad (8\text{-}9)$$

In this case, the test statistic follows the Student t distribution with $\nu = n - 1$ degrees of freedom. The same testing procedure outlined earlier again applies, but now we use the t test statistic instead of the Z test statistic.

■ **EXAMPLE 8.3**

The Gas Mileage of a New Car

A new car sticker claims gas usage under normal driving conditions is 35 miles per gallon (mpg) on the average, in city driving. Several months after the purchase of a new car a customer decides to check to see if she has been getting the appropriate mileage. From the time of her purchase she kept careful records of her odometer readings and the number of gallons required at each fill-up. She randomly selects the records for 9 fill-ups, and finds that the average for the 9 fill-ups is 33.4 mpg with a standard deviation 2.3 mpg. Does this indicate that she has been getting less than 35 mpg? Use a level of significance of .05 and assume that gas mileage is normally distributed.

Statistical Solution

Step 1
Set up H_o and H_A: First, state H_o. H_o reflects the assumption of no change from the expected gas mileage. This is symbolized by H_o: $\mu = 35$, where 35 is the gas mileage claimed on the sticker.

Now state H_A. H_A reflects the purchaser's concern. The purchaser is concerned that her gas mileage may be lower than expected. This is symbolized by H_A: $\mu < 35$.

In summary, we can write

$$H_o: \quad \mu = 35 \quad \text{(No change from expected)}$$
$$H_A: \quad \mu < 35 \quad \text{(Lower then expected)}$$

Step 2
Select a level of significance: In this case $\alpha = .05$.

Step 3
Determine the value of σ if possible: The value of σ is unknown. The standard deviation reported is calculated from a sample of 9 fill-ups, so the value given is the sample standard deviation S.

Step 4
Determine the sample size, n: The reported sample size is 9, so $n = 9$.

Step 5

Determine the suitability of a test statistic based on the normal distribution: The problem states that we should assume the population of gas mileages is normal, but the value of the standard deviation given is a sample value, not a population value, and the sample size $n = 9$ does not exceed 30. Therefore, the appropriate test statistic is the Student t statistic with $n - 1 = 9 - 1 = 8$ df.

Step 6

Write the expression for the test statistic: The test statistic is

$$t_8 = \frac{\bar{X} - 35}{S/\sqrt{9}}$$

Step 7

Determine the rejection region: The rejection region for the one-sided test is given by $t_8 < -t_{(.05,8)}$. From Appendix Table VII, $t_{(.05,8)} = 1.860$. So,

$$t_8 = \frac{\bar{X} - 35}{S/\sqrt{9}} < -t_{(.05,8)} = -1.860$$

The rejection region is defined to the left of $t_8 = -1.860$, and this is shown in Figure 8.10.

Step 8

Determine the values of the sample statistics, $\bar{X}$ and S: The problem states that the observed values of $\bar{X}$ and S are 33.4 and 2.3, respectively.

Step 9

Determine the value of the test statistic and apply the decision rule: Substituting 33.4 for $\bar{X}$ and 2.3 for S in the test statistic, the calculated t test statistic is found to be -2.087. Since the calculated t statistic is less than -1.860, it lies in the rejection region. So we reject the null hypothesis of no change.

Figure 8.10
Distribution of t test statistic
with $\mu = 35$

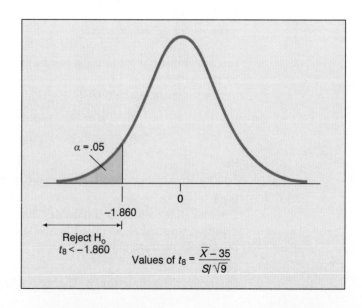

Step 10

Calculate the p-value: In this example, the p-value is given by

$$P(\bar{X} < 33.4 \mid \mu = 35) = P\left(t_8 < \frac{33.4 - 35}{2.3/\sqrt{9}}\right)$$

$$= P(t_8 < -2.087)$$

An evaluation of the exact probability of the final expression requires a more extensive table than provided for in this book, but a useful approximation can be obtained from Appendix Table VII. It can be seen from the table that the p-value lies between .025 and .05, and therefore is less than .05. The low p-value indicates that the observed result is a noticeable departure from the H_0 value of 35 and not likely due to chance. Also notice that if the originally chosen level of significance had been the more stringent value of .01 rather than .05, we would not have rejected H_0. This borderline case raises two issues. First, can we change the level of significance after seeing the results? To change the level of significance after seeing the sample results removes some of the objectivity from the investigation and subjects the investigator to the criticism that he or she is "fishing" for a particular result. The second point is that perhaps it is more informative to present the p-value in addition to stating whether the null hypothesis has been rejected or not rejected at the chosen significance level. This can avoid possible subjectiveness in presenting results. A more appropriate reaction to borderline cases, such as in this example, would be to consider further investigation with other independent samples.

Practical Interpretation

At the .05 level of significance we conclude that the new car owner has been getting less mileage than the sticker claimed. If the car has a new car 3 year warranty, should she take the car back to the dealer? She could show the service manager her records and her statistical analysis, and ask the service manager to have the engine checked for possible defects or faulty parts that may be affecting the car's gas mileage. However, before she takes this course of action, she should carefully evaluate whether she has been driving the car under "normal" driving conditions and whether 33.4 is sufficiently low, in a practical sense, to be due to possible defective or faulty engine parts or assembly.

● ●

PRACTICE EXERCISES

8.29 Suppose we wish to test the hypothesis that monthly charges made with VISA® cards average \$83, that is, H_0: $\mu = 83$. Assume a sample of size $n = 16$, and assume that we don't have a value for the population standard deviation.

a. Give the one-sided rejection region with the alternative that the monthly charges average less than \$83, that is, H_A: $\mu < 83$.

$$H_0: \quad \mu = 83$$
$$H_A: \quad \mu < 83$$

Use $\alpha = .05$.

b. Find the two-sided rejection region, again using $\alpha = .05$.

8.30 Repeat Practice Exercise 8.29, but this time let the alternative be that the charges average more than \$83. In that case,

$$H_0: \quad \mu = 83$$
$$H_A: \quad \mu > 83 .$$

with $n = 16$. If the sample standard deviation $S = 8$ and the sample mean $\bar{X} = 85.1$, then:

a. Should we reject H_o?
b. What is the p-value?

● ●

Flowchart I

Choosing the appropriate test statistic to use in a given situation can be a somewhat difficult task. The flowchart shown in Figure 8.11 summarizes the checkpoints involved in choosing the appropriate statistic. In addition, Table 8.3 illustrates the three possible alternative hypotheses along with their corresponding rejection and nonrejection regions.

TABLE 8.3 A Summary Table for the Three Possible Alternative Hypotheses for Testing a Mean Value		
H_A	Do not reject H_o if	Reject H_o if
$\mu > \mu_o$	$Z \leq +Z_\alpha$ $t_\nu \leq +t_{(\alpha,\nu)}$	$Z > +Z_\alpha$ $t_\nu > +t_{(\alpha,\nu)}$
$\mu < \mu_o$	$Z \geq -Z_\alpha$ $t_\nu \geq -t_{(\alpha,\nu)}$	$Z < -Z_\alpha$ $t_\nu < -t_{(\alpha,\nu)}$
$\mu \neq \mu_o$	$-Z_{\alpha/2} \leq Z \leq +Z_{\alpha/2}$ $-t_{(\alpha/2,\nu)} \leq t_\nu \leq +t_{(\alpha/2,\nu)}$	$Z < -Z_{\alpha/2}$ or $Z > +Z_{\alpha/2}$ $t_\nu < -t_{(\alpha/2,\nu)}$ or $t_\nu > +t_{(\alpha/2,\nu)}$

Note: $\nu = n - 1$ and represents the degrees of freedom.

Figure 8.11
Flowchart I for testing one population mean

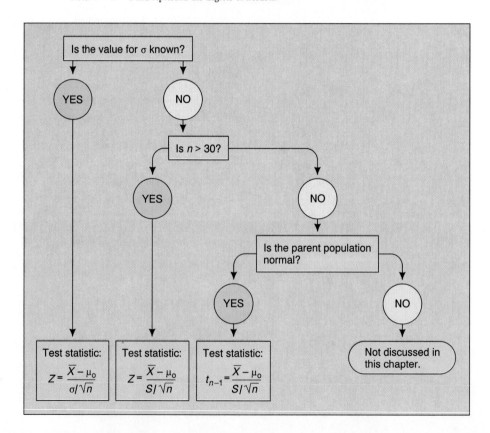

PRACTICE EXERCISE

8.31 Suppose a consumer agency states that the average selling price for a home electronic burglar alarm is $99, and suppose we wish to test this hypothesis versus the alternative that the average selling price is greater than $99. Then we have

$$H_o: \quad \mu = 99$$
$$H_A: \quad \mu > 99$$

Use $\alpha = .025$ and use the flowchart in Figure 8.11 or the summary table in Table 8.3 to determine the appropriate test statistic. Give the rejection region if:
a. $\sigma^2 = 36$ and $n = 25$
b. $S^2 = 36$ and $n = 25$
c. $S^2 = 36$ and $n = 36$

EXERCISES

▶ **8.4** Construct a power curve for the situation in Practice Exercise 8.26. (Hint: Try $\mu_A = 1210, 1205, 1195, 1185, 1180, 1175, 1170, 1165, 1160$.)

8.5 Construct a power curve for the situation in Practice Exercise 8.27. (Hint: Try $\mu_A = 37.5, 38.5, 39.5, 40$.)

8.6 Construct a power curve for the situation in Practice Exercise 8.28. (Hint: Try $\mu_A = 497.5, 500.5, 494.5, 503.5, 493, 505$.)

8.7 A synthetically produced growth hormone was administered to 16 randomly selected cows to determine whether the hormone would stimulate milk production. The sample results showed an average percent increase of 0.2768 with a standard deviation of 0.073335. Assuming that the percent change in milk production is normally distributed, does this sample result provide statistical evidence of an improvement in milk production (versus no improvement in milk production)? Use a level of significance of .05.

8.8 Suppose a government agency claims that VISA® credit card holders make an average monthly payment of $135, and suppose the sample in Exercise 7.17, repeated below, was taken to test this claim. For the sample of size 51, use the sample mean of $142.42 and the sample standard deviation of $26.98 to test the claim at a significance level of .01.

181.78	157.39	142.45	140.92	166.98	128.48	149.46	108.61	122.72	112.86
157.35	116.25	167.46	138.95	106.89	113.53	147.03	136.28	162.70	150.13
117.32	125.57	166.06	152.61	160.39	112.66	137.06	125.60	200.29	107.78
134.56	185.24	118.63	202.61	110.79	149.05	132.60	165.51	112.29	180.77
123.30	200.76	122.32	84.29	144.97	151.52	156.13	153.41	149.13	110.26
161.97									

▶ **8.9** An agency that monitors the legal profession claims that lawyers earn, on the average, more than $85,000 per year. Using the fact that the variance has remained stable at ($27,000)^2 and using the sample average of $101,500 (based on a sample of size 9), determine whether there is statistical support for the agency's claim. Use a significance level of .01.

8.10 Find the p-value for the results in:
a. Exercise 8.7.
b. Exercise 8.8.
c. Exercise 8.9.

▶ **8.11** With respect to Exercise 8.9, find the value of β if the true average of annual earnings is:
a. $90,000
b. $100,000

c. $110,000

d. Compare the three values of β obtained in parts a, b, and c. Is there a pattern?

8.12 In an attempt to determine whether global temperatures are increasing, a climatologist compares the average temperatures of 70 randomly selected regions in the world and, for each region, compares the average temperature over the last 30 years with the average temperature for the preceding 30 years. He records the differences by subtracting the preceding 30 years' average from the last 30 years' average. Thus, a positive difference for a region reflects an increase in the average temperature in that region in the last 30 years, and a negative difference reflects a corresponding decrease. For the 70 regions his results show an average increase of 0.83°F with a standard deviation of 0.21°F. At the .0122 level of significance does this result provide statistical evidence of an increase in the average global temperature in the last 30 years relative to the previous 30 year period?

8.13 A physician notes that one of her patients shows symptoms of a certain disease and directs the patient to get a blood test. Suppose the normal count for platelets in the blood is 200,000 per cubic millimeter (mm^3) with a standard deviation of 2000 per mm^3. The physician doesn't want to erroneously tell her patient that he has the disease, so she decides to use a very small value, .005, for the level of significance. But she also doesn't want to commit the error of telling her patient that all is well when, in fact, he has the disease; so she instructs the lab to make 100 independent determinations. If the lab results show that the patient's average count is 195,000 per mm^3, is this significantly lower than normal? Assume the lab measurements are normally distributed.

▶ **8.14** At a salesperson's convention, a saleswoman is told that the average time it takes a salesperson to make a sale is 2 hr with a standard deviation of 0.35 hr. She is also informed that the distribution of sales times is normal. To see if she fits the standard, she decides to check her records and randomly selects 16 sales times. If the average for the 16 observations is 2.45 hr, does this show a significant departure from the norm? Use a level of significance of .05.

8.15 In the past, a chemical plant has produced an average of 1200 lb of chemicals per day with a standard deviation of 300 lb. Records of the daily production show the distribution to be normal. A company executive suspects that the average daily production has dropped, and he selects a random sample of 16 operating days and finds an average of 1110 lb per day. Is this a significant decrease from the norm? Use a level of significance of .10.

8.16 A manufacturer of cooking oil claims that not more than 0.3 oz of her oil gets used up in frying 5 lb of chicken. In 25 independent tests, an average of 0.32 oz of oil, with a standard deviation of 0.07 oz, gets used up. Does the sample result provide sufficient evidence to reject the manufacturer's claim? Use a level of significance of .025, and assume that the amount of oil used up is normally distributed. What is the *p*-value in this case?

8.17 Suppose we are prepared to assume that the treadlife of tires produced by a certain manufacturer is normally distributed, and suppose the manufacturer claims that the tires have an average treadlife of at least 35,000 mi. If a consumer agency tests 49 randomly selected tires made by this manufacturer and finds an average of 33,000 mi with a standard deviation of 2300 mi, does this provide sufficient evidence to refute the manufacturer's claim? Use a level of significance of .01.

8.3

TEST OF HYPOTHESIS: ONE POPULATION PROPORTION

In testing hypotheses concerning one population proportion, the sample statistic computed from the sample is $\hat{p} = X/n$, where X represents the number of occurrences of a given type among n independent trials. The sampling distribution of X is binomial but, whenever possible, the distribution of $\hat{p}$ is approximated by a normal distribution. We noted in Chapter 6 that the sampling distribution of $\hat{p}$ can be approximated by a normal distribution when three conditions are met: $n > 30$, $np \geq 5$, and $n(1 - p) \geq 5$. If the normal approximation is justified, the following test statistic can be constructed:

Test Statistic for One Population Proportion

$$Z = \frac{\hat{p} - p_0}{\sqrt{\dfrac{p_0(1 - p_0)}{n}}} \qquad (8\text{-}10)$$

where p_0 is the hypothesized value of the population parameter p specified in H_0.

The test statistic in this form is distributed as the standard normal random variable Z.

There are two variants for the alternative hypothesis in testing a hypothesis on one population proportion. One variant deals with two-sided tests which, by definition, always concern both tails of the testing probability distribution. The second variant deals with one-sided tests, which may consider either the upper tail or the lower tail of the testing probability distribution. Let's first consider the one-sided tests and then the two-sided test.

For the one-sided upper tail test, the hypotheses are

$$H_0: \quad p = p_0$$
$$H_A: \quad p > p_0 \quad \text{Indicates an upper tail test.}$$

Using the expression of the test statistic given in formula (8-10) and fulfilling the condition $P(Z > +Z_\alpha) = \alpha$, the rejection region can be expressed as follows:

Rejection Region for One-Sided Upper Tail Test for One Population Proportion

Reject H_0 if

$$Z = \frac{\hat{p} - p_0}{\sqrt{\dfrac{p_0(1 - p_0)}{n}}} > +Z_\alpha \qquad (8\text{-}11)$$

where $+Z_\alpha$ is the value of Z for which the upper tail area equals α.

This is the region in which the calculated Z value exceeds $+Z_\alpha$, where $+Z_\alpha$ is the table value of Z and represents the point beyond which the upper tail area is α.

For the one-sided lower tail test, the null and alternative hypotheses are given as

$$H_o: \quad p = p_o$$
$$H_A: \quad p < p_o \quad \text{Indicates a lower tail test.}$$

For the specified level of significance, α, the rejection region is determined by fulfilling the condition $P(Z < -Z_\alpha) = \alpha$ when the normal distribution approximation may be used. Therefore, the rejection region is given by the following:

Rejection Region for One-Sided Lower Tail Test for One Population Proportion

Reject H_o if

$$Z = \frac{\hat{p} - p_o}{\sqrt{\dfrac{p_o(1 - p_o)}{n}}} < -Z_\alpha \tag{8-12}$$

For a two-sided test, both sides of the test statistic distribution must be considered. The hypotheses are

$$H_o: \quad p = p_o$$
$$H_A: \quad p \neq p_o$$

Notice that in a two-sided test, H_A states that p can be either greater than p_o or less than p_o. Thus, the rejection region is determined by

$$P(Z < -Z_{\alpha/2}) = \alpha/2$$
$$P(Z > +Z_{\alpha/2}) = \alpha/2$$

These expressions assume that the normal distribution approximation to the binomial distribution may be used. In this case, the rejection region is given by the following:

Rejection Region for Two-Sided Test for One Population Proportion

Reject H_o if

$$Z = \frac{\hat{p} - p_o}{\sqrt{\dfrac{p_o(1 - p_o)}{n}}} < -Z_{\alpha/2} \quad \text{or} \quad Z = \frac{\hat{p} - p_o}{\sqrt{\dfrac{p_o(1 - p_o)}{n}}} > +Z_{\alpha/2} \tag{8-13}$$

The rejection region is illustrated in Figure 8.12.

Now let's apply this procedure to determine the impact of a price reduction on peoples' perception of the quality of a product.

Figure 8.12
Approximate distribution
of test statistic

$$\frac{\hat{p} - p_o}{\sqrt{\dfrac{p_o(1 - p_o)}{n}}}$$

with $p = p_o$

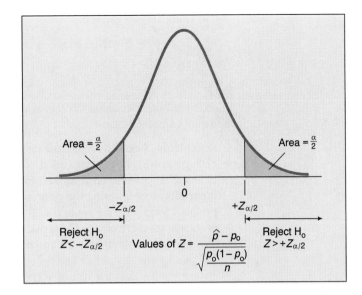

■ **EXAMPLE 8.4**

**A One-Sided Test:
Impact of Price on
Product Quality
Perceptions**

Suppose you are employed in the marketing research department of a medium-sized pharmaceutical company heavily involved in nonprescription over-the-counter consumer drugs. Your marketing manager insists that economic theory doesn't work in this business; that is, lowering the price of a product relative to the price charged by the competition is not a sure-fire way of increasing sales volume. The manager believes that the consumer's reaction is, "You get what you pay for," a lower price tag means a lower quality drug. But the company is committed to improving the market penetration (number of customers who use the product) of their brand of aspirin substitute. Previous marketing research shows that 30% of the aspirin substitute users regard the brand as inferior to the market leader. If a lower price strategy is implemented and this inferiority figure rises, then this marketing strategy will prove to be a disaster. To check this out, the marketing research department interviews a random sample of 140 aspirin substitute users who are willing to express their attitudes on whether or not they believe a lower price will be accompanied by lower quality control (and, hence, would be considered inferior to the market leader). If 63 of 140 persons interviewed believe it would, is this significant evidence that implementation of the lower price structure will increase the proportion of aspirin substitute users who will regard the brand as inferior to the market leader?

Statistical Solution

We shall now illustrate the hypothesis test procedure to resolve this issue.

Step 1
Set up H_o and H_A: First, state H_o. Usually, H_o incorporates the assumption of no change. In this example, we can hypothesize that $H_o: p = p_o$, where $p_o = .3$ is the proportion of persons in the population who, prior to the price cut, perceived the product as being inferior.

Now state H_A. H_A reflects the investigator's concern that lowering the price would result in an increase in the proportion of persons who perceive the product as being inferior. This is symbolized by writing $H_A: p > p_o$. That is, $H_A: p > .3$.

In summary, we can write

H_o: $p = .3$ (No change in consumer perception of inferiority)

H_A: $p > .3$ (An increase in consumer perception of inferiority)

Step 2

Select a level of significance: In this example we shall use .05 based on the following considerations:

a. Rejecting H_o would be a mistake resulting in a Type I error if truly there has been no change in the proportion of consumers who believe the product to be inferior. It would result in keeping the higher price under the mistaken impression that lowering the price would lower consumer esteem for the product. Such an error could cost the company an opportunity to make gains in its market penetration. Thus, the company would want to keep down the likelihood of committing such an error. Nevertheless, it must also consider the consequences and likelihood of committing a Type II error. Recall that for a fixed sample size, the risk of a Type II error must increase if we choose to decrease the risk of a Type I error.

b. Failing to reject H_o would be a mistake resulting in a Type II error if a price cut does lower consumer esteem for the product. The error would result from lowering the price under the mistaken impression that consumer esteem of the product is unchanged. Such an error could cause a loss in the product's market penetration. Clearly, the company would like to keep down the likelihood of committing that error as well.

c. As a compromise between the likelihood of committing Type I and Type II errors, it is decided to let $\alpha = .05$ for the maximum risk acceptable for committing a Type I error, even though a higher value of α would reduce the risk of committing a Type II error.

Step 3

Specify the sample size: The sample size of $n = 140$ is considered reasonable for economy and accuracy.

Step 4

Determine the appropriateness of the normal distribution approximation to the binomial distribution: In this example, $n = 140$ is greater than 30, and since $np_o = (140)(.3) = 42$ and $n(1 - p_o) = 98$ meet the conditions $np \geq 5$ and $n(1 - p_o) \geq 5$, the normal distribution approximation to the binomial distribution is appropriate. We can write the test statistic expression as

$$Z = \frac{\hat{p} - .3}{\sqrt{\frac{(.3)(.7)}{140}}}$$

Step 5

Determine the rejection region: Given $\alpha = .05$, the standard normal table shows that $Z_{.05} = 1.645$. The expression $P(Z > Z_\alpha) = \alpha$ becomes $P(Z > 1.645) = .05$. So the rejection region is defined as

$$Z = \frac{\hat{p} - .3}{\sqrt{\frac{(.3)(.7)}{140}}} > 1.645$$

Figure 8.13
Approximate distribution
of test statistic

$$\frac{\hat{p} - .30}{\sqrt{\dfrac{(.30)(1 - .3)}{140}}}$$

with $p = .3$ and $n = 140$

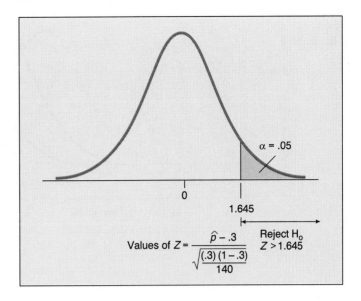

This is illustrated in Figure 8.13.

Step 6
Determine the value of the sample statistic, $\hat{p}$: The observed value of $\hat{p}$ is $\frac{63}{140} = .45$.

Step 7
Determine the value of the test statistic: Substituting .45 for $\hat{p}$ in the expression for the test statistic, we find the calculated Z test statistic value:

$$Z = \frac{.45 - .3}{\sqrt{\dfrac{(.3)(.7)}{140}}} = 3.87$$

Step 8
Apply the decision rule: Since 3.87 is greater than 1.645 (the beginning Z value of the rejection region), the calculated Z value falls in the rejection region. Therefore, H_o is rejected.

Step 9
Calculate the p-value: In this example H_o is true when $p = .3$, so the p-value is obtained from

$$P(\hat{p} > .45 \mid p = .3) = P\left(Z > \frac{.45 - .3}{\sqrt{\dfrac{(.3)(.7)}{140}}}\right)$$

$$= P(Z > 3.87)$$

$$= 0 \quad \text{To four decimal place accuracy}$$

This extremely low p-value suggests that the observed result is virtually impossible if the null hypothesis is true; therefore, the sample evidence strongly indicates that H_o is not true. The result strongly confirms the concern that

Figure 8.14
Description of H_o: $p_o \leq .3$

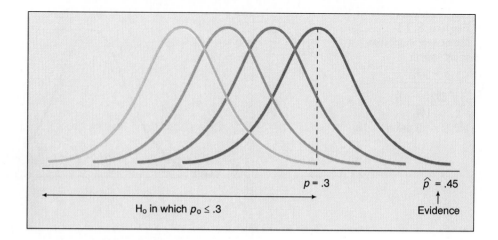

Practical Interpretation

lowering the price would lower the product's esteem among its potential customers. Would it thus be wise for the manufacturer to lower the price of the product? Marketing research would urgently recommend against it.

Practical Interpretation

At a .05 level of significance we conclude that lowering the price of the product would increase the proportion of consumers who regard the product as inferior to the market leader. Thus, marketing research would report to the manufacturer that lowering the price of the product would lower the product's esteem in the eyes of its potential customers, news that the manufacturer is undoubtedly hoping not to have to hear!

Comment

In Example 8.4 H_o stipulates that $p_o = .3$. However, the procedure and the test outcome would have been identical if H_o had stipulated $p_o < .3$. The reason for this is that evidence ($\hat{p} = .45$) that enables us to reject H_o for $p_o = .3$ implies that this same evidence must also enable us to reject H_o for any value of $p_o \leq .3$, as shown by Figure 8.14. Therefore, rejecting H_o: $p_o = .3$ is equivalent to rejecting H_o: $p_o \leq .3$, so we cover both cases by using the notation H_o: $p_o = .3$.

PRACTICE EXERCISES

8.32 Suppose we wish to test, with $\alpha = .05$, the hypothesis that 45% of the unskilled and semiskilled workers in this country belong to a union. Assume a normal approximation to the binomial sampling distribution is appropriate.

a. Test the null hypothesis,

H_o: $p = .45$

against the alternative that more than 45% of the workers belong to a union,

H_A: $p > .45$

Give the rejection region.

b. Test

$$H_o: \quad p = .45$$

against the alternative that fewer than 45% of the workers belong to a union,

$$H_A: \quad p < .45$$

Give the rejection region.

8.33 Suppose we wish to test, with $\alpha = 0.25$, the hypothesis that 63% of all the automobiles that travel the Los Angeles freeways are imports versus the alternative that fewer than 63% are imports. Suppose also that we see 40 imports in a random sample of 100 cars on the Los Angeles freeways. Then we have

$$H_o: \quad p = .63$$
$$H_A: \quad p < .63$$

with $\alpha = .025$, $n = 100$, and $X = 40$. Then:
a. Should we reject H_o?
b. What is the p-value?

● ●

The following example illustrates the use of a two-sided hypothesis test.

■ **EXAMPLE 8.5**

A Two-Sided Test: Memory Chip Production and Defective Rate

Computer technology changes rapidly. As soon as a semiconductor chip for a computer comes off the production line, a new, more powerful chip is designed that can deliver more computing power for less cost. Engineers are aware that altering chip design can cause a change in the proportion of defective chips manufactured. In many cases it is not possible to tell in advance whether the change of a chip design will increase or decrease the proportion of defective chips. Thus, quality control procedures are installed to detect any change that has occurred in the population proportion of defectives being produced. Once data has been obtained from sampling the production line, the next step is to formulate a hypothesis test. The null hypothesis would state no change, that is, $H_o: p = p_o$, where p is the true proportion of defective chips and p_o is the hypothesis value when no change occurs. The alternative hypothesis would claim any change from p_o, that is, $H_A: p \neq p_o$. The alternative hypothesis indicates that a two-sided hypothesis test will be conducted since it states a change in either direction.

Suppose the current production line of semiconductor chips for a certain type of computer is showing an average rate of 1% defectives. A new design developed by the company's engineers would greatly increase the memory capacity of the chip and permit the chip to perform more complex functions. A pilot production line for the new design is set up and put into operation. After 1 week, a random sample of 600 chips are examined for defects and 2 of the 600 chips are defective. Can we say that there has been a change in the average percentage of defectives produced? Use a level of significance of .02.

Statistical Solution

Step 1

Set up H_o and H_A: First, state H_o. In this example, H_o can be stated to reflect the assumption of "no change," where "no change" means that the proportion p of defectives for the new design chips remains the same as for the old design chips. In this case, $H_o: p = .01$ since the value of $p_o = .01$ is the proportion of defective chips associated with the old design.

Now state H_A: Usually, H_A reflects the investigator's concern. In this example, the investigator is concerned that some change in the proportion of defective chips has occurred. Of course, the investigator is hopeful that there will not be a significant increase in the proportion of defectives with the new design and would be delighted to find a decrease in the proportion of defectives with the new design. In either case, however, the investigator needs to be aware of the change. The concern about change in this case is expressed by writing $H_A: p \neq .01$.

In summary, we can write

$$H_o: p = .01 \quad \text{(No change in defective proportion)}$$
$$H_A: p \neq .01 \quad \text{(A real change in defective proportion)}$$

Step 2

Select a level of significance: In this case, $\alpha = .02$.

Step 3

Specify the sample size: The sample size is $n = 600$.

Step 4

Determine the appropriateness of using the normal distribution approximation to the binomial distribution: If appropriate, we'll use a test statistic based on the normal approximation to the binomial. Since $n = 600$, $np_o = 600(.01) = 6$, and $n(1 - p_o) = 600(.99) = 594$, the approximating conditions are met. Using the normal distribution approximation to the binomial distribution, we get the test statistic

$$Z = \frac{\hat{p} - .01}{\sqrt{\dfrac{(.01)(.99)}{600}}}$$

Step 5

Determine the rejection region: Define the rejection region in terms of the test statistic. Since α has been specified as .02, the upper and lower tail areas will each equal $\alpha/2$, or .01. Then, using the standard normal probability table (Appendix Table IV), we find the value of Z_α that satisfies $P(Z > +Z_{\alpha/2}) = .01$ is 2.326. Then, since $P(Z < -2.326) = P(Z > +2.326) = .01$, the rejection region is

$$Z = \frac{\hat{p} - .01}{\sqrt{\dfrac{(.01)(.99)}{600}}} < -2.326 \quad \text{or} \quad Z = \frac{\hat{p} - .01}{\sqrt{\dfrac{(.01)(.99)}{600}}} > +2.326$$

Note that a Type I error results if we reach the mistaken conclusion that there is a change in percentage of defectives with the new design when in fact there is no change. On the other hand, a Type II error results if we reach the mistaken conclusion that there is no change in the percentage of defectives with the new design when in fact there is a change.

Step 6

Determine the value of the sample statistic, $\hat{p}$: The observed value of $\hat{p}$ is $\frac{2}{600} = .00333$.

Step 7

Determine the value of the test statistic and apply the decision rule: Substituting .00333 for $\hat{p}$ in the expression for the test statistic yields

$$Z = \frac{.00333 - .01}{\sqrt{\dfrac{(.01)(.99)}{600}}} = -1.64$$

Since this value is not less than -2.326 (nor, of course, greater than $+2.326$), the calculated Z value doesn't fall in the rejection region. Therefore, H_o cannot be rejected.

Practical Interpretation

The conclusion, at the .02 level of significance, is that the changes introduced into the pilot production line have not discernibly changed the proportion of defective chips being produced. That is, the difference between the sample proportion defective rate of .00333 and the previously established defective rate of .01 is not statistically significant. Thus, it would appear that the company could go into production of the new, more powerful chip without an effective change in the rate of defectives produced. Although the mean defective rate did not decrease as the company hoped, it did not increase, and this is encouraging.

PRACTICE EXERCISES

8.34 Suppose we wish to test, with $\alpha = .05$, the hypothesis that 30% of the gamblers in Las Vegas win at the roulette table versus the alternative that this value is incorrect. Assume that a normal approximation to the binomial distribution is appropriate. Then we have

$$H_o: \quad p = .30$$
$$H_A: \quad p \neq .30$$

Give the rejection region.

8.35 Suppose we wish to test, with $\alpha = .01$, the hypothesis that 54% of all the automobiles that travel the Los Angeles freeways exceed the speed limit versus the alternative that this value is not true. Suppose also that we see 60 speeders in a random sample of 100 cars on the Los Angeles freeways. Then we have

$$H_o: \quad p = .54$$
$$H_A: \quad p \neq .54$$

with $n = 100$ and $X = 60$. Should we reject H_o?

SUMMARY OF HYPOTHESIS TESTS FOR ONE PROPORTION

When the normal distribution approximation to the binomial distribution is appropriate, the test statistic to use is

$$Z = \frac{\hat{p} - p_o}{\sqrt{\dfrac{p_o(1 - p_o)}{n}}}$$

where p_o is the hypothesized value for p in H_o. A summary of the three possible alternative hypotheses, and the corresponding nonrejection and rejection regions, is given in Table 8.4.

TABLE 8.4 A Summary Table for Testing an Hypothesis Concerning One Proportion		
H_A	**Do not reject H_o if**	**Reject H_o if**
$p > p_o$	Calculated Z value $\leq +Z_\alpha$	Calculated Z value $> +Z_\alpha$
$p < p_o$	Calculated Z value $\geq -Z_\alpha$	Calculated Z value $< -Z_\alpha$
$p \neq p_o$	$-Z_{\alpha/2} \leq$ Calculated Z value $\leq +Z_{\alpha/2}$	Calculated Z value $< -Z_{\alpha/2}$ or: Calculated Z value $> +Z_{\alpha/2}$

In each of the above three cases, the calculated Z value is obtained by substituting the observed (sample) value of $\hat{p}$ in the expression for the test statistic given by

$$Z = \frac{\hat{p} - p_o}{\sqrt{\frac{p_o(1 - p_o)}{n}}}$$

EXERCISES

8.18 A chain photo service claims that only 3% of its customers complain about the prints they get from the rolls of film they bring in for developing and printing. Suppose we interpret this claim to mean, "Not more than 3% of the customers complain." Use a level of significance of .025 to test this claim. Use the sample result of 5 complaints out of 196 randomly selected customers.

▶ **8.19** The Interstate Savings Institution claims that 94% of its depositors have both a savings account and a checking account with the institution. Suppose we interpret this claim to mean, "At least 94% of the depositors have both types of account." Use a level of significance of .05 to test this claim using the sample result of 226 depositors with both types of account, out of 234 randomly selected customers.

8.20 A compact disk (CD) club intends to send out mailers advertising 4 free CDs for joining, with the obligation of buying two additional CDs at regular club prices in the first year of membership. The company claims that it can make a profit if there is more than a 6% response by joining. But before the company embarks on a full-fledged mailing, it sends mailers to 350 randomly selected names from the mailing list it plans to use. If 22 people respond by joining, should the club consider this significant evidence that it can make a profit with such an advertising campaign? Use the .01 level of significance.

8.21 In a recent U.S. Supreme Court decision, the Court ruled that employees do not have to prove intentional bias in hiring and promotions decisions. Rather, an employee only needs to provide statistical evidence of underrepresentation of minority groups and women. Suppose a demographic study of all law school graduates in the past 10 years shows that 30% of the graduates were women. Now suppose a random sample of 400 law firm members (from throughout the United States) hired in the past 10 years shows 90 women among the 400. Does this provide statistical evidence of underrepresentation of women hired by law firms in the past 10 years? Use the .01 level of significance.

8.22 California winemakers claim that 70% of all wine consumed in the United States comes from California vineyards. In a survey across the nation, 530 randomly selected wine purchases showed 380 purchases of wine from California vineyards. At the .05 level of significance is there sufficient reason to doubt the California winemakers' claim?

8.23 Find the *p*-value for the results in:
   a. Exercise 8.18
   b. Exercise 8.19
   c. Exercise 8.20
   d. Exercise 8.21

8.24 Suppose that a federal food consumer agency has a rule that if a very large lot of fish stick packages has more than 5% of its packages adulterated with more than 100 parts per million (ppm) of insect parts and mouse waste, the entire lot should be scrapped. With respect to one very large lot of fish sticks, a federal inspector takes a random sample of 64 packages and finds 5 packages with more than 100 ppm in insect parts and mouse waste. Is this sufficient evidence to reject the lot? Use a level of significance of .01.

▶ **8.25** A pharmaceutical firm claims that a new drug can relieve the symptoms of flu without any undesirable side effects at least 98% of the time it is used in treating these symptoms. In a random sample of 225 subjects suffering the symptoms of flu, 217 showed relief without undesirable side effects. Is there sufficient evidence to reject the manufacturer's claim? Use a level of significance of .05. What is the *p*-value in this case?

8.26 A purchaser of drive belts for tape recorders is informed by a representative of manufacturer A that more than 97% of manufacturer A's drive belts will last 10,500 hr or more in constant use. Is there significant evidence, using a level of significance of .01, to support the representative's claim if 138 out of a random sample of 144 drive belts last at least 10,500 hr?

● ●

8.4

TEST OF HYPOTHESIS: TWO POPULATION MEANS (INDEPENDENT SAMPLES)

This section presents the procedure and the rationale of testing hypotheses concerning differences between two population means. The hypothesis testing procedure draws from the confidence interval procedures given in Section 7.5 of Chapter 7.

For a one-sided test of hypothesis we have:

$$H_o: \quad \mu_1 = \mu_2 \qquad \text{or equivalently} \qquad H_o: \quad \mu_1 - \mu_2 = 0$$
$$H_A: \quad \mu_1 < \mu_2 \qquad \text{or equivalently} \qquad H_A: \quad \mu_1 - \mu_2 < 0$$

or we have

$$H_o: \quad \mu_1 = \mu_2 \qquad \text{or equivalently} \qquad H_o: \quad \mu_1 - \mu_2 = 0$$
$$H_A: \quad \mu_1 > \mu_2 \qquad \text{or equivalently} \qquad H_A: \quad \mu_1 - \mu_2 > 0$$

where μ_1 represents the mean for the first population, and μ_2 represents the mean for the second population. The choice of first and second is arbitrary. However, the form of H_A must be in accordance with what the investigator seeks to prove if H_o is rejected.

For a two-sided test of hypothesis we have

$$H_o: \quad \mu_1 = \mu_2 \qquad \text{or equivalently} \qquad H_o: \quad \mu_1 - \mu_2 = 0$$
$$H_A: \quad \mu_1 \neq \mu_2 \qquad \text{or equivalently} \qquad H_A: \quad \mu_1 - \mu_2 \neq 0$$

To appropriately test hypotheses about two means, two basic questions must be resolved:

1. Are the values of the population variances known, or unknown? There are three cases:

   Case 1: The values of σ_1 and σ_2 are both known.

   Case 2: The values of σ_1 and σ_2 are assumed to be equal, but the common value is unknown.

   Case 3: The values of σ_1 and σ_2 are not equal, but their values are unknown.

   These three cases lead to different denominators in the expression for the test statistic.

2. May we legitimately assume sampling from either normally distributed or approximately normally distributed populations when the sample sizes are small? For large samples the test statistic is almost always the standard Z statistic, but for small samples the appropriate test statistic would be either the Z statistic or the t statistic only if the sampling is from a normally distributed or approximately normally distributed population.

   For all the cases discussed we will use the following standard notation:

   μ_1 and σ_1 represent the mean and standard deviation, respectively, for the first population;

   μ_2 and σ_2 represent the mean and standard deviation, respectively, for the second population;

   $\bar{X}_1$ and S_1 represent the sample point estimates of μ_1 and σ_1, respectively;

   $\bar{X}_2$ and S_2 represent the sample point estimates of μ_2 and σ_2, respectively;

   n_1 represents the size of the random sample taken from the first population, and n_2 represents the size of the random sample taken from the second population.

CASE 1: WHEN THE VALUES OF σ_1 AND σ_2 ARE BOTH KNOWN

When both populations are normally distributed and the population variances are known, then regardless of sample size, the test statistic will be distributed as a standard normal distribution. Assuming the null hypothesis is true so that H_o: $\mu_1 = \mu_2$ and substituting its equivalent expression, $\mu_1 - \mu_2 = 0$, into the Z statistic represented in Section 7.5 of Chapter 7, we obtain the following test statistic:

Test Statistic for Two Population Means:
Both Population Variances Known

$$Z = \frac{\bar{X}_1 - \bar{X}_2}{\sqrt{\dfrac{\sigma_1^2}{n_1} + \dfrac{\sigma_2^2}{n_2}}} \tag{8-14}$$

For the one-sided test in which H_A: $\mu_1 < \mu_2$, the rejection region is given by

$$Z < -Z_\alpha$$

For the one-sided test in which H_A: $\mu_1 > \mu_2$, the rejection region is given by

$$Z > +Z_\alpha$$

For the two-sided test in which H_A: $\mu_1 \neq \mu_2$, the rejection is given by

$$Z < -Z_{\alpha/2} \quad \text{or} \quad Z > +Z_{\alpha/2}$$

The following example illustrates the use of these formulas in a two-sided hypothesis test.

■ **EXAMPLE 8.6**

Pitch Characteristic of a Stretched Wire

If a wire is stretched between two clamps to a specified tension and then struck at its center, it will produce a note, or pitch, that can be measured in vibrations per second. Prior pitch experimentation indicates pitch measurements are normally distributed with a standard deviation of 2 vibrations per second. A manufacturer of wire for musical instruments is interested in using a wire made from a new material but wants assurance that the new type of wire has the same pitch characteristic as that of the wire currently being used. A random sample of 17 wires of the new type and a random sample of 23 wires of the current type are taken. Pitch measurements are independently made on the 40 wires. The mean for the 17 new type of wires is 41.86 vibrations per second, and the mean for the 23 current type of wires is 40.93 vibrations per second. Comparing the two populations from which the samples were drawn at the .05 level of significance, is there a significant difference in pitch between the two types of wire?

Statistical Solution

Step 1
Set up H_o and H_A: First, state H_o. H_o reflects the assumption of no difference in pitch between the new type of wire and the current type of wire. This is symbolized by H_o: $\mu_1 = \mu_2$.

Now, state H_A. H_A reflects the manufacturer's concern that the pitch of the new type of wire is different from that of the current type of wire. This is symbolized by H_A: $\mu_1 \neq \mu_2$.

In summary, we can write

$$H_o: \quad \mu_1 = \mu_2 \quad \text{(No difference in pitch exists.)}$$
$$H_A: \quad \mu_1 \neq \mu_2 \quad \text{(There is a real difference in pitch.)}$$

Step 2
Determine the level of significance: The problem sets α at .05.

Step 3
Determine the values of σ_1 and σ_2: The value of the standard deviation given may be understood as the population value gained from prior experience. This means that the population standard deviation σ_1 of pitch measurements of the new wire is the same as the population standard deviation σ_2 of the current type of wire. That is, the population standard deviations are $\sigma_1 = \sigma_2 = 2$.

Step 4
Determine the sample sizes: The example states that $n_1 = 17$ for the new type and $n_2 = 23$ for the current type.

Step 5
Determine the applicability of the standard normal distribution: Prior experience with pitch measurements indicates that they are normally distributed. This, together with the known values of σ_1 and σ_2, means that we can validly use a form of the standard Z statistic.

Step 6
Write the expression for the test statistic: The test statistic is

$$Z = \frac{\bar{X}_1 - \bar{X}_2}{\sqrt{\dfrac{4}{17} + \dfrac{4}{23}}}$$

Step 7
Determine the rejection region: Since H_A is stated by $\mu_1 \neq \mu_2$, this test is two-sided. The rejection region therefore is given by

$$Z < -Z_{.025} = -1.96 \quad \text{or} \quad Z > +Z_{.025} = +1.96$$

Notice that $Z_{\alpha/2} = Z_{.025}$ is the appropriate value to use rather than $Z_\alpha = Z_{.05}$.

Step 8
Determine the values of the sample statistics $\bar{X}_1$ and $\bar{X}_2$: The example states that $\bar{X}_1 = 41.86$ for the new wire and $\bar{X}_2 = 40.93$ for the current type.

Step 9
Calculate the value of the test statistic and apply the decision rule: The observed value of the test statistic is

$$Z = \frac{41.86 - 40.93}{\sqrt{\dfrac{4}{17} + \dfrac{4}{23}}}$$

$$= 1.45$$

Since the observed value of 1.45 is less than 1.96 and greater than -1.96, it does not lie in the rejection region, so we cannot reject H_o.

Step 10
Calculate the p-value: For this two-sided test the p-value is

$$P(Z < -1.45) + P(Z > +1.45) = 2(.0735) = .147$$

The probability is large enough to claim that the observed sample mean difference is due to sampling variation.

Practical Interpretation

At the .05 level of significance we conclude that there is not a statistically significant difference in pitch between the two types of wire. That is, the new type of wire appears to have the same pitch characteristic as that of the current type of wire. If the new type is cheaper to make but just as durable as the current type, then the manufacturer can make a greater profit by switching. However, if the manufacturer makes the switch because of this test result and if our test result is the consequence of a Type II error, then the manufacturer could end up with a large group of disgruntled musicians whose instruments are not "true." This is a risk the manufacturer must consider.

● ●

PRACTICE EXERCISE

8.36 Suppose we wish to test whether or not the rate of growth in the economies of cities in the eastern part of the United States is currently equal to that of cities in the western part of the United States. Assume it is known from past experience that the variability among western cities has been fairly close to $\sigma_1^2 = 121$ for the past 80 years, and the variability among eastern cities has been fairly close to $\sigma_2^2 = 81$ over the same period. Suppose we randomly select 9 western cities and 16 eastern cities, and determine their growth rates. And suppose we use $\alpha = .05$, $\sigma_1^2 = 121$, and $\sigma_2^2 = 81$.

a. Using the two-sided alternative,

$$H_o: \quad \mu_1 = \mu_2$$
$$H_A: \quad \mu_1 \neq \mu_2$$

What would be our rejection region?

b. If we use a one-sided alternative,

$$H_o: \quad \mu_1 = \mu_2$$
$$H_A: \quad \mu_1 < \mu_2$$

where μ_1 represents the average growth rate of western cities and μ_2 represents the average growth rate of eastern cities, what would be our rejection region?

c. If we use the following one-sided alternative:

$$H_o: \quad \mu_1 = \mu_2$$
$$H_A: \quad \mu_1 < \mu_2$$

where μ_1 represents the average growth rate of eastern cities and μ_2 represents the average growth rate of western cities, what would be our rejection region?

● ●

CASE 2: WHEN THE VALUES OF σ_1 AND σ_2 ARE UNKNOWN, BUT PRESUMED EQUAL

In this section we will presume the two population standard deviations are equal but unknown, and use the sample standard deviations S_1 and S_2 as substitutes for σ_1 and σ_2, respectively. By presuming $\sigma_1 = \sigma_2$ it follows that S_1 and S_2 are both estimates of the same value and can be pooled into a single estimate. We denote the pooled estimate as S_p (as in Section 7.5) and define it as follows:

Pooled Estimate of σ

$$S_p = \sqrt{\frac{(n_1 - 1)S_1^2 + (n_2 - 1)S_2^2}{n_1 + n_2 - 2}} \qquad (8\text{-}15)$$

Using S_p as a substitute for both σ_1 and σ_2, and assuming the populations are normal or approximately normal, we will now discuss the appropriate procedure to use when we have (1) a large sample and (2) a small sample.

Large Samples

When $n_1 + n_2 - 2 > 30$, the samples are considered large and the appropriate test statistic is the Z statistic defined as follows:

Test Statistic for Two Population Means, Both Population Variances Unknown, but Presumed Equal: Large Samples

$$Z = \frac{\bar{X}_1 - \bar{X}_2}{\sqrt{\dfrac{S_P^2}{n_1} + \dfrac{S_P^2}{n_2}}} = \frac{\bar{X}_1 - \bar{X}_2}{S_P \sqrt{\dfrac{1}{n_1} + \dfrac{1}{n_2}}} \qquad (8\text{-}16)$$

Once again the equivalency of H_o: $\mu_1 = \mu_2$ and H_o: $\mu_1 - \mu_2 = 0$ has been used to simplify the Z test statistic.

The rejection regions depend on whether a one-sided test or a two-sided test is being conducted. For a one-sided test with H_A: $\mu_1 < \mu_2$, the rejection region is given by

$$Z < -Z_\alpha$$

For a one-sided test with H_A: $\mu_1 > \mu_2$, the rejection region is given by

$$Z > +Z_\alpha$$

For a two-sided test, the rejection region is given by

$$Z < -Z_{\alpha/2} \qquad \text{or} \qquad Z > +Z_{\alpha/2}$$

Example 8.7 provides an illustration of a situation in which a hypothesis test using these formulas can help clarify an issue.

■ **EXAMPLE 8.7**

SAT Scores

Scholastic Aptitude Test (SAT) scores are often used to award student scholarships. A high score can be worth as much as $40,000 in financial aid to a student over a 4 year period. As a result, SAT preparation classes have sprung up throughout the country, advertising that they can properly prepare a student to take the test. Additionally, the claim these preparation classes make is that the average SAT score for their properly prepared students is a higher (variances unchanged) average than that for students who are not properly prepared. To test the claim, a group of educators takes a random sample of 50 SAT scores of students from SAT preparation classes, and independently takes a random sample of 50 students who had no such preparation. The mean and standard deviation of the SAT scores for the prepared students are 601 and 120, respectively; and the mean and standard deviation for the nonprepared students are 533 and 115, respectively. At the .05 level of significance, does this indicate a significantly higher average score for the students who are prepared for the SAT exam? Assume that SAT scores are normally distributed.

Statistical Solution

Step 1

Set up H_o and H_A: First, state H_o. H_o reflects the assumption of no difference in average SAT scores between students who have gone through SAT preparation classes and students who have not. This is symbolized by H_o: $\mu_1 = \mu_2$.

Now state H_A. H_A reflects the claim that SAT scores are higher for students who participate in SAT preparation classes. Suppose we select μ_2 to represent the average SAT scores for students with SAT preparation classes and μ_1 to represent the average SAT scores for students with no preparation classes, then the alternative hypothesis is stated as H_A: $\mu_1 < \mu_2$.

In summary, we can write

$$H_o: \quad \mu_1 = \mu_2 \quad \text{(No difference in mean SAT scores)}$$

$$H_A: \quad \mu_1 < \mu_2 \quad \text{(Higher mean SAT score for prepared students)}$$

Step 2
Determine the level of significance: This is set in the problem at $\alpha = .05$.

Step 3
Determine the values of σ_1 and σ_2: The problem statement, "No change in the variances" suggests that the two variances are equal, that is, $\sigma_1^2 = \sigma_2^2$ and $\sigma_1 = \sigma_2$. But since both σ_1 and σ_2 are unknown, we pool S_1 and S_2, the two sample standard deviation values given to get a single estimate, S_p, of the common standard deviation.

Step 4
Determine the sample sizes: Both n_1 and $n_2 = 50$.

Step 5
Determine the applicability of the normal distribution: The example states that we should assume SAT scores are normally distributed.

Step 6
Write the expression for the test statistic: The values for σ_1 and σ_2 are unknown, but assumed equal. With $n_1 + n_2 - 2 = 98 > 30$, the sample size is large. Given these conditions, the test statistic can be expressed as a Z statistic as follows:

$$Z = \frac{\bar{X}_1 - \bar{X}_2}{S_p\sqrt{\dfrac{1}{50} + \dfrac{1}{50}}}$$

Step 7
Determine the rejection region: The rejection region is given by $Z < -Z_{.05} = -1.645$.

Step 8
Determine the values of the sample statistics S_p, $\bar{X}_1$, and $\bar{X}_2$: Calculate the pooled sample standard deviation, S_p,

$$S_p = \sqrt{\frac{49(115)^2 + 49(120)^2}{50 + 50 - 2}}$$

$$= 117.527$$

and determine the values for $\bar{X}_1$ and $\bar{X}_2$:

$$\bar{X}_1 = 533 \quad \text{For the nonprepared students}$$

$$\bar{X}_2 = 601 \quad \text{For the prepared students}$$

Step 9

Determine the value of the test statistic and apply the decision rule: The calculated value of the test statistic is

$$Z = \frac{533 - 601}{117.527 \sqrt{\frac{1}{50} + \frac{1}{50}}}$$

$$= -2.89$$

The calculated Z statistic of -2.89 is less than -1.645, so it lies in the rejection region, and we reject H_o of no improvement.

Step 10

Calculate the p-value: The p-value is $P(Z < -2.89) = .0019$. The extremely low probability shows that the result is highly statistically significant. That is, such an observed difference is very unlikely if H_o is true.

Practical Interpretation

At the .05 level of significance we conclude that the prepared student SAT scores are statistically significantly higher than the scores for the nonprepared students. But the actual magnitude of the difference in the average scores may or may not have practical significance. Practical significance would be achieved if the difference brings the student into the range of scores that would receive financial aid or permit the student to gain admission into a school of choice. Practical significance does not follow automatically from statistical significance. Note also that it would be inadvisable to conclude that the preparation, in effect, improved the scores. It is possible that the students who elect to go through SAT preparatory classes have many more other advantages, including greater innate ability, than those who elect not to go through the preparatory classes. This line of reasoning suggests that the two populations of students could be very different from the beginning, and that the observed difference in their SAT score averages simply may reflect initial advantages one group has over the other.

PRACTICE EXERCISE

8.37 Suppose we wish to compare the average cost of buying a home in San Diego with the average cost of buying a home in Chicago. Assume that the variability in purchase costs are the same for both cities. That is, assume that $\sigma_1^2 = \sigma_2^2$. We randomly select 160 recent purchases in San Diego and 170 recent purchases in Chicago and record their sales prices. We find sample variances of $S_1^2 = 121$ for San Diego and $S_1^2 = 81$ for Chicago. Use $\alpha = .05$.

a. If we use a two-sided alternative,

$$H_o: \mu_1 = \mu_2$$
$$H_A: \mu_1 \neq \mu_2$$

what would be our rejection region?

b. Using a one-sided test,

$$H_o: \mu_1 = \mu_2$$
$$H_A: \mu_1 < \mu_2$$

where μ_1 represents the average purchase price in San Diego and μ_2 represents the average purchase price in Chicago, what would be our rejection region?

c. Using a one-sided test,

$$H_o: \mu_1 = \mu_2$$
$$H_A: \mu_1 > \mu_2$$

where μ_1 represents the average purchase price in San Diego and μ_2 represents the average purchase price in Chicago, what would be our rejection region?

Small Samples

When $n_1 + n_2 - 2 \leq 30$, the samples are considered small and the appropriate test statistic is the Student t statistic defined as follows:

Test Statistic for Two Population Means, Both Population Variances Unknown, but Presumed Equal: Small Samples

$$t_\nu = \frac{\bar{X}_1 - \bar{X}_2}{\sqrt{\frac{S_p^2}{n_1} + \frac{S_p^2}{n_2}}} = \frac{\bar{X}_1 - \bar{X}_2}{S_p \sqrt{\frac{1}{n_1} + \frac{1}{n_2}}} \tag{8-17}$$

The number of degrees of freedom for the Student t statistic is $\nu = n_1 + n_2 - 2$. Again assuming H_o is true, the equivalency of $H_o: \mu_1 = \mu_2$ and $H_o: \mu_1 - \mu_2 = 0$ is used to simplify the t_ν statistic. The rejection region for the one-sided test with $H_A: \mu_1 < \mu_2$ is given by

$$t_\nu < -t_{(\alpha, \nu)}$$

The rejection region for the one-sided test with $H_A: \mu_1 > \mu_2$ is given by

$$t_\nu > +t_{(\alpha, \nu)}$$

The rejection region for the two-sided test is given by

$$t_\nu < -t_{(\alpha/2, \nu)} \qquad \text{or} \qquad t_\nu > +t_{(\alpha/2, \nu)}$$

The following example demonstrates how the hypothesis testing procedure using these formulas helps resolve an issue.

■ **EXAMPLE 8.8**

Warm-up Exercises

Warm-up exercises are recommended to those individuals who run to maintain their health. Generally, it takes about 20 min of warm-up exercises to increase the range of motion of the various muscles used in running. Since some runners frequently experience interruptions in their routine, there is the question as to whether or not it is necessary to repeat the warm-up exercises after an interruption. A research group studied the length of time it takes a healthy male to lose the increase in the range of motion after a 20 min warm-up. Two different types of warm-up exercises were tried— a 20 min warm-up on an exercise bicycle and a 20 min warm-up of stretching and isometric exercises—and 10 healthy males were assigned to each type. The 10 healthy males who warmed up on an exercise bicycle took an average of 81 min, with a standard deviation of 8 min, to lose the increase in the range of motion. The 10 healthy males who warmed up with stretching and isometric exercises took an average of 98 min, with a standard deviation of 9 min, to lose the increase in the range of motion. At the .05 level of significance, is there a significant difference in the average time it takes to lose the increase in the range of motion associated with the two warm-up methods? Assume the time measurements are normally distributed and the population standard deviations for the two groups are equal.

Statistical Solution

Step 1

Set up H_o and H_A: First, state H_o. H_o reflects the assumption that there is no difference between the two types of warm-up exercises in the length of time it takes to lose the increase in range of motion. This is symbolized by H_o: $\mu_1 = \mu_2$.

Now state H_A. H_A reflects the investigator's concern that there may be a difference. It would be important to know about such a difference regardless of its direction, so the test is two-sided. This is symbolized by H_A: $\mu_1 \neq \mu_2$.

In summary, we write

$$H_o: \quad \mu_1 = \mu_2 \quad \text{(There is no difference between the two populations in mean time.)}$$

$$H_A: \quad \mu_1 \neq \mu_2 \quad \text{(There is a difference in mean time.)}$$

Step 2

Choose the level of significance: The problem sets α at .05.

Step 3

Determine the values of σ_1 and σ_2: In this example, only the sample standard deviations are given; the example states that the two population standard deviations can be assumed equal, that is, $\sigma_1 = \sigma_2$. But both σ_1 and σ_2 are unknown values. By pooling the two given sample standard deviations, we get a single estimate, S_p, of the common standard deviation value.

Step 4

Determine the sample sizes: The example states that $n_1 = n_2 = 10$.

Step 5

Determine the applicability of an appropriate test statistic: The example tells us to assume that time measurements are normally distributed, so either the Z distribution or the t distribution will be appropriate, depending on sample size and whether the values of both σ_1 and σ_2 are known. The values for σ_1 and σ_2 are unknown. With $n_1 + n_2 - 2 = 18 < 30$, the sample size is small. Under these conditions it is appropriate to formulate a Student t statistic with $n_1 + n_2 - 2 = 18$ d.f.

Step 6

Write the expression for the test statistic: The test statistic is

$$t_{18} = \frac{\bar{X}_1 - \bar{X}_2}{S_p \sqrt{\dfrac{1}{10} + \dfrac{1}{10}}}$$

Step 7

Determine the rejection region: The rejection region for rejecting H_o is given by

$$t_{18} < -t_{(.025,18)} = -2.101 \qquad \text{or} \qquad t_{18} > +t_{(.025,18)} = +2.101$$

Step 8

Determine the values of the sample statistics S_p, $\bar{X}_1$, and $\bar{X}_2$: Calculate the pooled standard deviation, S_p,

$$S_p = \sqrt{\frac{9(8)^2 + 9(9)^2}{10 + 10 - 2}}$$

$$= 8.5147$$

and determine the values for $\bar{X}_1$ and $\bar{X}_2$:

$$\bar{X}_1 = 81 \quad \text{For the exercise bicycle}$$
$$\bar{X}_2 = 98 \quad \text{For the stretching and isometric exercises}$$

Step 9

Determine the value of the test statistic and apply the decision rule: The computed t value of the test statistic is

$$t_{18} = \frac{81 - 98}{8.5147 \sqrt{\frac{1}{10} + \frac{1}{10}}}$$

$$= -4.464$$

Since the calculated value of the test statistic of -4.464 lies in the rejection region $t_{18} < -2.101$, the null hypothesis H_o of no difference is rejected.

Step 10

Calculate the p-value: The p-value is $P(|t_{18}| > 4.464) = 2P(t_{18} > 4.464)$. An exact evaluation of the probability requires a more complete table than provided in this book. Nevertheless, looking at the t table value, we can see that the p-value must be less than $2(.005)$. Thus, the result is highly statistically significant.

Practical Interpretation

At the .05 level of significance we conclude that the difference between the averages for the time measurements is statistically significant for the two warm-up methods. The males who warmed up with stretching and isometric exercises maintained an increase in range of motion longer than the males who warmed up on an exercise bicycle. However, since both groups maintained the increased range for more than an hour, there would be no practical significance to the difference between both groups if interruptions generally last less than an hour.

Comparing the last statement in Step 9 of Example 8.8 with the practical interpretation illustrates the distinction between our finding of a statistically significant difference and the practical implications of that difference. Finding a statistically significant difference cannot foretell whether that difference is enough to have any practical importance.

● ●

PRACTICE EXERCISE

8.38 We wish to compare the average price of unleaded regular gasoline in Boston with the average price of unleaded gasoline in Dallas. The price of unleaded regular gasoline at 9 randomly selected gas stations in Boston has a variance of $S_1^2 = 196$, and the price of unleaded in regular gasoline at 16 randomly selected gas stations in Dallas has a variance of $S_2^2 = 100$. Assume $\sigma_1^2 = \sigma_2^2$, and use $\alpha = .05$.

a. Use the two-sided test:

$$H_o: \quad \mu_1 = \mu_2 \quad \text{(The average price is the same in both cities.)}$$
$$H_A: \quad \mu_1 \neq \mu_2 \quad \text{(The average price is not the same in both cities.)}$$

What is the rejection region?

b. Using a one-sided test,

$$H_o: \quad \mu_1 = \mu_2$$
$$H_A: \quad \mu_1 < \mu_2$$

where μ_1 represents the average price in Boston and μ_2 represents the average price in Dallas), what is the rejection region?

c. Using a one-sided test,

$$H_o: \quad \mu_1 = \mu_2$$
$$H_A: \quad \mu_1 > \mu_2$$

where μ_1 represents the average price in Boston and μ_2 represents the average price in Dallas), what is the rejection region?

● ●

CASE 3: WHEN THE VALUES OF σ_1 AND σ_2 ARE UNKNOWN, BUT PRESUMED UNEQUAL

In this section we will assume that both populations are normally distributed, and that the values for the population standard deviations are unknown as in Case 2. However, we will also assume that the two population standard deviations cannot validly be presumed equal. The sample standard deviations S_1 and S_2 will serve as substitutes for σ_1 and σ_2, respectively. Two situations must be distinguished, one for large samples and one for small samples.

Large Samples

When $n_1 \geq 30$ and $n_2 \geq 30$, the samples are considered large and the following Z test statistic can be used:

Test Statistic for Two Population Means, Both Population Variances Unknown, but Presumed Unequal: Large Samples

$$Z = \frac{\bar{X}_1 - \bar{X}_2}{\sqrt{\dfrac{S_1^2}{n_1} + \dfrac{S_2^2}{n_2}}} \tag{8-18}$$

Since $H_o: \mu_1 = \mu_2$ is equivalent to $H_o: \mu_1 - \mu_2 = 0$, the Z statistic again incorporates the use of $\mu_1 - \mu_2 = 0$.

The rejection region for the one-sided test with H_A: $\mu_1 < \mu_2$ is given by

$$Z < -Z_\alpha$$

The rejection region for the one-sided test with H_A: $\mu_1 > \mu_2$ is given by

$$Z > +Z_\alpha$$

The rejection region for the two-sided test is given by

$$Z < -Z_{\alpha/2} \quad \text{or} \quad Z > +Z_{\alpha/2}$$

Let's now consider an application of these formulas in a hypothesis testing situation.

■ **EXAMPLE 8.9**

Ethnic Responses to Perfumes

A cosmetic firm conducted an experiment in its testing lab to determine ethnic differences in responses to concentrations of a specific perfume. Thirty-four members of one ethnic group and 37 members of a second ethnic group were independently exposed to increasing concentrations of the perfume until a reaction of pleasure was noted. The 34 members of the first ethnic group responded, on the average, to a concentration of 1.90 parts per million (ppm) with a standard deviation of 1.23 ppm. The 37 members of the second ethnic group responded, on the average, to a concentration of 1.95 ppm with a standard deviation of 0.54 ppm. At the .01 level of significance, is there a difference in response concentrations between the two ethnic groups? Assume the responses to concentrations are normally distributed. Prior experiences with such experiments have indicated different variabilities among different ethnic groups; hence, the population variances cannot validly be assumed equal.

Statistical Solution

Step 1
Set up H_o and H_A: First, state H_o. H_o reflects the assumption of no difference between the two ethnic groups in the average concentration eliciting a pleasurable response. This is symbolized by H_o: $\mu_1 = \mu_2$.
  Now state H_A. H_A reflects the search for a difference. This is symbolized by H_A: $\mu_1 \neq \mu_2$.
  In summary, we can write

H_o: $\mu_1 = \mu_2$ (Response concentrations are the same.)

H_A: $\mu_1 \neq \mu_2$ (Response concentrations are not the same.)

Step 2
Choose the level of significance: The problem sets $\alpha = .01$.

Step 3
Determine the values of σ_1 and σ_2: The example gives only the sample standard deviations and states that the population standard deviations cannot be assumed to be equal; this means we cannot set $\sigma_1 = \sigma_2$. The observed sample standard deviations S_1 and S_2 will be the estimates for the unknown and unequal values of σ_1 and σ_2.

Step 4
Determine the sample sizes: From the example we know that $n_1 = 34$ and $n_2 = 37$.

Step 5

Determine the applicability of an appropriate test statistic: The example tells us to assume that responses to concentrations are normally distributed. We don't know the values for σ_1 and σ_2, but we are told that they are not equal. We have $n_1 = 34 > 30$ and $n_2 = 37 > 30$. Under these conditions, a form of the standard normal Z statistic can be used.

Step 6

Write the expression for the test statistic: The test statistic is determined as

$$Z = \frac{\bar{X}_1 - \bar{X}_2}{\sqrt{\dfrac{S_1^2}{34} + \dfrac{S_2^2}{37}}}$$

Step 7

Determine the rejection region: The rejection region is defined by

$$Z < -2.576 \quad \text{or} \quad Z > +2.576$$

Step 8

Determine the values of the sample statistics: These are stated in the problem:

$$\bar{X}_1 = 1.90 \qquad \bar{X}_2 = 1.95$$
$$S_1 = 1.23 \qquad S_2 = 0.54$$

Step 9

Determine the value of the test statistic and apply the decision rule: The calculated value of Z is

$$Z = \frac{1.90 - 1.95}{\sqrt{\dfrac{(1.23)^2}{34} + \dfrac{(0.54)^2}{37}}}$$
$$= -0.218$$

Since the calculated Z value of -0.218 is not less than -2.576 (nor greater than $+2.576$), the calculated Z does not lie in the rejection region, and the null hypothesis of no difference is not rejected.

Step 10

Calculate the p-value: The p-value is $P(|Z| > 0.218) = 2(.4129) = .8258$, which is rather large. Thus, the observed difference is very likely the result of sampling variation, and we conclude that it is due to chance.

Practical Interpretation

At the .01 level of significance we conclude that there is no statistically discernible difference in response to the perfume concentrations. The experiment was part of an attempt to establish viable products for the two supposedly different market segments. But there was no such luck with this particular perfume.

PRACTICE EXERCISE

8.39 The cosmetic firm in Example 8.9 was also interested in determining whether there was a male versus female difference in response to the perfume. Assume that $\sigma_1^2 \neq \sigma_2^2$. The concentrations that elicited a response from 85 randomly selected men and 135 randomly selected women were recorded, and the respective sample variances were $S_1^2 = 5.43$ and $S_2^2 = 1.46$. Use $\alpha = .05$.

a. Using a two-sided test,

$$H_o: \quad \mu_1 = \mu_2$$
$$H_A: \quad \mu_1 \neq \mu_2$$

what would be our rejection region?

b. Using a one-sided test,

$$H_o: \quad \mu_1 = \mu_2$$
$$H_A: \quad \mu_1 > \mu_2$$

(where μ_1 represents the average response concentration of the men and μ_2 represents the average response concentration of the women), what would be our rejection region?

c. Using a one-sided alternative,

$$H_o: \quad \mu_1 = \mu_2$$
$$H_A: \quad \mu_1 < \mu_2$$

(where μ_1 represents the average response concentration of the men and μ_2 represents the average response concentration of the women), what would be our rejection region?

● ●

Small Samples

When either one (or both) of n_1 or n_2 is less than 30, we use the Student t statistic to test hypotheses for $\mu_1 - \mu_2$:

Test Statistic for Two Population Means, Both Population Variances Unkonwn, but Presumed Unequal: Small Samples

$$t_\nu = \frac{\bar{X}_1 - \bar{X}_2}{\sqrt{\dfrac{S_1^2}{n_1} + \dfrac{S_2^2}{n_2}}} \qquad (8\text{-}19)$$

where ν represents the number of degrees of freedom for the Student t statistic, and the value of ν is obtained either by using the smaller value of $n_1 - 1$ and $n_2 - 1$, or alternatively from the more complicated expression

$$\nu = \frac{\left(\dfrac{S_1^2}{n_1} + \dfrac{S_2^2}{n_2}\right)^2}{\dfrac{(S_1^2/n_1)^2}{n_1 - 1} + \dfrac{(S_2^2/n_2)^2}{n_2 - 1}} \qquad (8\text{-}20)$$

This expression generally does not yield an integer value; therefore, the value computed is rounded to the nearest integer according to the standard procedure for rounding. The choice of the smaller value of $n_1 - 1$ and $n_2 - 1$ is simpler and yields "conservative" results.

The test statistic reflects that H_0: $\mu_1 = \mu_2$ is equivalent to H_0: $\mu_1 - \mu_2 = 0$. The rejection region for the one-sided test with H_A: $\mu_1 < \mu_2$ is given by

$$t_\nu < -t_{(\alpha,\nu)}$$

The rejection region for the one-sided test with H_A: $\mu_1 > \mu_2$ is given by

$$t_\nu > +t_{(\alpha,\nu)}$$

The rejection region for the two-sided test is given by

$$t_\nu < -t_{(\alpha/2,\nu)} \qquad \text{or} \qquad t_\nu > +t_{(\alpha/2,\nu)}$$

The following application demonstrates the use of hypothesis testing with these formulas.

■ **EXAMPLE 8.10**

Optical Manufacturer's Eye Strain Research

The research department of a manufacturer of optical lenses is conducting experiments with color reversals to determine visual strain differences in men versus women. Seven groups of 4 men and five groups of 4 women were gathered to play bridge in separate, but equally esthetic, playing rooms. Ordinarily, bridge players are accustomed to a deck of 52 playing cards, 13 each of black-colored spades and clubs and 13 each of red-colored hearts and diamonds. Instead, the researchers gave each group of players a deck of playing cards with 13 each of red-colored spades and clubs and 13 each of black-colored hearts and diamonds. The players were asked to play bridge until one player in each foursome developed a headache. The length of time each foursome played before they had to quit was recorded. The seven groups of men averaged 1.49 hr, with a standard deviation of 0.22 hr, and the five groups of women averaged 2.34 hr with a standard deviation of 0.79 hr. Did the women play a significantly longer period of time than did the men? This one-sided question is the consequence of some initial theorizing (before the data were obtained) that women would adapt better to the color reversal than the men and, hence, be able to play longer. Assume playing times are normally distributed and use a level of significance of .01.

Statistical Solution

Step 1
Set up H_o and H_A: First, state H_o. H_o reflects the assumption that men and women have the same visual strain tolerances to color reversal in a deck of playing cards. This is symbolized by H_0: $\mu_{\text{men}} = \mu_{\text{women}}$, where the μ's represent the respective average playing times under stress conditions.

Now state H_A. H_A reflects the theorized assertion that there are different tolerances, with women having a greater resistance to visual strain induced by color reversal than men. This is symbolized by H_A: $\mu_{\text{men}} < \mu_{\text{women}}$.

Summarizing these considerations, we have

H_o: $\mu_{\text{men}} = \mu_{\text{women}}$ (Both playing times are, on average, the same.)

H_A: $\mu_{\text{men}} < \mu_{\text{women}}$ (Women, on average, play longer than men.)

Step 2
Choose the level of significance: This is stated in the problem as $\alpha = .01$.

Step 3
Determine the values of σ_1 and σ_2: The example provides no clue that the population standard deviations are equal, and we have no objective or theoretical

reasons to suppose they would be. Therefore, we must rely on the observed sample standard deviations S_1 and S_2 as estimates of the unequal and unknown values of σ_1 and σ_2.

Step 4

Determine the sample sizes: The example states that $n_{men} = 7$ and $n_{women} = 5$.

Step 5

Determine the applicability of an appropriate test statistic: Playing times are assumed normally distributed. The values for σ_1 and σ_2 are unknown and unequal. Both $n_{men} = 7$ and $n_{women} = 5$ are small. These conditions suggest that we can validly use a form of the Student t statistic.

Step 6

Write the expression for the test statistic: The test statistic is

$$t_\nu = \frac{\bar{X}_{men} - \bar{X}_{women}}{\sqrt{\dfrac{S_{men}^2}{7} + \dfrac{S_{women}^2}{5}}}$$

Step 7

Determine the rejection region: First, determine the number of degrees of freedom. Using the values as stated in the example,

$$S_{men} = 0.22 \qquad S_{women} = 0.79$$
$$n_{men} = 7 \qquad n_{women} = 5$$

ν equals the smaller of $7 - 1$ and $5 - 1$, so $\nu = 4$. Or, alternatively,

$$\nu = \frac{\left[\dfrac{(0.22)^2}{7} + \dfrac{(0.79)^2}{5} \right]^2}{\dfrac{\left[\dfrac{(0.22)^2}{7} \right]^2}{6} + \dfrac{\left[\dfrac{(0.79)^2}{5} \right]^2}{4}} = 4.45 \text{ (approx.)}$$

Since we must round to the nearest integer, the number of degrees of freedom we would use is $\nu = 4$.

The rejection region is given by $t_4 < -3.747$ (obtained from Appendix Table VII).

Step 8

Determine the values of $\bar{X}_{men}$ and $\bar{X}_{women}$: The example gives $\bar{X}_{men} = 1.49$ and $\bar{X}_{women} = 2.34$.

Step 9

Determine the value of the test statistic and apply the decision rule: The calculated value of the test statistic is

$$t_4 = \frac{1.49 - 2.34}{\sqrt{\dfrac{(0.22)^2}{7} + \dfrac{(0.79)^2}{5}}}$$
$$= -2.34$$

The calculated value of the test statistic, -2.34, is greater than the t value of -3.747. Therefore, it does not lie in the rejection region, and the null hypothesis of no difference cannot be rejected.

Step 10

Calculate the p-value: Since this is a one-sided test, the p-value is $P(t_4 < -2.34)$. To evaluate this probability requires a more extensive table than provided in this book. Nevertheless, it can be seen from Appendix Table VII that the p-value lies between .025 and .050. Notice that the relatively small size of the p-value alerts us to possibly reaching the conclusion that the difference is a departure from chance. For example, if a level of significance of .050 had originally been chosen, we would be rejecting H_o instead of not rejecting it. A more appropriate reaction to a small, but not quite significant, p-value is to consider further exploring the matter with other independent samples.

Practical Interpretation

At the .01 level of significance we conclude that the observed difference in time of play does not reflect a discernible real difference, but rather is of a magnitude small enough to be consistent with variability caused solely by chance factors. Thus, the researchers who hypothesized that women would adapt better to the color reversal would need to reexamine their arguments since the evidence doesn't substantiate the claim.

At this point it is worth noting that if a statistically significant difference between men and women had been established with regard to headaches and reversal of playing card colors, we would not have firmly established that the reversal of playing card colors is the source of the difference. From the design of the experiment as given, we could not exclude the possibility that men get headaches faster whether or not the colors are reversed.

PRACTICE EXERCISE

8.40 Suppose we want to compare the average intensity of light produced by fluorescent bulbs and by ordinary incandescent bulbs. The light intensities of independent random samples of 16 fluorescent bulbs and 25 incandescent bulbs of the same wattage are recorded, and their respective sample variances are $S_1^2 = 67$ and $S_2^2 = 129$. Use $\alpha = .05$ and assume that $\sigma_1^2 \neq \sigma_2^2$. Choose the degrees of freedom that would yield "conservative" results.

a. Using a two-sided test,

$$H_o: \quad \mu_1 = \mu_2$$
$$H_A: \quad \mu_1 \neq \mu_2$$

what would be our rejection region?

b. Using a one-sided test,

$$H_o: \quad \mu_1 = \mu_2$$
$$H_A: \quad \mu_1 < \mu_2$$

(where μ_1 represents the average light intensity produced by fluorescent bulbs and μ_2 represents the average light intensity produced by incandescent bulbs), what would be our rejection region?

c. Using a one-sided test,

$$H_o: \quad \mu_1 = \mu_2$$
$$H_A: \quad \mu_1 > \mu_2$$

(where μ_1 represents the average light intensity produced by fluorescent bulbs and μ_2 represents the average light intensity produced by incandescent bulbs), what would be our rejection region?

Flowchart II

The flowchart shown in Figure 8.15 provides steps that lead us to correctly choose the appropriate statistic for the given conditions. Table 8.5 presents the three possible alternative hypotheses for testing the equality of two means and the appropriate statistics that define the nonrejection and rejection regions.

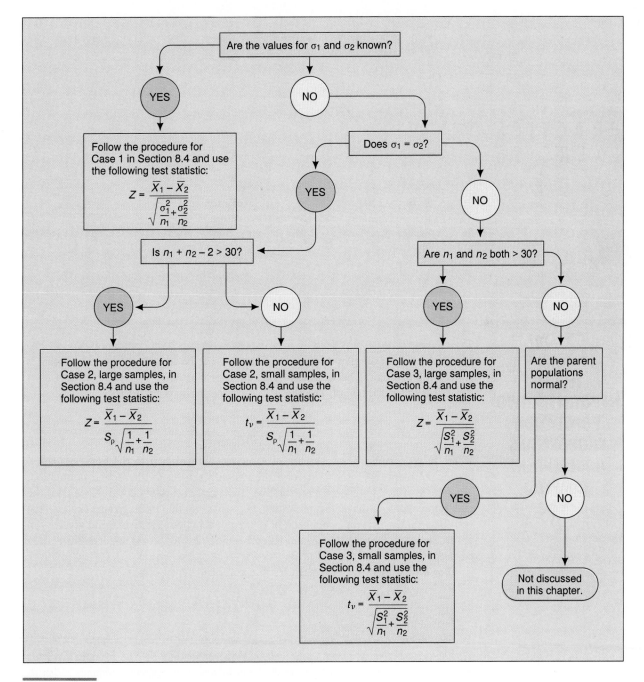

Figure 8.15
Flowchart II for testing the equality of two population means (independent samples)

	TABLE 8.5 A Summary Table for the Three Possible Alternative Hypotheses for Testing Two Means	
H_A	DO NOT REJECT H_o IF	REJECT H_o IF
$\mu_1 > \mu_2$	$Z \leq +Z_\alpha$ $t_\nu \leq +t_{(\alpha,\nu)}$	$Z > +Z_\alpha$ $t_\nu > +t_{(\alpha,\nu)}$
$\mu_1 < \mu_2$	$Z \geq -Z_\alpha$ $t_\nu \geq -t_{(\alpha,\nu)}$	$Z < -Z_\alpha$ $t_\nu < -t_{(\alpha,\nu)}$
$\mu_1 \neq \mu_2$	$-Z_{\alpha/2} \leq Z \leq +Z_{\alpha/2}$ $-t_{(\alpha/2,\nu)} \leq t_\nu \leq +t_{(\alpha/2,\nu)}$	$Z < -Z_{\alpha/2}$ or $Z > +Z_{\alpha/2}$ $t_\nu < -t_{(\alpha/2,\nu)}$ or $t_\nu > +t_{(\alpha/2,\nu)}$

PRACTICE EXERCISE

8.41 Suppose we have

$$H_o: \quad \mu_1 = \mu_2$$
$$H_A: \quad \mu_1 < \mu_2$$

with $\alpha = .05$, $n_1 = 6$, and $n_2 = 8$.

a. If $\sigma_1^2 = 22$ and $\sigma_2^2 = 71$, give the rejection region.

b. If $S_1^2 = 22$ and $S_2^2 = 71$, give the rejection region.

c. Suppose we change H_A to $H_A: \mu_1 > \mu_2$. How would this affect the rejection regions in parts a and b?

8.5

TEST OF HYPOTHESIS: TWO POPULATION PROPORTIONS (INDEPENDENT SAMPLES)

The confidence interval procedure for differences between two population proportions from independent samples discussed in Chapter 7 can be adapted to testing hypotheses concerning differences between two population proportions.

For a one-sided test of hypothesis, the competing hypotheses are

$$H_o: \quad p_1 = p_2$$
$$H_A: \quad p_1 < p_2$$

where p_1 represents the probability of a success with respect to the first population and p_2 represents the probability of a success with respect to the second population. The choice of first and second is arbitrary, so we can always choose the labels for the two populations to have the one-sided H_A stated in the form given. That is, the population for which the proportion of successes is hypothesized as being greater can always be labeled population 2, and its corresponding proportion of successes is then labeled p_2.

For a two-sided test of hypothesis, the competing hypotheses are

$$H_o: \quad p_1 = p_2$$
$$H_A: \quad p_1 \neq p_2$$

Regardless of whether a one-sided or a two-sided test is being considered, the null hypothesis states that $p_1 = p_2$. Then, under the assumption that the null hypothesis is true, we can pool the independent sample estimates of p_1 and p_2 into a single common estimate. The pooled estimate is denoted $\hat{p}_p$, and is calculated using the following expression:

Pooled Estimate of p

$$\hat{p}_{\mathrm{p}} = \frac{X_1 + X_2}{n_1 + n_2} \tag{8-21}$$

where

X_1 represents the number of "successes" among the n_1 trials from the first population;

X_2 represents the number of "successes" among the n_2 trials from the second population.

Additionally notice that H$_\mathrm{o}$: $p_1 - p_2 = 0$ can be used as an equivalent for the stated H$_\mathrm{o}$: $p_1 = p_2$. The use of $p_1 - p_2 = 0$ is helpful in simplifying the test statistic.

Suppose n_1, the number of independent trials from the first population, and n_2, the number of independent trials from the second population, are both greater than or equal to 30. Then the standard normal Z statistic can be used to test the hypotheses. Looking at the Z statistic given in Section 7.7 of Chapter 7, we can substitute the term $\hat{p}_{\mathrm{p}}$ for both $\hat{p}_1$ and $\hat{p}_2$ in the formulas for S_1 and S_2. Then setting $p_2 - p_2 = 0$, the expression for the test statistic can be written as follows:

Test Statistic to Test Two Population Proportions

$$Z = \frac{\hat{p}_1 - \hat{p}_2}{\sqrt{\hat{p}_{\mathrm{p}}(1 - \hat{p}_{\mathrm{p}})\left(\dfrac{1}{n_1} + \dfrac{1}{n_2}\right)}} \tag{8-22}$$

where $\hat{p}_1 = X_1/n_1$ and $\hat{p}_2 = X_2/n_2$.

For the one-sided test, the rejection region is given by

$$Z < -Z_\alpha$$

For the two-sided test, the rejection region is given by

$$Z < -Z_{\alpha/2} \qquad \text{or} \qquad Z > +Z_{\alpha/2}$$

From time to time we like to remind you that while you are just learning the power of statistical methods for the first time, statistical thinking and methods have a long history of useful business applications. The following example provides considerable insight into the usefulness of statistics in business a generation ago.

■ **EXAMPLE 8.11**
**The Shopping
List Study**

One of the classic studies in the marketing research literature is the famous "shopping list" study conducted by Professor Mason Haire of Harvard University.* A sample of 100 Boston women were personally interviewed. Each woman was given one of two types of grocery shopping lists and told to project herself into the situation until she

*Mason Haire, "Projective Techniques in Marketing Research," *Journal of Marketing*, vol. 14, 1950, pp. 649–656.

could "more or less characterize the woman who brought home the groceries. Then write a brief description of her personality and character."

The interviewed women were not aware of the existence of two lists and, more importantly, that the two shopping lists were identical except for the type of coffee. The coffee on one list was "Nescafe Instant Coffee," and on the other list it was "1 lb can of Maxwell House Coffee (Drip Grind)." The purpose of this shopping list approach was to isolate the attitude difference toward the two coffees. It was thought that there might be a possible stigma attached to the use of instant coffee. This notion of the shopping list arose because at that time, when directly questioned as to why they did not purchase instant coffee, women used the acceptable answer, "I don't like the flavor," and avoided the answer, "People will think I am lazy and not a good wife."

All responses were reported literally so that no interviewer bias would be read into them. Twenty-four (48%) of the 50 women in the group who were given the "Nescafe Instant" shopping list depicted the shopper by the word "lazy." Only 2 (4%) of the 50 women with the "Maxwell House (Drip Grind)" list characterized the shopper using the word "lazy." Could two random samples of 50 each produce such dramatically different rates of occurrence of the description "lazy" if in fact there were no differences in the populations from which the samples were drawn? The thrust of marketing research is to find answers to questions like this concerning important differences that might exist between brands and could be profitably exploited.

Statistical Solution

Step 1

Set up H_o and H_A: First, state H_o. H_o reflects the assumption of no difference in the proportion of "lazy" responses between the two shopping lists. This is symbolized by H_o: $p_1 = p_2$.

Now State H_A. H_A reflects the investigator's concern that there is a real difference in the population proportions of "lazy" responses between the two lists. This is symbolized by H_A: $p_1 \neq p_2$.

In summary, we can write

H_o: $p_1 = p_2$ (Rate of occurrence for both populations is the same.)

H_A: $p_1 \neq p_2$ (Rate of occurrence for both populations is not the same.)

Step 2

Choose the level of significance, α: It is important for the marketing researcher to understand why different consumers end up making different choices, and to find out how these differences among consumer attitudes and behavior can be exploited. For the two-sided test, a Type I error results in believing there is an exploitable difference in consumer attitudes toward users of instant coffee as compared to users of regular ground coffee when in fact there may be none. On the other hand, a Type II error results in missing an exploitable difference in attitudes—in this case an opportunity to appeal to consumers concerned about being considered lazy. Thus, if market penetration is a key objective, a firm may be willing to have a relatively high risk for committing a Type I error in order to keep down the risk for committing a Type II error.

Realizing this tradeoff between Type I and Type II error risk requires a compromise, it was decided to set the level of significance at .05.

Step 3

Determine the sample sizes: The problem states that $n_1 = 50$ and $n_2 = 50$.

Step 4

Check the validity of using the Z distribution: With both n_1 and n_2 larger than 30, the test statistic is

$$Z = \frac{\hat{p}_1 - \hat{p}_2}{\sqrt{\hat{p}_P(1 - \hat{p}_P)\left(\frac{1}{n_1} + \frac{1}{n_2}\right)}}$$

and is approximately distributed as the standard normal variable Z.

Step 5

Determine the rejection region: The rejection region is given by

$$Z = \frac{\hat{p}_1 - \hat{p}_2}{\sqrt{\hat{p}_P(1 - \hat{p}_P)\left(\frac{1}{n_1} + \frac{1}{n_2}\right)}} < -Z_{.025} = -1.96$$

or

$$Z = \frac{\hat{p}_1 - \hat{p}_2}{\sqrt{\hat{p}_P(1 - \hat{p}_P)\left(\frac{1}{n_1} + \frac{1}{n_2}\right)}} > +Z_{.025} = +1.96$$

Step 6

Determine the values of the sample statistics $\hat{p}_P$, $\hat{p}_1$, and $\hat{p}_2$: Calculate the pooled sample proportion, $\hat{p}_P$:

$$\hat{p}_P = \frac{24 + 2}{50 + 50} = .26$$

Calculate $\hat{p}_1 = \frac{24}{50} = .48$. Calculate $\hat{p}_2 = \frac{2}{50} = .04$.

Step 7

Determine the value of the test statistic: Substituting the calculated values of $\hat{p}_P$, $\hat{p}_1$, $\hat{p}_2$, and n_1 and n_2 into the test statistic, we find

$$Z = \frac{.48 - .04}{\sqrt{(.26)(.74)\left(\frac{1}{50} + \frac{1}{50}\right)}} = 5.02$$

Step 8

Decide whether or not to reject H_o: Since the value of the test statistic, 5.02, exceeds 1.96, it lies in the rejection region, so we reject H_o of no difference.

Step 9

Calculate the p-value: In this example, the p-value is found to be

$$P(Z > 5.02 | p_1 = p_2) = 0 \quad \text{To four decimal place accuracy}$$

Since we are dealing with a two-sided test, the p-value is defined as the probability of finding a value of Z either less than -5.02 or greater than $+5.02$, assuming the null hypothesis is true. Therefore, the p-value just determined must be doubled. But doubling a probability of 0 to four decimal places still yields a value close to 0. This very low probability means that the observed result is highly unlikely if H_o of no real difference is true. The evidence strongly suggests that there is a real difference in the two population proportions.

Practical Interpretation

At the .05 level of significance we conclude that the rates of occurrence of the description of "lazy" is significantly different in the response attitudes of the interviewees toward persons who purchase "Nescafe Instant" versus those who purchase "Maxwell House (Drip Grind)." Since the evidence indicates that shoppers who purchase instant coffee are considered "lazy," promotional advertisers of instant coffee must design ads that help neutralize or possibly change that image. On the other hand, promotions for non-instant coffees could stress the association of "lazy" with the use of instant coffee.

Comment

The original investigation was conducted many years ago. Later repetitions of the shopping list studies have indicated some dissipation of the "laziness" stigma applied to instant coffee users. Marketing researchers can track the changing attitudes toward women's (and men's) responsibilities to their families by comparing the results of shopping list studies conducted over time.

A summary of the two possible alternative hypotheses and the corresponding nonrejection and rejection regions is given in Table 8.6.

TABLE 8.6 A Summary Table for the Two Possible Alternative Hypotheses for Testing Two Proportions		
H_A	Do not reject H_o if	Reject H_o if
$p_1 < p_2$	Calculated Z value $\geq -Z_\alpha$	Calculated Z value $< -Z_\alpha$
$p_1 \neq p_2$	$-Z_{\alpha/2} \leq$ Calculated Z value $\leq +Z_{\alpha/2}$	Calculated Z value $< -Z_{\alpha/2}$ or: Calculated Z value $> +Z_{\alpha/2}$

In each of the above two cases, the calculated value of the test statistic is obtained by substituting the observed sample values of $\hat{p}_1$, $\hat{p}_2$, and $\hat{p}_p$ in the expression for the test statistic given by

$$Z = \frac{\hat{p}_1 - \hat{p}_2}{\sqrt{\hat{p}_p(1 - \hat{p}_p)\left(\frac{1}{n_1} + \frac{1}{n_2}\right)}}$$

PRACTICE EXERCISE

8.42 Generic aspirin tablets are claimed to be as good as any name brand aspirin tablets. A consumer agency, concerned with product safety, is aware that aspirin dosage can't be consistent if the tablets break up in their containers. The agency decides to test, with $\alpha = .05$, a particular generic aspirin tablet versus a specific name brand aspirin tablet. The agency purchases 56 containers (each containing 100 tablets) of the generic aspirin and 75 containers (each containing 100 tablets) of the name brand aspirin, and examines the containers to see what proportion of the containers in each group have broken aspirin tablets. Thus,

$$H_o: \quad p_1 = p_2$$
$$H_A: \quad p_1 \neq p_2$$

Use $\alpha = .05$, $n_1 = 56$, and $n_2 = 75$. Give the rejection region.

8.6

TEST OF HYPOTHESIS: PAIRED OBSERVATIONS

Often, researchers deal with observations from two populations that are related to each other and can be paired. One common case is "before" and "after" experiments in which observations are made on the same subjects before and after some treatment is applied. In these cases we can adapt the confidence interval procedure for $\mu_d = \mu_1 - \mu_2$ discussed in Section 7.6 to test hypotheses concerning differences between two population means.

By using the fact that H_o: $\mu_1 = \mu_2$ can be written equivalently as H_o: $\mu_1 - \mu_2 = 0$, and by setting the difference between the two population means equal to μ_d ($\mu_1 - \mu_2 = \mu_d$), we can express H_o: $\mu_1 = \mu_2$ as H_o: $\mu_d = 0$.

Then, when conducting a one-sided test of hypothesis, we can write

$$H_o: \quad \mu_d = 0$$
$$H_A: \quad \mu_d < 0$$

when μ_2 is expected to be greater than μ_1, or

$$H_o: \quad \mu_d = 0$$
$$H_A: \quad \mu_d > 0$$

when μ_2 is expected to be less than μ_1.

When conducting a two-sided test of hypothesis, we can write

$$H_o: \quad \mu_d = 0$$
$$H_A: \quad \mu_d \neq 0$$

The underlying assumption for both the one-sided and two-sided tests is that the two populations must be normally distributed. Given normality, the appropriate test statistic to use is given by:

Test Statistic for Paired Observations

$$t_{(n-1)} = \frac{\bar{d}}{S_d / \sqrt{n}} \tag{8-23}$$

where

$t_{(n-1)}$ is the Student t statistic with $n - 1$ degrees of freedom;

n represents the number of paired differences;

$d_i = X_{1,i} - X_{2,i}$ is the ith paired difference and $X_{1,i}$ and $X_{2,i}$ are the respective ith observations on population 1 and population 2 (there are n pairs in all);

$\bar{d} = \dfrac{\Sigma\, d_i}{n}$ where $\bar{d}$ is the observed mean of the paired differences;

$S_d = \sqrt{\dfrac{n\Sigma\, d_i^2 - (\Sigma\, d_i)^2}{n(n-1)}}$, where S_d is the standard deviation of the paired differences;

$\mu_d = \mu_1 - \mu_2$, the true mean difference.

The value of $\bar{d}$ represents a point estimate of μ_d, and S_d measures the observed variability of d in the sample.

The rejection region for the one-sided test with $H_A: \mu_d < 0$ is given by

$$t_{(n-1)} < -t_{(\alpha, n-1)}$$

The rejection region for the one-sided test with $H_A: \mu_d > 0$ is given by

$$t_{(n-1)} > +t_{(\alpha, n-1)}$$

The rejection region for the two-sided test is given by

$$t_{(n-1)} < -t_{(\alpha/2, n-1)} \qquad \text{or} \qquad t_{(n-1)} > +t_{(\alpha/2, n-1)}$$

The following example illustrates the use of the paired difference format for hypothesis testing.

■ **EXAMPLE 8.12**

Drug Effectiveness on the Span of Concentration

A drug experiment was performed on 10 consenting randomly selected female college students. The purpose of the experiment was to determine whether a certain drug can increase the span of concentration. The observed times, in consecutive minutes of concentration before fatigue or distraction, are given in Table 8.7. Do the data provide statistically significant evidence of an increase in concentration time? That is, is there significant evidence that $\mu_1 - \mu_2 < 0$ with the use of the drug? Use a level of significance of .01 and assume the "before" and "after" distributions of concentration times are normally distributed.

Statistical Solution

Step 1

Set up H_o and H_A: First, state H_o. H_o expresses the assumption that no change in

	TABLE 8.7 The Time (in Minutes) of Concentration Before Fatigue or Distraction			
STUDENT	**BEFORE DRUG INTAKE** $X_{1,i}$	**AFTER DRUG INTAKE** $X_{2,i}$	**PAIRED DIFFERENCES** d_i	d_i^2
1	45	47	−2	4
2	32	34	−2	4
3	58	60	−2	4
4	57	59	−2	4
5	60	63	−3	9
6	38	44	−6	36
7	47	49	−2	4
8	51	53	−2	4
9	42	46	−4	16
10	38	41	−3	9
			$\Sigma\, d_i = -28$	$\Sigma\, d_i^2 = 94$

$$\bar{d} = \frac{\Sigma\, d_i}{n} = \frac{-28}{10} = -2.8$$

$$S_d = \sqrt{\frac{n\Sigma\, d_i^2 - (\Sigma\, d_i)^2}{n(n-1)}} = \sqrt{\frac{10(94) - (-28)^2}{10(9)}} = 1.3166$$

the span of concentration has occurred. That is, the drug is ineffective. This is symbolized by H_o: $\mu_d = 0$.

Now state H_A. H_A reflects the investigator's search for a positive effect of the drug on the span of concentration. This is symbolized by H_A: $\mu_d < 0$.

Summarizing the two conditions, we write

H_o: $\mu_d = 0$ (The drug is ineffective.)

H_A: $\mu_d < 0$ (The drug is effective in increasing the concentration span.)

Step 2
Choose the level of significance: The problem states $\alpha = .01$.

Step 3
Determine the value of σ_d: The value of σ_d is unknown, and only an estimate, S_d, can be computed from the data given.

Step 4
Determine the number of pairs: There are $n = 10$ pairs in this example.

Step 5
Determine the applicability of an appropriate statistic: The example tells us that the distributions of the "before" and "after" concentration times can be assumed to be normally distributed. The value for σ_d is unknown. We have a small sample, since $n = 10$. These conditions meet the requirements for the valid use of the Student t statistic with 9 d.f.

Step 6
Write the expression for the test statistic: The test statistic is

$$ t_9 = \frac{\bar{d}}{S_d/\sqrt{10}} $$

Step 7
Determine the rejection region: The rejection region is given by $t_9 < -2.821$.

Step 8
Determine the values of the sample statistics: The computations given in Table 8.7 show that $\bar{d} = -2.8$ and $S_d = 1.3166$.

Step 9
Determine the value of the test statistic and apply the decision rule: The calculated t test statistic is

$$ t_9 = \frac{-2.8}{1.3166/\sqrt{10}} $$
$$ = -6.7 $$

Since the calculated t test statistic value of -6.7 is smaller than -2.821, it falls in the rejection region, so we can reject H_0 of no effectiveness.

Step 10
Calculate the p-value: The p-value is $P(t_9 < -6.7)$. To evaluate this probability precisely requires a more extensive table than provided in this book. But by reading Appendix Table VII, we can see that the p-value must be less than .005. The very low p-value indicates that it is very unlikely that the observed difference in concentration can be the result of simply a chance variation.

Practical Interpretation

At the .01 level of significance we conclude that the drug has been effective in increasing the average concentration time. However, the statistical significance may not represent a relevant real difference. The data suggest that the increase in concentration time is a matter of just a few minutes. The real-life question would be whether it is worth risking side effects from the drug for just a few more minutes of concentration time.

EXERCISES

▶ **8.27** A random sample of 61 automobiles of last year's model showed an average of 27.3 miles per gallon (mpg) with a standard deviation of 4.4 mpg. A random sample of 61 automobiles of this year's model showed an average of 32.5 mpg with a standard deviation of 3.5 mpg. Does this show a statistically significant increase in the average miles per gallon for the newer model automobiles? Use a significance level of .01. Assume that the miles per gallon for these automobiles is normally distributed.

8.28 A random sample of 22 policies from insurance company A showed an average net profit of $39 per policy with a standard deviation of $3.70. A random sample of 31 policies from insurance company B showed an average net profit of $47 with a standard deviation of $3.90. Use a significance level of .05, and assume the policy profits are normally distributed with equal variances for the two companies. Is there a statistically significant difference in the average profit they make from their policies?

▶ **8.29** A management team wishes to determine whether there is a statistically significant difference in the average longevity of two types of light bulbs. Among 10 type A bulbs, an average longevity of 4372 hr was recorded with a standard deviation of 66.5 hr; and 11 type B bulbs had an average longevity of 4191 hr with a standard deviation of 64.8 hr. Assume longevity is normally distributed, and assume the population variances are the same for both types of bulbs. Perform an appropriate statistical test at the .01 level of significance to advise the management team on the longevity of these two types of bulbs.

8.30 The computer chips from two suppliers are supposed to operate at the same average speed. However, a random sample of 12 chips from one supplier has an average speed of 8.1 megahertz (MHz) while a random sample of 12 chips from the second supplier has an average speed of 7.9 MHz. Does this result supply statistically significant evidence at the .02 level of significance that the average speeds of the chips from the two suppliers are not equal? Assume the speeds are normally distributed with the standard deviation for both populations of chips equal to 0.1 MHz.

8.31 The specifications for computer chips call for an average thickness of 2 mm and a standard deviation of 0.15 mm. Since samples from two suppliers do not yield precisely the required specified values, a computer manufacturer would like to determine whether there is a significant difference in the average thickness of chips provided by two suppliers. Use the sample results to advise the manufacturer if the sample results show that 15 chips from one supplier have an average thickness of 1.97 mm with a standard deviation of 0.23 mm, and 13 chips from the second supplier have an average thickness of 2.01 mm with a standard deviation of 0.14 mm. Assume the thicknesses are normally distributed, and use a significance level of .05.

▶ **8.32** The quality control manager of a manufacturing plant senses that the day shift may be producing a higher proportion of rejects than that produced by the night shift. To check this out she takes a random sample of 75 items produced by the day shift and finds 7 rejects; and she takes a random sample of 75 items produced by the night shift and finds 3 rejects. At the .01 level of significance, does this provide statistical evidence that the day shift is indeed producing a higher proportion of rejects?

8.33 A lawyer claims that jury composition in capital punishment trials has a consistently lower percentage of Hispanics than jury composition in civil cases. To illustrate his contention, he takes a random sample of 40 juries in capital punishment trials and finds 2 juries with at least one Hispanic member. He also takes a random sample of 54 juries in civil cases and finds 17 juries with at least one Hispanic member. Use these sample results to determine whether there is significant statistical evidence to support his claim. Use the .0073 level of significance.

8.34 There is always some political pressure to raise the minimum wage. Proponents argue that families supported by wage earners who earn the minimum wage live below the poverty level. Opponents argue that raising the minimum wage will result in inflation and/or the loss of jobs. A congressional representative decides to examine one particular aspect of this problem: Who are the people who work for the minimum wage? In a random sample of 150 minimum wage earners, 125 were young single persons (24 and under); and in a random sample of 175 wage earners earning above the minimum wage, 33 were young single persons (24 and under). Is there a statistically significant higher proportion of young single persons (24 and under) working at the minimum wage than at above the minimum wage? Use a significance level of .05.

8.35 Find the p-value for the results in:
  a. Exercise 8.32
  b. Exercise 8.33
  c. Exercise 8.34

8.36 One purpose of asking people to estimate the price of a new model automobile first with picture slides and then with direct contact exposure, is to simulate the conditions most consumers encounter with new automobiles: Most people are first exposed to magazine and TV pictures of new automobiles, and later come into direct contact with them. Another, and important, purpose is to determine whether consumers will reassess a higher value to an automobile when they have direct contact with the automobile after having been exposed to magazine and TV pictures. A random sample of 40 people showed an average higher reassessed value of $2085 and a standard deviation of $976. Use these results to determine whether there is statistically significant evidence of a higher reassessed value after direct contact. Assume the differences are normally distributed, and use the .0099 level of significance.

8.37 Find the p-value for the results in:
  a. Exercise 8.30
  b. Exercise 8.31

8.38 Two very reliable laboratories are asked to analyze food samples from a given manufacturer to determine the quantity of a certain chemical in the food. From past experience with substances of this type, it is known that laboratory 1 has a standard deviation of 0.0013 part per million (ppm), and laboratory 2 has a standard deviation of 0.0015 ppm. Laboratory 1 is given 34 food samples to analyze, and laboratory 2 is given 45 food samples to analyze. The mean obtained by laboratory 1 is 0.0061 ppm, and the mean obtained by laboratory 2 is 0.0069 ppm. At a level of significance of .02, is the difference in the means obtained by the two laboratories statistically significant?

8.39 Students' grades in a certain math course tend to be normally distributed with a mean of 57 and a standard deviation of 22. Two instructors decide to modify their instruction procedures, anticipating that they will raise the average but leave the variance unaffected. At the end of the semester, the average grade for a class of 21 with one instructor is 62.3 and the average grade for a class of 27 with the second instructor is 64.7. At the .05 level of significance, is the difference in the average grades between the two classes statistically significant?

8.40 A university investigation is conducted to determine whether car ownership is detrimental to academic achievement. A random sample of 20 students from among those who do not own cars have a grade-point average of 2.75 with a variance of 0.36; and a random sample of 20 students from among those who do own cars have a grade-point average of 2.51 with a variance of 0.40. Assume grade-point averages are normally distributed, and assume that the grade-point average population variances are the same for those who own cars as for those who do not own cars. Use the .10 level of significance to determine whether the grade-point average of students who own cars is statistically significantly lower than the grade-point average of students who do not own cars.

8.41 Two production lines produce the same type of wire, but there is some question as to whether or not there is a difference in the tensile strengths of the wires produced by these two lines. A random sample of 9 wires from one line has an average tensile strength of 10 with a standard deviation of 2.1, and a random sample of 8 wires from the second line has an average tensile strength of 11.4 with a standard deviation of 1.9. Assume tensile strength measurements are normally distributed, and assume the population of measurements for the two production lines have the same variance. Use the .02 level of significance to determine whether there is a statistically significant difference in average tensile strength for the two lines.

8.42 A consumer agency claims that the proportion of defective new microwave ovens of brand A is less than the proportion of defective microwave ovens of brand B. A random sample of 93 microwave ovens of brand A has 2 defective ovens; and a random sample of 69 microwave ovens of brand B has 6 defective ovens. At a level of significance of .05, do these sample results provide statistically significant evidence to support the consumer agency's claim?

8.43 On a question concerning library hours on a college campus, 35 out of 50 men interviewed favored a proposal to increase the hours of operation, whereas 61 of 80 women favored the proposal. At a level of significance of .02, does this indicate a statistically significant difference in the proportions of men and women who favor the proposal?

8.44 A quality control manager suspects that two production lines producing magnets are not producing the same proportions of defective magnets. If a random sample of 250 magnets from one production line has 11 defectives, and if a random sample of 300 magnets from the second production line has 17 defectives, does this provide statistically significant evidence to support the quality control manager's suspicion? Use a level of significance of .012.

▶ **8.45** A state consumer agency wishes to determine whether a particular auto repair shop, shop A, charges more for repairs, on the average, than shop B. The agency takes 6 cars in good working order and deliberately creates a different, but common, malfunction in each car. On different occasions, the agency submits each car to each auto repair shop and requests an estimate for cost of repair. It obtains the following results:

Car	Estimate Shop A	Estimate Shop B
1	$240	$205
2	90	100
3	390	275
4	115	100
5	160	130
6	135	140

At the .05 level of significance, would it be correct to say that shop A gives a statistically significant higher average estimate than shop B? Assume that the populations of estimate figures are normal.

● ●

8.7
TEST OF HYPOTHESIS: ONE POPULATION VARIANCE

The methodology of hypothesis testing can be applied to testing hypotheses about a population variance, provided the underlying population from which we sample is a normal population. The procedure used is an adaptation of the confidence interval procedure for a population variance described in Section 7.8. If σ_0^2 represents the null hypothesized value for σ^2, then the appropriate test statistic to use is the following:

Test Statistic to Test One Population Variance

$$\chi_{(n-1)}^2 = \frac{(n-1)S^2}{\sigma_0^2} \qquad (8\text{-}24)$$

The value n is the sample size, S^2 is the sample variance, and $\chi_{(n-1)}^2$ indicates that the statistic follows the chi-square distribution with $n-1$ degrees of freedom. The hypothesis testing procedure can be applied to one-sided and two-sided testing.

For a one-sided test of hypothesis there are two possibilities:

(1)　H_o:　$\sigma^2 = \sigma_0^2$

　　　H_A:　$\sigma^2 > \sigma_0^2$　(The true variance is greater than the hypothesized value.)

with the corresponding rejection region defined as:

Rejection Region for One-Sided Test of One Population Variance (1)

$$\frac{(n-1)S^2}{\sigma_0^2} > \chi_{(\alpha, n-1)}^2 \qquad (8\text{-}25)$$

(2)　H_o:　$\sigma^2 = \sigma_0^2$

　　　H_A:　$\sigma^2 < \sigma_0^2$　(The true variance is less than the hypothesized value.)

with the corresponding rejection region defined as:

Rejection Region for One-Sided
Test of One Population Variance (2)

$$\frac{(n-1)S^2}{\sigma_o^2} < \chi^2_{(1-\alpha, n-1)} \qquad (8\text{-}26)$$

For a two-sided test of hypothesis,

H_o: $\sigma^2 = \sigma_o^2$

H_A: $\sigma^2 \neq \sigma_o^2$ (The true variance is not equal to the hypothesized value.)

with the corresponding rejection region defined as:

Rejection Region for Two-Sided
Test of One Population Variance

$$\frac{(n-1)S^2}{\sigma_o^2} < \chi^2_{(1-\alpha/2, n-1)} \qquad \text{or} \qquad \frac{(n-1)S^2}{\sigma_o^2} > \chi^2_{(\alpha/2, n-1)} \qquad (8\text{-}27)$$

The following application is an example of hypothesis testing for a population variance.

■ **EXAMPLE 8.13**

**Hand Grenades and
Explosion Time
Variability**

Two boxes of hand grenades are identical in appearance, with both having identical 5 sec mean time to explosion from the moment the pins are pulled and the safety released. However, in one box all the grenades explode at exactly 5 sec, while in the other box they explode anywhere from 0 to 10 sec. If you were a combat soldier, would there be any doubt as to the box from which you would prefer to select your grenades?

Firms who receive a defense contract to manufacture hand grenades must continuously check that the manufactured grenades meet specifications. Suppose a quality control system is designed to monitor the variability (as measured by the standard deviation). The specification is that the variability of explosion time from the time the pin is pulled and the safety released should not exceed 0.01 sec. The standard testing procedure is to randomly select 25 grenades from the assembly line during each 8 hr shift and measure the time to explosion from the moment the pin is pulled and the safety released. The standard deviation for the 25 time measurements is then calculated and compared with 0.01 to determine whether there is too much variability. If the sample of 25 measurements from one 8 hr shift has a standard deviation of 0.02 sec, does this indicate that the grenades now being produced from this process may have too much variability? Assume the times to explosion are normally distributed and the level of significance α specified is .10, a value somewhat larger than usual. The choice of the large value for α is necessary because the manufacturer wishes to keep down the value of β, the risk of committing a Type II error. That is, to commit a Type II error in this case would mean that the manufacturer would ship out grenades with too much variability, and this would jeopardize the lives of users of these grenades. By selecting a large value for α, the manufacturer reduces the value of β, the probability of committing the Type II error. The reason for not choosing a value much greater than .10 for α is that the manufacturer does not wish to interrupt the process with too many false signals. That is, to commit a Type I error in this case would mean that the manufacturer would have to interrupt and correct a manufacturing process that has not gone awry, and such interruptions are costly. To interrupt the process because of too frequent false signals could cause the manufacuter to become noncompetitive in the marketplace.

Statistical Solution

Step 1
Set up H_o and H_A: First, state H_o. H_o reflects the assumption of no change from specifications in the variability of explosion time, which in this case requires the hypothesized standard deviation value of 0.01. This condition is symbolized by H_o: $\sigma = 0.01$, or, using the variance, by H_o: $\sigma^2 = (0.01)^2$.

Now, state H_A. H_A reflects the manufacturer's concern that the variability in the time to explosion may be greater than it should be. This condition is symbolized by H_A: $\sigma > 0.01$, or, equivalently, by H_A: $\sigma^2 > (0.01)^2$.

In summary, we can write

$$H_o: \quad \sigma^2 = (0.01)^2 \quad \text{(The variability is within specifications.)}$$
$$H_A: \quad \sigma^2 > (0.01)^2 \quad \text{(The variability is too large.)}$$

Step 2
Choose the level of significance: The problem states $\alpha = .10$.

Step 3
Determine the sample size: In this example, $n = 25$ grenades.

Step 4
Determine the applicability of an appropriate test statistic: The example tells us to assume that times to explosion are normally distributed. The example requires a test of the variability of the times to explosion. The number of degrees of freedom is equal to $n - 1 = 25 - 1 = 24$. Under these conditions it is appropriate to use the χ^2 statistic with 24 d.f.

Step 5
Write the expression for the test statistic: The test statistic is

$$\chi_{24}^2 = \frac{24S^2}{(0.01)^2}$$

Step 6
Determine the rejection region: The rejection region is given by

$$\frac{24S^2}{(0.01)^2} > \chi_{(.10,24)}^2 = 33.196$$

Step 7
Determine the value of the sample statistic: The problem states $S = 0.02$.

Step 8

Determine the value of the test statistic and apply the decision rule: The calculated value of the test statistic is

$$\frac{24(0.02)^2}{(0.01)^2} = 96$$

Since the calculated value of the test statistic, 96, exceeds the table value of 33.196 (Appendix Table VIIIb), its value lies in the rejection region. The null hypothesis H_o of variability within specification is rejected.

Step 9

Calculate the p-value: In this example, the p-value statement to be evaluated is

$$P(\chi_{24}^2 > 96 \mid \sigma = 0.01)$$

This requires finding the value for

$$P(\chi_{24}^2 > 96)$$

To obtain the precise value of this probability a more extensive table would be required than that provided in this text. Nevertheless, it can be seen from Appendix Table VIII, that the p-value must be much less than .005. This low probability indicates that it is very unlikely to find such a result if H_o is true.

Practical Interpretation

At the .10 level of significance we conclude that there is too much variability in the time to explosion for grenades produced by the manufacturing process. At this point the manufacturer must consider interrupting the process, and find and correct whatever is wrong with it. To do otherwise would jeopardize lives and, at the very least, bring the manufacturer into court on the charge of criminal negligence.

PRACTICE EXERCISE

8.43 Suppose that salaries among computer analysts are normally distributed, and suppose we wish to determine, with $\alpha = .025$ and with a sample of size $n = 20$, whether the variability σ among the salaries exceeds \$2100. In this case we have

$$H_o: \quad \sigma^2 = 4{,}410{,}000 = (2100)^2$$
$$H_A: \quad \sigma^2 > 4{,}410{,}000 = (2100)^2$$

Give the rejection region.

EXERCISES

8.46 An architect is concerned with suppliers meeting her specifications for drafting sheets. She specifies a standard deviation of 0.15 mm, and finds a random sample of 15 sheets from one of the suppliers has a standard deviaiton of 0.23 mm. She would like to know if this indicates a statistically significant higher value than her specification. If so, she will consider discontinuing business with this supplier. Perform an appropriate statistical test using a significance level of .025. Assume the measurements are normally distributed.

8.47 Suppose a young business couple believes that a standard deviation greater than \$350 would represent a fluctuation in daily receipts thay they would not be able to contend with, at least not at the start of their venture when they are most vulnerable to cash flow shortages. A random sample of 17 daily receipts from a franchise they are considering purchasing shows a variance of 155,236, and they would like to know if this reflects a standard deviation whose value is statistically significantly greater than $350. If that is the case, then they would have second thoughts about purchasing the franchise. Perform an appropriate statistical test using a significance level of .01 to advise the young couple. Assume the daily receipts are normally distributed.

▶ **8.48** A manufacturer believes that the treadlife of his premium tire is normally distributed with an average of 50,200 mi. He would like to guarantee the treadlife for 50,000 mi, but would be reluctant to do so if the standard deviation of the distribution of treadlife is greater than 250 mi. If a random sample of 71 tires has a standard deviation of 301 mi, does this provide sufficient evidence to cause the manufacturer to refrain from offering the guarantee? Assume treadlife is normally distributed, and use a level of significance of .05.

8.49 A manufacturer of odometers claims that mileage measurements indicate his instruments have a standard deviation of at most 0.29 mi per 10 mi traveled. An experiment consisting of eight runs over a measured 10 mi stretch is performed in order to check the manufacturer's claim. A sample standard deviation of 0.33 mi per 10 mi traveled is obtained. Does this provide sufficient evidence to indicate that the manufacturer underestimates the variability of his odometers? Assume the measurements are normally distributed, and use a level of significance of .05.

8.50 A certain missile guidance system is believed to be capable of guiding a missile to its target with a variance of 1.5 mi². Variances greater than this value are not desirable. A random sample of 20 of these guidance systems is tested and found to have a variance of 1.9 mi². Does this provide sufficient evidence to assert that the variance is in reality greater than 1.5 mi²? Assume the striking distance from the center of the target is normally distributed, and use a level of significance of .01.

● ●

8.8

TEST OF HYPOTHESIS: TWO POPULATION VARIANCES

The confidence interval procedure for the ratio of two population variances discussed in Section 7.9 can be adapted to test hypotheses concerning the equality of two population variances. The test of hypothesis can be conducted as a one-sided test or a two-sided test.

For a one-sided test of hypothesis, we have

$$H_o:\ \sigma_1^2 = \sigma_2^2$$
$$H_A:\ \sigma_1^2 > \sigma_2^2$$

where σ_1^2 represents the variance for the first population, and σ_2^2 represents the variance for the second population. Because the choice of first and second population is arbitrary, we will always label the population with the larger expected variance as population 1. This will ensure that the one-sided H_A is stated in the form above.

For a two-sided test of hypothesis, we have

$$H_o:\ \sigma_1^2 = \sigma_2^2$$
$$H_A:\ \sigma_1^2 \neq \sigma_2^2$$

The assumptions are that the two populations are normal or nearly normal, and the samples taken from each population are independent. If these conditions are valid, then the appropriate test statistic to use is given by the following:

Test Statistic to Test Two Population Variances

$$F_{(n_1-1,n_2-1)} = \frac{S_1^2}{S_2^2} \tag{8-28}$$

where

$F_{(n_1-1,n_2-1)}$ follows the F distribution with $n_1 - 1$ numerator degrees of freedom and $n_2 - 1$ denominator degrees of freedom;

S_1^2 represents the variance of a sample of size n_1 taken from a normal population whose variance is equal to σ_1^2;

S_2^2 represents the variance of a sample of size n_2 taken from a normal population whose variance is equal to σ_2^2;

the expression for F has been simplified and the variance terms σ_2^2 and σ_1^2 canceled, because H_o: $\sigma_2^2 = \sigma_1^2$ is equivalent to writing H_o: $\sigma_2^2/\sigma_1^2 = 1$.

The rejection region for the one-sided test is given by:

Rejection Region for One-Sided Test of Two Population Variances

$$F_{(n_1-1,n_2-1)} > F_{(\alpha,n_1-1,n_2-1)} \tag{8-29}$$

The rejection region for the two-sided test is found as follows, after determining which term, S_1^2 or S_2^2, has the larger value:

Rejection Region for Two-Sided Test of Two Population Variances

If S_1^2 has the larger value, then the test statistic is written as

$$F_{(n_1-1,n_2-1)} = \frac{S_1^2}{S_2^2} \quad \text{and } H_o \text{ is rejected if} \quad F_{(n_1-1,n_2-1)} > F_{(\alpha/2,n_1-1,n_2-1)} \tag{8-30}$$

If S_2^2 has the larger value, then the test statistic is written as

$$F_{(n_2-1,n_1-1)} = \frac{S_2^2}{S_1^2} \quad \text{and } H_o \text{ is rejected if} \quad F_{(n_2-1,n_1-1)} > F_{(\alpha/2,n_2-1,n_1-1)} \tag{8-31}$$

Now we'll use inequality (8-29) to perform a one-sided test of hypothesis.

■ **EXAMPLE 8.14**

Fruit Flies, Climate, and Wing Length

The state agriculture research group studying the characteristics of populations of a certain species of fruit fly known to cause fruit infestation is faced with the question of whether the variability in the wing length is greater for flies living in a warm climate than for flies living in a cold climate. In earlier experiments greater variability in wing length was found to be associated with greater variability in resistance to a particular insecticide. As part of an investigation, 31 females were collected in the warm climate and their wing lengths measured. The variance was found to be equal to 0.00038809. Thirty-one females were also collected in the cold climate and their wing lengths measured. The variance was found to be equal to 0.000144. Do the data provide significant evidence that wing length variability for this species of fruit fly is greater in the warmer climate? Use a level of significance of .01. Assume that wing length measurements are normally distributed in both populations.

Statistical Solution

Step 1

Set up H_o and H_A: First, state H_o.

$$H_o: \quad \sigma_1^2 = \sigma_2^2 \text{ (Variability for both fly populations is the same.)}$$

Now, state H_A.

$$H_A: \quad \sigma_1^2 > \sigma_2^2 \quad \text{(There is greater variability among warmer climate flies.)}$$

Step 2

Choose the level of significance: The problem states $\alpha = .01$.

Step 3

Determine the sample sizes: The example states that $n_1 = n_2 = 31$.

Step 4

Determine the applicability of an appropriate statistic: The example says to assume that wing length measurements are normally distributed. The two samples are taken independent of each other. The example requires a test of the ratio σ_1^2 to σ_2^2. The numerator degrees of freedom is $n_1 - 1 = 31 - 1 = 30$. The denominator degrees of freedom is $n_2 - 1 = 31 - 1 = 30$. These conditions validate the use of the F statistic with 30 d.f. for the numerator and 30 d.f. for the denominator.

Step 5

Write the expression for the test statistic: The test statistic to be calculated is

$$F_{(30,30)} = \frac{S_1^2}{S_2^2}$$

Step 6

Determine the rejection region: The rejection region is given by $F_{(30,30)} > F_{(.01,30,30)} = 2.39$.

Step 7

Establish the value of the sample statistics: The problem specifies $S_1^2 = 0.00038809$ and $S_2^2 = 0.000144$.

Step 8

Determine the value of the test statistic and apply the decision rule: The observed value of the test statistic is

$$F_{(30,30)} = \frac{0.00038809}{0.000144} = 2.695$$

Since the observed value of the test statistic of 2.695 exceeds 2.39, it lies in the rejection region, so we reject H_o of equality of variance.

Step 9

Calculate the p-value: The p-value is $P(F_{(30,30)} > 2.695)$. To evaluate the probability requires a more inclusive table than provided in this book. However, the p-value is less than .01, and this low probability value indicates that it is very unlikely that such a result would occur if H_o is true.

Practical Interpretation

At the .01 level of significance we conclude that wing length is more variable among fruit flies of the given species living in a warm climate than those living in a colder climate. This finding agrees with some researchers' expectations, since it is known that the wing not only enables the fruit fly to fly, but also functions to maintain body heat. Since longer wings cause more body heat loss, flies with longer wings would be handicapped in colder climates. So it was anticipated that the colder climate would restrict the maximum length of the wing and, as a result, restrict the overall variability in wing length. Moreover, in accordance with the fact that insecticide resistance variability is associated with wing length variability, we might expect that the flies in the warmer climates would show greater variability in their resistance to the insecticide.

P R A C T I C E   E X E R C I S E

8.44 Suppose we wish to test the hypothesis that salaries vary as much among computer analysts as among account executives versus the alternative that salaries vary more among computer analysts than among account executives. If we take a random sample of $n_1 = 16$ computer analyst salaries and a random sample of $n_2 = 26$ account executive salaries, then

$$H_o: \quad \sigma_1^2 = \sigma_2^2$$
$$H_A: \quad \sigma_1^2 > \sigma_2^2$$

Use $\alpha = .05$, $n_1 = 16$, and $n_2 = 26$. Give the rejection region.

E X E R C I S E S

▶ **8.51** Twenty-two insurance policies from company A have a standard deviation of $3.70, and 31 policies from insurance company B have a standard deviation of $3.90. Test the assumption that the population variances are equal versus the alternative that they are unequal with an appropriate statistical test. Use the .10 level of significance.

8.52 A random sample of 61 of last year's model of automobiles have a standard deviation of 4.4 miles per gallon (mpg), and a random sample of 61 of this year's model have a standard deviation of 3.5 mpg. Use an appropriate statistical test to determine whether it would be reasonable to assume equality of variance. Use the .02 level of significance.

8.53 Consistency in a product is important to the consumer, especially with high-priced items like automobiles. For example, it may be true that two different models of automobiles advertise the same average miles per gallon in highway driving, but a potential buyer might want to know just how close to the advertised mileage a selected automobile will actually operate. If with one model the buyer can supposedly get the advertised mileage, but with another model the mileage is rumored to be more variable, it is likely the buyer would purchase the first, and not the second, model. Now suppose in actual tests with 121 automobiles of model A and 121 automobiles of model B, both yield the same average miles per gallon but the sample standard deviation for model A is 3.3 mpg, and the sample standard deviation for model B is 7.2 mpg. At the .01 level of significance, would you conclude that model B automobiles are less consistent (i.e., more variable) in their mileage performance than model A automobiles?

8.54 In a test of fire resistance involving two types of fabric, 10 strips of each type of fabric were placed in an oven in random order and heated. The temperatures at which the strips started to burn were recorded. If the variances in the critical temperatures for the two types of fabric were 7.4 and 2.9, would you say that there is sufficient evidence to indicate the variability in the critical temperature distribution of the two types of fabric are not the same? Use a level of significance of .10, and assume the critical temperatures are normally distributed.

SUMMARY

Hypothesis testing is intimately associated with the scientific method. That is, an idea or concept about the reality of some phenomenon may be formalized into an hypothesis, the null hypothesis. A contradiction of the null hypothesis then becomes the alternative hypothesis. The concept in the null hypothesis is subject to test by examining and analyzing relevant sample data. When the results of the analysis are consistent with the null hypothesis concept, the concept is not rejected. But when the results of the analysis are not consistent with the null hypothesis concept, the concept is rejected in favor of the contradiction expressed in the alternative hypothesis. The process is dynamic: When a concept is not rejected it is still subject to further testing as new data become available; and when a concept is rejected a new concept is formulated and is subject to testing as new data come in. In other words, we evaluate ideas and concepts of reality (hypotheses) on the basis of observed relevant data. We adjust or reevaluate our ideas and concepts in light of new incoming data. The process is ongoing.

In this chapter we addressed the issue of hypothesis testing for values of population parameters: means, proportions, and variances. We showed how to set up appropriate null and alternative hypotheses for the particular situations we presented. Using observed data, we provided techniques for determining the plausibility of the population parameter value stated in the null hypothesis.

We must always keep in mind that testing hypotheses by sample data may lead us to draw incorrect conclusions. Because sample data vary, a sample result may lead to two possible types of error. A Type I error is committed when the sample result leads us to the mistaken conclusion to reject the null hypothesis when we shouldn't. A type II error is committed when the sample result leads us to the mistaken conclusion not to reject the null hypothesis when we should. These errors are always possible, but the techniques we have developed and applied in this chapter are designed to make them improbable, or even highly improbable.

Although we can never be certain about our conceptions about business phenomena, the scientific methodology of statistical hypothesis testing makes it possible for us to reach conclusions from observed data with a high degree of confidence.

KEY EQUATIONS

Test Statistic for One Population Mean: σ Known

$$Z = \frac{\bar{X} - \mu_o}{\sigma/\sqrt{n}} \tag{8-1}$$

Rejection Region for (One-Sided) Upper Tail Test, One Population Mean: σ Known

$$Z = \frac{\bar{X} - \mu_o}{\sigma/\sqrt{n}} > +Z_\alpha \tag{8-2}$$

Rejection Region for (One-Sided) Lower Tail Test, One Population Mean: σ Known

$$Z = \frac{\bar{X} - \mu_o}{\sigma/\sqrt{n}} < -Z_\alpha \tag{8-3}$$

Rejection Region for Two-Sided Test, One Population Mean: σ Known

$$Z = \frac{\bar{X} - \mu_o}{\sigma/\sqrt{n}} < -Z_{\alpha/2} \quad \text{or} \quad Z = \frac{\bar{X} - \mu_o}{\sigma/\sqrt{n}} > +Z_{\alpha/2} \tag{8-4}$$

Test Statistic for One Population Mean: σ Unknown, Large Sample

$$Z = \frac{\bar{X} - \mu_o}{S/\sqrt{n}} \tag{8-5}$$

Value of β for the One-Sided Test Where $H_o: \mu = \mu_o$ versus $H_A: \mu_A < \mu_o$

$$\beta = P\left(Z > \frac{\mu_o - \mu_A}{S/\sqrt{n}} - Z_\alpha\right) \tag{8-6}$$

Value of β for the One-Sided Test Where $H_o: \mu = \mu_o$ versus $H_A: \mu_A > \mu_o$

$$\beta = P\left(Z < \frac{\mu_o - \mu_A}{S/\sqrt{n}} + Z_\alpha\right) \tag{8-7}$$

Value of β for the Two-Sided Test Where $H_o: \mu = \mu_o$ versus $H_A: \mu_A \neq \mu_o$

$$\beta = P\left(\frac{\mu_o - \mu_A}{S/\sqrt{n}} - Z_{\alpha/2} < Z < \frac{\mu_o - \mu_A}{S/\sqrt{n}} + Z_{\alpha/2}\right) \tag{8-8}$$

Test Statistic for One Population Mean: σ Unknown, Small Sample

$$t_{(n-1)} = \frac{\bar{X} - \mu_o}{S/\sqrt{n}} \tag{8-9}$$

Test Statistic for One Population Proportion

$$Z = \frac{\hat{p} - p}{\sqrt{\dfrac{p_o(1 - p_o)}{n}}} \tag{8-10}$$

Rejection Region for One-Sided Upper Tail Test for One Population Proportion

$$Z = \frac{\hat{p} - p_o}{\sqrt{\dfrac{p_o(1 - p_o)}{n}}} > +Z_\alpha \tag{8-11}$$

Rejection Region for One-Sided Lower Tail Test for One Population Proportion

$$Z = \frac{\hat{p} - p_\circ}{\sqrt{\dfrac{p_\circ(1 - p_\circ)}{n}}} < -Z_\alpha \qquad (8\text{-}12)$$

Rejection Region for Two-Sided Test for One Population Proportion

$$Z = \frac{\hat{p} - p_\circ}{\sqrt{\dfrac{p_\circ(1 - p_\circ)}{n}}} < -Z_{\alpha/2} \qquad \text{or} \qquad Z = \frac{\hat{p} - p_\circ}{\sqrt{\dfrac{p_\circ(1 - p_\circ)}{n}}} > +Z_{\alpha/2} \qquad (8\text{-}13)$$

Test Statistic for Two Population Means: Both Population Variances Known

$$Z = \frac{\bar{X}_1 - \bar{X}_2}{\sqrt{\dfrac{\sigma_1^2}{n_1} + \dfrac{\sigma_2^2}{n_2}}} \qquad (8\text{-}14)$$

The rejection region is given by $Z < -Z_\alpha$ for the one-sided test with H_A: $\mu_1 < \mu_2$, and by $|Z| > Z_{\alpha/2}$ for the two-sided test.

Pooled Estimate of σ

$$S_p = \sqrt{\frac{(n_1 - 1)S_1^2 + (n_2 - 1)S_2^2}{n_1 + n_2 - 2}} \qquad (8\text{-}15)$$

Test Statistic for Two Population Means, Both Population Variances Unknown, but Presumed Equal: Large Samples

$$Z = \frac{\bar{X}_1 - \bar{X}_2}{\sqrt{\dfrac{S_p^2}{n_1} + \dfrac{S_p^2}{n_2}}} = \frac{\bar{X}_1 - \bar{X}_2}{S_p \sqrt{\dfrac{1}{n_1} + \dfrac{1}{n_2}}} \qquad (8\text{-}16)$$

The rejection region for the one-sided test with H_A: $\mu_1 < \mu_2$ is given by $Z < -Z_\alpha$, and the rejection region for the two-sided test is given by $|Z| > Z_{\alpha/2}$.

Test Statistic for Two Population Means, Both Population Variances Unknown, but Presumed Equal: Small Samples

$$t_\nu = \frac{\bar{X}_1 - \bar{X}_2}{\sqrt{\dfrac{S_p^2}{n_1} + \dfrac{S_p^2}{n_2}}} = \frac{\bar{X}_1 - \bar{X}_2}{S_p \sqrt{\dfrac{1}{n_1} + \dfrac{1}{n_2}}} \qquad (8\text{-}17)$$

The number of degrees of freedom for the Student t statistic is $\nu = n_1 + n_2 - 2$. The rejection region for the one-sided test with H_A: $\mu_1 < \mu_2$ is given by $t_\nu < -t_{(\alpha, \nu)}$, and the rejection region for the two-sided test is given by $|t_\nu| > t_{(\alpha/2, \nu)}$.

Test Statistic for Two Population Means, Both Population Variances Unknown, but Presumed Unequal: Large Samples

$$Z = \frac{\bar{X}_1 - \bar{X}_2}{\sqrt{\dfrac{S_1^2}{n_1} + \dfrac{S_2^2}{n_2}}} \qquad (8\text{-}18)$$

The rejection region for the one-sided test with H_A: $\mu_1 < \mu_2$ is given by $Z < -Z_\alpha$, and the rejection region for the two-sided test is given by $|Z| > Z_{\alpha/2}$.

Test Statistic for Two Population Means, Both Population Variances Unknown, but Presumed Unequal: Small Samples

$$t_\nu = \frac{\bar{X}_1 - \bar{X}_2}{\sqrt{\dfrac{S_1^2}{n_1} + \dfrac{S_2^2}{n_2}}} \tag{8-19}$$

where ν represents the number of degrees of freedom for the Student t statistic, and the value of ν we use is the smaller of $n_1 - 1$ and $n_2 - 1$, or is obtained via the expression

$$\nu = \frac{\left(\dfrac{S_1^2}{n_1} + \dfrac{S_2^2}{n_2}\right)^2}{\dfrac{(S_1^2/n_1)^2}{n_1 - 1} + \dfrac{(S_2^2/n_2)^2}{n_2 - 1}} \tag{8-20}$$

which is rounded to the nearest integer.

Pooled Estimate of p

$$\hat{p}_P = \frac{X_1 + X_2}{n_1 + n_2} \tag{8-21}$$

where X_1 represents the number of "successes" among the n_1 trials from the first population, and X_2 represents the number of "successes" among the n_2 trials from the second population.

Test Statistic to Test Two Population Proportions

$$Z = \frac{\hat{p}_1 - \hat{p}_2}{\sqrt{\hat{p}_P(1 - \hat{p}_P)\left(\dfrac{1}{n_1} + \dfrac{1}{n_2}\right)}} \tag{8-22}$$

where $\hat{p}_1 = X_1/n_1$ and $\hat{p}_2 = X_2/n_2$. For the one-sided test ($H_A: p_1 < p_2$), the rejection region is given by $Z < -Z_\alpha$. For the two-sided test, the rejection region is given by $|Z| > Z_{\alpha/2}$.

Test Statistic for Paired Observations

$$t_{(n-1)} = \frac{\bar{d}}{S_d/\sqrt{n}} \tag{8-23}$$

Test Statistic to Test One Population Variance

$$\chi^2_{(n-1)} = \frac{(n-1)S^2}{\sigma_0^2} \tag{8-24}$$

Rejection Region for One-Sided (Upper Tail) Test of One Population Variance

$$\frac{(n-1)S^2}{\sigma_0^2} > \chi^2_{(\alpha, n-1)} \tag{8-25}$$

Rejection Region for One-Sided (Lower Tail) Test of One Population Variance

$$\frac{(n-1)S^2}{\sigma_0^2} < \chi^2_{(1-\alpha, n-1)} \tag{8-26}$$

Rejection Region for Two-Sided Test of One Population Variance

$$\frac{(n-1)S^2}{\sigma_0^2} < \chi^2_{(1-\alpha/2, n-1)} \quad \text{or} \quad \frac{(n-1)S^2}{\sigma_0^2} > \chi^2_{(\alpha/2, n-1)} \tag{8-27}$$

Test Statistic to Test Two Population Variances

$$F_{(n_1-1, n_2-1)} = \frac{S_1^2}{S_2^2} \qquad (8\text{-}28)$$

Rejection Region for One-Sided Test of Two Population Variances

$$F_{(n_1-1, n_2-1)} > F_{(\alpha, n_1-1, n_2-1)} \qquad (8\text{-}29)$$

Rejection Region for Two-Sided Test of Two Population Variances

First, determine whether S_1^2 or S_2^2 has the larger value. Then:

If S_1^2 has the larger value, the test statistic is

$$F_{(n_1-1, n_2-1)} = \frac{S_1^2}{S_2^2} \qquad \text{and } H_o \text{ is rejected if} \qquad F_{(n_1-1, n_2-1)} > F_{(\alpha/2, n_1-1, n_2-1)} \qquad (8\text{-}30)$$

If S_2^2 has the larger value, the test statistic is

$$F_{(n_2-1, n_1-1)} = \frac{S_2^2}{S_1^2} \qquad \text{and } H_o \text{ is rejected if} \qquad F_{(n_2-1, n_1-1)} > F_{(\alpha/2, n_2-1, n_1-1)} \qquad (8\text{-}31)$$

PRACTICE EXERCISE ANSWERS

8.1 a. No; a calculated *p*-value of .001 means that there is only 1 chance in 1000 that an outcome as unusual as the observed $20,000 increase would occur if the true increase is $100,000.

   b. Yes; finding a *p*-value of .276 suggests that an outcome as unusual as the observed $20,000 increase could have occurred by chance as often as 27.6% of the time in 6 month trials like this one.

8.2 a. No; a *p*-value of .39 tells us that the observed 86% on-schedule rate could occur by chance as often as 39 times in 100 tries. Thus, the observed result is not unusual, and it would be consistent with the airline claim.

   b. The very low *p*-value of .00235 means that the chance of observing the sample result is only 235 out of 100,000 if it is true that planes arrive on schedule at least 95% of the time.

8.3 No; a *p*-value of .00085 means that there are only 85 chances in 100,000 that a sample would show an average of 2.3 ppm if the true average for the frozen fish sticks is 2 ppm. This result is too unusual to be consistent with the manufacturer's claim.

8.4 The alternative hypothesis should be expressed as:

   H_A: A computer with a powerful word processor will not increase student proficiency at reading and writing.

8.5 a. Since the null hypothesis simply states that the average return is 10%, the alternative hypothesis is that the return is not 10%:

   H_A: The broker's clients do not earn an average return of 10% per year on their investments.

   b. Since the claim is that the return is at least 10%, the alternative is that the return is not at least 10%:

   H_A: The broker's clients, on average, earn less than 10% per year on their investments.

    c. Since the claim is that the return is at most 10%, the alternative is that the return is not at most 10%:

        H_A: The broker's clients, on average, earn more than 10% per year on their investments.

8.6 The alternative hypothesis should be expressed as:

        H_A: A market crash will not follow if the index of 10 economic indicators turns negative.

8.7 a. The conclusion would be that a computer with a powerful word processor will not increase student proficiency at reading and writing.
    b. The conclusion would be that a computer with a powerful word processor will increase student proficiency at reading and writing.
    c. A Type I error is made if the null hypothesis is true but the decision is to reject it. The conclusion if the null hypothesis is rejected is that a computer with a powerful word processor will not increase student proficiency at reading and writing.
    d. A Type II error is made if the null hypothesis is false but the decision is to not reject it. The conclusion if the null hypothesis is not rejected is that a computer with a powerful word processor will increase student proficiency at reading and writing.

8.8 a. This would be a Type II error. The error could be serious if your return is much less than what you expected and if you could have earned a much higher return elsewhere.
    b. This is a Type I error. The error could be serious if you got a much lower return elsewhere than what you could have earned with this investment broker.

8.9 a. The other two possibilities are: you have a losing hand but you continue playing the hand; you have a losing hand and you fold.
    b. You could commit a Type II error if you continue playing the hand. You could commit a Type I error if you fold.

8.10 a. The null and alternative hypotheses are:

        H_o: You have the proper qualifications.

        H_A: You do not have the proper qualifications.

    b. If you do have the proper qualifications, then the null hypothesis is true. By rejecting a true null hypothesis a Type I error is made.

8.11 The necessary values are the Z values that leave area of $\alpha/2 = .005$ in each tail of the standard normal distribution. The values are $Z_c = -2.576$ and $Z_c = +2.576$.

8.12 The one-sided upper tail area above $Z = +1.96$ is $\alpha = .025$.

8.13 The one-sided lower tail area below $Z = -1.96$ is $\alpha = .025$.

8.14 The two-sided area is $P(Z > +2.04) + P(Z < -2.04) = 2(.5 - .4793) = .0414$.

8.15 a. Do not reject H_o, since 1.98 is not greater than 2.04.
    b. Reject H_o, since 10.98 is greater than 2.04.

8.16 a. Do not reject H_o, since -1.33 is not less than -2.04.
    b. Reject H_o, since -2.43 is less than -2.04.
    c. Do not reject H_o, since 1.98 is not less than -2.04.
    d. Do not reject H_o, since 10.98 is not less than -2.04.

8.17 Yes; a p-value of .0034 is less than the level of significance $\alpha = .05$. The null hypothesis would be rejected.

8.18 Rejecting the null hypothesis would lead to the conclusion that the company has committed fraud.

8.19 a. Rejecting the null hypothesis would lead to the conclusion that the weight is less than $\frac{1}{4}$ lb.

b. If we do not reject the null hypothesis, we would conclude that the weight of the meat in a $\frac{1}{4}$ lb burger is $\frac{1}{4}$ lb.

8.20 a. Rejecting the null hypothesis would lead to the conclusion that the company is not financially solvent.

b. If we do not reject the null hypothesis, we would conclude that the company is financially solvent.

c. Yes, it could be quite serious to the survival of the company if it is falsely accused of not being financially solvent.

d. Yes, it could be serious to investors who are led to believe the company is financially solvent when it isn't.

8.21 a. The null and alternative hypotheses are:

H_o: $p = .5$

H_A: $p > .5$

b. For a one-sided upper tail test and a 1% level of significance, Z_c is the value that cuts off 1% in the upper tail of the standard normal distribution. In other words, we need to find Z_c such that $P(Z > Z_c) = .01$. The needed value is $Z_c = 2.326$.

c. The rejection region is $Z > Z_\alpha = Z_{.01} = 2.326$.

d. The decision rule is to not reject the null hypothesis unless the standardized value of the test statistic is greater than 2.326.

e. Here, $n = 600$, $p = .5$, and $\hat{p} = \frac{338}{600} = .5633$, so the value of the test statistic is

$$Z = \frac{\hat{p} - p}{\sqrt{\dfrac{p(1 - p)}{n}}} = \frac{.5633 - .5}{\sqrt{\dfrac{(.5)(1 - .5)}{600}}} = 3.10$$

f. Since $Z = 3.10 > Z_c = 2.326$, the null hypothesis that the probability of heads on each toss is .5 is rejected.

g. The maximum level of significance at which H_o could be rejected is given by the p-value of the test statistic,

$$p\text{-value} = P(X \geq 338) = P(Z \geq 3.10) = .5 - .49903 = .00097$$

This means that H_o is rejected for levels of significance of 0.097% or greater, and H_o is not rejected for levels of significance below 0.097%.

8.22 a. Let

$$H_o: \quad \mu = 40 \quad \text{(Checks average \$40.)}$$
$$H_A: \quad \mu > 40 \quad \text{(Checks average more than \$40.)}$$

This is a one-sided test. Here, $n = 16$, $\sigma = 8$, and $\alpha = .05$, so $Z_\alpha = 1.645$. Thus, the null hypothesis is rejected if $Z > 1.645$. The rejection region is

$$Z = \frac{\bar{X} - \mu}{\sigma/\sqrt{n}} = \frac{\bar{X} - 40}{8/4} > 1.645$$

b. Let

$$H_o: \quad \mu = 40 \quad \text{(Checks average \$40.)}$$
$$H_A: \quad \mu \neq 40 \quad \text{(Checks do not average \$40.)}$$

This is a two-sided test. Here, $n = 16$, $\sigma = 8$, and $\alpha = .05$, so $Z_{\alpha/2} = 1.96$. Thus, the null hypothesis is rejected if $Z > +1.96$ or if $Z < -1.96$. The rejection region is

$$Z = \frac{\bar{X} - 40}{8/4} < -1.96 \quad \text{or} \quad Z = \frac{\bar{X} - 40}{8/4} > 1.96$$

8.23 a. Let

$$H_o: \quad \mu = 40 \quad \text{(Checks average \$40.)}$$
$$H_A: \quad \mu < 40 \quad \text{(Checks average less than \$40.)}$$

This is a one-sided test. Here, $n = 16$, $\sigma = 8$, $\bar{X} = 35$, and $\alpha = .05$, so $Z_\alpha = 1.645$. Thus, the null hypothesis is rejected if $Z < -1.645$. The sample outcome is

$$Z = \frac{\bar{X} - \mu}{\sigma/\sqrt{n}} = \frac{35 - 40}{8/4} = -2.5$$

so the null hypothesis is rejected at the .05 level of significance.

b. The p-value is $P(Z \le -2.5) = .5 - .4938 = .0062$.

8.24 a. Let

$$H_o: \quad \mu = 160 \quad \text{(Checks average \$160.)}$$
$$H_A: \quad \mu < 160 \quad \text{(Checks average less than \$160.)}$$

This is a one-sided test. Here, $n = 64$, σ is unknown, $S = 20$, and $\alpha = .05$, so $Z_\alpha = 1.645$. Thus, the null hypothesis is rejected if $Z < -1.645$. Even though the population standard deviation is unknown, a Z statistic is used because the sample size is larger than 30. The rejection region is

$$Z = \frac{\bar{X} - \mu}{S/\sqrt{n}} = \frac{\bar{X} - 160}{S/8} < -1.645$$

b. For a two-sided test, $\alpha = .05$, so $Z_{\alpha/2} = 1.96$. Thus, the null hypothesis is rejected if $Z < -1.96$ or if $Z > +1.96$. The rejection region is

$$Z = \frac{\bar{X} - 160}{S/8} < -1.96 \qquad \text{or} \qquad Z = \frac{\bar{X} - 160}{S/8} > +1.96$$

8.25 a. Let

$$H_o: \quad \mu = 160 \quad \text{(Checks average \$160.)}$$
$$H_A: \quad \mu > 160 \quad \text{(Checks average more than \$160.)}$$

This is a one-sided test. Here, $n = 64$, $S = 20$, $\bar{X} = 164.31$, and $\alpha = .05$, so $Z_\alpha = 1.645$. Thus, the null hypothesis is rejected if $Z > +1.645$. The test statistic is

$$Z = \frac{\bar{X} - \mu}{S/\sqrt{n}} = \frac{164.31 - 160}{20/8} = 1.724$$

so the null hypothesis is rejected at the .05 level of significance.

b. The p-value is $P(Z \ge 1.724) \approx .5 - .4573 = .0427$.

8.26 a. For this lower tail test, H_o is rejected if $\bar{X}$ falls sufficiently below $\mu_o = 1215$. For $\alpha = .05$, the lower limit before the null hypothesis is rejected is

$$\mu_o - 1.645(S/\sqrt{n}) = 1215 - 1.645(250/\sqrt{100}) = 1173.875$$

Thus,

$$\beta = P(\text{Type II error}) = P(H_o \text{ is not rejected, given } H_A \text{ is true})$$
$$= P(\bar{X} > 1173.875 | \mu_A = 1200)$$
$$= P\left(Z > \frac{1173.875 - \mu_A}{S/\sqrt{n}}\right) = P\left(Z > \frac{1173.875 - 1200}{250/\sqrt{100}}\right)$$
$$= P(Z > -1.05) \quad \text{(approx.)}$$
$$= .8531$$

b. The power of the test is $1 - \beta = 1 - .8531 = .1469$ (approx.).

c. $\beta = P(\text{Type II error}) = P(H_o \text{ is not rejected, given } H_A \text{ is true})$

$= P(\bar{X} > 1173.875 | \mu_A = 1190)$

$= P\left(Z > \dfrac{1173.875 - \mu_A}{S/\sqrt{n}}\right) = P\left(Z > \dfrac{1173.875 - 1190}{250/\sqrt{100}}\right)$

$= P(Z > -0.65)$ (approx.)

$= .7422$

The power of the test is $1 - \beta = 1 - .7422 = .2578$ (approx.).

d. Yes; notice that as the difference between μ_o and μ_A increased so did the power of the test to discriminate.

8.27 a. For this upper tail test, H_o is rejected if $\bar{X}$ falls sufficiently above $\mu_o = 37$. For $\alpha = .05$, the upper limit before the null hypothesis is rejected is

$$\mu_o + 1.645(S/\sqrt{n}) = 37 + 1.645(15/\sqrt{225}) = 38.645$$

Thus,

$\beta = P(\text{Type II error}) = P(H_o \text{ is not rejected, given } H_A \text{ is true})$

$= P(\bar{X} < 38.645 | \mu_A = 38)$

$= P\left(Z < \dfrac{38.645 - \mu_A}{S/\sqrt{n}}\right) = P\left(Z < \dfrac{38.645 - 38}{15/\sqrt{225}}\right)$

$= P(Z < 0.65)$ (approx.)

$= .7422$

b. The power of the test is $1 - \beta = 1 - .7422 = .2578$ (approx.).

c. $\beta = P(\text{Type II error}) = P(H_o \text{ is not rejected, given } H_A \text{ is true})$

$= P(\bar{X} < 38.645 | \mu_A = 39)$

$= P\left(Z < \dfrac{38.645 - \mu_A}{S/\sqrt{n}}\right) = P\left(Z < \dfrac{38.645 - 39}{15/\sqrt{225}}\right)$

$= P(Z < -0.36)$ (approx.)

$= .3594$

The power of the test is $1 - \beta = 1 - .3594 = .6406$ (approx.).

d. Yes; notice that as the difference between μ_o and μ_A increased so did the power of the test to discriminate.

8.28 a. For this two-sided test, H_o is not rejected if $\bar{X}$ is sufficiently close to $\mu_o = 499$. For $\alpha = .05$, the boundaries of the rejection region are $\mu_o \pm 1.960(S/\sqrt{n})$, so

$$499 + 1.960(36/\sqrt{144}) = 504.88$$
$$499 - 1.960(36/\sqrt{144}) = 493.12$$

Thus,

$\beta = P(\text{Type II error}) = P(H_o \text{ is not rejected, given } H_A \text{ is true})$

$= P(493.12 < \bar{X} < 504.88 | \mu_A = 496)$

$= P\left(\dfrac{493.12 - \mu_A}{S/\sqrt{n}} < Z < \dfrac{504.88 - \mu_A}{S/\sqrt{n}}\right)$

$= P\left(\dfrac{493.12 - 496}{15/\sqrt{144}} < Z < \dfrac{504.88 - 496}{36/\sqrt{144}}\right)$

$= P(-0.96 < Z < 2.96) = .8300$

b. The power of the test is $1 - \beta = 1 - .8300 = .1700$.

c.
$$\beta = P(\text{Type II error}) = P(H_o \text{ is not rejected, given } H_A \text{ is true})$$

$$= P(493.12 < \bar{X} < 504.88 | \mu_A = 502)$$

$$= P\left(\frac{493.12 - \mu_A}{S/\sqrt{n}} < Z < \frac{504.88 - \mu_A}{S/\sqrt{n}}\right)$$

$$= P\left(\frac{493.12 - 502}{15/\sqrt{144}} < Z < \frac{504.88 - 502}{36/\sqrt{144}}\right)$$

$$= P(-2.96 < Z < 0.96) = .8300$$

The power of the test is $1 - \beta = 1 - .8300 = .1700$.

d. No; they are equal since this is a two-sided test and the value of the difference between μ_o and the two alternate values of μ_A are equal.

8.29 a. Let

$$H_o: \quad \mu = 83 \quad \text{(Charges average \$83.)}$$
$$H_A: \quad \mu < 83 \quad \text{(Charges average less than \$83.)}$$

This is a one-sided test. Here, $n = 16$ (which is less than 30) and σ is unknown, so a t statistic with $n - 1 = 15$ d.f. must be used. $\alpha = .05$, so $t_{.05,15} = 1.753$; thus, the null hypothesis is rejected if $t_{15} < -1.753$. The rejection region is

$$t_{15} = \frac{\bar{X} - \mu}{S/\sqrt{n}} < -1.753$$

b. For the two-sided problem, the hypotheses are

$$H_o \quad \mu = 83 \quad \text{(Charges average \$83.)}$$
$$H_A: \quad \mu \neq 83 \quad \text{(Charges do not average \$83.)}$$

$\alpha = .05$, so $t_{\alpha/2,n-1} = t_{.025,15} = 2.131$; thus, the null hypothesis is rejected if $t_{15} < -2.131$ or if $t_{15} > +2.131$. The rejection region is

$$t_{15} = \frac{\bar{X} - \mu}{S/\sqrt{n}} < -2.131 \qquad \text{or} \qquad t_{15} = \frac{\bar{X} - \mu}{S/\sqrt{n}} > 2.131$$

8.30 a. Let

$$H_o: \quad \mu = 83 \quad \text{(Charges average \$83.)}$$
$$H_A: \quad \mu > 83 \quad \text{(Charges average more than \$83.)}$$

This is a one-sided test, where $n = 16$ (which is less than 30) and σ is unknown, so a t statistic with $n - 1 = 15$ d.f. must be used. $S = 8$, $\bar{X} = 85.1$, and $\alpha = .05$, so $t_{.05,15} = 1.753$; thus, the null hypothesis is rejected if $t_{15} > +1.753$. The test statistic is

$$t_{15} = \frac{\bar{X} - \mu}{S/\sqrt{n}} = \frac{85.1 - 83}{8/4} = 1.05$$

so the null hypothesis is not rejected at the .05 level of significance.

b. The p-value is $P(t_{15} \geq 1.05)$, which is greater than .10.

8.31 a. The population standard deviation is known, so a Z statistic is used. $\alpha = .025$, so $Z_\alpha = 1.96$, and H_o is rejected if

$$Z = \frac{\bar{X} - \mu}{\sigma/\sqrt{n}} = \frac{\bar{X} - 99}{6/5} > 1.96$$

b. The population standard deviation is unknown and the sample size is less than 30, so a t statistic with $n - 1 = 24$ d.f. is used. $\alpha = .025$, so $t_{\alpha,n-1} = t_{.025,24} = 2.064$, and H_o is rejected if

$$t_{24} = \frac{\bar{X} - \mu}{S/\sqrt{n}} = \frac{\bar{X} - 99}{6/5} > 2.064$$

c. The population standard deviation is unknown, but the sample size is larger than 30, so a Z statistic is used. $\alpha = .025$, so $Z_\alpha = 1.96$, and H_o is rejected if

$$Z = \frac{\bar{X} - \mu}{S/\sqrt{n}} = \frac{\bar{X} - 99}{6/6} > 1.96$$

8.32 a. The rejection region for $\alpha = .05$ and a one-sided upper tail hypothesis is $Z > Z_\alpha = Z_{.05} = +1.645$:

$$Z = \frac{\hat{p} - .45}{\sqrt{\dfrac{(.45)(.55)}{n}}} > +1.645$$

b. The rejection region for $\alpha = .05$ and a one-sided lower tail hypothesis is $Z < -Z_\alpha = -Z_{.05} = -1.645$

$$Z = \frac{\hat{p} - .45}{\sqrt{\dfrac{(.45)(.55)}{n}}} < -1.645$$

8.33 a. Let

$$H_o: \quad p = .63 \quad (63\% \text{ of the cars are imports.})$$
$$H_A: \quad p < .63 \quad (\text{Fewer than } 63\% \text{ of the cars are imports.})$$

This is a one-sided lower tail test. $\alpha = .025$, so $Z_\alpha = -1.96$; thus, the null hypothesis is rejected if $Z < -1.96$. Here, $n = 100$ and $\hat{p} = x/n = 40/100 = .4$, so

$$Z = \frac{\hat{p} - p}{\sqrt{\dfrac{p(1-p)}{n}}} = \frac{.4 - .63}{\sqrt{\dfrac{(.63)(.37)}{100}}} = -4.764$$

The observed value, -4.764, is less than -1.96, so the null hypothesis is rejected at the .025 level of significance.

b. The p-value, rounding off the Z value obtained above, is $P(Z \leq -4.76) = 0$ (approx.).

8.34 The rejection region for $\alpha = .05$ and a two-sided hypothesis is $|Z| > Z_{\alpha/2} = |Z_{.025}| = 1.96$:

$$|Z| = \left| \frac{\hat{p} - .30}{\sqrt{\dfrac{(.30)(.70)}{n}}} \right| > 1.96$$

8.35 Let

$$H_o: \quad p = .54 \quad (54\% \text{ of the cars exceed the speed limit.})$$
$$H_A: \quad p \neq .54 \quad (\text{More or less than } 54\% \text{ of the cars exceed the speed limit.})$$

This is a two-sided test. $\alpha = .01$, so $Z_{\alpha/2} = 2.576$; thus, the null hypothesis is rejected if $Z > 2.576$ or if $Z < -2.576$. Here, $n = 100$ and $\hat{p} = x/n = 60/100 = .6$, so

$$|Z| = \left| \frac{\hat{p} - p}{\sqrt{\dfrac{p(1-p)}{n}}} \right| = \left| \frac{.6 - .54}{\sqrt{\dfrac{(.54)(.46)}{100}}} \right| = 1.20$$

The observed value of 1.20 is not in the rejection region, so the null hypothesis is not rejected at the .01 level of significance.

8.36 a. Since both population standard deviations are known, the appropriate test statistic is the Z statistic. $Z_{\alpha/2} = 1.96$ for a two-sided test with $\alpha = .05$, so the rejection region is $|Z| > 1.96$, where

$$Z = \frac{\bar{X}_1 - \bar{X}_2}{\sqrt{\dfrac{\sigma_1^2}{n_1} + \dfrac{\sigma_2^2}{n_2}}} = \frac{\bar{X}_1 - \bar{X}_2}{\sqrt{\dfrac{121}{9} + \dfrac{81}{16}}}$$

b. This is a one-sided lower tail test, with $Z_\alpha = 1.645$ for $\alpha = .05$, so the rejection region is $Z < -1.645$, where

$$Z = \frac{\bar{X}_1 - \bar{X}_2}{\sqrt{\dfrac{\sigma_1^2}{n_1} + \dfrac{\sigma_2^2}{n_2}}} = \frac{\bar{X}_1 - \bar{X}_2}{\sqrt{\dfrac{121}{9} + \dfrac{81}{16}}}$$

c. This is also a one-sided lower tail test, but μ_1 now represents the mean growth rate of eastern cities and μ_2 represents the mean growth rate of western cities. $Z_\alpha = 1.645$ for $\alpha = .05$, so the rejection region is $Z < -1.645$, where

$$Z = \frac{\bar{X}_1 - \bar{X}_2}{\sqrt{\dfrac{\sigma_1^2}{n_1} + \dfrac{\sigma_2^2}{n_2}}} = \frac{\bar{X}_1 - \bar{X}_2}{\sqrt{\dfrac{81}{16} + \dfrac{121}{9}}}$$

8.37 The population standard deviations are unknown but presumed equal, and the sample sizes are large, so the test statistic is the Z statistic. The pooled estimated of $\sigma_1 = \sigma_2$ is

$$S_p = \sqrt{\frac{(n_1 - 1)S_1^2 + (n_2 - 1)S_2^2}{n_1 + n_2 - 2}} = \sqrt{\frac{(159)(121) + (169)(81)}{160 + 170 - 2}} = 10.0195$$

a. Since $\alpha = .05$ and this is a two-sided test, the rejection region is $|Z| > 1.96$, where

$$Z = \frac{\bar{X}_1 - \bar{X}_2}{S_p \sqrt{\dfrac{1}{n_1} + \dfrac{1}{n_2}}} = \frac{\bar{X}_1 - \bar{X}_2}{10.0195 \sqrt{\dfrac{1}{160} + \dfrac{1}{170}}}$$

b. Since $\alpha = .05$ and this is a one-sided lower tail test, the rejection region is $Z < -1.645$, where Z is given as shown in part a.

c. Since $\alpha = .05$ and this is a one-sided upper tail test, the rejection region is $Z > +1.645$, where Z is given as shown in part a.

8.38 The population standard deviations are unknown but presumed equal, but the sample sizes are small, so the test statistic is the t statistic with $n_1 + n_2 - 2 = 9 + 16 - 2 = 23$ d.f. The pooled estimated of $\sigma_1 = \sigma_2$ is

$$S_p = \sqrt{\frac{(n_1 - 1)S_1^2 + (n_2 - 1)S_2^2}{n_1 + n_2 - 2}} = \sqrt{\frac{(8)(196) + (15)(100)}{9 + 16 - 2}} = 11.5495$$

a. Since $\alpha = .05$ and this is a two-sided test, the rejection region is $|t_{23}| > 2.069$, where

$$t_{23} = \frac{\bar{X}_1 - \bar{X}_2}{S_p \sqrt{\dfrac{1}{n_1} + \dfrac{1}{n_2}}} = \frac{\bar{X}_1 - \bar{X}_2}{11.5495 \sqrt{\dfrac{1}{9} + \dfrac{1}{16}}}$$

b. Since $\alpha = .05$ and this is a one-sided lower tail test, the rejection region is $t_{23} < -1.714$, where t_{23} is given as shown in part a.

c. This is a one-sided upper tail test, so the rejection region is $t_{23} > +1.714$, where t_{23} is given as shown in part a.

8.39 The population standard deviations are unknown and presumed unequal, but the sample sizes are both larger than 30, so the test statistic is the Z statistic.

a. Since $\alpha = .05$ and this is a two-sided test, the rejection region is $|Z| > 1.96$, where

$$Z = \frac{\bar{X}_1 - \bar{X}_2}{\sqrt{\dfrac{S_1^2}{n_1} + \dfrac{S_2^2}{n_2}}} = \frac{\bar{X}_1 - \bar{X}_2}{\sqrt{\dfrac{5.43}{85} + \dfrac{1.46}{135}}}$$

b. Since $\alpha = .05$ and this is a one-sided upper tail test, the rejection region is $Z > +1.645$, where Z is given as shown in part a.

c. The Z statistic is the same as shown above in part a, but the test is a one-sided lower tail test. The rejection region is $Z < -1.645$.

8.40 The population standard deviations are unknown and presumed unequal, and the sample sizes are small, so the test statistic is the t statistic. The number of degrees of freedom can be chosen conservatively as the smaller of $n_1 - 1$ and $n_2 - 1$. This conservative approach yields $\nu = 15$ d.f. Note that the theoretically correct formula for ν generates a larger number of degrees of freedom:

$$\nu = \frac{[(S_1^2/n_1) + (S_2^2/n_2)]^2}{\dfrac{(S_1^2/n_1)^2}{n_1 - 1} + \dfrac{(S_2^2/n_2)^2}{n_2 - 1}} = \frac{[(67/16) + (129/25)]^2}{\dfrac{(67/16)^2}{15} + \dfrac{(129/25)^2}{24}} = 38.35$$

which is rounded to $\nu = 38$.

a. Since $\alpha = .05$ and this is a two-sided test, the rejection region, using $\nu = 15$ d.f., is $|t_{15}| > 2.131$, where

$$t_{15} = \frac{\bar{X}_1 - \bar{X}_2}{\sqrt{\dfrac{S_1^2}{n_1} + \dfrac{S_2^2}{n_2}}} = \frac{\bar{X}_1 - \bar{X}_2}{\sqrt{\dfrac{67}{16} + \dfrac{129}{25}}}$$

If $\nu = 38$ d.f. is used, the rejection region is $|t_{38}| > 2.021$ (this is an approximation, taken from the 40 d.f. row in the t table). One can see that the simpler conservative method gives a rejection region with an effective level of significance that is slightly smaller than α.

b. Since $\alpha = .05$ and this is a one-sided lower tail test, the rejection region using $\nu = 15$ d.f. is $t_{15} < -1.753$, where t_{15} is given as shown in part a.

c. $\alpha = .05$ and this is a one-sided upper tail test, so the rejection region is $t_{15} > +1.753$, where t_{15} is given as shown in part a.

8.41 a. Both sample sizes are small, but since both population standard deviations are known, the appropriate test statistic is the Z statistic. This is a one-sided lower tail test with $Z_\alpha = 1.645$ for $\alpha = .05$, so the rejection region is $Z < -1.645$, where

$$Z = \frac{\bar{X}_1 - \bar{X}_2}{\sqrt{\dfrac{\sigma_1^2}{n_1} + \dfrac{\sigma_2^2}{n_2}}} = \frac{\bar{X}_1 - \bar{X}_2}{\sqrt{\dfrac{22}{6} + \dfrac{71}{8}}}$$

b. The population standard deviations are unknown and presumed unequal, and the sample sizes are small, so the test statistic is the t statistic. The number of degrees of freedom can be conservatively estimated to be the smaller of $n_1 - 1$ and $n_2 - 1$. The conservative approach yields $\nu = 5$ d.f. Since $\alpha = .05$ and this is a lower-tail test, the rejection region is $t_5 < -2.015$, where

$$t_5 = \frac{\bar{X}_1 - \bar{X}_2}{\sqrt{\frac{S_1^2}{n_1} + \frac{S_2^2}{n_2}}} = \frac{\bar{X}_1 - \bar{X}_2}{\sqrt{\frac{22}{6} + \frac{71}{8}}}$$

Note that the theoretically correct formula for ν generates a larger number of degrees of freedom:

$$\nu = \frac{[(S_1^2/n_1) + (S_2^2/n_2)]^2}{\frac{(S_1^2/n_1)^2}{n_1 - 1} + \frac{(S_2^2/n_2)^2}{n_2 - 1}} = \frac{[(22/6) + (71/8)]^2}{\frac{(22/6)^2}{5} + \frac{(71/8)^2}{7}} = 11.28$$

which is rounded to $\nu = 11$.

c. In part a, the rejection region would be $Z > +1.645$; and in part b, the rejection region would be $t_5 > +2.015$. The form of the Z and t statistics would remain the same.

8.42 Let

$$H_o: \quad p_1 = p_2 \quad \text{(Both brands contain the same proportion of containers with broken aspirin tablets.)}$$

$$H_A: \quad p_1 \neq p_2 \quad \text{(The proportions are not the same.)}$$

Let X_1 be the number of containers in which broken tablets are found in the 56 bottles of generic aspirin sampled, and let X_2 be the number of containers in which broken tablets are found in the 75 bottles of the name brand aspirin. Then the pooled estimate of p is

$$\hat{p}_P = \frac{X_1 + X_2}{n_1 + n_2} = \frac{X_1 + X_2}{56 + 75}$$

$Z_{\alpha/2} = 1.96$ for a two-sided test with $\alpha = .05$, so the rejection region is $|Z| > 1.96$, where

$$|Z| = \left| \frac{\frac{X_1}{56} + \frac{X_2}{75}}{\sqrt{\hat{p}_P(1 - \hat{p}_P)\left(\frac{1}{56} + \frac{1}{75}\right)}} \right|$$

8.43 Let

$$H_o: \quad \sigma^2 = 4{,}410{,}000 = (2100)^2 \quad \text{(Variability is equal to \$2100.)}$$

$$H_A: \quad \sigma^2 > 4{,}410{,}000 = (2100)^2 \quad \text{(Variability exceeds \$2100.)}$$

A chi-square statistic with $n - 1$ degrees of freedom is used for this test. Here, $n = 20$ and $\alpha = .025$. The null hypothesis is rejected if $\chi_{19}^2 > \chi_{(\alpha, n-1)}^2 = \chi_{(.025, 19)}^2 = 32.8523$, where the test statistic is

$$\chi_{19}^2 = \frac{(n - 1)S^2}{\sigma_0^2} = \frac{(19)S^2}{4{,}410{,}000}$$

8.44 The test statistic for this one-sided test of two population variances is the F statistic, with $n_1 - 1 = 15$ d.f. and $n_2 - 1 = 25$ d.f. The null hypothesis is rejected if

$$F_{(n_1-1, n_2-1)} = \frac{S_1^2}{S_2^2} > F_{(\alpha, n_1-1, n_2-1)} = F_{(.05, 15, 25)} = 2.09$$

CHAPTER REVIEW EXERCISES

8.55 In a given sales region it is known that approximately 1 in 10 smokers favor a certain brand of cigarettes. After a promotional campaign in the given sales region, a random sample of 200 cigarette smokers were interviewed to determine the effectiveness of the campaign. The result of the survey showed that a total of 26 people expressed a preference for the above brand. Is there significant evidence that the campaign increased the proportion of smokers favoring this brand? Use a level of significance of .05. What is the actual *p*-value in this case?

8.56 A medical researcher believes that 9% of the people in a certain county are allergic to oranges. If 11 persons from a random sample of 100 persons living in the county are found to· be allergic to oranges, does this constitute significant evidence that the true proportion is different from 9%? Use a level of significance of .10.

8.57 A member of the Board of Education in a very large city believes that 40% of the students in the city's schools wear glasses or contact lenses. In a random sample of 60 students, 36 wore glasses or contact lenses. Does this provide significant evidence that the true percentage is different from 40%? Use a level of significance of .05. What is the *p*-value in this case?

▶ **8.58** A manufacturer of automatic washing machines sells a particular model in one of three colors: A, B, or C. She would like to know if customers have a preference for color A. She accesses records of automatic washing machine sales for the past 3 months, and takes a random sample of 300 machines. If 150 of these machines were of color A, does this indicate significant evidence that customers prefer color A? Use a level of significance of .025.

8.59 A claim is made that 36% of the men in the United States wear an 8C size shoe. To test this claim, 121 men are randomly selected. If 40 of these men are found to wear an 8C shoe, does this refute the claim? Use a level of significance of .02.

8.60 Suppose the weights of baseballs produced by a certain company are normally distributed, and suppose the baseballs are reputed to have an average weight of 6.3 oz. If a random sample of 10 baseballs is taken from the output of this company and found to have an average weight of 6.15 oz with a standard deviation of 0.5 oz, does this provide significant evidence that the reputed average weight for these baseballs is incorrect? Use a level of significance of .05. What is the *p*-value in this case?

8.61 Suppose the amount of delinquent property taxes is normally distributed, and suppose a politician claims that the average amount owed is not more than $400. If a county clerk takes a random sample of 9 records from the records of all delinquent accounts and finds the average amount owed is equal to $432.72 with a standard deviation of $90.24, does this provide significant evidence that the politician is underestimating the amount of delinquent property taxes? Use a level of significance of .01.

8.62 A market analyst claims that the average gain per stock for the past 6 months was $54. If a random sample of 10 stocks show gains (+) and losses (−) of +$55, +$66, −$61, +$48, −$50, +$45, +$57, +$71, +$56, and +$51 for the past 6 months, does this refute the market analyst's claim? Assume gain and loss amounts may be approximated by a normal distribution, and use a level of significance of .02.

8.63 A state inspector takes a random sample of sixteen 32 oz cans of pineapple and gets a sarnple mean of 31.2 oz with a sample standard deviation of 0.8 oz. Assuming the distribution of can weights is normal, does the inspector's sample supply sufficient evidence to conclude that the cans are being short-weighted? Use a level of significance of .05. What is the *p*-value in this case?

8.64 In testing an incoming coal shipment the amount of sulfur in three 1 g samples was measured as 2.20, 2.00, and 1.80 mg. Contract specifications state that the amount of sulfur per gram of coal must not exceed 1 mg. If we assume sulfur content is normally distributed, does the sample provide significant evidence that the shipment does not meet specifications? Use a level of significance of .01. What is the *p*-value in this case?

8.65 A cement manufacturer claims that concrete prepared from his product possesses a compressive strength, on average, of more than 40 kg/cm². A sample of size 20 using his cement produces a sample mean of 41.8 kg/cm² with a standard deviation of 16 kg/cm². Assuming compressive strength is normally distributed, determine whether the sample result provides significant support for the manufacturer's claim. Use a level of significance of .025.

8.66 A manufacturer of batteries claims that her batteries will operate continuously delivering 1.5 V for at least 20 hr. A government testing laboratory tests a random sample of 5 of her batteries and obtains the following times that the batteries could deliver 1.5 V: 19.0, 17.0, 22.3, 20.7, and 16.9 hr. Assuming that operating times are normally distributed, is there significant evidence that the batteries do not meet the manufacturer's claim? Use a level of significance of .05. What is the *p*-value in this case?

▶ **8.67** In a certain company a particular manufacturing process produces an average of 12.3 units per hour with a standard deviation of 1.4 units per hour. A new process is suggested, which is expensive to install but would be profitable if production could be increased to an average of more than 13.0 units per hour. In order to decide whether or not to make the change, the new process is put into effect on 16 different, randomly selected, occasions. Assuming the standard deviation remains the same, and the yield values are normally distributed, is there sufficient evidence to indicate the change to the new process would be profitable if the 16 observations on the new process yield an average of 13.1 units per hour? Use a level of significance of .05.
  a. What is the *p*-value in this case?
  b. Find the value of β if the true average yield for the new process is equal to 13.2 units per hour.
  c. What would it mean to the company to commit the error associated with β?

8.68 A construction company supplies its employees with gloves that have an average life of 90 days with a standard deviation of 18 days. A recommended new type of glove is claimed to last longer, although it is more expensive. The company figures the new glove would be cost effective if its average life exceeds 120 days. If a random sample of 36 of the new type of glove has an average life of 123 days, does this provide sufficient evidence that the new type of glove is cost effective? Assume the length of life for the new glove is a normally distributed random variable with the same standard deviation as for the original glove, and use a level of significance of .025.
  a. What is the *p*-value in this case?
  b. Find the value of β if the true average life for the new type of glove is equal to 121 days.
  c. What would it mean to the company to commit the error associated with β?

8.69 A certain large nationwide retailer claims that there is no difference in reliability between her "house" brand of electric toasters and those made by a "name" brand. In a random sample of 36 toasters of the house brand, 5 showed defective workmanship; and in a random sample of 36 toasters of the name brand, 3 showed defective workmanship. Does this provide significant evidence to assert that the house brand has a higher proportion of toasters with defective workmanship? Use a level of significance of .05.

8.70 If 300 castings produced on mold A contain 19 defectives while 250 castings on mold B contain 27 defectives, does this provide significant evidence to conclude that the percentage of defectives for the two molds is not the same? Use a level of significance of .10.

8.71 A market analyst believes that there is no difference in the proportions of individuals in two major cities who prefer detergent A to detergent B. If 245 out of a random sample of 500 from one city and 306 out of a random sample of 600 from the second city prefer detergent A, does this show sufficient evidence to refute the market analyst's belief? Use a level of significance of .0366.

8.72 It is claimed that individuals who have smoked two packs of cigarettes a day for at least 2 years have a higher incidence of lung cancer than nonsmokers. In a random sample of 225 individuals who smoked two packs a day for at least 2 years, 45 were found to have lung cancer, whereas in a random sample of 256 nonsmokers, 22 were found to have lung cancer. Does this provide significant evidence at a level of significance of .01 to support the claim?

8.73 A certain organization claims that proportionately more short people (i.e., people under 5′10″ tall) wear glasses or contact lenses than tall people. In a random sample of 72 tall people, 36 wore corrective lenses, whereas in a random sample of 84 short people, 42 wore corrective lenses. Does this provide significant evidence at a level of significance of .05 to substantiate the organization's claim?

▶ **8.74** A drug company produces two different kinds of cold relief medicines, and through experimentation has determined that they both give an average of 5 hr of relief, with a standard deviation of 1.5 hr for one and 2.3 hr for the second. A new ingredient is added to both medicines to increase the average number of hours of relief, and it is believed that the variance is not affected. A sample of 36 persons with colds are given the first drug, and they find relief for an average of 8.3 hr. An independent sample of 40 persons with colds are given the second drug, and they find relief for an average of 7.1 hr. At the .05 level of significance, do the persons using the first drug with the new ingredient get relief for a longer period of time than the persons using the second drug with the new ingredient?

8.75 An independent laboratory is asked to determine the quantity of a certain chemical in a drug made by two different pharmaceutical companies. From past experience with substances of this type, it is known that the laboratory's measurements for the chemical have a standard deviation of 0.00072 part per million (ppm). Thirty-seven samples from the first pharmaceutical company and 36 samples from the second pharmaceutical company are analyzed, and the respective means are found to be 0.0033 and 0.0028. Use the .05 level of significance to determine whether the difference between the two companies is statistically significant.

8.76 Fifty tires of each of two brands are tested for longevity, and the number of miles of wear is recorded for each tire. The 50 tires of brand A last an average of 30,500.6 mi with a standard deviation of 147.2 mi, and the 50 tires of brand B last an average of 33,617.8 mi, with a standard deviation of 157.5 mi. Assume tire wear is normally distributed. Use the .10 level of significance to determine whether there is a statistically significant difference in the average wear for the two brands of tires.

8.77 Length measurements on a random sample of 16 gila monsters (a lizard found in the Sonoran desert of Arizona, New Mexico, and Mexico) obtained in Arizona have an average of 19.5 in. with a standard deviation of 5 in.; and length measurements on a random sample of 25 gila monsters obtained in Mexico have an average of 21.3 in. with a standard deviation of 4.5 in. Assume the populations of length measurements are normally disributed with equal variances. Use the .05 level of significance to determine whether the average length of gila monsters in Mexico is statistically significantly greater than the average length of gila monsters in Arizona.

8.78 A certain stimulus is to be tested for its effect on blood pressure. Nine men have their blood pressures measured (in millimeters of mercury) before and after the stimulus, and the results are as follows:

Man	Before	After
1	120	127
2	124	128
3	130	131
4	118	127
5	140	132
6	128	128
7	140	136
8	135	133
9	126	128

At the .01 level of significance, would you say there is reason to believe that, on the average, the stimulus raises blood pressure? Assume the populations of blood pressure measurements are normally distributed.

▶ 8.79 An assembly operation in a manufacturing plant requires approximately a 1 month training period for a new employee to reach maximum efficiency. A new method of training is suggested, and a test is conducted to compare the two training methods. Two groups of 9 new employees are trained for a period of 3 weeks, one group using the new method and the other using the standard training method. The average length of assembly required by the 9 employees trained by the standard method is 35.22 min with a standard deviation of 4.94 min, and the average length of assembly time required by the 9 employees trained by the new method is 31.56 min with a standard deviation of 4.47 min. At the .05 level of significance, would you say that the data present sufficient evidence to indicate that the mean assembly time at the end of a 3 week training period is less for the new training procedure? Assume that the populations of assembly times are normally distributed, with equal variances.

8.80 To compare two different diets, a sample of 14 people is randomly selected from a population of overweight people who wish to lose weight. Seven are assigned to diet A, and the other 7 to diet B. After a 2 month period, the 7 persons on diet A lose an average of 12.7 lb with a standard deviation of 3.5 lb, and the 7 persons on diet B lose an average of 10.1 lb with a standard deviation of 4.2 lb. At the .10 level of significance, is there a significant difference in the average amount of weight loss over a 2 month period between the two diets? Assume the populations of weight losses are normally distributed, with equal variances.

8.81 A state agency wishes to determine whether the average mechanical aptitudes of students at two different schools are equal. An identical mechanical aptitude test is given to random samples of 15 students at each school. For one school, the 15 students have an average score of 89.2 with a standard deviation of 4.1; and for the second school, the 15 students have an average score of 92.3 with a standard deviation of 3.2. At the .01 level of significance, is there sufficient evidence that the average mechanical aptitude scores are not the same? Assume the mechanical aptitude scores are normally distributed, but not necessarily with equal variances.

8.82 A medical student conducts a diet study using 50 rats in group I and 40 rats in group II. Group I receives a diet containing a widely used food additive, and group II receives the same diet but without the food additive. After 5 weeks, the rats in group I gain an average of 5.3 oz with a standard deviation of 0.9 oz, and the rats in group II gain an average of 6.8 oz with a standard deviation of 2.5 oz. At the

.05 level of significance, is there sufficient evidence to conclude that the rats in group II gained more weight than the rats in group I? Assume the populations of weight gains are normally distributed, but not necessarily with equal variances.

8.83 The variance of an electrical characteristic of an electronic component is believed to be 0.67. A manufacturer of this component would like to maintain a reasonable amount of control over the production process so that the variance does not exceed 0.67, and to do this she specifies a sampling and test procedure to determine whether the variance exceeds 0.67. However, the manufacturer is also aware of the fact that production managers sometimes alter data in order to keep production flowing, and this could reflect a much smaller variance than expected. Thus, she decides to set up a two-sided test procedure. If a random sample of 31 components have a variance of 0.29, does this provide sufficient evidence to conclude that the production process is not under control? Assume the population of measurements is normal, and use a level of significance of .01.

▶ **8.84** A manufacturer of electronic components believes that the variance of the lifetime distribution of components she manufactures is less than that of her major competitor. If a random sample of 31 of her components has a variance of 21.7 and a random sample of 25 of her major competitor's components has a variance of 32.6, does this provide sufficient evidence to support her belief? Use a level of significance of .05, and assume the lifetime distribution of the electronic components is normal.

8.85 An insurance company claims that the variability in the life expectancies in one ethnic group (group B) is greater than that of another ethnic group (group A). If a random sample of 41 persons from group A has a variance of 136.9 and a random sample of 61 persons from group B has a variance of 204.5, does this provide sufficient evidence to support the insurance company's claim? Use a level of significance of .01, and assume life expectancies are normally distributed.

8.86 A neurologist notices that a certain type of mentally retarded person is capable of learning specific tasks, but cannot associate tasks according to principle. That is, a person with this type of mental retardation can be taught two very similar tasks, but each task must be taught step-by-step as though the two tasks have nothing in common. The normal person can be taught either one of the two tasks step-by-step, and can then be taught the other task simply by pointing out the principles behind the two tasks and by indicating the differences between them. This causes the neurologist to think that perhaps some part, or pattern, of the brain is linked with the ability to associate by principle. She then measures the amplitudes of a certain wave pattern on 41 mentally retarded persons and gets a variance of 17.3. Independently, she measures the amplitudes of the same wave pattern on 41 normal persons and gets a variance of 2.4. At a 2% level of significance, do the data provide sufficient evidence to conclude that the variances in the amplitudes of the wave pattern of the normal and mentally retarded persons are different? Assume the amplitudes are normally distributed.

8.87 As an executive in a large corporation, you have two secretaries who work directly for you. In the period of time that they have worked for you, you notice that you have a preference to give your work to secretary A rather than to secretary B. You wonder why, and you take a sample of 6 equivalent tasks you had assigned to each of the two secretaries. For the 6 tasks assigned to secretary A you find an average of 2.2 hr, with a standard deviation of 0.1 hr, to perform the task; and for the 6 tasks assigned to secretary B you find an average of 2.1 hr, with a standard deviation of 0.7 hr. Assume the times to perform the tasks are normal, and use a level of significance of .05.

a. Perform an appropriate test to determine whether the average times it takes the two secretaries to perform the equivalent tasks are equal.

b. Perform an appropriate test to determine whether secretary A is more consistent than secretary B in the times taken to perform the equivalent tasks.

c. Explain why the results in parts a and b could provide an objective measure of why you prefer to give your work to secretary A rather than to secretary B.

SOLVING APPLIED CASES
The Effect of Supermarket Shelf Position on Product Sales

Wheaties, Ultra-Bright, and Alberto VO-5. Do these and other brands achieve greater consumer sales if the products are displayed at eye level on supermarket shelves? If they do, supermarket retailers want to know so they can put their most profitable products on the "best" shelves. Manufacturers want to know too. They must decide whether or not to commit armies of sales representatives to the battle for the best supermarket shelf space.

The answer for both the retailer and the manufacturer rests on the shopping habits of consumers. If consumers are "product visibility" buyers or "impulse" buyers, brand exposure through eye-level shelf display will be a strong stimulant to sales. On the other hand, if "brand loyalty" dominates consumer thinking on what to buy, consumers will search for and select a brand regardless of its shelf position. With consumer behavior of the latter type, any attempt to improve profit by gaining eye-level shelf space for a particular brand will be a misdirected use of time, effort, and sales force resources.

An effective way to determine whether the position of the shelf space affects product sales is a statistical experiment. Such a study was conducted for several products at 24 different stores. The stores were first grouped into 12 pairs according to similarity of weekly sales. Then one of the stores in each pair was randomly picked to display the brand product on eye-level shelf space. The other store displayed the brand product on shelf space above or below eye level. The results for breakfast products are shown in Table 8.8.

TABLE 8.8   Packages of the Breakfast Product Sold in Test Store

STORE PAIR	SAMPLE 1 NON-EYE-LEVEL SHELF SPACE	SAMPLE 2 EYE-LEVEL SHELF SPACE	DIFFERENCE
1	71	111	−40
2	121	150	−29
3	133	130	3
4	126	154	−28
5	93	67	26
6	49	112	−63
7	109	84	25
8	96	123	−27
9	27	71	−44
10	58	62	−4
11	36	38	−2
12	37	51	−14

The null hypothesis tested is:

H_o: Sales of the product exposed on shelf space above or below eye level are at least as great as the sales of the brand when exposed on the eye-level shelf.

The alternative hypothesis is:

H_A: Sales of the product when displayed on shelf space above or below eye level are less than the sales associated with the product exposed on the eye-level position.

Symbolically, the two hypotheses can be expressed as

$$H_o: \quad \mu_d = \mu_1 - \mu_2 \geq 0$$
$$H_A: \quad \mu_d < 0$$

where μ_1 represents the average sales for product exposed on shelf space above or below eye level, and μ_2 represents the average sales for product exposed on the eye-level shelf.

The investigator has reason to believe that the observed differences, d_i, are drawn from a normal distribution. With this assumption, the paired t test discussed in Section 8.6 is an appropriate test procedure to determine whether there is a real difference in sales due to shelf exposure level.

Checkpoint Exercise

1. Using the paired difference procedure, do the data provide sufficient evidence to indicate that there exists a shelf position effect? Use a level of significance of .01.

WENDY'S DATABASE ANALYSIS

In these database exercises we will continue to make inferences as we did in Chapter 7 about the population of households using fast foods in Columbus, Ohio. Now, however, our attention turns to appropriate hypothesis tests.

Taste advantage claims of one hamburger over another dominate the television and other media advertising of the major hamburger chains. "Their brand is grilled, ours is open flame broiled," and so on. But despite the claims and counterclaims (perhaps even because of them), it is entirely possible that the perceived taste differences among brands observed in the customer sampling are so minimal that overall, taste is not a factor of discernible difference among brands for the population. Let's investigate this more closely by statistical analysis using the hypothesis testing procedure.

■ **PROBLEM 1**

Let's use the rating preference on hamburger taste given by each customer. By using the same customer's rating on each hamburger type we can apply the paired difference procedure to test the null hypothesis that the mean rating difference between Burger King and Wendy's is 0 with respect to the taste variable.

a. Use the MINITAB commands to create the taste difference variable C150 between Wendy's and Burger King by subtracting the Burger King taste variable C29 from the Wendy's taste variable C31. Using $\alpha = .01$, test the null hypothesis of no difference versus the two-sided alternative that some difference exists. That is,

$$H_o: \quad \mu_d = 0 \quad \text{(No difference exists.)}$$
$$H_A: \quad \mu_d \neq 0 \quad \text{(Some difference exists.)}$$

Use the MINITAB command TTEST. The appropriate MINITAB commands and the corresponding output are shown in Figure 8.16.

b. Interpret the hypothesis test result. Since the observed mean is a negative value, the subtraction of the responses of Burger King from Wendy's must have shown Burger King to have higher numerical responses on average, and therefore, lower taste ratings. The observed t value is -5.75. Since n is large, we use Appendix Table VI and $\pm Z_{\alpha/2} = \pm Z_{.005} = \pm 2.576$ as the critical values. Since the observed t value of -5.75 is less than the critical value -2.576, we reject H_o. This means that the observed mean difference of -0.48 is statistically signif-

```
MTB> subt c29 c31 c150

MTB> name c150 'taste B/W'

MTB> ttest 0 c150

TEST OF MU = 0.0000 VS MU N.E. 0.0000

                N        MEAN     STDEV     SE MEAN           T      P VALUE
tasteB/W       382     -0.4817    1.6373    0.0838       -5.75       0.0000
                                            Hypothesis Test for
                                            Difference between Means -
                                            Matched Pair
```

Figure 8.16
Hypothesis test for taste difference between Wendy's and Burger King

icantly different from 0. The *p*-value of 0 to four decimal places indicates that such a result is very unlikely if H_o is true. The mean value of -0.48 suggests that Wendy's enjoys approximately a half point rating advantage over Burger King on the taste dimension. From a practical perspective, Wendy's now knows it should continue to stress its taste superiority in its advertising directed against Burger King.

We now turn our attention to a factor that might help to discriminate between customers who have higher preference for Wendy's and those who don't.

■ **PROBLEM 2**

Use the two independent samples procedure to test the null hypothesis that there does not exist a difference in proportions between the high versus low preference Wendy's customers with respect to variable C135, the opportunity to garnish.

a. Use the MINITAB command CODE to recode variable C107 so that the high preference Wendy's customers can be separated from the low preference Wendy's customers:

Variable C107 Responses	Type of Customer	Coded
1–2	High preference (hp)	1
3–6	Low preference (lp)	0

Then perform the hypothesis test by using the MINITAB command TWOT. Using $\alpha = .01$, test the null hypothesis versus the alternative hypothesis:

$$H_o: \quad \mu_{hp} = \mu_{lp}$$
$$H_A: \quad \mu_{hp} \neq \mu_{lp}$$

Notice that this command is identical to the one used in the Wendy's database exercises in Chapter 7. Now we can see the full output given by this command as shown in Figure 8.17.

b. Interpret the hypothesis test result. The observed *t* value is 2.96. Since *n* is large, we consult Appendix Table VI and find the critical values $\pm Z_{\alpha/2} = \pm Z_{.005} = \pm 2.576$. Since the observed

```
MTB> code  (1:2)1 (3:6)0 c107 c200

MTB> code (2)0 c135 c201

MTB> name c200 'h/1prew'

MTB> name c201 'y/ngarn'

MTB> twot 99 c201 c200

TWO SAMPLE T FOR y/ngarn

h/1prew       N        MEAN        STDEV        SE MEAN
1            209       0.938       0.242        0.0167
0            118       0.822       0.384        0.0354

99 PCT CI FOR MU 1 - MU 0:  (0.01382, 0.2177)
TTEST MU 1 = MU 0 (VS NE): T=2.96 P=0.0035 DF=170
```

Figure 8.17
Hypothesis test of the difference in preference of high and low preference Wendy's
customers with respect to the opportunity to garnish

$t = 2.96$ exceeds 2.576, we can reject H_o and claim that the observed proportional difference is statistically significant. Here we see a case where the statistical significance may have no practical significance in terms of differentiating a marketing strategy for the two types of Wendy's customers, since the numerical difference between the means (0.938 versus 0.822) is only slightly larger than .1.

Wendy's Database Student Exercises

1. Use the paired difference procedure to test the null hypothesis that the mean rating difference between Burger King (BK) and Wendy's (W) is 0 using $\alpha = .05$. Consider the following variables:

Variable Name	Burger King	Wendy's
Cleanliness, BK − W	C35	C37
Convenience, BK − W	C41	C43
Price, BK − W	C47	C49
Service, BK − W	C53	C55
Popular with children, BK − W	C59	C61
Menu, BK − W	C65	C67

2. Use the two independent samples procedure to test the null hypothesis that there does not exist a difference in proportions between the high versus low preference McDonald's customers with respect to variable C135, the opportunity to garnish. Test at $\alpha = .01$ using the following steps:

```
MTB> code (1:2)1 (3:6)0 c106 c200
MTB> code (2)0 c135 c201
MTB> name c200 'h/1premd'

MTB> name c201 'y/ngarn'
MTB> twot 99 c201 c200
```

ANALYSIS OF VARIANCE

F
ast food chains are highly competitive, especially on quality, price, and service. Red ink will soon mar a company's profit and loss statement if the chain fails to respond effectively to consumers' increasing appetite for good quality food that is both tasty and healthful. Fast food chains are therefore listening and responding to the public's demand. For example, three prominent hamburger chains, McDonald's, Wendy's, and Burger King, now offer well-stocked salad bars and a variety of chicken items in addition to traditional choices.

Cooking oil is one item that has come under scrutiny by a public that is beginning to demand healthful food. French fries, a high profit margin item, are deep fried in hot oil. Newspaper health reports have informed the public that animal fat oil or liquid lard (both polysaturated oils loaded with cholesterol) are the hot cooking oils used in preparing french fries. The public has demanded a change. Not willing to jeopardize their important quality images (which once tarnished can't easily be repaired), the hamburger chains have responded and switched to vegetable oils, which are believed to be less harmful. But the change to vegetable oil brings up issues of cost and performance—two key factors that must be effectively balanced when vegetable cooking oil is purchased. Performance can be measured by the length of time the cooking oil maintains its cooking integrity before breaking down. Worn-out oil renders french fries rancid, but constantly changing worn-out oil is costly.

Headline Issue

THE HOT OIL PREDICAMENT AT FAST FOOD RESTAURANTS

Such consequences prompt the fast food chains to investigate carefully and thoroughly the cooking oil life of brands proposed by prospective suppliers. A chain's management must be able to experiment with the various cooking oils and to assess the quantitative results in order to make average life comparisons of the different cooking oils. They must ask themselves, "Are differences in the average cooking oil life small enough that they could be due merely to the normal variation in kitchen conditions that affect oil life at different franchises? Or are the differences significant enough to suggest that the oils themselves are different?" The *analysis of variance* technique presented in this chapter will help to answer these questions.

Overview

In Chapter 8 we introduced hypothesis tests for population means, proportions, and variances. In all three cases we limited the discussions to one or two populations. Now, in this chapter we introduce tests of hypotheses for means from more than two populations. The procedure we'll introduce utilizes measures of variability and the F statistic. Although it might appear strange to you that we'll test hypotheses about population means with measures of variability and the F statistic, the procedure is valid and it is powerful! It is called the *analysis of variance (ANOVA)* procedure, and it has been successfully applied in a wide variety of circumstances, even when some of the assumptions formally necessary for its application are not strictly met. In the examples in this chapter we presume that the assumption conditions are sufficiently satisfied so that we can apply the procedure and interpret the results.

The analysis of variance technique is directly linked to experimental design in statistical methodology. The development of formal experimental designs and analysis of variance, and their joint application over the past 50 years, have contributed significantly to advances in data analysis and to the performance of statistical investigations. A comprehensive treatment of the topic of experimental design is largely beyond the level of this text. Nevertheless, this chapter presents a two-way analysis of variance and raises the interaction issue to offer an informative first look at this important topic.

In the Comprehensive Case Study on quality control following Chapter 6, an important distinction was drawn between specific causes of process output variation and common causes. Specific causes can be corrected by finding out what has gone wrong with the process and correcting it. Common causes, on the other hand, are inherent in the system and can only be reduced by improving the process: using better materials, better machines, better trained and more careful employees, etc. In this chapter a manufacturing example will be used throughout the chapter to illustrate how the analysis of variance technique may be applied to discover sources of variability that might be eliminated from the manufacturing process and the process thereby improved.

9.1

INTRODUCTION: BACKGROUND OF THE HERZOG PROBLEM

Dr. Donald Herzog, an industrial engineer, has been called in as a consultant by an automobile manufacturer to solve a troubling problem. The problem occurred in the development of a new component of a part required for modern high-speed, high-compression automobile engines. The part in question is a multiple piece steel coil control device, called a segment. This segment is essentially a thin ribbon of steel coiled on edge in the form of a ring. An important feature of this coiling is its shape. It must be uniform. When placed in a cylindrical gauge, each point on the circumference of the ring must make contact with the surface of the gauge. Ideally, a light shining at one end of the gauge would be entirely blocked out by the coiled steel ring. Imperfectly shaped rings, on the other hand, do not entirely block the light; this condition is referred to as an "open light" condition.

A point measurement system was developed to obtain quantitative measurements of the amount of open light a ring permits to pass through. With such measurements available, the manufacturer can properly evaluate by statistical techniques the quality of material shipped by competing suppliers. Several reputable suppliers of steel, mills a, b, and c, deliver steel that meets all the chemical and physical property specifications for the segments. But feelings were expressed in the shop that differences in the rolling ability of the steels were responsible for producing defects known as "dog legs." Dog legs are straight sections on the circumference of the ring that create the objectionable open light condition.

The key question facing Herzog is, "Could differences in the steel purchased from different suppliers be a factor affecting the segments produced?" He finds in his investigation that steel is randomly assigned to the various plant machines and operators—that is, there is no particular pattern in the assignment of the steel rolls from supplier mills a, b, and c to the various operators and machines. He also finds that records are kept of the steel supplier identity and of the measurements taken on the open light condition of the segments produced. Table 9.1 gives results, adapted to a 0 base, for independent random samples of 10 measurements from each of the three steel suppliers; the higher the open light reading, the more troublesome the open light condition of the segment.

TABLE 9.1 Open Light Measurements, by Steel Supplier		
MILL a	**MILL b**	**MILL c**
20	15	18
19	17	16
16	6	12
12	19	26
29	0	21
7	1	29
5	11	19
22	11	25
22	2	10
12	19	19
Totals 164	101	195

Herzog's task is to evaluate the data for the open light condition. Specifically, Herzog is to determine whether there is a statistical basis for claiming that the distributions of open light measurements are the same for the steels supplied by these three suppliers. On the other hand, the presence of systematic differences in open light measurements in the steels supplied by the different suppliers would confirm a steel supplier effect.

HOW TO SET UP H_o AND H_A

To "prove" the presence of a steel supplier effect requires convincing data that refutes the hypothesis that no such effect exists. On the other hand, if the data are not convincing enough, the "no effect" hypothesis can't be refuted, and a steel supplier effect can't be supported. The formal statement of the hypothesis is the null hypothesis H_o. A rejection of the null hypothesis allows us to support the alternative hypothesis H_A. In the Herzog problem, the verbal description of the null hypothesis is:

H_o: The population means of open light measurements among the three suppliers are equal; that is, the open light measurements come from a population with the same mean, and therefore no distinct steel supplier effect exists.

In symbolic form we write $H_o = \mu_a = \mu_b = \mu_c$, where a, b, and c denote the three steel suppliers. The alternative hypothesis is:

H_A: The means among the three suppliers are not equal. A steel supplier effect exists.

In symbolic form, we write H_A: μ_a, μ_b, μ_c are not all equal.

Observed differences in the sample means of open light measurements among the three steel suppliers will be noticed regardless of which of these hypotheses is true. But are the differences statistically significant or simply due to sampling variation? If only sampling variability is at work to produce the observed differences in the sample means, then (with probability $1 - \alpha$) the testing should conclude that the null hypothesis can't be rejected. This means that the data are consistent with the stated null hypothesis of no steel supplier effect. On the other hand, when the differences observed in the sample means for the three steel suppliers are shown by testing to be statistically significantly different, then the null hypothesis should be rejected. Data inconsistent with the stated null hypothesis support the assertion that there is significant evidence of a steel supplier effect.

TESTING METHOD

Three steel suppliers are involved, so the null hypothesis proposes the equality of all three population means. Can the procedures discussed in Chapter 8 for testing the equality of two means be used? Perhaps we could test all possible pair combinations of the three means. Let's examine that approach on all the possible pairs of means.

1. There are three population means, μ_a, μ_b, μ_c.
2. To test the equality of all possible pair combinations of these three means would involve testing the following three null hypotheses:

$$H_{o1}: \mu_a = \mu_b \qquad H_{o2}: \mu_a = \mu_c \qquad H_{o3}: \mu_b = \mu_c$$

3. Now let the level of significance be $\alpha = .05$ for each pair tested. The probability, then, of not committing a Type I error is $1 - \alpha = .95$ *for each of the three tests.*
4. Assuming the three tests are independent of each other, the probability of not committing a Type I error *when all three tests are considered together* is equal to $(.95)^3$ $= .857$. Therefore, when all three cases are considered together, the probability of committing a Type I error in *at least one of the three tests* must be $1 - .857 = .143$.

With slightly more than a 14% chance of erroneously rejecting at least one of the three null hypotheses, the risk is higher than what was originally intended. Does this conclusion rest on the independence assumption of the three tests?

The assumption that the three tests are independent facilitates the probability calculation. But if the tests had not been independent, the same conclusion that the risk is higher would hold, although the probability would have been more difficult to calculate. Thus, pairwise comparisons of means as used in Chapter 8 would increase the risk of committing a Type I error in this type of example. Moreover, when there are more than three population means, the total number of pairwise comparisons is increased, thereby further increasing the gap between the actual and intended risk of Type I error. For example, with four population means and $\alpha = .05$ on each of the six pairwise comparisons, the total risk of Type I error would increase to .265.

Fortunately, the problem of a higher risk when several means are considered doesn't apply to the analysis of variance procedure. This is an important advantage.

9.2

ONE-WAY ANALYSIS OF VARIANCE (ANOVA)

The direction of our discussion so far has been to focus on a one-way classification of the open light measurements (according to the source of the steel supplied). The objective has been to detect whether there are significant differences in the mean open light readings. When the analysis is conducted on a measured characteristic categorized in only one way, it is called a *one-way analysis of variance (ANOVA)*. The analysis of data categorized in more than one way will be discussed in the next section on two-way analysis. The procedure in this section concerns only one-way analysis.

We need the following five conditions to perform a one-way ANOVA, and the problem discussed in Section 9.1 meets all these conditions:

Sampling Conditions

1. The measurements come from random samples from different populations.
2. The samples are independent.

Underlying Population Conditions

3. The populations are normally, or approximately normally, distributed.
4. The populations all have the same variance. That is, the variability of measurements must be the same for all populations.

Additivity Assumption (Effects of Individual Populations Relative to an Overall Average)

5. If a population effect on measurements does exist, then we assume each individual population's effect is additive; that is, it is a constant value that is added to or subtracted from an overall average for all the measurements.

Now, let's see how the open light data comply with these five conditions:

1. The open light measurements were made on random samples from three different steel suppliers.
2. The samples from the three steel suppliers were obtained independently of each other.
3. We can assume that each open light measurement is determined or affected by several factors and therefore is the resultant, or average, effect of those factors. This assumption, when valid, allows us to apply the central limit theorem and assert that open light measurements, as averages, are normally, or approximately normally, distributed.
4. We'll assume that the variability of the open light measurements is the same for the steels from the three suppliers unless we have prior evidence that this is not so.
5. By assuming additivity we assume that the discrepancies among the averages for the three steel suppliers can be viewed as an addition or subtraction from an overall average of all the measurements.

Given these five assumptions, we can proceed to perform an ANOVA on the open light data. First, however, some comments on the last three assumptions are in order. The normality assumption and the equality of variances assumption have been presumed to hold in the examples illustrated in this chapter, but when sufficient data are available the researcher should perform appropriate statistical tests to check that these conditions are not grossly violated. The procedures used to perform variance and normality tests are beyond the scope of this text, but can be found in advanced statistics texts. The additivity assumption is generally accepted as valid unless there is evidence or *a priori* information available to the contrary.

Next we must establish the null and alternative hypotheses. Let X_a, X_b, and X_c represent the respective open light measurements for rings made from the steel rolls received from suppliers a, b, and c. Let μ_a, μ_b, and μ_c represent the population means for X_a, X_b, and X_c, respectively. Then the null hpothesis and the alternative hypothesis can be stated as follows:

H_o: $\mu_a = \mu_b = \mu_c$ (Equal means indicate no steel supplier effect.)

H_A: μ_a, μ_b, μ_c and not all equal   (Unequal means indicate a steel supplier effect.)

We are now ready to outline the necessary calculations to test the hypothesis. Then we will explain the motive behind the calculations.

STATISTICAL SOLUTION

The following computational steps show how to calculate the statistic necessary for ANOVA testing of the null hypothesis stated above. The underlying rationale of the ANOVA procedure is also presented.

Computational Procedure for the Herzog Data

The computational procedure requires the calculation of the following three expressions: **total sum of squares (SST)**, **treatment sum of squares (SSTr)**, and **error sum of squares (SSE)**. (Each steel supplier represents a different "treatment.") These are calculated by performing the following operations using the data of Table 9.1:

Step 1
Square each observed value. Then add up all the squared values:

$$20^2 + 19^2 + \cdots + 10^2 + 19^2$$

This sum of squared values is 8836.

Step 2
a. Sum all the observed values, and then square the sum.

$$(20 + 19 + \cdots + 10 + 19)^2$$

This value is $(460)^2 = 211,600$.
b. Find the **correction term** by dividing the result in Step 2a by the total number of observations (30), to get $211,600/30 = 7053.333333$.

Step 3
Sum the observed values separately for each supplier, and then square each of these sums. Then divide each squared sum by the number of observed values for the corresponding supplier. Sum the resultant quotients:

$$\frac{164^2}{10} + \frac{101^2}{10} + \frac{195^2}{10} = \frac{75,122}{10} = 7512.2$$

The three key sums of squares can now be calculated:

Step 4

$$SST = \text{Result from Step 1 minus result from Step 2b}$$
$$= 8836 - 7053.333333 = 1782.666667$$

Step 5

$$SSTr = \text{Result from Step 3 minus result from Step 2b}$$
$$= 7512.2 - 7053.333333 = 458.866667$$

Step 6

$$SSE = SST - SSTr$$
$$= 1782.666667 - 458.866667 = 1323.8$$

Note that the sum of SSTr and SSE is SST. For this reason, SST is said to be *partitioned* into SSTr and SSE. The values for SSTr and SSE now permit us to calculate the **mean square for treatments (MSTr)** and the **mean square for error (MSE)**.

Step 7

The mean square for treatments (MSTr) adjusts SSTr for the number of degrees of freedom associated with the number of suppliers. In this case the number of suppliers is 3 and, hence, the number of degrees of freedom is equal to $3 - 1 = 2$. Thus, MSTr = SSTr/2, or

$$MSTr = \frac{SSTr}{2} = \frac{458.866667}{2} = 229.43333$$

Step 8

The mean square for error (MSE) is an adjustment of SSE for the remaining number of degrees of freedom. The number of degrees of freedom equals the total number of observations minus the number of suppliers. In this case the number of observations is 30, the number of suppliers is 3, and the number of degrees of freedom is equal to $30 - 3 = 27$. Thus, MSE = SSE/27, or

$$MSE = \frac{SSE}{27} = \frac{1323.8}{27} = 49.02963$$

Rationale for MSTr and MSE

What is the motive for finding the values for MSTr and MSE? To answer this question consider the following scenario: *What if the null hypothesis is true* and the three suppliers are supplying steel from the same distribution (mean and variance) of open light measurements? In this case *both MSTr and MSE are estimates of the common overall variance* σ^2, a fact we shall soon exploit. Let's consider first the term MSTr. Computationally, MSTr (even though we didn't calculate it this way) is the product of the sample size 10, and the sample estimate of $\sigma_{\bar{x}}^2$. The term $\sigma_{\bar{x}}^2$ is the value of the population variance of mean open light measurements, and it refers to mean open light measurements determined from the observed differences among the means of the three suppliers. Since the value of $\sigma_{\bar{x}}^2$ was shown in Chapter 6 to have the relationship $\sigma_{\bar{x}}^2 = \sigma^2/n$, it follows that when the null hypothesis is true, we have $\sigma_{\bar{x}}^2 = \sigma^2/10$ so that $10\sigma_{\bar{x}}^2 = \sigma^2$. In summary, if there is no true difference among the different suppliers' mean open light measurements, then MSTr will be an appropriate sample estimate of the common overall variability σ^2. But when there exists a true difference in the supplier steel types, then two sources of variability are present in MSTr: The common overall variability σ^2, plus any variability that results from the difference in the three steel supplier open light means.

The MSE is also a sample estimate of σ^2, the common overall variability. It is computed by pooling (averaging) the three individual supplier variances determined by the variation of the open light measurements around each steel supplier's sample mean. Whereas MSTr is affected by differences among μ_a, μ_b, and μ_c, MSE is not affected. This distinction is very important.

When H_o is true and there is no true difference in the three population means, then the two variance estimates, MSTr and MSE, should be equal except for sampling errors. We will use a ratio of the two variance estimates as an appropriate test statistic. Even though MSTr and MSE are estimates of the same population value, σ^2, when H_o is true, they are calculated by different methods and can have different sampling error influences. Therefore, their ratio is not necessarily equal to 1, even when H_o is true. The statistic will follow the F distribution (a distribution first discussed in Chapter 7 and subsequently used in Chapter 8 to test for the equality of variances). A one-sided test of H_o will be performed because when the null hypothesis H_o of equal means is true, the test statistic MSTr/MSE should differ from the value 1 only because of sampling error. On the other hand, when the null hypothesis is not true, the expectation is that MSTr will be greater than MSE because MSTr would be measuring real differences among the population means as well as sample variation. Thus, the calculated test statistic should be a value greater than 1 when H_o is not true. Since only values of MSTr/MSE greater than 1 can be considered consistent with H_A, our interest is in the upper tail of the F distribution. Making the appropriate numerical substitution for the Herzog problem, the computed F distribution test statistic is

$$F_{(2,27)} = \frac{\text{MSTr}}{\text{MSE}} = \frac{229.43333}{49.02963} = 4.679$$

At the 5% level of significance the F table (Appendix Table IXa) shows that $F_{(.05,2,27)} = 3.35$. So for α set at .05, the rejection region is defined as $F_{(2,27)} > 3.35$ and the decision rule would be to reject H_o if the calculated test statistic is greater than 3.35. Since 4.679 is greater than 3.35, it lies in the rejection region. Therefore, H_o is rejected. The rejection of H_o means refutation of the hypothesis that the open light means of the steels from the three suppliers are equal. So the alternative, H_A, a steel supplier effect, is supported.

Table 9.2 is an **analysis of variance (ANOVA) table** that condenses these computational results.

NOTE: The sample statistic is significant at the 5% level, but not at the 1% level. The reader can verify this by finding the value of $F_{(.01,2,27)}$ in Appendix Table IXb.

TABLE 9.2 ANOVA Table for the Open Light Data				
SOURCE OF VARIATION	**DEGREES OF FREEDOM**	**SUM OF SQUARES**	**MEAN SQUARES**	**CALCULATED F**
Suppliers **Error**	2 27	SSTr = 458.866667 SSE = 1323.8	MSTr = 229.43333 MSE = 49.02963	$\frac{\text{MSTr}}{\text{MSE}} = 4.679^*$
TOTALS	29	SST = 1782.666667		

*Represents significance at the 5% level.

OVERVIEW OF THE ONE-WAY ANOVA PROCEDURE

Several useful generalizations can be made from the Herzog example:

- There are three sources (suppliers) of the raw material used in the manufactured item.

- The manufactured item is measured for a particular characteristic—the open light condition.
- The concern is whether the effect of the raw materials from the three suppliers on the open light condition is uniform.

Suppose the raw mateials received from the three suppliers are truly equal in their propensity to produce defects that cause the open light condition. Then the characteristic measured—the amount of open light—will not (except by pure chance) differ significantly among the steels from the three suppliers. But what if, upon carrying out the statistical test, we find statistically significant results? That is, what if we find that the measured (open light) characteristic differs by a statistically significant amount among the steels from the three suppliers? In that case we come to a different conclusion. We conclude that the source populations of raw materials received from the three suppliers are not of uniform quality (at least as they affect the measured characteristic— open light).

Generalizing to *k* Populations

This line of reasoning can be extended to include more than three sources. The more general format would address the problem for k suppliers, or k conditions, in which k is geater than or equal to 2. In the language of experimental design, the k conditions are referred to as k treatments, or k groups, or k levels. An hypothesis test employing the F distribution is used to test the equality of the k means. Since the test on the means is actually conducted by comparing estimates of the population variance, the procedure is the analysis of variance.

Unequal Sample Sizes

On the issue of sample size, the Herzog example used three equal sized samples of 10 items manufactured from the raw material purchased from each of the three suppliers. Although it is necessary to sample at least 2 items in each group, there is no upper limit to the number of items from a group if the items are available. The sample could have been equal sized samples of 12, or 15, or 100 manufactured items; or we can even take samples of unequal sizes. The size of the sample is determined by practical reasons (e.g., availability and inspection cost). It may be that we can consider only 10 items manufactured from raw material purchased from one supplier, 17 items from another supplier, and 34 items from the third supplier as cost effective. In general terms, we can designate by the symbol n_1 the number of measurements from one supplier (treatment), by n_2 the number of measurements from a second supplier, and so on to n_k measurements from a kth supplier. Fortunately, the one-way ANOVA procedure is very flexible, both on how many populations (suppliers) we wish to consider, and also on how many measurements we will take from each population.

Summary of Conditions and Assumptions

Several conditions and assumptions are necessary for the ANOVA procedure to be appropriate. They are:

1. We have $k \geq 2$ populations.
2. We take a random sample of size n_j from the jth population for each of $j = 1, 2, \ldots, k$, where $n_j \geq 2$.

3. We define the k population means as $\mu_1, \mu_2, \ldots, \mu_k$. The null hypothesis we wish to test is given as $H_o: \mu_1 = \mu_2 = \cdots = \mu_k$. The alternative hypothesis is H_A: The means are not all equal.
4. The samples from each population are independent of each other.
5. The samples are taken from normally distributed populations (unless samples are large enough for the central limit theorem to be appropriate).
6. The populations all have the same variance, that is, $\sigma_1^2 = \sigma_2^2 = \cdots = \sigma_k^2$. (This equality of variance condition is referred to as **homoscedasticity**.)
7. Each population mean μ_j (for $j = 1, 2, \ldots, k$) may be viewed as a combination of two components: a common quantity (μ component) shared by all the population means, plus (or minus) a unique component τ_j specific to each jth population. Symbolically then, $\mu_j = \mu + \tau_j$. This condition asserts the assumption of additivity. We may describe τ_j as the unique additive effect that distinguishes one population mean from all the others.

The above formal requirements permit the valid application of the ANOVA procedure. But what if one or more of the requirements are not met? Would violating one or more of the requirements invalidate the procedure? Fortunately, the ANOVA procedure is quite *robust*. This term means that moderate violations of the assumptions don't undermine its use; the procedure can still be applied successfully, and useful conclusions can be drawn.

Summarizing the Computational Steps for Testing H₀

After the null and alternative hypotheses have been formulated, the computational procedure for the ANOVA can be implemented. The procedure consists of a series of sequential steps that enable us to organize the sample data, construct building block elements, calculate the test statistic, compare the test statistic to the rejection region, reach a decision on H_o, and make a statistical conclusion.

Step 1
Specify the null and alternative hypotheses:

H_o: $\mu_1 = \mu_2 = \cdots = \mu_k$ (The means for the k populations are all equal.)

H_A: The means are not all equal.

Step 2
List the values in a table (as in Table 9.1).

a. Each column represents a sample of measurements from a single population.
b. Find the column totals and list them.
c. Find the grand total (the total over all the measurements in the table).

Step 3
Find the value of the total sum of squares, SST.

Step 4
Find the value of the treatment sum of squares, SSTr.

Step 5
Find the error sum of squares, SSE (using SST − SSTr = SSE).

Step 6

Find the mean square for treatments (MSTr):

$$MSTr = \frac{SSTr}{k - 1} \tag{9-1}$$

where $k - 1$ represents the degrees of freedom for treatments.

Step 7

Find the mean square for error (MSE):

$$MSE = \frac{SSE}{\Sigma\, n_j - k} \tag{9-2}$$

where $\Sigma\, n_j - k$ represents the degrees of freedom for error.

Step 8

Find the calculated value of the test statistic:

$$F_{(k-1, \Sigma n_j - k)} = \frac{MSTr}{MSE} \tag{9-3}$$

where the test statistic is F distributed.

Step 9

Compare the calculated F test statistic with the table F value for the specified significance level α, taken from Appendix Table IXa or IXb.

Step 10

Apply the decision rule:

a. Reject H_o if the calculated F statistic is larger than the table F value.
b. Do not reject H_o if the calculated F statistic is not larger than the table F value.

Step 11

Reach a statistical conclusion.

The results of these steps are summarized in a generalized ANOVA table, Table 9.3.

TABLE 9.3 Generalized ANOVA Table				
SOURCE OF VARIATION	**DEGREES OF FREEDOM**	**SUM OF SQUARES**	**MEAN SQUARES**	**CALCULATED F**
Treatments	$k - 1$	SSTr	MSTr	$\dfrac{MSTr}{MSE} = F_{(k-1, \Sigma n_j - k)}$
Error	$\Sigma\, n_j - k$	SSE	MSE	
TOTALS	$\Sigma\, n_j - 1$	SST		

Notes: Compare $F_{(k-1, \Sigma n_j - k)}$ with $F_{(\alpha, k-1, \Sigma n_j - k)}$ specified at either the $\alpha = .01$ level or at the $\alpha = .05$ level. Reject H_o if $F_{(k-1, \Sigma n_j - k)} > F_{(\alpha, k-1, \Sigma n_j - k)}$.

A single asterisk placed after the calculated F value identifies significance at the 5% level (i.e., $\alpha = .05$). A double asterisk placed after the calculated F value identifies significance at the 1% level (i.e., $\alpha = .01$).

The ANOVA procedure discussed in this section is referred to as a *one factor completely randomized design*. In the Herzog example the suppliers are the one factor, and the different suppliers represent different levels of that factor. The design is completely randomized in that the steels purchased from the suppliers are randomly assigned to the various plant machines and operators. In a later section, we'll look at another experiment—a two factor completely randomized design—that also uses the ANOVA procedure.

The *p*-Value Interpretation

Some computer outputs provide the "prob-value," or *p*-value. As a result, the *p*-value, rather than the significance level, is used in relating the computer *F* test statistic to the appropriate *F* distribution. We must therefore consider how to interpret the *p*-value. The *p*-value is the probability of getting a computed *F* value as large as, or larger than, the value we actually obtained if the hypothesis is true. Thus, a *p*-value of .25 indicates that if the null hypothesis is true, then the probability of getting an *F* value as large as, or larger than, the one actually obtained is equal to .25. Some statisticians prefer the *p*-value terminology because it makes a statement of fact about the results without relying on an investigator's subjective rule for rejecting the null hypothesis.

PRACTICE EXERCISE

9.1 Suppose seven groups are under study, and independent random samples of size 4 are taken from each group. And suppose a single characteristic is measured on each item sampled. If the preliminary results of the data analysis show SST = 87 and SSTr = 74, then:

a. What assumptions need be made to complete the ANOVA?

b. Complete the ANOVA.

EXERCISES ▫ ▶ **9.1** In the manufacture of semiconductor chips, measurements of electrical leakage current can be an important indicator of the potential life expectancy of the chip. It is known that higher leakage current values are associated with earlier failure. So a range of values of the leakage current can be established and used to help identify chips that have a high probability of early failure. As part of quality control maintenance, a manufacturer of computers using a chip continually monitors the quality of incoming chips supplied by four different producers. The quality control group takes independent weekly random samples of 12 chips from each supplier to measure the leakage current of the sampled chips. This week's samples of leakage current measurements (in microamperes) on chips supplied by the four producers are given in the table. State H_o and H_A. Put your calculations in an ANOVA table. Does this week's sample reading present significant evidence at the .05 level of significance that the averages of the leakage current of the chips across the four suppliers are not all equal? Assume normality and homoscedasticity.

			SUPPLIER				
1		2		3		4	
1.16	1.26	1.50	1.93	1.39	1.71	1.24	1.08
1.62	1.17	1.65	1.54	1.33	1.36	1.32	1.15
1.39	1.22	1.80	1.48	1.44	1.19	1.25	1.41
1.37	1.30	1.96	1.61	1.17	1.10	1.56	1.84
1.29	1.21	1.93	1.77	1.35	1.49	1.62	.85
1.32	1.31	1.87	1.60	1.44	1.46	1.25	1.46

▫ **9.2** Three bankers are discussing the merits of their respective financing plans used to attract money into new and old accounts. Each claims success in attracting deposits. Suppose we take independent random samples of size 20 from deposits made to each bank during the past week, and the sample results are given in the table. State H_o and H_A. Put your calculations in an ANOVA table. Do the sample results provide significant evidence at the .01 level of significance that the average amounts of deposits to the three banks are not the same? Assume normality and homoscedasticity.

	BANKER					
1			**2**		**3**	
87.80	86.86	71.42	89.13	110.60	108.20
93.44	86.64	73.56	81.32	107.80	114.79
93.37	89.61	85.32	87.78	112.71	111.61
87.74	96.25	79.26	78.19	106.17	111.90
84.60	92.46	80.47	86.14	119.70	105.13
90.69	89.58	92.87	85.17	119.65	104.14
84.55	94.91	82.23	76.31	114.57	106.04
89.18	91.08	81.16	82.44	107.93	107.34
94.58	90.69	89.25	81.28	112.20	113.14
89.73	93.74	78.58	85.53	110.59	101.84

9.3 A company packages frozen shrimp at four different locations. Six packages selected at random from each of the four locations yield the following weights, in ounces:

LOCATION 1	12.00	12.05	12.04	12.07	12.05	12.03
LOCATION 2	11.96	11.98	11.96	11.97	12.00	11.95
LOCATION 3	12.04	12.03	11.96	11.98	12.03	12.02
LOCATION 4	11.98	12.05	11.98	12.06	12.02	12.03

Assume the populations of weights are normal with equal variances. State H_o and H_A. Use a level of significance of .05 and determine whether there is significant evidence of a difference in the average weights of the shrimp from the four different locations. Put the results in an ANOVA table and interpret the results.

9.4 In order to compare the mileage yields of four different kinds of gasoline, several tests are run using the gasolines in a single motorcycle. The following results are obtained (each figure represents the number of miles obtained with a gallon of the specified gasoline):

TYPE 1	TYPE 2	TYPE 3	TYPE 4
62	38	62	58
42	44	57	70
48	58	68	62
56	58	60	60
62	52	58	65

Assume the populations of mileage yields are normally distributed with equal variances. State H_o and H_A. At a level of significance of .01, is there significant evidence of a difference among the four types of gasoline in terms of the average miles per gallon? Put the results in an ANOVA table and interpret the results.

9.3

COMPARING PAIRS OF MEANS

The ANOVA procedure enables us to determine whether k means are all equal. But it does not provide us with an objective measure as to which means are statistically different from the others. Suppose we have rejected H_o in the ANOVA procedure. This means that at least one of the sample means must be statistically significantly different from the others. Intuitively it would then seem reasonable to conclude that the largest sample mean differs significantly from the smallest sample mean. This intuitive conclusion, however, is limited. What about the other means? Are any of these statistically significantly different from each other, or from the largest sample mean, or from the smallest sample mean? How many and which ones? We might like to answer these questions whenever H_o is rejected in an ANOVA procedure. But how can we answer these questions now that we have already ruled out using the procedures of Chapter 8 (based upon our discussion in Section 9.1)? Answers to these questions can be obtained using the methodology of *multiple comparisons*. Multiple comparison procedures permit testing various combinations of k means, with all combinations considered together at a single overall level of significance. Some of the more popular multiple comparison procedures (discussed in more advanced texts) include Duncan's multiple range test, Tukey's method, Scheffe's method, and the Newman–Keuls test. But these procedures should be used when, and only when, H_o is rejected in the ANOVA procedure.

9.4

TWO-WAY ANALYSIS OF VARIANCE: HERZOG REVISITED

So far our discussion of the Herzog problem has been limited to the sources of steel as a factor influencing the open light measurements. But typically in such situations there are additional factors that should be investigated. For instance, in the Herzog example, there are four rolling machines used in making the coiled steel segments. Although the machines are of the same design, they were purchased over a period of several years as production requirements increased. Consequently, there could be important differences among them. Then, again, each machine is operated by a different person, so the operator could have an effect on the measured characteristic. (But the same operator is always assigned to the same machine.) As a matter of fact, there is speculation in the shop that certain machines are better than others, and certain operators are more capable of producing superior results. So it seems plausible, but by no means certain, that different machine–operator combinations could have an influence on the number of ring defects.

To investigate these factors, a series of tests were designed. The operator regarded as most capable was assigned to the machine thought to be best. The operator regarded as second most capable was assigned to the machine thought to be second best, and so on. This gave four machine–operator combinations. The thinking was that if machine–operator combinations were really a factor influencing the open light measurements, it should show up with this design. The three steel types were assigned randomly to each of the four machine–operator combinations operating at normal production conditions. Table 9.4 shows the results for each steel type with each machine–operator combination. Each value in the table is an average of five rolls for each particular steel/machine–operator combination.

Two questions present themselves: (1) Is there a difference in the open light measurements among the three steel suppliers—that is, a steel type effect? (This question was first addressed in the one-way ANOVA.) (2) Is there a difference in the open

TABLE 9.4 Steel Suppliers, Machines, and Open Light Measurements					
STEEL	**MACHINE–OPERATOR COMBINATION**				**STEEL (ROW) TOTALS**
	1	**2**	**3**	**4**	
a	11.5	8.2	7.1	9.9	Row 1 total = 36.7
b	6.1	7.0	6.8	4.9	Row 2 total = 24.8
c	12.0	12.5	8.7	11.2	Row 3 total = 44.4
MACHINE (COLUMN) TOTALS	29.6 Column 1 total	27.7 Column 2 total	22.6 Column 3 total	26.0 Column 4 total	Grand total = 105.9

light measurements among the four machine–operator combinations, regardless of the particular steel type—that is, a machine–operator effect? Let's now consider both questions.

We'll represent the population average open light measurements for machine–operator combination number 1 by the symbol $\mu_{.1}$. The dot subscript preceding the numeral 1 indicates that we summed across the steel suppliers a, b, and c for the first machine–operator combination. Similarly, let $\mu_{.2}$, $\mu_{.3}$, and $\mu_{.4}$ represent the population open light measurement averages for machine–operator combinations 2, 3, and 4, respectively, each summed across steel suppliers, a, b, and c. Since these four population means are summed over the same three steel suppliers, we presume they now reflect only the averages for the four machine–operator combinations regardless of steel type.

In a like manner, let $\mu_{a.}$, $\mu_{b.}$, and $\mu_{c.}$ represent the population open light measurement averages for steel suppliers a, b, and c, respectively, each summed over the same four machine–operator combinations. We thus presume that they now reflect only the averages for the three steel suppliers (types) regardless of machine–operator combination. The notations for all the population means involved are given in Table 9.5.

TABLE 9.5 Notation for Population Means: Steel Supplier and Machine-Operator Combinations					
STEEL SUPPLIER	**MACHINE–OPERATOR COMBINATION**				**STEEL SUPPLIER POPULATION AVERAGE**
	1	**2**	**3**	**4**	
a	μ_{a1}	μ_{a2}	μ_{a3}	μ_{a4}	$\mu_{a.}$
b	μ_{b1}	μ_{b2}	μ_{b3}	μ_{b4}	$\mu_{b.}$
c	μ_{c1}	μ_{c2}	μ_{c3}	μ_{c4}	$\mu_{c.}$
MACHINE–OPERATOR POPULATION AVERAGE	$\mu_{.1}$	$\mu_{.2}$	$\mu_{.3}$	$\mu_{.4}$	—

Using these symbols, question (1) may be rephrased as a steel supplier effect regardless of the particular machine–operator combination. The null hypothesis is that of no differential effect; that is, no difference in mean open light readings among the three brands of steel.

Null hypothesis for steel supplier effect:

$$H_{o1}: \quad \mu_{a.} = \mu_{b.} = \mu_{c.}$$

Alternative hypothesis (1):

H_{A1}: The supplier means are not all equal.

Question (2) may be phrased as a machine–operator effect that applies regardless of the particular steel supplier type. The null hypothesis is that of no differential effect; that is, no difference in mean open light recordings among the four machine–operator combinations.

Null hypothesis for machine–operator effect:

H_{o2}: $\mu_{.1} = \mu_{.2} = \mu_{.3} = \mu_{.4}$

Alternative hypothesis (2):

H_{A2}: The machine–operator means are not all equal.

The proper application of the two-way ANOVA procedure to test these two sets of hypotheses rests on meeting the five assumptions listed in Section 9.2. That is, the samples should be random and independent, open light measurements should be normally, or approximately normally, distributed with the same variance for the various factor combinations, and the individual components (i.e., steel supplier effect and machine–operator effect) of an open light measurement should be additive.

The steps that follow are for the analysis of the data in Table 9.4. As before, the initial steps are designed to enable us to calculate the total sum of squares (SST); the **treatment sum of squares associated with rows (SSTr$_1$)**, steel; the **treatment sum of squares associated with columns (SSTr$_2$)**, machine–operator combinations; and the error sum of squares (SSE).

STATISTICAL SOLUTION

Step 1
Square each measurement in Table 9.4, and add up the squared values. The result is

$$11.5^2 + 6.1^2 + \cdots + 4.9^2 + 11.2^2 = 1005.75$$

Step 2
Find the value of the correction term.

a. Find (Grand total)^2 = $(105.9)^2$.
b. Divide the result in Step 2a by 12, the total number of measurements in Table 9.4:

$$\frac{(105.9)^2}{12} = 934.5675$$

Step 3
a. Square each column total, and divide each square by the corresponding number of observations in the column; then add them up, obtaining

$$\frac{(29.6)^2}{3} + \frac{(27.7)^2}{3} + \frac{(22.6)^2}{3} + \frac{(26.0)^2}{3} = 943.4033$$

b. Square each row total, and divide each square by the corresponding number of observations in the row; then add them up, obtaining

$$\frac{(36.7)^2}{4} + \frac{(24.8)^2}{4} + \frac{(44.4)^2}{4} = 983.3225$$

Step 4

$$SST = \text{Result from Step 1} - \text{Result from Step 2b}$$
$$= 1005.75 - 934.5675 = 71.1825$$

The total sum of squares from Step 4 is now partitioned into three components:

Step 5

$$SSTr_1 = \text{Result from Step 3b} - \text{Result from Step 2b}$$
$$= 983.3225 - 934.5675 = 48.755$$

Step 6

$$SSTr_2 = \text{Result from Step 3a} - \text{Result from Step 2b}$$
$$= 943.4033 - 934.5675 = 8.8358$$

Step 7

$$SSE = SST - SSTr_1 - SSTr_2$$
$$= 71.1825 - 48.755 - 8.8358 = 13.5917$$

Note that the values of $SSTr_1$, $SSTr_2$, and SSE must sum to SST. The values for $SSTr_1$, $SSTr_2$, and SSE now permit the calculation of independent estimates of the variability among steels, the variability among machine–operator combinations, and the common variability not associated with either steel type or machine–operator combination. The respective calculated variance estimates are denoted by the **mean squares for treatments associated with rows ($MSTr_1$),** the **mean squares for treatments associated with columns ($MSTr_2$),** and MSE. These values are obtained by adjusting each corresponding sum of squares for the appropriate number of degrees of freedom.

For $MSTr_1$, the appropriate number of degrees of freedom is equal to 1 less than the number of steel types, that is, $3 - 1 = 2$. For $MSTr_2$, the appropriate number of degrees of freedom is equal to 1 less than the number of machine–operator combinations, that is, $4 - 1 = 3$. And for MSE, the appropriate number of degrees of freedom is equal to 1 less than the total number of steel types times 1 less than the number of machine–operator combinations, that is, $(3 - 1)(4 - 1) = (2)(3) = 6$. Thus, we have the following:

Step 8

$$MSTr_1 = \frac{SSTr_1 \text{ from Step 5}}{\text{Number of steel types} - 1}$$
$$= \frac{48.755}{2} = 24.3775$$

Step 9

$$MSTr_2 = \frac{SSTr_2 \text{ from Step 6}}{\text{Number of machine–operator combinations} - 1}$$
$$= \frac{8.8358}{3} = 2.9453$$

Step 10

$$MSE = \frac{SSE \text{ from Step } 7}{(\text{Number of steel types} - 1)(\text{Number of machine–operators} - 1)}$$

$$= \frac{13.5917}{6} = 2.2653$$

The first null hypothesis to be tested is

$$H_{o1}: \quad \mu_{a.} = \mu_{b.} = \mu_{c.}$$

versus

$$H_{A1}: \quad \text{The steel type population means are not equal.}$$

The calculated F test statistic for 2 and 6 d.f. is

$$F_{(2,6)} = \frac{MSTr_1}{MSE} = \frac{24.3775}{2.2653} = 10.7613$$

Now compare this calculated value with the table F values in Appendix Tables IXa and IXb. Using $\alpha = .05$ and $\alpha = .01$ as levels of significance with $n_1 = 2$ and $n_2 = 6$, the values found in Tables IXa and IXb are $F_{(.05,2,6)} = 5.14$ and $F_{(.01,2,6)} = 10.9$. Thus, the calculated value of 10.7613 falls between the F values corresponding to $\alpha = .05$ and $\alpha = .01$. This indicates that the open light means of the three suppliers may be claimed to be statistically significantly different from each other at the .05 level of significance, but not quite at the .01 level.

To test the second set of hypotheses, we test

$$H_{o2}: \quad \mu_{.1} = \mu_{.2} = \mu_{.3} = \mu_{.4}$$

versus

$$H_{A2}: \quad \text{The machine–operator population means are not equal.}$$

The calculated F test statistic for 3 and 6 d.f. is

$$F_{(3,6)} = \frac{MSTr_2}{MSE} = \frac{2.9453}{2.2653} = 1.3002$$

Looking at the table F values at the $\alpha = .05$ and $\alpha = .01$ levels of significance, with $n_1 = 3$ and $n_2 = 6$, we find $F_{(.05,3,6)} = 4.76$ and $F_{(.01,3,6)} = 9.78$. The calculated F statistic value of 1.3002 does not exceed either value and therefore is not statistically significant at either level. We conclude that the evidence does not support the claim that there exists a machine–operator effect on the open light measurements. Putting this another way, we can say that the sample evidence doesn't support the shop speculation that certain operators working on certain machines tend to produce rings with fewer open light problems, that is, the observed difference is not large enough to be discernible statistically.

Table 9.6 summarizes the computational results of the above two-way ANOVA procedure.

TABLE 9.6 ANOVA Table for the Open Light Data of Table 9.4				
SOURCE OF VARIATION	**DEGREES OF FREEDOM**	**SUM OF SQUARES**	**MEAN SQUARES**	**CALCULATED F**
Suppliers	2	$SSTr_1 = 48.755$	$MSTr_1 = 24.3775$	$\dfrac{MSTr_1}{MSE} = 10.7613^*$
Machine–Operator	3	$SSTr_2 = 8.8358$	$MSTr_2 = 2.9453$	$\dfrac{MSTr_2}{MSE} = 1.3002$
Error	6	$SSE = 13.5917$	$MSE = 2.2653$	
TOTALS	11	$SST = 71.1825$		

*Represents significance at the 5% level.

GENERAL PROCEDURE

This section describes a general procedure for performing a two-way ANOVA where there are c columns of one factor and r rows of a second factor. The columns and rows therefore represent the various levels of the two different factors whose effects we wish to analyze. In this section, each row/column entry contains either a single observation or the average of several observations. The computational procedure for the two-way ANOVA is not difficult if the steps described below are carefully followed.

Step 1

Specify the two pairs of null and alternative hypotheses:

a. Null hypothesis for row effect:

$$H_{o1}: \quad \mu_{1.} = \mu_{2.} = \cdots = \mu_{r.} \quad \text{(The row means all are equal.)}$$

where $\mu_{r.}$ is the population mean for row r (the last row), versus alternate hypothesis (1):

$$H_{A1}: \quad \text{The row means are not equal.}$$

b. Null hypothesis for column effect:

$$H_{o2}: \quad \mu_{.1} = \mu_{.2} = \cdots = \mu_{.c} \quad \text{(The column means are all equal.)}$$

where $\mu_{.c}$ is the population mean for column c (the last column), versus alternate hypothesis (2):

$$H_{A2}: \quad \text{The column means are not equal.}$$

Step 2

List the measurements in a table (as in Table 9.4).

a. Each column contains sample measurements drawn from one population. Since there are c columns, we have c populations.
b. Find the column totals and list them.
c. Each row contains sample measurements drawn from one population. Since there are r rows, we have r populations.
d. Find the row totals and list them.
e. Find the grand total (the total over all the measurements in the table).

Step 3

Square each measurement in the table and add up the squared values.

Step 4

Find the value of the correction term. Square the value of the grand total (from Step 2e) and divide the result by the total number of measurements.

Step 5

Square each column total.

a. Divide the square of each column total by the corresponding number of observations, r, in that column.
b. Add up the values obtained in Step 5a.

Step 6

Square each row total.

a. Divide the square of each row total by the corresponding number of observations, c, in that row.
b. Add up the values obtained in Step 6a.

Step 7

Find the value of the total sum of squares (SST). Do this by subtracting the correction term (Step 4) from the sum of the squares obtained in Step 3.

Step 8

Find the value of the sum of squares for the treatments associated with the rows ($SSTr_1$). Do this by subtracting the correction term (Step 4) from the result obtained in Step 6b.

Step 9

Find the value of the sum of squares for the treatments associated with the columns ($SSTr_2$). Do this by subtracting the correction term (Step 4) from the result obtained in Step 5b.

Step 10

Find the error sum of squares (SSE) using the results from Steps 7–9:

$$SST - SSTr_1 - SSTr_2$$

Step 11

Find the mean square for the treatments associated with the rows ($MSTr_1$):

$$MSTr_1 = \frac{SSTr_1}{r - 1} \tag{9-4}$$

Step 12

Find the mean square for the treatments associated with the columns ($MSTr_2$):

$$MSTr_2 = \frac{SSTr_2}{c - 1} \tag{9-5}$$

Step 13

Find the mean square for error (MSE):

$$MSE = \frac{SSE}{(r - 1)(c - 1)} \tag{9-6}$$

Step 14

Find the calculated F statistics for the two treatments. Calculate the F statistic for the row effect:

$$F_{[r-1,(r-1)(c-1)]} = \frac{MSTr_1}{MSE} \tag{9-7}$$

Calculate the F statistic for the column effect:

$$F_{[c-1,(r-1)(c-1)]} = \frac{MSTr_2}{MSE} \qquad (9\text{-}8)$$

Step 15

Find the appropriate table F values from Tables IXa and IXb in the Appendix for the specified level of significance α, and the correct numerator and denominator degrees of freedom. Compare each table value with its corresponding calculated F statistic. Determine whether each calculated F statistic is larger than its corresponding table F value.

Step 16

Apply the decision rule:

a. Reject the appropriate null hypothesis if the calculated F statistic is greater than its corresponding table F value.
b. Do not reject the appropriate null hypothesis if the calculated F statistic is not greater than its corresponding table F value.

Step 17

Reach one of the following statistical conclusions about each null hypothesis:

a. The sample evidence indicates that the means can be claimed to be statistically significantly different at the α level of significance.
b. The sample evidence cannot support the claim that the means are statistically significantly different at the α level of significance.

These elements of a two-way ANOVA are summarized in the generalized two-way ANOVA table given in Table 9.7.

TABLE 9.7 Generalized Two-Way ANOVA Table				
SOURCE OF VARIATION	**DEGREES OF FREEDOM**	**SUM OF SQUARES**	**MEAN SQUARES**	**CALCULATED F**
Treatments (rows)	$r-1$	$SSTr_1$	$MSTr_1$	$\frac{MSTr_1}{MSE} = F_{[r-1,(r-1)(c-1)]}$
Treatments (columns)	$c-1$	$SSTr_2$	$MSTr_2$	$\frac{MSTr_2}{MSE} = F_{[c-1,(r-1)(c-1)]}$
Error	$(r-1)(c-1)$	SSE	MSE	
TOTALS	$rc-1$	SST		

Notes: Compare $F_{[r-1,(r-1)(c-1)]}$ with $F_{[\alpha,r-1,(r-1)(c-1)]}$. Reject H_{o1} if $F_{[r-1,(r-1)(c-1)]} > F_{[\alpha,r-1,(r-1)(c-1)]}$. Compare $F_{[c-1,(r-1)(c-1)]}$ with $F_{[\alpha,c-1,(r-1)(c-1)]}$. Reject H_{o2} if $F_{[c-1,(r-1)(c-1)]} > F_{[\alpha,c-1,(r-1)(c-1)]}$.
A single asterisk placed after the calculated F value identifies significance at the 5% level (i.e., $\alpha = .05$).
A double asterisk placed after the calculated F value identifies significance at the 1% level (i.e., $\alpha = .01$).

The ANOVA procedure discussed in this section is referred to as a *two factor completely randomized design*. In the example, the suppliers are one factor and the machine–operator combinations are the second factor. The different suppliers represent different levels of the supplier factor, and the different machine–operator combinations represent different levels of that factor. The design is completely randomized in that the steels purchased from the three suppliers are randomly assigned to the four plant machine–operator combinations. That is, the steels purchased from supplier a are randomly assigned to the four machine–operator combinations, and the same is true for the steels purchased from suppliers b and c.

NOTE: Before concluding this section it is important to point out that this two-way analysis implicitly assumed *no interaction* between the machine–operator combinations and the different suppliers of steel. By no interaction we mean that if a particular type of steel has a given effect on the open light reading for a particular machine–operator combination, it has that same given effect for all other machine–operator combinations. The no interaction condition is an implicit consequence of the additivity assumption. The analysis we presented would be flawed if there had been a significant interaction. The meaning and importance' of **interaction** is illustrated by the well-known toxic effect of combining alcohol and drugs. Excessive alcohol indulgence on a given occasion produces a slowing of reflexes, drowsiness, and possible stupor. A prescription antihistamine deadens sinus pain and likely will produce drowsiness. In combination, however, the effect of excessive alcohol indulgence and the use of a prescription antihistamine may cause some bodily functions to stop, and possibly result in death. The effect of an interaction in this case is critical, and obviously reflects a much greater response than the simple additivity assumption suggests.

Whenever it is plausible to rule out interaction in a two-way analysis, the ANOVA procedure described in this section provides a way to perform the appropriate analysis.

PRACTICE EXERCISE

9.2 Suppose seven groups and four different stress conditions are involved in a stress study. Four members are randomly selected from each group, for a total of 28 members. A random assignment is made of one of four different stress conditions to one member from each group; then another stress condition is randomly assigned to another member from each group; and so on. A single measurement is recorded for a particular stress reaction on each of the 28 sampled members. If the preliminary results of the data analysis show SST = 87, $SSTr_1$ (for groups) = 24, and $SSTr_2$ (for stress) = 50, then:

a. What assumptions do we need to make to complete the ANOVA?

b. Complete the ANOVA.

EXERCISES

9.5 In the manufacture of semiconductor chips, an impurity is diffused into selected exposed surfaces of the chip by passing a gas mixture over the chip for a specified period of time. The amount of deposition of the impurity (in microns) is a function of the temperature of the gas mixture and of the percent of concentration of the impurity in the gas mixture. However, it is believed that within the range of 600–700°C and within the range of 9–12% concentration, the amount of deposition is constant. If true, this would be important, because the production lines could then be permitted to vary within these tolerances. This, in turn, would cut down on production costs for controlling temperature and concentration. Suppose an experiment is conducted on 12 randomly selected chips to determine the amount of deposition at combinations of 600°C, 650°C, and 700°C with concentrations of 9%, 10%, 11%, and 12%; and suppose we get the following results (the body of the table shows the value of the amount of impurity deposition in microns):

TEMPERATURE	CONCENTRATION OF IMPURITY			
	9%	**10%**	**11%**	**12%**
600°C	1.75	5.31	5.04	6.08
650°C	5.99	4.66	5.34	4.11
700°C	3.40	4.99	4.28	5.10

State H_o and H_A. Put the results in an ANOVA table. Based on these sample results, use the .05 level of significance to determine whether there is significant evidence that the average amount of impurity deposition is different at the different temperatures or at the different concentrations. State a formal conclusion to the test. Assume normality and homoscedasticity.

▶ **9.6** The life of a cutting tool may depend on the type of metal used and on the speed of the lathe used in its manufacture. Six cutting tools, randomly selected from among those produced from two different metals at three different speeds, are tested. The results are given in the table below. (The life of a cutting tool is given in terms of the number of items it produces before it must be discarded or reworked.)

| SPEED OF LATHE | TYPE OF METAL | |
	A	B
1	31	19
2	22	14
3	21	5

State H_o and H_A. Put the results in an ANOVA table. Assume the lives of cutting tools are normally distributed with equal variances. At the .05 level of significance, is there sufficient evidence to indicate that:
a. The average lives of the cutting tools are different for the two metals?
b. The average lives of the cutting tools are different for the three speeds?

9.7 Two different fumigants, A and B, are being considered for use in granaries for the control of mice, roaches, grasshoppers, and other pests. Three levels of concentration for each fumigant are to be used in combination with each other. The combinations are tested in a laboratory on a specified number of these pests, and the number of deaths after a 1 hr period is recorded. Assume the numbers of deaths under the specified conditions may be reasonably approximated by normal distributions with equal variances. Suppose the total sum of squares is equal to 1561.49, the sum of squares for the three levels of fumigant A is equal to 319.38, and the sum of squares for the three levels of fumigant B is equal to 56.54. Use a level of significance of .05. State H_o and H_A, and put the ANOVA results in a table. Is there sufficient evidence to indicate that there is a significant difference in the average kill among the levels of concentration for:
a. Fumigant A? b. Fumigant B?

9.8 Do we get better gasoline mileage (miles per gallon, mpg) with premium gas versus regular gas at different speeds? In a preliminary study, 18 experienced drivers were randomly subdivided into 6 groups of 3. The first group was assigned to drive with regular gas at 55 miles per hour (mph), the second group was assigned to drive with regular gas at 65 mph, the third group was assigned to drive with regular gas at 75 mph, the fourth group was assigned to drive with premium gas at 55 mph, the fifth group was assigned to drive with premium gas at 65 mph, and the sixth group was assigned to drive with premium gas at 75 mph. Each driver went through five tank fill-ups, and the number of miles traveled divided by the number of gallons used is taken as the average miles per gallon for each driver. The table shows the averages for the 6 groups of drivers.

| TYPE OF GAS | SPEED | | |
	55 mph	65 mph	75 mph
Regular	35.83	32.00	23.57
Premium	36.97	31.43	26.47

State H_o and H_A. Put the results in an ANOVA table. Based on these sample results, use the .05 level of significance to determine whether there is significant evidence to say that:

a. The gas mileage is different at the different speeds.

b. The gas mileage is different for the two types of gasoline.

• •

9.5

SAMPLE COMPUTER OUTPUT

Let's consider a computer output, using MINITAB, for the Herzog data given previously in Table 9.4.

Data

All 12 data observations are read into the first MINITAB column C1. Columns two, C2, and three, C3, are reserved to identify machine–operator combinations and the steel type designation of each observation. Figure 9.1 shows the MINITAB naming of columns C1, C2, and C3 as "openlite" (open light), "mhoper" (machine–operator), and "steel" (type of steel), respectively. The data are then read in, row by row, for three variables. The first number in a row is the observed open light reading, the second number in a row identifies the machine–operator combination, and the third number identifies the type of steel. The 12 rows represent the 12 triples of data that are entered for the analysis. Although earlier in the chapter the steel suppliers were designated by the letters a, b, and c, note that MINITAB requires us to use the numerals 1, 2, and 3 instead.

Graph

The LPLOT MINITAB command produces a profile plot of three variables, as shown in Figure 9.2. This allows us to see, in picture form, the open light measurements for the various machine–operator/steel combinations. The variation in the machine–operator effect across the three steel types is shown clearly in Figure 9.2. In the figure, the machine–operator types are coded A, B, C, or D, and the three steel types are labeled 1, 2, and 3. Notice the letters do not align in the same order columnwise at each steel type. This indicates no consistent or systematic effect operating between the types of steel and the machine–operator combinations. However, there is a distinctly lower level of open light readings for the middle steel type. This suggests that the type of

Figure 9.1
MINITAB data entry for two-way ANOVA on Herzog data

```
MTB > name c1 'openlite' c2 'mhoper' c3 'steel'
MTB> read c1 c2 c3
DATA> 11.5 1 1
DATA> 6.1 1 2
DATA> 12 1 3
DATA> 8.2 2 1
DATA> 7 2 2
DATA> 12.5 2 3
DATA> 7.1 3 1
DATA> 6.8 3 2
DATA> 8.7 3 3
DATA> 9.9 4 1
DATA> 4.9 4 2
DATA> 11.2 4 3
DATA> end
        12 ROWS READ
```

steel is affecting the open light readings. The open light mean readings, 9.175, 6.200, and 11.100, for the three steel types as shown in Figure 9.2 confirm the lower level readings for middle steel type.

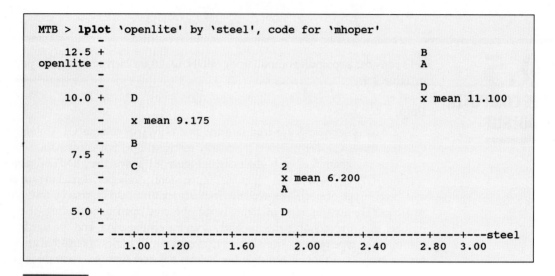

Figure 9.2
MINITAB output: Profile plot of Herzog data (Note: The number 2 in the middle column represents the B and C machine–operator combinations)

Two-Way ANOVA

Figure 9.3 shows the numerical results of the two-way ANOVA performed by MINITAB. The output shows calculated F values obtained from the MS (mean squares) values.

To test for

H_{o1}: $\mu_{a.} = \mu_{b.} = \mu_{c.}$

H_{A1}: The means of the three steel suppliers are not all equal.

Figure 9.3
MINITAB output: Two-way
ANOVA on Herzog data

```
MTB > anova 'openlite' = 'mhoper' 'steel'

Factor      Type Levels Values
mhoper      fixed     4     1     2     3     4
steel       fixed     3     1     2     3

Analysis of Variance for openlite

Source    DF       SS        MS       F      P
mhoper     3    8.836     2.945    1.30  0.358
steel      2   48.755    24.377   10.76  0.010
Error      6   13.592     2.265
Total     11   71.182
```

we use the calculated $F_{(2,6)}$ for steel effect computed by

$$F_{(2,6)} = \frac{\text{MSTr}_1(\text{steel})}{\text{MSE}} = \frac{24.377}{2.265} = 10.76$$

The calculated F test statistic can now be compared to the table F value given in Appendix Table IXa. By comparing the calculated F test statistic of 10.76 with the table F value of $F_{(.05,2,6)} = 5.14$, we can conclude that there is a statistically significant difference in the effect of the steel types on the open light measurements. We can reach the same conclusion by noting that the output tells us that the p-value equals .01. Since this p-value of .01 is less than the significance level of $\alpha = .05$, we can conclude that statistical significance exists due to the effect on the steel types. By using the p-value in testing for significance, we don't have to refer to Appendix Table IXa.

Similarly, testing for

H_{o2}: $\mu_{.1} = \mu_{.2} = \mu_{.3} = \mu_{.4}$

H_{A2}: The means for the machine–operator combinations are not all equal.

we use the calculated $F_{(3,6)}$ for machine–operator effect computed by

$$F_{(3,6)} = \frac{\text{MSTr}_2(\text{mhoper})}{\text{MSE}} = \frac{2.945}{2.265} = 1.30$$

On comparing the calculated F test statistic of 1.30 to the table F value of $F_{(.05,3,6)} = 4.76$ (or equivalently, noting that the p-value of 0.358 is not less than .05), we can conclude that there is no statistically significant difference in the effect of the machine–operator on the open light measurements. In summary, there is statistical evidence supporting a steel supplier effect, but a machine–operator effect cannnot be supported by the statistical evidence.

SUMMARY

While it is true that the ANOVA procedure is an extension to testing the equality of means to more than two populations, that attribute is only a small part of its importance. The ANOVA procedure is fundamental to statistical experimental design. There are volumes written on experimental designs and the ANOVA. Business, science, government agencies, and finance, to name a few, all use experimental designs of various types to analyze data and make sense of the daily bombardment of data.

There was a time before the ANOVA procedure was developed, and even afterward—before it was widely understood and used—when data were gathered in terms of "control" versus "experimental." These were the only populations under consideration. So if you wanted to know if changing a process by using different combinations of ingredients would affect its yield, a process would have to be set up to run one new combination (experimental) while running the current operating combination (control). Think of how time-consuming and costly this would be! For example, suppose there were six combinations; then the experiment would have to be run six times: one new combination versus the current operating combination, repeated six times. This procedure would not only be time-consuming and expensive, but it has the added disadvantage that you would not be able to compare the different combinations with each other. In order to compare them with each other, two of the combinations would have to be run at the same time, repeating this procedure for each pair of combinations. This would result in more time consumption and expense. And even if all these combinations were tried, you would not be able to determine whether the different ingredients interacted with each other to enhance or negate each other's effects on the yield. In one fell swoop, a properly designed experiment with the ANOVA procedure can put it all together and resolve these questions, at considerably less cost in time and money.

The ANOVA procedure is one of the most important tools available for data analysis. It permits and encourages setting up efficient procedures for experimentation and data analysis in all walks of life. It has had a major impact on the twentieth century.

KEY EQUATIONS

One-Way ANOVA

$$MSTr = \frac{SSTr}{k - 1} \qquad (9\text{-}1)$$

where $k - 1$ represents the degrees of freedom for treatments.

$$MSE = \frac{SSE}{\Sigma\, n_j - k} \qquad (9\text{-}2)$$

where $\Sigma\, n_j - k$ represents the degrees of freedom for error.

$$F_{(k-1,\Sigma n_j - k)} = \frac{MSTr}{MSE} \qquad (9\text{-}3)$$

where the test statistic has the F distribution.

Two-Way ANOVA (Without Interaction)

$$MSTr_1 = \frac{SSTr_1}{r - 1} \qquad (9\text{-}4)$$

where this represents a between-rows estimate of population variance σ^2, and r is the number of rows.

$$MSTr_2 = \frac{SSTr_2}{c - 1} \qquad (9\text{-}5)$$

where this represents a between-columns estimate of population variance σ^2, and c is the number of columns.

$$MSE = \frac{SSE}{(r - 1)(c - 1)} \qquad (9\text{-}6)$$

where this represents an estimate of σ^2 used in the denominator of the F ratio, r is the number of rows, and c is the number of columns.

$$F_{[r-1,(r-1)(c-1)]} = \frac{MSTr_1}{MSE} \quad \text{Rows effect} \qquad (9\text{-}7)$$

$$F_{[c-1,(r-1)(c-1)]} = \frac{MSTr_2}{MSE} \quad \text{Columns effect} \qquad (9\text{-}8)$$

PRACTICE EXERCISE ANSWERS

9.1 Let

$$H_o: \quad \mu_1 = \mu_2 = \mu_3 = \mu_4 = \mu_5 = \mu_6 = \mu_7$$
$$H_A: \quad \text{The means are not all equal.}$$

The appropriate test statistic is the F statistic with $k - 1 = 6$ numerator degrees of freedom and $n - k = 28 - 7 = 21$ denominator degrees of freedom. From the F tables, $F_{(.05,6,21)} = 2.57$ and $F_{(.01,6,21)} = 3.81$.

a. The problem states that samples are random and independent, but three more assumptions are needed. We need to assume that the characteristic measurements are

(1) normally distributed with the (2) same variance for each group, and (3) the groups have an additive effect on the overall mean for the particular characteristic measurement.

b.

SOURCE OF VARIATION	DEGREES OF FREEDOM	SUM OF SQUARES	MEAN SQUARES	CALCULATED F
Supplier	6	SSTr = 74	MSTr = 12.3333	$\frac{MSTr}{MSE} = 19.9246**$
Error	21	SSE = 13	MSE = 0.6190	
TOTALS	27	SST = 87		

**Represents significance at the 1% level.

9.2 a. We are given that the samples are random and independent, but to justify the ANOVA procedure we would have to assume that the characteristic measurements are normally distributed with the same variance for each combination of group and stress; and we would also have to assume that groups and stress each have an additive effect, without any interaction, on the overall mean for the particular measurement.

b.

SOURCE OF VARIATION	DEGREES OF FREEDOM	SUM OF SQUARES	MEAN SQUARES	CALCULATED F
Group	6	24	4.0	$\frac{MSTr}{MSE} = 5.539**$
Stress	3	50	16.6667	$\frac{MSTr}{MSE} = 23.078**$
Error	18	13	0.7222	
TOTALS	27	87		

**Represents significance at the 1% level.

For groups, the calculated F of 5.539 is compared to $F_{(.01,6,18)} = 4.01$; for stress, the calculated F of 23.078 is compared to $F_{(.01,3,18)} = 5.09$.

CHAPTER REVIEW EXERCISES

9.9 The engineering manager of Magnadynamics Electronic Division is trying to evaluate which of three engineering software packages to install for cost estimating on the work stations his engineers use. To test them, he acquires a copy of each software program. He then selects 12 engineers, randomly assigning 4 of the engineers to each of the 3 software programs, and measures the time required to perform specified cost estimates. The employees work independently of one another, so they don't have the opportunity to learn from one another. The estimating times (in minutes) are given in the table:

SOFTWARE A	SOFTWARE B	SOFTWARE C
62	51	51
55	57	43
69	66	69
79	68	54

a. State H_o and H_A.
b. Develop the ANOVA table.
c. Test the null hypothesis at the .05 level of significance and interpret the results.

□ ▶ **9.10** Three different textbooks are available for use in a certain course in economics. An instructor wishes to determine the effectiveness of each of these three texts. Since she teaches three sections of the course, she assigns a different text to each, and judges the texts on the basis of final examination scores for the three sections. Assume the scores are normally distributed with equal variances for the three sections. The final examination scores are given in the table:

TEXTBOOK 1	TEXTBOOK 2	TEXTBOOK 3
56	77	70
53	73	61
68	63	67
59	65	72
45	74	66
58	68	62
49	60	63

State H_o and H_A. At the .01 level of significance, is there sufficient evidence to indicate that the average scores associated with the three textbooks are different? Put the results in an ANOVA table and interpret the results.

9.11 A physical education instructor believes there is a statistical difference in a key physical characteristic measurement among successful baseball, football, and basketball athletes. He theorizes that a significant difference in this characteristic, along with several other key physical characteristics, would enable him to develop a distinctive physical profile of successful athletes in each sport. He assumes physical measurements are normally distributed and the variances of the physical characteristic measurements in each sport are the same. As a preliminary study, suppose he takes independent random samples of measurements on 10 baseball players, 10 football players, and 10 basketball players. The results are given in the table:

BASEBALL	FOOTBALL	BASKETBALL
63.6	60.5	62.6
67.8	57.9	64.7
62.0	60.9	60.4
65.2	66.3	65.4
61.1	62.0	71.3
66.2	61.8	67.8
60.6	61.0	64.4
63.1	60.2	65.5
59.0	68.9	64.3
54.5	60.1	75.9

At the .05 level of significance, is there a significant difference in this key physical characteristic measurement among successful baseball, football, and basketball athletes?

□ **9.12** When a certain impurity is diffused into selected exposed regions of a semiconductor chip, an important resulting characteristic is the resistivity (in ohm-centimeters) of the chip. Suppose an experiment is conducted on 18 randomly selected chips to determine the effect of 3 types of gas mixtures on resistivity. Six chips are randomly assigned to each gas mixture, and the results are given in the table (the body of the table shows the resistivity in ohm-centimeters):

	TYPE OF GAS	
A	**B**	**C**
0.72	0.66	0.47
0.83	0.85	0.79
1.05	0.95	0.79
0.88	0.58	0.94
0.93	1.20	1.02
0.68	1.06	0.62

At the .01 level of significance, is there a significant difference among the 3 types of gas?

9.13 A dean at a certain very large university wishes to determine whether the grade-point averages (GPAs) of students differ according to whether the student belongs to a sorority/fraternity, lives in a dorm, or commutes. To get an idea of what he might expect if he examines all the available data at the university, the dean randomly selects the records of 4 students who belong to a sorority or fraternity, 4 students who live in a dorm, and 4 students who commute, and he records their GPAs. The results are given in the table:

SORORITY/FRATERNITY	DORM	COMMUTE
2.27	2.23	2.55
2.07	2.45	2.46
2.28	2.86	2.71
2.29	2.76	2.83

At the .05 level of significance, is there a significant difference in GPAs among these three groups?

9.14 Suppose we have 5 different fertilizers to be tested for their effects on the yields of 6 varieties of oats, with the following results (the figures given are in terms of bushels per unit of area):

VARIETY	FERTILIZERS				
	1	**2**	**3**	**4**	**5**
1	131	205	274	299	337
2	84	176	287	291	318
3	121	179	271	293	328
4	77	190	275	298	332
5	131	196	262	299	333
6	106	194	239	317	344

Assume the yields are normally distributed with equal variances. State H_o and H_A. Put the results in an ANOVA table. At the .01 level of significance, is there sufficient evidence to indicate that:
a. The average yields are different among the fertilizers?
b. The average yields are different among the varieties of oats?

9.15 An experiment is designed to test 4 different fuels and 4 different automobiles for gas mileage. The results are (the figures are given in terms of miles per gallon):

AUTOMOBILE	FUEL			
	1	2	3	4
1	28.2	19.1	30.1	35.8
2	26.2	24.1	28.3	40.9
3	22.6	12.8	19.1	28.3
4	35.3	21.6	24.1	45.8

State H_o and H_A. Put the ANOVA results in a table. Assume miles per gallon are normally distributed with equal variances. At the .01 level of significance, is there sufficient evidence to indicate that:
a. The average miles per gallon for the 4 fuels are different?
b. The average miles per gallon for the 4 automobiles are different?

9.16 A group of psychologists intend to study the reaction effects of three drugs on three types of nervous disorders. Three subjects for each disorder are randomly assigned to each of the three drugs. That is, for the three subjects with nervous disorder type 1, one is randomly assigned one of the three drugs, another is randomly assigned one of the two remaining drugs, and the third is assigned the remaining drug; and so on. The subjects' reaction times (in seconds) to an experimental task is to be recorded. Assume the reaction times are normally distributed with equal variances, and use a level of significance of .05 to set up a procedure to analyze the data to be obtained from this experiment.
a. State the hypotheses to be tested.
b. Set up the appropriate ANOVA table.
c. State the critical regions.

9.17 A business executive asks her secretary to call 3 different travel agents and find out what price they can get on tickets of 5 airlines to a specified destination. The secretary gets the following information:

TRAVEL AGENT	AIRLINE				
	A	B	C	D	E
1	$130	$121	$160	$131	$171
2	123	113	158	106	165
3	121	112	164	102	149

At the .01 level of significance, is there a significant difference in ticket prices among:
a. Airlines?
b. Travel agents?

9.18 A consumer agency shops around to compare interest rates on home loans obtained from banks versus savings and loan institutions (S&Ls) in 5 major cities in the United States. The agency obtains the following averages:

INSTITUTION	CITY				
	A	B	C	D	E
Bank	9.25%	9.50%	9.00%	9.25%	9.75%
S&L	8.75%	9.00%	8.75%	8.75%	9.25%

At the .05 level of significance, is there a significant difference among:
a. Cities?
b. Banks and savings and loan institutions?

9.19 Five companies each offer 6 different guaranteed investment contracts for retirement plans. The current average rates of return (in percents) for the companies and their contracts are given in the table:

CONTRACT	COMPANY				
	A	B	C	D	E
1	13.3	15.5	9.1	10.3	11.2
2	9.0	16.6	8.0	7.6	8.6
3	12.6	11.5	12.1	10.2	11.4
4	7.7	16.3	8.3	8.1	7.9
5	12.9	15.4	10.5	9.5	10.4
6	10.6	13.9	9.8	9.9	11.1

At the .01 level of significance, is there a significant difference among:
a. Companies?
b. Contracts?

9.20 Four real estate agencies with offices in 4 cities were compared in terms of how long it took them to sell their listed homes. The averages (in weeks) for each agency in each city are given in the table:

CITY	AGENCY			
	A	B	C	D
1	28	19	31	40
2	27	25	30	42
3	19	12	19	44
4	31	16	19	26

At the .01 level of significance, is there a significant difference among:
a. Agencies?
b. Cities?

9.21 A study is being made of the amount of time sales representatives with a certain chinaware company spend on a sales call. The purpose is to determine whether schedules for sales calls should take into consideration the type of account being called upon. Twelve customer prospects are selected at random from each of 3 types of accounts in a large city. The number of minutes spent on each call is recorded in the table:

ACTIVE	INACTIVE	NEW PROSPECT
36	35	38
34	36	34
27	34	45
31	42	39
29	36	44
32	31	48
32	30	40
29	39	42
26	37	46
38	39	42
36	39	40
25	30	43

a. Assume sales call times for the 3 account types are normally distributed with equal variances. State H_o and H_A.

b. To test the hypothesis that the mean length of call is identical for all 3 types of account, construct an ANOVA table and test at the .01 level of significance. Interpret the results.

9.22 A manufacturer of laundry detergent wants to advertise that one of its brands makes clothes look "whiter" on average than other brands. However, this claim must first be substantiated before it is aired. A random sample of 36 consumers, 9 for each of 4 detergent brands, participate in the experiment. Each participant does a regular load of laundry using the assigned detergent (with brand unidentified). At the completion of the wash load, the consumer rates the laundry for whiteness on a scale of 1–10. This is repeated 4 times, the ratings are summed, and the results are recorded in the table:

BRAND A	BRAND B	BRAND C	BRAND D
32.0	31.4	30.9	33.1
34.5	32.6	29.4	36.8
29.5	35.1	33.1	36.2
32.2	36.8	32.7	34.5
28.7	29.5	31.5	35.9
28.9	33.4	29.6	35.4
30.9	35.2	35.3	33.6
31.4	30.7	31.2	31.4
27.1	34.9	32.0	29.8

a. State H_o and H_A.

b. Construct an ANOVA table and test the hypothesis H_o at the .05 level of significance.

c. Do the results substantiate the claim of a difference in whiteness as perceived by consumers? (Brand D is the brand in question.)

9.23 A large department store chain conducted an experiment to learn whether management style changes the productivity of its retail sales force. Sixteen sales representatives were randomly assigned to 4 different groups. The groups were given different managerial styles, and the output was subsequently measured. The data in the table represent the sales for a 1 month period in thousands of dollars.

STYLE A	STYLE B	STYLE C	STYLE D
388	375	436	475
496	450	421	490
452	333	508	515
470	468	497	509

a. State H_o and H_A, and construct the ANOVA table.

b. Test the null hypothesis at the .05 level of significance and interpret the results.

9.24 A firm is test marketing 3 alternative container sizes for its instant breakfast. The alternatives refer to different ways of boxing 144 packages in a case. Alternative 1 is a case of twenty-four 6 package boxes; alternative 2 is sixteen 9 package boxes; and alternative 3 is twelve 12 package boxes. Each alternative is placed in 9 stores and the sales measured over a period of 1 month. The sales (in cases per month) are given in the table:

ALTERNATIVE 1			ALTERNATIVE 2			ALTERNATIVE 3		
33	12	87	40	43	22	45	17	21
76	38	45	46	58	62	60	9	12
48	45	107	78	25	37	58	43	36

a. State H_o and H_A, and construct an ANOVA table.
b. Test at the .05 level the null hypothesis of no difference in mean sales among the three alternatives and interpret the results.

9.25 A manufacturer of billiard balls notices an article in a science magazine that states that certain chemical additives increase the elasticity of particular types of plastics. The manufacturer recognizes that if the elasticity (and, hence, the rebounding capabilities) of billiard balls could be increased, her customers would perceive the balls to be of higher quality. Assuming the additives would have only a modest cost, the quality increase would be substantial enough to allow her to increase the price of the balls and, therefore, her profits. She knows, however, that there is always some variation in elasticity among billiard balls. Her problem is to distinguish an increase in elasticity due to the additives, from an increase in elasticity that comes merely by chance. So she commissions an engineer to test 5 of the additives against a control, using 3 batches of the plastic melt in the production of the billiard balls. She wishes to determine which, if any, of the additives significantly (statistically and practically) improve the elasticity of her billiard balls. Each of the 3 batches is divided into 6 equal portions: one portion is randomly assigned to the control (i.e., it is left untouched); one portion is randomly assigned to additive A (i.e., additive A is added to this melt and then the melt continues through a process of conversion to billiard balls); one portion is randomly assigned to additive B; and so on. At the end of the experiment, the engineer measures the elasticity of the billiard balls produced and records, on a scale from 0 to 1 (higher fractions represent greater elasticity), the overall elasticity for each combination in the table:

BATCH	CONTROL	TYPE OF ADDITIVE				
		A	B	C	D	E
1	0.47	0.61	0.55	0.73	0.94	0.47
2	0.43	0.65	0.59	0.77	0.88	0.53
3	0.52	0.53	0.57	0.80	0.91	0.51

Assume the elasticity scores are normally distributed with equal variances for the control and the 5 types of chemical additives. Additionally, assume that the chemical additives, if effective, have an additive effect on the elasticity scores. State H_o and H_A. At the $\alpha = .01$ level of significance, is there significant evidence to indicate that the average elasticities are not the same for the control and the 5 additive types? That is, is there at least one additive that significantly (statistically and practically) improves the elasticity of the billiard balls? Put the results in an ANOVA table and interpret the results.

9.26 A fast food chain has options to purchase 4 different parcels of land for building one of their fast food outlets. An important concern of the fast food chain is the average daily traffic that passes by these locations: greater traffic means greater opportunity for sales. The food chain would also like to know if the average daily traffic is different for different days of the week. A statistical consulting firm gathers the data in the table (the data reflect the average daily traffic observed, in hundreds of cars, over a 5 week period):

	MONDAY	TUESDAY	WEDNESDAY	THURSDAY	FRIDAY	SATURDAY	SUNDAY
LOCATION 1	21.0	7.6	7.7	7.9	8.9	17.6	19.7
LOCATION 2	24.9	23.9	19.4	20.2	19.3	21.7	23.1
LOCATION 3	10.5	7.8	11.5	12.4	9.4	10.8	11.6
LOCATION 4	8.7	11.2	22.2	16.5	15.3	14.1	17.4

At the .01 level of significance, is there a significant difference among:
a. Days of the week?
b. Locations?
On the basis of these results, what would you recommend to the fast food chain?

9.27 An egg distributor wishes to determine whether there are differences in bacterial growth rates for eggs stored at different temperatures and different levels of humidity for a specified length of time. In particular, he wants to know what would happen at 5 different temperatures and 5 different levels of humidity. He sets up the equipment, randomly selects 50 eggs from his warehouse, and randomly assigns 2 eggs to each of the 25 treatment combinations. The averages are given in the following table (the averages reflect a measure of growth rate):

HUMIDITY	TEMPERATURE				
	0°C	3°C	6°C	9°C	12°C
5%	3.8	4.4	5.1	6.0	3.8
10%	2.0	3.6	8.1	6.1	4.1
15%	8.2	8.7	1.8	6.8	5.8
20%	5.7	3.8	5.9	3.6	4.4
25%	5.0	5.9	3.7	6.0	3.2

Assume that all the conditions necessary for the application of the ANOVA procedure are satisfied. Use the .01 level of significance to determine whether there is a significant difference in bacterial growth rate among temperatures and humidity levels. On the basis of these results, what would you recommend to the egg distributor?

SOLVING APPLIED CASES
Executive Transfers:
Silk Purse or Sow's Ear?

IBM—that means, "I've Been Moved!" For many years, transfers at IBM Corporation were so common that the company's initials became synonymous with executive relocation. Many other large corporations also transfer executives frequently among districts, often sweetening the moves with a promotion. Sales executives are particularly susceptible to transfers. But why play geographical musical chairs with executive talent? From the company's point of view the relocations appear to offer several advantages. Not the least of these is the assurance that their sales executives won't have time to develop strong personal ties with customers and then leave the company, taking the customers with them.

From the executive's point of view, the transfers are a two-edged sword. On the one hand, it provides an excellent opportunity to demonstrate that the good performance in the present position is real and not a fluke. On the other hand, it can be a performance trap because of the sales quota assigned to the territory. A key marketing decision by top management in designing sales territories of different sizes (say small, medium, large) is the appropriate sales quota of the territory. Within each size category, the intent is to make the sales potential as equal as possible. But what if the territory's sales potential has been overestimated? Overestimating a district's sales potential sets up a performance evaluation trap for the transferred sales executive. Transfer to a district destined (because of overestimated potential) to produce "below quota sales," no matter who heads it, is a sure way to deflate the corporate image of the executive. The consequence can be detrimental to both the individual and the structure of corporate management. Superior sales performance may go unrecognized, the executive reward systems become disrupted, and the confidence of the best performers become undermined. But how can a corporation find out whether different territories really do have the same sales potential?

One way to learn about the effect, if any, of territory design on sales is to compile and analyze sales data of sales executives in different districts. The data in Table 9.8 are the sales performance records of 8 sales executives, each of whom has been transferred among the same 4 sales districts.

TABLE 9.8	Sales Performance of 8 Sales Executives (in Millions of Dollars)			
SALES EXECUTIVE	**SALES DISTRICT**			
	Pittsburgh	**Dallas**	**Los Angeles**	**Kansas City**
1	2	3	13	1
2	12	11	13	10
3	10	3	11	9
4	4	12	10	11
5	10	4	5	3
6	10	4	7	3
7	14	4	7	2
8	3	2	4	13

Looking at the data, we see that Kansas City generally represents the lowest sales performance regardless of sales executive. Therefore, executives slated for transfer to the Kansas City district may have second thoughts about the desirability of accepting a transfer to that district. But to make certain we aren't being too hasty in condemning such a transfer, we ought to consider the possibility of chance variation. To test this possibility, and to test for differences in the capabilities of the sales executives, we formulate the following two pairs of null and alternative hypotheses:

H_{o1}: Sales potential of the 4 districts are identical.

H_{A1}: Sales potential of the 4 districts are not identical.

H_{o2}: The sales executives have equal capability.

H_{A2}: The sales executives do not have equal capability.

If the assumptions of the ANOVA are met, a two-way ANOVA can be carried out on the data to test these hypotheses. This is asked for in the exercises that follow.

Checkpoint Exercises

1. Assume that all the conditions to validate the ANOVA procedure have been met. Use the two-way ANOVA procedure to test both pairs of hypotheses given in the text, just above. Use $\alpha = .05$.

2. Use the following MINITAB output to confirm your results in Exercise 1. Report your interpretation of the results.

```
MTB > LPLOT 'SALES' BY 'EXEC', CODED FOR 'CITY'

         -
   15.0+
         -                                                   A
 SALES   -     C     C                                              D
         -           A
         -           B     C     B
   10.0+ -           D     A     C     A     A
         -                 D
         -
         -                                   C     C
    5.0+ -                       C
         -                 A     B     B     B     C
         -     B     B     D     D     D     A
         -     A                             D     B
         -     D
    0.0+
         --------+---------+---------+---------+---------+---------+-------EXEC
               1.5       3.0       4.5       6.0       7.5
```

```
MTB > ANOVA 'SALES' = 'EXEC' 'CITY'

Factor    Type Levels Values
EXEC      fixed     8   1    2    3    4    5    6    7    8
CITY      fixed     4   1    2    3    4

Analysis of Variance for SALES

Source    DF        SS          MS       F       P
EXEC       7     148.88      21.27    1.32   0.288
CITY       3      56.63      18.88    1.17   0.343
Error     21     337.38      16.07
Total     31     542.88
```

WENDY'S DATABASE ANALYSIS

In previous Wendy's database exercises, we examined the importance of various fast food restaurant attributes with respect to consumer brand choice. For example, we found taste to be very important, and on this attribute McDonald's is perceived more favorable than Burger King. Now, in this section we shall consider the elements that constitute what is meant by customer brand preference.

Wendy's serves only fresh hamburgers, while McDonald's and Burger King use frozen patties. Wendy's promotes its fresh hamburgers as a distinctive feature of the chain. If there is a consumer segment that places high value on having fresh rather than frozen meat in their hamburgers, and if members of that segment become aware of Wendy's feature, we might expect that segment to become Wendy's customers.

As a measure of the importance consumers place on meat freshness, question 79 asks for the importance of food taste versus meat freshness. A higher score indicates a willingness to sacrifice taste, if necessary, for freshness. If Wendy's has found a winning issue here, might we not expect a tendency for freshness advocates to align themselves with Wendy's rather than with McDonald's or Burger King?

To explore this issue we sorted the respondents according to their top preference among fast food restaurants. Among those who rate Wendy's number 1, do we find a stronger tendency to want freshness than among those who rate McDonald's or Burger King number 1? An affirmative answer to this question would establish preference for meat freshness as a feature differentiating the Wendy's user profile from the profiles of McDonald's and Burger King users.

The difference in profile, in turn, would indicate that at least on this particular dimension, Wendy's seems to cater to a distinct clientele—"Wendy's kind of people."

The MINITAB command COPY with the subcommand USE is used to sort the respondents according to their favorite fast food restaurant and obtain their ratings on freshness.

		Freshness Rating	Freshness Ratings of Respondents Rating Burger King #1
Command:	COPY	C79	C151;
Subcommand:	USE C105 = 1.		(Respondents rating Burger King #1)

		Freshness Rating	Freshness Ratings of Respondents Rating McDonald's #1
Command:	COPY	C79	C153;
Subcommand:	USE C106 = 1.		(Respondents rating McDonald's #1)

		Freshness Rating	Freshness Ratings of Respondents Rating Wendy's #1
Command:	COPY	C79	C155;
Subcommand:	USE C107 = 1.		(Respondents rating Wendy's #1)

Columns C151, C153, and C155 are new columns and contain the data for our study. The use of the subcommand USE of the COPY command first locates in column C105 persons who rate Burger King #1; then it identifies their corresponding freshness preference (C79), and then stores the chosen data in C151. This procedure is repeated for the McDonald's and Wendy's data, storing the corresponding McDonald's data in C153, and storing the corresponding Wendy's data in C155. We can label the brands with the following MINITAB commands:

**Freshness Preference Ratings Data
for Persons Rating Brand as #1**

NAME C151 'BKING1'
NAME C153 'MCDON1'
NAME C155 'WENDYS1'

As a preliminary check, we can calculate the mean rating on the freshness–taste tradeoff question:

Mean Freshness Preference Ratings

MEAN C151
MEAN C153
MEAN C155

The MINITAB response in Figure 9.4 shows Wendy's with a higher mean, 2.308, versus 2.231 and 2.083 for McDonald's and Burger King, respectively. So at least in our sample, Wendy's lovers have a stronger preference for freshness.

Figure 9.4
MINITAB commands for data handling

```
MTB > copy c79 c151;
SUBC> use c105=1.
MTB > copy c79 c153;
SUBC> use c106=1.
MTB > copy c79 c155;
SUBC> use c107=1.


MTB> name c151 'BKING1' c153 'MCDON1' c155 'WENDYS1'
MTB> mean c151
   MEAN =  2.083
MTB> mean c153
   MEAN =  2.231
MTB  mean c155
   MEAN =  2.308
```

But can we generalize this to the entire population? Could the difference among the sample means simply be due to sampling variability? To answer this question, we can test the hypotheses:

H_o: There is no difference among the population mean ratings of the brands.

versus

H_A: There is a difference among the population mean ratings of the brands.

Assuming the underlying assumptions of the ANOVA procedure have been met, let's perform an ANOVA test setting α at the .05 level of significance. The MINITAB command is:

Command: AOVO C151 C153 C155   MINITAB command to perform one-way ANOVA on data in columns C151, C153, C155

The computer output is given in Figure 9.5, and it shows a calculated F test statistic of 0.99. For 2 d.f. in the numerator and 343 d.f. in the denominator, the F table value at α = .05 lies between 3.00 and 3.07. Thus, we do not reject H_o, since the computed F test statistic of 0.99 is not in the rejection region, and, equivalently, the p-value of .373 is not less than .05. The results of the testing show that in spite of the fact that Wendy's had a higher mean value, the evidence is not strong at all in favor of a real "freshness" influence. Indeed, the evidence is consistent with the idea that variation among the mean ratings is due to sampling error.

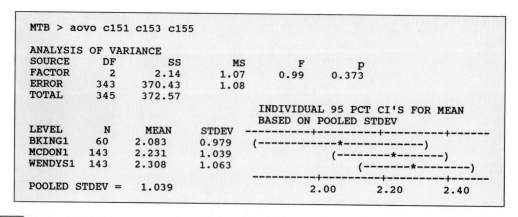

Figure 9.5
MINITAB output: ANOVA on Wendy's

Wendy's Database Student Exercises

1. Develop variable C151 'BKING1', C153 'MCDON1', and C155 'WENDYS1' from variables C105, C106, and C107 on the variable C74, which reflects the respondent attitude toward french fries, a key menu item. Use the MINITAB commands given below. Then comment on the means for C151, C153, and C155.

```
MTB> copy c74 c151;
SUBC> Use c105=1.
MTB> copy c74 c153;
SUBC> Use c106=1.
MTB> copy c74 c155;
SUBC> Use c107=1.
```

2. Perform an ANOVA on C151, C153, and C155 using the command shown below, and comment on the results.

```
MTB> AOVO c151 c153 c155
```

THE REGRESSION AND CORRELATION MODELS

Headline Issue

BETA ANALYSIS: WALL STREET'S NEW AGE TOOL

Beta analysis as an investment tool has come of age. Never heard of beta analysis? It's one of Wall Street's favorite systems of quantifying one important type of investment risk, called *market risk*, faced by holders of common stocks. At the heart of beta analysis are calculated quantities called *beta values*, which tell the investor how much market risk the price of a particular stock is subject to. The market risk represents the sensitivity of the price of a stock to general marketwide price movement. On October 19, 1987, when the stock market crashed, virtually every stock price was affected—but not equally. Some stock prices are much more affected by general market movements than others. Generally, a substantial portion of the price movement facing a stock is due to market risk. For this reason the beta value of a stock should be considered when investment decisions are made.

How can investors find out how much of a market risk they are taking on a particular stock? Investment firms such as Value Line and Merrill Lynch include beta values in their evaluation reports of individual companies. For instance, the Value Line reports presented in Figure 10.1 for IBM and Lotus show their calculated beta values of .95 and 1.40, respectively.

An investor who holds shares in a stock portfolio of several companies can easily calculate the beta value of the stock portfolio. It is simply a weighted average of the individual beta values. The weight given each stock's beta value depends on the percentage of the total amount of portfolio funds invested in the common stock of that company. Portfolio beta values are often used for comparing the market risk of publicly traded stock mutual funds. These mutual funds often publish their portfolio beta values to help investors (and their advisors) determine which mutual funds best match the market risk objectives of the investor. Without the portfolio beta values, it would be more difficult to compare the market risk of different mutual funds, because they may hold common stocks in hundreds of different companies.

But how are the beta values calculated? They are calculated by using *regression analysis,* an important statistical method discussed in this chapter. To find a beta value for a particular stock, the regression analysis is performed on a sample of historical price changes found for the stock and for the general market over the same period of time. This provides a beta estimate for the individual stock, and we are able to judge the reliability of the beta estimate by constructing a confidence interval for the true beta value.

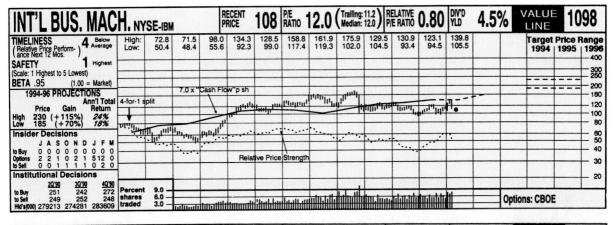

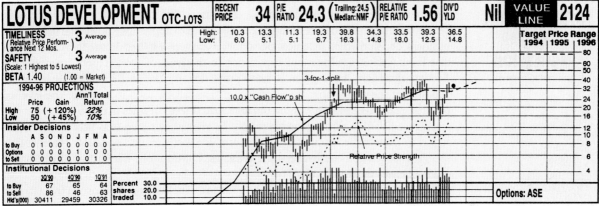

Figure 10.1
Value line beta values for IBM and Lotus

Overview

High on the list of important statistical tools used by management are *regression analysis* and *correlation analysis*. To find the nature of the statistical relationship between two or more quantitative variables, regression analysis is a popular choice. For instance, in business planning, management will typically employ regression analysis to uncover the nature of the statistical relationship between the cost variable and the sales variable. Given a specific level of anticipated sales, the estimated relationship can be used to forecast and budget cost.

Correlation analysis, on the other hand, is not concerned with the nature of the relationship or with predicting one variable from knowledge of the other. The aim of correlation analysis is to provide a measure of the strength of the co-movement between values of two variables. Correlation measures are important to investment managers in evaluating the potential benefits of diversifying between various investment vehicles. More specifically, correlation analysis provides a measure of the degree of linear association (correlation) between the investment returns obtained from various investment vehicles such as stocks and bonds.

This chapter begins with a discussion of regression analysis, including graphic devices called *scatter diagrams*, then deals with fitting a *regression line* to observed sample data, judging the appropriateness of the regression line fitted to the observed data, and predicting the next value of one of the variables given information on the value of the other variable. Regression analysis also can be used for statistical inference. When certain assumptions necessary for statistical inference can be made, regression analysis can be used as a powerful estimating and predicting tool.

Our discussion of correlation analysis follows, including calculation of a correlation measure that describes the strength of the linear association between two variables and how to perform an hypothesis test on the correlation measure.

A case study at the end of this chapter presents a business situation in which the estimated regression line is used for the purpose of prediction and estimation.

10.1
INTRODUCTION TO LINEAR REGRESSION

Managers are constantly called upon to estimate the relationship between the levels of business performance or activity and various levels of inputs or resources used. They often rely on *regression analysis* for the estimation. The purpose of the estimate is to better understand the nature of the relationship and to apply this knowledge to improve business decisions. For instance, personnel managers want to know the relationship that links worker aptitude and experience to the level of worker performance. Production managers, once given a sales projection by the firm's marketing research department, need to know the relationship that can be used to estimate the level of material required in inventory for the anticipated level of sales activity.

The estimation of a relationship may be viewed as a two-step process. The first step is to express the relationship in the form of a mathematical equation; the equation specifies the relationship between the variables. For example, the form might be linear or exponential or logarithmic. The second step is to use sample data to estimate values that specifically define the nature of the equation. The method we'll use in this chapter to estimate the values results in an estimated equation which is called the regression equation. When only two variables are under investigation, the expression is a **simple regression equation.** One variable, the Y variable, is designated as the variable being estimated or predicted; the Y variable is thus referred to as the **dependent variable.** The other variable, the X variable, is the variable doing the estimating or predicting; the X variable is called the **independent, predictor, or explanatory variable.**

The equation is the one that "best" describes the relationship for the observed sample data. Once the specific regression equation has been estimated, it can be used to predict or estimate the Y variable from known or given values of the X variable. (If the regression equation contains two or more independent variables, such as X_1 and X_2, the estimated regression equation is called a *multiple regression equation*. Multiple regression will be discussed in Chapter 11.)

We begin our discussion by introducing a graphical device, called the *scatter diagram,* that is useful in revealing the nature of the relationship between the variables X and Y involved in regression analysis.

SCATTER DIAGRAMS AND THE NATURE OF THE RELATIONSHIP BETWEEN X AND Y

A **scatter diagram** is a graph on which the individual X, Y observations are plotted. It is constructed to provide a visual impression of the data. A scatter diagram is a helpful aid for evaluating the form, type, and strength of the relationship between X and Y.

Form

The form of the relationship may be **linear** or **nonlinear.** The form is linear if the value of Y changes by a constant amount for each unit increase in X. Consider an example from economics. Suppose the number of pineapples demanded, Y, increases by a constant amount for each unit decrease in price, X; quantity is then linearly related to price. On the other hand, if Y changes by increasing amounts or by decreasing amounts for each unit increase in X, the relationship is nonlinear. In managerial accounting, we generally find that the unit cost of output falls rapidly at low output levels, then more slowly as output expands. Thus, the relationship between unit cost and output shows a nonlinear form. The patterns of observations in Figures 10.2a and 10.2b are linear forms, whereas Figures 10.2c and 10.2d are nonlinear patterns. A circular pattern of observations, as shown in Figure 10.2e, describes a situation in which there appears to be no relationship at all between X and Y.

Type of Relationship

Two types of relationships can exist between variables X and Y: **direct (positive) relationships** and **inverse (negative) relationships.** A direct relationship exists if the value of one variable increases as the value of the other variable also increases. In the inverse relationship, the value of one variable decreases as the value of the other increases. Direct linear and direct nonlinear relationships are shown in Figures 10.2a and 10.2c, respectively. Inverse linear and inverse nonlinear relationships are shown in Figures 10.2b and 10.2d, respectively.

Strength

How much coordination is there between changes in X and changes in Y? The degree of coordination reflects the strength of the relationship. The stronger the relationship, the more closely coordinated are the changes. In the extreme case where the coordination is perfect, the graph of the relationship between X and Y follows exactly a linear or nonlinear path, with every observation on X and Y falling exactly on the curve. The scatter diagrams in Figures 10.2a and 10.2d show strong relationships between X and Y, since the points are tightly clustered along their respective paths. In contrast, Figures 10.2b and 10.2c show weaker relationships, since the points in these graphs show a wider scatter about their respective paths.

Relationships between X and Y may exist for various reasons. One reason may be *causality;* that is, there may be a cause and effect relationship between X and Y. In that case, a change in the value of X is said to produce, or cause, an observed change in the value of Y. For example, the frequency and amount of rain causes fluctuations in the sales of umbrellas (but certainly not vice versa!). However, observed changes in both X and Y may be caused by a third element. For instance, increases in sales of in-ground residential swimming pools may be found to be strongly associated with increases in the sales of expensive automobiles. But no one should seriously claim that one is caused by the other! In this particular example, the cause more likely is a third variable, such as the level of spendable income. The point is that simply labeling one of the variables X and the other Y should not lead us to say that changes in X cause changes in Y, or vice versa. Thus, scatter diagrams are properly used to detect association, but they cannot be used to judge cause and effect. Moreover, while the form (linear versus nonlinear) and type (direct versus inverse) of the relationship often may be determined from the scatter diagram, visual impressions of the strength of the relationship need to be supplemented by a numerical measure. A measure of the strength of the linear relationship between X and Y is a correlation measure, which we will discuss in Section 10.13.

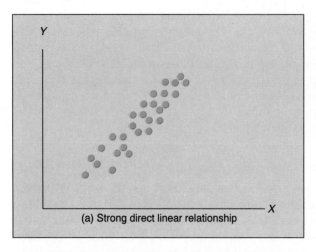

(a) Strong direct linear relationship

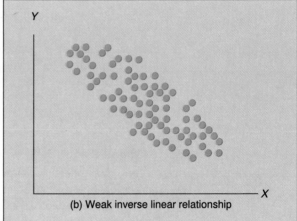

(b) Weak inverse linear relationship

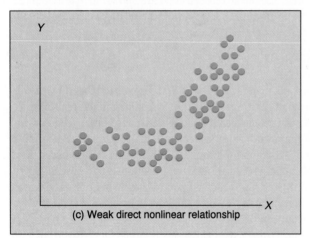

(c) Weak direct nonlinear relationship

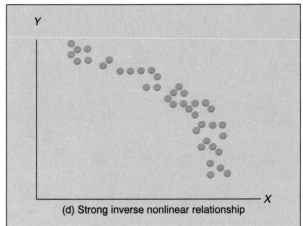

(d) Strong inverse nonlinear relationship

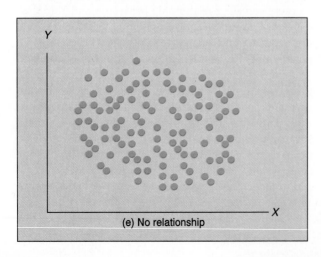

(e) No relationship

Figure 10.2
Scatter diagrams showing different types of relationships

10.2

THE FITTED REGRESSION LINE AND ITS MATHEMATICS

When the scatter diagram of observed X, Y values shows a linear form, it is appropriate to describe the flow of the data points by a straight line, as shown in Figure 10.3 This line, called the **fitted regression line**, estimates an average relationship between X and Y for the observed values of X and Y.

The mathematical expression for the fitted regression line is:

Fitted Regression Line Equation

$$\hat{Y} = a + bX \qquad\qquad (10\text{-}1)$$

where

$\hat{Y}$ (read, "Y hat") is the value of Y read off the fitted regression line; it represents the vertical height of the fitted regression line at a given X value;

a is the value of $\hat{Y}$ where $X = 0$; thus, it is the value of $\hat{Y}$ at the point where the fitted regression line meets the Y axis; it is called the **Y intercept**;

b is the value of the **slope** of the line; it represents the estimated average change in the value of $\hat{Y}$, the dependent variable, for each unit change in X, the independent variable.

A fitted regression line showing the a and b components is presented in Figure 10.4.

Once specific values of a and b have been determined for the fitted equation $\hat{Y} = a + bX$, new values of X can be inserted into the equation to generate the corresponding $\hat{Y}$ values. Note that once the a and b terms have been calculated for an equation, these values remain numerically fixed in determining the value of $\hat{Y}$ for a given value of X.

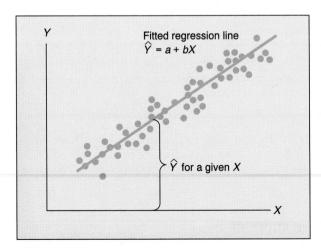

Figure 10.3
Scatter diagram with fitted regression line

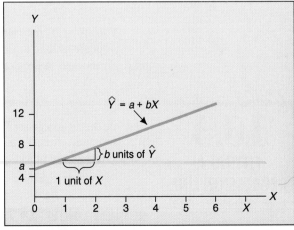

Figure 10.4
Equation for fitted regression line $\hat{Y} = 5 + bX$

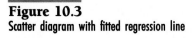

REGRESSION COEFFICIENTS

The diagram in Figure 10.4 shows that by moving 1 unit to the right on the X axis, $\hat{Y}$ increases by an amount b; these two changes define the slope of the regression line. The slope b and the intercept a are collectively termed the **regression coefficients,** but a is often called the **regression constant** and b the **slope coefficient.**

The sign of the value of b indicates whether the relationship between X and $\hat{Y}$ is direct or inverse. The relationship is direct when the value of b is positive; the relationship is inverse when the value of b is negative. Suppose that for the linear relationship shown in Figure 10.4 the value of b is 2. Since the value of b is positive, the relationship between X and $\hat{Y}$ is direct and we know that an increase of 1 unit in X will result in an increase of 2 units in $\hat{Y}$.

USING THE FITTED REGRESSION LINE TO FIND $\hat{Y}$ FOR A PARTICULAR X

Assume that X and $\hat{Y}$ are related by a fitted regression equation of the form $\hat{Y} = a + bX$ and that we have already determined from observed sample data the values of a and b for the equation. Let's suppose $a = 4$ and $b = 2$. Using just two simple steps, we demonstrate the general procedure for finding the value of $\hat{Y}$ for any given X. For example, what is the value of $\hat{Y}$ for $X = 3$?

Step 1
Specify the regression equation. Write the regression equation for the fitted regression line in general form and then substitute the a and b values already determined. This gives the equation of the fitted regression line:

$$\hat{Y} = a + bX$$
$$\hat{Y} = 4 + 2X$$

Step 2
Substitute the stated value for X into the equation and solve for $\hat{Y}$. For $X = 3$:

$$\hat{Y} = 4 + 2(3)$$
$$= 10$$

When $X = 3$, the value of $\hat{Y}$ on the fitted regression line is 10. This procedure is appropriate as long as the X value we used is somewhere within the observed range of X values used to develop the fitted regression equation.

10.3
FITTING A REGRESSION LINE

How do we fit a regression line to observed data? In this section, we shall set down a criterion and discuss the procedure that fits a regression line to meet this criterion. We'll illustrate the procedure using observed data for the following business example.

BUSINESS CONTEXT OF THE RELATIONSHIP

Suppose a specialist in human resources development is hired as a consultant to evaluate and compare the content of the executive jobs at a growing software development firm. In evaluating the jobs, several job content components are considered. Included among these might be technical know-how, amount of managerial responsibility, etc. For each particular job, points are assigned to each component; then the points assigned to the individual components are summed. For example, the national sales manager job might be evaluated as 2 points for technical know-how and 5 points for managerial responsibility, for a total of 7 points. The overall (total) points assigned to a job becomes the "jobscore rating" of the particular job, reflecting the consultant's evaluation of the content for that job. The higher the jobscore rating, the greater the consultant's perception of the overall content of the job.

After the ratings are assigned, a pairing is made of every job's jobscore rating, variable X, and the salary paid to the person holding that job, variable Y (measured in tens of thousands of dollars). Each (X, Y) pairing represents a bivariate (two variable) quantitative observation—two numerical measurements on the same job. The entire collection of observations (pairings) represents the observed set of bivariate data.

The purpose of the investigation of salary and jobscore rating is to establish the statistical relationship that exists (if any) between jobscore and salary. Is job content as represented by the jobscore assigned by the consultant a good predictor of salary? If it is, management can be confident that salary differences are explainable in terms of differences in job content rather than factors unrelated to the job (favoritism, etc.). Table 10.1 lists six observations, including X_i, as the jobscore for the ith job, and Y_i, the salary (in tens of thousands of dollars) for the ith job. The scatter diagram for the data is shown in Figure 10.5.

TABLE 10.1	Data for Jobscores and Salaries	
OBSERVATION *i*	**JOBSCORE (POINTS)** X_i	**SALARY (x $10,000)** Y_i
1	4	6
2	6	9
3	3	5
4	5	6
5	8	10
6	7	9

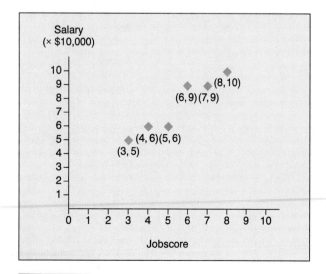

Figure 10.5
Scatter diagram for salary and job content score

LEAST SQUARES CRITERION

The regression equation fitted to the observed set of data should describe the flow of the observations. Thus, if the flow of points is upward to the right on the scatter diagram, the slope should be a positive value. The fitting procedure we shall use also meets a specific condition called the **least squares criterion**, which we will state shortly. The regression equation that meets this criterion for our observed data set is graphed as an upward sloping line in Figure 10.6, along with the six data points. Each observed value of Y has a subscript identifying the number of the observation. Thus, Y_2 indicates the value of the Y coordinate of the second observation in Table 10.1. Also, each observed Y has a corresponding $\hat{Y}$, or *fitted Y value,* read off the regression line. Thus, $\hat{Y}_2$ indicates the fitted Y value for the second observation.

Figure 10.6 shows the fitted regression line over the observed range of X, that is, from the smallest value of X observed to the largest value observed. From the line, we can find the fitted Y value for any X we wish to specify in the observed range of X. This means that for any value of X within this range, the fitted Y value stands for the *regression line prediction* of the Y value. However, let's for the moment consider only the six pairs of (X, Y) values actually observed. Here is an important point to remember: *The fitted value $\hat{Y}$ is generally only a "best guess" prediction of what the observed Y value should be for an observed X value.*

Look again at Figure 10.6, where the six points are scattered around the regression line. Our measure of the scatter is the vertical discrepancy between the observed Y value and $\hat{Y}$. This difference, $Y - \hat{Y}$, is called the *error* and is denoted by the letter e.

Least Squares Criterion

> The least squares criterion requires that the fitted regression line be that line that minimizes the sum of the squares of the vertical differences, or errors, for all the observed values of Y_i.

Figure 10.6
The least squares line

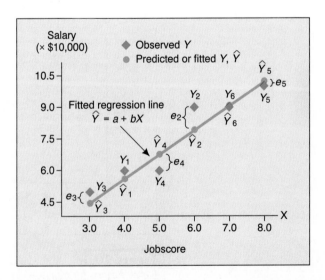

Jobscore

In mathematical terms, this says that the sum $\Sigma(Y_i - \hat{Y}_i)^2$ must be set to a minimum. Alternatively, we can say that the task of the fitted line is to minimize the sum of e_i^2. For simplicity, we will now drop the subscript i with the understanding that all the differences $Y - \hat{Y}$ are to be squared and summed in order to meet the least squares criterion. In summary, by the least squares criterion, the regression line must [for the set of (X, Y) pairs actually observed] minimize

$$\Sigma(Y - \hat{Y})^2 \quad \text{or} \quad \Sigma\, e^2 \quad \text{where } e = Y - Y$$

The values of the regression coefficients a and b needed to meet this criterion determine the least squares regression line $\hat{Y} = a + bX$ shown in Figure 10.6. To introduce a and b into the expression to be minimized, we substitute $a + bX$ for $\hat{Y}$, obtaining

$$\Sigma[Y - (a + bX)]^2 = \Sigma(Y - a - bX)^2$$

Given observed data on X and Y, the two unknowns in the equation are a and b. Only one combination of values for a and b will meet the minimization requirement. That combination is found by solving two simultaneous equations, known as the **normal equations,** for a and b.* These two equations are

$$\Sigma\, Y = na + b(\Sigma\, X)$$
$$\Sigma\, XY = a\,\Sigma X + b(\Sigma\, X^2)$$

where n is equal to the number of paired observations on X and Y.

Isolating a and b in these normal equations results in the following two formulas:

$$b = \frac{n\,\Sigma\, XY - \Sigma\, X\,\Sigma\, Y}{n\,\Sigma\, X^2 - (\Sigma\, X)^2}$$

$$a = \frac{\Sigma\, Y}{n} - \frac{b\,\Sigma\, X}{n}$$

Note that we have stated the formula for b first; this corresponds to the sequence in which the calculations must be carried out, since the value of b is needed to solve for a. These formulas for a and b also can be expressed more simply as follows:

Computational Formulas for Least Squares Estimates

$$b = \frac{\Sigma\, XY - n\bar{X}\bar{Y}}{\Sigma\, X^2 - n\bar{X}^2} \qquad\qquad (10\text{-}2)$$

$$a = \bar{Y} - b\bar{X} \qquad\qquad (10\text{-}3)$$

where $\bar{X}$ and $\bar{Y}$ are the computed means for X and Y.

The formula for the regression constant can be rewritten as $\bar{Y} = a + b\bar{X}$. This form helps us recognize that the computed least squares regression line will always pass through the point $(\bar{X}, \bar{Y})$. This point is located where the horizontal mean line $\bar{Y}$ crosses the vertical mean line $\bar{X}$, as shown in Figure 10.7.

*Through differential calculus we are able to determine the normal equations for a and b such that $\Sigma(Y - a - bx)^2$ will be minimized for the observed set of data.

Figure 10.7
Computed regression line
passes through the point
$(\bar{X}, \bar{Y})$

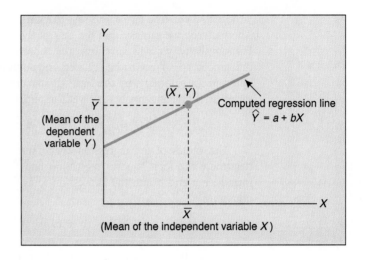

ILLUSTRATING THE LEAST SQUARES SOLUTION

Now let's calculate the regression coefficients a and b. The preliminary computations are presented in Table 10.2.

TABLE 10.2	Calculating Regression Statistics			
OBSERVATION	JOBSCORE X	SALARY Y	XY	X^2
1	4	6	24	16
2	6	9	54	36
3	3	5	15	9
4	5	6	30	25
5	8	10	80	64
6	7	9	63	49
Totals	$\Sigma X = 33$	$\Sigma Y = 45$	$\Sigma XY = 266$	$\Sigma X^2 = 199$

$$\bar{X} = \frac{\Sigma X}{n} = \frac{33}{6}$$

$$\bar{Y} = \frac{\Sigma Y}{n} = \frac{45}{6}$$

Using the appropriate values computed in Table 10.2 and substituting these values into the computational formula (10-2) for b, we get

$$b = \frac{\Sigma XY - n\bar{X}\bar{Y}}{\Sigma X^2 - n\bar{X}^2}$$

$$= \frac{266 - 6\left(\frac{33}{6}\right)\left(\frac{45}{6}\right)}{199 - 6\left(\frac{33}{6}\right)^2}$$

$$= \frac{18.5}{17.5} = 1.057143$$

Then, using formula (10-3), we have

$$a = \bar{Y} - b\bar{X}$$
$$= \left(\tfrac{45}{6}\right) - 1.057143\left(\tfrac{33}{6}\right)$$
$$= 1.685716$$

Thus, the fitted regression line is given by the equation

$$\hat{Y} = 1.686 + 1.057X$$

This regression equation (stated in rounded terms) describes an average relationship between jobscore and salary for the observed data.* Since units of Y represent $10,000, the value of Y must be multiplied by $10,000 to express the fitted salary in dollar terms. The practical interpretation of the regression coefficients would be: The Y intercept value a of $16,860 ($1.686 \times $10,000$) represents an estimate of the average salary attributable to factors other than jobscore, for example, years of experience, personality, etc. The slope value b of $10,570 ($1.057 \times $10,000$) represents the consultant's estimate of the average salary increase for each unit increase in jobscore assigned by the consultant. Note that the regression coefficient only *measures* the average salary differential per unit difference in job content; it does *not imply a value judgment* about what the salary differential ought to be per unit difference in jobscore.

INTERPRETING THE FITTED REGRESSION EQUATION: FITTED *Y* VALUES

How closely do the fitted salary levels from the regression line correspond to the observed salary levels for the jobs studied? To answer this question we will have to determine the fitted value $(\hat{Y})$ for each observed value of X.

Let's use the equation for the fitted regression line to find the fitted salary $(\hat{Y})$ for an observed value of X, say $X = 4$. We should be aware at this point that although we can calculate the fitted salary level for any chosen X value, an appropriate approach is to limit the value of X to the range of the observed X's used to estimate the regression equation. In this problem, the range of the observed X values is $X = 3$ to $X = 8$, so $X = 4$ is within the range. At a jobscore of 4, then, the fitted salary computed from the regression equation is

$$\hat{Y} = 1.686 + 1.057(4) = 5.914$$

That is, at $X = 4$, the fitted Y value $(\hat{Y})$ is 5.914, which in dollar terms means $59,140. The difference between the actual salary $Y = 6$ (or $60,000) and the fitted salary, $\hat{Y} = 5.914$ determines the observed error, $Y - \hat{Y} = 0.086$, or in dollar terms, $10,000 \times 0.086 = $860.

REGRESSION RESIDUALS

In regression analysis the observed error difference is represented by $e = Y - \hat{Y}$, and e is called a **residual.** To find the remaining residuals for the jobscore example, we simply compute $\hat{Y}$ for each of the observed jobscore values, as shown in column 3 of

*The amount of rounding used to express the regression equation will vary. Typically coefficients are shown with two or three digits beyond the decimal point.

Table 10.3; and then find the values of the residuals, $Y - \hat{Y}$, as given in column 4 of Table 10.3. Squaring the residuals gives us column 5 of Table 10.3. We see that the sum of the squared residuals is equal to 1.9428, shown at the bottom of column 5.

TABLE 10.3 Comparison of the Observed and Fitted Values of Salary				
COLUMN 1 OBSERVED JOBSCORE X	**COLUMN 2** OBSERVED SALARY Y	**COLUMN 3** FITTED SALARY $\hat{Y}$	**COLUMN 4** RESIDUAL VALUES $e = Y - \hat{Y}$	**COLUMN 5** RESIDUALS SQUARED $(Y - \hat{Y})^2$
4	6	5.914	+0.086	0.0074
6	9	8.028	+0.972	0.9448
3	5	4.857	+0.143	0.0204
5	6	6.971	−0.971	0.9428
8	10	10.142	−0.142	0.0202
7	9	9.085	−0.085	0.0072
			$\Sigma(Y - \hat{Y}) = +0.003$	$\Sigma(Y - \hat{Y})^2 = 1.9428$

What is the significance of the value 1.9428? *Because the values for a and b were determined by the least squares criterion, the value 1.9428 is the minimum value of $\Sigma(Y - \hat{Y})^2$ obtainable by fitting a straight line to the six pairs of (X, Y) values in the data set.* If we used any other pair of values for a and b, the sum of the squared deviations would be greater than 1.9428. Also, *the sum of the unsquared deviations (column 4), except for rounding errors, should always be 0; that is, $\Sigma(Y - \hat{Y}) = 0$. This means that the negative predictive errors using the regression line will always balance out the positive predictive errors.* In any set of computations, the sum may differ slightly from 0 due to rounding errors, as in Table 10.3, where the sum in column 4 totaled + 0.003 rather than 0.

PRACTICE EXERCISE

10.1 The following data set describes a statistical relationship between entrance test scores, X, of six production line workers, and their subsequent productivity test scores, Y:

	OBSERVATION					
	1	2	3	4	5	6
Y	27	45	51	9	33	51
X	7	15	13	3	10	12

The fitted regression line was found by the method of least squares to be

$$\hat{Y} = 1 + 3.5X$$

a. Find $\Sigma(Y - \hat{Y})^2$ (or Σe^2).
b. Show that the fitted regression line passes through the point $(\bar{X}, \bar{Y})$.

INTERPOLATION: PREDICTING WITHIN THE OBSERVED X RANGE

Once a regression equation has been fitted, management can use it to "interpolate" a $\hat{Y}$ value; that is, find the $\hat{Y}$ value on the fitted regression line for any chosen X value.

Prediction of Y is permissible as long as the prediction is based on the values of X within the observed range of X.

For example, suppose the human resource consultant assigned a jobscore of 6.5 to a newly created executive position, that is, $X = 6.5$. Then, by interpolation, the fitted $\hat{Y}$ value is $\hat{Y} = 1.686 + 1.057(6.5) = 8.557$. This means that the $\hat{Y}$ value of 8.557 is the fitted salary value read from the regression line for a job score of 6.5. The implication is that for a 6.5 jobscore, a salary of \$85,570 ($8.557 \times \$10,000$) is consistent with the relationship that exists between salary and jobscore as described by the regression equation.

EXERCISES

▶ **10.1** A small random sample of 3 Kray supercomputers showed the following figures for major breakdowns and years in service:

	OBSERVATION		
	1	2	3
MAJOR BREAKDOWNS **Y**	3	2	5
YEARS IN SERVICE **X**	3	1	4

a. Compute ΣX^2.
b. Compute ΣXY.
c. Write the normal equations, substituting the numerical values of n, ΣX, ΣY, ΣX^2, and ΣXY as required.
d. Find the value of b.
e. Find the value of a.
f. Is the relationship direct or inverse?
g. Calculate the value of $\hat{Y}$ corresponding to $X = 1$.
h. Using the result of part g, by how much does $\hat{Y}$ err as an estimate of Y?
i. Estimate the value of Y for $X = 2$.

10.2 A South-Mart research analyst investigating the relationship between shopping center traffic and a retail store's weekly sales developed an index for weekly sales over 5 randomly selected weeks, as given in the table.

	OBSERVATION				
	1	2	3	4	5
SALES INDEX **Y**	50	30	90	80	60
TRAFFIC INDEX **X**	4	1	8	5	3

a. Calculate ΣY.
b. Calculate ΣX^2.
c. Calculate ΣXY.
d. Write the normal equations, substituting the numerical values of n, ΣX, ΣY, ΣX^2, and ΣXY as required.
e. Find the value of b.
f. Find the value of a.
g. Is the relationship direct or inverse?

h. Calculate $\hat{Y}$ for $X = 3$.

i. By how much does your answer to part h err as an estimate of Y?

j. Estimate Y for $X = 6$.

10.3 Adam Car Rental Agency studied the following data collected on a sample of 5 cars:

CAR	MILES DRIVEN (IN THOUSANDS OF MILES) X	MAINTENANCE COST (IN HUNDREDS OF DOLLARS) Y
1	20	3
2	70	12
3	50	7
4	30	5
5	30	7

In the fitted regression equation of Y on X:

a. What is b, the slope coefficient?

b. What is a, the Y intercept?

c. For a 1000 mi increase in miles driven, what is the estimated change in maintenance cost?

▶ **10.4** Holding goods in inventory is costly because inventoried goods are susceptible to breakage and other forms of physical damage. Typically, the amount of damage increases with the level of inventory, but some of the damage is unrelated to the amount of inventory. The following data show a company's inventory damage experience:

	OBSERVATION						
	1	2	3	4	5	6	7
DAMAGE (THOUSAND DOLLARS) Y	80	100	70	60	50	70	100
INVENTORY (MILLION DOLLARS) X	11	15	13	10	7	9	13

Using regression analysis, the relationship between damage and inventory level can be estimated.

a. Determine the fitted regression equation $\hat{Y} = a + bX$.

b. With an increase in inventory investment of $1 million, how much, on average, will be the change in damaged inventory?

c. Interpolate the amount of damage for an inventory level of $8 million.

10.5 A management study of employee willingness to relocate led to the data given in the table for a random sample of 7 employees. The variable X represents number of years in the present position, and the variable Y represents an index of willingness to relocate, with $Y = 0$ meaning no willingness to relocate.

	OBSERVATION						
	1	2	3	4	5	6	7
Y	9	0	1	3	2	6	4
X	3	6	7	6	5	2	1

a. Plot the points in a scatter diagram and check for the linearity assumption.
b. Use the least squares criterion to determine the fitted linear regression equation relating willingness to relocate, Y, to years in present position, X.
c. Is the relationship direct or inverse?
d. For $X = 4$, calculate $\hat{Y}$.
e. Over what range of X values would interpolated values of $\hat{Y}$ be permissible?

10.6 Low-involvement consumer purchases of items such as floor wax, dishwashing detergent, and ballpoint pens are a challenge to the creativity of marketers trying to generate enthusiasm for their brands. On the one hand, consumers may pay little attention to advertising for these products; on the other hand, the brand they choose is often the first brand that comes to mind in connection with that product category. Thus, a brand's share of the market in its product class is often directly related to its "share of mind," the consumer's degree of brand awareness. The data in the table represent market share, Y, and brand awareness index values, X, for 5 low-involvement consumer brands.

| | OBSERVATION | | | | |
	1	2	3	4	5
Y	25	35	50	65	70
X	2.5	4	5	7.5	8

a. Plot the points in a scatter diagram and check for the linearity assumption.
b. Use the least squares criterion to determine the fitted linear regression equation.
c. Is the relationship direct or inverse?
d. For $X = 7$, calculate $\hat{Y}$.
e. Over what range of X values would interpolation of $\hat{Y}$ values be permissible?

10.7 The advertising manager for the Green Giant brand of frozen mixed fruit sponsors a consumer panel study to determine the productivity of advertising for the brand. A regression equation (known as an advertising response function) is computed, using a family's dollar purchases of the brand as the variable Y and the number of exposure opportunities to Green Giant brand advertising as the variable X. The range of interpolation is $0 < X < 15$. The computed regression equation is $\hat{Y} = 3.15 + 0.16X$.

a. What is the average change in a family dollar's purchases of the Green Giant brand associated with 1 additional exposure opportunity to Green Giant advertising?
b. For a family having 10 exposure opportunities to Green Giant advertising, what is the estimated family dollar purchase of the Green Giant brand?
c. Suppose a family is not exposed to Green Giant brand advertising. What is the family's expected dollar purchase of Green Giant brand?

10.4

STANDARD DEVIATION OF RESIDUALS

Recall that the difference between the actual Y value and its corresponding value on the regression line, $\hat{Y}$, is called the error, or residual, term e; that is, $Y - \hat{Y} = e$. Two summary statistics that measure the spread and size of e are the **error variance S_e^2 and the standard deviation of residuals S_e. The formula for the error variance is**

$$S_e^2 = \frac{\Sigma(Y - \hat{Y})^2}{n - 2}$$

Dividing the term $\Sigma(Y - \hat{Y})^2$ by $n - 2$ provides an average of the squared residuals. By taking the square root of this average, we get the definitional formula for the standard deviation of the residuals, S_e:

$$S_e = \sqrt{\frac{\Sigma(Y - \hat{Y})^2}{n - 2}}$$

CALCULATING S_e

The numerator of the standard deviation of residuals is the expression $\Sigma(Y - \hat{Y})^2$. The value of this term for the jobscore example was calculated in Table 10.3 and is repeated here in Table 10.4 for convenience.

		TABLE 10.4	Calculations for S_e	
X	**Y**	**$\hat{Y}$**	**$e = Y - \hat{Y}$**	**$(Y - \hat{Y})^2$**
4	6	5.914	+0.086	0.0074
6	9	8.028	+0.972	0.9448
3	5	4.857	+0.143	0.0204
5	6	6.971	−0.971	0.9428
8	10	10.142	−0.142	0.0202
7	9	9.085	−0.085	0.0072
			$\Sigma(Y - \hat{Y})^2 =$	1.9428

From the table we see that $\Sigma(Y - \hat{Y})^2$ has a value of 1.9428. Since there are $n = 6$ observations, the value of the standard deviation of residuals is

$$S_e = \sqrt{\frac{\Sigma(Y - \hat{Y})^2}{n - 2}}$$

$$= \sqrt{\frac{1.9428}{6 - 2}} = 0.6969$$

This means that the size of the standard deviation of the fitting error for these 6 observations is 0.6969, or, in dollar terms, ($10,000 \times 0.6969$) = $6969.

Since the purpose of fitting a regression line is to predict values of Y, the standard deviation of residuals as a measure of fit should, and does, suggest something about the predictive accuracy of the fitting process. Knowing that the value of S_e reflects the amount of fitting or predictive error, we are led to an important conclusion: The smaller the value of the standard deviation of residuals S_e, the better the predictive accuracy of the fitting process.

Computational Method for Calculating S_e

The calculation of S_e above required several steps: first, calculating a value of $\hat{Y}$ for each X value in the data set; second, finding the differences, $Y - \hat{Y}$, and squaring them to obtain $\Sigma(Y - \hat{Y})^2$; and finally, summing the squared differences. This lengthy series of calculations can be avoided by a computational approach that uses only the original data and the regression coefficients a and b.

Computational Formula for S_e

$$S_e = \sqrt{\frac{\Sigma\,Y^2 - a\,\Sigma\,Y - b\,\Sigma\,XY}{n-2}} \qquad \text{(10-4)}$$

All the terms in the numerator of this expression, except $\Sigma\,Y^2$, were already calculated for the jobscore example in the process of determining the Y intercept and slope of the regression line. Thus, from Table 10.2, we have $\Sigma\,Y = 45$ and $\Sigma\,XY = 266$, which gave us $a = 1.685716$ and $b = 1.057143$. Table 10.5 repeats these computations and adds the column needed for $\Sigma\,Y^2$. Since we have $n = 6$ observations in the data set,

$$S_e = \sqrt{\frac{\Sigma\,Y^2 - a\,\Sigma\,Y - b\,\Sigma\,XY}{n-2}}$$

$$= \sqrt{\frac{359 - (1.685716)(45) - (1.057143)(266)}{6-2}}$$

$$= \sqrt{\frac{1.9428}{4}} = 0.6969$$

This is the same result (as it must be except for rounding differences) as found using the definitional formula.

	TABLE 10.5	**Computations for S_e**			
OBSERVATION	**X**	**Y**	**XY**	**X²**	**Y²**
1	4	6	24	16	36
2	6	9	54	36	81
3	3	5	15	9	25
4	5	6	30	25	36
5	8	10	80	64	100
6	7	9	63	49	81
	$\Sigma X = 33$	$\Sigma Y = 45$	$\Sigma XY = 266$	$\Sigma X^2 = 199$	$\Sigma Y^2 = 359$

Before exploring the interpretation and usefulness of S_e, let's take another look at its square, the error variance, which we mentioned briefly at the beginning of this section.

THE ERROR VARIANCE, S_e^2

There are situations in which the use of the error variance S_e^2 is preferred to the standard deviation of residuals. For example, the error variance is a useful statistical measure in finance where diversified investment portfolios are evaluated on the basis of the error variance of investment returns (price changes).

The error variance for the salary–jobscore data is calculated as follows:

$$S_e^2 = \frac{\Sigma(Y - \hat{Y})^2}{n-2}$$

$$= \frac{1.9428}{4} = 0.4857$$

PRACTICE EXERCISE

10.2 As financial manager, you are asked to develop a financial index that indicates an investment project's potential cash flow level and stability. The objective of the financial index is to provide a way of predicting the investment project's ultimate profitability from the financial index. The following data are collected for 8 recently completed investment projects. The data report their investment profitability, Y, and the financial index, X.

		PROJECT							
		A	**B**	**C**	**D**	**E**	**F**	**G**	**H**
PROFITABILITY Y		41	25	52	42	30	49	30	18
FINANCIAL INDEX X		8	5	10	8	6	9	7	3

a. Calculate $\Sigma(Y - \hat{Y})^2$.
b. Calculate the error variance, S_e^2.
c. Calculate the standard deviation of residuals, S_e.

10.5
THE COEFFICIENT OF DETERMINATION, r2: ANOTHER MEASURE OF REGRESSION LINE FIT

We have calculated the standard deviation of residuals, S_e, to measure the fit of the regression line to the scatter of observed data. But there is another measure of regression line fit called the **coefficient of determination, r^2**. This measure requires computation of $\Sigma(\hat{Y} - \bar{Y})^2$, which is the amount of variation of the $\hat{Y}$'s (fitted Y's) around the mean value, $\bar{Y}$. Also required is the computation of $\Sigma(Y - \bar{Y})^2$, the total amount of variation of the observed Y values around the mean value, $\bar{Y}$. The definitional formula for r^2 is the ratio of these two variations:

$$r^2 = \frac{\Sigma(\hat{Y} - \bar{Y})^2}{\Sigma(Y - \bar{Y})^2}$$

The square root of r^2 is the value r, which is called the *coefficient of correlation* and measures the degree of linear association between X and Y. We will have more to say about the meaning and calculation of r in Section 10.13.

TOTAL VARIATION

In Figure 10.8 the green data point represents an observed Y value at a given X. Directly below this point is a point on the fitted regression line; this orange point represents the fitted Y value ($\hat{Y}$) corresponding to the observed Y value. The mean value, $\bar{Y}$, for all the Y values is shown in Figure 10.8 as a horizontal line. By drawing a vertical dashed line from the observed Y value to the $\bar{Y}$ line, we can visually portray the size of the overall deviation $Y - \bar{Y}$. The longer this line segment, the greater the amount of overall deviation. The overall deviations for the jobscore data are portrayed in Figure 10.9.

The term in the denominator of the definitional formula for r^2 is computed from the overall deviations. We obtain this denominator by squaring each overall deviation term and summing all the squares. This quantity is called the **total sum of squares**, or **total variation**, and is denoted by **SST**:

$$\text{SST} = \Sigma(Y - \bar{Y})^2$$

Figure 10.8
Overall deviation, explained portion, and unexplained portion for one observed value of Y

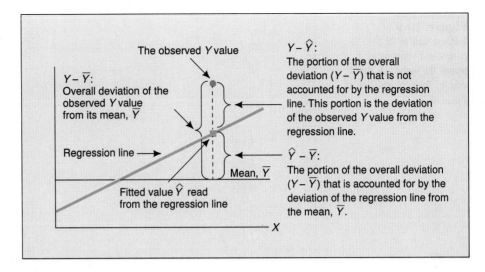

Explained Variation

Now consider in Figure 10.8 the portion of the vertical dashed line from the orange point (on the regression line) down to $\bar{Y}$, shown as the difference $\hat{Y} - \bar{Y}$. This portion represents the part of the observed overall deviation that is accounted for by $\hat{Y}$, the position or height of the point on the regression line. By squaring these differences for all observations and summing the squared values, we obtain the numerator of r^2. This sum in the numerator of r^2 is called the **explained variation**; it is also called the **sum of squares due to regression** and is denoted by **SSR**:

$$SSR = \Sigma(\hat{Y} - \bar{Y})^2$$

Unexplained Variation

In Figure 10.8 the segment $Y - \hat{Y}$ represents the residual—that is, the portion of the observed overall deviation unaccounted for by the height of the point on the regression line. These residuals are shown in Figure 10.9b for all the jobscore observations. By squaring each difference and summing the squares, we obtain the quantity called the **unexplained variation**, or **error sum of squares**, denoted by **SSE**:

$$SSE = \Sigma(Y - \hat{Y})^2$$

This unexplained variation is also referred to as **residual variation**. Note that SSE = Σe^2.

CALCULATING r^2

Algebraically, the total variation can be partitioned into the explained and unexplained components (a mathematical proof is not within the intended scope of this book):

Partitioning the Total Variation

$$\Sigma(Y - \bar{Y})^2 = \Sigma(\hat{Y} - \bar{Y})^2 + \Sigma(Y - \hat{Y})^2$$

$$\begin{pmatrix} \text{Total} \\ \text{variation} \end{pmatrix} = \begin{pmatrix} \text{Explained} \\ \text{variation} \end{pmatrix} + \begin{pmatrix} \text{Unexplained} \\ \text{variation} \end{pmatrix}$$

$$SST \quad = \quad SSR \quad + \quad SSE$$

Figure 10.9
A comparison of (b) the unexplained variation of Y around the regression line $\hat{Y}$ with (a) the total variation of Y around $\bar{Y}$

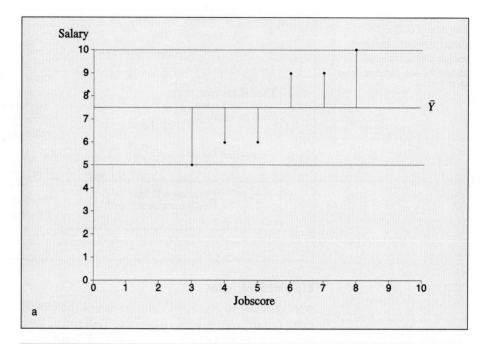

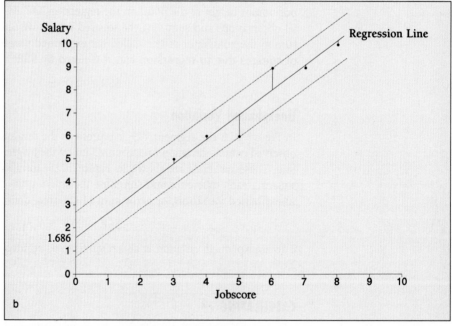

The value of r^2 is simply the ratio of the explained component to the total variation:

$$r^2 = \frac{\text{Explained variation}}{\text{Total variation}}$$

$$= \frac{\Sigma(\hat{Y} - \bar{Y})^2}{\Sigma(Y - \bar{Y})^2} = \frac{\text{SSR}}{\text{SST}}$$

It follows that r^2 can be interpreted as the proportion of the total variation of Y explained by the fitted regression line. It also follows that:

1. Since SSR cannot exceed SST, and since neither SST nor SSR can ever be negative, the value of r^2 must be between 0 and 1.
2. If $r^2 = 1$, then all the variation in Y is explained by the regression line.
3. At the other extreme, if $r^2 = 0$, then none of the variation of Y is explained by the regression line.

Additionally, it is instructive to note that the proportion of total variation unexplained by the regression line must be equal to $1 - r^2$. That is,

$$1 - r^2 = 1 - \frac{\text{Explained variation}}{\text{Total variation}}$$

$$= 1 - \frac{\text{SSR}}{\text{SST}}$$

$$= \frac{\text{Unexplained variation}}{\text{Total variation}}$$

$$= \frac{\text{SSE}}{\text{SST}}$$

Rearranging terms to isolate the r^2 value, we recognize that an alternative way to calculate the r^2 value is to use the SSE and SST terms:

$$r^2 = 1 - \frac{\text{Unexplained variation}}{\text{Total variation}}$$

$$= 1 - \frac{\text{SSE}}{\text{SST}}$$

In Y terms this becomes

$$r^2 = 1 - \frac{\Sigma(Y - \hat{Y})^2}{\Sigma(Y - \bar{Y})^2}$$

But to illustrate the calculation of r^2, let's return to the definitional formula of r^2 and compute r^2 using the SSR and SST terms. These calculations are presented in Table 10.6 for the jobscore–salary data set.

TABLE 10.6 Computation of Explained Variation and Total Variation				
JOBSCORE X	SALARY Y	PREDICTED SALARY $\hat{Y}$	EXPLAINED DEVIATION SQUARED $(\hat{Y} - \bar{Y})^2$	TOTAL DEVIATION SQUARED $(Y - \bar{Y})^2$
4	6	5.914	$(5.914 - 7.5)^2$	$(6 - 7.5)^2$
6	9	8.028	$(8.028 - 7.5)^2$	$(9 - 7.5)^2$
3	5	4.857	$(4.857 - 7.5)^2$	$(5 - 7.5)^2$
5	6	6.971	$(6.971 - 7.5)^2$	$(6 - 7.5)^2$
8	10	10.142	$(10.142 - 7.5)^2$	$(10 - 7.5)^2$
7	9	9.085	$(9.085 - 7.5)^2$	$(9 - 7.5)^2$
	$\Sigma Y = 45$		$\Sigma(\hat{Y} - \bar{Y})^2 = 19.557$	$\Sigma(Y - \bar{Y})^2 = 21.500$

$\bar{Y} = \dfrac{45}{6} = 7.5$

$r^2 = \dfrac{\Sigma(\hat{Y} - \bar{Y})^2}{\Sigma(Y - \bar{Y})^2} = \dfrac{19.557}{21.500} = 0.91$

The high r^2 value of 0.91 means that the fitted regression line has been very helpful in accounting for the variation in Y. The r^2 value shows that 91% of the total variation in salary Y has been explained by a linear relationship between salary Y and jobscore X. Taking the square root of r^2, we obtain the correlation coefficient $r = 0.95$. The value of r measures the strength of the linear association between the variables X and Y, which in this case are the variables jobscore and salary.

Shortcut Computational Formula for r^2

For computational ease, there is a shortcut formula for r^2 that uses values already computed.

Computational Formula for r^2

$$r^2 = \frac{a \sum Y + b \sum XY - n\bar{Y}^2}{\sum Y^2 - n\bar{Y}^2} \qquad \text{(10-5)}$$

Let's compute r^2 by the shortcut computational formula for the jobscore–salary problem. First, we repeat the results from Table 10.5 in Table 10.7 for convenience. Then, from the computed regression equation, $\hat{Y} = 1.686 + 1.057X$, we use the values $a = 1.686$ and $b = 1.057$. Inserting these a and b values, along with the computations from Table 10.7, into formula (10-5), we have

TABLE 10.7	Computations for Shortcut Formula for r^2				
OBSERVATION	**X**	**Y**	**XY**	**X²**	**Y²**
1	4	6	24	16	36
2	6	9	54	36	81
3	3	5	15	9	25
4	5	6	30	25	36
5	8	10	80	64	100
6	7	9	63	49	81
	$\sum X = 33$	$\sum Y = 45$	$\sum XY = 266$	$\sum X^2 = 199$	$\sum Y^2 = 359$

$$r^2 = \frac{a \sum Y + b \sum XY - n\bar{Y}^2}{\sum Y^2 - n\bar{Y}^2}$$

$$= \frac{1.686(45) + 1.057(266) - 6(7.5)^2}{359 - 6(7.5)^2}$$

$$= \frac{19.532}{21.5} = 0.91$$

The r^2 value of 0.91 is equal to the result previously calculated by the definitional formula.

PRACTICE EXERCISE

10.3 The data in the table (repeated from Practice Exercise 10.2) compare a project's profitability with an index of cash flow.

		PROJECT						
	A	**B**	**C**	**D**	**E**	**F**	**G**	**H**
PROFITABILITY Y	41	25	52	42	30	49	30	18
FINANCIAL INDEX X	8	5	10	8	6	9	7	3

a. Calculate the total sum of squares (total variation), SST.
b. Calculate the sum of squares due to regression (explained variation), SSR.
c. Calculate the coefficient of determination, r^2.

COMPARING r^2 and S_e

There is an important distinction between r^2 and S_e. Each measure is designed to convey a different aspect of the regression line fit, so the two measures are not substitutes for each other. We shall contrast the different dimensions of fit by comparing r^2 and S_e for regression lines fitted to two different data sets. The scatter diagrams and regression lines for the two data sets are shown in Figures 10.10a and 10.10b. We see that the data in Figure 10.10a have an S_e value of 1.254 as compared to an S_e of 4.317 for the data set shown in Figure 10.10b.

Looking at the r^2 values for the same two data sets, we find $r^2 = 0.23$ for Figure 10.10a and $r^2 = 0.53$ for Figure 10.10b.

Now, recall that higher values of r^2 indicate greater explanatory power and lower values of S_e indicate greater predictive reliability. The fitted regression line in Figure 10.10a explains only 23% of the variation in Y for that data set, compared to 53% for

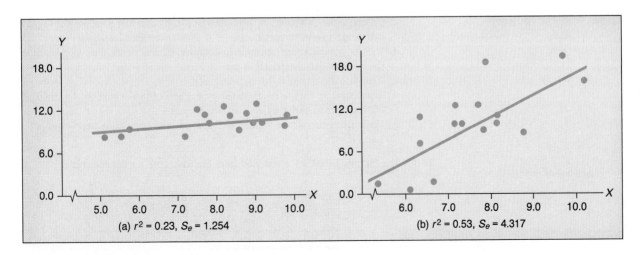

(a) $r^2 = 0.23$, $S_e = 1.254$ (b) $r^2 = 0.53$, $S_e = 4.317$

Figure 10.10
A comparison of the scatter for different values of S_e and r^2

the regression line in Figure 10.10b. Thus, the fitted regression line in Figure 10.10a has greater predictive reliability (measured by its lower S_e) but less explanatory power (measured by its lower r^2) than the one in Figure 10.10b. This shows that the r^2 value provides a dimension of fit separate from the S_e measure of fit. In comparing regression equations, we can be misled if we assume that the regression equation with the higher r^2 value must also be the regression equation with the lower predictive error. The value of r^2 does not provide complete information on predictive reliability. Likewise, S_e does not provide complete information on explanatory power. Both r^2 and S_e are needed to provide a complete picture of the explanatory power and predictive accuracy attained by a fitted regression line to observed data. Unfortunately, this fact is frequently overlooked in statistical reporting.

EXERCISES

▶ **10.8** The following data set is repeated from Exercise 10.1 for convenience:

	OBSERVATION		
	1	2	3
MAJOR BREAKDOWNS Y	3	2	5
YEARS IN SERVICE X	3	1	4

 a. Calculate $\hat{Y}$ for $X = 4$.
 b. Calculate the residual term $Y - \hat{Y}$ for $X = 4$.
 c. Calculate ΣY^2.
 d. Calculate $\Sigma(Y - \hat{Y})^2$.
 e. Calculate the error variance, S_e^2.
 f. Calculate the standard deviation of residuals, S_e.

10.9 Use the data set from Exercise 10.8 for the following:
 a. Compute the total variation, $\Sigma(Y - \bar{Y})^2$.
 b. Compute the explained variation, $\Sigma(\hat{Y} - \bar{Y})^2$.
 c. Compute the coefficient of determination, r^2, by dividing your answer to part b by your answer to part a.
 d. Use the computational formula to compute r^2, and verify that your result is the same as that computed in part c.
 e. Compute the unexplained variation, $\Sigma(Y - \hat{Y})^2$.
 f. Compute $1 - r^2$, the unexplained proportion of total variation, by dividing your answer to part e by your answer to part a.
 g. Verify that your answer to part f will give you the same value for r^2 as in parts c and d.

10.10 The following data set is repeated from Exercise 10.2 for convenience.

	OBSERVATION				
	1	2	3	4	5
SALES INDEX Y	50	30	90	80	60
TRAFFIC INDEX X	4	1	8	5	3

a. Calculate $\hat{Y}$ for $X = 5$.
b. Calculate the residual term $Y - \hat{Y}$ for $X = 5$.
c. Calculate ΣY^2.
d. Write the computational expression for $\Sigma(Y - \hat{Y})^2$, and determine its value by substituting the required numerical values.
e. Calculate the error variance, S_e^2.
f. Calculate the standard deviation of residuals, S_e.

10.11 Use the data set in Exercise 10.10 for the following:
a. Compute the total variation, $\Sigma(Y - \bar{Y})^2$.
b. Compute the explained variation, $\Sigma(\hat{Y} - \bar{Y})^2$.
c. Compute the coefficient of determination, r^2 (divide your answer to part a into your answer to part b).
d. Use the computational formula to compute r^2, and verify that your result is the same as that computed in part c.

10.12 In Exercise 10.7 (Green Giant brand), of the following statistics

$$r^2, \quad S_e, \quad 1 - r^2, \quad a, \quad b$$

. a. Which would measure the explanatory power, that is, the proportion of variation in Green Giant sales explained by exposure to Green Giant advertising?
b. Which would be the best measure of predictive reliability, that is, the regression equation's ability to predict Green Giant sales?
c. Which would be the unexplained variation in Green Giant sales attributable to estimation errors (using $\hat{Y}$ to estimate sales) measured as a proportion of the total variation of Y?

□ ▶ **10.13** A supermarket chain conducted a marketing research experiment to determine the relationship between the number of "facings" (i.e., the number of packages on the shelf facing the shopper) of a natural food breakfast cereal and its weekly sales. The amount of space allocated to the brand was varied every week. This was done by changing the number of packages facing the shopper among 2, 4, and 6 facings in a random pattern over 12 weeks. The space allotted to competing brands was kept at 2 facings each. Let variable X represent the number of facings and variable Y the number of packages sold. The data are given in the table.

						OBSERVATION						
	1	**2**	**3**	**4**	**5**	**6**	**7**	**8**	**9**	**10**	**11**	**12**
Y	469	371	145	397	324	229	385	211	436	248	368	230
X	6	4	2	6	4	2	4	2	6	2	6	4

a. Compute the fitted regression line.
b. What is the estimated sales for 4 facings? 5 facings?
c. Interpret r^2 in the context of this problem.

□ ▶ **10.14** Lehman's, a diversified department store, wishes to predict its need for temporary help. Located in the Water Tower complex in downtown Chicago, Lehman's uses many part-time clerical and sales employees to supplement the regular staff during busy selling periods. The supplementary work force is hired by the personnel manager as needed on a weekly basis. The reason for this is twofold: first, competent people are hard to get on a daily basis, especially on short notice; second, the consumer reaction to purchase offers may be immediate or may take several days, and specials are commonly extended for the week. Harry Speer, a marketing consultant with Market Planning Associates, is brought in to identify a way of predicting weekly sales. "Accurate forecasts of weekly sales will hold down the cost of hiring unnecessary help, yet it will let us take advantage of sales opportunities," explained the personnel manager. Speer thought a while and came up with the suggestion that weekly expenditures on advertising should provide a useful predictor of the fluctuation in weekly sales. Listed below are the weekly records on sales and advertising. Variable Y represents weekly sales in thousands of dollars, and variable X represents weekly media advertising in thousands of dollars.

	OBSERVATION							
	1	2	3	4	5	6	7	8
Y	80	110	90	150	75	135	70	125
X	2	5	3	8	2	6	1	4

a. Speer suggested that simple linear regression can be used effectively to predict sales from the knowledge of next week's media advertising. Calculate and interpret the values of a and b for the least squares regression line.
b. As a personnel manager, you decide to check on the appropriateness of Speer's suggestion. Plot the observations. Then, on the same graph, plot the least squares regression line for the observed values of X. Evaluate.
c. What did you find is the typical size error in predicting sales?
d. What proportion of the variation in weekly sales were explained by the variation in weekly media advertising?
e. For a week when $4000 is spent on media advertising, what would you predict to be the sales estimate?

10.15 Management's expectations for control over manufacturing overhead costs are commonly conveyed to each of the firm's cost centers by the use of a "flexible budget," which shows cost expectations for various output levels at the cost center. Up to now, MCI ELectronics, a computer disk manufacturer, has been run by engineers with little background in financial control. Their procedure for estimating the budget for manufacturing overhead cost was to laboriously estimate each cost item at the anticipated volume for the period (a so-called "static budget" budget). Although for the most part, this approach was accurate, preparation time was lengthy and therefore expensive. Besides, the process diverted the engineers' attention away from their engineering responsibilities. Suppose you are hired to develop a flexible budget system capable of estimating the changing or variable cost as computer disk production rises and falls. Assume that, in general, the total overhead varies with direct machine hours. You gather the historical data given in the table on overhead costs and direct machine hours over a certain range of production. Variable Y represents total overhead costs in units of $10,000, and variable X represents direct machine hours in thousands of hours.

	OBSERVATION				
	1	2	3	4	5
TOTAL OVERHEAD COSTS (× $10,000) Y	25	35	50	65	70
DIRECT MACHINE HOURS (× 1000) X	2.5	4	5	7.5	8

a. Check on linearity by plotting the paired XY observations with the cost variable

   Y on the vertical axis and the machine hours variable X on the horizontal axis. Comment.

b. Compute the fitted regression line.

c. The slope b of the fitted regression line represents the average change in total overhead cost per unit change in direct machine hours. In financial terms, b measures variable overhead cost per machine hours. Interpret the calculated value.

d. Estimate the total overhead cost corresponding to 6000 direct machine hours.

e. What proportion of the variation in total overhead cost is explained by the variation in direct machine hours?

10.16 Overland Express realizes a market opportunity exists in serving market segments abandoned by the large commercial truck carriers. The plan is to link land delivery services and commuter airlines. Overland will provide a dependable delivery truck service for small packages arriving on these new commuter airlines. The task of the firm's cost accountant is to devise a rate schedule to charge for the service. This requires estimates that account for two cost factors: truck operating costs and labor costs. Since operating costs rise the farther away the delivery address, charges are distance-based. The accountant therefore needs a cost estimate for each extra delivery mile. For truck operating costs, truck dealerships and government statistics indicate a 55¢ per mile cost for the truck type considered. The accountant will use this figure as a reliable truck operating cost. Therefore, regression analysis will not be needed in determining truck operating costs. For labor costs, costs vary with labor time usage, assuming a fixed wage per hour. Overland must estimate the extra labor time, on average, it takes to deliver an extra delivery mile. This is the central problem addressed by regression analysis. The data on 10 deliveries are given in the table. Variable Y represents labor time usage and variable X represents number of miles traveled.

| | PACKAGE NUMBER | | | | | | | | | |
	1	2	3	4	5	6	7	8	9	10
LABOR TIME USAGE Y	9	20	20	16	23	19	20	30	33	27
DELIVERY DISTANCE X	3	6	8	9	11	11	13	14	15	16

a. Check on linearity by plotting the paired XY observations with the labor time usage variable Y on the vertical axis and delivery distance variable X on the horizontal axis. Comment.

b. Compute the fitted regression line.

c. Graph the computed regression line on the scatter diagram.

d. Predict the labor time usage that it will take to deliver a package a distance of 6 mi.

e. Estimate the change in labor time usage for a 1 unit change (i.e., a 1 mi increase) in delivery distance.

f. Estimate the average labor time usage for delivery that is attributable to factors other than delivery distance.

g. What proportion of the observed variation in labor time usage is explained by the variation in the values of the delivery distance variable?

h. What statistic do we use as a measure of the average prediction error?

i. What is the value of this statistic?

10.6
REGRESSION MODEL

Before beginning our discussion of the regression model, let's briefly recall some of the features of regression analysis we have just demonstrated:

1. Finding a and b, the coefficients of the "best fitting straight line," according to the least squares criterion
2. Evaluating the regression line fit, using the measures S_e and r^2
3. Finding $\hat{Y}$, the fitted Y value, from the regression line for any X value in the observed range of X

These features summarize the basic descriptive results obtained in the regression analysis. However, the *estimated regression line* is viewed as a *sample regression line* from which we make inferences about the *population regression line*. The population regression line is a key component of the hypothesized regression model. We'll now introduce the basic assumptions required to draw such inferences.

BASIC ASSUMPTIONS FOR INFERENCE

Several assumptions are necessary for making inferences about the regression model:

1. **Random sample.** The observed data on Y comprise a random sample from the population of Y values at each given X.
2. **Linearity.** The mean value of Y, $\mu_{Y.X}$, is a linear function across the values of X, as shown in Figure 10.11. The line represented by this equation is the **population (true) regression line**.

Population Regression Line Equation

$$\mu_{Y.X} = A + BX \qquad (10\text{-}6)$$

where $\mu_{Y.X}$ stands for the mean value of Y at a given value of X; and A and B are the true Y intercept and slope parameters, respectively, of the population regression line.

If we assume the term E represents the random element of Y that causes Y to fall above or below $\mu_{Y.X}$, we can hypothesize a *regression model* that generates the Y values, expressed as follows:

Regression Model

$$Y = A + BX + E \qquad \text{or} \qquad Y = \mu_{Y.X} + E \qquad (10\text{-}7)$$

3. **Normality and mean zero.** At any value of X, the E's are normally distributed, or at least nearly normally distributed, with a mean of 0 and a standard deviation of σ_E.

4. **Homoscedasticity.** Across all values of X, the probability distribution of the E values has a constant standard deviation, σ_E. Thus, we should find a constant vertical scatter or dispersion of data points all along the population regression line.

Figure 10.11
Population regression line and scatter assuming normality

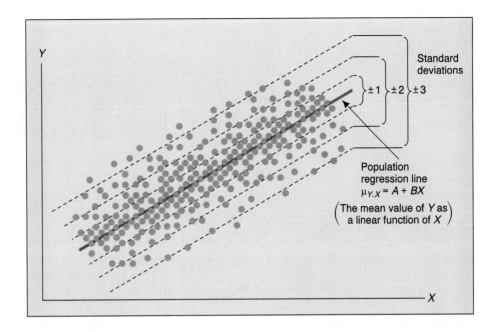

5. **Independence of E's.** The E's are expected to be statistically independent of each other. That is, all E's and, in particular, successive E's, are expected to be unrelated in size and/or sign.

Figure 10.12 shows five scatter diagrams. Only the observed pattern in Figure 10.12a would appear to be consistent with all the assumptions about the population. Figures 10.12b–e each show a pattern that violates at least one of the five assumptions. Figure 10.12e shows a pattern that clearly violates assumption 4, the homoscedasticity assumption.

BACKGROUND FOR MAKING REGRESSION INFERENCES

Let's suppose that the five assumptions just stated hold. Then the observed data on X and Y, to which we fitted a regression line, may be viewed as only one set of the many possible sets of sample data that could come from the population. If we consider the many possible sets of sample data and their fitted regression lines, we can imagine a family of possible fitted regression lines. This family, along with the observed fitted regression line, is illustrated in Figure 10.13.

Figure 10.13 portrays a variety of possible fitted regression lines with differing a and b values [all generated by the same underlying (true) population regression line]. This illustrates the extent of the *sampling variability* that exists for the fitted regression line. This sampling variability must be taken into account when the fitted regression line is used to make inferences about (1) the population regression coefficient, B; (2) the mean value of Y on the population regression line at a particular X value; or (3) a new value of Y at a particular X value.

Given that the five assumptions hold, particularly the assumptions that E has a normal distribution with a constant variance (homoscedasticity), the computed value

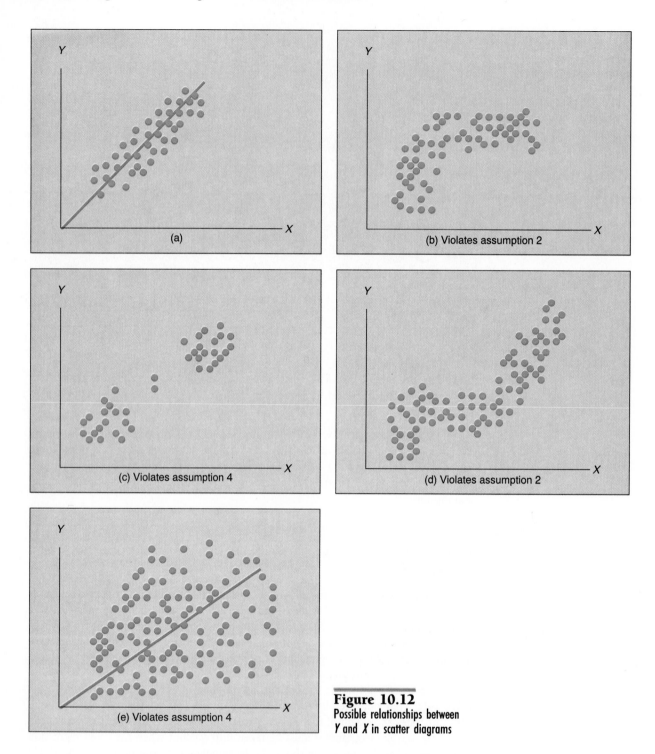

Figure 10.12
Possible relationships between
Y and X in scatter diagrams

of S_e is an estimate of the unknown population value σ_E. This S_e value plays a key role in defining the sampling distribution of the statistic needed for conducting hypothesis tests and constructing confidence intervals in subsequent sections.

Figure 10.13
A few of the family of fitted regression lines possible from sample data

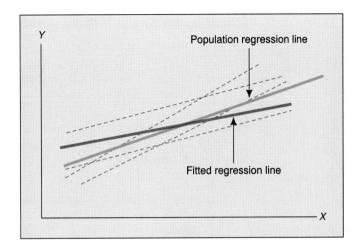

E X E R C I S E   **10.17** For each assumption given below, indicate whether that particular assumption is necessary for valid regression analysis inference. (Answer "Yes" or "No.")
  a. The values of X are normally distributed.
  b. At any given X, the values of Y are a random sample from the population of Y values at that X.
  c. At any given X, the E's are roughly normally distributed.
  d. The values of X are affected by the E's.
  e. The values of the E's are affected by the X values.
  f. Successive E values are independent.
  g. The standard deviation of the distribution of E at a given X value is the same as that at any other X value.
  h. $\mu_{Y.X}$ is a linear function of X.

10.7
INFERENCES ABOUT THE POPULATION REGRESSION COEFFICIENT

Is it plausible that the b value calculated for the fitted regression line could be obtained as a sampling result from a population in which the Y values are not related to the X values? In other words, is the evidence about the calculated b value sufficient to conclude that there exists a true linear relationship between X and Y? If we can confidently claim that X and Y are related in the population, then how accurate an estimate of B, the true slope of the population regression line, is b? The first question about a linear relationship between X and Y can be answered by a hypothesis test in which the null hypothesis sets B equal to 0. The second question can be answered by constructing a confidence interval estimate for B from the calculated value of b. Both procedures rely on the use of the sample statistic S_b, a measure estimating the sampling variability of b, which we will now discuss.

ESTIMATED STANDARD DEVIATION OF THE REGRESSION COEFFICIENT, S_b

The value of S_b, the **estimated standard deviation of the regression (slope) coefficient,** can be calculated from the following formula:

Estimated Standard Deviation of the Regression Coefficient

$$S_b = \sqrt{\frac{S_e^2}{\Sigma(X - \bar{X})^2}} \tag{10-8}$$

where S_e^2 is the estimated error variance and $\Sigma(X - \bar{X})^2$ is the sum of squares for X.

From the numerical results of the jobscore–salary data, we can determine the value of S_b as follows:

Step 1
Calculate S_e^2. In Section 10.4 we have already calculated this value to be 0.4857.

Step 2
Calculate $\Sigma(X - \bar{X})^2$. The computationally equivalent formula for $\Sigma(X - \bar{X})^2$ is $\Sigma X^2 - n\bar{X}^2$. Using this form, we calculate

$$\Sigma X^2 - n\bar{X}^2 = 199 - 6\left(\tfrac{33}{6}\right)^2 = 17.50$$

Step 3
Substitute the results of Steps 1 and 2 into the numerator and denominator, respectively, of the expression for S_b:

$$S_b = \sqrt{\frac{0.4857}{17.50}} = 0.1666$$

Therefore, the value of the estimated standard deviation of the slope coefficient S_b is 0.1666.

HYPOTHESIS TESTING OF *B*

In the null hypothesis we state that the population slope B equals a particular value B_0; that is, $H_0: B = B_0$. Then, adopting the hypothesis testing procedure described in Chapter 8, we test the null hypothesis using the following test statistic:

Test Statistic for the Population Regression Coefficient

$$t_{n-2} = \frac{b - B_0}{S_b} \tag{10-9}$$

where

b is the estimated regression coefficient (slope term);

S_b is the estimated standard deviation of the regression coefficient b;

B_0 is the hypothesized value of the slope of the population regression line;

t_{n-2} is the test statistic, which follows a Student t distribution with $n - 2$ degrees of freedom.

The value of the test statistic when calculated for sample data in regression analysis is generally referred to as the *t value*, *observed t*, or *t ratio*. The most common test sets B_0 equal to 0 to test whether there exists a linear relationship between X and Y.

Two-Sided Test of B_o

Suppose we are testing the null hypothesis that the slope is 0 versus the alternative hypothesis that either a positive or negative linear relationship exists. Then we require an alternative hypothesis for a two-sided test. Setting the value of B_o at 0, we have

H_o: $B = 0$ (No linear relationship exists.)

H_A: $B \neq 0$ (There exists either a positive or a negative linear relationship.)

The alternative hypothesis H_A reflects the fact that the alternatives to no linear relationship are either a direct (positive B) linear relationship or an inverse (negative B) linear relationship. For a two-sided test of the null hypothesis H_o, we use the following hypothesis testing procedure.

Step 1

Determine the rejection region. For a specified significance level α and $n - 2$ degrees of freedom, the rejection region for a two-sided test is defined as those values of the test statistic t_{n-2} that meet the condition

$$t_{n-2} < -t_{(\alpha/2, n-2)} \qquad \text{or} \qquad t_{n-2} > +t_{(\alpha/2, n-2)}$$

where $t_{(\alpha/2, n-2)}$ cuts off $\alpha/2$ in each tail of the t distribution and is the t table value for $n - 2$ degrees of freedom. (See Table VII.) The rejection region for this two-sided test is pictured in Figure 10.14.

Step 2

Compute the value of the test statistic for the sample. The test statistic is the observed t value calculated from

$$t_{n-2} = \frac{b - B_o}{S_b}$$

This value can be easily found once we have the values b and S_b. Moreover, since in this particular case B_o is set to 0, the test statistic generally can be read directly from the computer output of a regression analysis (e.g., in MINITAB's regression analysis output, after executing the command REGRESS, the test statistic is shown as the "t-ratio" and in business MYSTAT it is shown simply as "T"). In other words, since H_o: $B = 0$ is such an important test, computer output automatically reports the t ratio for $(b - 0)/S_b$.

Step 3

Determine whether the observed value of the test statistic is in the rejection region. Compare the observed test statistic with

$$+t_{(\alpha/2, n-2)} \qquad \text{and} \qquad -t_{(\alpha/2, n-2)}$$

Figure 10.14
The slope is considered nonzero if the observed $t_{(n-2)}$ falls in the area beyond $\pm\, t_{(\alpha/2, n-2)}$

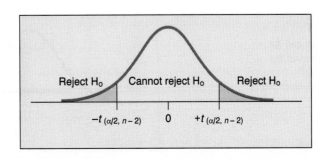

Step 4

Draw a conclusion about H_o. If the test statistic lies in the rejection region, we reject H_o and conclude that B is significantly different from 0. Otherwise, we conclude that B is not statistically significantly different from 0.

Let's go through this step-by-step approach for a two-sided test based on the jobscore–salary problem. We'll use $\alpha = .05$ as the level of significance. We have

H_o: $B = 0$ (No linear relationship exists between salary and jobscore.)

H_A: $B \neq 0$ (Some linear relationship, either direct or inverse, exists between salary and jobscore.)

Step 1

Determine the rejection region. With a sample size of $n = 6$, the degrees of freedom $\nu = n - 2 = 6 - 2 = 4$ d.f. The rejection region is defined as those values of the test statistic t_{n-2} that meet the condition

$$t_{n-2} < -t_{(\alpha/2, n-2)} \qquad \text{or} \qquad t_{n-2} > +t_{(\alpha/2, n-2)}$$

With α specified at .05, the t table value for $t_{(\alpha/2, n-2)}$ is $t_{(.025, 4)} = 2.776$. (See Table VII.) So the rejection region for H_o is

$$t_4 < -2.776 \qquad \text{or} \qquad t_4 > +2.776$$

This rejection region for H_o is pictured in Figure 10.15.

Step 2

Compute the value of the test statistic. The observed value of the test statistic is computed from the observed value of the slope coefficient b and its estimated standard error, S_b. The value of b was previously computed in Section 10.3 and found to be 1.057. The value of S_b computed earlier in this section was found to be 0.1666. Thus, the observed value of the test statistic is

$$t_{n-2} = \frac{b - B_o}{S_b}$$

$$= \frac{1.057 - 0}{0.1666}$$

$$= 6.35$$

Step 3

Determine whether the test statistic is in the rejection region. Since the observed value of the test statistic, 6.35, is greater than 2.776, it lies in the rejection region.

Figure 10.15

The rejection region and the position of the observed test statistic

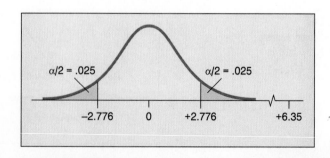

$\alpha/2 = .025$ $\alpha/2 = .025$

−2.776   0   +2.776   +6.35

Step 4

Draw a conclusion. The sample evidence on b is strong enough to conclude at a level of significance of .05 that H_o should be rejected.

By rejecting H_o, we reach the practical interpretation that there exists a linear relationship between salary and jobscore. Therefore, we can confidently use the estimated relationship to predict salary, given the jobscore value.

One-Sided Tests

As with hypothesis tests for means, proportions, and standard deviations, one-sided tests of hypotheses on B are also possible. For the one-sided test, the null hypothesis is stated as before:

$$H_o: \quad B = 0 \quad \text{(No linear relationship exists.)}$$

For the alternative hypothesis we have either Case 1 or Case 2.

Case 1

$$H_A: \quad B > 0 \quad \text{(A positive linear relationship exists.)}$$

Case 2

$$H_A: \quad B < 0 \quad \text{(A negative linear relationship exists.)}$$

For Case 1, a one-sided test in which the alternative hypothesis is $H_A: B > 0$, the rejection region is defined in terms of values of the test statistic t_{n-2}. To reject H_o, the test statistic must meet the condition

$$t_{n-2} > +t_{(\alpha, n-2)}$$

where $t_{(\alpha, n-2)}$ is the t table value for $n - 2$ degrees of freedom that cuts off α in the right tail of the distribution. (See Table VII.)

For Case 2, a one-sided test in which the alternative hypothesis is $H_A: B < 0$, the rejection region is defined as those values of the test statistic t_{n-2} that meet the condition

$$t_{n-2} < -t_{(\alpha, n-2)}$$

where $-t_{(\alpha, n-2)}$ is the negative of the t table value for $n - 2$ degrees of freedom that cuts off α in the left tail of the distribution.

Confidence Interval for *B*

We can also draw inferences about B by constructing a confidence interval for B. The procedure for constructing a confidence interval for B at the $1 - \alpha$ confidence level uses the t distribution with $\nu = n - 2$ degrees of freedom. The upper and lower limits of this interval are given by the following expressions:

1 − α Confidence Interval for B

Upper confidence limit (UCL) for B:
$$b + t_{(\alpha/2, n-2)} S_b$$

Lower confidence limit (LCL) for B: (10-10)

$$b - t_{(\alpha/2, n-2)} S_b$$

where the value of b is considered a point estimate of B, and the confidence interval is an interval estimate of B.

Let's use the jobscore–salary regression example, where $b = 1.057$ and $S_b = 0.1666$, to construct a 95% confidence interval for B.

1. Compute the upper confidence limit for B:

$$\text{UCL} = 1.057 + 2.776(0.1666) = 1.519$$

2. Compute the lower confidence limit for B:

$$\text{LCL} = 1.057 - 2.776(0.1666) = 0.595$$

Thus, we can conclude that we are 95% confident that the interval from 0.595 to 1.519 contains the true value of B. The process of constructing a 95% confidence interval assures us that, on average, 95 times out of 100 these intervals contain the population value B. In reporting the results, a more practical interpretation may be desirable. We might say that we are fairly sure that the true relationship between salary and jobscore is such that with each additional unit increase in jobscore, the increase in annual salary is some amount between $5,950 and $15,190.

PRACTICE EXERCISE

10.4 The data in the table (repeated from Practice Exercise 10.2) compare a project's profitability with an index of cash flow.

				PROJECT				
	A	**B**	**C**	**D**	**E**	**F**	**G**	**H**
PROFITABILITY **Y**	41	25	52	42	30	49	30	18
FINANCIAL INDEX **X**	8	5	10	8	6	9	7	3

The regression equation is $\hat{Y} = -0.09722 + 5.138888X$, and $S_b = 0.491504$ and $S_e = 2.949026$.
a. At the 5% level of significance, test H_o: $B = 0$.
b. Find the 95% confidence interval for B.

EXERCISES

10.18 A store manager ran an experiment in which she varied the price of her most popular brand of TV set from month to month. Over a 6 month period, she recorded monthly the price of the TV set, X, and the number of TV sets sold for each month, Y, as shown in the table:

			OBSERVATION			
	1	**2**	**3**	**4**	**5**	**6**
Y	6	25	20	10	14	19
X	400	350	370	390	380	360

Use the resulting regression equation, $\hat{Y} = 152.8 - 0.3657X$, and calculated $S_e = 1.679$ for the following:
a. Calculate $\Sigma(X - \bar{X})^2$.
b. Calculate S_b.

   c. For H_o: $B = 0$ versus H_A: $B \neq 0$, using $\alpha = .01$, determine the rejection region for H_o.

   d. Calculate the t statistic.

   e. What conclusion about H_o follows from your answers to parts c and d?

   f. Would your answer to part e differ if $\alpha = .05$?

   g. What are the upper and lower limits for the 99% confidence interval for B?

   h. Make an inferential statement about your results in part g.

▶ **10.19** A car rental agency collected data on a sample of 5 cars, including the number of miles driven (in thousands of miles), X, and maintenance costs (in hundreds of dollars), Y. The data are shown in the table:

| | OBSERVATION | | | | |
	1	2	3	4	5
Y	6	15	2	8	10
X	30	80	10	50	50

From this data set, we find that $\hat{Y} = 0.1765 + 0.1824X$ and $S_e = 0.886$.

   a. Calculate $\Sigma(X - \bar{X})^2$.

   b. Calculate S_b, the standard error of the regression coefficient.

   c. For H_o: $B = 0$ versus H_A: $B > 0$, using $\alpha = .05$, determine the rejection region for H_o.

   d. Calculate the test statistic t.

   e. What conclusion about H_o follows from your answer to parts c and d?

   f. Would your answer to part e differ if $\alpha = .01$?

   g. What are the upper and lower limits for the 95% confidence interval for B?

10.20 Data were collected by an insurance company concerned with setting fire insurance rates on residential property. A sample of 25 fire damaged residential homes was obtained. Then a simple linear regression equation $\hat{Y} = a + bX$ was fitted to analyze the relationship between Y = Fire damage (in thousands of dollars) and X = Distance from fire station (in miles). The following statistics were computed: $b = 1$, $S_e = 10$, and $\Sigma(X - \bar{X})^2 = 100$. Consider testing H_o: $B = 0$ versus H_A: $B \neq 0$, and answer the following questions.

   a. At $\alpha = .05$, what is the rejection region for H_o?

   b. What is the formula for the t statistic used in this hypothesis test?

   c. What is the value of the calculated t?

   d. What conclusion is reached about H_o?

10.21 Five 1991 graduates of Robins College were randomly selected, and the following data were collected:

GRADUATE	GRADE-POINT AVERAGE X	STARTING SALARY (IN THOUSANDS OF DOLLARS) Y
1	3.8	25
2	2.1	13
3	2.9	15
4	3.2	20
5	2.4	18

Consider the linear model $Y = A + BX + E$.

   a. What is the 95% confidence interval for B?

b. For a hypothesis test of H_o: $B = 0$ versus H_A: $B > 0$, using a significance level of .05, what is the region of rejection?

c. For the observed data, what is the value of the t statistic for testing H_o: $B = 0$ versus H_A: $B > 0$?

d. What should we conclude about H_o?

10.22 A large home furnishings retailer believes expenditures on home furnishings are related to new family formations. Data on expenditures for a specific category of home furnishings are collected along with data on the number of marriages for a sample of 9 counties in the United States. The data are given in the table.

	COUNTY								
	1	2	3	4	5	6	7	8	9
HOME FURNISHINGS EXPENDITURES (IN MILLIONS) *Y*	9.5	12.0	11.6	14.7	11.1	12.7	16.5	16.0	9.6
MARRIAGES (IN HUNDREDS) *X*	55.5	90.3	35.0	93.1	33.5	75.2	99.5	110.9	25.1

a. Calculate the fitted regression equation.

b. Test H_o: $B = 0$ against H_A: $B \neq 0$ using $\alpha = .05$.

c. Determine the 95% confidence interval for the average increase in home furnishings expenditures associated with each additional 100 marriages.

10.8
CONFIDENCE INTERVAL FOR µY.Xo, THE POPULATION MEAN OF Y at Xo

Having dealt with making inferences about the value of the population regression coefficient B, we now turn our attention to another important inferential issue in regression. Our objective is to construct a confidence interval for the population mean of Y at X_o. This value is expressed by the symbol $\mu_{Y.X_o}$. The confidence interval for $\mu_{Y.X_o}$ is constructed using the point estimate $\hat{Y}_o$, which is the fitted Y value read off the regression line at X_o (see Figure 10.16a). To build a confidence interval, we also need a measure of the sampling variability of $\hat{Y}_o$ values. Figure 10.16b indicates the different $\hat{Y}_o$ values at the X_o value where several fitted regression lines have been fitted to different possible sets of X, Y data.

ESTIMATED STANDARD DEVIATION OF A FITTED Y VALUE, $S_{\hat{Y}.X_o}$

A sample statistic that estimates the sampling variability of $\hat{Y}$ at the point X_o is the *estimated standard deviation of a fitted Y value*, $S_{\hat{Y}.X_o}$. This is also the value that helps us account for the size of the estimation error we face when we use $\hat{Y}_o$ at X_o to estimate $\mu_{Y.X_o}$. The notation X_o in the subscript is used to indicate that the value of $S_{\hat{Y}.X_o}$ changes with the specific value of X_o chosen. The formula for the standard deviation of a fitted Y value is given by:

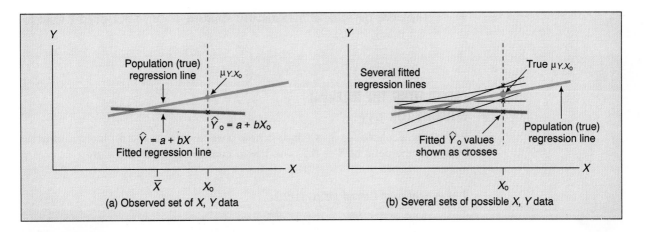

Figure 10.16
(a) One observed $\hat{Y}_0$ as an estimate of $\mu_{Y.X_0}$ (b) Host of $\hat{Y}_0$ values as possible estimates of $\mu_{Y.X_0}$

Estimated Standard Deviation of a Fitted Y Value at X_0

$$S_{\hat{Y}.X_o} = S_e \sqrt{\frac{1}{n} + \frac{(X_o - \bar{X})^2}{\Sigma(X - \bar{X})^2}} \qquad (10\text{-}11)$$

The first term under the radical shows us that $S_{\hat{Y}.X_o}$ depends on n, the sample size. More specifically, reductions of $S_{\hat{Y}.X_o}$ are proportional to $\sqrt{n}$. From the second term under the radical, we see that $S_{\hat{Y}.X_o}$ also depends on how close X_o is to $\bar{X}$. The closer the particular value of X_o is to $\bar{X}$, the smaller will be the value of $S_{\hat{Y}.X_o}$.

We'll use the jobscore–salary data to illustrate the calculation of the value of $S_{\hat{Y}.X_o}$. We must choose a particular value of X, say $X = 6.5$. Also, note that we have $\bar{X} = 5.5$.

Step 1
Calculate $(X_o - \bar{X})^2$. With X_o at 6.5, we have $(X_o - \bar{X})^2 = (6.5 - 5.5)^2 = 1$.

Step 2
Substitute the known values into the remaining terms for $S_{\hat{Y}.X_o}$ and solve. The value of S_e (calculated in Section 10.4) is equal to 0.6969, and the value of the variation in X, $\Sigma(X - \bar{X})^2$, is computationally equivalent to the formula $\Sigma(X - \bar{X})^2 = \Sigma X^2 - n\bar{X}^2$. The latter value was obtained in Section 10.7 and found to be 17.50. Inserting these values for our sample size n of 6, we have

$$S_{\hat{Y}.X_o} = S_e \sqrt{\frac{1}{n} + \frac{(X_o - \bar{X})^2}{\Sigma(X - \bar{X})^2}}$$

$$= 0.6969 \sqrt{\frac{1}{6} + \frac{(6.5 - 5.5)^2}{17.50}}$$

$$= 0.6969 \sqrt{\frac{1}{6} + \frac{1}{17.50}}$$

$$= 0.6969 \sqrt{0.1667 + 0.0571}$$

$$= 0.3297$$

Therefore, the value of the estimated standard deviation of a fitted Y value at $X = 6.5$ is $S_{\hat{Y} \cdot X_0} = 0.3297$.

CALCULATING THE INTERVAL ESTIMATE FOR $\mu_{Y \cdot X_0}$

With $S_{\hat{Y} \cdot X_0}$ calculated for $X = 6.5$, it is now possible to construct an interval estimate of $\mu_{Y \cdot X_0}$ at the point of $X = 6.5$. The **$1 - \alpha$ confidence interval for $\mu_{Y \cdot X_0}$** is:

$1 - \alpha$ Confidence Interval for $\mu_{Y \cdot X_0}$ at X_0

$$\text{Upper confidence limit (UCL)} = \hat{Y}_0 + t_{(\alpha/2, n-2)} S_{\hat{Y} \cdot X_0} \qquad \textbf{(10-12)}$$

$$\text{Lower confidence limit (LCL)} = \hat{Y}_0 - t_{(\alpha/2, n-2)} S_{\hat{Y} \cdot X_0}$$

The 95% confidence interval for $\mu_{Y \cdot X_0}$ at $X = 6.5$ jobscore is calculated as follows:

Step 1

Determine the value of the fitted Y value at $X = 6.5$. Using the fitted regression line computed in Section 10.3, we find

$$\hat{Y}_0 = a + bX$$
$$= 1.686 + 1.057X$$
$$= 1.686 + 1.057(6.5)$$
$$= 8.5565$$

Step 2

Compute the upper confidence limit for $\mu_{Y \cdot X_0}$ at $X = 6.5$. Finding from Table VII that $t_{.025, 4} = 2.776$, we can write

$$\text{UCL} = \hat{Y}_0 + t_{(.025, 4)} S_{\hat{Y} \cdot X_0}$$
$$= 8.5565 + 2.776(0.3297)$$
$$= 9.4717$$

Step 3

Compute the lower confidence limit for $\mu_{Y \cdot X_0}$ at $X = 6.5$:

$$\text{LCL} = \hat{Y}_0 - t_{(.025, 4)} S_{\hat{Y} \cdot X_0}$$
$$= 8.5565 - 2.776(0.3297)$$
$$= 7.6413$$

Thus, we can conclude at the 95% confidence level that at $X = 6.5$ the interval from 7.6413 to 9.4717 contains the point $\mu_{Y \cdot X_0}$ through which the population regression line passes. The practical interpretation is that we are 95% sure that for executives with a jobscore of 6.5, the interval from \$76,413 to \$94,717 covers their true average salary.

10.5 The data in the table below (repeated from Practice Exercise 10.2) compare a project's profitability with an index of cash flow.

				PROJECT				
	A	**B**	**C**	**D**	**E**	**F**	**G**	**H**
PROFITABILITY **Y**	41	25	52	42	30	49	30	18
FINANCIAL INDEX **X**	8	5	10	8	6	9	7	3

The regression equation is $\hat{Y} = -0.09722 + 5.138888X$, and $S_b = 0.491504$ and $S_e = 2.949026$.

a. At $X = 7$, find the estimated standard deviation of the fitted Y value $(\hat{Y})$.

b. At $X = 7$, find the 95% confidence interval for fitted Y value $(\hat{Y})$.

▶ **10.23** The data set in the table (repeated from Exercise 10.18) shows the recorded monthly price of the TV set, X, and the number of TV sets sold for each month over a 6 month period:

			OBSERVATION			
	1	**2**	**3**	**4**	**5**	**6**
Y	6	25	20	10	14	19
X	400	350	370	390	380	360

The regression equation is $\hat{Y} = 152.8 - 0.3657X$, $S_e = 1.679$, and $\Sigma(X - \bar{X})^2 = 1750$.

a. Calculate $S_{\hat{Y}.X}$ for $\bar{X} = 375$ (the mean of X).

b. Calculate $S_{\hat{Y}.X}$ for $X = 360$.

c. Calculate $S_{\hat{Y}.X}$ for $X = 390$.

d. Calculate the point estimates of $\mu_{Y.X}$ at $X = 360$, $X = 375$, and $X = 390$.

e. Calculate the upper and lower limits of the 95% confidence interval for $\mu_{Y.X}$ at $X = 360$, $X = 375$, and $X = 390$.

f. Compare the widths of the confidence intervals computed in part e at $X = 375$ and at $X = 360$. At which of these values of X is the width larger? Comment.

10.24 The data set in the table (repeated from Exercise 10.19) represents a car rental agency's recordings on two variables for a sample of 5 cars. The two variables are number of miles driven (in thousands of miles), X, and maintenance costs (in hundreds of dollars), Y.

			OBSERVATION		
	1	**2**	**3**	**4**	**5**
Y	6	15	2	8	10
X	30	80	10	50	50

The regression equation is $\hat{Y} = 0.1765 + 0.1824X$, $S_e = 0.886$, and $\Sigma(X - \bar{X})^2 = 2720$.

a. Calculate $S_{\hat{Y} \cdot X}$ for $\bar{X} = 44$ (the mean of X).
b. Calculate $S_{\hat{Y} \cdot X}$ for $X = 30$.
c. Calculate $S_{\hat{Y} \cdot X}$ for $X = 80$.
d. Calculate the point estimates of $\mu_{Y \cdot X}$ at $X = 30$, $X = 44$, and $X = 80$.
e. Calculate the upper and lower limits of the 99% confidence interval for $\mu_{Y \cdot X}$ at $X = 30$, $X = 44$, and $X = 80$.
f. Compare the widths of the confidence intervals computed in part e at $X = 44$ and at $X = 80$. At which of these values of X is the estimation error larger?

10.9

PREDICTION INTERVAL OF A NEW Y VALUE AT Xo

The $\hat{Y}_o$ value from the fitted regression line also can serve as the *point prediction of a new Y value* for a specific value of X_o. Using $\hat{Y}_o$ to predict the Y value will likely result in some amount of *prediction error*, $Y - \hat{Y}_o$. In view of the prevalence of these errors, how accurate is $\hat{Y}_o$ as a prediction of Y?

The accuracy of $\hat{Y}_o$ as a prediction of Y depends on the amount of random error inherent in the sampling to obtain $\hat{Y}_o$. A statistic that helps us determine the size of the prediction error when using $\hat{Y}_o$ for a given X_o to predict a new Y value is the *estimated standard deviation of prediction*, $S_{\text{NEW} \cdot X_o}$. The notation X_o in the subscript tells us that the value of $S_{\text{NEW} \cdot X_o}$ (and thus the prediction error) changes with the value of X_o at which the prediction of a new Y value is being made. The value of $S_{\text{NEW} \cdot X_o}$ is given by the following formula:

Estimated Standard Deviation of Prediction of a New Y Value at X_o

$$S_{\text{NEW} \cdot X_o} = S_e \sqrt{\frac{1}{n} + \frac{(X_o - \bar{X})^2}{\Sigma(X - \bar{X})^2} + 1} \qquad (10\text{-}13)$$

The smaller the value of $S_{\text{NEW} \cdot X_o}$, the more accurate and more reliable the prediction. Let's calculate $S_{\text{NEW} \cdot X_o}$ for the jobscore problem at $X = 6.5$:

$$S_{\text{NEW} \cdot X_o} = S_e \sqrt{\frac{1}{n} + \frac{(X_o - \bar{X})^2}{\Sigma(X - \bar{X})^2} + 1}$$

$$= 0.6969 \sqrt{\frac{1}{6} + \frac{(6.5 - 5.5)^2}{17.50} + 1}$$

$$= 0.6969 \sqrt{0.1667 + 0.0571 + 1}$$

$$= 0.7709$$

Therefore, the value of the estimated standard deviation of prediction at $X = 6.5$ is 0.7709.

CALCULATING THE PREDICTION INTERVAL FOR A NEW Y VALUE

Let's now use the calculated $S_{\text{NEW} \cdot X_o}$ value at $X = 6.5$ and determine the prediction interval for a new Y value at $X = 6.5$. The **prediction interval of a new Y value** is:

$1 - \alpha$ Prediction Interval for a New Y Value at X_o

$$\text{Upper prediction limit (UPL)} = \hat{Y}_o + t_{(\alpha/2,n-2)}S_{NEW.X_o} \qquad (10\text{-}14)$$
$$\text{Lower prediction limit (LPL)} = \hat{Y}_o - t_{(\alpha/2,n-2)}S_{NEW.X_o}$$

The prediction interval of a new value of Y at $X = 6.5$ jobscore with a 95% reliability level is computed as follows:

Step 1
Determine the value of the fitted Y value at $X = 6.5$. This was computed in Section 10.8: $\hat{Y} = 8.5565$.

Step 2
Compute the upper prediction limit (UPL) for a new Y value at $X = 6.5$. Finding from Table VII that $t_{.025,4} = 2.776$, we can write

$$\text{UPL} = \hat{Y}_o + t_{(.025,4)}S_{NEW.X_o}$$
$$= 8.5565 + (2.776)(0.7709)$$
$$= 10.6965$$

Step 3
Compute the lower prediction limit (LPL) for a new Y value at $X = 6.5$:

$$\text{LPL} = \hat{Y}_o - t_{(.025,4)}S_{NEW.X_o}$$
$$= 8.5565 - (2.776)(0.7709)$$
$$= 6.4165$$

Thus, given $X = 6.5$, the prediction interval for a new Y value is the range of values between 6.4165 and 10.6965. The chances are 95 out of 100 that an interval constructed according to this procedure will include the new Y value. The practical interpretation of the prediction level would be: We are 95% sure that a newly assigned executive with a jobscore of 6.5 will receive a salary between $64,165 and $106,965.

PRACTICE EXERCISE

10.6 The data in the table (repeated from Practice Exercise 10.2) compare a project's profitability with an index of cash flow.

	PROJECT							
	A	B	C	D	E	F	G	H
PROFITABILITY Y	41	25	52	42	30	49	30	18
FINANCIAL INDEX X	8	5	10	8	6	9	7	3

The regression equation is $\hat{Y} = -0.09722 + 5.138888X$, and $S_b = 0.491504$ and $S_e = 2.949026$.

a. At $X = 7$, find the estimated standard deviation of prediction.

b. At $X = 7$, find the 95% prediction interval for a new Y value.

●●●●●●●●●●●●●●●●●●●●●●●●●●●●●●●●●●●●●●●

EXERCISES

10.25 The data set in the table is repeated from Exercise 10.18 for convenience.

	OBSERVATION					
	1	**2**	**3**	**4**	**5**	**6**
Y	6	25	20	10	14	19
X	400	350	370	390	380	360

We have the fitted regression equation $\hat{Y} = 152.8 - 0.3657X$, $S_e = 1.679$, and $\Sigma(X - \bar{X})^2 = 1750$.
  a. Calculate $S_{NEW.X_0}$ at $\bar{X} = 375$ (the sample mean value of X).
  b. Calculate $S_{NEW.X_0}$ at $X = 360$.
  c. Calculate $S_{NEW.X_0}$ at $X = 390$.
  d. Calculate the point forecast of Y at $X = 360$, $X = 375$, and $X = 390$.
  e. Calculate the upper and lower limits for the 95% prediction interval for Y at $X = 360$, $X = 375$, and $X = 390$.
  f. What is the width of the prediction interval at $X = 375$? Is the width smaller, larger, or the same at $X = 360$?

10.26 The data set in the table is repeated from Exercise 10.19.

	OBSERVATION				
	1	**2**	**3**	**4**	**5**
Y	6	15	2	8	10
X	30	80	10	50	50

We have the fitted regression equation $\hat{Y} = 0.1765 + 0.1824X$, $S_e = 0.886$, and $\Sigma(X - \bar{X})^2 = 2720$.

  a. Calculate $S_{NEW.X_0}$ for $\bar{X} = 44$ (the sample mean value of X).
  b. Calculate $S_{NEW.X_0}$ for $X = 30$.
  c. Calculate $S_{NEW.X_0}$ for $X = 80$.
  d. Calculate the point forecast of Y at $X = 30$, $X = 44$, and $X = 80$.
  e. Calculate the upper and lower limits for the 99% prediction interval for Y at $X = 30$, $X = 44$, and $X = 80$.
  f. What is the width of the prediction interval at $X = 44$? Is the width smaller, larger, or the same at $X = 80$?

10.27 A simple linear model $Y = A + BX + E$ was used to help predict $Y =$ Number of hot dogs sold (in thousands) from $X =$ Number of advance tickets sold (in thousands) for a football stadium concession company. From past data taken from the sales of 15 football games, the following statistics were computed: $\bar{X} = 50$, $a = -18.5$, $b = 0.87$, $\Sigma(X - \bar{X})^2 = 500$, and $\Sigma(Y - \hat{Y})^2 = 21.55$.
  a. What is the value of S_e?
  b. Give a point estimate of the mean number of hot dogs sold when advance ticket sales are 45 thousand.
  c. Give a 95% confidence interval for the mean number of hot dogs sold when advance ticket sales are 45 thousand.
  d. Give a 95% prediction interval for the number of hot dogs sold at next Sunday's game, when it is known that 45 thousand tickets have been sold.

▶ **10.28** The following statistics were gathered by a manager of a factory that produces replacement parts. Orders were taken and lots of varying sizes were produced to fill the orders. Data were recorded for a sample of 20 past orders with $X =$ Lot size and Y = Work hours required to produce the lot. A linear regression equation $\hat{Y} = a + bX$ was fitted, with $a = 11$, $b = 2$; and $S_e = 3$, $\Sigma(X - \bar{X})^2 = 10{,}000$, and $\bar{X} = 50$ were calculated.

a. Give a point estimate of the mean work hours required to produce lots of size 80.

b. Give a 95% confidence interval for the mean work hours required to produce lots of size 80.

c. Give a 95% prediction interval for the work hours required to produce a new lot of size 80.

d. For what lot size will the prediction interval be smallest?

10.29 Motor freight charges typically reflect two components: (1) a distance-related "line haul" charge and (2) a nondistance-related "terminal" charge. A regression analysis was performed with Y = delivery freight rates in dollars per 100 lb of freight and X = distance in miles from origin. The following regression equation and related statistics were obtained: $\hat{Y} = 1.09 + 0.0067X$, $S_e = 0.153$, $\Sigma(X - \bar{X})^2 = 507{,}681.33$, $\bar{X} = 155.4$, for $n = 100$.

a. Determine the 90% confidence interval for the mean total freight bill, given a distance of 300 mi.

b. Determine the 90% prediction interval for a new total freight bill, given a distance of 300 mi.

c. Determine the 90% confidence interval for B, the average line haul charge per mile of delivery.

10.10

COMPARING CONFIDENCE INTERVALS AND PREDICTION INTERVALS

In Sections 10.8 and 10.9 we constructed two different intervals. Both intervals start with the same point estimate $\hat{Y}_0$ at the particular X_0 value. But since the values of $S_{\hat{Y}.X_0}$ and $S_{NEW.X_0}$ differ at the same value of X_0, the intervals surrounding the point estimate also differ in width. The relationship linking these two standard deviations is given by

$$S_{NEW.X_0} = \sqrt{S_e^2 + S_{\hat{Y}.X_0}^2}$$

This formula shows that the value of $S_{NEW.X_0}$ depends on both the values of $S_{\hat{Y}.X_0}$ and the estimated standard deviation of residuals, S_e. Since the value of $S_{NEW.X_0}$ always exceeds the corresponding value of $S_{\hat{Y}.X_0}$ at any level, the prediction interval for a new Y value is always wider than the confidence interval for $\mu_{Y.X_0}$. Both these intervals have varying widths, depending on the various levels of X. Figure 10.17 shows that the confidence and prediction intervals both widen at X levels distant from $\bar{X}$. The outer band represents the 95% prediction band for individual new Y values. The inner band is the 95% confidence band estimating $\mu_{Y.X}$. The narrower width of the inner band at all levels of X reflects the fact that there is less uncertainty in estimating a mean $\mu_{Y.X}$ compared to predicting a new individual Y value.

E X E R C I S E   **10.30** The data set in the table is repeated from Exercise 10.18:

	OBSERVATION					
	1	2	3	4	5	6
Y	6	25	20	10	14	19
X	400	350	370	390	380	360

Figure 10.17
Confidence band for the mean of Y and prediction band for new Y value across the range of X

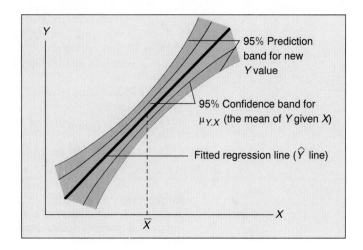

We have the fitted regression equation $\hat{Y} = 152.8 - 0.3657X$, $S_e = 1.679$, and $\Sigma(X - \bar{X})^2 = 1750$.

a. Construct a graph showing the regression line within the range of interpolation (i.e., from $X = 350$ to $X = 400$).

b. Plot on the graph the upper and lower limits of the 95% confidence interval for $\mu_{Y.X}$ at $X = 360$, $X = 375$, and $X = 390$. (These were calculated in Exercise 10.23, part e.)

c. Connect the three upper limit points with a smooth curve. Also connect the three lower limit points with a smooth curve. Shade in the area between the upper limit curve and the lower limit curve. The shaded area represents the 95% confidence band for $\mu_{Y.X}$.

d. Plot on the graph the upper and lower limits of the 95% prediction interval for a new Y at $X = 360$, $X = 375$, and $X = 390$. (These were calculated in Exercise 10.25 part e.)

e. Connect the three upper prediction limit points with a smooth curve. Also connect the three lower prediction limit points with a smooth curve. The area between these two curves represents the 95% prediction band for a new Y forecast.

f. Is there any X value for which the 95% confidence interval for $\mu_{Y.X}$ is wider than the 95% prediction interval for Y?

g. Use the values previously calculated (in Exercises 10.23 and 10.25) for $S_{\text{NEW}.X_0}$ and $S_{\hat{Y}.X}$ at $X = 360$, $X = 375$, and $X = 390$, and the formula $S_{\text{NEW}.X_0} = \sqrt{S_e^2 + S_{\hat{Y}.Y_0}^2}$ to verify that the error variance (S_e^2) remains a constant value over the range of X.

10.11

SAMPLE COMPUTER OUTPUT

If it were necessary to hand calculate the various regression statistics for an ample number of observations, the time required and the drudgery of the task would probably discourage the effort. Fortunately, statistical software packages are available on personal computers and minicomputers to carry out nearly all the calculations.

MINITAB and business MYSTAT computer output for the regression analysis of the jobscore–salary problem are presented in Figure 10.18 and Figure 10.19.

The boxed areas on the MINITAB output will be used to point out the various statistical concepts we have discussed in this chapter. For example, in the first boxed area, the values of the regression constant a and the regression slope coefficient b, used in the linear regression equation, are shown under "COEF" in the output. We

Figure 10.18
MINITAB: Regression results for jobscore–salary data

```
MTB > regress 'salary' 1 'jobscore';
SUBC> predict for X=6.5.

The regression equation is
salary = 1.69 + 1.06 jobscore
                                     observed t-ratio
Predictor      Coef       Stdev    t-ratio      p
Constant      1.6857←a   0.9594←Sₐ   1.76      0.154
jobscore      1.0571←b   0.1666←Sᵦ   6.35      0.003
  ↙Sₑ
s = 0.6969     R-sq = 91.0%    R-sq(adj) = 88.7%

Analysis of Variance

SOURCE       DF        SS        MS        F         p
Regression    1      19.557    19.557    40.26    0.003
Error         4       1.943     0.486
Total         5      21.500

Obs. jobscore  salary      Fit  Stdev.Fit  Residual  St.Resid
  1     3.00     5.00     4.857    0.504     0.143     0.30
  2     4.00     6.00     5.914    0.379     0.086     0.15
  3     5.00     6.00     6.971    0.296    -0.971    -1.54
  4     6.00     9.00     8.029    0.296     0.971     1.54
  5     7.00     9.00     9.086    0.379    -0.086    -0.15
  6     8.00    10.00    10.143    0.504    -0.143    -0.30

   Fit  Stdev.Fit       95% C.I.            95% P.I.
 8.557     0.330   ( 7.641,  9.473)   ( 6.416, 10.698)
```

Figure 10.19
Business MYSTAT: Regression results for jobscore–salary data

```
DEP VAR:SALARIES    N:   6   MULTIPLE R:  .954   SQUARED MULTIPLE R:   .910
ADJUSTED SQUARED MULTIPLE R:  .887      STANDARD ERROR OF ESTIMATE:      0.697

  VARIABLE    COEFFICIENT   STD ERROR   STD COEF TOLERANCE    T    P(2 TAIL)
CONSTANT           1.686      0.959      0.000    .         1.757    0.154
JOBSCORE           1.057      0.167      0.954    .100E+01  6.345    0.003

                        ANALYSIS OF VARIANCE

  SOURCE    SUM-OF-SQUARES   DF  MEAN-SQUARE    F-RATIO      P

REGRESSION       19.557       1     19.557      40.265     0.003
 RESIDUAL         1.943       4      0.486
```

find that $a = 1.6857$ and $b = 1.0571$. Thus, the linear regression equation using these MINITAB regression coefficients is

$$\hat{Y} = a + bX$$
$$= 1.6857 + 1.0571X$$

The regression equation printed in the MINITAB output uses rounded values of a and b, and is shown as

$$salary = 1.69 + 1.06 \text{ jobscore}$$

The value of S_b used in making inferences about B is 0.1666, found in the second row of the column headed "Stdev." The observed t value used in testing the null hypothesis for this coefficient is given in the column "t-ratio," and the probability of finding a t ratio that extreme under the null hypothesis is shown in the column headed "p." The standard deviation of residuals, S_e, is shown as simply $S = 0.6969$ and r^2 is shown as $R\text{-}sq = 91.0\%$.

In the second boxed area, the MINITAB regression output shows the observation, ordered according to the size of the X variable, jobscore. The changing values of the estimated standard deviation of the fitted Y values, $S_{\hat{Y}.X_o}$, for the observed X values of jobscore are found under the column "Stdev.Fit." The computer printout confirms the fact that the values for $S_{\hat{Y}.X_o}$ become larger, the more distant the observed X is from the mean value $\bar{X} = 5.5$. The value of $S_{\hat{Y}.X_o}$ for $X = 6.5$, which we calculated in Section 10.8, isn't one of the values found in this "Stdev.Fit" column, because it isn't an observed X value from the data set used to fit the regression line.

In order to obtain from MINITAB values for $\hat{Y}_o$, $S_{\hat{Y}.X_o}$, the 95% confidence interval for $\mu_{Y.X}$, and the 95% prediction interval for a new Y value at the X value of 6.5, we must use the subcommand PREDICT specifying $X = 6.5$, after the main REGRESS command. These results are shown on the last line of the second boxed area. The computer output shows:

1. The fitted Y value at $X = 6.5$ is 8.557, under the column heading "Fit."
2. The value of $S_{\hat{Y}.X}$ at $X = 6.5$ is 0.330, under the column heading "Stdev.Fit."
3. The 95% confidence interval for $\mu_{Y.X}$ at $X = 6.5$ is found to be from 7.641 to 9.473.
4. The 95% prediction interval for Y at $X = 6.5$ is found to be from 6.416 to 10.698.

As expected, the prediction interval is wider than the confidence interval.

Since the other computer output items (e.g., adjusted R^2 and analysis of variance) are more relevant to multiple regression, we shall defer any discussion until Chapter 11.

10.12

LIMITATIONS AND CAUTIONS WHEN PERFORMING REGRESSION ANALYSIS

Appropriately used, regression analysis provides the means for making predictions and describing the relationship between the variables. But when improperly used, its application can lead to poor decisions with serious consequences.

Three issues are of particular concern in applying the fitted regression line:

Issue 1

Is it legitimate to extrapolate the fitted linear equation outside the observable range of X used in fitting the equation?

No matter how well a linear regression line fits the observed points, we should not assume that the linear relationship will hold for X values outside the range of observed X values. In the following example we see that this is a particular concern to accountants estimating cost–volume relationships.

■ **EXAMPLE 10.1**

Linear Extrapolation of Nonlinear Costs

Cost analysts often feel they are on safe ground in making the simplifying assumption that total costs and sales volume over a specific range of activity are linearly related. But there are sound economic reasons for expecting that over an extended volume

Figure 10.20
Nonlinear cost curve

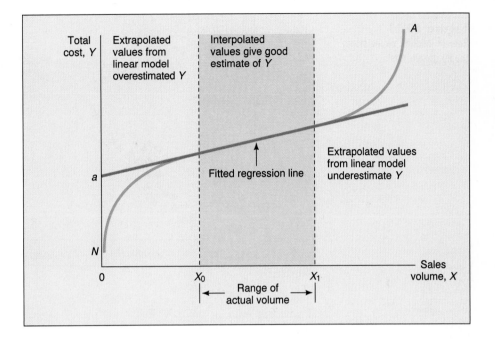

range the cost–volume relationship is nonlinear. A plausible nonlinear cost structure is shown in Figure 10.20 by the curve NA.

If prediction of costs is restricted to the range of actual volume, X_0 to X_1, the fitted regression line aa' represents the relationship and should be useful in predicting Y, showing prediction errors with a random behavior. But for values of X larger than X_1, the use of aa' to extrapolate cost Y should show serious prediction errors with a nonrandom pattern. Cost would be underestimated and by a larger amount the further X is beyond X_1. The analyst blindly extrapolating the linear regression line probably is doing so out of ignorance, unaware of the nonlinearity and the large prediction error being made. Thus, extrapolation is hazardous unless tied to specific knowledge of the nature of the underlying function at the outside regions.

Issue 2

Can you give economic meaning to the value of a, the Y intercept?

There are circumstances in economic theory in which there is a legitimate economic meaning for the value of Y at $X = 0$. However, that economic meaning may not always be given to the a value, the extrapolation of the fitted regression to $X = 0$. The following example illustrates how our inclination to assign economic meaning to the calculated Y intercept may lead us astray when the data do not include any X values near 0.

■ **EXAMPLE 10.2**

Misinterpreting the *Y* Intercept

Suppose the orange dots in Figure 10.21 represent the observed sample data. The fitted regression line (shown as a solid line) is computed, and a is the estimated Y intercept—where the extrapolated regression line meets the Y axis. But, in reality, the population relationship between X and Y includes the green points, which reach the

Figure 10.21
Rate of inflation versus money
supply growth rate

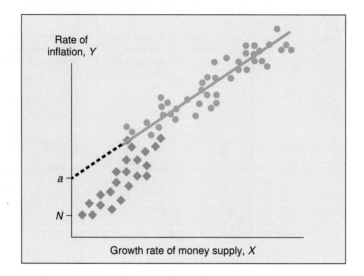

Y intercept value at point N. Economic theory suggests that for the two economic variables shown in Figure 10.21, the value of N has a legitimate economic interpretation as the average rate of growth of inflation not related to X, the rate of growth of the money supply. If the value a of the sample computed regression line had been accepted as an appropriate estimate of N, there would be a gross overestimation of the value of N. In this situation, linear extrapolation of an underlying curvilinear relationship is the culprit. Analysts should not hastily use the intercept term as representing a meaningful figure, when it is merely a mechanical extrapolation to $X = 0$ well beyond the observed sample range of X.

Issue 3
Can we interpret the nonexistence of a linear relationship as indicating no relationship at all?

A low r^2 value is indicative of a weak or a nonexistent linear relationship. However, if the two variables are meaningfully but nonlinearly related, we must be aware that a low r^2 value will also be the result. By checking the scatter diagram of the data to see the form of the relationship we avoid reaching the premature judgment that no relationship at all exists when a low r^2 is observed or reported.

10.13
CORRELATION ANALYSIS

We now recognize that regression analysis is the proper tool when our interest is in using the X value to estimate or predict the value of Y, or we want to numerically measure the responsiveness of Y to changes in X. But what if our interest is simply the measurement of strength and direction of the linear association between X and Y? That is, suppose we want only a numerical measure that summarizes to what extent the linear movement of the two variables coincide. **Correlation analysis** fulfills this role. Whereas in regression analysis, only Y is the random variable, in correlation analysis, both X and Y are random variables.

PEARSON'S *r*

The most widely used measure of the strength and direction of the linear association between two quantitative variables is the linear correlation coefficient, ρ (Greek letter rho). The symbol ρ is assigned to the population parameter. The computed estimate of ρ from sample data is given the symbol r and is called **Pearson's coefficient of linear correlation,** or simply, the **correlation coefficient** or the **Pearson *r*.** The calculated sign and value of r therefore provide a sample summary measure that reports the direction and strength of the linear association between observed sample values of X and Y.

The possible values of r range from -1.00 to $+1.00$ and indicate the different degrees of linear association that may be found. The extreme values, -1.00 and $+1.00$, indicate perfect negative correlation and perfect positive correlation, respectively. What does a particular r value imply about the scatter of observations in a scatter diagram? Let's examine Figure 10.22. Various scatter diagrams are given in this figure, along with their associated Pearson r values. As we can see, perfect correlation (positive or negative) means that all the observations lie on a straight line. The move away from the perfect positive correlation is shown in Figures 10.22c and d. As the relationship passes from a strong positive r $(r = +0.83)$ to $r = 0.00$, the scatter changes from an elongated oval shape with little vertical scatter (Figure 10.22c) to a circular shape with very wide vertical scatter (Figure 10.22d). A circular shape with very wide vertical scatter indicates no linear relationship exists; therefore, we have no correlation with an r value equal to 0. The process is similar starting from a strong negative correlation. Figure 10.22e shows the scatter of a situation where weak negative correlation exists.

The sign of r can be positive or negative and always conveys the direction of the relationship. Positive r indicates the variables tend to move in the same direction, and negative r means the variables tend to move in opposite directions.

The definitional formula for the Pearson r correlation coefficient is:

Pearson r Correlation Coefficient

$$r = \frac{\Sigma(X - \bar{X})(Y - \bar{Y})}{\sqrt{\Sigma(X - \bar{X})^2}\,\sqrt{\Sigma(Y - \bar{Y})^2}} \qquad (10\text{-}15)$$

Consider the data plotted in Figure 10.23 on the yearly profits for a company's two divisions, division A (variable X) and division B (variable Y). The flow and scatter of the observations suggest that the relationship between the two variables is strong and positive. Table 10.8 provides the necessary calculations to compute the r value.

Comparing the computed r value of 0.962 with the range of possible values (-1.0 to $+1.0$), we can say that the correlation between X and Y is positive and strong. In practice, this means that whenever an economic force affects the divisional profits of one division, it will likely affect the divisional profits of the other division in the same way. From this perspective, the company is not highly diversified.

The square of the coefficient of correlation is the coefficient of determination r^2, introduced in Section 10.5. The latter statistic is cited in regression analysis to indicate the amount of explanatory power the fitted regression line (expressed in terms of the independent variable X) provides about the dependent variable Y. In correlation analysis,

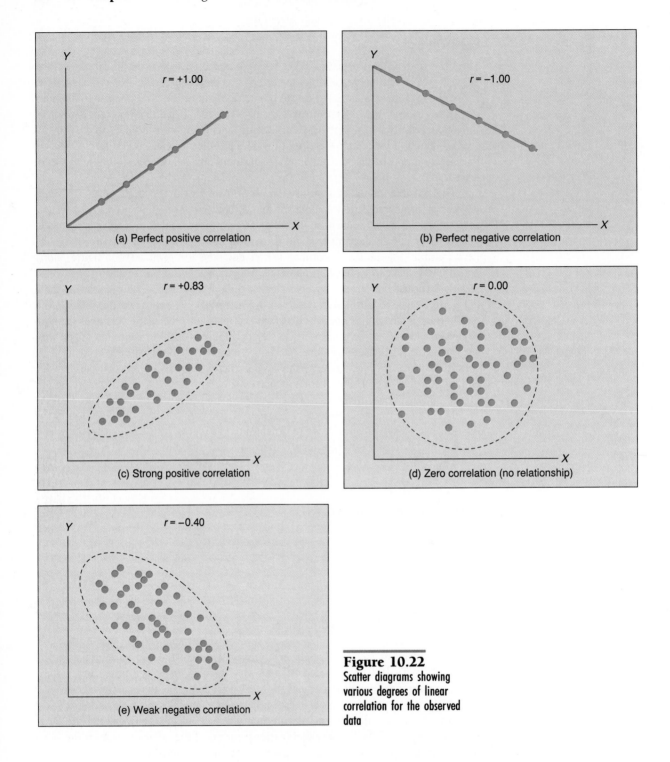

Figure 10.22
Scatter diagrams showing various degrees of linear correlation for the observed data

the reported coefficient r refers to the degree of linear association between the two variables X and Y, neither of which is classified as the independent or dependent variable.

Let's now turn to the preferred computational formula for calculating r; it relies on simpler computational quantities.

Figure 10.23
Scatter diagram of profits of
Division A and Division B

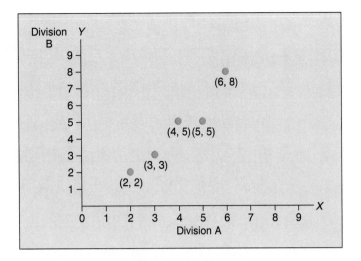

	TABLE 10.8	Application of the Definitional Formula for Calculating *r* Values between the Yearly Profits of Division A (*X* Variable) and Division B (*Y* Variable)					
YEAR	**X**	**Y**	**X − X̄**	**Y − Ȳ**	**(X − X̄)(Y − Ȳ)**	**(X − X̄)²**	**(Y − Ȳ)²**
1	4	5	0	+0.4	0	0	0.16
2	6	8	+2	+3.4	+6.8	4	11.56
3	2	2	−2	−2.6	+5.2	4	6.76
4	5	5	+1	+0.4	+0.4	1	0.16
5	3	3	−1	−1.6	+1.6	1	2.56
	$\Sigma X = 20$	$\Sigma Y = 23$			$\Sigma(X − \bar{X})(Y − \bar{Y}) = 14.0$	$\Sigma(X − \bar{X})^2 = 10$	$\Sigma(Y − \bar{Y})^2 = 21.20$

$$\bar{X} = \frac{20}{5} = 4.0, \bar{Y} = \frac{23}{5} = 4.6$$

$$r = \frac{\Sigma(X − \bar{X})(Y − \bar{Y})}{\sqrt{\Sigma(X − \bar{X})^2}\ \sqrt{\Sigma(Y − \bar{Y})^2}} = \frac{14.0}{\sqrt{10}\ \sqrt{21.20}} = \frac{14.0}{\sqrt{212}} = 0.962$$

Computational Formula for *r*

A computational formula that provides the same numerical answer (except for rounding) as the definitional formula is:

Computational Formula for r

$$r = \frac{\Sigma XY − n\bar{X}\bar{Y}}{\sqrt{\Sigma X^2 − n\bar{X}^2}\ \sqrt{\Sigma Y^2 − n\bar{Y}^2}} \qquad (10\text{-}16)$$

Table 10.9 shows the calculation of the necessary terms for use in the computational formula. Note that the numerical value obtained from the computational formula is identical to the numerical value obtained from the definitional formula.

		TABLE 10.9	Application of the Computational Formula for Calculating r Values between the Yearly Profits of Division A (X Variable) and Division B (Y Variable)			
YEAR	**X**	**Y**	**XY**	**X²**	**Y²**
1	4	5	20	16	25
2	6	8	48	36	64
3	2	2	4	4	4
4	5	5	25	25	25
5	3	3	9	9	9
	$\Sigma X = 20$	$\Sigma Y = 23$	$\Sigma XY = 106$	$\Sigma X^2 = 90$	$\Sigma Y^2 = 127$

$$\bar{X} = \frac{20}{5} = 4, \bar{Y} = \frac{23}{5} = 4.6$$

$$r = \frac{\Sigma XY - n\bar{X}\bar{Y}}{\sqrt{\Sigma X^2 - n\bar{X}^2} \sqrt{\Sigma Y^2 - n\bar{Y}^2}}$$

$$= \frac{106 - 5(4)(4.6)}{\sqrt{90 - 5(4)^2} \sqrt{127 - 5(4.6)^2}}$$

$$= \frac{14}{\sqrt{10} \sqrt{21.2}} = 0.962$$

Relationship between r and b

Turning our attention to the computational formulas for the regression slope coefficient b and the linear correlation coefficient r, we can see that the numerators are identical and some similar terms appear in the denominator. Compare

$$b = \frac{\Sigma XY - n\bar{X}\bar{Y}}{\Sigma X^2 - n\bar{X}^2} \quad \text{and} \quad r = \frac{\Sigma XY - n\bar{X}\bar{Y}}{\sqrt{\Sigma X^2 - n\bar{X}^2} \sqrt{\Sigma Y^2 - n\bar{Y}^2}}$$

This appearance of similar quantities in the two formulas hints that a relationship exists between the two formulas. The relationship is given by

$$r = b\left(\frac{\sqrt{\Sigma X^2 - n\bar{X}^2}}{\sqrt{\Sigma Y^2 - n\bar{Y}^2}}\right) = b\frac{\sqrt{SS_X}}{\sqrt{SS_Y}}$$

This expression linking r and b means that an hypothesis test using one statistic (r or b) has an equivalence to an hypothesis test using the other statistic. This is understandable because if there is no correlation in the population ($\rho = 0$), the population regression line has a slope of 0 ($B = 0$). Therefore, an hypothesis test of no linear relationship can be performed using either the null hypothesis H_o: $B = 0$ or H_o: $\rho = 0$. Both will result in identical values of the t statistic and thus the identical inferential conclusion about whether X and Y are linearly related to the population. As a matter of practice, the hypothesis approach using $B = 0$ is more commonly used to test a linear relationship, since regression analysis answers more questions about the nature of the relationship between X and Y.

PRACTICE EXERCISE

10.7 From a sample of 6 Oklahoma counties, data were obtained on the number of golf courses, X, and the divorce rate (percent), Y:

		OBSERVATION				
	1	**2**	**3**	**4**	**5**	**6**
Y	25	30	25	50	22	10
X	5	10	6	15	4	2

    a. Calculate $\Sigma(X - \bar{X})^2$.
    b. Calculate $\Sigma(Y - \bar{Y})^2$.
    c. Calculate the product $(X - \bar{X})(Y - \bar{Y})$ for the second observation.
    d. Calculate $\Sigma(X - \bar{X})(Y - \bar{Y})$.
    e. Calculate Pearson's r using the definitional formula.
    f. Is the association positive or negative?

10.14

INFERENCES ABOUT THE POPULATION CORRELATION COEFFICIENT

The sample linear correlation coefficient r is used as a basis for significance testing about the population value ρ. Statistical inferences about ρ rest on some formal assumptions. In correlation analysis, we assume that both X and Y (1) are random variables and (2) are drawn from a joint, normally distributed population.

    Let's now examine the procedures for making inferences about ρ, the population correlation coefficient, from the value of r.

HYPOTHESIS TESTING

To test the null hypothesis of no correlation in the population, that is, H_o: $\rho = 0$, we use the test statistic

$$t_{n-2} = \frac{r - 0}{S_r}$$

where $S_r = \sqrt{(1 - r^2)/(n - 2)}$, and represents the estimate of the standard deviation of the sample correlation coefficient. We therefore can write:

Test Statistic for a Zero Population Correlation Coefficient

$$t_{n-2} = r\sqrt{\frac{n - 2}{1 - r^2}} \tag{10-17}$$

The null and alternative hypotheses are stated as:

        H_o: $\rho = 0$ (No linear correlation exists.)
        H_A: $\rho \neq 0$ (Positive or negative linear correlation exists.)

The alternative hypothesis H_A reflects the fact that the alternatives to no linear correlation are either a positive linear correlation or negative linear correlation. This implies a two-sided test of H_o.

    Let's apply the following four-step procedure to the data set given in Table 10.8 on yearly divisional profits.

Step 1

Determine the rejection region. For a significance level of α, the rejection region is defined as those values of the test statistic t_{n-2} that meet the condition

$$t_{n-2} < -t_{(\alpha/2, n-2)} \qquad \text{or} \qquad t_{n-2} > +t_{(\alpha/2, n-2)}$$

For the data set given in Table 10.8, $n - 2 = 3$. Using the $\alpha = .05$ level of significance, the value of t from Table VII is $t_{(.025, 3)} = 3.182$. This means the rejection region is

$$t_{n-2} < -3.182 \qquad \text{or} \qquad t_{n-2} > +3.182$$

Step 2

Compute the value of the test statistic. The observed t statistic is found from formula (10-17):

$$t_{n-2} = r\sqrt{\frac{n-2}{1-r^2}}$$

$$= 0.962\sqrt{\frac{5-2}{1-(0.962)^2}}$$

$$= 6.08$$

Step 3

Determine whether the statistic is in the rejection region. Since the observed value $6.08 > +3.182$, it lies in the rejection region.

Step 4

Draw a conclusion. We reject H_o at a significance level of .05 and conclude that a linear correlation exists between X and Y. In practical terms, this means that there is strong statistical evidence that there exists a linear association between the profits of division A and the profits of division B.

DEMYSTIFYING "NONSENSE" CORRELATIONS

A clear distinction must be made between correlation in a sample (measured by r) and correlation in the population (measured by ρ). A "nonsense" correlation situation arises when a notable numerical value is found for the sample correlation coefficient even though the two variables in the population being investigated are in fact unrelated. Consider a set of yearly observations made over a 5 year period on the numbers of sightings of UFOs in the United States and the annual number of ounces of gold mined in South Africa. Suppose one finds a positive value of 0.55 for the sample correlation coefficient. Despite the high sample correlation found over these relatively few sample observations, the conclusion that the two populations are related is unwarranted. The point to recognize is that finding a strong correlation in the sample does not automatically imply that there must be a meaningful or practical interpretation to the correlation.

PRACTICAL IMPORTANCE VERSUS STATISTICAL SIGNIFICANCE

Suppose the linear relationship between X and Y is found to be statistically significant. Does it follow that the relationship is strong enough to also be practically important? When statistical testing for the existence of a population linear correlation from sample information produces statistical significance, it may not have practical significance.

Let us illustrate. Suppose an industrial psychologist develops a learning procedure to increase word processing workers' productivity and the learning procedure is administered to a huge sample of 40,000 workers. Suppose also that the sample correlation between time spent in the learning procedure and productivity is 0.02. Then the observed t statistic is

$$t = 0.02 \sqrt{\frac{39{,}998}{1 - (0.02)^2}} = 4.0$$

This very high observed t value would lead us to reject a null hypothesis H_o of no population correlation, even at the $\alpha = .001$ level. Hence, we would declare the result "highly statistically significant." Yet, the test accounts for only $r^2 = (0.02)^2 = 0.004$, or only 0.4% of the variation observed in workers' productivity. From a practical perspective, the learning procedure offers virtually no explanatory power of the observed variation in workers' productivity. Thus, the "high statistical significance" has no practical importance. The time spent in the learning procedure is virtually worthless as a practical indicator of productivity. The point to recognize is that the practical significance of correlation analysis depends on (1) the magnitude of the estimated value of the correlation coefficient and (2) the level of statistical significance. Focusing on one factor and neglecting the other can lead the investigator astray.

DO NOT CONFUSE ASSOCIATION WITH CAUSATION

Causality cannot be assumed to exist merely from the fact that two variables are strongly correlated. Correlated changes in X and Y may be induced indirectly by a third variable that affects both X and Y simultaneously. The identity of this third variable may or may not be known.

■ **EXAMPLE 10.3**
The Stork Did It

Many advertisements of baby products can be found showing a stork carrying a baby. Where did this notion that storks deliver babies come from? Reported studies of the stork populations in Belgian towns have indicated a high (positive) correlation between the number of storks and the number of childbirths. The sample correlation was so statistically significant and was so close to 1 that the investigators could not explain its value away as a mere quirk of sampling variation (as in the case of the "nonsense" correlation case discussed earlier in this section). But does statistically significant correlation prove that storks really do bring babies? Consider the following alternative explanation.

Storks are said to like to nest on chimneys of buildings. The larger the population of a town, the more chimneys there are to attract a large number of storks. According to this explanation, the observed (statistically significant) correlation between storks and babies is not because more (or fewer) storks "cause" more (or fewer) babies. The observed correlation is indirectly induced by a third intervening variable: population. Diagrammatically:

The correlation value calculated in observational business studies should be interpreted as an index of the strength of the association between two variables, not as an indicator of whether there is cause and effect between them. However, when a controversial issue is being considered, there is a tendency to claim causality from mere correlation. For example, in two protracted cases of alleged salary discrimination against women in Illinois (Harris Trust, a large Chicago Bank, and United Airlines), it was clearly established (among other things) that men were paid more than women with comparable numbers of years of service. The plaintiffs charged discrimination. The defendants claimed that other factors, rather than gender discrimination, were the underlying reasons for the observed pay level differential. When a strong correlation (association) is found between gender and salary, can gender discrimination be claimed? More specifically, do gender differences cause salary differences? Explain what you think are plausible alternative explanations for salary differentials, other than gender discrimination?

EXERCISES

10.31 The data set in the table (repeated from the Practice Exercise 10.7) is a random sample collected on the number of golf courses, X, and the divorce rate (percent), Y, in 6 Oklahoma counties.

	OBSERVATION					
	1	2	3	4	5	6
Y	25	30	25	50	22	10
X	5	10	6	15	4	2

Test the null hypothesis H_o: $\rho = 0$ against the alternative hypothesis H_A: $\rho \neq 0$ for $\alpha = .05$.

a. For a level of significance of $\alpha = .05$, find the table value of t that determines the rejection region of H_o.
b. Calculate the observed t value.
c. Which of the following conclusions about H_o follows from your answers to parts a and b?
(1) Increased golf playing causes increased divorce rates.
(2) Divorced men play more golf than do married or single men.
(3) Urbanized counties have more golf courses and higher divorce rates, which cause the number of golf courses and the divorce rate to be correlated.
(4) The observed association between the number of golf courses and divorce rate is spurious and simply due to sampling error.
(5) The number of golf courses and the divorce rate are positively associated, but the cause cannot be inferred from the data.

10.32 A car dealer wishes to understand the relationship between the number of sales people on duty during the week, X, and the number of cars sold during the week, Y. He has the following data on a random sample of 5 weeks:

	OBSERVATION				
	1	2	3	4	5
Y	2	5	8	5	3
X	6	4	2	3	5

    a. Calculate the terms ΣX, ΣY, ΣXY, ΣX^2, and ΣY^2.

    b. Calculate $\bar{X}$ and $\bar{Y}$.

    c. Calculate Pearson's r using the computational formula.

    d. Is the association positive or negative?

10.33 Given the data in Exercise 10.32:

    a. Test the null hypothesis H_o: $\rho = 0$ against the alternative hypothesis H_A: $\rho \neq 0$, for a level of significance of $\alpha = .10$. Find the table value of t that determines the region of rejection of H_o.

    b. Calculate the observed t value.

    c. What conclusion about H_o follows from your answer to parts a and b?

▶ **10.34** Some college admissions experts place a great deal of emphasis on high school grade-point averages; others place stronger emphasis on SAT (or ACT) scores; still others believe grade-point averages and college entrance tests largely measure the same thing. Sample bivariate data are given below:

				STUDENT			
	1	**2**	**3**	**4**	**5**	**6**	**7**
SAT SCORE	479	632	395	551	412	370	455
HIGH SCHOOL GPA	2.8	3.5	2.7	4.0	2.9	2.1	3.0

    a. Compute r.

    b. Test H_o: $\rho = 0$ against H_A: $\rho \neq 0$ at the $\alpha = .05$ level of significance.

    c. What practical conclusion follows from your results in part b?

10.35 A society of bird watchers has collected data from several large European cities on stork sittings and human births to test the widely expressed belief that where there are storks there will also be babies. The data are given in the table.

				CITY			
	1	**2**	**3**	**4**	**5**	**6**	**7**
BABIES	21	10	5	22	9	36	25
STORKS	36	32	23	41	30	55	44

    a. Compute the Pearson coefficient of linear correlation, r.

    b. Test H_o: $\rho = 0$ against H_A: $\rho > 0$ at the $\alpha = .10$ level of significance.

    c. Is it plausible to say that the observed sample correlation is a sampling fluke?

    d. If the observed sample correlation is not spurious, does it follow that storks do bring babies? Explain.

10.36 Television commercials have long been suspected of having adverse effects on children who view them. A study of school children correlated attitudes toward cold medicines and viewing of television commercials for cold medicines. Part of the study examined children who received cold medicine but were given little or no parental guidance about taking cold medicines and the way they are advertised. Another part of the study examined only children who also received cold medicine but with close parental guidance and supervision. Correlations were computed for four questions that the children answered concerning their attitudes when they have a cold, and for a fifth question concerning frequency of usage. The results are given in the table. At $\alpha = .05$, which, if any, of the sample linear correlations are statistically significant?

Correlation with Exposure to TV Cold Medicine Commercials		
ATTITUDE	**NO PARENTAL GUIDANCE GROUP** ($n = 132$) r	**STRONG PARENTAL GUIDANCE GROUP** ($n = 55$) r
(1) When I have a cold, cold medicine can make me feel better.	0.06	0.29
(2) When I have a cold, I like to take cold medicine.	0.13	0.26
(3) When I have a cold, I want to take cold medicine.	0.44	0.23
(4) When I have a cold, I ask my parents for cold medicine.	0.39	0.34
(5) Frequency of usage	0.12	0.23

10.37 Anthony's Sea Food Grotto is a popular restaurant. Its owners wish to learn more about the segment of the population that frequently patronizes better quality restaurants. A correlation study was conducted of eating out frequency (better restaurants) against several other variables. The results are given in the table. At $\alpha = .05$, which of the variables are significantly correlated with eating out frequency?

	r ($n = 200$)
Age	0.16
Household income	0.35
Education	0.41
Family size	−0.23
Newspaper reading	0.20
TV viewing	−0.15
Magazine reading	0.52
Book reading	0.11
Sports participation	−0.34
Spectator sports interest	−0.15
Fishing or hunting activity	−0.10
Movie attendance	0.22
Beer consumption	−0.19
Wine consumption	−0.19
Liquor consumption	0.09
Church attendance	0.05
Charitable contributions	0.37

SUMMARY

Regression analysis and correlation analysis are powerful tools for business management. Although both analyze the relationships between two quantitative variables, the purpose of the analysis determines which form is appropriate. Regression analysis is performed when the prediction of the value of one variable, given a specific value for the other variable, is required. Another purpose of regression analysis is to estimate the average amount of change in one variable, given a specific amount of change in the value of the other. Sometimes the goal is to measure the average amount of co-movement in the two variables, without reference to particular values of either variable. In that case, correlation analysis is the appropriate tool.

Regression analysis and correlation analysis have always been held in high regard by business, but now their application is becoming more common as a result of the advent of computers and the availability of reliable statistical software. Importantly, the computational burden has been eliminated and access to statistical software has become affordable. For less than $15, you can buy a hand-held electronic calculator preprogrammed to compute basic regression and correlation analysis statistics. With the cost minimal, the busy work removed, and the description of the statistical relationship between two variables within reach, it now becomes important to know the limitations of the analysis and the interpretation of the results. So we'll conclude this chapter by providing some guidelines to follow and some pitfalls to watch out for.

First, since the formulas presented in this chapter deal with linear relationships between two variables, the first check is the plausibility of the linearity assumption.

Second, if you assume your observed data are a sample from a population, it's important to recognize that the computed correlation coefficient and the fitted regression line are only estimates. Reliable statements about the true regression equation and population correlation coefficient can be made only if the inferential procedures discussed in the chapter are performed.

Third, to decide whether statistical significance is linked to practical importance, look at the size of the correlation coefficient or the regression coefficient to see if it is large enough to have meaningful business implications.

Fourth, finding both statistical significance and practical importance doesn't necessarily lead to conclusions about causality. It's possible that changes in both of the variables studied could be caused by another variable that wasn't studied.

Although these limitations reduce to some extent the value of regression and correlation analysis, these tools continue to be put to good use every day in the business world. The Chapter Review Exercises illustrate some applications you probably wouldn't think of on your own.

Figure 10.24 presents a flowchart to guide you through the steps you need to perform regression analyses.

KEY EQUATIONS

Where appropriate, two formulas are shown: one in computational terms and the other expressed in compact sum of squares (SS) notation commonly found in computer output. This notation is summarized below:

Summation Terms:

For X,

$$SS_X = \Sigma(X - \bar{X})^2 = \Sigma X^2 - n\bar{X}^2$$

For XY,

$$SS_{XY} = \Sigma(X - \bar{X})(Y - \bar{Y}) = \Sigma XY - n\bar{X}\bar{Y}$$

Variation Terms

For total variation,

$$SST = \Sigma(Y - \bar{Y})^2$$

For explained (regression) variation,

$$SSR = \Sigma(\hat{Y} - \bar{Y})^2$$

For unexplained (error) variation,

$$SSE = \Sigma(Y - \hat{Y})^2$$

Fitted Regression Line Equation by Least Squares Method

$$\hat{Y} = a + bX \tag{10-1}$$

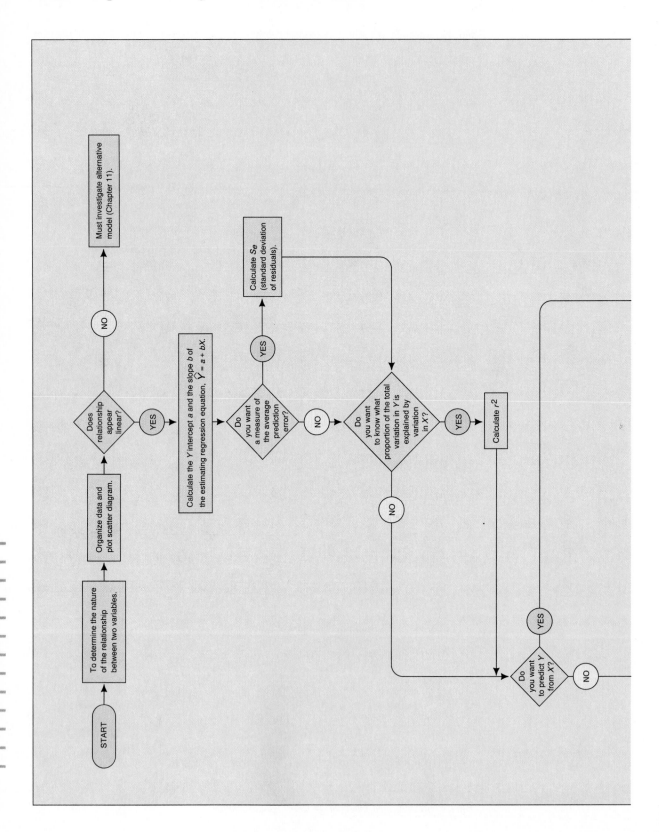

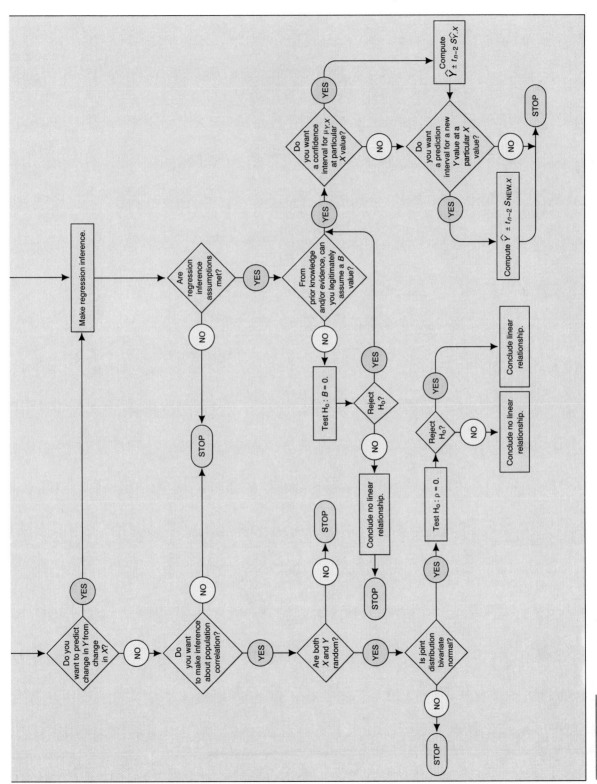

Figure 10.24 Flowchart for performing regression analyses

Computational Formulas for Least Squares Estimates

$$b = \frac{\sum XY - n\bar{X}\bar{Y}}{\sum X^2 - n\bar{X}^2} \quad \text{or} \quad b = \frac{SS_{XY}}{SS_X} \tag{10-2}$$

$$a = \bar{Y} - b\bar{X} \tag{10-3}$$

Computational Formula for Standard Deviation of Residuals

$$S_e = \sqrt{\frac{\sum Y^2 - a\sum Y - b\sum XY}{n - 2}} \quad \text{or} \quad S_e = \sqrt{\frac{SSE}{n - 2}} \tag{10-4}$$

Computational Formula for Coefficient of Determination

$$r^2 = \frac{a\sum Y + b\sum XY - n\bar{Y}^2}{\sum Y^2 - n\bar{Y}^2} \quad \text{or} \quad r^2 = \frac{SSR}{SST} \tag{10-5}$$

Population Regression Line Equation

$$\mu_{Y.X} = A + BX \tag{10-6}$$

Regression Model

$$Y = A + BX + E = \mu_{Y.X} + E \tag{10-7}$$

Estimated Standard Deviation of the Regression (Slope) Coefficient

$$S_b = \sqrt{\frac{S_e^2}{\Sigma(X - \bar{X})^2}} \tag{10-8}$$

Test Statistic for the Population Regression Coefficient

$$t_{n-2} = \frac{b - B_o}{S_b} \tag{10-9}$$

$1 - \alpha$ Confidence Interval for B

$$\text{Upper confidence limit (UCL)} = b + t_{(\alpha/2, n-2)}S_b \tag{10-10}$$
$$\text{Lower confidence limit (LCL)} = b - t_{(\alpha/2, n-2)}S_b$$

Estimated Standard Deviation of a Fitted Y Value at X_o

$$S_{\hat{Y}.X_o} = S_e \sqrt{\frac{1}{n} + \frac{(X_o - \bar{X})^2}{\Sigma(X - \bar{X})^2}} \tag{10-11}$$

$1 - \alpha$ Confidence Interval for $\mu_{Y.X_o}$ at X_o

$$\text{Upper confidence limit (UCL)} = \hat{Y}_o + t_{(\alpha/2, n-2)}S_{\hat{Y}.X_o} \tag{10-12}$$
$$\text{Lower confidence limit (LCL)} = \hat{Y}_o - t_{(\alpha/2, n-2)}S_{\hat{Y}.X_o}$$

Estimated Standard Deviation of Prediction of a New Y Value at X_o

$$S_{NEW.X_o} = S_e \sqrt{\frac{1}{n} + \frac{(X_o - \bar{X})^2}{\Sigma(X - \bar{X})^2} + 1} \tag{10-13}$$

$1 - \alpha$ Prediction Interval for a New Y Value at X_o

$$\text{Upper prediction limit (UPL)} = \hat{Y}_o + t_{(\alpha/2, n-2)}S_{NEW.X_o} \tag{10-14}$$
$$\text{Lower prediction limit (LPL)} = \hat{Y}_o - t_{(\alpha/2, n-2)}S_{NEW.X_o}$$

Pearson r Correlation Coefficient

Definitional formula:

$$r = \frac{\Sigma(X - \bar{X})(Y - \bar{Y})}{\sqrt{\Sigma(X - \bar{X})^2} \, \sqrt{\Sigma(Y - \bar{Y})^2}} \tag{10-15}$$

Computational formula:

$$r = \frac{\Sigma XY - n\bar{X}\bar{Y}}{\sqrt{\Sigma X^2 - n\bar{X}^2} \, \sqrt{\Sigma Y^2 - n\bar{Y}^2}} \tag{10-16}$$

Test Statistic for a Zero Population Correlation Coefficient

$$t_{n-2} = r\sqrt{\frac{n - 2}{1 - r^2}} \tag{10-17}$$

PRACTICE EXERCISE ANSWERS

10.1 a.

X	Y	$\hat{Y}$	$e = Y - \hat{Y}$	$(Y - \hat{Y})^2$
7	27	25.5	1.5	2.25
15	45	53.5	−8.5	72.25
13	51	46.5	4.52	0.25
3	9	11.5	−2.5	6.25
10	33	36.0	−3.0	9.00
12	51	43.0	8.0	64.00
60	216	216.0	0.0	174.00

$\Sigma(Y - \hat{Y})^2 = \Sigma e^2 = 174$

b. Using the above data, $\bar{X} = \Sigma \dfrac{X}{n} = \dfrac{60}{6} = 10$ and $\bar{Y} = \Sigma \dfrac{Y}{n} = \dfrac{216}{6} = 36$. The regression equation is $\hat{Y} = 1 + 3.5X$. When $X = \bar{X} = 10$, $\hat{Y} = 1 + 3.5(10) = 36 = \bar{Y}$.

10.2 a.

X	Y	$\hat{Y}$	$e = Y - \hat{Y}$	$(Y - \hat{Y})^2$
8	41	41.0142	−0.0142	0.0002
5	25	25.5975	−0.5975	0.3570
10	52	51.2920	0.7080	0.5013
8	42	41.0142	0.9858	0.9718
6	30	30.7364	−0.7364	0.5423
9	49	46.1531	2.8469	8.1048
7	30	35.8753	−5.8753	34.5191
3	18	15.3197	2.6803	7.1840
56	287	287.0024	−0.0024	52.1805

$\Sigma(Y - \hat{Y})^2 = 52.1805$

b. $S_e^2 = \dfrac{\Sigma(Y - \hat{Y})^2}{n - 2} = \dfrac{52.1805}{8 - 2} = 8.69675$

c. $S_e = \sqrt{\dfrac{\Sigma(Y - \hat{Y})^2}{n - 2}} = \sqrt{\dfrac{52.1805}{8 - 2}} = \sqrt{8.69675} = 2.949$

10.3 a.

X	Y	$\hat{Y}$	$(\hat{Y} - \bar{Y})^2$	$(Y - \bar{Y})^2$
8	41	41.0142	26.41	26.266
5	25	25.5975	105.63	118.266
10	52	51.2920	237.68	260.016
8	42	41.0142	26.41	37.516
6	30	30.7364	26.40	34.516
9	49	46.1531	105.64	172.266
7	30	35.8753	0	34.516
3	18	15.3197	422.52	319.516
56	287	287.0024	950.69	1002.87

$$\bar{Y} = \frac{287}{8} = 35.875$$

a. $\text{SST} = \Sigma(Y - \bar{Y})^2 = 1002.87$
b. $\text{SSR} = \Sigma(\hat{Y} - \bar{Y})^2 = 950.69$

c. $r^2 = \dfrac{\text{SSR}}{\text{SST}} = \dfrac{950.69}{1002.87} = 0.94797$

10.4 a. H_o: $B = 0$
   H_A: $B \neq 0$

   The sample size is $n = 8$ and $\alpha = .05$, so the critical value is $t_{(\alpha/2, n-2)} = t_{(.025,6)} = 2.447$. H_o is rejected if $t_6 < -2.447$ or $t_6 > +2.447$. The test statistic is $t_6 = (b - 0)/S_b = 5.138888/0.491504 = 10.4554$. Since $10.4554 > +2.447$, we reject the null hypothesis and conclude that the slope is significantly different than 0.

b. For 95% confidence, the appropriate t value is $t_{(\alpha/2, n-2)} = t_{(.025,6)} = 2.447$. The confidence interval is

$$\text{UCL} = b + t_{(\alpha/2, n-2)}S_b = 5.138888 + 2.447(0.491504) = 6.3416$$
$$\text{LCL} = b - t_{(\alpha/2, n-2)}S_b = 5.138888 + 2.447(0.491504) = 3.9362$$

10.5 a. Using the data provided, we find that $\bar{X} = \Sigma \dfrac{X}{n} = \dfrac{56}{8} = 7$. For $X = 7$, $(X - \bar{X})^2 = (7 - 7)^2 = 0$. The standard deviation of the fitted Y value for $X = 7$ is

$$S_{\hat{Y}.X} = S_e\sqrt{\frac{1}{n} + \frac{(X - \bar{X})^2}{\Sigma(X - \bar{X})^2}} = 2.959026\sqrt{\frac{1}{8} + \frac{0}{\Sigma(X - \bar{X})^2}} = 1.042638$$

b. At $X = 7$, the value of $\hat{Y}$ is $\hat{Y} = -0.09722 + 5.138888(7) = 35.875$. The limits of the 95% confidence interval are

$$\text{UCL} = \hat{Y} + t_{(\alpha/2, n-2)}S_{\hat{Y}.X} = 35.875 + 2.447(1.042638) = 38.42633$$
$$\text{LCL} = \hat{Y} - t_{(\alpha/2, n-2)}S_{\hat{Y}.X} = 35.875 - 2.447(1.042638) = 33.32366$$

10.6 a. Using the data provided, we find that $\bar{X} = \Sigma \dfrac{X}{n} = \dfrac{56}{8} = 7$. For $X = 7$, $(X - \bar{X})^2 = (7 - 7)^2 = 0$. The standard deviation of the prediction for $X = 7$ is

$$S_{\text{NEW}.X} = S_e\sqrt{\frac{1}{n} + \frac{(X - \bar{X})^2}{\Sigma(X - \bar{X})^2} + 1}$$

$$= 2.949026\sqrt{\frac{1}{8} + \frac{0}{\Sigma(X - \bar{X})^2} + 1} = 3.127914$$

b. At $X = 7$, the value of $\hat{Y}$ is $\hat{Y} = -0.09722 + 5.138888(7) = 35.875$. The limits of the 95% prediction interval are

$$\text{UPL} = \hat{Y} + t_{(\alpha/2, n-2)}S_{\text{NEW}.X} = 35.875 + 2.447(3.127914) = 43.52900$$
$$\text{LPL} = \hat{Y} - t_{(\alpha/2, n-2)}S_{\text{NEW}.X} = 35.875 - 2.447(3.127914) = 28.22099$$

10.7

OBSERVATION	X	Y	XY	X²	Y²
1	5	25	125	25	625
2	10	30	300	100	900
3	6	25	150	36	625
4	15	50	750	225	2500
5	4	22	88	16	484
6	2	10	20	4	100
	42	162	1433	406	5234

$$\bar{X} = \Sigma \frac{X}{n} = \frac{42}{6} = 7 \text{ and } \bar{Y} = \Sigma \frac{Y}{n} = \frac{162}{6} = 27$$

X − X̄	(X − X̄)²	Y − Ȳ	(Y − Ȳ)²	(X − X̄)(Y − Ȳ)
−2	4	−2	4	4
3	9	3	9	9
−1	1	−2	4	2
8	64	23	529	184
−3	9	−5	25	15
−5	25	−17	289	85
0	112	0	860	299

a. $\Sigma(X - \bar{X})^2 = 112$
b. $\Sigma(Y - \bar{Y})^2 = 860$
c. For the second observation, $(X - \bar{X})(Y - \bar{Y}) = (3)(3) = 9$.
d. $\Sigma(X - \bar{X})(Y - \bar{Y}) = 299$
e. $r = \dfrac{\Sigma(X - \bar{X})(Y - \bar{Y})}{\sqrt{\Sigma(X - \bar{X})^2}\sqrt{\Sigma(Y - \bar{Y})^2}} = \dfrac{299}{\sqrt{112}\sqrt{860}} = 0.963413$
f. The association is positive because $r > 0$.

CHAPTER REVIEW EXERCISES

10.38 The marketing department of California's Sealand Resorts is studying the relationship between the number of daily visitors that come to the amusement park and the various advertising media that have been employed. The department decided to vary the number of television commercials shown locally over 10 consecutive weekend nights. The data on the number of commercials, X, and the number of visitors (thousands), Y, on the day after each was shown are given in the table.

					OBSERVATION					
	1	2	3	4	5	6	7	8	9	10
Y	7.2	7.5	10.3	9.4	12.9	14.0	15.4	16.2	19.9	20.0
X	2	2	3	3	4	4	5	5	6	6

a. Plot the points on a scatter diagram and check for the linearity assumption.
b. Use the least squares method to determine the fitted linear regression equation.
c. Calculate the standard deviation of residuals, S_e.
d. Calculate the error variance, S_e^2.
e. Compute the coefficient of determination, r^2.
f. Is the relationship direct or inverse?
g. For $X = 4$, calculate $\hat{Y}$.

10.39 The human resources director for a company is interested in the relationship between this year's salary increase for a salesperson, X, and the subsequent year's improvement in sales performance, Y. A sample of 6 salespeople who performed satisfactorily was selected, and the information about their salary increases (in thousand dollars) and their increases in sales performance (in percentages) are given in the table.

| | **OBSERVATION** | | | | | |
	1	2	3	4	5	6
Y	5	6	6	9	9	10
X	3	4	5	6	7	8

a. Plot the points on a scatter diagram and check for the linearity assumption.
b. Use the least squares method to determine the fitted linear regression equation.
c. Calculate the standard deviation of residuals, S_e.
d. Calculate the error variance, S_e^2.
e. Compute the coefficient of determination, r^2.
f. Is the relationship direct or inverse?
g. For $X = 4$, calculate $\hat{Y}$.

10.40 Forecasted inventory requirements are almost always linked to the level of anticipated sales. One forecasting procedure is known as the *percent of sales method*. In this method, a constant percentage of next year's anticipated sales level is used to determine the level of inventory to purchase. The production manager at a rapidly growing company that uses this system believes that at low levels of target sales he can concentrate on a few fast turnover products, thereby holding inventory requirements to a minimum. But to attract more customers, a broader product line is needed, including slower-moving items. This, he feels, tends to raise inventory requirements as a percentage of sales. He wants to try an alternative approach by applying regression analysis to find the relationship between anticipated sales (in millions of dollars), X, and the inventory level (thousands of units), Y, over 10 quarters. The fitted value of Y corresponding to anticipated sales would be the forecast inventory requirement.

| | **OBSERVATION** | | | | | | | | | |
	1	2	3	4	5	6	7	8	9	10
Y	9	20	20	16	23	19	20	30	33	27
X	3	6	13	9	11	11	8	14	15	16

a. Plot the points on a scatter diagram and check for the linearity assumption.
b. Use the least squares method to determine the linear regression equation.
c. Draw the least squares regression line on your scatter diagram.
d. Draw another line through the origin and the point $(\bar{X}, \bar{Y})$. This line corresponds to the assumption of a constant percentage.
e. Which of the two lines appears to best fit the data?

10.41 For the data given in Exercise 10.40:
  a. Calculate the standard deviation of residuals, S_e.
  b. Calculate the error variance, S_e^2.
  c. Compute the coefficient of determination, r^2.
  d. Is the relationship direct or inverse?
  e. For $X = 4$, calculate $\hat{Y}$.
  f. For $X = 6$, calculate $\hat{Y}$; the total deviation, $Y - \bar{Y}$; residual deviation, $Y - \hat{Y}$; and explained deviation, $\hat{Y} - \bar{Y}$.
  g. For what range of X values would the corresponding predictions of Y not be subject to extrapolation error?

□ **10.42** Use the following data set to answer the questions below.

OBSERVATION	Y	X
1	403	4,560
2	461	4,962
3	506	5,728
4	507	6,477
5	665	8,480
6	1,087	17,924
7	1,165	17,524
8	1,278	20,181
9	1,438	21,752
10	1,216	24,106

  a. Plot the points on a scatter diagram and check the linearity assumption.
  b. Use the least squares method to determine the fitted linear regression equation.
  c. Draw the least squares regression line on the scatter diagram.
  d. Calculate the error variance, S_e^2.
  e. Calculate the standard deviation of residuals, S_e.
  f. Compute the coefficient of determination, r^2.
  g. Is the relationship direct or inverse?

10.43 For the data given in Exercise 10.42:
  a. Calculate the ratio $\bar{Y}/\bar{X}$.
  b. Draw a straight line through this point $(\bar{X}, \bar{Y})$ and the origin. For $X = 5728$, calculate $\hat{Y}$ and the residual deviation, $Y - \hat{Y}$, using the least squares regression line determined in Exercise 10.42.
  c. Calculate $Y^* = 5728 \,(\bar{Y}/\bar{X})$, and use this as an alternative prediction of Y for $X = 5728$.
  d. Compare the residual deviation for the method in part c with that obtained in part b. Can you explain what this new estimator represents and why it doesn't give as accurate a prediction?

▶ **10.44** The following data were collected over a 7 month period for the investment return on Hybratech stock, X, and the market return index, Y.

	OBSERVATION						
	1	2	3	4	5	6	7
Y	12	13	11	15	13	15	16
X	3	4	6	4	8	9	7

  a. Calculate the terms ΣX, ΣY, ΣXY, ΣY^2, and ΣX^2.
  b. Compute the values of $\bar{X}$ and $\bar{Y}$.
  c. Determine the Pearson correlation, r.
  d. Is the association positive or negative?

10.45 Use the data in Exercise 10.44 and the hypotheses H_o: $\rho = 0$ versus H_A: $\rho \neq 0$.
  a. Calculate the t test statistic.
  b. At the $\alpha = .01$ level of significance, find the t table values that determine the rejection region of H_o.
  c. What decision about H_o follows from your answers in parts a and b?

10.46 Use the following data set:

	OBSERVATION							
	1	2	3	4	5	6	7	8
Y	8	2	6	4	8	4	4	2
X	5	5	6	6	5	6	4	5

  a. Calculate $\Sigma(Y - \bar{Y})^2$.
  b. Calculate $\Sigma(X - \bar{X})^2$.
  c. Calculate $\Sigma(X - \bar{X})(Y - \bar{Y})$.
  d. Calculate the Pearson r.
  e. Is the association positive or negative?

10.47 Use the data given in Exercise 10.46 and the hypotheses H_o: $\rho = 0$ versus H_A: $\rho \neq 0$.
  a. Calculate the t test statistic.
  b. At the $\alpha = .05$ level of significance, find the t table values that determine the rejection region of H_o.
  c. What decision about H_o follows from your answers in parts f and g?

▶ **10.48** "We gotta hold onto our older workers," demanded the foreman of plant 2 to Joe Purvis, the personnel manager. "They know the job, and besides, they come to work everyday. Just look at the records; you'll see what I mean." After venting a few more complaints, the foreman left. Joe sipped his morning coffee a few more times, turned to his files, and pulled at random a few records on workers in plant 2. Compiling the information, he came up with the data given in the table.

	EMPLOYEE						
	1	2	3	4	5	6	7
DAYS ABSENT OVER LAST YEAR	10	0	1	4	3	7	5
NUMBER OF YEARS EMPLOYED WITH THE COMPANY	3	6	7	7	5	2	1

  a. As a check on linearity, plot the points with days absent, Y, on the vertical axis and number of years employed, X, on the horizontal axis. Assess the resulting scatter diagram.
  b. Compute the least squares regression equation.
  c. Draw the fitted regression line on the scatter diagram.
  d. The personnel manager noted the positive value of the intercept coefficient and said, "This equation is useless because according to it, people who haven't started to work yet (i.e., $X = 0$) have (on average) already accumulated a poor absenteeism record." Do you agree that this is a correct interpretation of the Y intercept term? If not, why not?

10.49 Using the data set and regression results from Exercise 10.48, answer the following questions.
  a. Calculate S_b.

b. For H_o: $B = 0$ versus H_A: $B \neq 0$, and for $\alpha = .01$, determine the rejection region for H_o.

c. Calculate the t statistic.

d. What conclusion about H_o follows from your answers to parts b and c?

e. Would your answer to part d differ if $\alpha = .05$?

f. What are the upper and lower limits for the 99% confidence interval for B?

g. Make an inferential statement about your results in part f.

10.50 Using the data set and regression results from Exercise 10.48, answer the following questions.

a. Calculate $S_{\hat{Y}.X_o}$ at $X = 5$ and at $X = 2$.

b. Calculate the point estimates of $\mu_{Y.X}$ at $X = 5$ and at $X = 2$.

c. Calculate the upper and lower limits for the 95% confidence interval for $\mu_{Y.X}$ at $X = 5$ and $X = 2$.

d. Why is the width of the confidence interval at $X = 5$ not the same as at $X = 2$?

e. Make an inferential statement about your results in part d.

10.51 Using the data set and regression results from Exercise 10.48, answer the following questions.

a. Calculate $S_{NEW.X}$ at $X = 5$ and $X = 2$.

b. Calculate the point forecast of a new Y value at $X = 5$ and at $X = 2$.

c. Why are the results in part b the same as your results in part c of Exercise 10.50?

d. Calculate the upper and lower limits for the 95% prediction interval for a new Y value at $X = 5$ and at $X = 2$.

e. What is the width of the prediction interval at $X = 5$? Is the width smaller, larger, or the same at $X = 2$?

f. Make an inferential statement about your results in part e.

10.52 The data set in the table is repeated from Exercise 10.14 for convenience.

		OBSERVATION						
	1	2	3	4	5	6	7	8
Y	80	110	90	150	75	135	70	125
X	2	5	3	8	2	6	1	4

The regression equation is $\hat{Y} = 57.09 + 12.2X$ and $S_e = 9.428$.

a. Calculate $\Sigma(X - \bar{X})^2$.

b. Calculate S_b.

c. For H_o: $B = 0$ versus H_A: $B \neq 0$, and for $\alpha = .05$, determine the rejection region for H_o.

d. Calculate the t statistic.

e. What conclusion about H_o follows from your answers to parts c and d?

f. Would your answer to part e differ if $\alpha = .01$?

g. What are the upper and lower limits for the 95% confidence interval for B?

h. Make an inferential statement about your results in part g.

10.53 Using the data set and regression results given in Exercise 10.52, answer the following questions.

a. Calculate $S_{\hat{Y}.X}$ at $X = 4$ and at $X = 2$.

b. Calculate the point estimate of $\mu_{Y.X}$ at $X = 4$ and at $X = 2$.

c. Calculate the upper and lower limits for the 99% confidence interval for $\mu_{Y.X}$ at $X = 4$ and at $X = 2$.

d. Why is the width of the interval smaller at $X = 4$ than at $X = 2$?

e. Where is the width of the confidence interval for $\mu_{Y.X}$ the narrowest?

f. Make an inferential statement about your results in part c.

10.54 Using the data set and regression results given in Exercise 10.52, answer the following questions.

a. Calculate $S_{NEW.X}$ at $X = 4$ and at $X = 2$.

b. Calculate the point forecast of a new Y value at $X = 4$ and at $X = 2$. Why is it the same as your point estimate of $\mu_{Y.X}$ in part b of Exercise 10.53?

c. Calculate the upper and lower limits for the 95% prediction interval for a new Y value at $X = 4$ and at $X = 2$.

d. Why is the width of the prediction interval at $X = 4$ narrower than at $X = 2$?

e. Where is the width of the prediction interval the narrowest? How does this compare with your answer to part e of Exercise 10.53?

▶ **10.55** Using the data set provided in Exercise 10.39 and the following regression results, answer the questions below. The regression equation is $\hat{Y} = 1.686 + 1.057X$, and $S_e = 0.6969$.

a. Calculate $\Sigma(X - \bar{X})^2$.

b. Calculate S_b.

c. For $H_o: B = 0$ versus $H_A: B \neq 0$, and for $\alpha = .02$, determine the rejection region for H_o.

d. Calculate the t statistic.

e. What conclusion about H_o follows from your answers to parts c and d?

f. Would your answer to part e differ if $\alpha = .10$?

g. What are the upper and lower limits for the 98% confidence interval for B?

h. Make an inferential statement about your results in part g.

i. Explain why your results in part g confirm your conclusion in part e.

10.56 Using the data set provided in Exercise 10.39 and the regression results given in Exercise 10.55, answer the following questions.

a. Calculate $S_{\hat{Y}.X}$ at $X = 5$ and at $X = 6$.

b. Calculate the point estimate of $\mu_{Y.X}$ at $X = 5$ and at $X = 6$.

c. Explain why the $S_{\hat{Y}.X}$ results at $X = 5$ and at $X = 6$ are identical, yet the results for the point estimate of $\mu_{Y.X}$ at $X = 5$ and at $X = 6$ differ.

d. Calculate the upper and lower limits for the 98% confidence interval for $\mu_{Y.X}$ at $X = 5$ and at $X = 6$. What feature do these two intervals have in common besides the confidence level?

e. Where is the width of the confidence interval for $\mu_{Y.X}$ the narrowest?

f. Make an inferential statement about your results in part e.

▶ **10.57** Again using the data set provided in Exercise 10.39 and the regression results given in Exercise 10.55, answer the following questions.

a. Calculate $S_{NEW.X}$ at $X = 4$ and at $X = 7$.

b. Calculate the point forecast of a new Y value at $X = 4$ and at $X = 7$.

c. Explain why the $S_{NEW.X}$ results at $X = 4$ and at $X = 7$ are identical but the results for the point estimates of a new Y value at $X = 4$ and at $X = 7$ differ.

d. Calculate the upper and lower limits for the 98% prediction interval for an individual Y at $X = 4$ and at $X = 7$. What feature besides the confidence level do these intervals have in common?

e. Make an inferential statement about your results in part d.

f. Where is the prediction interval of a new Y value narrowest? How do these results compare with your answer to part e in Exercise 10.56?

10.58 A sample of 20 manufacturing companies was selected. For each sampled company, $X =$ Advertising expenditures (in thousands of dollars) and $Y =$ Gross sales (in millions of dollars) were recorded. Using the regression model $Y = A + BX + E$, the observed data gave the following regression equation statistics: $b = 0.03$, $S_e = 2$, $\Sigma(X - \bar{X})^2 = 40,000$.

a. For two firms differing by $1000 in advertising expenditures, what will be the estimated gross sales difference, on average?

b. What is the value of S_b?

c. Construct a 95% confidence interval for B.

10.59 Real estate appraisers depend on an appraisal tool called the *depth table* to calculate the value placed on additional lot depth. Data are collected on sales price per square foot for parcels of land differing in depth, but alike in all other important respects. Regression analysis is used to estimate the relationship between price per square foot and lot depth. The data in the table were collected.

DEPTH (IN FEET) X	SALE PRICE (DOLLARS PER SQUARE FOOT) Y	DEPTH (IN FEET) X	SALE PRICE (DOLLARS PER SQUARE FOOT) Y
20	1.05	120	3.10
30	1.38	130	3.70
40	1.90	140	3.43
50	1.80	150	3.46
60	1.88	160	3.98
70	2.38	170	3.90
80	2.45	180	4.55
90	2.37	190	4.25
100	2.00	200	4.49
110	2.86	210	4.35

a. Determine the fitted regression equation $\hat{Y} = a + bX$.

b. At $\alpha = .01$, test the two-sided hypothesis that sales price per square foot is unrelated to lot depth.

c. Find the 95% confidence interval for the additional amount of sales price per foot of depth.

d. For lots 175 ft deep, find the 99% confidence interval for mean price per square foot.

e. For a lot 175 ft deep, find the 99% prediction interval for sales price per square foot.

10.60 Consumer purchase decisions are generally viewed as a series of very complex processes involving many steps and several factors. This process complexity may obscure the fact that there may be an underlying simplicity to a successful brand strategy. Advertising agencies say that a brand's success is often explained by a single factor: the degree of *top-of-mind brand awareness* achieved. Top-of-mind brand awareness refers to the percentage of consumers who name this brand first when asked about brands in this product category. A regression analysis of market share versus brand awareness leads to the fitted regression equation

$$\hat{Y} = -5.20 + 0.64X$$

where $\hat{Y}$ is the brand's fitted market share and X is the level of consumer awareness achieved by the brand. From computer output, the following statistics are obtained: $S_e = 3.179$, $\Sigma(X - \bar{X})^2 = 3084.115$, $\bar{X} = 24.256$, $n = 25$, and $r^2 = 0.87$.

a. Compute S_b.

b. At $\alpha = .05$, test H_o: $B = 0$ versus H_A: $B > 0$.

c. For an awareness level of 35%, determine the 90% confidence interval for mean market share.

d. For an awareness level of 35%, determine the 90% prediction interval for mean market share.

e. If a brand wanted to increase its market share by 5%, what would be the estimated increase in brand awareness required?

f. Do you agree that increased brand awareness is an important key to increased market share? Explain.

10.61 The Technant Company produces high-technology components for 9 customers in a specialized industrial market segment. These companies are a small but representative fraction of the market segment. In making plans to achieve greater penetration of this market segment, Technant needs to estimate the market potential in this segment for the component parts it produces. Unfortunately, this market potential for components is not a published statistic, nor is it directly calculable. So Technant will have to estimate it based on knowledge of its 9 customer companies. A statistic that is available for all 9 customer companies and also for all the industry categories is employment. If Technant's sales can be related to its employment, then employment can be used to estimate potential sales in companies Technant doesn't currently sell to and then market potential can be estimated. For the 9 customers, we related actual Technant sales, Y, to customer company employment, X, by the regression equation $\hat{Y} = a + bX$. In the equation, we'll let the value of $\hat{Y}$ represent the estimated Technant sales potential for a company (in the market segment) that has X employees, whether or not that company is currently a Technant customer. The value of b represents the average additional Technant sales potential per additional customer employee. The value of a represents the average Technant sales to the customer company that is unrelated to customer employment. The data in the table give the number of employees and Technant sales for each customer. Employment data are available from government sources by industry category (e.g., average employees per firm, number of firms, etc.), so the equation (once determined from data on present customers) can then be applied to potential new customers as well.

				CUSTOMER NO.					
	1	**2**	**3**	**4**	**5**	**6**	**7**	**8**	**9**
TECHNANT SALES, Y (THOUSAND DOLLARS)	9.8	14.7	48.1	27.8	59.8	77.1	52.3	74.6	69.7
CUSTOMER EMPLOYEES, X	110	204	395	612	707	738	902	1045	1250

a. Determine the fitted regression equation.
b. At $X = 1000$ employees, what is the 95% confidence interval for $\mu_{Y \cdot X}$?
c. The U.S. Census of manufacturers reports that there are, on average, 830 employees for the 1000 companies that are prospective customers of Technant. Calculate potential Technant sales to a company that is a prospective customer and has 830 employees.
d. Estimate Technant sales potential among all 1000 companies that are prospective customers.

10.62 The Jackson Advertising Agency collects data on the relationship between consumer awareness of newly introduced personal care products and the number of advertising impressions purchased by the advertiser. A regression analysis of percent awareness, Y, on millions of impressions, X, gave the following regression equation and related statistics: $\hat{Y} = 20 + 0.4X$, and $S_e = 2$, $\Sigma(X - \bar{X})^2 = 40,000$, $\bar{X} = 110$, and $n = 100$.
a. For 100 million impressions, what is the 95% confidence interval for consumer awareness?
b. For 100 million impressions, what is the 95% prediction interval for consumer awareness of the new product?
c. What is the estimated mean increase in awareness for each additional 1 million impressions purchased, b?

d. What is the 95% confidence interval for B, the true mean increase estimated in part c?

10.63 The Levitt Consumer Research group collects data on the relationship between sales of newly introduced personal care products and the level of consumer awareness attained by the new product. Data were collated for a particular new brand. A regression analysis of sales (in millions of dollars) on awareness (in percent) gave the following regression equation and related statistics: $\hat{Y} = 20 + 1X$, and $S_e = 3$, $\Sigma(X - \bar{X})^2 = 10,000$, $\bar{X} = 60$, and $n = 81$.

a. For consumer awareness of 60%, what is the 90% confidence interval for mean sales?

b. For consumer awareness of 60%, what is the 90% prediction interval for sales of the new brand?

c. What is the 90% confidence interval for B, the mean increase in sales per additional percentage point of consumer awareness.

10.64 The Johnson Beauty Care Corporation expects profits (before deduction of advertising expenditures) from its new personal care product to equal 20% of sales. Assume the new product's advertising budget is $5 million and that advertising impressions are expected to cost $0.20 each. An estimate of profits was made using the following procedure:

a. Obtain an awareness estimate using the regression equation between awareness and impressions provided by its Jackson Advertising Agency in Exercise 10.62.

b. With your result from part a, use the regression equation between sales and awareness provided by the Levitt Consumer Research group in Exercise 10.63 to predict sales.

c. Determine expected profit from your predicted sales result from part b.

▶ **10.65** A hosiery mill conducted a study over the relevant range of pantyhose output of the relationship between cost and output. The following fitted regression equation resulted: $\hat{Y} = 2936 + 1.998X$, where $Y =$ Monthly cost of production in thousand dollars and $X =$ Dozens of pairs produced. Other statistics computed were $n = 43$, $S_e = 6110$, $r = 0.973$, and $S_b = 0.034$.

a. Find the 95% confidence interval for B.

b. What is the estimated incremental cost of an order for 1000 dozens of pairs of pantyhose?

c. What is the 95% confidence interval for the incremental cost of 1000 dozens of pairs of pantyhose?

10.66 The Sargeant Company systematically recorded the amount of new business that was obtained when salespeople were added or removed from sales territories. This made it possible to construct an index showing how new business responded to changes in the number of salespeople. Consider the case where a territory is cut in half; the ratio of the number of salespeople after the change to the number before the change is 2.0. Or if a sales force of 10 is reduced by 2, the ratio is 0.8. This salespeople ratio is the variable X; the ratio of new business after the change to business before the change is the variable Y. For example, suppose placing 2 salespeople in a territory results in 40% more new business than would be generated by a single salesperson; the new business ratio Y is 1.4 and the corresponding salesperson ratio X is 2.0. A regression analysis of the new business ratio on the salesperson ratio led to the following fitted regression equation and related statistics: $\hat{Y} = 0.5 + 0.4X$, and $S_e = 0.2$, $\Sigma(X - \bar{X})^2 = 2.5$, $\bar{X} = 1$, and $n = 25$.

a. For a salesperson ratio of 1.5, what is the 95% confidence interval for the mean new business ratio?

b. For a salesperson ratio of 1.5, what is the 95% confidence interval for the new business ratio?

SOLVING APPLIED CASES

This case uses business dialog to show how the regression line proves to be a very useful device for making predictions that will save time and money.

Using Regression Analysis to Estimate Daily Order Receipts

You are hired as a consultant to the operations manager (OM) at a plant of one of the large mail order houses that competes with Sears and JC Penney's. The plant, depending on the season, handles between 1000 and 4000 orders in a 10, 15, or 20 minute cycle. This means that during each cycle anywhere from 1000 to 4000 orders are being processed, assembled, and shipped through the same operational channels and by the same personnel. Any bottlenecking of machines and people because of poor planning will cause an overlapping of the cycles and result in complete chaos. Early knowledge of the number of orders to be processed on a particular day is essential in organizing a daily work plan. A method of forecasting each day's orders has been implemented, but it has been unsatisfactory.

Key Thought

Production bottlenecks are caused by inability to match available help with demand.

YOU: What is the nature of the problem that got you started using this forecasting method?

OM: Lack of a workable approach to cope with the tremendous daily fluctuation in the volume of orders to be processed. We were having bottlenecks on some days that caused complete chaos. On the other days we had people standing around idle. Corporate office budgets a certain number of people based on the anticipated total volume for a 3 or 4 month period, but our big problem is the day to day fluctuation. The orders don't come in at a steady rate.

YOU: Can't you borrow people from some other department to help on your busy days and pay them back on slack days?

OM: Yes. Of course, we have to let the managers of the other departments know at the beginning of the day how much help we need from them, so they can make the necessary adjustments in their own plans for that day.

YOU: So why were the day to day fluctuations a problem for you?

OM: Because we didn't know at the beginning of the day how much help we'd be needing.

YOU: Is that what led to your present forecasting method?

Key Thought

Forecasting volume by relating orders to weight of the mail.

OM: Yes. We started to keep a diary of the weight of each day's mail, X, and number of orders, Y, that resulted. We figured more mail meant more orders and we realized we would have to devise some way to forecast orders. At the end of 2 months we wanted to know on average, over the 2 months, how many orders there were per pound of mail. So for the number of mailbags we received over the 2 months, we totaled up the number of orders, ΣY, and the number of pounds of mail, ΣX. Dividing each figure by n gave us the average number of orders per mailbag and the average number of pounds of mail per mailbag. That is,

$$\frac{\Sigma Y}{n} = \frac{\text{Total number of orders}}{\text{Number of mailbags}}$$
$$= \text{Average number of orders} = \bar{Y} \text{ per bag}$$
$$\frac{\Sigma X}{n} = \frac{\text{Total weight of mail}}{\text{Number of mailbags}}$$
$$= \text{Average weight of mail} = \bar{X} \text{ per bag}$$

Dividing the two averages, $\bar{Y}$ and $\bar{X}$, gives us another average.

YOU: What was that average you calculated?

OM: Rounded, we got 33. We call this W, for the weight factor in estimating our orders. From the records, we found $\bar{Y} = 13,230$ and $\bar{X} = 400$. Then,

$$W = \frac{\bar{Y}}{\bar{X}} = \frac{(\Sigma\,Y)/n}{(\Sigma\,X)/n} = \frac{13,230}{400} = 33.08$$

You can think of W as the number of orders per pound of mail, on average.

YOU: I see how you can interpret W as the number of orders, on average, per pound of mail, but how do you use this average to forecast orders?

Key Thought

The estimating equation (pre-regression).

OM: Every morning we weigh the mail and multiply the weight by 33 to estimate the number of orders we'll have to process. From that, we determine how many people we'll need that day. For example, if the mail weighs 200 lb, we'll estimate 6600 orders; if the mail weighs 500 lb, we'll estimate 16,500 orders. (Note: The formula used is $Y^* = WX$, where Y^* is the estimated number of orders.)

YOU: Did this forecasting method solve the problem?

OM: It helped, but not as much as we thought it would. For some reason, we are still making big errors in estimating orders. That's why you were called in.

YOU: Let me guess. Are you having trouble with your forecasts on days when the mail is especially heavy? On those days, do you usually underestimate and ask for less help than you actually need?

OM: Yes. How could you know?

YOU: And on days when the mail is lighter than usual, you quite often overestimate your actual needs?

OM: Don't keep me in suspense. Tell me what is going on!

YOU: I think your estimating equation can be improved. An estimating equation of the form $\hat{Y} = a + bX$ may give smaller errors. The term b will relate changes in orders to changes in weight in mailbags.

Key Thought

Developing the regression line estimating equation.

OM: How do we find out whether this type equation will help?

YOU: We'll start by graphing the data you collected. Let's plot daily observations: the daily number of orders on the vertical axis and mail weight for the same day on the horizontal axis. We call this graph a scatter diagram, or scatterplot.

OM: What will the a term represent?

YOU: There may be mail in the mailbags that aren't orders, and it is this factor that causes you to underestimate your need for help on days when the mail is especially heavy, and to overestimate your need for help when the mail is lighter than usual. The a term will reflect this factor.

OM: How are the a and b values determined?

YOU: If the flow of the data follows a linear pattern, we can use a statistical technique called linear regression analysis to obtain that estimation line, which I'm convinced will improve your forecasts.

After running the regression analysis, here's what the computer printout showed. The fitted regression equation came out to be

$$\hat{Y} = -8.15 + 5.345X$$

where X = Weight of mailbags ($\times$ 100 lb) and $\hat{Y}$ = Thousands of orders. Thus, according to this equation, orders increase, on average, by 5345 for each 100 lb increase in the weight of the mailbags, or by 53.45 orders for each additional pound of mail.

Look at the scatter diagram. On it, I've drawn your pre-regression estimation line and the fitted regression line (see Figure 10.25). You can see that the fitted regression line provides a better fit to the data you've collected. More importantly, you'll be able to make much more accurate forecasts of orders using the regression equation.

OM: So I shouldn't use our average of 33 orders per pound of mail in forecasting anymore?

Key Thought

Interpreting the regression equation.

YOU: Right. On an average day (400 lb of mail), you'll still estimate 13,230 orders just as before, but (based on the slope coefficient of 5345 orders for each additional 100 lb of mail) for each pound of mail above 400 you'll now add approximately 53 orders to your estimate

Figure 10.25
Comparison of pre–regression line and regression prediction line

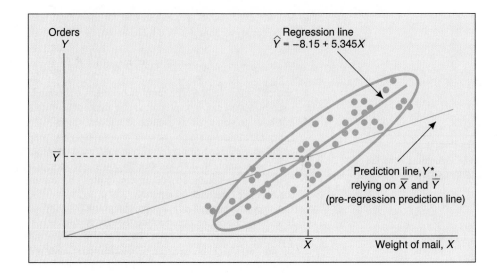

rather than 33. Likewise, you'll deduct 53 orders from the 13,230 for every pound of mail below 400. What this means is that on that 500 lb day you'll estimate 18,575 orders rather than the 16,500 you told me. On the 200 lb days you'll estimate 2480 rather than the 6600 orders you told me. I think the new forecasts will make your life a lot easier around here.

OM: I agree, but why are your regression equation estimates so much more accurate?

YOU: Your old method assumes that orders are proportional to the weight of the mailbags. The forecast is doubled only when the weight of the bags is doubled. The regression estimate doesn't assume this. It recognizes that the bags contain mail other than orders and that changes in the amount of this mail aren't necessarily linked to the number of orders.

OM: You said the *a* term in the estimation equation reflects this factor. If that's so, I don't understand the meaning of a negative value for *a*.

YOU: I said the term *reflects* this factor. I didn't say that it *measures* how much of this type of mail you have. The *a* term is merely an extrapolation of the straight line estimating equation to the Y axis, where X = 0. You don't actually have any days when mailbag weight is 0. Even on days when there are very few orders, the mailbags may be heavy with mail that has nothing to do with new orders.

Checkpoint Exercises

1. On a day when the mailbags weigh 600 lb, what is the estimated number of orders, determined from the least squares fitted regression equation? From the pre-regression estimating equation?
2. Which method of estimation gave the larger estimate in Exercise 1?
3. On a day when mailbags weigh 300 lb, what is the estimated number of orders determined from the fitted regression equation? From the pre-regression estimating equation?
4. Which method of estimation gave the larger estimate in Exercise 3?
5. Suppose one observed data point in Figure 10.25 showed that at X = 500 lb, Y = 18,200 orders. What would be the estimation error if Y had been estimated by using the fitted regression equation at X = 500? Using the pre-regression estimating equation?
6. Compute the absolute difference between the pre-regression estimation error and the fitted regression line estimation error from Exercise 5 (i.e., compute Y^* pre-regression $- \hat{Y}$ regression).
7. Would you expect the difference found in Exercise 6 to be larger or smaller than a difference computed for a data point having X = 600? X = 450? Explain.

WENDY'S DATABASE ANALYSIS

Importance of Food Taste

Fast food restaurants are in business to sell food profitably. Intense competition in the fast food industry forces every brand to pay close attention to the taste of the food they serve. Three of the major brands in the survey—Wendy's, McDonald's, and Burger King—are perceived as serving food that tastes very good. This can be seen from Figure 10.26 which presents food taste images for the brands. Wendy's has the most favorable image on food taste as measured by its mean rating, but the mean ratings of McDonald's and Burger King are only slightly less favorable. This slim Wendys' advantage on food taste image raises several important questions.

1. Food taste image and brand preference: How close is the relationship?

First, what is the relationship between a brand's image on food taste and the preference of

```
MTB > mean c103 k1
   MEAN    =      4.2552
MTB > mean c104 k2
   MEAN    =      4.0911
MTB > mean c105 k3
   MEAN    =      3.0052
MTB > mean c106 k4
   MEAN    =      2.2429
MTB > mean c107 k5
   MEAN    =      2.5351
MTB > mean c108 k6
   MEAN    =      4.7812
MTB > stack k1-k6 c200
MTB > print c200


C200
    4.25521    4.09115    3.00518    2.24289    2.53506    4.78125


MTB > mean c27 k27
   MEAN    =      3.5659
MTB > mean c28 k28
   MEAN    =      3.3290
MTB > mean c29 k29
   MEAN    =      2.4231
MTB > mean c30 k30
   MEAN    =      2.0895
MTB > mean c31 k31
   MEAN    =      1.9661
MTB > mean c32 k32
   MEAN    =      3.8061
MTB > stack k27-k32 c201
MTB > name c200 'meanpref' c201 'meantast'
MTB > print c200-c201

   ROW   meanpref   meantast

     1    4.25521    3.56589    BORDEN BURGER
     2    4.09115    3.32902    HARDEE'S
     3    3.00518    2.42308    BURGER KING
     4    2.24289    2.08951    MC DONALDS
     5    2.53506    1.96615    WENDY'S
     6    4.78125    3.80612    WHITE CASTLE
```

Figure 10.26
MINITAB output for mean ratings on preference and food taste for six brands

consumers for that brand? We know (from the responses to question 21) that consumers rate food taste as important, but they rate other variables as important, too. With food taste being only one of many factors influencing food choice, what can be said about the importance of a highly favorable image on food taste? Is it essential or unimportant in achieving consumer preference over other brands? Has any brand achieved a strong consumer preference rating without a highly favorable image on food taste?

Some of these questions can be answered by comparing the mean preference ratings of the six brands with their images (mean rating) on food taste. A scatter diagram is useful for this purpose. To construct the scatter diagram the six brand means on food taste must be put into one column and the six brand means on brand preference must be put into another column. The MINITAB worksheet shown in Figure 10.26 indicates the commands required for the mean values on brand preference and on food taste to be computed, put into columns C200 and C201, and named "meanpref" and "meantast," respectively. The MINITAB command PLOT then produces the scatter diagram of the mean ratings, as shown in Figure 10.27.

From the diagram it is apparent that the two variables are positively related. Not a single brand has achieved a high preference rating without having a good food taste image.

To describe the relationship in quantitative terms, we can determine the regression equation relating "meanpref" and "meantast." This is done using the command REGRESS, as shown in Figure 10.28.

The value of r^2 reported in Figure 10.28 is 0.975, or 97.5%, meaning that 97.5% of the variation among brands in their mean preference ratings is explained by the variation in their mean ratings on food taste. So the explanatory power of the regression equation is very high. What about the fit of the regression line? Recalling that S on output is S_e, the small S_e value of 0.1833 indicates a very close fit of the fitted regression line to the data points. The MINITAB output gives the equation for the fitted regression line as

$$\text{Fitted mean preference} = -0.160 + 1.27(\text{Mean taste})$$

The slope coefficient (b value) of 1.27 is noteworthy. It indicates that, on average, a 1 unit difference between brands in their mean food taste ratings is associated with a difference of 1.27 in their mean preference ratings. A 1 unit difference in mean food taste ratings is well within

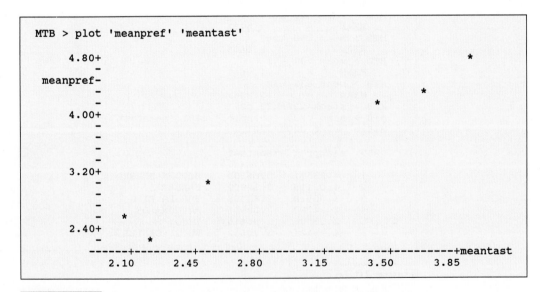

Figure 10.27
MINITAB scatter diagram of mean preference ratings versus mean food taste ratings

```
MTB > regress 'meanpref' 1 'meantast'

The regression equation is
meanpref = - 0.160 + 1.27 meantast

Predictor        Coef        Stdev      t-ratio        p
Constant       -0.1603       0.3028       -0.53      0.625
meantast        1.2732       0.1025       12.42      0.000

s = 0.1833      R-sq = 97.5%      R-sq(adj) = 96.8%

Analysis of Variance

SOURCE          DF           SS          MS          F         p
Regression       1        5.1820      5.1820     154.31     0.000
Error            4        0.1343      0.0336
Total            5        5.3163
```

Figure 10.28
MINITAB regression analysis of mean preference versus mean food taste ratings

the actually observed range of 3.81–1.97 for the six brands. Yet the corresponding difference of 1.27 in mean preference ratings is substantial enough to reverse the positions of a competing pair of brands and probably make corporate heads roll in the fast food chain that loses market position. So the *b* value indicates that a small difference in food taste can have a powerful influence on brand preference.

2. How pervasive is Wendy's taste image?

Knowing the importance of food taste image in explaining brand preference, how can Wendy's fragile lead in mean ratings on food taste be improved? Two approaches can be contrasted.

- *Across-the-board approach.* Wendy's can try to improve every fast food user's image of Wendy's food taste, even if only by a small amount.

- *Targeted conversion approach.* Wendy's can concentrate efforts on converting selected groups of consumers who presently rate another brand more favorably than Wendy's but might be good candidates for conversion.

Which approach is better? To help examine this issue about the food taste variable we must look at the rating difference given by each individual consumer to Wendy's and its competitor. If we find that nearly everyone's preference ratings among the brands on food taste are identical, this would be an argument in favor of the across-the-board approach. But if we find strong disagreement among consumers on brand food taste ratings, this would be an argument in favor of the targeted conversion approach.

We start by creating a new variable, DIFTASTE, representing each individual respondent's difference between his or her Wendy's rating and McDonald's rating on the food taste attribute (responses are listed in columns 31 and 30, respectively). To construct and name the variable DIFTASTE in MINITAB, we use the commands LET and NAME, as shown in Figure 10.29. The assigned column of the newly created rating difference data is C151. The command to construct the histogram for these differences is HIST 'DIFTASTE'. The histogram for the difference in food taste ratings between Wendy's and McDonald's is shown in Figure 10.29.

```
MTB > let c151 = c31-c30
MTB > name c151 'diftaste' #wendys rating minus mcdon rating
MTB > hist 'diftaste'

Histogram of diftaste   N = 381   N* = 25
Each * represents 5 obs.

Midpoint   Count
      -5       4  *
      -4       2  *
      -3      13  ***
      -2      30  ******
      -1      87  ******************
       0     155  *******************************
       1      46  *********
       2      21  *****
       3      14  ***
       4       7  **
       5       2  *

MTB > describe 'diftaste'

                 N       N*     MEAN    MEDIAN   TRMEAN    STDEV   SEMEAN
diftaste       381       25  -0.1207   0.0000  -0.1370   1.5117   0.0774

               MIN      MAX       Q1       Q3
diftaste   -5.0000   5.0000  -1.0000   0.0000
```

Figure 10.29
MINITAB histogram and mean of DIFTASTE (Wendy's rating minus McDonald's rating)

From the spread of the DIFTASTE histogram it appears that considerable rating variation exists among the individual fast food consumers who rated Wendy's and McDonald's. Moreover, the spread of DIFTASTE makes it evident that there is not a clear consensus among fast food consumers that Wendy's has better tasting food than McDonald's. Quite the contrary, nearly as many people rated McDonald's taste over Wendy's as the other way around. These are the consumers Wendy's must concentrate on to improve their image of Wendy's. It begins to look as though the targeted conversion approach might be better than the across-the-board approach. But wait. There are some other issues we need to look into.

The consumers who have a better image of McDonald's food than Wendy's have maintained their brand perceptions in spite of intensive Wendy's advertising campaigns. Wendy's pursues a policy and advertising campaign to make customers aware that Wendy's uses only fresh meat rather than frozen patties; cooks the hamburger only on order rather than precooking in large batches; allows for individual garnishing in a much simpler way; and makes Wendy's "frosty" shakes thicker than McDonald's. All these features were designed to gain for Wendy's a taste advantage over McDonald's—one sufficient to offset Wendy's higher menu prices. Then, what causes so many people to rate McDonald's taste higher than Wendy's? Do they really prefer McDonald's food? Or are they simply unfamiliar with Wendy's food, in which case targeted promotional efforts might help familiarize them with Wendy's advantages?

3. Brand familiarity: Is it related to food taste image?

Among the three brands, Wendy's, McDonald's, and Burger King, consumers are least familiar with Wendy's—it has the worst rating on mean familiarity. Is Wendy's food taste image, good as it is, being hurt by Wendy's comparative unfamiliarity? Could it be that as consumers become more familiar with Wendy's, they are more likely to recognize the Wendy's difference?

To compare food taste image with familiarity by brand, we will need the mean familiarity rating for each of the six brands. Using the MINITAB commands MEAN and STACK once again, the mean familiarity was found for each brand, as shown in Figure 10.30. The PLOT command was then used to obtain the scatter diagram of mean taste versus mean familiarity shown.

The MINITAB command REGRESS permits us to investigate the relationship between each brand's food taste ratings and each brand's familiarity ratings. From Figure 10.31 we obtain the following regression equation describing the relationship:

$$\text{Fitted mean taste} = 0.01 + 1.22(\text{Mean familiarity})$$

The positive b value of 1.22 indicates that greater familiarity is indeed associated with more favorable ratings of food taste. On average, each 1 point difference in mean familiarity between brands is associated with an improvement of 1.22 points in food taste rating between brands.

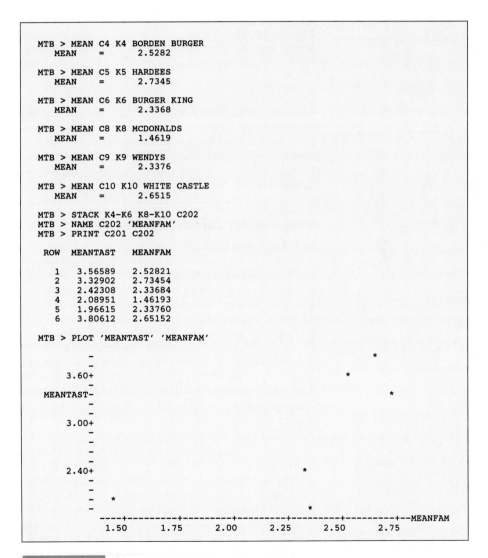

Figure 10.30
MINITAB calculations and scatter diagram of mean taste ratings versus mean familiarity ratings

```
MTB > regress 'meantast' 1 'meanfam'

The regression equation is
meantast = 0.01 + 1.22 meanfam

Predictor      Coef      Stdev     t-ratio        p
Constant      0.005      1.471       0.00      0.997
meanfam      1.2204      0.6183       1.97      0.120

s = 0.6363     R-sq = 49.3%     R-sq(adj) = 36.7%

Analysis of Variance

SOURCE         DF          SS          MS          F          p
Regression      1      1.5773      1.5773       3.90      0.120
Error           4      1.6196      0.4049
Total           5      3.1969
```

Figure 10.31
MINITAB regression output for mean taste ratings versus mean familiarity ratings

Here we see that familiarity appears to breed affection, not contempt. Consumers give high food taste ratings to the brands with which they are more familiar. The value of r^2 is 0.493, so the variation in mean familiarity rating accounts for 49.3% of the variation in mean food taste ratings.

These findings suggest an interesting question: If Wendy's could somehow close the "familiarity gap" with McDonald's, would its mean food taste ratings improve? The answer depends on the presumed direction of causality between familiarity and food taste ratings. In principle, an improved food taste image could either lead to greater familiarity or follow from it.

Brand Familiarity and Locational Convenience

Some insight into the direction of causality can be achieved by considering the linkage between familiarity and the locational convenience of fast food restaurants. McDonald's has many more outlets than Wendy's, a factor favoring McDonald's and likely contributing to its better rating than Wendy's on convenient location. But does this greater convenience image affect familiarity? If Wendy's familiarity rating is statistically related to its rating on locational convenience, then the relative inconvenience of Wendy's locations becomes important. It quite plausibly explains the "familiarity gap" between Wendy's and McDonald's.

To study the relationship between familiarity and convenience, the mean convenience ratings must be computed. The MINITAB commands MEAN and STACK are again used to obtain the mean rating on convenience, "meanconv." The results and a scatter diagram of "meanfam" and "meanconv" are shown in Figure 10.32. The MINITAB command REGRESS is again used to obtain the regression analysis. Figure 10.33 shows the regression equation describing the relationship to be

Fitted mean familiarity = 0.425 + 0.663(Mean convenience)

The equation indicates that, on average, each 1 point difference in convenience rating among the brands is associated with an improvement of 0.663 point in familiarity ratings among the brands. The explanatory power of the equation, measured by r^2, is 0.777. This means that the variation in mean convenience accounts for 77.7% of the variation in mean familiarity ratings. This equation helps us understand the path of effects—namely, that the path starts with greater convenience and leads to greater patronage and onto greater familiarity. It would be difficult to claim the reverse path from a business perspective; that is, it would be difficult to claim that greater patronage leads to greater convenience.

What Has Been Learned, and a Next Step

Why is Wendy's food perceived overall as best tasting among the fast food brands according to its mean rating, yet actually rated worse than McDonald's by about half of the consumers? At least part of the explanation now appears linked to the fact that Wendy's outlets are less conveniently reached than McDonald's. This comparative inconvenience leads to fewer Wendy's visits and consequently less familiarity with Wendy's. Lesser familiarity means fewer opportunities for consumers to recognize and appreciate whatever food taste advantages Wendy's offers.

What remedy should Wendy's pursue, if management accepts this line of reasoning? One tactic Wendy's should consider is the construction of new Wendy's outlets. Greater locational convenience would lead to more familiarity and, in turn, an improved food taste image among its target customers. Given the close relationship between food taste image and brand preference, an improved food taste image ought to move Wendy's higher on the all-important customer preference scale.

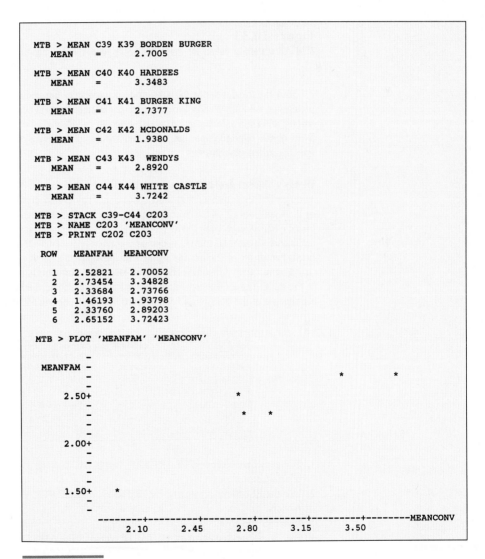

Figure 10.32
MINITAB calculations and scatter diagram of mean familiarity ratings versus mean convenience ratings

```
MTB > regress 'meanfam' 1 'meanconv'

The regression equation is
meanfam = 0.425 + 0.663 meanconv

Predictor        Coef       Stdev     t-ratio         p
Constant       0.4249      0.5224        0.81     0.462
meanconv       0.6632      0.1775        3.74     0.020

s = 0.2428      R-sq = 77.7%      R-sq(adj) = 72.2%

Analysis of Variance

SOURCE          DF          SS          MS         F        p
Regression       1     0.82320     0.82320     13.97    0.020
Error            4     0.23574     0.05894
Total            5     1.05895
```

Figure 10.33
MINITAB regression output for mean familiarity ratings versus mean convenience ratings

But do these relationships among convenience, familiarity, food taste image, and brand preference hold for Wendy's most important customers—its heavy users? Additional verification among this key customer group is requested in the following exercises. Validation among heavy users of the relationships just described would further substantiate Wendy's consideration of opening additional outlets.

Wendy's Student Exercises

The heavy user group of fast food customers are defined as those respondents who answer 1 or 2 on question 2 of the Wendy's questionnaire. For this heavy user group, the mean ratings for (1) heavy user preference (HUPREF), (2) heavy user taste (HUTASTE), (3) heavy user familiarity (HUFAM), and (4) heavy user convenience (HUCONV) were computed and are listed below for all six of the brands studied in the survey.

Figure 10.34 illustrates the use of MINITAB commands to obtain the mean ratings given in the table. The COPY command shows how to segregate the heavy user group; also illustrated are the use of the MEAN and STACK commands to obtain HUPREF and HUTASTE.

BRAND	HUPREF	HUTASTE	HUFAM	HUCONV
Borden Burger	4.39	3.67	2.53	2.78
Hardee's	4.07	3.22	2.59	3.34
Burger King	2.86	2.22	2.07	2.34
McDonald's	2.14	1.99	1.26	1.81
Wendy's	2.44	1.74	2.10	2.90
White Castle	5.02	3.95	3.67	3.56

1. Plot a scatter diagram of HUPREF versus HUTASTE. Do the points suggest a linear relationship?
2. Use the REGRESS command for HUPREF on HUTASTE. What is the regression equation? r_2? S_e?
3. Interpret the equation found in Exercise 2.
4. Plot a scatter diagram of HUTASTE versus HUFAM. Do the points suggest a linear relationship?
5. Use the REGRESS command for HUTASTE on HUFAM. What is the regression equation? r^2? S_e?

```
MTB > RETRIEVE 'WENDYS406'
MTB > NAME C2 'HVY'
MTB > COPY C27-C32 C156-C161;
SUBC> USE 'HVY'=1,2.
MTB > COPY C103-C108 C168-C173;
SUBC> USE 'HVY'=1,2.

MTB > MEAN C168 K1
   MEAN    =        4.3908
MTB > MEAN C169 K2
   MEAN    =        4.0686
MTB > MEAN C170 K3
   MEAN    =        2.8629
MTB > MEAN C171 K4
   MEAN    =        2.1437
MTB > MEAN C172 K5
   MEAN    =        2.4425
MTB > MEAN C173 K6
   MEAN    =        5.0230
MTB > STACK K1-K6 C200
MTB > NAME C200 'HUPREF'
```

Mean Preference Rating for Borden Burger Among Heavy User	= 4.3908
Mean Preference Rating for Hardee's Among Heavy User	= 4.0686
Mean Preference Rating for Burger King Among Heavy User	= 2.8629
Mean Preference Rating for McDonald's Among Heavy User	= 2.1437
Mean Preference Rating for Wendy's Among Heavy User	= 2.4425
Mean Preference Rating for White Castle Among Heavy User	= 5.0230

```
MTB > MEAN C156 K1
   MEAN    =        3.6685
MTB > MEAN C157 K2
   MEAN    =        3.2203
MTB > MEAN C158 K3
   MEAN    =        2.2247
MTB > MEAN C159 K4
   MEAN    =        1.9944
MTB > MEAN C160 K5
   MEAN    =        1.7429
MTB > MEAN C161 K6
   MEAN    =        3.9489
MTB > STACK K1-K6 C201
MTB > NAME C201 'HUTASTE'
```

Mean Taste Rating for Borden Burger Among Heavy User	= 3.6685
Mean Taste Rating for Hardee's Among Heavy User	= 3.2203
Mean Taste Rating for Burger King Among Heavy User	= 2.2247
Mean Taste Rating for McDonald's Among Heavy User	= 1.9944
Mean Taste Rating for Wendy's Among Heavy User	= 1.7429
Mean Taste Rating for White Castle Among Heavy User	= 3.9489

Figure 10.34
MINITAB commands used to segregate heavy user group and obtain the mean ratings of HUPREF and HUTASTE for the six brands

6. Interpret the equation determined in Exercise 5.
7. Plot a scatter diagram of HUFAM versus HUCONV. Do the points suggest a linear relationship?
8. Use the REGRESS command for HUFAM on HUCONV. What is the regression equation? r^2? S_e?
9. Interpret the equation determined in Exercise 8.
10. What conclusions do you draw from your findings?

WENDY'S DATABASE ANALYSIS, Continued

Introduction: Regression Inference

We have found that a relationship between brand preference and brand food taste for Wendy's data was found effective for prediction. Let's now investigate that relationship from the standpoint of regression inference.

The regression equation investigated for brand preference and brand food taste showed that a brand's mean food taste image can be useful as a predictor variable of a brand's mean preference rating. Well over 90% of the variation in mean preference ratings of a brand was explained by variation in a brand's mean food taste ratings ($r^2 = 0.975$). But, with only six observations to work with in the sample (six brands), is the relationship found in the sample statistically reliable? Is the relationship statistically significant (not merely a sampling fluke), so that we can conclude that there exists a relationship in the population?

Regression Inference: Testing the Relationship between Brand Preference Rating and Brand Food Taste Image

Suppose we accept as a working premise that the required assumptions for regression inference are met. Then, values given in the Wendy's MINITAB regression output can be used to test the null hypothesis of no population relationship between mean preference rating for a brand and the brand's mean food taste image. Let's test the relationship at the $\alpha = .01$ level of significance. That is,

$$H_o: \quad B = 0 \quad \text{(There exists no relationship.)}$$

$$H_A: \quad B \neq 0 \quad \text{(There exists a relationship.)}$$

With $\alpha = .01$, $\alpha/2 = .005$, and we find from the t table (Table VII) that, at $n - 2 = 4$ d.f., $t_{.005,4} = 4.604$. So the rejection region is

$$t_{n-2} < -4.604 \quad \text{or} \quad t_{n-2} > +4.604$$

The MINITAB regression output reports the values $b = 1.2732$, $S_b = 0.1025$, and

$$t \text{ ratio} = \frac{b - 0}{S_b}$$

$$= \frac{1.2732}{0.1025} = 12.42.$$

Since the observed t value of 12.42 greatly exceeds 4.604, we reject H_o and conclude that the results are highly statistically significant. That is, the statistical evidence strongly suggests that mean brand preference ratings are directly related to a brand's food taste image. It also means that despite the small number of data points, the relationship found in the sample between these two variables is not likely to be a sampling fluke.

Regression Inference: Interval Estimation of the Mean Preference Rating, Given the Food Taste Rating

Turning to estimation, we can see that the observable range for ratings (image) of food taste is from 1.97 (the best image) for Wendy's to 3.81 (the worst image) for White Castle. Within what range or for what interval estimate are we confident to find the mean preference rating of a brand, given its food taste rating?

Since we have found a statistically reliable relationship between food taste rating and preference rating, we can use the relationship to good advantage. In particular, we can use it for the purpose of estimating the preference rating for a given value of food taste rating. Let's use the brand's mean rating, $X = 2.2$, to obtain an interval estimate for the mean taste preference rating, Y. Using the PREDICT subcommand, MINITAB will compute both the 95% confidence interval for the mean of all Y's, $\mu_{Y.X}$ and the 95% prediction interval for an individual new Y value at $X = 2.2$. The commands are as follows:

MTB > **regress** 'meanpref' 1 'meantast';

SUBC > **predict** $X = 2.2$.

MINITAB output then shows, after the regression results, the following extra lines:

FIT	STDEV.FIT	95% C.I.	95% P.I.
2.6406	0.1011	(2.3599, 2.9214)	(2.0594, 3.2218)

From this output we see that at $X = 2.2$, the fitted value is $\hat{Y} = 2.6406$. That is, the fitted mean preference rating (the point estimate of $\mu_{Y.X}$ at $X = 2.2$) is the value 2.6406. The "Stdev.Fit" value of $S_{\hat{Y}.X}$ is 0.1011 at $X = 2.2$; the 95% confidence interval estimate is the range 2.36–2.92 (rounded). In other words, we can conclude from the MINITAB output that with 95% confidence, the interval between 2.36 and 2.92 contains the true value of the mean brand preference rating when mean food taste has a value of 2.2. With respect to prediction, the MINITAB output tells us that 95% of the time, we can expect to find an individual brand mean preference rating to have a value from 2.06 to 3.22 (rounded) when mean food taste has a value of 2.2. The wider range for an individual Y value versus the range for the mean of all Y's reflects the greater uncertainty associated with predicting an individual value.

Wendy's Student Exercises

Let's now look further into the relationship between brand preference ratings and brand food taste image for the heavy user customer group.

The data in the table report for heavy users the mean preference (HUPREF) and the mean food taste image (HUTASTE) across the six brands

BRAND	HUPREF	HUTASTE
Borden Burger	4.39	3.67
Hardee's	4.07	3.22
Burger King	2.86	2.22
McDonald's	2.14	1.99
Wendy's	2.44	1.74
White Castle	5.02	3.95

Using the MINITAB command REGRESS, with its subcommand PREDICT, the following selective results were obtained:

```
MTB>REGRESS 'hupref' 1 'hutaste';
SUBC>PREDICT X=2.2.
The regression equation is:
  hupref = .057 + 1.23 hutaste
```

Predictor	Coef	Stdev	t-ratio
Constant	0.0572	0.3446	
hutaste	1.2256	0.1178	

S=0.2463   R-sq=96.4%   R-sq(Adj)=95.5%

Fit	Stdev. Fit	95% C.I.	95% P.I.
	0.123	( )	( )

11. Calculate the missing t ratios and test the null hypothesis of no relationship ($B = 0$) setting $\alpha = .05$.

12. From the results in Exercise 11, make a concluding statement about the relationship between brand preference and brand taste for the heavy user group.

13. Calculate the missing fitted value for the prediction at $X = 2.2$.

14. Determine the 95% confidence interval for the mean of Y at $X = 2.2$, and draw a conclusion.

15. Determine the 95% prediction interval for an individual new Y value at $X = 2.2$, and draw a conclusion. (*Hint:* To determine $S_{NEW.X}$, use the relationship between $S_{NEW.X}$ and S_e and $S_{\hat{Y}.X}$ described in Section 10.10.)

MULTIPLE REGRESSION AND MODELING

THE DOMESDAY PROJECT: USING STATISTICAL ANALYSIS TO REWRITE ELEVENTH CENTURY ECONOMIC HISTORY

Computer power is creating a new window to view economic history. Greater computing power, along with the lesser cost of processing massive amounts of data, have encouraged the investigation of new questions and the reexamination of old ones. Dramatic benefits may result from being able to deal systematically with large amounts of data by modern statistical analysis. One unusual example is the Domesday (pronounced "doomsday") Project.

In 1085, William of Normandy, eager to have an accurate accounting of the wealth of the kingdom of England, which he had conquered 20 years earlier, commissioned a complete census of the English land under his rule. Detailed information about the ownership of land, the extent of ownership, and the valuation of the ownership was gathered and recorded on parchment.

Completed in 1086, it represented then, as it still does today, the definitive document for settling legal disputes on property rights. Hence, the parchment book holding these recordings gained the widespread reputation as the "last judgment," or "Domesday book."

The Domesday book is a motherlode of England's political and economic statistics from that time. Now these statistics have been converted into a computer database, and intense statistical investigation is being conducted. The results of the statistical analyses on the Domesday statistics are forcing economic historians to modify their understanding of the economic forces at work in eleventh century England. Major research projects using the Domesday statistical database are underway at the University of California at Santa Barbara, and in Australia at Flinders.

The relationship between taxation and wealth during the Domesday era was explored by applying modern statistical analysis to the Domesday database. Was the amount of tax levied on an English manor linked to the economic ability (wealth) of the manor to pay the tax? Or only to the political power of the manor's owner? Historians had long believed that only political power mattered.

Now, putting computer power to work, the issue has been examined by means of *multiple regression equations*, and some interesting results have been produced. The number of plough teams, laborers, slaves, pastures, meadows, mills, horses, and other individual factors that define manorial economic resources, are stated as explanatory variables. The tax assessments imposed by King William are used as the dependent variable. The evidence from the multiple regression equations is now clear: Considered collectively, these economic resources were a major determinant explaining the level of taxes levied on the English manors. The economic wherewithal to pay, not merely political power, was a major consideration for William's administrators in deciding the amount of the tax and on whom the tax burden should fall.*

In this chapter we'll discuss the basic methodology of multiple regression analysis and the applications of this methodology to business. The applied cases at the end of the chapter further emphasize how multiple regression's versatility can help tackle important business problems.

Overview

This chapter extends to more than two variables the regression ideas introduced in Chapter 10, where a simple regression equation linked a dependent variable Y to an independent variable X. When simple regression is inadequate, we may include in a *multiple regression equation* two or more explanatory variables, say X_1 and X_2. By doing this, we hope to improve the accuracy of predicting Y or to provide a numerical estimate of the responsiveness of Y to the various factors that affect it.

Among the types of questions we shall try to explore in this chapter are the following:

- What will happen to Y if there is a 3 unit increase in X_1 and simultaneously a 2 unit decrease in X_2?
- Which of the estimated regression coefficients are statistically significant?
- What is the prediction gain achieved by including more than one explanatory variable?
- How can we accommodate qualitative variables (such as gender) and deal with nonlinear patterns in the data?
- What special statistical problems or concerns should we be aware of when multiple regression is used?

11.1 INTRODUCTION

The computer has opened the door to the use of *multiple regression* techniques to explore highly complex business issues. Readily available computer programs now solve—in just a few seconds—multiple regression equations that previously were too burdensome or too time-consuming to solve. Here are a few situations that demonstrate the value of multiple regression as an analytical tool in examining business issues. In all three situations, a knowledge of what constitutes a multiple regression equation and how it works is necessary.

- Ford Motor of Dearborn has decided to determine an equation linking the sales of its new high-performance cars with two key determinants of car purchases: the price of the car and the target consumer's personal income.

*The following articles by John McDonald and Graeme Snooks describe the computer analysis of the Domesday book: Statistical analysis of Domesday Book (1086), *Journal of the Royal Statistical Society*, Series A (General) *148*, Pt. 2, 1985, 147–160. The determinants of manorial income in Domesday England: Evidence from Essex, *Journal of Economic History*, 45, Sept. 1985, 541–555. Were the tax assessments of Domesday England artificial? The case of Essex, *Economic History Review*, 2nd Series, 38(3), Aug. 1985, 352–372.

- Boston's Strategic Planning Institute is a business think-tank. One of its research projects is to investigate the link between the amount of a firm's executive compensation (dependent variable) and such characteristics (explanatory variables) as the size of the company's assets, the company's 5 year sales growth rate, and the company's 3 year average return on equity. The relationship between these variables and the level of executive compensation is expressed by a multiple regression equation that will be published and used by corporate sponsors.

- Price Waterhouse is one of the "big four" accounting firms that is also strong in consulting services. A client of its New York management consultant group wants Price Waterhouse to evaluate and improve the client company's cost accounting regression equation. That equation links company operating costs to its level of output and its mix of product lines.

11.2
MULTIPLE REGRESSION EQUATION

A multiple linear regression equation consists of one dependent Y variable and several independent X variables, called **explanatory variables** or **predictor variables**. If there are k explanatory variables, $X_1, X_2, \ldots, X_i, \ldots, X_k$, then the fitted multiple regression equation is given as follows:

Fitted Multiple Regression Equation

$$\hat{Y} = a + b_1 X_1 + b_2 X_2 + \cdots + b_i X_i + \cdots + b_k X_k \qquad (11\text{-}1)$$

where $\hat{Y}$ is the estimated (or fitted) value of the variable Y, X_i is the ith explanatory variable, b_i is the value of its corresponding regression coefficient, and a is the Y intercept. The equation shows that a value of $\hat{Y}$ is determined by the value of a and the aggregate of the products of the X_i's and their corresponding b_i coefficients. This chapter discusses the development of the multiple regression equation when there are two explanatory variables, X_1 and X_2; that is,

$$\hat{Y} = a + b_1 X_1 + b_2 X_2$$

The conclusions we shall reach for the case including two explanatory variables are generalizable to situations where there are more than two explanatory variables.

SCATTER DIAGRAM

In the case of two explanatory variables, each joint sample observation will have a value for Y, along with corresponding values for X_1 and X_2. A three-dimensional scatter diagram is needed to graph such sample observations, as shown in Figure 11.1.

FITTED REGRESSION PLANE

We found in Chapter 10, on simple regression, that the fitted relationship between Y and X is graphed as a line in two dimensions. The fitted relationship between observed sample values of Y, X_1, and X_2 is a fitted plane in a three-dimensional space. The

Figure 11.1
Fitted regression plane through sample observations

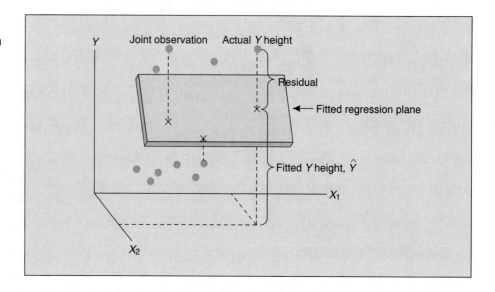

fitted multiple regression equation is therefore the equation for the plane. The fitted plane extends over the observed range of X_1 and X_2. The height of the plane at any pair of (X_1, X_2) coordinates is the value $\hat{Y}$ (see Figure 11.1). Suppose the fitted regression equation is

$$\hat{Y} = 40 + 3X_1 + 5X_2$$

Then, for $X_1 = 30$ and $X_2 = 20$, the equation is

$$\hat{Y} = 40 + 3(30) + 5(20) = 230$$

Thus, the $\hat{Y}$ value on the regression plane at coordinates $X_1 = 30$ and $X_2 = 20$ is 230.

The fitted multiple regression equation represents an average relationship among the three variables. Given the assumptions of the linear model, the $\hat{Y}$ values on the regression plane represent estimates of the "typical Y" values over the observed ranges of X_1 and X_2.

REGRESSION PLANE FITTED BY LEAST SQUARES

How do we fit a regression plane? The most widely used method employed to fit the regression plane is the least squares method.

Least Squares Criterion

The least squares regression plane fitted to the observed data minimizes the sum of the squared vertical distances of the Y observations from the surface of the plane.

If we define the difference between Y and the corresponding $\hat{Y}$ as e, then the least squares condition minimizes $\Sigma\, e^2$.

Figure 11.1 shows a fitted least squares plane. The e values are indicated in the figure by the vertical dashed lines connecting the actual Y observations to the small crosses on the plane. Note that (1) the set of $\hat{Y}$'s (the crosses) are all on the surface of the fitted regression plane, and (2) the $\hat{Y}$ values also represent the least squares estimates of the actual Y observations for the given (X_1, X_2) coordinates of the observed sample data.

It is always permissible to use the fitted regression equation to determine the value of $\hat{Y}$ within the range of observed X_1 values and within the range of observed X_2 values. If we assume that the fitted regression equation is also valid beyond the observed ranges, then we may use the equation for extrapolation.

11.3

FITTING THE MULTIPLE REGRESSION EQUATION

The basic procedure used for calculating the coefficients a, b_1, and b_2 of the fitted least squares regression plane is similar to the procedure for calculating the coefficients a and b in a simple linear regression. That is, from a set of normal equations we determine the coefficients a, b_1, and b_2 using the quantities calculated from the observed values of X_1, X_2, and Y. The normal equations are solved simultaneously to obtain the one unique set of values of the regression coefficients that satisfy the least squares criterion. The number of normal equations equals the number of unknown coefficients. In this case, there are three unknowns, so there are three normal equations:*

$$\sum Y = na + b_1 \sum X_1 + b_2 \sum X_2$$
$$\sum X_1 Y = a \sum X_1 + b_1 \sum X_1^2 + b_2 \sum X_1 X_2$$
$$\sum X_2 Y = a \sum X_2 + b_1 \sum X_1 X_2 + b_2 \sum X_2^2$$

Ordinarily, we need a computer to solve these equations. Almost all statistical software packages include a multiple regression option. We'll now present the MINITAB regression output for a business problem and examine the meaning of the calculated intercept term a and the regression coefficients b_1 and b_2.

COMPUTER OUTPUT AND THE INTERPRETATION OF REGRESSION RESULTS

Suppose a real estate broker wishes to build a predictive model evaluating the price of coastline housing tracts in his county in southern California. From county records, he obtains a random sample of 10 properties and their selling price per lot (in hundreds of thousands of dollars). After visiting the properties, the broker assigns points on a scale of 0–5 for the property's view of the ocean. The higher the score, X_1, the more attractive the view. Additionally, he rates the property's distance from the ocean, X_2, in terms of city blocks. A property directly on the ocean is given a 0 value. The 10 observations are listed in Table 11.1. The table shows Y as the price per lot variable, X_1 as the view rating variable, X_2 as the block distance from the ocean variable.

Figure 11.2 shows the MINITAB regression analysis output using the REGRESS command on the data given in Table 11.1. The coefficient values are listed under the

---

*The three normal equations are conditions that result from applying differential calculus to the mathematical task of finding the minimum of $\Sigma(Y - a - b_1 X_1 - b_2 X_2)^2$.

	TABLE 11.1 Data on Property Valuation		
OBSERVATION	PRICE PER LOT (× $100,000) Y	VIEW RATING X_1	BLOCK DISTANCE FROM OCEAN X_2
1	1	0	2
2	1	1	4
3	1	0	3
4	2	2	4
5	2	1	3
6	3	3	1
7	4	4	2
8	4	2	0
9	6	4	1
10	6	3	0

column COEF for the predictors (i.e., the explanatory variables). The value of coefficient a is labeled "Constant," coefficient b_1 is labeled "View," and coefficient b_2 is labeled "Dist."

```
MTB > regress 'Price' 2 'View' 'Dist'

The regression equation is
Price = 2.60 + 0.800 View - 0.600 Dist
Predictor       Coef        Stdev       t-ratio           p
Constant      2.6000       0.7521          3.46       0.011
View          0.8000       0.2047          3.91       0.006
Dist         -0.6000       0.2047         -2.93       0.022

S = 0.7928      R-sq = 87.1%     R-sq(adj) = 83.4%

Analysis of Variance

SOURCE          DF           SS           MS         F         P
Regression       2       29.600       14.800     23.55     0.001
Error            7        4.400        0.629
Total            9       34.000

SOURCE          DF       SEQ SS
View             1       24.200
Dist             1        5.400
```

Obs.	View	Price	Fit	Stdev.Fit	Residual	St.Resid
1	0.00	1.000	1.400	0.480	−0.400	−0.63
2	1.00	1.000	1.000	0.434	0.000	0.00
3	0.00	1.000	0.800	0.434	−0.200	−0.30
4	2.00	2.000	1.800	0.480	1.200	0.32
5	1.00	2.000	1.600	0.324	0.400	0.55
6	3.00	3.000	4.400	0.320	0.400	−1.93
7	4.00	4.000	4.600	0.480	0.600	−0.95
8	2.00	4.000	4.200	0.480	0.200	−0.32
9	4.00	6.000	5.200	0.434	−0.800	1.21
10	3.00	6.000	5.000	0.434	−1.000	−1.51

Figure 11.2
MINITAB regression results for property valuation

Thus, the value of a is 2.6000, b_1 is 0.8000, and b_2 is -0.6000. Substituting these values of a, b_1, and b_2 into the multiple regression equation, we obtain

$$\hat{Y} = a + b_1X_1 + b_2X_2$$
$$\hat{Y} = 2.6000 + 0.8000X_1 - 0.6000X_2$$

Notice that MINITAB states the multiple regression equation using rounded coefficients but we will not follow this convention in stating multiple regression equations since it produces inaccurate predictions.

This is the equation for the least squares plane used to represent the average relationship among the property's view rating, X_1, distance from the ocean, X_2, and selling price, Y.

INTERPRETATION OF THE REGRESSION COEFFICIENTS

Similar to simple regression, the value of a represents the Y intercept and the b_i values represent slopes. That is, b_1 is the slope of the regression plane in the X_1 direction, and b_2 is the slope of the plane in the X_2 direction. Thus, the value of a is the value of $\hat{Y}$ (estimated price) when both X_1 and X_2 are simultaneously 0; and the coefficients b_1 and b_2 describe how changes in X_1 and X_2, respectively, affect the value of $\hat{Y}$. The coefficient b_1 is interpreted as the change in $\hat{Y}$ for a unit change in X_1 with X_2 held constant. For example, holding block distance constant, fitted price will increase by 0.8000 unit (or \$80,000) for each additional unit increase in view rating. Likewise, b_2 is interpreted as the change in $\hat{Y}$ for a unit change in X_2 with X_1 held constant. Thus, holding view rating constant, we find that for each additional increase of 1 block in distance, there will be a fall in fitted price of 0.6000 unit (or \$60,000).

FORECASTING A NEW *Y* VALUE

Suppose that, for possible investment purposes, the real estate broker wants to predict the lot price for a new development tract on the coastline. He has decided to give the lot a 3 rating for view, and the property is 2 blocks from the ocean; that is, $X_1 = 3$ and $X_2 = 2$. Inserting these values into the fitted regression equation, we get

$$\hat{Y} = 2.6000 + 0..8000X_1 - 0.6000X_2$$
$$= 2.6000 + 0.8000(3) - 0.6000(2)$$
$$= 2.6000 + 2.4000 - 1.2000$$
$$= 3.8000$$

Therefore, the lot price for this combination of view and distance from the ocean estimated from the regression equation is 3.8000, or \$380,000. This estimate is based on the assumption that the new development tract can be interpreted as equivalent to a random selected property from the set of properties used to construct the fitted regression equation.

A MEASURE OF FIT: THE STANDARD DEVIATION OF RESIDUALS, S_e

How well did the least squares regression equation fit the data points? The general formula for S_e for k explanatory variables is:

Standard Deviation of Residuals

$$S_e = \sqrt{\frac{\sum (Y - \hat{Y})^2}{n - k - 1}} \tag{11-2}$$

The **standard deviation of residuals, S_e,** summarizes (as in simple regression) the overall fitting accuracy. The denominator in the formula represents the number of degrees of freedom, which is reduced by 1 for each additional explanatory variable.*

In Figure 11.2 we have highlighted by a box the first Y value ("Price"), its corresponding fitted Y value ("Fit"), and the first residual ("Residual"), which the output shows has a value of -0.400. Notice the observations are listed according to the values of the dependent variable, Price, and because of space limitations only the values of the first independent variable, View, are shown.

How was the residual value of -0.400 computed? By matching the first Y value, $Y_1 = 1.000$, to the corresponding first fitted Y value, $\hat{Y}_1 = 1.400$. The computer calculated the first fitted Y value by substituting into the fitted regression equation the data point coordinates, $X_{1,1} = 0$, $X_{2,1} = 2$ of the first observation; that is,[†]

$$\hat{Y}_1 = 2.6000 + 0.8000(0) - 0.6000(2) = 1.400$$

Now the calculation for e_1 follows as

$$\text{First residual} = e_1 = Y_1 - \hat{Y}_1$$
$$= 1.000 - 1.400$$
$$= -0.400$$

The S_e value (as in simple regression) is given in MINITAB output as the symbol "s." We can find the value for S_e manually by the following computational steps:

Step 1

Square each residual, $(Y - \hat{Y})^2$.

Step 2

Sum the squared values, $\sum (Y - \hat{Y})^2$.

---

*Note that $n - (k + 1) = n - k - 1$. The $n - k - 1$ expression then indicates that the number of observations, n, is reduced by the required number of numerical estimates $(k + 1)$ for fitting the multiple regression equation to the data. These include k numerical estimates required for the b coefficients (one for each of the k explanatory variables) plus a numerical estimate for a, the constant term in the equation. In the property valuation problem, $k + 1 = 3$, since numerical estimates of the three coefficients a, b_1, and b_2 are required.

†Note: The subscript on the Y_1 value indicates the first Y observation. To indicate the corresponding X_1 and X_2 values, we add a second subscript to obtain $X_{1,1}$ and $X_{2,1}$. Notice that adding a second subscript to represent the observations position adds clutter to the notation, so ordinarily we shall not use it unless we wish to refer to a specific observation.

Step 3

Calculate the degrees of freedom, $n - k - 1$.

Step 4

Divide the result in Step 2 by the result in Step 3.

Step 5

Take the square root of the value found in Step 4.

For our example, $n - k - 1 = 10 - 2 - 1 = 7$, and the result is

$$S_e = \sqrt{\frac{\sum (Y - \hat{Y})^2}{n - k - 1}}$$

$$= \sqrt{\frac{4.4}{7}}$$

$$= 0.7928$$

As we can see, the value of S_e obtained by hand calculation matches the value of s in the computer output shown in Figure 11.2.

Similar to simple regression, the value of S_e is a key quantity in calculating the widths of the prediction intervals for new Y values.

Effect on S_e of Additional Explanatory Variables

In the property valuation multiple regression equation, we used two explanatory variables. If another explanatory variable becomes available for inclusion, how can we tell whether its inclusion in the equation improves the fit for statistical prediction? The answer lies with S_e. If a gain in prediction reliability has been made by including another variable in the equation, we can expect a lowered value of S_e. Therefore, the statistical guideline to follow is: *A variable should be included in the equation for the prediction of Y if its addition (to the other explanatory variables) lowers S_e.* Otherwise, it should not be retained for predictive purposes. From a practical perspective, the benefits of the addition must match the cost of obtaining the data on the new variable in question.

ANOTHER MEASURE OF FIT: THE COEFFICIENT OF MULTIPLE DETERMINATION

Along with the S_e measure of fit that helps us judge the predictive ability of the fitted equation, there is another statistical measure of fit—the **coefficient of multiple determination**, R^2. The value of R^2 measures the explanatory power of the multiple regression equation. The definition for R^2 follows directly from the one used in Chapter 10 for a simple regression (r^2):

Coefficient of Multiple Determination

$$R^2 = \frac{\sum (\hat{Y} - \bar{Y})^2}{\sum (Y - \bar{Y})^2} \tag{11-3}$$

$$= \frac{\text{Explained portion of total variation of } Y}{\text{Total variation of } Y}$$

Like r^2 in simple regression, the R^2 value is a ratio that is often expressed in decimal form. The decimal fraction tells us what proportion of the total variation of Y about its mean $\bar{Y}$ (the denominator term) is explained by variation of the regression equation value $\hat{Y}$ about the mean $\bar{Y}$ (the numerator term). In this sense, R^2 is a statistic that measures the degree of explanatory power achieved by the fitted regression equation. If the regression equation explains all the variation, then $R^2 = 1$; but if it explains none of the variation, then $R^2 = 0$. Thus, the better the explanatory power of the regression equation, the closer R^2 is to 1.

The value of R^2 also can be reported in percentage terms. The MINITAB output shown in Figure 11.2 shows the R^2 value in percentage terms as 87.1%. This tells us that 87.1% of the total variation in lot prices is explainable by the variation in the view rating variable and in the distance variable of the regression equation.

ADJUSTED R^2, R_a^2

Mathematically, the R^2 statistic can never decrease in value when another explanatory variable is added to the current explanatory variables—not even when the newly included variable is a "nonsense" variable. The tendency for R^2 to show an increase with any added variable is a failing of the R^2 statistic that prompts the use of the **adjusted R^2 statistic, R_a^2**. Like R^2, the R_a^2 statistic is a ratio, but, unlike the unadjusted R^2, both the numerator and denominator of R_a^2 have been "adjusted for degrees of freedom." This degrees of freedom adjustment enables us to detect whether the addition of an independent variable has contributed significantly to the explanation of the dependent variable Y. If the newly included independent variable has contributed significantly, R_a^2 will increase.

In measuring the gain in explanatory power of the equation when entering another explanatory variable, we use the following rules:

1. Use R_a^2, not R^2.
2. If R_a^2 increases, the variable has brought a significant increase in explanatory power, otherwise R_a^2 will remain the same or decrease.

The adjusted R^2 is generally given alongside the R^2 value on computer output. In the MINITAB output for the property valuation data, the adjusted R^2 is 83.4% and is shown in Figure 11.2 alongside the standard R^2 value of 87.1%.

What about the other statistics found in MINITAB output under the headings "Analysis of Variance," "t-ratio," and "Stdev.Fit"? These numbers will be needed shortly to draw inferential conclusions about the population multiple regression parameters and to construct prediction intervals for new Y values—topics covered in the next few sections.

PRACTICE EXERCISE

11.1 A sales manager for an industrial chemical company believes that sales of individual salespeople, Y, are related to the potential volume of business in each salesperson's territory, X_1, and each salesperson's effort, X_2. Potential business is measured by the percentage of national sales of this type of chemicals that are made in the sales region by all sellers. Sales effort is measured by number of calls on customer accounts. Presented in the table are data on the dependent variable, Y, and the two explanatory variables, X_1 and X_2. The computer output gives the following values for the regression coefficients: $a = -13.824566$, $b_1 = 1.999461$, and $b_2 = 0.212167$.

OBSERVATION	Y	X_1	X_2
1	10	3.0	90
2	11	0.5	115
3	23	1.5	150
4	35	8.0	152
5	26	5.0	140
6	32	5.5	160
7	30	9.5	112
8	39	9.0	170
9	15	6.0	80
10	34	5.0	185
Totals	255	53.0	1354

a. Write the multiple regression equation.
b. Interpret the value obtained for b_1.
c. For $X_1 = 3$ and $X_2 = 120$, what is the value of $\hat{Y}$?
d. What is the value of S_e?
e. What is the value of R^2?

EXERCISES

11.1 A real estate developer wanted to construct a multiple regression equation to use for estimating the selling price of wooded lots for vacation homes near a New Hampshire ski resort. To do so, she recorded data on the following variables for each of 28 lots recently sold:

Y = Sale price of the wooded lot (in $1000 units)
X_1 = Area of the lot (in hundreds of square feet)
X_2 = Elevation of the lot
X_3 = Slope of the lot

Using a computer software regression analysis program, the real estate developer obtained the output in the table below:

Sample size	20
R^2	0.90
Standard deviation of residuals	0.53
Mean of price variable	5.23
Standard deviation of price variable	1.27
Standard deviation of fitted Y at mean value of $X_1X_2X_3$	0.11
Standard deviation of prediction at mean value of $X_1X_2X_3$	0.54

Individual Analysis of Variables				
VARIABLE	**MEAN**	**STANDARD DEVIATION**	**COEFFICIENT, b**	**STANDARD ERROR OF b**
Constant	—	—	0.604	—
Area, X_1	16.38	3.09	0.124	0.048
Elevation, X_2	5.49	3.22	0.251	0.070
Slope, X_3	175.24	23.57	0.007	0.008

a. Give the prediction equation that the real estate developer would use to relate selling price to the area, elevation, and slope of a wooded lot near the ski resort.

b. A prospective financier for the project tells the developer, "I don't think the price you can get for a lot has much to do with the size of the lot, its elevation, or its slope." Formulate a response to the financier using the R^2 statistic.

c. Interpret the regression coefficients for area, elevation, and slope.

d. Interpret the value given for the standard deviation of residuals, S_e.

□ ▶ **11.2** "High employee turnover is hurting us badly," said Iris Korne, the personnel manager at Continuous Lens, a growing contact lens producer on the West Coast. "I bet it's having a negative impact on our productivity; besides, it's disruptive to be continually recruiting and training new personnel. Maybe we're hiring too many of the wrong type of employee—the type who just have little company loyalty." After some further thought on the matter, Korne decides that an in-house study of current and former employee traits may give some insight into the kind of individual that should be sought. The data in the table were collected, and then a multiple regression analysis was run, giving the following coefficient values: $a = -4.672$, $b_1 = 0.013$, and $b_2 = 0.068$.

a. Write the multiple regression equation.

b. Interpret the regression coefficients a, b_1, and b_2.

c. Describe how Korne might use the multiple regression equation for prediction.

EMPLOYEE	GROUP ORIENTATION INDEX X_1	GROUP SERVICE INDEX X_2	YEARS WITH CONTINUOUS LENS Y
A	85	70	1
B	120	125	4
C	125	135	6
D	100	80	2
E	110	90	3
F	90	75	2
G	130	150	8
H	115	110	5

□ **11.3** For the regression equation and data set given in Exercise 11.2:

a. Compute and interpret the coefficient of multiple determination, R^2.

b. What is the value of the standard deviation of residuals, S_e, and how might Korne use it?

□ **11.4** A controversy developed in the fast food industry over the relative importance to business of having numerous store outlets versus spending on television advertising. Data were collected for a given metropolitan area on customer patronage, Y, number of television commercials per day, X_1, and the number of restaurants, X_2. The table shows the data for 15 restaurants of a fast food chain in a particular metropolitan area. Computer multiple regression output gave the following coefficient values: $a = -2018.214$, $b_1 = 145.643$, and $b_2 = 32.065$.

a. Write the multiple regression equation fitted to the data.

b. Interpret the value of b_2.

c. For a value of $X_1 = 10$ and $X_2 = 50$, what is the value of $\hat{Y}$?

OBSERVATION	Y	X_1	X_2
1	1500	16	33
2	900	16	25
3	675	12	30
4	750	14	29
5	450	07	53
6	2400	16	61
7	500	06	52
8	430	12	19
9	540	07	41
10	825	13	33
11	627	12	27
12	650	12	36
13	770	15	23
14	950	14	22
15	1200	12	35

    d. Calculate the value of S_e.

    e. Calculate the value of R^2 and interpret.

11.5 One viewpoint held about the fast food industry in the past was that if you saturated the area with stores, you didn't need to do much advertising. This viewpoint was predicated on the belief that customer patronage is normally motivated by convenience. Another viewpoint was that if you saturated the airways with television advertising, you didn't need to build so many stores, because customers would seek you out. This view was predicated on the belief that brand loyalty could be built. A third viewpoint was that both numerous stores and heavy television advertising were necessary for success, because television advertising could build name recognition and might be necessary to help remind customers looking for a fast food restaurant of the advertised brand's key benefits. But according to this view, television blitzes couldn't move people to go out of their way to find the advertised brand, so convenient locations were also necessary. A fourth viewpoint claimed that emphasis on both numerous stores and heavy television advertising was misguided. "If you serve good food at low prices in a good atmosphere, customers will flock to your restaurant." What insight on these alternative viewpoints are gained from the regression equation calculated in Exercise 11.4?

● ●

11.4

INFERENCES IN MULTIPLE REGRESSION

The fitted regression plane can be used to make inferences about the population regression plane. Suppose the fitted multiple regression plane

$$\hat{Y} = a + b_1X_1 + b_2X_2$$

is considered a sample estimate of the true but unknown population regression plane, defined as follows:

$$\mu_{Y.X_1X_2} = A + B_1X_1 + B_2X_2$$

Then the value of an individual Y observation can be defined as the sum of population regression plane height at the (X_1, X_2) coordinates, $\mu_{Y.X_1X_2}$, and a random element, E. That is,

$$Y = \mu_{Y.X_1X_2} + E$$

In this expression, $\mu_{Y.X_1X_2}$ represents the *systematic component* of Y, and E represents its *random component*. Expressed in terms of the independent variables X_1 and X_2, the equation becomes what is called the multiple regression model:

Multiple Regression Model

$$Y = A + B_1X_1 + B_2X_2 + E \qquad\qquad (11\text{-}4)$$

The assumptions for the multiple regression model are similar to those we discussed in Chapter 10 for simple regression inference.

1. **Random sample.** At any given set of values for X_1 and X_2, the observed data on Y are a random sample from the population of Y values at those given values of X_1 and X_2.
2. **Linearity.** At any pair of values for X_1 and X_2, the mean value of Y ($\mu_{Y.X_1X_2}$) is a linear function of the values of X_1 and X_2.
3. **Normality.** At any pair of values for X_1 and X_2, the values of $E = Y - \mu_{Y.X_1X_2}$ are normally distributed, or at least approximately normally distributed.
4. **Homoscedasticity.** Across all values of X_1 and X_2, the probability distribution of the E values has a constant standard deviation.
5. **Independence.** The E values are not statistically linked with each other.

To make inferences about the population regression slope values (B_1 and B_2), we use the fitted multiple regression plane slope values (b_1 and b_2) along with their respective standard deviations (S_{b_1} and S_{b_2}).

The first inferential procedure we'll discuss concerns the significance of the population regression equation as a whole. The purpose is to establish whether the regression equation has explanatory power. If it does, then inferences about the individual B_i's may be considered. Generally speaking, the regression equation will have explanatory power if the population regression plane is tilted rather than horizontal. The direction of tilt is immaterial.

INFERENCE ABOUT THE REGRESSION EQUATION AS A WHOLE

The test of the explanatory power of the regression equation as a whole is performed through the ANOVA table using the F distribution. The null hypothesis H_o being tested claims that none of the explanatory variables used in the regression analysis have any explanatory power. If all the B_i coefficients of the explanatory variables equal 0, then the population regression plane is horizontal (no tilt) and the true population ρ^2 equals 0.

$$H_o: \quad B_1 = B_2 = \cdots = B_k = 0 \quad (Y \text{ is not related to any } X.)$$
$$H_A: \quad \text{At least one } B_i \neq 0 \qquad (Y \text{ is related to at least one } X.)$$

The observed F value is computed from quantities provided in the ANOVA table in the MINITAB output. The procedure will be outlined later in this section. Rejection of H_o means that the aggregate effect of the X_i's does provide a statistically significant explanation of the variability in the dependent variable Y.

Let us illustrate, using a level of significance of $\alpha = .01$, the procedure for testing H_o for the property valuation problem.

Step 1

Determine the rejection region. At the $\alpha = .01$ significance level for 2 and 7 d.f. in the numerator and denominator, respectively, the F table (Table IXb) shows a 9.95 value. Thus, the rejection region is $F_{(2,7)} > 9.95$.

Step 2

Determine the value of the test statistic. Looking at Figure 11.2 for the MINITAB output for the property valuation problem, we see that the ANOVA is given in the typical tabular form. The table reports an observed F value of 23.55, with the p-value for the observed F value equal to .001. To obtain this observed test statistic value, divide MSR by MSE:

$$F_{(2,7)} = \frac{MSR}{MSE} = \frac{14.800}{0.629} = 23.55$$

Step 3

Determine whether the test statistic is in the rejection region. Since our observed F value of 23.55 is greater than 9.95, it is in the rejection region. Note that we could also reach this conclusion directly from the MINITAB output by observing that the p-value of .001 reported for the F statistic is less than the $\alpha = .01$ level of significance.

Step 4

Draw a conclusion about H_o. We can declare that the regression analysis as a whole is significant at the $\alpha = .01$ level (i.e., highly significant). Thus, the regression equation with the view ratings and distance from the ocean as explanatory variables offers a statistically significant explanation of lot price variability.

We can generalize the procedure for the F test of the null hypothesis as follows:

Step 1

Determine the rejection region. Given the specified level of α and the k and $n - k - 1$ values for the degrees of freedom, the F table value is $F_{(\alpha,k,n-k-1)}$. Therefore, the rejection region is defined as all values of the F distribution for k and $n - k - 1$ degrees of freedom that are greater than the critical value $F_{(\alpha,k,n-k-1)}$. That is,

$$F_{(k,n-k-1)} > F_{(\alpha,k,n-k-1)}$$

Step 2

Determine the value of the test statistic. The test statistic is the observed F value calculated from quantities provided in the ANOVA table, which is found in typical regression output following the standard format shown in Table 11.2. (This format is similar to that presented in Chapter 9.)

TABLE 11.2 Typical Format of ANOVA Table for Regression Output				
Source	**D.F.**	**SS**	**MS**	**F RATIO OBSERVED**
Regression	k	SSR	$MSR = SSR/k$	
Error	$n - k - 1$	SSE	$MSE = SSE/(n - k - 1)$	$F_{(k,n-k-1)} = MSR/MSE$
Total	$n - 1$	SST	$SST/n - 1$	
where $SSR = \Sigma(\hat{Y} - \bar{Y})^2$, $SSE = \Sigma(Y - \hat{Y})^2$, and $SST = \Sigma(Y - \bar{Y})^2$.				
MSR = Mean square due to regression, and MSE = Mean square due to error				

The ANOVA table shows that the observed F value is a ratio of two MS (mean square) terms. Each MS term is a sum of squares divided by its degrees of freedom.

F Test Statistic for Testing Significance of the Regression Equation as a Whole

$$F_{(k,n-k-1)} = \frac{MSR}{MSE} \tag{11-5}$$

Step 3

Determine whether the test statistic is in the rejection region. Compare the observed test statistic, $F_{(k,n-k-1)}$, with $F_{(\alpha,k,n-k-1)}$.

Step 4

Draw a conclusion about H_o. The decision rule is:

a. Reject H_o if the observed value of the test statistic is in the rejection region, and conclude that at least one of the B_i's is nonzero. That is, Reject H_o if

$$F_{(k,n-k-1)} > F_{(\alpha,k,n-k-1)}$$

b. Do not reject H_o if

$$F_{(k,n-k-1)} \leq F_{(\alpha,k,n-k-1)}$$

By rejecting H_o, we are asserting that the statistical evidence is strong enough to claim that the regression equation offers statistically significant explanatory power of the variability of Y.

When a p-value for the observed F value is provided by the computer regression program, the p-value should be interpreted as the area in the right-hand tail of the F distribution beyond the observed F value. When we find a p-value smaller than the given significance level, it indicates that the observed F falls in the rejection region defined by the significance level and we should reject H_o.

Note that when our main focus is on reliable predictions of Y, it is preferred that an F test for the overall significance of the regression equation be taken before performing hypothesis tests about the individual regression parameters. If we cannot reject the null hypothesis and confirm the overall significance of the regression equation, then there is no need to test the significance of the individual B_i's, because there is insufficient reliability for the equation as a whole. Even when our focus is an accurate estimation of a particular regression parameter, an F test should be conducted before testing the significance of the particular coefficient.

PRACTICAL VERSUS STATISTICAL SIGNIFICANCE IN REGRESSION INFERENCE

There is a distinct and important difference between statistical significance and practical significance that we should keep in mind. Statistical significance can be attained even when there is little practical significance to the variable(s) considered. Suppose, in the aggregate, a fitted regression equation has statistical significance. Despite this statistical significance, the regression equation may not be helpful for practical implementation. Here are two reasons why, despite statistical significance, implementation of the regression equation may not be practical:

1. The regression equation may not contain variables that are of practical interest. ("What do I care if my snow sled sales are significantly related to the number of inches of snow this season?" says a retail store manager, "I have to order the sleds before I know how much snow we'll have.")
2. The explanatory variables in a regression equation may exert only a minimal effect (but not 0 effect) on the dependent variable, for example, if the price of Christmas tree lights are included as an independent variable explaining the volume of sales of Christmas trees. Even if the price of Christmas tree lights doubles, the adverse impact on tree sales would be minimal and so for practical purposes not merit consideration in the equation.

Although our attention has been focused on understanding the statistical interpretation of the observed F value, in each business situation the practical significance validates the statistical interpretation that follows.

PRACTICE EXERCISE

11.2 Below are the partial multiple regression results obtained from MINITAB output for Practice Exercise 11.1 relating sales volume to territory potential and number of sales calls made:

Analysis of Variance			
SOURCE	D.F.	SS	MS
Regression	2	962.71	481.36
Error	7	11.79	1.68
Total	9	974.50	

SOURCE	D.F.	SEQ SS
X_1	1	489.65
X_2	1	473.06

a. What is the observed value of F?
b. At $\alpha = .01$, is the explanatory power of the equation significant?

INFERENCES ABOUT INDIVIDUAL COEFFICIENTS

When the five assumptions made at the beginning of this section hold, the procedure for making inferences about the individual population regression coefficients of a multiple regression is very similar to that followed in Chapter 10 for simple regression. The procedure requires the b_i value, its corresponding sample standard deviation, S_{b_i}, and the t value from Table VII in the Appendix. Again, because the computations required for obtaining S_{b_i} terms of each coefficient are too complicated to obtain easily by hand, we rely on the computer output for their values.

Testing the Significance of the Individual Coefficients

We can test for the statistical significance of any observed b_i value. For instance, by formulating the null hypothesis $H_o: B_i = B_{i,o}$ and setting $B_{i,o} = 0$, we are testing whether the observed b_i value differs statistically from 0. If we reject the null hypothesis statement that B_i is 0, we refute the statement that no linear statistical relationship exists between Y and X_i. We shall use the property valuation problem to illustrate the computational procedure for testing the significance of the individual regression coefficients.

Looking back at the MINITAB output of Figure 11.2 for the property valuation problem, we find for each predictor (explanatory) variable, its b_i value, standard deviation, t statistic, and p-value of the t statistic, as before. For example, for the distance variable, these values are -0.6000, 0.2047, -2.93, and 0.022, respectively.

Let's set $\alpha = .05$ to test the null hypothesis that $B_1 = 0$ versus the alternate hypothesis that $B_1 \neq 0$ for the explanatory variable VIEW, X_1. We proceed as follows:

Step 1
Determine the rejection region. For a two-sided test at $\nu = n - k - 1 = 7$ d.f., the t table value (from Table VII) shows that $t_{(.025,7)} = 2.365$. So the rejection region for a two-sided hypothesis test is

$$t_7 < -2.365 \qquad \text{or} \qquad t_7 > +2.365$$

Step 2
Compute the value of the test statistic. For the variable VIEW, the MINITAB output in Figure 11.2 shows a b_1 value of 0.80, a value of 0.2047 for S_{b_1}, and a t ratio of 3.91 (calculated by dividing $b_1 = 0.80$ by $S_{b_1} = 0.2047$). Remember that the computer output gives an observed t test statistic assuming the null hypothesis that $B_1 = 0$ is true.

Step 3
Determine whether the test statistic is in the rejection region. The observed t ratio of 3.91 is greater than 2.365 and therefore lies in the rejection region. The same conclusion can be reached by observing that the p-value of .006 given in the MINITAB output for the VIEW coefficient is less than the set $\alpha = .05$ level of significance.

Step 4
Draw a conclusion. Since the observed value of the test statistic lies in the rejection region, we reject H_o and conclude that the VIEW variable, X_1, in the presence of X_2, has a statistically significant influence on lot price.

Let's now set $\alpha = .05$ and test $H_o: B_2 = 0$ versus $H_A: B_2 \neq 0$ for the explanatory DIST variable X_2, the block distance from the ocean:

Step 1

Determine the rejection region. For a two-sided test and $\nu = n - k - 1 = 7$ d.f., the t table value is $t_{(.025,7)} = 2.365$, as before. Therefore, the rejection region is again $t_7 < -2.365$ or $t_7 > +2.356$.

Step 2

Compute the value of the test statistic. From the MINITAB output we find that $b_2 = -0.60$, $S_{b_2} = 0.2047$, and the observed value of the t statistic is -2.93 (found in the third row of the "t-ratio" column).

Step 3

Determine whether the test statistic is in the rejection region. The observed t ratio of -2.93 is less than -2.365 and therefore lies in the rejection region. This conclusion could also be reached by noting that the p-value of .022 given in the MINITAB output for the distance coefficient is less than $\alpha = .05$.

Step 4

Draw a conclusion. We reject H_o and conclude that the block distance variable, X_2, in the presence of X_1, has a statistically significant (depressing) influence on lot price.

Generalizing the procedure for testing the significance of the individual coefficients, we have:

Step 1

Determine the rejection region. For a specified significance level of α and for $\nu = n - k - 1$ degrees of freedom, the rejection region for a two-sided test is defined as those values of the test statistic $t_{(n-k-1)}$ that meet the condition

$$t_{(n-k-1)} < -t_{(\alpha/2,n-k-1)} \qquad \text{or} \qquad t_{(n-k-1)} > +t_{(\alpha/2,n-k-1)}$$

where $t_{(\alpha/2,n-k-1)}$ is the t table value for $n - k - 1$ degrees of freedom that cuts off an area equal to $\alpha/2$ in each tail of the t distribution.

Step 2

Compute the value of the test statistic. The test statistic is the computed t value:

$$t_{(n-k-1)} = \frac{b_i - B_{i,o}}{S_{b_i}}$$

where $B_{i,o}$ is the value of B_i specified in the null hypothesis. This value will be assumed to be 0 in our hypothesis testing (unless specified otherwise). As has been mentioned, the observed statistic provided by the MINITAB computer output assumes that $B_i = 0$.

Step 3

Determine whether the test statistic is in the rejection region. Compare the observed test statistic, $t_{(n-k-1)}$, with $t_{(\alpha/2,n-k-1)}$ and $-t_{(\alpha/2,n-k-1)}$.

Step 4

Draw a conclusion about H_o. If the test statistic lies in the rejection region, we reject H_o and conclude that B_i is significantly different from 0. Otherwise, H_o cannot be rejected.

Confidence Intervals for B_i

We can construct $1 - \alpha$ confidence intervals for any B_i value. The procedure for constructing a confidence interval for B_i at the $1 - \alpha$ confidence level uses the t distribution with $\nu = n - k - 1$ degrees of freedom. The upper and lower limits of this interval are given by the following expressions:

$1 - \alpha$ Confidence Interval for Individual Coefficients for B_i

Upper confidence limit (UCL) for B_i:

$$b_i + t_{(\alpha/2, n-k-1)}S_{b_i}$$

Lower confidence limit (LCL) for B_i: (11-6)

$$b_i - t_{(\alpha/2, n-k-1)}S_{b_i}$$

Let's construct a 95% confidence interval for B_1 in the property valuation problem.

1. Compute the upper confidence limit for B_1:

$$\text{UCL} = 0.80 + (2.365)(0.2047) = 1.28$$

2. Compute the lower confidence limit for B_1:

$$\text{LCL} = 0.80 - (2.365)(0.2047) = 0.32$$

Thus, we can be 95% confident that the interval from 0.32 to 1.28 contains the true value of B_1. A practical interpretation would be that we are fairly confident that with each additional unit increase in the view rating, holding block distance from the ocean constant, there will be an increase in lot price between \$32,000 and \$128,000. Thus, our high level of confidence requires a rather wide price range.

PRACTICE EXERCISE

11.3 The calculation procedure for a 95% confidence interval for B_2 would follow exactly the same format as shown above for B_1. Using the computer results shown in Figure 11.2, construct the 95% confidence interval for B_2. Give it a practical interpretation.

CONFIDENCE INTERVAL FOR $\mu_{Y.X_1X_2}$

As in simple regression, we can construct a confidence interval for $\mu_{Y.X_1X_2}$ (the population mean of Y at given X_1 and X_2 values). The form of the $1 - \alpha$ confidence interval for $\mu_{Y.X_1X_2}$ is:

$1 - \alpha$ Confidence Interval for $\mu_{Y.X_1X_2}$

$$\hat{Y} \pm t_{(\alpha/2, \nu)}(\text{Standard deviation of fitted } Y) \qquad (11\text{-}7)$$

The procedure for calculating a 95% confidence interval for $\mu_{Y.X_1X_2}$ at $X_1 = 3$ and $X_2 = 2$ for the property valuation example follows:

Step 1

Determine the t table value $t_{(\alpha/2,\nu)}$ for $\alpha/2 = .025$ and $\nu = n - k - 1 = 10 - 2 - 1 = 7$ d.f. From the table, $t_{(.025,7)} = 2.365$, as before.

Step 2

Determine the value of the standard deviation of fitted Y. The value of the standard deviation of the fitted Y is specific to the values of X_1 and X_2 being considered. The computations for the standard deviation of the fitted Y for a multiple regression equation are computationally burdensome and are not ordinarily done by hand. Fortunately, many computer packages have options to compute such interval estimates. For example, MINITAB uses the REGRESS command with the PREDICT subcommand. The MINITAB regression results, boxed in Figure 11.3, show that at $X_1 = 3$ and $X_2 = 2$, the standard deviation of fitted Y (Stdev.Fit) = 0.324.

Step 3

Determine the upper and lower confidence interval limits for $\mu_{Y.X_1X_2}$. The MINITAB regression output in Figure 11.3 gives 3.8 as the "Fit" value for $\hat{Y}$ at

```
MTB > regress 'PRICE' 2 'VIEW' 'DIST'
SUBC> predict 3,2.

The regression equation is
SALARY = 2.60 + 0.800 VIEW - 0.600 DISTANCE

Predictor        Coef        Stdev        t-ratio          p
Constant       2.6000       0.7521           3.46      0.011
VIEW           0.8000       0.2047           3.91      0.006
DISTANCE      -0.6000       0.2407          -2.93      0.022

s = 0.7928       R-sq = 87.1%    R-sq(adj) = 83.4%

Analysis of Variance

SOURCE          DF           SS           MS          F        p
Regression       2       29.600       14.800      23.55    0.001
Error            7        4.400        0.629
Total            9       34.000

SOURCE          DF       SEQ SS
VIEW             1       24.200
DISTANCE         1        5.400

Obs.    VIEW      PRICE       Fit Stdev.Fit     Residual    St.Resid
  1     0.00      1.000      1.400     0.480       -0.400       -0.63
  2     1.00      1.000      1.000     0.434        0.000        0.00
  3     0.00      1.000      0.800     0.434        0.200        0.30
  4     2.00      2.000      1.800     0.480        0.200        0.32
  5     1.00      2.000      1.600     0.324        0.400        0.55
  6     3.00      3.000      4.400     0.324       -1.400       -1.93
  7     4.00      4.000      4.600     0.480       -0.600       -0.95
  8     2.00      4.000      4.200     0.480       -0.200       -0.32
  9     4.00      6.000      5.200     0.434        0.800        1.21
 10     3.00      6.000      5.000     0.434        1.000        1.51

   Fit     Stdev.Fit          95% C.I.          95% P.I.
  3.800        0.324      (3.034,   4.566)   (1.774,   5.826)
```

Figure 11.3
MINITAB regression output for property valuation problem

$X_1 = 3$ and $X_2 = 2$. Thus, the 95% confidence interval for mean lot price for a lot with a view rating of 3 and block distance rating of 2 is constructed around 3.8, and is computed by $3.8 \pm (2.365)(0.324)$, with upper and lower confidence limits of

$$UCL = 3.8 + (2.365)(0.324) = 4.566$$
$$LCL = 3.8 - (2.365)(0.324) = 3.034$$

The MINITAB output in Figure 11.3 also shows these values of 3.034–4.566 for the 95% confidence interval.

Thus, we are 95% confident that for $X_1 = 3$ and $X_2 = 2$, the interval from 3.034 to 4.566 contains the point $\mu_{Y.X_1X_2}$ through which the population regression plane passes. From a practical perspective, the real estate broker is now fairly sure that the mean lot price for a lot with a view rating of 3 at a distance of 2 blocks from the ocean, should be between $303,400 and $456,600.

PREDICTION INTERVAL FOR A NEW *Y* VALUE

Procedurally, the prediction of a new Y value from a multiple regression equation is similar to prediction using a simple regression equation. The form of the $1 - \alpha$ prediction interval for a new Y value is:

1 − α Prediction Interval for New Y Value

$$\hat{Y} \pm t_{(\alpha/2,\nu)}(\text{Standard deviation of prediction}) \tag{11-8}$$

The formula for the standard deviation of prediction for a multiple regression equation is generally a complex and difficult formula to calculate directly. However, there is a way to obtain it indirectly (if need be) from the relationship:

$$\text{Standard deviation of prediction} = \sqrt{S_e^2 + (\text{Standard deviation of fitted } Y)^2}$$

Using this relationship, we can compute the prediction interval following this procedure:

Step 1
Determine S_e. For our property valuation problem, we have already found that $S_e = 0.7928$ (s in the MINITAB output).

Step 2
Determine the standard deviation of fitted Y. In the above discussion, we determined that at $X_1 = 3$ and $X_2 = 2$, the estimated standard deviation of fitted $Y = 0.324$.

Step 3
Calculate the standard deviation of prediction. At $X_1 = 3$ and $X_2 = 2$, we estimate

$$\text{Standard deviation of prediction} = \sqrt{S_e^2 + (\text{Standard deviation of fitted } Y)^2}$$
$$= \sqrt{(0.7928)^2 + (0.324)^2}$$
$$= 0.8564$$

Now we can calculate the prediction interval for a new Y value.

Step 4

Determine the upper and lower prediction interval limits. For $X_1 = 3$ and $X_2 = 2$, using the value of $\hat{Y} = 3.8$ and the t table value of $t_{(.025,7)} = 2.365$, the 95% prediction interval is $3.8 \pm (2.365)(0.8564)$, which gives upper and lower prediction limits of

$$\text{UPL} = 3.8 + (2.365)(0.8564) = 5.825$$
$$\text{LPL} = 3.8 - (2.365)(0.8564) = 1.775$$

These values of 1.775–5.825 for the upper and lower limits of the 95% prediction interval agree (except for rounding error) with the results in the MINITAB output shown in Figure 11.3. Thus, we can conclude at the 95% confidence level that for $X_1 = 3$ and $X_2 = 2$, an individual lot price will fall between 1.775 and 5.825. In practical terms, the real estate broker is now fairly sure that an individual lot with a view rating of 3 and at a distance of 2 blocks from the ocean should have a lot price between \$177,500 and \$582,500. This suggests that a lot price with a view rating of 3 and a 2 block distance priced above \$582,500 would be excessive, whereas a lot price below \$177,500 may offer a good investment opportunity. Note that the interval obtained for the 95% confidence interval for the mean, $\mu_{Y \cdot X_1 X_2}$ is narrower than the prediction interval for the individual Y value. This smaller range indicates that there is greater certainty about the average lot price than about the price of an individual lot.

EXERCISES

11.6 In Exercise 11.1, a computer regression analysis was run for price, Y, on three variables thought to affect the price of a "view" lot: area (X_1), elevation (X_2), and slope (X_3). The computer output is repeated below:

Sample size	20
R^2	.90
Standard deviation of residuals	.53
Price mean	5.23
Price standard deviation	1.27
Standard deviation of fitted Y at mean value of $X_1 X_2 X_3$	.11
Standard deviation of prediction at mean value of $X_1 X_2 X_3$	.54

Individual Analysis of Variables				
VARIABLE	MEAN	STANDARD DEVIATION	COEFFICIENT, b	STANDARD ERROR OF b
Constant	—	—	0.604	—
Area, X_1	16.38	3.09	0.124	0.048
Elevation, X_2	5.49	3.22	0.251	0.070
Slope, X_3	175.24	23.57	0.007	0.008

a. Test each null hypothesis, $H_o: B_1 = 0$, $H_o: B_2 = 0$, and $H_o: B_3 = 0$, all at $\alpha = .05$.

b. For each statistically significant variable found in part a, determine 95% confidence intervals for their true regression coefficient values.

c. Determine the 95% confidence interval for the mean price of lots having area, elevation, and slope at the mean values given in the computer output.

d. Determine the 95% prediction interval corresponding to the confidence interval determined in part c.

11.7 For the real estate problem discussed in Exercise 11.6, you had a theory that sloping lots were preferred over those with lesser slope. Do the computer regression results provide sufficient evidence to indicate that sales price increases as the slope increases? (*Hint:* Test H_o: $B_3 = 0$ against the one-sided alternative H_A: $B_3 > 0$. Use $\alpha = .05$.)

☐ ▶ **11.8** The human resources director of the Sure-Hands Insurance Company wishes to find out whether the sales talent of sales representatives can be predicted from their education and age. If found useful, these criteria would provide a valuable aid in screening the candidates for employment. As a start, 10 sales representatives are selected at random and are rated by their supervisor as to sales ability, education, and age. The rating on sales ability covers a 7 point scale, from "poor" (0) to "excellent" (6). The education scale varies from "none" (0) to "has master's degree" (4). The age scale extends from "age 20–29" (0) to "age 60–69" (4). The results are shown in the table.

SALES REP	SALES ABILITY Y	EDUCATION X_1	AGE X_2
1	1	0	2
2	2	1	3
3	4	2	0
4	6	3	0
5	1	0	3
6	2	2	4
7	6	4	1
8	1	1	4
9	4	4	2
10	3	3	1
Totals	30	20	20

a. A multiple linear regression equation was computed by the method of least squares to estimate sales potential from education and age. Show all relevant statistics, including the equation of $\hat{Y}$.

b. What is the meaning of the regression coefficient b_1 in this particular case?

c. From the partial multiple regression results compute F for the regression equation as a whole, and test the null hypothesis of no explanatory power at $\alpha = .05$.

Analysis of Variance			
SOURCE	**D.F.**	**SS**	**MS**
Regression	2	29.600	14.800
Error	7	4.400	0.629
Total	9	34.000	

SOURCE	**D.F.**	**SEQ SS**
Education	1	24.200
Age	1	5.400

d. Compute S_{b_1} and S_{b_2}; then test H_o: $B_1 = 0$ and H_o: $B_2 = 0$ at $\alpha = .1$.

11.5
REGRESSION MODELING

Our discussion of multiple regression so far has been limited to estimation for a linear equation and for quantitative data. But the relationship between Y and X_i explanatory variables may be nonlinear. Moreover, the data set for some of the X_i explanatory variables may be qualitative. The techniques that handle these situations require:

- Altering the form of the regression equation
- Altering the type and number of explanatory variables included in the equation

The process of adapting the regression equation to deal with these situations is called **modeling**. Let's now look at a model that accounts for qualitative data.

MODELING WITH DUMMY VARIABLES

A regression equation that includes a **dummy variable** is a model designed to deal with qualitative data. A dummy variable is a variable with just two possible values, 0 or 1. When the particular quality considered is present, the dummy variable takes the value 1; otherwise it takes the value 0. Let X_i represent a dummy explanatory variable, and let b_i be the coefficient of X_i. The product $b_i X_i$ has the value b_i when $X_i = 1$ (quality present); otherwise, the product has a value of 0. That is, $b_i X_i = 0$ when $X_i = 0$ (quality absent). Simply said, b_i is the estimated quantitative impact on Y of the presence of a qualitative factor.

The use of the dummy variable estimating technique in a multiple regression analysis has become an important tool in analyzing employment discrimination. The issue has even received U.S. Supreme Court attention, as noted from the following quotation from the *Los Angeles Times* (June 30, 1988, p. 1):

> **STATISTICS HELD PROOF OF BIAS IN WORKPLACE**
> The [Supreme] Court ruled that civil rights plaintiffs in virtually all job discrimination cases—particularly those involving white-collar professional and managerial jobs—can use statistical analyses to prove their claims, a powerful weapon that formerly could be used only in some cases.

Let's now see how multiple regression with a dummy variable can be used to analyze employment discrimination complaints. Suppose a manufacturer of office machines pays its computer service and repair personnel an hourly wage rate that is established upon hiring and is increased periodically in accordance with company policy. Female workers contend that the entry wage structure discriminates against them. Their contention is that entry wage, in reality, is affected not only by prior experience, but also by gender. They think that if a man and a woman were to be hired at the same time, and they had equal prior experience, the women would be offered a lower starting salary. Management is willing to investigate the validity of the charge and provides the data given in Table 11.3.

The table gives the entry wage rate (in dollars per hour) of all the recently hired employees, along with their gender and months of prior experience. In looking over the data, the director of personnel calculates the average entry wage for the men and for the women. She immediately notices that the average is lower for the women than for the men, although not by much ($10.53 compared to $10.78 hr). Since prior experience affects the entry wage rate, it could be that the men who were hired had more experience than the women. The personnel director calculates the average prior experience for men and for women and learns that the women actually averaged more experience than the men who were hired (8.3 months compared to 5.8 months).

TABLE 11.3 Data for Job Discrimination			
OBSERVATION	**ENTRY WAGE** $/hr	**PRIOR EXPERIENCE** Months	**GENDER**
1	9.5	1	Male
2	10.6	5	Male
3	11.1	7	Male
4	12.3	13	Male
5	10.4	3	Male
6	8.2	0	Female
7	10.7	8	Female
8	11.8	15	Female
9	11.4	10	Female

However, she has only 9 observations, so it might be argued that these results are a sampling fluke, attributable to a sample too small to give a reliable indication of discrimination. If the entry wage rate does depend on both gender as well as prior experience, we would expect a scatter diagram of entry wage rate (on the vertical axis) against previous experience (on the horizontal axis) to provide some informal visual evidence of this. It should show a path of points flowing upward to the right, with a lower line drawn through the points representing women and a higher line drawn through the points representing men. Figure 11.4 is the scatter diagram for the personnel director's data, and it does show this pattern. But where is the statistical smoking gun? How can she use the data to statistically test for discrimination against the female workers?

This is where multiple regression comes in. It will allow the personnel director to study the effect of gender, taking into account the different prior experience of the male and female workers. Experience, expressed in months, is naturally quantitative and so can be used "as is" as an explanatory variable in multiple regression analysis. Gender, on the other hand, is a qualitative feature, with two categories, male and female. To be useful in regression, the qualitative information must be converted to a 0–1 dummy explanatory variable, X_2. Let's arbitrarily designate the presence of a female by $X_2 = 1$, and so assign $X_2 = 0$ for males (absence of a female). The data entries for the computer to perform the regression computations are given in Table 11.4.

Figure 11.4
Scatter diagram of job discrimination data

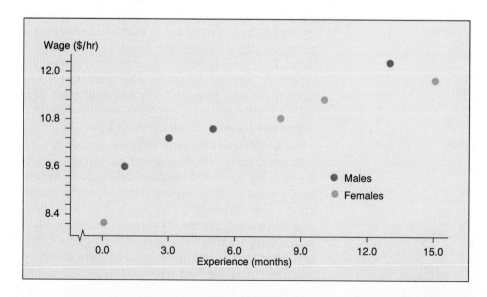

TABLE 11.4 Data for Performing Job Discrimination Regression			
OBSERVATION	WAGE/HR	EXPERIENCE	GENDER
1	9.5	1	0
2	10.6	5	0
3	11.1	7	0
4	12.3	13	0
5	10.4	3	0
6	8.2	0	1
7	10.7	8	1
8	11.8	15	1
9	11.4	10	1

Fitting a multiple regression equation to the data in Table 11.4, we use the equation form

$$\hat{Y} = a + b_1 X_1 + b_2 X_2$$

where X_1 is a quantitative variable for experience and X_2 is the dummy variable for gender. If there is no discrimination, b_2 should not differ significantly from 0. When we apply this equation to predict the entry salary for a new computer repair person, we use the following equations:

$$\hat{Y} = a + b_1 X_1 + b_2(0) = a + b_1 X_1 \qquad \text{For a male}$$
$$\hat{Y} = a + b_1 X_1 + b_2(1) = (a + b_2) + b_1 X_1 \quad \text{For a female}$$

This means that for men and women with the same length of prior experience, we predict an entry wage differential of b_2. Remember that the coefficient value, b_2, is only a sample estimate for the true value, B_2, of the population regression.

If discrimination against women exists, then B_2 should be negative. This would indicate that women with the same length of prior experience as men receive, on average, lower entry wage rates.

We can test the following competing hypotheses:

$$H_0: \quad B_2 = 0 \quad \text{(Null hypothesis of no gender discrimination)}$$
$$H_A: \quad B_2 < 0 \quad \text{(Women discriminated against)}$$

The MINITAB regression output for the data of Table 11.4 is given in Figure 11.5.

```
MTB > regress c1 2 c2 c3

The regression equation is
wage/hr = 9.40 + 0.238 expernc - 0.838 gender

Predictor        coef          Stdev        t-ratio           p
Constant       9.4000         0.1987          47.31       0.000
expernc        0.23793        0.02310         10.30       0.000
gender        -0.8379         0.2272          -3.69       0.010

s = 0.3280      R-sq = 94.7%    R-sq(adj) = 92.9%
```

Figure 11.5
MINITAB regression results for job discrimination problem

From the stated regression equation we see that the gender variable has a b_2 coefficient of -0.8379. This negative value is consistent with the charge of discrimination, but is the result statistically significant? Let's test H_o using a significance level of $\alpha = .01$.

Step 1

Determine the rejection region. From the statement of H_A, this is a one-sided hypothesis test. To determine the rejection region, we obtain the t value from the t table (Table VII, Appendix) for $\nu = n - k - 1 = 9 - 2 - 1 = 6$ d.f. at $\alpha = .01$. This t value is -3.143. The rejection region at $\alpha = .01$ then is $t_\nu < -3.143$.

Step 2

Compute the value of the test statistic:

$$t_\nu = \frac{b_2 - B_{2,0}}{S_{b_2}} = \frac{b_2 - 0}{S_{b_2}}$$

The value of the observed t ratio is given in the MINITAB output (Figure 11.5) as -3.69.

Step 3

Determine whether the test statistic is in the rejection region. Since the observed t ratio of -3.69 is less than -3.143, it lies in the rejection region. This conclusion also could be ascertained by noting that the two-sided p-value of .010 shown in the MINITAB output in Figure 11.5 gives a one-sided p-value of .005, which is less than $\alpha = .01$.

Step 4

Draw a conclusion about H_o. The sample evidence on b_2 is strong enough to conclude at a level of significance of $\alpha = .01$ that we should reject H_o. By rejecting H_o, we can reach the practical interpretation that the company does pay women lower entry wages than men at the same prior experience level for a position and this may be due to sex discrimination.

PRACTICE EXERCISE

11.4 Suppose we have data on hourly wages (in dollars), Y, years of nursing experience, X_1, and shift worked, X_2, for 5 nurses, as given in the table.

	ORIGINAL DATA		
Nurse	Wage Rate ($/hr), Y	Years of Experience, X_1	Shift Worked, X_2
1	12	3	Night shift
2	11	2	Night shift
3	10	3	Day shift
4	10	1	Night shift
5	8	1	Day shift

a. Convert the qualitative variable on shift worked into a 0–1 dummy explanatory variable, designating the presence of the night shift by $X_2 = 1$.
b. What would be the general equation to predict Y for the day shift? For the night shift?
c. Estimate the hourly wage differential between the night shift and the day shift.

QUALITATIVE VARIABLES WITH MORE THAN TWO CATEGORIES

The dummy variable technique shown so far was for qualitative features with only two categories. But this approach also can accommodate qualitative data with several categories. For example, suppose a manufacturing production line produces type A, type B, and type C silicon computer chips. Then the qualitative variable "type of chip" has three mutually exclusive categories. To deal with the three categories, we require two 0–1 dummy variables, which we represent by X_2 and X_3. Arbitrarily, let X_2 denote the presence and absence of type B chip, and we let X_3 denote the presence and absence of type C. Each dummy variable must have either 0 or 1 as its value. For each observation on a computer chip type, only one of the two dummy variables can have a 1 for the presence of that category of computer chip. Thus, there are three possible pairs of values that the variables X_2 and X_3 can have, $(0, 0)$, $(1, 0)$, and $(0, 1)$, with the following meanings:

1. To designate a type A chip, assign the value 0 to X_2 and 0 to X_3.
2. To designate a type B chip, assign the value 1 to X_2 and 0 to X_3.
3. To designate a type C chip, assign the value 0 to X_2 and 1 to X_3.

In this scheme, type A has been designated the *base category*, because when type A is present, the two dummy variables X_2 and X_3 are both assigned the value 0. Thus, the Y intercept for type A is simply the value a in the regression equation. When type B is present, the dummy variable X_2 is assigned the value 1 and the dummy variable X_3 is 0. The Y intercept for type B then is $a + b_2$. When type c is present, $X_2 = 0$ and $X_3 = 1$, and the Y intercept for type C is $a + b_3$.

An interesting illustration of the use of this approach is the Chiquita Banana example given at the end of this chapter.

To summarize, to deal with qualitative data composed of k categories in regression analysis, we introduce $k - 1$ dummy (0–1) variables into the regression equation and assign values as follows:

1. Designate one of the categories the *base category*. Do not introduce a dummy variable for this category.
2. For each of the other $k - 1$ categories, introduce a dummy explanatory variable into the regression equation. Thus, the number of dummy variables must be $k - 1$; that is, 1 less than the number of categories.
3. For each observation on the dependent variable Y, assign a value (either 0 or 1) to each dummy variable.
   a. Only one dummy variable can be assigned the value 1.
   b. The dummy variable that is assigned the value 1 is the one representing the category that is present.
   c. If the observation has the quality designated as the base category, then all the dummy variables are assigned the value 0.

PRACTICE EXERCISE

11.5 An automobile parts and accessories chain collected data on the relationship between sales of individual stores and three explanatory variables: median income in the trade area, number of automobiles registered in the trade area, and location of the store. The latter variable is qualitative, with three categories: suburban free-standing, suburban shopping center, and urban location. Data on the location variable are given below for 8 stores:

Store Number	Location
1	Urban
2	Suburban free-standing
3	Suburban free-standing
4	Urban
5	Suburban shopping center
6	Suburban free-standing
7	Urban
8	Suburban shopping center

A regression analysis will be run of store sales, Y, on median income, X_1, number of automobiles registered, X_2, and location, represented by two dummy variables X_3 and X_4. Find the values of X_3 and X_4 for each store. Let the base location category be designated as urban; then let X_3 represent the suburban free-standing category and let X_4 represent the suburban shopping center category.

CURVE FITTING AND DATA TRANSFORMATION

There are many business situations in which the underlying relationship between X and Y is nonlinear. Two alternative statistical approaches deal with the nonlinearity: *curve fitting* and *data transformation*.

Curve Fitting

The curve fitting approach deals directly with the nonlinearity of the data by fitting an equation with nonlinear terms to the original data. A second-degree (parabolic) equation is a commonly used mathematical form for nonlinear curve fitting:

Parabolic Equation

$$\hat{Y} = a + b_1X + b_2X^2 \qquad (11\text{-}9)$$

A fitted parabolic curve is an appropriate fit to observed data on X and Y when the nonlinearity follows either of the patterns shown in Figure 11.6. The variable X^2

Figure 11.6
Scatter diagrams for two situations in which a second-degree parabolic regression analysis might be appropriate

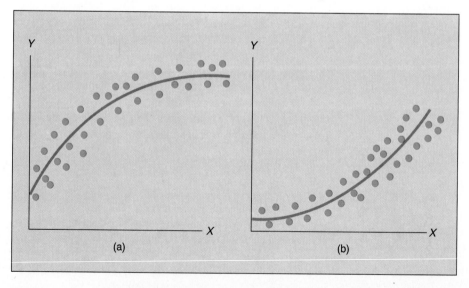

(a) (b)

is generated from the observed data on the independent variable X by squaring every X observation. The insertion of the X^2 term into the regression equation as X_2 allows the equation to capture the curvature of the relationship. So defining $X_1 = X$ and $X_2 = X^2$, we have the form of a linear multiple regression equation with two explanatory variables. As before, we can apply the least squares method to the data on the three variables Y, X_1, and X_2, and solve for the fitted multiple regression equation:

$$\hat{Y} = a + b_1X_1 + b_2X_2$$

We then obtain least squares estimates a, b_1, and b_2 that minimize the sum of the squared errors.

Let's now look at a business situation in which fitting a parabolic equation seems sensible. Suppose a sales manager is concerned that his salespeople are experiencing "burnout," that is, a decline in productivity associated with prolonged assignment to the same territory. From his records, the manager has compiled the data in Table 11.5 on the sales force. The scatter diagram for the data in Table 11.5 is given in Figure 11.7.

TABLE 11.5 Comparison of Sales and Time Spent in the Same Territory		
SALESPERSON	**SALES** (× $1000) **Y**	**YEARS SPENT IN SAME TERRITORY** **X**
1	195	1.1
2	402	4.4
3	473	3.6
4	102	0.8
5	298	4.5
6	237	1.5
7	265	1.4
8	263	5.5
9	345	2.2
10	533	3.0

Figure 11.7
Scatter diagram

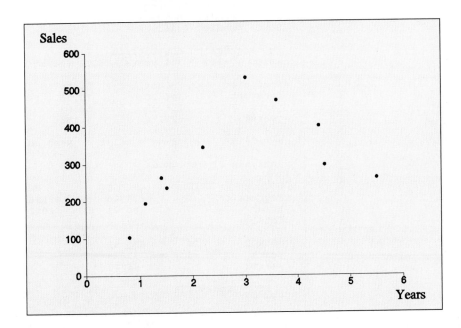

The drift of data points in the scatter diagram does not follow a linear pattern, but rather a nonlinear pattern. The pattern suggests that at low values of years spent in the same territory, additional years produce additional sales. But at higher values of years spent in the same territory, additional years bring a sales decline. Is a parabolic curve an appropriate fit to the data? We can follow the steps given below to find the equation of the parabola fit to the data.

Step 1

Define the "years" variable as X_1 of a multiple regression equation.

Step 2

Square each value of the "years" variable X_1 and define "years squared" as variable X_2 in the multiple regression equation. By using MINITAB's LET command we can instruct the computer to create the YEARSQ variable.

Step 3

Run a multiple regression analysis of variable Y on variables X_1 and X_2. The MINITAB output is shown in Figure 11.8.

The fitted parabolic equation, constructed from the coefficients, is

$$\hat{Y} = -144.10 + 354.05X_1 - 52.176X_2$$

This regression equation has an R^2 value of 86.3%, which means that the parabolic model fits the data quite well. Further checking of the computer output for information on the standard statistical tests, we find that the regression coefficient of both years (X_1) and years squared (X_2) have very high absolute t values of 6.26 and $|-5.70|$, respectively. The latter t value is convincing statistical evidence that X_2 belongs in the regression model. But is statistical evidence the decisive factor? We might ask whether it confirms or contradicts our preconceived ideas about the relationship between the two variables.

Figure 11.8
MINITAB regression output for salespeople's burnout problem

```
MTB > let c4=(c3)**2
MTB > name c4 'yearsq'
MTB > regress 'sales' 2 'years' 'yearsq';
SUBC> predict 4 16.

The regression equation is
sales = -144 + 354 years - 52.2 yearsq

Predictor        Coef       Stdev      t-ratio         p
Constant      -144.10       70.76       -2.04     0.081
years          354.05       56.56        6.26     0.000
yearsq        -52.176        9.157      -5.70     0.000

s = 54.47      R-sq = 86.3%    R-sq(adj) = 82.4%

Analysis of Variance

SOURCE        DF          SS          MS          F         P
Regression     2      131395       65698      22.14     0.001
Error          7       20771        2967
Total          9      152166

SOURCE        DF      SEQ SS
years          1       35053
yearsq         1       96343

   Fit   Stdev.Fit          95% C.I.              95% P.I.
437.3        25.9       (376.0,   498.6)     (   294.6,    580.0)
```

Recall our motivation for trying a parabolic model. It was our original idea that burnout existed; it was also our thinking that the parabolic model could accommodate a downward bending curve that burnout would imply. Since the statistical evidence confirms this reasoning, then $X_2 = X^2$ should certainly be retained in the model.

Given the relationship expressed in the multiple regression equation, what level of sales would management predict for a salesperson who has spent 4 years in the same territory?

Step 1

Determine the values of X_1 and X_2: X_1 is given as 4, so $X_2 = 4^2 = 16$.

Step 2

Substitute the values for X_1 and X_2 into the fitted parabolic equation:

$$\hat{Y} = -144.10 + 354.05X_1 - 52.176X_2$$
$$= -144.10 + 354.05(4) - 52.176(16)$$
$$= 437.3 \text{ (Rounded)}$$

Thus, for a salesperson with 4 years in the same territory, the prediction of sales is 437.3, that is, \$437,300. Using the MINITAB REGRESS command with the PREDICT subcommand, the same numerical prediction of 437.3 was obtained for $X_1 = 4$ and $X_2 = 16$. The value 437.3 appears on the last line under the heading "Fit" in Figure 11.8.

The observed relationship is consistent with the burnout hypothesis; this can be verified by substituting into the equation different values of X_1 and the corresponding values of X_2. For the first 3 years, sales Y increases with years X_1. After the third year, an additional year begins to have a negative effect on sales, slowly at first, then more rapidly. So a salesperson with 4 years in the same territory is close to the burnout stage when sales will decline sharply. For example, at 5 years, predicted sales will decline to 329. On this basis, management should consider making a territorial change or some other corrective measure for that particular salesperson.

Data Transformation

Sometimes the underlying nonlinear relationship between X and Y requires a **data transformation** to permit linear estimation. For example, suppose the underlying relationship or model has the following equation form:

$$Y = AB^X$$

This is called an *exponential model*, because X appears as an exponent. In this case, a *logarithmic data transformation* produces a linear expression. For instance, by taking the logarithms of both sides of the expression for the exponential model, the equation can be rewritten as

$$\log Y = \log A + (\log B)X$$

If we let $Y^* = \log Y, A^* = \log A$, and $B^* = \log B$, we can then express the last equation as

$$Y^* = A^* + B^*X$$

With this new formulation, linear regression analysis can be tried on the transformed variable Y^* and variable X to estimate the coefficients A^* and B^*.

Predictions of the original dependent variable Y, given a value of X, require two steps: First, we substitute the given value of X into the equation to obtain the estimate $\hat{Y}^*$, and, second, we find the antilog of $\hat{Y}^*$ to obtain $\hat{Y}$ in original units. This will be our prediction of Y, given the value of X.

PRACTICE EXERCISE

11.6 Don Mann, owner of a large New Hampshire dairy farm, has completed a cost study of his production operation. A regression analysis of total variable costs on milk production led to the following equation:

$$\hat{Y} = 15{,}800 + 2.2X - 0.001X^2$$
$$\quad\quad (7{,}000) \quad (0.30) \quad (0.0009)$$

Milk production (in gallons) is represented by X, estimated cost (in dollars) is represented by $\hat{Y}$. The numbers in parentheses are the standard deviations of the regression coefficients. The value of R^2 for the equation is 0.88, and the standard deviation of residuals is 33.
a. What would be the estimated cost of producing 1000 gal?
b. At a production level of 1000 gal, what would be the estimated increase in cost for a 1 gal increase in production?

EXERCISES

▶ **11.9** Data were gathered on three variables for single-family homes recently sold in a particular subdivision: (1) sales price of the home, (2) number of square feet of floor space in the home, and (3) type of home. The latter variable had three categories: (a) ranch, (b) split-level, and (c) two-story. Data for the first 6 observations are given in the table.

SALES PRICE (× $1000) Y	SQUARE FEET (× 1000) X_1	TYPE OF HOME
72.9	1.6	Two-story
94.7	2.1	Split-level
83.1	1.8	Split-level
65.0	1.4	Ranch
91.4	2.0	Two-story
78.2	1.6	Ranch

a. How many 0–1 dummy variables are needed to handle the types of homes?
b. Using ranch style as the base category, construct 0–1 dummy variables for these 6 observations.
c. Suppose the effect of split-level style is estimated by the multiple regression analysis to average $3000 more than the base category (holding square footage constant), and the effect of two-story is estimated to average $5000 less than the base category (holding square footage constant). The constant term is 13,752 and the square footage coefficient is 36.8. Write the multiple regression equation.

11.10 Z. A. Malik operates a pearl-diving operation near Tahiti. He hires local divers and sells both the oyster meat and the pearls from the catch. Over the past month he has gone pearl hunting 9 times in the same general area, taking with him all the divers who showed up for each trip. A record of the number of divers and weight of oysters recovered is given in the table.

TRIP NUMBER	NUMBER OF DIVERS	WEIGHT OF OYSTERS RECOVERED lb
1	6	70
2	10	123
3	18	167
4	7	84
5	13	163
6	4	33
7	15	177
8	16	171
9	9	114

    a. Fit a parabolic curve to the data.
    b. Calculate R^2.
    c. Estimate the mean weight of oysters recovered using 10 divers.

11.11 A multiple regression analysis was run of salespeople's monthly sales at a retail sporting goods store, Y, on months employed at the store, X_1, and gender, X_2. Data on the first 6 employees are given in the table.

MONTHLY SALES (× $1000)	MONTHS EMPLOYED	GENDER
7.3	6	Female
8.5	13	Male
9.4	15	Male
13.6	30	Female
10.2	18	Female
6.0	5	Male

    a. List the values of Y, X_1, and X_2 for these 6 employees. Let "Male" be the base category of the 0–1 dummy variable X_2.
    b. Suppose the multiple regression equation for the entire set of data from which the 6 observations given in the table is

$$\hat{Y} = 0.25 + 0.22X_1 + 0.81X_2$$

Estimate the differential sales of women, holding months employed constant.

11.6

RESIDUAL ANALYSIS: CHECKING MODEL ADEQUACY

In this chapter some alternative models for regression analysis have been proposed: dummy variables, nonlinear terms, log transformation. In choosing an appropriate model, we should consider the following features:

1. **Simplicity.** First select the simplest form of the equation for the business situation.
2. **Statistical fit and significance.** Use R_a^2 and S_e to check for statistical fit, and test the significance overall (using ANOVA) and for individual coefficients.
3. **Model adequacy.** This feature refers to meeting the residual assumptions of the linear regression model first described in Section 11.4. The guideline is to check first for adequacy of the simplest model.

    Let's now examine the model adequacy feature. Suppose we have selected the simplest equation form thought to be appropriate for the business situation. And then on performing the regression analysis for the model, we obtain a high R^2 value for the statistical measure of fit and statistically significant t ratios for the regression coefficients. How do we now check for model adequacy? We judge model adequacy by examining the behavior of the regression residuals in a process often called *diagnostic checking*.

RESIDUAL PLOTS: THE IMPORTANCE OF RANDOMLY DISTRIBUTED RESIDUALS

Diagnostic checking typically includes a visual check of a *residual plot* to examine the behavior of the residuals and determine whether they follow any of several possible patterns. A residual plot is similar to a scatter diagram, but instead of plotting the original data points, the points plotted are joint observations of the residual value (vertical axis) and fitted Y values, $\hat{Y}$ (horizontal axis). Figure 11.9 is an example of a residual plot. Examining residual plots permits us to detect disruptive departures from the regression model error assumptions of constant variance and statistical independence. Serious violations of these key assumptions about the behavior of residuals become apparent on the residual plot. More specifically, an error assumption is violated when the pattern of the residuals is not evenly and randomly distributed around a horizontal line drawn across the scatter at the 0 residual level.

This expectation about the pattern of the residuals is consistent with the structure of the linear regression model, which can be expressed in terms of a systematic component ($\mu_{Y.X_1X_2}$) and a random component (E):

$$Y = \mu_{Y.X_1X_2} + E$$

The fitted multiple regression equation estimates the first term $\mu_{Y.X_1X_2}$, which represents the systematic determinants of Y in the data. If this is done satisfactorily, the remaining E terms should behave randomly. But if the fitted regression equation fails to adequately capture the systematic component of Y, these systematic factors remain in the residuals and the residuals do not behave randomly. In that case, we can conclude that model adequacy has not yet been achieved.

Figure 11.9
Residual plot: Residuals plotted against fitted Y

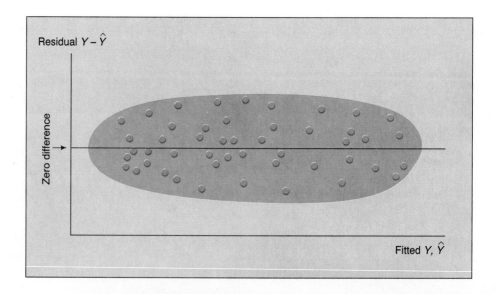

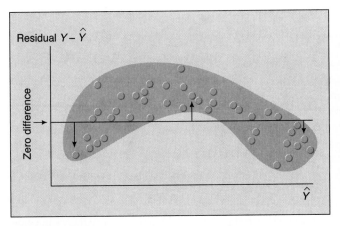

Figure 11.10
Residual plot showing nonrandom behavior: When residuals are bow-shaped, the model requires an X^2 term to make it parabolic.

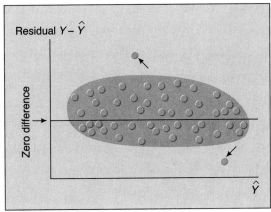

Figure 11.11
Residual plot showing nonrandom behavior: The arrows indicate outliers, which suggest the data should be checked before accepting the regression results.

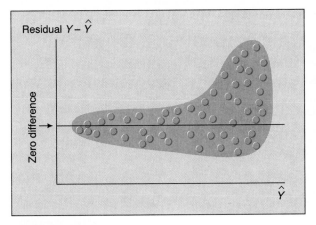

Figure 11.12
Residual plot showing nonrandom behavior: Residuals with a bow shape and increasing variability (i.e., the error increases as Y increases) indicate that a log transformation of Y is required.

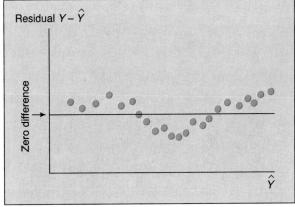

Figure 11.13
Residual plot showing nonrandom behavior: Serial correlation in the residuals. When one residual is high (low), the next tends to be high (low).

But what residual patterns should we expect to see in the residual plot when visually checking for the nonrandom behavior of residuals?

DETECTING MODEL INADEQUACIES

Figures 11.10–11.13 show residual plots in which the patterns of the residuals in some way viclate the regression model assumptions and show nonrandom behavior. Such violations reflect model inadequacies. These types of residual patterns can appear in the residual plot whether simple regression model or multiple regression model violations occur. Figure 11.13 illustrates *serial correlation*, a model inadequacy that is so important in business applications of regression analysis that we discuss it in more detail below.

SERIAL CORRELATION: FALSE
SIGNALS OF REGRESSION RELIABILITY

The pattern of the residuals shown in Figure 11.13 warrants special comment. The series of consecutive residuals in Figure 11.13 exhibits statistical dependency, which on a residual plot is seen as a wavelike pattern with nearby residuals appearing similar in size and/or sign. Statistical dependency in the residuals surfaces when the original data are recorded in consecutive time periods (time series data), and one or more important determinants affecting Y are not specified in the regression equation. This forces the systematic pattern to reside in the residuals from period to period. This tendency of consecutive residuals to be statistically dependent, producing a trend or cyclical pattern, is called *serial correlation.*

The statistical consequence of strong serial correlation is that the computed value S_e (the estimated standard deviation of residuals) is, on average, lower than the value it should be (σ_E). (The proof that S_e will consistently underestimate its true value σ_E is beyond the scope of this text.) Since the estimated standard deviation of prediction directly depends on S_e, it also will be underestimated. Consequently, the prediction interval for a new individual Y value constructed from the standard deviation of prediction will be narrower than it should be, overstating predictive accuracy. Thus, the presence of serial correlation undermines the reliability of the prediction interval constructed for new Y values.

The second statistical consequence of serial correlation is that the conventional t ratio test will no longer be dependable as a test for the statistical significance of regression coefficients. This is because the computed standard deviation of the regression coefficient, S_{b_i}, depends on the value S_e. A low value of S_e will produce a low computed value of S_{b_i} and in turn inflate the t ratio (the regression coefficient divided by S_{b_i}). An inflated t ratio could make a nonsignificant result appear statistically significant. Thus, the presence of serial correlation will jeopardize significance testing of the regression coefficients.

Since the serial correlation problem affects both our predictive ability and testing for statistical significance, we need a numerical index that will signal the presence and magnitude of the serial correlation problem.

Durbin–Watson Statistic: An Index of
Serial Correlation

The **Durbin–Watson (DW) statistic,** named after the two statisticians who devised it, can indicate, in most cases, the extent of the serial correlation problem. Values of the DW statistic range between 0 and 4; a value close to 2 indicates that successive residuals are statistically independent and not plagued by serial correlation. The basic guidelines in interpreting the DW statistic are:

1. A DW value below 1.5 or above 2.5 indicates that the presence of serial correlation is likely disrupting our prediction reliability and statistical significance testing.
2. A DW value between 1.5 and 2.5 indicates that the presence of serial correlation may not be disruptive.

Figure 11.14 presents a chart showing these guidelines. The Durbin–Watson statistic is a generally available statistic with most computer regression programs and should be reported when time series data are under analysis. In MINITAB, the Durbin–Watson statistic is obtained by using the REGRESS command followed by the subcommand DW.

Figure 11.14
Measuring the extent of serial correlation

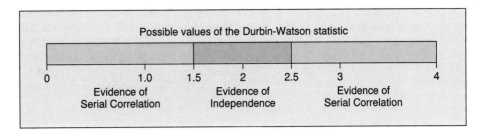

EXERCISES

11.12 Make a residual plot from the following table:

$\hat{Y}$	1	2	3	4	5	6	7	8	9	10	11	12
$Y - \hat{Y}$	3	1	0	0	−1	−2	−3	−1	0	0	1	2

Based upon your analysis of residuals, does a linear or curvilinear equation appear to be more appropriate? Explain.

11.13 Make a residual plot from the following table:

$\hat{Y}$	1	2	3	4	5	6	7	8	9	10	11	12
$Y - \hat{Y}$	0	1	2	1	0	−1	−3	−1	0	1	3	1

$\hat{Y}$	13	14	15	16	17	18	19	20	21	22	23	24
$Y - \hat{Y}$	0	−1	−2	−1	0	1	2	1	0	−1	−2	1

Are the residuals more suggestive of a problem caused by (a) curvilinearity, or (b) serial correlation? Explain.

▶ **11.14** In the late 1960s, A. W. Phillips investigated the relationship linking the inflation rate and unemployment rate. He suggested that there is a trade-off between inflation and unemployment, which is defined by a simple curvilinear relationship now called the *Phillips curve*. In other words, unemployment would be "bought" at the price of high inflation. (In recent years, this idea has been severely criticized.) A regression analysis of the percentage of unemployment was run on the percentage of inflation, using annual data for an 18 year period. The variables were expressed as logarithms (with base e). Computer output reported the following results: $\hat{Y} = 3.121 - 1.407X$, $R^2 = 0.197$, $R_a^2 = 0.147$, $S_b = 0.709$, $S_e = 0.601$, and Durbin–Watson statistic = 0.855.
   a. Comment on the explanatory power of the equation, and evaluate the significance of the explanatory variable at the $\alpha = .01$ level.
   b. What problem with residuals is suggested by the value of the Durbin–Watson statistic? Explain.

11.15 A multiplant company has one particular plant with a history of unusually high employee grievances of all kinds. The plant manager, suspected of being a poor administrator, invariably blames the weather for the high rate of grievances at the plant. Essentially, he argues that large deviations from ideal humidity cause employees to become disgruntled and dream up a wide variety of imaginary grievances. The only way to stop the grievances, he says, is to air-condition the plant, which he happens to know is virtually impossible. The vice–president in charge of industrial relations thinks the solution to the problem may be to find a new plant manager. To check out the situation, she has data collected on employee grievances and on the deviation of humidity from ideal. Then she computes the least squares regression line. The computed r^2 is very low ($r^2 = 0.005$ for the equation $\hat{Y} = 25.8 - 0.355X$), and the standard deviation of the slope coefficient is several times the value of the coefficient. Based on this information, the vice-president draws up the plant manager's pink slip for dismissal. The plant manager appeals and asks for the data (given in the table). He questions the suitability of a linear regression.

DAY	DEVIATION OF HUMIDITY INDEX FROM IDEAL	NUMBER OF EMPLOYEE GRIEVANCES
1	−2	6
2	+3	11
3	+7	51
4	+2	6
5	0	2
6	−9	83
7	+6	38
8	−5	27
9	+4	18
10	−5	27
11	−1	3
12	−3	11
13	+7	51

a. Draw a scatter diagram of the data.
b. Using the least squares regression equation given, find the value of $\hat{Y}$ for each observation (day).
c. Compute the residuals for each observation (day).
d. Plot the residuals on a scatter diagram. What problem is suggested by the pattern of residuals?
e. Fit a parabolic curve to the data. How good is the fit?
f. Comment on the importance of the regression residual checking in analyzing this problem.

11.7 OTHER MODELING ISSUES

Before concluding our discussion of modeling, two other statistical issues need to be considered: *multicollinearity* and *selection of independent variables*.

MULTICOLLINEARITY

The condition of **multicollinearity** exists in multiple regression when the X_i explanatory variables are not statistically independent; that is, one or more of the X_i explanatory variables are interdependent (highly correlated) with one or more of the other X_i explanatory variables. This situation may pose a problem, depending on whether the purpose of the regression analysis is the estimation of the regression coefficients or the prediction of Y. Multicollinearity may seriously impede reliable estimation of the regression coefficients, while having little effect on the prediction of Y.

Let's look at a numerical example to illustrate the impact of high multicollinearity on regression results. Suppose for the past 12 quarters, the national sales manager of Glitz Jewelry, a wholesale jeweler, has been observing the fluctuation of its customer sales with the fluctuation in the wholesale prices of gold and silver. Over 3 years, the manager has collected the data in Table 11.6 on Glitz nationwide jewelry sales, the wholesale price of gold, and the wholesale price of silver.

	TABLE 11.6 Data on Glitz Jewelry		
QUARTER	NATIONAL JEWELRY SALES (MILLION DOLLARS) Y	WHOLESALE PRICE OF GOLD ($/OZ) X_1	WHOLESALE PRICE OF SILVER ($/OZ) X_2
1	229	417	6.0
2	263	360	5.5
3	332	279	4.5
4	283	291	3.5
5	216	369	6.0
6	292	342	4.0
7	331	279	3.0
8	246	429	6.5
9	260	306	4.0
10	442	252	3.0
11	266	336	4.0
12	284	333	5.0

In Figure 11.15, the MYSTAT output for the correlation among the three variables shows that there exists a moderately strong negative correlation ($r_{Y.X_1} = -0.782$) between the dollar volume of jewelry sales and the wholesale price of gold and a similar moderately strong negative correlation ($r_{Y.X_2} = -0.721$) between jewelry sales and the wholesale price of silver. The strong negative correlation indicates that each price variable can be viewed as an important determinant of jewelry sales.

Figures 11.16 and 11.17 are MYSTAT outputs of the individual regression analyses of jewelry dollar sales on the price of gold and on the price of silver, respectively. For the regression analysis of jewelry dollar sales on the price of gold, we find an observed t value of -3.972. At $\alpha = .01$, the t table value for 10 d.f. is 3.169. Since the absolute value of the observed $t, |-3.972|$, exceeds 3.169, we can assert that the wholesale price of gold is a highly significant explanatory variable for jewelry sales. (Or, equivalently, we can reach this conclusion because the p-value, shown in the computer output under "$P(2$ TAIL)," of .003 is less than .01.) In addition, the value of S_e (standard error of estimate) equals 39.327, and the r^2 value of 0.612 indicates that about 61% of the variation in jewelry sales can be explained by the variation in gold price.

For the regression analysis on the price of silver (Figure 11.17), the observed t value of -3.286 for the price of silver indicates that the silver price is also a highly significant explanatory variable of jewelry dollar sales. The value S_e is 43.781, and the

Figure 11.15
MYSTAT correlation matrix for Glitz Jewelry data

```
PEARSON CORRELATION MATRIX

                      JEWELRY          GOLD         SILVER

        JEWELRY         1.000
           GOLD        -0.782         1.000
         SILVER        -0.721         0.895         1.000


Number of observations:    12
```

```
DEP VAR: JEWELRY   N:   12   MULTIPLE R:  .782   SQUARED MULTIPLE R:   .612
ADJUSTED SQUARED MULTIPLE R: .573   STANDARD ERROR OF ESTIMATE:      39.327


   VARIABLE   COEFFICIENT  STD ERROR   STD COEF TOLERANCE    T     P(2 TAIL)
  CONSTANT       571.964     72.634       0.000  .          7.875    0.000
     GOLD        -0.856       0.216      -0.782  .100E+01   -3.972   0.003




                         ANALYSIS OF VARIANCE


    SOURCE    SUM-OF-SQUARES    DF  MEAN-SQUARE     F-RATIO      P


  REGRESSION    24401.958       1    24401.958      15.778    0.003
  RESIDUAL      15466.042      10     1546.604
```

Figure 11.16
MYSTAT regression analysis of jewelry sales on price of gold

```
DEP VAR: JEWELRY    N:   12   MULTIPLE R:  .721    SQUARED MULTIPLE R: .519
ADJUSTED SQUARED MULTIPLE R: .471    STANDARD ERROR OF ESTIMATE:    43.781


   VARIABLE    COEFFICIENT   STD ERROR    STD COEF TOLERANCE    T    P(2 TAIL)
  CONSTANT       452.288       51.861       0.000  .          8.721   0.000
    SILVER       -36.063       10.974      -0.721  .100E+01   -3.286  0.008




                         ANALYSIS OF VARIANCE


    SOURCE    SUM-OF-SQUARES    DF   MEAN-SQUARE     F-RATIO       P


  REGRESSION    20700.063       1    20700.063      10.799     0.008
  RESIDUAL      19167.937      10     1916.794
```

Figure 11.17
MYSTAT regression analysis of jewlery sales on price of silver

r^2 value of 0.519 indicates that nearly 52% of the variation in jewelry sales can be attributed to the variation in the price of silver.

With both explanatory variables highly significant individually, we can try to use both of them in a multiple regression analysis to isolate the net effect of each price, given the presence of the other price in the equation. Additionally, the presence of both prices in the equation should be useful in predicting Y, the level of jewelry sales.

The MYSTAT output in Figure 11.18 shows that taken as a whole the multiple regression equation is significant at $\alpha = .05$ (the p-value of .014 is less than .05). But, checking the p-values for the variables in the multiple regression under "P(2 TAIL)," we see that even at $\alpha = .1$, neither variable is a significant explanatory variable (with p-values of .171 and .830).

```
DEP VAR: JEWELRY    N:  12   MULTIPLE R: .784    SQUARED MULTIPLE R: .614
ADJUSTED SQUARED MULTIPLE R: .528    STANDARD ERROR OF ESTIMATE:    41.342


     VARIABLE    COEFFICIENT   STD ERROR    STD COEF TOLERANCE    T    P(2 TAIL)
     CONSTANT       562.054      88.533       0.000  .          6.348   0.000
         GOLD        -0.756       0.508      -0.691 0.1991316  -1.488   0.171
       SILVER        -5.135      23.222      -0.103 0.1991316  -0.221   0.830




                         ANALYSIS OF VARIANCE


      SOURCE    SUM-OF-SQUARES    DF   MEAN-SQUARE      F-RATIO         P


   REGRESSION      24485.542      2    12242.771        7.163        0.014
     RESIDUAL      15382.458      9     1709.162
```

Figure 11.18
MYSTAT multiple regression analysis of jewelry sales on price of gold and price of silver

What seemed to be a promising undertaking (including both variables in one equation), has turned out to be unsuccessful. The fault lies with the high multicollinearity between X_1 and X_2. This multicollinearity can be spotted in Figure 11.15, which tells us that the pairwise correlation between the price of gold and the price of silver is 0.895. With only a few available observations (12 in this case), the high collinearity undermines the reliable estimation of the values of b_1 and b_2, the *net* effect of X_1 and X_2 on Y. Fortunately, we are still able to use the multiple regression analysis to make relatively precise predictions of Y. The S_e value, which determines the width of the prediction interval of Y, was found to be 41.342 in the multiple regression— only a slightly higher value than the S_e achieved (39.327) with the simple regression using gold price as an explanatory variable. With b_1 and b_2 imprecise as estimates, we dare not use b_1 and b_2 values of the multiple regression to estimate the impact on jewelry dollar sales of a change in the price of gold or silver, respectively. For instance, the interpretation of the coefficient of silver ($b_2 = -5.135$) in the multiple regression would be that jewelry sales would rise by $5.135 million for a $1 drop in the price of silver. But the imprecision of that 5.135 estimate is defined by its standard error, which is 23.222, that is, about 23.222 million—a value over four times the size of the coefficient!

Two important conclusions can now be reached:

1. **Estimation of the true regression coefficients B_1 and B_2.** If the purpose of the regression analysis is to measure the separate effects of X_1 and X_2 on Y by estimating the regression coefficients, then very high correlation between X_1 and X_2 does pose a problem. High multicollinearity will tend to result in imprecise estimates of the regression coefficients. It will cause the standard error of the regression coefficients to inflate, which lowers the t values for the regression coefficients and generally renders them insignificant. In fact, in severe cases of multicollinearity, statistically separating out the effects of X_1 and X_2 on Y will be virtually impossible.

2. **Prediction of Y.** If the prediction of Y is the main purpose of the regression analysis, then even very high interdependence among the X_i variables will not seriously disrupt the predictive accuracy of the regression equation as a whole. To judge predictive accuracy, we use the regression statistic S_e, and this regression statistic will be relatively unchanged by high interdependence among the X_i's. If we are dealing with time series data, we are especially likely to encounter multicollinearity. If our task is to forecast a future Y value, we assume that the structure and intensity of the multicollinearity between the explanatory variables remains unchanged into the forecasting period.

We should also keep in mind in dealing with multicollinearity that the difficulty of obtaining reliable estimates b_1 and b_2 in the presence of high interdependence between X_1 and X_2 generally cannot be resolved by dropping X_2 and reestimating the regression for b_1 (or by dropping X_1 and reestimating the regression for b_2). It requires either an alternative means of specifying or estimating the effect on Y of at least one of the independent variables, or else additional data sufficient for the net effect of each variable to be discerned.

SELECTING EXPLANATORY VARIABLES FOR THE REGRESSION EQUATION

Another modeling issue that arises in statistical applications is how to select the best set of explanatory variables when the investigator has a dozen or more explanatory variables available for inclusion in the regression model. More concisely, with model simplicity as an objective, how do we screen the variables efficiently?

If the purpose of the analysis is to obtain a prediction model that accurately predicts Y, then we need a mechanical approach that best sorts out a particular set of explanatory variables that best predicts Y. One such selection procedure is called *backward elimination*. This procedure uses S_e as the measure of the predictive ability of a regression equation, and relies on the changes in the value of S_e as a criterion for eliminating an explanatory variable. For instance, if upon elimination of an explanatory variable the value of S_e falls, the predictive ability of the regression equation has been enhanced.

Backward elimination starts with a full multiple regression model of all the available explanatory variables under consideration. It uses the guiding rule: *Do not eliminate an explanatory variable having the correct sign and an absolute t value above 1, since S_e would increase by the deletion.*

If by chance all the variables of the full model have the correct sign and absolute t values above 1, no further steps are needed. All the explanatory variables are kept in the predictive equation. But, generally, this is not the case, and one or more independent variables have absolute t values below 1. In that case, we use the following procedure:

Step 1
The first variable deleted is the one with the smallest absolute t value below 1. This elimination should lower S_e, indicating an overall improvement in predictive ability.

Step 2
Rerun the regression with the one variable removed and again apply the guiding rule. After a regression is run with the remaining variables, the absolute t values are again examined. If all absolute t values exceed 1, we have found the best set

of explanatory variables. If at least one variable has an absolute t value less than 1, return to Step 1.

This weeding out procedure of variables with $|t| < 1$ leaves an equation of remaining explanatory variables, all with $|t| > 1$. Any additional deletions at this point would cause S_e to increase and violate our guiding rule.

Computer regression programs (such as MINITAB) are generally designed to automatically perform (at the user's option) the backward elimination procedure, using a *stepwise regression* routine. This makes the procedure very accessible and convenient to use. Alternative mechanical selection procedures are also available. Some of these are particularly useful if parameter estimation is an important issue in variable selection, along with the best prediction of Y. However, a thorough discussion of all these approaches and the issues involved is beyond the scope of this book.

SUMMARY

In this chapter we have discussed the multiple regression model, which is an important and valuable extension of the simple regression model developed in Chapter 10. Simple regression analysis required us to specify that Y is related to only one independent variable X, whereas the multiple regression model allows us the flexibility to account for the effect of several independent variables in determining the value of Y.

If the purpose of the multiple regression equation is the prediction of the value of Y, our attention is focused on judging the reliability of the equation as a whole in predicting Y, and not on the reliability of the individual regression coefficients. If a set of potentially useful independent variables is available for inclusion in the multiple regression equation, the first task is to include the entire set of available independent variables in the regression equation and conduct an F test for overall significance of the entire set of X variables. If the equation is found to have overall significance, our attention can turn to judging the merit of retaining individual variables. The ability of an equation to predict Y improves with the lowering of the standard deviation of residuals, S_e, of the regression, so if the elimination of a variable lowers S_e, the variable should be left out of the equation. On the other hand, if the value of S_e rises with elimination of the variable, the variable should be retained. The guiding rule is to retain a variable as long as it has a logically correct sign and an absolute t value above 1. The exclusion of variables should proceed in a stepwise fashion. At each step the variable with the lowest absolute $|t|$ value below 1 should be eliminated. Fortunately, the existence of multicollinearity between the independent variables will not disrupt the predictive ability of the regression equation as a whole. The explanatory power of multiple regression equations is best measured by the adjusted multiple R^2, R_a^2.

When the purpose of the multiple regression analysis is to reliably estimate the values of individual regression coefficients, the first step again is to conduct an F test for overall significance of the multiple regression equation. If the F test concludes statistical significance of the equation as a whole, then each individual regression coefficient can be judged by its t value and whether the coefficient possesses a logically correct sign. Statistical significance of the individual coefficient is difficult to achieve in the presence of high multicollinearity because it depresses the absolute t value of the coefficient.

The legitimacy of using the t values to draw inferences about the statistical significance of the regression coefficients rests on whether the estimation is in conformity with the regression model assumptions of constant variance and randomness of the error term. One way model adequacy is judged is by visually examining the behavior of the regression residuals on a scatter plot. Multiple regressions using data that are collected chronologically (time series data) typically produce serially correlated residuals, that violate the randomness assumption. To detect the severity of the problem the Durbin–Watson statistic is used in conjunction with a visual examination of the residual scatter plot. Sometimes, model inadequacy in the behavior of the residuals of a linear multiple regression can be corrected by fitting a parabolic equation or by a data transformation such as the logarithmic transformation.

The usefulness of a model and a model's explanatory power can be improved by including in the model an additional explanatory variable. For instance, in our employment discrimination example, our main interest was the reliable estimation of the coefficient of the gender variable. By adding the prior experience variable, we not only improved the explanatory power of the equation but also reduced the standard deviation of residuals, which in turn helped obtain a reliable estimate of the gender variable. This example illustrates the use of a dummy variable to estimate the quantitative effect of gender, a qualitative variable.

KEY EQUATIONS

Fitted Multiple Regression Equation

$$\hat{Y} = a + b_1 X_1 + b_2 X_2 + \cdots + b_k X_k \tag{11-1}$$

Standard Deviation of Residuals

$$S_e = \sqrt{\frac{\Sigma(Y - \hat{Y})^2}{n - k - 1}} = \sqrt{\frac{\text{SSE}}{n - k - 1}} \tag{11-2}$$

Coefficient of Multiple Determination

$$R^2 = \frac{\Sigma(\hat{Y} - \bar{Y})^2}{\Sigma(Y - \bar{Y})^2} = \frac{\text{SSR}}{\text{SST}} \tag{11-3}$$

Multiple Regressior Model

$$Y = A + B_1 X_1 + B_2 X_2 + E \tag{11-4}$$

F Test Statistic for Testing Significance of the Regression Equation as a Whole

$$F_{(k, n-k-1)} = \frac{\text{MSR}}{\text{MSE}} \tag{11-5}$$

$1 - \alpha$ Confidence Interval for Individual Coefficients B_i

Upper confidence limit (UCL) for B_i:

$$b_i + t_{(\alpha/2, \nu)} S_{b_i}$$

Lower confidence limit (LCL) for B_i: $\tag{11-6}$

$$b_i - t_{(\alpha/2, \nu)} S_{b_i}$$

where $\nu = n - k - 1$ degrees of freedom.

$1 - \alpha$ Confidence Interval for $\mu_{Y.X_1 X_2}$

$$\text{UCL} = \hat{Y} + t_{(\alpha/2, \nu)}(\text{Standard deviation of fitted } Y) \tag{11-7}$$

$$\text{LCL} = \hat{Y} - t_{(\alpha/2, \nu)}(\text{Standard deviation of fitted } Y)$$

(*Note:* "Std dev. Fit" (or similar) is given as part of the output of many computer statistical software packages.)

$1 - \alpha$ Prediction Interval for New Y Value

$$\text{UPL} = \hat{Y} + t_{(\alpha/2, \nu)}(\text{Standard deviation of prediction}) \tag{11-8}$$

$$\text{LPL} = \hat{Y} - t_{(\alpha/2, \nu)}(\text{Standard deviation of prediction})$$

(*Note:* The standard deviation of prediction can be obtained as part of the regression output of a computer statistical software package, e.g., MINITAB.)

Parabolic Regression Equation

$$\hat{Y} = a + b_1X + b_2X^2 \tag{11-9}$$

PRACTICE EXERCISE ANSWERS

11.1 a. The multiple regression equation is $\hat{Y} = -13.824566 + 1.999461X_1 + 0.212167X_2$.
b. A one point increase in the percentage of national sales occurring in the district (X_1), with the number of sales calls (X_2) held constant, is associated with an average increase in Y of 1.999461 units.
c. If $X_1 = 3$ and $X_2 = 120$, the value of $\hat{Y}$ is $\hat{Y} = -13.824566 + 1.999461(3) + 0.212167(120) = 17.63386$.

d.

OBSERVATION	Y	X_1	X_2	$\hat{Y}$	$Y - \hat{Y}$	$(Y - \hat{Y})^2$
1	10	3.0	90	11.2689	-1.26885	1.60999
2	11	0.5	115	11.5744	-0.57438	0.32991
3	23	1.5	150	20.9997	2.00031	4.00126
4	35	8.0	152	34.4205	0.57948	0.33580
5	26	5.0	140	25.8761	0.12387	0.01534
6	32	5.5	160	31.1192	0.88080	0.77581
7	30	9.5	112	28.9330	1.06697	1.13843
8	39	9.0	170	40.2390	-1.23899	1.53509
9	15	6.0	80	15.1456	-0.14557	0.02119
10	34	5.0	185	35.4236	-1.42365	2.02678
	255	53.0	1354	255.0000	0	11.78960

$$S_e = \sqrt{\frac{\Sigma(Y - \hat{Y})^2}{n - k - 1}} = \sqrt{\frac{11.78960}{10 - 2 - 1}} = 1.29778$$

e.

OBSERVATION	Y	$\hat{Y}$	$\bar{Y}$	$(\hat{Y} - \bar{Y})^2$	$(Y - \bar{Y})^2$
1	10	11.2689	25.5	202.526	240.25
2	11	11.5744	25.5	193.923	210.25
3	23	20.9997	25.5	20.253	6.25
4	35	34.4205	25.5	79.576	90.25
5	26	25.8761	25.5	0.141	0.25
6	32	31.1192	25.5	31.575	42.25
7	30	28.9330	25.5	11.786	20.25
8	39	40.2390	25.5	217.238	182.25
9	15	15.1456	25.5	107.214	110.25
10	34	35.4236	25.5	98.479	72.25
				962.711	974.50

$$R^2 = \frac{\Sigma(\hat{Y} - \bar{Y})^2}{\Sigma(Y - \bar{Y})^2} = \frac{962.711}{974.5} = 0.9879$$

11.2 The regression equation is $\hat{Y} = -13.825 + 1.9995X_1 + 0.21217X_2$. The following results are taken from the MINITAB output for this problem:

PREDICTOR	COEFFICIENT	STANDARD DEVIATION	t-RATIO	p
Constant	-13.825	1.795	-7.70	0.000
X_1	1.9995	0.1456	13.73	0.000
X_2	0.21217	0.01266	16.76	0.000
$S = 1.298$	$R^2 = 98.8\%$	$R^2(adj) = 98.4\%$		

Analysis of Variance					
SOURCE	**d.f.**	**SS**	**MS**	**F**	**p**
Regression	2	962.71	481.36	285.80	0.000
Error	7	11.79	1.68		
Total	9	974.50			
SOURCE	**d.f.**	**SEQ SS**			
X_1	1	489.65			
X_2	1	473.06			

a. The observed F value is 285.80.

b. In this problem there were 10 observations and 2 independent variables, so the explanatory power of the regression equation is significant if $F > F_{(.01,2,7)} = 9.55$. Since the observed F of 285.80 is greater than the critical F of 9.55, the equation does have significant explanatory power.

11.3 The limits of the confidence interval for B_2 are given by

$$b_2 \pm t_{(\alpha/2, n-k-1)} S_{b_2} = b_2 \pm t_{(.025,7)} S_{b_2} = -0.600 \pm 2.365(0.2047)$$

Thus, UCL $= -0.116$ and LCL $= -1.084$. We are 95% confident that with each additional block of distance from the ocean, holding the view rating constant, there will be a decrease in lot price of between \$116,000 and \$1,084,000.

11.4 a.

NURSE	WAGE RATE ($/HR) Y	YEARS OF EXPERIENCE X_1	SHIFT X_2
1	12	3	1
2	11	2	1
3	10	3	0
4	10	1	1
5	8	1	0

b. Day shift, $\hat{Y} = 6.5 - 1.25X_1$; night shift, $\hat{Y} = (6.5 + 1.67) - 1.25X_1$

c. \$1.67/hr

11.5 The base location category is urban, so the dummy variables X_3 and X_4 are defined as follows:

$$X_3 = \begin{cases} 1 & \text{if suburban free-standing} \\ 0 & \text{otherwise} \end{cases}$$

$$X_4 = \begin{cases} 1 & \text{if suburban shopping center} \\ 0 & \text{otherwise} \end{cases}$$

The values of X_3 and X_4 are listed below:

Store Number	X_3	X_4
1	0	0
2	1	0
3	1	0
4	0	0
5	0	1
6	1	0
7	0	0
8	0	1

11.6 a. When production is 1000 gal, estimated cost is

$$\hat{Y} = 15{,}800 + 2.2(1000) - 0.001(1000)^2 = \$17{,}000.00$$

b. When production is 1001 gal, estimated cost is

$$\hat{Y} = 15{,}800 + 2.2(1001) - 0.001(1001)^2 = \$17{,}000.20$$

So the incremental cost of the production increase from 1000 to 1001 gal is $0.20.

CHAPTER REVIEW EXERCISES

11.16 Suppose the computed multiple regression equation is

$$\hat{Y} = 52 + 1.7X_1 - 7.0X_2 + 4.0X_3$$

a. For values of $X_1 = 6$, $X_2 = 2$, and $X_3 = 1$, what is the predicted value of Y?
b. What two statistics measure the fit of the regression equation to the sample data?
c. What statistic measures the reliability of the coefficient of X_1?

▶ **11.17** Data on three variables are summarized in the following sums of squares and cross products. There were 5 data points.

$$\sum Y = 12 \qquad \sum X_1 = 10 \qquad \sum X_2 = 12 \qquad \sum X_1^2 = 22$$
$$\sum X_2^2 = 40 \qquad \sum YX_1 = 28 \qquad \sum YX_2 = 37 \qquad \sum X_1X_2 = 26$$

a. Write the normal equations to determine the net regression coefficients b_1 and b_2.
b. Given the following solution for the multiple regression equation,

$$\hat{Y} = -1.783 + 1.54X_1 + 0.457X_2$$
$$S_{b_1} = 0.6248 \qquad \text{and} \qquad S_{b_2} = 0.2640$$

interpret the meaning of the coefficients.
c. Using the standard errors of the regression coefficients as shown in part b, compute the t ratios.
d. Determine which variable is more significant statistically. Explain.

11.18 A small manufacturer of men's ties experienced a very high rate of absenteeism among its workers, and the absenteeism has tended to fluctuate considerably from week to week. The president of the company believes union organizers are the source of the absenteeism problem. Absenteeism and employee complaints have been encouraged by the organizers to apply pressure to management. A measure of the activity of the organizers is provided by the number of union-supported complaints appearing in the employee suggestion box each week. The plant manager believes the absenteeism results from the president's policy of not increasing the work force during peak demand periods. Any increase in demand must be met through overtime. The plant manager claims the workers "just don't want to work more than 45 hr a week." Excessive overtime assignments lead many workers to stay home rather than accumulate extra work hours. You decide to try to find out which factor is the more influential in causing the fluctuations in absenteeism—union organizers or overtime assignments. Accordingly, you compile the appropriate data over the past 4 weeks and set up the multiple regression equation, with Y the number of work hours absent in a given week, X_1 the total number of overtime hours required in that week, and X_2 the number of union-supported complaints in the suggestion box that week. The data (all figures are in hundreds) are summarized in the following sums of squares and cross products:

$$\sum Y = 18 \qquad \sum X_1 = 10 \qquad \sum X_2 = 9 \qquad \sum X_1^2 = 30$$
$$\sum X_2^2 = 23 \qquad \sum YX_1 = 48 \qquad \sum YX_2 = 43 \qquad \sum X_1X_2 = 22$$

a. Write the normal equations to determine the regression coefficients b_1 and b_2.
b. Given the following solution for the multiple regression equation,

$$\hat{Y} = 0.407 + 0.704X_1 + 1.037X_2$$
$$S_{b_1} = 0.046 \quad \text{and} \quad S_{b_2} = 0.053$$

interpret the meaning of the coefficients.
c. Using the standard errors of the coefficients as shown in part b, determine which variable is more significant statistically.

11.19 An advertising agency sponsors a consumer panel study to determine the productivity of advertising for a client's brand of frozen mixed fruit. A multiple regression equation known as an *advertising response function* is computed, regressing a family's dollar purchases of the brand (Y) on two explanatory variables: the number of exposure opportunities to the brand's advertising, X_1, and the number of exposure opportunities to a competing brand's advertising, X_2. The computed regression equation is

$$\hat{Y} = 0.22 + 0.235X_1 - 0.110X_2$$

a. What interpretation should be given to the two regression coefficients in the advertising response function?
b. For a family having 10 exposure opportunities to the brand's advertising and none to the competitor's advertising, what is the estimated expenditure on the brand?
c. Suppose a family is given 5 exposure opportunities to the brand's advertising, the competing brand retaliates by advertising its own brand enough so that 2 of its ads are seen by this same family. What is the expected expenditure of the family on the client's brand?
d. Does advertising of a brand of frozen mixed fruit appear to stimulate sales of that brand only, or does it stimulate sales of competing brands as well? (*Hint:* Interpret the coefficient of X_2.)

11.20 A company sells women's hosiery in special display racks directly to supermarkets and variety stores. This company wants to determine the relationship, if any, between the percentage of stores who agree to carry its product (Y) and two explanatory variables: price, X_1, and years of experience of the salesperson, X_2. Thirty salespeople employed by the company are randomly assigned to sell the product to retail dealers, 6 salespeople for each of 5 different prices, ranging from 63¢ to $2.49 per pair. Each salesperson makes a sales presentation to 40 prospective new dealers, and the percentage of new accounts is recorded. The 30 observations (6 salespeople for each of 5 prices) are used to determine the least squares regression equation,

$$\hat{Y} = -28 - 1.2X_1 + 12X_2$$

with $S_{b_1} = 0.4$, $S_{b_2} = 3.0$, $F = 29.8$, and $R^2 = 0.88$.
a. Interpret the values of b_1 and b_2.
b. Using an F test and the 5% level of significance, test the hypothesis that the equation has explanatory power useful for predicting Y.
c. Do the data support the conclusion that higher prices decrease dealer willingness to carry the product? Explain.

d. Does the evidence indicate that additional experience increases the ability of salespeople to secure additional dealers? Explain.

11.21 Data on the supply of milk produced by a firm per month, Y, over the past 10 months at various prices, X_1, are given in the table. During the first, second, and third months, the firm sustained a strike in some of its plants.

Milk Supply (thousand of gallons) at Various Prices										
	MONTH									
	1	**2**	**3**	**4**	**5**	**6**	**7**	**8**	**9**	**10**
PRICE/GALLON DOLLARS	1.93	1.95	1.96	1.88	1.88	1.90	1.93	1.94	1.96	1.97
QUANTITY	80	87	94	113	116	118	121	123	126	128

a. Run a regression analysis of Y on X_1 and X_2, letting X_2 be a 0–1 dummy explanatory variable for which $X_2 = 1$ during the month of the strike and $X_2 = 0$ otherwise.
b. Test the strike variable, X_2, for statistical significance at $\alpha = .01$.

11.22 Twelve randomly selected families were surveyed on their consumption expenditure, Y, their disposable income, X_1, and the sex of the head of the household, X_2. The data collected are presented in the table, with the consumption and disposable income expressed in thousands of dollars.

	FAMILY											
	1	**2**	**3**	**4**	**5**	**6**	**7**	**8**	**9**	**10**	**11**	**12**
Y	18.5	11.3	12.1	15.2	8.7	16.8	13.5	9.7	17.8	11.1	14.3	20.0
X_1	22.5	14.0	13.0	17.5	9.4	20.6	16.5	10.7	22.4	12.3	16.8	23.0
X_2	M	M	F	M	F	M	M	F	M	F	F	M

a. Let X_2 be a 0–1 dummy explanatory variable in which $X_2 = 1$ for families headed by a female and $X_2 = 0$ otherwise. Regress consumption, on income and sex.
b. Is the dummy variable statistically significant at the 5% level?

11.23 An automobile manufacturer wants to express the gasoline mileage ratings, Y, of automobiles as a function of their engine size, X. A sample of 50 automobiles of varying engine sizes is selected, and the miles per gallon rating of each is determined. A parabolic regression model is proposed, and the fitted regression equation is

$$\hat{Y} = 43.1 - 8.3X - 0.18X^2$$

where the size X of the engine is measured in hundreds of cubic inches. Other relevant statistics are $S_{b_2} = 0.0032$ and $R^2 = 0.91$.
a. Sketch the regression curve (between $X = 1$ and $X = 4$).
b. Is there evidence that the quadratic (X^2) term in the model improves the prediction of the miles per gallon rating Y? Use the .05 level of significance.
c. Use the model to estimate the mean miles per gallon rating for all cars with 300 in.[3] engines ($X = 3.0$).
d. Suppose the limits of a 95% confidence interval for the quantity estimated in part c are from 16.01 to 17.15. Interpret this interval.
e. Suppose you purchase an automobile with a 300 in.[3] engine and determine that the miles per gallon rating is 15.4. Is the fact that this value lies below the confidence interval given in part d surprising? Explain.

11.24 Many companies sponsor job-related safety programs in order to reduce accidents on the job. Suppose it is hypothesized that serious accidents become more likely near the end of the work day, when workers are fatigued, rather than near the beginning of the day. A nonlinear model is proposed to investigate the fatigue hypothesis. Accident reports over the past year are sampled, and the number of hours the employee had worked before the accident occurred (X) and the number of days lost from work (Y) are recorded. A total of 80 accident reports are examined. The fitted regression equation is

$$\hat{Y} = 12.5 + 0.23X - 0.0035X^2$$

with $R^2 = 0.044$.

a. Use the regression equation to predict the number days lost from work for an employee who has an accident after 7 hrs of work.

b. Does the low value of R^2 necessarily mean that no fatigue factor exists? Explain.

❑ ▶ **11.25** System Design Inc. produces electronic modules and is keeping records on the hours to failure, Y, of units tested. In addition, for each module tested, data are kept on the frequency of exposure to power surges of more than 8 volts, X_1, the power level at which each part is used in a machine, X_2, and the number of quality control steps during manufacture, X_3. The records for 14 electronic modules tested are given in the table.

UNIT	Y	X_1	X_2	X_3
1	55	8	700	13
2	65	8	1100	17
3	90	4	1600	18
4	40	9	400	10
5	75	5	1300	19
6	60	7	800	11
7	100	3	1500	23
8	80	5	1400	20
9	45	8	500	14
10	95	3	1700	24
11	50	9	600	12
12	70	6	900	15
13	65	6	1000	16
14	85	4	1800	21

a. Enter the data in your computer and use a scatter diagram to see if Y and X_1 and/or Y and X_2 are linearly related.

b. Use a regression analysis program to calculate the regression equation and its related statistics.

c. Test for the overall significance of the whole regression equation at the $\alpha = .05$ level.

d. Test the statistical significance of each explanatory variable at the $\alpha = .05$ level.

e. Predict the value of Y for $X_1 = 5$, $X_2 = 1200$, and $X_3 = 18$ using the equation you choose in part d.

❑ **11.26** Wilkinson Shoe Company manufactured men's shoes and distributed them in 11 sales territories covering 43 states. The company wanted a measure of territory sales potential that could be used in comparing territories and in evaluating the performance of the salesperson assigned to the territory. Data were compiled for each territory on four variables that were thought to be linked to sales: X_1, percentage of U.S. footwear sales; X_2, number of accounts serviced; X_3, percentage of U.S. personal income; and X_4, percentage nonwhite population. Data on the variables, as well as territory sales, Y (in thousands of dollars), are given in the table.

TERRITORY	Y	X₁	X₂	X₃	X₄
1	1352	8.6	239	7.1	12.1
2	336	5.0	125	8.2	9.5
3	682	7.6	204	11.4	13.1
4	147	2.1	76	5.0	4.2
5	378	3.5	125	4.4	12.6
6	732	7.0	157	8.1	5.5
7	1031	8.8	153	12.6	12.7
8	498	6.3	125	9.9	4.2
9	826	10.2	181	10.7	13.3
10	357	5.3	182	14.1	24.7
11	119	3.9	67	7.4	14.4

a. Enter the data into your computer and use your regression analysis program to determine the regression equation and related statistics.
b. What percentage of the variation in sales among territories is explained by the equation?
c. Which explanatory variables are significant at $\alpha = .10$?
d. Compute $\hat{Y}$ for each territory and interpret this value as the estimated sales "norm" for the territory. This norm would be used in establishing sales quotas for the territory that would be consistent with quotas established for other territories.
e. Describe the variation in estimated sales potential among the territories.
f. Interpret the regression coefficient for each variable in terms of the impact of the variable on estimated sales potential.
g. Compute the regression residuals and interpret each residual as the deviation in performance of the salesperson in that territory from the norm for that territory.
h. In which territories did performance exceed or fall below the sales norm by a noteworthy amount, that is, by greater than one S_e from the norm?

□ 11.27 The data given in the table were compiled by a company on 11 of its salespeople.

SALESPERSON	TRAVEL COST DOLLARS	NUMBER OF CALLS MADE	NIGHTS AWAY FROM HOME	NUMBER OF ACCOUNTS
1	5,485	410	85	268
2	5,560	396	123	136
3	6,212	783	130	255
4	5,268	624	169	245
5	6,157	618	165	266
6	5,730	536	171	218
7	5,998	568	130	226
8	10,406	632	142	210
9	8,592	458	209	107
10	6,397	736	163	98
11	7,765	635	171	352

a. Regress travel cost on the other variables, and obtain the estimated regression equation and the associated statistics (S_e, R^2, R_a^2).
b. One executive has complained that she doesn't believe that the travel costs are primarily attributable to objective factors such as the number of accounts,

how many calls are actually made, and how many nights the salespeople are away from home. Use the R^2 statistic to respond to her charge.

c. Give a practical interpretation to the value of a in the regression equation.

d. Compute the regression residuals. Pick out the salespeople you might investigate further concerning their travel expenses.

e. Estimate the travel expense for a salesperson who is expected to call upon 200 accounts, making 600 calls, and being away from home 150 nights. Is this estimate useful for decision making?

11.28 The data in the table were compiled on the entertainment expenses of the same 11 company salespeople discussed in Exercise 11.27.

						Salesperson					
	1	2	3	4	5	6	7	8	9	10	11
ENTERTAINMENT EXPENSE Dollars	963	742	961	682	637	713	614	829	854	770	1285

a. Regress entertainment expense on number of accounts and number of sales calls made. Data on the latter two variables are given in Exercise 11.27.

b. Interpret the coefficients of the regression equation.

c. What percentage of entertainment expenses is accounted for by variation in number of accounts and number of sales calls?

d. Interpret the value of a in the regression equation.

e. Compute the regression residuals. Which salespeople would you single out for additional explanation of their entertainment expenses?

11.29 An automobile manufacturer has 20 franchised dealers in a large metropolitan area. To study factors influencing the amount of customer traffic, data were collected on customer traffic, the amount of newspaper and TV advertising by each dealer, the size of their physical facilities, and whether their location was in an urban area or in a suburban area. The data are given in the table.

DEALER	CUSTOMER TRAFFIC (NUMBER PER WEEK)	ADVERTISING (× $100)	SIZE (ACRE LOTS)	URBAN (0)/ SUBURBAN (1)
1	90	0	1.3	1
2	550	0	2.0	1
3	380	4.0	2.1	1
4	180	10.0	1.5	1
5	200	11.0	1.0	0
6	660	17.0	1.9	0
7	310	19.0	1.0	1
8	220	31.0	1.5	1
9	790	32.0	2.0	0
10	720	38.0	2.0	1
11	360	41.0	1.6	1
12	1040	48.0	2.8	0
13	840	53.0	1.4	1
14	220	54.0	2.3	1
15	510	57.0	1.7	1
16	690	59.0	1.9	0
17	980	57.0	2.8	1
18	630	73.0	2.5	0
19	700	67.0	2.4	0
20	1030	69.0	2.0	1

a. Enter the data into a computer.
b. Compute the multiple regression equation and related statistics (R^2, S_e, F, t ratios).
c. Interpret the regression coefficient of each variable.
d. What percentage of variation in customer traffic is accounted for by the explanatory variables?
e. Which variables are significant at $\alpha = .05$?

□ ▶ 11.30 The table lists the sales price, Y, and four assumed related explanatory variables, X_1, X_2, X_3, and X_4, for each of 40 single-family residences sold by a real estate agent the previous month. Which variables would you include in the regression equation if you wanted to estimate the market value of:

SALES PRICE (× $1000) Y	SQUARE FEET (× 100) X_1	NUMBER OF STORIES X_2	NUMBER OF BATHROOMS X_3	AGE (YEARS) X_4
33.1	8.9	1	1	2
45.3	9.5	1	1	6
45.8	12.4	2	1.5	5
48.3	10.5	1	1	11
41.7	10.7	1	1.5	15
54.0	13.8	2	1.5	10
54.1	12.6	2	1.5	11
54.4	12.9	2	1.5	8
54.9	15.5	2	1	9
57.3	16.5	1	1.5	15
59.5	16.0	2	1	11
59.9	16.7	2	1	12
60.3	17.5	2	2	13
60.8	17.9	2	1.5	18
61.0	19.0	2	1	22
63.5	17.6	1	1	17
66.1	18.1	2	1.5	5
66.5	17.0	3	2	2
66.8	20.4	2	1.5	16
66.9	20.0	2	1.5	12
69.2	21.9	2	1.5	10
69.5	20.6	2	1.5	11
72.9	19.9	1	1.5	13
75.0	21.8	2	2	8
75.1	20.5	1	2	9
76.6	22.2	2	1.5	10
78.9	22.0	2	2.5	6
81.8	22.5	2	1.5	17
84.0	24.3	2	1.5	17
84.7	23.5	2	2.5	12
89.0	25.0	2	1.5	11
92.0	25.4	1	1	12
99.8	25.1	2	2	8
105.3	26.8	2	2.5	6
107.1	22.7	2	2	18
114.0	25.6	2	2	10
118.4	24.0	2	2	13
119.0	31.2	3	2.5	25
123.0	21.6	2	2.5	18
155.0	40.8	3	4	12

a. Enlarging an existing house to add one bathroom?
b. Adding one bathroom without enlarging the house?

c. Suppose older houses generally have fewer bathrooms for a given house size than do newer houses. What effect, if any, would this have on the reliability of the coefficients b_3 and b_4 in a regression equation with the four given independent variables?

d. Suppose age of the house is thought to have an important influence on the market value of the house. A regression analysis of Y on X_1, X_2, X_3, and X_4 gives coefficients for X_1, X_2, and X_3 that are highly statistically significant. The coefficient of X_4 is not significant, having a t value well below 1. Would you include X_4 in a regression equation used to predict selling price of a house? Explain.

e. Should your answer to part d depend on the sign of b_4? Explain.

11.31 Refer to the data set in Exercise 11.30.

a. Fit a multiple linear regression equation,

$$\hat{Y} = a + b_1X_1 + b_2X_2 + b_3X_3 + b_4X_4$$

using a standard computer regression analysis program.

b. Interpret the computer output for this analysis.

c. Use the computed multiple regression equation to estimate selling price for each of 5 residences currently on the market. The data are given in the table:

RESIDENCE	SQUARE FEET (× 100)	NUMBER OF STORIES	NUMBER OF BATHROOMS	AGE (YEARS)
i	X_1	X_2	X_3	X_4
1	20.4	2	2	17
2	15.8	2	1.5	6
3	19.2	1	1.5	4
4	21.7	3	2	22
5	30.0	2	2.5	11

Data for Exercises 11.32–11.36: A food products manufacturer developed a new highly nutritional snack bar that could be used as a diet food. Early product and concept tests were encouraging, but Bill Wilkinson, the product manager, wanted a 6 month market test before nationwide introduction of the product. An experiment was designed to study the effect of price, advertising, and location of the product within the store. Three price levels were tested, two levels of advertising (high and low), and two locations (placing the product in the diet food section versus the snack food section). Prices and locations were varied across stores within cities, while advertising was varied across cities. Each experimental unit included three stores in the same city. In selecting cities and stores for the tests, an attempt was made to match experimental units and cities on such variables as store size, number of checkout counters, and store neighborhood characteristics. Because it was not certain that adequate matches had been achieved, measurements were also obtained on average family income of families in each store's trading area and also on the average weekly dollar sales of all stores in an experimental unit. The data from the test are given in the table. The price stipulated is for a box of 10 bars (in dollars). A high level of advertising is represented by 1 and a low level by 0; in-store location at the diet food section is represented by 1 and location at the snack food section is represented by 0. Family income and store sales volume are reported in thousands of dollars.

11.32 a. Using price, advertising, and location for independent variables, write the general form of the regression equation.

b. For an experimental unit in which advertising is at a high level, the in-store location is in the diet section, and retail price is set at $5.80 per box, what would be the data values representing the independent variables?

c. Suppose the experimental unit described in part b is located in city 2. If the

UNIT	CITY NUMBER	AVERAGE UNIT SALES PER MONTH	PRICE	ADVERTISING	LOCATION WITHIN STORE	AVERAGE ANNUAL FAMILY INCOME	STORE SALES VOLUME
		Y	P	A	L	I	V
1	3	620	4.80	0	0	36.5	34
2	4	776	4.80	0	0	41.5	41
3	1	955	4.80	1	0	34.5	32
4	2	669	4.80	1	0	32.5	28
5	3	623	4.80	0	1	36.5	34
6	4	542	4.80	0	1	41.5	41
7	1	596	4.80	1	1	34.5	23
8	2	1208	4.80	1	1	32.5	37
9	3	475	5.80	0	0	32.5	33
10	4	544	5.80	0	0	42.0	39
11	1	472	5.80	1	0	32.5	30
12	2	697	5.80	1	0	31.0	27
13	3	582	5.80	0	1	32.5	37
14	4	706	5.80	0	1	42.0	43
15	1	482	5.80	1	1	32.5	30
16	2	388	5.80	1	1	31.0	19
17	3	413	6.80	0	0	36.0	32
18	4	556	6.80	0	0	40.5	42
19	1	294	6.80	1	0	33.0	29
20	2	378	6.80	1	0	30.5	24
21	3	395	6.80	0	1	36.0	32
22	4	382	6.80	0	1	40.5	36
23	1	355	6.80	1	1	33.0	29
24	2	373	6.80	1	1	31.0	24

instructions for data input to the computer stipulate that the dependent variable be entered first, and then the price variable, advertising variable, and location variable, what would be the data input for this experimental unit?

11.33 a. Suppose the regression output of sales on price, advertising, and location is as given below. What would be the predicted sales level for an experimental unit in which there is a high level of advertising, packages are located in the diet section, and retail price is set at $5.80 per box?

Constant: 1590.795, S_e: 155.9904, R^2: 0.511608,
Number of observations: 24,   d.f.: 20

	Price	Advertising	Location
X coefficient(s)	−177.687	21.08333	−18.0833
Standard deviation of coefficient(s)	38.99760	63.68282	63.68282

b. By how much would the predicted sales volume decline if advertising were set at the lower spending level?
c. What would be the change in predicted sales volume from the level predicted in part a if in-store location were changed from the diet section to the snack food section?
d. Which regression coefficient(s) are statistically significant at the .05 level? Do these variables have the logically correct sign?

11.34 It was felt that the effect of some of the independent variables might be obscured by extraneous variation in family income and size of store (measured by sales volume) among the experimental units. Therefore, a second regression run was made including the two additional independent variables as a control measure. The regression output is given below.

Constant: 1017.813, S_e: 121.2849, R^2: 0.734277,
Number of observations: 24, d.f.: 18

	Price	Advertising	Location	Income	Store Size
X Coefficient(s)	−149.295	184.9942	−3.54549	−16.3578	27.71252
Standard deviation of coefficient(s)	31.49299	81.16495	49.67041	11.64137	7.295026

a. For the experimental unit in city 2 having a high level of advertising, location within the diet section, and a retail price of $5.80 per box, what is the predicted level of sales?

b. What would be the predicted decline in unit sales if advertising spending were reduced to the lower level?

c. What would be the change in predicted sales volume if in-store location is changed to the snack food section?

d. Which regression coefficient(s) are statistically significant at the .05 level? Do these variables have the logically correct sign?

e. Compare your answers to parts a–d of this problem with your answers to parts a–d of Exercise 11.33. What has been the impact of adding the two additional variables?

11.35 The family income variable is not statistically significant in Exercise 11.34, and it does not have the logically correct sign. Drop this variable from the regression equation and rerun the regression using price, advertising, location, and store sales volume as independent variables. Interpret your output and compare your results to the results from Exercises 11.33 and 11.34.

11.36 The regression residuals are given below for the equation determined in Exercise 11.35. Check the residuals to identify observations that don't seem to fit the model (if any). If there are observations that don't seem to fit, explain why.

UNIT	OBSERVED Y	PREDICTED Y	RESIDUAL
1	620	642.6	−22.6
2	776	754.3	21.7
3	955	805.0	150.0
4	669	727.1	−58.1
5	623	639.1	−16.1
6	542	750.8	−208.8
7	596	552.2	43.8
8	1208	972.9	235.1
9	475	531.4	−56.4
10	544	541.4	2.6
11	472	633.2	−161.2
12	697	574.8	122.2
13	582	638.7	−56.7
14	706	648.7	57.3
15	482	529.7	−147.7
16	388	349.7	38.3
17	413	296.9	116.1
18	556	499.8	56.2
19	294	448.0	−154.0
20	378	350.6	27.4
21	395	293.4	101.6
22	382	330.1	51.9
23	355	444.5	−89.5
24	373	338.9	34.1

SOLVING APPLIED CASES

In the following business situation, multiple regression is used to improve the business analysis. The case illustrates how qualitative variables with more than two categories can be handled and interpreted by the dummy variable technique.

Demand Analysis for Chiquita Bananas

Hoping to carve out a market niche and to avoid an intense price war with Ecuadorian bananas, the United Fruit Company developed a strategy to market a superior quality banana at a premium price under the brand name "Chiquita" banana. To achieve superior quality, a higher-cost shipping method must be used. To minimize in-transit damage that would impair quality, bananas have to be boxed at the tropical plantations instead of using the traditional method of shipping bananas on the stem. The boxing method reduces breakage, bruising, and deterioration. In general, this procedure entails a more stringent quality control program than has existed in the industry. But will consumers perceive this quality difference and pay extra for the Chiquita bananas? With the cooperation of a supermarket chain, United Fruit Company conducted a market research study encompassing 14 locations.

The effects on consumer sales for several combinations of three banana quality levels and three price premium levels were researched with the price levels quantified in the following way:

Price Premium	Coded Price Value, X_3
2¢ per pound below prevailing retail (discount)	-2
Prevailing retail price	0
2¢ per pound above prevailing retail (premium)	$+2$

The marketing results received from the 14 locations appear in Table 11.7.

TABLE 11.7	Market Research Study on Banana Sales		
LOCATION	**SALES IN POUNDS PER WEEK PER THOUSAND CUSTOMERS**	**QUALITY**	**PRICE**
1	390	Superior–boxed	+2
2	388	Superior–boxed	+2
3	278	Creamed–stem	+2
4	316	Creamed–stem	+2
5	578	Superior–boxed	0
6	598	Superior–boxed	0
7	490	Creamed–stem	0
8	512	Creamed–stem	0
9	228	Regular–stem	0
10	392	Regular–stem	0
11	452	Creamed–stem	−2
12	602	Creamed–stem	−2
13	390	Regular–stem	−2
14	420	Regular–stem	−2

To perform a statistical analysis on the data, it was decided to use multiple regression with both price premium and banana quality as explanatory variables. The dummy variable technique was applied to the quality levels. Boxed bananas were recorded as the superior quality. Bananas shipped on the stem were either creamed or regular, creamed being the higher quality of the two. Since there were three levels of banana quality, two 0–1 dummy variables were required to identify the quality levels. Regular–stem was assigned the base category, with creamed–stem indicated by one dummy, X_1, and superior–boxed indicated by the other dummy, X_2. That is, regular–stem is indicated by 0 being assigned to both X_1 and X_2; creamed–stem is indicated by assigning 1 to X_1 and 0 to X_2; and superior–boxed is indicated by assigning 0 to X_1 and 1 to X_2. For example, consider the first store location where superior–boxed bananas were sold; there, the dummy variable X_1 would get a 0, but X_2 (for the superior–boxed category) would get a 1. In stores where regular–stem bananas were sold, both X_1 and X_2 would be 0.

	TABLE 11.8 Dummy Variables for Quality			
LOCATION	SALES IN POUNDS PER WEEK PER THOUSAND CUSTOMERS Y	CREAMED X_1	SUPERIOR X_2	PRICE X_3
1	390	0	1	+2
2	388	0	1	+2
3	278	1	0	+2
4	316	1	0	+2
5	578	0	1	0
6	598	0	1	0
7	490	1	0	0
8	512	1	0	0
9	228	0	0	0
10	392	0	0	0
11	452	1	0	-2
12	602	1	0	-2
13	390	0	0	-2
14	420	0	0	-2

Look at Table 11.8, where we now show the quality levels in a dummy variable format. The two dummy variables account for the three qualitative levels. Figure 11.19 shows the multiple regression results of sales (dependent variable), on the three independent variables: dummy X_1 (for creamed quality), dummy X_2 (for superior quality), and X_3 (price premium). The fitted multiple regression equation, constructed from the coefficients, is

$$\hat{Y} = 294.67 + 147.00X_1 + 256.67X_2 - 62.83X_3$$

All the signs of the explanatory variables meet with our expectations. Both dummy variables X_1 and X_2 have positive signs, indicating higher quality levels than the base category; the price

Figure 11.19
MINITAB regression results for Chiquita Banana case

```
MTB >regr c1 3 c2-c4

The regression equation is
sales = 295 + 147 creamed + 257 superior - 62.8 price

                                St. Dev.      T-Ratio =
Column          Coefficient     of Coef.      Coef/S.D.              p
                294.67          35.68         8.26              0.000
Creamed         147.00          44.73         3.29              0.008
Superior        256.67          53.94         4.76              0.000
Price           -62.83          13.49         -4.66             0.000

s = 66.07


R-Squared = 74.9 percent
R-Squared = 67.4 Percent, Adjusted for D.F.

Analysis of Variance

 Due To      DF        SS        MS=SS/DF           F              p
Regression    3     130269        43423          9.95          0.002
Residual     10      43649         4365
Total        12     173918
```

variable X_3 has the expected negative sign for its inverse effect on sales. For a two-sided significance test at $\alpha = .01$ and $\nu = 10$ d.f., we determine the rejection region by obtaining from the t table (Appendix Table VII) the value $t_{(.005,10)} = 3.169$. Thus, the rejection region is

$$t_\nu < -3.169 \quad \text{or} \quad t_\nu > 3.169$$

The observed t values are 3.29, 4.76, and -4.66 for X_1, X_2, and X_3, respectively. Since the observed t value for each dummy variable exceeds 3.169, and since the t value for price is less than -3.169, the value of the test statistic is in the rejection region for all three of the variables. Thus, we conclude that the regression coefficient for each variable is highly significant, and from a statistical viewpoint, all the variables should remain in the model.

How can we use the fitted regression model to estimate demand? For example, how does the estimated demand for superior quality boxed bananas at a 2¢ per pound price premium compare with estimated demand for creamed quality at the prevailing price? The answer will be revealed by the dummy variable coefficients. Let's see how to interpret the pair of dummy variables indicating quality levels.

For superior quality demand, the dummy variable X_2 in the equation has a value of 1 and dummy variable X_1 has a value of 0. The multiple regression equation that estimates demand for superior–boxed at a 2¢ per pound price premium is

$$\hat{Y} = 294.67 + 147.00X_1 + 256.67X_2 - 62.83X_3$$
$$= 294.67 + 147.00(0) + 256.67(1) - 62.83(+2)$$
$$= 426.4 \quad \text{(Rounded)}$$

For creamed quality demand, dummy variable X_1 has a value of 1 and dummy variable X_2 has a value of 0. The multiple regression equation for estimating creamed–stem demand at the prevailing price is

$$\hat{Y} = 294.67 + 147.00X_1 + 256.67X_2 - 62.83X_3$$
$$= 294.67 + 147.00(1) + 256.67(0) - 62.83(0)$$
$$= 442 \quad \text{(Rounded)}$$

At the 2¢ per pound premium price for the superior–boxed bananas, note that the demand (426.4) is not as high as for creamed bananas (442) at the prevailing price. Note also, though, that with the price premium removed, demand for superior–boxed substantially exceeds demand for creamed–stem bananas:

$$\hat{Y} = 294.67 + 147.00X_1 + 256.67X_2 - 62.83X_3$$
$$= 294.67 + 147.00(0) + 256.67(1) - 62.83(0)$$
$$= 552 \quad \text{(Rounded)}$$

Checkpoint Exercise

1. A follow-up marketing research study of 14 similar locations was conducted. The objective was to introduce some additional price variation and determine the stability of results of the first study. The price levels used are listed below:

Price Premium	Coded Price Value
2¢ per pound below prevailing retail (discount)	−2
Prevailing retail price	0
3¢ per pound above prevailing retail (premium)	+3

The follow-up market research results are shown in Table 11.9:

TABLE 11.9	Follow-Up Market Research Study on Banana Sales		
LOCATION	SALES IN POUNDS PER WEEK PER THOUSAND CUSTOMERS	QUALITY	PRICE
1	542	Creamed–stem	0
2	648	Superior–boxed	0
3	347	Creamed–stem	+3
4	465	Superior–boxed	+3
5	349	Regular–stem	0
6	612	Creamed–stem	−2
7	519	Regular–stem	−2
8	534	Regular–stem	−2
9	687	Creamed–stem	−2
10	430	Regular–stem	0
11	567	Creamed–stem	0
12	464	Superior–boxed	+3
13	366	Creamed–stem	+3
14	658	Superior–boxed	0

For the three quality levels, construct dummy variables that can be used as independent variables in a multiple regression model; assign the base category to the regular–stem type of banana.

a. Fit a multiple regression equation to the data in Table 11.9 using sales as the dependent variable and with price and the quality dummy variables as explanatory variables. Analyze the findings. Do the findings of the follow-up study confirm or contradict the conclusion reached in the first study?

b. How does the estimated demand of superior–boxed bananas at the prevailing price compare with the estimated demand of regular–stem at 2¢ below the prevailing price?

WENDY'S DATABASE ANALYSIS

In Chapter 10, the Wendy's Database Analysis investigated the relationship between brand preference and food taste image. For the 406 surveyed respondents, consumers' fast food brand preference was shown to be directly related to consumers' image of a brand's food taste. This relationship was statistically significant, but only one independent variable, brand food taste image, was tested. Now we are in a position to deal with several independent variables simultaneously by multiple regression analysis. The multiple regression will include, in addition to brand food taste image, two other explanatory variables: brand convenience image and brand menu price image.

The form of the multiple regression equation to be fitted is

$$\hat{Y} = a + b_1X_1 + b_2X_2 + b_3X_3$$

where X_1 = Brand food taste image, X_2 = Brand convenience image, and X_3 = Brand menu price image. An illustration of the MINITAB commands used to construct the four variables to be used in the multiple regression are given in Figure 11.20. Note that the six observations on each variable are the arithmetic means for the six brands. Thus, variable X_1, for brand food taste image, is identified as "meantast," variable X_2, for brand convenience image, is identified as "meanconv," etc. The MINITAB commands to perform the regression analysis, along with the results, are given in Figure 11.21.

```
MTB > mean c27 k1
    MEAN    =      3.5659  Mean of Food Taste Rating for Borden Burger
MTB > mean c28 k2
    MEAN    =      3.3290   "   "   "   "   "   "   "   " Hardee's
MTB > mean c29 k3
    MEAN    =      2.4231   "   "   "   "   "   "   "   " Burger King
MTB > mean c30 k4
    MEAN    =      2.0895   "   "   "   "   "   "   "   " McDonld's
MTB > mean c31 k5
    MEAN    =      1.9661   "   "   "   "   "   "   "   " Wendy's
MTB > mean c32 k6
    MEAN    =      3.8061   "   "   "   "   "   "   "   " White Castle
MTB > stack k1-k6 c201
MTB > name c201 'meantast'

MTB > mean c39 k7
    MEAN    =      2.7005  Mean of Convenience Rating for Borden Burger
MTB > mean c40 k8
    MEAN    =      3.3483   "   "       "       "   " Hardee's
MTB > mean c41 k9
    MEAN    =      2.7377   "   "       "       "   " Burger King
MTB > mean c42 k10
    MEAN    =      1.9380   "   "       "       "   " McDonald's
MTB > mean c43 k11
    MEAN    =      2.8920   "   "       "       "   " Wendy's
MTB > mean c44 k12
    MEAN    =      3.7242   "   "       "       "   " White Castle
MTB > stack k7-k12 c202
MTB > name c202 'meanconv'

MTB > mean c45 k13
    MEAN    =      2.9372  Mean of Menu Price Rating for Borden Burger
MTB > mean c46 k14
    MEAN    =      2.7513   "   "   "   "   "   "   " Hardee's
MTB > mean c47 k15
    MEAN    =      3.0761   "   "   "   "   "   "   " Burger King
MTB > mean c48 k16
    MEAN    =      2.4884   "   "   "   "   "   "   " McDonald's
MTB > mean c49 k17
    MEAN    =      4.0814   "   "   "   "   "   "   " Wendy's
MTB > mean c50 k18
    MEAN    =      1.7080   "   "   "   "   "   "   " White Castle
MTB > stack k13-k18 c203
MTB > name c203 'meanpric'

MTB > mean c103 k19
    MEAN    =      4.2552  Mean of Preference Ratings for Borden Burger
MTB > mean c104 k20
    MEAN    =      4.0911   "   "       "       "   " Hardee's
MTB > mean c105 k21
    MEAN    =      3.0052   "   "       "       "   " Burger King
MTB > mean c106 k22
    MEAN    =      2.2429   "   "       "       "   " McDonald's
MTB > mean c107 k23
    MEAN    =      2.5351   "   "       "       "   " Wendy's
MTB > mean c108 k24
    MEAN    =      4.7812   "   "       "       "   " White Castle
MTB > stack 19-k24 c204
MTB > name c204 'meanpref'
```

Figure 11.20
MINITAB commands to construct the variable "meantast," "meanconv," "meanpric," and "meanpref"

```
MTB > regress 'meanpref' 3 'meantast' 'meanconv' 'meanpric'

The regression equation is
meanpref = - 0.915 + 1.15 meantast + 0.320 meanconv + 0.0668 meanpric

Predictor        Coef       Stdev     t-ratio        p
Constant       -0.9154      0.2697      -3.39      0.077
meantast        1.14773     0.06841     16.78      0.004
meanconv        0.31984     0.07197      4.44      0.047
meanpric        0.06683     0.05387      1.24      0.341

s = 0.06969     R-sq = 99.8%     R-sq(adj) = 99.5%

Analysis of Variance

SOURCE         DF          SS          MS          F          p
Regression      3       5.3066      1.7689     364.20      0.003
Error           2       0.0097      0.0049
Total           5       5.3163

SOURCE         DF       SEQ SS
meantast        1       5.1820
meanconv        1       0.1171
meanpric        1       0.0075
```

Figure 11.21
MINITAB output for Wendy's multiple regression

Regression Statistics and Interpretation of the Results

a. **The fitted multiple regression equation.** The fitted multiple regression equation is given in the output as

$$\text{meanpref} = -0.915 + 1.15 \text{ meantast} + 0.320 \text{ meanconv} + 0.0668 \text{ meanpr}$$

b. **Explanatory power.** The explanatory power of this equation, measured by the adjusted R_a^2 of 99.5%, is very high. But could this explanatory power be a sampling fluke, since only six observations (one for each brand) were available to calculate the R^2 statistic? By testing the statistical significance of the regression equation as a whole, we can address this issue.

c. **Significance of the regression equation considered as a whole.** For this test, we follow the procedure described in Section 11.4.

Step 1

Determine the rejection region. Using a significance level of $\alpha = .01$, the value $F_{(.01,3,2)} = 99.2$ is found from the F table (Table IXb, Appendix). Thus, values of observed F larger than 99.2 are in the rejection region.

NOTE: The discrepancy between the F ratio calculated here and the F value of 364.22 shown in the MINITAB output is due to rounding error in stating the MS terms.

Step 2

Calculate the test statistic. From the MINITAB ANOVA table, we find values for MSR and MSE and for the observed F ratio:

$$F_{(3,2)} = \frac{\text{MSR}}{\text{MSE}} = \frac{1.7689}{0.0049}$$

$$= 361$$

Step 3

Determine whether the test statistic is in the rejection region. We see that the observed F statistic of 361 is greater than 99.2 and therefore falls in the rejection region.

Step 4

Draw a conclusion. Since the observed F value falls in the rejection region, we reject H_o

and conclude that the regression equation as a whole—including taste, convenience, and price—is highly significant in determining customer preference.

d. **Predictive reliability.** The low value of 0.06969 for the standard deviation of residuals, S_e, relative to the mean brand preference ratings, will be beneficial in forming narrow prediction intervals of new mean brand preference ratings.

e. **Significance of individual coefficients.** The coefficient of the brand food taste image variable (meantast) has the correct sign, and its high t value of 16.78 allows us to conclude that its coefficient is statistically significant. The brand convenience variable (meanconv) has a t value of 4.44 and is also statistically significant. But the coefficient of the brand menu price image variable (meanpric) has a low t value of 1.24; it is not statistically significant even at the $\alpha = .10$ significance level.

f. **Interpretation of coefficients.** Looking at the computed regression coefficients, we see the meantast coefficient $(b_1) = 1.14774$. This tells us that an increase of 1 unit in meantast ratings (i.e., toward a more favorable brand food taste image), holding meanconv and meanpr ratings constant, leads, on average, to an increase in a brand's meanpref ratings of 1.14774 units. This means that any improvements in a brand's food taste image could lead to even greater increases in the preference ratings for that brand among consumers. The coefficient of meanconv, on the other hand, indicates that an increase of 1 unit in meanconv could lead, on average, to a much smaller 0.31984 unit increase in meanpref, holding meantast and meanpr constant. The coefficient of meanpr indicates that a 1 unit improvement in that variable leads, on average, to a positive but small 0.06683 increase in meanpref, holding meantast and meanconv constant. We can conclude from a comparison of the three coefficients that a franchise could obtain a much more favorable impact on the consumer preference rating for its brand by increasing its brand's food taste image than by obtaining a similar increase in either its brand's convenience image or menu price image.

g. **The meaning of the coefficients—multiple versus simple regression.** The coefficient value $(+1.14774)$ for the meantast variable in the multiple regression equation is smaller than the coefficient value $(+1.2732)$ of the meantast variable from the simple regression of meantast on meanpref performed in Chapter 10. The larger 1.2732 value of the simple regression equation is plausible, since it represents the gross effect of meantast on meanpref, whereas the 1.14774 value represents the net effect of meantast on meanpref. The gross value of meantast captures not only the effect of taste on preference but also factors not included in the simple regression equation that are related to taste such as convenience and menu price. The multiple regression equation, on the other hand, has the capability of holding these factors constant by including them in the regression equation, and thus can separate out the net effects of all three variables on brand preference—something that was not possible with simple regression analysis.

Wendy's Student Exercises

For the heavy user group (i.e., those who answer 1 or 2 on question 2 of the Wendy's questionnaire), the mean ratings for (1) heavy user preference (HUPREF), (2) heavy user, food taste image (HUTASTE), (3) heavy user convenience image (HUCONV), and (4) heavy user menu price image (HUPRICE) were computed and are listed below for the six brands of fast food chains studied. The mean values were obtained in the same way as explained in the Wendy's Student Exercises in Chapter 10.

BRAND	HUPREF	HUTASTE	HUCONV	HUPRICE
Borden Burger	4.39	3.67	2.78	3.02
Hardee's	4.07	3.22	3.34	2.75
Burger King	2.86	2.22	2.34	3.15
McDonald's	2.14	1.99	1.81	2.52
Wendy's	2.44	1.74	2.90	4.09
White Castle	5.02	3.95	3.56	1.71

1. Use the REGRESS command for HUPREF on HUTASTE, HUCONV, and HUPRICE.
   a. What is the fitted regression equation?
   b. What is S_e?
   c. What is R^2?

2. Comment on the S_e and R^2 values found in Exercises 1b and 1c.

3. Comment on the magnitude and the statistical significance of the regression coefficients.

4. Interpret the coefficients. Compare the magnitudes of the coefficients and draw a conclusion from the comparison.

CHI-SQUARE ANALYSIS

Headline Issue

THE BIG BUSINESS OF COLLEGE ATHLETICS: THE EXPLOITED COLLEGE ATHLETE?

College athletics, particularly football and basketball, are big business at many major universities. Packed stadiums and alumni contributions linked to the athletic programs are a significant source of revenue for universities and colleges with notable sports programs. For the few fortunate major universities and colleges that have national or regional fan support, the revenue pot is sweetened further by television networks that pay large sums for the rights to televise their football and basketball games. To ensure a constant supply of talent for these sports, universities and colleges offer thousands of athletic scholarships yearly (often for free tuition, room and board). But recent headlines indicate that college athletes may pay a high price for the benefits received. The articles report that a majority of these athletes either fail to graduate or don't get the education they thought they should have gotten. Cases have been cited of athletes who graduate but are functionally illiterate—that is, they simply can't read.

To document this situation, the U.S. General Accounting Office published a report based on sample data provided by the NCAA (National Collegiate Athletic Association). The report compared graduation rates of athletes versus all students at NCAA member schools. Part of this report surfaced in the sports section of the *Los Angeles Times* on January 9, 1990, as one of two major articles featured under the headline, "Colleges Play Numbers Game With Athletes." The article provides two of the tables from the General Accounting Office report and a very detailed interpretation of the report. One table compares the graduation rates of basketball players versus all students, for the same 97 schools; and the other table compares the graduation rates of football players versus all students, for the same 103 schools. The graduation rates are based on a 5-year completion period. The rates are computed by dividing the number of students and student athletes who entered the school in the 1982–1983 academic year into the number of those same students and student athletes who had graduated by August 31, 1987 (5 years later). Table 12.1 compares the graduation rates of football players to the rates for all students at 103 division I-A member schools. Division I-A is the category that includes schools with the most comprehensive sports programs. Under the "Football" and "All students" headings, the table lists the number of schools that reported particular graduation rates for the reporting period. For example, on the first line, 5 schools reported that from 0% to 20% of all their students graduated within the 5 year period; 14 schools reported that from 0% to 20% of their football players graduated within the same 5 year period.

Note that 5 of the 103 schools had graduation rates of 20% or less for all students, whereas 14 of the 103 schools had graduation rates of 20% or less for football players. Thus, there were 9 more schools that had extremely low graduation rates for football players than had this extremely low rate for all students.

TABLE 12.1 Graduation Rates: Football Players Compared to All Students at 103 Division I-A Schools

PERCENT GRADUATED WITHIN 5 YEARS		FOOTBALL PLAYERS	ALL STUDENTS
0 to 20	(extremely low)	14	5
21 to 40	(low)	39	30
41 to 60	(moderate)	31	42
61 to 80	(good)	13	20
81 to 100	(excellent)	6	6
		103	103

Examining the remaining rows of the table line by line, we see that:

- Football players had low graduation rates of 21–40% in 39 schools, whereas these low rates applied to all students in only 30 schools. In this category also, we see that 9 more schools had low graduation rates for football players than had this low rate for all students.

- Football players had moderate graduation rates of 41–60% in 31 schools, but these moderate rates applied to 42 schools for all students. Thus, 11 fewer schools had moderate graduation rates for football players.

- Football players had good graduation rates of 61–80% in 13 schools, but these good rates applied to 20 schools for all students. Thus, 7 fewer schools had good graduation rates for football players.

- Football players and all students had excellent graduation rates of 81–100% in 6 schools. Thus, excellent graduation rates at 6 schools applied equally to football players and to all students.

Does this evidence suggest that football players are being exploited? Since football players show low and extremely low graduation rates in more schools, and high graduation rates in fewer schools than all students, exploitation of football players appears plausible. But does the appearance of lower graduation rates for football players hold up under statistical testing? Is the discrepancy between graduation rates statistically significant? Or can it merely be attributed to random sampling error—a peculiarity of the particular students during those 5 years at the 103 schools in the sample? The *chi-square technique* described in this chapter will give us an objective evaluation of whether the discrepancies are real or attributable to sampling error and an objective determination of the likelihood of our conclusion being wrong.

Overview

The hypothesis testing procedures discussed in Chapters 8 and 9 are classified as parametric procedures because of two characteristics they have in common. First, they address solely the issue of hypothesis tests for population parameters such as the population mean and the population variance—meaningful measures only if the data are interval scaled. Second, their application requires the assumption of a particular parametric family of distributions. For example, in the case of small samples, the application of the parametric Student *t* test statistic assumes the underlying population is normally distributed. When the necessary underlying conditions are met, the parametric procedures efficiently utilize the data; but the restrictive focus and assumptions of parametric tests limit their applicability.

Fortunately, other hypothesis testing techniques are available, which are either free of the restrictive assumption of a normal population distribution and/or enable us to deal with a wide variety of data, including nominal scale data and ordinal scale data. One of these techniques, the *chi-square technique,* will be discussed in this chapter; others will be discussed in Chapter 13.

Our discussion in this chapter will illustrate two uses of the *chi-square distribution.* The first use of the chi-square distribution tests for the independence of nominal scale data on two categorical variables. The second use tests for goodness of fit of a sample frequency distribution to an actual or theoretical statistical distribution. Both of these applications of the chi-square distribution are encountered frequently in statistical analyses of data.

12.1

ANALYSIS OF CATEGORICAL DATA

In analyzing a set of data on two categorical variables, we usually want to know whether a relationship exists. For example, suppose a random sample of households is selected and individually cross-classified according to (1) the brand of laundry detergent most frequently used in the household versus (2) the occupational status of the primary wage earner. The cross-classified sample data are given in Table 12.2. Suppose you are asked to determine whether the cross-classified sample data offers sufficient evidence to claim that an association (dependence) exists between the two variables in the population. That is, does occupational status affect the brand of detergent most frequently used? To conduct a test of the null hypothesis of no association between the variables (statistical independence), what statistic should be calculated to conduct the test?

When two categorical variables are statistically independent in the population, some cross-classified category combinations will have greater probability of occurrence than others. Assuming independence and using these probabilities, estimated theoretical expected frequencies can be derived for each category combination of the sample data. The test statistic compares the estimated theoretical frequency of each category combination to the corresponding observed frequency of each category combination. Statistically significant differences between the two frequencies cause us to reject the null hypothesis of independence. The observed frequencies for testing association are presented in a table known as a **contingency table**. Table 12.2 is the contingency table for the data on laundry detergent brand and occupational status.

		OCCUPATIONAL STATUS			
		Blue-Collar Worker	**White-Collar Worker**	**Does Not Work Outside Home**	**TOTALS**
BRAND OF	**A**	20	80	30	130
LAUNDRY	**B**	90	30	20	140
DETERGENT	**C**	15	25	100	140
TOTALS		125	135	150	410

TABLE 12.2 Contingency Table of Brand of Laundry Detergent and Occupational Status (Observed Frequencies; Number of Observations)

CONTINGENCY TABLES

The general form of a contingency table is presented in Table 12.3. The table shows the category combinations for two categorical variables, say A and B, where variable A has r categories and variable B has c categories. Each cross-classification of the categories forms a cell of the table. The number of cells in a table is determined by how many categories there are for each of the two categorical variables. If one variable, A, has r categories and the other variable, B, has c categories, then the total number of cross-classification cells is the product, $r \times c$.

TABLE 12.3	An r x c Two-Way Contingency Table				
	CATEGORICAL VARIABLE B				**TOTALS**
	1	**2**	**...**	**c**	
1	O_{11}	O_{12}	...	O_{1c}	$O_{1.}$
2	O_{21}	O_{22}	...	O_{2c}	$O_{2.}$
CATEGORICAL . **VARIABLE A** . .	. . .	. . .	O_{ij}	. . .	. . .
r	O_{r1}	O_{r2}	...	O_{rc}	$O_{r.}$
TOTALS	$O_{.1}$	$O_{.2}$	...	$O_{.c}$	n

Note that the categories for variable A are shown as row headings and the categories for variable B are shown as column headings in Table 12.3. Letting i denote the row category and j denote the column category, each cell is then denoted by a particular ij combination. Thus, cell ij refers to the cross-classification of the ith category of variable A and the jth category of variable B.

Each observation in the sample is classified into only one of the cells. The total number of sample observations that fall into each cell is the *observed frequency* of that cell, O_{ij}. The cells and their respective observed frequencies are popularly called *cross-tabulations*, or simply "cross-tabs." It should be noted that the contingency tables can be used with any kind of data: nominal, ordinal, interval, or ratio. However, the range of interval or ratio-scaled data must be subdivided to form categories. For example, the range of salary data (measured on a ratio scale) may be divided into high, medium, low categories for reporting in a contingency table.

Table 12.3 also gives the row and column totals. The row totals are shown as $O_{i.}$ terms, where $i = i, ..., r$. For instance, the $O_{i.}$ term equals $O_{11} + O_{12} + \cdots + O_{1c}$; that is, $O_{1.}$ is the sum of the observed frequencies across the c columns for the first row. The column totals are shown as $O_{.j}$ terms, where $j = 1, \ldots, c$. For instance, the $O_{.1}$ term equals $O_{11} + O_{21} + \cdots + O_{r1}$; this is the sum of the observed frequencies down the r rows for the first column. To indicate the sum of the observed frequencies in all the cells (across all c columns and r rows), we write

$$\sum_{i=1}^{r} \sum_{j=1}^{c} O_{ij}$$

which, for the sake of brevity of notation, we state simply as $\Sigma\Sigma\, O_{ij}$. Since summing the frequency of observations across all rows and all columns must include all the observations, this summation operation must yield the total number of observations; that is, $\Sigma\Sigma\, O_{ij} = n$.

PRACTICE EXERCISE

12.1 A contingency table is constructed, which cross-classifies two categorical variables: marital status and type of residence. The marital status categories are single (never married), presently married, presently divorced, widow (or widower). The type of residence categories are single-family home, high-rise apartment (or high-rise condominium), low-rise apartment (or low-rise condominium), mobile home, other.
   a. How many cells are in the contingency table?
   b. How many cells would there be if each of the marital status categories were split into two new categories, indicating the presence or absence of children?

ASSOCIATION IN A CONTINGENCY TABLE: THE "HOLLYWOOD SQUARES" PROBLEM

Let's consider the problem facing the sponsor of the "Hollywood Squares" TV program and illustrate the use of the contingency table in performing a **chi-square test for association**.

The "Hollywood Squares" television program is supported by the advertising budget of a leading liquid starch producer. However, the effectiveness of the ads for the liquid starch brand aired on the program has been questioned. Do the ads help the sales of the advertised brand? To find out, a random sample of consumers is surveyed. The consumers are asked questions on both viewership of "Hollywood Squares" and usage of liquid starch. The survey produces 289 viewers and 1331 nonviewers. A contingency table showing the observed frequencies of the six cross-classification cells is given in Table 12.4.

		VIEWERSHIP		TOTALS
		Viewer	Nonviewer	
BRAND USAGE	Use Advertised Brand A	76	204	280
	Use Another Brand, B	80	402	482
	Do Not Use Product, N	133	725	858
	TOTALS	289	1331	1620

TABLE 12.4 Usage of Advertised Brand of Liquid Starch versus Viewership of "Hollywood Squares"

The advertiser wants to use the random sample survey data to determine whether viewership of "Hollywood Squares" and usage of the advertised brand are statistically linked. Suppose the usage of the advertised brand is not associated with viewership. Then the money spent to sponsor the program can be viewed as ineffective and wasteful of the manufacturer's advertising budget.

Calculating the Expected Cell Frequencies

To determine whether there is any apparent association between viewership and usage of the advertised brand, we must compare the observed cell frequencies to the cell frequencies we would expect if there is no relationship between the two variables. The *expected frequency* of each cell is calculated by the three steps below:

Step 1
Determine the relative frequency for each column. From the last row of Table 12.4, we see that the 1620 survey respondents are split into two categories, 289 viewers and 1331 nonviewers. We calculate this split in relative frequency terms:

$$\text{Viewer relative frequency:} \quad \frac{289}{1620} = .178395$$

$$\text{Nonviewer relative frequency:} \quad \frac{1331}{1620} = .821605$$

Step 2
Determine the expected frequency for each column in row 1. Take the relative frequency for each column calculated in Step 1 and multiply it by, O_1, the total frequency in row 1. The expected frequency for each cell presumes no association exists between the two categorical variables.

Row 1 expected viewer frequency: .178395(280) = 49.9506
Row 1 expected nonviewer frequency: .821605(280) = 230.0494

Step 3
Determine the expected frequency for each column for the remaining rows. Repeat the procedure in Step 2 for rows 2 and 3:

Row 2 expected viewer frequency: .178395(482) = 85.9864
Row 2 expected nonviewer frequency: .821605(482) = 396.0136
Row 3 expected viewer frequency: .178395(858) = 153.0629
Row 3 expected nonviewer frequency: .821605(858) = 704.9371

In Table 12.5 the observed and expected frequencies are shown for each cell in the contingency table.

TABLE 12.5	Expected Frequencies (Bracketed) versus Observed Frequencies	
	VIEWERSHIP	
	Viewer	**Nonviewer**
BRAND USAGE A	76 [49.9506]	204 [230.0494]
B	80 [85.9864]	402 [396.0136]
N	133 [153.0629]	725 [704.9371]

Summing the expected frequency values in the table across rows and down columns of the cells must give (except for rounding errors) the same row and column totals shown in Table 12.4. That is, the sum of the expected frequencies in any row (or column) must equal the sum of the observed frequencies for that row (or column).

PRACTICE
EXERCISE

12.2 Department stores are usually concerned about the image of their store as perceived by customers and by prospective customers who do not shop there. In response to a market survey, the results in the table were obtained for a particular department store.

| | | RESPONDENT CLASSIFICATION | |
		Customers of This Store	Noncustomers of This Store
RESPONSE	At This Store	13	15
	Elsewhere, or No Response	175	290

a. Calculate the relative frequency split between columns.
b. Calculate the estimated expected cell frequencies.
c. Verify that the sum of the expected cell frequencies for each row is equal to the sum of the observed frequencies for that row.
d. Verify that the sum of the expected cell frequencies for each column is equal to the sum of the observed frequencies for that column.

12.2

CHI-SQUARE TEST PROCEDURE FOR ASSOCIATION

The hypothesis testing procedure begins with a statement of the null hypothesis H_o and its alternative H_A:

H_o: The two categorical variables are statistically independent, meaning that there is no statistical association between them in the population. (In the "Hollywood Squares" problem, H_o should state that there is no statistical association between the brand usage variable and the "Hollywood Squares" viewership variable.)

H_A: There is an association in the population between the two categorical variables. (In the "Hollywood Squares" problem, H_A should state that the viewership variable is statistically associated with the brand usage variable.)

A chi-square (χ^2) distribution is used to test H_o. This family of distributions was first introduced in Chapter 7. There exists one chi-square distribution, χ^2_ν, for each degree of freedom, ν. The probability associated with a particular chi-square value depends upon the χ^2 distribution specified. As Figure 12.1 suggests, when the degrees of freedom are small, the shape of the distribution is skewed to the right. As the degrees of freedom increase, the shape becomes more symmetrical until, at large values for ν, the distribution attains a shape that is approximately normal.

After the hypothesis statements, the elements and procedure needed for a chi-square test of H_o, are as follows:

Step 1
Select a level of signifance. This value is chosen prior to conducting the test. Let's say $\alpha = .05$ was chosen.

Step 2
Calculate the degrees of freedom. The number of degrees of freedom is determined from the number of rows and number of columns in the contingency table:

Figure 12.1
Three different chi-square
distributions

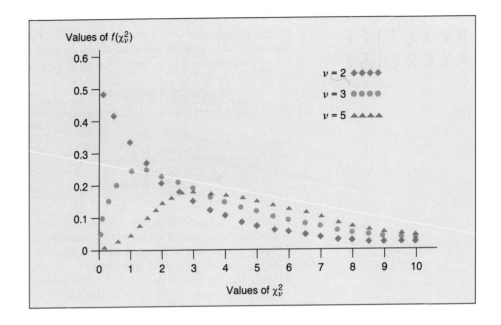

$$\nu = (r - 1)(c - 1)$$

where r is the number of rows and c is the number of columns.

In the "Hollywood Squares" example, the number of degrees of freedom is

$$\nu = (r - 1)(c - 1) = (3 - 1)(2 - 1) = 2$$

Step 3
Determine the rejection region. For the given significance level α and degrees of freedom $\nu = (r - 1)(c - 1)$, find the value of $\chi^2_{(\alpha, \nu)}$

Appendix Table VIIIb shows the χ^2 values for α ranging from .100 to .005. A portion of Table VIIIb is shown here in Table 12.6. It gives the table values with 2 d.f. for selected values of α.

TABLE 12.6 Chi-Square Values for Selected Values of α, Where $\nu = 2$	
At α value	$\chi^2_{(\alpha, 2)}$
.100	4.60517
.050	5.99147
.025	7.37776
.010	9.21034
.005	10.5966

For $\alpha = .05$, Table 12.6 shows a $\chi^2_{(.05, 2)}$ value of 5.99147. Therefore, the rejection region for the "Hollywood Squares" example is the range of test statistic values beyond 5.99147.

Step 4

Determine the value of the test statistic. To calculate the test statistic, first find the difference between the observed frequency, O_{ij}, in each cell and the expected frequency, E_{ij}, computed for the same cell; then square the difference. Divide the squared difference in each cell by the expected frequency for that cell.

For example, the result of these operations for the observed and expected frequencies shown in the top left cell (row 1, column 1) of the contingency table, Table 12.5, is

$$\frac{(O_{11} - E_{11})^2}{E_{11}} = \frac{(76 - 49.9506)^2}{49.9506} = 13.5848$$

Now, sum the results for all the cells. The mathematical expression for the test statistic is given below:

Chi-Square Test for Association

$$\text{Test statistic} = \sum\sum \frac{(O_{ij} - E_{ij})^2}{E_{ij}} \tag{12-1}$$

where the *observed cell frequencies* (O_{ij}) are obtained directly from the contingency table, and the *expected cell frequencies* (E_{ij}) are obtained by the procedure described in Section 12.1. The double summation $\sum\sum$ indicates that the calculation must be made for all the contingency table cells in a given row and for all rows.

For the "Hollywood Squares" example, the test statistic is calculated as follows:

$$\text{Test statistic} = \sum\sum \frac{(O_{ij} - E_{ij})^2}{E_{ij}}$$

$$= \frac{(O_{11} - E_{11})^2}{E_{11}} + \frac{(O_{12} - E_{12})^2}{E_{12}}$$

$$+ \frac{(O_{21} - E_{21})^2}{E_{21}} + \frac{(O_{22} - E_{22})^2}{E_{22}}$$

$$+ \frac{(O_{31} - E_{31})^2}{E_{31}} + \frac{(O_{32} - E_{32})^2}{E_{32}}$$

$$= \frac{(76 - 49.9506)^2}{49.9506} + \frac{(204 - 230.0494)^2}{230.0494}$$

$$+ \frac{(80 - 85.9864)^2}{85.9864} + \frac{(402 - 396.0136)^2}{396.0136}$$

$$+ \frac{(133 - 153.0629)^2}{153.0629} + \frac{(725 - 704.9371)^2}{704.9371}$$

$$= 13.5848 + 2.9497 + 0.4168 + 0.0905 + 2.6298 + 0.5710$$

$$= 20.2426$$

The distribution of this test statistic is closely approximated by a chi-square distribution with $(r - 1)(c - 1)$ degrees of freedom whenever the sample size $n \geq 25$, and the expected cell value exceeds 5 for all cells.

Figure 12.2
Chi-square hypothesis test at the .05 level of significance for 2 d.f., showing the rejection region (shaded) and the observed value of the test statistic, 20.2426

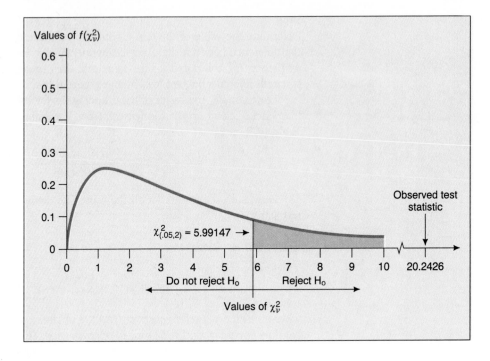

Step 5

Determine whether the test statistic is in the rejection region and apply the decision rule. Compare the calculated value of the test statistic to $\chi^2_{(.05,2)}$. If the value of the test statistic is greater than $\chi^2_{(.05,2)}$, it lies in the rejection region.

In the "Hollywood Squares" example, $n = 1620$ is greater than 25 and the smallest expected cell value 49.9506 is greater than 5, so the χ^2 test is applicable. We find that

$$\sum\sum \frac{(O_{ij} - E_{ij})^2}{E_{ij}} > \chi^2_{(.05,2)}$$

$$20.2426 > 5.99147$$

so the test statistic does lie in the rejection region, as shown in Figure 12.2. Thus, we can reject H_o and conclude that brand usage and viewership are statistically associated.

Analysis After Rejecting H_o

From the chi-square test above, we were able to reject the null hypothesis of independence (no association) and conclude that brand usage is associated with "Hollywood Squares" viewership. But that conclusion doesn't tell us anything about the *nature* of the relationship between viewership and brand usage. Is the relationship positive or negative? Strong or weak? Finding a positive association is a necessary condition for viewership of "Hollywood Squares" to be considered effective in stimulating the usage of the advertised brand. And, of course, a strong association is more encouraging than a weak one. Some insight into the nature of the association that links viewership and usage can be acquired by comparing the observed and expected frequencies for individual cells in the contingency table given in Table 12.5.

Consider the three cells in the viewer column. The observed frequency for the top cell substantially exceeds the expected frequency; that is, 76 viewers use brand A, while only 49.9506 would have been expected to use brand A. This suggests a favorable viewership effect. Also pointing toward a favorable viewership effect is the fact that the observed frequencies of both competing brand users (middle cell in the viewer column) and nonusers (bottom cell) of liquid starch fell below the values expected for their respective cells. Taken together, these results suggest the practicality of sponsoring the "Hollywood Squares" program if viewership can reasonably be taken as the cause of the higher usage. Of course, the additional profit contributed by the increase in brand usage must exceed the cost of sponsoring the program in order for the association to be of practical importance.

PRACTICE EXERCISE

12.3 A department store manager wishes to analyze the data obtained from a market survey on the department store's image. The results from the survey in Practice Exercise 12.2 are repeated below for convenience.

Question 1: Where Would a Construction or Mill Worker Buy Casual Shoes?		
	RESPONDENT CLASSIFICATION	
	Customers of This Store	**Noncustomers of This Store**
RESPONSE At This Store	13	15
Elsewhere, or No Response	175	290

a. Using the results obtained from Practice Exercise 12.2, calculate the chi-square test statistic for the data.
b. Test for association at $\alpha = .10$.

EXERCISES

12.1 How many degrees of freedom does a χ^2 distribution have if it is based on a cross-classification of two categorical variables, one with 6 categories and the other with 4 categories?

12.2 The table presents data for various age groups on the number of arrests for driving under the influence of alcohol or any other controlled substance during the past 5 years.

		NUMBER OF ARRESTS			
		0	**1–2**	**3–4**	**5 or more**
AGE (YEARS)	**16–25**	16	12	12	10
	26–45	22	8	6	4
	46–75	34	10	8	3

a. Calculate the E_{ij}'s, given the independence assumption.
b. Before running a chi-square test, are there any preliminary indications of a lack of independence? What are they?
c. Test for independence of age and frequency of arrests at the 10% level of significance.
d. Comment on the relationship between repeat offenders and age.

12.3 Random samples of people within four geographic areas of a city were asked how often they went to a church or other religious event in the past year. The frequencies are shown in the table. Use a chi-square test statistic to perform an hypothesis test on whether the response frequencies in the various attendance categories differ significantly among the four groups. Use the $\alpha = .05$ level of significance.

| | | NUMBER OF TIMES ATTENDED | | | |
		0	1–15	16–35	36 or more
	1	56	47	13	12
GEOGRAPHIC	2	43	26	17	13
AREA	3	24	41	19	6
	4	24	29	18	9

12.4 A police department collected data for four regions of the city on the occurrence of various crimes. The department wanted to determine whether the type of crime was independent of the city region. The data are reported in the table.

| | | NUMBER OF CRIMES | | |
		Homicides	Assault and Battery	Grand Larceny
	1	16	257	210
REGION	2	19	172	297
	3	8	108	126
	4	13	191	189

a. Calculate the chi-square statistic.
b. Determine whether there is significant dependence between the regions and the types of crime. Use $\alpha = .05$.

12.5 From the market survey conducted by the department store first mentioned in Practice Exercise 12.2, the additional data given in the table were obtained.

Question 2: Where Would a Banker or Draftsman Buy Casual Shoes?			
		RESPONDENT CLASSIFICATION	
		Customers of This Store	Noncustomers of This Store
RESPONSE	At This Store	111	119
	Elsewhere, or No Response	77	186

a. Calculate the chi-square test statistic.
b. Test H_o of no association at $\alpha = .05$, and comment.

12.6 From the market survey conducted by the department store first mentioned in Practice Exercise 12.2, the additional data given in the table below were obtained.

Question 3: Where Would a Doctor or Lawyer Buy Casual Shoes?			
		RESPONDENT CLASSIFICATION	
		Customers of This Store	Noncustomers of This Store
RESPONSE	At This Store	124	147
	Elsewhere, or No Response	64	258

a. Calculate the chi-square test statistic for the new data.
b. It is argued that the observed relationships in the data set could well be attributable solely to sampling variation and that a relationship would not be observed in a larger sample. Using the $\alpha = .05$ level of significance and the computed chi-square test statistic, test the plausibility of this argument.
c. What can you conclude about the image of this department store from the market survey results?

12.7 Suppose a contingency table is constructed that cross-classifies a population of cigarette smokers according to (1) gender and (2) whether or not the person smokes the Marlboro brand. A second contingency table is constructed for this same population using occupational status rather than gender as a variable cross-classified against Marlboro use. The data are given in the table.

Population of Cigarette Smokers						
MARLBORO STATUS	**(A) GENDER**		**TOTALS**	**(B) OCCUPATIONAL STATUS**		**TOTALS**
	Male	Female		Blue-Collar	White-Collar	
Smoke Marlboro	400	50	450	250	200	450
Do Not Smoke Marlboro	800	750	1550	750	800	1550
TOTALS	1200	800	2000	1000	1000	2000

a. What numerical calculations would you make to gain an impression on whether smoking the Marlboro brand is associated with gender? Occupational status?
b. Assume that smoking status of the Marlboro brand is found to be associated both with gender and with occupational status. What numerical comparisons would you make to determine whether smoking of the Marlboro brand is more strongly associated with gender than with occupational status?
c. Based upon the given contingency tables, perform a chi-square test on whether there is an association between Marlboro smoking and (1) gender and (2) occupational status.

12.3

TESTS OF GOODNESS OF FIT

A chi-square analysis can be used to test the **goodness of fit** of a sample frequency distribution to a population distribution hypothesized to have generated the sample data. That is, we can answer the question, "Is the distribution of frequencies in this sample a plausible outcome of random sampling from the particular population in question?" The population from which the sample is hypothesized to have been drawn has in some cases a known percentage distribution (e.g., 20% in this class, 40% in that class, etc.). An example might be the age or income distributions of the population of the United States. Percentage distributions of this population are known from U.S. Bureau of the Census reports. If we compare the age distribution in any particular sample drawn randomly from this population with known population distribution, we will invariably find some differences. But are these differences small enough to be in conformity with what a process of random sampling should generate? If so, we can regard the sample as representative of the population, so that conclusions we reach from studying the people in the sample can be generalized to the population. The goodness of fit methodology also applies to cases where we have no empirical knowledge of the percentage breakdown among categories of the hypothesized population, but we wish to assume a particular form of theoretical distribution (such as uniform, binomial, Poisson, normal, etc.).

Whether the hypothesized population distribution is known empirically or is specified to be from one of the theoretical families of distributions, a null hypothesis is required. The null hypothesis is that there exists no significant difference between the sample relative frequency distribution and the corresponding empirical or theoretical population distribution. If the null hypothesis is true, we should find a high degree of conformity between the observed sample frequencies and the comparable expected frequencies for a sample of the same size drawn from the hypothesized population. If the null hypothesis is true, the slight differences that we observe can be attributed to sampling variation. We test the hypothesis by comparing the computed chi-square test statistic to the table value. We now illustrate this goodness of fit test procedure—first, with an empirically known population; next, with a discrete theoretical population distribution; and then, with a continuous theoretical population distribution.

EMPIRICALLY KNOWN POPULATION DISTRIBUTION

Suppose a firm is planning to produce and distribute fresh pasta nationwide. The firm commissions a study to survey different size households on their preference for package size—a factor the firm feels is important in successfully promoting fresh pasta. A sample of 1000 households are interviewed about the package size preference. But is the sample representative of the population of the United States? Because pasta purchasing patterns are thought to be related to the number of persons in the household, the sample design takes on added importance. There is some concern that the sample design might not have produced a sample that is representative of the distribution of household size in the United States, as reported by the U.S. Bureau of the Census. Thus, the null hypothesis is:

H_o: The sample distribution of household size is in conformity with the distribution of household sizes in the United States.

H_A: The sample distribution of household size is not in conformity with the distribution of household size in the United States.

Table 12.7 presents the household size distribution for the sample and for the United States.

TABLE 12.7 Hypothetical Percentage Distribution of 1000 Families in the Sample and All U.S. Households by Number of Persons in Household			
SIZE OF HOUSEHOLD Persons	NUMBER OF FAMILIES	SAMPLE %	CENSUS ESTIMATE FOR U.S. HOUSEHOLDS %
1	182	18.2	17.0
2	318	31.8	30.3
3	270	27.0	25.2
4	95	9.5	10.5
5	75	7.5	8.0
6	47	4.7	5.0
7 or more	13	1.3	4.0
	1000	100.0	100.0

With H_o and H_A stated, the goodness of fit test procedure is as follows:

Step 1

Select a level of significance. Let's set the level of significance at $\alpha = .01$.

Step 2

Calculate the (estimated) expected sample frequencies, E_i. Under the null hypothesis, E_i is the product of the sample size n and the population percentage in the ith class. That is,

$$E_i = n(\text{Population percentage in the ith class})$$

where $n = 1000$. For example, consider the first class (only 1 person in the household). In the U.S. population, 17.0% of households fall into this class. Therefore, the estimated expected sample frequency for this first class is $1000(17.0\%)$, or 170 households. Following the same procedure, the expected sample frequencies for the seven classes are

$$E_1 = 1000(17.0\%) = 170$$
$$E_2 = 1000(30.3\%) = 303$$
$$E_3 = 1000(25.2\%) = 252$$
$$E_4 = 1000(10.5\%) = 105$$
$$E_5 = 1000(8.0\%) \;\; = \;\; 80$$
$$E_6 = 1000(5.0\%) \;\; = \;\; 50$$
$$E_7 = 1000(4.0\%) \;\; = \;\; 40$$

$$\text{Total} \quad \overline{1000}$$

Step 3

Determine the applicability of the chi-square distribution. The sample size of $n = 1000$ is large, and the expected sample frequency is 5 or more in each of the $k = 7$ classes. Therefore, the chi-square distribution is applicable.

Step 4

Determine the degrees of freedom. The test statistic is distributed approximately as chi-square, with degrees of freedom of

$$\nu = k - 1 = 7 - 1 = 6$$

Step 5

Write the expression for the test statistic. The test statistic for the goodness of fit test is:

Test Statistic for Chi-Square Goodness of Fit

$$\sum_{i=1}^{k} \frac{(O_i - E_i)^2}{E_i} \tag{12-2}$$

Step 6

Determine the rejection region. At the .01 level of significance, the χ^2 value from Appendix Table VIIIb is $\chi^2_{(.01,6)} = 16.8119$. So the rejection region is

$$\text{Test statistic} > 16.8119$$

That is, the rejection region is the range of test statistic values beyond 16.8119.

Step 7

Determine the calculated value of the test statistic. The value of the test statistic is

$$\sum_{i=1}^{k} \frac{(O_i - E_i)^2}{E_i} = \frac{(O_1 - E_1)^2}{E_1} + \frac{(O_2 - E_2)^2}{E_2} + \frac{(O_3 - E_3)^2}{E_3} + \frac{(O_4 - E_4)^2}{E_4}$$

$$+ \frac{(O_5 - E_5)^2}{E_5} + \frac{(O_6 - E_6)^2}{E_6} + \frac{(O_7 - E_7)^2}{E_7}$$

$$= \frac{(182 - 170)^2}{170} + \frac{(318 - 303)^2}{303} + \frac{(270 - 252)^2}{252} + \frac{(95 - 105)^2}{105}$$

$$+ \frac{(75 - 80)^2}{80} + \frac{(47 - 50)^2}{50} + \frac{(13 - 40)^2}{40}$$

$$= 0.847 + 0.743 + 1.286 + 0.952 + 0.313 + 0.180 + 18.225$$

$$= 22.546$$

Step 8

Determine whether the test statistic lies in the rejection region and apply the decision rule. The calculated test statistic of 22.546 exceeds the table value of 16.8119, so it lies in the rejection region. Thus, on the basis of our calculations, we can say that at the .01 level of significance, the value of the calculated χ^2 is too large to have occurred because of sampling variation alone. Therefore, we reject the null hypothesis, and claim that there exists a statistically significant difference between the two distributions.

Practical Interpretation

It seems that the sample underrepresents the largest household sizes (7 or more), enough so that the evidence indicates the results as a whole are not representative of the U.S. population. Such discrepancies could introduce a bias in the consumer preference data on package size, so some adjustment seems to be in order in the sampling design.

A DISCRETE THEORETICAL POPULATION DISTRIBUTION: THE DISCRETE UNIFORM DISTRIBUTION

One of the simplest applications of the goodness of fit procedure tests whether the observed data are a sample from a discrete, uniformly distributed population. The toss of a fair coin or the toss of a balanced die are examples of a population that is uniformly distributed. The test statistic is the same as shown in equation (12-2). The statistic is constructed by comparing, over the k classes, the number of sample observations in each class (denoted by O_i) to the corresponding estimated expected sample frequency (E_i). However, in the case of a uniform distribution, the E_i are obtained by dividing the total number of observations, n, equally among the k classes. That is,

$$E_i = \frac{n}{k} \qquad \text{where} \quad n = \sum_{i=1}^{k} O_i$$

The number of degrees of freedom is the number of classes (or groups) minus 1. That is, if there are k classes, then $\nu = k - 1$.

For example, suppose a personnel director is attempting to evaluate the possibility of seasonal influences on the number of employee resignations. Specifically, he is interested in determining whether employee resignations are equally distributed over the year, or if there is a particular season of the year when employees resign more often. A random sample of records gives the following information:

Season	Number of Resignations
Winter	10
Spring	22
Summer	19
Fall	9
Total	60

More than two-thirds of the resignations occurred during the spring and summer seasons for this particular sample of 60 persons. Is this strong evidence that resignations are not uniformly distributed across the year? After specifying the desired level of significance α, we can test for a significant deviation between the observed distribution and the assumed theoretical distribution stated in the null hypothesis.

H_o: The population from which the observed sample is drawn is a discrete uniform distribution. (That is, the proportion of resignations is not associated with the season of the year, but is distributed evenly over the seasons of the year.)

H_A: The population from which the observed distribution is drawn shows an association between resignations and the particular season. (The proportion of resignations is not uniformly distributed over the seasons of the year.)

Having established H_o and H_A, let's follow the procedure below to test goodness of fit and H_o.

Step 1
Select a level of significance. In this example, let's use $\alpha = .05$.

Step 2
Calculate the expected frequencies. Under the null hypothesis, the estimated expected frequency for each category is $E_i = n/k$, where $n = $ Number of observations $= 60$ and $k = $ Number of seasons $= 4$. Thus, the expected frequencies are:

Winter $\quad E_1 = \frac{60}{4} = 15$

Spring $\quad E_2 = \frac{60}{4} = 15$

Summer $E_3 = \frac{60}{4} = 15$

Fall $\qquad E_4 = \frac{60}{4} = 15$

Total $\quad 60$

Step 3

Determine the applicability of the chi-square distribution. Since the sample of $n = 60$ is large and every cell has an expected frequency of 5 of more, the chi-square distribution is applicable.

Step 4

Determine the degrees of freedom. The test statistic is distributed approximately as a chi-square distribution with $k - 1$ degrees of freedom. In this particular case, $k - 1 = 4 - 1 = 3$.

Step 5

Determine the rejection region. Having set the level of significance α at .05, we find that the χ^2 value from Appendix Table VIIIb is $\chi^2_{(.05,3)} = 7.815$ (rounded). Thus, the rejection region is

$$\text{Test statistic} > 7.815$$

That is, the rejection region is the area in the range of test statistic values beyond 7.815.

Step 6

Determine the value of the test statistic. The value of the test statistic is

$$\sum_{i=1}^{k} \frac{(O_i - E_i)^2}{E_i} = \frac{(O_1 - E_1)^2}{E_1} + \frac{(O_2 - E_2)^2}{E_2} + \frac{(O_3 - E_3)^2}{E_3} + \frac{(O_4 - E_4)^2}{E_4}$$

$$= \frac{(10 - 15)^2}{15} + \frac{(22 - 15)^2}{15} + \frac{(19 - 15)^2}{15} + \frac{(9 - 15)^2}{15}$$

$$= 8.40$$

Step 7

Determine whether the test statistic lies in the rejectioin region and apply the decision rule. The test statistic value of 8.40 is greater than the table value of 7.815, so it lies in the rejection region and we therefore reject H_o. Thus, at the .05 level of significance, the value of the test statistic is statistically significant. This means that the number of resignations does vary significantly from a uniform distribution.

Practical Interpretation

The personnel director should be aware that rejection of the uniform distribution implies that there does exist a seasonal pattern to the number of employees who resign. Adjustments for this seasonality should be made in evaluating a trend.

A CONTINUOUS THEORETICAL POPULATION DISTRIBUTION: THE NORMAL DISTRIBUTION

The goodness of fit test for normality is an extremely important and useful application of the chi-square distribution. As with other goodness of fit tests, a frequency distribution of observed data is compared with a theoretical distribution of expected frequencies. The normal distribution is continuous, so the frequencies refer to data grouped into classes. In computing the theoretical expected frequencies for a class, we must find the area under the hypothetical normal curve between the upper and lower boundaries of the class. This calculation is straightforward if the population parameters μ and σ have been specified. However, since μ and σ often are not specified, we can use the sample statistics $\bar{X}$ and S to represent μ and σ, respectively, with an appropriate adjustment to degrees of freedom.

Table 12.8 presents a frequency distribution of lifetimes for a sample of 500 critical components in electronic facsimile (fax) machines. The sample mean and sample standard deviation of the 500 items are determined from the raw data to be $\bar{X} = 130$ and $S = 20$, respectively. The null hypothesis to be tested is that the data in the population are normally distributed. The alternative hypothesis is that the population data are not normally distributed. The procedure for testing the null hypothesis is presented below.

TABLE 12.8 Frequency Distribution for Life of Components	
LIFE OF COMPONENTS Hours	O_i
Less than 90	0
90 but under 110	75
110 but under 130	225
130 but under 150	125
150 but under 170	50
170 but under 190	25
190 or over	0

Step 1
Select the level of significance. Let's use $\alpha = .01$.

Step 2
Calculate Z values corresponding to the class limits. The class limits are 90, 110, 130, 150, 170, and 190. The Z value corresponding to $X = 90$ is

$$Z = \frac{X - \bar{X}}{S} = \frac{90 - 130}{20} = -2$$

The Z values corresponding to $X = 110$, 130, 150, 170, and 190 are calculated the same way, giving $Z = -1$, 0, 1, 2, 3, respectively.

Step 3
Calculate the expected frequencies for the classes. To find the expected frequency for the class bounded by, say $X = 170$ and $X = 190$, we need to convert the lower and upper limits to Z values, in this case $Z = 2$ and $Z = 3$, respectively. Then using the standard normal distribution table, we find the area under the curve between $2 < Z < 3$ is $p(2 < Z < 3) = .4987 - .4772 = .0215$. (See Appendix Table IV.) This area is multiplied by the sample size of 500, to give 10.75 as the expected frequency of the class. Table 12.9 gives the expected frequencies for all the classes. Note that two open-ended classes are added to accommodate the tails of the normal distribution.

TABLE 12.9		Expected Frequencies for Life of Components			
LIFE OF COMPONENTS Hours	O_i	**X Range**	**Corresponding Z Range**	**Corresponding Normal Curve Area**	E_i
Less than 90	0	$X < 90$	$Z < -2$	.0228	11.40
90 but under 110	75	$90 \leq X < 110$	$-2 \leq Z < -1$	.1359	67.95
110 but under 130	225	$110 \leq X < 130$	$-1 \leq Z < 0$	.3413	170.65
130 but under 150	125	$130 \leq X < 150$	$0 \leq Z < 1$	.3413	170.65
150 but under 170	50	$150 \leq X < 170$	$1 \leq Z < 2$	.1359	67.95
170 but under 190	25	$170 \leq X < 190$	$2 \leq Z < 3$	.0215	10.75 ⎫
190 or over	0	$190 \leq X$	$3 \leq Z$	.0013	0.65 ⎬ 11.40
	500				500.00

Step 4

Combine any class having an expected frequency less than 5 with an adjacent class. The open-ended class "190 or over" has an expected frequency less than 5, so it is combined with the next lower class (170 but under 190), giving 11.40 as the expected frequency of the combined class.

Step 5

Calculate the degrees of freedom. The degrees of freedom is given by $\nu = k - 1 - m$, where k is the number of classes and m is the number of parameters estimated. For this example, $\nu = 6 - 1 - 2 = 3$ d.f., since two parameters, the mean and the standard deviation, were estimated.

CAUTION: While this adjustment in degrees of freedom applies to the estimation of the mean and standard deviation of the normal distribution, it does not apply to all distributions.

Step 6

Write the expression for the test statistic:

$$\chi^2 = \sum_{i=1}^{k} \frac{(O_i - E_i)^2}{E_i}$$

Step 7

Determine the rejection region. We find from Appendix Table VIIIb that $\chi^2_{(.01,3)} = 11.345$ (rounded). Thus, the rejection region is

$$\text{Test statistic} > 11.345$$

Step 8

Calculate the value of the test statistic and apply the decision rule. The value of the test statistic is

$$\chi^2 = \sum_{i=1}^{k} \frac{(O_i - E_i)^2}{E_i} = 62.620$$

The computations are given in Table 12.10.

Since the test statistic value of 62.620 is greater than the table value of 11.345, it lies in the rejection region. Thus, we reject H_o and conclude that the population from which this sample was drawn is not normally distributed.

TABLE 12.10		Chi-Square Calculations		
LIFE OF COMPONENTS **Hours**	O_i	E_i	$O_i - E_i$	$(O_i - E_i)^2/E_i$
Less than 90	0	11.40	−11.40	11.400
90 but under 110	75	67.95	7.05	0.731
110 but under 130	225	170.65	54.35	17.310
130 but under 150	125	170.65	−45.65	12.212
150 but under 170	50	67.95	−17.95	4.742
170 or over	25	11.40	13.60	16.225
				$\chi^2 = 62.620$

Practical Interpretation

The test statistic is so much larger than the rejection region bounding value of 11.345 that we can be virtually certain of our conclusion in this case. By comparing the observed frequency to the expected frequency in Table 12.10, we see some upper tail skewness of the observed data with the observed frequency of 25, more than twice the size of the expected frequency of 11.4 for the 170 or over category. This result tells management to pursue the cause of this better than expected high level of component life.

In this section we have limited our discussion of the chi-square goodness of fit test to the uniform and normal distributions. However, other distributions also can be fitted to grouped data to determine the goodness of fit. In each case, the value of the parameters of the distributions tested must be either hypothesized or estimated from the data so that the expected (theoretical) frequencies can be calculated. But in all such instances, we must be careful to determine the correct number of degrees of freedom. Although we could subtract 1 d.f. for each estimated parameter for the normal distribution, this is not necessarily true for other distributions.

PRACTICE EXERCISE

12.4 The financial manager in charge of the accounts receivable department is concerned about the current economic slowdown, because customers sometimes wait longer to pay their bills. She wishes to check on this year's performance of the department by comparing the current outstanding accounts with records from the past few years. Historical records show the following percentages in the respective classifications:

Age of Accounts Receivable	Percent of Total Receivables
Less than 30 days	50%
Between 30 and 60 days	25%
Between 60 and 90 days	15%
Over 90 days	10%

To avoid the time required for a complete audit of the accounts receivable, the financial manager chooses a random sample of 60 accounts and finds 28, 17, 10, and 5 accounts, respectively, in the above categories.

a. Use a chi-square test, and calculate the chi-square test statistic.

b. Using the $\alpha = .05$ level of significance, what can the financial manager conclude?

● ●

EXERCISES

▶ **12.8** The data given below report the number of books borrowed from a public library during the 5 days of a particular week. Treat the data as a random sample from the population of days that book borrowing occurs. Test the hypothesis that the number of books borrowed is not associated with a particular day of the week. Use a significance level of $\alpha = .10$. Repeat the test at the .05 level of significance.

Day	Number of Books Borrowed
Monday	138
Tuesday	105
Wednesday	120
Thursday	112
Friday	147

▢ **12.9** People from a large eastern city, a large western city, and a large midwestern city were asked whether they subscribe to a particular cable news network and/or a particular cable sports network. The observed frequencies are given in the table.

TYPE OF CABLE SUBSCRIPTION	EASTERN	WESTERN	MIDWESTERN
Both news and sports	7	9	9
News only	12	18	5
Sports only	9	8	3
Neither	22	25	23

a. Can you conclude that the proportions in the various subscription categories differ among the three cities? Use a chi-square test and $\alpha = .10$.
b. Which categories contribute most heavily to the chi-square test statistic? What does this lead you to believe?

▢ **12.10** At four major North American airports, data were collected on the number of cars rented from the four car rental companies located at these airports. (Assume in this problem that only four car rental companies exist.) The data shown in the table represent a random sample.

Market Share of Four Car Rental Companies (Percent)				
		RENTAL COMPANY		
	1	2	3	4
AIRPORT 1	68	73	45	29
AIRPORT 2	54	67	51	33
AIRPORT 3	69	85	44	41
AIRPORT 4	51	72	28	15

a. Calculate the appropriate chi-square statistic.
b. Is there enough evidence to conclude at the $\alpha = .10$ level of significance that at these airports the market share (percentage of market) of these four rental companies differs significantly in aggregate?
c. What type of test (independence or goodness of fit) did you use?
d. What is the relevant population in this problem, and in what sense do we have only a sample from this population?

▶ **12.11** An aptitude test for graduate study in management was taken by applicants to a particular graduate program. A frequency distribution of test scores is given below for a random sample of 100 applicants:

Test Score	Frequency
Below 300	1
300 but less than 350	8
350 but less than 400	15
400 but less than 450	18
450 but less than 500	25
500 but less than 550	22
550 but less than 600	5
600 or over	6

The sample mean is 464 and the standard deviation is 89. Using the estimated mean and standard deviation, may we conclude that the applicant data are normally distributed? Use the .05 level of significance.

▶ **12.12** A random sample of 500 failed transmissions revealed the following distribution of mileage at time of failure:

Mileage (Thousand Miles)	Frequency
40 but less than 50	8
50 but less than 60	12
60 but less than 70	90
70 but less than 80	174
80 but less than 90	186
90 but less than 100	30

a. Compute the mean and standard deviation of this frequency distribution.
b. At the .01 level of significance, test the hypothesis that the data fit a normal distribution.

12.13 A random sample of 500 car batteries revealed the following distribution of battery life (in years):

Years	Frequency
Less than 1	28
1 but less than 2	54
2 but less than 3	124
3 but less than 4	166
4 but less than 5	80
5 but less than 6	48

a. Compute the mean and standard deviation of this frequency distribution.
b. At the .05 level of significance, test the hypothesis that the data fit a normal distribution.

● ●

12.4
SAMPLE COMPUTER OUTPUT

Various statistical analysis software programs are available to perform the required computations for several nonparametric tests. Here, we'll use MINITAB computer output for a chi-square analysis to perform an hypothesis test for association. We'll use the contingency table of brand of laundry detergent and occupational status shown in Table 12.2 and test at the $\alpha = .01$ level of significance. Table 12.2 is reproduced here as Table 12.11.

TABLE 12.11	Contingency Table of Brand of Laundry Detergent and Occupational Status (Observed Frequencies; Number of Observations)			
	OCCUPATIONAL STATUS			
	Blue-Collar Worker	**White-Collar Worker**	**Does Not Work Outside Home**	**TOTALS**
BRAND OF A	20	80	30	130
LAUNDRY B	90	30	20	140
DETERGENT C	15	25	100	140
TOTALS	125	135	150	410

Figure 12.3
(a) MINITAB output for chi-square test for contingency table of brand of laundry detergent and occupational status, (b) Business MYSTAT: Chi-square statistic for laundry detergent data

```
MTB > read c1-c3
DATA> 20 80 30
DATA> 90 30 20
DATA> 15 25 100
DATA> end
     3 ROWS READ
MTB > chisquare c1-c3

Expected counts are printed below observed counts

          C1        C2        C3      Total
   1      20        80        30       130
        39.63     42.80     47.56

   2      90        30        20       140
        42.68     46.10     51.22

   3      15        25       100       140
        42.68     46.10     51.22

Total    125       135       150       410

ChiSq =  9.726 + 32.321 +  6.484 +
        52.454 +  5.621 + 19.029 +
        17.954 +  9.656 + 46.458 = 199.704
  df = 4
a
```

TABLE OF	BRAND$	(ROWS) BY	OCCUP$	(COLUMNS)
FREQUENCIES	Blue	White	Wkhom	TOTAL
A	20	80	30	130
B	90	30	20	140
C	15	25	100	140
TOTAL	125	135	150	410

TEST STATISTIC	VALUE	DF	PROB
PEARSON CHI-SQUARE	199.704	4	.000

b

Working in MINITAB, the nine observed cell frequencies of the contingency table are placed in the first three columns of MINITAB by using the READ command and entering the frequencies as indicated in the data lines in the top portion of Figure 12.3.

A statement of the null and alternative hypotheses is:

H_o: No association exists between the occupational status and the brand of laundry detergent.

H_A: There exists an association between the occupational status and the brand of laundry detergent.

To perform an hypothesis test on the two categorical variables, we require a contingency table and its test statistic, which has a chi-square distribution. By using the MINITAB CHISQUARE command on the data located in C1–C3, we obtain a printout of the contingency table with the observed cell frequencies that were read into MINITAB. Printed directly below the observed cell values are their corresponding estimated expected cell frequencies. The CHISQUARE command also prints out the elements of the chi-square test statistic, the value of the test statistic, and the appropriate degrees of freedom (denoted on the output by "df" rather than ν). In this case, $\nu = $ df $= 4$.

For $\alpha = .01$ and $\nu = 4$, the χ^2 table in Appendix Table VIIIb has a value of 13.2767. Thus, the rejection region for H_o is in the right tail beyond the value 13.2767. The computer output shows the value of the chi-square test statistic to be 199.704. This result lies well into the rejection region and is highly statistically significant, thereby enabling us to reject the null hypothesis of no association. Practically speaking, the association found between occupational status and the use of the advertised brand of detergent will help the advertiser direct marketing efforts.

We can obtain the chi square statistic (along with its p value) from business MYSTAT. Figure 12.3b is the statistical output from business MYSTAT for the laundry detergent data of Table 12.11.

SUMMARY

The contingency table is a valuable tool for analyzing relationships between two categorical variables. However, sampling variation may cause a relationship in the sample contingency table data even when there is no relationship between the two variables in the population from which the sample was drawn. To test for the existence of a relationship in the bivariate population, we can use the chi-square test for association. If the null hypothesis of no association is rejected, we can presume that the relationship found in the contingency table is not a sampling fluke. However, the chi-square statistic is not a good measure of the strength of association between two variables. Especially when the sample is very large, it is possible to have results that are highly statistically significant, but have little practical significance. Checking the relationship found in the contingency table will usually provide insight as to whether a relationship that is statistically significant is strong enough to have any practical value.

As we have discussed in this chapter, the chi-square statistic also can be used to test for goodness of fit of sample data to an hypothesized population distribution. Rather than assuming a population is normally distributed, for example, we can test the normality assumption.

The chi-square tests considered in this chapter are our first introduction to nonparametric procedures. That is, neither of the chi-square tests stipulated a particular parametric family of population distributions, such as the normal distribution family. In the next chapter we will discuss several other nonparametric procedures that have proven useful when parametric procedures are not applicable.

KEY EQUATIONS

Chi-Square Test for Association

$$\text{Test statistic} = \sum\sum \frac{(O_{ij} - E_{ij})^2}{E_{ij}} \tag{12-1}$$

where the observed cell frequencies (O_{ij}) are obtained directly from the contingency table, and the estimated expected cell frequencies (E_{ij}) are obtained by the procedure described in Section 12.1.

Test Statistic for Chi-Square Goodness of Fit

$$\text{Test statistic} = \sum_{i=1}^{k} \frac{(O_i - E_i)^2}{E_i} \tag{12-2}$$

PRACTICE EXERCISE ANSWERS

12.1 a. There are 4 marital status categories and 5 residence categories, so there are 20 cells in the 4 × 5 contingency table.

b. The new table would be a 4 × 5 × 2 table, with 40 cells.

12.2 a. There are a total of 13 + 175 + 15 + 290 = 493 responses to this market survey. Of these, 13 + 175 = 188 are customers of this store; the remaining 15 + 290 = 305 are noncustomers. The relative frequency split is

$$\text{Customer relative frequency:} \quad \frac{188}{493} = .38134$$

$$\text{Noncustomer relative frequency:} \quad \frac{305}{493} = .61866$$

b. The expected cell frequencies for each row are found by multiplying the column relative frequencies found in part a by the total frequency in the row.

$$\text{Row 1 expected customer frequency:} \quad .38134(28) = \quad 10.68$$
$$\text{Row 1 expected noncustomer frequency:} \quad .61866(28) = \quad 17.32$$
$$\text{Row 2 expected customer frequency:} \quad .38134(465) = 177.32$$
$$\text{Row 2 expected noncustomer frequency:} \quad .61866(465) = 287.68$$

c. For row 1: 10.68 + 17.32 = 28; for row 2: 177.32 + 287.68 = 465.

d. For column 1: 10.68 + 177.32 = 188; for column 2: 17.32 + 287.68 = 305.

12.3 a. The chi-square test statistic is given by

$$\sum\sum \frac{(O_{ij} - E_{ij})^2}{E_{ij}} = \frac{(O_{11} - E_{11})^2}{E_{11}} + \frac{(O_{12} - E_{12})^2}{E_{12}} + \frac{(O_{21} - E_{21})^2}{E_{21}} + \frac{(O_{22} - E_{22})^2}{E_{22}}$$

$$= \frac{(13 - 10.68)^2}{10.68} + \frac{(15 - 17.32)^2}{17.32} + \frac{(175 - 177.32)^2}{177.32} + \frac{(290 - 287.68)^2}{287.68}$$

$$= 0.504 + 0.311 + 0.030 + 0.019$$

$$= 0.864$$

b. This table has 2 rows and 2 columns, so $\nu = (2 - 1)(2 - 1) = 1$ d.f. The rejection region is

$$\sum\sum \frac{(O_{ij} - E_{ij})^2}{E_{ij}} > \chi^2_{(.10,1)} = 2.706$$

Since the calculated chi-square value of 0.864 is less than 2.706, the null hypothesis that there is no association between survey response and respondent classification cannot be rejected.

12.4 a. Suppose the manager establishes as a null hypothesis that the population from which the sample is drawn has the same distribution of age of accounts receivable as in preceding years. If the null hypothesis is true, the 60 observations in the sample should have the same pattern of variation as historical records:

Age of Accounts Receivable	Historical Distribution	Expected Frequencies in Sample of Size 60	Actually Observed
Less than 30 days	50%	30	28
Between 30 and 60 days	25%	15	17
Between 60 and 90 days	15%	9	10
Over 90 days	10%	6	5

There are 4 classes, so we use the chi-square distribution with $4 - 1 = 3$ d.f. The test statistic is

$$\sum \frac{(O_i - E_i)^2}{E_i} = \frac{(O_1 - E_1)^2}{E_1} + \frac{(O_2 - E_2)^2}{E_2} + \frac{(O_3 - E_3)^2}{E_3} + \frac{(O_4 - E_4)^2}{E_4}$$

$$= \frac{(28 - 30)^2}{30} + \frac{(17 - 15)^2}{15} + \frac{(10 - 9)^2}{9} + \frac{(5 - 6)^2}{6}$$

$$= 0.1333 + 0.2667 + 0.1111 + 0.1667$$

$$= 0.6778$$

b. The test statistic value of 0.6778 is less than the value of 7.815 from the chi-square distribution table for 3 d.f. and $\alpha = .05$, so we do not reject the null hypothesis that the distribution of this year's accounts is the same as the distribution of accounts in the preceding years. Therefore, the financial manager can conclude that the current economic slowdown has not significantly affected the accounts receivable.

CHAPTER REVIEW EXERCISES

12.14 A mail order clothing retailer is considering including in its fall catalog a swatch of cloth for its new all wool shirt-jacket. The retailer feels that a substantial increase would occur in the proportion of orders from those mailed a catalog with a cloth swatch. It is decided to test this marketing idea on the next fall catalog mailing. One thousand catalogs with cloth swatch included are mailed to a random sample of prospective customers. From this group, 185 eventually place an order for the shirt-jacket. With the cloth swatch excluded, identical catalogs are sent to another random sample of 1000 prospective customers. From this group, 132 orders are received. The table shows the difference in response.

		ORDER STATUS	
		Purchased	Not Purchased
CATALOG STATUS	Cloth Included	184	815
	No Cloth	132	868

a. Determine the rejection region for a chi-square test of association. Use the $\alpha = .01$ level of significance.
b. Compute the chi-square test statistic.
c. Test H_0 and reach a practical conclusion.

❑ **12.15** A breakfast cereal manufacturer wants to know whether individual preferences for types of breakfast cereal sweetener are associated with the age of the buyer. In an urban survey of consumers, sweetener preferences were matched to the consumers' age group. From a random sample of 500 responses, the results are given in the table.

		AGE (YEARS)			
		0–10	**11–18**	**19–60**	**Over 60**
CEREAL STATUS	Sugar Sweetened	50	60	50	40
	Fruit Sweetened	20	40	10	30
	Natural	30	50	90	30
	TOTALS	100	150	150	100

a. Specify the rejection region for a chi-square test for association using the $\alpha = .10$ level of significance.
b. Calculate the chi-square test statistic.
c. Test H_o and reach a practical interpretation.

▶ **12.16** The LWL (League of Women Lobbyists) is interested in the impact on women voters of some reading material they mailed out advocating more militancy on women's rights issues. The particular issue the LWL is concerned about is whether mandatory quotas for minorities (women included) will be supported by women voters. To determine women voter opinion on this issue prior to the LWL mailing, a sample of 320 eligible voters were canvassed for their reaction on the quota issue. After the reading material had been mailed and the individuals had a chance to consider the material, their opinion was again solicited on this issue. The data are summarized in the table. (Note that in the case of no change in a woman's reaction she must be placed in either the upper right-hand cell or the lower left-hand cell.)

		AFTER THE MAILING	
		Against Proposal	Favor Proposal
BEFORE THE MAILING	Favor Proposal	30	135
	Against Proposal	80	75

a. State the rejection region for a chi-square test for a "before and after" effect at the .05 level of significance.
b. Calculate the chi-square test statistic.
c. Test H_o and reach a practical suggestion for the LWL.

❑ **12.17** A large insurance company is computerizing its operations and has installed a workstation system in one of its main offices. A series of training sessions has been undertaken to acquaint all employees with workstation systems. Management believes that the age of the employee affects the success of the training sessions. A random sample of employees who have completed the training sessions are given 1 hr to perform a certain set of tasks at the workstation. The results are graded to determine whether the training sessions have been successful. The results are given in the table.

		AGE		
		21–29	30–39	40–49
TRAINING	Success	80	80	75
SESSION STATUS	Failure	50	65	55

a. Determine the rejection region for a chi-square test, testing whether there is an association between training session success/failure and age at the .01 level of significance.
b. Calculate the chi-square statistic.
c. Test H_o and decide whether management's belief is substantiated.

12.18 A computer chip manufacturer issues a money-back guarantee to its customers. The money is returned if less than 99% of any given lot of its computer chips meet the stated specifications. A random sample of 500 chips were selected from a lot by an end user (customer). Testing revealed that 460 were acceptable and 40 were not.
a. Define the null and alternative hypotheses and set up the rejection region based on the chi-square statistic.
b. Does the end user have evidence to refute the manufacturer's claim at the .01 level of significance?

12.19 Suppose the audit team of the Resolution Trust (a government agency formed to deal with troubled financial institutions) is examining a S&L (savings and loan institution) to check on the status of the loans in its commercial lending portfolio. Loans are classified as *current* if all payments are up to date, *late* if the payment is 1–45 days overdue, and *delinquent* if the payment is more than 45 days overdue. The industry guidelines used by the Trust for the proportions in each of the three categories are .80, .15, and .05, respectively. Suppose a random sample of 300 loans from the portfolio are examined. Of these 300 loans, 225 are found current, 30 are late, and 45 are delinquent.
a. Define the null and alternative hypotheses and set up the rejection region.
b. Using $\alpha = .05$ as the level of significance, test whether the Trust has sufficient evidence to claim that the S&L has deviated significantly from the industry guidelines.

▶ 12.20 A random sample of first-year students in public and private colleges located in Orange County, California, were polled on whether their intended college major was business administration. The survey showed the results given in the following table:

Sample of First-Year Students Planning to Major in Business						
FAMILY INCOME	MEN		WOMEN		TOTAL	
	Number	%	Number	%	Number	%
Under $25,000	122	5.5	127	7.2	249	6.2
$25,000–50,000	1,176	52.5	956	54.6	2,132	53.4
$50,000–100,000	940	42.0	670	38.2	1,610	40.4
	2,238	100.0	1,753	100.0	3,991	100.0

Compare these results with the empirical data obtained from tabulations done by a U.S. Government agency for the nation (the population):

Population of First-Year Students Planning to Major in Business			
FAMILY INCOME	**MEN** %	**WOMEN** %	**TOTAL** %
Under $25,000	2.5	4.8	3.6
$25,000–50,000	50.6	52.1	51.3
$50,000–100,000	46.9	43.1	45.1
	100.0	100.0	100.0

a. Calculate the value of the chi-square test statistic.
b. Test the hypothesis that the Orange County first-year students planning to major in business come from family income backgrounds different from those of first-year students in the nation as a whole who plan to major in business. Use $\alpha = .01$.
c. What conclusion can be reached?

12.21 A survey of 230 entering students at a public university is taken to determine whether their degree of computer literacy depends on the income level of their families. The data in the table are collected.

		COMPUTER LITERACY			
		Low	Medium Low	Medium High	High
FAMILY INCOME (THOUSAND DOLLARS)	Under 25	15	13	8	6
	25–50	25	42	36	15
	50 or more	17	22	16	15

a. Determine the rejection region for a chi-square test for association. Use $\alpha = .05$ as the level of significance.
b. Calculate the chi-square test statistic.
c. Test H_o.

12.22 A controversy developed over the relationship between the age of a driver and proneness to automobile accidents. A survey was taken of drivers 21 years of age or older, with the results shown in the table. At issue is whether the results provide any basis for concluding that in the population there is an association between age of driver and number of accidents.

		AGE OF DRIVER (YEARS)			
		21–30	31–45	46–60	Over 60
NUMBER OF ACCIDENTS	0	785	813	782	652
	1	74	60	55	50
	2	29	27	22	13
	3 or more	11	12	6	9

a. Using $\alpha = .05$, what is the rejection region for the chi-square test?
b. What is the value of the test statistic?
c. Test H_o.

12.23 A survey of 200 users of hair shampoo led to the contingency table given here. Don Miller, a marketing planner with a personal care products company, noted in the survey that more women than men are heavy users and more men than women are light users.

Usage of Hair Shampoo				
		GENDER		Totals
		Male	Female	
USAGE RATE	Light	48	32	80
	Medium	38	42	80
	Heavy	14	26	40
	TOTALS	100	100	200

a. Is the percentage of heavy users who are women the same as the percentage of women who are heavy users? If not, compare the two percentages.

b. If Miller wants to target a new shampoo at the heavy user segment, which of the two percentages in part a is more pertinent? Would your answer change if Miller wants to target a shampoo especially for women?

c. Considering the possibility that the observed relationship in the sample between gender and usage rate might just be a sampling fluke, use the chi-square distribution to test the hypothesis of no association between usage rate and gender at the $\alpha = .05$ level of significance.

12.24 Frustrated marketers have long noticed that some eventual purchasers of their products are very difficult to reach with information the marketer feels prospective buyers should have before a decision is made. Yet other buyers are easy to reach; many go out of their way to seek out pertinent information for evaluating products and brands. Why are some buyers so difficult and others so easy to reach? According to one theory, it is the inexperienced buyers of the product who are easiest to reach because they know they need the information. The "old hands" have often settled into a routine pattern of acquiring the product and are not on the lookout for information to the same extent as inexperienced buyers. The contingency table presents data from a study on the amount of information sought by automobile buyers having different degrees of previous automobile buying experience. In the table, previous buying experience includes any brand.

Amount of Information Sought by Automobile Buyers (1)					
		AMOUNT OF INFORMATION-SEARCH EFFORT			
		Very Little	Some	Moderate	Very Intensive
NUMBER OF AUTOMOBILES PREVIOUSLY PURCHASED	0–2	4	10	8	9
	3–5	16	14	14	10
	6 or more	16	13	16	16

a. Calculate the value of the chi-square test statistic.

b. Test the hypothesis of no association at the $\alpha = .10$ level of significance.

c. Do the data provide evidence supporting the theory that persons with more car buying experience tend to put forth less effort searching for information when they shop for a new car? Explain.*

12.25 Refer to Exercise 12.24.* A second set of data is given below from the same study. Here, however, the definition of previous buying experience is restricted to the same brand as presently purchased.

*Data in Exercises 12.24 and 12.25 are reported in Peter Bennett and Robert Mandell, "Prepurchase Information Seeking Behavior of New Car Purchasers—The Learning Hypothesis," *Journal of Marketing Research*, vol. 6 (November 1969), pp. 430–433.

Amount of Information Sought by Automobile Buyers (2)					
		AMOUNT OF INFORMATION-SEARCH EFFORT			
		Very Little	**Some**	**Moderate**	**Very Intensive**
NUMBER OF AUTOMOBILES	**0**	5	20	27	28
PREVIOUSLY PURCHASED	**1–2**	15	17	11	13
(SAME BRAND)	**3 or more**	16	10	10	4

a. Calculate the value of the chi-square test statistic.

b. Test the hypothesis of no association at the $\alpha = .01$ level of significance.

c. Do the data provide evidence that the more times a buyer of a particular brand of new car has purchased this same brand in the past, the less is the effort that tends to be put into shopping for the new car? Explain.

12.26 A marketing researcher wants to know whether brand loyalty for a certain brand of hair care products is related to the hair color of the user. A random sample of 230 users was surveyed with the results shown in the table.

		BRAND LOYALTY			**TOTALS**
		Highly Loyal	**Moderately Loyal**	**Brand Switcher**	
HAIR COLOR	**Blonde**	30	42	18	90
	Brunette	14	20	31	65
	Other	34	25	16	75
	TOTALS	78	87	65	230

a. Determine the rejection region for a chi-square test using $\alpha = .05$ as the level of significance.

b. Calculate the test statistic and apply the decision rule.

c. What are the practical implications of your findings?

12.27 An advertising executive wants to know whether the preferred business publication (*Business Week, Forbes, Fortune,* etc.) is related to the type of college degree held by a purchaser. The data in the table were collected.

PUBLICATION	**TECHNICAL DEGREE**	**NO TECHNICAL DEGREE**	**TOTALS**
A	15	15	30
B	25	20	45
C	30	25	55
D	20	15	35
	90	75	165

a. Determine the rejection region for a chi-square test using $\alpha = .01$ as the level of significance.

b. Calculate the test statistic and apply the decision rule.

▶ 12.28 A marketing researcher wants to know whether the preferences stated in a survey of computer publication readers could plausibly be attributed to random variation. Computer executives were asked to identify one of four computer publications as their first choice. The researcher thinks that the forced-choice situation could have resulted in random selection of a publication, and if this is the case, the rankings of preferences in the survey would be meaningless. The survey data are given in the table.

PUBLICATION	FREQUENCY
A	45
B	30
C	55
D	35
	165

a. Use the uniform population distribution to test the hypothesis of random choices. Let $\alpha = .05$.

b. Would you reach the same conclusion using $\alpha = .01$?

12.29 A study of patient attitudes toward nursing homes resulted in the data in the table.

NURSING HOME RELIGIOUS AFFILIATION	PATIENT SATISFACTION RATING		
	Low	Medium	High
Church supported	16	68	135
Nonsectarian	85	131	160

a. State the rejection region for testing the null hypothesis that nursing home religious affiliation is not associated with patient satisfaction rating.

b. Calculate the test statistic and apply the decision rule using $\alpha = .05$.

12.30 The study of patient attitudes toward nursing homes also gave the results in the table below.

NUMBER OF NEW FRIENDS MADE	PATIENT SATISFACTION RATING		
	Low	Medium	High
None	31	28	15
"Just a few"	31	21	60
"Quite a few"	37	96	225

a. State the rejection region for testing the null hypothesis that number of new friends made is not associated with patient satisfaction rating.

b. Calculate the test statistic and apply the decision rule using $\alpha = .05$.

SOLVING APPLIED CASES
Target Marketing at Sure-Foot Bicycle

Spending the advertising budget on an audience composed of people who aren't good prospects for the company's products would be foolish. So it is the job of the advertising manager to make sure the audience of the company's advertising messages includes a good proportion of people who use, or at least might potentially use, the product the company sells.

Suppose you are the advertising manager of Sure-Foot Bicycle, a large bicycle manufacturer. You face a decision of whether or not to advertise heavily in the specialty magazine, *Cycling*. Table 12.12 shows four cross-classification cells, one for each possible combination of purchasing status in the target market of prospective bicycle purchasers and readership status of *Cycling* magazine.

TABLE 12.12	Cross-Classification of Purchasing Status and *Cycling* Reader		
		READERSHIP STATUS	
		Reader	**Not Reader**
PURCHASING STATUS	**Prospect**	Prospect/reader match	Unreached prospect
	Not Prospect	Wasted advertising	No gain/no loss

The four cross-classification cells of the two categorical variables, "purchasing status" and "readership status," in Table 12.12 have totally different implications for the advertiser.

1. The top left entry shows a match between readers and prospects. That is, prospective purchasers are reached by the advertising. The more people found in this cell, the more productive are advertising expenditures.
2. The bottom left entry represents people who are reached by the advertising but who are not prospective purchasers. Unfortunately, the advertiser is charged for the magazine's total circulation and that includes the people in this cell. This cell represents wasted advertising dollars, so the fewer the people in this cell, the better the situation for the advertiser.
3. The top right entry represents an unreached segment of the target market of prospective purchasers. Because they don't read *Cycling,* these people can't be reached by advertising in the magazine. It is also advantageous for the advertiser if the number of people in this cell is minimal.
4. The bottom right entry represents a cell of no particular interest to the advertiser. These are people who don't read *Cycling* and therefore won't be exposed to advertising in it, and who are not in the market for a bicycle anyway. No advertising dollars will be spent reaching these nonprospects. The number of people in this cell is of no concern to the advertiser.

To uncover whether there is an underlying relationship or association between the target market variable and the audience variable, you commission a market research study. A research firm is hired to conduct a random sample survey of consumers on (1) their bicycle purchasing status during the coming year and (2) their *Cycling* readership. The data for the 2050 respondents are organized into a contingency table showing the observed frequencies for the four cross-classifications, and the results are given in Table 12.13.

TABLE 12.13	Contingency Table for Purchasing Status and Readership Status for *Cycling* Magazine (for a Random Sample of 2050 Respondents)			
		READERSHIP STATUS		**TOTALS**
		Reader	**Not Reader**	
PURCHASING STATUS	**Plan to Purchase**	45	368	413
	Not Planning to Purchase	163	1474	1637
	TOTALS	208	1842	2050

Now, you want to determine whether there is any apparent statistical association between purchasing status and readership status. To find out, you must compare the observed cell frequencies to the cell frequencies expected if there is no relationship between the two variables. The computation of the expected cell frequencies is summarized in Table 12.14.

TABLE 12.14	Computation of Expected Frequencies and Readership for Purchase Status		
	READERSHIP STATUS		TOTALS
	Reader	Non Reader	
PURCHASING STATUS — Plan to Purchase	(208/2050)(413) = 41.9044	(1842/2050)(413) = 371.0956	413.0000
Not Planning to Purchase	(208/2050)(1637) = 166.0956	(1842/2050)(1637) = 1470.9044	1637.0000
TOTALS	208.0000	1842.0000	2050

The null hypothesis H_o, in this case, is that there is no difference in purchasing plans between readers and nonreaders of *Cycling* magazine. Let's suppose you have decided to test H_o at the .01 level of significance. The table contains 2 rows and 2 columns, so we have $\nu = (2 - 1)(2 - 1) = 1$ d.f. The chi-square table, Appendix Table VIIIb, shows a $\chi^2_{(.01,1)}$ value of 6.63490; therefore, the rejection region is the range of values beyond 6.63490. The next step is to calculate the chi-square test statistic by comparing the expected cell frequencies to the corresponding observed cell frequencies. The expected and observed frequencies are shown in Table 12.15.

TABLE 12.15	Expected Frequencies (Bracketed) and Observed Frequencies	
PURCHASING STATUS — Plan to Purchase	45 [41.9044]	368 [371.0956]
Not Planning to Purchase	163 [166.0956]	1474 [1470.9044]

The calculated test statistic is

$$\sum\sum \frac{(O_{ij} - E_{ij})^2}{E_{ij}} = \frac{(45 - 41.9044)^2}{41.9044} + \frac{(368 - 371.0956)^2}{371.0956}$$

$$+ \frac{(163 - 166.0956)^2}{166.0956} + \frac{(1474 - 1470.9044)^2}{1470.9044}$$

$$= 0.2287 + 0.0258 + 0.0577 + 0.0065$$

$$= 0.3187$$

Because the calculated test statistic value of 0.3187 is less than 6.63490, it does not lie in the rejection region. Since we can't reject the null hypothesis, we can't claim that there is a statistical association between *Cycling* readership and bicycle purchasing plans. If there is any relationship at all between bicycle purchasing status and readership status, it is too weak to be distinguished from random sampling variation. From a practical perspective this suggests to you as advertising manager that perhaps the money considered for *Cycling* advertising may be better spent elsewhere. Perhaps you should consider advertising in a more widely circulated general-purpose magazine (such as *Time* or *Sport*) that reaches a wider audience and therefore offers a larger target market. These magazines usually offer a much lower cost per thousand readers than specialty magazines like *Cycling*. So, if *Cycling* can't show a significant association between purchasing status and readership, the better media placement may be in the lower-cost (per reader) general-purpose magazine.

Checkpoint Exercises

Sure-Foot Shoe Company is introducing a new running shoe and is very anxious to advertise it so that the maximum target market is reached. You are told by your ad agency that *Running* magazine would be one of the best advertising media to reach prime prospects for the new running shoe. An extensive random sample market survey is conducted by the magazine and 7983 responses are received. The contingency table shows the observed results.

| | | READERSHIP | | TOTALS |
		Reader	Not Reader	
PURCHASING STATUS	**Plan to Purchase**	244	3212	3456
	Not Planning to Purchase	254	4273	4527
	TOTALS	498	7485	7983

1. Calculate the contingency table for the expected frequencies if no association exists between readership and purchasing status.
2. Using $\alpha = .05$, test the hypothesis that no association exists between readership and purchasing plans.
3. What practical conclusion can be suggested?

WENDY'S DATABASE ANALYSIS

A hamburger chain strives to earn the reputation of providing the "best buy" on key items thought to attract consumers to the chain's restaurants. One key item is the hamburger itself. Question 124 (we'll name it BURGVAL) asks consumers to choose the burger that gives them the most for their money. On this criterion, Wendy's single burger rates third behind top-rated Burger King and McDonald's.

At issue, however, are the factors that contribute to the perception of value. For example, at McDonald's and Burger King, burgers are garnished before delivery to the customer. But at Wendy's, customers select and put on their own garnishes. Most people say they enjoy this feature, but a minority say they don't (question 135).

Is Preference for Self-Garnishing Associated With Perception of Burger Value?

Is preference for this feature independent of the perception of value? Or is it related to perceived value? That is, are people more likely to perceive Wendy's single burger as offering the most for their money if they prefer to garnish their own burgers? We can investigate this issue by first constructing a contingency table and then conducting a chi-square test for association on the frequencies in the table.

Figure 12.4 presents MINITAB commands and output for the contingency table and for the chi-square test. The rows represent preference among burgers and the columns represent the status of one's preference for self-garnishing. Also reported on the MINITAB output is the value of the chi-square test statistic.

Let's test the null hypothesis of no association using $\alpha = .05$ as the level of significance. Since there are 4 rows and 2 columns, the number of degrees of freedom is

$$\nu = (r - 1)(c - 1) = (4 - 1)(2 - 1) = 3$$

The rejection region is thus

$$\text{Test statistic} > \chi^2_{(.05,3)}$$

From the table of chi-square values, Appendix Table VIIIb, the region of rejection is

$$\text{Test statistic} > 7.81473$$

The reported test statistic from the MINITAB output is 2.079. Since this is less than 7.81473, we can't reject H_o. The evidence doesn't support the view that a customer's attitude toward self-garnishing affects the perception of which brand offers the best burger buy.

Figure 12.4
Contingency table and chi-square test statistic for BURGVAL and GARNISH

```
MTB > TABLE 'BURGVAL' BY 'GARNISH';
SUBC> CHISQUARE 2.


ROWS:      BURGVAL          COLUMNS:    GARNISH
               1                2          ALL

  1            94                7         101
             90.84            10.16      101.00

  2            81                9          90
             80.85             9.05       90.00

  3           102               15         117
            105.23            11.77      117.00

  4            18                1          20
             17.99             2.01       20.00

 ALL          295               33         328
            295.00            33.00      328.00
 CHI-SQUARE =                  2.079     WITH D.F. = 3


     CELL CONTENTS --
                            COUNT
                            EXP FREQ
```

Is Brand Preference Associated with Perception of "Most for the Money"?

In Figure 12.5, MINITAB commands and output for a second contingency table are shown. A new variable, BRANPREF, is created from the responses to questions 105–107 for Burger King, McDonald's, and Wendy's, respectively. BRANPREF indicates which of the three brands the respondent most prefers. The contingency table cross-classifies BURGVAL against BRANPREF. People have preferences for particular fast food brands, and they also have perceptions about which burger offers the "most for the money." But the question is whether the brand preferences and perceptions of burger value are associated. That is, are people more likely to prefer the fast food chain that sells the burger they believe offers the most for the money? A chi-square test for association can help answer this question.

Let's test the null hypothesis of no association at $\alpha = .05$ between BURGVAL and BRANPREF. Since there are 3 burgers and 3 fast food chains being considered, the degrees of freedom are

$$\nu = (r - 1)(c - 1) = (3 - 1)(3 - 1) = 4$$

The region of rejection is thus

$$\text{Test statistic} > \chi^2_{(.05,4)}$$

The value of $\chi^2_{(.05,4)}$ is read from the chi-square table (Appendix Table VIIIb) as 9.48773. Thus, the rejection region is

$$\text{Test statistic} > 9.48773$$

The test statistic is reported on the MINITAB output in Figure 12.5 as 169.219. Since this is greater than 9.48773, H_o is rejected. Practically speaking, we conclude that BRANPREF and BURGVAL are associated variables. That is, there is a relationship between which burger is thought to offer the most for the money and which burger chain the customer prefers to patronize.

Wendy's Student Exercise

The chi-square test for association can be used to investigate other possible relationships that Wendy's might want to explore. The exercises below consider a few of the more obvious relationships of interest.

```
MTB > retreive 'wendys406'
MTB > copy c124 into c205;
SUBC> use c105=1.
MTB > copy c124 into c206;
SUBC> use c106=1.
MTB > copy c124 into c207;
SUBC> use c107=1.
MTB > stack c205 c206 c207 into c209
MTB > copy c209 into c210;
SUBC> omit c209=4.
MTB > name c210 'burgval'
MTB > copy c205 into c305;
SUBC> omit c205=4.
MTB > count c305
MTB > copy c206 into c306;
SUBC> omit c206=4.
MTB > count c306
MTB > copy c207 into c307;
SUBC> omit c207=4.
MTB > count c307
MTB > set c211
DATA> 60(1), 142(2), 134(3)
DATA> end
MTB > name c211 'branpref'
MTB > table 'burgval' by 'branpref';
SUBC> chisquare 2.


     ROWS: burgval      COLUMNS: branpref

                 1         2         3       ALL

      1          2        16        81        99
             17.81     41.65     39.54     99.00

      2          5        78        21       104
             18.71     43.76     41.54    104.00

      3         52        44        29       125
             22.48     52.59     49.92    125.00

    ALL         59       138       131       328
             59.00    138.00    131.00    328.00

    CHI-SQUARE =   169.219    WITH D.F. =      4
        CELL CONTENTS --
                       COUNT
                       EXP FREQ
```

Figure 12.5
Contingency table and chi-square test statistic for **BURGVAL** and **BRANPREF**

1. Is gender a factor in the perception of which burger offers the "best buy?" To find out:
   a. Construct a contingency table using variables 124 (BURGVAL) and 137 (GENDER).
   b. Use a chi-square test for association with $\alpha = .01$ to test H_o.
2. Is marital status a factor in the perception of which burger offers the best buy? To find out:
   a. Construct a contingency table using variables 124 (BURGVAL) and 136 (MARITAL). Question 124 on the Wendy's questionnaire asked respondents to designate which of four hamburger chains provides the best value. A response of 4 in column 124 indicates a

designation of Hardee's as the best value. If a row is included in the contingency table for Hardee's, some expected cell frequencies will be below 5, violating one of the assumptions needed for the use of the chi-square test for association. To avoid this problem, we omit Hardee's responses from consideration in forming the contingency table for the remaining franchises. To accomplish this, we omit rows of columns 124 and 136 for which the entry in column 124 is 4. Use the following MINITAB commands:

```
MTB>    copy C124, C136, C204, C206;
SUBC>   omit C124 = 4.
MTB>    table C204   C206;
SUBC>   chisquare 2.
```

b. Use a chi-square test for association with $\alpha = .01$ to test H_o.

NONPARAMETRIC METHODS

Headline Issue

TECHNICAL STOCK MARKET PATTERNS: WINNING STRATEGIES OR BLIND ALLEYS?

Among the various types of financial market analysts that reside on Wall Street, technicians are the most exotic. They religiously plot daily price and volume data on traded stocks, producing zigzagging price and volume charts. The purists of the technician cult are convinced that there are underlying detectable patterns in price and volume movement that have implications for future price changes. Charting, they believe, allows the trained eye to spot these patterns early in their formation, so that a stock can be bought or sold before the signalled price change occurs. One of the price patterns technicians look for is the "head and shoulders" pattern pictured in Figure 13.1. As the name suggests, it resembles the head and shoulders of a person, with a high point in the middle and a slightly lower hump on each side. To detect this and other distinctive patterns, with their implicit buy and sell signals, pure technicians rely solely on their observational powers, avoiding any formal statistical testing.

To the purists, it is not important to know what, if any, financial event is the source of the pattern. In contrast to the purists, there is a group of "notable event" technicians who approach technical pattern detection more scientifically. Their belief is that certain types of financial events possess relevant investor information. Frequently cited examples are the announcement of a dividend change or a stock split, which supposedly triggers the price and volume activity that cause distinctive patterns in subsequent price movement. The first step in an analysis by a notable event technician is to apply a statistical test to determine whether the price pattern produced by a particular type of financial event is not simply a random price movement. A pattern of random price movements would have no implication for future price changes.

To recognize randomness in price movements, notable event technicians always arrange the price changes chronologically. Those savvy in statistical methodology use the *runs test* to detect whether random movements are present once the data has been arranged chronologically. This test is noteworthy, because it is a nonparametric method with no parametric counterpart. Moreover, it can be applied without making restrictive assumptions about the shape of the underlying population distribution generating the data. This is the first nonparametric test we will study in this chapter.

Overview

This chapter continues our discussion of nonparametric methods begun in Chapter 12 with the chi-square technique. Each of the **nonparametric** tests presented in this chapter possesses one or more of the following features:

Figure 13.1
Bar chart of "head and shoulders" top formation

- It can be used for analyzing business data that are ordinally scaled.

- It represents a direct alternative to a parametric test and thus can be used when the restrictive assumptions of the parametric test cannot be met or plausibly assumed.

- It offers a way to perform an hypothesis test for situations for which no parametric test is appropriate.

A nonparametric technique that exemplifies the third feature is the *runs test*, discussed in Section 13.1. The runs test is designed to detect random versus nonrandom movement in data that are arranged chronologically.

In Section 13.2, we discuss the *Wilcoxon rank sum test*, a nonparametric technique designed for comparing two populations when the samples are independent. The parametric counterpart of this test is the hypothesis test of $\mu_1 = \mu_2$ when σ_1^2 and σ_2^2 are unknown but equal and when samples are independent. Section 13.3 deals with the *Wilcoxon signed-rank test* and the *sign test*; these tests are designed to compare two populations from which matched-pair samples have been drawn. In Section 13.4, we discuss the *Kruskal–Wallis test* for a comparison of more than two populations. The parametric counterpart is an hypothesis test of $\mu_1 = \mu_2 = \cdots = \mu_k$, which is handled by the ANOVA technique discussed in Chapter 9. The chapter concludes with Section 13.5, in which we investigate *rank correlation*; this method is used to measure the degree of correlation or association between ranks on two variables for which we have ordinal scaled data (rather than interval scaled data). The parametric counterpart, applicable when the degree of correlation is sought between interval scaled data, is the coefficient of correlation discussed in Chapter 10.

13.1

RUNS TEST FOR SEQUENTIAL RANDOMNESS

We conveniently assumed in the previous inferential chapters (Chapters 7–12) that successive observed values of X are independent. That is, each observed X value neither influences nor is influenced by any other X value. On the basis of this assumption, we have performed probability calculations, assigned confidence levels to statistical inference, and specified levels of significance in conducting hypothesis testing. When we are random sampling from a population, the assumption of independence is plausible. Otherwise, it may not be. For example, chronologically collected business data (stock prices, interest rates, unemployment rates, etc.) should not be presumed independent. When independence is in doubt, a test for independence must be conducted.

Testing for independence (or randomness) requires examining the pattern of the variation of sequential values of X. If the independence (randomness) assumption holds, the observed variation shown by sequential values of X can be attributed solely to random factors, a situation we call *sequential randomness*. But what if we find nonrandom movement in the pattern of successive X values? Then the independence (randomness) assumption must be discarded, and we have statistical *dependence* (nonrandomness). Statistical dependence is typically associated with time-ordered observations; it occurs because successive chronological observations often share common influences that persist from time period to time period. This dependency is particularly pronounced when the time periods between observations are short. For example, when a "hot spell" hits, ice cream sales reach a high dollar volume on successive days. There is a statistical dependency between sales volume on consecutive days, but the dependency might disappear if we use a longer time frame, say, year to year rather than day to day sales.

On Wall Street, analysts are constantly checking different situations to detect whether randomness is lacking in price changes. The Headline Issue presented at the beginning of this chapter is one example of the search for nonrandomness. Let's now see what is meant statistically by randomness and how we can test for it by a nonparametric procedure.

RUNS ABOVE AND BELOW THE MEDIAN

What is sequential randomness? When dealing with sample (quantitative) data, a useful starting point is to divide the data into opposite numerical categories, for example, high versus low values. The classification of an observation into a category will depend on the value of the observation relative to the median value of the data. Since the median is the middle value, half the observed values are expected to be above the median and half below. For example, with a consecutive series of stock price changes, each period's stock price change can be classified either as above the median or below the median change. If a period's stock price change is above the median stock price change (or for that matter, above any other designated dividing line), the period's price change is assigned a plus sign (+). Those below are assigned a negative sign (−). Such a classification scheme will transform the quantitative price change data into a string of plus and minus categorical designations. To illustrate,

The brackets identify a streak of a particular category. The streak, called a **run,** is an important notion in testing for randomness. The test for randomness is called the **runs test,** and the number of runs produced by the sequence of observations is the statistic used to judge whether randomness (or lack of it) exists in the sequence of observations. The number of runs in a nonrandom sequence tends to be very different from the number of runs in a random sequence of the same length. Sometimes, a nonrandom sequence produces a much smaller number of runs than would be expected from a random sequence, and at other times, a much larger number of runs.

Trend versus Sawtooth Patterns

At one extreme, there are nonrandom patterns that show *trends*—strong persistent movements in the same direction that continue for many periods. This kind of a systematic pattern produces very few runs. For example, in the following sequence of 30 observations there are only two runs; one run is a long trend of 15 positives, the other an equally long run of 15 negatives:

First run

$$\boxed{+\ +\ +\ +\ +\ +\ +\ +\ +\ +\ +\ +\ +\ +\ +}\ \boxed{-\ -\ -\ -\ -\ -\ -\ -\ -\ -\ -\ -\ -\ -\ -}$$

Second run

At the other end of the spectrum, there are nonrandom movements that produce a systematic data pattern of *abrupt direction reversals* (like a sawtooth). This kind of a rigid pattern results in an overabundance of runs. For example, in the following sequence of 13 observations there is a sawtooth pattern of 13 runs (identified by the numbers above and below the runs of + and − signs). This is the maximum number of runs possible for any sequence of 13 observations, since in this particular case every observation constitutes a run.

We shall denote the number of runs by R, the number of observations in the smaller of the plus and minus categories by n_1, and the number in the larger of these categories by n_2. In the above example, there are 6 minuses and 7 pluses, so $n_1 = 6$ and $n_2 = 7$.

The number of runs for any sample sequence falls between two limits. The minimum runs count is 2, and the maximum runs count is $2n_1 + 1$. For example, in a sequence of observations in which $n_1 = 6$, the highest possible runs count is

$$\text{Maximum } R = 2n_1 + 1$$
$$= 2(6) + 1 = 13$$

Thus, the expression is consistent with the sawtooth sequence shown above of 13 alternating pluses and minuses, which generates the maximum number of runs possible.

In summary, a random sequence will tend to produce a runs count that lies somewhere between the maximum and minimum extremes—larger than the extremely small number of runs associated with trend movements, but smaller than the extremely large number of runs associated with frequent sawtooth reversals of direction. A nonrandom sequence, on the other hand, will tend to produce a runs count closer to one of the extremes. We'll now conduct an hypothesis test based upon the number of runs.

THE RUNS TEST

The sampling distribution of the number of runs (the R test statistic) for repeated samples of n observations drawn from a random process follows the hypergeometric distribution—a specific distribution not studied in this text. Although the direct calculation of probabilities for R values requires the hypergeometric distribution, a standard normal table can provide approximate values for these probabilities. *The normal distribution is a very good approximation of the probability sampling distribution of R if n_1 and n_2, the number of observations in each of the two categories, are both greater than 10.*

The sampling distribution of R has a mean and standard deviation given as follows:

Runs Test (Normal Approximation)

Mean value of R:

$$\mu_R = \frac{2n_1 n_2}{n_1 + n_2} + 1 \tag{13-1}$$

Standard deviation of R:

$$\sigma_R = \sqrt{\frac{2n_1 n_2(2n_1 n_2 - n_1 - n_2)}{(n_1 + n_2)^2(n_1 + n_2 - 1)}} \tag{13-2}$$

where n_1 is the number of observations in the smaller of two designated categories, and n_2 is the number of observations in the larger category.

If we determine that the normal approximation is a good approximation of the probability sampling distribution, the values of μ_R and σ_R will serve as the mean and standard deviation of the approximating normal distribution.

The null and alternative hypotheses state the competing beliefs about the nature of the process generating the observed runs.

H_o: The sequence is in conformity with a random process—there is no sequential pattern.

H_A: The sequence is in conformity with a nonrandom process—there is a sequential pattern.

The test statistic used in testing the null hypothesis is the standard normal variable, Z, for the difference between the observed number R and expected number μ_R of runs, given that H_o holds.

Test Statistic for Runs Test

$$Z = \frac{R - \mu_R}{\sigma_R}$$

(13-3)

A two-sided test is usually employed, since a departure from randomness can result in either too few or too many runs.

USING THE RUNS TEST
WITH QUANTITATIVE DATA

Consider the following manufacturing plant data on the number of improperly assembled units for 30 consecutive days of output:

DAY	1	2	3	4	5	6	7	8	9	10	11	12	13	14	15
UNITS	2	3	5	7	3	5	6	1	4	6	3	7	3	6	8
DAY	16	17	18	19	20	21	22	23	24	25	26	27	28	29	30
UNITS	4	8	9	4	6	3	8	7	8	10	5	6	4	8	11

Let's now perform the runs test for sequential randomness on the frequency of improperly assembled units. We'll use $\alpha = .05$ as the level of significance.

Step 1
Determine the median. The median value is 6, the middle value of this set of 30 numbers.

Step 2
Convert the observations into a sequence of plus and minus categories, and determine n_1 and n_2. Assigning a $+$ for values above the median value of 6 and assigning a $-$ for values below the median, we have:

Units: 2 3 5   7   3 5 1 4 3   7   3   8   4   8 9   4 3   8 7 8 10   5 4   8 11

Category: |– – –| |+| |– – – – –| |+| |–| |+| |–| |+ +| |– –| |+ + + +| |– –| |+ +|

NOTE: We ignored observations at the median value of 6. Thus, observations for days 7, 10, 14, 20, and 27 are ignored. This leaves us with 25 observations in the sequence to test for randomness.

The value of n_1 = Number of +'s (i.e., number of observations with values higher than 6) and n_2 = Number of –'s. By counting, we find $n_1 = 11$ and $n_2 = 14$.

Step 3

Determine μ_R and σ_R:

$$\mu_R = \frac{2n_1n_2}{n_1 + n_2} + 1 = \frac{2(11)(14)}{11 + 14} + 1$$

$$= \frac{308}{25} + 1 = 13.32$$

$$\sigma_R = \sqrt{\frac{2n_1n_2(2n_1n_2 - n_1 - n_2)}{(n_1 + n_2)^2(n_1 + n_2 - 1)}}$$

$$= \sqrt{\frac{2(11)(14)[2(11)(14) - 11 - 14]}{(11 + 14)^2(11 + 14 - 1)}}$$

$$= 2.4106$$

Step 4

Determine the rejection region. Since both n_1 and n_2 are greater than 10, the condition necessary to use the normal approximation for the sampling distribution of R is satisfied. For the level of significance $\alpha = .05$, the rejection region would cut off $\alpha/2 = .025$ in each tail of the standard normal Z distribution. (See Appendix Table VI.) Since $Z_{.025} = 1.96$,

$$Z < -1.96 \quad \text{or} \quad Z > 1.96$$

defines the rejection region.

Step 5

Determine the test statistic, Z. We first count the number of runs, and obtain R = 12:

|– – –| |+| |– – – – –| |+| |–| |+| |–| |+ +| |– –| |+ + + +| |– –| |+ +|
  1   2   3   4   5   6   7   8   9   10   11   12

Then the value of the test statistic is

$$Z = \frac{R - \mu_R}{\sigma_R}$$

$$= \frac{12 - 13.32}{2.4106} = -.5476$$

Step 6

Determine whether the test statistic falls in the rejection region and draw a statistical conclusion. Since the observed test statistic value of $-.5476$ is not less than -1.96, the value does not lie in the lower tail of the two-sided rejection region and the null hypothesis of sequential randomness cannot be rejected. We can therefore conclude at the $\alpha = .05$ level of significance that the sequence appears to be in conformity with a random process.

Practical Interpretation

From a practical standpoint there is no evidence of any noteworthy pattern to the occurrences of improperly assembled units. The quality control manager can interpret this as evidence that improper assembly occurs randomly and is not due to any systematic problem. Provided the values of the mean and standard deviation are in accordance with established guidelines, the assembly process may be considered to be in control.

USING THE RUNS TEST WITH QUALITATIVE DATA

We have discussed and illustrated the runs test using quantitative data, but this test also can be applied to qualitative data. Suppose a baseball statistician examines the sequence of wins and losses for a particular team over a randomly selected 40 game period. Representing a win by W and a loss by L, the sequence is

L L W L W W L W L W L L W W W L W L L W

L W L L W L L W W L W W L W L W W W L W

If we arbitrarily denote one of the two possibilities by a $+$ and the other by a $-$, we can proceed with the runs test as before. Let's denote a win by a $+$ and a loss by a $-$; then we have

$$\underline{-\ -}\ \ \boxed{+}\ \ \underline{-}\ \ \boxed{+\ +}\ \ \underline{-}\ \ \boxed{+}\ \ \underline{-}\ \ \boxed{+}\ \ \underline{-\ -}\ \ \boxed{+\ +\ +}\ \ \underline{-}\ \ \boxed{+}\ \ \underline{-\ -}\ \ \boxed{+}$$

$$\underline{-}\ \ \boxed{+}\ \ \underline{-\ -}\ \ \boxed{+}\ \ \underline{-\ -}\ \ \boxed{+\ +}\ \ \underline{-}\ \ \boxed{+\ +}\ \ \underline{-}\ \ \boxed{+}\ \ \underline{-}\ \ \boxed{+\ +\ +}\ \ \underline{-}\ \ \boxed{+}$$

We count 21 $+$'s, 19 $-$'s, and 28 runs. Thus, $n_1 = 19$, $n_2 = 21$, and $R = 28$. From this point the analysis proceeds as with quantitative data. The values of μ_R, σ_R, and the test statistic are computed as follows:

$$\mu_R = \frac{2n_1 n_2}{n_1 + n_2} + 1$$

$$= \frac{2(19)(21)}{19 + 21} + 1 = 20.95$$

$$\sigma_R = \sqrt{\frac{2n_1 n_2 (2n_1 n_2 - n_1 - n_2)}{(n_1 + n_2)^2 (n_1 + n_2 - 1)}}$$

$$= \sqrt{\frac{2(19)(21)[2(19)(21) - 19 - 21]}{(19 + 21)^2 (19 + 21 - 1)}}$$

$$= \sqrt{9.6937} = 3.11346$$

$$Z = \frac{R - \mu_R}{\sigma_R}$$

$$= \frac{28 - 20.95}{3.11346} = 2.264$$

Using the commonly selected value of $\alpha = .05$, the rejection region would be

$$Z < -1.960 \quad \text{or} \quad Z > 1.960$$

Since the value of 2.264 lies in the rejection region, the null hypothesis of randomness in the sequence of wins and losses is rejected.

PRACTICE EXERCISE

13.1 For the most recent 2 month period, the production manager at a manufacturing plant has the following sequential information on the quality of the daily assembly line output of mobile phone units. Quality is designated as above (category +) or below (category −) the established acceptable median number of faulty units.

First month: + + − − − + − + − − − + + + − + + − − + − − −

Second month: + + − − + + − − + + − − − − + + + + − + − + − +

a. Using $\alpha = .05$, test whether the sequence indicates a departure from randomness.
b. Why would the production manager be concerned about whether the series suggests randomness or not?

EXERCISES

13.1 The quality control division of a textile manufacturer took a sample of 22 bolts of cloth from the manufacturing process at periodic intervals. The number of defects found in each sample were recorded and are chronologically presented rowwise in the table. The process is regarded as in control if the variation of defects is random and out of control if the variation is not random.

	NUMBER OF DEFECTS										
ROW 1	7	6	10	6	4	5	7	8	12	8	15
ROW 2	6	14	10	10	7	5	9	6	10	4	8

a. Determine the median of this data set, and assign a + to values above the median and a − to values below the median.
b. What are the values of n_1 and n_2?
c. What are the values of μ_R and σ_R?
d. Determine R and test the randomness hypothesis at the $\alpha = .05$ level of significance.

13.2 An automobile industry supplier produces pistons for a particular automobile engine model. Samples of size 15 were periodically drawn from the production process and measurements taken on a critical dimension. The results for 25 consecutive sample means (chronologically arranged rowwise) are given in the table. One of the signals that alert the quality control department of an emerging quality problem is nonrandom variation of the sample means. Test the randomness hypothesis at the $\alpha = .05$ level of significance.

	SAMPLE MEAN				
ROW 1	84.61	85.72	85.24	85.18	85.44
ROW 2	85.46	85.32	85.40	85.44	85.08
ROW 3	85.50	85.80	85.22	85.04	85.72
ROW 4	85.01	84.82	85.46	85.60	85.78
ROW 5	84.93	85.27	85.12	85.37	84.88

13.3 An "index" mutual fund holds a portfolio consisting of the 500 stocks in the Standard & Poor's 500 stock index. The data in the table give the market return annually on an investment in this index fund over a 25 year period. Using the $\alpha = .01$ level of significance, test the hypothesis that these annual returns (chronologically presented rowwise) are randomly distributed.

	ANNUAL INVESTMENT RETURN (PERCENT)				
ROW 1	20.5	18.7	6.6	−7.2	23.8
ROW 2	37.2	−26.5	−14.7	19.0	14.3
ROW 3	4.0	−8.5	11.1	24.0	−10.1
ROW 4	12.5	16.5	22.8	8.7	26.9
ROW 5	0.5	12.0	43.4	−10.8	6.6

13.4 Monthly dollar sales of the Lydia E. Pinkham vegetable tonic are reported in the table for a 36 month period of general price stability in the economy. Considerable variation in the monthly sales is evident, but are the changes random in nature, and hence unpredictable? Or do the changes follow a systematic (i.e., nonrandom) pattern? Test the sequence (chronologically presented rowwise) for randomness at the $\alpha = .05$ level of significance. If you reject H_o, comment on some of the possible reasons for nonrandomness.

	MONTHLY SALES (THOUSAND DOLLARS)					
ROW 1	1482	1442	1648	1530	1501	1416
ROW 2	1373	1621	1749	710	1387	1021
ROW 3	1759	1626	2270	1375	1281	1018
ROW 4	1421	1415	1503	1885	1185	954
ROW 5	1235	1160	1542	1563	1402	1287
ROW 6	1378	1391	1328	1073	1070	726

13.5 The residuals from a regression analysis (chronologically arranged rowwise) have the following values:

ROW 1	−1.6	−10.9	+5.8	+13.8	−10.0	−0.6	−5.6	−3.6
ROW 2	−4.1	+14.4	−8.7	+7.8	−6.2	+3.2	+4.9	+4.7
ROW 3	+4.7	+8.6	−2.2	−8.1	−0.9	−4.8	+0.5	−1.1

Using $\alpha = .05$, can we conclude from the data that the residuals are random? (Note: Random residuals are consistent with the claim of statistical independence.)

13.6 A salesperson for Avon Products makes 50 calls over a period of several days. She is successful on calls numbered 1, 3, 7, 9, 11, 14, 15, 21, 22, 28, 35, 36, 37, 47, and 49.

a. Denote a successful call by + and an unsuccessful call by −. Count the number of runs in this salesperson's sequence of 50 successes and failures. Does there appear to be any evidence of nonrandomness? If so, what type?

b. Perform a runs test on the data. Do the results differ significantly from randomness at $\alpha = .05$?

13.7 A Ralph's supermarket manager is examining records of the daily fresh fish deliveries to the store for the past 2 months. The following arrival sequence indicates whether the delivery to the store occurred during the scheduled 6:00–8:00 am period. The symbol E represents early or on-time arrival, and L indicates a late arrival.

Month 1: E L E E L L E E E L E L L E E E L E L L E E

Month 2: E L L E E E L E E L E L E L E L L L E E L L E E E L L E

a. Perform a runs test on the data. Do the results give an indication of a departure from randomness? Use $\alpha = .01$ as the significance level.

b. Why should the store manager be concerned about the nonrandomness of the arrival times?

▶ **13.8** A trade association for the electric utility industry is investigating the firms Grace Nuclear and Wilcox Interstate, the two major suppliers of turbine generators. The charge is price fixing. The association suspects that the firms have agreed not to undercut each other on price and to divide the market by some predetermined formula for assigning customers to the firms. To accomplish their objectives, it is suspected that the firms have arranged a bid submission game plan. One firm would put in an unacceptably high bid, opening the way for the other firm to get the contract at a comfortably high price level. Is there any information the trade association can examine and test to uncover any pattern that exists for past winners of large contracts for turbines? The sequence of winning bids follows (read from left to right):

G W G W W G G W W G W G W G G W G G W G W G W

If a disconcerting pattern is found, a complaint may be filed with the Justice Department.
a. Is the exact sequence of bids a critical information element for answering the issue of price fixing?
b. Use a runs test to test at $\alpha = .05$ the hypothesis that the winning bidder sequence follows a random pattern.
c. If the randomness hypothesis is rejected and a type I error has not been made, can you suggest an alternative explanation to conspiracy?
d. If the turbine suppliers are conspiring to fix prices, will the randomness hypothesis necessarily be rejected? Explain.

13.2
WILCOXON RANK SUM TEST: TWO INDEPENDENT SAMPLES

In Chapter 8 we dealt with two types of parametric tests for comparing the means of two populations. In the first type of test, known formally as a *completely randomized design*, we independently drew one random sample from each of the two populations and compared the means of the two samples using either a Z test or a t test. In the second type of test, called a *matched-pairs test*, we drew one sample of elementary units from a population and then took two measurements on each elementary unit. For example, one measurement might be taken before administering the experimental treatment and the other taken after administering an experimental treatment. In this section, we consider a nonparametric alternative to the first type of test. In the next section, we consider nonparametric matched-pairs tests.

From Chapter 8, recall the following two parametric tests of the first type (completely randomized design) for comparing two independent samples of quantitative data:

1. **For large samples: the Z test.** The parametric Z test (based on the standardized normal distribution) tests for the difference between two population means when (a) we have large independent random samples and (b) the data are measured on an interval scale.

2. **For small samples: the Student t test.** The parametric Student t test tests for the difference between two population means when we have (a) small independent random samples with (b) interval scaled data from (c) two normally distributed populations with (d) equal and unknown variances.

Both these large and small parametric tests require quantitative data on an interval scale. This requirement and the requirement in the small sample case that the populations be normal (or nearly normal) limit the applicability of these tests. What if the available data are not quantitative? Or, in the small sample case, what if the two populations are not expected to be normally distributed? If either of these conditions are present, the formal large and small sample parametric testing procedure requirements are not met, and a nonparametric alternative should be considered. For the case of two independent samples, an alternative is the **Wilcoxon rank sum test.** The following example describes a situation in which the Wilcoxon rank sum test is an appropriate procedure.

The length of an automobile's useful life is an issue that car manufacturers have to take seriously. Several automobile makers, such as Volvo and Mercedes-Benz, have successfully marketed their claims of how many miles satisfied owners have driven cars that are still running satisfactorily. Owners of Japanese makes sometimes assert that Japanese brands last many miles longer than their American counterparts. How can a manufacturer determine the road life (in miles driven) of the major components of the cars it produces compared to a competitive brand? One way is to survey the automobile repair shops.

Suppose Ford wants to find out if the transmissions on its brand S compact last as long as the transmissions on the GM brand M compact. A visit by the Ford product researcher to local shops where transmissions are repaired gives the sample data shown in Table 13.1. The sample collected includes all automobiles of the two models that, according to their owners, are in the shop for their first major transmission repair.

TABLE 13.1 Odometer Reading at Time of Repair (Thousands of Miles)			
BRAND S Sample Size 18		**BRAND M** Sample Size 17	
99.2	113.9	107.0	79.7
100.8	102.5	75.6	106.9
96.7	83.8	102.9	86.8
94.5	87.4	101.5	106.8
80.0	94.9	105.5	83.6
89.4	90.2	77.4	88.7
119.0	92.6	81.7	91.7
82.8	87.0	93.1	99.3
94.9	81.8	81.3	
Mean: 93.967		**Mean: 92.324**	

This is an independent sample design, since the two samples are taken from different populations. Because the samples are small, we might expect the Student t test to be appropriate. Similar auto longevity studies, however, suggest that the underlying distribution is highly skewed to the right, with some autos reaching unusually high mileage before major transmission repairs are required. Therefore, the parametric Student t test requirement of sampling from a normal population is not a reasonable assumption.

The nonparametric Wilcoxon rank sum test does not require sampling from a normal population. It can be used with skewed distributions, provided the variances and the shapes of the two distributions are the same. The competing hypotheses for the Wilcoxon test are:

H_o: There is no difference in the population between brands S and M in mean mileage at first major transmission repair; that is, $\mu_S = \mu_M$.

H_A: $\mu_S \neq \mu_M$

Let's choose $\alpha = .05$ as the desired level of significance.

To test H_o using the Wilcoxon rank sum test, the Wilcoxon test statistic W must be computed. The following procedure is used:

Step 1

Pool the samples, arraying the values of both sets of observations from low to high (columns 1 and 4 of Table 13.2).

TABLE 13.2 Observations, Pooled and Ranked							
COLUMN 1 OBSERVATION		**COLUMN 2 BRAND S**	**COLUMN 3 BRAND M**	**COLUMN 4 OBSERVATION**		**COLUMN 5 BRAND S**	**COLUMN 6 BRAND M**
1000 Miles	Model	Rank	Rank	1000 Miles	Model	Rank	Rank
75.6	M		1	93.1	M		19
77.4	M		2	94.5	S	20	
79.7	M		3	94.9	S	21.5	
80.0	S	4		94.9	S	21.5	
81.3	M		5	96.7	S	23	
81.7	M		6	99.2	S	24	
81.8	S	7		99.3	M		25
82.8	S	8		100.8	S	26	
83.6	M		9	101.5	M		27
83.8	S	10		102.5	S	28	
86.8	M		11	102.9	M		29
87.0	S	12		105.5	M		30
87.4	S	13		106.8	M		31
88.7	M		14	106.9	M		32
89.4	S	15		107.0	M		33
90.2	S	16		113.9	S	34	
91.7	M		17	119.0	S	35	
92.6	S	18					

Step 2

Identify each arrayed value with a brand of car, as shown in the table.

Step 3

Rank the low to high arrayed values, giving the lowest value a rank of 1, and assign each rank to the rank column designated for its brand. For example, start with the rank of 1. Since this observation (with value 75.6) is a brand M car, the number 1 is listed in the column for brand M ranks (column 3). How are ties handled in computing the rankings? *Ties are given a rank equal to the average rank of the tied observations.* That is, if three observations tie for ranks 4, 5, and 6, each observation is given rank 5. In Table 13.2, two observations are tied for ranks 21 and 22, so each is given rank 21.5.

If the mean mileage life of brand S and brand M transmissions don't differ significantly, the rankings should be more or less evenly dispersed between the two brands. But if there is a brand effect on mileage life, the automobiles of the brand with longer mileage life should have higher rankings. A visual examination of the rankings doesn't clearly show whether the observed differences are due to the brands or simply to typical sampling variation.

Step 4

Compute the Wilcoxon statistic W. The value of W is the sum of the ranks for the brand with the smaller sample size. If the two samples are of the same size, it doesn't matter which one is used to compute W. In this case, brand M has the smaller sample size (17 cars). Its rank sum is:

$$W = 1 + 2 + 3 + \cdots + 33 = 294$$

Step 5

Determine the rejection region. Let n_1 represent the size of the smaller sample and n_2 the size of the larger sample. For samples where both n_1 and n_2 are 10 or more, the distribution of W can be approximated by the normal curve. Since in this example $n_1 = 17$ and $n_2 = 18$, we can use the normal approximation. The test statistic Z and the standardized normal probability table are then used to determine the rejection region. The form of the alternative hypothesis H_A determines whether the rejection region is one-sided or two-sided. In this particular example, H_A indicates that we use a two-sided rejection region,

$$Z < -Z_{\alpha/2} \quad \text{or} \quad Z > Z_{\alpha/2}$$

For $\alpha = .05$, we have $\alpha/2 = .05/2 = .025$, and from the normal table $Z_{.025} = 1.96$. Therefore, the rejection region is

$$Z < -1.96 \quad \text{or} \quad Z > 1.96$$

Step 6

Compute the standardized normal test statistic, Z. Under the assumptions that H_o is true and that both n_1 and n_2 are 10 or more, the distribution of W can be approximated by the normal curve with mean and standard deviation determined as follows:

Wilcoxon Rank Sum Test (Normal Approximation)

Mean value of W:

$$\mu_W = \frac{n_1(n_1 + n_2 + 1)}{2} \tag{13-4}$$

Standard deviation of W:

$$\sigma_W = \sqrt{\frac{n_1 n_2 (n_1 + n_2 + 1)}{12}} \tag{13-5}$$

In the automobile transmission life example,

$$\mu_W = \frac{17(17 + 18 + 1)}{2}$$

$$= 306$$

$$\sigma_W = \sqrt{\frac{(17)(18)(17 + 18 + 1)}{12}}$$

$$= 30.299$$

where $n_1 = 17$ and $n_2 = 18$ are the respective sizes of the smaller and larger samples.

To calculate the standardized normal test statistic Z, the following expression is used:

Test Statistic for Wilcoxon Rank Sum Test

$$Z = \frac{W - \mu_W}{\sigma_W}$$

(13-6)

Thus, the value of the Z test statistic is

$$Z = \frac{W - \mu_W}{\sigma_W} = \frac{294 - 306}{30.299} = -.396$$

Step 7

Determine whether the value of the test statistic is in the rejection region and draw a conclusion. The computed test statistic $Z = -.396$ is greater than -1.96, so it does not fall in the rejection region. Therefore, H_o, the null hypothesis that the two brands have equal mean transmission longevity, cannot be rejected. This means that the observed sample is consistent with the null hypothesis of equal mean mileage to the first major transmission repair for the two brands. This suggests that the observed greater average mileage of brand S cars ($\bar{X}_S = 93{,}967$) over brand M cars ($\bar{X}_M = 92{,}324$) in the two samples is not sufficiently large to rule out the plausibility of H_o and that the difference is due merely to sampling variation.

Practical Interpretation

The finding of no significant difference between the two brands of cars implies that the mileage differences among cars of the same brand can reasonably be thought to account for what on the surface appears to be a difference in mean life between the brands. Our testing suggests that the longer mean life to first major transmission repair of Ford's brand S cars in the sample can be attributable to inescapable random variation that comes with sampling.

PRACTICE EXERCISE

13.2 A rental car company owns a fleet of cars consisting of two different models. Looking at the repair bills (in dollars) for model A and model B, the manager finds the following:

Model A ($n = 11$)		Model B ($n = 15$)		
51.00	320.43	435.00	75.00	54.60
157.83	291.32	321.00	107.50	106.21
231.24	105.59	44.85	241.75	148.00
200.70	636.51	84.00	58.20	186.00
135.36	288.00	96.00	51.99	60.00
212.61				

a. Arrange the data from low to high, rank the arrayed data, and calculate the Wilcoxon rank sum test statistic.

b. For $\alpha = .01$, use the Wilcoxon rank sum test to test the hypothesis that there is no difference in the population between model A and model B in mean repair bills.

● ●

EXERCISES   ▢ ▶ **13.9** A sample of credit card purchase amounts is gathered from each of two competing department stores. The data are shown in the table.

PURCHASE AMOUNTS FOR STORE 1	PURCHASE AMOUNTS FOR STORE 2
Dollars	Dollars
27.95	16.63
26.53	35.38
54.78	26.53
29.86	15.43
10.54	68.34
15.65	14.33
14.21	76.25
23.27	35.12
78.32	23.15
25.47	15.07
22.50	30.48

a. Arrange the data from low to high, rank the arrayed data, and calculate the Wilcoxon rank sum W.
b. Calculate μ_W and σ_W.
c. Use the rank sum test to test whether the mean of one store's credit card purchase amounts is significantly different from that of the other store's. Use $\alpha = .10$.
d. Run a Student t test on the data. Do you get the same conclusion as in part c?
e. For these particular data, why might the Student t test be inappropriate?

▢ **13.10** Steel mill R and steel mill L are alternate suppliers of specially ordered alloy steel. Two independent random samples of 10 orders each are taken from the two suppliers. The number of days that lapse between the placement of the order and the receipt of shipment is recorded. The results and their rankings are given in the table.

	STEEL MILL																			
	R	R	R	R	L	R	R	R	L	L	R	L	R	L	R	L	R	L	L	L	L	L
DAYS	28	29	31	32	33	34	35	36	38	41	42	44	45	47	49	51	53	54	57	60
RANKING	1	2	3	4	5	6	7	8	9	10	11	12	13	14	15	16	17	18	19	20

a. Calculate the value of the Wilcoxon rank sum test statistic.
b. What is the value of the standard normal statistic?
c. Use the $\alpha = .05$ level of significance to test the null hypothesis of no difference between the suppliers in the distribution of time until an order is received.

▢ **13.11** Dale Max, owner of an apartment building, wants to know whether there is any difference in the length of time tenants obtained through two different real estate agents stay before moving out. Records on 11 tenants obtained through each agent are given in the table. Assume that the data can be regarded as independent random samples. Test the null hypothesis of no difference at the $\alpha = .10$ level of significance.

	LENGTH OF TENANCY Months										
AGENT A	8	19	15	11	23	10	16	20	18	18	12
AGENT B	15	19	16	13	17	20	18	22	19	18	14

⌨   **13.12** Marcia Katz, owner of a popular Denver restaurant, has noticed that on some days seating of persons with lunch hour reservations backs up. She suspects that this is due to slower turnover of tables when the tables are occupied by groups of four or more persons. If her suspicion proves correct, she feels that she should take fewer reservations on days when reservations include an above average number of groups of four or more. To check out her suspicion, she recorded the occupied table time for 15 randomly selected groups of four or more patrons. Occupied table time was also recorded for 15 randomly selected groups of three or fewer patrons. The results are given in the table. Test for the null hypothesis at the .01 level of significance.

		MINUTES TABLE WAS OCCUPIED														
NUMBER OF PERSONS	**3 or Less**	47	65	39	72	60	54	81	47	56	42	38	45	51	66	48
AT TABLE	**4 or More**	38	49	94	63	78	56	42	59	70	52	111	59	68	76	45

• •

13.3

WILCOXON SIGNED-RANK TEST AND THE SIGN TEST: MATCHED PAIRS

We used the Wilcoxon rank sum test to test the difference between means of two independent samples. But when testing the difference between means for a matched pair of samples, two other nonparameteric techniques are widely used. The choice between them depends upon the measurement scale of the data. The **Wilcoxon signed-rank test** requires the matched pairs of differences to be interval scaled measurements. The two-sample **sign test** is less restrictive, since the matched pairs of differences need only be ordinal scale (ranked) measurements.

WILCOXON SIGNED-RANK TEST

The Wilcoxon rank sum test for independent samples from two populations ranked the values of two pooled sets of observations. Now, in dealing with two sets of observations that are paired and differenced, the absolute values of the paired differences must be ranked. The population distribution of paired differences should be symmetrically distributed, but it doesn't have to be a normal curve.

To illustrate the Wilcoxon signed-rank test, we shall revisit the marketing experiment first described at the end of Chapter 8, in the applied cases, "The Effect of Supermarket Shelf Position on Product Sales." But now we shall remove the restriction that the population be normally distributed.

It is well known that supermarket retailers try to put their most profitable products on the "best" shelves. It is also well known that food producers are constantly trying to obtain the best supermarket shelf space for their products. But do consumers buy what attracts their attention, or do they search for and select a favorite brand regardless of its shelf position?

To study the problem across a variety of buying situations, 24 different stores were selected. The stores were grouped into 12 pairs according to similarity of weekly sales. Then one of the stores in each pair was randomly selected to display a particular brand of product on eye-level shelf space. These were the sample 1 stores. The other store in the pair displayed the same brand of product on shelf space above or below eye level. These were the sample 2 stores. The results for a breakfast product brand are shown in Table 13.3.

TABLE 13.3 Packages of the Breakfast Product Sold in Test Stores							
COLUMN 1	**COLUMN 2**	**COLUMN 3**	**COLUMN 4** **SIGNED** **DIFFERENCE**	**COLUMN 5** **ABSOLUTE VALUE** **OF DIFFERENCE**	**COLUMN 6**	**COLUMN 7** **POSITIVE** **DIFFERENCE**	**COLUMN 8** **NEGATIVE** **DIFFERENCE**
	SAMPLE 1	**SAMPLE 2**					
Pair	**Eye-Level** **Shelf Space**	**Non-Eye-Level** **Shelf Space**	**d**	**$|d|$**	**Ranks of** **Column 5**		
1	111	71	40	40	10	10	
2	150	121	29	29	9	9	
3	130	133	−3	3	2		2
4	154	126	28	28	8	8	
5	67	93	−26	26	6		6
6	112	49	63	63	12	12	
7	84	109	−25	25	5		5
8	123	96	27	27	7	7	
9	71	27	44	44	11	11	
10	62	58	4	4	3	3	
11	38	36	2	2	1	1	
12	51	37	14	14	4	4	
						65	$V = 13$

The competing hypotheses to be tested are

$$H_o: \quad \mu_1 = \mu_2$$
$$H_A: \quad \mu_1 > \mu_2$$

Since the stores in a given pair are matched on weekly sales, we have a randomized block design, rather than a completely randomized design. In this situation, a matched-pair test is preferable because of its lower sampling variability, which is attributable to "blocking out" the effect on mean differences of extraneous variation in store size.

Choosing the level of significance at $\alpha = .05$, we follow the procedure given below for computing the Wilcoxon signed-rank statistic, denoted by V.

Step 1
Determine the difference for each matched pair formed from the two samples:

$$d_i = X_{1i} - X_{2i} \qquad i = 1, \ldots, 12 \text{ pairs}$$

where

X_{1i} is the measurement from the sample 1 store of the ith pair,

X_{2i} is the measurement from the sample 2 store of the ith pair.

For each pair given in Table 13.3, the difference between the sample observations in columns 2 and 3 gives the signed difference in column 4. For example, the first pair, $X_{11} = 111$ (from sample 1) and $X_{21} = 71$ (from sample 2), gives the signed difference $d_1 = 111 - 71 = 40$. The positive value indicates that higher sales occurred with the eye-level shelf position.

Step 2
Take the absolute value of the differences (ignore signs), $|d_i|$. Thus, $|d_1| = |40| = 40$, which is shown in column 5. Note that for the third store pair we have $|d_3| = |-3| = 3$.

Step 3
Rank the absolute values of the differences. Establish column 6, with the ranks assigned to the 12 absolute differences given in column 5. Start with a rank of 1 for the lowest value of $|d_i|$.

Step 4
Establish two groups (according to the sign of the d_i terms) and assign each rank to one of the two groups. Form the two groups according to the sign of the d_i terms given in column 4, one group for positive d_i and the other for negative d_i. Now place each rank shown in column 6 into one of the two groups. For example, d_1 has a positive signed difference of 40 and a rank of 10, so rank 10 is assigned to the positive difference group (column 7).

Step 5
Sum the ranks assigned to the signed differences in each group (the positive group and the negative group). The smaller sum is V. In this example, the sum of the three ranks under the negative differences (column 8) is smaller, so $V = 2 + 6 + 5 = 13$.

Step 6
Determine the rejection region. For very small samples, V is the test statistic and special tables (not included in this text) for its distribution must be consulted. However, it has been shown that for most sample sizes we encounter (10 or more), the sampling distribution for V can be approximated by a normal distribution. Since V is always the smaller of the two sums computed, the testing must always be done on the lower tail, regardless of whether the hypothesis about μ is one-sided or two-sided. Using the normal distribution approximation for V, the one-sided rejection region is $Z < -Z_\alpha$ and the two-sided rejection region is $Z < -Z_{\alpha/2}$. Since n in this case equals 12, we can use Z and the standard normal probability table values to determine the rejection region. (See Appendix Table VI.) The alternative hypothesis H_A suggests that a one-sided probability be used to determine the rejection region. For $\alpha = .05$, Appendix Table VI shows $Z_{.05} = 1.645$; therefore, the rejection region is $Z < -1.645$.

Step 7
Compute the standardized normal test statistic, Z. Under the assumption that H_o is true, the distribution of V can be approximated by the normal curve with mean and standard deviation determined from the following formulas:

Wilcoxon Signed-Rank Test (Normal Approximation)

Mean value of V:

$$\mu_V = \frac{n(n + 1)}{4}$$ (13-7)

Standard deviation of V:

$$\sigma_V = \sqrt{\frac{n(n + 1)(2n + 1)}{24}}$$ (13-8)

From these formulas, we can compute the Z test statistic. The result is the following expression:

Test Statistic for Wilcoxon Signed-Rank Test

$$Z = \frac{V - \mu_V}{\sigma_V} \qquad (13\text{-}9)$$

In the example on shelf space, the value of the Z distributed test statistic is

$$Z = \frac{13 - \dfrac{12(13)}{4}}{\sqrt{\dfrac{(12)(13)(25)}{24}}}$$

$$= -2.040$$

Step 8

Determine whether the value of the test statistic is in the rejection region and draw a conclusion. Since the computed test statistic value of $Z = -2.040$ is less than -1.645, the test statistic lies in the rejection region and we reject H_o. Therefore, we can conclude that there is a statistically significant difference between the mean sales of the sample 1 (eye-level shelf space) stores and the mean sales of the sample 2 (non-eye-level shelf space) stores.

Practical Interpretation

It does seem that eye-level shelf positions stimulate sales for the breakfast product, but whether the amount of sales stimulation is worth fighting over is a question that has not been answered by the test. For a cereal company, that is a managerial issue requiring a comparison of the cost and effort needed to get the better space versus the expected additional sales that would result. The statistical analysis has encouraged this comparison by establishing the reality of a shelf location effect.

Although the situation did not arise in the above example, there is the possibility of tied ranks in performing the Wilcoxon signed-rank test. *Ties in determining the ranks are resolved by assigning to each tied difference the average of the tied ranks.* For example, if two differences were tied for the 4th and 5th ranked positions, they would both be assigned a rank of 4.5. *When differences of 0 occur, they are simply eliminated and the number of pairs reduced accordingly.*

**PRACTICE
EXERCISE**

13.3 A blindfold test is performed on 10 individuals who are asked to rate on a scale of 1–10 their preference for two competing cola drinks. Half the individuals are given cola A first, and the other half are given cola B first. The results are shown in the table. Use the Wilcoxon signed-rank test to test at the $\alpha = .05$ level of significance whether one cola is preferred to the other.

	INDIVIDUAL									
	1	**2**	**3**	**4**	**5**	**6**	**7**	**8**	**9**	**10**
COLA A	6	4	9	7	6	9	10	10	7	9
COLA B	8	9	3	6	3	2	2	1	3	1

SIGN TEST

In the Wilcoxon signed-rank example just completed, the paired difference terms d_i were interval measurements calculated by comparing product sales made at paired stores. But suppose the paired differences were measured on an ordinal scale, as would have been the case if the only information reported was which store had the higher sales. Then the Wilcoxon signed-rank test could not be used, since the numerical values of d_i could not be calculated. But since + and − signs can be assigned even when the measurements compared are ordinal, the nonparametric sign test can be used. Let's now take a look at the rationale behind the sign test and its procedure.

A simple idea underlies the sign test. Assume first that no real difference exists between two populations and that random drawings of values are made from each population. In this case, a comparison of the paired values, one from each population, should show that chances are equal that the larger of the two values will be from one population as from the other. More specifically, matching the observations from populations A and B, and assigning a plus sign when the difference $A − B$ has a positive value, we expect the probability of assigning a plus sign to any pairing to be .5 (ties aren't used). In a sample of n pairs (excluding ties), the sampling distribution for the number of plus signs will be binomial with $p = .5$ and $n =$ Number of pairs sampled. For large samples, the normal distribution approximation to the binomial distribution may be utilized. Thus, for a sample of size n, the mean and standard deviation of the number of plus signs are given by:

Sign Test (Normal Approximation)

$$\mu = np = n(.5) = .5n \tag{13-10}$$
$$\sigma = \sqrt{np(1 − p)} = \sqrt{n(.5)(.5)} = .5\sqrt{n} \tag{13-11}$$

From these equations, we can compute the test statistic, which is the value of the standardized normal variable Z for X plus signs, obtained from the following formula:

Test Statistic for the Sign Test

$$Z = \frac{X − \mu}{\sigma} = \frac{X − .5n}{.5\sqrt{n}} = \frac{2X − n}{\sqrt{n}} \tag{13-12}$$

Now let's illustrate the numerical calculations in a real estate example that requires a sign test.

Dan Rivetti, a real estate broker, has reciprocal listing agreements with two other brokers in his community. When Rivetti secures a listing on a home, the other two brokers are quickly informed so that they can try to sell it. Rivetti would like to know whether there is any real difference between these two brokers in the mean number of days it takes to sell the listed houses. The faster a buyer can be found, the greater the probability that Rivetti can sell the house and earn the commission before his listing expires. If there is a difference, he might be inclined to stress closer cooperation with, and courtesies for, the faster selling broker, even if this means somewhat impaired relations with the other broker.

The last 30 sales made through these two brokers are selected as a random sample of reciprocal listings. Note that Rivetti's problem differs in an important way from our previous problems in which a pair of measurements were matched. In this case, a measurement is available on only one member of the pair, namely the broker who actually sold the house. We know how many days it took that broker to sell the house, but we don't know how long it would have taken the other broker to sell the house. However, we do know that it would have taken longer. Thus, the sign of the pairing can be determined, even though the amount of the difference can't. For instance, suppose broker L sold a house in 14 days. Then broker M would have taken more than 14 days, indicated by 14+. Table 13.4 shows the comparative success of the two brokers for the 30 listings. A plus sign in the L − M column means that broker M sold the house first; a minus sign indicates that broker L sold the house first.

TABLE 13.4 Length of Time to Sell a House (Days)			
LISTING	BROKER L	BROKER M	L − M
1	14	14+	−
2	22+	22	+
3	9+	9	+
4	27	27+	−
5	16+	16	+
6	13+	13	+
7	36+	36	+
8	25	25+	−
9	17	17+	−
10	3	3+	−
11	22+	22	+
12	19	19+	−
13	34+	34	+
14	29	29+	−
15	15+	15	+
16	11	11+	−
17	42	42+	−
18	5+	5	+
19	19	19+	−
20	23+	23	+
21	12+	12	+
22	11+	11	+
23	18	18+	−
24	26+	26	+
25	20	20+	−
26	39	39+	−
27	7+	7	+
28	13	13+	−
29	25	25+	−
30	16	16+	−

The null and alternative hypotheses may be stated as follows:

H_o: On the average, there is no difference in the length of time it takes the two brokers to sell a house; that is, H_o: $\mu_L = \mu_M$.

H_A: The length of time it takes the two brokers to sell a house is not the same on the average; that is, H_A: $\mu_L \neq \mu_M$.

We use a two-sided test, because if there is a difference, we don't have advance knowledge as to which broker would sell the house faster.

Choosing $\alpha = .05$ as the level of significance, we follow the procedure outlined below. This procedure is based on the number of plus signs that result from the sampling.

Step 1

Determine the rejection region. For a two-sided null hypothesis, the rejection region is given by $Z < -Z_{\alpha/2}$ or $Z > Z_{\alpha/2}$. (See Table VI.) For $\alpha = .05$, the rejection region is

$$Z < -1.96 \qquad \text{or} \qquad Z > 1.96$$

Step 2

Compute the test statistic. In this sample there are 14 plus signs. For a value of $X = 14$, the computed Z value is

$$Z = \frac{2X - n}{\sqrt{n}} = \frac{2(14) - 30}{\sqrt{30}} = \frac{-2}{5.477} = -.365$$

Step 3

Determine whether the test statistic is in the rejection region and draw a conclusion. Since the computed test statistic value of $Z = -.365$ is not less than -1.96, it is not in the rejection region and we cannot reject H_o. The observed difference is not statistically significant, so the evidence is supportive of the view that there is no true mean difference between the brokers.

Practical Interpretation

Practically speaking, Rivetti should not pursue a policy that shows favoritism to either broker.

We have illustrated the sign test for a problem in which only ordinal data were available. (Remember, the data were ordinal in this example because although we knew which broker was able to sell a particular property more quickly, we didn't know how much more quickly.) It is with ordinal data that the sign test is most useful, but this test also can be used with interval data when the assumptions required for the parametric matched-pairs test described in Chapter 8 are not met. In particular, if the matched-pair differences are far from being normally distributed, the sign test still can be used. However, the Wilcoxon signed-rank test is preferred in this situation, because it uses the magnitude information that the interval scale provides whereas the sign test disregards it. Thus, the Wilcoxon test is more likely than the sign test to reject a false null hypothesis when differences measured on an interval scale are available.

● ●

PRACTICE
EXERCISE

13.4 A blindfold test is performed on 40 persons who frequently purchase dark imported beer. The subjects are asked to taste two brands of dark beer and record their preference. One brand is the leading imported brand, and the other (the test brand) is a brand under consideration by an importer. Half the subjects taste the leading imported beer first; the other half taste the test brand first. The results show that 15 subjects prefer the leading imported brand and 25 subjects prefer the alternative brand. Use the sign test to test at the .05 level of significance whether one beer brand is preferred over the other.

● ● ● ● ● ● ● ● ● ● ● ● ● ● ● ● ● ■ ● ● ■ ● ● ● ● ● ● ● ● ● ● ●

EXERCISES   ❑

13.13 Many tennis players don't like having to play at night on a lighted court. To test whether playing under the lights really makes a difference, 20 players of varying abilities are given 100 balls to hit during the day and another 100 to hit at night under the lights. (To minimize extraneous sources of variation, the balls are fed to each player by a ball machine.) At each session, a recording is made of the number of shots each player returns into a target area. These results are shown in the table.

PLAYER	SHOTS IN TARGET DURING THE DAY	SHOTS IN TARGET AT NIGHT
1	35	26
2	25	28
3	12	10
4	32	19
5	10	29
6	14	19
7	30	22
8	21	23
9	26	9
10	32	42
11	16	20
12	21	15
13	10	21
14	16	13
15	25	10
16	25	11
17	15	14
18	9	21
19	18	11
20	32	16

a. Use the Wilcoxon signed-rank test to test whether players tend to perform differently during the day than at night. Use $\alpha = .05$ for a two-sided test.
b. Why is a matched-pairs test necessary for this problem?
c. Why is a one-sided test probably preferred to the two-sided test performed in part a? Modify the alternative hypothesis to make it one-sided, and perform a hypothesis test on the data in the table at the .05 level of significance.

❑ ▶ **13.14** A group of 12 executives are asked to rate the effectiveness of widely used computer spreadsheet software as it relates to their particular companies. The executives are then given a crash course in spreadsheet usage, after which they are again asked to rate the effectiveness of the technique. The results are shown in the table. Each rating is on a scale of 0–100. Use the Wilcoxon signed-rank test to determine whether there is a significant difference between the ratings before and after the course. Use $\alpha = .05$.

EXECUTIVE	RATING BEFORE COURSE	RATING AFTER COURSE
1	65	70
2	45	70
3	55	75
4	70	55
5	35	70
6	25	35
7	30	75
8	80	40
9	45	75
10	65	70
11	75	80
12	45	95

13.15 Arnie's and Bixby's are two fast food restaurants located across the street from one another. They are extremely competitive and closely monitor each other's business in terms of number of customers served. The number of customers served at each restaurant on 15 randomly selected days are observed, and the data are listed in the table.

DAY	ARNIE'S RESTAURANT	BIXBY'S RESTAURANT
1	225	236
2	386	399
3	265	280
4	206	196
5	265	286
6	342	330
7	405	456
8	266	259
9	276	282
10	345	276
11	195	209
12	279	291
13	164	173
14	305	289
15	167	175

a. Why is a matched-pairs test appropriate here?
b. Use the Wilcoxon signed-rank test to test whether Arnie's serves more customers than Bixby's. Use $\alpha = .01$.

13.16 A group of 12 married couples are asked to rate a newly introduced luxury automobile on a scale of 1–20. The husbands and wives gave the separate ratings shown in the table. Is the difference between the mean rating of the husbands and their wives significant? Use a Wilcoxon signed-rank test and $\alpha = .05$.

COUPLE NUMBER	HUSBAND'S RATING	WIFE'S RATING
1	12	14
2	17	10
3	10	14
4	9	20
5	12	20
6	16	16
7	19	16
8	7	17
9	10	12
10	13	14
11	17	11
12	8	13

▶ **13.17** An advertiser ran a test on 50 male subjects to determine whether the use of decorative (i.e., attractive) female models has an effect on how well men remember the advertising message. Each subject was shown two types of ads for similar products and was then asked several questions about each ad. One of the ads used a decorative female model; the other did not. Based on the answers to these questions, each subject received a pair of scores, one for each type of ad. The results of the test showed that 17 of the subjects scored higher on the ad using the decorative female model, 30 scored higher on the other ad, and 3 scored equally well on both ads.

  a. Test the null hypothesis at $\alpha = .05$ that, on average, the two types of ads produce equal scores on this test of recall. Use the sign test.

  b. The test was repeated using 50 female subjects. The results showed that 32 of the subjects scored higher on the ad using the decorative female model, 13 scored higher on the other ad, and 5 scored equally well on both ads. Test the null hypothesis at $\alpha = .05$.

  c. With the data given, could you use any other statistical test? Explain.

▢ **13.18** A real estate brokerage chain wants to learn whether husbands or wives tend to keep up more on trends in home values. A total of 18 married couples were given a 50 question test on current home value trends in their local area. The scores are reported in the table.

HUSBAND'S SCORE	WIFE'S SCORE	HUSBAND'S SCORE	WIFE'S SCORE
35	32	35	37
24	19	22	21
25	36	33	26
43	45	42	36
32	36	33	21
19	29	40	32
27	18	25	10
23	40	15	40
31	11	21	35

  a. Use the sign test to test whether husbands differ significantly from their wives in their knowledge of current home values as determined from the items asked on this test. Use $\alpha = .05$.

  b. Repeat part a, but now use the Wilcoxon signed-rank test.

▶ **13.19** A group of 100 people are asked to rate their impressions of the "ethical responsibility" of a well-known investment company. These 100 people are then provided with some in-depth information about the company prepared by the Securities and Exchange Commission, and they listen to several addresses given by financial journalists and by company executives. Finally, they are asked to reassess their original ratings. Let X be the number who revise their ratings upward, and let Y be the number who revise their ratings downward. (Assume that everyone's ratings change, so that $X + Y = 100$.) The null hypothesis tested is whether the in-depth information has had any effect.

a. What values do you expect X and Y to have if the null hypothesis is true?
b. Using the sign test, how much must X and Y differ before the (two-sided) alternative hypothesis will be accepted at $\alpha = .05$?
c. Why might a one-sided test be preferred over a two-sided test? What would the null and alternative hypotheses be for the one-sided test?

13.4

KRUSKAL-WALLIS TEST: COMPARING MORE THAN TWO POPULATION MEANS

The Wilcoxon rank sum test described in Section 13.2 is an appropriate test for comparing the means of two populations when the normality assumption necessary for a Student t test cannot be justified. But when three or more populations are involved, we use an extension of the Wilcoxon rank sum test, called the **Kruskal–Wallis test**. This test is the nonparametric counterpart to the parametric F test used for the one-way ANOVA discussed in Chapter 9.

Let m denote the number of populations. The null hypothesis claims that all of the m populations possess the same mean. The alternative hypothesis therefore states that the means of the different populations are not all equal. Under the null hypothesis, the Kruskal–Wallis test statistic, H, is given as follows:

Kruskal–Wallis Test Statistic

$$H = \frac{12}{n(n + 1)}\left(\sum_{j=1}^{m} \frac{T_j^2}{n_j} \right) - 3(n + 1) \qquad \textbf{(13-13)}$$

where

  m = Number of populations

  n_j = Number of observations in the jth population

  $n = \sum n_j$, the total number of observations in all the populations

  T_j = Sum of ranks for each population (the ranks are for the pooled sample and therefore range from 1 to n)

The sampling distribution of H is approximately a chi-square distribution with $m - 1$ degrees of freedom. The approximation is reasonably accurate if the sample size for each group is at least 5. Like its parametric counterpart, the Kruskal–Wallis test is applicable to completely randomized designs. In essence, we independently draw one random sample from each of m populations and compare the means of the samples. We'll now demonstrate the Kruskal–Wallis test procedure.

Suppose Marc Peter, a real estate economist for the home building industry, is presented with the data in Table 13.5. This table reports the average annual percentage change in value of 20 randomly selected single-family homes in California. The homes are from a particular geographical area and are classified in four categories according to materials and construction quality of the home (from A, the highest quality, to D, the lowest quality). Marc is asked to test whether better quality homes appreciate in value faster than lower quality homes, as is often claimed. He can apply the Kruskal–Wallis test to find an answer.

TABLE 13.5　Average Annual Percentage Change in Value of 20 Homes in Four Quality Categories (Ranks Shown in Parentheses; $n_A = n_B = n_C = n_D = 5$)			
QUALITY (A = HIGHEST, D = LOWEST)			
A	**B**	**C**	**D**
16　(1)	21 (11)	31 (19.5)	19　(6)
22 (13.5)	27 (17)	20　(8.5)	19　(6)
21 (11)	17　(2.5)	23 (15)	30 (18)
26 (16)	18　(4)	17　(2.5)	19　(6)
22 (13.5)	31 (19.5)	20　(8.5)	21 (11)
$T_A = 55$	$T_B = 54$	$T_C = 54$	$T_D = 47$
$T_A^2 = 3025$	$T_B^2 = 2916$	$T_C^2 = 2916$	$T_D^2 = 2209$
$\dfrac{T_A^2}{n_A} = 605$	$\dfrac{T_B^2}{n_B} = 583.2$	$\dfrac{T_C^2}{n_C} = 583.2$	$\dfrac{T_D^2}{n_D} = 441.8$

The competing null and alternative hypotheses are:

H_o:　No difference exists among the mean rates of appreciation and value of homes of different construction quality; that is, $\mu_A = \mu_B = \mu_C = \mu_D$.

H_A:　The mean rates of appreciation in value of homes of different construction quality are not all the same.

Choosing $\alpha = .05$ for the level of significance, Marc follows the steps below to reach a solution.

Step 1
Determine the degrees of freedom. Since there are four quality categories $m = 4$ and $\nu = m - 1 = 4 - 1 = 3$.

Step 2
Determine the rejection region. Since the sample size of each group is at least 5, the sampling distribution follows approximately a chi-square distribution. The rejection region is $\chi^2 > \chi^2_{(\alpha,\nu)}$.

From the chi-square table (Appendix Table VIIIb), $\chi^2_{(.05,3)}$ has a value of 7.81473. Therefore, when values of the test statistic exceed 7.81473, they fall in the right tail and are in the rejection region.

Step 3
Determine the value of the test statistic. Using the values shown in Table 13.5, we calculate

$$H = \frac{12}{n(n+1)}\left(\sum_{j=1}^{m} \frac{T_j^2}{n_j}\right) - 3(n+1)$$

$$= \frac{12}{20(21)}(605 + 583.2 + 583.2 + 441.8) - 3(21)$$

$$= 0.2343$$

Step 4

Determine whether the value of the test statistic is in the rejection region and draw a conclusion. Since $H = 0.2343$ is less than 7.81473, it does not lie in the rejection region and we can't reject H_o.

Practical Interpretation

Home builders in this geographical area who claim that higher quality construction enhances the prospects for appreciation in value are making unfounded statements, since the evidence presented doesn't substantiate their claims.

PRACTICE EXERCISE

13.5 A manufacturer of men's dress shirts wants to determine whether different brands of shirts differ from one another with respect to durability. Six dress shirts of each of four brands are tested by being subjected to simulated wearing conditions. This test includes stretching, stains and spills, and many washings. At the end of the test each dress shirt is rated on a 30 point scale for overall appearance. Assume that the normality assumption required for a parametric F test isn't justified. The results are shown in the table. Do there appear to be significant differences among the four brands? Use the Kruskal–Wallis test at the $\alpha = .05$ significance level.

BRAND 1	BRAND 2	BRAND 3	BRAND 4
21	19	16	20
28	16	19	19
22	17	16	15
16	15	18	24
24	14	21	22
18	20	17	25

EXERCISES

🖥 ▶ **13.20** Three different models of light trucks are tested for their ability to withstand the impact of a collision. Several trucks of each model are crashed into a wall at a speed of 30 mph, and the resulting damage is rated on a scale of 0–10 (10 being the worst damage). The results are shown in the table. On average, the model 1 trucks sustained the most damage. But is there enough evidence to conclude that these three models differ, on the average, with respect to their ability to withstand the impact of a collision? Use a Kruskal–Wallis test with $\alpha = .05$.

MODEL 1	MODEL 2	MODEL 3
4	5	3
3	6	4
5	4	3
6	5	4
7	4	2
9	6	4

🖥 **13.21** Steel mill U is a third source of supply of alloy steel, along with mills R and L described in Exercise 13.10. A random sample of 10 orders is taken from this supplier, and the number of days until receipt of the shipment is recorded. Using $\alpha = .01$ as the level of significance, test the hypothesis of no difference among the three suppliers in the distribution of time until an order is received. The number of days elapsed until the 10 sample orders were received from mill U are as follows: 17, 19, 42, 24, 37, 38, 39, 26, 49, 50.

13.22 In Section 13.3, we investigated the effect of supermarket shelf position on product sales. Suppose the experiment was altered to include a third location, namely, a special display at the end of an aisle, producing the data given in the table.

	Aisle Display Effect on Sales (Number of Packages Sold)		
STORE GROUP	SALES AT END AISLE LOCATION	SALES AT EYE-LEVEL	SALES AT NON-EYE-LEVEL
1	121	111	71
2	159	150	121
3	132	130	133
4	160	154	126
5	73	67	93
6	120	112	49
7	89	84	109
8	136	123	96
9	82	71	27
10	66	62	58
11	71	38	36
12	53	51	37

a. Use the Kruskal–Wallis test to test the null hypothesis using $\alpha = .01$ as the level of significance.
b. The two-sample test used in Section 13.3 on the supermarket shelf position data was based on matched pairs. The Kruskal–Wallis test used here for the three-sample case assumes independent samples. Is there any disadvantage in treating the samples as independent? Explain.

13.23 In Section 13.2, the longevity of automobile transmission life was compared for two brands of automobiles using the Wilcoxon rank sum test. This test is not applicable if more than two brands are to be compared. Suppose 18 observations on a third brand, F, are collected with the following results.

Brand F Mileage (in Thousands)

82.4	88.1	82.8	91.3	106.6	88.5
104.4	103.6	111.4	115.0	76.7	84.9
102.6	96.0	78.5	93.7	94.2	82.9

a. What nonparametric test would be appropriate to test the null hypothesis of no difference in mean mileage longevity among the three brands?
b. Conduct the test identified in part a using $\alpha = .05$ as the level of significance. Data on the other two brands of cars are given in Table 13.1.

13.5
RANK CORRELATION

The **Spearman rank correlation** procedure has been widely used for more than three-quarters of a century for studying the association between two variables. It is simple to use, easy to understand, and requires only the order of magnitude of the values, instead of the measured amounts required by its parametric counterpart (the Pearson r, which was described in Chapter 10). More specifically, the Spearman rank correlation method is commonly used because (1) it does not require interval data and (2) it makes no assumption about the shape of the distribution of either variable being correlated. It requires only that the observations on each variable be contained within a range of values.

TYPE OF RELATIONSHIP AND THE SPEARMAN RANK CORRELATION COEFFICIENT

The Spearman rank correlation coefficient, r_S, is a valid measure of association when the relationship between the two variables under consideration is (1) consistently (monotonic) increasing (one variable increases and the other variable also increases) or (2) consistently (monotonic) decreasing (one variable increases and the other decreases). *This means that the rank correlation applies even when the relationship is nonlinear, but not when the relationship changes direction.*

To illustrate these relationships, let's look at three examples: the first one is monotonic decreasing, the second is monotonic increasing, and the third is not monotonic. In the first two examples, the rank correlation coefficient provides a meaningful measure of association. In these situations, the more restrictive parametric counterpart (the coefficient of correlation studied in Chapter 10), on the other hand, would require both interval data and a linear relationship, and therefore would not be applicable. Neither the rank correlation coefficient nor the parametric counterpart (Pearson r) is applicable in the third example.

- **Curvilinear demand function.** A particular demand function shows constant declines in price leading to changing increases in quantity demanded. This means the demand function is curvilinear, so the Pearson (linear) coefficient r (from Chapter 10) is not applicable. However, even though the relationship is not linear, a given price change always leads to a demand quantity change in the opposite direction, so this is a *monotonic decreasing* relationship. Therefore, the rank correlation coefficient r_S is a valid ordinal measure of the association between price and demand quantity changes.

- **Ordinal evaluation of medical school applicants.** A faculty admissions committee and an advisory committee of practicing physicians independently ranked 22 applicants to medical school. This is a monotonic relationship (presumably, *monotonic increasing*), so the rank correlation coefficient does establish a measure of the ordinal association between the preferences of the two committees. But it does not convey how strong the preference of either committee was for the top ranked candidates versus the other candidates, so the linear (Pearson) correlation coefficient is not applicable.

- **Humidity and employee grievances.** A parabola (approximately U-shaped) describes the relationship between humidity and employee complaints in a factory. In one portion of the parabola, an increase in humidity leads to a decrease in complaints, whereas in another portion of the parabola, an increase in humidity leads to an increase in complaints. Therefore, the relationship is *not monotonic*, and the rank correlation coefficient cannot be relied upon to give a valid measure of association.

INFERENCE ABOUT RANK CORRELATION COEFFICIENT

Many inexpensive electronic pocket calculators have a correlation coefficient key. If the data entered are ranks, this key computes the value of r_S. If you don't have a calculator, you can compute the Spearman rank correlation coefficient by the following quick and easy shortcut formula, as long as neither variable has any repeated values (i.e., no tie rankings are used):

Spearman Rank Correlation Coefficient

$$r_S = 1 - \frac{6 \sum d_i^2}{n(n^2 - 1)} \tag{13-14}$$

Here, d_i is the difference between ranks of the two variables for each individual or object and n is the number of paired ranks.

The sampling distribution of r_S is symmetrical about 0. It approaches the normality distribution as the sample size becomes large. For samples of size 10 or more, the standardized normal distribution can be used to test the significance of r_S. The null hypothesis of no association between the two variables can be tested by computing a test statistic which has an approximately standard normal distribution.

$$Z = \frac{r_S - 0}{\text{Standard error of } r_S}$$

where

$$\text{Standard error of } r_S = \sqrt{\frac{1}{n - 1}}.$$

This gives the following:

Test Statistic for Rank Correlation Coefficient (Large Sample)

$$Z = r_S \sqrt{n - 1} \tag{13-15}$$

The calculation of r_S and its use in testing the null hypothesis is illustrated in the following example of executive succession.

Suppose that Dennis Briscoe, an executive career consultant, is investigating whether corporate executives who attain positions of high responsibility for their age follow a particular route to the top. Do internal promotions within the same organization provide a speedy path to the top? Or does the outside promotional route, with timely switches from one organization to another, offer the best strategy to the executive suite? Or is executive ladder climbing generally unrelated to the particular route traveled?

A survey was sent to a panel of notable executive career researchers asking them to rank 10 executives on two variables: (1) achievement level with respect to age and (2) advancement by internal promotion within a single organization versus advancement by switching jobs. The ranks ranged from 1 to 10, with 1 assigned the highest value. On the second variable, the executive thought to have advanced most through internal promotion was assigned a value of 1; and the executive thought to have relied least on internal promotion was assigned a value of 10. The data are given in Table 13.6.

	TABLE 13.6 Rank, by Category			
EXECUTIVE	EXECUTIVE LADDER CLIMBING SPEED	RELIANCE UPON INTERNAL PROMOTIONS	d	d^2
A	7	6	1	1
B	8	8	0	0
C	9	10	−1	1
D	3	4	−1	1
E	2	2	0	0
F	6	3	3	9
G	10	9	1	1
H	4	7	−3	9
I	5	5	0	0
J	1	1	0	0
				$\Sigma\, d^2 = 22$

Do the data confirm an association between how fast the executive ladder is climbed and the means of climbing it? Let's define the set of competing hypotheses for the proposed relationship, then obtain a rank correlation coefficient, and perform an hypothesis test for the proposed relationship. Statements for the null and alternative hypotheses are:

H_o: The population rank correlation coefficient value is 0. No correlation exists between (1) the rank on the speed with which the executive has climbed the executive ladder and (2) the rank in using internal promotions to climb the ladder. That is, H_o: Population rank correlation = 0.

H_A: Executive ladder climbing speed is correlated with the degree of reliance on internal promotion. That is, H_A: Population rank correlation ≠ 0.

Let's test the null hypothesis at the $\alpha = .01$ level of significance. Since $n = 10$, a Z test statistic can be used.

Step 1
Determine the rejection region. The alternative hypothesis H_A suggests a two-sided rejection region:

$$Z < -Z_{\alpha/2} \quad \text{or} \quad Z > Z_{\alpha/2}$$

For $\alpha = .01$, we have $\alpha/2 = .005$, and from the Z table (Appendix Table VI), the value of $Z_{.005} = 2.576$. Therefore, the two-sided rejection region is

$$Z < -2.576 \quad \text{or} \quad Z > 2.576$$

Step 2
Compute d_i and d_i^2. These values are given in Table 13.6.

Step 3

Compute the value of r_S:

$$r_S = 1 - \frac{6 \sum d_i^2}{n(n^2 - 1)}$$

$$= 1 - \frac{(6)(22)}{10(100 - 1)}$$

$$= 1 - 0.1333$$

$$= 0.8667$$

Step 4

Determine the value of the test statistic:

$$Z = r_S \sqrt{n - 1}$$

$$= 0.8667 \sqrt{10 - 1}$$

$$= 2.600$$

Step 5

Determine whether the value of the test statistic is in the rejection region and draw a conclusion. The test statistic value of 2.600 is greater than 2.576 and therefore is in the rejection region; thus H_o is rejected. With the result highly significant at the $\alpha = .01$ level, we conclude that executive ladder climbing speed and reliance upon internal promotions are statistically associated.

Practical Interpretation

Practically speaking, the high positive value of r_S of 0.8667 indicates a strong positive association between the ranked variables. This suggests that Briscoe should advise his clients that internal promotions, rather than switching, may be the faster route to the top.

Although we used hypothetical data in the above example and intended only to demonstrate the use of rank correlation and its computational procedure, the conclusions reached are from an actual study.

The rank correlation value r_S may be found by using the MINITAB system. We simply enter the paired ranking into two columns, and then determine the correlation. The MINITAB output for the executive succession data is given in Figure 13.2.

Figure 13.2
MINITAB for rank correlation

```
MTB > read c1c2
DATA> 7 6
DATA> 8 8
DATA> 9 10
DATA> 3 4
DATA> 2 2
DATA> 6 3
DATA> 10 9
DATA> 4 7
DATA> 5 5
DATA> 1 1
DATA> end
     10 ROWS READ

MTB > corr c1 c2

Correlation of C1 and C2 = 0.867
```

● ●

PRACTICE EXERCISE

13.6 Ten graduate business schools were ranked by business school deans on the basis of the quality of the faculty and the quality of instruction. These same schools were ranked by business executives in terms of where they would most prefer new employees to have obtained an MBA degree. The results are shown in the table.

SCHOOL	BUSINESS SCHOOL DEANS Rank	EXECUTIVES Rank
A	3	2
B	6	5
C	1	4
D	9	6
E	8	1
F	4	10
G	10	8
H	7	7
I	2	3
J	5	9

a. Calculate r_s.
b. Test the null hypothesis of no rank correlation using the .05 level of significance.

● ●

EXERCISES

❑ **13.24** The data in the table were collected from 16 men. They show the annual salary and the value of the automobile owned for each man.

SALARY	AUTOMOBILE VALUE	SALARY	AUTOMOBILE VALUE
$25,400	$ 8,350	$29,350	$15,800
46,700	11,200	52,400	6,700
19,430	5,400	46,130	17,430
28,250	9,650	27,500	7,200
65,620	18,820	21,650	5,610
43,100	12,500	57,320	11,450
18,560	6,900	42,890	18,668
37,800	10,300	68,520	24,350

a. Rank the 16 salaries and the 16 automobile values, and then calculate the Spearman rank correlation coefficient.
b. Test the null hypothesis of no correlation in the populations. Use $\alpha = .05$ as the level of significance.

❑ ▶ **13.25** A test is given to graduating seniors at an engineering college. This test is divided into two parts: One part concerns the student's technical knowledge, and the second part tests leadership qualities that might eventually lead to management positions. The results of the test for 12 graduating seniors are shown in the table. Find the Spearman rank correlation coefficient for the data, and interpret the results.

TECHNICAL KNOWLEDGE	LEADERSHIP ABILITY	TECHNICAL KNOWLEDGE	LEADERSHIP ABILITY
23	31	21	33
43	38	36	43
25	36	40	49
27	29	27	30
30	37	48	42
46	39	30	36

13.26 Preference for a type of wine and the price of the wine were the factors measured in a consumer wine tasting experiment conducted to determine the extent of association in a particular target market. The wines were tasted and ranked in order of descending preference without knowledge of price. A dummy label was affixed over the bottle label to avoid any bias due to brand effect. The results are given in the table.

	Wine Ranked by Taste, Price Unknown	
WINE	**RANK BY TASTING PANEL**	**PRICE**
A	9	$2.45
B	8	4.50
C	3	2.75
D	6	3.80
E	4	6.00
F	1	9.25
G	7	5.50
H	2	8.00
I	5	7.00
J	10	2.95

a. Compute the rank correlation coefficient for the data.
b. Test the null hypothesis of no association at the .01 level of significance.

13.27 A rerun of the wine tasting experiment described in Exercise 13.26 was performed, except that the subjects were permitted to see a "suggested list price" on the dummy label. The results are given in the table below.

	Wine Ranked by Taste, Price Known	
WINE	**RANK BY TASTING PANEL**	**PRICE**
A	9	$2.45
B	5	4.50
C	10	2.75
D	8	3.80
E	4	6.00
F	1	9.25
G	6	5.50
H	2	8.00
I	3	7.00
J	7	2.95

a. Compute the rank correlation coefficient for the data.
b. Test the null hypothesis of no association at the $\alpha = .01$ level of significance.
c. What is the rank correlation between the rankings by the panel with price known (this problem) and with price unknown (Exercise 13.26)?

SUMMARY

Nonparametric tests differ from parametric tests in that they are not necessarily concerned with population parameters, or do not depend for their validity upon the data being interval scaled or upon specifid assumptions (for example, normality) about the distribution of population values. Nevertheless, nonparametric methods should be restricted to those situations in which assumptions required for their parametric counterparts are not met. Parametric tests, when feasible, offer greater efficiency.

The type of nonparametric test to be used depends on the hypothesis to be tested. To test for sequential randomness in chronologically ordered data, the runs test is appropriate. To test for ordinal association between two variables, the Spearman rank correlation coefficient is computed and tested for significance. To test the null hypothesis of no difference between or among means of different populations, the choice depends on (1) how many populations are compared and (2) whether the data were collected from independent samples (completely randomized design) or a matched-pair (randomized block) design.

For matched samples from two populations, the Wilcoxon signed-rank test should be used if the data are measured on an interval or ratio scale. If the data are measured only on an ordinal scale, the sign test is used. The sign test is particularly valuable in what might be termed "ruined samples" of the type illustrated by the real estate broker example in Section 13.3. Once the number of days required to sell the house is known for the broker who makes the sale, it "ruins" the opportunity for the investigator to learn how many days it might have taken the other broker to sell it. The sign test requires knowing only which broker made the sale. It is therefore advantageously used to test the null hypothesis of no difference between the two brokers in mean selling time. The parametric counterpart to both the Wilcoxon signed-rank test and the sign test is the t test.

We also consider tests for independent samples from two populations and for more than two populations. The former was handled by the use of the Wilcoxon Rank Sum test and the latter by the Kruskal–Wallis test.

Finally, we note that the chi-square test discussed in Chapter 12 is also considered a nonparametric test. It was given a separate chapter because of its prevalent use in statistical practice.

KEY EQUATIONS

Runs Test (Normal Approximation)

Mean value of R:

$$\mu_R = \frac{2n_1 n_2}{n_1 + n_2} + 1 \tag{13-1}$$

Standpard deviation of R:

$$\sigma_R = \sqrt{\frac{2n_1 n_2 (2n_1 n_2 - n_1 - n_2)}{(n_1 + n_2)^2 (n_1 + n_2 - 1)}} \tag{13-2}$$

Test Statistic for Runs Test

$$Z = \frac{R - \mu_R}{\sigma_R} \tag{13-3}$$

Wilcoxon Rank Sum Test (Normal Approximation)

Mean value of W:

$$\mu_W = \frac{n_1(n_1 + n_2 + 1)}{2} \tag{13-4}$$

Standard deviation of W:

$$\sigma_W = \sqrt{\frac{n_1 n_2 (n_1 + n_2 + 1)}{12}} \tag{13-5}$$

Test Statistic for Wilcoxon Rank Sum Test

$$Z = \frac{W - \mu_W}{\sigma_W} \tag{13-6}$$

Wilcoxon Signed-Rank Test (Normal Approximation)

Mean value of V:

$$\mu_V = \frac{n(n + 1)}{4} \tag{13-7}$$

Standard deviation of V:

$$\sigma_V = \sqrt{\frac{n(n + 1)(2n + 1)}{24}} \tag{13-8}$$

Test Statistic for Wilcoxon Signed-Rank Test

$$Z = \frac{V - \mu_V}{\sigma_V} \tag{13-9}$$

Sign Test (Normal Approximation)

$$\mu = .5n \tag{13-10}$$
$$\sigma = .5\sqrt{n} \tag{13-11}$$

Test Statistic for the Sign Test

$$Z = \frac{2X - n}{\sqrt{n}} \tag{13-12}$$

Kruskal–Wallis Test Statistic

$$H = \frac{12}{n(n + 1)}\left(\sum_{j=1}^{m} \frac{T_j^2}{n_j}\right) - 3(n + 1) \tag{13-13}$$

Spearman Rank Correlation Coefficient

$$r_S = 1 - \frac{6 \sum d_i^2}{n(n^2 - 1)} \tag{13-14}$$

Test Statistic for Rank Correlation Coefficient (Large Sample)

$$Z = r_S\sqrt{n - 1} \tag{13-15}$$

PRACTICE EXERCISE ANSWERS

13.1 a. The sequence for the 2 month period contains 23 +'s and 24 −'s so let $n_1 = 23$ and $n_2 = 24$. Then

$$\mu_R = \frac{2n_1 n_2}{n_1 + n_2} + 1 = \frac{2(23)(24)}{23 + 24} + 1 = \frac{1104}{47} + 1 = 24.49$$

$$\sigma_R = \sqrt{\frac{2n_1 n_2(2n_1 n_2 - n_1 - n_2)}{(n_1 + n_2)^2(n_1 + n_2 - 1)}} = \sqrt{\frac{2(23)(24)[2(23)(24) - 23 - 24]}{(23 + 24)^2(23 + 24 - 1)}} = 3.3888$$

Since both n_1 and n_2 are greater than 10, a normal approximation may be used for the sampling distribution of R. For $\alpha = .05$, the rejection region is $Z < -1.96$ or $Z > 1.96$. There are 25 runs in this sequence, so the test statistic is

$$Z = \frac{R - \mu_R}{\sigma_R} = \frac{25 - 24.49}{3.3888} = .15$$

Since $-1.96 < .15 < 1.96$, the hypothesis that the pattern is in conformity with a random process is not rejected.

b. If the series shows nonrandom behavior, the manager might face a systematic source of variation that could lead to the production process being out of control. Corrective action may be necessary.

13.2 a.

RANKED DATA	MODEL A	MODEL B	RANKED DATA	MODEL A	MODEL B
44.85		1	148.00		14
51.00	2		157.83	15	
51.99		3	186.00		16
54.60		4	200.70	17	
58.20		5	212.61	18	
60.00		6	231.24	19	
75.00		7	241.75		20
84.00		8	288.00	21	
96.00		9	291.32	22	
105.59	10		320.43	23	
106.21		11	321.00		24
107.50		12	435.00		25
135.36	13		636.51	26	

Car model A has the smaller sample size, so the Wilcoxon statistic W is the sum of the ranks for model A cars: $W = 186$.

b. There are 11 model A cars and 15 model B cars, so let $n_1 = 11$ and $n_2 = 15$. Both samples are larger than 10, so the normal approximation may be used. Using $\alpha = .01$, the rejection region is $Z < -Z_{\alpha/2} = -2.576$ or $Z > Z_{\alpha/2} = 2.576$. The value of the test statistic is $Z = (W - \mu_W)/\sigma_W$, where

$$\mu_W = \frac{n_1(n_1 + n_2 + 1)}{2} = \frac{11(11 + 15 + 1)}{2} = 148.5$$

$$\sigma_W = \sqrt{\frac{n_1 n_2(n_1 + n_2 + 1)}{12}} = \sqrt{\frac{(11)(15)(11 + 15 + 1)}{12}} = 19.267$$

so the test statistic is

$$Z = \frac{W - \mu_W}{\sigma_W} = \frac{186 - 148.5}{19.267} = 1.946$$

Since the test statistic doesn't fall in the rejection region, the null hypothesis that there is no difference in repair bills between car models is not rejected.

13.3

INDIVIDUAL	COLA A	COLA B	d_i	$|d_i|$	RANK	POSITIVE DIFFERENCE	NEGATIVE DIFFERENCE
1	6	8	−2	2	2		2
2	4	9	−5	5	5		5
3	9	3	6	6	6	6	
4	7	6	1	1	1	1	
5	6	3	3	3	3	3	
6	9	2	7	7	7	7	
7	10	2	8	8	8.5	8.5	
8	10	1	9	9	10	10	
9	7	3	4	4	4	4	
10	9	1	8	8	8.5	8.5	
						48	7

Since the sum of the negative difference ranks is the smaller of the two sums, we set $V = 7$. Since the sample size is 10, we can use the normal distribution approximation for V. The two-sided rejection region for $\alpha = .05$ is $Z < -Z_{\alpha/2} = -1.96$ or $Z > Z_{\alpha/2} = 1.96$. The value of the test statistic is

$$Z = \frac{V - \dfrac{n(n + 1)}{4}}{\sqrt{\dfrac{n(n + 1)(2n + 1)}{24}}} = \frac{7.0 - \dfrac{10(11)}{4}}{\sqrt{\dfrac{10(11)(21)}{24}}} = -2.089$$

Since the test statistic value of −2.089 lies within the rejection region, the null hypothesis is rejected. Therefore, we can conclude that there is a statistically significant difference between the mean ratings of the two colas.

13.4 For $\alpha = .05$, the rejection region is defined by $Z < -Z_{\alpha/2} = -1.96$ or $Z > Z_{\alpha/2} = 1.96$. Let R designate the leading import and S designate the test brand. Then the null and alternative hypotheses are

H_o: $\mu_R = \mu_S$ (There is no difference in the mean brand preferences.)

H_A: $\mu_R \neq \mu_S$ (There is a difference in the mean brand preferences.)

Fifteen of the 40 subjects preferred the leading brand, so let $X = 15$ and $n = 40$. For $X = 15$, the test statistic is

$$Z = \frac{2X - n}{\sqrt{n}} = \frac{2(15) - 40}{\sqrt{40}} = -1.581$$

Since the test statistic doesn't fall in the rejection region, the null hypothesis that the two mean ratings are equal can't be rejected. There isn't a statistically significant difference in brand preferences at the $\alpha = .05$ level.

13.5 The null and alternative hypotheses are:

H_o: The mean durability ratings are equal for the four brands; that is, $\mu_1 = \mu_2 = \mu_3 = \mu_4$.

H_A: The means are not all the same.

BRAND 1		BRAND 2		BRAND 3		BRAND 4	
Durability	**Rank**	**Durability**	**Rank**	**Durability**	**Rank**	**Durability**	**Rank**
21	17.5	19	13.0	16	5.5	20	15.5
28	24.0	16	5.5	19	13.0	19	13.0
22	19.5	17	8.5	16	5.5	15	2.5
16	5.5	15	2.5	18	10.5	24	21.5
24	21.5	14	1.0	21	17.5	22	19.5
18	10.5	20	15.5	17	8.5	25	23.0
	98.5		46.0		60.5		95.0

There are four categories, so the number of degrees of freedom is $4 - 1 = 3$. Since the sample size of each group is greater than 5, the sampling distribution follows approximately a chi-square distribution. For $\alpha = .05$, the rejection region for the null hypothesis is $\chi^2 > \chi^2_{(.05,3)} = 7.81473$. The value of the test statistic is

$$H = \frac{12}{n(n+1)}\left(\sum_{j=1}^{4}\frac{T_j^2}{n_j}\right) - 3(n+1)$$

$$= \frac{12}{24(25)} \times \left[\frac{(98.5)^2}{6} + \frac{(46.0)^2}{6} + \frac{(60.5)^2}{6} + \frac{(95.0)^2}{6}\right] - 3(25)$$

$$= 6.678$$

Since $6.678 < 7.81473$, the null hypothesis is not rejected. Therefore, there is not significant evidence at the $\alpha = .05$ level that there is a difference in average durability between brands.

13.6 a.

SCHOOL	BUSINESS SCHOOL DEANS Rank	EXECUTIVES Rank	d_i	d_i^2
A	3	2	1	1
B	6	5	1	1
C	1	4	−3	9
D	9	6	3	9
E	8	1	7	49
F	4	10	−6	36
G	10	8	2	4
H	7	7	0	0
I	2	3	−1	1
J	5	9	4	16
				$\sum d_i^2 = 126$

The value for r_S is

$$R_S = 1 - \frac{6\sum d_i^2}{n(n^2 - 1)}$$

$$= 1 - \frac{(6)(126)}{10(100 - 1)}$$

$$= 1 - 0.764 = 0.236$$

b. The hypothesis test is

H_o: Population rank correlation = 0.
H_A: Population rank correlation ≠ 0.

The two-sided rejection region for $\alpha = .05$ is $Z < -Z_{\alpha/2} = -1.96$ or $Z > Z_{\alpha/2} = 1.96$. The test statistic is

$$Z = r_s\sqrt{n-1} = 0.236\sqrt{10-1} = 0.708$$

The test statistic doesn't lie in the rejection region, so the null hypothesis of no rank correlation isn't rejected. We conclude that there is no statistically significant correlation between the rankings assigned by deans and those assigned by executives.

CHAPTER REVIEW EXERCISES

13.28 Judy Mersino, a ski resort operator, wants to know whether snow occurs randomly at her particular location. During the months of January and February, the days on which it snowed (S) or did not snow (NS) were observed and recorded in the table.

DATE	WEATHER	DATE	WEATHER	DATE	WEATHER
1/1	NS	1/21	NS	2/10	NS
1/2	S	1/22	NS	2/11	NS
1/3	S	1/23	NS	2/12	S
1/4	S	1/24	S	2/13	S
1/5	NS	1/25	S	2/14	NS
1/6	NS	1/26	NS	2/15	NS
1/7	S	1/27	S	2/16	NS
1/8	S	1/28	NS	2/17	NS
1/9	NS	1/29	S	2/18	NS
1/10	NS	1/30	S	2/19	NS
1/11	NS	1/31	S	2/20	NS
1/12	NS	2/1	NS	2/21	S
1/13	S	2/2	NS	2/22	NS
1/14	S	2/3	S	2/23	NS
1/15	S	2/4	NS	2/24	NS
1/16	S	2/5	NS	2/25	NS
1/17	NS	2/6	S	2/26	S
1/18	NS	2/7	S	2/27	NS
1/19	S	2/8	S	2/28	NS
1/20	NS	2/9	NS		

a. Count the number of runs.
b. Are there more or less than the expected number of runs, given sequential randomness?
c. Does this sequence indicate a pattern of sequential nonrandomness in the weather that is significant at $\alpha = .05$?

13.29 How does the way a product is promoted affect customer reaction to the product? To find out, Pat Johnson, the manufacturer of a new consumer product, asks 32 subjects to rate the product from 0 to 100. Before the experiment is performed, half the subjects are shown a fairly technical, facts-oriented description of the product, while the other half are shown a less technical, more emotionally oriented description. The ratings in the table are obtained.

FACTS-ORIENTED GROUP RATINGS	EMOTIONALLY ORIENTED GROUP RATINGS
76	57
56	49
87	70
37	66
48	71
56	51
68	49
72	55
85	59
61	50
75	60
54	48
69	87
55	45
85	55
51	62

a. Is a test based on independent samples or matched pairs more appropriate?
b. Use the appropriate Wilcoxon test to determine whether a significant difference between the mean ratings exists at $\alpha = .05$.

13.30 Evelyn Pequez manages the hair salon operations for a large chain of moderate-priced department stores. She has decided to launch an advertising campaign to attract customers to the chain's hair salon services. Three types of advertising are being considered: type A, informational; type B, symbolic association; and type C, repeat assertion. Pequez randomly chooses 21 of the discount stores and divides these into three groups of 7 stores each. The stores are told to use the advertising method assigned to their group. After 1 month, the percentage increases in hair salon sales are measured; these are shown in the table. Use a nonparametric test to determine whether the three types of advertising methods produce significantly different increases in hair salon sales. Use the $\alpha = .10$ significance level.

Percent Increase		
ADVERTISING TYPE A	ADVERTISING TYPE B	ADVERTISING TYPE C
8.1	5.1	10.0
6.2	4.7	6.1
9.3	6.8	7.7
4.6	4.9	7.1
10.3	6.9	5.4
9.8	3.5	8.8
8.3	7.6	6.9

13.31 A group of 30 women with above average cholesterol levels is split into two groups of 15 each. Each woman in group 1 is matched as closely as possible with a woman in group 2 with respect to weight, initial cholesterol level, and other relevant physical characteristics. Each of the two groups then goes on a different type of cholesterol reduction diet for a 1 month period. The cholesterol reductions are shown in the table. Does the Wilcoxon signed-rank test indicate that the two diets produce significantly different results at the $\alpha = .05$ level?

Reduction in Cholesterol Level			
GROUP 1	GROUP 2	GROUP 1	GROUP 2
13	9	9	19
5	7	11	16
10	11	8	19
6	9	15	19
12	19	13	12
15	7	20	8
11	17	5	19
19	10		

SOLVING APPLIED CASES

The case presented in this section pinpoints the value of having nonparametric methods available to handle the different types of data found in the business world. This case illustrates the use of the sign test, which enables us to analyze sample evidence on bond rating assignments done by the two rating agencies, Moody's and Standard & Poor's.

Bond Rating Services: Are Moody's and Standard & Poor's Equally Conservative?

Tens of thousands of corporate and municipal bonds are periodically rated for "investment quality" by two rating services: Moody's and Standard & Poor's. A simplified description of the rating categories is given in Table 13.7. Note that the ratings are not quantitative. We can tell which of two ratings is greater and which lesser, but not by how much. This means that the data are ordinal scaled, but not interval scaled.

TABLE 13.7 Comparison of Bond Rating Categories		
QUALITY CHARACTERIZATION	MOODY'S	STANDARD & POOR'S
Prime	Aaa	AAA
Excellent	Aa	AA
Upper medium	A, A-1	A
Lower Medium	Baa, Baa-1	BBB
Marginally speculative	Ba	BB
Very speculative	B, Caa	B
Default	Ca, C	D

Are the two rating services equally conservative in rating investment quality? To find out, an hypothesis test can be conducted on the mean difference in ratings published by the two organizations. If the null hypothesis of no difference is rejected, then the rating service with the lower mean rating would be judged more conservative. It is possible to conduct the test by drawing independent samples of ratings from each service. But because each bond issue is rated by both services, sampling variability can be reduced by using a test based on matched pairs rather than independent samples. We have discussed three matched-pairs tests: the paired sample t test (in Chapter 8), the Wilcoxon signed-rank test, and the sign test. Our first choice among these (because of its lesser sampling variability) would be the t test, if its assumptions of interval scaled normally distributed data are met. However, the difference between a Moody's rating and the corresponding Standard & Poor's rating is not an interval measurement. Therefore, the paired sample t test is not appropriate. Its nonparametric counterpart, the Wilcoxon signed-rank test, relaxes the normality assumption but still requires interval scaled data and therefore is inappropriate. We are left with the sign test, which does not require interval scaled data.

Table 13.8 presents bond rating data on 493 industrial bonds that were issued between January and December; of these, 430 were given the same quality rating by both agencies. However, 63 of the bonds were rated higher by one agency than the other. Even a small systematic difference in rating quality assignments between the two agencies would be an important fact for the financial community to be aware of. So let's investigate whether one service tends to give higher ratings than the other. To do this, we shall state and test the null hypothesis of no systematic difference in rating quality assignments between the two agencies.

TABLE 13.8 Distribution of the New Issues Sample by Rating

		STANDARD & POOR'S RATING					
		AAA	AA	A	BBB	BB	B
	Aaa	31	1				
	Aa	3	65	12			
MOODY'S	A		13	155	7		
RATING	Baa			9	9	5	
	Ba					36	7
	B					6	104

The test does not consider ties, so we must eliminate all the cases in which Moody's and Standard & Poor's assigned the same quality rating. Table 13.9 presents the data from Table 13.8 with the equal rating diagonal element removed and replaced by asterisks. If H_o is true (i.e., there is no underlying systematic difference in ratings between Moody's and Standard & Poor's), the probability p of Moody's assigning a higher rating (ties having been eliminated) is .5. The sampling (probability) distribution for the number of higher Moody's ratings, denoted by a plus sign, will be binomial with $p = .5$ and $n = 63$ (the number of bond pairings sampled for which ratings assigned were not the same).

TABLE 13.9 Distribution of the New Issues Sample by Rating

		STANDARD & POOR'S RATING					
		AAA	AA	A	BBB	BB	B
	Aaa	*	1				
	Aa	3	*	12			
MOODY'S	A		13	*	7		
RATING	Baa			9	*	5	
	Ba					*	7
	B					6	*

Using the sign test procedure, let's test H_o with $\alpha = .05$ as the level of significance.

Step 1
Determine the value of μ and σ for the sampling distribution. With $p = .5$, we'll consider the sample size of $n = 63$ to be large enough to use the normal distribution approximation, and since np is greater than 5, the normal distribution will approximate the binomial with mean of

$$\mu = np = 63(.5) = 31.5$$

and standard deviation of

$$\sigma = \sqrt{np(1 - p)} = \sqrt{(31.5)(.5)} = 3.969$$

Step 2

Determine the rejection region. Using $\alpha = .05$ as the level of significance, the rejection region cuts off $\alpha/2 = .025$ in each tail of the distribution. Since $Z_{.025} = 1.96$, the rejection region is

$$Z < -1.96 \quad \text{or} \quad Z > 1.96$$

Step 3

Determine the value of X. The value of X, the number of plus signs, represents the number of times the Moody's rating exceeds the Standard & Poor's rating. There are 32 plus signs, counted as shown below:

+ = Moody's > S & P	Frequency
Aaa > AA	1
Aa > A	12
A > BBB	7
Baa > BB	5
Ba > B	7
$X = 32$	

Step 4

Determine the test statistic, Z. The value of the test statistic is

$$Z = \frac{X - \mu}{\sigma} = \frac{X - np}{\sqrt{np(1 - p)}}$$

$$= \frac{32 - 31.5}{3.969} = .126$$

Step 5

Determine whether the value of the test statistic is in the rejection region and draw a conclusion. Since .126 is less than 1.96, the test statistic does not lie in the rejection region and therefore, H_o cannot be rejected. The observed differences in ratings are not statistically significant and can be attributed to sampling variation.

Practical Interpretation

We can conclude that there is no evidence of a systematically higher rating being given by one rating service as compared to the other. This relieves the financial bond markets of the concern that a pronounced bias in the rating agency exists.

Checkpoint Exercises

A follow-up study of the bond rating services the next year led to the data given in the table.

Distribution of the New Issues Sample by Rating							
		STANDARD & POOR'S RATING					
		AAA	AA	A	BBB	BB	B
	Aaa	45	1				
	Aa	5	57	16			
MOODY'S	A		22	128	10		
RATING	Baa			16	12	6	
	Ba				10	30	5
	B					4	92

1. Using the sign test and $\alpha = .01$, what is the rejection region?
2. What is the value of the test statistic?
3. Test H_o and draw a conclusion.

WENDY'S DATABASE ANALYSIS

We shall now continue our investigation of factors that differentiate the clientele of the fast food chains. We'll focus on one particular characteristic—family size—or more specifically, the number of children 18 or under living in the house.

Almost from its inception nearly four decades ago, McDonald's has been identified as a "family" restaurant. For many years that image was cultivated through Ronald McDonald, the clown figure heavily promoted by McDonald's. To a degree, most other fast food chains also targeted families, although Wendy's, with its "old-fashioned" theme, clearly emphasized an adult ambience. Might we not expect to find larger families aligning themselves with McDonald's and families with fewer children patronizing Wendy's or possibly White Castle?

To explore this issue, we sorted the respondents according to their top preference among fast food restaurants. Among those who rate Wendy's number 1, do we find a tendency toward fewer children in the household? An affirmative answer to this question would establish number of children as a factor differentiating the Wendy's user profile from those of McDonald's and Burger King. Are there "Wendy's kind of people"? The difference in profile, in turn, would suggest that at least on this dimension Wendy's has a special appeal to a particular clientele.

The MINITAB commands to sort the respondents according to their favorite fast food chain and then to access their family sizes are listed below:

		Number of children	Number of children for respondents rating McDonald's #1
COMMAND:	COPY	C138	C151;
SUBCOMMAND:	USE C106 = 1.	(Respondents rating McDonald's #1)	

		Number of children	Number of children for respondents rating Wendy's #1
COMMAND:	COPY	C138	C153;
SUBCOMMAND:	USE C107 = 1.	(Respondents rating Wendy's #1)	

		Number of children	Number of children for respondents rating White Castle #1
COMMAND:	COPY	C138	C155;
SUBCOMMAND:	USE C108 = 1.	(Respondents rating White Castle #1)	

Columns C151, C153 and C155 are new columns and contain the data for our study. The use of the subcommand USE of the COPY command locates in column 106 persons who rate McDonald's number one, identifies their corresponding number of children (column 138), and then stores the data in column 151. For the Wendy's and White Castle data, the corresponding data are stored in columns 153 and 155, respectively. We can now label the brands with the following MINITAB commands:

NAME C151 'McDon1'
NAME C153 'Wendys1'   Number of children for
NAME C155 'WCastl1'   persons rating brand as #1

As a preliminary check, we can calculate the mean number of children:

Mean C151
Mean C153   Mean number of children, by brand
Mean C155

The MINITAB response in Figure 13.3 shows McDonald's with a higher mean, 1.2276, versus 1.0278 and 1.2000 for Wendy's and White Castle, respectively.

So, at least in our sample, Wendy's lovers have fewer children. But can we generalize this to the entire population? Could the difference among the sample means simply be due to sampling variability? To answer this question we can test the following null and alternative hypotheses:

H_o: There is no difference among the population mean ratings of the brands.

H_A: There is a difference among the population mean ratings of the brands.

The distribution of number of children is not normally distributed, being skewed to the right. Without the normality assumption needed for the ANOVA method discussed in Chapter 9, we must rely on the nonparametric Kruskal–Wallis test. To perform this test, we must stack the number of children into one column and create a restaurant code in another. We can accomplish this by using the command STACK and the subcommand SUBSCRIPTS:

MTB> STACK C151 C153 C155 C156;
SUB C> Subscripts C157.

We have now stacked columns 151, 153, and 155 in a single column, C156. Also, the subcommand SUBSCRIPTS creates a column of coded values. For example, the McDonald's responses will be given 1's, the Wendy's block of responses will be given 2's, and the White Castle responses will be given 3's. Now a Kruskal–Wallis test can be performed:

MTB> Kruskal-Wallis C156 C157

The computer output is displayed in Figure 13.3 and shows a calculated H test statistic of 3.10. If the distribution of the test statistic H is very close to the chi-square distribution, with $m - 1$ degrees of freedom, and if every sample size is at least 5, then it is permissible to use

Figure 13.3
MINITAB for Kruskal-Wallis on Wendy's

```
MTB > copy c138 c151;
SUBC> use c106=1.
MTB > copy c138 c153;
SUBC> use c107=1.
MTB > copy c138 c155;
SUBC> use c108=1.
MTB > name c151 'mcdonl'
MTB > name c153 'wendysl'
MTB > name c155 'wcastll'
MTB > mean 'mcdonl'
    MEAN    =        1.2276
MTB > mean 'wendysl'
    MEAN    =        1.0278
MTB > mean 'wcastll'
    MEAN    =        1.2000
MTB > stack c151 c153 c155 c156;
SUBC> subscripts c157.
MTB > kruskal-wallis c156 c157

LEVEL     NOBS    MEDIAN    AVE. RANK    Z VALUE
    1      145   1.00E+00       161.6       1.72
    2      144   1.00E+00       145.1      -1.40
    3       15   0.00E+00       136.1      -0.74
OVERALL   304                   152.5

H = 3.10  d.f. = 2  p = 0.213
H = 3.45  d.f. = 2  p = 0.178 (adj. for ties)
```

the chi-square distribution in stating the decision rule. Since there are three populations under consideration, $m - 1 = 3 - 1 = 2$ d.f. For 2 d.f., the chi-square table value at $\alpha = .05$ is 5.991. (See Appendix Table VIIIb.) Thus, the calculated H test statistic of 3.10 is not in the rejection region and we cannot reject H_o. The results of the testing indicate that in spite of the fact that Wendy's has a lower mean value, the evidence is not convincing that Wendy's has a distinct small family appeal. It is plausible that the observed mean difference found in the samples was due to sampling error.

Wendy's Database Student Exercises

1. Create the column C160 as the sum of columns C139, C140, and C141. The new column represents the number of children under the age of 12. Use the MINITAB command

   MTB> Let C160 = C139 + C140 + C141

2. Develop variables C151, 'Bking1', C153 'McDon1', and C155 'Wendys1' from variables C105, C106, and C107 on the variable C160. Use the MINITAB command COPY and subcommand USE. Then, by using MINITAB command STACK, develop one column (C156) that contains the data for number of children under 12 and, by using subcommand SUBSCRIPTS, develop another column that gives a code of 1, 2, or 3 for each of the three restaurants:

   MTB> Copy C160 C151;
   SUBC> Use C105 = 1.
   MTB> Copy C160 C153;
   SUBC> Use C106 = 1.
   MTB> Copy C160 C155;
   SUBC> Use 107 = 1.
   MTB> Stack C151 C153 C155 C156;
   SUBC> Subscripts C157.

   Then find the mean of C151, C153 and C155 and comment.

3. Perform a Kruskal–Wallis test on C156 and C157, using

   MTB> Kruskal–Wallis C156 C157

   and comment on the results.

INDEX NUMBERS

The dynamics of presidential campaigns in the United States often present an opportunity for candidates to be "creative" with statistics. The 1976 presidential campaign was no exception. Jimmy Carter, Democratic nominee for President of the United States, devised a new statistic, which he called the "misery index." This index, defined as the sum of the nation's unemployment rate and the inflation rate, was used against Gerald Ford, the incumbent President. Carter claimed that it was during Ford's term in office that the misery index soared to an unacceptable double-digit value. Carter was elected. Four years later, during the 1980 presidential election, it was President Carter who was now on the defensive. Ronald Reagan, the Republican challenger, attacked Carter on his own statistical creation. With the misery index hovering around the 20% mark in the closing days of the campaign, Reagan hammered home the point that by applying Carter's own inspired index, President Carter didn't deserve to be re-elected. Carter's misery index had boomeranged, and he lost the 1980 election.

Is the misery index a valid measure of economic prosperity? What would it have been during the Great Depression? What is its value now? In this chapter we'll learn how to construct various types of indexes and determine just what can be properly said by using indexes.

Headline Issue

MISERY INDEX

BOOMERANGS

Overview

Times change. To keep abreast of change, government officials, business managers, and investors have become avid index watchers. Numerous indexes—gold price index, housing starts index, unemployment index, industrial production index, to name a few—provide their followers with a report card on the past plus a prospectus about the future. In this chapter, our focus will be on the general principles of index construction. Perhaps because of increased concern about inflation and its consequences, no index attracts more attention than the Consumer Price Index discussed in Section 14.4. In the applied case at the end of the chapter, we'll see how index numbers are used in accounting as an important way of adjusting financial statements to reflect changes in general purchasing power of the dollar.

14.1

INDEX NUMBERS AND INDEX SERIES

An index in its simplest form requires a ratio comparison of two values of the same series during different time periods. For example, suppose the average price in one year of a dozen large grade A eggs is $1.20. Five years later, the price has increased to $1.56. Dividing $1.56 by $1.20 gives 1.30 as the ratio of prices between the ending and beginning time periods. The denominator of the ratio ($1.20 in this case) is the value of the series for the *base period*. This value is designated as the standard against which the values of all other periods are measured. The numerator of the ratio is the value of the series for a *particular period*. This value is being compared to the base period value. The ratio is generally multiplied by 100 to show the particular period value as a percent of the base period value. The result is the *index value*.

Thus, we can find an index value following two steps:

Step 1
Find the index ratio. This ratio is the particular period value divided by the base period value of the series:

$$\text{Index ratio} = \frac{\text{Particular period value of the series}}{\text{Base period value of the series}}$$

Step 2
Multiply the index ratio by 100 to get the index value:

$$\text{Index value} = \text{Index ratio} \times 100$$

Let's look at an example. Suppose the 1990 value of the series is to serve as the base period. Then the ratio for a particular year, say 1992, would be formed as follows:

Step 1 $\quad \dfrac{\text{1992 value of the series}}{\text{1990 (base period) value of the series}} = \text{Index ratio for 1992}$

Step 2 $\quad\quad \text{Index ratio for 1992} \times 100 = I_{1992}$

The calculated I_{1992} is the index value, or **index number**, for 1992 that would be cited in newspapers and used by business economists to show how a particular variable has changed from 1990 to 1992. An index value of 115, for example, would indicate a 15% increase in the variable between 1990 and 1992. If the original values of a particular series over time (called a *time series*) are converted to index numbers with a common base period, the new series is called an **index time series**.

14.2
SIMPLE INDEXES OF PRICE

Index time series can be constructed for a single item, such as a pound of coffee, or for a collection of items, such as a weekly grocery store shopping list. If the index is for only one item, it's called a *simple index*. If the measurement is on price, the index is a *simple price index*. Let's construct a simple price index for gold, supposing the prices for the past 13 years are those given in Table 14.1.

TABLE 14.1 Gold Price Index		
START OF THE YEAR	**GOLD PRICE** Dollars/Ounce	**GOLD PRICE INDEX** Base Year 1
Year 1	40.80	100.0
Year 2	58.10	142.4
Year 3	97.20	238.2
Year 4	159.10	390.0
Year 5	161.10	394.9
Year 6	124.00	303.9
Year 7	147.70	362.0
Year 8	190.00	465.7
Year 9	300.00	735.3
Year 10	508.50	1246.3
Year 11	589.75	1445.5
Year 12	397.50	974.3
Year 13	452.50	1109.1

The index series helps create, without graphics, a quick mental image of the relative change in gold price. Knowing that the index is 1109 in year 13 compared to the base period value of 100, we quickly realize that gold showed an elevenfold increase in price:

Step 1 $\text{Index ratio} = \dfrac{\text{Particular period value of the series}}{\text{Base period value of the series}}$

$$= \frac{452.50}{40.80}$$

$$= 11.091$$

Step 2   Index value = Index ratio × 100 = 11.091 × 100 = 1109.1

The base year can be set to coincide with an important event (such as a government decision to deregulate the price of gold). In this way, ratio comparisons of subsequent prices can be made directly with the price in the year the important event took place.

PRACTICE EXERCISE

14.1 For a particular firm, dollar sales volumes (in millions of dollars) are given in the table.

YEAR	1	2	3	4	5	6	7
SALES	105	108	106	119	138	160	180

a. Using year 1 as the base year, what is the simple sales index?
b. Since the firm went international in year 4, use year 4 as the base year and calculate the simple sales index.

EXERCISES

▶ **14.1** Consider the time series of gold prices given in the table.

YEAR	GOLD PRICE Dollars/Ounce
1	300.00
2	508.50
3	589.75
4	397.50

a. Using year 1 as the base year, what is the simple price index for year 3?
b. Using year 3 as base year, what is the simple price index for year 4?
c. Suppose, using year 1 as the base year, that the simple gold price index for year 5 is 150. What would be the price of gold in year 5?
d. Suppose, using year 1 as the base year, that the simple gold price index for year 0 is 63.3. If the base year is switched to year 0, what will the simple gold price index for year 3 become?

14.2 Consider the following price data on coal:

YEAR	1	2	3
PRICE PER TON	$8.00	$7.80	$8.10

a. Using year 1 as the base year, construct the simple price index series.
b. Using year 3 as the base year, construct the simple price index series.

● ●

14.3

SIMPLE AGGREGATIVE INDEXES

The most widely used indexes are **aggregate price indexes,** that is, indexes that measure price changes for more than one commodity or item at a time. Millions of Americans are familiar with the *Consumer Price Index (CPI)*, an index published monthly by the U.S. Bureau of Labor Statistics. This index is used as the country's monthly report card on inflation. (We'll have more to say about this in Section 14.4.)

Inflation is the economic condition of rising prices. But to the general population, the idea of inflation simply means "prices of everything are rising rapidly." To measure "how rapidly" prices are rising, we can look at changes in an aggregate price index and examine the behavior of the "average price." Like any other average, the value of an aggregate price index refers not to the behavior of each and every specific item considered, but to the behavior of the collection of items taken as a whole. It may be that during a rise in an aggregate index the prices of some goods actually fall. In fact, during the general inflation of the last two decades, the prices of certain calculators, digital watches, and personal computers, to name just a few items, have declined dramatically. The proper way, then, to view the movement in the value of an aggregate price index is as a gauge of "general price level movement" and not as a yardstick for any one item.

How workable is the concept of a general price level and its changes when we try to measure it? Suppose an individual wishes simply to compare today's food prices with yesterday's food prices. Certainly this could be done on an item by item basis—couldn't it? For example, someone attempting to compare today's grocery prices with those paid 5 years ago might write down the prices given in Table 14.2.

	TABLE 14.2 Consumer Shopping List			
ITEM	**TODAY'S PRICE**	**PRICE 5 YR AGO**	**PRICE CHANGE**	**INDIVIDUAL PRICE INDEX**
	Dollars	**Dollars**	**Dollars**	
Chicken (lb)	0.79	0.59	0.20	134
T-bone steak (lb)	3.29	1.79	1.50	184
Ground beef (lb)	1.39	0.99	0.40	140
Bacon (lb)	1.69	1.19	0.50	142
Loaf of bread (lb)	0.89	0.62	0.27	144
Coffee (lb)	2.75	1.00	1.75	275
Sugar (lb)	0.24	0.17	0.07	141
Eggs (dozen)	0.89	0.73	0.16	122
Milk (gal)	1.69	1.29	0.40	131
Potatoes (lb)	0.25	0.20	0.05	125
Margarine (lb)	0.59	0.39	0.20	151
Apples (lb)	0.49	0.39	0.10	126
	$14.95	$9.35		

There are 12 food items on this list. The items have different prices, and they all changed in price over 5 years. Most of the price changes are different too. A simple price index series was constructed for the 12 items and is shown in the last column of the table. Inflation could possibly be measured by reporting the changes in all 12 indexes, but ordinarily this would not be done. It is too difficult to try to see a pattern in 12 individual comparisons as a measure of inflation. Instead, the information contained in all the individual price indexes is condensed and summarized into a single aggregate price index. This way, inflation can be measured by a single comparison that is easy to understand. This advantage often far outweighs the potential disadvantage that the changes in the series may not directly apply to any particiular product included in the aggregate. But what sort of aggregate indexes can we now devise?

CONSTRUCTION OF A SIMPLE (UNWEIGHTED) AGGREGATE INDEX

The simple aggregate index, I_{BT}, of all commodities in the market basket is a ratio of the aggregate price of the market basket computed at two different points in time. The numerator of the ratio is the sum of the prices in a particular year (often called "today's" year), ΣP_T. The denominator of the ratio is the sum of the prices in the base year, ΣP_B. The ratio is then multiplied by 100 to obtain the index value. Follow these computational steps:

Step 1
Compute

$$\Sigma P_T = \text{Sum of prices today of a market basket}$$

Step 2
Compute

$$\Sigma P_B = \text{Sum of prices in the base period of this same market basket}$$

Step 3
Compute

$$I_{BT} = \text{Simple aggregate index}$$

$$I_{BT} = \frac{\Sigma P_T}{\Sigma P_B} \times 100$$

If we make 5 years ago the base period, and use the figures in Table 14.2, today's prices have an index number computed as follows:

Step 1

$$\Sigma P_T = \$14.95$$

Step 2

$$\Sigma P_B = \$9.35$$

Step 3

$$I_{BT} = \frac{14.95}{9.35} \times 100 = 159.89$$

This index (159.89) provides a useful summary measure describing the average price change in the items included in the index. We can use it to describe how prices in general have changed or how a change in the price of one item compares to the average price change of all items included in the index.

However, it is important to recognize that a simple aggregate price index can present a misleading picture of the impact of inflation on the consumer market basket. Why? Because it neglects the use of *expenditure weights*, which are needed to account for the frequency of purchase of the various items. That is, all items are not purchased with the same frequency, nor are they all equally important to the consumer. Even for two items purchased with the same frequency, a 10% decline on a $1 item doesn't begin to offset a 10% increase on an item costing $1000. The decrease on the $1 item amounts to only 10¢ while the increase on the $1000 item is $100.

One solution to the problem is to provide a weighting scheme and form a *weighted aggregate index*, which we'll discuss in the next section.

PRACTICE EXERCISE

14.2 Consider the appliance prices in the table. Use the data for 10 years ago as the base year to calculate the requested index number.

YEAR	APPLIANCE PRICES (STANDARD MODEL; DOLLARS)		
	Washer	Dryer	Dishwasher
Now	323	260	310
5 yr ago	327	250	268
10 yr ago	310	223	255

a. What is the simple aggregate index number for appliance prices of 10 years ago, using 10 years ago as the base year?
b. What is the simple aggregate index number for appliance prices of 5 years ago, using 10 years ago as the base?

EXERCISES

14.3 Consider the meat prices (dollars per pound) in the table. Use the data, with year 1 as the base year, to calculate the index numbers.

YEAR	MEAT		
	Chicken	Ham	Ground Beef
1	0.98	2.00	1.49
2	1.31	2.09	1.62
3	1.53	2.15	1.69

a. What is the simple aggregate index number for meat prices of year 2?
b. What is the simple aggregate index number for meat prices of year 3?

14.4 For the meat prices given in Exercise 14.3 and using year 1 as the base year:
a. Compute the simple price indexes for chicken, for ham, and for ground beef.
b. Plot the indexes on a graph, connecting points in the same index series with straight lines.

c. Plot the simple aggregate meat price index series on the graph from part b. Compare the movement of the individual series to the movement of the aggregate series.

14.5 Recompute the simple aggregate series in Exercise 14.3 using year 3 as the base year.

▶ **14.6** Consider the price data given in the table on units of three types of fuel.

YEAR	GASOLINE	OIL	COAL
1	0.50	2.00	8.00
2	1.00	3.00	7.80
3	1.25	3.20	8.10

a. Using year 1 as the base year, what are the simple indexes of gas, oil, and coal for year 3?
b. What is the simple aggregate index for year 3?
c. Which fuel most greatly influences the simple aggregate index?

14.4

WEIGHTED AGGREGATE PRICE INDEXES

We shall consider two types of weighted aggregate indexes: the *Laspeyres type of index*, which is used in the Consumer Price Index, and the *Paasche type of index*.

LASPEYRES WEIGHTED AGGREGATE PRICE INDEX

The impact of inflation is most commonly measured by answering the following question: How much would it cost today, relative to the base period, to purchase the same market basket of goods that was purchased in the base period? The price index that is used to answer this question is called the **Laspeyres weighted aggregate index**. A Laspeyres price index is constructed by (1) choosing quantities purchased in the base period as weights and (2) holding these weights constant in computing the index for subsequent periods. The Laspeyres index for the current period is calculated as follows:

Laspeyres Weighted Aggregate Price Index

$$L_{0,1} = \frac{\sum p_1 q_0}{\sum p_0 q_0} \times 100 \qquad (14\text{-}1)$$

where p_0 and q_0 are base year prices and quantities, respectively, and p_1 represents current year prices.

Suppose that a consumer's total budget consists of 5 items. The expenditures on these 5 items for a period of 4 years are shown in Table 14.3.

The Laspeyres index for the data in Table 14.3 for 1991, with base year 1989, uses the actual expenditures for 1989 in the denominator but does not use the actual expenditures for 1991 in the numerator. The numerator weights 1991 prices by 1989 quantities for a value of $12,897.50.

TABLE 14.3	Prices and Quantities Purchased by Consumer With Hypothetical 5 Item Market Basket, 1989-1992							
ITEM	**1989**		**1990**		**1991**		**1992**	
	p_{1989}	q_{1989}	p_{1990}	q_{1990}	p_{1991}	q_{1991}	p_{1992}	q_{1992}
Automobile, each	$7,000.00	1	$7,400.00	1	$7,900.00	0	$8,400.00	1
Rent, per month	280.00	12	305.00	12	325.00	12	360.00	12
Bread, per loaf	0.70	250	0.75	275	0.82	275	0.88	300
Movie tickets, each	2.75	10	3.00	6	3.25	10	3.50	10
Suits, each	185.00	4	195.00	4	215.00	3	235.00	1
Total expenditures	11,302.50		12,064.25		4,803.00		13,254.00	

Note: Subscripts represent years, and p and q represent prices and quantities, respectively. The totals are calculated by summing the pq products, that is, Σpq.

The Laspeyres index for the data in Table 14.3 for 1991, with base year 1989, is computed as follows:

$$L_{1989,1991} = \frac{\Sigma\, p_{1991}q_{1989}}{\Sigma\, p_{1989}q_{1989}} \times 100$$

$$= \frac{7,900.00(1) + 325.00(12) + 0.82(250) + 3.25(10) + 215.00(4)}{7,000.00(1) + 280.00(12) + 0.70(250) + 2.75(10) + 185.00(4)} \times 100$$

$$= 114.11$$

Note that the index for 1991 is determined *as if* a car had been purchased. Therefore, even though total expenditures dropped to only $4803 in 1991 (a car was not purchased), the Laspeyres index increased from 100 to 114.11.

The index value of 114.11 tells the consumer that it would cost 14.11% more to purchase the identical market basket in 1991 as was purchased in 1989. The calculated Laspeyres index series for the data in Table 14.3 is:

Laspeyres Series	**1989**	**1990**	**1991**	**1992**
(Base Year 1989):	100.0	106.68	114.11	123.11

This sequence of the index tells us that prices of the market basket are rising, but more importantly, that they are rising faster from year to year.

PAASCHE INDEX

The **Paasche weighted aggregate index** defines the market basket using current period quantities as weights, rather than past (base) period quantities. The Paasche index relates the actual current period expenditure, $\Sigma\, p_1q_1$, in the numerator to a contrived base period expenditure, $\Sigma\, p_0q_1$.

Paasche Weighted Aggregate Price Index

$$P_{0,1} = \frac{\Sigma\, p_1q_1}{\Sigma\, p_0q_1} \times 100 \qquad (14\text{-}2)$$

By using current period weights, the Paasche index tells us how much it currently costs to obtain the standard of living indicated by today's market basket relative to how much it would have cost to obtain today's market basket in the base period.

The Paasche index is frequently employed to show the decline in the purchasing power of the dollar, as in the statement, "The same goods that it takes $1 to buy in 1992 could have been purchased for 52¢ in 1977."

Using the data in Table 14.3, the Paasche index for 1991, with base year 1989, is found as follows:

$$P_{1989,1991} = \frac{\sum p_{1991}q_{1991}}{\sum p_{1989}q_{1991}} \times 100 = \frac{4803}{4135} \times 100 = 116.15$$

We can say, "The same goods that it took $1 to buy in 1991 could have been purchased for $\frac{100}{116.15} = 86$¢ in 1989."

The Paasche indexes for each of the 4 years are:

Paasche Series	1989	1990	1991	1992
(Base Year 1989):	100.00	106.68	116.15	122.92

The Paasche index number of 116.15 also says that it cost 16.15% more to purchase the market basket of the current period (in this case, 1991) than that same market basket would have cost in the base year (in this case, 1989).

● ●

PRACTICE EXERCISE

14.3 Consider the meat prices (dollars per pound) and consumption quantities (pounds per month for a typical family) in the table. Use the data, with year 1 as the base year, to calculate the index numbers.

YEAR	CHICKEN		HAM		GROUND BEEF	
	Price	Quantity	Price	Quantity	Price	Quantity
1	0.98	10	2.00	1	1.49	8
2	1.31	8	2.09	2	1.62	9
3	1.53	7	2.15	3	1.69	9

a. What is the Laspeyres index for meat prices of year 2?
b. What is the Laspeyres index for meat prices of year 3?
c. What is the Paasche index for meat prices of year 2?
d. What is the Paasche index for meat prices of year 3?

● ●

CONSUMER PRICE INDEX

Governments in many countries, including the United States, publish and announce a Laspeyres type of index that measures price changes over time on a market basket of goods.

In the United States, the Consumer Price Index is a Laspeyres index that is used to track price changes for a specified market basket. By tracking the Consumer Price Index (CPI), a consumer can gauge whether the purchasing power of the dollar has increased or eroded. Since over the past 20 years there has been a persistent trend toward erosion, the CPI has been viewed as the major indicator and describer of inflation. Interest on the movement of the CPI is of interest not only to the consumer but also to the business manager. A clear understanding of price movements and their structure is an essential element in formulating a relevant and effective business plan. Let us now look at the composition and construction of this index.

In the United States, the CPI measures prices on a diverse market basket of some 400 goods and services, including food, housing, clothing, transportation, health, and recreation. Prices for each item in this market basket are computed monthly, by city, state, and region. The CPI is computed from these data using base period purchase quantities as weights.

The market basket is defined for the "typical" or "average" middle-income urban family. The set of items included in the CPI and their weights are revised infrequently— every 10 years in the United States and every 7 years in Canada.

Constructing the CPI requires the following steps:

Step 1
Select the appropriate items for the market basket.

Step 2
Select the appropriate weights for the items in the market basket.

Step 3
Select an appropriate base period.

To maintain the validity of the CPI over a number of years, some important problems must be overcome. Currently, the CPI is based on moderate-income urban families. But, has the typical family changed? How much distortion occurs during the years between official revisions of the CPI (only then are new consumption patterns incorporated into the index)? Have definitional changes occurred with respect to such terms as "food away from home"? How important are qualitative changes, and does the revised CPI incorporate these differences? (For example, is the color television set used in the CPI the same quality or type in 1992 as it was in 1982? If we are getting a better quality television set today, the higher price we pay may largely be attributable to the higher quality of the product, rather than to inflationary pressures.)

Although the CPI was never intended as the official measure of inflation, it has come to be used as such by the general public. Labor contracts, pension-plan payments, and federal Social Security benefits include "cost of living" increases that are based on the CPI, on the presumption that it defines the level of inflation.

Let's take a look at the CPIs from 1980 to 1989 shown in Table 14.4. Notice that the base years of the index are 1982–1984, a 3 year period. The use of a period of years as a base provides an averaging effect on year-to-year variations. That is, any particular year may have relatively unique influences present, but when a three-to-five year base period is used, these will tend to be evened out. One use of this table is to deflate the annual values of prices or wages. This removes the effect of inflation, making comparisons more realistic. For example, suppose that a worker in 1985 earned $6.25/hr and in 1989 earned $7.10/hr. To determine whether the worker's purchasing power really increased, we deflate both figures by dividing by the CPI for each year and then multiply the results by 100. Table 14.5 presents the figures. The deflated wages are now being measured in 1982–1984 dollars for both years, and we can see that the worker earns slightly less (in purchasing power) in 1989 than in 1985.

TABLE 14.4 Consumer Price Index (CPI)*	
YEAR	**CPI**
1980	82.4
1981	90.9
1982	96.5
1983	99.6
1984	103.9
1985	107.6
1986	109.6
1987	113.6
1988	118.8
1989	122.7

*Base years of the index: 1982–1984 = 100

TABLE 14.5 Computation of Deflated Wages			
YEAR	**HOURLY WAGE**	**CPI**	**DEFLATED WAGE**
1985	$6.25	107.6	$5.81
1989	$7.10	122.7	$5.79

DEFLATING THE GNP

The *gross national product* (GNP)* is perhaps the best known and most widely used measure of economic activity in the United States. It measures the value of all the goods and services produced by the economy for the year. When the economy is growing, this shows up in the form of a large increase in the GNP. When the GNP starts to level off, that's a sure sign of a slowdown in the economy. However, since the GNP measures the value of goods and services (that is, their total dollar value), changes in the GNP reflect quantity changes as well as price changes. Thus, changes in the GNP reflect (1) changes in the real level of output and (2) price changes (inflation).

During inflationary times, it's important to know how much of the change in GNP is due to real output change, or growth in the economy, and how much is due to inflated prices. A measure known as the "constant dollar" GNP, or the "price-deflated" GNP, can be constructed to remove the inflationary component. The GNP implicit price deflator is used for this purpose.

The most comprehensive general price level index in the United States is the GNP Implicit Price Deflator. It measures expenditures on this year's market basket of goods and services at the prices prevailing in a base period (such as 1982). Because the quantity weights are for the current year rather than the base year, the GNP Implicit Price Deflator measured in this way is a Paasche type of index rather than a Laspeyres index. Its values for 1980–1989 are shown in the third column of Table 14.7. Comparing these values to the corresponding CPI values, we can see that the two indexes are very similar, but not identical. The differences are due to the broader inclusion of items in the GNP deflator and to the fact that quantity weights are based on the current year's market basket for the GNP deflator rather than some past year's market basket (as with the CPI).

*A new measure, GDP (gross domestic product), is now being reported in place of GNP

■ **EXAMPLE 14.1**

Finding Real GNP

The data for the GNP of the United States for the years 1980–1989 are shown in Table 14.6. We shall use the GNP implicit price deflator in Table 14.7 to deflate these figures to 1982 dollars.

TABLE 14.6 U.S. Gross National Product (GNP)	
YEAR	GNP
	Billion Dollars
1980	2,732.0
1981	3,052.6
1982	3,166.0
1983	3,405.7
1984	3,772.2
1985	4,014.9
1986	4,240.3
1987	4,526.7
1988	4,909.0
1989	5,389.5

Source: U.S. Department of Commerce, Bureau of the Census, *Statistical Abstracts of the United States: 1990.*

Solution

To convert the GNP to 1982 (sometimes referred to as "constant 1982") dollars, we will divide the GNP in Table 14.7 by its associated GNP implicit price deflator.

TABLE 14.7 Constant Dollar GNP and GNP Implicit Price Deflator				
YEAR	GNP	GNP IMPLICIT PRICE DEFLATOR	REAL GNP	CPI
	Current (Billion) Dollars		1982 Constant (Billion) Dollars	
1980	2,732.0	85.7	3,199.5	82.4
1981	3,052.6	94.0	3,240.7	90.9
1982	3,166.0	100.0	3,166.0	96.5
1983	3,405.7	103.9	3,299.7	99.6
1984	3,772.2	107.7	3,503.5	103.9
1985	4,014.9	110.9	3,600.7	107.6
1986	4,240.3	113.9	3,733.5	109.6
1987	4,526.7	117.7	3,845.3	113.6
1988	4,909.0	121.3	3,987.5	118.8
1989	5,398.5	127.0	4,245.8	122.7

The GNP in current dollars gives the impression that the economy has grown very rapidly in the period 1980–1989, but when measured in 1982 constant dollars, the growth is much more modest. This conclusion would not change if we had used a year other than 1982 as our basis.

COMPUTATION DIFFERENCES IN LASPEYRES AND PAASCHE INDEX SERIES

Like the Laspeyres index, the Paasche index is a ratio of weighted aggregate expenditures on a specific market basket of goods and services.

However, in a Laspeyres index series, the denominator used to compute each index in the series is the same—it represents expenditures on the base period market basket at prices prevailing at that time. The reason the denominator never changes is that a Laspeyres series uses fixed weights, namely, the quantities for the base period. Thus, finding succeeding values in the series simply requires computing a new numerator each year, updating expenditures on the same market basekt to reflect the new price level.

On the other hand, in a Paasche index series, the denominator used to compute each index in the series is not the same. In a Paasche series, the market basket changes each year to reflect changes in the pattern of consumption that have taken place over the year. Thus, the Paasche index series does not have fixed quantity weights, so the denominator in the index has to change each year to reflect expenditures on the shifting market basket. Consequently, computations involved in obtaining a Paasche series are not quite as simple as for a Laspeyres series. Both numerator and denominator must be recomputed for each year. This difference between the way a Laspeyres index (CPI) and a Paasche index (GNP implicit price deflator) are constructed accounts in part for the differences between the two indexes given in Table 14.7.

● ●

EXERCISES

14.7 Consider the meat prices (dollars per pound) and consumption quantities (pounds per month for a typical family) in the table. Use the data, with year 1 as the base year, to calculate the index numbers.

YEAR	CHICKEN		HAM		GROUND BEEF	
	Price	Quantity	Price	Quantity	Price	Quantity
1	1.42	9	1.79	3	1.25	12
2	1.49	10	2.19	1	1.43	13
3	1.53	12	2.15	1	1.69	11

a. What is the Laspeyres index for meat prices of year 2?
b. What is the Laspeyres index for meat prices of year 3?
c. What is the Paasche index for meat prices of year 2?
d. What is the Paasche index for meat prices of year 3?

▶ **14.8** Consider the prices (in dollars) and quantities (in millions) of materials given in the table.

MATERIAL	YEAR 1		YEAR 2	
	Price	Quantity	Price	Quantity
Bottles	0.25	1.7	0.29	2.0
Caps	0.02	2.0	0.03	2.2
Labels	0.01	1.7	0.02	2.0
Cartons	0.03	0.5	0.05	0.7

    a. Compute the Laspeyres index using year 1 as the base period.

    b. Compute the Paasche index using year 1 as the base period.

    c. Why is the reported overall price increase different for the two methods used in parts a and b?

14.5

ISSUES IN CONSTRUCTING AN INDEX SERIES

In choosing between Laspeyres and Paasche indexes, consider the advantages and disadvantages of each. For example, *a Laspeyres index will tend to somewhat overstate the effect of inflation, because it is based on the fixed weight applicable to the base period market basket.* As prices of some items increase more than others, consumers can be expected to try to substitute (wherever possible) items that have comparable benefits but have not increased as much in price. The Laspeyres index doesn't allow for this favorable substitution effect. For precisely the opposite reason, *the Paasche index, which is based on current period weights, tends to somewhat understate the impact of inflation.*

Also, note that the Laspeyres index is less costly to construct, because it is based on fixed weights of the base period, which are typically changed infrequently. A Paasche index series, because of its shifting weights, will be more of a nuisance and more costly to update; but precisely because the weights are always current, the cost of revising and tabulating the quantity weights each period may be worth the effort.

The base period used in constructing either index must be selected with care. When base period updating is infrequent, the selection of a base period becomes even more important. For example, neither peak nor trough periods of fluctuation should be selected. Instead, a period that is considered the norm for consumption should be chosen as the base.

Finally, note that index numbers don't reflect changes in the quality of the items they measure. If there has been a substantial change in the quality of an important item (or items) in the index, then the changes in index values either understate or overstate the real price level changes that have occurred. This is a more serious problem for finished goods, such as pocket calculators, than for basic commodities, such as coal and oil.

14.6

MINITAB CONSTRUCTION OF AN INDEX SERIES

Statistical software packages can be used to calculate index series values. Generally, only a few simple commands are necessary once the data are input. MINITAB programs to compute Laspeyres and Paasche indexes are found in the MINITAB supplement for this text.

SUMMARY

The past two decades have seen high levels of inflation. Because of this, corporate management, government bureaucrats, and financial advisers now require up-to-date information on overall price changes in the economy and price changes on specific goods and services they deal with or manufacture. This need is partially fulfilled by the U.S. Bureau of Labor Statistics, which monthly constructs and distributes two key indexes on price movements: the Consumer Price Index, discussed in this chapter, and another index, called the *Producer Price Index*. This need for this flow of information is continous. Managers who know how to use such information and successfully incorporate the rate of inflation into their investment strategy could very well provide their companies with the extra margin that makes the difference between corporate failure and financial success. For example, the financial manager who estimates the cost of capital in a noninflationary environment to be 10% per year and concludes that the average inflation over the next 5 years will be 6%, will need to use 16% in evaluating the firm's critical long-term projects. If the inflation was underestimated, the firm would face the difficult task of having to "catch up" for several years. Officials in business and government who fail to foresee inflationary changes will find themselves in financial difficulties due to the differences between estimated and actual expenditures.

KEY EQUATIONS

Laspeyres Weighted Aggregate Price Index

$$L_{0,1} = \frac{\sum p_1 q_0}{\sum p_0 q_0} \times 100 \tag{14-1}$$

where p_0 and q_0 are base year prices and quantities, respectively, and p_1 represents current year prices.

Paasche Weighted Aggregate Price Index

$$P_{0,1} = \frac{\sum p_1 q_1}{\sum p_0 q_1} \times 100 \tag{14-2}$$

where q_1 represents current year quantities.

PRACTICE EXERCISE ANSWERS

14.1 a. Using year 1 as the base year:

YEAR	SALES	SIMPLE INDEX
1	105	$\frac{105}{105} \times 100 = 100.00$
2	108	$\frac{108}{105} \times 100 = 102.86$
3	106	$\frac{106}{105} \times 100 = 100.95$
4	119	$\frac{119}{105} \times 100 = 113.33$
5	138	$\frac{138}{105} \times 100 = 131.43$
6	160	$\frac{160}{105} \times 100 = 152.38$
7	180	$\frac{180}{105} \times 100 = 171.43$

b. Using year 4 as the base year:

YEAR	SALES	SIMPLE INDEX
1	105	$\frac{105}{119} \times 100 = 88.24$
2	108	$\frac{108}{119} \times 100 = 90.76$
3	106	$\frac{106}{119} \times 100 = 89.08$
4	119	$\frac{119}{119} \times 100 = 100.00$
5	138	$\frac{138}{119} \times 100 = 115.97$
6	160	$\frac{160}{119} \times 100 = 134.45$
7	180	$\frac{180}{119} \times 100 = 151.26$

14.2 a. The simple aggregate index number for appliance prices of 10 years ago, using 10 years ago as the base year, is 100. This is true by definition, since the desired period is the base period.

b. The simple aggregate index number for appliance prices of 5 years ago is

$$I_B = \frac{\sum P_{\text{Desired period}}}{\sum P_{\text{Base period}}} \times 100 = \frac{\sum P_{5 \text{ yr ago}}}{\sum P_{10 \text{ yr ago}}} \times 100$$

$$= \frac{327 + 250 + 268}{310 + 223 + 255} \times 100 = 107.23$$

14.3 a. The Laspeyres index for meat prices of year 2, using year 1 as the base year, is

$$L_{1,2} = \frac{\sum p_2 q_1}{\sum p_1 q_1} \times 100 = \frac{1.31(10) + 2.09(1) + 1.62(8)}{0.98(10) + 2.00(1) + 1.49(8)} \times 100$$

$$= \frac{28.15}{23.72} \times 100 = 118.68$$

b. The Laspeyres index for meat prices of year 3, using year 1 as the base year, is

$$L_{1,3} = \frac{\sum p_3 q_1}{\sum p_1 q_1} \times 100 = \frac{1.53(10) + 2.15(1) + 1.69(8)}{0.98(10) + 2.00(1) + 1.49(8)} \times 100$$

$$= \frac{30.97}{23.72} \times 100 = 130.56$$

c. The Paasche index for meat prices of year 2, using year 1 as the base year, is

$$P_{1,2} = \frac{\sum p_2 q_2}{\sum p_1 q_2} \times 100 = \frac{1.31(8) + 2.09(2) + 1.62(9)}{0.98(8) + 2.00(2) + 1.49(9)} \times 100$$

$$= \frac{29.24}{25.25} \times 100 = 115.80$$

d. The Paasche index for meat prices of year 3, using year 1 as the base year, is

$$P_{1,3} = \frac{\sum p_3 q_3}{\sum p_1 q_3} \times 100 = \frac{1.53(7) + 2.15(3) + 1.69(9)}{0.98(7) + 2.00(3) + 1.49(9)} \times 100$$

$$= \frac{32.37}{26.27} \times 100 = 123.22$$

CHAPTER REVIEW EXERCISES

14.9 Consider the price data given in the table on units of three types of fuel.

YEAR	NATURAL GAS ($ per kilotherm)	OIL ($ per barrel)	COAL ($ per ton)
1	6.72	2.52	0.58
2	7.02	2.61	0.50
3	8.00	2.75	0.60

a. Using year 1 as the base year, what are the simple price indexes of gas, oil, and coal for year 3?

b. What is the simple aggregate price index for year 3?

c. Which fuel most greatly influences the simple aggregate price index?

14.10 Consider the fish and meat prices (dollars per pound) and consumption quantities (pounds per month for a typical family) in the table. Use the data, with year 1 as base year, to calculate the index numbers.

YEAR	FISH		RED MEAT		WHITE MEAT	
	Price	Quantity	Price	Quantity	Price	Quantity
1	1.98	12	2.00	2	1.79	15
2	1.81	15	2.20	18	1.85	19
3	1.64	19	2.10	6	1.92	21

a. What is the simple aggregate index number for fish and meat prices of year 2?
b. What is the simple aggregate index number for fish and meat prices of year 3?

14.11 For the data given in Exercise 14.10, and again using year 1 as the base period, what is the Laspeyres index for fish and meat prices of:
a. Year 2?
b. Year 3?

14.12 For the data given in Exercise 14.10, and using year 1 as the base year, what is the Paasche index for fish and meat prices of:
a. Year 1?
b. Year 2?
c. Year 3?

14.13 An automobile manufacturer reported sales information (in thousands of dollars) for year 1 and price information (in dollars) for years 1 and 2 (the current model year) as shown in the table.

MODEL	YEAR 1		YEAR 2
	Sales	Price	Price
A	800	10,000	11,000
B	300	12,000	13,000
C	50	20,000	20,500
D	100	14,000	14,500

a. Compute the simple aggregate price index for year 2, using year 1 as the base.
b. Compute the Laspeyres index value for year 2, using year 1 as the base and assuming no change in quantities between the two years.
c. If the manufacturer wanted to report the lower average price increase, which method should be used? Explain.
d. If a government agency wants to estimate the inflationary impact of the price changes, which method should be used? Explain.

14.14 The automobile manufacturer in Exercise 14.13 included a driver-side air bag as standard equipment in all its car models in year 2. The air bags were not available on any of the models in year 1.
a. Would the inclusion of the air bags change the value of either the simple or weighted aggregate price index for year 2? Explain.
b. Suppose the air bags had been available as optional equipment in year 1 at a price of $1000. Would inclusion as standard equipment in year 2 change the value of either the simple or weighted aggregate index? Explain.

14.15 An investor owns a portfolio of common stock in three companies: A, B, and C. Their prices at three points in time are given in the table. Use Period 1 as the base period.

STOCK	PRICE		
	Period 1	Period 2	Period 3
A	20	25	35
B	120	60	140
C	40	35	45

    a. Construct a simple price index series for each individual stock.
    b. Construct a simple aggregate price index series for the aggregate of all three stocks.
    c. Plot on a graph all the index series constructed in parts a and b.
    d. Comment on the movements of each individual stock index compared to the movement of the aggregate stock price index.

14.16 The simple aggregate stock price index computed in Exercise 14.15 is similar to the *Dow-Jones Index*, a well-known stock market price index, in that both are unweighted simple price aggregates.
    a. Do you see any problem with this type of stock index as a measure of stock price changes? Explain.
    b. The *Standard & Poor's 500*, another well-known stock price index, weights the price of each stock in the index by the number of shares of that stock. As an investor, would you have any preference as to the type of index used in reporting stock market price movements? Explain.

SOLVING APPLIED CASES
Constant Dollar Accounting

When price inflation soars, accounting statements listing corporate assets and profits come under criticism by financial analysts and investors, who rely on these statements to evaluate corporate strength and performance. Their criticism is directed at the accounting principle that requires assets to be recorded on financial statements at the actual purchase price even during inflationary times. This means that recently acquired assets are recorded in terms of inflated dollars, not in the same purchasing power dollars used to record previous assets. This accounting procedure inflates the aggregate value figure of the firm's assets compared to the aggregate figure that would be obtained if all the firm's assets were recorded at the same purchasing power. Reported profits likewise are inflated, because revenues immediately reflect the current price inflation, but costs generally reflect previous lower prices. This phenomenon leaves investors unsure about how much of reported rising profits are due to inflation and how much are truly due to expanded corporate operations.

    Supppose that on January 1, a company was organized and on that date sold common stock for a total of $10,000 to purchase land costing $10,000. On December 31 of the same year, the company sold the land for $12,000 and used that entire amount to retire all the common stock. At that time, the company terminated its operations. Following conventional accounting principles, the company's income statement for the year would show a $2,000 profit, the difference between the selling price of $12,000 and the purchase cost of $10,000. However, if general price inflation over the year was 30%, the reported $2,000 profit would be very misleading, because the purchasing power of the $12,000 received at the end of the year would be less than the purchasing power of the $10,000 invested at the beginning of the year. Thus, if price inflation is significant, profits can't be determined simply by comparing nominal dollars paid at one point in time to nominal dollars received at a later point in time, because the dollars don't have the same purchasing power.

    Constant dollar accounting is an approach accountants have developed to deal with the price inflation problem. The objective of constant dollar accounting is to report the elements of financial statements in constant dollars, that is, dollars that have the same purchasing power. Amounts that conventionally would have been shown and compared in nominal dollars are now converted to constant dollar amounts. This conversion is achieved by using a general price level index that measures inflation, such as the CPI. A financial statement currently stated in nominal amounts is converted to constant dollar amounts using the following general formula:

$$\text{Constant dollar amount} = (\text{Nominal dollar amount})\left(\frac{\text{CPI of current period}}{\text{CPI of previous period}}\right)$$

The ratio of CPIs is called a *conversion factor*, because it converts nominal dollar amounts to constant dollar amounts. In the example above, suppose the CPI on January 1 was 100 and the CPI on December 31 was 130. Then the acquisition price of the land expressed in constant dollars is

$$(\$10,000)\left(\frac{130}{100}\right) = \$13,000$$

Thus, comparing this $13,000 (constant dollar) acquisition cost to the $12,000 sale price gives a loss of $1,000, rather than a gain of $2,000.

Constant dollar accounting may be applied to physical assets, accounts receivable or payable, notes receivable or payable, or any other item that represents a fixed number of dollars to be received or paid.

A Numerical Illustration

The use of several price indexes for constant dollar accounting can be demonstrated by comparing two annual income statements, one prepared conventionally (without adjustment for price inflation) and the other using constant dollars. On an income statement, an accountant determines profitability of the company over the stated period by comparing revenue and expenses.

Table 14.8 presents a conventional income statement for the I. V. Carrier Corporation. As can be seen from the net income figure, the company earned $100,000 over the year.

TABLE 14.8 Conventional Income Statement for I. V. Carrier Corporation, 1991		
Sales revenue		$400,000
Cost of goods sold (expense)		
Beginning inventory	$100,000	
Purchases	210,000	
Goods available	$310,000	
Ending inventory	90,000	220,000
Gross profit on sales		$180,000
Operating expenses		80,000
Net income		$100,000

Now let's assume that substantial price inflation occurred during the year, with the CPI increasing from 130.0 at the beginning of the year to 157.3 at the end of the year, averaging 143.0 during the year. Based on these values, an accountant would compute the following conversion factors to restate the conventional income statement information in constant dollars:

Conversion Factors

January 1 index	$\frac{157.3}{130.0} = 1.21$	
Average index for 1991	$\frac{157.3}{143.0} = 1.10$	
December 31 index	$\frac{157.3}{157.3} = 1.00$	

If we assume that revenues were received and expenses incurred evenly throughout the year, then any conversion factor based on the average index value for the year is acceptable.

The constant dollar version of the income statement is shown in Table 14.9, along with the conversion factor used for each changed value.

TABLE 14.9 Constant Dollar Income Statement for I. V. Carrier Corporation, 1991		
Sales ($400,000 × 1.10)		$440,000
Cost of goods sold		
Beginning inventory ($100,000 × 1.21)	$121,000	
Purchases ($210,000 × 1.10)	231,000	
Goods available	$352,000	
Ending inventory ($90,000 × 1.10)	99,000	253,000
Gross profit on sales		$187,000
Operating expenses ($80,000 × 1.10)		88,000
Net income		$ 99,000

Note that the conversion factor of 1.10 is applied to purchases on the assumption that they were made throughout the year. The conversion factor of 1.10 is also applied to the ending inventory value on the assumption that the amount accumulated in ending inventory is the result of purchases and shipments through the year. A comparison of the net income figures in Tables 14.8 and 14.9 shows that the constant dollar income statement has a smaller net income. This result is to be expected during an inflationary period, because the conventional income statement will not take full account of the fact that inflation has appreciated items held in inventory. This causes the conventional income statement to show a lower cost of goods sold ($220,000) compared to the constant dollar amount ($253,000). The full recognition of inflation in the cost of goods sold amount in the constant dollar income statement properly deflates the net income figure. For additional considerations in constant dollar accounting, an accounting textbook should be consulted.

Checkpoint Exercise

1. The income statement for the Stamm Company for 1991, stated in conventional terms, is given below. The CPI at the beginning of the year was 120, the CPI at the end of the year was 144, and the average CPI during the year was 132. Construct the corresponding constant dollar income statement for 1991.

Conventional Income Statement for Stamm Company, 1991		
Sales revenue		$600,000
Cost of goods sold (expense)		
Beginning inventory	$200,000	
Purchases	380,000	
Goods available	$580,000	
Ending inventory	240,000	340,000
Gross profit on sales		$260,000
Operating expenses		90,000
Net income		$170,000

TIME SERIES AND FORECASTING

15

Headline Issue

A BIG BAND FAN: A RESEARCH ANALYST USES THE MOVING AVERAGE*

Buy low, sell high. That's the one sure way you can make money in the stock market. But it's not easy. Professional investors often can't distinguish an expensive market from an undervalued one. An indicator or signal that causes one analyst to buy might prompt another to sell. As a group, individual investors are notorious for picking the wrong periods to enter and exit the market.

David Vomund, an analyst at Target, Inc., a Pleasanton, California, based company that publishes financial newsletters, including the *Ruff Times,* offers some suggestions on how individuals can improve their timing skills:

Small investors often buy near market tops and sell near market bottoms. That is why their actions are one of the most reliable reverse market indicators. They buy or sell based on emotions. As the market rises, they chase strength fearing they will be left behind; when the market drops, they sell because of gloomy headlines.

A basic tool I use to avoid buying high and selling low is a trading band. A trading band has an upper and lower limit containing a moving average of an investment. To determine the upper and lower limits, adjust the moving average as much as necessary to parallel its extremes—points at which the price reverses direction. I run a trading band on the New York composite index by using a 30-day moving average and shifting it upward by 6% and downward by 4%. The results are shown in Figure 15.1. Notice how many times the market has reversed direction when it approached the high or low end of the trading band.

The strategy behind the trading band is simple—buy only when the market nears the bottom of the band [as it did in early January 1991] and sell when it nears the top. This strategy works best with stock mutual funds that allow investors to switch without charge.

Mutual fund timing is an inexact science, and the risk of missing a stock rally outweighs the risk of a correction. For this reason, I keep a portion of my portfolio in funds that have good long-term track records and low expenses, and are well-diversified, ... I hold these funds, no matter how bleak the outlook. The trading bands provide me with buying points for these funds.

The remaining portion of the portfolio goes toward market timing, buying near the bottom band and selling near the top band. More aggressive funds are used [for that].

Vomund uses a personal computer spreadsheet program to figure out *moving averages*. Hand-held calculators also can do the job. Moving averages help show trends

*From "A Big Band Fan: A Research Analyst Uses Moving Average," *Personal Investor,* Sept. 1990, p. 38. Reprinted by permission of Plaza Communications, Inc.

by "smoothing out" daily fluctuations. They can be constructed for any time period you like—from a few days to several years.

In this chapter we will discuss how to construct the moving average series and illustrate the purpose it serves in economic and financial analysis.

Overview

Forecasting is an art. It requires the analyst to blend a statistical analysis of past data with good business judgment. The *classical time series model* offers a framework to conduct a statistical analysis of past data. The model states that the data series can be decomposed into a long-term trend component and a short-term seasonal component. An analysis of the data series may reveal the period to period movement of each component series. This decomposition and analysis procedure accomplishes two objectives: It isolates the dominant component(s) of the data series, and it reveals the individual behavior of each underlying component from period to period. Once the statistical structure of each component has been revealed, a manager can project (extrapolate) the value of that component for several periods ahead. By combining each projected component into an aggregate figure, we can make a forecast. For example, if the trend component projects an increase of 35 units and the seasonal component projects an increase of 7 units, the aggregate of these two projections would be an increase of 42 units. But this aggregate statistical forecast is usually modified by the manager's or analyst's judgment. Management is always on the lookout for any new factors that may be affecting current values or that may affect future values. For example, the Persian Gulf crisis might have prompted a downward revision of, say, 9 units in the forecast. The better the insight of management about new external factors, the more relevant the modification.

In another approach, decomposition using the classical time series model is avoided altogether. This alternate statistical approach to forecasting relies solely on the movement of the undecomposed past series. In this case, the manager or analyst focuses on

Figure 15.1
Moving average and its upper
and lower limits

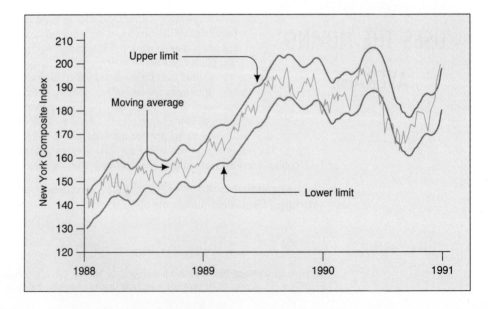

discovering a mathematical equation that accurately captures the underlying pattern of behavior of the undecomposed series over the past periods considered. The aim is to find an equation that portrays the underlying system that generates the series and that is capable of projecting values for the series several periods ahead. The decision of whether to use decomposition approach or the mathematical equation approach generally rests with the approach that can more accurately forecast the level of the series for the coming periods.

This chapter begins with a discussion and analysis of the classical time series model, and presents a decomposition of actual data into the trend, seasonal, cyclical, and irregular components. The chapter continues with a discussion of one technique tailored for short-term forecasting (*exponential smoothing*) and one designed for long-term forecasting (*trend projection*). We conclude with a comment on forecasting by using a structural equation that incorporates economic and technical variables hypothesized to generate the series.

15.1
SEQUENTIAL PATTERNS: DATA COLLECTED OVER TIME

Observations collected over successive time periods are called a **time series** and are denoted by the symbol Y_t. If collected over n periods, the entire set of Y_t observations is designated by the expression

$$Y_t \qquad \text{where } t = 1, \ldots, n$$

Time series observations are frequently examined for time-related patterns. When we conclude that there exists a time-related pattern between successive values of Y_t, this means that we can specify the path and the magnitude of Y from its time (t^{th}) period of occurrence. We call such a Y_t series **statistically time-dependent.**

Our goal in analyzing a statistically time-dependent Y_t series is to isolate and identify the structure of the time-related patterns embedded in the series. The application of techniques used to do this is referred to as **time series analysis.** Two main purposes are achieved by performing this type of analysis:

1. One purpose is descriptive. That is, we specify the structure or model that describes the time-dependent patterns in the historical data. One such model, defined with four components, is discussed in Section 15.2.
2. Another purpose is predictive. That is, we apply techniques that identify patterns we can use for predicting future values of Y_t. These techniques include methods for projecting long-run trends (Sections 15.3 and 15.7), a method for adjusting seasonal influences (Section 15.5), and a method for short-term forecasting (Section 15.6). The last method, called *exponential smoothing,* offers a way to adapt the forecast when a sudden shift in the Y_t series occurs from an otherwise trendless level.

15.2
THE CLASSICAL TIME SERIES MODEL

Business managers often use an analysis of time series data as an aid in making decisions. In making these decisions, they should not forget that time-dependent patterns in data are the result of a host of persistent, recurring, and newly evolving causal forces. In business, causal forces are separated into two categories: long-term and short-term.

We often assume that various types of short-term and long-term forces are present when an economic or business data series is graphed over several time periods, as shown in Figure 15.2. The observed pattern of a time-ordered data series is traditionally

Figure 15.2
Time-related pattern of Y_t
series

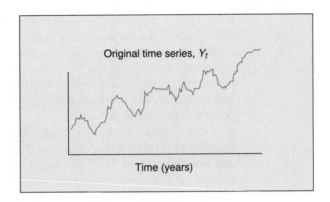

regarded as a composite of the following four long-term and short-term statistical components: *trend component, seasonal component, cyclical component,* and *irregular component.*

Any specific time series may include any or all of the four components listed above. The conceptual framework in which all four components are included is called the *classical time series model.* This model therefore provides an important starting point for decomposing a specific time series into its various components. Figure 15.3 illustrates the decomposition of the original time series graphed in Figure 15.2.

Now, let's take a look at the various features of the four time series components.

TREND COMPONENT

The trend, sometimes called **secular trend**, indicates a sustained pattern of steadily increasing or steadily decreasing values over a prolonged period of time. Some long-term forces that produce trends are:

- Cultural forces (such as greater acceptability of women in the work force)
- Demographic forces (such as population shifts, exemplified by the aging of the post-World War II "baby boom" generation and the consequent shifts in their product buying patterns)
- Economic forces (such as growth in disposable income and the steadily increasing competitive strength of Pacific Rim countries)
- Technological forces (such as the expansion of microchip technology)

Trends in economic data are considered long-run movements that last several years, generally from 3 to 15 years. The trend component is generally graphed as a smooth curve, rising or falling steadily over successive time periods. The smooth curve may have a linear or nonlinear shape, as shown in Figure 15.4.

SEASONAL COMPONENT

When time series data show fluctuations that recur in a stable, periodic fashion (usually from year to year), **seasonal variation** is present. Although the term *seasonal* commonly refers to the four quarters or the 12 months of a year, it could just as well refer to the 7 days of a week, etc. Two conditions are required for the periodicity to exist in the

Figure 15.3
Original time series Y_t and its various components

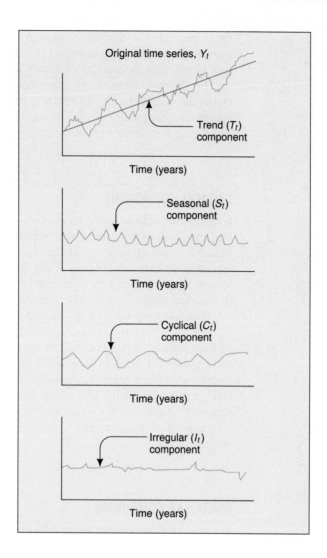

Figure 15.4
Different types of increasing, or positive, trends

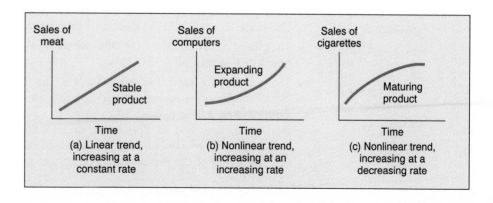

data series: (1) the time lapse between occurrences must be identical (days, weeks, months, etc.) and (2) the extreme (high or low) observation should recur at the same time period (always Saturday or always July, etc.).

To illustrate: Suppose we chart quarterly textbook sales over several years. We expect the conditions for periodicity to be met, since (1) quarters are equal lengths of time and (2) the peaks and the low points will consistently be found in the fall quarter and during the summer quarter, respectively.

CYCLICAL COMPONENT

Cyclical fluctuation occurs in the time series when there is a prolonged, recurring but erratic wavelike pattern that doesn't fit the periodicity definition of seasonal variation. Although cycles are classified as long-term movements, they are not generally regarded as stable components of the classical time series model; only the trend and seasonality components are considered stable. Hence, cycles, if they exist, are part of the residual component left after trend and seasonality have been filtered out.

A well-known example of the cyclical component is the so-called *business cycle,* which reflects the fact that business activity experiences long wavelike movements that go from peak to trough and back to peak again. A business cycle may last a relatively short span of 2 years or persist for as long as 15 years. For example, the Great Depression, which began in the early 1930s, persisted until the end of that decade. One complete oscillation of a typical business cycle is often described as having four economic phases: recovery, boom, recession, and depression. Recovery and boom comprise the *expansionary phases;* recession and depression comprise the *contractionary phases.*

IRREGULAR COMPONENT

The **irregular component** is caused by factors that are very transitory and very often nonrecurring. These factors run the gamut from bizarre conditions of nature, such as hurricanes, floods, and blights, to unpredictable situations such as wars, strikes, and global political crises. For example:

- The southern corn blight in 1969–1970 caused corn prices to jump 50% above the previous year's prices; a similar supply disruption accompanied the great drought of 1988.

- The rapid build-up of the U.S. trade imbalance during 1985–1986 caused the U.S. dollar to drop 50% in value against the Japanese yen in just 1 year.

- The glut of oil throughout the 1980s saw oil prices drop from $25 a barrel to near $15 a barrel.

- The potential shortage of oil attributable to the Persian Gulf crisis of 1990 (when Iraq invaded and took over Kuwait) saw oil prices skyrocket from approximately $18 to close to $40 a barrel in a matter of weeks. By the time the United States and its allies began the military bombardment of Iraq in early 1991, concerns over oil supply had eased considerably, and within the first few weeks of the Persian Gulf War, prices were back down to around $25 per barrel.

At times, just one random event (such as corn blight) can cause a rapid rise or fall in the time series; at other times, a series of unpredictable happenings (such as action by OPEC, plus a huge new oil find at Prudhoe Bay) act in tandem to trigger the dramatic rise or fall. "Black Monday," the October 19, 1987, stock market crash, appears to have been triggered by the questionable activity surrounding Wall Street dealers and the state of the economy.

ADDITIVE AND MULTIPLICATIVE COMPONENT MODELS

There are two versions of the classical time series model. In one version, the dependent variable Y_t is composed of four additive components, which, when added together, give Y_t.

Additive Component Model

$$Y_t = T_t + S_t + C_t + I_t \tag{15-1}$$

where

t = Time period (the first time period is generally assigned the value of 1, that is, $t = 1$; the second time period has $t = 2$, etc.)

Y_t = Value of the time series at time t

T_t = Value of the trend component at time t

S_t = Value of the seasonal component at time t

C_t = Value of the cyclical component at time t

I_t = Value of the irregular component at time t

Suppose Y_t represents quarterly sales and has a value of 150. The decomposition would lead to four components, which, when added together, give 150; for example, one decomposition might be:

$$\text{Trend} \quad T_t = 100$$
$$\text{Seasonal} \quad S_t = -5$$
$$\text{Cyclical} \quad C_t = 30$$
$$\text{Irregular} \quad I_t = 25$$

Thus,

$$Y_t = T_t + S_t + C_t + I_t$$
$$= 100 - 5 + 30 + 25 = 150$$

In this case, the seasonal influence shows a value of -5, suggesting that this particular season has a depressing effect on sales.

A shortcoming of the additive model is that changes in the magnitude of the seasonal and cyclical components are assumed to be unaffected by changes in the magnitude of the trend component. For example, if sales double or triple due to long-term growth, it is likely that the gap between seasonal peaks and troughs will also become larger. For this reason, another version of the classical time series model, the multiplicative component model, is more commonly used than the additive model to analyze time series data.

The multiplicative model expresses the value of the dependent variable Y_t as the product of the components.

Multiplicative Component Model

$$Y_t = T_t \cdot S_t \cdot C_t \cdot I_t \qquad (15\text{-}2)$$

This is called the *classical multiplicative component time series model*. In this model, the trend component T_t is measured in the same units as Y_t. However, the S_t, C_t, and I_t components are measured in relative terms, with values above 1.00 indicating a seasonal, cyclical, or irregular effect above the trend. Suppose Y_t has a value of 200. One possible multiplicative decomposition might be:

$$\text{Trend} \quad T_t = 160$$
$$\text{Seasonal} \quad S_t = 1.25$$
$$\text{Cyclical} \quad C_t = 0.75$$
$$\text{Irregular} \quad I_t = 1.3333$$

Thus,

$$Y_t = T_t \cdot S_t \cdot C_t \cdot I_t$$
$$= (160)(1.25)(0.75)(1.3333) = 200$$

In Sections 15.3–15.5, we'll illustrate the traditional decomposition of time series data into the specific multiplicative components.

15.3
TREND ANALYSIS WITH ANNUAL DATA

The secular trend represents the long-term component of a time series. The trend component is attributable to underlying factors that exert influence over an extended period of time. In this section we shall illustrate mathematical trend fitting based on regression analysis using the method of least squares, a topic first discussed in Chapter 10. The trend values are the fitted values of the regression equation. Trend fitting often uses annual data. *As long as all four seasons are included in each annual observation, an analysis of the annual data is conducted without regard to how seasonality may be changing. In effect, each annual observation is assumed to be the net effect of the yearly cycle of seasons.*

There are three main purposes for finding the secular trend:

1. **Describing an historical pattern.** Frequently, we can use a past trend to evaluate past performance of a person or a policy. For example, a hospital administrator may evaluate the effectiveness of a marketing program by examining its past admissions trends.

2. **"What if" projection of past trend into the future.** Knowledge of the past can tell us a great deal about the future. Examining the growth rate of a state's population, for example, can help us estimate the school population for some future time period.

3. **Eliminating the trend component from a series.** We may find it easier to study the other three components of the time series (seasonal, cyclical, irregular) when the trend component has been eliminated. For instance, removing the trend component and the cyclical-irregular component from the original data helps us isolate the seasonal component.

USING TIME AS A PREDICTOR VARIABLE

The time variable t is typically used as the predictor variable when a linear trend is assumed and a fitted regression line equation is estimated by the method of least squares. The linear trend equation fitted to the actual Y_t series is stated as:

Fitted Linear Trend Equation

$$\hat{Y}_t = a + bt \tag{15-3}$$

where

$\hat{Y}_t$ = Level of fitted Y at time period t

b = Trend slope (the rise in the fitted Y per time period)

a = Intercept term (i.e., the value of the fitted Y if the fitted trend line is extrapolated to $t = 0$)

In fitting a trend line, the predictor variable t serves as a surrogate. It represents the net effect of all causal factors that aren't explicitly expressed in the equation but influence the Y_t series to rise or fall each period. For example, a trend line $\hat{Y}_t = a + bt$ fitted to a Y_t series of air-conditioner sales might use t as a surrogate variable for the net effect of factors such as population and disposable income that aren't expressed in the equation. Assuming these two factors are increasing with time, then using values of t to capture the net effect of the factors will produce a fitted trend equation with a positive value of b. On the other hand, a trend line $\hat{Y} = a + bt$ can be fitted to a Y_t series of declining cigarette sales in the United States. Here, the use of values of t would reflect the net effect of the factors that are depressing sales, such as U.S. government advertisements on health hazards of smoking, medical literature against smoking, smoking cessation clinics, regulations banning smoking in many public places, and higher excise taxes on "sin products." In this case, the value of the coefficient b is negative.

To illustrate the procedure for fitting a trend line, we consider a company's shipments of 8 oz jars of mayonnaise, salad dressing, and related products. The data for 10 years are presented in Table 15.1.

The scatter diagram given in Figure 15.5 shows the shipment data from Table 15.1 plotted against time. Looking at the diagram, we see that a downward trend occurs in the shipment percentage. So, assuming a linear trend line is appropriate, we expect the fitted linear trend equation to have a negative b coefficient.

TABLE 15.1　Shipments of Mayonnaise, Salad Dressing, and Related Products	
YEAR	**PERCENT OF TOTAL SHIPMENTS**
1	14.0
2	13.3
3	13.3
4	12.8
5	12.8
6	13.2
7	13.0
8	12.8
9	12.4
10	12.0

Figure 15.5
Scatter diagram of mayonnaise shipments

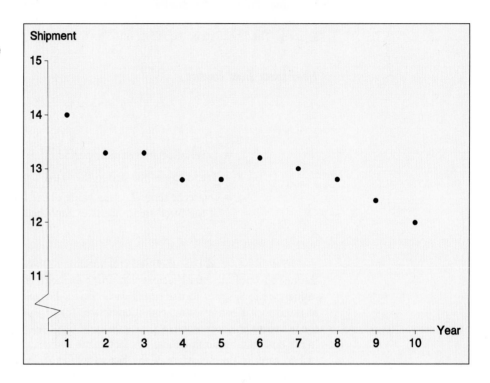

The formulas for computing the a and b regression coefficients, first given in Chapter 10, are shown again below, but with t replacing X and Y_t replacing Y_i:

$$b = \frac{\sum tY_t - n\bar{t}\bar{Y}}{\sum t^2 - n\bar{t}^2} \qquad a = \bar{Y} - b\bar{t}$$

where

n = Number of periods

$\bar{Y}$ = Average value of the Y_t time series; that is, $\bar{Y} = \sum Y_t/n$

$\bar{t}$ = Average value of t; that is, $\bar{t} = \sum t/n$

The preliminary computations needed for determining the coefficients a and b of the trend equation for the data in Table 15.1 are presented in Table 15.2.

TABLE 15.2 Worksheet for Trend Equation Calculations			
t	Y_t	tY_t	t^2
1	14.0	14.0	1
2	13.3	26.6	4
3	13.3	39.9	9
4	12.8	51.2	16
5	12.8	64.0	25
6	13.2	79.2	36
7	13.0	91.0	49
8	12.8	102.4	64
9	12.4	111.6	81
10	12.0	120.0	100
Totals 55	129.6	699.9	385

We then perform the following calculations:

$$\bar{t} = \frac{\sum t}{n} = \frac{55}{10} = 5.5$$

$$\bar{Y} = \frac{\sum Y_t}{n} = \frac{129.6}{10} = 12.96$$

$$b = \frac{\sum tY_t - n\bar{t}\bar{Y}}{\sum t^2 - n\bar{t}^2}$$

$$= \frac{699.9 - 10(5.5)(12.96)}{385 - 10(5.5)^2} = -0.15636$$

$$a = \bar{Y} - b\bar{t} = 12.96 - (-0.15636)(5.5) = 13.8200$$

Thus, the fitted linear trend equation is

$$\hat{Y}_t = a + bt$$

$$= 13.8200 - 0.15636t$$

USING MINITAB

Trend analysis can be done easily by using MINITAB or other regression analysis software. Regression analysis requires the values of Y_t be entered as the dependent variable and the values of t be entered as the only predictor variable. Figure 15.6 shows the computer estimated version of the trend equation at the top of the MINITAB output. The exact figures are given in the column headed "COEF."

The trend coefficient of -0.15636 (the same as calculated above) indicates that there was a decline in the percentage of mayonnaise shipped in 8 oz jars averaging 0.15636% per year. The values for the trend component for each year are given in Table 15.3. These are the values shown on the MINITAB output under the column "FIT."

"WHAT IF" LINEAR TREND PROJECTIONS

Once the trend equation has been determined, we can use it to project future values of the series under the assumption that this trend continues into the future. That is,

Figure 15.6
MINITAB trend equation of mayonnaise data

```
MTB > regress 'Shipment' 1 'Time';
SUBC> predict t=11.

The regression equation is
shipment = 13.8 - 0.156 Time

Predictor       Coef       Stdev      t-ratio        p
Constant      13.8200      0.1972       70.07     0.000
Time         -0.15636      0.03179      -4.92     0.000

s = 0.2887      R-sq = 75.2%     R-sq(adj) = 72.0%

Analysis of Variance

SOURCE         DF          SS           MS         F          p
Regression      1       2.0171       2.0171     24.20     0.000
Error           8       0.6669       0.0834
Total           9       2.6840

Obs.    Time   shipment        Fit Stdev.Fit   Residual    St.Resid
   1     1.0    14.0000    13.6636    0.1697     0.3364        1.44
   2     2.0    13.3000    13.5073    0.1439    -0.2073       -0.83
   3     3.0    13.3000    13.3509    0.1210    -0.0509       -0.19
   4     4.0    12.8000    13.1945    0.1030    -0.3945       -1.46
   5     5.0    12.8000    13.0382    0.0927    -0.2382       -0.87
   6     6.0    13.2000    12.8818    0.0927     0.3182        1.16
   7     7.0    13.0000    12.7255    0.1030     0.2745        1.02
   8     8.0    12.8000    12.5691    0.1210     0.2309        0.88
   9     9.0    12.4000    12.4127    0.1439    -0.0127       -0.05
  10    10.0    12.0000    12.2564    0.1697    -0.2564       -1.10


    Fit   Stdev.Fit          95% C.I.             95% P.I.
12.1000      0.1972   (11.6450,12.5550)   (11.2934,12.9066)
```

TABLE 15.3 Trend Components for Mayonnaise Shipments	
YEAR t	**TREND COMPONENT** $\hat{Y}$
1	13.6636
2	13.5073
3	13.3509
4	13.1945
5	13.0382
6	12.8818
7	12.7255
8	12.5691
9	12.4127
10	12.2564

we start by saying, "What if this trend continues into the future?" Then we ask for the estimated value of the time series a specified number of years into the future. This is determined in two steps:

Step 1
Let the value of t equal the time period for which a trend projection is desired.

Step 2
Insert the numerical value for t into the trend equation.

For example, to find the trend projection of mayonnaise shipments for the next period (year 11):

Step 1
Let $t = 11$.

Step 2
$$\hat{Y}_t = 13.8200 - 0.15636t$$
$$= 13.8200 - 0.15636(11)$$
$$= 12.1000$$

That is, the projected shipments on a linear trend basis for year 11 are 12.1000% of total shipments. The value can be obtained directly from the MINITAB computer output using the PREDICT subcommand after the REGRESS command, as shown in Figure 15.6. Notice that the value 12.1000 is found on the last line directly under the first column "FIT."

NONLINEAR TREND FITTING

Linear trend fitting by regression analysis is by far the most popular trend fitting approach for time series data. But for some time series data, fitting a nonlinear trend by regression analysis may be more appropriate. For instance, in the introductory stages of the personal computer (PC) life cycle, when PCs were just beginning to catch on, PC sales showed an increasing amount of growth with each period. On a graph, this appears as a sharply rising curve, as shown in Figure 15.4b. Statistical software packages can readily accommodate both the linear and the nonlinear fitting approaches under the regression analysis option. The quadratic trend equation is one of the most common nonlinear trend equations fitted.

Fitted Quadratic Trend Equation

$$\hat{Y}_t = a + b_1t + b_2t^2 \tag{15-4}$$

where

$$a = \text{Estimated } Y \text{ intercept}$$
$$b_1 = \text{Estimated linear effect on } Y$$
$$b_2 = \text{Estimated curvilinear effect on } Y$$

One nonlinear trend equation that deals with situations of constant percentage growth (e.g., compounding effect of growth) is the exponential trend equation.

Exponential Trend Equation

$$\hat{Y}_t = kc^t \tag{15-5}$$

where

$$k = \text{Estimated } Y \text{ intercept}$$
$$(c - 1) \times 100\% = \text{Estimated compound growth rate (in percent per period)}$$

It is possible to find the coefficients k and c for the exponential trend equation using conventional least squares analysis. First, we must obtain a logarithm transformation on both sides of the equation to obtain the log linear equation:

$$\log \hat{Y}_t = \log k + (\log c)t$$

Now, a linear regression of $\log \hat{Y}_t$ on t will produce a fitted linear regression equation:

Regression Version of Exponential Trend Equation

$$\log \hat{Y}_t = a + bt$$
$$a = \log k \quad \text{and} \quad b = \log c$$

(15-6)

The antilogs of the coefficients a and b are the values of k and c, respectively:

$$k = \text{antilog } a \quad \text{and} \quad c = \text{antilog } b$$

An illustration of quadratic trend fitting is given in the Wendy's analysis section at the end of this chapter. Figures 15.4b and 15.4c show two nonlinear growth trends.

PRACTICE EXERCISE

15.1 The table gives annual company sales data (in millions of dollars) for a 10 year period.

YEAR	1	2	3	4	5	6	7	8	9	10
SALES	17.0	18.4	17.0	20.9	18.3	20.1	22.0	22.2	19.6	23.4

You may wish to use the computer, if available, to answer the following questions.
a. Fit a linear trend equation to the data.
b. What is the trend line value ($\hat{Y}_t$) for year 6?
c. Find the linear trend projection of shipments for year 11.

EXERCISES ▫

15.1 Annual data on shipments of mayonnaise, salad dressing, and related products in 16 oz containers are given in the table.

YEAR	1	2	3	4	5	6	7	8	9	10
SHIPMENTS Percentage of the total	13.7	14.0	13.6	14.0	15.3	15.9	16.9	17.5	18.6	20.9

You may wish to use the computer, if available, to answer the following questions.
a. Construct a time plot (scatter diagram) of the data.
b. Fit a linear trend equation to the data.
c. What is the trend line value ($\hat{Y}_t$) for year 9?
d. Find the linear trend projection of shipments for year 11.

◻ **15.2** The data in the table refer to the percent of external sources of funds for the corporate nonfinancial sector.

YEAR	1	2	3	4	5	6	7	8	9	10
PERCENT	35	41	52	48	68	72	66	72	77	85

You may wish to use the computer, if available, to answer the following questions.
a. Fit a linear trend equation to the data.
b. Find the linear trend projection for year 11.

◻ **15.3** The table lists debt/equity (D/E) ratios for a 20 year period for manufacturing corporations in the United States.

YEAR	D/E RATIO	YEAR	D/E RATIO
1	0.209	11	0.273
2	0.232	12	0.308
3	0.246	13	0.345
4	0.244	14	0.370
5	0.239	15	0.402
6	0.245	16	0.437
7	0.250	17	0.444
8	0.251	18	0.435
9	0.253	19	0.439
10	0.254	20	0.469

You may wish to use the computer, if available, to answer the following questions.
a. Plot this series on a scatter diagram.
b. Fit the trend line to the data, and draw in this trend on your chart.
c. Briefly describe the financial trend.

◻ ▶ **15.4** The table gives the sales (in millions of dollars) of a large fertilizer company.

YEAR	1	2	3	4	5	6	7
SALES	536	569	583	588	614	616	628

You may wish to use the computer, if available, to answer the following questions.
a. Determine the linear trend equation.
b. What is the trend component for year 5?
c. Find the linear trend projection for year 8.

· ·

15.4

ISOLATING AND REMOVING TREND FROM ANNUAL DATA: CYCLICAL-IRREGULAR RELATIVES

The cyclical and irregular components of a time series can be found by removing the trend component T_t from the classical time series model. Starting with annual data (no seasonal component), the trend component T_t is estimated by $\hat{Y}_t$, which is calculated by the linear trend equation using the method of least squares. The trend component may be removed from the original data Y_t through division as follows:

Step 1
Start with the multiplicative model (no seasonal component, since annual data are used), $Y_t = T_t \cdot C_t \cdot I_t$.

Step 2
Divide the actual value of the series, Y_t, by the least squares method estimate of the trend, $\hat{Y}_t$:

$$\frac{Y_t}{\hat{Y}_t} = \frac{T_t \cdot C_t \cdot I_t}{\hat{Y}_t}$$

Step 3
The division by $\hat{Y}_t$ eliminates T_t from the numerator of the equation, and we obtain

$$\frac{Y_t}{\hat{Y}_t} = C_t \cdot I_t$$

Thus, the ratio of the observed value to the fitted trend value $Y_t/\hat{Y}_t$ yields the cyclical and irregular components. This ratio is computed for each year in the series and is called the *cyclical–irregular relative*.

Cyclical–Irregular (C–I) Relatives (No Seasonal Component)

$$C_t \cdot I_t = \frac{Y_t}{\hat{Y}_t} \tag{15-7}$$

The term *relative* given to the derived cyclical–irregular components reflects the fact that the results are numerical values around a base of 1.0. Each cyclical–irregular relative indicates the proportionate effects of the combined cyclical and irregular activities in determining each Y value of the series. For example, the cyclical–irregular relatives for the mayonnaise shipments example are displayed in Table 15.4 for the 10 year period. The year 1 value of 1.02462 indicates that year 1 mayonnaise sales are buoyed 2.462% above the trend line due to cyclical–irregular influences. In year 2, cyclical–irregular influences have depressed sales to only 98.465% of that year's trend line value.

TABLE 15.4 Cyclical–Irregular Component for Mayonnaise Shipments			
COLUMN 1 YEAR	COLUMN 2 SHIPMENT Y_t	COLUMN 3 FITTED $\hat{Y}_t$	COLUMN 4 C–I RELATIVE $Y_t/\hat{Y}_t$
1	14.0	13.6636	1.02462
2	13.3	13.5073	0.98465
3	13.3	13.3509	0.99619
4	12.8	13.1945	0.97010
5	12.8	13.0382	0.98173
6	13.2	12.8818	1.02470
7	13.0	12.7255	1.02157
8	12.8	12.5691	1.01837
9	12.4	12.4127	0.99897
10	12.0	12.2564	0.97908

For each year in the series, the observed value (column 2) is divided by the fitted value representing the trend (column 3). This division yields the cyclical–irregular

(C–I) relative (column 4). Remember that with annual data there can be no seasonal component, so only the trend and cyclical–irregular components of the time series can be present.

PRACTICE EXERCISE

15.2 For the data given in Practice Exercise 15.1 and repeated below, calculate the cyclical–irregular relative for each year.

YEAR	1	2	3	4	5	6	7	8	9	10
SALES	17.0	18.4	17.0	20.9	18.3	20.1	22.0	22.2	19.6	23.4

EXERCISES

▶ **15.5** The data in the table, on shipments of mayonnaise, salad dressing, and related products in 16 oz containers, are repeated from Exercise 15.1.

YEAR	1	2	3	4	5	6	7	8	9	10
SHIPMENTS Percentage of the total	13.7	14.0	13.6	14.0	15.3	15.9	16.9	17.5	18.6	20.9

Calculate the cyclical–irregular relative for each year.

15.6 The table gives the number of employees in nonagricultural establishments in tens of thousands:

YEAR	1	2	3	4	5	6	7
EMPLOYEES	529	514	534	544	542	558	570

You may wish to use the computer, if available, to answer the following questions.
a. What is the trend equation?
b. Calculate the cyclical–irregular relative for each year.

15.7 The data in the table report sales of General Mills Corporation.

YEAR	SALES Million Dollars	YEAR	SALES Million Dollars
1	576	9	885
2	546	10	1,092
3	524	11	1,185
4	541	12	1,901
5	559	13	1,662
6	525	14	2,000
7	603	15	2,309
8	669		

You may wish to use the computer, if available, to answer the following questions.
a. Calculate the trend equation for years 1–8.
b. Calculate the cyclical–irregular relatives for years 1–8.
c. Calculate the trend equation for years 9–15.
d. Compare the two trend equations.

15.5
SEASONAL VARIATION

Seasonal variation exists when repetitive and predictable fluctuations occur around the trend line. To study seasonal variation, we must record data at consecutive time periods smaller than 1 year: days, weeks, months, bimonths, or quarters.

There are three main reasons for studying seasonal variation:

- **Establishing the pattern of past change.** To learn whether the volatility of the series within the year is normal, we compare the current movement of the series to the movement in the previous years for the same periods. For example, if a university wants to know whether the slump in the current summer enrollment is normal, it can examine the seasonal pattern established from previous years for the summer and make the comparison.

- **Projecting past patterns into the future.** In the same way that long-range projections require secular trend analysis, short-range projections require seasonal analysis. To illustrate, suppose we start with a "what if" approach to obtain a year long enrollment trend at the university. Then semester by semester enrollment projections can be made by adjusting for the normal pattern of seasonal variation between semesters that has been observed in the past.

- **Eliminating seasonal variation from the series.** Pronounced seasonal patterns in the data may mask other important changes that are occurring in the series. In order to determine whether these other changes are more or less than expected, data must be purged of the seasonal variation (**deseasonalized**) to allow other patterns to become observable.

STEPS IN MEASURING SEASONAL VARIATION: THE RATIO-TO-MOVING AVERAGE METHOD

Seasonal variation is measured by an index, and the major computational procedure for determining **seasonal indexes** is the **ratio-to-moving average method**. This method requires five intermediate calculations, which we shall now list, briefly discuss, and then illustrate using data.

Step 1
Moving totals: The ratio-to-moving average method begins by computing *moving totals* for the original data. Each moving total is a partial summation of the original data, generally for 1 year duration (e.g., 12 months, 6 bimonths, 4 quarters). The choice of 1 year as the duration is designed to encompass all the seasons.

Step 2
Centered moving totals: Each moving total is identified with a specific point in time that is half the duration encompassed by the moving total. For instance, the halfway point for a 4-quarter moving total that starts in the first quarter would be identified with a point at the end of June and the beginning of July. This point is not aligned with either quarter 2 or quarter 3, but is positioned at the boundary of both quarters 2 and 3. A centering procedure is used to realign each moving total so that it coincides with an actual time period of the original data (e.g., quarter 1, quarter 2, etc.).

Step 3

Moving averages: Each moving total is converted to a corresponding **moving average** by dividing the number of periods encompassed in the moving total into the total. Averaging reduces the moving totals to a basis comparable to the original data. Note that the totaling and averaging procedures have now eliminated the seasonal component, and the moving averages now represent only the combined trend–cyclical components of the data.

Step 4

Original-to-moving average ratios: By dividing each term of the original data (containing all four components) by the corresponding moving average term (containing only trend and cyclical components), we are removing the trend and cyclical components from the original data; we are left with the seasonal–irregular components:

$$\frac{\text{Original data}}{\text{Moving average}} = \frac{T_t \cdot C_t \cdot S_t \cdot I_t}{T_t \cdot C_t} = S_t \cdot I_t$$

Step 5

Seasonal indexes: By averaging the original-to-moving average ratios for the same season, we minimize the irregular influence, giving results that represent the "pure" seasonal effect, S_t. These are the seasonal indexes.

Now, let's use the ratio-to-moving average method on the data on Sunburst Travel Agency bookings given in Table 15.5. Suppose Sunburst's management wants to establish the seasonal pattern of its travel bookings.

TABLE 15.5 Time Series for Sunburst Travel Bookings (Number of Bookings per Quarter)				
		YEAR		
		1	**2**	**3**
QUARTER	**I**	3253	4056	3882
	II	2879	3619	2639
	III	2279	3336	2278
	IV	4002	3412	2473

Step 1. Moving Totals

The first step in studying seasonal variation is to group observations into moving totals containing k terms of the original series, where k is the number of periods covering the seasons. In our example, $k = 4$ (4 quarters). The term *moving* comes from the fact that successive moving totals are constructed by moving along the original series, dropping and adding one term at a time. Each moving total therefore will have some terms in common with other moving totals.

Let's look at the composition of the series of moving totals, each constructed from k terms of the original time series, which has n observations, $Y_1, Y_2, \ldots, Y_n$:

First moving total: $Y_1 + Y_2 + \cdots + Y_k \quad \rightarrow k$ terms

Second moving total: $Y_2 + Y_3 + \cdots + Y_{k+1} \rightarrow k$ terms

Third moving total: $Y_3 + Y_4 + \cdots + Y_{k+2} \rightarrow k$ terms

.

.

.

Last moving total: $Y_{n-k+1} + \cdots + Y_n \quad \rightarrow k$ terms

For our Sunburst data, $n = 12$ (total number of quarterly bookings for 3 years) and $k = 4$, so we can form $n - k + 1 = 12 - 4 + 1 = 9$ moving totals; the last moving total includes observations Y_9, Y_{10}, Y_{11}, and Y_{12}. Illustrative calculations for the data in Table 15.5 are given below:

First moving total: $3253 + 2879 + 2279 + 4002 = 12{,}413$

Second moving total: $2879 + 2279 + 4002 + 4056 = 13{,}216$

Third moving total: $2279 + 4002 + 4056 + 3619 = 13{,}956$

.

.

.

Last moving total: $3882 + 2639 + 2278 + 2473 = 11{,}272$

As you can see, the first two moving totals share in common the three terms 2879, 2279, and 4002. The 9 moving totals for the travel bookings example are given in column 3 of Table 15.6.

TABLE 15.6 Calculating the 4 Quarter Centered Moving Average

COLUMN 1 TIME PERIOD	COLUMN 2 BOOKINGS	COLUMN 3 MOVING TOTAL	COLUMN 4 CENTERED MOVING TOTAL	COLUMN 5 CENTERED MOVING AVERAGE
1	3253			
2	2879			
		12,413		
3	2279		12,814.5	3203.63
		13,216		
4	4002		13,586.0	3396.50
		13,956		
5	4056		14,484.5	3621.13
		15,013		
6	3619		14,718.0	3679.50
		14,423		
7	3336		14,336.0	3584.00
		14,249		
8	3412		13,759.0	3439.75
		13,269		
9	3882		12,740.0	3185.00
		12,211		
10	2639		11,741.5	2935.38
		11,272		
11	2278			
12	2473			

Step 2. Centered Moving Totals

From column 3 of Table 15.6 we see that the location of each moving total (length $k = 4$) is not aligned with a particular quarter, but is instead stranded halfway between 2 quarters. The procedure for bringing each moving total into alignment with a nearby quarter is known as *centering the moving total*.

The centering procedure for a moving total is only necessary when the number of terms k included in the moving total is even. When the number of terms k is odd, the moving total naturally aligns with a particular period. Generally, seasonal patterns occur annually, with an even number of seasonal periods over the year cycle. For example, there are 4 seasonal periods if the data are collected quarterly; 6 seasonal periods if the data are collected bimonthly; and 12 seasonal periods if the data is collected monthly. Thus, data collected on a quarterly, bimonthly, or monthly basis will require centering.

We'll now illustrate the procedure for centering the moving totals for the 12 quarters of data shown in Table 15.6. By adding successive pairs of moving total terms and dividing by 2, we get the centered moving total series found in column 4 of the table:

$$\frac{12{,}413 + 13{,}216}{2} = 12{,}814.5 \quad \text{Third quarter, year 1}$$

$$\frac{13{,}216 + 13{,}956}{2} = 13{,}586.0 \quad \text{Fourth quarter, year 1}$$

$$\vdots$$

$$\frac{12{,}211 + 11{,}272}{2} = 11{,}741.5 \quad \text{Second quarter, year 3}$$

As a result of the averaging, every centered value is now aligned with a particular quarterly period. For example, 12,814.5 is aligned with period $t = 3$; 13,856.0 is aligned with period $t = 4$, etc.

Step 3. Centered Moving Average Series

To find the centered moving averages, we divide the centered moving totals by k (in this case, $k = 4$) to obtain the series shown in column 5 of Table 15.6:

$$\frac{12{,}814.5}{4} = 3203.63$$

$$\frac{13{,}586.0}{4} = 3396.50$$

$$\vdots$$

$$\frac{11{,}741.5}{4} = 2935.38$$

Denoting the centered moving average series by Y_t^*, we have

$$Y_t^* = \frac{\text{Centered moving total}}{k}$$

The graphs of Y_t^* and the original series Y_t are presented in Figure 15.7. The graphs show that over the period portrayed, neither series consistently trends upward or downward; but in terms of variability, the moving average series has a

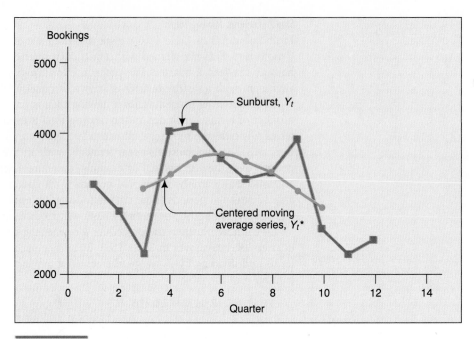

Figure 15.7
Sunburst original series and centered moving average series

much reduced variability as compared to the original data series. This reduced variability occurs because Y_t^* doesn't contain a pronounced seasonal component. Remember, each moving average value is the result of averaging a first quarter value, a second quarter value, a third quarter value, and a fourth quarter value. The fact that all 4 quarters are always included in the average means that the highs and lows of seasonal influences have been balanced out by the process of creating the moving averages.

In general, in creating a moving average series, the averaging procedure smoothes out seasonal as well as irregular components. In our four component model, this leaves remaining in the moving average series only the trend and cyclical components. More specifically, in terms of the four component multiplicative model first discussed in Section 15.2, the moving average series Y_t^* can be shown to be

$$Y_t^* = \frac{Y_t}{S_t \cdot I_t} = \frac{T_t \cdot C_t \cdot S_t \cdot I_t}{S_t \cdot I_t} = T_t \cdot C_t$$

Notice, in Table 15.6, that there are no moving average terms for the first 2 quarters ($t = 1$ and $t = 2$) nor for the last 2 quarters ($t = 11$ and $t = 12$). The first term in the moving average series is Y_3^*. The last moving average term is Y_{10}^*. The formation of a quarterly moving average series results in $n - k = 12 - 4 = 8$ moving average terms.

Finally, a helpful reminder: When the averaging procedure contains an odd number of terms, centering is not necessary. In the practice exercise that follows, you are asked to construct a moving average series based on an odd number of periods.

PRACTICE EXERCISE

15.3 Listed below are the daily sales (in thousands of dollars) of a convenience store for 14 consecutive days (read from left to right).

6.23   5.53   5.99   7.73   9.06   9.34   6.00

6.45   5.93   6.17   8.17   9.30   9.83   6.43

a. Compute the 7 period moving average centered on day 10.
b. Compute the last term in the 7 period moving average series.

Step 4. Computing the Original-to-Moving Average Ratio

Let's now continue with the quarterly travel bookings data to illustrate the computation of the original-to-moving average ratios. This step requires the division of each original data value by the corresponding calculated moving average value.

a. Obtain Y_t and Y_t^* values. Reprinted in columns 2 and 3 of Table 15.7 are the original sales and moving averages Y_t and Y_t^*, previously given in columns 2 and 5 of Table 15.6.

TABLE 15.7 Calculation of Original-to-Moving Average Ratios			
COLUMN 1 TIME PERIOD t	COLUMN 2 BOOKINGS Y_t	COLUMN 3 CENTERED MOVING AVERAGE Y_t^*	COLUMN 4 ORIGINAL-TO-MOVING AVERAGE RATIO Y_t/Y_t^*
1	3253	—	—
2	2879	—	—
3	2279	3203.63	0.71138
4	4002	3396.50	1.17827
5	4056	3621.13	1.12009
6	3619	3679.50	0.98356
7	3336	3584.00	0.93080
8	3412	3439.75	0.99193
9	3882	3185.00	1.21884
10	2639	2935.38	0.89903
11	2278	—	—
12	2473	—	—

b. Divide each value of the Y_t series by the corresponding value of the Y_t^* series. This division produces the original-to-moving average ratio: Y_t/Y_t^*.

It is important to remember that the ratio factors out the trend and cyclical components, leaving a composite of the seasonal–irregular components. Considering the four component multiplicative model, the ratio of Y_t and Y_t^* represents

$$\frac{Y_t}{Y_t^*} = \frac{T_t \cdot C_t \cdot S_t \cdot I_t}{T_t \cdot C_t} = S_t \cdot I_t$$

The figures in column 4 of Table 15.7 are the original-to-moving average ratios for the travel bookings data; these figures are obtained by dividing each value in column 2 by the corresponding value in column 3. For instance, starting with the third quarter of year 1, the first ratio value is

$$\frac{Y_3}{Y_3^*} = \frac{2279}{3203.63} = 0.71138$$

With the trend and cycle components factored out of the original data and only the seasonal and irregular components remaining, the next step is to deal effectively with the irregularity, so that the seasonal component can be measured.

Step 5. Calculating the Seasonal Indexes

The purpose of the last step in the ratio-to-moving average method is to reduce the irregular component and to isolate the pure seasonal component. The end results are seasonal indexes that measure the seasonal effect. Table 15.8 displays the procedure for computing seasonal indexes from the original-to-moving average ratios.

TABLE 15.8 Calculating the Seasonal Indexes			
FIRST QUARTER	**SECOND QUARTER**	**THIRD QUARTER**	**FOURTH QUARTER**
	Original-to-Moving Average Ratios		
1.12009	0.98356	0.71138	1.17827
1.21884	0.89903	0.93080	0.99193
2.33893	1.88259	1.64218	2.17020
Arithmetic Means			
1.16947	0.94130	0.82109	1.08510

Sum of means = 1.16947 + 0.94130 + 0.82109 + 1.08510 = 4.01696
Adjustment factor = 0.99578
Seasonal indexes
  Q_1: 1.16947 × 0.99578 = 1.16453
  Q_2: 0.94130 × 0.99578 = 0.93732
  Q_3: 0.82109 × 0.99578 = 0.81763
  Q_4: 1.08510 × 0.99578 = 1.08052

Four steps are required in the calculations:

a. Sort the original-to-moving average ratios according to season. Using column 4 of Table 15.7, arrange the same quarter ratios into separate columns as shown in Table 15.8. This places all the first quarter ratios in the first column, all the second quarter ratios in the second column, etc.

b. Average the ratios for each season. Three types of averaging procedures can be used: (1) the median value for each column, (2) the simple arithmetic mean, or (3) a **modified mean** in which the highest valued original-to-moving average ratio and the lowest valued for each season are eliminated. Whenever possible, the modified mean approach is preferred because it eliminates extreme relative values and is less affected by skewness than the median. It avoids the problem of extreme values that would have a disproportionate impact on the straightforward arithmetic mean. With only two observations for each quarter for the travel bookings data, the use of the modified mean is not feasible, so a simple arithmetic mean is used for the average shown in Table 15.8.

   c. Calculating an adjustment factor. The multiplicative decomposition model requires that the value measuring the typical seasonal influence average to 1.00; that is, the sum of the four seasonal indexes must equal 4.00. This requirement guarantees that the seasonal effect evens out over the year, as it should. When the sum doesn't equal 4.00, an adjustment is necessary. Looking at Table 15.8, we find the sum of the arithmetic means is slightly greater than 4.00 (in this case, due to rounding), so an adjustment is required. We obtain an adjustment factor by adding the means for all the seasons and then dividing the sum into the number of seasons. Hence, the adjustment factor formula is

$$\text{Adjustment factor} = \frac{\text{Number of seasons in year}}{\text{Sum of means}}$$

For the travel bookings data, the adjustment factor is calculated as follows:

$$\text{Sum of means} = 1.16947 + 0.94130 + 0.82109 + 1.08510 = 4.01696$$

$$\text{Adjustment factor} = \frac{\text{Number of seasons in year}}{\text{Sum of means}}$$

$$\frac{4}{4.01696} = 0.99578$$

    This result is shown on Table 15.8.

   d. Calculating seasonal indexes. Applying the adjustment factor to the mean, we obtain an adjusted mean measure of the seasonal effect. We call this measure the *seasonal index*. In short, the seasonal index formula is

$$\text{Seasonal index} = (\text{Seasonal mean}) \cdot (\text{Adjustment factor})$$

For the first quarter, the seasonal index is found to be

$$(\text{Seasonal mean}) \cdot (\text{Adjustment factor}) = \text{Seasonal index}$$
$$(1.16947)(0.99578) = 1.16453$$

Table 15.8 shows all four seasonal indexes for the travel bookings data. Note that the sum of the indexes after rounding must equal 4.00.

INTERPRETATION OF THE SEASONAL INDEXES

How should the seasonal indexes for particular periods be interpreted? An index above 1.00 means that a season exerts an above average seasonal effect. Values below 1.00 indicate a below average seasonal effect. A percentage conversion can aid interpretation of a seasonal index. For example, when the difference between a particular seasonal index and 1.00 is multiplied by 100, it gives the percentage by which that season exceeds or falls below the (moving) annual average season. To illustrate, consider the value of 1.16453 calculated for the first quarter seasonal index. A percentage conversion indicates that travel bookings for the first quarter average 16.453% more than the annual average for all seasonal periods. This is nearly 35% [(1.16453 − 0.81763) × 100] above the lowest seasonal index, which occurs in the third quarter.

Uses of Seasonal Indexes

Seasonal indexes are used in several ways: to obtain *seasonal weights,* which reveal the seasonal pattern of past change and help assess current changes; to eliminate seasonal variations from a series; and to project past seasonal patterns into the future.

Seasonal weights. Seasonal indexes transformed into *seasonal weights* can help us evaluate the pattern of past changes in a series. The computation of seasonal weights is simple; we divide each seasonal index by the number of seasons in the year. That is,

$$\text{Seasonal weight for season} = \frac{\text{Seasonal index for season}}{\text{Number of seasons in year}}$$

The **seasonal weight** is the proportion of the yearly total associated with a particular season. Looking at the travel bookings data of Table 15.8, the seasonal weight for the first quarter is

$$\text{Seasonal weight for first quarter} = \frac{\text{First quarter seasonal index}}{\text{Number of seasons}}$$

$$= \frac{1.16453}{4} = 0.291133$$

Multiplying the seasonal weight by 100 converts it to a *seasonal percentage*. Thus, the seasonal percentage for the first quarter is $0.291133 \times 100 = 29.1133\%$, or approximately 29%, of the yearly travel bookings. Comparing this 29% figure to the simple (unweighted) average of 25% for each of the four seasons, we realize immediately the importance of the first quarter for travel bookings compared to the rest of the year.

■ **EXAMPLE 15.1**

Using Seasonal Weights as Performance Benchmarks

Suppose the Pontiac Division of General Motors, in reviewing its plans for spring car production, has just received the January sales figures for current models. January sales amounted to only 6% of the total sales planned for the year. Is this bad? Are consumers purchasing fewer cars than GM had planned? Should production be cut back? Not necessarily. You can't make a determination until you compare the 6% figure against the percentage typical for the same month. Suppose the seasonal weight converted to percentage of yearly sales that normally are made in January is 9%. This can be viewed as the benchmark percentage. Now we can compare 6%—the actual sales expressed as a percent of the sales planned for the year—against the January norm given by the seasonal weight of 9%. This calculation quickly reveals that actual sales this January were only 6%/9%, or 2/3, of the level implied by that norm. Clearly, this tells management that actual sales are behind the benchmark percentage set for January. At this pace, Pontiac will fail to meet its sales objectives for the year. It is management's responsibility to take notice and find out why.

The removal of seasonality to establish a norm against which realized results can be compared is very important in the financial world. The applied case at the end of this chapter illustrates how such a removal helps refine a Wall Street investment strategy.

Let's pause for a moment to review briefly what we have covered about seasonal indexes and indicate where we will go from here. We have shown how seasonal indexes can be obtained with the ratio-to-moving average method. We also showed how to determine seasonal weights, which serve as norms. Now, we turn to another use of seasonal indexes: how to *deseasonalize* the original data. Then we'll find out what managerial questions are best answered with deseasonalized data.

Deseasonalizing data. Seasonal indexes are effective means of removing seasonal influences from data; this process is called *deseasonalizing* the data. Deseasonalized data can then be used to detect the trend, cyclical, and irregular components that remain. Again consider the components of the multiplicative model.

Step 1
Specify the components of the multiplicative model:

$$Y_t = T_t \cdot C_t \cdot S_t \cdot I_t$$

Step 2
Divide the original value of Y_t by the seasonal component, so that seasonality is removed:

$$\frac{Y_t}{S_t} = \frac{T_t \cdot C_t \cdot S_t \cdot I_t}{S_t}$$

Step 3
The result of the division is a deseasonalized sales series Y_t^d, which represents the trend, cyclical, and irregular components:

$$Y_t^d = T_t \cdot C_t \cdot I_t$$

The deseasonalized sales series is obtained by dividing actual sales by the appropriate seasonal index for the period; that is,

$$\text{Deseasonalized sales} = \frac{\text{Actual sales}}{\text{Seasonal index}}$$

For example, suppose the actual sales are 140, and the seasonal index is 1.25; the deseasonalized sales value is

$$\frac{\text{Actual sales}}{\text{Seasonal index}} = \text{Deseasonalized sales}$$

$$\frac{140}{1.25} = 112.0$$

The deseasonalized values for the travel bookings data are shown in column 5 of Table 15.9. The value for the first quarter of year 1 is obtained as follows:

$$\text{Deseasonalized sales} = \left(\frac{\text{Actual bookings}}{\text{First quarter}} \right) \div \text{Seasonal index}$$

$$= 3253 \div 1.16453$$

$$= 2793.40$$

With seasonality removed, the deseasonalized bookings shown in column 5 reflect the level of bookings due to the trend and cyclical–irregular components.

Projecting past seasonal patterns into the future. After a trend projection has been made, seasonal indexes and seasonal weights can be applied in two ways:

- Suppose we are using annual data and make a trend projection for next year based on the past annual data. We may want to make a *seasonal projection* for a particular season within the year.

		TABLE 15.9 Deseasonalizing the Data		
COLUMN 1 YEAR	**COLUMN 2 QUARTER**	**COLUMN 3 ACTUAL BOOKINGS**	**COLUMN 4 SEASONAL INDEX**	**COLUMN 5 DESEASONALIZED BOOKINGS**
1	I	3253	1.16453	2793.40
	II	2879	0.93732	3071.52
	III	2279	0.81763	2787.32
	IV	4002	1.08052	3703.77
2	I	4056	1.16453	3482.95
	II	3619	0.93732	3861.01
	III	3336	0.81763	4080.09
	IV	3412	1.08052	3157.74
3	I	3882	1.16453	3333.53
	II	2639	0.93732	2815.47
	III	2278	0.81763	2786.10
	IV	2473	1.08052	2288.71

- Suppose we are using monthly or quarterly data. We may make a trend projection for the next month or quarter; then extrapolate the projected value to an annual level.

Let's consider each application. Suppose annual sales for next year have been projected at $3.0 million, but we want a projection for the second quarter. Assume that the seasonal index for the second quarter is 1.20. The **seasonal projection** is determined as follows:

Step 1
Divide the annual projection by the number of seasons in the year to get the deseasonalized projection for a period:

$$\frac{\$3.0 \text{ million}}{4 \text{ quarters}} = \$0.75 \text{ million per quarter}$$

Step 2
Multiply the deseasonalized projection for a period by the seasonal index for that period to obtain the seasonalized projection:

$$\$0.75 \text{ million} \times 1.20 = \$0.9 \text{ million}$$

This is the second quarter sales projection.

Note that the net effect of these two steps also could be achieved by multiplying the projected annual sales by the seasonal weight. Thus, if the seasonal weight (in this case, $\frac{1.20}{4} = 0.30$) is known, the two-step procedure described above can be avoided.

Now let's consider projecting current monthly sales to an annual rate. Suppose January sales were projected to be $2.2 million, and the seasonal index for January is 1.32. The **annualization of projected sales** for a particular month (January) is determined as follows:

Step 1
Divide the January seasonal index of 1.32 by 12 months to get the seasonal weight for January:

$$\frac{1.32}{12} = 0.11$$

Step 2
Divide actual January sales by the seasonal weight for January to project an annualized sales figure consistent with the January pace:

$$\frac{\$2.2 \text{ million}}{0.11} = \$20 \text{ million}$$

This is the projected sales level for the year that would be consistent with the January level of $2.2 million.

TREND ANALYSIS WITH QUARTERLY OR MONTHLY DATA

In Section 15.3 we discussed the trend analysis procedure based on annual data, and so seasonality wasn't a concern. However, when data are quarterly, bimonthly, or monthly, seasonality is present and the question arises as to whether to perform trend analysis before or after deseasonalizing the data. The classical procedure for decomposing a time series requires that the data be deseasonalized before determining the trend component. Thus, in the Sunburst travel bookings problem, trend analysis would be conducted on the deseasonalized series given in Table 15.9, not on the raw data. Since the cyclical–irregular component is determined only after the trend component has been calculated, the sequence of analysis must proceed in the following order:

1. Deseasonalize the data.
2. Determine the trend component.
3. Determine the cyclical–irregular component.

PRACTICE EXERCISE

15.4 The table gives hypothetical data on air-conditioner sales in thousand units.

		YEAR				
		1	2	3	4	5
QUARTER	1	5	6	7	8	9
	2	12	13	14	15	16
	3	16	17	18	19	20
	4	7	8	9	10	11

a. Construct the 4-quarter moving total series.
b. Center the moving total series.
c. Construct the 4-quarter moving average series.
d. How many terms are in the series in part c?
e. Find the original-to-moving average ratio.
f. Find the seasonal indexes (use the arithmetic mean method).
g. Deseasonalize the sales data.
h. Find the cyclical–irregular relatives.
i. Find the seasonal weights.
j. What is the deseasonalized projection for quarter 2 of year 6?
k. What is the seasonalized projection for quarter 2 of year 6?

EXERCISES

▶ **15.8** Consider the time series of prime interest rates given in the table.

TIME PERIOD	INTEREST RATE
	Percent
Year 1: Winter	17
Spring	16
Summer	15
Fall	15
Year 2: Winter	18
Spring	16
Summer	15
Fall	17
Year 3: Winter	20
Spring	19
Summer	17
Fall	18
Year 4: Winter	19
Spring	17
Summer	16
Fall	17

a. Compute a 4-quarter moving total series for the data.
b. Center the moving totals computed in part a.
c. Compute a centered 4-quarter moving average series.
d. What is the value for summer of year 1 of the centered moving average series?
e. What can be said about a comparison of the original year 2, year 3, and year 4 winter interest rates with the corresponding year 2, year 3, and year 4 winter 4-quarter moving averages?
f. What is the 4-quarter moving average for fall of year 3?

15.9 Consider the table of soft drink sales (in millions of dollars) and corresponding 4-quarter moving averages.

TIME PERIOD	SALES	MOVING AVERAGE
1987: Fall	13	—
1988: Winter	10	—
Spring	13	14.25
Summer	20	14.625
Fall	15	15.0
1989: Winter	11	15.5
Spring	15	16.125
Summer	22	16.625
Fall	18	16.75
1990: Winter	12	16.625
Spring	15	16.635
Summer	21	16.125
Fall	17	16.0
1991: Winter	11	16.125
Spring	15	—
Summer	22	—

a. What is original-to-moving average ratio for summer 1988?
b. What is the adjustment factor (using an arithmetic mean) for computing the seasonal indexes?

c. What is the seasonal index for winter?
d. What is the seasonal weight for winter?
e. Project the total of 1992 sales, assuming that actual winter 1992 sales of $12 million set the norm for annual sales.

15.10 Consider the portion of a times series shown in the table for lumber sales with ratio to seasonal indexes as listed. (Note: The seasonal indexes were computed from a longer time series.)

TIME PERIOD	LUMBER SALES Million Dollars
1990: Winter	10
Spring	15
Summer	22
Fall	13
1991: Winter	8
Spring	13
Summer	19
Fall	13
Seasonal indexes	
Winter:	0.75
Spring:	0.98
Summer:	1.37
Fall:	0.90

a. What is the deseasonalized value for winter 1991?
b. What is the deseasonalized value for summer 1991?
c. After adjusting for season, which of the 1991 quarters had the most unusually large lumber sales?
d. If lumber sales of winter 1992 were $9 million, and if you assume winter 1992 sales are related to annual sales by its seasonal weight, what would you project the total 1992 lumber sales to be?

15.11 A construction company has completed the number of construction projects listed in the table over the past 12 bimonthly periods.

	J/F	M/A	M/J	J/A	S/O	N/D
YEAR 1	8	7	9	11	9	7
YEAR 2	9	11	12	14	11	10

a. Compute a 6 bimonth moving total series for the data.
b. Center the moving totals computed in part a.
c. Compute a centered 6 bimonth moving average series.
d. What is the value for S/O year 1 of the centered moving average series?
e. Construct a graph showing the centered moving average series versus the original series.

15.12 For the data in Exercise 15.11:
a. What is the original-to-moving average ratio for S/O year 1?
b. What is the adjustment factor (using an arithmetic mean) for computing the seasonal indexes?
c. What is the seasonal index for S/O?
d. What is the seasonal weight for S/O?

e. What is the deseasonalized value for S/O of year 1?

f. Which bimonthly period is the seasonal peak? Which one is the seasonal low point?

• •

15.6
SHORT-TERM FORECASTING BY EXPONENTIAL SMOOTHING

Forecasts of future values of a time series based on least squares trend projections assume that (1) there is a trend to project, (2) it will remain stable, and (3) it has an important enough bearing on the value of the series to be worth projecting. Let's now turn to the situation in which either there is no trend, or an existing trend has already been removed from the data series. We shall also assume for simplicity that the data are not affected by seasonal influences. The key feature of the series is that it fluctuates randomly for some period of time around a particular level. However, from time to time an event occurs that causes the series to adjust or gradually shift to a new level, which could be either higher or lower than the existing level. Because this pattern doesn't exhibit a steady trend or regular seasonal fluctuations, it requires a different method of analysis.

One method of forecasting for this type of time series data is the **exponential smoothing method.** This method smoothes the random variation in the time series data for the purpose of making forecasts of the next observations in the series. The basic form of the method is popularly used for short-term forecasting, particularly in situations where the trend and the seasonal influences are not major factors influencing the series. Its growing use owes much to the method's ability to provide inexpensive forecasts that quickly reflect permanent changes in the underlying conditions generating the values of the series. The method's simplicity and low cost of implementation become valuable features when forecasts are required quickly for a large number of different data series.

PERMANENT VERSUS TRANSITORY SHIFTS IN RETAILER DEMAND

Supermarkets, discount stores, and some other retail businesses generally carry 10,000 or more different items of merchandise in their inventory. Typically, the items have a price tag of only a few dollars or less, so the per unit profit is quite small. Many of the items have high turnover and require frequent reordering.

Retailers aim to keep enough inventory on hand to meet customer demand until the next reordering cycle. But limited storeroom space and high holding costs discourage retailers from carrying too large a stock of any one individual item. To establish a satisfactory inventory level requires the retailer to project demand for a particularly short period of time—a week, perhaps a month. But for many of these products the demand fluctuations are substantial, making forecasting by trend analysis not very feasible, since trend analysis assumes steady changes from period to period.

Since the sources that cause fluctuations in retail demand usually are too numerous to analyze individually, we conveniently categorize the sources into (1) factors that exert their influence on sales for extended periods of time and (2) those exerting influence for only brief periods of time. The first type produce long-term demand shifts, whereas the second type produce transitory demand shifts:

- **Long-term demand shifts.** A tract of new family homes has been sold and occupied in the neighborhood. This would be a source of a long-term, relatively permanent upward shift in the demand for food items.
- **Transitory demand shifts.** Shifts in demand with only brief staying power are associated with special deals on food items at a competitive store, or cents-off coupons mailed to consumers by the food manufacturer. A gasoline shortage may lead to temporary demand shifts with customers less inclined to make frequent shopping trips for the duration of the shortage.

What should the retailer's inventory policy be in this environment in which a particular random factor can exert a dominant influence, even temporarily swamping a permanent gradual upward or downward shift in demand that might be occurring? Should time and money be spent predicting sales of individual brands?

This is where exponential smoothing is applied, since it requires storage of only two numbers, and computers can easily handle forecast updating for several thousand products. Moreover, the forecasting process is mechanical; it doesn't depend on human intervention. Retailers require an inexpensive means of quickly detecting the more permanent shifts in demand and a way to filter out the disruptive impact of transitory random factors. Exponential smoothing fits this requirement and for that reason has become a popular planning tool for the retail trade.

EXPONENTIAL SMOOTHING VERSUS MOVING AVERAGES

In studying the moving average method, we found that the method produces smoothed values of the time series by averaging equally weighted data blocks of the original series; each block of data covers an equal period of time (1 year in our illustration). The exponential approach likewise smoothes. It averages the original data to produce a smoothed sequence of values, but differs from the moving average method of smoothing in two important respects:

1. All the previous values of the sequence are incorporated into a smoothed value.
2. As the number of terms incorporated in a smoothed value increases, the influence of the most recent actual value in determining the smoothed value also increases.

EXPONENTIALLY SMOOTHED DATA

Let the actual value of the data series at time sequence t be Y_t and the corresponding smoothed value be S_t. For the first period $t = 1$, it follows that S_1 will be the first actual value of the sequence, Y_1. Thus, let

$$S_1 = Y_1$$

For $t \geq 2$, each of the smoothed values S_t is computed from the most recent actual data value Y_t and the previous smoothed value S_{t-1}. The S_{t-1} term is a surrogate for all the previous Y values before Y_t. For $t \geq 2$, we thus have the smoothing formula:

$$S_t = wY_t + (1 - w)S_{t-1}$$

where w is a **smoothing constant**, or weight assigned to the actual data value Y_t. The value of w is chosen by the forecaster and must be in the range from 0 to 1. When w

= 0, no weight is applied to the actual value for period t; when $w = 1$, full weight is attached to the actual value; and the values of w between 0 and 1 give only partial weight to the Y_t value. Note that the remaining weight once w is set is $1 - w$ and is attached to S_{t-1}.

Table 15.10 illustrates the exponential smoothing method for computer-simulated data exhibiting a large positive shift in period 4. To start the process, the actual figure for period 1 is used as the smoothed value for period 1. Arbitrarily setting the smoothing constant at $w = 0.3$, the calculations for the first three smoothed values are

$$S_1 = Y_1 = 1000$$

$$S_2 = 0.3(1020) + (1 - 0.3)(1000)$$

$$= 306 + 700 = 1006$$

$$S_3 = 0.3(950) + (1 - 0.3)(1006)$$

$$= 285 + 704.2 = 989.20$$

TABLE 15.10	Illustration of Exponential Smoothing $(w = 0.3)$	
PERIOD t	ACTUAL DEMAND Y_t	EXPONENTIALLY SMOOTHED DEMAND S_t
1	1000	1000
2	1020	1006
3	950	989.20
4	1410	1115.44
5	1380	1194.81
6	1400	1256.37
7	1430	1308.46
8	1390	1332.92

FORECASTING WITH EXPONENTIAL SMOOTHING

To forecast future observations, we rely on the previous smoothed value. Thus, the forecast for the period t, F_t, uses S_{t-1}, the smoothed value for period $t - 1$, and the forecast for period $t + 1$, F_{t+1} uses S_t. That is,

$$S_{t-1} = F_t \quad \text{and} \quad S_t = F_{t+1}$$

To obtain a forecasting equation in terms of Y_t, recall the exponential smoothing formula $S_t = wY_t + (1 - w)S_{t-1}$.

Now substitute the value of F_t and F_{t-1} for S_{t-1} and S_t. We have

$$F_{t+1} = wY_t + (1 - w)F_t$$

Rearranging terms to obtain an expression for F_{t+1}, we obtain:

Exponential Smoothing Forecast Equation

$$F_{t+1} = F_t + w(Y_t - F_t) \tag{15-8}$$

The expression on the right-hand side of the equal sign shows that the forecast for period $t + 1$ takes into account the forecast made for period t, F_t, and partly adjusts for the forecast error between the actual value Y_t and the forecast F_t in period t. How much of a partial adjustment is indicated by the weight w? Using the data on demand shown in Table 15.10, we shall illustrate the calculations for forecasts based upon exponential smoothing. To begin, in Table 15.11, we note that the forecast for period 2 is the actual value for period 1. That is,

$$F_2 = Y_1 = 1000$$

TABLE 15.11 Forecasting by Exponential Smoothing ($w = 0.3$)			
PERIOD t	ACTUAL DEMAND Y_t	FORECAST FOR PERIOD t (MADE IN PERIOD $t - 1$) F_t	ERROR $Y_t - F_t$
1	1000	—	—
2	1020	1000	20
3	950	1006	−56
4	1410	989.20	420.8
5	1380	1115.44	Overall 264.56
6	1400	1194.81	declining 205.19
7	1430	1256.37	error 173.63
8	1390	1308.46	81.54
9		1332.92	

The next forecasts for periods 3 and 4 are computed as follows:

$$F_3 = F_2 + w(Y_2 - F_2)$$
$$= 1000 + 0.3(1020 - 1000) = 1006$$
$$F_4 = F_3 + w(Y_3 - F_3)$$
$$= 1006 + 0.3(950 - 1006) = 989.20$$

How can we interpret the results? Suppose that we are in period 8; it can be seen from Table 15.11 that the forecast made last period was 1308.46, but the actual result was a higher value, 1390. So our next forecast (for period 9) now made in period 8 will show an increase of $0.3(1390 - 1308.46)$. That is, $F_9 = 1308.46 + 0.03(1390 - 1308.46)$. The new forecast of 1332.92 reflects this upward adjustment.

Exponential smoothing is an *adaptive* forecasting process. Each forecast is a revision of the previous forecast, recognizing and adapting to the error just made ($Y_t - F_t$). The smoothing constant w indicates the degree of adaptation. (The factors that go into assigning the constant w are discussed later in this section.)

The adaptive feature is illustrated by the error shown in the last column of Table 15.11. Note that after the large error in period 4, subsequent errors diminish as the forecasts adapt to the errors made.

To summarize, we obtain exponential smoothed forecasts as follows:

Step 1

Choose a smoothing constant, w. The value must be between 0 and 1; the closer to 1, the more weight is put on current data, the less on previous forecasts.

Step 2

Let the initial forecast for period 2 be the first period's actual demand, Y_1; that is, let $F_2 = Y_1$.

Step 3

Compute the forecast for period 3 using the forecast for period 2 with an adjustment for error term:

$$F_3 = F_2 + w(Y_2 - F_2)$$

Step 4

Compute the forecast for each subsequent period using the forecasting equation:

$$F_{t+1} = F_t + w(Y_t - F_t)$$

It is interesting to note that a prediction can be made only to the next time period, because the forecasting equation requires Y_t, the actual value for the latest time period.

Figure 15.8 shows that exponential smoothing can be done using the business MYSTAT program. As we can see, the computer forecasts match (after rounding) the results calculated by hand and shown in column 3 of Table 15.11.

PRACTICE EXERCISE

15.5 The number of customers for 5 consecutive days are given below for a fruit and produce market:

124   121   110   124   119

Using $w = 0.1$:
a. Determine F_2 and S_2.
b. Determine F_3 and S_3.
c. What is the forecast error for period 3?
d. What is the forecast for period 6?

APPLICATION OF EXPONENTIAL SMOOTHING

Basic exponential smoothing serves as a forecasting model in situations where demand, subject to random variation, suddenly shifts to a new permanent level about which the random variation now takes place. Let's denote by Y_{old} the level at which demand fluctuated prior to the permanent upward shift. After the permanent shift, demand fluctuates around Y_{new}. The goal of the basic exponential smoothing model is to distinguish between:

1. A *permanent shift* in demand to a new level (Y_{old} to Y_{new}), as shown in Figure 15.9
2. A *transitory movement* due to a dominant random event; that is, fluctuations around Y_{old} or, later, around Y_{new} (shown in Figure 15.10)

How is a permanent shift distinguished from transitory movement? The determination is not made in a single time period, but rather by stages. Assume a permanent shift occurs to a new level, and the model revises subsequent forecasts in the direction of the shift. With the actual values now fluctuating near Y_{new} (as shown in Figure 15.10), large positive forecast errors will occur at first. These lead to a sequence of upward revisions on subsequent forecasts, driving F_t closer to Y_{new}. Eventually, this adjustment process brings the forecasts, F_t, in line with the new permanent level, Y_{new}.

Figure 15.8
Business MYSTAT: Exponential
smoothing results

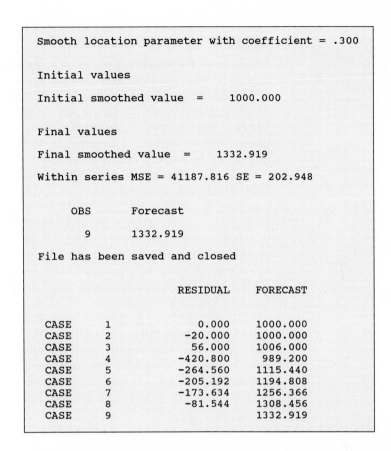

```
Smooth location parameter with coefficient = .300

Initial values

Initial smoothed value  =    1000.000

Final values

Final smoothed value  =    1332.919

Within series MSE = 41187.816 SE = 202.948

        OBS        Forecast

         9        1332.919

File has been saved and closed

                            RESIDUAL      FORECAST

    CASE      1                0.000      1000.000
    CASE      2              -20.000      1000.000
    CASE      3               56.000      1006.000
    CASE      4             -420.800       989.200
    CASE      5             -264.560      1115.440
    CASE      6             -205.192      1194.808
    CASE      7             -173.634      1256.366
    CASE      8              -81.544      1308.456
    CASE      9                          1332.919
```

Figure 15.9
Response of exponentially
smoothed forecast to shift in
mean sales level

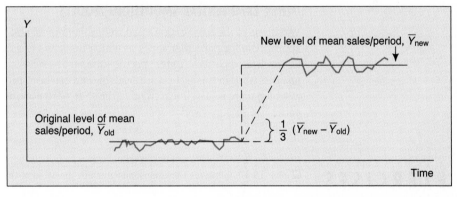

Figure 15.10
Effect of smoothing constant on
forecast response to permanent
shifts

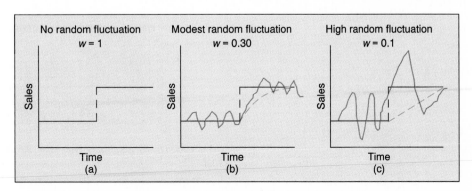

CHOOSING THE SMOOTHING CONSTANT

Regulation of the adjustment process is accomplished by the smoothing constant w. This is the value that determines how quickly the revised forecast adapts to the shift in demand. Figure 15.9 shows that for $w = 0.33$, each new forecast will move up $\frac{1}{3}$ of the distance between the current forecast and the new permanent level Y_{new}. The size of w depends upon the degree of random fluctuation in the series. Thus, expectations about the volatility of the series play an important role in choosing w. The value of w should be inversely related to volatility.

Figures 15.10a–c show three types of fluctuation. With no random fluctuation (part a), the entire observed error, $Y_t - F$, is considered information and the proper adjustment is an immediate jump to the new permanent level. A weight of one ($w = 1$) is assigned to reflect this situation. However, when the series shows volatility, low values of w are assigned. Low w values indicate less sensitivity to the observed error in the belief that much of it is random fluctuation and as such should not be considered as evidence of a shift to a permanent new level. Values between 0.1 and 0.3 have worked best in most situations with values around 0.10 and 0.15 most appropriate for series with high volatility.

One rule of thumb suggests we set w approximately equal to what we consider to be the probability that a shift will be permanent. Then, we compute forecast errors using this w, after which higher and lower values of w can be tried and their forecast errors computed and recorded. The errors resulting from each w value are then squared and the squared errors averaged to give the *mean squared error* of the forecast. The w value producing the lowest mean squared error is then taken as the best choice.

OTHER EXPONENTIAL SMOOTHING MODELS

Variations of the basic exponential smoothing model also exist. These variants are more appropriate for particular series in which the shifts to a new permanent plateau follow a complicated pattern. Three specific variants of the basic exponential smoothing model just described in this section are available and can be appropriately matched to situations in which there is (1) a linear trend to the shift, (2) a nonlinear trend, or (3) a pronounced pattern of seasonal variation.

● ●

EXERCISES ❏ **15.13** Consider the time series given in the table of the demand (in megatons) for iron ore.

PERIOD	DEMAND	PERIOD	DEMAND
1979	3000	1985	3000
1980	3050	1986	2900
1981	3200	1987	2700
1982	3100	1988	2500
1983	3000	1989	2200
1984	3200		

a. Using exponential smoothing with $w = 0.4$, what is the smoothed value for 1980?

b. Using exponential smoothing with $w = 0.4$, what is the smoothed value for 1989?

c. Using exponential smoothing with $w = 0.4$, what is the projected value for 1990?

d. Using exponential smoothing with $w = 0.7$, what is the projected value for 1990?

15.14 Consider the time series given in the table of sales of yachts:

MONTH	1	2	3	4	5	6	7
UNITS SOLD	12	11	12	14	15	17	16

Using exponential smoothing with $w = 0.3$:

a. What is the smoothed value for month 7?

b. What is the forecast for month 8?

c. Compute the error for each month.

▶ **15.15** Maintenance expenses for a public school system (in thousands of dollars) over a 10 month period are given in the table.

MONTH	1	2	3	4	5	6	7	8	9	10
EXPENSE	2.0	3.0	1.0	3.0	3.0	1.5	1.0	2.0	1.7	1.5

Using exponential smoothing with $w = 0.2$:

a. Compute the forecast expense for month 8, F_8.

b. Compute the error for each month.

c. Square the value of each error term, and then sum the squares and find their mean. This value is the mean squared error, or MSE.

d. Compare the MSE using $w = 0.4$ with your answer to part c.

● ●

15.7

FORECASTING TIME SERIES USING REGRESSION ANALYSIS

Our discussion of regression analysis in Chapters 10 and 11 explained the development of a regression equation in which one or several independent (predictor) variables are used to predict the value of the dependent variable Y. Assuming the data used to estimate the regression equation were time series data, the resulting regression equation could be recognized and employed as a forecasting tool, forecasting future values of Y_t.

One approach in developing a regression equation for forecasting is to build a regression equation composed of $X_1, \ldots, X_k$ independent variables that are believed to be determinants of Y. In this sense, the X variables represent the underlying structure that determines Y. Regression equations of this type developed for forecasting are called **structural regression models,** or simply, structural models. The general form for such equations is

Structural Regression Model

$$\hat{Y}_t = a + b_1 X_{1,t} + b_2 X_{2,t} + \cdots + b_k X_{k,t} \qquad (15\text{-}9)$$

A second approach toward using a regression equation for forecasting relies on previous values of the Y series alone to serve as the predictor variables of Y_t. That is:

$$\hat{Y}_t = a + b_1 Y_{t-1} + b_2 Y_{t-2} + \cdots + b_k Y_{t-k}$$

This form of construction of the regression equation hypothesizes that there is a systematic pattern that connects the current value of Y_t to previous Y levels Y_{t-1}, Y_{t-2}, etc. The variables included in the regression equation and the values of the estimated regression coefficients specify the nature of that relationship.

In its simplest form, the regression model includes only one predictor variable, Y_{t-1}. When the regression equation is of this type, it is called an **autoregressive model.** (The word *autoregression* means regressing on itself.)

Autoregressive Model

$$\hat{Y}_t = a + b Y_{t-1} \qquad\qquad (15\text{-}10)$$

Autoregressive models recognize the fact that consecutive time series values of Y_t are correlated and attempt to use this information in formulating a forecasting model.

It is informative to note that structural models and autoregressive models may be viewed as competing approaches to improved forecasting. Because structural models require collecting information on several variables and are usually more costly and more time-consuming to construct, devoting resources to building a structural model may not be justified. It may make sense to use the less demanding autoregressive model. For this reason, the autoregressive model is often set up as the benchmark to beat for forecasting performance. A structural model that can't beat a simple autoregressive model isn't worth maintaining. Even if the structural model turns out to give better results, the expenditure of considerable time, effort, and cost may outweigh the forecasting gain.

SUMMARY

In this chapter we have examined the components of the classical time series model: trend, seasonality, and cyclical–irregularity. Assuming past trend and seasonal variation extend into the future, we have described a procedure for developing projections. While we know that the irregular and cyclical components will continue to play a role in the future, their erratic nature makes them difficult to model and use in forecasting. The decomposition of the classical model into its components is an appropriate way of describing the component movement in past time series data. But the sole use of a model to forecast can be naive and result in considerable forecasting error. Management should combine the forecasts of any statistical procedure with the knowledge of other factors that bear on the future of their business. In particular, an informed management should be asking, "How regular and lasting have been the past trends? What do we know about how they might be changing?"

Modern forecasting techniques have tried to improve the accuracy of forecasts without requiring great insight into the sources of change. The exponential smoothing model discussed in Section 15.6 is a basic example of these methods. More advanced approaches include the autoregressive model, which has been growing in popularity and serves as a benchmark measure for judging the gain from forecasting on the basis of business variables.

KEY EQUATIONS

Additive Component Model

$$Y_t = T_t + S_t + C_t + I_t \tag{15-1}$$

Multiplicative Component Model

$$Y_t = T_t \cdot S_t \cdot C_t \cdot I_t \tag{15-2}$$

Fitted Linear Trend Equation

$$\hat{Y}_t = a + bt \tag{15-3}$$

Fitted Quadratic Trend Equation

$$\hat{Y}_t = a + b_1 t + b_2 t^2 \tag{15-4}$$

Exponential Trend Equation

$$\hat{Y}_t = kc^t \tag{15-5}$$

Regression Version of Exponential Trend Equation

$$\log \hat{Y}_t = a + bt \tag{15-6}$$

where $a = \log k$ and $b = \log c$.

Cyclical–Irregular (C–I) Relatives (No Seasonal Component)

$$C_t \cdot I_t = \frac{Y_t}{\hat{Y}_t} \tag{15-7}$$

Exponential Smoothing Forecast Equation

$$F_{t+1} = F_t + w(Y_t - F_t) \tag{15-8}$$

Structural Regression Model

$$\hat{Y}_t = a + b_1 X_{1,t} + b_2 X_{2,t} + \cdots + b_k X_{k,t} \tag{15-9}$$

Autoregressive Model

$$\hat{Y}_t = a + bY_{t-1} \tag{15-10}$$

PRACTICE EXERCISE ANSWERS

15.1 a. The regression equation is SALES $= 16.6533 + 0.5885t$.

PREDICTOR	COEFFICIENT	STANDARD DEVIATION	t-RATIO	p
Constant	16.6533	0.9703	17.16	0.000
t	0.5885	0.1564	3.76	0.006
s = 1.420		$R^2 = 63.9\%$	R^2(adj) $= 59.4\%$	

b. $\hat{Y}_6 = 16.6533 + 0.5885(6) = 20.1843$

c. The forecast for $t = 11$ is $\hat{Y}_{11} = 16.6533 + 0.5885(11) = 23.1268$

15.2

YEAR	SALES		C-I RELATIVE
t	Y_t	$\hat{Y}_t$	$Y_t/\hat{Y}_t$
1	17.0	17.2418	0.98597
2	18.4	17.8303	1.03195
3	17.0	18.4188	0.92297
4	20.9	19.0073	1.09958
5	18.3	19.5958	0.93388
6	20.1	20.1842	0.99583
7	22.0	20.7727	1.05908
8	22.2	21.3612	1.03927
9	19.6	21.9497	0.89295
10	23.4	22.5382	1.03824

15.3 a. The 7 day moving average centered on day 10 requires that the 7 values centered at day 10 be averaged:

$$Y_{10}^* = \frac{Y_7 + Y_8 + Y_9 + Y_{10} + Y_{11} + Y_{12} + Y_{13}}{7}$$

$$= \frac{6.00 + 6.45 + 5.93 + 6.17 + 8.17 + 9.30 + 9.83}{7} = 7.4071$$

b. The last term in the 7 day moving average series is Y_{11}^*:

$$Y_{11}^* = \frac{Y_8 + Y_9 + Y_{10} + Y_{11} + Y_{12} + Y_{13} + Y_{14}}{7}$$

$$= \frac{6.45 + 5.93 + 6.17 + 8.17 + 9.30 + 9.83 + 6.43}{7} = 7.4686$$

15.4 a–c.

TIME PERIOD	SALES	4 QUARTER MOVING TOTAL	CENTERED MOVING TOTAL	MOVING AVERAGE
Year 1: Q_1	5			
Q_2	12			
Q_3	16	40	40.5	10.125
Q_4	7	41	41.5	10.375
Year 2: Q_1	6	42	42.5	10.625
Q_2	13	43	43.5	10.875
Q_3	17	44	44.5	11.125
Q_4	8	45	45.5	11.375
Year 3: Q_1	7	46	46.5	11.625
Q_2	14	47	47.5	11.875
Q_3	18	48	48.5	12.125
Q_4	9	49	49.5	12.375
Year 4: Q_1	8	50	50.5	12.625
Q_2	15	51	51.5	12.875
Q_3	19	52	52.5	13.125
Q_4	10	53	53.5	13.375
Year 5: Q_1	9	54	54.5	13.625
Q_2	16	55	55.5	13.875
Q_3	20	56		
Q_4	11			

d. There are 20 data points, so there are $20 - 4 = 16$ data points in the 4 quarter moving average series.

e.

TIME PERIOD	SALES Y_t	4 QUARTER MOVING AVERAGE Y_t^*	ORIGINAL-TO-MOVING AVERAGE RATIO Y_t/Y_t^*
Year 1: Q_1	5		
Q_2	12		
Q_3	16	10.125	1.5802
Q_4	7	10.375	0.6747
Year 2: Q_1	6	10.625	0.5647
Q_2	13	10.875	1.1954
Q_3	17	11.125	1.5281
Q_4	8	11.375	0.7033
Year 3: Q_1	7	11.625	0.6022
Q_2	14	11.875	1.1789
Q_3	18	12.125	1.4845
Q_4	9	12.375	0.7273
Year 4: Q_1	8	12.625	0.6337
Q_2	15	12.875	1,1650
Q_3	19	13.125	1.4476
Q_4	10	13.375	0.7477
Year 5: Q_1	9	13.625	0.6606
Q_2	16	13.875	1.1532
Q_3	20		
Q_4	11		

f. First, find the adjustment factor by sorting the original–to–moving average ratios by season and then averaging the ratios for each season:

	Q_1	Q_2	Q_3	Q_4
	0.5647	1.1954	1.5802	0.6747
	0.6022	1.1789	1.5281	0.7033
	0.6337	1.1650	1.4845	0.7273
	0.6606	1.1532	1.4476	0.7477
Means:	0.6153	1.1731	1.5101	0.7133

The adjustment factor is found by dividing the number of periods in the year by the sum of the means:

$$\text{Sum of means} = 4.0118$$

$$\text{Number of periods} = 4$$

$$\text{Adjustment factor} = \frac{\text{Number of seasons}}{\text{Sum of means}} = \frac{4}{4.0118} = 0.9971$$

The seasonal indexes are:

Q_1: Seasonal index = Mean × Adjustment factor = 0.6153 × 0.9971 = 0.6135

Q_2: Seasonal index = Mean × Adjustment factor 1.1731 × 0.9971 = 1.1697

Q_3: Seasonal index = Mean × Adjustment factor = 1.5101 × 0.9971 = 1.5057

Q_4: Seasonal index = Mean × Adjustment factor = 0.7133 × 0.9971 = 0.7112

g.

TIME PERIOD	SALES	DESEASONALIZED SALES
Year 1: Q_1	5	5/0.6135 = 8.15
Q_2	12	12/1.1697 = 10.26
Q_3	16	16/1.5057 = 10.63
Q_4	7	7/0.7112 = 9.84
Year 2: Q_1	6	6/0.6135 = 9.78
Q_2	13	13/1.1697 = 11.11
Q_3	17	17/1.5057 = 11.29
Q_4	8	8/0.7112 = 11.25
Year 3: Q_1	7	7/0.6135 = 11.41
Q_2	14	14/1.1697 = 11.97
Q_3	18	18/1.5057 = 11.95
Q_4	9	9/0.7112 = 12.65
Year 4: Q_1	8	8/0.6135 = 13.04
Q_2	15	15/1.1697 = 12.82
Q_3	19	19/1.5057 = 12.62
Q_4	10	10/0.7112 = 14.06
Year 5: Q_1	9	9/0.6135 = 14.67
Q_2	16	16/1.1697 = 13.68
Q_3	20	20/1.5057 = 13.28
Q_4	11	11/0.7112 = 15.47

h. The $\hat{Y}_t$ values in the table are found from the trend equation using the deseasonalized data above. The deseasonalized linear trend regression equation is

$$\hat{Y}_t = 8.9729 + 0.28796t$$

PREDICTOR	COEFFICIENT	STANDARD DEVIATION	t-RATIO	p
Constant	8.9729	0.2860	31.37	0.000
t	0.28796	0.02387	12.06	0.000
s = 0.6157		R^2 = 89.0%	R^2(adj) = 88.4%	

t	Y_t	$\hat{Y}_t$	C-I RELATIVES $Y_t/\hat{Y}_t$
1	8.15	9.2609	0.88005
2	10.26	9.5488	1.07448
3	10.63	9.8368	1.08064
4	9.84	10.1247	0.97188
5	9.78	10.4127	0.93924
6	11.11	10.7007	1.03825
7	11.29	10.9886	1.02743
8	11.25	11.2766	0.99764
9	11.41	11.5646	0.98663
10	11.97	11.8525	1.00991
11	11.95	12.1405	0.98431
12	12.65	12.4284	1.01783
13	13.04	12.7164	1.02545
14	12.82	13.0044	0.98582
15	12.62	13.2923	0.94942
16	14.06	13.5803	1.03532
17	14.67	13.8683	1.05781
18	13.68	14.1562	0.96636
19	13.28	14.4442	0.91940
20	15.47	14.7321	1.05009

i. The seasonal weights are

Q_1: Seasonal weight $= \dfrac{\text{Seasonal index}}{\text{Number of seasons in year}} = \dfrac{0.6135}{4} = 0.1534$

Q_2: Seasonal weight $= \dfrac{1.1697}{4} = 0.2924$

Q_3: Seasonal weight $= \dfrac{1.5057}{4} = 0.3764$

Q_4: Seasonal weight $= \dfrac{0.7112}{4} = 0.1778$

j. Quarter 2 of year 6 is time period 22. The deseasonalized projection is found from the deseasonalized trend line regression equation:

$$\hat{Y}_t = 8.9729 + 0.28796t$$

$$\hat{Y}_{22} = 8.9729 + 0.28796(22) = 15.3080$$

k. The seasonalized projection is found by multiplying the deseasonalized forecast by the appropriate seasonal index:

$$\text{Seasonalized projection} = (\hat{Y}_{22})(\text{Seasonal index for } Q_2)$$

$$= 15.3080(1.1697) = 17.9058$$

15.5

DAY t	CUSTOMERS Y_t	EXPONENTIALLY SMOOTHED ($w = 0.1$) S_t	FORECAST VALUE ($w = 0.1$) F_t
1	124	124.00	—
2	121	123.70	124.00
3	110	122.33	123.70
4	124	122.50	122.33
5	119	122.15	122.50
6			122.15

a. $F_2 = 124.00$; $S_2 = 123.70$
b. $F_3 = 123.70$; $S_3 = 122.33$
c. The forecast error for period 3 is $Y_3 - F_3 = 110 - 123.70 = -13.70$.
d. $F_6 = S_5 = 122.15$

CHAPTER REVIEW EXERCISES

15.16 Construct a 4 quarter moving average series to isolate the main movements in the Whisker Brush Co. sales data given in the table.

QUARTER	YEAR		
	1	2	3
1	1401	1415	1455
2	1421	1438	1482
3	1457	1507	1527
4	1438	1493	1500

Actual Sales of Whisker Brush Co. (Not Seasonally Adjusted, 100s of units)

15.17 For the Whisker Brush Co. data given in Exercise 15.16:
  a. Construct a ratio-to-moving average series using the moving average series computed in Exercise 15.16.
  b. Construct seasonal indexes for the data using the arithmetic mean method.
  c. Construct a deseasonalized series.
  d. Both the moving average series and the deseasonalized series remove the seasonal effect. Which one of the two series still includes the random effect? Explain.
  e. Comment on the sales history of the Whisker Brush brand using the deseasonalized data series.

15.18 Using the deseasonalized Whisker Brush Co. sales series computed in Exercise 15.17 and an exponential smoothing model:
  a. With $w = 0.4$, compute the forecast sales in the last quarter of year 3.
  b. With $w = 0.04$, compute the forecast error for the last quarter of year 3.
  c. With $w = 0.04$, compute the forecast of deseasonalized sales in the first quarter of year 4.
  d. Use the seasonal indexes computed in Exercise 15.17 and the forecast of deseasonalized sales computed in part c above to determine the forecast of actual sales for the first quarter of year 4.

⌑ **15.19** Best Foods, a manufacturer of salad dressing, contracts with your market research firm for an objective study to assess trends in container preferences among customers. You decide to examine reports on shipments of mayonnaise, salad dressing, and related products. The table gives the information you found.

Shipments of Mayonnaise, Salad Dressing, and Related Products by Size of Container (Percent of Shipment)										
YEAR CONTAINER SIZE	1	2	3	4	5	6	7	8	9	10
32 oz	37.3	37.7	38.7	39.4	38.8	39.0	38.3	39.8	40.3	39.1

  a. Construct a time plot (scatter diagram) of the shipment data.
  b. Compute the linear trend equation for the shipment data by the least squares procedure.
  c. What has been the average annual increase in percentage of shipments accounted for by 32 oz containers over the 10 year period?
  d. What is the trend component for year 7?
  e. Find the projection of shipments for year 11.

15.20 The table gives information on shipments of mayonnaise, salad dressing, and related products (percent of total shipments in this product category) for 128 oz containers.

YEAR	1	2	3	4	5	6	7	8	9	10
SHIPMENT	22.7	22.5	21.8	21.6	21.0	20.6	19.8	19.3	18.3	17.5

  a. Construct a time plot (scatter diagram) of the shipment data.
  b. Compute the linear trend equation for the shipment data by the least squares method.
  c. What has been the average annual increase in percentage of shipments accounted for by 128 oz containers over the 10 year period?
  d. What is the trend component for year 9?
  e. Find the projection of shipments for year 11.

15.21 For the data given in Exercise 15.20:
   a. Find the cyclical–irregular relative for year 9.
   b. Construct a time plot (scatter diagram) of the cyclical–irregular relatives.

15.22 For the data given in Exercise 15.19:
   a. Find the cyclical–irregular relative for year 7.
   b. Construct a time plot (scatter diagram) of the cyclical–irregular relatives.

15.23 Compare your answers for Exercises 15.19–15.22. Recommend which container size should be sold and in which proportions for year 11. Explain your recommendations.

15.24 At one time, Camel brand cigarettes were the top-selling brand in the United States. In recent decades, however, sales have fallen drastically from their all-time highs. Annual sales for a 25 year period are given in the table.

YEAR	SALES Billion Dollars	YEAR	SALES Billion Dollars
1	99.0	14	48.1
2	84.0	15	44.9
3	77.0	16	40.1
4	72.5	17	35.3
5	66.0	18	32.9
6	62.5	19	31.6
7	63.5	20	29.9
8	66.5	21	29.9
9	67.0	22	28.9
10	66.0	23	27.4
11	63.0	24	26.0
12	52.5	25	24.3
13	49.1		

   a. Construct a time plot (scatter diagram) of the data.
   b. Construct a least squares trend equation for the years 1–11, inclusive.
   c. Construct a least squares trend equation for the years 12–25.
   d. In year 12, the U.S. Surgeon General issued a report linking cigarette smoking to increased risk of cancer. This report is widely thought to have adversely affected sales of cigarettes, particularly nonfilter brands such as Camel. Does the adverse effect appear to be a short-lived phenomenon, or more persistent in nature? Explain the criterion you used in drawing your conclusion.

15.25 Consider the data on unemployment rates in the table.

TIME PERIOD	UNEMPLOYMENT %
1987: Jan.–Feb.	9
Mar–Apr.	8
May–June	10
July–Aug.	12
Sept.–Oct.	10
Nov.–Dec.	8
1988: Jan.–Feb.	10
Mar–Apr.	12
May–June	13
July–Aug.	15
Sept.–Oct.	12
Nov.–Dec.	11

a. Constructing a 5 period moving average, what is the smoothed value for Mar.–Apr. 1988?
b. Constructing a 6 period moving average, what is the smoothed value for Mar.–Apr. 1988?
c. To eliminate a seasonal effect, how many periods should be averaged over in the moving average?

□ **15.26** Consider the time series in the table.

PERIOD	DEMAND	PERIOD	DEMAND
1	3000	7	2600
2	3150	8	2550
3	3050	9	2450
4	3100	10	2500
5	3000	11	2300
6	2500		

Using exponential smoothing with:
a. $w = 0.3$, what is the smoothed value for period 2?
b. $w = 0.3$, what is the smoothed value for period 11?
c. $w = 0.3$, what is the forecast error for period 11?
d. $w = 0.3$, what is the forecast for period 12?
e. $w = 0.8$, what is the forecast for period 12?

□ **15.27** The manager of a recently opened supermarket specializing in natural foods is reviewing the stores's 4 months of sales history in preparation for merchandise and employment planning. The first month of sales were affected by grand opening promotions to introduce the store to customers in the trade area. Sales in the subsequent 3 months exhibited considerable growth, although there was substantial variation from day to day. The manager felt the daily sales history reflected normal shopping patterns within the week, combined with rapidly increasing market penetration as the store and its policies became better known in the community. To plan merchandise and employment requirements effectively, the store manager needs to get some dimensions on the sales growth picture. The data on daily sales (expressed in thousands of dollars) for the last 3 months are given in the table.

WEEK	SUNDAY	MONDAY	TUESDAY	WEDNESDAY	THURSDAY	FRIDAY	SATURDAY
1	4.80	5.01	4.88	5.04	6.59	7.39	7.58
2	4.97	5.18	4.89	5.28	6.83	7.74	7.80
3	5.31	5.55	5.23	5.32	6.97	7.85	8.30
4	5.51	5.78	5.43	5.65	7.20	8.36	8.38
5	5.84	5.85	5.53	5.76	7.59	8.78	8.81
6	5.77	6.23	5.53	5.99	7.73	9.06	9.34
7	6.00	6.45	5.93	6.17	8.17	9.30	9.83
8	6.20	6.45	6.02	6.01	8.24	9.37	9.94
9	6.43	6.65	6.26	6.49	8.37	9.95	10.40
10	6.92	6.91	6.49	6.56	8.85	10.67	10.38
11	6.92	7.23	6.55	6.58	8.93	10.46	10.75
12	7.14	7.58	7.09	7.15	9.37	10.76	11.25
13	7.17	7.48	7.31	7.48	9.35	11.10	11.24

a. Construct a 7 day moving average to reveal how rapidly and how steadily sales have been growing during the last 3 months.

b. Plot the computed moving average values on a chart. (Note: If a computer is not available, consider only the last 5 weeks.)
c. What do you conclude about the sales growth pattern exhibited by the moving average sales?

15.28 For daily sales of the natural food store given in Exercise 15.27:
a. Compute daily indexes for each day of the week using the ratio-to-moving average method.
b. On which days of the week should the manager schedule the most employees and plan to have the greatest stock of merchandise available on the shelves for customer purchases?

15.29 Refer to the data in Exercise 15.27. The store manager is aware that existing trade area competitors are trying retaliatory promotions to keep their own customers from straying. "Have they had any measurable effect on the new stores' sales?" is the question the store manager needs to answer.
a. Deseasonalize the sales data by dividing the actual sales by the daily index for that day (computed in Exercise 15.28) for the last 3 weeks.
b. Plot the results of part a, with deseasonalized sales on the vertical axis and the time period on the horizontal axis.
c. Compute the least squares trend line from the deseasonalized data.
d. Compute the residuals of the trend line determined in part c.
e. Explain how the residuals computed in part d reflect the possible impact of a competitor's retaliatory promotions.

15.30 Monthly data on patient hours in the maternity department of a hospital for a 5 year period are given in the table.

MONTH	YEAR				
	1	2	3	4	5
1	3935	3866	4024	3217	2929
2	3850	3264	3416	3106	3137
3	3580	3585	3671	3196	2975
4	4240	4308	3762	3118	3274
5	4605	4078	4444	3305	3422
6	4660	4369	5375	4667	4507
7	4377	4281	3752	3555	3254
8	3972	3423	2884	3101	3425
9	3523	4097	3324	3507	2983
10	3675	3646	3133	3131	2724
11	3679	3603	3048	3639	2974
12	3573	3848	3163	2762	2561

a. Compute 12 month moving averages for the data.
b. Plot the moving average series on a chart.
c. Compute ratio-to-moving averages for the data.
d. Compute seasonal indexes.
e. Interpret the seasonal indexes.
f. Compute the trend in the moving average series.

▶ **15.31** Consider the data in the table on quarterly unit sales of used jet aircraft by an airplane broker.

		YEAR		
		1	**2**	**3**
QUARTER	Winter	1	2	3
	Spring	2	4	5
	Summer	4	6	7
	Fall	2	5	4

a. How many values would there be in a 4 quarter moving average series for the data?
b. Construct a moving total series. What are the first and last values in this series?
c. Center the moving totals and then construct a centered moving average series. What are the first and last values in this series?
d. Find the seasonal indexes for each season.
e. Construct the deseasonalized series. What is the first value in this series?
f. Use the least squares method to find the linear trend equation.
g. Find the trend components for each period. What is the trend component of the summer quarter of year 3?
h. Find the cyclical–irregular relatives. What is the value of this component for winter of year 1?
i. What is the deseasonalized sales projection for winter of year 4?
j. Seasonalize your projection in part i.

15.32 Consider the quarterly absenteeism record (in days) of Jonathan Cutler given in the table.

		YEAR		
		1	**2**	**3**
QUARTER	**1**	2	3	5
	2	3	3	6
	3	5	6	6
	4	4	5	7

a. How many values would there be in a 4 quarter moving average series for the data?
b. Construct a moving total series. What are the first and last values in this series?
c. Center the moving totals and then construct a centered moving average series. What are the first and last values in this series?
d. Find the seasonal indexes for each quarter.
e. Construct the deseasonalized series. What is the first value in this series?
f. Use the least squares method to find the linear trend equation.
g. Find the trend components for each period. What is the trend component of the third quarter of year 3?
h. Find the cyclical–irregular relatives. What is the value of this component for the first quarter of year 1?
i. What is the deseasonalized absenteeism projection for the first quarter of year 4?
j. Seasonalize your projection in part i.

15.33 Given in the table are monthly data of Skyline Brands for a 3 year period.

YEAR 1		YEAR 2		YEAR 3	
Jan.	30	Jan.	35	Jan.	39
Feb.	35	Feb.	38	Feb.	40
Mar.	38	Mar.	39	Mar.	43
Apr.	39	Apr.	42	Apr.	46
May	42	May	47	May	53
June	45	June	49	June	54
July	50	July	52	July	56
Aug.	35	Aug.	35	Aug.	40
Sept.	32	Sept.	33	Sept.	39
Oct.	30	Oct.	32	Oct.	38
Nov.	31	Nov.	33	Nov.	39
Dec.	29	Dec.	34	Dec.	41

a. Compute the 12 month moving totals.
b. Compute the centered moving totals.
c. Compute the centered moving average series.
d. Compute the original–to–moving average ratios.
e. Compute the seasonal indexes using the modified mean method.
f. Compute the deseasonalized series.
g. What is the (seasonalized) trend projection for January of year 4?

▶ **15.34** A quarterly time series of profits for Rosebud Oil Company was first smoothed by applying a 4 period moving average. Seasonal indexes were calculated and given as winter = 1.21, spring = 0.81, summer = 1.15, fall = 0.83. Then, a least squares trend analysis was used to fit the following equation to the deseasonalized sales:

$$\hat{Y}_t^d = 200 + 100t + t^2$$

a. Which of the following can be said about Rosebud's profits?
   A. Profits are decreasing steadily.
   B. Profits are increasing steadily.
   C. Profits were first increasing but later decreased.
   D. Profits are increasing more and more rapidly as time goes on.
   E. None of the above.
b. What is the deseasonalized trend projection for period 25, the winter season, not adjusting for season?
c. What is the projection for winter period 25 adjusting for winter season?
d. What is the projection for spring period 26 adjusting for spring season?

15.35 Suppose you are a well-known consultant on executive compensation and have been called in by a conglomerate's board of directors to mediate an executive compensation dispute. John Wilson, recently hired president of one of the corporate conglomerate's subsidiaries, is claiming that he is entitled to a substantial bonus for third quarter profits. The third quarter represents Wilson's first quarter at the helm. His compensation contract specifies that he is eligible for a substantial bonus as soon as the profit picture of the subsidiary improves. Wilson attributes the sharp profit rise of the third quarter over the profits earned in the second quarter by his predecessor to his "bold initiatives and necessary actions" upon taking over the reins of the company. The corporate board has another view of third quarter profits. Current third quarter profits are down from the third quarter of last year. The board feels this is a better measure of Wilson's early performance as president, and using that measure, profits haven't improved.
a. Is Wilson's interpretation of profit improvement as the increase over the preceding quarter wrong?

b. Is the corporate board of directors' interpretation of profit improvement as the increase over the previous year's third quarter wrong?

c. You must recommend a different basis for measuring profit—one that neither Wilson nor the board used. Can you suggest an approach that overcomes the major deficiencies of the comparison with the preceding quarter or with the previous year's quarter? Explain.

15.36 How's business? "We don't mind letting our sales figures speak for themselves," answered Phil Washington, an executive in charge of marketing for the 52 unit chain of 4 Day Tire Stores. "The tire business is supposed to be in a decline, but we haven't noticed it." The possibility of an eventual down-turn was somewhat disconcerting to Doris Carr, another executive in the company, whose responsibilities are in the area of financial control and forecasting. "Perhaps we are getting more than our fair share," Carr beamed aloud, "but we ought to model our past growth so that we can better forecast our future growth. Let's see what we can find in our most recent quarterly figures." Doris Carr wants to try forecasting from the data in the table by computer regression analysis using the deseasonalized sales trend line approach.

Quarterly Sales ($) for 4 Day Tire Stores (Period in Parentheses)					
LAST 8 YEARS	QUARTER 1	QUARTER 2	QUARTER 3	QUARTER 4	TOTALS
1	(1) 3,907,138	(2) 4,167,928	(3) 4,273,815	(4) 3,938,207	16,287,088
2	(5) 3,966,566	(6) 4,553,981	(7) 5,125,848	(8) 4,404,604	18,050,999
3	(9) 3,466,812	(10) 5,332,532	(11) 6,391,050	(12) 5,291,252	21,471,646
4	(13) 5,563,955	(14) 6,789,784	(15) 7,830,159	(16) 7,493,172	27,677,070
5	(17) 8,358,342	(18) 10,995,111	(19) 12,437,812	(20) 13,495,637	45,286,902
6	(21) 11,499,374	(22) 13,874,356	(23) 14,948,274	(24) 14,762,919	55,084,923
7	(25) 13,926,279	(26) 15,567,652	(27) 16,301,650	(28) 17,640,253	63,435,834
8	(29) 17,055,684	(30) 19,180,347	(31) 22,118,258	(32) 21,984,673	80,338,962

a. Compute the centered four quarter moving average series.

b. Using the ratio-to-moving average method, calculate the seasonal indexes.

c. Compute the deseasonalized sales series.

d. Compute the deseasonalized sales trend line, $\hat{Y}_t^d = a + b_1 t + b_2 t^2$, eliminating t^2 if its inclusion doesn't improve (lower) the standard deviation of the residuals.

e. With the deseasonalized sales trend equation determined in part d, project the quarterly sales trend line to obtain a forecast for the next quarter period. Now apply the appropriate seasonal index to the forecast to arrive at the seasonally adjusted forecast for the next period.

15.37 Refer to the quarterly sales data of 4 Day Tire Stores in Exercise 15.36. Another forecasting technique that Doris Carr wished to evaluate is the technique of exponential smoothing.

a. Calculate the exponential smoothing forecasts F_t using the exponential weight $w = 0.1$.

b. Compute the forecast error for the last 8 quarters.

c. Calculate the exponential smoothing forecasts F_t using the exponential weight $w = 0.4$.
d. Compute the forecast errors for the last 8 quarters.
e. Repeat parts a and b using $w = 0.8$.
f. Plot the original series and the forecasts based on the smoothing factors 0.1, 0.4, and 0.8. Discuss. Does one value of w consistently produce forecasts that tend to be low? Is there a tendency to overshoot at the turning points?

SOLVING APPLIED CASES

In this section we consider a case situation in which the importance of properly handling seasonal variation becomes apparent.

Earnings Seasonality and the Low Price–Earnings Strategy

On Wall Street, everyone talks about *P-E ratios*. The P-E (price–earnings) ratio is a financial statistic obtained by dividing the current market price of a stock by its earnings over some designated time period, usually a year. Some security analysts pursue a low P-E ratio investment strategy. These analysts believe it worthwhile to identify low P-E ratio stocks. Their thinking is that these stocks, as a group, promise better than average price appreciation prospects.

The P-E (Price–Earnings) Ratio

A P-E ratio is the ratio of the current market price of a firm's stock (in the numerator) to the firm's earnings over some fixed time period, usually 1 year (in the denominator).

$$\text{P-E ratio} = \frac{\text{Current market price of firm's stock}}{\text{Firm's earnings per fixed time period}}$$

Bargain Stocks: The Low Price–Earnings Strategy

According to the low P-E ratio strategy, firms currently with low P-E ratios are prime, undervalued candidates for price appreciation. When the earnings strength of one of these firms is discovered by the market, the stock price will rise to reflect the earnings expectations. This price rise represents capital gains for investors who were among the first to see the earnings strength, buy the stock, and gain from the price rise.

Annualized Earnings

But what earnings number should be used in forming this investment ratio? Earnings for the latest quarter? Or earnings over an entire year? And if the latter, then for what year? Last year's actual earnings? An average of earnings for the past several years? Or a projection of earnings for this next year based on the latest (quarterly) earnings report? Since most analysts would argue for the latter approach, let's discuss its use.

Firms listed on stock exchanges issue financial reports of quarterly earnings per share. But P-E ratio calculations conventionally require a 12 month (annual) earnings figure. So, to use the current quarterly (3 month) earnings figure as the relevant earnings information, we first need to annualize the quarterly earnings figure for use in the denominator of the P-E ratio. This is done by multiplying the quarterly earnings by 4. If earnings for the current period are $1, the corresponding annualized earnings are $4. Starting with the quarterly earnings per share figures shown in column 3 in Table 15.12 we multiply these figures by 4 to annualize the earnings. The results of this annualization procedure are shown in Table 15.12 for the first two quarters of 1987. For example, the annualized earnings corresponding to the first quarter of 1987 are 4($1.98) = $7.92; the annualized earnings corresponding to the second quarter of 1987 are 4($0.78) = $3.12, etc. The remainder of the annualized earnings are determined in the same way.

		TABLE 15.12 Quarterly Earnings and Their Annualized Counterparts	
COLUMN 1 YEAR	COLUMN 2 QUARTER	COLUMN 3 EARNINGS PER SHARE Dollars	COLUMN 4 ANNUALIZED EARNINGS PER SHARE Dollars
1987	1	1.98	7.92
	2	0.78	3.12
	3	0.48	
	4	1.76	
1988	1	2.10	
	2	0.80	
	3	0.58	
	4	2.02	
1989	1	2.10	
	2	0.75	
	3	0.56	
	4	1.84	
1990	1	2.50	
	2	0.78	
	3	0.62	
	4	2.10	
1991	1	2.75	
	2	1.05	
	3	0.70	
	4	2.50	

But are these simply constructed annualized earnings figures appropriate to perform effective P-E ratio analyses for determining which stocks to buy? The problem is that quarterly earnings figures typically are subject to strong seasonal influence, and annualizing the quarterly figures simply reinforces that influence. For instance, if annualization is based upon earnings for a peak quarter, the annualized figure will be too high. If based on earnings for a trough quarter, the annualized earnings will be too low, etc. The naive financial analyst who uses annualized earnings for P-E ratio analysis without adjusting for these seasonal influences is really in for a surprise!

One solution is to deseasonalize the earnings figures that are to be used in the denominator of the P-E ratio. By deseasonalizing, the disruptive influences of seasonality and random factors from quarterly earnings are eliminated. In the financial jargon, this is known as *normalizing*. Normalized earnings are the values security analysts use to construct P-E ratios.

We'll now illustrate the use of time series techniques that allow us to obtain normalized quarterly earnings—the component of quarterly earnings that remains once the disruptive seasonal and random components of earnings have been removed.

Normalized Quarterly Earnings
Deseasonalization of the original (unadjusted) quarterly earnings series to obtain a normalized series can be accomplished by the centered ratio-to-moving average method. Table 15.13 shows the calculations.

Column 5 Values in column 4 are divided by 4 to give the centered moving average values, Y_t^*.

Column 6 Column 2 values are divided by their corresponding column 5 values. This gives the original-to-moving average ratio series (Y_t/Y_t^*) shown in column 6.

The seasonal indexes are calculated in Table 15.14 using the ratio-to-moving average series. Then, in Table 15.15, we obtain the normalized (i.e., deseasonalized) quarterly earnings series. To do this, we take the original quarterly earnings series in column 2, and divide that series by the appropriate seasonal index, to obtain the deseasonalized series shown in column 3. The

TABLE 15.13	Seasonal Relatives Series for Quarterly Earnings				
COLUMN 1 QUARTER t	COLUMN 2 UNADJUSTED QUARTERLY EARNINGS PER SHARE Y_t, Dollars	COLUMN 3 4 QUARTER MOVING TOTAL	COLUMN 4 4 QUARTER CENTERED MOVING TOTAL	COLUMN 5 4 QUARTER CENTERED MOVING AVERAGE Y_t^*	COLUMN 6 ORIGINAL-TO-MOVING AVERAGE RATIO Y_t / Y_t^*
1	1.98				
2	0.78				
3	0.48	5.00	5.06	1.265	0.3794
4	1.76	5.12	5.13	1.2825	1.3723
5	2.10	5.14	5.19	1.2975	1.6185
6	0.80	5.24	5.37	1.3425	0.5959
7	0.58	5.50	5.50	1.375	0.4218
8	2.02	5.50	5.475	1.36875	1.4758
9	2.10	5.45	5.44	1.36	1.5441
10	0.75	5.43	5.34	1.335	0.5618
11	0.56	5.25	5.45	1.3625	0.4110
12	1.84	5.65	5.665	1.41265	1.2992
13	2.50	5.68	5.71	1.4275	1.7513
14	0.78	5.74	5.87	1.4675	0.5315
15	0.62	6.00	6.125	1.53125	0.4049
16	2.10	6.25	6.385	1.59625	1.3156
17	2.75	6.52	6.56	1.64	1.6768
18	1.05	6.60	6.80	1.7	0.6176
19	0.70	7.00			
20	2.50				

TABLE 15.14	Calculating Seasonal Indexes			
YEAR	Q_1	Q_2	Q_3	Q_4
1	—	—	(L)0.3794	1.3723
2	1.6185	0.5959	(H)0.4218	(H)1.4758
3	(L)1.5441	0.5618	0.4110	(L)1.2992
4	(H)1.7513	(L)0.5315	0.4049	1.3156
5	1.6768	(H)0.6176		
	Modified Means			
	1.6477	0.5789	0.4080	1.3440

Sum of means = 3.9786
Adjustment factor = $\frac{4.0000}{3.9786}$ = 1.00538
Seasonal indexes
  Q_1: 1.6477 × 1.00538 = 1.6566
  Q_2: 0.5789 × 1.00538 = 0.5820
  Q_3: 0.4080 × 1.00538 = 0.4102
  Q_4: 1.3440 × 1.00538 = 1.3512
                     4.0000

Note: The (L) and (H) symbols designate the high and low figures eliminated in each column.

values in column 3 are the normalized quarterly earnings per share we seek; changes in these figures represent earnings changes not attributable to seasonal factors. An annualized projection made using this deseasonalization procedure will give an appropriate value for the denominator of a projected P-E ratio. For example, dividing the quarterly EPS figure by its seasonal index and multiplying values in this series by 4 gives the normalized annualized earnings per share series, the first two values of which are given in column 4 of Table 15.15. Now compare these two values in column 4 of Table 15.15 to their counterparts (before deseasonalization) in column 4 of Table 15.12. We see that normalizing has substantially reduced the first value but raised the second. In the Checkpoint Exercises that follow, you will be asked to continue this process.

TABLE 15.15 Normalized (Deseasonalized) Quarterly Earnings per Share (EPS)			
COLUMN 1 QUARTER	COLUMN 2 UNADJUSTED QUARTERLY EPS Dollars	COLUMN 3 NORMALIZED QUARTERLY EPS Dollars	COLUMN 4 NORMALIZED ANNUALIZED EPS Dollars
1	1.98	1.20	4.78
2	0.78	1.34	5.36
3	0.48	1.17	
4	1.76	1.30	
5	2.10	1.27	
6	0.80	1.37	
7	0.58	1.41	
8	2.02	1.49	
9	2.10	1.27	
10	0.75	1.29	
11	0.56	1.37	
12	1.84	1.36	
13	2.50	1.51	
14	0.78	1.34	
15	0.62	1.51	
16	2.10	1.55	
17	2.75		
18	1.05		
19	0.70		
20	2.50		

Checkpoint Exercises

1. Complete the procedure begun in column 3 of Table 15.15.

2. Complete the procedure begun in column 4 of Table 15.15.

3. Compare the normalized values of column 4 of Table 15.15 to their counterparts (before deseasonalization) in column 4 of Table 15.12. Comment.

WENDY'S TIME SERIES ANALYSIS

The performance of Wendy's sales over a decade from 1976 to 1985 had been very impressive, going from $65.6 million in 1976 to $1,128.6 million in 1985. But starting in 1986 there has been a series of disappointing years. Wendy's first encountered difficulties with the introduction of a new breakfast line, and then competition in the hamburger business heated up. Wendy's ill-fated omelet breakfast line was unpopular, being perceived as expensive, slow to prepare, and difficult to eat. By concentrating its resources on the morning menu to stimulate breakfast sales, Wendy's allowed the competition in the "hamburger wars," with their aggressive advertising, to erode Wendy's basic hamburger business. After stalling in 1986 ($1,128.6 million in 1985 to $1,149.7 million in 1986), Wendy's sales actually showed a decline from 1987 to 1990 as shown in Table 15.16. How much of a sales shortfall does this represent compared to Wendy's good years?

A starting point in developing a plan for renewed growth is for Wendy's to evaluate how much damage they have suffered. To find out, Wendy's must calculate how much successful growth they have been experiencing historically, prior to the recent stagnation; then, they must project that growth to the 1986 period and compare the 1986 projection to the actual 1986 figure. With shortfall figures available, Wendy's can see how much of a recovery is needed to put them back on track. The path of growth of Wendy's sales for the 10 years from 1976–1985 can be seen from the graph presented in Figure 15.11.

TABLE 15.16	Wendy's Annual Sales Data		
YEAR	**SALES**	**YEAR**	**SALES**
	Million Dollars		**Million Dollars**
1976	65.6	1984	944.8
1977	114.2	1985	1128.6
1978	197.7	1986	1149.7
1979	274.0	1987	1058.9
1980	350.0	1988	1062.6
1981	490.4	1989	1069.7
1982	607.6	1990	1025.0
1983	720.4		

Is a linear trend a proper fit for the data despite the curvature observed? That is, are sales, on average, increasing a given amount on a yearly basis? To find out a linear trend regression is performed with sales the dependent variable, Y, and time the independent variable, t. The values of t start at $t = 1$ for 1976 and continue to $t = 10$ for 1985. The fitted linear trend equation would be

$$\hat{Y} = a + bt$$

where $\hat{Y}$ = Sales trend figures and t = Time, $t = 1, \ldots, 10$.

Figure 15.11
Wendy's sales growth, 1976–1985

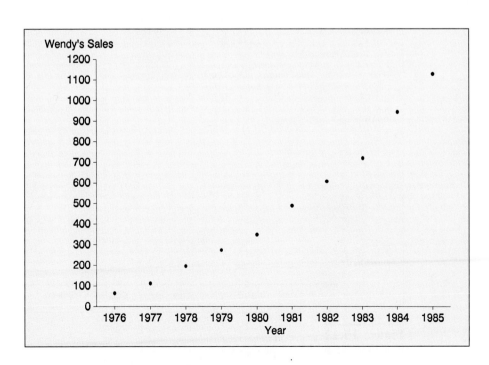

The MINITAB regression results in Figure 15.12 appear to show that the variable time explains Wendy's dollar sales very well. The computed t ratio for the time coefficient has an impressive value of 14.05 and r^2 (adjusted) is 95.6%. Although these statistics appear to indicate a good fit between sales and the passage of time, can the relationship be used to reliably predict sales for a given time period? That judgment depends on the behavior of the regression residuals. If the residuals follow a random pattern, the t ratio, the r^2 value, and the estimated trend equation may be relied upon for predicting new Y values.

Figure 15.12 also shows the residual plot for the linear trend regression with the residuals (standardized for ease of presentation) on the vertical axis and fitted Y on the horizontal axis. The obvious horseshoe shape of the path of the plotted residuals tells us that the linear fit is grossly inappropriate, despite the high t value and high r^2.

Recognizing that fitting a linear trend is inadequate, how do we go about fitting a trend? Looking at Figure 15.11, we see that Wendy's sales over the years 1976–1985 tend to curve up, suggesting that perhaps Wendy's sales are growing at an increasing pace from year to year. To model this curvature, a quadratic trend equation, $\hat{Y} = a + b_1 t + b_2 t^2$, with the prediction variable time, t, and time squared, t^2, was fitted to the 10 years of sales data. Figure 15.13 shows the multiple regression commands and results for the quadratic trend fitting.

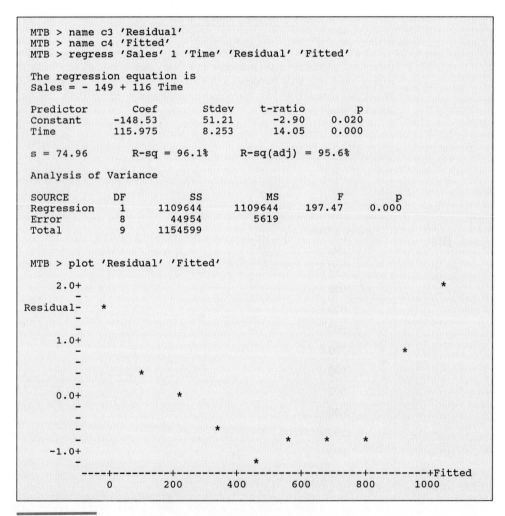

Figure 15.12
MINITAB for Wendy's linear trend regression

```
MTB > let c3=c2**2
MTB > name c3 'Timesq'
MTB > name c4 'Residual'
MTB > name c5 'Fitted'
MTB > regress 'Sales' 2 'Time' 'Timesq' 'Residual' 'Fitted';
SUBC> predict 11,121.

The regression equation is
Sales = 48.0 + 17.7 Time + 8.93 Timesq

Predictor        Coef        Stdev      t-ratio          p
Constant        48.02        23.55         2.04      0.081
Time           17.696         9.836        1.80      0.115
Timesq         8.9345        0.8715       10.25      0.000

s = 20.02        R-sq = 99.8%       R-sq(adj) = 99.7%

Analysis of Variance

SOURCE          DF           SS           MS          F          p
Regression       2       1151792       575896    1436.17      0.000
Error            7          2807          401
Total            9       1154599

     Fit  Stdev.Fit          95% C.I.            95% P.I.
 1323.75       23.55    (1268.04,1379.46)   (1250.63,1396.87) X

X  denotes a row with X values away from the center

MTB > plot 'Residual' 'Fitted'


    1.2+
       -               *
Residual-                  *            *                  *        *
       -
       -
    0.0+
       -          *                           *
       -                        *
       -      *
       -
   -1.2+
       -
       -
       -
       -
   -2.4+                                           *
       -
       +---------+---------+---------+---------+---------+--Fitted
       0        200       400       600       800      1000
```

Figure 15.13
MINITAB for Wendy's quadratic trend regression

Testing the significance of the regression coefficient for the t^2 variable by a one-sided hypothesis test at the $\alpha = .01$ significance level, we find the calculated t ratio of 10.25 far exceeds the Appendix Table VII value of $t_{(.01,7)} = 2.998$. Testing the significance of the whole equation at the $\alpha = .01$ level of significance, we find that the calculated F of 1436.17 far exceeds the Appendix Table IXb value of $F_{(.01,2,7)} = 9.55$. Compared to the previous linear trend fitting, the quadratic trend fitting shows positive gains on two fronts: (1) a dramatic reduction from 74.96 to 20.02 in the value of S_e, the standard deviation of residuals (a key component in constructing prediction intervals of new Y values) and (2) an improvement in the explanatory power (R^2 adjusted) of the fitted equation from 96.1% to 99.7%. (Note: A model of only the t^2 variable also shows improvement over the linear trend model, but the gains are more modest.)

But are the gains in these regression measures of fit (r^2 and S_e) still window dressing? Again, that issue rests on the behavior of the residuals. A close look at the residual plot in Figure 15.13 shows the residuals behaving more in conformity with the assumption of random behavior. With random behavior of the residuals confirmed, we can validly use the fitted quadratic equation for forecasting.

Let's now make a point prediction of Wendy's 1986 sales, assuming that Wendy's maintained its 1976–1985 growth trend into 1986. Using the just estimated quadratic trend equation to represent the 10 year growth trend, we can obtain a sales forecast by plugging into the fitted equation the values of t and t^2 for 1986. For 1986, $t = 11$ and $t^2 = 121$; therefore,

$$\hat{Y}_{11} = 48.02 + 17.696t + 8.9345t^2$$
$$= 48.02 + 17.696(11) + 8.9345(121)$$
$$= 48.02 + 194.66 + 1081.0745 = 1323.75$$

Comparing this forecast figure of 1323.75 to the actual 1986 Wendy's sales figure of $1,149.7 million, we notice that the gap is $174.05 million ($1,323.75 - 1,149.7$). When compared to the level of 1985 sales in percentage terms, the dollar gap becomes $(174.05/1323.75) \times 100 = 13.1\%$. If management's goal is to make up the gap, it can now start planning for the resources necessary.

The same forecasting result on Wendy's projected 1986 sales can be obtained from MINITAB. This was done in Figure 15.13 by executing the subcommand PREDICT after the REGRESS command and specifying the values for t and t^2. The numerical prediction 1323.75 is shown on the last line of the MINITAB output under the heading "FIT," along with its 95% prediction interval.

Wendy's Student Exercises

1. Assume that Wendy's had maintained its 1976–1985 growth path into 1990. Based on the quadratic trend equation fitted for Wendy's sales for the years 1976–1985, make a point prediction for 1990 sales.

2. Compare the actual 1990 Wendy's sales figure of $1,025.0 million to the point prediction made in Exercise 1. Calculate the size of the sales gap that has developed in absolute terms and also in percentage terms relative to the 1985 sales figure.

DECISION 16 THEORY

Headline Issue

THE INVENTORY CURSE: PRAYING FOR A BLIZZARD

by Jeff Lyons

"Lookit all this stuff," Feinstein said. Inside all the boxes were 20,000 pairs of men's, ladies', and children's winter footwear, all rubberized and waterproof. Enough galoshes, rubbers, and boots to keep every person in a good-sized town as dry as toast while winter storms rage around them.

Twenty thousand pairs of winter footwear that Jack Feinstein is about to get stuck with because the deity that makes it snow has been taking the season off this year.

"I need a big snow," Feinstein said mournfully. "Seven, 8, 9 inches, maybe. I'm not hoping for 90 inches, like last year. Just one good blizzard."

In July, when he ordered $250,000 worth of rubber footwear from his suppliers, most of whom are foreign importers, things looked bullish. Another snowy winter seemed in the offing, and the retail shoe stores Feinstein sells to were almost sure to have customers beating their doors down for galoshes and boots.

In addition, Feinstein reasoned happily, the stores were starting from scratch. They had no leftover stock from last year because the horrible winter had left their shelves cleaned out.

What Feinstein expected were big initial orders and then a season of steady profitable repeat orders. What he got was $140,000 worth of initial orders and then nothing.

"I haven't had an order in ages," he said. He dug into an open carton and pulled out a blue pair of "Moon Boots," huge things manufactured in Korea. He ran his fingers slowly over the ridged black soles, with a "why me?" expression on his face.

"In the shoe business," he said, "the stores buy their opening needs and they expect the wholesaler to hold their stock for them the rest of the season."

"If there's a lot of play, with customers demanding a certain item, they call the wholesaler up and reorder. If there's no play," he sighed, gesturing sweepingly at his floor full of inventory, "then the wholesaler's left holding the bag. That's me."

Jack Feinstein knows well the dire consequences that can follow from decisions made in the face of uncertainty. He can't control the weather, and the galoshes manufacturers won't wait until winter for his order. So he has to decide in the summer how many pairs to order for the following winter, take his chances on the winter weather, and live with his decision even if it means he's the one left "holding the bag." If he wants to be a wholesaler in the shoe business, Jack Feinstein has to accept this business uncertainty. How he deals with the inescapable uncertainty, though, can greatly influence his success as a wholesaler. Fortunately, Jack Feinstein can be helped in his ordering and inventory decisions by modern business decision theory.

Overview

Important analytical techniques have been developed to handle many types of management decisions. One pivotal tool is *decision theory analysis,* or DTA, as it has come to be known in management circles. It is of particular importance because of its flexibility and basic simplicity.

We shall return to Jack Feinstein's problem in the applied case at the end of this chapter. By learning the methods of decision theory analysis discussed in this chapter, you should be able to handle basic decision problems of the kind encountered by Feinstein. That is, you should be able to correctly balance the unwelcome risk of leftover inventory against the risk of running short of inventory, and thereby maximize the opportunity for profit available to you. You should also be able to incorporate the possibility of new information into your decision analysis, and determine how much it would be worth paying to receive it.

16.1
INTRODUCTION

Five essential elements comprise every decision theory problem. One element is the set of decision choices available to the decision maker. These choices are called **acts.** Another element is the set of possible occurrences that the chosen act must anticipate; these are the **events** of a decision problem. Corresponding to the events are their respective *event probabilities.* The fourth element is the consequence, or result, of a particular combination of act and event; this consequence is called a **payoff.** The last element is the *objective of the decision maker.* Let's look at these elements in the context of a simple, but classic, decision problem: whether or not to carry an umbrella. Table 16.1 displays the elements of the problem. The acts are indicated by the column headings; events are indicated by the row headings; payoffs are represented by the four entries in the table. This display is called a *payoff table.*

TABLE 16.1　Payoff Table for Umbrella Decision		
	ACT	
	A_1 **Carry Umbrella**	**A_2** **Don't Carry Umbrella**
EVENT　E_1 **Rainy Day**	Nuisance of umbrella, stay dry, C_1	No umbrella nuisance, get wet, C_2
E_2 **Not Rainy Day**	Nuisance of umbrella, stay dry, C_1	No umbrella nuisance, stay dry, C_3

In analyzing the decision problem, explicit answers must be given to the following five questions:

1. **What acts (decision choices) are available to the decision maker?** The acts are A_1, carry the umbrella, and A_2, don't carry it.
2. **What are the events (possible occurrences) that can directly affect the decision at hand?** The events are E_1, rain, and E_2, no rain.
3. **What probabilities are assigned to the events?** These probabilities depend on the weather forecast for the day.
4. **What are the payoffs (monetary or other consequences) corresponding to each act–event combination?** There are four combinations of acts and events, and each one has a different payoff. The payoffs are shown in the four entries

comprising the body of Table 16.1. The act–event combinations and their payoffs are:

a. *Carrying the umbrella on a rainy day:* The payoff is that the decision maker incurs the nuisance of carrying the umbrella, but stays dry. This combination is represented by the upper left-hand entry of Table 16.1 and is denoted C_1.

b. *Not carrying the umbrella on a rainy day:* The payoff is that the nuisance of the umbrella is avoided, but the decision maker gets wet. This combination is represented by the upper right-hand entry of Table 16.1 and is denoted C_2.

c. *Carrying the umbrella on a day with no rain:* The payoff is that the decision maker stays dry, but incurs the nuisance of carrying the umbrella. This combination is represented by the lower left-hand entry of Table 16.1. The payoff is identical to that which follows from carrying the umbrella on a rainy day, so we denote it by C_1.

d. *Not carrying the umbrella on a day with no rain:* The payoff is that the decision maker avoids the nuisance of carrying the umbrella and stays dry. This combination is represented by the lower right-hand entry of Table 16.1 and is denoted by C_3.

5. **What decision criterion will be used?** The decision criterion in this example will depend on the decision maker's attitude toward staying dry versus not incurring the nuisance of carrying an umbrella. For example, one criterion might be to choose the act that minimizes the risk of getting wet. In most of the remainder of this chapter, monetary values will be a key factor in the decision criterion.

16.2
HOW DECISION THEORY ANALYSIS WORKS

The approach to decision theory analysis (DTA) described in this chapter is one made popular by business decision theorists at the Harvard Business School. It utilizes the *decision tree technique.* A decision tree is a graphic device presenting the series of decision choices available to the decision maker together with the events that are related to these choices. The decision tree consists of *forks* and *branches* that relate events to acts. The branches on the decision tree indicate the acts and events being considered. Each branch represents a particular act or a particular event. Thus, in the umbrella problem, we'll have one set of branches denoting whether we carry the umbrella (A_1) or don't carry it (A_2). We'll have a second set of branches denoting the weather: rain (E_1), no rain (E_2).

A fork is the point on the decision tree at which we find two or more branches, indicating the act or event alternatives at a particular point on the tree. The symbol used for the fork indicates whether the branches emerging from it represent acts or events, so we can have **act forks** or **event forks.** A box is used to indicate act choices, and a circle to represent event possibilities. In Figure 16.1, the box represents the choice between carry the umbrella (act A_1) and don't carry the umbrella (act A_2). The circle represents the alternative event possibilities, rain (event E_1) or no rain (event E_2).

The set of acts or events that each fork represents are both mutually exclusive and exhaustive. For example, the events E_1, rainy day, and E_2, not rainy day, are mutually exclusive because they can't occur simultaneously. They are exhaustive because one of them must occur. When an event fork has several branches, it resembles a hand-held fan, and thus is referred to as an *event fan.* Listed on every branch exiting from an event fork (fan) is a probability; it is the probability of the event identified at the end of the branch. Since these events are mutually exclusive and exhaustive, it follows that

Figure 16.1
Illustration of the act fork and event fork used in decision trees

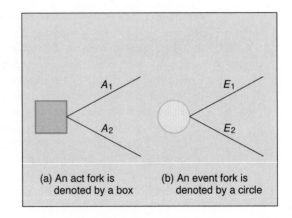

(a) An act fork is denoted by a box

(b) An event fork is denoted by a circle

Figure 16.2
A decision tree with one act fork and two event forks leading to five payoff possibilities

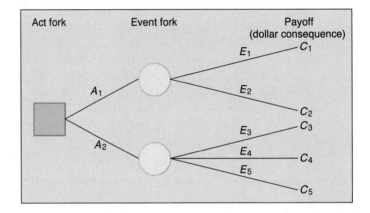

the event probabilities shown on the branches exiting from each event fork must sum to 1. Note, however, that these probabilities are difficult to assess in many cases; indeed, making good probability assessments is often the most difficult step in finding a solution to the decision problem.

Each act–event branch path ends (on the right-hand side) in a *consequence*. In most business decision problems, the consequences are expressible in financial terms, which we shall describe as a *dollar consequence* or payoff. The simple decision tree shown in Figure 16.2 has one act fork (with branches A_1 and A_2) and two event forks (one with branches E_1 and E_2, the other with branches E_3, E_4, and E_5). At the end of each branch path is its dollar consequence (labeled C_1–C_5).

Let's look at an example involving a hypothetical, but realistic, business decision.

■ **EXAMPLE 16.1**

Decision on a California Real Estate Opportunity

A California real estate broker has an interesting land acquisition opportunity. The broker has been offered a parcel of prime land at an advantageous price of $500,000, with a $100,000 down payment. This land is ideally suited for commercial development, but is presently restricted to residential use. The broker assesses the chances as only 50-50 that the local government will rezone the parcel for commercial development. In case of a rezoning denial, the parcel would not be purchased and the down payment of $100,000 would be forfeited. Since other potential buyers in the area have been contacted also, the broker feels an immediate decision must be made. Previous sales figures on comparable parcels of land suggest that it could be resold to investors for $800,000 if the local government will rezone for commercial development. Thus, the profit on purchase and resale would be $800,000 − $500,000 = $300,000. The decision is whether to buy the property. We shall assume that further negotiation with the seller will not improve the terms of the offer.

The elements of the decision in this problem are as follows:

Acts	**Events**
A_1 = Buy parcel	E_1 = Rezoning application approved
A_2 = Don't buy parcel	E_2 = Rezoning application denied

Payoffs (Dollar Consequences)

A_1 and $E_1 \rightarrow C_1$: $300,000   The last two combinations would never take
A_1 and $E_2 \rightarrow C_2$:   −$100,000   place, because the rezoning application would
A_2 and $E_1 \rightarrow C_3$: $0   be submitted only if the parcel is purchased.
A_2 and $E_2 \rightarrow C_4$: $0   However, the payoffs are included for
completeness.

Probabilities of Events

$P(E_1) = .5$
$P(E_2) = .5$ Reflecting the 50-50 chance

A decision tree for this real estate problem is shown in Figure 16.3. The act fork branches on the tree indicate the choice between buying or not buying the land. The event fork branches indicate the approval or denial of the rezoning to commercial development. Note that there is no event fork for the act branch, A_2, since this act has a dollar consequence of $0 regardless of what decision the local government would render on a rezoning application.

CONSTRUCTING THE DECISION TREE

Assigning a 50-50 chance to approval of rezoning implies that if the parcel is purchased, there is a 50% chance of obtaining $300,000 profit (i.e., if rezoning is approved) against an equal chance of losing $100,000 (i.e., if rezoning is denied). The elements of a simple decision problem like this one can be displayed in a payoff table, as in Table 16.2. However, to analyze the decision problem we shall use the decision tree in Figure 16.3.

Figure 16.3
Decision tree illustrating the act-event forks and dollar consequences

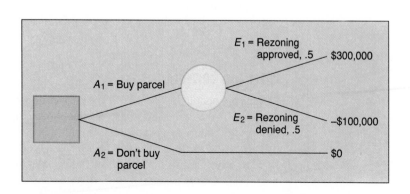

TABLE 16.2 Payoff Table for Decision Tree of Figure 16.3			
PROBABILITY	**EVENT**	**ACT**	
		A_1 Buy Parcel	A_2 Don't Buy Parcel
.5	E_1: Rezoning approved	Profit: $300,000.00	Profit: $0
.5	E_2: Rezoning denied	Profit: $-$100,000.00	Profit: $0

We can summarize the steps in constructing a decision tree as follows:

Step 1
Draw a square representing the act fork and from it exiting to the right in a fan shape draw one straight line (branch) for each mutually exclusive action possibility. Label each branch according to the act it represents. In Figure 16.3, the two act branches are labeled "Buy Parcel" and "Don't Buy Parcel."

Step 2
At the end of each act branch draw a circle representing the event fork (if any) for that act. From this event fork circle, exiting to the right in fan shape, draw one branch for each event possibility that meets the following two conditions:
   a. it affects the consequences of the action taken, but
   b. is not under the control of the decision maker.
Label each event branch.
In Figure 16.3 there is only one circle representing an event fork. From this circle two event branches exit. One branch is labeled "Rezoning Approved" and the other is labeled "Rezoning Denied."

Step 3
Assign to each event the probability that best represents the event's chance of occurrence. Put this probability directly above the branch representing that event. Check to be sure that the sum of probabilities assigned to the branches on an event fan equals one. Do this for every event fork. In Figure 16.3, both event branches have a .50 probability written above them, reflecting the 50-50 probability split between rezoning approved and rezoning denied.

Step 4
At the right end of each act-event branch put the dollar consequence (payoff) corresponding to its act and event combination. In Figure 16.3, the dollar consequences shown are $300,000, $-$100,000 and $0, the same values shown in the cells of Payoff Table 16.2.

DECISION CRITERIA
Which act should be preferred? The answer depends on the criterion used to compare payoffs. In the real estate example, the choice among decision criteria should reflect the broker's attitude toward the different financial consequences the payoffs represent. Listed below are four different decision criteria that exemplify different rules decision makers might follow in a given situation, depending upon their attitudes toward risk.

Maximize the minimum payoff. This criterion is pessimistic. It focuses only on the worst scenarios; that is, on the worst possible consequences of each act. It assumes that one of these worst payoffs will occur and then says "pick the best of the worst." This criterion is known as the **maximin** criterion. You can also think of it as the "play it safe" criterion. Believers in Murphy's Law (whatever can go wrong will go wrong) would probably appreciate the maximin criterion. In the real estate example, the maximin criterion tells the broker not to buy the parcel, since the payoff ($0) for that act is greater than the $-\$100,000$ minimum payoff for the other act (buy the parcel).

Advocates of the maximin approach could point to the savings and loan industry as an example of what can happen when businesses expose themselves to great risk and don't prepare for the worst. After deregulation of the industry, many savings and loan companies chased high interest returns, seemingly disregarding the high-risk nature of their investments. Failures have been widespread and taxpayers are bailing the industry out at a cost of hundreds of billions of dollars.

Maximize the maximum payoff. This criterion is optimistic. It focuses only on the best possible scenario; that is, it focuses only on the best possible consequences of each act. It assumes that one of these will be the payoff. This criterion is known as the **maximax** criterion. You can also think of it as the "go for broke" criterion. In the real estate example, the maximax criterion tells the broker to buy the parcel, since the maximum payoff for that act ($300,000) is greater than the maximum payoff for the other act. You might hear a proponent of the maximax approach say something like, "There are winners and losers in life and the winners are people who go for an opportunity whenever they see it, and then put everything they have behind their drive to bring the opportunity to fruition." Clearly, the maximax approach is for risk takers, people who are willing to shrug off even great risk to keep a steady eye on their goal. In this respect, a maximax advocate might be likened to a high-wire trapeze artist, who knows that too much looking at the ground below will cause the very fall that must be avoided.

Minimize the maximum regret. In between the extremes of maximin and maximax, the broker might consider a third alternative known as the **minimax regret** criterion. With this criterion, we take a "what if" approach to each event; that is, we ask, "If this event occurs, which act would leave us best off and which worst off?" Then, taking a pessimistic perspective, we determine the difference in payoffs between the two, called our (hindsight) *regret.* For example, in the umbrella problem, we would take each event separately:

Event E_1: Rain	**Regret**
Act A_1: Carry umbrella	None
Act A_2: Don't carry umbrella	Get wet

Event E_2: No Rain	**Regret**
Act A_1: Carry umbrella	Incur nuisance of carrying umbrella
Act A_2: Don't carry umbrella	None

The regret idea goes beyond Murphy's Law (whatever can go wrong will go wrong); it assumes that fate always is cruel to the decision maker. That is, fate waits until the decision maker has chosen an act and then selects the event that will have the worst consequence for the decision maker. The solution is to choose the act that will minimize the maximum regret. In the umbrella problem, the solution depends on whether you think it is worse to get wet or to incur the nuisance of carrying an umbrella.

In the real estate example, suppose we choose act A_1, buy parcel. There is no regret for the act–event combination A_1 and E_1, rezoning approved, since buying the parcel is the best act if rezoning is approved. There is a regret of $100,000 for the act–event combination A_1 and E_2, rezoning denied. This regret occurs because the $100,000 down payment is forfeited in the event of denial of rezoning. Thus, we have

Act A_1: Buy Parcel

Event	Regret
E_1: Rezoning approved	None
E_2: Rezoning denied	$100,000

Now we turn to act A_2, don't buy parcel. There is a regret of $300,000 for the act–event combination A_2 and E_1, rezoning approved. This represents the lost opportunity to make $300,000, given rezoning approval. ("Now that I find out that rezoning was approved, I sure wish I had bought the parcel!") The act–event combination A_2 and E_2, rezoning denied, has no regret, since not buying represents the best act in the case of rezoning denial. Thus, we have

Act A_2: Don't Buy Parcel

Event	Regret
E_1: Rezoning approved	$300,000
E_2: Rezoning denied	None

Now, for each act we identify the maximum regret. Thus, for the act A_1, buy parcel, the maximum regret is $100,000, occurring if rezoning is denied. For the act A_2, don't buy parcel, the maximum regret is $300,000, occurring if rezoning is approved.

Maximum Regret

Act A_1: Buy parcel	$100,000
Act A_2: Don't buy parcel	$300,000

Therefore, A_1, buy parcel, with maximum regret of $100,000, is the act that minimizes the maximum regret.

Expectation rule. A feature common to the first three approaches is that they all reach a decision about what to do without any weighing of the probabilities of what might happen. That is, they ignore the probabilities of what could actually occur. However, a decision maker might believe in "playing the averages" and be neutral toward taking risks. This risk posture leads to the **expectation rule of monetary consequences.** The major part of this chapter will be devoted to the application of this rule.

In the real estate problem, the optimal action depends upon the decision criterion used. If the broker wants to "play it safe" by maximizing the minimum payoff (maximin), then the parcel should not be purchased. [The worst (and only) loss is $0 if the parcel isn't purchased, compared to a worst payoff of −$100,000 if the parcel is purchased.] The maximum payoff is $300,000 if the parcel is purchased compared to $0 gain if it is not purchased. On the other hand, if the broker wants to "go for broke" (maximax), the parcel should be acquired, because the maximum payoff from this act ($300,000) exceeds the maximum payoff of $0 obtainable from choosing the other action (i.e., don't buy). The minimax regret approach leads to the same decision. If the broker wants to "play the averages" (expectation rule), further calculations are required. These are explained in the next section.

Whichever decision criterion is used, the objective of the decision theory analysis is to determine which act is most advantageous according to that criterion. This act is called the *optimal act*. Note that in the case of the maximin, maximax, and minimax regret criteria, probabilities aren't relevant. Only with the expectation rule do probabilities enter into the decision.

PRACTICE EXERCISE

16.1 For the following payoff table:
   a. What is the maximax decision?
   b. What is the maximin decision?
   c. What is the minimax regret decision?

		ACT			
		1	2	3	4
	1	45	−35	0	120
EVENT	2	20	−20	10	80
	3	75	−85	40	30

EXPECTATION RULE

If we use this widely followed criterion for solving DTA problems, we choose the act that produces the highest expected value of payoff. Computationally, the expected value of an act is analogous to the calculation for the expected value of a discrete random variable X. From Chapter 5, we know this expected value is given by

$$E(X) = \Sigma\ [XP(X)]$$

where the product of the value of the variable and its probability are summed over the possible values of X. Using profit as the payoff resulting from an act, the expected profit of an act is found by calculating

$$E(\text{Profit}) = \Sigma[(\text{Profit})(\text{Probability of that profit})]$$

where the summation is taken over each event branch of the event fork circle following the act. This expected profit is called the **expected monetary value (EMV)** of the act.

Before beginning our formal analysis of the decision tree, we must recognize that the EMV of an act can be expressed in terms of the decision tree. To find the EMV of an act, we find the EMV of the event fan branches exiting from the square representing the act fork. (The event fan corresponds to the right-hand side of the above equation.) This interpretation of EMV in terms of event fans is necessary to understand the intermediate steps in the calculation of the EMV of an act.

We can write the expression for the EMV of a particular event fork along a path originating with act i as:

Expected Monetary Value

$$\text{EMV} = \sum_{j=1}^{k} \pi_{i,j} p_{i,j} \qquad (16\text{-}1)$$

where

$\pi_{i,j}$ represents the profit if act i is chosen and event j occurs; thus, $\pi_{i,j}$ is a *conditional* profit.

$p_{i,j}$ is the probability of the occurrence of event possibility j, given the selection of act i; thus, $p_{i,j}$ is a *conditional* probability.

To solve a decision problem using the expectation rule, we find the act with the highest EMV—this is the optimal act. Five steps are required:

Step 1

Starting at the extreme right end of the uppermost decision tree fork, compute the expected dollar consequence that corresponds to that event fork. This is accomplished as follows:

a. For each branch exiting from the event fork, find the product of the probability for each branch and its dollar consequence. For example, the uppermost branch in Figure 16.3 has a product of

$$(.5)(\$300,000) = \$150,000$$

The lower branch on that same event fork has a product of

$$(.5)(-\$100,000) = -\$50,000$$

b. Sum the products obtained in Step 1a. This sum is the EMV for the event fork. For the event fork following the act A_1, buy parcel, in Figure 16.3, the sum is $\$150,000 + (-\$50,000) = \$100,000$. The EMV calculations can be summarized as

$$\text{EMV} = \pi_{1.1} p_{1.1} + \pi_{1.2} p_{1.2}$$
$$= (\$300,000)(.5) + (-\$100,000)(.5) = \$100,000$$

Step 2

Replace the event fork by its EMV. Do this by putting the EMV calculated in Step 1b inside the circle representing the event fork. This substitution is accomplished in Figure 16.4 by placing the calculated EMV of $\$100,000$ in the event fork circle and then eliminating the two branches exiting to the right from this event fork. Thus, the encircled value ($\$100,000$) is the expected payoff for the act branch A_1 leading into the event fork. In the real estate example, there is only one event fork (local governmental approval or denial of the rezoning) on the tree. If there had been several event forks on this tree, the same procedure would have been repeated on each fork.

Figure 16.4
Reduced decision tree by
applying the expectation rule

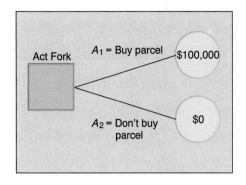

Step 3

Moving leftward on the decision tree, repeat Steps 1 and 2 for each event fork encountered enroute to an act fork. That is, replace every event fork by its EMV, taking care to place the EMV in the event fork's circle of origin. In the real estate problem, there are no other event forks corresponding to the A_1, buy parcel, branch so this step is not needed.

Step 4

When an act fork is encountered, select the act having the highest EMV value inside the event fork circle at the end points of the branches. This act is optimal at that fork, and the encircled value is its EMV. This is the "best" action to take, according to the expectation rule.

Step 5

Return to the right end of the decision tree and repeat Steps 1–4 as necessary, moving down the tree until all event forks have been assigned an EMV, and the optimal act overall has been chosen. Note that the EMV of the act A_2, don't buy parcel (with no event fork), is a certain value of $0. Therefore, $0 is circled for this act. The act fork in the real estate example now consists of a branch with an EMV of $100,000 and a branch with an EMV of $0. Applying the decision rule, act A_1, buy parcel, maximizes the EMV and so is the optimal course of action. The analysis of the problem is now complete.

**PRACTICE
EXERCISE**   16.2

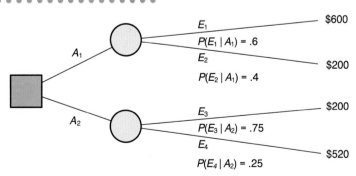

Given this decision tree:
a. What is the EMV of the upper event fork?
b. What is the EMV of act A_1?
c. What is the EMV of the lower event fork?
d. What is the EMV of act A_2?
e. Using the expectation rule, which is the optimal act?

E X E R C I S E S

16.1 Consider the following decision tree associated with a boxing promoter's decision of whether to schedule a championship match in an open-air stadium or an indoor arena.

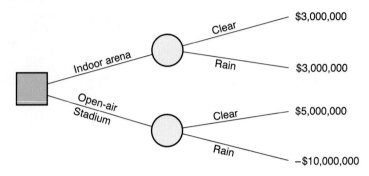

a. If $P(\text{Clear}) = .9$, what is the EMV of scheduling the open-air stadium?
b. If $P(\text{Clear}) = .9$, then, using the expectation rule, what is the best action?
c. What is the EMV of the optimal act?

▶ **16.2** The table condenses a business decision tree that includes an initial act fork followed by event alternatives. Values in the table represent profits (in thousands of dollars) corresponding to particular act–event combinations.

PROBABILITY	EVENT	ACT		
		A_1 BUY	A_2 LEASE	A_3 DON'T BUY OR LEASE
.3	E_1: Low demand	200	240	0
.3	E_2: Moderate demand	210	200	0
.4	E_3: High demand	160	120	0

a. Construct the decision tree from the information summarized in the table.
b. Applying the expectation rule, which act is optimal?
c. Since A_3, don't buy or lease, never gives a profit, should it always be eliminated as a possible choice?

16.3 The values in the table are the relevant conditional profits (in dollars) for a decision tree in which the starting act fork has three acts. Each act is subsequently followed by the three events of the event fork and its probabilities.

PROBABILITY	EVENT	ACT		
		A_1	A_2	A_3
.2	E_1	320	350	0
.2	E_2	220	40	356
.6	E_3	80	0	270

a. Draw the decision tree for the information presented in the table.
b. Determine the EMV for each act.
c. Applying the expectation rule, what is the optimal act (highest expected profit)?

▶ **16.4** The payoff table shows the dollar consequences corresponding to the combinations of three decision choices that are available and four events that are possible.

		ACTS		
		1	2	3
EVENT	1	45	−10	80
	2	10	0	40
	3	15	25	20
	4	5	−10	150

a. What is the maximin decision?
b. What is the maximax decision?
c. What is the minimax regret decision?

16.5 A gambler makes a bet where he loses $200 with probability .25, he loses $100 with probability .35, he wins $100 with probability .3, and he wins $600 with probability .1. The EMV is his decision criterion.
a. Draw a decision tree for this problem.
b. Should he make the bet? Explain.

16.6 Herb Lefkowicz is marketing manager of a company considering two new products for introduction to the industrial fasteners market. Development costs for product 1 are $95,000, and for product 2, the costs are $70,000. The success of these products depends on the general strength of the economy and on the consumers' reaction to the products. Three events summarize the possibilities: E_1 (good), E_2 (fair), and E_3 (poor). The company's profits after introducing product 1 only, product 2 only, or both products, are shown in the table (in thousands of dollars). The probabilities of the events are also shown. The company has four options: introduce neither product, introduce product 1 only, introduce product 2 only, or introduce both products.

PROBABILITY	EVENT	ACT			
		A_1 Neither	A_2 1 Only	A_3 2 Only	A_4 Both
.2	E_1	0	250	210	400
.5	E_2	0	120	160	195
.3	E_3	0	60	55	100

a. Construct a payoff table for this problem.
b. Construct a decision tree.
c. What is the best decision using the EMV as the criterion?
d. What is the EMV?

16.7 Banana Republic Engineering Company is trying to decide whether to ship some equipment now or wait until the threat of a dock strike is over. The relevant cost considerations involve two components: shipping costs and delay costs. These are shown in the table. The probabilities of a dock strike or no dock strike are p and $1 − p$, as indicated.

	SHIP NOW	WAIT
p: STRIKE	$6000	$600
$1 − p$: NO STRIKE	$1000	$1200

a. Convert the cost table to a payoff table by multiplying each cost by −1.
b. For which values of p does shipping now maximize the company's EMV (i.e., minimize its expected cost)?

16.3
GAMBLING AGAINST TIME: WAITING FOR DEFINITIVE INFORMATION

The decision analysis presented in Section 16.2 assumed that the decision had to be made quickly. It was based on the assumption that if the land is to be purchased by the broker, the decision to do so must be made now or the property may be lost to other potential buyers. In different situations, the pressure to make a decision quickly may not be as great. In these cases, the decision maker will want to consider the option of postponing the decision until crucial information has been obtained that will remove uncertainty from the decision. In the real estate problem, this postponement would certainly be the sensible thing to do if the offer on the property will remain open until the local government has decided whether to approve the rezoning application. That is the hitch, however; the seller may say that the offer will still be open only if someone hasn't accepted it first. In that case, uncertainty about whether the purchase offer will still be available should be incorporated into the decision analysis. This additional decision option (postponement) creates a new and different decision situation for analysis.

■ **EXAMPLE 16.2**

Question First, Act Later?

The California real estate broker wishes to incorporate into the decision analysis the possibility of applying for rezoning before acting on the purchase of the parcel. The broker knows that she is taking the risk that the deal will no longer be open by the time the rezoning answer comes. In fact, she thinks there is only a 30% chance that the government's rezoning decision will come while the opportunity to purchase the parcel is still available. Thus, by postponing the purchase decision until she has an answer on rezoning there is a 70% chance the answer won't do her any good. She will be closed out of the deal. However, on the positive side, the uncertainty surrounding two key events will be resolved before the broker acts on the parcel. That is, (1) the government will have either approved or refused the rezoning application, so this uncertainty will be resolved; and (2) it will be known whether the offer to buy the parcel is still open, so this source of uncertainty is also removed.

Let's consider the impact of having these two sources of uncertainty eliminated.

CONSTRUCTING THE DECISION TREE

The broker's new decision situation can be pictured by the decision tree shown in Figure 16.5. To the original decision tree given in Figure 16.3 we have added a new branch path, an information gathering route, which, if undertaken, precedes the buy–don't buy decision. Thus, the new decision tree has an act fork square with three branches (rather than two) existing from it—buy, don't buy, and wait for definitive information. The latter branch leads to an event fork (circle b) with two branches: information is favorable (rezoning approved) and information is unfavorable (rezoning denied).

What actions and what payoffs follow from these respective events? Let's evaluate the branch paths representing the act "wait for definitive information" shown in Figure 16.5. First, consider the combination of rezoning approval and of the offer to buy the parcel still open (shown in Figure 16.5 by the uppermost branch exiting from event fork circle d). This is the best of all worlds. The broker can now achieve a $300,000

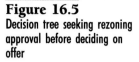

Figure 16.5
Decision tree seeking rezoning approval before deciding on offer

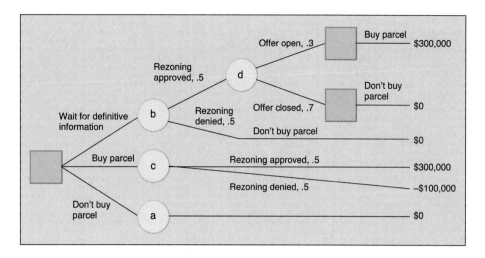

payoff of buying the property and reselling it after being rezoned for commercial development. While the "don't buy" alternative would still be available, it would not make sense to choose it, given that rezoning is approved (this is why no act branch is shown for it on the decision tree).

Second, suppose the offer to buy the parcel is no longer open; then there is really no longer a decision to make. The parcel is not purchased and the payoff is $0. This is shown by the bottom branch exiting from event circle d.

Third, suppose that after deciding to wait for definitive information, the news is unfavorable. That is, the local government denies the rezoning request (this is shown by the "rezoning denied" branch on event fork b in Figure 16.5). The real estate broker then quite obviously turns down the opportunity to acquire the parcel. This is why the "rezoning approval" branch leads directly to a decision to buy the parcel, and why the "rezoning denied" branch leads directly to a decision not to buy. Note that there is no need to evaluate a possible act if we are satisfied in advance that it is not going to be selected. Moreover, if the act is not going to be evaluated, it is not necessary to include it on the decision tree.

FOLDING BACK: THE KEY TO DECISION TREE ANALYSIS

The optimal act can be determined by the same procedure we followed in our earlier example. That is, we replace the branches from an event fork by the EMV of the event fork. Note, however, that the path of branches representing the new "wait for definitive information" option includes two event forks (circles b and d) in Figure 16.5.

Using the event probabilities shown in Figure 16.5, we can evaluate the series of events and decisions by a process known as *folding back the tree*. This process applies the expectation rule to successive stages of the decision tree. Working from right to left, the objective is to determine the optimal act by a process of elimination. The solution process is the same as that followed in the earlier version of this problem.

Step 1

The first event fork considered is the event fork d shown in Figure 16.5. It has two branches, so the expected value for this event fork is

$$\text{EMV of fork d} = .3(\$300,000) + .7(0)$$
$$= \$90,000$$

Step 2

The EMV of $90,000 is inserted inside the circle of event fork d and the two branches exiting from the circle are removed. This is shown on the right end of the uppermost branch path in Figure 16.6. Thus, the event fan is replaced by the EMV of $90,000.

Step 3

Now, moving left, the next event fan encountered is event fan b. The expected value operation is again repeated at this stage and computed to be

$$\text{EMV of fork b} = .5(\$90,000) + .5(0)$$
$$= \$45,000$$

Step 4

The EMV of $45,000 now summarizes event fork b and is placed in the circle of event b; the two branches of event b are now eliminated, as shown in Figure 16.7.

Step 5

For the bottom two branches of the decision tree in Figure 16.7, we use the decision tree and values shown in Figure 16.4 for the earlier version of this problem.

Step 6

Now that all event forks have been reduced to their respective EMVs, the broker faces a choice among three acts with their respective EMVs:

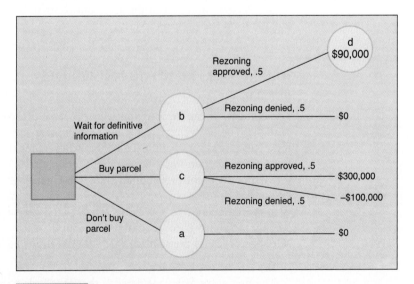

Figure 16.6
Reduced decision tree applying the expectation rule: Intermediate stage

Figure 16.7
Reduced decision tree applying
the expectation rule: Final stage

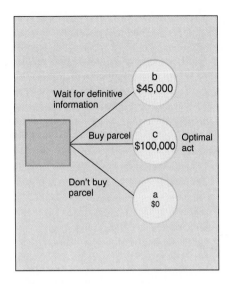

1. "Wait for Definitive Information" (i.e., rezoning approval) with an EMV of +$45,000
2. "Buy Parcel" now with an EMV of +$100,000
3. "Don't Buy Parcel" with a zero EMV

Following the expectation rule, we select the act with the highest EMV. From Figure 16.7, we can see that the act "buy parcel" (without waiting) is preferable.

From the decision tree, we see that given the decision criterion of maximizing expected monetary value, the broker should not delay the purchase until learning the results of the rezoning application. Instead, the broker should plan to buy the parcel immediately. Before concluding this problem, however, we should note that this particular real estate decision is not a repetitive situation. We must understand, therefore, that the $100,000 EMV is not the result of averaging outcomes from numerous repetitions of the identical decision situation. This $100,000 EMV results from *weighing* the possible outcomes by their respective probabilities in this *particular* decision situation. However, if we always follow the expectation rule in whatever decision situations we encounter, the aggregate of the actual outcomes should approach the sum of the EMVs for all the decision situations considered as a whole.

In this section, we have expanded our consideration of decision problems to include situations in which one of the decision alternatives is to wait for definitive information on the outcome of the crucial event. Next, in Section 16.4, we shall discuss how much value to place on the definitive information.

PRACTICE EXERCISE

16.3 A new product can be introduced in either the "basic" version or "deluxe" version, but not both. The success of either version depends on the strength of the economy, where $P(\text{Strong}) = .7$ and $P(\text{Weak}) = .3$. The anticipated payoffs (in millions of dollars) are strong economy, basic version: $4; strong economy, deluxe version: $7; weak economy, basic version: $5; weak economy, deluxe version: $2. It is also possible to delay a decision until the current recessionary period has ended. However, this delay will necessitate a crash development program costing $2 million.
  a. Draw the decision tree.
  b. What is the EMV of the optimal act?

EXERCISES

16.8 An airline ticket to a distant destination can be purchased now for $400 round trip, with full refund privileges if it is not used. It can be purchased for $250 now if refund privileges in the event of non-use are forfeited. The decision to purchase can be postponed until it is learned definitively when (or whether) the planned trip will be taken. However, the price of the ticket will be $500 at that time.

   a. Multiply the cost figures by −1 to get payoffs.

   b. Which act maximizes the EMV if the probability that the trip will be taken is .6?

   c. What is its EMV?

▶ **16.9** Refer to Exercise 16.2. Suppose it is possible to postpone the decision until it is definitively known which event (E_1, E_2, or E_3) will occur. However, there is a 70% chance that act A_1, buy, will no longer be available, and there is a 20% chance that the act A_2, lease, will no longer be available.

   a. Construct the new decision tree.

   b. Applying the expectation rule, which act is optimal? What is its EMV?

16.10 Refer to Exercise 16.3. Suppose it is possible to postpone the decision until it is definitively known which act (E_1, E_2, or E_3) will occur. However, by that time, acts A_1 and A_2 will not be open, and act A_3 has a 50% chance of still being available.

   a. Construct the new decision tree.

   b. Applying the expectation rule, which act is optimal?

16.4

EXPECTED VALUE OF PERFECT INFORMATION

Information is valuable in a decision situation it if reduces uncertainty. Sometimes, valuable information can be obtained without cost merely by waiting. This was the case in the California real estate problem described in Sections 16.2 and 16.3. There, the real estate broker considered trying to improve her EMV by waiting until she had (free) definitive information on the rezoning application. (The local government didn't charge a fee for considering the rezoning application.) As it turned out, she was better off not waiting. The point is, however, that valuable information isn't always obtainable free of charge, and it sometimes carries a very stiff price tag.

When is better information not worth its cost? We need a way to place a monetary value on information so that its value can be compared to its price tag. One feasible approach is to compare the price of the information to a standard known as the **expected value of perfect information (EVPI)**. The EVPI is the upper limit on the amount that should be paid for information that completely eliminates our uncertainty about the consequences of our decision choices. Thus, the EVPI serves as a benchmark in assessing the value of an actual research study or advice from a consultant. Information from these sources typically falls short of eliminating all uncertainty; therefore, its worth can't exceed the EVPI value. Thus, the EVPI serves as an upper spending limit for new information. Any research project or consultant's advice with a price tag higher than the EVPI value is overpriced for the decision at hand. In a later section, we shall learn how to place a value on the information itself, but for now, we'll concentrate on finding the upper limit on the value of information.

To calculate the EVPI we must first define a new concept, *perfect foresight,* which refers to knowing in advance which events will occur, even though we don't have any influence over the occurrence of the events. For example, suppose we know that 70%

of days are sunny and 30% are rainy. The person who not only knows this but also knows which of the days will be sunny and which will be rainy has what we call perfect foresight.

For the real estate broker problem, perfect foresight corresponds to someone being able to accurately foretell what the government decision will be on the rezoning application. Let's suppose this someone is an urban planning consultant who is certain to find out whether or not the government will rezone the parcel. The first step in calculating the EVPI is to find the **expected value of perfect foresight (EVPF)**; this is the payoff achievable with perfect foresight.

The EVPF is the expected value of the optimal course of action, given that perfect foresight will be acquired prior to the time the course of action must be chosen. This EVPF must be compared with the EMV of the optimal course of action when that action is chosen without acquiring additional information; let's now call this EMV the **expected value of current information (EVCI)**. For the real estate problem, this is what was calculated in Section 16.2 as $100,000. The difference between the EVPF and the EVCI is the gain in expected value from acquiring perfect information. That difference is the EVPI:

Expected Value of Perfect Information

$$\text{EVPI} = \text{EVPF} - \text{EVCI} \qquad (16\text{-}2)$$

EXPECTED VALUE OF PERFECT FORESIGHT

The calculation of the EVCI refers to the broker's expectation prior to acquiring the planning consultant's opinion on what the government will decide. However, the planning consultant is assumed to have perfect foresight into the government's reaction to the rezoning request, so the consultant presumably can (and will, for a fee) tell the broker with certainty what the rezoning decision will be. Thus, we may ask, "What is the probability that the consultant will say that E_1 will occur? That E_2 will occur?" Since the consultant doesn't control the local government's decision on rezoning, the probabilities of rezoning approval (E_1) and rezoning denial (E_2) aren't changed by what the consultant says, so both $P_{1.1}$ and $P_{1.2}$ will still be .5. However, if the consultant (having perfect foresight) says E_1 will occur, then the broker will choose A_1, since this act–event combination ($E_1 \mid A_1$) gives $300,000 profit. If the consultant says that E_2 will occur, this will cause the broker to choose A_2, which gives a $0 profit. Linking the probabilities of E_1 and E_2 with the profit consequences implies that $300,000 and $0 will each have a .5 probability of occurring. These conditions are expressed in Table 16.3.

TABLE 16.3	Data for Determining the EVPF		
IF THIS EVENT OCCURS	**THEN THE BEST ACT IS**	**THE PROFIT WILL BE**	**THE PROBABILITY OF THIS PROFIT IS**
E_1	A_1	$300,000	.5
E_2	A_2	$0	.5

The EVPF computation is simply the EMV that follows from choosing the best act knowing the event fork outcome, weighted by the probability of occurrence of the event. That is,

$$\$300,000(.5) = \$150,000 \quad \text{If rezoning is approved}$$
$$+\$0(.5) = \qquad\quad 0 \quad \text{If rezoning is denied}$$

$$\overline{\qquad\qquad\qquad}$$
$$\text{EVPF} = \$150,000$$

CALCULATION OF THE EVPI

We must first calculate the EVCI, the expected value of the optimal action assuming that the rezoning decision is not known in advance. As we mentioned earlier, for the real estate problem, this calculation has already been made in Section 16.2, where we found EMV = $100,000. We now call this EMV the EVCI to distinguish it from other EMVs.

Substituting the values found for the EVPF and the EVCI into the formula for the EVPI, we have

$$\text{EVPI} = \text{EVPF} - \text{EVCI}$$
$$= \$150,000 - \$100,000$$
$$= \$50,000$$

Thus, no matter how prophetic a consultant or research service claims to be, $50,000 is the most that should be paid for the information provided.

PRACTICE EXERCISE

16.4 The Bituminous Coal Company holds an option to buy a large land tract. The value of the land depends on the extent and location of its coal deposits. The payoff table (in millions of dollars) is given here. Assume that the probabilities of surface coal, underground coal, and no coal are .2, .3, and .5, respectively.

		ACT	
		Buy	**Don't Buy**
	Surface Coal	3	0
EVENT	**Underground Coal**	2	0
	No Coal	−3	0

a. Which act maximizes the EMV?
b. Find the EVPF.
c. Find the EVPI.

EXERCISES

16.11 Refer to Exercise 16.1.
a. What is the EVPF?
b. What is the EVPI?

▶ **16.12** Refer to Exercise 16.4. Assume that events E_1, E_2, E_3, E_4 have probabilities .1, .3, .5, and .1, respectively.
a. What is the optimal act using the expectation rule?
b. What is the EVPF?
c. What is the EVPI?

16.13 Refer to Exercise 16.6.
   a. What is the EVPF?
   b. What is the EVPI?

●●●

16.5
SEEKING IMPERFECT INFORMATION

The EVPI calculation described in Section 16.4 places an upper limit on the monetary worth of perfect foresight. Thus, even if the information obtainable leads to perfect foresight about the outcome of the event set in the real estate problem, the broker should pay at most $50,000 for the information. Thus, for information that leads to less than perfect foresight, we know its value to the broker must be less than $50,000. But how much less? Can the broker determine how much value to place on a proposal? Surely, the price paid ought to depend on how good the information is; that is, on how much it reduces the uncertainty. In this section, we consider the procedure for determining the value of imperfect information. The procedure is developed around the following alternate version of the real estate example.

■ **EXAMPLE 16.3**

Is Imperfect Information Worth Its Price?

Suppose a well-known local lobbyist proposes to "sound out," for a $1000 fee, the local government's position on the rezoning application in the real estate problem we've been analyzing. The lobbyist is not able to influence the decision, but through good contacts in the government is often able to get informal opinions on an application from technical staff members. These informal opinions serve as leading indicators as to which way the decision will go. The lobbyist says, "I can't guarantee that my interpretation of their informal opinions will prove to be correct, but I have a good track record on my predictions." There is some concern that the lobbyist might be very conservative in predicting approval, but he said that in situations like this one, "I've predicted approval 55% of the time, and on those occasions I've been right 82% of the time. I think that's an excellent batting average." The question is, "Should the broker pay $1000 to hire the lobbyist?"

SIMPLIFYING THE DECISION TREE

The decision tree shown in Figure 16.8 is an augmented version of Figure 16.5; it incorporates a new act–event branch path for use of the lobbyist. The bottom segment is identical to Figure 16.5, but with two act branches marked with double slashes, which indicate that these two branches have already been eliminated from further consideration. (Remember that using the expectation rule at a given act fork, all act branches except one will be ruled out.) Looking at this bottom segment (where the lobbyist isn't used), the broker sees that her best act is "buy," with an EMV of $100,000. We now look at the top segment to consider the analysis if she decides to use the lobbyist.

First, the objective of the real estate broker in hiring the lobbyist must be understood. We assume that the lobbyist's recommendations are a basis for action. It would make little sense to incur the cost of the lobbyist if the broker is going to disregard the recommendation and follow a course of action she has already chosen. The impli-

Figure 16.8
Augmented decision tree:
Using a lobbyist for a $1000
fee

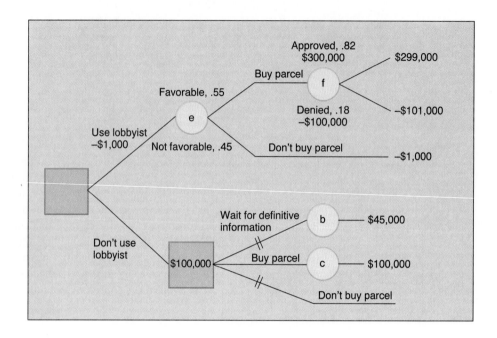

cation of this logic is that a favorable opinion from the lobbyist will cause the broker to buy the land parcel. Therefore, it is unnecessary to show on the decision tree a "don't buy" branch as a possibility following a favorable lobbyist's opinion. Likewise, a "buy" branch as a possibility is ruled out and not shown if the lobbyist's report is unfavorable to the purchase. Figure 16.9 shows in less cluttered form the augmented decision tree of Figure 16.8. All the branch paths to the right of the "don't use lobbyist" branch have been removed; the EMV of that branch is shown as $100,000. We now turn to the calculation of the EMV for the "use lobbyist" branch.

ADDITIONAL PROBABILITY CALCULATIONS

Given that a lobbyist will be hired, does the broker need to come up with any new probabilities? Yes, because with two additional event forks, there is an assessment required of two additional sets of probabilities:

1. The probabilities on event fork e; that is, the chances that the lobbyist's report will be favorable and the chances that it will be unfavorable.
2. The probabilities on event fork f; that is, if the report is favorable, we need to know the chances that the government will approve the rezoning, and the chances that it will deny the rezoning. Note that these are conditional probabilities (e.g., rezoning approval, given a favorable lobbyist's report).

Is there a redundancy here? After all, the broker already assessed the rezoning approval possibility as having .5 probability. Why ask for that probability again? The reason we must recompute it is that one is a conditional and the other is an unconditional probability. The .5 probability value initially assessed (in the absence of the lobbyist's report) measures the uncertainty surrounding government approval without the benefit of knowing that the lobbyist's report was favorable. Aided by the information of a favorable report, the probability of approval is a conditional probability that will

Figure 16.9
Reduced decision tree: Using a lobbyist

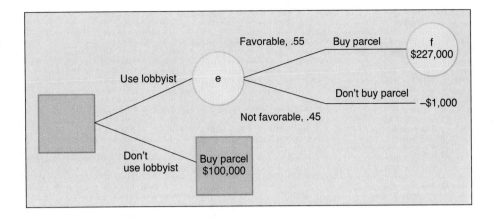

be higher than .5. We call this a *posterior probability*. Thus, there is no redundancy using the two probabilities of approval, because they refer to different situations.

A favorable lobbyist's report provides information that revises upward the chances that the forthcoming government decision will be an approval. Thus, the probability assigned to the event "rezoning approved" is always conditional (dependent) on the information available about the event. That is, there is no reason why P(Rezoning approved) should equal P(Rezoning approved, given a favorable lobbyist's report). On a decision tree, this means all the events and acts to the left of the event circle in question and on the same branch of the tree provide relevant information about the exiting branch probability. Consequently, the event "rezoning approved" may, and probably will, have a different chance of occurring, depending upon where on the decision tree its event circle appears. For example, in Figure 16.8, we see that the branch exiting from event circle c shows P(Rezoning approved) = .5, whereas the branch exiting from event circle f shows P(Rezoning approved, given a favorable lobbyist's report) = .82. There is no contradiction between these different probabilities for approval, because they are based on different states of pre-existing information.

ACCOUNTING FOR THE COST OF INFORMATION

The lobbyist's report to the broker, if favorable, causes the broker to believe that rezoning approval is more probable (.82) than was indicated by the .5 value used prior to receiving the report. Subtracting the $1000 lobbyist's fee from all the dollar consequences, introduces the lobbyist's cost explicitly into the problem. The effect of the lobbyist's fee can be seen in the reduced payoffs shown at the right end positions of the tree in Figure 16.8.

REDUCING THE TREE

The process of reducing the tree is the result of choosing the highest EMV on each decision action fork. The lower part of the decision tree that carries over from Figure 16.5 is shown in skeletal form in Figure 16.9 by the box showing $100,000. This refers to the EMV of $100,000 computed earlier for the act "buy parcel."

Calculating the expected value that will replace the f event fork, we find

$$\text{EMV for fork } f = \$299{,}000(.82) - \$101{,}000(.18) = \$227{,}000$$

which we find encircled in fork f in Figure 16.9.

For event e, the expected value is

$$\text{EMV fork } e = \$227{,}000(.55) - \$1000(.45) = \$124{,}400$$

The end result is the decision tree in Figure 16.10.

Comparing the act "use lobbyist," with its expected value of $124,400, to the series of acts "don't use lobbyist" followed by "buy parcel," with expected value $100,000, shows that using the lobbyist and paying the $1000 fee provides a greater expected gain than if the service and imperfect information were foregone.

EXPECTED VALUE OF SAMPLE INFORMATION

Acquisition of the lobbyist's opinion has raised the EMV from $100,000 to $124,400. Clearly, the lobbyist's opinion is valuable, far more so than the $1000 fee charged. The added value is referred to as the **expected value of sample information (EVSI)**. We can measure the intrinsic value of the lobbyist's opinion by the increase achieved in the EMV.

Expected Value of Sample Information

$$
\begin{aligned}
\text{EVSI} &= (\text{EMV with information}) - (\text{EMV without information}) \\
&= \$124{,}400 - \$100{,}000 \\
&= \$24{,}400
\end{aligned}
\tag{16-3}
$$

Thus, the lobbyist's opinion is actually worth $24,400 more than the broker has to pay for it, or a total of $25,400.

LACK OF INFORMATION AND DELAYED PERFECT INFORMATION VERSUS IMPERFECT CURRENT INFORMATION

Information is not gathered in a vacuum. It is gathered for a purpose—to minimize the uncertainty surrounding a decision. In the real estate problem, two sources of information were considered. First, was the option of waiting for an answer from the local government on the rezoning application before deciding whether to buy the

Figure 16.10
Final reduced decision tree:
Using a lobbyist

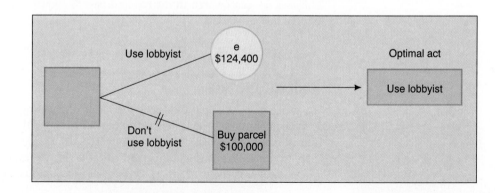

parcel. This approach provides definitive information, but delays the decision. Second, was the lobbyist's opinion about what the rezoning decision would be. Note that the use of either source involves a deliberate information gathering decision. That is, the information is not gathered merely for the sake of having it. It is gathered only if it is believed the information gathered will increase the EMV of the decision payoff.

The two sources of improved information differ in both timing and quality of information gathered. Hiring the lobbyist provides information quickly but supplies only imperfect information, which may substantially reduce, but will never totally eliminate, the risk that the act chosen is the wrong decision. We noted earlier that in spite of the imperfection of the lobbyist's information and its associated cost, its immediate availability made it quite attractive. On the other hand, the information obtained through formal application for rezoning was perfect (and therefore definitive), but suffered because it took so long to obtain it.

In the real estate example, the information provided by the lobbyist reduced the uncertainty enough to be worth the $1000 asking price. But the key point to bear in mind is that information that avoids costly decision errors is the kind of information that will be valuable to the decision maker.

PRACTICE EXERCISE

16.5 A brand manager wished to determine whether her company should market a new personal care product. The present value of future profits from a successful new personal care brand is $1,400,000, but failure of the brand would result in a loss of $500,000. Marketing the product would not affect profits from the company's other products. The manager believes that the probability of success is .4. However, before making her decision, the manager can spend $60,000 for a consumer testing program. Based upon the outcome of previous consumer tests, the outcome of the consumer testing will be favorable with probability .4 and unfavorable with probability .6. Given a favorable test outcome, the probability of eventual product success is judged to be .8. Given an unfavorable test, the probability of eventual success is judged to be only .25.
a. Construct a decision tree.
b. Given that the EMV is the decision criterion, what strategy should the manager use, and what is the optimal EMV?
c. What are the EVSI and EVPI?

EXERCISE

16.14 A publishing company is trying to decide whether to publish a new nursing textbook. After reading the manuscript, the editor in charge assessed the chances of success as given in the table, along with the payoffs if the book is published.

Current Assessments		
STATE	**PROBABILITY**	**PAYOFF (IF PUBLISHED)**
Very successful	.2	$110,000
Moderate success	.3	20,000
Very little success	.5	−60,000

The editor may postpone the publishing decision until the company can collect information about the chances of the book's success by doing an in-depth survey of college and university nursing instructors. The results of similar surveys (for health care books) taken in the past are also given in the table below. (For example, in similar surveys, 13 of the 31 books that turned out to be very successful were predicted by the survey results to be only moderately successful.)

Historical Frequencies: Surveys Versus Actual		ACTUAL		
		Very Successful	Moderate Success	Very Little Success
SURVEY INDICATION	Very Successful	16	14	3
	Moderate Success	13	20	12
	Very Little Success	2	6	10

a. Construct a decision tree that can be used to solve the company's problem. (Use the EMV criterion.)
b. What is the most the company should be willing to pay for the survey?
c. If the actual cost of the survey is $4000, what action should the company take?

● ●

16.6

DECISION MAKING BY UTILITY THEORY

We use the expectation rule to maximize the expected payoff among the alternative actions available. There are situations, however, in which the application of the expectation rule would lead the business manager astray. The major disadvantage of the expectation rule is that it downplays possible consequences that are far from the expected value. Following the expectation rule, we might never purchase insurance, nor bet on lotteries, for example.

Suppose the chief financial officer of a major airline has forecast this coming year's income statement and has recognized that, because of the recent unanticipated hikes in aviation fuel prices (from 87¢ a gallon to $1.07 a gallon), operating expenses will be considerably over budget and will devastate the hoped-for rate of return that he knows stockholders are expecting. Seriously disappointing current stockholders will likely cut off future investment money from prospective stockholders, and this money is needed to remain competitive by updating the firm's fleet. So, the financial officer is exploring different ways to cut costs. One option for paying expenses without causing a reduction in operating service is to cut the insurance expense line on the income statement. The air traffic records indicate that the chance of an airplane crash where the plane would be lost is only 2 in 1000. The expected loss on a $50 million plane would be $.002 \times \$50,000,000 = \$100,000$ expected loss per plane.

The insurance premium on each plane itself (passenger liability aside) has been costing the company $250,000. On the basis of the expectation rule (calculations shown in Table 16.4), the expected loss of $250,000 for the insurance premium exceeds the expected loss of $100,000 for an airline crash. This suggests that the insurance should be dropped if maximizing the EMV is the decision criterion.

TABLE 16.4	Decision Table for Purchasing Airplane Insurance			
PROBABILITY	**EVENT**		**ACT**	
			A_1 Buy Insurance	A_2 Don't Buy Insurance
.002	E_1 = Crash		−$250,000	−$50,000,000
.998	E_2 = No crash		−$250,000	$0

$A_1 = .002(-250,000) + .998(-250,000) = -250,000$
$A_2 = .002(-50,000,000) + .998(0) = -100,000$

If this suggestion is followed for its fleet of 100 planes, the company would show an immediate $25 million reduction in the insurance expense line on the income statement and an improved profit picture. But what if the unexpected happens and 1 or possibly 2 planes crash during the year? The impact of a $50 or $100 million capital loss would assuredly devastate whatever meager profits were forecast, disillusion current and prospective stockholders, put the firm's financial picture in comparatively poor light versus its competitors, and probably cripple the firm's immediate chance of raising new capital for replacement and modernization. A predictable consequence would be the resignation of the financial manager. Despite the favorable impact on the reported income statement if no crash occurs, not buying insurance places in jeopardy the short-run viability of the firm. Because of the dire consequences possible if the expectation rule is used as the decision criterion, the act that maximizes the EMV ought to be discarded in this situation.

EXPECTED UTILITY CONCEPT

Observation of the current management environment suggests that not every financial manager is an EMV maximizer; otherwise, we would see many more managerial shake-ups and a higher frequency of corporate bankruptcies. The vast majority of financial managers seem to follow a risk aversion policy. This leads them to buy insurance to avoid catastrophic losses from unpredictable and uncontrollable events. There are, however, financial managers who neither maximize the EMV nor are risk averters; instead, they commit capital to ventures that offer high speculative gain. They seem to seek out high-risk situations. What explains their behavior? The **expected utility** concept is introduced into decision making to add additional insight. Suppose a financial manager accurately assesses the probability of various profit outcomes. Subsequently, the financial manager assigns values, or *utilities,* to the different possible amounts of profit. In this case, utility refers to the degrees of pleasure or displeasure associated with outcomes. The utilities assigned and the different profit possibilities can be graphed as a *utility function,* which maps out the levels of utility associated with different amounts of profit attained.

THREE TYPES OF UTILITY FUNCTIONS

Basically, three types of managers can be identified: those who take a risk aversion posture, those who view risk neutrally, and those who can be labeled risk lovers. The three types have distinct attitudes toward profitability and risk. Suppose all three types have zero utility at zero profits, as shown in Figure 16.11.

Figure 16.11
Three types of utility curves

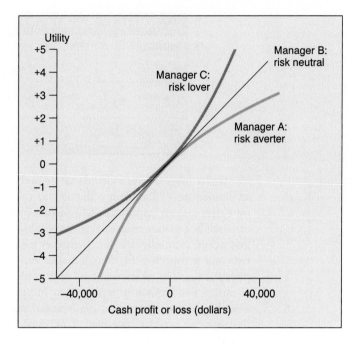

1. **Risk averters.** A deliberating, conservative manager is shown by curve A and is categorized as risk averse. The zero profit benchmark is located at the middle of the horizontal axis. A move to the right from the zero profit mark generates positive utility, but the utility gains are less than the utility loss suffered if an equal amount of profit is lost. Risk averse managers regret their losses much more than they enjoy their gains. Their utility function increases at a slower and slower pace with each increment in profit. Type A managers will reject investment opportunities in which substantial losses can occur.

2. **Risk neutral.** Manager B is indifferent to risk. The utility function of this type of manager increases by a constant amount with each increment in profit. A move to the right from the 0 point brings a positive utility amount equal to the utility loss associated with a move an identical distance to the left from 0. This manager can use the EMV criterion, since it is equivalent to the expected utility criterion if the manager is risk neutral.

3. **Risk lovers.** Finally, the type C manager is a risk lover, because the satisfaction that comes with high profits is more rewarding than the displeasure that comes from similar size losses. We can see from Figure 16.11 that a gain in profits from the 0 profit brings type C managers a higher utility than a loss of the same amount would have decreased it. Type C managers are more likely to take on boom or bust ventures that have very high profit potential—for example, genetic engineering projects, deep sea ore mining, and oil exploration.

P R A C T I C E
E X E R C I S E

16.6 Assume that the utility function for an investor is $U(X)$, where X is expressed in thousands of dollars. Given that the following utilities and outcome probabilities for the project are supplied, what decision—go or no go—would maximize the investor's expected utility?

X	U(X)	P(X)
−10,000	−0.733	.15
−1,000	−0.649	.10
−100	−0.051	.15
0	0	.10
2,300	0.683	.30
2,400	0.698	.20

● ●

EXERCISES

▶ **16.15** The following potential payoffs have been assessed for an investment:

Payoff	Probability
−$2000	.2
0	.1
2000	.3
4000	.2
6000	.1
8000	.1

An investor assesses her utility for various amounts of money, X, as follows:

X	U(X)
−$2000	0
−1000	0.18
0	0.31
1000	0.43
2000	0.55
3000	0.66
4000	0.77
6000	0.93
8000	1.08

a. Graph the investor's utility function and interpret the shape of the curve.
b. Three options are open to the investor: (1) She can make the investment, (2) she can turn down the investment opportunity, or (3) she can find a partner in the investment (where she gains or loses only half of the amounts shown, with the same probabilities). Which of the three actions would maximize her expected utility? Explain.

16.16 An author of a new CBT (computer-based training) course is trying to decide which of two computer courseware companies, A or B, to sign with. Company A will sell the CBT course for $250, and it will pay the author a flat 15% on each course sold. The table gives company A's estimate of the distribution of copies it will be able to sell over the useful lifetime of the course. Company B, on the other hand, will sell the course for $240. It will pay the author 13% on each of the first 2000 copies sold and 19% on each additional copy sold. Its estimate of the distribution of sales is also shown in the table.

COPIES SOLD	PROBABILITY	
	Assessed by A	Assessed by B
1000	.35	.40
2000	.25	.20
3000	.25	.20
4000	.10	.10
5000	.05	.10

a. If the author wishes to maximize her expected profit, what courseware company should she choose?

b. Now assume that the author is quite risk averse and has the following utility function:

$$U(X) = -(X - b)^2$$

where X is measured in thousands of dollars and b is a given constant. What is the author's best decision when $b = 220$?

16.17 In order to discover an executive's utility function, a consultant uses the following procedure. She explains to the executive that he (the executive) can choose between the following two options: (I) receive $100 for certain, or (II) gamble on winning Y dollars or 0 dollars. The gamble in II is very simple. There is a jar with marbles, R of which are red and $100 - R$ of which are blue. The executive must close his eyes and select one of the marbles at random. If he selects a red one, he wins Y dollars; otherwise, he wins 0 dollars. Now, the consultant explains that she will specify the number R, and then the executive must supply the value Y such that he is indifferent between options I and II. This procedure is repeated with several values of R, and the following responses are given:

Consultant's R	Executive's Y
20	$580
40	280
60	180
80	135

a. If the executive's utility function is $U(X)$, and we specify that $U(0) = 0$ and $U(100) = 1$, evaluate the utility of the four other dollar values.

b. Do the executive's responses indicate that he is risk averse? Why or why not?

c. If the executive is risk averse, what must be true of his response Y when $R = 75$? Be specific.

● ●

SUMMARY

Decision theory analysis begins with the choice of a criterion to be used in deciding among possible courses of action. Several criteria (maximax, minimax, minimax regret) depend only on the individual's attitude toward risk and not on the probabilities of the possible events. However, for most business decisions it is important to consider the probabilities of the various event possibilities as well as their consequences. For this purpose, the expectation rule, with its criterion of maximizing expected monetary value (EMV) proves useful.

The expectation rule requires a decision maker to clearly delineate the decision options available and to assess the probability of the possible consequences for each of these options. Then, a decision tree is used to successively eliminate inferior decisions. Folding back the tree is a procedure for analyzing complicated decision situations. It involves starting at the right-hand side of a decision tree and working toward the left, through the tree branches, to find the EMV of each act.

In many situations, it is possible to acquire additional information that will enable the decision maker to make a better choice among the available options. If the information is not free of charge, we need to compare the cost of acquiring it against the expected value of perfect information, or better yet, against the expected value of the sample information provided.

Much of the information required in formal decision analysis may be difficult to acquire. Probability assessments, for example, may be little more than informed speculation. Nevertheless, the discipline of spelling out the elements of a decision tree can yield insights into the decision situation that aren't obvious. For this reason, even informally thinking through a decision situation along the lines of decision theory analysis may avoid many of the surprise pitfalls of "seat of the pants" decision making.

KEY EQUATIONS

Expected Monetary Value

$$EMV = \sum_{j=1}^{k} \pi_{i,j} p_{i,j} \qquad (16\text{-}1)$$

Expected Value of Perfect Information

$$EVPI = EVPF - EVCI \qquad (16\text{-}2)$$

Expected Value of Sample Information

$$EVSI = (EMV \text{ with information}) - (EMV \text{ without information}) \qquad (16\text{-}3)$$

PRACTICE EXERCISE ANSWERS

16.1

		ACT			
		1	**2**	**3**	**4**
	1	45	−35	0	120
EVENT	**2**	20	−20	10	80
	3	75	−85	40	30
Column Maximum		75	−20	40	120
Column Minimum		20	−85	0	30

a. The largest maximum outcome is 120. The choice using the maximax decision criterion is act 4.

b. The largest minimum outcome is 30. The choice using the maximin decision criterion is act 4.

c.

		ACT			
		1	**2**	**3**	**4**
	1	75	155	120	0
EVENT	**2**	60	100	70	0
	3	0	160	25	45
Column Maximum		75	160	120	45

The smallest maximum regret is 45. The choice using the minimax regret decision criterion is act 4.

16.2 a. The EMV of the upper event fork is

$$EMV = P(E_1|A_1) \cdot E_1 + P(E_2|A_1) \cdot E_2$$
$$= (.6)(\$600) + (.4)(\$200) = \$440$$

b. The EMV of act A_1 is the same as in part a, since the upper event fork is the same as act A_1.

$$EMV = P(E_1|A_1) \cdot E_1 + P(E_2|A_1) \cdot E_2$$
$$= (.6)(\$600) + (.4)(\$200) = \$440$$

c. The EMV of the lower event fork is

$$EMV = P(E_3|A_2) \cdot E_3 + P(E_4|A_2) \cdot E_4$$
$$= (.75)(\$200) + (.25)(\$520) = \$280$$

d. The EMV of act A_2 is the same as in part c, since the lower event fork is the same as act A_2.

$$EMV = P(E_3|A_2) \cdot E_3 + P(E_4|A_2) \cdot E_4$$
$$= (.75)(\$200) + (.25)(\$520) = \$280$$

e. Act A_1 has the higher expected monetary value, so choose A_1.

16.3 a. A decision to delay means that subsequent development will occur during a strong economy, but payoffs will be reduced by $2 million. The decision tree is:

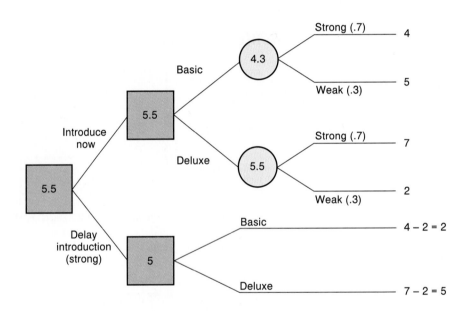

b. The optimal act is to introduce the deluxe version now, with EMV = $5.5 (million).

16.4 a. For the "buy" act: EMV = $3(.2) + 2(.3) + (-3)(.5) = -0.3$
For the "don't buy" act: EMV = 0

The "don't buy" act maximizes the EMV. (Note this maximum EMV is defined to be the EVCI.)

b.

IF THE PERFECT FORECAST IS	THEN THE BEST ACT IS	PAYOFF WILL BE	PROBABILITY OF THIS OUTCOME IS
Surface coal	Buy	3	.2
Underground coal	Buy	2	.3
No coal	Don't buy	0	.5

So, EVPF = $3(.2) + 2(.3) + 0(.5) = 1.2$.

c. EVPI = EVPF − EVCI = 1.2 − 0 = 1.2

16.5 a. All values in the decision tree are expressed in thousands of dollars.

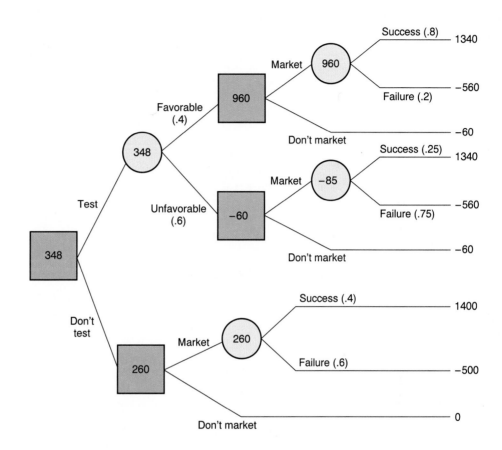

b. The optimal strategy is to test; then to market if the test result is favorable, and not market if the test result is unfavorable. This optimal strategy has EMV = $348,000.

c. EVSI is the difference between the EMV with sample information and the EMV without sample information. With sample information, the EMV in the tree above is $348,000. This value has already been reduced by $60,000 to reflect the cost of the information. The EMV with sample information, regardless of the cost of the information, is thus $348,000 + $60,000 = $408,000. Without information, the EMV was $260,000. Therefore, EVSI = $408,000 − $260,000 = $148,000. To determine EVPF, consider the following table:

IF THE PERFECT FORECAST IS	THEN THE BEST ACT IS	PAYOFF WILL BE	PROBABILITY OF THIS OUTCOME IS
Success	Market without testing	$1,400,000	.4
Failure	Don't market, no test	$0	.6

EVPF = $1,400,000(.4) + $0(.6) = $560,000

So, EVPI = EVPF − EVCI = $560,000 − $348,000 = $212,000.

16.6 a. The inventor has two options: to proceed or not to proceed. If the decision is not to proceed, the outcome is $X = 0$, with $U(X) = U(0) = 0$. If the decision is to proceed, the outcomes, utilities, and probabilities are as shown in the following table:

X	U(X)	P(X)
−10,000	−0.733	.15
−1,000	−0.649	.10
−100	−0.051	.15
0	0	.10
2,300	0.683	.30
2,400	0.698	.20

The expected utility if the inventor proceeds is

$$E(U) = \Sigma U(X) \cdot P(X)$$

$$= (-0.733)(.15) + (-0.649)(.10) + \cdots + (0.698)(.20) = .162$$

Since $.162 > 0$, the inventor should proceed.

CHAPTER REVIEW EXERCISES

16.18 The table condenses a business decision tree that includes an initial act fork followed by event alternatives. Values in the table represent profits (in thousands of dollars) corresponding to particular act–event combinations.

Expected Profits				
PROBABILITY	**EVENT**		**ACT**	
		A_1 Buy	A_2 Lease	A_3 Don't Buy or Lease
.3	E_1: Low demand	100	120	0
.3	E_2: Moderate demand	105	100	0
.4	E_3: High demand	80	60	0

a. Construct the decision tree from the information summarized in the table.
b. Applying the expectation rule, which act is optimal?
c. Since A_3, "don't buy or lease," never gives a profit, should it always be eliminated as an act to choose?

16.19 The values in the table are the relevant conditional profits (in dollars) for a decision tree in which the starting act fork has three acts. Each act is subsequently followed by the three events of the event fork and its probabilities.

Conditional Profits				
PROBABILITY	**EVENT**	A_1	A_2	A_3
.2	E_1	160	180	0
.2	E_2	120	20	180
.6	E_3	40	0	140

a. Draw the decision tree for the information presented in the table.
b. Determine the EMV for each act.
c. Applying the expectation rule, what is the optimal act (highest expected profit)?

16.20 Computech is a pioneering high-technology firm located in Silicon Valley, California. It has been very successful introducing a personal home microcomputer, System 5. It is now considering moving into the profitable commercial word processing business, which is in its infancy stage of growth. Since the technology for a word processor is essentially the same as for the microcomputer it now produces, Computech feels that its only current resource commitment would be taking out a lease option on additional plant capacity. If the economy becomes depressed, demand for commercial word processors will also be sluggish. In that case, Computech will not exercise the lease option, forfeiting the money it paid to obtain the option. A healthy economy with expanding business needs will show a strong demand for word processors. The lease option is expected to cost $25,000, and the chances of a low demand from a weak economy are assessed at .4; on the other hand, a .6 chance is given for high demand from a strong economy with a prospect of $75,000 profit.

a. Set up a decision tree with act–event forks and monetary consequences.
b. Formulate a summary table for the decision tree.
c. Using the expectation rule, select the optimal act.

16.21 Refer to Exercise 16.20. The corporate vice-president of finance at Computech has another plan for the expansion into word processing. The vice-president feels that Computech should redirect its efforts toward government purchasing by the GAO (Government Accounting Office), which would yield the same $75,000 profit prospect if successful. The new administration's push toward efficiency in government and its promise to trim down the use of government personnel should present Computech with a selling opportunity. Since Computech has done research for the government before, it knows how to deal with government machinery and the bidding process. The chance of winning the GAO bid is estimated as .7. This approach offers Computech three possibilities: (1) lease option; (2) don't lease option; (3) seek bid approval before finalizing the lease option. Although the latter act seems to suggest wisely, "look before you leap," the approach is flawed. Currently, little excess plant capacity is to be found in Silicon Valley because of the high level of growth going on. The competition for facilities, combined with the time lapse before the government acts on the bid, significantly reduces Computech's chances to purchase the lease option to .5.

a. Draw a decision diagram for this decision situation.
b. Use the folding back procedure to choose the best act.
c. Calculate the EVPF and explain what it means.
d. Calculate the EVPI and explain what it means.

SOLVING APPLIED CASES
Using Incremental Analysis in Decision Making

For certain types of problems the decision tree analysis can be greatly simplified. Consider the circumstance confronting Jack Feinstein, the galoshes wholesaler described in the introduction to this chapter. Orders for galoshes from his suppliers must be placed in the summer before he knows what demand the winter weather will bring. How many pairs of galoshes should be ordered? A straightforward decision tree approach to the number of galoshes ordered could conceivably be used, but there is a much simpler approach. The simplification involves the following key ideas:

1. Break the overall problem of how many pairs to order into a series of smaller problems: Should I order the first pair? If so, should I order a second? If so, should I order a third, etc.? Thus, there will be one small decision tree for each problem being considered.

2. Each decision tree will have one act fork with two branches (order, don't order) and one event fork with two branches (demanded, not demanded) to the right of each branch off the act fork.

3. The payoffs (dollar consequences) at the ends of the branch paths of any tree are identical to the payoffs for every other tree.
4. The probability assigned to the "order" branch of a decision tree will decline with each successive tree.

The dollar consequences reflect the loss on every available but undemanded pair and the unrealized profit potential on every demanded but unavailable pair. This unrealized profit potential is called an *opportunity loss*. The decision tree for a given pair of galoshes will show three opportunity losses, one at the end of each branch path. These opportunity losses are the same on every tree. Under these conditions, the proper decision question to ask for, say, the qth pair of galoshes is, "Should this qth pair be ordered?" If the answer is "yes," then proceed to ask and answer this same question for the $(q + 1)$th pair. Stop at the first pair of galoshes at which this question receives a "no" answer.

Supporting Jack Feinstein's profit picture is a $6 per pair profit margin for each sold pair prior to the February closing out date. Losses amount to $2 per pair on every unsold pair in stock at that date, because to sell enough galoshes to reduce his inventory sufficiently, substantial price markdowns will be necessary after that date. For each pair of galoshes considered, the decision tree will resemble Figure 16.12.

Figure 16.12
Decision tree for qth pair of galoshes

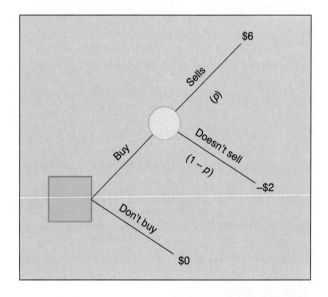

From the expectation rule, the event fork is replaced by the EMV:

$$\text{EMV} = p_q(\$6) + (1 - p_q)(-\$2)$$
$$= 8p_q - 2$$

where p_q is the probability of selling the qth pair before the February 1 closing date.

Should the qth pair of galoshes be ordered? That depends on whether the EMV of the act "buy" is greater than that of the act "don't buy," that is, when $\text{EMV}_{\text{buy}} > \text{EMV}_{\text{don't buy}}$. When will that happen, given that $\text{EMV}_{\text{don't buy}} = 0$? It will happen whenever

$$8p_q - 2 > 0$$
$$8p_q > 2$$
$$p_q > \frac{2}{8}$$
$$p_q > .25$$

This inequality puts a specific requirement on the value of p_q. It must exceed .25 for the "buy" act to be preferred. Thus, the qth pair of galoshes should be ordered only if there is at least a .25 chance of selling the pair before the markdown date in February.

What about the $(q + 1)$th pair of galoshes? Following the same logic as for the qth unit, the signal should again be "order" whenever p_{q+1} exceeds .25. But here is an important question: Could p_{q+1} exceed p_q? That would be a bit farfetched. If the probability of demand of at least q galoshes doesn't exceed .25, then certainly the probability that demand equals an even higher value $(q + 1)$ can't exceed .25 either. So, if the best decision on the qth unit is not to buy, the best decision on subsequent units must also be not to buy.

Stepping back a bit, we can see that a positive decision ("buy") on the qth pair of galoshes implies that the decision on the $(q - 1)$th pair must also be positive (buy that pair, too). This must be true once it is recognized that the probability that galoshes demand exceeds $q - 1$ pairs can't be less than the probability that demand exceeds an even larger qth number of pairs. Suppose q is 7. The probability that demand exceeds $q - 1 = 6$ can't be less than the probability of demand exceeding $q = 7$. So it is a principle of incremental analysis that a favorable decision on buying the qth item implies a favorable decision on any lower number of items. Thus, a favorable decision on the 7th item implies a favorable decision on buying items 1–6 also. Similarly, the decision not to buy the qth item implies that the decision on any larger number of items also must be negative (not to buy). Thus, if the decision on the 7th item is not to buy, then the decision on the 8th, 9th, etc., items also must be not to buy. With this principle in mind, a very simple decision criterion can be given to Jack Feinstein for use in buying galoshes.

What stop–go rule results? Assigning K_o as the loss on any unsold pair and K_u as the profit foregone by not having on-hand a pair that could have been sold, the rule suggests to continue to buy, up to and including the last (highest) value of q at which p_q equals or exceeds the ratio $K_o/(K_u + K_o)$. The value of q at this point is the $(1 - p_q)$ fractile of the probability distribution for demand. At this point, $p_q = K_o/(K_u + K_o)$. Expressing the stop–go rule in terms of a fractile of the distribution for the demand, it indicates that the quantity indicated by the $K_u/(K_u + K_o)$ fractile of the probability distribution should be ordered.

The procedure for determining how many items to order is summarized by the following steps:

Step 1
Determine K_o, the loss on any unsold item. In the galoshes problem, $K_o = \$2$.

Step 2
Determine K_u, the profit foregone by not having on-hand an item that could have been sold. In Feinstein's case, $K_u = \$6$ per pair.

Step 3
Calculate the ratio $K_u/(K_u + K_o)$. In the galoshes problem, this ratio is $6/(6 + 2) = .75$.

Step 4
Order the quantity of items that corresponds to the fractile of the demand distribution determined in Step 3. In Feinstein's case, he should order the quantity of galoshes that corresponds to the .75 fractile (75th percentile) of his demand distribution.

How many pairs should Feinstein have ordered if he assigned the demand for his galoshes as a normal distribution with a mean of 40,000 pairs and a standard deviation of 15,000 pairs? The .75 fractile of a normal distribution (from the table of areas under the standardized normal distribution) occurs at 0.67 standard deviation above the mean. Thus, a prudent move on Feinstein's part would have been an order of

$$\text{Mean} + .67(\text{Value of standard deviation}) = 40{,}000 + (.67)(15{,}000) = 50{,}050 \text{ pairs}$$

That is, the optimal stock of galoshes for the coming winter season is 50,050 pairs.

Checkpoint Exercise

1. A merchant carries a certain type of perishable goods in inventory. Each item costs $9 and sells for $15. At the end of the day, any unsold items must be thrown away (become valueless). Demand for this item is given by the distribution in the table. Assume that future customer demand is not altered by a stock-out during this period.

DEMAND	PROBABILITY
0	0
1	.3
2	.4
3	.2
4	.1
5 or more	0
	1.0

   a. What must the probability be for selling an item in order to have an expectation of profit (positive EMV) on ordering it?
   b. How many items should the merchant stock in order to maximize expected monetary value?
   c. What is the expected monetary value?

2. Management of the Top-Value Liquor Company wants to determine the optimal stock level for Beefeater's Gin, a popular brand with strong brand loyalty. Management believes stock-out cost is equal to the gross profit of $10 per case, on the assumption that customers will simply buy Beefeater's elsewhere, if Top-Value is temporarily out of stock. The cost of Beefeater's is $56 per case. Holding charges over the order cycle are comprised of interest cost ($2.25 per case) for financing $56 per case and shelf space rent ($0.46 per case). There are no obsolescence or deterioration costs. The probability distribution for Beefeater demand is estimated to have a mean of 134 cases. Errors are normally distributed, with mean 0 and standard deviation equal to 46 cases.

   a. What is the value of K_u, the foregone profit (opportunity loss) per case understocked?
   b. What is the value of K_o?
   c. What is the optimal stock level, expressed as a fractile of the probability distribution for demand?
   d. How many cases should be on-hand at the beginning of the order cycle?
   e. What would be the loss per case from overstocking, if the cost per case were $39? (Hint: Interest costs vary with case cost, but shelf space rent is a fixed cost per case.)

APPENDIX TABLES

TABLE I	Table of Random Digits								
57323	99793	10404	96963	94149	09436	81289	21954	61399	86562
34720	06356	13309	04958	72741	75575	56567	21262	77996	05409
07578	65410	00035	32693	98319	68032	28659	80408	27007	63030
47371	37336	22937	51738	37503	89855	45893	74636	29767	52720
75165	97575	83615	07281	58542	36009	59936	18517	73157	11300
04885	81136	90574	88200	34719	33343	91636	24256	34494	31587
83239	54826	75030	75527	97006	47758	42133	19846	64341	70126
66474	06298	38096	44376	26037	63524	62251	88179	23447	34741
87329	30156	01551	50210	65238	34063	01982	09946	32295	47462
79155	84829	48006	33146	60458	69990	05107	28048	82959	22878
78986	67245	27473	25972	56124	65964	78422	24307	21716	11185
48528	89326	57091	61161	30877	68643	23416	46300	38171	39607
81006	92708	24803	09953	06949	38763	85506	82871	16774	23654
46570	62179	45157	39433	70012	25561	44522	58486	16495	91575
82073	60459	92791	53955	11120	36410	14834	22564	11477	07221
33835	66284	64182	70403	76105	01726	62048	19155	27851	22094
12640	75442	76862	68499	33486	57958	09867	95452	61593	64290
21169	93933	69194	76324	89108	02521	47389	88952	84196	61334
96268	83080	76688	17712	61708	43603	48754	11164	25733	26622
23625	85536	27462	62992	88022	75867	83873	65408	17795	82751
94668	37558	66240	14759	16472	23333	50819	06367	95422	45043
31377	07132	84367	03961	31082	64493	72267	82722	61919	77949
27290	95250	76361	89702	08367	88061	08887	26817	77449	64561
96474	56573	07318	94244	11211	39106	85678	68921	37696	15046
19982	08416	70690	39842	54764	43373	62609	51968	73501	33840
93680	47532	69086	33632	42387	56096	93777	48942	13020	41687
15302	75898	21162	37786	66961	86425	54004	75370	47379	26955
25188	10433	98394	63340	13059	51567	99759	15205	97136	06467
97521	53578	46447	18822	78202	50881	27649	56352	10471	11864
50659	09388	66058	59280	32170	32237	61958	90519	92639	23562
07479	15283	61125	14652	17993	19537	93660	64835	22592	79821
64529	34694	22619	38324	48400	75378	09240	36861	98773	72209
48766	41753	28432	77542	01540	51697	35739	36545	27139	41492
62371	43589	54464	76751	76286	99431	53709	81291	36388	18239
39778	15508	71011	89910	57399	58438	85383	52950	08688	55506
03572	40870	80928	43010	44354	46546	62850	55804	69579	56033
48323	14620	62144	87071	34851	35772	58560	87164	60469	44358
73561	94254	15586	79022	80518	35385	02413	16608	97986	86378
40933	90142	33973	05994	41921	00538	51677	61707	31505	83978
01687	16267	82704	10086	38959	31971	63458	48903	91708	78642
63237	85898	17680	04691	05891	99990	17838	32989	18486	48168
32710	07942	46986	40972	93529	95560	69704	76599	82420	77828
01698	69360	77089	88169	67613	10902	86726	33163	67216	79745
03257	24670	57515	58366	72192	84483	85997	95869	29868	84265
53952	37074	63163	49843	38295	57415	01467	44343	99594	69159
29491	05725	55666	61541	93590	52618	77207	58627	09852	45554
20765	57055	76350	16220	13411	94537	88567	51673	18179	81825
51533	72854	25221	27548	48080	83387	14392	75371	55010	31938
36917	25339	57165	74158	75581	71166	59216	87606	04612	89915
57055	76561	84511	36351	35237	93892	93545	89497	78415	94475

				TABLE I Continued					
03148	04871	61554	65808	36972	31671	33367	09094	40339	41308
82169	55226	96435	66876	17340	00680	73972	81624	95444	53887
16714	53179	65824	88444	02673	47945	00824	04294	31704	13228
53508	39120	92541	36133	88096	30989	94866	48540	74109	98631
17646	23475	64745	79630	95824	53242	21881	89124	11343	18128
56147	64618	35986	66218	44003	59241	54121	53548	24324	16876
64294	79929	84285	27244	36433	82159	11379	06001	07266	12668
81843	61626	76247	88647	26484	65160	88418	83431	38116	80065
53662	66084	86887	33168	34637	45619	41139	16275	44743	27228
97204	77979	37865	69822	70419	11068	07929	34631	22064	25608
15860	54477	16417	87557	52300	47163	13865	31098	24637	06156
45516	16545	93161	19971	05222	68838	76589	94721	49634	92586
36290	90912	83649	92655	24334	53518	32398	91154	39304	87475
99417	85600	18282	12195	48137	34230	70013	97229	54763	30726
50946	69272	50662	21769	68381	02501	40191	49152	03082	34558
82590	42192	53419	87590	14257	14346	91700	49126	74218	64798
42846	48465	34252	97674	79457	18736	00909	86524	98611	54202
54795	87060	12961	59512	61453	89954	29561	75207	43710	49689
71641	81366	53406	55225	98537	15832	85052	46183	94424	59956
07088	64503	54101	95094	29899	06566	30991	36591	93945	63813
18496	15508	20749	78586	76780	26182	35955	22051	64431	78864
14173	33399	83276	82126	01674	26977	86600	83694	90405	18504
32254	73230	67352	52741	17197	74849	91663	96798	72708	61946
48649	31472	25294	56777	15852	71195	24282	16451	53940	20170
22451	33300	05786	36637	66954	51134	72260	66958	32093	62888
03392	31564	66318	30553	11981	33829	76034	19441	00634	59284
35774	35665	22015	53319	15756	84202	19887	59426	40044	32325
51196	09824	92181	14344	78464	65711	18340	40568	21574	37776
01863	97563	03162	40921	67197	68041	04586	47038	91526	27566
69750	55831	34595	88748	80398	47008	65935	14625	72974	63589
40318	90386	77022	95695	49915	96827	18290	82176	57965	85947
50314	97594	32442	28729	44841	40791	40876	21037	22818	21660
69855	64585	84752	38688	37362	70779	32085	33610	23101	65816
32782	80175	62904	19197	52940	09085	82005	13643	99665	14096
82415	57720	32125	05918	90919	54748	53037	88527	29275	91618
22392	33237	32573	12505	48481	89035	42519	08446	77558	20072
92113	35065	03210	81591	19652	83958	06640	02184	61085	38973
83807	04152	69923	12793	40150	31977	97418	91353	08907	70766
21435	67406	22074	07477	06107	71310	56939	83058	07865	18174
94774	71688	79126	86939	78564	50984	97128	33269	78401	87753
44515	35938	14533	95777	18190	37792	09581	98809	98406	00387
33236	30784	64950	99609	82066	19467	11280	70842	68265	41641
62960	73668	67954	51325	51737	08115	02683	91157	42577	84435
45562	91946	91963	44875	61486	56735	85029	97822	68556	24484
88453	05332	29046	85758	91592	99631	20821	29257	81925	73603
06480	40914	94059	40045	86873	70833	87507	18286	27588	49392
49252	04549	04404	95052	62013	25190	66006	12177	99175	97842
04160	79335	96970	80580	35614	03203	23961	95669	08698	95687
08126	27332	31788	15863	03388	97377	30859	62194	54165	48989
50715	31189	21558	52500	50265	38393	88608	47563	73791	18570

TABLE I	Continued								
35857	05881	56987	67626	91552	65227	25956	35367	98342	70449
65755	72241	90415	98071	53962	59714	72801	40823	24553	85828
38153	19407	16237	91592	01375	95309	71852	41520	81157	79864
97688	55671	01053	92304	64759	91865	19153	06674	99502	17278
47573	93053	59381	38182	99692	00201	59267	32347	46673	61985
49038	88784	39307	20261	89987	52459	35632	58977	97722	37701
02450	49641	34841	62921	63491	14884	41721	16410	88097	69795
76620	26203	80035	11163	84709	83234	40610	84462	20074	77735
55556	75074	34125	11814	44923	44702	13899	81894	79284	90456
81869	36582	26227	03448	59866	96840	35803	64665	97811	28603
29137	18688	97870	41342	19480	19071	37891	76719	00339	40151
81493	16953	62106	93856	84084	64161	46975	29936	14002	56781
87941	85345	66034	98019	05113	98087	44807	38114	54473	58202
51450	05667	89494	20117	45306	61000	10529	05306	88764	08546
96684	16409	13041	63794	72479	01423	40060	13694	50569	50620
10961	80756	60878	21433	41310	53493	87731	31789	04235	98404
05772	62112	43024	00738	50512	01421	68758	32132	73638	26087
54213	73522	98985	21933	90610	33414	19134	71000	69178	51174
46335	27688	75266	14787	89625	45675	45501	70686	27912	85607
25987	51987	32526	38002	28218	31193	62673	15291	58002	04745
59317	34130	50457	49452	18570	77734	26461	92754	26756	85131
19261	04405	92915	12487	34629	30015	49956	30029	38740	55835
91160	03233	58059	76021	41850	80031	70454	25257	81762	74726
34738	47059	05894	53370	74197	78952	44471	40301	28675	53335
36055	12201	48331	53079	99805	20856	30417	31031	30642	62847
52461	78934	08126	73361	58133	07688	06798	35647	29612	12277
74924	00082	72793	56368	16185	05981	60104	50736	99566	08682
86914	23052	73371	12208	70818	70922	56054	90908	99915	52815
79746	95993	99342	48774	06259	47572	19512	99950	65329	43547
93194	06949	66210	47646	22387	18062	69684	06439	58635	15507
52733	00447	95450	64911	99501	57621	62926	93166	00783	45761
70968	79352	42678	75484	19698	09591	41384	20018	77067	16737
93354	29790	75204	80578	41467	33787	71157	07642	75165	06201
07449	51775	20034	90992	13532	91324	22096	79243	02108	28969
05375	09190	11211	65612	52025	97267	23441	79237	86581	02790
03632	00330	26495	63881	67953	35619	35774	09008	73970	76267
09230	91978	07279	48465	36036	68075	66544	00313	25969	26545
35158	70007	26827	99964	47956	05511	55553	33819	14550	80562
08061	25904	75123	33840	74809	13685	85405	53975	59952	00235
17195	48074	46701	30907	86106	76089	93771	35152	14134	71002
24793	30890	50219	81774	12450	31948	21318	06994	21962	33025
40820	21424	64737	80123	89997	20493	64279	69293	01048	05464
76140	94450	45620	09687	82193	22839	05614	48144	83997	30215
34763	80580	16138	03468	18284	61269	27396	48852	23638	25777
54484	97576	67979	11227	26645	36822	28787	75708	49563	29843
51093	97935	64385	92783	44946	72086	24074	17419	63802	83648
05886	84043	44538	01351	51232	62591	40477	92753	06866	16617
38616	11167	21390	71310	76239	58367	22169	25948	12390	40680
09592	75140	95410	58377	76847	64799	57570	46548	49610	79171
08763	06504	35347	13735	15119	11191	00695	27439	24803	30733

TABLE I	**Continued**								
03044	24543	42072	79680	70019	78779	49306	90771	42022	35701
15560	51758	26977	64554	78236	24705	69695	99867	98919	08229
79087	54861	30935	17900	56066	84900	74827	20818	83319	38587
87053	04176	89256	50025	76731	18316	84391	78194	13870	29285
99080	60895	93811	24691	04617	00386	02141	30979	38443	40015
59715	81017	90024	09811	47574	28723	70418	30220	74729	05715
79610	76039	47334	75630	10614	88086	15794	65536	22233	01084
58011	80929	14172	77487	91825	27074	34459	26623	52078	85294
27351	96471	87733	33042	66295	67504	75683	89734	79295	03989
72708	79171	34745	61582	45778	56342	03275	80997	19954	33064
25169	04815	97967	57868	45665	67943	75752	21144	25093	23829
60262	53357	11413	16880	60053	32878	62011	44181	53124	93003
41548	56333	82614	64215	45209	13979	03694	49679	92492	92512
73539	59264	07430	36096	53409	76609	20240	81729	38628	88424
04159	12662	68478	49198	07870	45549	39237	25887	59740	56033
53767	57263	24011	03912	57514	73856	23916	68222	19320	55887
11057	02428	00784	77994	26033	37912	00656	22127	90684	43070
64894	23508	18287	40240	43033	84697	84851	57728	27921	09503
93325	26084	23637	36975	64523	57582	59426	13394	32554	06762
90468	51031	95933	41140	43608	19773	46944	79775	42240	51084
77363	03452	30358	53617	24194	02208	37612	64459	20987	21080
05307	78531	27936	77670	25855	01373	10692	00706	26943	44746
39296	03736	98571	67191	71198	41520	57326	69046	20424	68993
37294	49408	20049	99094	73162	01789	07572	54060	03831	97125
38095	82253	49106	95403	33066	49865	43033	29705	00537	42666
81801	29595	31364	70338	65143	55347	14579	55032	70167	26651
38320	27407	83640	35075	44338	00758	87455	68754	61716	83161
98098	92320	67132	67437	91291	22481	81568	41805	21903	82901
55704	21352	35263	99814	31774	72663	66281	33235	85421	07441
24948	16939	68622	55229	99696	77373	61871	83968	24902	41572
89263	90153	10494	06029	00555	54896	53185	02515	84821	39567
04002	19290	32247	08352	38913	44192	63586	07500	72659	70244
43531	00594	34216	18877	09467	24260	47346	16222	95813	37488
62043	10474	76404	96587	23886	70299	93954	42006	17843	95723
02455	74749	56588	53680	94361	23392	10699	69200	80699	43901
60746	27343	72901	00768	30981	63382	80418	84708	77483	20102
64233	34664	44774	00783	14465	09805	46428	25449	65136	98953
71597	01733	13727	08095	10483	25994	30097	15417	75958	28088
87621	00725	85032	74684	27267	00850	60825	75215	66928	96224
20210	38640	00185	34785	60340	48689	55062	14429	88350	63982
96858	88390	32067	37656	86493	59218	39596	14775	86475	51302
87073	51240	21891	34431	97567	50891	94034	83024	56657	43740
77694	12353	22939	94349	63524	67863	60161	65357	01754	23801
79269	79797	95723	77898	94504	54574	80223	71330	18165	65646
05425	15357	67120	17879	01863	68392	79358	82454	53388	03437
49242	88862	80962	26949	30827	56264	94866	80287	63328	47643
36078	57123	95248	64479	45423	22949	34756	56824	16858	17698
83851	13020	90959	47839	47863	33916	41292	91331	23391	40033
52176	93521	54383	45258	85524	75057	96733	22736	66880	53651
02795	85459	63621	86521	26416	64783	93141	83453	85880	11638

TABLE II Cumulative Binomial Probability Tables

Table values give the probability that the random variable X assumes a value less than or equal to x: $P(X \leq x|n, p)$. Example: $P(X \leq 5|n = 7, p = .7) = .671$

$n = 1$

x	.01	.05	.10	.20	.30	.40	p .50	.60	.70	.80	.90	.95	.99
0	.990	.950	.900	.800	.700	.600	.500	.400	.300	.200	.100	.050	.010

$n = 2$

x	.01	.05	.10	.20	.30	.40	p .50	.60	.70	.80	.90	.95	.99
0	.980	.903	.810	.640	.490	.360	.250	.160	.090	.040	.010	.003	.000
1	1.000	.998	.990	.960	.910	.840	.750	.640	.510	.360	.190	.097	.020

$n = 3$

x	.01	.05	.10	.20	.30	.40	p .50	.60	.70	.80	.90	.95	.99
0	.970	.857	.729	.512	.343	.216	.125	.064	.027	.008	.001	.000	.000
1	1.000	.993	.972	.896	.784	.648	.500	.352	.216	.104	.028	.007	.000
2	1.000	1.000	.999	.992	.973	.936	.875	.784	.657	.488	.271	.143	.030

$n = 4$

x	.01	.05	.10	.20	.30	.40	p .50	.60	.70	.80	.90	.95	.99
0	.961	.815	.656	.410	.240	.130	.063	.026	.008	.002	.000	.000	.000
1	.999	.986	.948	.819	.652	.475	.313	.179	.084	.027	.004	.000	.000
2	1.000	1.000	.996	.973	.916	.821	.688	.525	.348	.181	.052	.014	.001
3	1.000	1.000	1.000	.998	.992	.974	.938	.870	.760	.590	.344	.185	.039

$n = 5$

x	.01	.05	.10	.20	.30	.40	p .50	.60	.70	.80	.90	.95	.99
0	.951	.774	.590	.328	.168	.078	.031	.010	.002	.000	.000	.000	.000
1	.999	.977	.919	.737	.528	.337	.188	.087	.031	.007	.000	.000	.000
2	1.000	.999	.991	.942	.837	.683	.500	.317	.163	.058	.009	.001	.000
3	1.000	1.000	1.000	.993	.969	.913	.812	.663	.472	.263	.081	.023	.001
4	1.000	1.000	1.000	1.000	.998	.990	.969	.922	.832	.672	.410	.226	.049

TABLE II Continued

n = 6

x	.01	.05	.10	.20	.30	.40	p .50	.60	.70	.80	.90	.95	.99
0	.941	.735	.531	.262	.118	.047	.016	.004	.001	.000	.000	.000	.000
1	.999	.967	.886	.655	.420	.233	.109	.041	.011	.002	.000	.000	.000
2	1.000	.998	.984	.901	.744	.544	.344	.179	.070	.017	.001	.000	.000
3	1.000	1.000	.999	.983	.930	.821	.656	.456	.256	.099	.016	.002	.000
4	1.000	1.000	1.000	.998	.989	.959	.891	.767	.580	.345	.114	.033	.001
5	1.000	1.000	1.000	1.000	.999	.996	.984	.953	.882	.738	.469	.265	.059

n = 7

x	.01	.05	.10	.20	.30	.40	p .50	.60	.70	.80	.90	.95	.99
0	.932	.698	.478	.210	.082	.028	.008	.002	.000	.000	.000	.000	.000
1	.998	.956	.850	.577	.329	.159	.063	.019	.004	.000	.000	.000	.000
2	1.000	.996	.974	.852	.647	.420	.227	.096	.029	.005	.000	.000	.000
3	1.000	1.000	.997	.967	.874	.710	.500	.290	.126	.033	.003	.000	.000
4	1.000	1.000	1.000	.995	.971	.904	.773	.580	.353	.148	.026	.004	.000
5	1.000	1.000	1.000	1.000	.996	.981	.938	.841	.671	.423	.150	.044	.002
6	1.000	1.000	1.000	1.000	1.000	.998	.992	.972	.918	.790	.522	.302	.068

n = 8

x	.01	.05	.10	.20	.30	.40	p .50	.60	.70	.80	.90	.95	.99
0	.923	.663	.430	.168	.058	.017	.004	.001	.000	.000	.000	.000	.000
1	.997	.943	.813	.503	.255	.106	.035	.009	.001	.000	.000	.000	.000
2	1.000	.994	.962	.797	.552	.315	.145	.050	.011	.001	.000	.000	.000
3	1.000	1.000	.995	.944	.806	.594	.363	.174	.058	.010	.000	.000	.000
4	1.000	1.000	1.000	.990	.942	.826	.637	.406	.194	.056	.005	.000	.000
5	1.000	1.000	1.000	.999	.989	.950	.855	.685	.448	.203	.038	.006	.000
6	1.000	1.000	1.000	1.000	.999	.991	.965	.894	.745	.497	.187	.057	.003
7	1.000	1.000	1.000	1.000	1.000	.999	.996	.983	.942	.832	.570	.337	.077

n = 9

x	.01	.05	.10	.20	.30	.40	p .50	.60	.70	.80	.90	.95	.99
0	.914	.630	.387	.134	.040	.010	.002	.000	.000	.000	.000	.000	.000
1	.997	.929	.775	.436	.196	.071	.020	.004	.000	.000	.000	.000	.000
2	1.000	.992	.947	.738	.463	.232	.090	.025	.004	.000	.000	.000	.000
3	1.000	.999	.992	.914	.730	.483	.254	.099	.025	.003	.000	.000	.000
4	1.000	1.000	.999	.980	.901	.733	.500	.267	.099	.020	.001	.000	.000
5	1.000	1.000	1.000	.997	.975	.901	.746	.517	.270	.086	.008	.001	.000
6	1.000	1.000	1.000	1.000	.996	.975	.910	.768	.537	.262	.053	.008	.000
7	1.000	1.000	1.000	1.000	1.000	.996	.980	.929	.804	.564	.225	.071	.003
8	1.000	1.000	1.000	1.000	1.000	1.000	.998	.990	.960	.866	.613	.370	.086

TABLE II   Continued

n = 10

x	.01	.05	.10	.20	.30	.40	p .50	.60	.70	.80	.90	.95	.99
0	.904	.599	.349	.107	.028	.006	.001	.000	.000	.000	.000	.000	.000
1	.996	.914	.736	.376	.149	.046	.011	.002	.000	.000	.000	.000	.000
2	1.000	.988	.930	.678	.383	.167	.055	.012	.002	.000	.000	.000	.000
3	1.000	.999	.987	.879	.650	.382	.172	.055	.011	.001	.000	.000	.000
4	1.000	1.000	.998	.967	.850	.633	.377	.166	.047	.006	.000	.000	.000
5	1.000	1.000	1.000	.994	.953	.834	.623	.367	.150	.033	.002	.000	.000
6	1.000	1.000	1.000	.999	.989	.945	.828	.618	.350	.121	.013	.001	.000
7	1.000	1.000	1.000	1.000	.998	.988	.945	.833	.617	.322	.070	.012	.000
8	1.000	1.000	1.000	1.000	1.000	.998	.989	.954	.851	.624	.264	.086	.004
9	1.000	1.000	1.000	1.000	1.000	1.000	.999	.994	.972	.893	.651	.401	.096

n = 11

x	.01	.05	.10	.20	.30	.40	p .50	.60	.70	.80	.90	.95	.99
0	.895	.569	.314	.086	.020	.004	.000	.000	.000	.000	.000	.000	.000
1	.995	.898	.697	.322	.113	.030	.006	.001	.000	.000	.000	.000	.000
2	1.000	.985	.910	.617	.313	.119	.033	.006	.001	.000	.000	.000	.000
3	1.000	.998	.981	.839	.570	.296	.113	.029	.004	.000	.000	.000	.000
4	1.000	1.000	.997	.950	.790	.533	.274	.099	.022	.002	.000	.000	.000
5	1.000	1.000	1.000	.988	.922	.753	.500	.247	.078	.012	.000	.000	.000
6	1.000	1.000	1.000	.998	.978	.901	.726	.467	.210	.050	.003	.000	.000
7	1.000	1.000	1.000	1.000	.996	.971	.887	.704	.430	.161	.019	.002	.000
8	1.000	1.000	1.000	1.000	.999	.994	.967	.881	.687	.383	.090	.015	.000
9	1.000	1.000	1.000	1.000	1.000	.999	.994	.970	.887	.678	.303	.102	.005
10	1.000	1.000	1.000	1.000	1.000	1.000	1.000	.996	.980	.914	.686	.431	.105

n = 12

x	.01	.05	.10	.20	.30	.40	p .50	.60	.70	.80	.90	.95	.99
0	.886	.540	.282	.069	.014	.002	.000	.000	.000	.000	.000	.000	.000
1	.994	.882	.659	.275	.085	.020	.003	.000	.000	.000	.000	.000	.000
2	1.000	.980	.889	.558	.253	.083	.019	.003	.000	.000	.000	.000	.000
3	1.000	.998	.974	.795	.493	.225	.073	.015	.002	.000	.000	.000	.000
4	1.000	1.000	.996	.927	.724	.438	.194	.057	.009	.001	.000	.000	.000
5	1.000	1.000	.999	.981	.882	.665	.387	.158	.039	.004	.000	.000	.000
6	1.000	1.000	1.000	.996	.961	.842	.613	.335	.118	.019	.001	.000	.000
7	1.000	1.000	1.000	.999	.991	.943	.806	.562	.276	.073	.004	.000	.000
8	1.000	1.000	1.000	1.000	.998	.985	.927	.775	.507	.205	.026	.002	.000
9	1.000	1.000	1.000	1.000	1.000	.997	.981	.917	.747	.442	.111	.020	.000
10	1.000	1.000	1.000	1.000	1.000	1.000	.997	.980	.915	.725	.341	.118	.006
11	1.000	1.000	1.000	1.000	1.000	1.000	1.000	.998	.986	.931	.718	.460	.114

TABLE II Continued

n = 13

x	.01	.05	.10	.20	.30	.40	p .50	.60	.70	.80	.90	.95	.99
0	.878	.513	.254	.055	.010	.001	.000	.000	.000	.000	.000	.000	.000
1	.993	.865	.621	.234	.064	.013	.002	.000	.000	.000	.000	.000	.000
2	1.000	.975	.866	.502	.202	.058	.011	.001	.000	.000	.000	.000	.000
3	1.000	.997	.966	.747	.421	.169	.046	.008	.001	.000	.000	.000	.000
4	1.000	1.000	.994	.901	.654	.353	.133	.032	.004	.000	.000	.000	.000
5	1.000	1.000	.999	.970	.835	.574	.291	.098	.018	.001	.000	.000	.000
6	1.000	1.000	1.000	.993	.938	.771	.500	.229	.062	.007	.000	.000	.000
7	1.000	1.000	1.000	.999	.982	.902	.709	.426	.165	.030	.001	.000	.000
8	1.000	1.000	1.000	1.000	.996	.968	.867	.647	.346	.099	.006	.000	.000
9	1.000	1.000	1.000	1.000	.999	.992	.954	.831	.579	.253	.034	.003	.000
10	1.000	1.000	1.000	1.000	1.000	.999	.989	.942	.798	.498	.134	.025	.000
11	1.000	1.000	1.000	1.000	1.000	1.000	.998	.987	.936	.766	.379	.135	.007
12	1.000	1.000	1.000	1.000	1.000	1.000	1.000	.999	.990	.945	.746	.487	.122

n = 14

x	.01	.05	.10	.20	.30	.40	p .50	.60	.70	.80	.90	.95	.99
0	.869	.488	.229	.044	.007	.001	.000	.000	.000	.000	.000	.000	.000
1	.992	.847	.585	.198	.047	.008	.001	.000	.000	.000	.000	.000	.000
2	1.000	.970	.842	.448	.161	.040	.006	.001	.000	.000	.000	.000	.000
3	1.000	.996	.956	.698	.355	.124	.029	.004	.000	.000	.000	.000	.000
4	1.000	1.000	.991	.870	.584	.279	.090	.018	.002	.000	.000	.000	.000
5	1.000	1.000	.999	.956	.781	.486	.212	.058	.008	.000	.000	.000	.000
6	1.000	1.000	1.000	.988	.907	.692	.395	.150	.031	.002	.000	.000	.000
7	1.000	1.000	1.000	.998	.969	.850	.605	.308	.093	.012	.000	.000	.000
8	1.000	1.000	1.000	1.000	.992	.942	.788	.514	.219	.044	.001	.000	.000
9	1.000	1.000	1.000	1.000	.998	.982	.910	.721	.416	.130	.009	.000	.000
10	1.000	1.000	1.000	1.000	1.000	.996	.971	.876	.645	.302	.044	.004	.000
11	1.000	1.000	1.000	1.000	1.000	.999	.994	.960	.839	.552	.158	.030	.000
12	1.000	1.000	1.000	1.000	1.000	1.000	.999	.992	.953	.802	.415	.153	.008
13	1.000	1.000	1.000	1.000	1.000	1.000	1.000	.999	.993	.956	.771	.512	.131

TABLE II Continued

n = 15

x	.01	.05	.10	.20	.30	.40	p .50	.60	.70	.80	.90	.95	.99
0	.860	.463	.206	.035	.005	.000	.000	.000	.000	.000	.000	.000	.000
1	.990	.829	.549	.167	.035	.005	.000	.000	.000	.000	.000	.000	.000
2	1.000	.964	.816	.398	.127	.027	.004	.000	.000	.000	.000	.000	.000
3	1.000	.995	.944	.648	.297	.091	.018	.002	.000	.000	.000	.000	.000
4	1.000	.999	.987	.836	.515	.217	.059	.009	.001	.000	.000	.000	.000
5	1.000	1.000	.998	.939	.722	.403	.151	.034	.004	.000	.000	.000	.000
6	1.000	1.000	1.000	.982	.869	.610	.304	.095	.015	.001	.000	.000	.000
7	1.000	1.000	1.000	.996	.950	.787	.500	.213	.050	.004	.000	.000	.000
8	1.000	1.000	1.000	.999	.985	.905	.696	.390	.131	.018	.000	.000	.000
9	1.000	1.000	1.000	1.000	.996	.966	.849	.597	.278	.061	.002	.000	.000
10	1.000	1.000	1.000	1.000	.999	.991	.941	.783	.485	.164	.013	.001	.000
11	1.000	1.000	1.000	1.000	1.000	.998	.982	.909	.703	.352	.056	.005	.000
12	1.000	1.000	1.000	1.000	1.000	1.000	.996	.973	.873	.602	.184	.036	.000
13	1.000	1.000	1.000	1.000	1.000	1.000	1.000	.995	.965	.833	.451	.171	.010
14	1.000	1.000	1.000	1.000	1.000	1.000	1.000	1.000	.995	.965	.794	.537	.140

n = 16

x	.01	.05	.10	.20	.30	.40	p .50	.60	.70	.80	.90	.95	.99
0	.851	.440	.185	.028	.003	.000	.000	.000	.000	.000	.000	.000	.000
1	.989	.811	.515	.141	.026	.003	.000	.000	.000	.000	.000	.000	.000
2	.999	.957	.789	.352	.099	.018	.002	.000	.000	.000	.000	.000	.000
3	1.000	.993	.932	.598	.246	.065	.011	.001	.000	.000	.000	.000	.000
4	1.000	.999	.983	.798	.450	.167	.038	.005	.000	.000	.000	.000	.000
5	1.000	1.000	.997	.918	.660	.329	.105	.019	.002	.000	.000	.000	.000
6	1.000	1.000	.999	.973	.825	.527	.227	.058	.007	.000	.000	.000	.000
7	1.000	1.000	1.000	.993	.926	.716	.402	.142	.026	.001	.000	.000	.000
8	1.000	1.000	1.000	.999	.974	.858	.598	.284	.074	.007	.000	.000	.000
9	1.000	1.000	1.000	1.000	.993	.942	.773	.473	.175	.027	.001	.000	.000
10	1.000	1.000	1.000	1.000	.998	.981	.895	.671	.340	.082	.003	.000	.000
11	1.000	1.000	1.000	1.000	1.000	.995	.962	.833	.550	.202	.017	.001	.000
12	1.000	1.000	1.000	1.000	1.000	.999	.989	.935	.754	.402	.068	.007	.000
13	1.000	1.000	1.000	1.000	1.000	1.000	.998	.982	.901	.648	.211	.043	.001
14	1.000	1.000	1.000	1.000	1.000	1.000	1.000	.997	.974	.859	.485	.189	.011
15	1.000	1.000	1.000	1.000	1.000	1.000	1.000	1.000	.997	.972	.815	.560	.149

TABLE II Continued

n = 17

x	.01	.05	.10	.20	.30	.40	p .50	.60	.70	.80	.90	.95	.99
0	.843	.418	.167	.023	.002	.000	.000	.000	.000	.000	.000	.000	.000
1	.988	.792	.482	.118	.019	.002	.000	.000	.000	.000	.000	.000	.000
2	.999	.950	.762	.310	.077	.012	.001	.000	.000	.000	.000	.000	.000
3	1.000	.991	.917	.549	.202	.046	.006	.000	.000	.000	.000	.000	.000
4	1.000	.999	.978	.758	.389	.126	.025	.003	.000	.000	.000	.000	.000
5	1.000	1.000	.995	.894	.597	.264	.072	.011	.001	.000	.000	.000	.000
6	1.000	1.000	.999	.962	.775	.448	.166	.035	.003	.000	.000	.000	.000
7	1.000	1.000	1.000	.989	.895	.641	.315	.092	.013	.000	.000	.000	.000
8	1.000	1.000	1.000	.997	.960	.801	.500	.199	.040	.003	.000	.000	.000
9	1.000	1.000	1.000	1.000	.987	.908	.685	.359	.105	.011	.000	.000	.000
10	1.000	1.000	1.000	1.000	.997	.965	.834	.552	.225	.038	.001	.000	.000
11	1.000	1.000	1.000	1.000	.999	.989	.928	.736	.403	.106	.005	.000	.000
12	1.000	1.000	1.000	1.000	1.000	.997	.975	.874	.611	.242	.022	.001	.000
13	1.000	1.000	1.000	1.000	1.000	1.000	.994	.954	.798	.451	.083	.009	.000
14	1.000	1.000	1.000	1.000	1.000	1.000	.999	.988	.923	.690	.238	.050	.001
15	1.000	1.000	1.000	1.000	1.000	1.000	1.000	.998	.981	.882	.518	.208	.012
16	1.000	1.000	1.000	1.000	1.000	1.000	1.000	1.000	.998	.977	.833	.582	.157

n = 18

x	.01	.05	.10	.20	.30	.40	p .50	.60	.70	.80	.90	.95	.99
0	.835	.397	.150	.018	.002	.000	.000	.000	.000	.000	.000	.000	.000
1	.986	.774	.450	.099	.014	.001	.000	.000	.000	.000	.000	.000	.000
2	.999	.942	.734	.271	.060	.008	.001	.000	.000	.000	.000	.000	.000
3	1.000	.989	.902	.501	.165	.033	.004	.000	.000	.000	.000	.000	.000
4	1.000	.998	.972	.716	.333	.094	.015	.001	.000	.000	.000	.000	.000
5	1.000	1.000	.994	.867	.534	.209	.048	.006	.000	.000	.000	.000	.000
6	1.000	1.000	.999	.949	.722	.374	.119	.020	.001	.000	.000	.000	.000
7	1.000	1.000	1.000	.984	.859	.563	.240	.058	.006	.000	.000	.000	.000
8	1.000	1.000	1.000	.996	.940	.737	.407	.135	.021	.001	.000	.000	.000
9	1.000	1.000	1.000	.999	.979	.865	.593	.263	.060	.004	.000	.000	.000
10	1.000	1.000	1.000	1.000	.994	.942	.760	.437	.141	.016	.000	.000	.000
11	1.000	1.000	1.000	1.000	.999	.980	.881	.626	.278	.051	.001	.000	.000
12	1.000	1.000	1.000	1.000	1.000	.994	.952	.791	.466	.133	.006	.000	.000
13	1.000	1.000	1.000	1.000	1.000	.999	.985	.906	.667	.284	.028	.002	.000
14	1.000	1.000	1.000	1.000	1.000	1.000	.996	.967	.835	.499	.098	.011	.000
15	1.000	1.000	1.000	1.000	1.000	1.000	.999	.992	.940	.729	.266	.058	.001
16	1.000	1.000	1.000	1.000	1.000	1.000	1.000	.999	.986	.901	.550	.226	.014
17	1.000	1.000	1.000	1.000	1.000	1.000	1.000	1.000	.998	.982	.850	.603	.165

TABLE II Continued

n = 19

x	.01	.05	.10	.20	.30	.40	p .50	.60	.70	.80	.90	.95	.99
0	.826	.377	.135	.014	.001	.000	.000	.000	.000	.000	.000	.000	.000
1	.985	.755	.420	.083	.010	.001	.000	.000	.000	.000	.000	.000	.000
2	.999	.933	.705	.237	.046	.005	.000	.000	.000	.000	.000	.000	.000
3	1.000	.987	.885	.455	.133	.023	.002	.000	.000	.000	.000	.000	.000
4	1.000	.998	.965	.673	.282	.070	.010	.001	.000	.000	.000	.000	.000
5	1.000	1.000	.991	.837	.474	.163	.032	.003	.000	.000	.000	.000	.000
6	1.000	1.000	.998	.932	.666	.308	.084	.012	.001	.000	.000	.000	.000
7	1.000	1.000	1.000	.977	.818	.488	.180	.035	.003	.000	.000	.000	.000
8	1.000	1.000	1.000	.993	.916	.667	.324	.088	.011	.000	.000	.000	.000
9	1.000	1.000	1.000	.998	.967	.814	.500	.186	.033	.002	.000	.000	.000
10	1.000	1.000	1.000	1.000	.989	.912	.676	.333	.084	.007	.000	.000	.000
11	1.000	1.000	1.000	1.000	.997	.965	.820	.512	.182	.023	.000	.000	.000
12	1.000	1.000	1.000	1.000	.999	.988	.916	.692	.334	.068	.002	.000	.000
13	1.000	1.000	1.000	1.000	1.000	.997	.968	.837	.526	.163	.009	.000	.000
14	1.000	1.000	1.000	1.000	1.000	.999	.990	.930	.718	.327	.035	.002	.000
15	1.000	1.000	1.000	1.000	1.000	1.000	.998	.977	.867	.545	.115	.013	.000
16	1.000	1.000	1.000	1.000	1.000	1.000	1.000	.995	.954	.763	.295	.067	.001
17	1.000	1.000	1.000	1.000	1.000	1.000	1.000	.999	.990	.917	.580	.245	.015
18	1.000	1.000	1.000	1.000	1.000	1.000	1.000	1.000	.999	.986	.865	.623	.174

n = 20

x	.01	.05	.10	.20	.30	.40	p .50	.60	.70	.80	.90	.95	.99
0	.818	.358	.122	.002	.001	.000	.000	.000	.000	.000	.000	.000	.000
1	.983	.736	.392	.069	.008	.001	.000	.000	.000	.000	.000	.000	.000
2	.999	.925	.677	.206	.035	.004	.000	.000	.000	.000	.000	.000	.000
3	1.000	.984	.867	.411	.107	.016	.001	.000	.000	.000	.000	.000	.000
4	1.000	.997	.957	.630	.238	.051	.006	.000	.000	.000	.000	.000	.000
5	1.000	1.000	.989	.804	.416	.126	.021	.002	.000	.000	.000	.000	.000
6	1.000	1.000	.998	.913	.608	.250	.058	.006	.000	.000	.000	.000	.000
7	1.000	1.000	1.000	.968	.772	.416	.132	.021	.001	.000	.000	.000	.000
8	1.000	1.000	1.000	.990	.887	.596	.252	.057	.005	.000	.000	.000	.000
9	1.000	1.000	1.000	.997	.952	.755	.412	.128	.017	.001	.000	.000	.000
10	1.000	1.000	1.000	.999	.983	.872	.588	.245	.048	.003	.000	.000	.000
11	1.000	1.000	1.000	1.000	.995	.943	.748	.404	.113	.010	.000	.000	.000
12	1.000	1.000	1.000	1.000	.999	.979	.868	.584	.228	.032	.000	.000	.000
13	1.000	1.000	1.000	1.000	1.000	.994	.942	.750	.392	.087	.002	.000	.000
14	1.000	1.000	1.000	1.000	1.000	.998	.979	.874	.584	.196	.011	.000	.000
15	1.000	1.000	1.000	1.000	1.000	1.000	.994	.949	.762	.370	.043	.003	.000
16	1.000	1.000	1.000	1.000	1.000	1.000	.999	.984	.893	.589	.133	.016	.000
17	1.000	1.000	1.000	1.000	1.000	1.000	1.000	.996	.965	.794	.323	.075	.001
18	1.000	1.000	1.000	1.000	1.000	1.000	1.000	.999	.992	.931	.608	.264	.017
19	1.000	1.000	1.000	1.000	1.000	1.000	1.000	1.000	.999	.988	.878	.642	.182

TABLE II Continued

n = 21

x	.01	.05	.10	.20	.30	.40	*p* .50	.60	.70	.80	.90	.95	.99
0	.810	.341	.109	.009	.001	.000	.000	.000	.000	.000	.000	.000	.000
1	.981	.717	.365	.058	.006	.000	.000	.000	.000	.000	.000	.000	.000
2	.999	.915	.648	.179	.027	.002	.000	.000	.000	.000	.000	.000	.000
3	1.000	.981	.848	.370	.086	.011	.001	.000	.000	.000	.000	.000	.000
4	1.000	.997	.948	.586	.198	.037	.004	.000	.000	.000	.000	.000	.000
5	1.000	1.000	.986	.769	.363	.096	.013	.001	.000	.000	.000	.000	.000
6	1.000	1.000	.997	.891	.551	.200	.039	.004	.000	.000	.000	.000	.000
7	1.000	1.000	.999	.957	.723	.350	.095	.012	.001	.000	.000	.000	.000
8	1.000	1.000	1.000	.986	.852	.524	.192	.035	.002	.000	.000	.000	.000
9	1.000	1.000	1.000	.996	.932	.691	.332	.085	.009	.000	.000	.000	.000
10	1.000	1.000	1.000	.999	.974	.826	.500	.174	.026	.001	.000	.000	.000
11	1.000	1.000	1.000	1.000	.991	.915	.668	.309	.068	.004	.000	.000	.000
12	1.000	1.000	1.000	1.000	.998	.965	.808	.476	.148	.014	.000	.000	.000
13	1.000	1.000	1.000	1.000	.999	.988	.905	.650	.277	.043	.001	.000	.000
14	1.000	1.000	1.000	1.000	1.000	.996	.961	.800	.449	.109	.003	.000	.000
15	1.000	1.000	1.000	1.000	1.000	.999	.987	.904	.637	.231	.014	.000	.000
16	1.000	1.000	1.000	1.000	1.000	1.000	.996	.963	.802	.414	.052	.003	.000
17	1.000	1.000	1.000	1.000	1.000	1.000	.999	.989	.914	.630	.152	.019	.000
18	1.000	1.000	1.000	1.000	1.000	1.000	1.000	.998	.973	.821	.352	.085	.001
19	1.000	1.000	1.000	1.000	1.000	1.000	1.000	1.000	.994	.942	.635	.283	.019
20	1.000	1.000	1.000	1.000	1.000	1.000	1.000	1.000	.999	.991	.891	.659	.190

n = 22

x	.01	.05	.10	.20	.30	.40	*p* .50	.60	.70	.80	.90	.95	.99
0	.802	.324	.098	.007	.000	.000	.000	.000	.000	.000	.000	.000	.000
1	.980	.698	.339	.048	.004	.000	.000	.000	.000	.000	.000	.000	.000
2	.999	.905	.620	.154	.021	.002	.000	.000	.000	.000	.000	.000	.000
3	1.000	.978	.828	.332	.068	.008	.000	.000	.000	.000	.000	.000	.000
4	1.000	.996	.938	.543	.165	.027	.002	.000	.000	.000	.000	.000	.000
5	1.000	.999	.982	.733	.313	.072	.008	.000	.000	.000	.000	.000	.000
6	1.000	1.000	.996	.867	.494	.158	.026	.002	.000	.000	.000	.000	.000
7	1.000	1.000	.999	.944	.671	.290	.067	.007	.000	.000	.000	.000	.000
8	1.000	1.000	1.000	.980	.814	.454	.143	.021	.001	.000	.000	.000	.000
9	1.000	1.000	1.000	.994	.908	.624	.262	.055	.004	.000	.000	.000	.000
10	1.000	1.000	1.000	.998	.961	.772	.416	.121	.014	.000	.000	.000	.000
11	1.000	1.000	1.000	1.000	.986	.879	.584	.228	.039	.002	.000	.000	.000
12	1.000	1.000	1.000	1.000	.996	.945	.738	.376	.092	.006	.000	.000	.000
13	1.000	1.000	1.000	1.000	.999	.979	.857	.546	.186	.020	.000	.000	.000
14	1.000	1.000	1.000	1.000	1.000	.993	.933	.710	.329	.056	.001	.000	.000
15	1.000	1.000	1.000	1.000	1.000	.998	.974	.842	.506	.133	.004	.000	.000
16	1.000	1.000	1.000	1.000	1.000	1.000	.992	.928	.687	.267	.018	.001	.000
17	1.000	1.000	1.000	1.000	1.000	1.000	.998	.973	.835	.457	.062	.004	.000
18	1.000	1.000	1.000	1.000	1.000	1.000	1.000	.992	.932	.668	.172	.022	.000
19	1.000	1.000	1.000	1.000	1.000	1.000	1.000	.998	.979	.846	.380	.095	.001
20	1.000	1.000	1.000	1.000	1.000	1.000	1.000	1.000	.996	.952	.661	.302	.020
21	1.000	1.000	1.000	1.000	1.000	1.000	1.000	1.000	1.000	.993	.902	.676	.198

TABLE II Continued

n = 23

x	.01	.05	.10	.20	.30	.40	p .50	.60	.70	.80	.90	.95	.99
0	.794	.307	.089	.006	.000	.000	.000	.000	.000	.000	.000	.000	.000
1	.978	.679	.315	.040	.003	.000	.000	.000	.000	.000	.000	.000	.000
2	.998	.895	.592	.133	.016	.001	.000	.000	.000	.000	.000	.000	.000
3	1.000	.974	.807	.297	.054	.005	.000	.000	.000	.000	.000	.000	.000
4	1.000	.995	.927	.501	.136	.019	.001	.000	.000	.000	.000	.000	.000
5	1.000	.999	.977	.695	.269	.054	.005	.000	.000	.000	.000	.000	.000
6	1.000	1.000	.994	.840	.440	.124	.017	.001	.000	.000	.000	.000	.000
7	1.000	1.000	.999	.928	.618	.237	.047	.004	.000	.000	.000	.000	.000
8	1.000	1.000	1.000	.973	.771	.388	.105	.013	.001	.000	.000	.000	.000
9	1.000	1.000	1.000	.991	.880	.556	.202	.035	.002	.000	.000	.000	.000
10	1.000	1.000	1.000	.997	.945	.713	.339	.081	.007	.000	.000	.000	.000
11	1.000	1.000	1.000	.999	.979	.836	.500	.164	.021	.001	.000	.000	.000
12	1.000	1.000	1.000	1.000	.993	.919	.661	.287	.055	.003	.000	.000	.000
13	1.000	1.000	1.000	1.000	.998	.965	.798	.444	.120	.009	.000	.000	.000
14	1.000	1.000	1.000	1.000	.999	.987	.895	.612	.229	.027	.000	.000	.000
15	1.000	1.000	1.000	1.000	1.000	.996	.953	.763	.382	.072	.001	.000	.000
16	1.000	1.000	1.000	1.000	1.000	.999	.983	.876	.560	.160	.006	.000	.000
17	1.000	1.000	1.000	1.000	1.000	1.000	.995	.946	.731	.305	.023	.001	.000
18	1.000	1.000	1.000	1.000	1.000	1.000	.999	.981	.864	.499	.073	.005	.000
19	1.000	1.000	1.000	1.000	1.000	1.000	1.000	.995	.946	.703	.193	.026	.000
20	1.000	1.000	1.000	1.000	1.000	1.000	1.000	.999	.984	.867	.408	.105	.002
21	1.000	1.000	1.000	1.000	1.000	1.000	1.000	1.000	.997	.960	.685	.321	.022
22	1.000	1.000	1.000	1.000	1.000	1.000	1.000	1.000	1.000	.994	.911	.693	.206

n = 24

x	.01	.05	.10	.20	.30	.40	p .50	.60	.70	.80	.90	.95	.99
0	.786	.292	.080	.005	.000	.000	.000	.000	.000	.000	.000	.000	.000
1	.976	.661	.292	.033	.002	.000	.000	.000	.000	.000	.000	.000	.000
2	.998	.884	.564	.115	.012	.001	.000	.000	.000	.000	.000	.000	.000
3	1.000	.970	.786	.264	.042	.004	.000	.000	.000	.000	.000	.000	.000
4	1.000	.994	.915	.460	.111	.013	.001	.000	.000	.000	.000	.000	.000
5	1.000	.999	.972	.656	.229	.040	.003	.000	.000	.000	.000	.000	.000
6	1.000	1.000	.993	.811	.389	.096	.011	.001	.000	.000	.000	.000	.000
7	1.000	1.000	.998	.911	.565	.192	.032	.002	.000	.000	.000	.000	.000
8	1.000	1.000	1.000	.964	.725	.328	.076	.008	.000	.000	.000	.000	.000
9	1.000	1.000	1.000	.987	.847	.489	.154	.022	.001	.000	.000	.000	.000

TABLE II Continued													

n = 24

x	.01	.05	.10	.20	.30	.40	p .50	.60	.70	.80	.90	.95	.99
10	1.000	1.000	1.000	.996	.926	.650	.271	.053	.004	.000	.000	.000	.000
11	1.000	1.000	1.000	.999	.969	.787	.419	.114	.012	.000	.000	.000	.000
12	1.000	1.000	1.000	1.000	.988	.886	.581	.213	.031	.001	.000	.000	.000
13	1.000	1.000	1.000	1.000	.996	.947	.729	.350	.074	.004	.000	.000	.000
14	1.000	1.000	1.000	1.000	.999	.978	.846	.511	.153	.013	.000	.000	.000
15	1.000	1.000	1.000	1.000	1.000	.992	.924	.672	.275	.036	.000	.000	.000
16	1.000	1.000	1.000	1.000	1.000	.998	.968	.808	.435	.089	.002	.000	.000
17	1.000	1.000	1.000	1.000	1.000	.999	.989	.904	.611	.189	.007	.000	.000
18	1.000	1.000	1.000	1.000	1.000	1.000	.997	.960	.771	.344	.028	.001	.000
19	1.000	1.000	1.000	1.000	1.000	1.000	.999	.987	.889	.540	.085	.006	.000
20	1.000	1.000	1.000	1.000	1.000	1.000	1.000	.996	.958	.736	.214	.030	.000
21	1.000	1.000	1.000	1.000	1.000	1.000	1.000	.999	.988	.885	.436	.116	.002
22	1.000	1.000	1.000	1.000	1.000	1.000	1.000	1.000	.998	.967	.708	.339	.024
23	1.000	1.000	1.000	1.000	1.000	1.000	1.000	1.000	1.000	.995	.920	.708	.214

n = 25

x	.01	.05	.10	.20	.30	.40	p .50	.60	.70	.80	.90	.95	.99
0	.778	.277	.072	.004	.000	.000	.000	.000	.000	.000	.000	.000	.000
1	.974	.642	.271	.027	.002	.000	.000	.000	.000	.000	.000	.000	.000
2	.998	.873	.537	.098	.009	.000	.000	.000	.000	.000	.000	.000	.000
3	1.000	.966	.764	.234	.033	.002	.000	.000	.000	.000	.000	.000	.000
4	1.000	.993	.902	.421	.090	.009	.000	.000	.000	.000	.000	.000	.000
5	1.000	.999	.967	.617	.193	.029	.002	.000	.000	.000	.000	.000	.000
6	1.000	1.000	.991	.780	.341	.074	.007	.000	.000	.000	.000	.000	.000
7	1.000	1.000	.998	.891	.512	.154	.022	.001	.000	.000	.000	.000	.000
8	1.000	1.000	1.000	.953	.677	.274	.054	.004	.000	.000	.000	.000	.000
9	1.000	1.000	1.000	.983	.811	.425	.115	.013	.000	.000	.000	.000	.000
10	1.000	1.000	1.000	.994	.902	.586	.212	.034	.002	.000	.000	.000	.000
11	1.000	1.000	1.000	.998	.956	.732	.345	.078	.006	.000	.000	.000	.000
12	1.000	1.000	1.000	1.000	.983	.846	.500	.154	.017	.000	.000	.000	.000
13	1.000	1.000	1.000	1.000	.994	.922	.655	.268	.044	.002	.000	.000	.000
14	1.000	1.000	1.000	1.000	.998	.966	.788	.414	.098	.006	.000	.000	.000
15	1.000	1.000	1.000	1.000	1.000	.987	.885	.575	.189	.017	.000	.000	.000
16	1.000	1.000	1.000	1.000	1.000	.996	.946	.726	.323	.047	.000	.000	.000
17	1.000	1.000	1.000	1.000	1.000	.999	.978	.846	.488	.109	.002	.000	.000
18	1.000	1.000	1.000	1.000	1.000	1.000	.993	.926	.659	.220	.009	.000	.000
19	1.000	1.000	1.000	1.000	1.000	1.000	.998	.971	.807	.383	.033	.001	.000
20	1.000	1.000	1.000	1.000	1.000	1.000	1.000	.991	.910	.579	.098	.007	.000
21	1.000	1.000	1.000	1.000	1.000	1.000	1.000	.998	.967	.766	.236	.034	.000
22	1.000	1.000	1.000	1.000	1.000	1.000	1.000	1.000	.991	.902	.463	.127	.002
23	1.000	1.000	1.000	1.000	1.000	1.000	1.000	1.000	.998	.973	.729	.358	.026
24	1.000	1.000	1.000	1.000	1.000	1.000	1.000	1.000	1.000	.996	.928	.723	.222

n = 50												
x	.01	.05	.10	.20	.30	.40	**p** .50	.60	.70	.80	.90	.95	.99
0	.605	.077	.005	.000	.000	.000	.000	.000	.000	.000	.000	.000	.000
1	.911	.279	.034	.000	.000	.000	.000	.000	.000	.000	.000	.000	.000
2	.986	.541	.112	.001	.000	.000	.000	.000	.000	.000	.000	.000	.000
3	.998	.760	.250	.006	.000	.000	.000	.000	.000	.000	.000	.000	.000
4	1.000	.896	.431	.018	.000	.000	.000	.000	.000	.000	.000	.000	.000
5	1.000	.962	.616	.048	.001	.000	.000	.000	.000	.000	.000	.000	.000
6	1.000	.988	.770	.103	.002	.000	.000	.000	.000	.000	.000	.000	.000
7	1.000	.997	.878	.190	.007	.000	.000	.000	.000	.000	.000	.000	.000
8	1.000	.999	.942	.307	.018	.000	.000	.000	.000	.000	.000	.000	.000
9	1.000	1.000	.975	.444	.040	.001	.000	.000	.000	.000	.000	.000	.000
10	1.000	1.000	.991	.584	.079	.002	.000	.000	.000	.000	.000	.000	.000
11	1.000	1.000	.997	.711	.139	.006	.000	.000	.000	.000	.000	.000	.000
12	1.000	1.000	.999	.814	.223	.013	.000	.000	.000	.000	.000	.000	.000
13	1.000	1.000	1.000	.889	.328	.028	.000	.000	.000	.000	.000	.000	.000
14	1.000	1.000	1.000	.939	.447	.054	.001	.000	.000	.000	.000	.000	.000
15	1.000	1.000	1.000	.969	.569	.096	.003	.000	.000	.000	.000	.000	.000
16	1.000	1.000	1.000	.986	.684	.156	.008	.000	.000	.000	.000	.000	.000
17	1.000	1.000	1.000	.994	.782	.237	.016	.000	.000	.000	.000	.000	.000
18	1.000	1.000	1.000	.997	.859	.336	.032	.001	.000	.000	.000	.000	.000
19	1.000	1.000	1.000	.999	.915	.446	.059	.001	.000	.000	.000	.000	.000
20	1.000	1.000	1.000	1.000	.952	.561	.101	.003	.000	.000	.000	.000	.000
21	1.000	1.000	1.000	1.000	.975	.670	.161	.008	.000	.000	.000	.000	.000
22	1.000	1.000	1.000	1.000	.988	.766	.240	.016	.000	.000	.000	.000	.000
23	1.000	1.000	1.000	1.000	.994	.844	.336	.031	.000	.000	.000	.000	.000
24	1.000	1.000	1.000	1.000	.998	.902	.444	.057	.001	.000	.000	.000	.000
25	1.000	1.000	1.000	1.000	.999	.943	.556	.098	.002	.000	.000	.000	.000
26	1.000	1.000	1.000	1.000	1.000	.969	.664	.156	.006	.000	.000	.000	.000
27	1.000	1.000	1.000	1.000	1.000	.984	.760	.234	.012	.000	.000	.000	.000
28	1.000	1.000	1.000	1.000	1.000	.992	.839	.330	.025	.000	.000	.000	.000
29	1.000	1.000	1.000	1.000	1.000	.997	.899	.439	.048	.000	.000	.000	.000
30	1.000	1.000	1.000	1.000	1.000	.999	.941	.554	.085	.001	.000	.000	.000
31	1.000	1.000	1.000	1.000	1.000	.999	.968	.664	.141	.003	.000	.000	.000
32	1.000	1.000	1.000	1.000	1.000	1.000	.984	.763	.218	.006	.000	.000	.000
33	1.000	1.000	1.000	1.000	1.000	1.000	.992	.844	.316	.014	.000	.000	.000
34	1.000	1.000	1.000	1.000	1.000	1.000	.997	.904	.431	.031	.000	.000	.000
35	1.000	1.000	1.000	1.000	1.000	1.000	.999	.946	.553	.061	.000	.000	.000
36	1.000	1.000	1.000	1.000	1.000	1.000	1.000	.972	.672	.111	.000	.000	.000
37	1.000	1.000	1.000	1.000	1.000	1.000	1.000	.987	.777	.186	.001	.000	.000
38	1.000	1.000	1.000	1.000	1.000	1.000	1.000	.994	.861	.289	.003	.000	.000
39	1.000	1.000	1.000	1.000	1.000	1.000	1.000	.998	.921	.416	.009	.000	.000
40	1.000	1.000	1.000	1.000	1.000	1.000	1.000	.999	.960	.556	.025	.000	.000
41	1.000	1.000	1.000	1.000	1.000	1.000	1.000	1.000	.982	.693	.058	.001	.000
42	1.000	1.000	1.000	1.000	1.000	1.000	1.000	1.000	.993	.810	.122	.003	.000
43	1.000	1.000	1.000	1.000	1.000	1.000	1.000	1.000	.998	.897	.230	.012	.000
44	1.000	1.000	1.000	1.000	1.000	1.000	1.000	1.000	.999	.952	.384	.038	.000
45	1.000	1.000	1.000	1.000	1.000	1.000	1.000	1.000	1.000	.982	.569	.104	.000
46	1.000	1.000	1.000	1.000	1.000	1.000	1.000	1.000	1.000	.994	.750	.240	.002
47	1.000	1.000	1.000	1.000	1.000	1.000	1.000	1.000	1.000	.999	.888	.459	.014
48	1.000	1.000	1.000	1.000	1.000	1.000	1.000	1.000	1.000	1.000	.966	.721	.089
49	1.000	1.000	1.000	1.000	1.000	1.000	1.000	1.000	1.000	1.000	.995	.923	.395

Statistics for Business Decision Making, by Olson and Picconi. (Scott, Foresman & Company, 1983.) With permission.

TABLE III Cumulative Probability Values for the Poisson Distribution

$P(X \leq x \mid \lambda)$; Example: $P(X \leq 4 \mid \lambda = 1.8) = .9636$

x	0.1	0.2	0.3	0.4	0.5	0.6	0.7	0.8	0.9	1.0
0	0.9048	0.8187	0.7408	0.6703	0.6065	0.5488	0.4966	0.4493	0.4066	0.3679
1	0.9953	0.9825	0.9631	0.9384	0.9098	0.8781	0.8442	0.8088	0.7725	0.7358
2	0.9998	0.9989	0.9964	0.9921	0.9856	0.9769	0.9659	0.9526	0.9371	0.9197
3	1.0000	0.9999	0.9997	0.9992	0.9982	0.9966	0.9942	0.9909	0.9865	0.9810
4	1.0000	1.0000	1.0000	0.9999	0.9998	0.9996	0.9992	0.9986	0.9977	0.9963
5	1.0000	1.0000	1.0000	1.0000	1.0000	1.0000	0.9999	0.9998	0.9997	0.9994
6	1.0000	1.0000	1.0000	1.0000	1.0000	1.0000	1.0000	1.0000	1.0000	0.9999
7	1.0000	1.0000	1.0000	1.0000	1.0000	1.0000	1.0000	1.0000	1.0000	1.0000

x	1.1	1.2	1.3	1.4	1.5	1.6	1.7	1.8	1.9	2.0
0	0.3329	0.3012	0.2725	0.2466	0.2231	0.2019	0.1827	0.1653	0.1496	0.1353
1	0.6990	0.6626	0.6268	0.5918	0.5578	0.5249	0.4932	0.4628	0.4338	0.4060
2	0.9004	0.8795	0.8571	0.8335	0.8088	0.7834	0.7572	0.7306	0.7038	0.6767
3	0.9743	0.9662	0.9569	0.9463	0.9344	0.9212	0.9068	0.8913	0.8748	0.8571
4	0.9946	0.9923	0.9893	0.9857	0.9814	0.9763	0.9704	0.9636	0.9559	0.9473
5	0.9990	0.9985	0.9978	0.9968	0.9955	0.9940	0.9920	0.9896	0.9868	0.9834
6	0.9999	0.9997	0.9996	0.9994	0.9991	0.9987	0.9981	0.9974	0.9966	0.9955
7	1.0000	1.0000	0.9999	0.9999	0.9998	0.9997	0.9996	0.9994	0.9992	0.9989
8	1.0000	1.0000	1.0000	1.0000	1.0000	1.0000	0.9999	0.9999	0.9998	0.9998
9	1.0000	1.0000	1.0000	1.0000	1.0000	1.0000	1.0000	1.0000	1.0000	1.0000

x	2.1	2.2	2.3	2.4	2.5	2.6	2.7	2.8	2.9	3.0
0	0.1225	0.1108	0.1003	0.0907	0.0821	0.0743	0.0672	0.0608	0.0550	0.0498
1	0.3796	0.3546	0.3309	0.3084	0.2873	0.2674	0.2487	0.2311	0.2146	0.1991
2	0.6496	0.6227	0.5960	0.5697	0.5438	0.5184	0.4936	0.4695	0.4460	0.4232
3	0.8386	0.8194	0.7993	0.7787	0.7576	0.7360	0.7141	0.6919	0.6696	0.6472
4	0.9379	0.9275	0.9162	0.9041	0.8912	0.8774	0.8629	0.8477	0.8318	0.8153
5	0.9796	0.9751	0.9700	0.9643	0.9580	0.9510	0.9433	0.9349	0.9258	0.9161
6	0.9941	0.9925	0.9906	0.9884	0.9858	0.9828	0.9794	0.9756	0.9713	0.9665
7	0.9985	0.9980	0.9974	0.9967	0.9958	0.9947	0.9934	0.9919	0.9901	0.9881
8	0.9997	0.9995	0.9994	0.9991	0.9989	0.9985	0.9981	0.9976	0.9969	0.9962
9	0.9999	0.9999	0.9999	0.9998	0.9997	0.9996	0.9995	0.9993	0.9991	0.9989
10	1.0000	1.0000	1.0000	1.0000	0.9999	0.9999	0.9999	0.9998	0.9998	0.9997
11	1.0000	1.0000	1.0000	1.0000	1.0000	1.0000	1.0000	1.0000	0.9999	0.9999
12	1.0000	1.0000	1.0000	1.0000	1.0000	1.0000	1.0000	1.0000	1.0000	1.0000

TABLE III Continued

λ	3.1	3.2	3.3	3.4	3.5	3.6	3.7	3.8	3.9	4.0
0	0.0450	0.0408	0.0369	0.0334	0.0302	0.0273	0.0247	0.0224	0.0202	0.0183
1	0.1847	0.1712	0.1586	0.1468	0.1359	0.1257	0.1162	0.1074	0.0992	0.0916
2	0.4012	0.3799	0.3594	0.3397	0.3208	0.3027	0.2854	0.2689	0.2531	0.2381
3	0.6248	0.6025	0.5803	0.5584	0.5366	0.5152	0.4942	0.4735	0.4533	0.4335
4	0.7982	0.7806	0.7626	0.7442	0.7254	0.7064	0.6872	0.6678	0.6484	0.6288
5	0.9057	0.8946	0.8829	0.8705	0.8576	0.8441	0.8301	0.8156	0.8006	0.7851
6	0.9612	0.9554	0.9490	0.9421	0.9347	0.9267	0.9182	0.9091	0.8995	0.8893
7	0.9858	0.9832	0.9802	0.9769	0.9733	0.9692	0.9648	0.9599	0.9546	0.9489
8	0.9953	0.9943	0.9931	0.9917	0.9901	0.9883	0.9863	0.9840	0.9815	0.9786
9	0.9986	0.9982	0.9978	0.9973	0.9967	0.9960	0.9952	0.9942	0.9931	0.9919
10	0.9996	0.9995	0.9994	0.9992	0.9990	0.9987	0.9984	0.9981	0.9977	0.9972
11	0.9999	0.9999	0.9998	0.9998	0.9997	0.9996	0.9995	0.9994	0.9993	0.9991
12	1.0000	1.0000	1.0000	0.9999	0.9999	0.9999	0.9999	0.9998	0.9998	0.9997
13	1.0000	1.0000	1.0000	1.0000	1.0000	1.0000	1.0000	1.0000	0.9999	0.9999
14	1.0000	1.0000	1.0000	1.0000	1.0000	1.0000	1.0000	1.0000	1.0000	1.0000

λ	4.1	4.2	4.3	4.4	4.5	4.6	4.7	4.8	4.9	5.0
0	0.0166	0.0150	0.0136	0.0123	0.0111	0.0101	0.0091	0.0082	0.0074	0.0067
1	0.0845	0.0780	0.0719	0.0663	0.0611	0.0563	0.0518	0.0477	0.0439	0.0404
2	0.2238	0.2102	0.1974	0.1851	0.1736	0.1626	0.1523	0.1425	0.1333	0.1247
3	0.4142	0.3954	0.3772	0.3595	0.3423	0.3257	0.3097	0.2942	0.2793	0.2650
4	0.6093	0.5898	0.5704	0.5512	0.5321	0.5132	0.4946	0.4763	0.4582	0.4405
5	0.7693	0.7531	0.7367	0.7199	0.7029	0.6858	0.6684	0.6510	0.6335	0.6160
6	0.8736	0.8675	0.8558	0.8436	0.8311	0.8180	0.8046	0.7908	0.7767	0.7622
7	0.9427	0.9361	0.9290	0.9214	0.9134	0.9049	0.8960	0.8867	0.8769	0.8666
8	0.9755	0.9721	0.9683	0.9642	0.9597	0.9549	0.9497	0.9442	0.9382	0.9319
9	0.9905	0.9889	0.9871	0.9851	0.9829	0.9805	0.9778	0.9749	0.9717	0.9682
10	0.9966	0.9959	0.9952	0.9943	0.9933	0.9922	0.9910	0.9896	0.9880	0.9863
11	0.9989	0.9986	0.9983	0.9980	0.9976	0.9971	0.9966	0.9960	0.9953	0.9945
12	0.9997	0.9996	0.9995	0.9993	0.9992	0.9990	0.9988	0.9986	0.9983	0.9980
13	0.9999	0.9999	0.9998	0.9998	0.9997	0.9997	0.9996	0.9995	0.9994	0.9993
14	1.0000	1.0000	1.0000	0.9999	0.9999	0.9999	0.9999	0.9999	0.9998	0.9998
15	1.0000	1.0000	1.0000	1.0000	1.0000	1.0000	1.0000	1.0000	0.9999	0.9999
16	1.0000	1.0000	1.0000	1.0000	1.0000	1.0000	1.0000	1.0000	1.0000	1.0000

				TABLE III	Continued				

x \ λ	5.1	5.2	5.3	5.4	5.5	5.6	5.7	5.8	5.9	6.0
0	0.0061	0.0055	0.0050	0.0045	0.0041	0.0037	0.0033	0.0030	0.0027	0.0025
1	0.0372	0.0342	0.0314	0.0289	0.0266	0.0244	0.0224	0.0206	0.0189	0.0174
2	0.1165	0.1088	0.1016	0.0948	0.0884	0.0824	0.0768	0.0715	0.0666	0.0620
3	0.2513	0.2381	0.2254	0.2133	0.2017	0.1906	0.1801	0.1700	0.1604	0.1512
4	0.4231	0.4061	0.3895	0.3733	0.3575	0.3422	0.3272	0.3127	0.2987	0.2851
5	0.5984	0.5809	0.5635	0.5461	0.5289	0.5119	0.4950	0.4783	0.4619	0.4457
6	0.7474	0.7324	0.7171	0.7017	0.6860	0.6703	0.6544	0.6384	0.6224	0.6063
7	0.8560	0.8449	0.8335	0.8217	0.8095	0.7970	0.7842	0.7710	0.7576	0.7440
8	0.9252	0.9181	0.9106	0.9026	0.8944	0.8857	0.8766	0.8672	0.8574	0.8472
9	0.9644	0.9603	0.9559	0.9512	0.9462	0.9409	0.9352	0.9292	0.9228	0.9161
10	0.9844	0.9823	0.9800	0.9775	0.9747	0.9718	0.9686	0.9651	0.9614	0.9574
11	0.9937	0.9927	0.9916	0.9904	0.9890	0.9875	0.9859	0.9840	0.9821	0.9799
12	0.9976	0.9972	0.9967	0.9962	0.9955	0.9949	0.9941	0.9932	0.9922	0.9912
13	0.9992	0.9990	0.9988	0.9986	0.9983	0.9980	0.9977	0.9973	0.9969	0.9964
14	0.9997	0.9997	0.9996	0.9995	0.9994	0.9993	0.9991	0.9990	0.9988	0.9986
15	0.9999	0.9999	0.9999	0.9998	0.9998	0.9998	0.9997	0.9996	0.9996	0.9995
16	1.0000	1.0000	1.0000	0.9999	0.9999	0.9999	0.9999	0.9999	0.9999	0.9998
17	1.0000	1.0000	1.0000	1.0000	1.0000	1.0000	1.0000	1.0000	1.0000	0.9999
18	1.0000	1.0000	1.0000	1.0000	1.0000	1.0000	1.0000	1.0000	1.0000	1.0000

x \ λ	6.1	6.2	6.3	6.4	6.5	6.6	6.7	6.8	6.9	7.0
0	0.0022	0.0020	0.0018	0.0017	0.0015	0.0014	0.0012	0.0011	0.0010	0.0009
1	0.0159	0.0146	0.0134	0.0123	0.0113	0.0103	0.0095	0.0087	0.0080	0.0073
2	0.0577	0.0536	0.0498	0.0463	0.0430	0.0400	0.0371	0.0344	0.0320	0.0296
3	0.1425	0.1342	0.1264	0.1189	0.1119	0.1052	0.0988	0.0928	0.0871	0.0818
4	0.2719	0.2592	0.2469	0.2351	0.2237	0.2127	0.2022	0.1920	0.1823	0.1730
5	0.4298	0.4141	0.3988	0.3837	0.3690	0.3547	0.3407	0.3270	0.3137	0.3007
6	0.5902	0.5742	0.5582	0.5423	0.5265	0.5108	0.4953	0.4799	0.4647	0.4497
7	0.7301	0.7160	0.7018	0.6873	0.6728	0.6581	0.6433	0.6285	0.6136	0.5987
8	0.8367	0.8259	0.8148	0.8033	0.7916	0.7796	0.7673	0.7548	0.7420	0.7291
9	0.9090	0.9016	0.8939	0.8858	0.8774	0.8686	0.8596	0.8502	0.8405	0.8305
10	0.9531	0.9486	0.9437	0.9386	0.9332	0.9274	0.9214	0.9151	0.9084	0.9015
11	0.9776	0.9750	0.9723	0.9693	0.9661	0.9627	0.9591	0.9552	0.9510	0.9466
12	0.9900	0.9887	0.9873	0.9857	0.9840	0.9821	0.9801	0.9779	0.9755	0.9730
13	0.9958	0.9952	0.9945	0.9937	0.9929	0.9920	0.9909	0.9898	0.9885	0.9872
14	0.9984	0.9981	0.9978	0.9974	0.9970	0.9966	0.9961	0.9956	0.9950	0.9943
15	0.9994	0.9993	0.9992	0.9990	0.9988	0.9986	0.9984	0.9982	0.9979	0.9976
16	0.9998	0.9997	0.9997	0.9996	0.9996	0.9995	0.9994	0.9993	0.9992	0.9990
17	0.9999	0.9999	0.9999	0.9999	0.9998	0.9998	0.9998	0.9997	0.9997	0.9996
18	1.0000	1.0000	1.0000	1.0000	0.9999	0.9999	0.9999	0.9999	0.9999	0.9999
19	1.0000	1.0000	1.0000	1.0000	1.0000	1.0000	1.0000	1.0000	1.0000	0.9999
20	1.0000	1.0000	1.0000	1.0000	1.0000	1.0000	1.0000	1.0000	1.0000	1.0000

TABLE III	Continued								

x \ λ	7.1	7.2	7.3	7.4	7.5	7.6	7.7	7.8	7.9	8.0
0	0.0008	0.0007	0.0007	0.0006	0.0006	0.0005	0.0005	0.0004	0.0004	0.0003
1	0.0067	0.0061	0.0056	0.0051	0.0047	0.0043	0.0039	0.0036	0.0033	0.0030
2	0.0275	0.0255	0.0236	0.0219	0.0203	0.0188	0.0174	0.0161	0.0149	0.0138
3	0.0767	0.0719	0.0674	0.0632	0.0591	0.0554	0.0518	0.0485	0.0453	0.0424
4	0.1641	0.1555	0.1473	0.1395	0.1321	0.1249	0.1181	0.1117	0.1055	0.0996
5	0.2881	0.2759	0.2640	0.2526	0.2414	0.2307	0.2203	0.2103	0.2006	0.1912
6	0.4349	0.4204	0.4060	0.3920	0.3782	0.3646	0.3514	0.3384	0.3257	0.3134
7	0.5838	0.5689	0.5541	0.5393	0.5246	0.5100	0.4956	0.4812	0.4670	0.4530
8	0.7160	0.7027	0.6892	0.6757	0.6620	0.6482	0.6343	0.6204	0.6065	0.5926
9	0.8202	0.8096	0.7988	0.7877	0.7764	0.7649	0.7531	0.7411	0.7290	0.7166
10	0.8942	0.8867	0.8788	0.8707	0.8622	0.8535	0.8445	0.8352	0.8257	0.8159
11	0.9420	0.9371	0.9319	0.9265	0.9208	0.9148	0.9085	0.9020	0.8952	0.8881
12	0.9703	0.9673	0.9642	0.9609	0.9573	0.9536	0.9496	0.9453	0.9409	0.9362
13	0.9857	0.9841	0.9824	0.9805	0.9784	0.9762	0.9739	0.9714	0.9687	0.9658
14	0.9935	0.9927	0.9918	0.9908	0.9897	0.9886	0.9873	0.9859	0.9844	0.9827
15	0.9972	0.9968	0.9964	0.9959	0.9954	0.9948	0.9941	0.9934	0.9926	0.9918
16	0.9989	0.9987	0.9985	0.9983	0.9980	0.9978	0.9974	0.9971	0.9967	0.9963
17	0.9996	0.9995	0.9994	0.9993	0.9992	0.9991	0.9989	0.9988	0.9986	0.9984
18	0.9998	0.9998	0.9998	0.9997	0.9997	0.9996	0.9996	0.9995	0.9994	0.9993
19	0.9999	0.9999	0.9999	0.9999	0.9999	0.9999	0.9998	0.9998	0.9998	0.9997
20	1.0000	1.0000	1.0000	1.0000	1.0000	0.9999	0.9999	0.9999	0.9999	0.9999
21	1.0000	1.0000	1.0000	1.0000	1.0000	1.0000	1.0000	1.0000	1.0000	1.0000

x \ λ	8.1	8.2	8.3	8.4	8.5	8.6	8.7	8.8	8.9	9.0
0	0.0003	0.0003	0.0002	0.0002	0.0002	0.0002	0.0002	0.0002	0.0001	0.0001
1	0.0028	0.0025	0.0023	0.0021	0.0019	0.0018	0.0016	0.0015	0.0014	0.0012
2	0.0127	0.0118	0.0109	0.0100	0.0093	0.0086	0.0079	0.0073	0.0068	0.0062
3	0.0396	0.0370	0.0346	0.0323	0.0301	0.0281	0.0262	0.0244	0.0228	0.0212
4	0.0941	0.0887	0.0837	0.0789	0.0744	0.0701	0.0660	0.0621	0.0584	0.0550
5	0.1822	0.1736	0.1653	0.1573	0.1496	0.1422	0.1352	0.1284	0.1219	0.1157
6	0.3013	0.2896	0.2781	0.2670	0.2562	0.2457	0.2355	0.2256	0.2160	0.2068
7	0.4391	0.4254	0.4119	0.3987	0.3856	0.3728	0.3602	0.3478	0.3357	0.3239
8	0.5786	0.5647	0.5508	0.5369	0.5231	0.5094	0.4958	0.4823	0.4689	0.4557
9	0.7041	0.6915	0.6788	0.6659	0.6530	0.6400	0.6269	0.6137	0.6006	0.5874
10	0.8058	0.7955	0.7850	0.7743	0.7634	0.7522	0.7409	0.7294	0.7178	0.7060
11	0.8807	0.8731	0.8652	0.8571	0.8487	0.8400	0.8311	0.8220	0.8126	0.8030
12	0.9313	0.9261	0.9207	0.9150	0.9091	0.9029	0.8965	0.8898	0.8829	0.8758
13	0.9628	0.9595	0.9561	0.9524	0.9486	0.9445	0.9403	0.9358	0.9311	0.9262
14	0.9810	0.9791	0.9771	0.9749	0.9726	0.9701	0.9675	0.9647	0.9617	0.9585
15	0.9908	0.9898	0.9887	0.9875	0.9862	0.9847	0.9832	0.9816	0.9798	0.9780
16	0.9958	0.9953	0.9947	0.9941	0.9934	0.9926	0.9918	0.9909	0.9899	0.9889
17	0.9982	0.9979	0.9976	0.9973	0.9970	0.9966	0.9962	0.9957	0.9952	0.9947
18	0.9992	0.9991	0.9990	0.9989	0.9987	0.9985	0.9983	0.9981	0.9978	0.9976
19	0.9997	0.9996	0.9996	0.9995	0.9995	0.9994	0.9993	0.9992	0.9991	0.9989
20	0.9999	0.9999	0.9998	0.9998	0.9998	0.9997	0.9997	0.9997	0.9996	0.9996
21	1.0000	0.9999	0.9999	0.9999	0.9999	0.9999	0.9999	0.9999	0.9998	0.9998
22	1.0000	1.0000	1.0000	1.0000	1.0000	1.0000	1.0000	0.9999	0.9999	0.9999
23	1.0000	1.0000	1.0000	1.0000	1.0000	1.0000	1.0000	1.0000	1.0000	1.0000

TABLE III			Continued						

x \ λ	9.1	9.2	9.3	9.4	9.5	9.6	9.7	9.8	9.9	10.0
0	0.0001	0.0001	0.0001	0.0001	0.0001	0.0001	0.0001	0.0001	0.0001	0.0000
1	0.0011	0.0010	0.0009	0.0009	0.0008	0.0007	0.0007	0.0006	0.0005	0.0005
2	0.0058	0.0053	0.0049	0.0045	0.0042	0.0038	0.0035	0.0033	0.0030	0.0028
3	0.0198	0.0184	0.0172	0.0160	0.0149	0.0138	0.0129	0.0120	0.0111	0.0103
4	0.0517	0.0486	0.0456	0.0429	0.0403	0.0378	0.0355	0.0333	0.0312	0.0293
5	0.1098	0.1041	0.0987	0.0935	0.0885	0.0838	0.0793	0.0750	0.0710	0.0671
6	0.1978	0.1892	0.1808	0.1727	0.1650	0.1575	0.1502	0.1433	0.1366	0.1301
7	0.3123	0.3010	0.2900	0.2792	0.2687	0.2584	0.2485	0.2388	0.2294	0.2202
8	0.4426	0.4296	0.4168	0.4042	0.3918	0.3796	0.3676	0.3558	0.3442	0.3328
9	0.5742	0.5511	0.5479	0.5349	0.5218	0.5089	0.4960	0.4832	0.4705	0.4579
10	0.6941	0.6820	0.6699	0.6576	0.6453	0.6330	0.6205	0.6080	0.5955	0.5830
11	0.7932	0.7832	0.7730	0.7626	0.7520	0.7412	0.7303	0.7193	0.7081	0.6968
12	0.8684	0.8607	0.8529	0.8448	0.8364	0.8279	0.8191	0.8101	0.8009	0.7916
13	0.9210	0.9156	0.9100	0.9042	0.8981	0.8919	0.8853	0.8786	0.8716	0.8645
14	0.9552	0.9517	0.9480	0.9441	0.9400	0.9357	0.9312	0.9265	0.9216	0.9165
15	0.9760	0.9738	0.9715	0.9691	0.9665	0.9638	0.9609	0.9579	0.9546	0.9513
16	0.9878	0.9865	0.9852	0.9836	0.9823	0.9806	0.9789	0.9770	0.9751	0.9730
17	0.9941	0.9934	0.9927	0.9919	0.9911	0.9902	0.9892	0.9881	0.9869	0.9857
18	0.9973	0.9969	0.9966	0.9962	0.9957	0.9952	0.9947	0.9941	0.9935	0.9928
19	0.9988	0.9986	0.9985	0.9983	0.9980	0.9978	0.9975	0.9972	0.9969	0.9965
20	0.9995	0.9994	0.9993	0.9992	0.9991	0.9990	0.9989	0.9987	0.9986	0.9984
21	0.9998	0.9998	0.9997	0.9997	0.9996	0.9996	0.9995	0.9995	0.9994	0.9993
22	0.9999	0.9999	0.9999	0.9999	0.9998	0.9998	0.9998	0.9998	0.9997	0.9997
23	1.0000	1.0000	1.0000	0.9999	0.9999	0.9999	0.9999	0.9999	0.9999	0.9999
24	1.0000	1.0000	1.0000	1.0000	1.0000	1.0000	1.0000	1.0000	0.9999	0.9999
25	1.0000	1.0000	1.0000	1.0000	1.0000	1.0000	1.0000	1.0000	1.0000	1.0000

x \ λ	11.0	12.0	13.0	14.0	15.0	16.0	17.0	18.0	19.0	20.0
0	0.0000	0.0000	0.0000	0.0000	0.0000	0.0000	0.0	0.0	0.0	0.0
1	0.0002	0.0001	0.0000	0.0000	0.0000	0.0000	0.0000	0.0000	0.0000	0.0
2	0.0012	0.0005	0.0002	0.0001	0.0000	0.0000	0.0000	0.0000	0.0000	0.0000
3	0.0049	0.0023	0.0011	0.0005	0.0002	0.0001	0.0000	0.0000	0.0000	0.0000
4	0.0151	0.0076	0.0037	0.0018	0.0009	0.0004	0.0002	0.0001	0.0000	0.0000
5	0.0375	0.0203	0.0107	0.0055	0.0028	0.0014	0.0007	0.0003	0.0002	0.0001
6	0.0786	0.0458	0.0259	0.0142	0.0076	0.0040	0.0021	0.0010	0.0005	0.0003
7	0.1432	0.0895	0.0540	0.0316	0.0180	0.0100	0.0054	0.0029	0.0015	0.0008
8	0.2320	0.1550	0.0998	0.0621	0.0374	0.0220	0.0126	0.0071	0.0039	0.0021
9	0.3405	0.2424	0.1658	0.1094	0.0699	0.0433	0.0261	0.0154	0.0089	0.0050
10	0.4599	0.3472	0.2517	0.1757	0.1185	0.0774	0.0491	0.0304	0.0183	0.0108
11	0.5793	0.4616	0.3532	0.2600	0.1847	0.1270	0.0847	0.0549	0.0347	0.0214
12	0.6887	0.5760	0.4631	0.3585	0.2676	0.1931	0.1350	0.0917	0.0606	0.0390
13	0.7813	0.6815	0.5730	0.4644	0.3632	0.2745	0.2009	0.1426	0.0984	0.0661
14	0.8540	0.7720	0.6751	0.5704	0.4656	0.3675	0.2808	0.2081	0.1497	0.1049
15	0.9074	0.8444	0.7636	0.6694	0.5681	0.4667	0.3714	0.2866	0.2148	0.1565
16	0.9441	0.8987	0.8355	0.7559	0.6641	0.5660	0.4677	0.3750	0.2920	0.2211
17	0.9678	0.9370	0.8905	0.8272	0.7489	0.6593	0.5640	0.4686	0.3784	0.2970
18	0.9823	0.9626	0.9302	0.8826	0.8195	0.7423	0.6549	0.5622	0.4695	0.3814
19	0.9907	0.9787	0.9573	0.9235	0.8752	0.8122	0.7363	0.6509	0.5606	0.4703

	TABLE III	**Continued**								
λ x	11.0	12.0	13.0	14.0	15.0	16.0	17.0	18.0	19.0	20.0
20	0.9953	0.9884	0.9750	0.9521	0.9170	0.8682	0.8055	0.7307	0.6472	0.5591
21	0.9977	0.9939	0.9859	0.9711	0.9469	0.9108	0.8615	0.7991	0.7255	0.6437
22	0.9989	0.9969	0.9924	0.9833	0.9672	0.9418	0.9047	0.8551	0.7931	0.7206
23	0.9995	0.9985	0.9960	0.9907	0.9805	0.9633	0.9367	0.8989	0.8490	0.7875
24	0.9998	0.9993	0.9980	0.9950	0.9888	0.9777	0.9593	0.9317	0.8933	0.8432
25	0.9999	0.9997	0.9990	0.9974	0.9938	0.9869	0.9747	0.9554	0.9269	0.8878
26	1.0000	0.9999	0.9995	0.9987	0.9967	0.9925	0.9848	0.9718	0.9514	0.9221
27	1.0000	0.9999	0.9998	0.9994	0.9983	0.9959	0.9912	0.9827	0.9687	0.9475
28	1.0000	1.0000	0.9999	0.9997	0.9991	0.9978	0.9950	0.9897	0.9805	0.9657
29	1.0000	1.0000	1.0000	0.9999	0.9996	0.9989	0.9973	0.9940	0.9881	0.9782
30	1.0000	1.0000	1.0000	0.9999	0.9998	0.9994	0.9985	0.9967	0.9930	0.9865
31	1.0000	1.0000	1.0000	1.0000	0.9999	0.9997	0.9992	0.9982	0.9960	0.9919
32	1.0000	1.0000	1.0000	1.0000	0.9999	0.9999	0.9996	0.9990	0.9978	0.9953
33	1.0000	1.0000	1.0000	1.0000	1.0000	0.9999	0.9998	0.9995	0.9988	0.9973
34	1.0000	1.0000	1.0000	1.0000	1.0000	1.0000	0.9999	0.9997	0.9994	0.9985
35	1.0000	1.0000	1.0000	1.0000	1.0000	1.0000	0.9999	0.9999	0.9997	0.9992
36	1.0000	1.0000	1.0000	1.0000	1.0000	1.0000	1.0000	0.9999	0.9998	0.9996
37	1.0000	1.0000	1.0000	1.0000	1.0000	1.0000	1.0000	1.0000	0.9999	0.9998
38	1.0000	1.0000	1.0000	1.0000	1.0000	1.0000	1.0000	1.0000	1.0000	0.9999
39	1.0000	1.0000	1.0000	1.0000	1.0000	1.0000	1.0000	1.0000	1.0000	0.9999
40	1.0000	1.0000	1.0000	1.0000	1.0000	1.0000	1.0000	1.0000	1.0000	1.0000

Statistics for Business Decision Making, by Olson and Picconi. (Scott, Foresman & Company, 1983.) With permission.

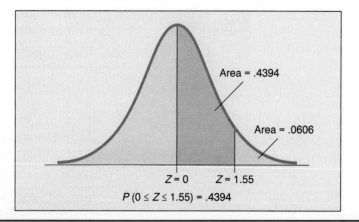

P (0 ≤ Z ≤ 1.55) = .4394

	TABLE IV	Areas under the Normal Curve								

Each entry is the proportion of the total area under the normal curve that lies under the segment between the mean and Z standard deviations from the mean. Example: $X - \mu = 31$ and $\sigma = 20$, so $Z = (X - \mu)/\sigma = 1.55$. The required area is .4394. The area in the tail beyond the point $X - \mu = 31$ is then $.5000 - .4394 = .0606$.

Z	.00	.01	.02	.03	.04	.05	.06	.07	.08	.09
0.0	.0000	.0040	.0080	.0120	.0160	.0199	.0239	.0279	.0319	.0359
0.1	.0398	.0438	.0478	.0517	.0557	.0596	.0636	.0675	.0714	.0753
0.2	.0793	.0832	.0871	.0910	.0948	.0987	.1026	.1064	.1103	.1141
0.3	.1179	.1217	.1255	.1293	.1331	.1368	.1406	.1443	.1480	.1517
0.4	.1554	.1591	.1628	.1664	.1700	.1736	.1772	.1808	.1844	.1879
0.5	.1915	.1950	.1985	.2019	.2054	.2088	.2123	.2157	.2190	.2224
0.6	.2257	.2291	.2324	.2357	.2389	.2422	.2454	.2486	.2518	.2549
0.7	.2580	.2612	.2642	.2673	.2704	.2734	.2764	.2794	.2823	.2852
0.8	.2881	.2910	.2939	.2967	.2995	.3023	.3051	.3078	.3106	.3133
0.9	.3159	.3186	.3212	.3238	.3264	.3289	.3315	.3340	.3365	.3389
1.0	.3413	.3438	.3461	.3485	.3508	.3531	.3554	.3577	.3599	.3621
1.1	.3643	.3665	.3686	.3708	.3729	.3749	.3770	.3790	.3810	.3830
1.2	.3849	.3869	.3888	.3907	.3925	.3944	.3962	.3980	.3997	.4015
1.3	.4032	.4049	.4066	.4082	.4099	.4115	.4131	.4147	.4162	.4177
1.4	.4192	.4207	.4222	.4236	.4251	.4265	.4279	.4292	.4306	.4319
1.5	.4332	.4345	.4357	.4370	.4382	.4394	.4406	.4418	.4429	.4441
1.6	.4452	.4463	.4474	.4484	.4495	.4505	.4515	.4525	.4535	.4545
1.7	.4554	.4564	.4573	.4582	.4591	.4599	.4608	.4616	.4625	.4633
1.8	.4641	.4649	.4656	.4664	.4671	.4678	.4686	.4693	.4699	.4706
1.9	.4713	.4719	.4726	.4732	.4738	.4744	.4750	.4756	.4761	.4767
2.0	.4772	.4778	.4783	.4788	.4793	.4798	.4803	.4808	.4812	.4817
2.1	.4821	.4826	.4830	.4834	.4838	.4842	.4846	.4850	.4854	.4857
2.2	.4861	.4864	.4868	.4871	.4875	.4878	.4881	.4884	.4887	.4890
2.3	.4893	.4896	.4898	.4901	.4904	.4906	.4909	.4911	.4913	.4916
2.4	.4918	.4920	.4922	.4925	.4927	.4929	.4931	.4932	.4934	.4936
2.5	.4938	.4940	.4941	.4943	.4945	.4946	.4948	.4949	.4951	.4952
2.6	.4953	.4955	.4956	.4957	.4959	.4960	.4961	.4962	.4963	.4964
2.7	.4965	.4966	.4967	.4968	.4969	.4970	.4971	.4972	.4973	.4974
2.8	.4974	.4975	.4976	.4977	.4977	.4978	.4979	.4979	.4980	.4981
2.9	.4981	.4982	.4982	.4983	.4984	.4984	.4985	.4985	.4986	.4986
3.0	.49865	.4987	.4987	.4988	.4988	.4989	.4989	.4989	.4990	.4990
3.1	.49903	.4991	.4991	.4991	.4992	.4992	.4992	.4992	.4993	.4993
3.2	.4993129	.4993	.4994	.4994	.4994	.4994	.4994	.4995	.4995	.4995
3.3	.4995166	.4995	.4995	.4996	.4996	.4996	.4996	.4996	.4996	.4997
3.4	.4996631	.4997	.4997	.4997	.4997	.4997	.4997	.4997	.4998	.4998

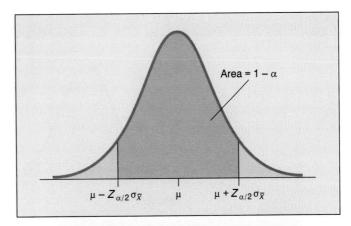

TABLE V Values of $Z_{\alpha/2}$ for $1 - \alpha$ Confidence Interval Estimation		
CONFIDENCE LEVEL $1 - \alpha$	**$\alpha/2$**	**VALUES OF $Z_{\alpha/2}$**
.80	.100	1.282
.90	.050	1.645
.95	.025	1.960
.98	.010	2.326
.99	.005	2.576

TABLE VI   Values of Z_α and $Z_{\alpha/2}$ for One-Sided and Two-Sided Tests of Hypotheses

One-Sided Tests

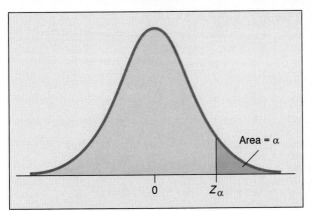

Two-Sided Tests

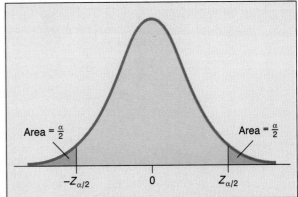

SIGNIFICANCE LEVEL α	VALUE OF Z_α
.100	1.282
.050	1.645
.025	1.960
.010	2.326
.005	2.576

SIGNIFICANCE LEVEL α	VALUE OF $Z_{\alpha/2}$
.100	1.645
.050	1.960
.025	2.240
.010	2.576
.005	2.810

TABLE VII   The *t* Table

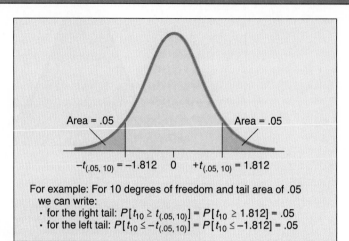

For example: For 10 degrees of freedom and tail area of .05
we can write:
- for the right tail: $P[t_{10} \geq t_{(.05, 10)}] = P[t_{10} \geq 1.812] = .05$
- for the left tail: $P[t_{10} \leq -t_{(.05, 10)}] = P[t_{10} \leq -1.812] = .05$

Area under one tail

d.f.	0.45	0.4	0.35	0.3	0.25	0.2	0.15	0.1	0.05	0.025	0.010	0.005	0.0005
1	.158	.325	.510	.727	1.000	1.376	1.963	3.078	6.314	12.706	31.821	63.657	636.619
2	.142	.289	.445	.617	.816	1.061	1.386	1.886	2.910	4.303	6.965	9.925	31.598
3	.137	.277	.424	.584	.765	.978	1.250	1.638	2.353	3.182	4.541	5.841	12.941
4	.134	.271	.414	.569	.741	.941	1.190	1.533	2.132	2.776	3.747	4.604	8.610
5	.132	.267	.408	.559	.727	.920	1.156	1.476	2.015	2.571	3.365	4.032	6.859
6	.131	.265	.404	.553	.718	.906	1.134	1.440	1.943	2.447	3.143	3.707	5.959
7	.130	.263	.402	.549	.711	.896	1.119	1.415	1.895	2.365	2.998	3.499	5.405
8	.130	.262	.399	.546	.706	.889	1.108	1.397	1.860	2.306	2.896	3.355	5.041
9	.129	.261	.398	.543	.703	.883	1.100	1.383	1.833	2.262	2.821	3.250	4.781
10	.129	.260	.397	.542	.700	.879	1.093	1.372	1.812	2.228	2.764	3.169	4.587
11	.129	.260	.396	.540	.697	.876	1.088	1.363	1.796	2.201	2.718	3.106	4.437
12	.128	.259	.395	.539	.695	.873	1.083	1.356	1.782	2.179	2.681	3.055	4.318
13	.128	.259	.394	.538	.694	.870	1.079	1.350	1.771	2.160	2.650	3.012	4.221
14	.128	.258	.393	.537	.692	.868	1.076	1.345	1.761	2.145	2.624	2.977	4.140
15	.128	.258	.393	.536	.691	.866	1.074	1.341	1.753	2.131	2.602	2.947	4.073
16	.128	.258	.392	.535	.690	.865	1.071	1.337	1.746	2.120	2.583	2.921	4.105
17	.128	.257	.392	.534	.689	.863	1.069	1.333	1.740	2.110	2.567	2.898	3.965
18	.127	.257	.392	.534	.688	.862	1.067	1.330	1.734	2.101	2.552	2.878	3.922
19	.127	.257	.391	.533	.688	.861	1.066	1.328	1.729	2.093	2.539	2.861	3.883
20	.127	.257	.391	.533	.687	.860	1.064	1.325	1.725	2.086	2.528	2.845	3.850
21	.127	.257	.391	.532	.686	.859	1.063	1.323	1.721	2.080	2.518	2.831	3.819
22	.127	.256	.390	.532	.686	.858	1.061	1.321	1.717	2.074	2.508	2.819	3.792
23	.127	.256	.390	.532	.685	.858	1.060	1.319	1.714	2.069	2.500	2.807	3.767
24	.127	.256	.390	.531	.685	.857	1.059	1.318	1.711	2.064	2.492	2.797	3.745
25	.127	.256	.390	.531	.684	.856	1.058	1.316	1.708	2.060	2.485	2.787	3.725
26	.127	.256	.390	.531	.684	.856	1.058	1.315	1.706	2.056	2.479	2.779	3.707
27	.127	.256	.389	.531	.684	.855	1.057	1.314	1.703	2.052	2.473	2.771	3.690
28	.127	.256	.389	.530	.683	.855	1.056	1.313	1.701	2.048	2.467	2.763	3.674
29	.127	.256	.389	.530	.683	.854	1.055	1.311	1.699	2.045	2.462	2.756	3.659
40	.126	.255	.388	.529	.681	.851	1.050	1.303	1.684	2.021	2.423	2.704	3.551
60	.126	.254	.387	.527	.679	.848	1.046	1.296	1.671	2.000	2.390	2.660	3.460
120	.126	.254	.386	.526	.677	.845	1.041	1.289	1.658	1.980	2.358	2.617	3.373
(Normal Distribution) inf.	.126	.253	.385	.524	.674	.842	1.036	1.282	1.645	1.960	2.326	2.576	3.291

This table is reprinted from *Table III* of Fisher and Yates: *Statistical Tables for Biological, Agricultural, and Medical Research*, published by Longman Group Ltd. London (previously published by Oliver and Boyd Ltd., Edinburgh) and by permission of the authors and publishers.

TABLE VIIIa   Percentiles of the Chi-Square Distribution: Values of $\chi^2_{(1-\alpha,\nu)}$

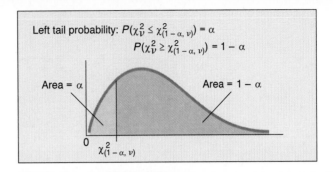

Left tail probability: $P(\chi^2_\nu \le \chi^2_{(1-\alpha,\nu)}) = \alpha$
$P(\chi^2_\nu \ge \chi^2_{(1-\alpha,\nu)}) = 1 - \alpha$

Area = α Area = $1 - \alpha$

$0 \quad \chi^2_{(1-\alpha,\nu)}$

d.f. (ν)	$1 - \alpha = .995$	.990	.975	.950	.900
1	0.0000393	0.0001571	0.0009821	0.0039321	0.0157908
2	0.0100251	0.0201007	0.0506356	0.102587	0.210720
3	0.0717212	0.114832	0.215795	0.351846	0.584375
4	0.206990	0.297110	0.484419	0.710721	1.063623
5	0.411740	0.554300	0.831211	1.145476	1.61031
6	0.675727	0.872085	1.237347	1.63539	2.20413
7	0.989265	1.239043	1.68987	2.16735	2.83311
8	1.344419	1.646482	2.17973	2.73264	3.48954
9	1.734926	2.087912	2.70039	3.32511	4.16816
10	2.15585	2.55821	3.24697	3.94030	4.86518
11	2.60321	3.05347	3.81575	4.57481	5.57779
12	3.07382	3.57056	4.40379	5.22603	6.30380
13	3.56503	4.10691	5.00874	5.89186	7.04150
14	4.07468	4.66043	5.62872	6.57063	7.78953
15	4.60094	5.22935	6.26214	7.26094	8.54675
16	5.14224	5.81221	6.90766	7.96164	9.31223
17	5.69724	6.40776	7.56418	8.67176	10.0852
18	6.26481	7.01491	8.23075	9.39046	10.8649
19	6.84398	7.63273	8.90655	10.1170	11.6509
20	7.43386	8.26040	9.59083	10.8508	12.4426
21	8.03366	8.89720	10.28293	11.5913	13.2396
22	8.64272	9.54249	10.9823	12.3380	14.0415
23	9.26042	10.19567	11.6885	13.0905	14.8479
24	9.88623	10.8564	12.4011	13.8484	15.6587
25	10.5197	11.5240	13.1197	14.6114	16.4734
26	11.1603	12.1981	13.8439	15.3791	17.2919
27	11.8076	12.8786	14.5733	16.1513	18.1138
28	12.4613	13.5648	15.3079	16.9279	18.9392
29	13.1211	14.2565	16.0471	17.7083	19.7677
30	13.7867	14.9535	16.7908	18.4926	20.5992
40	20.7065	22.1643	24.4331	26.5093	29.0505
50	27.9907	29.7067	32.3574	34.7642	37.6886
60	35.5346	37.4848	40.4817	43.1879	46.4589
70	43.2752	45.4418	48.7576	51.7393	55.3290
80	51.1720	53.5400	57.1532	60.3915	64.2778
90	59.1963	61.7541	65.6466	69.1260	73.2912
100	67.3276	70.0648	74.2219	77.9295	82.3581

This table is based on Table 8 of the *Biometrika Tables for Statisticians*, vol. 1, by Pearson, E. S., and Hartley, H. O., Cambridge University Press, 1966, by permission of the *Biometrika* trustees.

TABLE VIIIb   Percentiles of the Chi-Square Distribution: Values of $\chi^2_{(\alpha,\upsilon)}$

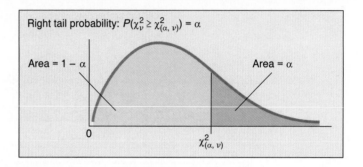

Right tail probability: $P(\chi^2_\upsilon \geq \chi^2_{(\alpha,\upsilon)}) = \alpha$

Area = $1 - \alpha$ Area = α

0 $\chi^2_{(\alpha,\upsilon)}$

d.f. (ν)	$\alpha = .100$	.050	.025	.010	.005
1	2.70554	3.84146	5.02389	6.63490	7.87944
2	4.60517	5.99147	7.37776	9.21034	10.5966
3	6.25139	7.81473	9.34840	11.3449	12.8381
4	7.77944	9.48773	11.1433	13.2767	14.8602
5	9.23635	11.0705	12.8325	15.0863	16.7496
6	10.6446	12.5916	14.4494	16.8119	18.5476
7	12.0170	14.0671	16.0128	18.4753	20.2777
8	13.3616	15.5073	17.5346	20.0902	21.9550
9	14.6837	16.9190	19.0228	21.6660	23.5893
10	15.9871	18.3070	20.4831	23.2093	25.1882
11	17.2750	19.6751	21.9200	24.7250	26.7569
12	18.5494	21.0261	23.3367	26.2170	28.2995
13	19.8119	22.3621	24.7356	27.6883	29.8194
14	21.0642	23.6848	26.1190	29.1413	31.3193
15	22.3072	24.9958	27.4884	30.5779	32.8013
16	23.5418	26.2962	28.8454	31.9999	34.2672
17	24.7690	27.5871	30.1910	33.4087	35.7185
18	25.9894	28.8693	31.5264	34.8053	37.1564
19	27.2036	30.1435	32.8523	36.1908	38.5822
20	28.4120	31.4104	34.1696	37.5662	39.9968
21	29.6151	32.6705	35.4789	38.9321	41.4010
22	30.8133	33.9244	36.7807	40.2894	42.7956
23	32.0069	35.1725	38.0757	41.6384	44.1813
24	33.1963	36.4151	39.3641	42.9798	45.5585
25	34.3816	37.6525	40.6465	44.3141	46.9278
26	35.5631	38.8852	41.9232	45.6417	48.2899
27	36.7412	40.1133	43.1944	46.9630	49.6449
28	37.9159	41.3372	44.4607	48.2782	50.9933
29	39.0875	42.5569	45.7222	49.5879	52.3356
30	40.2560	43.7729	46.9792	50.8922	53.6720
40	51.8050	55.7585	59.3417	63.6907	66.7659
50	63.1671	67.5048	71.4202	76.1539	79.4900
60	74.3970	79.0819	83.2976	88.3794	91.9517
70	85.5271	90.5312	95.0231	100.425	104.215
80	96.5782	101.879	106.629	112.329	116.321
90	107.565	113.145	118.136	124.116	128.299
100	118.498	124.342	129.561	135.807	140.169

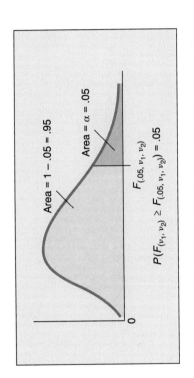

Area = 1 − .05 = .95

Area = α = .05

$F_{(.05,\, \nu_1,\, \nu_2)}$

$P(F_{(\nu_1,\, \nu_2)} \geq F_{(.05,\, \nu_1,\, \nu_2)}) = .05$

TABLE IXa F Distribution: Upper 5% Points

Values of $F_{(.05,\, \nu_1,\, \nu_2)}$

ν_2 \ ν_1	1	2	3	4	5	6	7	8	9	10	12	15	20	24	30	40	60	120	∞
1	161	200	216	225	230	234	237	239	241	242	244	246	248	249	250	251	252	253	254
2	18.5	19.0	19.2	19.2	19.3	19.3	19.4	19.4	19.4	19.4	19.4	19.4	19.4	19.5	19.5	19.5	19.5	19.5	19.5
3	10.1	9.55	9.28	9.12	9.01	8.94	8.89	8.85	8.81	8.79	8.74	8.70	8.66	8.64	8.62	8.59	8.57	8.55	8.53
4	7.71	6.94	6.59	6.39	6.26	6.16	6.09	6.04	6.00	5.96	5.91	5.86	5.80	5.77	5.75	5.72	5.69	5.66	5.63
5	6.61	5.79	5.41	5.19	5.05	4.95	4.88	4.82	4.77	4.74	4.68	4.62	4.56	4.53	4.50	4.46	4.43	4.40	4.37
6	5.99	5.14	4.76	4.53	4.39	4.28	4.21	4.15	4.10	4.06	4.00	3.94	3.87	3.84	3.81	3.77	3.74	3.70	3.67
7	5.59	4.74	4.35	4.12	3.97	3.87	3.79	3.73	3.68	3.64	3.57	3.51	3.44	3.41	3.38	3.34	3.30	3.27	3.23
8	5.32	4.46	4.07	3.84	3.69	3.58	3.50	3.44	3.39	3.35	3.28	3.22	3.15	3.12	3.08	3.04	3.01	2.97	2.93
9	5.12	4.26	3.86	3.63	3.48	3.37	3.29	3.23	3.18	3.14	3.07	3.01	2.94	2.90	2.86	2.83	2.79	2.75	2.71
10	4.96	4.10	3.71	3.48	3.33	3.22	3.14	3.07	3.02	2.98	2.91	2.85	2.77	2.74	2.70	2.66	2.62	2.58	2.54
11	4.84	3.98	3.59	3.36	3.20	3.09	3.01	2.95	2.90	2.85	2.79	2.72	2.65	2.61	2.57	2.53	2.49	2.45	2.40
12	4.75	3.89	3.49	3.26	3.11	3.00	2.91	2.85	2.80	2.75	2.69	2.62	2.54	2.51	2.47	2.43	2.38	2.34	2.30
13	4.67	3.81	3.41	3.18	3.03	2.92	2.83	2.77	2.71	2.67	2.60	2.53	2.46	2.42	2.38	2.34	2.30	2.25	2.21
14	4.60	3.74	3.34	3.11	2.96	2.85	2.76	2.70	2.65	2.60	2.53	2.46	2.39	2.35	2.31	2.27	2.22	2.18	2.13
15	4.54	3.68	3.29	3.06	2.90	2.79	2.71	2.64	2.59	2.54	2.48	2.40	2.33	2.29	2.25	2.20	2.16	2.11	2.07
16	4.49	3.63	3.24	3.01	2.85	2.74	2.66	2.59	2.54	2.49	2.42	2.35	2.28	2.24	2.19	2.15	2.11	2.06	2.01
17	4.45	3.59	3.20	2.96	2.81	2.70	2.61	2.55	2.49	2.45	2.38	2.31	2.23	2.19	2.15	2.10	2.06	2.01	1.96
18	4.41	3.55	3.16	2.93	2.77	2.66	2.58	2.51	2.46	2.41	2.34	2.27	2.19	2.15	2.11	2.06	2.02	1.97	1.92
19	4.38	3.52	3.13	2.90	2.74	2.63	2.54	2.48	2.42	2.38	2.31	2.23	2.16	2.11	2.07	2.03	1.98	1.93	1.88
20	4.35	3.49	3.10	2.87	2.71	2.60	2.51	2.45	2.39	2.35	2.28	2.20	2.12	2.08	2.04	1.99	1.95	1.90	1.84
21	4.32	3.47	3.07	2.84	2.68	2.57	2.49	2.42	2.37	2.32	2.25	2.18	2.10	2.05	2.01	1.96	1.92	1.87	1.81
22	4.30	3.44	3.05	2.82	2.66	2.55	2.46	2.40	2.34	2.30	2.23	2.15	2.07	2.03	1.98	1.94	1.89	1.84	1.78
23	4.28	3.42	3.03	2.80	2.64	2.53	2.44	2.37	2.32	2.27	2.20	2.13	2.05	2.01	1.96	1.91	1.86	1.81	1.76
24	4.26	3.40	3.01	2.78	2.62	2.51	2.42	2.36	2.30	2.25	2.18	2.11	2.03	1.98	1.94	1.89	1.84	1.79	1.73
25	4.24	3.39	2.99	2.76	2.60	2.49	2.40	2.34	2.28	2.24	2.16	2.09	2.01	1.96	1.92	1.87	1.82	1.77	1.71
27	4.21	3.35	2.96	2.73	2.57	2.46	2.37	2.31	2.25	2.20	2.13	2.06	1.97	1.93	1.88	1.84	1.79	1.73	1.67
30	4.17	3.32	2.92	2.69	2.53	2.42	2.33	2.27	2.21	2.16	2.09	2.01	1.93	1.89	1.84	1.79	1.74	1.68	1.62
40	4.08	3.23	2.84	2.61	2.45	2.34	2.25	2.18	2.12	2.08	2.00	1.92	1.84	1.79	1.74	1.69	1.64	1.58	1.51
60	4.00	3.15	2.76	2.53	2.37	2.25	2.17	2.10	2.04	1.99	1.92	1.84	1.75	1.70	1.65	1.59	1.53	1.47	1.39
120	3.92	3.07	2.68	2.45	2.29	2.18	2.09	2.02	1.96	1.91	1.83	1.75	1.66	1.61	1.55	1.50	1.43	1.35	1.25
∞	3.84	3.00	2.60	2.37	2.21	2.10	2.01	1.94	1.88	1.83	1.75	1.67	1.57	1.52	1.46	1.39	1.32	1.22	1.00

Degrees of Freedom for Numerator, ν_1

Degrees of Freedom for Denominator, ν_2

From Merrington, M. and Thompson, C. M., "Tables of percentage points of the inverted beta (F) distrubution." *Biometrika*, vol. 33, 1943, p. 73, with corrections obtained from *Biometrika Tables for Statisticians*, vol. 2, Table 5, 1972, by permission of the *Biometrika* trustees.

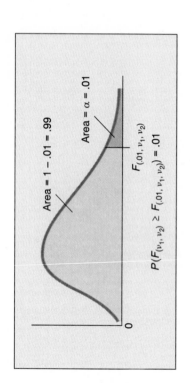

Area = 1 − .01 = .99

Area = α = .01

$F_{(.01, \nu_1, \nu_2)}$

$P(F_{(\nu_1, \nu_2)} \geq F_{(.01, \nu_1, \nu_2)}) = .01$

TABLE IXb F Distribution: Upper 1% Points

Values of $F_{(.01, \nu_1, \nu_2)}$

ν_2	Degrees of Freedom for Numerator, ν_1																		
	1	2	3	4	5	6	7	8	9	10	12	15	20	24	30	40	60	120	∞
1	4,052	5,000	5,403	5,625	5,764	5,859	5,928	5,982	6,023	6,056	6,106	6,157	6,209	6,235	6,261	6,287	6,313	6,339	6,366
2	98.5	99.0	99.2	99.2	99.3	99.3	99.4	99.4	99.4	99.4	99.4	99.4	99.4	99.5	99.5	99.5	99.5	99.5	99.5
3	34.1	30.8	29.5	28.7	28.2	27.9	27.7	27.5	27.3	27.2	27.1	26.9	26.7	26.6	26.5	26.4	26.3	26.2	26.1
4	21.2	18.0	16.7	16.0	15.5	15.2	15.0	14.8	14.7	14.5	14.4	14.2	14.0	13.9	13.8	13.7	13.7	13.6	13.5
5	16.3	13.3	12.1	11.4	11.0	10.7	10.5	10.3	10.2	10.1	9.89	9.72	9.55	9.47	9.38	9.29	9.20	9.11	9.02
6	13.7	10.9	9.78	9.15	8.75	8.47	8.26	8.10	7.98	7.87	7.72	7.56	7.40	7.31	7.23	7.14	7.06	6.97	6.88
7	12.2	9.55	8.45	7.85	7.46	7.19	6.99	6.84	6.72	6.62	6.47	6.31	6.16	6.07	5.99	5.91	5.82	5.74	5.65
8	11.3	8.65	7.59	7.01	6.63	6.37	6.18	6.03	5.91	5.81	5.67	5.52	5.36	5.28	5.20	5.12	5.03	4.95	4.83
9	10.6	8.02	6.99	6.42	6.06	5.80	5.61	5.47	5.35	5.26	5.11	4.96	4.81	4.73	4.65	4.57	4.48	4.40	4.31
10	10.0	7.56	6.55	5.99	5.64	5.39	5.20	5.06	4.94	4.85	4.71	4.56	4.41	4.33	4.25	4.17	4.08	4.00	3.91
11	9.65	7.21	6.22	5.67	5.32	5.07	4.89	4.74	4.63	4.54	4.40	4.25	4.10	4.02	3.94	3.86	3.78	3.69	3.60
12	9.33	6.93	5.95	5.41	5.06	4.82	4.64	4.50	4.39	4.30	4.16	4.01	3.86	3.78	3.70	3.62	3.54	3.45	3.36
13	9.07	6.70	5.74	5.21	4.86	4.62	4.44	4.30	4.19	4.10	3.96	3.82	3.66	3.59	3.51	3.43	3.34	3.25	3.17
14	8.86	6.51	5.56	5.04	4.70	4.46	4.28	4.14	4.03	3.94	3.80	3.66	3.51	3.43	3.35	3.27	3.18	3.09	3.00
15	8.68	6.36	5.42	4.89	4.56	4.32	4.14	4.00	3.89	3.80	3.67	3.52	3.37	3.29	3.21	3.13	3.05	2.96	2.87
16	8.53	6.23	5.29	4.77	4.44	4.20	4.03	3.89	3.78	3.69	3.55	3.41	3.26	3.18	3.10	3.02	2.93	2.84	2.75
17	8.40	6.11	5.19	4.67	4.34	4.10	3.93	3.79	3.68	3.59	3.46	3.31	3.16	3.08	3.00	2.92	2.83	2.75	2.65
18	8.29	6.01	5.09	4.58	4.25	4.01	3.84	3.71	3.60	3.51	3.37	3.23	3.08	3.00	2.92	2.84	2.75	2.66	2.57
19	8.19	5.93	5.01	4.50	4.17	3.94	3.77	3.63	3.52	3.43	3.30	3.15	3.00	2.92	2.84	2.76	2.67	2.58	2.49
20	8.10	5.85	4.94	4.43	4.10	3.87	3.70	3.56	3.46	3.37	3.23	3.09	2.94	2.86	2.78	2.69	2.61	2.52	2.42
21	8.02	5.78	4.87	4.37	4.04	3.81	3.64	3.51	3.40	3.31	3.17	3.03	2.88	2.80	2.72	2.64	2.55	2.46	2.36
22	7.95	5.72	4.82	4.31	3.99	3.76	3.59	3.45	3.35	3.26	3.12	2.98	2.83	2.75	2.67	2.58	2.50	2.40	2.31
23	7.88	5.66	4.76	4.26	3.94	3.71	3.54	3.41	3.30	3.21	3.07	2.93	2.78	2.70	2.62	2.54	2.45	2.35	2.26
24	7.82	5.61	4.72	4.22	3.90	3.67	3.50	3.36	3.26	3.17	3.03	2.89	2.74	2.66	2.58	2.49	2.40	2.31	2.21
25	7.77	5.57	4.68	4.18	3.86	3.63	3.46	3.32	3.22	3.13	2.99	2.85	2.70	2.62	2.53	2.45	2.36	2.27	2.17
27	7.68	5.49	4.60	4.11	3.78	3.56	3.39	3.26	3.15	3.06	2.93	2.78	2.63	2.55	2.47	2.38	2.29	2.20	2.10
30	7.56	5.39	4.51	4.02	3.70	3.47	3.30	3.17	3.07	2.98	2.84	2.70	2.55	2.47	2.39	2.30	2.21	2.11	2.01
40	7.31	5.18	4.31	3.83	3.51	3.29	3.12	2.99	2.89	2.80	2.66	2.52	2.37	2.29	2.20	2.11	2.02	1.92	1.80
60	7.08	4.98	4.13	3.65	3.34	3.12	2.95	2.82	2.72	2.63	2.50	2.35	2.20	2.12	2.03	1.94	1.84	1.73	1.60
120	6.85	4.79	3.95	3.48	3.17	2.96	2.79	2.66	2.56	2.47	2.34	2.19	2.03	1.95	1.86	1.76	1.66	1.53	1.38
∞	6.63	4.61	3.78	3.32	3.02	2.80	2.64	2.51	2.41	2.32	2.18	2.04	1.88	1.79	1.70	1.59	1.47	1.32	1.00

Degrees of Freedom for Denominator, ν_2

ANSWERS TO SELECTED ODD-NUMBERED EXERCISES

1

CHAPTER REVIEW EXERCISES

1.1 Answers will vary.

1.3 The selection of a random sample of 225 people is an example of statistical design. 217 of the 225 subjects showed relief is an example of statistical description, since the original set of data has been condensed into this summary statement. The generalization that the drug can relieve flu symptoms 96% of the time is an example of statistical inference.

1.5 The 5 cigarettes must be assumed to be chosen at random.

1.7 a. Brand preference between Peak and Shell antifreeze is done with an ordinal scale, since preference indicates relative order of rank.
b. A compilation of total Peak antifreeze sales is done with a ratio scale, since a natural zero point exists.
c. An interval scale, since no natural zero point exists.

1.9 a. The variables in the profile are categorical. The scale for comparison of A and B for each attribute is an ordinal scale. Only rankings matter, so we can't say that store B's employees are about 50% more helpful than store A's employees.
b. It would appear that store A's singular advantage is that it carries higher quality merchandise. However, price, service, helpful employees, and friendly atmosphere are clearly store B's advantage. If the quality of store B's merchandise is adequate, then store B is in a very competitive position.

CHAPTER

2

EXERCISES

2.1 a and c.

LOWER CLASS BOUNDARY	CLASS MIDPOINT	UPPER CLASS BOUNDARY	TALLY	FREQUENCY	RELATIVE FREQUENCY
4.085	4.435	4.785	|||	3	.0638
4.785	5.135	5.485	‖‖ ||	7	.1489
5.485	5.835	6.185	‖‖ ‖‖		11	.2340
6.185	6.535	6.885	‖‖ ‖‖		11	.2340
6.885	7.235	7.585	‖‖ ||	7	.1489
7.585	7.935	8.285	‖‖ ||	7	.1489
8.285	8.635	8.985			1	.0213
				Total 47	

b and d.

LOWER LIMIT OF CLASS INTERVAL	CUMULATIVE "LESS THAN" FREQUENCIES	CUMULATIVE "LESS THAN" RELATIVE FREQUENCIES
4.09	0	.0000
4.79	3	.0638
5.49	10	.2128
6.19	21	.4468
6.89	32	.6809
7.59	39	.8298
8.29	46	.9787
8.99	47	1.0000

e. (i) From the raw data we see that all 47 respondents were overcharged. (ii) 22 of the 47 (approx. 46.8%) were overcharged from $5.49 to $6.88. (iii) No one was overcharged by less than $4.09 nor more than $8.99. (Actually, from looking at the raw data when setting up these tables, we could see that none were overcharged less than $4.42, and none more than $8.63.) (iv) Approx. 68% were overcharged by up to $6.88. (v) Approx. 78% were overcharged by $5.49 or more.

2.3 a and c.

LOWER CLASS LIMIT	CLASS MIDPOINT	UPPER CLASS LIMIT	TALLY	FREQUENCY	RELATIVE FREQUENCY
36.9	42.35	47.8	|	1	.0270
47.9	53.35	58.8	||	2	.0541
58.9	64.35	69.8	₩₩ ₩₩ ||||	14	.3784
69.9	75.35	80.8	₩₩ ||||	9	.2432
80.9	86.35	91.8	₩₩ |	6	.1622
91.9	97.35	102.8	₩₩	5	.1351
				Total 37	

b and d.

LOWER LIMIT OF CLASS INTERVAL	CUMULATIVE "LESS THAN" FREQUENCIES	CUMULATIVE "LESS THAN" RELATIVE FREQUENCIES
36.9	0	.0000
47.9	1	.0270
58.9	3	.0811
69.9	17	.4595
80.9	26	.7027
91.9	32	.8649
102.9	37	1.0000

e. (i) In 34 of the 37 fields (approx. 92%), 58.9% or more of the young working professionals had used a resume service. (ii) In 23 of the 37 fields (approx. 62%), 58.9–80.8% of the young working professionals had used a resume service. (iii) A large percentage of the young working professionals have used a resume service, but we don't know the percentage of young professionals still seeking jobs who have also used a resume service.

2.5   a.

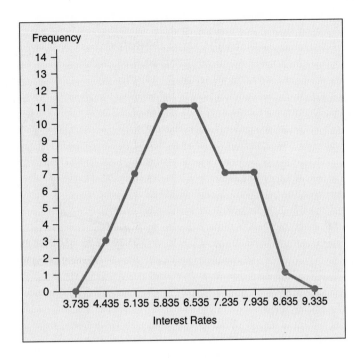

b.

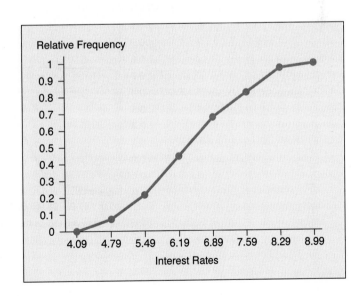

c. Similar: (i) The peak of overcharges ranges from $5.50 to $6.50. (ii) None of the 47 persons was overcharged by less than $4.00. (iii) None of the 47 persons was overcharged by more than $9.00. (iv) Halfway up the ogive (at a relative frequency of 0.5) we see that approximately half the 47 persons were overcharged from $4.00 to $6.00, and the other half from $6.00 to $9.00.

2.7   a.

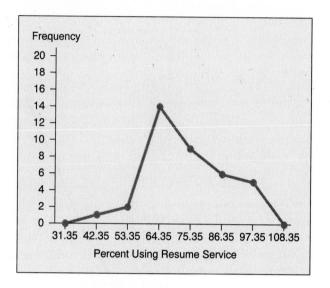

b.

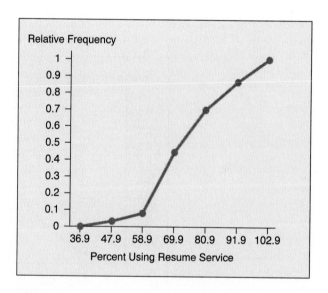

c. Similar: (i) Approx. 64% of the young working professionals in 14 fields had used a resume service. (ii) Halfway up the ogive (representing half the professional fields) we see that in half of the 37 fields, approx. 37–69% of the young working professionals had used a resume service, and in the other half, 69% or more had used a resume service.

2.9   a.

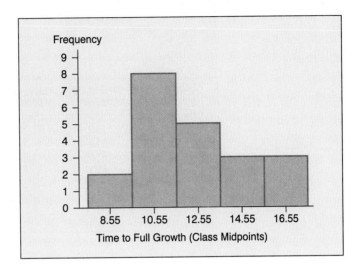

b. No; the histogram, frequency table, and frequency polygon provide similar information.

2.11   a.

4	78 42 50
5	79 55 67 63 84 25 28 13 62 00 20 64 22 12 61 95
6	90 25 45 28 28 15 33 39 19 42 83 29 33 13 97 96
7	62 06 76 32 80 79 20 30
8	63 18 11 17

b. They don't alter the earlier impressions, but they do provide additional insight: (i) From the stem-and-leaf plot we can see that more than half (32 out of 47, or 68.1%) of the 47 accounts were overcharged from $5.00 to $7.00. (ii) More observations lie in the lower portion of the stem-and-leaf plot. This suggests a slight asymmetry to the right (skewed to the right). It indicates that the overcharges are more concentrated at the low end.

2.13   a. To make a stem-and-leaf plot with as wide a range as from 38.3 to 99.6, we shall ignore the decimal portion of each value. That is, we shall treat 38.3 as 38, 54.2 as 54, and so on.

3	8
4	
5	4 6
6	1 0 1 9 3 7 0 8 2 9 7 5 7 1
7	0 3 3 6 3 0 6 8
8	9 3 7 0 8
9	9 0 7 7 0 2 4

b. They don't alter the earlier impressions, but they do provide some additional insights. From the stem-and-leaf plot we see that there is only one profession where less than 54% of the young working professionals had used a resume service. It suggests that the use of resumes may be the exception in that field, rather than the rule.

CHAPTER REVIEW EXERCISES

2.15 a. $R = L - S = 57 - 37 = 20$

b.

LOWER CLASS BOUNDARY	UPPER CLASS BOUNDARY	CLASS MIDPOINT	TALLY	FREQUENCY
35.5	39.5	37.5	|	1
39.5	43.5	41.5	|	1
43.5	47.5	45.5	ﾊﾄ	5
47.5	51.5	49.5	ﾊﾄ ﾊﾄ	10
51.5	55.5	53.5	ﾊﾄ ﾊﾄ ||	12
55.5	59.5	57.5	|	1
				30

c.

LOWER LIMIT OF CLASS INTERVAL	CUMULATIVE "LESS THAN" FREQUENCY
36	0
40	1
44	2
48	7
52	17
56	29
60	30

d.

CLASS INTERVAL	FREQUENCY	RELATIVE FREQUENCY
35.5–39.5	1	1/30 = .0333
39.5–43.5	1	1/30 = .0333
43.5–47.5	5	5/30 = .1667
47.5–51.5	10	10/30 = .3333
51.5–55.5	12	12/30 = .4000
55.5–59.5	1	1/30 = .0333
	30	1.000

e.

LOWER LIMIT OF CLASS INTERVAL	CUMULATIVE "LESS THAN" FREQUENCY	CUMULATIVE "LESS THAN" RELATIVE FREQUENCY
36	0	0/30 = .0000
40	1	1/30 = .0333
44	2	2/30 = .0667
48	7	7/30 = .2333
52	17	17/30 = .5667
56	29	29/30 = .9667
60	30	30/30 = 1.000

2.17 a. (1) There are 9 classes, each with equal length 4 units.

  (2) Class limits: (3) Class midpoints:

   14.6–18.5   16.55
   18.6–22.5   20.55
   22.6–26.5   24.55
   26.6–30.5   28.55
   30.6–34.5   32.55
   34.6–38.5   36.55
   38.6–42.5   40.55
   42.6–46.5   44.55
   46.6–50.5   48.55

 b. (1) No; 17 is within the class from 14.55 to 18.55. Of the 4 values in this class, we can't tell how many may be above or below 17. (2) Yes. (3) No. (4) Yes. (5) Yes. (6) Yes.

2.19 a. (1) There are 8 classes, each with length 3 mm.

  (2) Class boundaries: (3) Class midpoints:

   0.5– 3.5   2
   3.5– 6.5   5
   6.5– 9.5   8
   9.5–12.5   11
   12.5–15.5   14
   15.5–18.5   17
   18.5–21.5   20
   21.5–24.5   23

 b. (1) No; 17 is within the class from 16 to 18. (2) No. (3) Yes; since class limits are expressed with the same number of decimal places as the raw data, we know that the raw data must be expressed with zero decimal places. Thus, there are no values between 18 and 19. The number of values less than 19 is equal to the number less than or equal to 18, which is 64 of 69. (4) Yes. (5) Yes. (6) No. (7) Yes. (8) No.

2.21 a. There are 5 classes with an equal length of 3 units.

 b. Class midpoints: c. Class limits:

   1   0– 2
   4   3– 5
   7   6– 8
   10   9–11
   13   12–14

2.23 a.

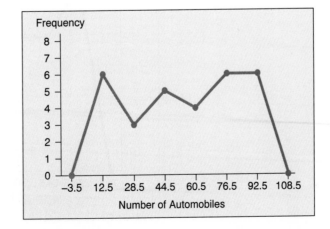

b.

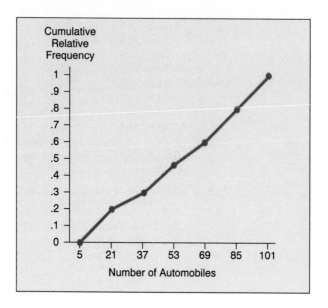

2.25 a.

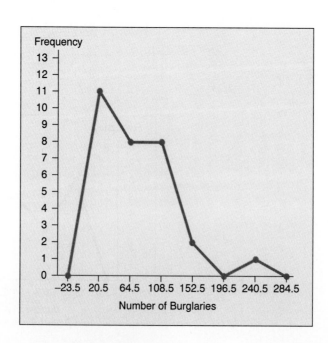

b.

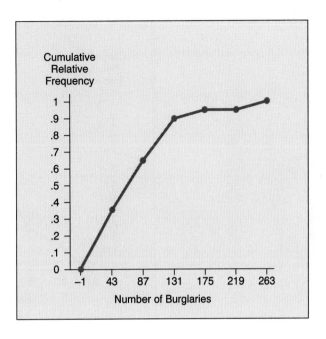

2.27 a.

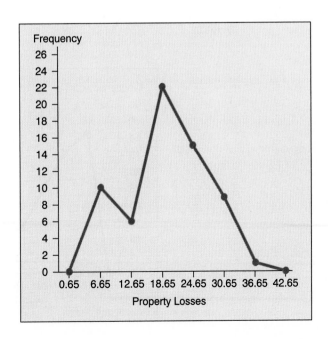

b.

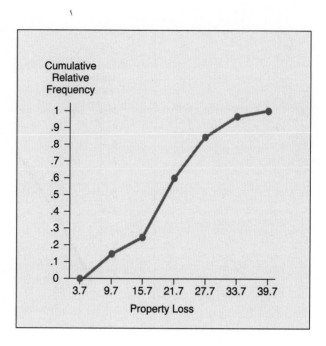

2.29 a.

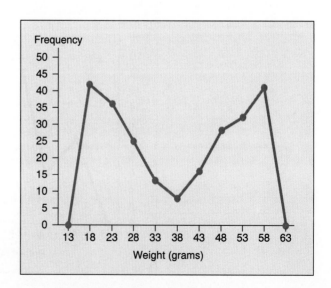

b.

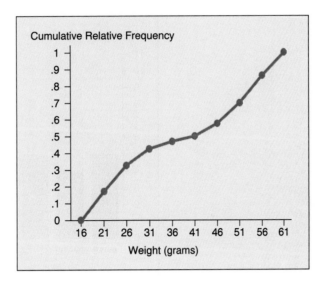

2.31 a.

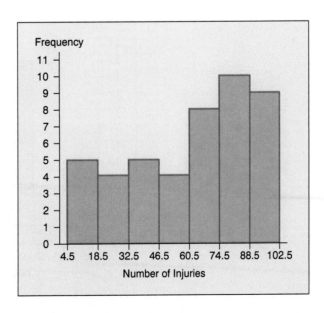

b.

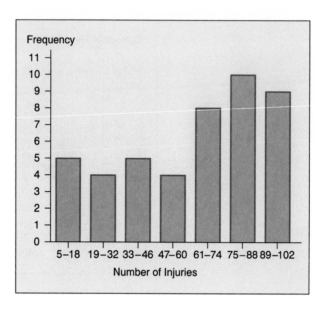

2.33 a.

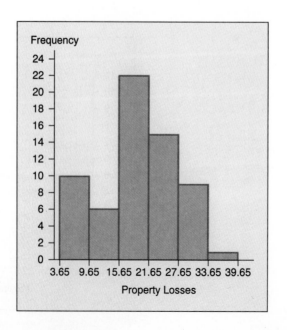

b.

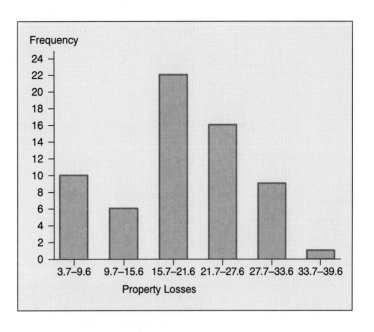

2.35

TYPE OF TREE	NUMBER	RELATIVE FREQUENCY	PIE CHART DEGREES
Acacia	50	50/500 = .10	36
Eucalyptus	100	100/500 = .20	72
Mulberry	125	125/500 = .25	90
Podocarpus	75	75/500 = .15	54
Sycamore	150	150/500 = .30	108
	500	1.00	360

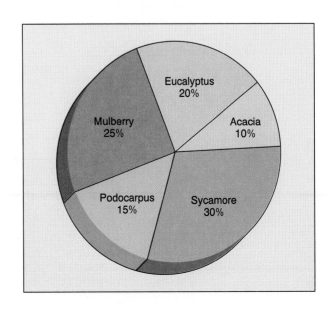

2.37

```
0 | 6
1 | 00479
2 | 16
3 | 08
4 | 235
5 | 06
6 | 048
7 | 0039
8 | 146
9 | 04559
```

2.39 a. Stem-and-leaf display, with stem interval 50 units, and rounding to a leaf unit of 10 units:

```
0 | 0001
0 | 5779
1 | 233
1 | 566778888889999
2 | 0002233
2 | 689
3 | 12
3 | 7
```

b.

LOWER CLASS BOUNDARY	UPPER CLASS BOUNDARY	CLASS MIDPOINT	FREQUENCY
−0.5	52.5	26	1
52.5	105.5	79	3
105.5	158.5	132	4
158.5	211.5	185	17
211.5	264.5	238	5
264.5	317.5	291	3
317.5	370.5	344	2
			39

c. The stem-and-leaf display provides essentially the same information as the frequency table. An advantage of the stem-and-leaf plot is that the original data values (although perhaps rounded, as in this example) are not lost within each class. The distribution of values within each class can be seen.

2.41 a.

```
           Female           Male
              987 | 1 | 134899
       9988655432 | 2 | 01122234455556667788
       8764322210 | 3 | 0001334455567789
             7410 | 4 | 0123445688
                0 | 5 | 257
                  | 6 | 3
```

b.

CLASS BOUNDARIES	MALE FREQUENCY	FEMALE FREQUENCY
9.5–19.5	6	3
19.5–29.5	20	10
29.5–39.5	16	10
39.5–49.5	10	4
49.5–59.5	3	1
59.5–69.5	1	0
	56	28

c. The stem-and-leaf plot allows the advantage of looking at the individual ages within each class. Notice that the oldest and youngest males in the race were 63 and 11, so the range is 52. Females were from 50 to 17, for a range of 33. It is not possible to specify these differences as precisely with frequency tables.

d. Males:

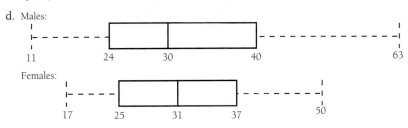

11   24   30   40   63

Females:

17   25   31   37   50

e. Yes; The boxplots not only show the spread but also more easily show where the values in the middle of the distribution lie. For males, the middle half of ages lies between about 24 and 40 years, while for females the middle half falls in the range between about 25 and 37 years. The age distribution of females is less dispersed than the age distribution of males.

2.43 a. Energy companies   Pharmaceutical companies

8876542	0	
97633211000	1	014
88650	2	89
97710	3	3689
5221	4	579
44	5	125
2	6	2
	7	6
0	8	59
	9	8

b.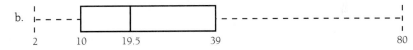

2   10   19.5   39   80

c. Energy companies tend to have cash turnover values that are smaller than those of pharmaceutical companies. Half of the pharmaceutical companies sampled had turnover values below 46, half had values above 46. The midpoint for energy companies is only 19.5. In fact, the boxplot for energy companies shows that over 75% of turnover values are below 40.

CHAPTER 3

EXERCISES

3.1 a. The mean, to the nearest dollar, is $\mu = \$275,098$; the median is $\$277,340$; there is no single modal value.

b. Range $= \$99,567$; MAD $= (558,758/29) = 19,267.52$; $\sigma^2 = 587,654,058$; $\sigma = \$24,241.58$; Coefficient of variation $= (\sigma/\mu)(100) = (24,242/275,097)(100) = 8.8\%$.

c. $k = 1.8$; therefore at least $1 - 1/(1.8)^2 = .69$, or 69% of the 29 values should lie between $275,097 - (1.8)(24,242) = 231,461.4$ and $275,097 + (1.8)(24,242) = 318,732.6$. That is, at least 20 of the 29 values should lie between $\$231,461$ and $\$318,732$. When we count the number of raw data values that are greater than $\$231,461$ and less than $\$318,732$, we find that 27 out of the 29 values (or 93%) lie in that interval. The Chebyshev theorem provided a conservative estimate.

d. (i) The mean and median values are fairly close, and the average annual gross income from these 29 families is $275,097. (ii) MAD and σ are fairly close in value. Also, by using σ and μ together in Chebyshev's theorem we can conservatively estimate that at least 69% of the 29 annual gross incomes should lie in the interval from $231,461 to $318,732. (iii) Since the value of the coefficient of variation is fairly small, there isn't very much variation among the incomes, relative to their size. For example, the standard deviation of $24,242 for incomes in the $275,097 bracket is a small variation as compared with a standard deviation of $24,242 for incomes in the $50,000 bracket.

3.3 a. The mean is $\bar{X} = 12.31$; the median is 11.6; there are three modes: 10.6, 10.8, and 13.1.

b. Range = 9.2; MAD = $(43.83/21) = 2.087$; $S^2 = 6.3729$; $S = 2.5245$; Coefficient of variation = $(S/\bar{X}) = (2.5245/12.31)(100) = 20.5\%$.

c. $k = 1.5$; therefore at least $1 - 1/(1.5)^2 = .56$, or 56% of the 21 values should lie between $12.31 - (1.5)(2.5245) = 8.523$ and $12.31 + (1.5)(2.5245) = 16.097$. That is, at least 12 of the 21 values should lie between 8.5 and 16.1. When we count the number of raw data values that are greater than 8.5 and less than 16.1, we find that 18 of the 21 values (or 85.7%) lie in that interval. The Chebyshev theorem provided a conservative estimate.

d. (i) For these experimental catfish, the average length of time to full growth is 12.31 months. This is approx. 6 months earlier than normal. (ii) Using $\bar{X}$ and S together in Chebyshev's theorem, we could conservatively estimate that at least 56% of the 21 catfish took from 8.5 months to 16.1 months to reach full growth. This is measurably faster than normal. (iii) The coefficient of variation shows that the variability is 20.5% the value of the mean. This much variability is moderate. The values are therefore moderately consistent, but perhaps not sufficiently consistent to make the procedure economically feasible.

e. The impressions are not changed, but now we have a quantitative measure of the faster growth, and a measure of its consistency.

3.5 a. The mean is $\bar{X} = 74.08$; the median is 70.7; there are three modes: 60.9, 67.9, and 73.2.

b. Range = 61.3; MAD = $(422.96/37) = 11.43$; $S^2 = 198.8538$; $S = 14.10$; Coefficient of variation = $(14.10/74.08)(100) = 19.03\%$.

c. At least 29 of the 37 values should lie between 43.1 and 105. We find that 36 of the 37 values (or 97.3%) lie in that interval.

d. (i) 74.08% is the average percentage of working young professionals who had used a resume service. (ii) Using $\bar{X}$ and S in Chebyshev's theorem we could conservatively estimate that from 43% to 100% of the young professionals hired by at least 79% of the 37 professions had used a resume service as an aid in getting the job. (iii) The coefficient of variation shows that the variability is 19.03% the value of the mean. This moderate variability indicates that the 37 professions do not attach the same level of importance to professionally done resumes. If the value of the coefficient of variation had been a small value (say, 1% or less), it would indicate that the 37 professions attach a uniform level of importance to professionally done resumes. If the average success rate is high (say, 74.08%) for getting a job with a professionally prepared resume, and if the coefficient of variation is small (say, 1% or less), a school counselor would then make very strong recommendations to graduating seniors to use a professional resume service.

e. We obtained considerable visual information in Chapter 2 such as

58.9% or more of the young working professionals had used a resume service;

58.9–80.8% of the young working professionals in 23 fields had used a resume service;

approximately 64% of the young working professionals in 14 fields had used a resume service;

and in half the 37 fields approximately 37–69% of the young working professionals had used a resume service.

From the numerical procedures in this chapter, we see that in half the 37 fields, exactly 70.7% of the young working professionals had used a resume service. We also see that in 36 of the 37 fields, at least 43.1% of the young working professionals had used a resume service. In addition, the value of the coefficient of variation indicates that the 37 professions do not attach the same level of importance to professionally done resumes.

CHAPTER REVIEW EXERCISES

3.7 The population consists of:
  a. Electrocardiograms of all people who run regularly along Mission Bay in San Diego.
  b. Electrocardiograms of all people who run regularly on the boardwalk in Rockaway Beach in New York.
  c. Electrocardiograms of all people who run regularly along Lake Shore Drive in Chicago.
  d. Electrocardiograms of all people who run regularly in the United States.

3.9 a. This data set is bimodal. The modes are 49 and 53.
  b. The median is 51.
  c. The mean is $\mu = 50$.

3.11 a. This data set is trimodal. The modes are 22, 83, and 92.
  b. The median is 47.5.
  c. The mean is $\mu = 49.767$.

3.13 a. The range is 20.
  b. $\sigma^2 = 19.267$.
  c. $\sigma = \sqrt{19.267} = 4.389$

3.15 a. The range is 94.
  b. $\sigma^2 = 902.0$
  c. $\sigma = \sqrt{902.0} = 30.033$

3.17 a. At least 81.096% of all observations must lie within 2.3 standard deviations of the mean. 96.667% of the observations (29 of 30) actually lie within this range.
  b. At least 69.136% of all observations must lie within 1.8 standard deviations of the mean. 96.667% of the observations (29 of 30) actually lie within this range.

3.19 a. At least 88.587% of the observations must lie within the interval 5.108–21.092.
  b. At least 73.696% of the observations must lie within the interval 7.808–18.392.
  c. At least 84.621% of the observations must lie within the interval 6.215–19.985.
  d. At least 41.728% of the observations must lie within the interval 9.563–16.637.

3.21 Approx. 65% of any set of measurements must lie within 1.69 standard deviations of their mean.

3.23 a. The 133 tax returns would be a sample if they represented only some of the tax returns prepared by their tax preparer.
  b. The 133 tax returns would be a population if they were the complete collection of all tax returns prepared by that tax preparer.

3.25 a. The median is −4.95.
  b. The mean is $\bar{X} = -1.81$.

3.27 a. The median is 42.
  b. The mean is $\bar{X} = 41.692$.

3.29 a. The sample mean is $\bar{X} = 2.938$. The sample standard deviation is $S = .6305$.
   b. At least 31.699% of the sample values must lie within 1.21 standard deviations of the sample mean. 76% of the sample values (38 of 50) fall within this range.

3.31 a. $\bar{X}_g = 11.870$
   b. $S_g^2 = 17.762$
   c. $S_g = \sqrt{17.762} = 4.2145$

3.33 a. $\bar{X}_g = 34.066$
   b. $S_g^2 = 79.720$
   c. $S_g = \sqrt{79.720} = 8.9286$

CHAPTER

4

EXERCISES

4.1 a. $A = \{234{,}994,\ 237{,}949,\ 246{,}746,\ 247{,}604,\ 247{,}919,\ 248{,}426,\ 250{,}356,\ 258{,}180,\ 259{,}456\}$

   b. $B = \{247{,}604,\ 247{,}919,\ 248{,}426,\ 250{,}356,\ 258{,}180,\ 259{,}456,\ 264{,}455,\ 264{,}916,\ 266{,}364,\ 272{,}290,\ 272{,}333,\ 277{,}340,\ 277{,}534,\ 278{,}391,\ 279{,}043\}$

   c. $C = \{264{,}455,\ 264{,}916,\ 266{,}364,\ 272{,}290,\ 272{,}333,\ 277{,}340,\ 277{,}534,\ 278{,}391,\ 279{,}043,\ 281{,}118,\ 285{,}085,\ 285{,}983,\ 286{,}789,\ 287{,}280,\ 292{,}394\}$

   d. $D = \{272{,}290,\ 272{,}333,\ 277{,}340,\ 277{,}534,\ 278{,}391,\ 279{,}043,\ 281{,}118,\ 285{,}085,\ 285{,}983,\ 286{,}789,\ 287{,}280,\ 292{,}394,\ 300{,}649,\ 302{,}751,\ 317{,}594,\ 319{,}331,\ 334{,}561\}$

   e. $C' = \{234{,}994,\ 237{,}949,\ 246{,}746,\ 247{,}604,\ 247{,}919,\ 248{,}426,\ 250{,}356,\ 258{,}180,\ 259{,}456,\ 300{,}649,\ 302{,}751,\ 317{,}594,\ 319{,}331,\ 334{,}561\}$

   f. $D' = \{234{,}994,\ 237{,}949,\ 246{,}746,\ 247{,}604,\ 247{,}919,\ 248{,}426,\ 250{,}356,\ 258{,}180,\ 259{,}456,\ 264{,}455,\ 264{,}916,\ 266{,}364\}$

   g. $C \cup D = \{264{,}455,\ 264{,}916,\ 266{,}364,\ 272{,}290,\ 272{,}333,\ 277{,}340,\ 277{,}534,\ 278{,}391,\ 279{,}043,\ 281{,}118,\ 285{,}085,\ 285{,}983,\ 286{,}789,\ 287{,}280,\ 292{,}394,\ 300{,}649,\ 302{,}751,\ 317{,}594,\ 319{,}331,\ 334{,}561\}$

   h. $C \cap D = \{272{,}290,\ 272{,}333,\ 277{,}340,\ 277{,}534,\ 278{,}391,\ 279{,}043,\ 281{,}118,\ 285{,}085,\ 285{,}983,\ 286{,}789,\ 287{,}280,\ 292{,}394\}$

   i. $(C \cup D)' = \{234{,}994,\ 237{,}949,\ 246{,}746,\ 247{,}604,\ 247{,}919,\ 248{,}426,\ 250{,}356,\ 258{,}180,\ 259{,}456\}$

   j. $(C \cap D)' = \{234{,}994,\ 237{,}949,\ 246{,}746,\ 247{,}604,\ 247{,}919,\ 248{,}426,\ 250{,}356,\ 258{,}180,\ 259{,}456,\ 264{,}455,\ 264{,}916,\ 266{,}364,\ 300{,}649,\ 302{,}751,\ 317{,}594,\ 319{,}331,\ 334{,}561\}$

   k. $C' \cap D = \{300{,}649,\ 302{,}751,\ 317{,}594,\ 319{,}331,\ 334{,}561\}$

   l. $(C \cap D) \cup (C' \cap D) = \{272{,}290,\ 272{,}333,\ 277{,}340,\ 277{,}534,\ 278{,}391,\ 279{,}043,\ 281{,}118,\ 285{,}085,\ 285{,}983,\ 286{,}789,\ 287{,}280,\ 292{,}394,\ 300{,}649,\ 302{,}751,\ 317{,}594,\ 319{,}331,\ 334{,}561\}$
   It is equal to D.

   m. $C' \cap D' = \{234{,}994,\ 237{,}949,\ 246{,}746,\ 247{,}604,\ 247{,}919,\ 248{,}426,\ 250{,}356,\ 258{,}180,\ 259{,}456\}$
   It is equal to $(C \cup D)'$

   n. $C' \cup D' = \{234{,}994,\ 237{,}949,\ 246{,}746,\ 247{,}604,\ 247{,}919,\ 248{,}426,\ 250{,}356,\ 258{,}180,\ 259{,}456,\ 264{,}455,\ 264{,}916,\ 266{,}364,\ 300{,}649,\ 302{,}751,\ 317{,}594,\ 319{,}331,\ 334{,}561\}$
   It is equal to $(C \cap D)'$

   o. $A \cap D = \varnothing$; the result is the empty set. The sets A and D are mutually exclusive.

4.3

```
┌─────────────────────────────────────────────────────────────────────┐
│ S                                                                     │
│            ┌──────────────────────────────────────────────┐          │
│            │ A       234,994        237,949      246,746   │          │
│     ┌──────┼────────────────────────────────────┐         │          │
│     │ B    │    247,604      247,919     248,426 │         │          │
│     │      │    250,356      258,180     259,456 │         │          │
│     │    ┌─┼────────────────────────────────────┼──┐      │          │
│     │    │ │   264,455      264,916     266,364  │  │      │          │
│     │  ┌─┼─┼────────────────────────────────────┼──┼──────┼────────┐ │
│     │  │ │ │   272,290      272,333     277,340  │  │      │        │ │
│     │  │ │ │   277,534      278,391     279,043  │  │      │        │ │
│     └──┼─┼─┴────────────────────────────────────┘  │      │        │ │
│        │ │     281,118      285,085     285,983     │      │        │ │
│        │ │     286,789      287,280     292,394     │      │        │ │
│        │ │ C                                        │      │        │ │
│        │ └──────────────────────────────────────────┘     │        │ │
│        │       300,649      302,751     317,594            │        │ │
│        │       319,331      334,561                        │        │ │
│        │ D                                                 │        │ │
│        └──────────────────────────────────────────────────┘        │ │
│                                                                     │ │
└─────────────────────────────────────────────────────────────────────┘
```

4.5 $P(A \cap B) = .52 - .49 = .03$

4.7 a. $\frac{12}{17}$
    b. $\frac{12}{15}$
    c. 0
    d. 0
    e. No.
    f. No.

4.9 a. $P(A|B) = .001/.05 = .02$
    b. $P(B|A) = .001/.02 = .05$
    c. $P(A'|B) = .049/.05 = .98$. Yes; it is equal to $1 - P(A|B)$.
    d. $P(B'|A) = .019/.02 = .95$. Yes; it is equal to $1 - P(B|A)$.
    e. $P(A|B') = .019/.95 = .01$. No; it is not equal to $1 - P(A|B)$.
    f. $P(B|A') = .049/.98 = .05$. No, it is not equal to $1 - P(B|A)$.

CHAPTER REVIEW EXERCISES

4.11 A = {Penny, Nickel, Dime, Quarter, Half dollar, Silver dollar}

4.13 A = {12, 13, 14, 15, . . .}

4.15 A = {(H, H), (H, T), (T, H), (T, T)}

4.17 a. Event A will occur.
  b. Event C will occur.
  c. Event A or C have the potential to occur in this setting.
  d. Neither A nor C occurs.
  e. Event A can occur.

4.19 a.

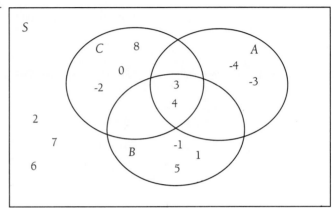

  b. A' = {−2, −1, 0, 1, 2, 5, 6, 7, 8}
  c. B' = {−4, −3, −2, 0, 2, 6, 7, 8}
  d. $A \cap C$ = {3, 4}
  e. $A \cup C$ = {−4, −3, −2, 0, 3, 4, 8}
  f. $B \cap C$ = {3, 4}
  g. $B \cup C$ = {−2, −1, 0, 1, 3, 4, 5, 8}
  h. $A \cap B \cap C$ = {3, 4}
  i. $A \cup B \cup C$ = {−4, −3, −2, −1, 0, 1, 3, 4, 5, 8}
  j. $A \cap B'$ = {−4, −3}
  k. $A \cup B'$ = {−4, −3, −2, 0, 2, 3, 4, 6, 7, 8}
  l. $A' \cap B$ = {−1, 1, 5}
  m. $A' \cup B$ = {−2, −1, 0, 1, 2, 3, 4, 5, 6, 7, 8}
  n. $B' \cap C$ = {−2, 0, 8}
  o. $B' \cup C$ = {−4, −3, −2, 0, 2, 3, 4, 6, 7, 8}
  p. $A' \cap C$ = {−2, 0, 8}
  q. $A' \cup C$ = {−2, −1, 0, 1, 2, 3, 4, 5, 6, 7, 8}
  r. $A' \cap B'$ = {−2, 0, 2, 6, 7, 8}
  s. $A' \cup B'$ = {−4, −3, −2, −1, 0, 1, 2, 5, 6, 7, 8}
  t. Yes; $(A \cup B)'$ = $A' \cap B'$ = {−2, 0, 2, 6, 7, 8}.
  u. Yes.
  v. Yes.
  w. Yes.
  x. Yes.
  y. Yes.
  z. Yes.

4.21 Let R = Republican, D = Democrat, I = Independent, N = None of these.
  a. S = {(R, R), (R, D), (R, I), (R, N), (D, R), (D, D), (D, I), (D, N), (I, R), (I, D), (I, I),
    (I, N), (N, R), (N, D), (N, I), (N, N)}
  b. {(D, D), (D, I), (D, N), (I, D), (I, I), (I, N), (N, D), (N, I), (N, N)}
  c. {(R, R), (R, I), (R, N), (I, R), (I, I), (I, N), (N, R), (N, I), (N, N)}
  d. {(I, I), (I, N), (N, I), (N, N)}

4.23 a. .3   b. .2   c. .4   d. .1
     e. .7   f. .6   g. .8

4.25 a. .15   b. .07   c. .07   d. .05   e. .06
   f. .01   g. .01   h. .17   i. .16   j. .13
   k. .18   l. .83   m. .95   n. .84   o. .94
   p. .87   q. .99   r. .82   s. .99

4.27 a. .4   b. .7   c. .9   d. .1
     e. .6   f. .7   g. .8

4.29 No.

4.31 a. $\frac{1}{3}$ b. $\frac{1}{3}$ c. $\frac{2}{3}$ d. $\frac{1}{9}$ e. $\frac{1}{9}$
   f. $\frac{1}{9}$ g. $\frac{5}{9}$ h. $\frac{8}{9}$ i. $\frac{8}{9}$ j. $\frac{1}{3}$
   k. $\frac{1}{6}$ l. $\frac{1}{6}$ m. $\frac{1}{3}$ n. $\frac{1}{3}$ o. $\frac{1}{3}$
   p. Yes.   q. No.   r. No.

4.33 No.

4.35 No. The sum of the probabilities exceeds 1.

4.37 a. .92   b. .78   c. .98   d. .32
     e. .7556   f. .9714   g. .2444   h. .2
     i. .8

4.39
  a. $P(B|A) + P(B'|A) = \dfrac{P(B \cap A)}{P(A)} + \dfrac{P(B' \cap A)}{P(A)} = \dfrac{P(B \cap A) + P(B' \cap A)}{P(A)} = \dfrac{P(A)}{P(A)} = 1$
  b. Similar procedure as in Part a.

4.41

$$P(A) = .10 \begin{cases} P(B|A) = .85 \\ P(B'|A) = .15 \end{cases}$$

$$P(A') = .90 \begin{cases} P(B|A') = .20 \\ P(B'|A') = .80 \end{cases}$$

$$P(A|B') = .0204$$

4.43 Let A = {A person has the disease} and let B = {The test is positive}. The problem provides the following: $P(A) = .01$, $P(B|A) = .98$, $P(B'|A') = .90$. The following tree can be completed:

$$P(A) = .01 \begin{cases} P(B|A) = .98 \\ P(B'|A) = .02 \end{cases}$$

$$P(A') = .99 \begin{cases} P(B|A') = .10 \\ P(B'|A') = .90 \end{cases}$$

The problem requests $P(A|B)$: $P(A|B) = .0901$.

4.45 Let A = {The resident works in the factory} and let B = {The resident is female}. Then $P(A'|B') = .4$.

4.47 Let A = {The coin is fair} and let B = {Two tosses yield 2 heads}.
   a. $P(B) = P(A)P(B|A) + P(A')P(B|A') = \left(\frac{3}{7}\right)\left(\frac{1}{4}\right) + \left(\frac{4}{7}\right)(1.0) = \frac{19}{28} = .6785$
   b. $P(A|B) = .1579$
   c. $P(A|B') = 1.0$
   d. $P(A|\text{Tail on any toss}) = 1.0$

4.49 a. The investor examines records of similar schemes and considers the schemes to all have the same chance of success.
   b. The investor uses the relative frequency of successes in a sample of similar schemes.
   c. The investor is impressed with the scheme as presented, makes no further investigation, and makes a decision; or the investor is impressed with the person presenting the scheme and makes a decision based on the impression.

4.51 By rejecting 4 applicants and interviewing the remaining 2, the employer is basing the hiring decision on a subjective judgment that the candidates don't have equal potential.

CHAPTER

5

EXERCISES

5.1 Since the events A, B, and C are independent, we have:
   a. $P(A' \cap B' \cap C') = P(A')P(B')P(C') = (.99)(.997)(.975) = .96235425$; this represents the probability that none of the three features go wrong in a sales presentation.
   b. $P(A \cap B' \cap C') = (.01)(.997)(.975) = .00972075$
   c. $P(A' \cap B \cap C') = (.99)(.003)(.975) = .00289575$
   d. $P(A' \cap B' \cap C) = (.99)(.997)(.025) = .02467575$
   e. $P(A \cap B \cap C') = (.01)(.003)(.975) = .00002925$
   f. $P(A \cap B' \cap C) = (.01)(.997)(.025) = .00024925$
   g. $P(A' \cap B \cap C) = (.99)(.003)(.025) = .00007425$
   h. $P(A \cap B \cap C) = (.01)(.003)(.025) = .00000075$; this represents the probability that all three features go wrong.

5.3

VALUES OF X $(X = x)$	PROBABILITY $P(X = x)$
0	.96235425
1	.03729225
2	.00035275
3	.00000075

5.5 a. $P(X = 0) = .818$
   b. $P(X < 2) = P(X \le 1) = .983$
   c. $P(X \le 2) = .999$
   d. $\mu = np = 0.2$
   e. $\sigma = \sqrt{np(1 - p)} = .0445$

5.7 a. $P(X = 0) = .6703$
   b. $P(X \ge 1) = 1 - P(X = 0) = 1 - .6703 = .3297$
   c. $\mu = \lambda = 0.4$
   d. $\sigma = \sqrt{\lambda} = 0.6325$

5.9 $P(X < 3) = .8686$

5.11 a. $P(X > 2.779) = P(Z > -1.7) = .5 + .4554 = .9554$
b. $P(X > 3.221) = P(Z > 1.7) = .5 - .4554 = .0446$
c. $P(2.779) < X < 3.26) = P(-1.7 < Z < 2) = .4554 + .4772 = .9326$
d. $P(X < 3.182) = .9192$

5.13 a. $P(X = 12) = P(11.5 < X < 12.5) = P(-0.18 < Z < 0.12) = .0714 + .0478 = .1192$
b. $P(X = 15) = .0812$
c. $P(7 \leq X \leq 11) = P(6.5 < X < 11.5) = .3840$
d. $P(9 \leq X \leq 13) = .5249$
e. $P(X < 10) = P(X \leq 9.5) = .2148$

CHAPTER REVIEW EXERCISES

5.15 a.

x = Number of a's	0	1	2	3
$P(X = x)$	$\frac{1}{5}$	$\frac{1}{5}$	$\frac{2}{5}$	$\frac{1}{5}$

b. $E(X) = 1.6$
c. $\sigma^2 = 1.04$

5.17 a.

x = Sum of element values	5	6	7	9	12
$P(X = x)$	$\frac{1}{8}$	$\frac{2}{8}$	$\frac{1}{8}$	$\frac{1}{8}$	$\frac{3}{8}$

b. $E(X) = 8.625$
c. $\sigma^2 = 7.9844$

5.19

x	$P(X = x)$
3	$\frac{2}{56}$
4	$\frac{2}{56}$
5	$\frac{4}{56}$
6	$\frac{4}{56}$
7	$\frac{6}{56}$
8	$\frac{6}{56}$
9	$\frac{8}{56}$
10	$\frac{6}{56}$
11	$\frac{6}{56}$
12	$\frac{4}{56}$
13	$\frac{4}{56}$
14	$\frac{2}{56}$
15	$\frac{2}{56}$

5.21 a.

x = SUM OF AGES	PROBABILITY
58	$\frac{2}{20} = .1$
63	$\frac{2}{20} = .1$
67	$\frac{2}{20} = .1$
70	$\frac{2}{20} = .1$
74	$\frac{2}{20} = .1$
79	$\frac{4}{20} = .2$
83	$\frac{2}{20} = .1$
88	$\frac{2}{20} = .1$
95	$\frac{2}{20} = .1$

b. $E(X) = 75.6$
c. $\sigma^2 = 118.44$; $\sigma = \sqrt{118.44} = 10.88$

5.23 a. .0892
b. $E(X) = 5.4298$
c. $\sigma = \sqrt{2.7437} = 1.656$
d. 2.118 min at least 75% of the time.

5.25 a. $P(X = 0) = \dfrac{15!}{0!(15 - 0)!}(.2)^0(.8)^{15} = (.8)^{15} = .03518$
b. $P(X = 1) = .13194$
c. $P(X = 7) = .0138$
d. $P(X = 12) = .000000954$
e. $P(X = x) = \dfrac{15!}{x!(15 - x)!}(.2)^x(.8)^{15-x}$ for $x = 0, 1, 2, \ldots, 15$
f. $\mu = (15)(.2) = 3$; $\sigma = \sqrt{\sigma^2} = \sqrt{np(1 - p)} = \sqrt{(15)(.2)(.8)} = 1.5492$
g. The number of Democrats in the survey will be between 1 and 5, inclusive.

5.27 a. $P(X = 0) = .210$ b. $P(X = 1) = .367$ c. $P(X \leq 1) = .577$
d. $P(X < 1) = .210$ e. $P(X \geq 0) = 1$ f. $P(X > 0) = .790$
g. $P(X > 1) = .423$ h. $P(X \geq 1) = .790$

5.29 a. $P(X = 5) = .148$ b. $P(X \leq 5) = .247$ c. $P(X \geq 5) = .901$
d. $P(X > 5) = .753$ e. $P(X = 9) = .089$ f. $P(X \leq 9) = .970$
g. $P(X < 9) = .881$ h. $P(X \geq 9) = .119$ i. $P(X > 9) = .030$
j. $P(X = 10) = .026$ k. $P(X \leq 10) = .996$ l. $P(X < 10) = .970$
m. $P(X \geq 10) = .030$ n. $P(X > 10) = .004$

5.31 a. $P(X = 0) = .086$ b. $P(X = 1) = .236$ c. $P(X = 6) = .010$
d. $P(X = 9) = 0$ e. $P(X \geq 2) = .678$ f. $P(X \leq 2) = .617$
g. $P(X < 2) = .322$ h. $P(X > 2) = .383$
i. $P(X \leq 7) = 1.0$ (approx.)
j. $P(X = x) = \dfrac{11!}{x!(11 - x)!}(.2)^x(.8)^{11-x}$ for $x = 0, 1, 2, \ldots, 11$
k. $\mu = (11)(.2) = 2.2$; $\sigma = \sqrt{(11)(.2)(.8)} = 1.32665$

5.33 a. $\dfrac{207!}{0!(207-0)!}(.1)^0(.9)^{207}$ (approx. 3.37×10^{-10})

b. $\dfrac{207!}{100!(207-100)!}(.1)^{100}(.9)^{107}$ (approx. 1.2865×10^{-44})

c. $\displaystyle\sum_{x=150}^{207}\binom{207}{x}(.1)^x(.9)^{207-x}$

d. $\displaystyle\sum_{x=0}^{87}\binom{207}{x}(.1)^x(.9)^{207-x}$

e. $\displaystyle\sum_{x=0}^{119}\binom{207}{x}(.1)^x(.9)^{207-x}$

f. $\displaystyle\sum_{x=171}^{207}\binom{207}{x}(.1)^x(.9)^{207-x}$

g. $P(X=x) = \dfrac{207!}{x!(207-x)!}(.10)^x(.90)^{207-x}$ for $x = 0, 1, 2, \ldots, 207$

h. $\mu = 20.7$; $\sigma^2 = 18.63$

i. From 14 to 28 (approx.)

5.35 a. $\dfrac{1100^{1000}e^{-1100}}{1000!}$

b. $\displaystyle\sum_{x=1000}^{550,000}\dfrac{1100^x e^{-1100}}{x!} = 1 - \sum_{x=0}^{999}\dfrac{1100^x e^{-1100}}{x!}$

c. $\displaystyle\sum_{x=0}^{1199}\dfrac{1100^x e^{-1100}}{x!}$

d. $\mu = np = (550,000)(.002) = 1100$; $\sigma^2 = np = 1100$

5.37 a. .16152

b. .19436

c. .52651

d. $P(X=x) = \dfrac{(3.8)^x e^{-3.8}}{x!}$ for $x = 0, 1, 2, \ldots$

5.39 a. .26997

b. .08122

c. .12530

d. $P(X=x) = \dfrac{(1.9)^x e^{-1.9}}{x!}$ for $x = 0, 1, 2, \ldots$

5.41 a. .8187   b. .8187   c. .9825

d. .0175   e. .1813   f. .0001

g. .9999   h. 1.0   i. 0

j. .0001

5.43 a. .1823   b. .7626   c. .5803

d. .2374   e. .4197   f. .3999

g. .2176   h. .3687   i. .1864

5.45 a. .4394   b. .4394   c. .4946

d. .4946   e. .4998   f. .4998

g. .2088   h. .2088   i. .3686

j. .4564   k. .4990   l. .4932

m. .4750   n. .4901   o. .4505

p. .4949

5.47 a. $P(-1.46 < Z < -.32) = P(-1.46 < Z < 0) - P(-.32 \leq Z < 0) = .3024$
b. .3997
c. $P(.19 < Z < 1.46) = P(0 < Z < 1.46) - P(0 < Z \leq .19) = .3526$

d. .0502	e. .0222	f. .0222
g. .2751	h. .2751	i. .0122
j. .0122	k. .0478	l. .2217

5.49 a. $P(Z < -1.96) = P(Z < 0) - P(-1.96 \leq Z < 0) = .5 - .4750 = .0250$

b. .0495	c. .0051	d. .0099
e. .0010	f. .0028	g. .4247
h. .3745	i. .0721	j. .0132

k. $P(Z > -1.96) = P(-1.96 < Z < 0) + P(Z \geq 0) = .4750 + .5 = .9750$

l. .9505	m. .9949	n. .9901
o. .9990	p. .9972	q. .5753
r. .6255	s. .9279	t. .9868

5.51

a. $a = 1.96$	b. $a = 2.33$	c. $a = 1.65$
d. $a = 2.57$	e. $a = -1.96$	f. $a = -2.33$
g. $a = -1.65$	h. $a = -2.57$	

5.53

a. $a = 1.96$	b. $a = 2.33$	c. $a = 1.65$
d. $a = 2.57$	e. $a = 1.57$	f. $a = 2.06$

5.55 a. $P(5.35 < X < 14.65) = P(-1.55 < Z < 1.55) = .8788$
b. $P(2.35 < X < 17.65) = P(-2.55 < Z < 2.55) = .9892$

c. .9500	d. .9010	e. .9802
f. .9898		

5.57 a. $P(2.35 < X < 5.05) = P(-2.55 < Z < -1.65) = .0441$

b. .0199	c. .0507	d. .0382
e. .1486	f. .1871	

5.59 a. $P(X > 14.65) = P(Z > 1.55) = .0606$

b. .9946	c. .0250	d. .9991
e. .1922	f. .9949	g. .0436
h. .9750		

5.61

a. $a = 4.12$	b. $a = 3.01$	c. $a = 5.05$
d. $a = 2.29$	e. $a = 13.03$	f. $a = 15.88$
g. $a = 14.95$	h. $a = 16.99$	

5.63 a. $P(X > 84) = P(Z > -3.0) = .99865$
b. .6106
c. $a = 90.75$

5.65 $P(A < 30.7) = P(Z < -2.0) = .0228$; $P(B < 30.7) = P(Z < -1.6) = .0548$. So brand A provides fewer batteries with a life expectancy of less than 30.7 months.

5.67 Known: $P(X > 89.99) = .1335$; standardized: $P(Z > (89.99 - \mu)/9) = .1335$; so $\mu = 80$.

5.69 Known: $P(X > 100) = .0250$; standardized: $P(Z > (100 - \mu)/5) = .0250$; so $\mu = 90.2$. Now, we want to find $P(X > 79.7)$: $P(X > 79.7) = P(Z > (79.7 - 90.2)/5) = .9821$.

5.71 a. Approximate $P(17 \leq X \leq 19)$ by evaluating:
$P(16.5 < Y < 19.5) = P(-.40 < Z < .40)$ (approx.)
$= .3108$
b. .6554
c. .4483

5.73 a. Approximate $P(40 < X < 43)$ by evaluating:
$$P(40.5 < Y < 42.5) = P(-.76 < Z < -.34) \text{ (approx.)}$$
$$= .1433$$

b. .5517

c. .0386

d. .4681

e. 40% of the 90 mufflers in the sample = 36 mufflers; $P(Y > 36.5) = .9452$.

f. .9857

5.75 a. Approximate $P(59 \le X \le 67)$ by evaluating:
$$P(58.5 < Y < 67.5 = P(-1.36 < Z < .52) \text{ (approx.)}$$
$$= .6116$$

b. .0485

c. .3015

d. .0869

5.77 a. $P(X < .24980) = P(Z < -1.0) = .1587$

b. $(.1587)(.1587) = .0252$

5.79 a. $P(X \le 80)$ can be approximated by evaluating:
$$P(Y < 80.5) = P(Z < 3.42) \text{ (approx.)}$$
$$= .9997$$

b. .9198

CHAPTER

6

EXERCISES

6.1 The calling service should first determine the range of seven-digit telephone numbers in the directory. Then it should use a random number generator or a table of random numbers to generate 10,000 seven-digit numbers within the directory's range. The 10,000 generated seven-digit numbers are then programmed into the electronic device for automatic dialing.

6.3 The calling service should first check the telephone directory white pages and list all the three-digit prefixes. Then it should randomly select several of the three-digit prefixes and, for each selected prefix, determine the range of the last four digits. For each prefix, it should use a random number generator or a table of random numbers to generate the last four digits within the range of the last four digits for each of the selected prefixes. The last four digits are then matched with their corresponding three-digit prefixes, and the resultant 10,000 telephone numbers should be programmed into the electronic device for automatic dialing:

6.5 $\mu_{\bar{X}} = \mu = \$38.60$; $\sigma_{\bar{X}}^2 = \dfrac{\sigma^2}{n}\left(\dfrac{N-n}{N-1}\right) = 6.3$

6.7 $\mu_{\bar{X}} = \mu = 0.33$; $\sigma_{\bar{X}} = \sigma/\sqrt{n} = 0.02/ = 0.01$

6.9 a. $P(\bar{X} < 317,393) = .9719$

b. $P(\bar{X} > 307,963) = .9857$

c. $P(311,528 < \bar{X} < 317,071) = .2389 + .4616 = .7005$

d. $P(315,484 < \bar{X} < 319,808) = .4985 - .3599 = .1386$

CHAPTER REVIEW EXERCISES

6.11 First, define the population to be all the clinic's emergency records during the last month. One procedure for selecting a random sample from this population is to sequentially number all the records, and use a computer or random number table to generate random numbers (within the range of numbered records) to define a sample of the required size.

6.13 a. An example of a systematic sampling procedure is the selection of every 5th record for examination.

b. (1) A stratified random sample may involve a random selection of a few records from each of the 10 clinics in the county. These randomly selected groups of records from the 10 clinics are then combined to form the sample.

(2) A cluster sampling method may involve a random selection of a few clinics from the 10 in the city, and then a random selection of records from just those few clinics.

6.15 $\mu_{\bar{X}} = 4.5$; $\sigma_{\bar{X}}^2 = 3.6667$

6.17 $\mu_{\bar{X}} = 4.5$; $\sigma_{\bar{X}}^2 = 4.2499957$; using the approximate formula, $\sigma_{\bar{X}}^2 = 8.5/2 = 4.25$

6.19 a. $\mu = 5$

b. $\sigma^2 = 8$

c. The ordered samples of size 2 (without replacement) are (1, 3), (1, 5), (1, 7), (1, 9), (3, 1), (3, 5), (3, 7), (3, 9), (5, 1), (5, 3), (5, 7), (5, 9), (7, 1), (7, 3), (7, 5), (7, 9), (9, 1), (9, 3), (9, 5), (9, 7).

d. The means of the samples from part c are, respectively, 2, 3, 4, 5, 2, 4, 5, 6, 3, 4, 6, 7, 4, 5, 6, 8, 5, 6, 7, 8.

e. The mean of the 20 values in part d is $\mu = 5$.

f. The variance of the values in part d is $\sigma^2 = 3$; the variance obtained from the exact formula is

$$\sigma_{\bar{X}}^2 = \frac{\sigma^2}{n}\left(\frac{N-n}{N-1}\right) = \frac{8}{2}\left(\frac{3}{4}\right) = 3.0$$

6.21 a. 71

b. 1.72727

c. If the sample is of size 22, the mean of the distribution of sample means remains the same, $\mu_{\bar{X}} = \mu = 71$.

d. If the sample is of size 22, the variance of the distribution of sample means becomes $\sigma_{\bar{X}}^2 = \sigma^2/n = 19/22 = 0.86364$, which is half of the variance for samples of size 11.

6.23 a. $P(\bar{X} < 23.8) = .0228$ b. $P(\bar{X} > 24.2) = .0228$
c. $P(\bar{X} < 24.165) = .9505$ d. $P(\bar{X} < 23.804) = .0250$
e. $P(\bar{X} > 24.257) = .0051$ f. $P(\bar{X} < 24.305) = .9989$

6.25 a. $P(\bar{X} > 1.031) = 0$ b. $P(\bar{X} < 1.003) = .8413$
c. $P(\bar{X} < 0.994) = .0228$ d. $P(\bar{X} > 0.9925) = .9938$
e. $P(\bar{X} > 1.00588) = .0250$ f. $P(\bar{X} < 1.00528) = .9608$

6.27 a. $P(62.55 < \bar{X} < 68.10) = .9292$

b. If $P(\bar{X} > A) = .9505$, then $A = (-1.65)(1.5) + 65 = 62.525$.

c. $P(\bar{X} \geq 62) = .9772$

d. $P(\bar{X} > 61.49) = .9904$

e. If $50.15 = \mu - k\sigma$, then $k = (65 - 50.15)/9 = 1.65$. If $79.85 = \mu + k\sigma$, then $k = (79.85 - 65)/9 = 1.65$. Using Chebyshev's theorem with $k = 1.65$, at least 63.269% of the observations must lie within the interval $50.15 to $79.85. If normally distributed, $P(50.15 < X < 79.85) = .9010$.

f. If $62 = \mu_{\bar{X}} - k\sigma_{\bar{X}}$, then $k = (65 - 62)/1.5 = 2.0$. If $68 = \mu_{\bar{X}} + k\sigma_{\bar{X}}$, then $k = (68 - 65)/1.5 = 2.0$. Using Chebyshev's theorem with $k = 2.0$, at least $1 - 1/(2)^2$, or 75% of the observations must lie within the interval $62 to $68. If normally distributed, $P(62 < \bar{X} < 68) = .9544$.

6.29 a. $P(\bar{X} < 15.6) = .0000317$

b. $P(15.7 < \bar{X} < 16.7) = .99865$

c. $P(\bar{X} \leq 16.17) = .9554$

d. $P(\bar{X} \geq 15.935) = .7422$

e. If $P(\bar{X} > W) = .9901$, then $W = (-2.33)(0.1) + 16 = 15.767$.

f. $P(\bar{X} < 15.91) = .1841$

6.31 a. On average, 4 tires in the samples of size 400 should have defective sidewalls.
b. The proportion is .01, or 1%.

6.33 a. 1
b. .04, or 4%
c. $\sigma_{\hat{p}} = 0.99876$

6.35 a. $P(X > 3) = .8159$
b. $P\left(\dfrac{X}{500} < .014\right) = .8159$

6.37 a. 3.0 date shakes will be sold.
b. They should expect to sell .02, or 2%, date shakes on any given day.
c. $P\left(\dfrac{X}{n} > .01\right) = .8078$

CHAPTER

7

EXERCISES

7.1 a. $P(Z > Z_{.0475}) = .0475$
b. $P(Z > Z_{.01}) = .01$
c. $P(Z > Z_{.005}) = .005$
d. $P(Z < Z_{.05}) = 1 - .05 = .95$
e. $P(Z < Z_{.01}) = 1 - .01 = .99$
f. $P(Z < Z_{.005}) = 1 - .005 = .995$
g. $P(Z > -Z_{.05}) = 1 - .05 = .95$
h. $P(Z > -Z_{.01}) = 1 - .01 = .99$
i. $P(Z > - Z_{.005}) = 1 - .005 = .995$
j. $P(Z < - Z_{.05}) = .05$
k. $P(Z < -Z_{.01}) = .01$
l. $P(Z < -Z_{.005}) = .005$

7.3 a. $Z_{.025} = 1.960$
b. $Z_{.0051} = 2.57$
c. $Z_{.0495} = 1.65$
d. $Z_{.4522} = 0.12$
e. $Z_{.0027} = 2.78$

7.5 Upper confidence limit = 4.05; lower confidence limit = -0.05

7.7 Upper confidence limit = 113.72; lower confidence limit = 106.28

7.9 a. $P(t_7 < 1.415) = .90$
b. $P(t_7 < 3.499) = .995$
c. $P(t_7 < -1.415) = .10$
d. $P(t_7 < -3.499) = .005$
e. $P(-1.415 < t_7 < 1.415) = P(t_7 < 1.415) - P(t_7 < -1.415) = .90 - .10 = .80$
f. $P(-3.499 < t_7 < 3.499) = P(t_7 < 3.499) - P(t_7 < -3.499) = .995 - .005 = .99$
g. $P(-3.499 < t_7 < 2.365) = P(t_7 < 2.365) - P(t_7 < -3.499) = .975 - .005 = .97$
h. $P(-3.499 < t_7 < 2.998) = P(t_7 < 2.998) - P(t_7 < -3.499) = .990 - .005 = .985$
i. $P(1.415 < t_7 < 2.365) = P(t_7 < 2.365) - P(t_7 < 1.415) = .975 - .90 = .075$
j. $P(2.998 < t_7 < 3.499) = P(t_7 < 3.499) - P(t_7 < 2.998) = .995 - .99 = .005$

7.11 Upper confidence limit = 121.53; lower confidence limit = 116.47

7.13 Upper confidence limit = 4.11534; lower confidence limit = 2.88466; since this 99% confidence interval doesn't include 4.2, the food component need not be stricken from the diet.

7.15 Upper confidence limit = 8.9144; lower confidence limit = 8.4657

7.17 With 99% confidence, the average monthly payments for VISA® credit card holders is approximately from $132.69 to $152.15. This could be a useful statistic in gauging the nation's private sector indebtedness.

7.19 Upper confidence limit = $122,434; lower confidence limit = $80,566

7.21 Use $n = 8$.

7.23 Upper confidence limit = 0.9854; lower confidence limit = 0.9463

7.25 Upper confidence limit $= 0.58423$; lower confidence limit $= 0.54777$; yes, it is reasonable to suppose that the legislation will pass since we are 90% confident that the true proportion of voters who favor the bill is between 0.54777 and 0.58423.

7.27 The opinion survey should take a random sample of size 619.

7.29 Upper confidence limit $= 0.0001$; lower confidence limit $= -0.0017$; 0 is in this interval, so it is reasonable to assert that the two labs are in agreement.

7.31 Upper confidence limit $= -\$6.25$; lower confidence limit $= -\$9.75$

7.33 Upper confidence limit $= 0.295$; lower confidence limit $= 0.105$

7.35 Upper confidence limit $= \$2443.95$; lower confidence limit $= \$1726.05$

7.37 Upper confidence limit $= 1.8142$; lower confidence limit $= -0.1742$; 0 is in this interval, so it is reasonable to assert that the two production lines produce the same average magnetic strength.

7.39 Upper confidence limit $= 0.03654$; lower confidence limit $= -0.04302$; the interval contains 0, so it is reasonable to conclude that the proportion of students who can't pass the hearing test is the same for both universities.

7.41 Upper confidence limit $= 0.1327$; lower confidence limit $= -0.0260$

7.43 a. $P(\chi_9^2 > 1.735) = .995$
b. $P(\chi_9^2 > 21.666) = .01$

7.45 Upper confidence limit $= 21.9375$; lower confidence limit $= 9.0324$

7.47 Upper confidence limit $= 0.0175$; lower confidence limit $= 0.0025$

7.49 Upper confidence limit $= 359,568.3632$; lower confidence limit $= 86,106.4849$

7.51 Upper confidence limit $= 2.914$; lower confidence limit $= 0.795$; the claim that the variance ratio is equal to 1 is consistent with the data, since a ratio of 1 falls within this 90% confidence interval.

7.53 Upper confidence limit $= 6.68$; lower confidence limit $= 0.33$

CHAPTER REVIEW EXERCISES

7.55 a. $P(Z > Z_{.0475}) = .0475$
b. $P(Z > Z_{.0129}) = .0129$
c. $P(Z > Z_{.025}) = .025$
d. $P(Z < Z_{.0475}) = 1 - .0475 = .9525$
e. $P(Z < Z_{.0129}) = 1 - .0129 = .9871$
f. $P(Z < Z_{.025}) = 1 - .025 = .975$
g. $P(Z > -Z_{.0475}) = 1 - .0475 = .9525$
h. $P(Z > -Z_{.0129}) = 1 - .0129 = .9871$
i. $P(Z > -Z_{.025}) = 1 - .025 = .975$
j. $P(Z < -Z_{.0475}) = .0475$
k. $P(Z < -Z_{.0129}) = .0129$
l. $P(Z < -Z_{.025}) = .025$

7.57 a. $Z_{.0475} = 1.67$
b. $Z_{.0129} = 2.23$
c. $Z_{.0099} = 2.33$
d. $Z_{.2946} = 0.54$

7.59 Upper confidence limit $= 3.656$; lower confidence limit $= -1.004$

7.61 Upper confidence limit $= 7.962$; lower confidence limit $= 7.878$; it is not reasonable to label the cans as containing 8 oz of nuts.

7.63 Upper confidence limit = 6.539; lower confidence limit = 5.961; although the mean weight of balls produced by the company may or may not be in this interval, we are 93.28% confident that this interval contains the true mean.

7.65 a. $P(t_7 > 2.365) = .025$
b. $P(t_7 > 1.415) = .10$
c. $P(t_7 > 2.998) = .01$
d. $P(t_7 > 3.499) = .005$

7.67 a. $P(t_{16} > 2.921) = .005$
b. $P(t_{16} < 2.921) = .995$
c. $P(-1.746 < t_{16} < 2.583) = .99 - .05 = .94$
d. $P(-2.921 < t_{16} < -1.337) = .10 - .005 = .095$
e. $P(2.120 < t_{16} < 2.583) = .99 - .975 = .015$

7.69 Upper confidence limit = −265.73; lower confidence limit = −404.29; although the mean gambling gain or loss may or may not be in this interval, we are 99.50% confident that this interval contains the true mean. Thus we are very confident that this gambler has an average loss, not a gain.

7.71 Upper confidence limit = 158.024; lower confidence limit = 148.276

7.73 Upper confidence limit = 23.8123; lower confidence limit = 22.4077; although the mean length may or may not be in this interval, we are 90% confident that this interval contains the true mean.

7.75 Upper confidence limit = 24.97274; lower confidence limit = 24.02726

7.77 Upper confidence limit = 8.355; lower confidence limit = 6.445; we can't say that the fuses don't meet specifications. An average time of 7 sec is within the 90% confidence interval, so the sample data aren't inconsistent with a claim that the fuses meet specifications.

7.79 Use $n = 2165$.

7.81 $E = 1.288$

7.83 Use $n = 34$.

7.85 Use $n = 9$.

7.87 Upper confidence limit = 0.12372; lower confidence limit = 0.06378; although the true proportion of cars exceeding the speed limit may or may not be in this interval, we are 90% confident that this interval contains the true proportion.

7.89 Upper confidence limit = 0.03628; lower confidence limit = 0.00372

7.91 Use $n = 3382$.

7.93 Use $n = 196$.

7.95 Use $n = 87$.

7.97 Upper confidence limit = −4344.016; lower confidence limit = −6615.984; this interval doesn't contain 0, so it is not reasonable to conclude that the average salaries are equal.

7.99 Upper confidence limit = 4.8899; lower confidence limit = 0.5101; this interval doesn't contain 0, so it is not reasonable to conclude that the average sugar content per box is the same for both brands.

7.101 Upper confidence limit = 9.516; lower confidence limit = 5.684; this interval doesn't contain 0, so it is reasonable to conclude that the average contamination levels are not equal.

7.103 Upper confidence limit = 2.4286; lower confidence limit = −1.0286; 0 is in this interval, so it is reasonable to assert that the two shifts are operating equally.

7.105 Upper confidence limit = 1.649; lower confidence limit = −0.739; this interval contains 0, so it is reasonable to conclude that the average gains of the two account executives are the same.

7.107 Upper confidence limit = −0.04503; lower confidence limit = −0.22479; the interval doesn't contain 0, so it is not reasonable to conclude that the proportion favoring the proposal is the same for men and women.

7.109 Upper confidence limit = 0.13977; lower confidence limit = −0.11197; the interval contains 0 so it is reasonable to conclude that the proportion of adulterated packages is the same from each manufacturer.

7.111 Upper confidence limit = 0.11397; lower confidence limit = −0.11397; the interval contains 0, so it is reasonable to conclude that the proportion of mercury contaminated cans is the same for both brands.

7.113 a. $P(\chi_9^2 > 23.589) = .005$
b. $P(\chi_9^2 > 2.088) = .99$

7.115 a. $P(\chi_{21}^2 < 11.591) = 1 - .95 = .05$
b. $P(\chi_{21}^2 > 35.479) = .025$
c. $P(\chi_{15}^2 < 5.229) = 1 - .99 = .01$
d. $P(\chi_{15}^2 > 30.578) = .01$
e. $P(7.015 < \chi_{18}^2 < 34.805) = .99 - .01 = .98$
f. $P(0.412 < \chi_5^2 < 12.832) = .995 - .025 = .97$
g. $P(42.557 < \chi_{29}^2 < 49.588) = .05 - .01 = .04$
h. $P(4.075 < \chi_{14}^2 < 5.629) = .995 - .975 = .02$

7.117 Upper confidence limit: 47.0768; lower confidence limit = 11.8027; we are 99% confident that the true variance lies between 11.8027 and 47.0768.

7.119 Upper confidence limit = 0.0163; lower confidence limit = 0.0058; the value of 0.008 is within this confidence interval, so the results of this sample don't contradict an assumption that the variance doesn't exceed 0.008.

7.121 Upper confidence limit = 0.2927; lower confidence limit = 0.0657; this doesn't include the value 1, so it is reasonable to conclude that the variance in wave amplitude is greater for mentally retarded persons.

CHAPTER

8

EXERCISES

8.1 a. This outcome would best be described as a matter of coincidence.
b. The outcome is likely a matter of significance.
c. What is the probability that 10 or more will survive if the treatment is ineffective?

$P(X \geq 10) = 1 - P(X \leq 9) = 1 - 1.0000 = 0$ (to at least four decimal places)

This gives very strong evidence that the treatment is a significant factor for survival.

8.3 a. Failing to reject a false null hypothesis is a Type II error.
b. This would cause people to spend money on a part that is not needed.
c. Rejecting a true null hypothesis is a Type I error.
d. Making a Type I error would mean not replacing a faulty part and getting exhaust in the car when using the heater or air conditioner. The consequences of breathing carbon monoxide in the exhaust could be fatal.

8.5 The power curve for the situation in Practice Exercise 8.27 is given below, along with approximate values of β and $1 - \beta$ for selected alternative values of μ_A.

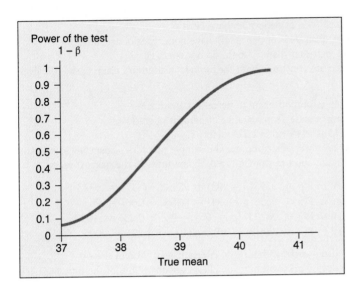

μ_A	Z (Approx.)	β	$1 - \beta$
37.0	1.65	0.9505	0.0495
37.2	1.45	0.9265	0.0735
37.4	1.25	0.8944	0.1056
37.6	1.05	0.8531	0.1469
37.8	0.85	0.8023	0.1977
38.0	0.65	0.7422	0.2578
38.2	0.45	0.6736	0.3264
38.4	0.25	0.5987	0.4013
38.6	0.05	0.5199	0.4801
38.8	−0.16	0.4364	0.5636
39.0	−0.36	0.3594	0.6406
39.2	−0.56	0.2877	0.7123
39.4	−0.76	0.2236	0.7764
39.6	−0.96	0.1685	0.8315
39.8	−1.16	0.1230	0.8770
40.0	−1.36	0.0869	0.9131
40.2	−1.56	0.0594	0.9406
40.4	−1.76	0.0392	0.9608
40.6	−1.96	0.0250	0.9750

8.7 H_o: $\mu = 0$ (There is no improvement in milk production.)
H_A: $\mu > 0$ (There is an improvement in milk production.)
Decision: Since 15.1 is greater than 1.753, reject H_o.
Interpretation: The sample increase in milk production of 0.2768% is statistically significant at the .05 level of significance. This amount of increase may or may not be practically significant.

8.9 H_o: $\mu = \$85,000$ (The agency's claim is not true.)
H_A: $\mu > \$85,000$ (The agency's claim is true.)
Decision: Since 1.833 is less than 2.326, do not reject H_o.
Interpretation: At the .01 level of significance the data don't provide statistically significant support for the agency's claim, and we can presume the value of $101,500 is attributable to sampling error.

8.11 a. $\beta = P(\bar{X} \leq 105,934 \,|\, \mu = 90,000) = P(Z \leq 1.77) = .9616$
b. $\beta = P(\bar{X} \leq 105,934 \,|\, \mu = 100,000) = P(Z \leq 0.66) = .7454$
c. $\beta = P(\bar{X} \leq 105,934 \,|\, \mu = 110,000) = P(Z \leq -0.45) = .3264$
d. Yes, there is a pattern. In general, the greater the difference between the hypothesized value and the alternative value, the smaller is the value of β.

8.13 H_o: $\mu = 200,000$ (Blood platelet count is normal.)
H_A: $\mu < 200,000$ (Blood platelet count is lower than normal.)
Decision: Since −25.0 is less than −2.576, reject H_o.
Interpretation: The platelet count is significantly lower than normal.

8.15 H_o: $\mu = 1200$ (Production level has not dropped.)
H_A: $\mu < 1200$ (Production level has dropped.)
Decision: Since −1.2 is not less than −1.282, do not reject H_o.
Interpretation: There is not significant evidence to indicate that the production level has dropped.

8.17 H_o: $\mu = 35,000$ (The manufacturer's claim is true.)
H_A: $\mu < 35,000$ (The manufacturer's claim is not true.)
Decision: Since −6.087 is less than −2.326, reject H_o.
Interpretation: There is sufficient evidence to reject the manufacturer's claim.

8.19 H_o: $p = .94$ (At least 94% of depositors have both types of account.)
H_A: $p < .94$ (Fewer than 94% of depositors have both types of account.)
Decision: Since 1.662 is greater than -1.645, do not reject H_o.
Interpretation: The data are consistent with the savings institution's claim at the .05 level of significance.

8.21 H_o: $p = .30$ (Hiring is proportionate to percent of graduates.)
H_A: $p < .30$ (Hiring is underrepresentative of percent of graduates.)
Decision: Since -3.273 is less than -2.326, reject H_o.
Interpretation: At the .01 level of significance the sample provides statistically significant evidence of underrepresentation of women hired by law firms in the past 10 years.

8.23 a. The p-value is equal to $P(\hat{p} \geq .0255 | p = .03) = P(Z \geq -0.37) = .6443$
b. The p-value is equal to $P(\hat{p} \leq .9658 | p = .94) = P(Z \leq -1.66) = .9515$
c. The p-value is equal to $P(\hat{p} \geq .062857 | p = .06) = P(Z \geq 0.23) = .4090$
d. The p-value is equal to $P(\hat{p} \leq .255 | p = .30) = P(Z \leq -3.27) = .0005$

8.25 H_o: $p = .98$ (The drug works without side effects at least 98% of the time.)
H_A: $p < .98$ (The drug works without side effects less than 98% of the time.)
Decision: Since $-1.6671 < -1.645$, reject H_o.
Interpretation: At the .05 level of significance the sample provides statistically significant evidence that the drug showed relief without side effects less than 98% of the time.

8.27 H_o: $\mu_{new} = \mu_{old}$ (The average miles per gallon is the same for both years.)
H_A: $\mu_{new} > \mu_{old}$ (The newer model yields more miles per gallon than the older model.)
Decision: Since 7.224 is greater than 2.326, reject H_o.
Interpretation: At the .01 level of significance the sample difference in gas mileage provides statistically significant evidence that the newer model yields higher average gas mileage.

8.29 H_o: $\mu_A = \mu_B$ (The average longevity is the same for both types of bulbs.)
H_A: $\mu_A \neq \mu_B$ (The average longevity is not the same for both types of bulbs.)
Decision: Since 6.314 is greater than 2.861, reject H_o.
Interpretation: At the .01 level of significance we conclude that type A bulbs have a longer average life than type B bulbs.

8.31 H_o: $\mu_1 = \mu_2$ (The average thickness is the same for sheets from both suppliers.)
H_A: $\mu_1 \neq \mu_2$ (The average thickness is not the same from both suppliers.)
Decision: Since 0.564 is less than 2.179, do not reject H_o.
Interpretation: At the .05 level of significance the sample result doesn't show a statistically significant difference in the average thickness of the sheets from the two suppliers. The manufacturer is free to choose either supplier if only the average thickness specification is considered.

8.33 H_o: $p_{cap} = p_{civ}$ (The proportion of capital punishment juries with at least one Hispanic member is equal to the proportion of civil case juries with at least one Hispanic member.)
H_A: $p_{cap} < p_{civ}$ (The proportion of capital punishment juries with at least one Hispanic member is less than the proportion of civil case juries with at least one Hispanic member.)
Decision: Since -3.16 is less than -2.44, reject H_o.
Interpretation: At the .0073 level of significance the data provide statistically significant evidence to support the lawyer's claim that proportionately fewer capital punishment juries have at least one Hispanic member than do civil case juries.

8.35 a. The p-value is equal to $P(Z \geq 1.309) = .0951$
b. The p-value is equal to $P(Z \leq -3.16) = .0008$
c. The p-value is equal to $P(Z \geq 11.594) = 0$ (approx.)

8.37 a. The p-value is equal to $P(Z \geq 4.899) = 0$ (approx.)
b. The p-value is equal to $P(t_{12} > 0.564) = .29$ (approx.)

8.39 H_o: $\mu_1 = \mu_2$ (The means of the two classes are the same.)
H_A: $\mu_1 \neq \mu_2$ (The means are different.)
Decision: Since -0.3749 is not less than -1.960 nor greater than $+1.960$, do not reject H_o.
Interpretation: We conclude that the grades in the two classes are not statistically significantly different.

8.41 H_o: $\mu_1 = \mu_2$ (The mean tensile strengths of the two production lines are equal.)
H_A: $\mu_1 \neq \mu_2$ (The means are not equal.)
Decision: Since -1.434 is not less than -2.602 nor greater than $+2.602$, do not reject H_o.
Interpretation: We conclude that there is no significant difference in the average tensile strengths between the two lines.

8.43 Let p_1 and p_2 be the proportions of men and women, respectively, who favor the proposal.
H_o: $p_1 = p_2$ (The two proportions are the same.)
H_A: $p_1 \neq p_2$ (The proportions of men and women favoring the proposal differ.)
Decision: Since $|0.7889| < 2.326$, do not reject H_o.
Interpretation: We conclude that there is no difference in the proportions of men and women who favor the proposal.

8.45 H_o: $\mu_d = \mu_B - \mu_A = 0$ (There is no difference between the paired observations.)
H_A: $\mu_d < 0$ (The mean estimate from shop A is higher.)
Decision: Since -1.619 is not less than -2.015, do not reject H_o.
Interpretation: The sample doesn't provide significant evidence that shop A estimates are higher, on average, than shop B estimates.

8.47 H_o: $\sigma^2 = (\$350)^2$ (The standard deviation is not greater than $350.)
H_A: $\sigma^2 > (\$350)^2$ (The standard deviation is greater than $350.)
Decision: Since 20.2757 is less than 31.9999, do not reject H_o.
Interpretation: The sample result is not significant at the .01 level of significance and so the data are consistent with the hypothesis that the standard deviation does not exceed $350. We would advise the young couple that they could contend with the fluctuations in daily receipts.

8.49 H_o: $\sigma^2 = (0.29)^2$ (The manufacturer's claim is accurate.)
H_A: $\sigma^2 > (0.29)^2$ (The manufacturer underestimates the variability.)
Decision: Since 9.064 is not greater than 14.0671, do not reject H_o.
Interpretation: There is not significant evidence to indicate that the manufacturer underestimates the variability of his odometer.

8.51 H_o: $\sigma_A^2 = \sigma_B^2$ (The two population variances are equal.)
H_A: $\sigma_A^2 \neq \sigma_B^2$ (The two population variances are not equal.)
Decision: Since 1.111 is less than 2.01, do not reject H_o.
Interpretation: At the .10 level of significance, the sample result is consistent with the assumption that the two population variances are equal.

8.53 H_o: $\sigma_A^2 = \sigma_B^2$ (Both models are equally consistent in gas mileage; i.e., the variances are equal.)
H_A: $\sigma_A^2 < \sigma_B^2$ (Model B is less consistent in gas mileage; i.e., model B variance is greater than model A variance.)
Decision: Since 4.76 is greater than 1.53, reject H_o.
Interpretation: At the .01 level of significance, the data indicate that model B automobiles are less consistent in their mileage performance than model A automobiles.

CHAPTER REVIEW EXERCISES

8.55 H_o: $p = .10$ (Campaign did not increase the proportion favoring this brand.)
H_A: $p > .10$ (Campaign increased the proportion favoring this brand.)
Decision: Since 1.4142 is less than 1.645, do not reject H_o.
Interpretation: There is not sufficient evidence to indicate that the campaign increased the proportion of smokers favoring this brand.
The p-value is $P(Z \geq 1.41) = .5 - .4207 = .0793$ (approx.)

8.57 H_o: $p = .40$ (40% wear glasses.)
H_A: $p \neq .40$ (Proportion is different from 40%.)
This is a two-sided test; $\alpha = .05$ so $Z_{\alpha/2} = 1.960$; thus, the null hypothesis is rejected if $Z < -1.960$ or if $Z > +1.960$. We have $n = 60$ and $\hat{p} = \frac{36}{60} = .60$, so the test statistic is

$$Z = \frac{\hat{p} - p}{\sqrt{\dfrac{p(1-p)}{n}}} = \frac{.60 - .40}{\sqrt{\dfrac{(.40)(.60)}{60}}} = 3.1623$$

Since $3.1623 > 1.960$, we reject the null hypothesis and conclude that the true proportion is different from 40%. The p-value is $2P(Z \geq 3.16) = 2(.5 - .4992) = .0016$ (approx.).

8.59 H_o: $p = .36$ (Claim is true.)
H_A: $p \neq .36$ (True proportion is different from 36%.)
The value -0.6742 is not in the rejection region (i.e., $|Z| > 2.236$), so we can't reject the null hypothesis at the 2% level of significance. Sample evidence doesn't provide significant evidence to refute the claim.

8.61 H_o: $\mu = 400$ (Politician's claim is true.)
H_A: $\mu > 400$ (Politician's claim is not true.)
Decision: Since 1.0878 < 2.896, do not reject H_o.
Interpretation: The sample result doesn't provide significant evidence that the politician underestimated the amount of delinquent property taxes.

8.63 H_o: $\mu = 32$ (Cans are correctly filled.)
H_A: $\mu < 32$ (Cans are being short-weighted.)
Since $t_{15} = -4.0 < -1.753$, the null hypothesis is rejected at the .05 level of significance, and we conclude that there is sufficient evidence that the cans are being short-weighted. The p-value is determined by evaluating $P(t_{15} \leq -4.0)$. Notice that $P(t_{15} \leq -4.073) = .0005$, so we can say that the p-value for this problem is approx. .0005.

8.65 H_o: $\mu = 40$ (Manufacturer's claim is not true.)
H_A: $\mu > 40$ (Manufacturer's claim is true.)
Since 0.5031 is not greater than 2.093, we can't reject the null hypothesis, and we conclude that the sample doesn't provide significant support for the manufacturer's claim.

8.67 The company does not want to change its process unless it has significant evidence that output will be increased to more than 13.0 units per hour.
H_o: $\mu = 13$ (Output does not increase to more than 13 units per hour.)
H_A: $\mu > 13$ (Output has increased to more than 13 units per hour.)
Since 0.2857 is less than 1.645, we cannot reject the null hypothesis at the .05 level of significance, and we conclude that there is not significant evidence to indicate that a change to the new process would be profitable.
a. The p-value can be approximated by rounding off the Z value calculated above and evaluating $P(Z \geq 0.29)$: $P(Z \geq 0.29) = .5 - .1141 = .3859$.
b. $\beta = .8577$

c. A Type II error in this setting is failing to recognize that the new process has increased output to more than 13 units per hour. Thus, it would mean that the company would fail to adopt the new process when, in fact, the change to the new process would be profitable.

8.69 H_o: $p_1 = p_2$ (The two brands have equal proportions defective.)
H_A: $p_1 < p_2$ (The house brand has a higher proportion defective.)
Decision: Since $-0.750 > -1.645$, do not reject H_o.
Interpretation: The sample result does not provide significant evidence that the house brand has a higher proportion of defective toasters.

8.71 H_o: $p_1 = p_2$ (The two proportions are the same.)
H_A: $p_1 \neq p_2$ (The proportions differ.)
Decision: Since $|-0.6606| < 2.09$, do not reject H_o.
Interpretation: We conclude that there is no significant difference between the two cities in their preference for detergent A versus detergent B.

8.73 H_o: $p_1 = p_2$ (The two proportions are the same.)
H_A: $p_1 < p_2$ (The proportion of short people wearing corrective lenses is larger.)
Decision: Since $0 > -1.645$, do not reject H_o.
Interpretation: We conclude that the proportion of corrective lens wearers among short people is not greater than among tall people.

8.75 H_o: $\mu_1 = \mu_2$ (The means of the two companies are the same.)
H_A: $\mu_1 \neq \mu_2$ (The means are different.)
Decision: Since $|2.9664| > 1.96$, we reject H_o.
Interpretation: We conclude that the difference between the two companies is significant.

8.77 H_o: $\mu_1 = \mu_2$ (The average lengths of the two groups are equal.)
H_A: $\mu_1 < \mu_2$ (The average length in Mexico is greater than the average length in Arizona.)
Decision: Since $-1.1966 > -1.645$, do not reject H_o.
Interpretation: Conclude that the average length of gila monsters in Mexico is not greater than the average length of gila monsters in Arizona.

8.79 H_o: $\mu_1 = \mu_2$ (Mean assembly times are the same.)
H_A: $\mu_1 > \mu_2$ (The new method reduces mean assembly time.)
Decision: Since $1.648 < 1.746$, do not reject H_o.
Interpretation: The samples do not provide significant evidence that the mean assembly time is less with the new training period.

8.81 H_o: $\mu_1 = \mu_2$ (Mean scores are the same.)
H_A: $\mu_1 \neq \mu_2$ (Mean scores differ between the two schools.)
Since $|-2.308|$ is not greater than 2.977, we cannot reject the null hypothesis at the .01 level of significance. The samples do not provide significant evidence of a difference in the average mechanical aptitudes at the two schools.

8.83 H_o: $\sigma^2 = 0.67$ (The process is in control.)
H_A: $\sigma^2 \neq 0.67$ (The process is not under control.)
Decision: Since $12.986 < 13.7867$, we reject H_o.
Interpretation: Conclude that the production process is not in control.

8.85 H_o: $\sigma_2^2 = \sigma_1^2$ (The variances are equal.)
H_A: $\sigma_2^2 < \sigma_1^2$ (The variance of group B is greater.)
Decision: Since $1.494 < 2.02$, do not reject H_o.
Interpretation: Conclude that the samples do not provide significant evidence to support the insurance company's claim.

8.87 a. H_o: $\mu_1 = \mu_2$ (The average times to perform tasks are equal.)
H_A: $\mu_1 \neq \mu_2$ (The average times to perform tasks are not equal.)
Decision: Since $|0.3464| < 2.571$, do not reject H_o.
Interpretation: We conclude that there is not significant evidence of a difference in the average time it takes the two secretaries to perform the 6 tasks.

b. H_o: $\sigma_2^2 = \sigma_1^2$ (The variances are equal.)
H_A: $\sigma_2^2 < \sigma_1^2$ (The variance of secretary B is greater.)
Decision: Since $49 > 5.05$, we reject H_o.
Interpretation: We conclude that secretary A is more consistent than secretary B.

c. Although the result of part a indicates that there is no significant difference in the mean time to perform tasks between secretaries, part b shows that there is significant evidence that the variability of time to perform tasks is greater for secretary B. The executive may prefer secretary A because of the reduced uncertainty about the time needed to complete assigned tasks.

CHAPTER 9

EXERCISES

9.1 H_o: $\mu_1 = \mu_2 = \mu_3 = \mu_4$ (Average leakage currents from four suppliers are all equal.)
H_A: Average leakage currents from four suppliers are not equal.

SOURCE OF VARIATION	DEGREES OF FREEDOM	SUM OF SQUARES	MEAN SQUARES	CALCULATED F
Supplier	3	1.3575167	0.452506	12.62**
Error	44	1.57755	0.035853	
Totals	47	2.9350667		

**Represents significance at the 1% level.

At the .05 level of significance we can conclude that the average leakage currents of the chips from the four suppliers are not all equal.

9.3 H_o: $\mu_1 = \mu_2 = \mu_3 = \mu_4$
H_A: The four means are not all equal.

SOURCE OF VARIATION	DEGREES OF FREEDOM	SUM OF SQUARES	MEAN SQUARES	CALCULATED F
Location	3	0.0156	0.0052	$\frac{MSTr}{MSE} = 6.753$**
Error	20	0.0154	0.00077	
Totals	23	0.031		

**Represents significance at the 1% level.

This F value is significant at the 5% level of significance, so we reject the null hypothesis and conclude that there is a significant difference in the mean weights at the different locations.

9.5 H_{o1}: $\mu_{.1} = \mu_{.2} = \mu_{.3} = \mu_{.4}$
H_{A1}: The impurity concentration population means are not equal.
We cannot reject H_{o1} and we therefore conclude that there is not a significant difference in the outcomes across the 4 impurity concentrations.
H_{o2}: $\mu_{1.} = \mu_{2.} = \mu_{3.}$
H_{A2}: The temperature population means are not equal.
We cannot reject H_{o2} and we therefore conclude that there is no significant difference in the outcome for the 3 temperatures.

SOURCE OF VARIATION	DEGREES OF FREEDOM	SUM OF SQUARES	MEAN SQUARES	CALCULATED F
Temperature	2	0.7736	0.3868	$\frac{MSTr_1}{MSE} = 0.209$
Impurity concentration	3	3.7334	1.2445	$\frac{MSTr_2}{MSE} = 0.672$
Error	6	11.1113	1.8519	
Totals	11	15.6183		

9.7 H_{o1}: $\mu_{.1} = \mu_{.2} = \mu_{.3}$
H_{A1}: The fumigant A population means are not equal.
H_{o2}: $\mu_{1.} = \mu_{2.} = \mu_{3.}$
H_{A2}: The fumigant B population means are not equal.

SOURCE OF VARIATION	DEGREES OF FREEDOM	SUM OF SQUARES	MEAN SQUARES	CALCULATED F
Fumigant A	2	319.38	159.69	$\frac{MSTr_A}{MSE} = 0.539$
Fumigant B	2	56.54	28.27	$\frac{MSTr_B}{MSE} = 0.0954$
Error	4	1185.57	296.3925	
Totals	8	1561.49		

a. We cannot reject H_{o1}, and we therefore conclude that there is no significant difference in the average kill among the concentrations of fumigant A.
b. We cannot reject H_{o2}, and we therefore conclude that there is no significant difference in the average kill among the three concentrations in fumigant B.

CHAPTER REVIEW EXERCISES

9.9 a. H_o: $\mu_A = \mu_B = \mu_C$ (The software packages do not differ in mean time to perform tasks.)
H_A: The three means are not all equal.

b.

SOURCE OF VARIATION	DEGREES OF FREEDOM	SUM OF SQUARES	MEAN SQUARES	CALCULATED F
Software	2	288.167	144.0835	$\frac{MSTr}{MSE} = 1.510$
Error	9	858.5	95.3889	
Totals	11	1146.667		

c. We cannot reject the null hypothesis, and we therefore conclude that there isn't a significant difference in the mean times to perform tasks among software packages.

9.11 H_o: $\mu_1 = \mu_2 = \mu_3$ (Average physical characteristics are equal across sports.)
H_A: Average physical characteristics are not equal.

SOURCE OF VARIATION	DEGREES OF FREEDOM	SUM OF SQUARES	MEAN SQUARES	CALCULATED F
Sport	2	112.4	56.2	3.74*
Error	27	406.1	15.0	
Totals	29	518.5		

*Represents significance at the 5% level.

At the .05 level of significance we can conclude that the average physical characteristics across sports are not the same.

9.13 H_o: $\mu_1 = \mu_2 = \mu_3$ (Average GPAs are equal across groups.)
H_A: Average GPAs are not equal.

SOURCE OF VARIATION	DEGREES OF FREEDOM	SUM OF SQUARES	MEAN SQUARES	CALCULATED F
Sport	2	0.3904	0.1952	4.81*
Error	9	0.3648	0.0405	
Totals	11	0.7552		

*Represents significance at the 5% level.

At the .05 level of significance we can conclude that the average GPAs across groups are not the same.

9.15 H_{o1}: $\mu_{.1} = \mu_{.2} = \mu_{.3} = \mu_{.4}$
H_{A1}: The fuel population means are not equal.
H_{o2}: $\mu_{1.} = \mu_{2.} = \mu_{3.} = \mu_{4.}$
H_{A2}: The automobile population means are not equal.

SOURCE OF VARIATION	DEGREES OF FREEDOM	SUM OF SQUARES	MEAN SQUARES	CALCULATED F
Automobile	3	280.312	93.437	$\dfrac{\text{MSTr}_1}{\text{MSE}} = 7.267^{**}$
Fuel	3	697.232	232.411	$\dfrac{\text{MSTr}_2}{\text{MSE}} = 18.075^{**}$
Error	9	115.725	12.858	
Totals	15	1093.269		

**Represents significance at the 1% level.

a. We reject H_{o1} and conclude that there is a significant difference in the miles per gallon for the 4 fuels.
b. We reject H_{o2} and conclude that there is a significant difference in the miles per gallon for the 4 automobiles.

9.17 H_{o1}: $\mu_{.1} = \mu_{.2} = \mu_{.3} = \mu_{.4} = \mu_{.5}$
      H_{A1}: The airline population means are not all equal.
      H_{o2}: $\mu_{1.} = \mu_{2.} = \mu_{3..}$
      H_{A2}: The travel agent means are not all equal.

SOURCE OF VARIATION	DEGREES OF FREEDOM	SUM OF SQUARES	MEAN SQUARES	CALCULATED F
Travel Agent	2	454.53	227.27	$\dfrac{\text{MSTr}_1}{\text{MSE}} = 4.433$
Airline	4	7042.27	1760.57	$\dfrac{\text{MSTr}_2}{\text{MSE}} = 34.341^{**}$
Error	8	410.13	51.27	
Totals	14	7906.93		

**Represents significance at the 1% level.

a. The null hypothesis, H_{o1}, is rejected, and we conclude that there is a significant difference in the outcomes across the 5 airlines.
b. We cannot reject H_{o2}, and we therefore conclude that there is no significant difference in the outcome for the 3 travel agents.

9.19 H_{o1}: $\mu_{1.} = \mu_{2.} = \mu_{3.} = \mu_{4.} = \mu_{5.}$
      H_{A1}: The company population means are not all equal.
      H_{o2}: $\mu_{.1} = \mu_{.2} = \mu_{.3} = \mu_{.4} = \mu_{.5} = \mu_{.6}$
      H_{A2}: The contract population means are not all equal.

SOURCE OF VARIATION	DEGREES OF FREEDOM	SUM OF SQUARES	MEAN SQUARES	CALCULATED F
Company	4	123.79	30.95	$\dfrac{\text{MSTr}_1}{\text{MSE}} = 12.09^{**}$
Contract	5	22.57	4.51	$\dfrac{\text{MSTr}_2}{\text{MSE}} = 1.76$
Error	20	51.16	2.56	
Totals	29	197.51		

**Represents significance at the 1% level.

a. We reject H_{o1}, and conclude that there is a significant difference in the rates of return for the 5 companies.

b. We fail to reject H_{o2}, and conclude that there is not a significant difference in the rates of return for the 6 contracts.

9.21 a. H_o: $\mu_1 = \mu_2 = \mu_3$ (Average times spent on sales calls are equal.)
H_A: Average times spent on sales calls are not equal.

b.

SOURCE OF VARIATION	DEGREES OF FREEDOM	SUM OF SQUARES	MEAN SQUARES	CALCULATED F
Account Type	2	667.1	333.5	21.12**
Error	33	521.2	15.8	
Totals	35	1188.2		

**Represents significance at the 1% level.

At the .01 level of significance we can conclude that the average number of minutes per sales calls of different types are not all equal.

9.23 a. H_o: $\mu_1 = \mu_2 = \mu_3 = \mu_4$ (Average productivity ratings are all equal.)
H_A: Average productivity ratings are not all equal.

SOURCE OF VARIATION	DEGREES OF FREEDOM	SUM OF SQUARES	MEAN SQUARES	CALCULATED F
Style	3	17,039	5680	2.72
Error	12	25,074	2089	
Totals	15	42,112		

b. We cannot reject the null hypothesis, and we conclude that there is no significant difference in mean productivity for the 4 management styles.

9.25 H_o: $\mu_{control} = \mu_A = \mu_B = \mu_C = \mu_D = \mu_E$ (Average elasticities are the same for each additive.)
H_A: Average elasticity means are not all equal.

SOURCE OF VARIATION	DEGREES OF FREEDOM	SUM OF SQUARES	MEAN SQUARES	CALCULATED F
Additive	5	0.42633	0.08527	$\frac{MSTr}{MSE} = 55.41$**
Error	12	0.01847	0.00154	
Totals	17	0.44480		

**Represents significance at the 1% level.

The null hypothesis is rejected at the 1% level of significance, and we therefore conclude that there is at least one additive that results in a mean billiard ball elasticity that is significantly different from the others.

9.27

SOURCE OF VARIATION	DEGREES OF FREEDOM	SUM OF SQUARES	MEAN SQUARES	CALCULATED F
Temperature	4	5.62	1.405	0.366
Humidity	4	9.692	2.423	0.632
Error	16	61.368	3.8355	
Totals	24	76.68		

The calculated F values for temperature and humidity are low, and both have values less than $F_{(.05,4,16)}$. Since these values are well below 3.07, we conclude that there is no significant difference in bacterial growth rates between temperatures and humidity levels. The egg distributor can permit storage tolerances with temperatures ranging from 0°C to 12°C, and humidity levels ranging from 5% to 25%, with the knowledge that these ranges will not have a significant effect on bacterial growth rates.

CHAPTER 10

EXERCISES

10.1   a. $\Sigma X^2 = 26$
b. $\Sigma XY = 31$
c. $10 = 3a + 8b$
$31 = 8a + 26b$
d. $b = 13/14$
e. $a = \frac{6}{7}$
f. Direct
g. $\hat{Y} = 1.786$
h. $Y - \hat{Y} = .214$
i. $\hat{Y} = 2.714$

10.3   a. $b = 0.15625$
b. $a = 0.55$
c. Increases maintenance cost by $15.63

10.5   a. Data points fall in a wide, generally linear, downward-sloping band.
b. $\hat{Y} = 7.5456 - 0.9273X$
c. Inverse
d. $\hat{Y} = 3.836$
e. $1 \leq X \leq 7$

10.7   a. An average $0.16 increase in expenditure.
b. $\hat{Y} = \$4.75$
c. $\hat{Y} = \$3.15$

10.9   a. SST $= \Sigma(Y - \bar{Y})^2 = 4.6667$
b. SSR $= \Sigma(\hat{Y} - \bar{Y})^2 = 4.0239$
c. $r^2 = .862$
d. $r^2 = 4.0245/4.6673 = .862$
e. SSE $=$ SST $-$ SSR $= .6428$
f. $1 - r^2 =$ SSE/SST $= .138$
g. $1 - r^2 = 1 - .862 = .138$

10.11 a. SST $= \Sigma(Y - \bar{Y})^2 = 2280$
b. SSR $= \Sigma(\hat{Y} - \bar{Y})^2 = 1939.7185$
c. $r^2 = .851$
d. $r^2 = 1939.71/2280 = .851$

10.13 a. $\hat{Y} = 108.5 + 52.312X$
b. When $X = 4$, $\hat{Y} = 317.75$; when $X = 5$, $\hat{Y} = 370.06$.
c. $r^2 = .763$; so 76.3% of the variation in weekly sales is explained by variation in the number of facings allocated.

10.15 a. The relationship appears to be linear.
b. $\hat{Y} = 4.954 + 8.1567X$
c. On average, each 1000 hr increase in direct machine hours is associated with an additional $81,567 overhead cost.
d. $\hat{Y} = \$538,942$
e. $r^2 = .982$

10.17 a. No   b. Yes   c. Yes   d. No
e. No   f. Yes   g. Yes   h. Yes

10.19 a. $\Sigma(X - \bar{X})^2 = 2720$
b. $S_b = 0.017$
c. H_o is rejected if $t_{n-2} > 2.353$.
d. $t_{n-2} = 10.73$
e. Reject H_o.
f. Still reject H_o.
g. UCL $= 0.236$, LCL $= 0.128$

10.21 a. UCL $= 12.268$, LCL $= -0.053$
b. H_o is rejected if $t_{n-2} > 2.353$.
c. $t_{n-2} = 3.155$
d. We reject H_o

10.23 a. $S_{\hat{Y} \cdot X_o} = 0.685$
b. $S_{\hat{Y} \cdot X_o} = 0.912$
c. $S_{\hat{Y} \cdot X_o} = 0.912$
d. $\hat{Y} = 21.148$
$\hat{Y} = 15.663$
$\hat{Y} = 10.177$
e. UCL $= 23.680$, LCL $= 18.616$;
UCL $= 17.565$, LCL $= 13.761$;
UCL $= 12.709$, LCL $= 7.645$
f. The width at $(X = 375) = 3.804$;
at $(X = 360) = 5.064$;
smallest at $\bar{X}$.

10.25 a. $S_{NEW \cdot X_o} = 1.814$
b. $S_{NEW \cdot X_o} = 1.911$
c. $S_{NEW \cdot X_o} = 1.911$
d. $\hat{Y} = 21.15$,
$\hat{Y} = 15.66$,
$\hat{Y} = 10.18$
e. For $X = 360$, UPL $= 26.45$ and LPL $= 15.85$;
for $X = 375$, UPL $= 20.70$ and LPL $= 10.62$,
for $X = 390$, UPL $= 15.48$ and LPL $= 4.88$.
f. For $X = 375$, interval width is 10.08;
for $X = 360$, interval width is larger, 10.60

10.27 a. $S_e = 1.2875$
b. $\hat{Y} = 20{,}650$ hot dogs
c. UCL $= 21.60$, LCL $= 19.70$
d. UPL $= 23.59$, LPL $= 17.71$

10.29 a. UCL $= 3.157$, LCL $= 3.043$
b. UPL $= 3.358$, LPL $= 2.842$
c. UCL $= .00705$, LCL $= .00635$

10.31 a. H_o is rejected if $t_{n-2} < -2.776$ or $t_{n-2} > 2.776$.
b. $t_{n-2} = 7.188$
c. 1. Does not follow.
2. Does not follow.
3. Does not follow.
4. Does not follow.
5. True.

10.33 a. H_o is rejected if $t_{n-2} < -2.353$ or $t_{n-2} > 2.353$.
b. $t_{n-2} = -6.102$
c. H_o: $\rho = 0$ is rejected.

10.35 a. $r = .979$
b. We reject H_o, since $10.738 > 1.476$.
c. No; highly statistically significant.
d. No; there is no causality implied in correlation analysis.

10.37 The critical value for $\alpha = .05$ is 1.960. H_o: $\rho = 0$ is rejected if $t_{n-2} < -1.960$ or $t_{n-2} > 1.960$. Significantly associated with eating out frequency are age, household income, education, family size, newspaper reading, TV viewing, magazine reading, sports participation, spectator sports interest, movie attendance, beer consumption, wine consumption, and charitable contributions.

CHAPTER REVIEW EXERCISES

10.39 b. $\hat{Y} = 1.686 + 1.057X$
c. $S_e = 0.6969$
d. $S_e^2 = (0.6969)^2 = 0.4857$
e. $r^2 = .910$
f. Slope is positive, so direct relationship.
g. $\hat{Y} = 5.914$

10.41 a. $S_e = 3.924$
b. $S_e^2 = 15.398$
c. $r^2 = .718$
d. Direct relationship
e. $\hat{Y} = 12.30$
f. $\hat{Y} = 15.15$, $Y - \bar{Y} = -1.7$, $Y - \hat{Y} = 4.85$, $\hat{Y} - \bar{Y} = -6.55$
g. $3 \leq X \leq 16$

10.43 a. $\bar{Y}/\bar{X} = 0.06626$
b. $\hat{Y} = 501.6$, $Y - \hat{Y} = 4.4$
c. $Y^* = 379.54$, $Y - Y^* = 126.46$
d. Y^* is not as accurate as $\hat{Y}$, which is based on the average change in Y per unit change in X.

10.45 a. $t_{n-2} = 0.830$
b. H_o is rejected if $t_{n-2} < -4.032$ or $t_{n-2} > 4.032$.
c. We cannot reject H_o.

10.47 a. $t_{n-2} = 0.104$
b. H_o is rejected if $t_{n-2} < -2.447$ or $t_{n-2} > 2.447$.
c. We cannot reject H_o.

10.49 a. $S_b = 0.4694$
b. H_o is rejected if $t_{n-2} < -4.032$ or $t_{n-2} > 4.032$.
c. $t_{n-2} = -2.02$
d. We cannot reject H_o.
e. H_o would still not be rejected.
f. UCL = 0.945, LCL = -2.841
g. 99% confident that the true slope B is in the interval from -2.841 to 0.945.

10.51 a. For $X = 5$, $S_{NEW \cdot X_o} = 3.011$; for $X = 2$, $S_{NEW \cdot X_o} = 3.208$.
b. The point estimates are $\hat{Y} = 3.744$, $\hat{Y} = 6.524$.
c. The point estimates are the same; uncertainty about the estimates differs.
d. UPL = 11.485, LPL = -3.997; UPL = 14.772, LPL = -1.724
e. At $X = 5$, 15.482; at $X = 2$, 16.496. The width at $X = 5$ is smaller because $X = 5$ is closer to $\bar{X}$ than $X = 2$.
f. 95% sure new Y value will be between -3.997 and 11.485.
95% sure new Y value will be between -1.724 and 14.772.

10.53 a. For $X = 4$, $S_{\hat{Y} \cdot x_o} = 3.339$; for $X = 2$, $S_{\hat{Y} \cdot x} = 4.376$.
b. $\hat{Y} = 105.89$, $\hat{Y} = 81.49$
c. UCL = 118.27, LCL = 93.51;
UCL = 97.71, LCL = 65.27
d. Estimation error at $X = 4$ is smaller because 4 is closer to the mean $\bar{X}$.
e. The width is narrowest at $\bar{X} = 3.875$.
f. 99% confident mean Y value (when $X = 4$) falls in the interval from 93.51 to 118.27.
99% confident mean Y value (when $X = 2$) falls in the interval from 65.27 to 97.71.

10.55 a. $\Sigma(X - \bar{X})^2 = 17.5$
b. $S_b = 0.1666$
c. H_o is rejected if $t_{n-2} < -3.747$ or $t_{n-2} > 3.747$.
d. $t_{n-2} = 6.345$
e. We reject H_o.
f. H_o would still be rejected.
g. UCL = 1.681, LCL = 0.433
h. 98% confident true slope B is in the interval from 0.433 to 1.681.
i. Highly confident that B is different from zero since $B = 0$ is not a point within the constructed confidence interval.

10.57 a. For $X = 4$; $S_{NEW \cdot X_o} = 0.793$; for $X = 7$, $S_{NEW \cdot X_o} = 0.793$.
b. $\hat{Y} = 5.914$,
$\hat{Y} = 9.085$
c. The $S_{NEW \cdot X}$ values are the same because they were calculated for X values that were equally distant from $\bar{X}$. The point estimates were obtained from different points along the fitted regression line, and so are not the same.
d. For $X = 4$, UPL = 8.885 and LPL = 2.943;
for $X = 7$, UPL = 12.056 and LPL = 6.114.
e. We are 98% sure that at $X = 4$ a new Y value will be between 2.943 and 8.885.
f. Prediction interval narrowest at $\bar{X} = 5.5$; same value for the confidence interval.

10.59 a. $\hat{Y} = 0.881 + 0.01811X$
b. $t_{n-2} = 17.61$, the critical t value is $t_{(.005,18)} = 2.878$. H_o is rejected since $17.61 > 2.878$.
c. UCL = 0.020275, LCL = 0.015951
d. UCL = 4.30, LCL = 3.80
e. UPL = 4.85, LPL = 3.25

10.61 a. $\hat{Y} = 11.19 + 0.05588X$
b. UCL = 83.37, LCL = 50.76
c. $\hat{Y} = 57.57$
d. Potential sales are 1000($57,570) = $57,570,000.

10.63 a. UCL = 80.548, LCL = 79.452
b. UPL = 84.965, LPL = 75.035
c. UCL = 1.04935, LCL = 0.95065

10.65 a. UCL = 2.0646, LCL = 1.9314
b. $1.998(1000) = $1998
c. Multiplying part a by 1000, UCL = $2064.6 and LCL = $1931.4.

CHAPTER 11

EXERCISES

11.1 a. $\hat{Y} = .604 + .124X_1 + .251X_2 + .007X_3$
b. 90% of the variability in selling price is explained by variation in size, elevation, and slope.
c. On average, the sales price increases by $124 for each additional 100 ft² of area, holding all other variables constant. On average, the sales price increases by $251 for each additional unit of elevation, holding all other variables constant. On average, the sales price increases by $7 for each additional unit of slope, holding all other variables constant.
d. $530 is a measure which reflects the size of the fitting error between Y and $\hat{Y}$.

11.3 a. Adjusted R^2 value is .883, which means that over 88% of the variation in service years across these employees is associated with the variation present in their two indexes.
b. Use this as a measure of service life unpredictability still remaining.

11.5 An increase by 1 in the number of commercials per day, holding the number of restaurants constant, is associated with an average increase in customer patronage of 145.643 patrons. This is much larger than the average impact on patronage from an extra restaurant, holding commercials constant. Both coefficients are positive, however. This supports the view that both the number of restaurants and advertising exposure are important, but advertising does have a strong brand loyalty effect.

11.7 There are 16 d.f., so the rejection region for a one-sided test is $t > t_{(.05,16)} = 1.746$. The observed value of the test statistic is $t = .007/.008 = .875$. The observed t value is not in the rejection region, so we may not reject the null hypothesis. There isn't significant evidence that sales price increases as the slope increases.

11.9 a. Three categories exist, so two dummy variables are needed.
b. Let X_2 represent two-story homes, and let X_3 represent split-level homes.

Observation	X_2	X_3
1	1	0
2	0	1
3	0	1
4	0	0
5	1	0
6	0	0

c. $\hat{Y} = 13,752 + 36.8X_1 - 5.000X_2 + 3.000X_3$

11.11 a.

Observation	Y	X_1	X_2
1	7.3	6	1
2	8.5	13	0
3	9.4	15	0
4	13.6	30	1
5	10.2	18	1
6	6.0	5	0

b. The coefficient for the gender dummy variable is .81. The coefficient indicates that females, on average, generate $810 more in sales than males, if all other variables are held constant.

11.13 The residuals suggest a serial correlation problem because of their cyclic pattern.

11.15 b.–c. The regression equation is Griev = 25.8 − 0.355HumDev.

ROW	GRIEV Y	RESIDUAL $Y - \hat{Y}$	FITTED $\hat{Y}$
1	6	−20.5105	26.5105
2	11	−13.7377	24.7377
3	51	27.6805	23.3195
4	6	−19.0923	25.0923
5	2	−23.8014	25.8014
6	83	54.0075	28.9925
7	38	14.3260	23.6740
8	27	−0.5742	27.5742
9	18	−6.3832	24.3832
10	27	−0.5742	27.5742
11	3	−23.1560	26.1560
12	11	−15.8651	26.8651
13	51	27.6805	23.3195

d. The pattern of residuals suggests that the data would best be described by a nonlinear equation.

e. Griev = 2.00 − 0.000000HumDev + 1.00HumDevSQ

f. Without performing regression diagnostics the vice-president would have concluded that employee grievances were due to poor management and would have fired the plant manager. Further exploration strongly supported the plant manager's claim that humidity deviations from the ideal was an important factor in explaining the number of grievances. Using the correct regression model increased R^2 from 0.5% to 100% and drastically changed the implications for decision making.

CHAPTER REVIEW EXERCISES

11.17 a. The normal equations are

$$\Sigma Y = na + b_1 \Sigma X_1 + b_2 \Sigma X_2 \Rightarrow 12 = 5a + 10b_1 + 12b_2$$

$$\Sigma X_1Y = a \Sigma X_1 + b_1 \Sigma X_1^2 + b_2 \Sigma X_1 X_2 \Rightarrow 28 = 10a + 22b_1 + 26b_2$$

$$\Sigma X_2Y = a \Sigma X_2 + b_1 \Sigma X_1X_2 + b_2 \Sigma X_2^2 \Rightarrow 37 = 12a + 26b_1 + 40b_2$$

b. $b_1 = 1.54$: A 1 unit increase in X_1, holding X_2 constant, is associated with an average increase in Y of 1.54 units. $b_2 = 0.457$: A 1 unit increase in X_2, holding X_1 constant, is associated with an average increase in Y of 0.457 unit. $a = -1.783$: The computed regression plane crosses the Y axis at -1.783. This may have no valid interpretation if the origin lies outside the range of the data used in the sample.

c. For b_1, $t = b_1/S_{b_1} = 1.54/0.6248 = 2.465$; for b_2, $t = b_2/S_{b_2} = 0.457/0.2460 = 1.731$.

d. Variable X_1 is statistically more significant since it has the larger t value; b_1 is over 2.4 standard deviations from 0, b_2 is only about 1.7 standard deviations from 0.

11.19 a. Among families exposed to the same amount of our competitor's advertising, the estimated average increase in a family's dollar purchases of our brand per additional exposure to our own advertising is $0.235. Among families exposed to the same amount of our own advertising, the estimated average decrease in a family's dollar purchases of our brand per additional exposure to competitive brand advertising is $0.110.

b. The estimated expenditure is $\hat{Y} = 0.22 + 0.235(10) - 0.110(0) = \$2.57$.

c. The estimated expenditure is $\hat{Y} = 0.22 + 0.235(5) - 0.110(2) = \$1.175$.

d. The negative sign of b_2 indicates that the competitor's advertising reduces our sales, and the positive sign of b_1 indicates that our own advertising increases our sales. Taken together, this means that advertising stimulates our brand sales, but not competitive brand sales. In marketing terminology, this situation is referred to as *selective demand stimulation*.

11.21 a. PRICE $= 1.31 + 0.00507$QUANTITY $+ 0.195$STRIKE

b. The t value for b_2 is 6.01, which is greater than $t_{(.005,7)} = 3.499$, so the STRIKE variable is significantly different from 0 at the $\alpha = .01$ level.

11.23 b. Yes; the t statistic for X^2 is $0.18/0.0032 = 56.25$, which is larger than the critical Z value of 1.96. The Z value is used since the sample size is larger than 30. Recall that generally a variable with a t value over 1 will improve prediction.

c. The estimate for $X = 3$ is $\hat{Y} = 43.1 - 8.3(3) - 0.18(3)^2 = 16.58$ mpg.

d. UCL $= 17.15$, LCL $= 16.01$; we are 95% confident that the true mean mileage lies within the interval 16.01–17.15.

e. No; the interval in part c is an interval for the *mean* mileage for all cars having 300 in.^{3} engines. The prediction interval for the mileage of *individual* cars would be wider.

11.25 b. The regression equation is $\hat{Y} = 76.9 - 4.89X_1 + 0.0139X_2 + 0.432X_3$.

c. The F statistic is 67.02, with a p-value of 0.000. Therefore, the regression equation is significant at the $\alpha = .05$ level. The critical F value for $\alpha = .05$ and 3 and 10 d.f. is 3.71.

d. Only variable X_1 is significant at the $\alpha = .05$ level. The t value for X_2 is 1.69. Although X_2 is not statistically significant at the $\alpha = .05$ level, the t value larger than 1 suggests that the variable will improve the overall explanatory power of the equation if left in the equation. The new regression equation is $\hat{Y} = 83.62 - 5.227X_1 + 0.016248X_2$.

e. $\hat{Y} = 83.62 - 5.227(5) + 0.016248(1200) = 76.98$

11.27 a. The regression equation is TravCost $= 4010 + 0.95$Calls $+ 15.2$Nights $- 0.76$Accounts. The MINITAB output is:

Predictor	Coef	Stdev	t-ratio	p
Constant	4010	3838	1.04	0.331
Calls	0.955	4.798	0.20	0.848
Nights	15.18	18.18	0.84	0.431
Accounts	−0.762	7.860	−0.10	0.925

s = 1784   R-sq = 12.0%   R-sq(adj) = 0.0%

b. The adjusted R^2 is 0%, so none of the variation in travel costs is explained. Thus, the executive's complaint is a valid one.

c. The value of a is 4010. The value has no meaningful interpretation outside the range of data collected, and simply represents the height of the regression surface at the origin.

d. RESIDUAL
```
  -2.25
 -591.46
 -324.52
-1716.48
 -745.01
-1221.41
 -355.36
 3797.15
 1053.50
 -715.36
  821.20
```

Large positive residuals indicate that costs were substantially above the regression estimates. The two largest positive residuals are attributed to salespersons 8 and 9.

e. The predicted value is TravCost = $6708. Realize, however, that this estimate is highly variable since the regression equation had no explanatory power, and is not useful for decision making.

11.29 b. The regression equation is Traffic = $-21 + 0.431$Advert + 244Size $- 66$Suburban.

Predictor	Coef	Stdev	t-ratio	p
Constant	-21.5	233.1	-0.09	0.928
Advert	0.4307	0.2537	1.70	0.109
Size	244.0	120.1	2.03	0.059
Suburban	-65.9	111.4	-0.59	0.563

s = 228.0   R-sq = 51.0%   R-sq(adj) = 41.9%

Analysis of Variance

SOURCE	DF	SS	MS	F	p
Regression	3	867203	289068	5.56	0.008
Error	16	831897	51994		
Total	19	1699100			

SOURCE	DF	SEQ SS
Advert	1	601168
Size	1	247854
Suburban	1	18181

c. The coefficient for advertising is 0.431. On average and holding the levels of other variables constant, a 1 unit increase in the amount of newspaper and TV advertising increases customer traffic by 0.431 person. The coefficient for size is 244. On average and holding the levels of other variables constant, a 1 unit increase in the size of the dealer's physical facilities increases customer traffic by 244 people. The coefficient for suburban is -66. This variable is a dummy variable. On average and holding the levels of other variables constant, a dealer in a suburban area experiences customer traffic that is 66 persons lower than dealers in urban areas.

d. Adjusted R^2 is .419, so 41.9% of the variation in customer traffic is explained by variation in the values of these three independent variables.

e. The critical t value for $n - k - 1 = 20 - 3 - 1 = 16$ d.f. and $\alpha = .05$ is $t_{(.025,16)}$ = 2.120. None of these variables are significant at the .05 level. The closest is the size variable, which is significant at the .059 level.

f. This model is not best for prediction. The model has one variable (suburban) that has a t value less than 1 (in absolute value). The model is likely to be improved for prediction if this variable is removed.

Traffic $= -95 + 0.444$Advert $+ 258$Size

Predictor	Coef	Stdev	t-ratio	p
Constant	−94.6	193.7	−0.49	0.631
Advert	0.4438	0.2479	1.79	0.091
Size	257.5	115.7	2.23	0.040

$s = 223.6$ R-sq $= 50.0\%$ R-sq(adj) $= 44.1\%$

Analysis of Variance

SOURCE	DF	SS	MS	F	p
Regression	2	849022	424511	8.49	0.003
Error	17	850078	50005		
Total	19	1699100			

SOURCE	DF	SEQ SS
Advert	1	601168
Size	1	247854

Notice that the standard deviation of residuals has decreased slightly from 228.0 to 223.6, the adjusted R^2 has increased from 41.9% to 44.1%, and the F statistic has risen from 5.56 to 8.49. The two remaining variables are now both significant at the 10% level.

11.31 a. The regression equation is PRICE $= -3.35 + 2.63$SQFT $- 1.72$STORIES $+ 15.0$BATHS $+ 0.425$AGE.

Predictor	Coef	Stdev	t-ratio	p
Constant	−3.355	6.882	−0.49	0.629
SQFT	2.6326	0.4526	5.82	0.000
STORIES	−1.716	3.570	−0.48	0.634
BATHS	14.983	4.492	3.34	0.002
AGE	0.4255	0.3465	1.23	0.228

$s = 9.938$ R-sq $= 86.5\%$ R-sq(adj) $= 85.0\%$

Analysis of Variance

SOURCE	DF	SS	MS	F	p
Regression	4	22197.4	5549.4	56.19	0.000
Error	35	3456.7	98.8		
Total	39	25654.1			

b. Of the four explanatory variables, only STORIES has a t value below 1 and therefore is likely to be unimportant for prediction. Results show that selling price can be expected to increase $2632.60, on average, for each additional 100 ft^2 of home area, assuming all other variables are held constant. On average, and all else held constant, selling price decreases $1716 for each additional story, increases $14,983 for each additional bathroom, and increases $425.50 for each additional year of age. The constant term is negative, and has no meaningful interpretation since the origin is outside the range of the data. Adjusted R^2 is .850, so 85% of the variation in selling price is explained by variation in SQFT, STORIES, BATHS, and AGE. The regression model is significant, the F value is 56.19. The standard deviation of residuals is 9.938, which is relatively small compared to the average magnitude of the values of the dependent variable (PRICE).

c. Residence number 1 has estimated price

$$\text{PRICE} = -3.35 + 2.63(20.4) - 1.72(2) + 15.0(2) + 0.425(17) = 84.12 \text{ (in thousands of dollars)}$$

Using the regression equation computed above, the estimated selling prices can be found by using the MINITAB subcommand PRED:

$$\text{MTB} > \text{regr cl 4 c2-c5;}$$

$$\text{SUBC}> \text{pred 20.4,2,2,17;}$$

In addition to the regression output above, the following output is obtained:

Fit	Stdev.Fit	95% C.I.	95% P.I.
84.12	2.92	(78.18, 90.05)	(63.08, 105.15)

11.33 a. Using the regression output provided, the regression equation is $\hat{Y} = 1590.795 - 177.687P + 21.08333A - 18.0833L$, so the predicted sales level when $P = 5.8$, $A = 1$, and $L = 1$ is $\hat{Y} = 1590.795 - 177.687(5.8) + 21.08333(1) - 18.0833(1) = 563.2105$

b. If $A = 0$, the predicted value would fall by the amount of the coefficient of the advertising variable. The decrease would be 21.08333 units per month.

c. If $L = 0$, the average unit sales would increase by the coefficient of the location variable. The increase would be 18.0833 units per month.

d. The t ratios and p values are

Predictor	Coef	Stdev	t-ratio	p
Constant	1590.8	232.8	6.83	0.000
PRICE	−177.69	39.00	−4.56	0.000
ADVERT	21.08	63.68	0.33	0.744
LOCATION	−18.08	63.68	−0.28	0.779

Only the PRICE variable is significant at the $\alpha = .05$ level. The sign of the price variable is logically correct, since an increase in price should reduce the quantity demanded per period, all else held constant. The coefficient of the ADVERTISING variable is positive but insignificant. The sign suggests that increases in advertising would increase average sales. The LOCATION variable is negative, indicating that a movement from the diet food section to the snack food section would increase sales. The sign is consistent with the notion that the demand for this good as a snack food is significantly higher than the demand for this good as a diet food.

11.35 a. The regression equation is $\hat{Y} = 591 - 147P + 227A - 7.0L + 22.1V$.

Predictor	Coef	Stdev	t-ratio	p
Constant	591.4	338.4	1.75	0.097
PRICE	−147.30	32.26	−4.57	0.000
ADVERT	227.33	77.39	2.94	0.008
LOCATION	−7.03	50.86	−0.14	0.891
VOLUME	22.097	6.258	3.53	0.002

$s = 124.4$ R-sq = 70.5%   R-sq(adj) = 64.3%

All the coefficients of the variables except LOCATION are now significant at the α = .05 level. The signs of the significant variables are logically consistent with marketing theory. The model may still be improved if the LOCATION variable is removed, since that variable has a *t* ratio less than 1. The size of the coefficient for the advertising variable has changed dramatically since the result presented in Exercise 11.33.

CHAPTER 12

EXERCISES

12.1 $(6 - 1)(4 - 1) = 15$

12.3 The chi-square test statistic = 19.256. The calculated chi-square value of 19.256 is greater than 16.9190, so the null hypothesis that there is no association between church attendance and area is rejected.

12.5 a. The chi-square test statistic = 18.742.
b. The calculated chi-square value of 18.742 is greater than 3.84146, so the null hypothesis that there is no association between respondent classification and response is rejected.

12.7 a. The chi-square statistic for the gender contingency table.
b. The size of the chi-square statistics—the larger the chi-square statistic, the more significant the association.
c. For gender: Since the calculated chi-square value of 201.912 is greater than 3.84146, the null hypothesis of no association is rejected. For occupational status: Since the calculated chi-square value of 7.168 is greater than 3.84146, the null hypothesis of no association is rejected.

12.9 a. The null hypothesis is rejected if test statistic > $\chi^2_{(.10,6)} = 10.6446$. The test statistic is = 6.677. The null hypothesis that the proportions in the various subscription categories is the same across the three cities cannot be rejected at the α = .10 level.
b. The "neither" category contributes most.

12.11 The test statistic = 4.743. Since 4.743 is not in the rejection region, the null hypothesis that the population from which this sample is drawn is normally distributed is not rejected.

12.13 a. The mean for this data set is $\bar{X} = 3.22$.
The standard deviation is $S = 1.2857$.
b. The test statistic = 21.853. Since 21.853 is in the rejection region, the null hypothesis that the population from which this sample is drawn is normally distributed is rejected.

CHAPTER REVIEW EXERCISES

12.15 a. The rejection region is $\Sigma\Sigma[(O_{ij} - E_{ij})^2/E_{ij}] > \chi^2_{(.10,6)} = 10.6446$.
b. The chi-square test statistic is 47.5.
c. Since the calculated chi-square value of 47.5 is greater than 10.6446, the null hypothesis that there is no association between age group and sweetener preferences is rejected.

12.17 a. The rejection region is $\Sigma\Sigma[(O_{ij} - E_{ij})^2/E_{ij}] > \chi^2_{(.01,2)} = 9.21034$.
b. The chi-square test statistic = 1.149.
c. Since the calculated chi-square value of 1.149 is not greater than 9.21034, the null hypothesis that there is no association between training session success/failure and age is not rejected.

12.19 a. H_o: The population from which the sample was drawn is in conformity with industry guidelines.

H_A: The population from which the sample was drawn is not in conformity with industry guidelines.

b. The test statistic value of 65.9375 is greater than 5.99147, so we reject the null hypothesis and conclude that the S&L has deviated significantly from industry guidelines.

12.21 a. The rejection region, using $\alpha = .05$, is $\chi^2 > \chi^2_{(.05,6)} = 12.5916$.

b. The chi-square test statistic $= 7.130$.

c. Since the calculated test statistic value of 7.130 is less than 12.5916, the null hypothesis that there is no association between computer literacy and family income is not rejected.

12.23 a. No; considering only heavy users, 65%; considering only females, 26%.

b. If the target is heavy users, the pertinent percentage is 65%. If women, the 26% would be pertinent.

c. Since the calculated test statistic value of 7.0 is greater than 5.99147, the null hypothesis that there is no association between gender and usage rate is rejected.

12.25 a. The chi-square test statistic $= 26.07$.

b. Since the calculated test statistic value of 26.07 is greater than 16.8119, the null hypothesis that there is no association between search effort and number of previous purchases of the same brand is rejected.

c. Yes; since we rejected the null hypothesis, we conclude that there is a difference in the amount of effort people exert in shopping for a new car between consumers with different amounts of experience buying the same brand.

12.27 a. The rejection region, using $\alpha = .01$, is $\chi^2 > \chi^2_{(.01,3)} = 11.3449$.

b. Since the calculated test statistic value of 0.364 is less than 11.3449, the null hypothesis that there is no association between first-choice publication mentions and type of college degree is not rejected.

12.29 a. The rejection region, using $\alpha = .05$, is $\chi^2 > \chi^2_{(.05,2)} = 5.99147$.

b. Since the calculated test statistic value of 29.853 is greater than 5.99147, the null hypothesis that there is no association between patient satisfaction rating and nursing home affiliation is rejected.

CHAPTER 13

EXERCISES

13.1 a. The median is midway between 7 and 8, or 7.5.

b. $n_1 = 11$, $n_2 = 11$

c. $\mu_R = 12.0$, $\sigma_R = 2.2887$

d. For $\alpha = .05$, the rejection region is $Z < -1.960$ or $Z > 1.960$. There are 12 runs in this series, so the test statistic is

$$Z = \frac{R - \mu_R}{\sigma_R} = \frac{12 - 12.0}{2.2887} = 0$$

Zero is not in the rejection region, so the hypothesis that the pattern is in conformity with a random process is not rejected.

13.3 The median is 12.0; $n_1 = 12$, $n_2 = 12$; $\mu_R = 13.0$; $\sigma_R = 2.3956$. The rejection region is $Z < -2.576$ or $Z > 2.576$. There are 14 runs in this series, so

$$Z = \frac{R - \mu_R}{\sigma_R} = \frac{14 - 13.0}{2.3956} = 0.4174$$

Since the test statistic is not in the rejection region, the hypothesis that the pattern is in conformity with a random process is not rejected.

13.5 The median is -1.0; $\mu_R = 11.917$; $\sigma_R = 2.3783$. The rejection region is $Z < -1.960$ or $Z > 1.960$. There are 13 runs, so $Z = 0.4554$. Since $-1.960 < 0.4554 < 1.960$, the null hypothesis is not rejected.

13.7 $n_1 = 21$, $n_2 = 27$; $\mu_R = 24.625$; $\sigma_R = 3.3723$. The rejection region is $Z < -2.576$ or $Z > 2.576$, and $R = 27$ runs, so

$$Z = \frac{R - \mu_R}{\sigma_R} = \frac{27 - 24.625}{3.3723} = 0.7043$$

Since the test statistic value is not in the rejection region, the null hypothesis is not rejected.

13.9 a. $W = 120.5$
b. $\mu_W = 126.5$; $\sigma_W = 15.229$
c. The rejection region is $Z > Z_{.05} = 1.645$ or $Z < -1.645$.

$$Z = \frac{W - \mu_W}{\sigma_W} = \frac{120.5 - 126.5}{15.229} = -0.394$$

The test statistic is not in the rejection region, so the null hypothesis is not rejected.
d. The calculated t statistic is -0.29 and the p-value is 0.78, so the null hypothesis is not rejected at the $\alpha = .10$ level. This is the same conclusion reached in part c.
e. The sample sizes from each store are small, and the underlying populations are not known to be normal.

13.11 $W = 112.5$; $\mu_W = 126.5$; $\sigma_W = 15.229$. The rejection region is $Z > Z_{.05} = 1.645$ or $Z < -1.645$.

$$Z = \frac{W - \mu_W}{\sigma_W} = \frac{112.5 - 126.5}{15.229} = -0.919$$

The test statistic is not in the rejection region, so the null hypothesis is not rejected.

13.13 a. $V = 97.0$

$$\mu_V = \frac{n(n + 1)}{4} = \frac{20(21)}{4} = 105$$

$$\sigma_V = \sqrt{\frac{n(n + 1)(2n + 1)}{24}} = \sqrt{\frac{(20)(21)(41)}{24}} = 26.786$$

The test statistic is

$$Z = \frac{V - \mu_V}{\sigma_V} = \frac{97.0 - 105}{26.7867} = -0.299$$

The rejection region, using $\alpha = .05$, is $Z > Z_{.025} = 1.960$ or $Z < -1.960$. Since the test statistic value of -0.299 does not fall in the rejection region, we cannot reject the null hypothesis.
c. The rejection region for a one-sided lower tail test (still using $\alpha = .05$) is $Z < -Z_{.05} = -1.645$. Since the observed test statistic value of -0.299 does not fall in the rejection region, we still cannot reject the null hypothesis.

13.15 b. Rejection region for $\alpha = .01$; $Z < -Z_{.05} = -2.326$; $\mu_V = 60$; $\sigma_V = 17.607$.

$$Z = \frac{V - \mu_V}{\sigma_V} = \frac{41.5 - 60}{17.607} = -1.051$$

Since the test statistic value of -1.051 does not fall in the rejection region, we cannot reject the null hypothesis.

13.17 a. 50 subjects were tested, but 3 scored equally well on both ads, so the number of pairs with non-zero differences is $n = 47$.

$$Z = \frac{2X - n}{\sqrt{n}} = \frac{2(17) - 47}{\sqrt{47}} = -1.896$$

The rejection region for $\alpha = .05$ is $Z > Z_{.025} = 1.960$ or $Z < -1.960$. Since the test statistic of -1.896 is not in the rejection region, the null hypothesis is not rejected.

b. $n = 45$, $X = 32$; $Z = 2.832$. The rejection region for $\alpha = .05$ is $Z > Z_{.025} = 1.960$ or $Z < -1.960$. Since the test statistic of 2.832 is in the rejection region, the null hypothesis is rejected.

13.19 a. If the information has no effect, any increases in ratings would be offset by other decreases, so X and Y should have equal size: $X = 50$ and $Y = 50$.

b. The two-sided null hypothesis is rejected if $X \geq 60$ or if $X \leq 40$. This implies that X and Y must differ by at least 20 before the alternative hypothesis will be accepted at $\alpha = .05$.

13.21 There are three categories, so the number of degrees of freedom is $3 - 1 = 2$. For $\alpha = .01$, the rejection region for the null hypothesis is $\chi^2 > \chi^2_{(.01,2)} = 9.21034$. The value of the test statistic is $H = 8.82$. Since $8.82 < 9.21034$, the null hypothesis is not rejected.

13.23 a. The appropriate test is the Kruskal–Wallis test. There are three categories, so the number of degrees of freedom is $3 - 1 = 2$. For $\alpha = .05$, the rejection region for the null hypothesis is $\chi^2 > \chi^2_{(.05,2)} = 5.99147$. The value of the test statistic is $H = .1718$. Since $.1718 < 5.99147$, the null hypothesis is not rejected.

13.25 $r_S = 1 - \dfrac{6 \Sigma d_i^2}{n(n^2 - 1)} = 1 - \dfrac{6(66)}{12(144 - 1)} = .769$

13.27 a. $r_S = .964$.

b. The rejection region, using $\alpha = .01$, is $Z > Z_{.005} = 2.576$ or $Z < -2.576$. The value of the test statistic is $Z = r_S \sqrt{n - 1} = .964 \sqrt{10 - 1} = 2.892$. The test statistic value of 2.892 is in the rejection region, so the null hypothesis is rejected.

c. $r_S = .5394$.

CHAPTER REVIEW EXERCISES

13.29 a. A test based on independent samples is appropriate.

b. $W = 299.5$; $\mu_W = 264$; $\sigma_W = 26.533$. Using $\alpha = .05$, the rejection region is $Z > Z_{.05} = 1.960$ or $Z < -1.960$; $Z = 1.338$. The test statistic is not in the rejection region, so the null hypothesis is not rejected.

13.31 $V = 42.0$; the rejection region is $Z < -Z_\alpha = -1.645$. The value of the test statistic is $Z = -1.022$. Since $-1.022 > -1.645$, the null hypothesis that there is no statistically significant difference between the mean cholesterol reductions is not rejected.

CHAPTER

14

EXERCISES

14.1 a. 196.58
b. 67.40
c. $450.00
d. 310.56

14.3 a. 112.30
b. 120.13

14.5 The simple aggregate index for meat prices of year 1, using year 3 as the new base year, is 83.24. The simple aggregate index for meat prices of year 2, using year 3 as the base year, is 93.48. The simple aggregate index for meat prices of year 3 is 100.00, since year 3 is the new base year.

14.7 a. 112.04
b. 122.17
c. 110.67
d. 120.01

CHAPTER REVIEW EXERCISES

14.9 a. Gas index, year 3: 119.05; oil index, year 3: 109.13; coal index, year 3: 103.45.
b. 115.58
c. Gas is the fuel that most greatly influences the simple aggregate price index, since its price is the largest. The magnitude of its price increase swamps the changes in price from the other two fuels.

14.11 a. 98.64
b. 96.47

14.13 a. 105.36
b. 108.39
c. The lower average price increase is reported when the simple aggregate price index is used.
d. The Laspeyres index is a better measure of the inflationary impact of the price changes because it is a weighted index.

14.15 a.

Stock A		Price Index (Base period = period 1)
Period 1	20	100
Period 2	25	125
Period 3	35	175

Stock B		
Period 1	120	100.00
Period 2	60	50.00
Period 3	140	116.67

Stock C		
Period 1	40	100.0
Period 2	35	87.5
Period 3	45	112.5

b. Period 1: 100.0; period 2: 66.7; period 3: 122.2.

CHAPTER 15

EXERCISES

15.1 b. The regression equation is $\hat{Y} = 11.8467 + 0.76242t$

s = 0.8222   R-sq = 89.9%   R-sq(adj) = 88.6%

c. When $t = 9$, $\hat{Y}_9 = 11.8467 + 0.76242(9) = 18.708$.

d. The forecast for $t = 11$ is $\hat{Y}_{11} = 11.8467 + 0.76242(11) = 20.233$.

15.3 b. $\hat{Y} = 0.16737 + 0.014269t$

s = 0.03109   R-sq = 88.6%   R-sq(adj) = 88.0%

c. The ratio of debt to equity has increased over these 20 years at an average rate of .014269 per year.

15.5 $\hat{Y} = 11.8467 + 0.76242t$

a.

t	C–I Relatives = $Y_t / \hat{Y}_t$
1	1.08652
2	1.04700
3	0.96222
4	0.93983
5	0.97709
6	0.96826
7	0.98349
8	0.97514
9	0.99420
10	1.07340

15.7 a. $\hat{Y} = 516.61 + 11.393t$

s = 43.05   R-sq = 32.9%   R-sq(adj) = 21.7%

b.

t	C–I Relatives = $Y_t / \hat{Y}_t$
1	1.09091
2	1.01225
3	0.95137
4	0.96233
5	0.97460
6	0.89749
7	1.01114
8	1.10078

c. $\hat{Y} = -1237.3 + 234.46t$

s = 176.3   R-sq = 90.8%   R-sq(adj) = 89.0%

15.9 a. 1.3675

b. 1.0010

c. 0.7053

d. 0.1763

e. $68.07 million

15.11 a–c.

TIME PERIOD	CONSTRUCTION PROJECTS	6 BIMONTH MOVING TOTAL	CENTERED MOVING TOTAL	MOVING AVERAGE
Jan.–Feb. Y1	8			
Mar.–Apr. Y1	7			
May–June Y1	9	51	51.5	8.583
July–Aug. Y1	11	52	54.0	9.000
Sept.–Oct. Y1	9	56	57.5	9.583
Nov.–Dec. Y1	7	59	60.5	10.083
Jan.–Feb. Y2	9	62	63.0	10.500
Mar.–Apr. Y2	11	64	65.5	10.917
May–June Y2	12	67		
July–Aug. Y2	14			
Sept.–Oct. Y2	11			
Nov.–Dec. Y2	10			

d. 9.0

15.13 a. 3020.00
   b. 2517.05
   c. 2517.05
   d. 2314.58

15.15 a. $F_8 = 1.93$ (thousands of dollars)

b.

Month	Forecast Error $Y_t - F_t$
1	—
2	1.00
3	−1.20
4	1.04
5	0.83
6	−0.83
7	−1.17
8	0.07
9	−0.25
10	−0.40

c. MSE = .7217
d. MSE = .8295; a larger MSE results when $w = .4$ is used.

CHAPTER REVIEW EXERCISES

15.17 a.

Quarter	Ratio-to-Moving Average
3	1.0182
4	1.0022
5	0.9804
6	0.9874
7	1.0264
8	1.0096
9	0.9786
10	0.9945

b.

	Q_1	Q_2	Q_3	Q_4
Arithmetic mean:	0.9795	0.9910	1.0223	1.0059
Seasonal indexes:	0.9798	0.9913	1.0226	1.0062

c.

Quarter	Deseasonalized Sales
1	1429.88
2	1433.47
3	1424.80
4	1434.84
5	1444.17
6	1450.62
7	1473.69
8	1489.72
9	1485.00
10	1495.01
11	1493.25
12	1496.71

d. The deseasonalized series

15.19 b. The regression equation is $32OZ = 37.61 + 0.223TIME$

$s = 0.6462$ R-sq = 55.1%   R-sq(adj) = 49.5%

c. .223 percentage points per year
d. $\hat{Y}_7 = 37.6 + 0.223(7) = 39.2$
e. 40.053

15.21 a. 0.98890

15.23 The trend equations show that the proportion of shipments accounted for by 32 oz containers has grown over the last 10 years, while the proportion of shipments accounted for by 128 oz containers has declined over the past 10 years. The trend projections for year 11 can be used to plan shipments in year 11. An appropriate recommendation to the firm would be to plan to have 40.07% of all shipments be of 32 oz containers and 17.36% of all shipments be of 128 oz containers. Other sizes (perhaps 8 or 16 oz containers) will account for the remainder of the shipments.

15.25 a. 11.6
b. 11.5
c. A 6 period moving average will cover 1 year and smooth yearly seasonality.

15.27 a. NATURAL FOOD SALES (in thousands), first 15 Days

Day	Moving Average (7 Day)
1	—
2	—
3	—
4	5.90
5	5.92
6	5.95
7	5.95
8	5.98
9	6.02
10	6.07
11	6.10
12	6.15
13	6.20
14	6.25
15	6.25

c. The moving average shows that sales are following a steady linear growth pattern over time.

15.29 a. The deseasonalized series is computed by dividing the original sales values by the appropriate daily index. The last 3 weeks include periods 71–91.

Day	Deseasonalized Data
71	8.21
72	8.26
73	8.06
74	7.87
75	8.17
76	8.35
77	8.35
78	8.47
79	8.66
80	8.72
81	8.55
82	8.57
83	8.59
84	8.74
85	8.50
86	8.54
87	8.99
88	8.95
89	8.55
90	8.86
91	8.74

c. The regression equation (for data in rows 71–91 only) is $\hat{Y} = 5.441 + 0.0379\text{Day}$.

$s = 0.1718$ R-sq $= 66.3\%$ R-sq(adj) $= 64.6\%$

d.

Day	Residual
1	0.079308
2	0.091424
3	−0.146459
4	−0.374342
5	−0.112226
6	0.029892
7	−0.007991
8	0.074125
9	0.226242
10	0.248360
11	0.040477
12	0.022593
13	0.004710
14	0.116827
15	−0.161057
16	−0.158939
17	0.253178
18	0.175294
19	−0.262589
20	0.009528
21	−0.148355

e. We can examine the residuals for the days corresponding to retaliatory promotions by competitors. If the retaliation had a serious impact on your business, those residuals should be negative. The stronger the competitive impact, the larger should be the magnitude of the negative residuals.

15.31 a. 8
   b. The first moving total is $1 + 2 + 4 + 2 = 9$. The last moving total is $3 + 5 + 7 + 4 = 19$.
   c. The first centered total (for Y1 Summer) is $(9 + 10)/2 = 9.5$, giving a moving average of 2.375. The last centered total is $(20 + 19)/2 = 19.5$, giving a moving average of 4.875.
   d. Seasonal Index$_{Fall}$ = 0.8875; Seasonal Index$_{Winter}$ = 0.6040; Seasonal Index$_{Spring}$ = 1.0100; Seasonal Index$_{Summer}$ = 1.4987
   e. 1.6556
   f. $\hat{Y}_t^d = 1.6217 + 0.3227t$
   g. $\hat{Y}_t^d = 1.6217 + 0.3227(11) = 5.1714$
   h. 0.85148
   i. 5.8168
   j. 3.5133

15.33 a.–d. First year answers:

MONTH	SALES	12 MONTH MOVING TOTAL	CENTERED MOVING TOTAL	12 MONTH MOVING AVERAGE	SEASONAL–IRREGULAR RELATIVES
1	30				
2	35				
3	38				
4	39				
5	42				
6	45	436	438.5	36.5417	1.36830
7	50	441	442.5	36.8750	0.94915
8	35	444	444.5	37.0417	0.86389
9	32	445	446.5	37.2083	0.80627
10	30	448	450.5	37.5417	0.82575
11	31	453	455.0	37.9167	0.76484
12	29	457			

e. Seasonal Index

January:	0.92924
February:	0.97515
March:	1.01798
April:	1.08448
May:	1.22159
June:	1.24655
July:	1.34505
August:	0.91658
September:	0.84608
October:	0.80140
November:	0.81935
December:	0.79658

f. First year only:

Month	Deseasonalized Sales
1	32.2844
2	35.8919
3	37.3288
4	35.9619
5	34.3814
6	36.0996
7	37.1733
8	38.1854
9	37.8215
10	37.4345
11	37.8349
12	36.4056

g. 43.057

15.35 a. It may be wrong to claim a profit improvement by comparing third-quarter profits to second quarter profits. It may be that this firm is in an industry in which significant seasonality is present.

b. Seasonality is included when this year's third quarter is compared to last year's third quarter, but underlying trends may not be considered. If the industry is declining, a decrease in profit since last year may be expected.

c. Isolate both the seasonality and trend components, and judge Mr. Wilson's effectiveness by comparing the current profit with a projection that includes trend and seasonal adjustments.

15.37 a.–b. Last 8 quarters:

QUARTER	SALES	EXPONENTIALLY SMOOTHED FORECAST, $w = .1$ (MADE IN PERIOD $t - 1$)	FORECAST ERROR
25	13,926,279	9,721,652	4,204,627
26	15,567,652	10,142,114	5,425,538
27	16,301,650	10,684,668	5,616,982
28	17,640,253	11,246,366	6,393,887
29	17,055,684	11,885,755	5,169,929
30	19,180,347	12,402,748	6,777,599
31	22,118,258	13,080,508	9,037,750
32	21,984,673	13,984,283	8,000,390

c.–d. Last 8 quarters:

QUARTER	SALES	EXPONENTIALLY SMOOTHED FORECAST, $w = .4$ (MADE IN PERIOD $t - 1$)	FORECAST ERROR
25	13,926,279	13,987,604	−61,325
26	15,567,652	13,963,074	1,604,578
27	16,301,650	14,604,905	1,696,745
28	17,640,253	15,283,603	2,356,650
29	17,055,684	16,226,263	829,421
30	19,180,347	16,558,031	2,622,316
31	22,118,258	17,606,958	4,511,300
32	21,984,673	19,411,478	2,573,195

e. Last 8 quarters:

QUARTER	SALES	EXPONENTIALLY SMOOTHED FORECAST, $w = .8$ (MADE IN PERIOD $t - 1$)	FORECAST ERROR
25	13,926,279	14,740,761	−814,482
26	15,567,652	14,089,175	1,478,477
27	16,301,650	15,271,957	1,029,693
28	17,640,253	16,095,711	1,544,542
29	17,055,684	17,331,345	−275,661
30	19,180,347	17,110,816	2,069,531
31	22,118,258	18,766,441	3,351,817
32	21,984,673	21,447,895	536,778

f. The weight $w = .1$ consistently generated forecasts that were low. The weight $w = .8$ generated forecasts that tended to overshoot the turning points in the actual sales series.

CHAPTER 16

EXERCISES

16.1 a. $3,500,000
  b. The EMV of scheduling in the indoor arena is $3,000,000. The open-air stadium has the higher expected monetary value and should be chosen using the expectation rule.
  c. $3,500,000

16.3 b. $E(A_1) = 156$; $E(A_2) = 78$; $E(A_3) = 233.2$.
  c. Act A_3

16.5 b. If the gambler uses the expectation rule, the bet will be accepted, since the gamble has a positive expected value of $5.00. If the expectation rule is not used, the gambler must decide if the positive expected value is sufficiently high to offset the risk of a potential loss of $100 or $200.

16.7 a. The payoff table is

	SHIP NOW	WAIT
p STRIKE	−6000	−$600
$1 - p$ NO STRIKE	−$1000	−$1200

  b. Values of p below 0.0357 (3.57%) make "ship now" the optimal act.

16.9 b. The optimal decision is to decide now and buy. The EMV is 187.

16.11 a. EVPF = 4,800,000
  b. EVPI = 1,300,000

16.13 a. EVPF = 92
  b. EVPI = 23.5

16.15 b. Option 1, make the investment: $E(U) = .549$. Option 2, turn down the investment: the outcome is 0, so the expected utility is $U(0) = .31$. Option 3, find a partner and split the payoff: $E(U) = .449$. Option 1 maximizes her expected utility.

16.17 a. $U(580) = 5$; $U(280) = 2.5$; $U(180) = 1.67$; $U(135) = 1.25$.
  b. Yes, the executive is risk averse. A doubling of utility from 1.25 to 2.5 requires that the monetary value more than double, from 135 to 280.

c. If the executive were risk neutral, the relationship between monetary outcome and utility would be linear. $R = 60$ generates a response of 180, and $R = 80$ gives 135. Then the monetary response for $R = 75$ would be greater than 135 by one-fourth of the distance between 135 and 180, for a response of 146.25. Since we know that the executive is risk averse, we know that the monetary response must be greater than 146.25 to compensate for the executive's aversion to risk.

CHAPTER REVIEW EXERCISES

16.19 b. $E(A_1) = 80$; $E(A_2) = 40$; $E(A_3) = 120$.

c. Act A_3 generates the largest expected profit.

16.21 b. Using backward induction (folding back the tree), the best act is to buy the option now (EMV = $27,500).

c. EVPF = $35,000

d. EVPI = $7500

INDEX

ABOUT THE AUTHORS

Mario J. Picconi is Professor of Business at the University of San Diego. He received his MBA from the University of Chicago and his Ph.D. from Rutgers University, where he was an NDEA fellow specializing in business statistics and econometrics.

He has taught the introductory business statistics course to undergraduates and graduates in a one- and two-semester format for over 20 years. As consultant for IBM, he helped design computer-assisted courseware in business mathematics and statistics. He has also served as a statistical consultant to Security Pacific Bank investment research division.

His quantitative research has appeared in journals of various business disciplines, including the *Journal of Accounting Research*, *Journal of Marketing Research*, and *Journal of Portfolio Management*. In addition, he has participated in and chaired sessions on the teaching of business statistics at the national and regional meetings of decision sciences. For the past three years he has been co-chair of the local chapter of the American Statistical Association.

Albert Romano is Professor of Mathematics at San Diego State University, where he has taught for the past 27 years. He earned his M.A. from Washington University and his Ph.D. from Virginia Polytechnic Institute.

During his 27 years of tenure at San Diego State, he has taught a wide variety of statistics courses, including introductory statistics, probability, statistical methods, use of computers, mathematical statistics, linear statistical models and experimental design, and quantitative business courses.

Before entering academia, he served as a professional statistician for quality control at Motorola, where he devised testing procedures for reliability analysis. Subsequently, he received a postdoctoral fellowship to do statistical research at the National Bureau of Standards in Washington, D.C. He has remained an active statistical consultant since that time and his experiences are reflected in the text applications. He has been a member of the American Statistical Association and the Institute of Mathematical Statistics for over 30 years.

Charles Olson holds MBA degrees from Boston University and the University of Chicago. Since 1973 he has been Professor of Business Administration at Governor's State University in suburban Chicago.

In addition to university teaching and research, Olson has worked as an industrial engineer, research analyst, and statistical consultant in industry and government agencies. Some of his research topics have been land use and transportation planning, econometric studies of industrial agglomeration, advertising and store location, and financial market prognostication.